JANE'S SURFACE SKIMMERS
1979

ANTI-MISSILE and ANTI-AIRCRAFT DEFENCE

BREDA

40L70 TWIN MOUNTING

- *600 rds/min*
- *proximity fuse ammunition*
- *736 ready-use rounds*
- *above or below deck installation*

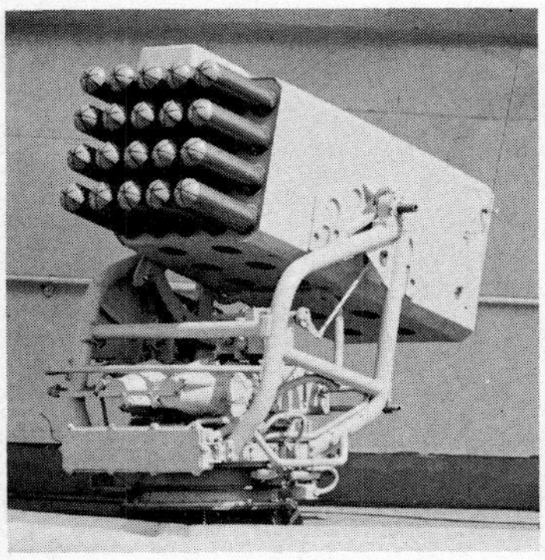

BREDA NAVAL ROCKET LAUNCHER

40 L 70 SINGLE NAVAL GUN with 144 round AFD

BREDA ANTI TANK WEAPON 'FOLGORE'

BREDA SHOTGUNS

BREDA

BREDA MECCANICA BRESCIANA S.p.A.
2, VIA LUNGA (25100) BRESCIA ITALY - TEL. (030) 31 40 61 - TELEX 30 056 BREDARMI

Alphabetical list of advertisers

Classified list of advertisers

The companies advertising in this publication have informed us that they are involved in the fields of manufacture indicated below

ACV manufacturers
Bell Aerospace Textron
British Hovercraft Corporation
Vosper Thornycroft

ACV operators
British Rail Hovercraft

ACV research and design
Bell Aerospace Textron
British Hovercraft Corporation
ELSAG
Vosper Thornycroft

Diesel engines
Mitsui Engineering
Motoren-und Turbinen-Union
Zahnradfabrik

Electronic equipment
ELSAG
SEPA
SMA
Vosper Thornycroft

Finished machine parts
British Hovercraft Corporation

Glass fibre resins
British Hovercraft Corporation

Guided missile ground handling equipment
OTO Melara

Guns and mountings
Breda Meccanica
OTO Melara

Hovercraft command staff training
Bell Aerospace Textron
British Hovercraft Corporation

Hovercraft consultants
Bell Aerospace Textron
British Hovercraft Corporation
Vosper Thornycroft

Hovercraft interior design
Bell Aerospace Textron
British Hovercraft Corporation
Vosper Thornycroft

Hovercraft interior furnishings
British Hovercraft Corporation
Vosper Thornycroft

Hovercraft manufacturers
Bell Aerospace Textron
British Hovercraft Corporation
Mitsui Engineering
Vosper Thornycroft

Hoverpallet manufacturers
British Hovercraft Corporation

Hydrofoil boats and ships
Cantiere Navaltecnica
Cantieri Navali Riuniti
Grumman
Vosper Thornycroft

Hydrofoil interior design
Cantiere Navaltecnica
Cantieri Navali Riuniti
Vosper Thornycroft

Hydrofoil interior furnishing
Cantiere Navaltecnica
Vosper Thornycroft

Hydrofoil missile / gun boats combat systems
OTO Melara
SMA

Hydrofoil missile / gun boats
Cantiere Navaltecnica
Cantieri Navali Riuniti
OTO Melara
Vosper Thornycroft

Hydrofoil research and design
Cantiere Navaltecnica
Cantieri Navali Riuniti

Hydrofoil seating
Cantiere Navaltecnica

Instruments, electronic
Bell Aerospace Textron
British Hovercraft Corporation
SEPA

Instruments, navigation
Bell Aerospace Textron

Instruments, test equipment
British Hovercraft Corporation

Patrol boats
Bell Aerospace Textron
Cantiere Navaltecnica
Cantieri Navali Riuniti
Mitsui Engineering
Vosper Thornycroft

Patrol boats combat systems
OTO Melara
SMA
Vosper Thornycroft

Radar
Bell Aerospace Textron
ELSAG
SMA

Radio navigation equipment
Bell Aerospace Textron
ELSAG

Reverse-reduction gears
Vosper Thornycroft

Rocket launchers
Breda Meccanica

Simulators
SEPA

Skirt materials
Avon Industrial Polymers
Bell Aerospace Textron
British Hovercraft Corporation
Northern Rubber

Speed control devices
British Hovercraft Corporation
SEPA

Surveillance systems
SEPA
SMA

Transmission systems
British Hovercraft Corporation

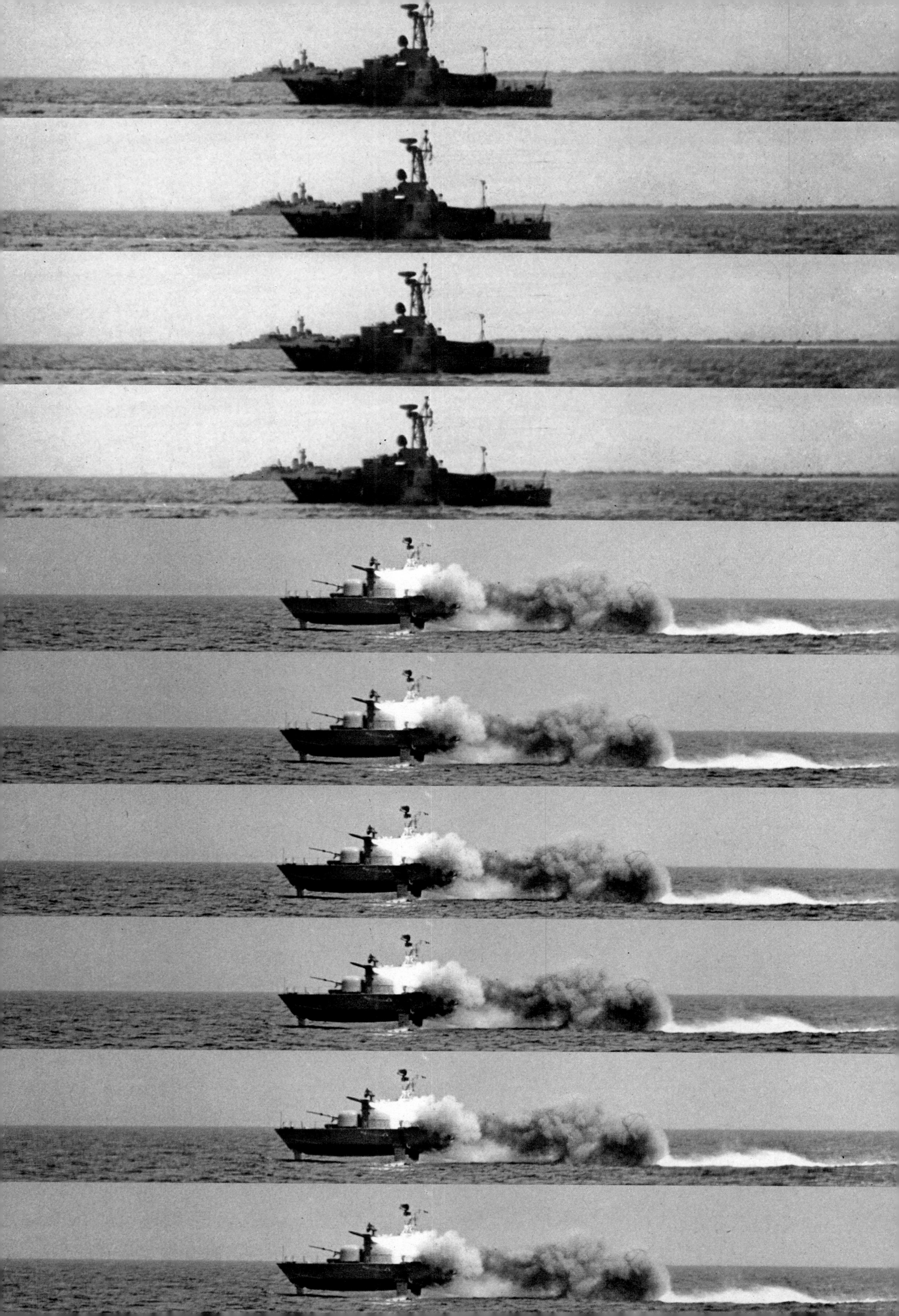

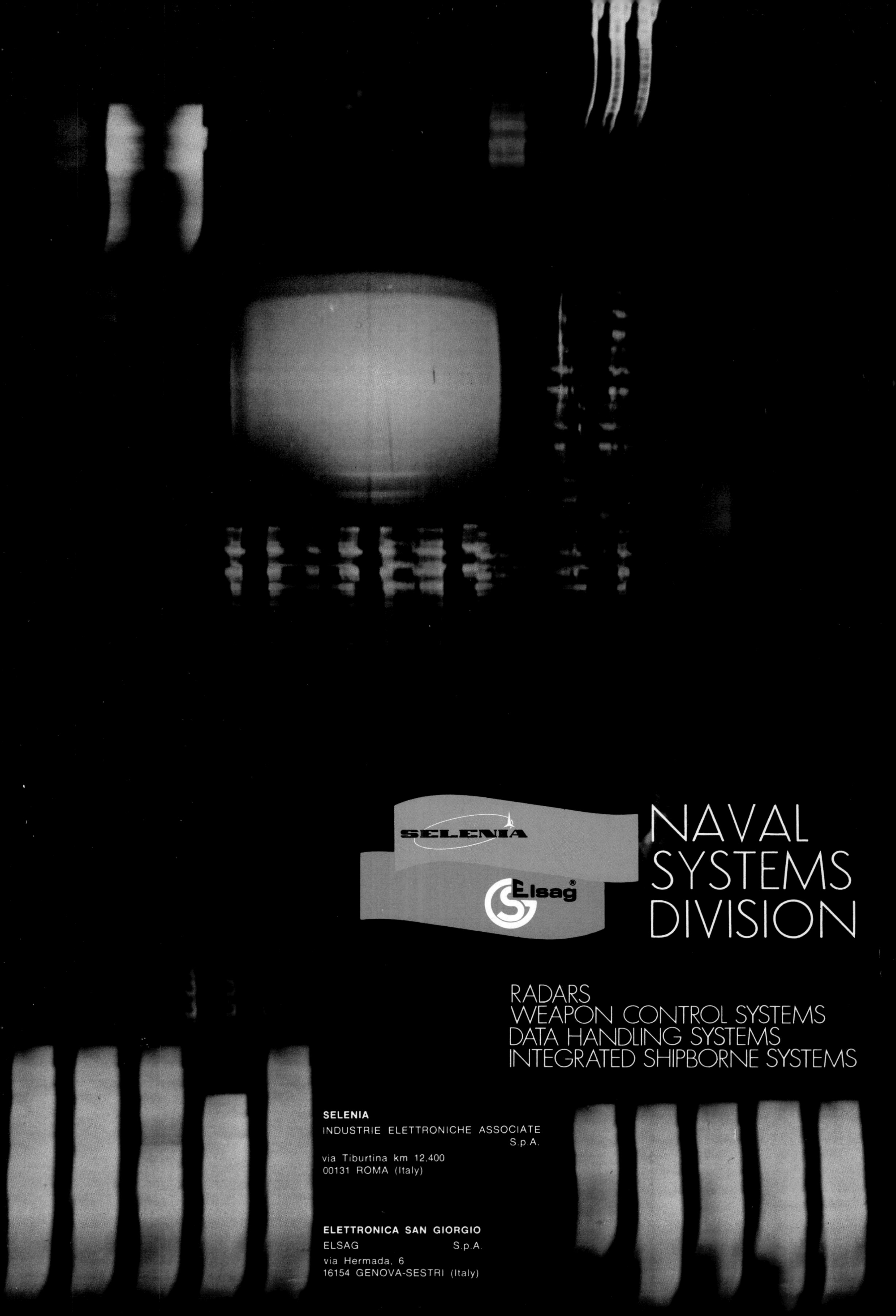
SELENIA
Elsag
NAVAL SYSTEMS DIVISION
RADARS
WEAPON CONTROL SYSTEMS
DATA HANDLING SYSTEMS
INTEGRATED SHIPBORNE SYSTEMS
SELENIA
INDUSTRIE ELETTRONICHE ASSOCIATE S.p.A.
via Tiburtina km 12.400
00131 ROMA (Italy)
ELETTRONICA SAN GIORGIO
ELSAG S.p.A.
via Hermada, 6
16154 GENOVA-SESTRI (Italy)

Make a quick getaway on the largest hovercraft in the world.

Seaspeed makes short work of getting you across the channel. In little more than half an hour, you can go Dover-Calais, or Dover-Boulogne. And you'll travel on the largest hovercraft in the world.

Seaspeed's Super 4 has a carrying capacity of 416 passengers and 55 cars. The first Super 4 came into operation last year, and a second is scheduled for service from 1st June '79.

Also operating now is the new French-owned N500, which takes 400 passengers and 60 cars.

All flights take off from the new International Hoverport at Dover, where modern facilities ensure quick and efficient take-offs.

Seaspeed is the quickest way across the channel.

Now that there are new hovercraft and a new Hoverport, going Seaspeed is more comfortable and more luxurious than ever.

Seaspeed HOVERCRAFT

Hover over from Dover

Ask your travel agent for details.

WHO NEEDS WINGS TO FLY?
ROYAL NAVY
Certainly not the VT.2 Hovercraft – this British invention is carried to a highly versatile conclusion by Vosper Thornycroft in a logistic role or as a missile platform.
If your tactical requirement is for a multi-role vessel, look at the VT.2, with its go-anywhere practicality.
To 'FLY NAVY' is true of the VT.2, chartered three times by the Royal Navy for operational and tactical exercises, including the first circumnavigation of the British Isles adding yet another unusual dimension to the Service.
VT.2, can manoeuvre in any depth of water, has a capacity to carry 130 fully armed men complete with back-up equipment and land them dry shod inland, close to their objective.
In a ship to shore ferry role – a fast turn round is achieved because the VT.2 has a ramp and top hatch facility for ease of loading and offloading.
VT.2's low magnetic and acoustic signature, together with a near immunity to underwater shock, makes it ideal in a mine countermeasures role where its high manoeuvrability is an additional advantage.
Maximum speed: 60 knots.
Typical average range: 500 nautical miles at 50 knots.
Its principal dimensions: length 99ft. (30m); beam 43½ft. (13m); cushion depth 5½ft. (1.7m).
This, then is the VT.2, a highly versatile craft and remember, you don't need wings to fly –
VOSPER THORNYCROFT
Vosper Thornycroft (UK) Limited,
Southampton Road, Paulsgrove, Portsmouth PO 4QA.
Telephone: Cosham (07018) 79481. Telex: 86115.
Cables: Repsov, Portsmouth.
A Member of British Shipbuilders

FOR SEAWORTHY HYDROFOILS-
HYDROFOILWORTHY SYSTEMS

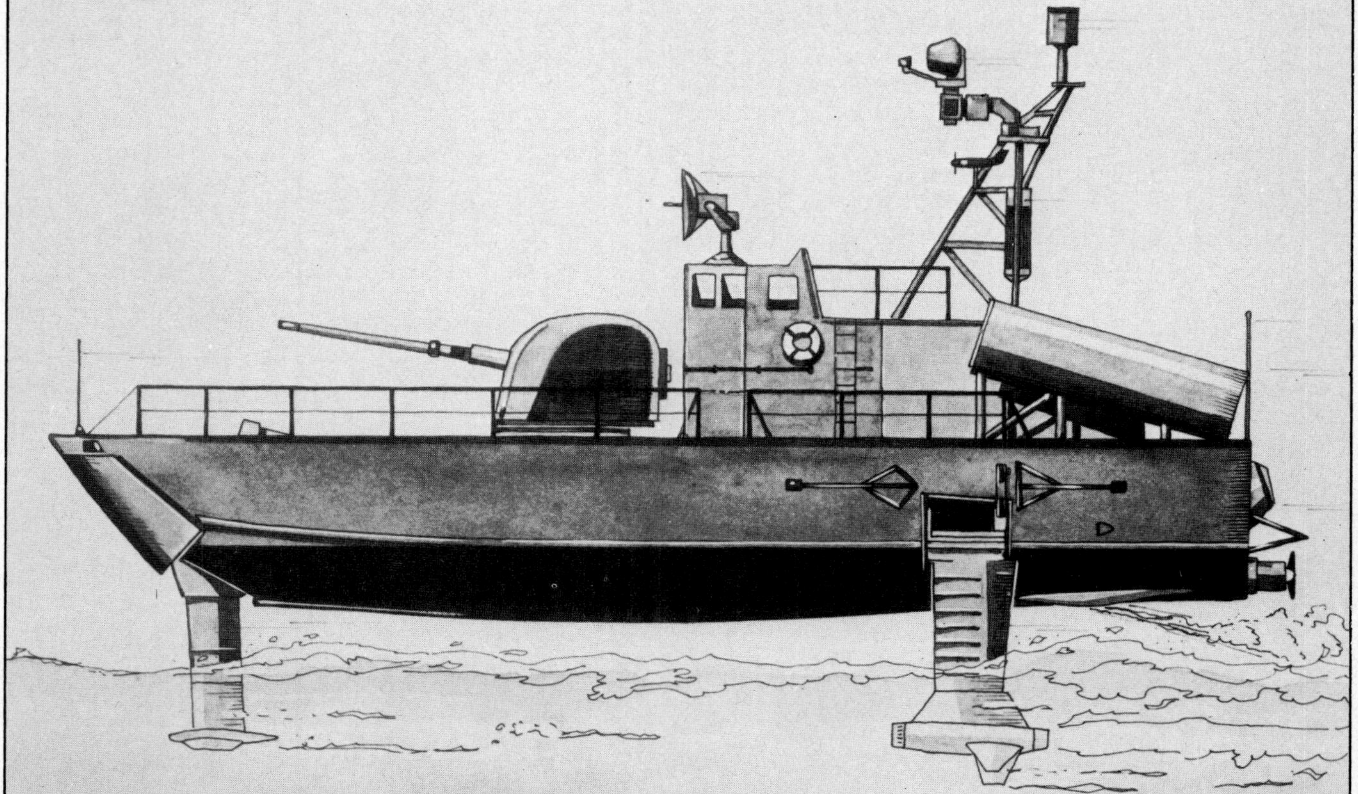

SEPA AN700
HYDROFOIL AUTOMATIC ATTITUDE CONTROL

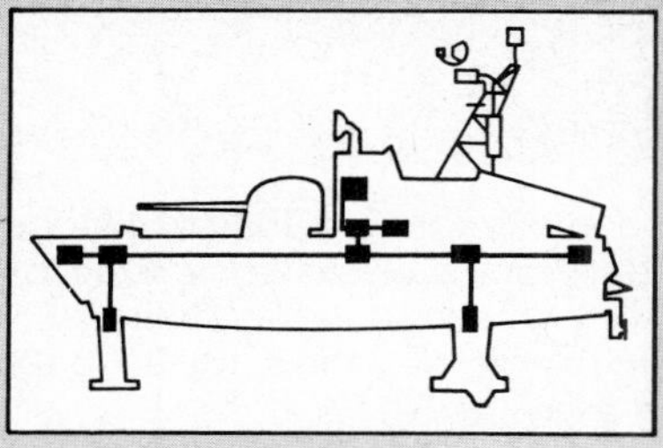

Derived from a well proven SEPA experience in seaborne automation, AN 700 is an attitude control system specifically designed for all-weather high performance hydrofoils with the task of providing precise fast acting, easy to maintain trouble-free foil control under extreme manoeuvring conditions.

Its main characteristics are:

- ☐ *Automatic-sea, airborne mode change over sequences*
- ☐ *Roll and pitch control to better than 0,5 degree with sea force 4 and 40 knots speed*
- ☐ *Automatic height above the water control with both platforming and contouring modes*
- ☐ *Automatic banking during turns*
- ☐ *Automatic hull trim*
- ☐ *Single lever control*
- ☐ *U.S. Navy Mil standard construction*
- ☐ *Design to low life-cost*
- ☐ *Built-in automatic test facilities.*

Società di Elettronica per l'Automazione S.p.A.
Lungo Stura Lazio 45 -10156 Torino (Italy)
Tel. (011) 262.3333 (5 linee r.a.) Telex 23527 Sepa

SEPA

User size electronics

dolci italia

The Bell-Halter 110 SES demonstration boat. The B-H 110 has a maximum deck load of 49 tons and a displacement of 138 tons. Construction is of marine aluminium and although its initial propulsion system is sized for a performance of 40 knots, the hull has been designed for speeds up to 60-70 knots. The B-H 110 can be used in offshore services, ferry boat, US Coast Guard and fast patrol boat applications. After initial dockside and underway trials, the B-H 110 will begin a demonstration programme in early 1979

JANE'S SURFACE SKIMMERS
Hovercraft and Hydrofoils

TWELFTH EDITION

COMPILED AND EDITED BY
ROY McLEAVY

1979

ISBN 0 354 00579 0

JANE'S YEARBOOKS

LONDON

P420
IS OUR PRIDE,
THE LATEST
OF A LONG SERIES.

CONTENTS

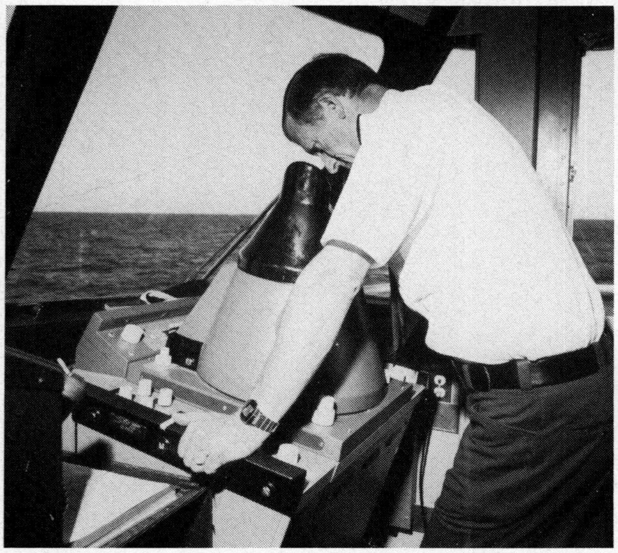

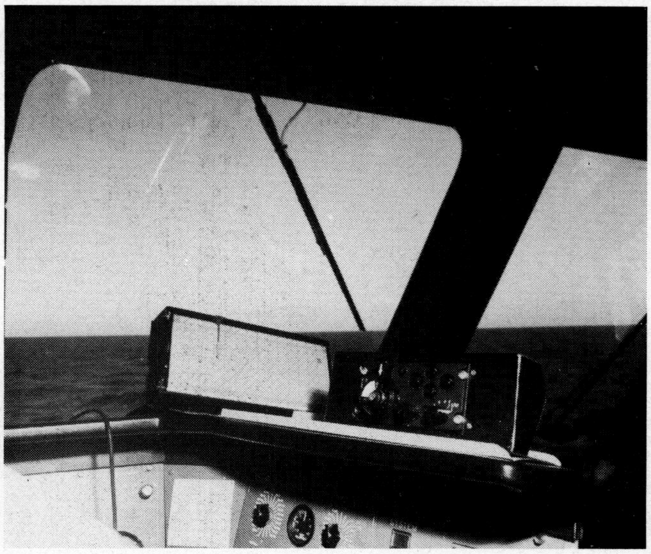

FOREWORD

Hovering off the beaten track

With notably few exceptions the output of the hovercraft industry over the past twenty years has been directed towards the transport requirements of the modern world. Today, however, an exciting new market is beckoning: one that promises to lift the industry out of its present financial doldrums and provide it with a firm base for future expansion. To meet its requirements, a dramatic turn-about from current design philosophy is needed, calling for the technology to be stretched to new limits, but its rewards should far outweigh any of the returns of the past.

The market offering the glittering prospects is the Third World. Although the production of fast ferries and warships will continue to make a valuable contribution to turnover in the years ahead, analysts believe the major proportion of the industry's income will be derived from harnessing the hovercraft's unique characteristics to the needs of emergent countries. By the early 1980s hovercraft are likely to be employed throughout Africa, Central and South America, South-east Asia, on the islands of the Pacific and across the Chinese mainland in such diverse applications as amphibious trucks and freighters, personnel transport, self-propelled and towed barges, excavator and drill platforms, rice harvesters, cattle waggons, ambulances, rescue vehicles and mobile laboratories and hospitals.

It is now widely recognised that the hovercraft, with its unlimited cross-country capabilities, is the only transport system capable of penetrating deep into the world's hinterlands at an acceptable cost per ton-kilometre. Many opportunities to exploit hover technology in the utilisation of natural resources have been lost in the past due to a lack of funds. Paradoxically those who most needed the hovercraft were those who could least afford it. That situation is now changing. International funding and a huge variety of aid programmes sponsored by overseas governments are available today to assist the Third World in solving problems of hunger, disease and economic development. Agencies such as the World Bank and the International Development Association (IDA) are two of many organisations which are contributing vast sums annually towards transportation projects in developing countries around the world. In 1978 out of a total funding of US $8, 410·7 million, US $1,092·9 million was supplied for transport projects; in 1977 the equivalent figure was US $1,047·6 million. In addition, separate funding was made available by the World Bank for the development of rural areas, agriculture, irrigation schemes, tourism and water supplies. In many of these areas, too, hovercraft might well have a useful role.

Now, it is not so much the difficulty of obtaining funds as identifying and establishing the priorities for the respective development programmes. In general Third World countries have no developed areas outside their capitals and possibly a major town or port. Natural resources are therefore invariably at some distance from roads and are probably deep in remote regions well off the beaten track. Experience has shown that the capital costs of projects involving building and industrial construction in these localities is two to three times greater than that of similar projects in developed areas, and the cost of transport is as much as 60% of the total sum. The vast difference in capital cost arises from the fact that often no workable transport system exists and that traditional vehicles are generally unsuitable to meet the climatic, terrain and soil conditions.

Roads and railways are attractive economically only in more developed areas with a reasonable traffic flow. In remote areas, where the terrain may well vary from swampland to hard rock, roads and railways cannot be built at a reasonable price and, because of the scanty traffic flow, would never pay a reasonable return on investment. Because it can cope with any reasonably flat terrain, regardless of soil characteristics and seasonal conditions, the amphibious hovercraft fits admirably into the overall pattern of development in remote areas. Additionally, rigid sidewall hovercraft, which are of more simple construction, and easier to control, can be employed in countries where rivers abound, especially in regions lacking other forms of rapid transportation.

Not only can the hovercraft be applied to solving acute problems such as opening-up new energy, mineral and food resources, it can also provide developing countries with additional employment and a basis for the acquisition of new skills. Craft intended for use in the Third World will need to be simple, rugged, versatile and cheap. Compared with helicopters and STOL or V/STOL aircraft which have obvious but less widespread applications in remote areas, the level of skill required in building a hovercraft is far lower, making it an ideal candidate for local construction. Manufacturers will be faced with the choice of either exporting the finished craft or building them on site. Most are likely to opt for a technology-transfer arrangement under which craft will be built locally by company-supported and supervised native labour from materials and components shipped in. Imported items will include engines, machinery, instrumentation and skirt materials. In a typical case, hovercraft could be employed to revolutionise the transportation system used in the extraction of chemicals, minerals, oil or gas in four basic cycles:

First, light ACVs would survey the area, then bring in personnel to establish the selected site.

Second, hovertransporters and platforms would bring in drilling equipment and machinery.

Third, hoverpallets and ACV conveyor systems would be provided to aid movement on site.

Finally, 50- to 300-ton hoverfreighters would undertake the movement of the extracted matter from the site to the port or terminal for shipment.

Although craft designed for use in remote areas will employ much of the technology spawned during the past decade, it will also call for new efforts to be exerted to provide lower operating costs and increased reliability. Far greater use is likely to be made of high-speed diesels, and where gas-turbines are employed they are likely to be derivatives of industrialised gas-turbines, whenever suitable units are available. Where diesels are specified, performance is likely to be reduced slightly due to their greater weight, and there will also be a moderate sacrifice in payload as a percentage of all-up weight. Nevertheless, life between major overhauls will be extended and the need for complex maintenance facilities and highly skilled engineers permanently on site will be reduced. The basic hulls or raft structures will be heavier and more rugged and will be fabricated in welded light metal for cheaper construction and easier maintenance. Lift and propulsion systems will be much the same as those in current use, but where air propellers are used, they will be ducted in the interests of both safety and noise reduction. Skirt systems are likely to be of a simpler design than those in vogue at present.

Although the experience of United Kingdom manufacturers is still unmatched, their drive to sell the growth potential of the hovercraft and its relevant technologies to the Third World will almost certainly stir up stiff competition. The USA, Canada, France, Japan, China and the Soviet Union have all designed and built craft of various capacities which could find applications in this kind of environment. Lively debates will undoubtedly ensue over the forms the first generation Third World hovercraft will take and where and when the first major sales breakthrough will be made.

In the meantime encouraging progress is continuing to be made in developed countries. One of the industry's major triumphs is the overwhelming success of the English Channel hoverferry services operated by Hoverlloyd, British Rail and, more recently, SNCF. During the first ten years of full cross-Channel operation these companies carried between them more than 13 million passengers. In 1978 1·88 million passengers and 300,000 vehicles were carried. Not only is the traffic increasing, it is also broadening in its scope. Businessmen use it more and more frequently, as do the vans and smaller commercial vehicles of the international commercial undertakings.

Awareness of the immense benefits that craft such as BHC's SR.N4s are bringing to the fast ferry scene is growing in varying degrees throughout the shipping world. Apart from its very high mechanical reliability, the N4 has proved to be extremely manoeuvrable, even in particularly adverse weather. All the earlier snags that once beset SR.N4s have been virtually ironed out, including the failure of skirt components. Skirt technology has now reached a stage where potential failures and components that require replacement can be identified and forecast during routine examinations.

Among the major events on the Channel hover scene in 1978 were the introduction into service of British Rail's new SR.N4 Mk III, renamed the Super 4, the launching of SEDAM's N 500-02 Naviplane, and the opening of British Rail Seaspeed's new hovercraft terminal at Dover. British Rail's 300-ton Super 4, *The Princess Anne,* is the world's biggest hovercraft. A lengthened and refitted BHC SR.N4 Mk 1, it entered service on 9 July 1978. Features of this latest model include a lengthened hull, widened superstructure and uprated engines. As a result of these modifications the N4's revenue-earning capability has been

Strongest

Avon skirt systems are the only ones used to endure the extreme operating conditions experienced by the Vosper VT2 high speed amphibious military craft.

Hottest

Avon supplied the skirt system for the 30 ton Mackace hover platform used for potash exploration in the extreme heat of Jordan's Dead Sea.

Coldest

Operating in temperatures well below zero, Avon skirt materials are used on the Hoverlift 50 ton Pioneer hover ferry bridging the Peace River in Northern Alberta, Canada.

Biggest

Ferrying refinery plant in the Persian Gulf, the world's largest hover transporter, Mackace's 750 ton Sea Pearl uses Avon skirt materials and components.

Fastest

Carrying millions of passengers and cars across the English channel every year, BHC N4 hovercraft regularly cruise at speeds in excess of 60mph, safe and secure on Avon skirt components.

Highest

Avon skirts are used on the Hovermarine HMII hover ferry in daily operation on the world's highest altitude water, Lake Titicaca in Bolivia, South America.

The world's toughest conditions. The world's toughest skirts.

In service throughout the world, today's hovercraft operate in places where other craft couldn't survive.

To do this they have to be tough.

And their component parts have to be tough.

Components like skirts and skirt systems.

Tough enough to take the heat of the Gulf, and the Arctic cold of the Yukon.

Tough enough not to be torn apart by jagged salt mountains in the Dead Sea.

Or pounded apart by the wild waters of the Channel.

Tough enough to survive high speed, high altitude and extreme humidity. And tackle sand, rock, concrete and water with the same easy confidence.

Toughness that requires special technology. The sort of technology that only comes from a 100 years' experience of polymer engineering and the total resources of a £120m. world-wide group, comprising more than 80 companies.

The sort of technology only Avon can offer. Avon Industrial Polymers. Makers of the toughest skirt systems in the world.

AVON

Avon Hovercraft Skirts

Avon Industrial Polymers (Melksham) Limited
Melksham, Wiltshire SN12 8AA. Telex 44142.

Hovercraft Skirts, Flexible Containers for Fuels and Fluids, Diving Suits and Inflatable Plugs for Jet Engines.

increased by 70% while its operating costs have risen by only 15%. Seaspeed's second SR.N4, *The Princess Margaret*, is undergoing similar conversion to Mk III standard and will be returned from BHC as a Super 4 in time for the 1979 summer season.

SEDAM's impressive-looking N 500-02 Naviplane, owned by SNCF, began operating in conjunction with British Rail's SR.N4 service under the Seaspeed banner on 5 July 1978. Unfortunately, its introduction was accompanied by a variety of teething problems affecting its skirt, engines and control system, but these should have been remedied in time for the 1979 peak season. The SNCF board has taken the decision in principle to order N 500-03 and an option is also believed to have been taken on N 500-04.

When British Rail's SR.N4 *The Princess Margaret* rejoins the fleet in June 1979, Seaspeed's three hovercraft will provide an annual passenger-carrying capacity for 3 million passengers and 400,000 vehicles. To accommodate the increased size of the craft and increasing traffic a new purpose-built terminal complex was opened in 1978 occupying 15 acres of reclaimed land between the Prince of Wales Pier and the North Pier in Western Docks, Dover.

Further evidence of the success of the cross-Channel hovercraft service was provided during 1978 by Hoverlloyd's Chief Executive, James Hodgson, who said that his company was operating at 'very near capacity'. He revealed that Hoverlloyd faces the prospect of a declining share of cross-Channel traffic due to lack of capacity. For this reason the company is to begin a programme of adding craft year by year, building up to about 10 in the late 1980s. Hoverlloyd reported a profit of £1·5 million for 1977 and a far bigger return is anticipated for 1978.

Similar successes, but on a more modest scale, are reported by commercial hovercraft operators elsewhere, including the British Isles, Portugal, Japan and Hong Kong. These services are operated in the main by SR.N6s, HM.216s and 218s and MV-PP5s. The Hong Kong and Yaumati Ferry Co, probably the largest private ferry operator in the world, employs, in conjunction with its conventional ferries, a fleet of eight Hovermarine sidewall hovercraft, which carry annually about 1·3 million passengers. Two more craft are due for delivery during 1979, providing ten hovercraft and making it the largest fleet of commercial hovercraft in use outside the Soviet Union. On 17 November 1978 the company opened the first hovercraft service between Hong Kong and Canton, People's Republic of China, using two HM.2s. Eventually up to five of these craft will be employed on this route. A licence has been received from China to operate this service for up to five years.

Hovermarine has become one of the world's biggest hovercraft builders. It has completed 50 craft and has another 10 on order. Apart from Hong Kong, fleets of HM.2s are operated in Brazil, the Philippines, Portugal, Venezuela and the Netherlands. Individual HM.2s are operated in many other countries. Under active development is the 309-ton Hovermarine 600 series Hoverfreighter and car ferry and during 1978 a deep cushion concept research and development programme was initiated. Work on the 280-passenger Hovermarine HM.5 was re-started early in 1979 and the company hopes that the prototype will begin its trials by the middle of the year. It is expected that the first HM.5 will be delivered to Hong Kong. Sales prospects for the craft in the 1980s are said to be 'very strong'.

Another part of the world in which increasing attention is being focused on hovercraft is the People's Republic of China. Research programmes have been underway since 1970, and at least seven prototypes have been built, one of which is being operated out of Chungking on a scheduled passenger ferry service. While China's immediate plans appear to include importing craft to meet its civil and military needs, there is no doubt that in the long term it will undertake the construction of its own designs. Priority is being given to vehicles of 10 to 55 tons which are needed for a variety of military and civil applications, including the operation of fast passenger ferry services over river networks with route distances of up to 240 to 320km (150 to 200 miles).

Substantial growth in commercial activities is also reported from the Soviet Union. Experience with the Zarnitsa, Orion and Rassvet sidewall hovercraft has been so encouraging that the Central Scientific Research Institute has produced designs for a series of sidewall hoverfreighters, the first of which is likely to be of similar configuration to the Turist, a mixed-traffic craft for 100 to 120 passengers and 15 cars. Soviet designers are closely examining the possibility of building large sea-going freighters employing sidewalls, presumably along the lines of projected SES craft. Forecasts have been made within the Soviet Union that hovercraft with a cargo-carrying capacity of 5,000 to 10,000 tons and a speed of 100 knots might well see commercial service in the early decades of the next century.

Military hovercraft

Confirmation of the importance attached to hovercraft by the Soviet armed forces for amphibious operations was seen in the announcement in 1978 that the Soviet Navy's latest and largest amphibious landing ship, the Ivan Rogov, is capable of carrying three Gus amphibious assault ACVs. Each of these craft can carry a fully-armed platoon onto a landing beach at speeds of up to 92km/h (57mph). Production of Gus continues and it is thought that 30 to 35 are in service with the Soviet Marine Infantry. Gus and the 270-ton Aist amphibious logistic supply craft are the only two military hovercraft in the world in series production. Both types are seen in increasing numbers, especially off East Germany's island of Rügen, a Warsaw Pact training and testing zone. In exercises held in conjunction with Polish and East German marines Aist has delivered main battle tanks, self-propelled guns and mechanised infantry to beach-heads. About fifteen Aists are now in service. Capable of crossing sea areas, bogs, rivers and canals previously considered natural defensive areas, Aist adds considerable weight to the mobility, flexibility and striking power of the forces of the Warsaw Pact countries in the Baltic.

The first nation to recognise the potential of the hovercraft for a variety of military roles was the United Kingdom. But despite the commendable initiative displayed by the British defence authorities in the 1960s, when the ACV was assessed for anti-submarine warfare, fishery protection and logistic support duties, no government policy on military hovercraft development has become evident. Even the current mine-countermeasures trials, which have been underway for seven years, have failed to secure a craft requirement.

The continued indifference to the hovercraft within government circles is due largely to the failure of a small number of sceptics in key ministerial positions to recognise it as a high-dividend investment instead of an area of government expenditure. In stark contrast to the no-policy attitude in the United Kingdom, the requirement by NATO in Europe for versatile, amphibious vehicles has never been greater. Its existing amphibious craft are either obsolete or inadequate for today's demands, especially in the light of increased Warsaw Pact activities in the Baltic area. It is astonishing that despite the vital need by the United Kingdom's partners in NATO, the British Ministry of Defence has not been more active in encouraging new designs which will meet NATO's needs in the North Sea and Baltic waters for mine countermeasure, patrol and surveillance duties. The availability of such designs would undoubtedly lead to their adoption by NATO countries in both Northern and Southern Europe in the drive for the standardisation of craft and equipment. In this way the British funding of both the design and construction of suitable craft would be more than recouped by the sale of identical craft, both within NATO and possibly to other countries with which the United Kingdom has co-operative defence agreements.

Although most of the Soviet Navy's hovercraft activity so far has been in the Baltic region along NATO's northern flank, it is not unlikely that in the foreseeable future they will appear in the Mediterranean. Such a development might easily require a military hovercraft presence there by NATO. At the moment the only NATO country with a hovercraft in the Mediterranean is Italy, which has a single SR.N6 based on Venice.

Advocates of the surface effect ship (SES) in the US Navy are having their problems, too. Prospects for a continuation of design and engineering work on the 3,000-ton 3KSES are certainly not as bright as they might be, and recent reports suggest that it could soon be a victim of the Carter Administration's war on inflation. A last-minute appeal against killing the programme has been sent to Harold Brown, the US Defence Secretary, by Admiral Elmo R Zumwalt, the dynamic former Chief of Naval Operations to whom credit is generally given for initiating the concept. The 100-knot SES programme, which is a key element in the US Navy's long term planning to improve fleet effectiveness, has many supporters, both in the US Navy and in Congress. The Defence Secretary's chief criticism of the 3KSES is that the US Navy had not made a solid case for a mission for it. The truth is that the 3KSES was designed principally as a sea going research platform, which would enable the SES concept to be tested in a number of military configurations, one of which was that of an anti-submarine-warfare frigate for convoy escort duties. But, as Zumwalt pointed out in his letter, the speed of the SES, even in this early configuration, would lend itself not only to the effective utilisation of short take-off and landing (STOL) aircraft, but also to large remotely-piloted vehicles (RPVs). RPVs, he stated, could be recovered by the SES at an essentially zero speed differential. Among the naval missions possible for such a

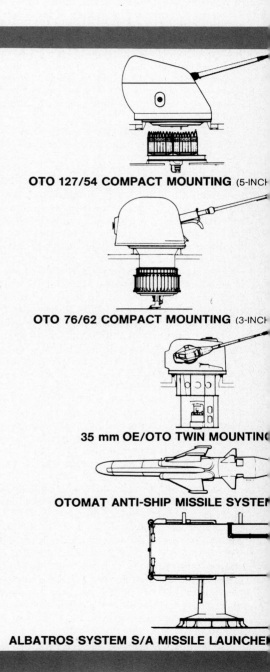

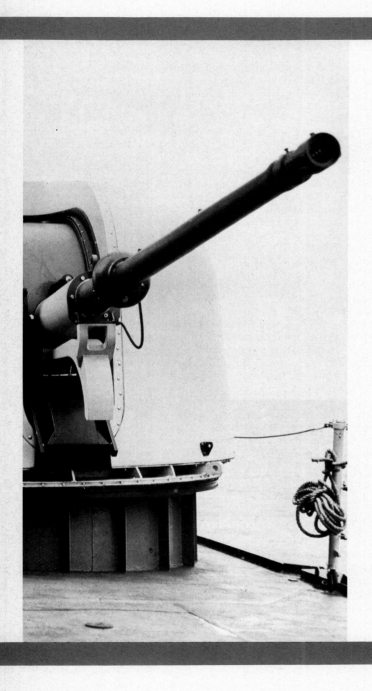

vessel equipped with large RPVs are surface-subsurface surveillance, airborne early warning, over-the-horizon targetry, reconnaissance and damage assessment. Weapon delivery with the RPV-SES combination would be via cruise missiles targeted by the RPV employing the surface-launched/air-targeted (SLAT) concept. In the light of Zumwalt's letter, and not forgetting the growing Soviet interest in large seagoing SES designs, affirmed in a statement by Admiral of the Fleet Sergey Georgievich Gorshkov, it seems just possible that the 3KSES might still have a chance of making the 1980 defence budget.

In the meantime a growing number of smaller navies is turning to small and medium-size hovercraft to replace ageing patrol boats and destroyers. Many of the craft will be armed with anti-ship missiles which will enable them to face very much larger displacement vessels on equal terms. Considerable interest is being shown by the navies of the emerging countries in the BH.7, the SR.N4, Hovermarine's M527, M533 and M539 and Vosper Thornycroft's new 18-metre fast patrol craft.

Hydrofoils

Hydrofoil operations continue to expand the world over. Among the major developments of 1978 were a spate of new Jetfoil sales, including a fast patrol variant for the Royal Navy; the announcement by Boeing of a project for a 600-ton hydrofoil car ferry; the extension of Supramar's design range and the introduction of two new hydrofoils by the Soviet Union: one a 400-ton fast patrol craft, the other a Kometa replacement.

Jetfoil sales, which started 1978 at ten, are reported to have risen to nineteen. Contracts have been signed for fifteen of these craft, and commitments have been made for a further four. Ten Jetfoils are currently in service, five with Far East Hydrofoil Co, Hong Kong; two with Turismo Margarita CA, Venezuela; two with Sado Kisen Kaisha, Japan and one with P&O Jet Ferries, England. During 1978 Boeing announced an order by B + I Lines of Dublin, Ireland, for a Jetfoil to operate between Dublin and Liverpool starting in April 1980; and an order from Jetlink Ferries Ltd, England, for a craft to operate between Brighton and Dieppe. Both operators have options on second craft.

In addition, the Royal Navy placed an order for the first Jetfoil fast patrol hydrofoil for use in fisheries protection in the North Sea. Designated Patrol Hydrofoil 0001, PH01, it is being built on the commercial Jetfoil production line. Externally the craft is similar to the projected Offshore Jetfoil in which the upper passenger deck has been removed to provide an open load deck. In this instance the deck will be occupied by two semi-inflatable dinghies on davits. It will displace 117 tons and carry light weapons. Power for foilborne operation will be provided by two Allison gas-turbines, in addition to which two Allison diesels will be installed for hullborne operation, giving increasing on-station time and overall endurance. Delivery is scheduled for October 1979.

Jetfoil 011, which was built for Sado Kisen and launched in June 1978, was the first of five Jetfoil Model 929-115s under construction. These incorporate a number of design improvements which, according to Boeing, add significantly to performance, payload and reliability. Trials with the first two craft of the new series indicate that their performance is equal to or better than that predicted.

By 20 August 1978 Jetfoils had logged 178,389,734 passenger miles during 41,873 hours underway with a dispatch reliability of 98·6%. Discussions for future sales are being held with potential operators in Scandinavia and the Mediterranean. Jetfoils are also being considered for offshore oil rig support in the North Sea.

During 1978 Boeing submitted a proposal for a 600-ton hydrofoil passenger/car ferry to a number of operators. The biggest hydrofoil yet designed for commercial operation, it is envisaged in two configurations: the 9BB-600, a short-haul version, and the 9BB-601, a long-haul auto/passenger ferry. Deck arrangements vary considerably between the two, but both are based on a catamaran hull configuration, are waterjet-propelled and have retractable, tandem foil systems. Vehicle loading arrangements include through-loading on the main deck and further vehicle capacity on laterally-hinged, variable outer extensions at A deck level, on both sides of the superstructure, permitting both outer extensions to be lowered and raised as required for loading and off-loading in both directions. Maximum payload of the 9BB-601 would be 100 cars and 400 passengers. Length overall would be 54 metres, maximum beam 19·5 metres, and draft, foils retracted, 2·5 metres.

Apart from the construction of further Jetfoils and the first of the five 235-tonne PHM production craft, Boeing has also undertaken the conceptual design of an 890-tonne hydrofoil frigate for the US Navy's Advanced Naval Vehicles Concepts (ANVCE) office. Designed for task force and convoy protection, it is regarded as the smallest practical size for a vessel likely to be capable of undertaking all the tasks required for sea control duties. In addition it would give the US Navy an opportunity to study the virtues of a craft of this size and its ability to undertake its own anti-submarine attacks without the aid of helicopters. The project, designated HYD-7, has variable-geometry foils which provide it with a normal maximum speed in sub-cavitating mode of 50 knots and a sprint speed, in super-cavitating mode, of around 75 knots. A triple mode operational capability is therefore available; hullborne, with a speed of 16 knots and a range of 1,450n miles; foilborne, sub-cavitating mode with a speed in excess of 45 knots and a range of 1,400n miles and finally, foilborne, supercavitating mode, with a speed of 75 knots and a range of 850n miles. Payload would be between 110 and 150 tonnes, depending on weapons carried.

Restricted budgets, inflation and a general manpower shortage have prompted an increasing number of navies to adopt the 'more and smaller' policy for their sea defences. Development of the naval hydrofoil over the past decade has been far more successful than anyone expected and it is now regarded as an attractive investment. 50-knot missile-armed hydrofoils cost less than the frigates and destroyers they replace and, in addition to being much faster, second generation craft, because of their auto-stabilisation systems, reduce their speed only slightly in the higher sea states. Their high speed simplifies patrolling long coastlines and the availability of greater numbers provides additional firing points in the event of a conflict. Cost effectiveness studies conducted by the US Navy show the PHM, for example, to be superior to P-3C aircraft, carrier aircraft and surface ships, such as the FFG, in performing close-surveillance and quick-reaction/counter-strike missions. Also, because of its all-weather, high-speed capability, it can perform anti-submarine missions that no conventional surface ships can execute. Senior officers of the US Navy report that the PHM has converted many of their colleagues who were unable to conceive the tremendous improvements that hydrofoils offer in operating capability or believed that such technology could provide an effective and reliable system suitable for operating with the US Fleet. "Almost to a man, such sceptics have undergone a complete change of views when actually confronted with the operating hardware at sea", says one official report. During 1978 PHM-1 Pegasus was deployed to Hawaii for extended Fleet exercises. It is anticipated that it will be transferred to the Atlantic for operations in Europe during 1979.

A second military hydrofoil in series production in the USA is a variant of the Grumman Flagstaff Mk II which has been ordered by the Israeli Navy. Capable of 52 knots, this new model is designed for a variety of naval and military roles and can be fitted with a wide range of weapons. Typical armament would include missiles of the Harpoon and Gabriel type, an Emerlec 30mm gun forward and two 20mm cannon mounts in port and starboard gun tubs behind the bridge. In addition to the original order, thought to be for four craft, Israel has acquired a licence to build a further batch of six or more Flagstaffs at the Israel Shipyards, Haifa. It is understood that Israeli craft will also be available for export, although the markets will be subject to approval by the US government.

The United Kingdom and Israel are the latest countries to order naval hydrofoils and there are indications that at least another seven will soon follow suit, among them Australia, Canada, France, Japan, Denmark, the Netherlands, and Sweden. Increasing numbers of emergent countries are being supplied with Hu Chwan (White Swan) hydrofoil torpedo-boats by the People's Republic of China, which is also in series production in Romania.

Among the latest hydrofoils to be introduced to the military and para-military market is a range of Supramar craft, some of which are adapted from the company's highly successful commercial designs. In addition to the Supramar PAT 20, MT 80 and MT 250, described in earlier editions, Supramar is offering the following:

PAT 70, a military version of the PT 50 Mk II.

NAT 85, a missile-armed fast patrol boat derived from the PTS 75 Mk III.

NAT 90, an alternative model to the NAT 85, with waterjet propulsion and fully retracting foils.

NAT 190, a 180-ton fast strike craft variant of the PTS 150 Mk III. Weapons would include Exocet MM 38 missiles fired from three launchers and two 40mm Bofors L/70 automatic twin mounts.

Supramar's licensees include Vosper Private Limited, the Singapore-based associate of Vosper Limited, Supramar Pacific Shipbuilding Limited, Hong Kong, and Hitachi Zosen, Japan.

Further evidence of the importance being attached to the hyd-

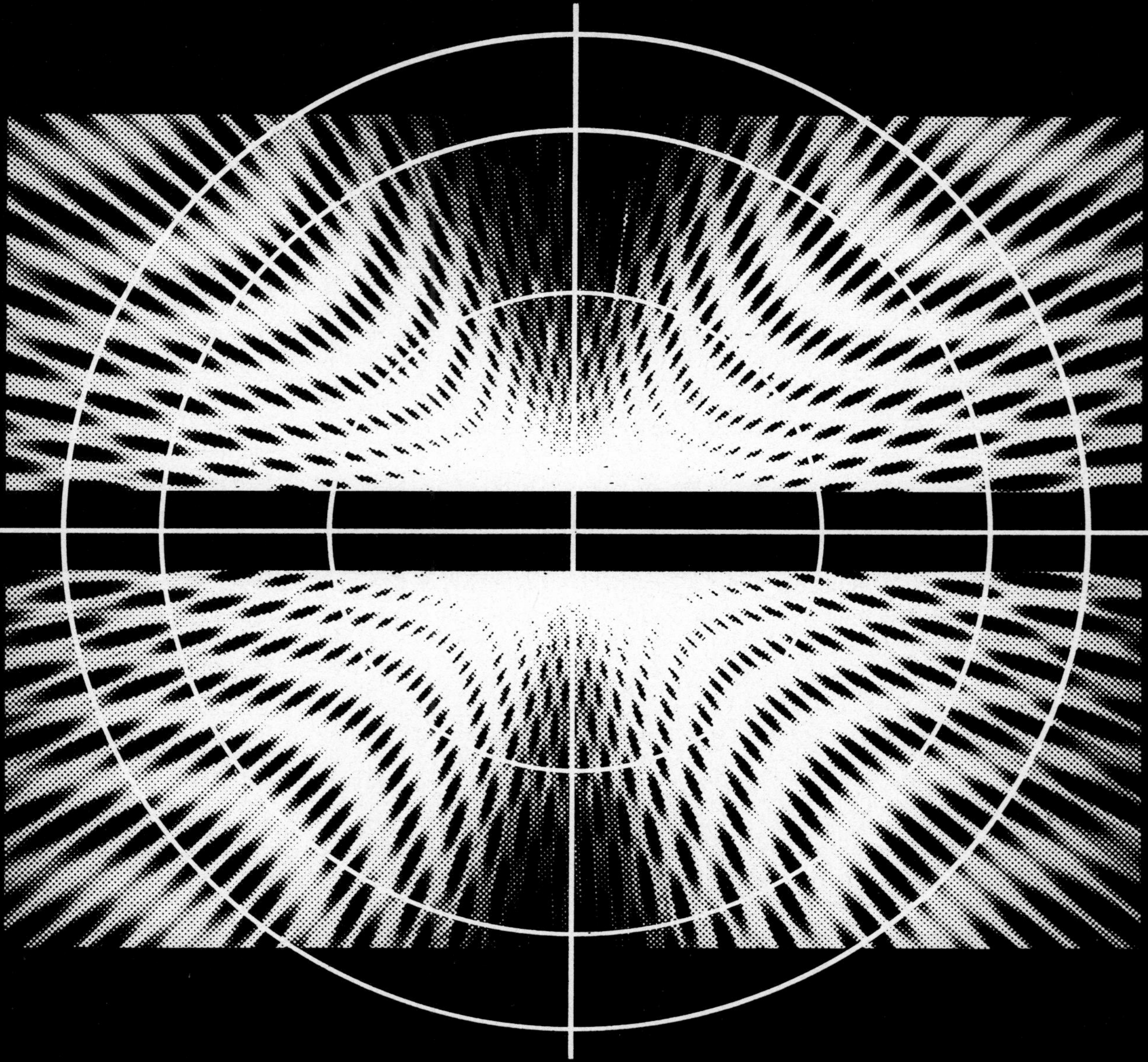

rofoil for defence applications by the Soviet Union is the appearance of yet another large naval craft, this time a fast patrol boat, known by the NATO codename Babochka (Butterfly). With an overall length of 50 metres (164 feet) and an all-up weight of 400 tonnes, Babochka is the biggest military hydrofoil in operational service anywhere in the world. Evidently designed for anti-submarine warfare duties, its power for foilborne operation is supplied by three gas-turbines thought to be comparable in size to the 28,000bhp Rolls-Royce Marine Olympus. Judging from its size the craft is almost certainly intended for operation on the open seas. Few details of the foil system are discernable from published photographs, but it may well be of surface-piercing design. The main armament appears to be anti-submarine torpedoes in two triple mounts forward of the superstructure and two 30mm L/65 fully-automatic twin mounts for anti-aircraft defence.

The Soviet Union is continuing the development of its range of commercial hydrofoils. One of the most successful designs, the 60-ton Kometa, has been exported to eleven countries. By early 1978 export orders totalled 52. Inter-Governmental Maritime Consultative Organisation (IMCO) recommendations on fire safety are being taken into account which will simplify certification by the regulatory organisations in the countries importing these craft in the future. At present the standard Kometa-M seats 116 to 120, but because of the additional weight of air-conditioning equipment the tropicalised Kometa-MT seats only 102. One of the features of the latest models is the relocation of the engine room aft to reduce the noise in the passenger saloons and the employment of a vee-drive instead of the existing inclined shaft. The arrangement is expected to be similar to that on the Voskhod-2. The revised deck configuration allows more seats to be fitted.

These modifications are also incorporated in the recently announced Kometa derivative, the Albatros. The prototype of this 150-seater is due to be launched at the Poti shipyard on the Black Sea early in 1979. Two newly-designed diesels will give the craft a top speed in excess of 50 knots. Among the various innovations introduced are a new foil system with automatic lift control, the use of new materials in the hull structure and a more rational cabin layout allowing the seating capacity to be increased by more than 40%. Overall dimensions will remain exactly the same as those of the Kometa-M.

Demand for hydrofoils is likely to continue into the foreseeable future. Despite the world's current economic uncertainties the future of these craft has never been more encouraging.

Roy McLeavy
January 1979

ACKNOWLEDGEMENTS

The Editor would like to express his gratitude to the following correspondents for their readiness to supply information and their many helpful suggestions.

Baron Hanns von Schertel, Supramar; R Wheeler, G D Elsley and Mike McSorley, British Hovercraft Corporation; Dr Leopoldo Rodriquez and Giovanni Falzea, Cantiere Navaltecnica; Donald J Norton, Bell Aerospace Textron; Alan Bingham, Vosper Thornycroft; Peter Mantle; Capt T M Barry, USN; Dr William R Bertelsen, Bertelsen Manufacturing Company; L Flammand, Bertin & Cie; M W Beardsley, Skimmers Inc; Franklin A Dobson, Dobson Products Co; Nigel Seale, Coelacanth Gemco; T Akao, Hitachi Shipbuilding and Engineering; Neil MacDonald, Hovercraft Development Ltd; R V Taylor, Taylorcraft Transport Pty; A Bordat, Société Nationale Industrielle Aérospatiale; David Staveley, Missionary Aviation Fellowship; Audoin de Dampierre, Dubigeon-Normandie; C D J Bland and P H Winter, Air Vehicles Ltd; Andre Clodong, United Aircraft of Canada; Leo D Stolk, Stolkraft Pty Ltd; Chuck Srock, Scorpion Inc; Richard Catling, Rolls-Royce (1971) Ltd; W G Eggington and Jacqueline Jenerette, Rohr Industries Inc; B H Wright, Rolair; Kenneth Cook, Hydrofoils Inc; Masahiro Mino, Nihon University; Mike Pinder, Pindair Ltd; Georges Hennebutte, Ets Georges Hennebutte; Charles G Pieroth, Grumman Aerospace, Marine Division; C F de Jersey, De Havilland Aircraft of Canada; Robert Bateman, P B Dakan and Bob Edwards, Boeing Marine Systems; Milton Bade, Arctic Engineers & Constructors; Ralph Wortmann, AiResearch Mfg; Christopher Fitzgerald, Neoteric Engineering; Masaya Nakamura, Nakamura Seisakusho Co Ltd; R D Hunt, Geoff Parkes and C H Harcourt, Hoverlift Systems Ltd; H F Lentge, Seaglide Ltd; M Ishibashi, Mitsui Engineering & Shipbuilding; R C Gilbert, Air Cushion Equipment (1976) Ltd; Fred Herman, Aerojet-General Corporation; Kip McCollum, Osprey Hovercraft Ltd; D G Kinner, Mears Construction Ltd; Syoichi Fukumitsu, Kanazawa Institute of Technology; Donald E Kenney, Bell-Halter; Marilyn Walsh, Aero-Go Inc; Jukka Tervamäki; R J Windt, Universal Hovercraft; Esko Hietanen, Pintaliitäjäpalvelu; Jalmari Lukkarila; Paul W Esterle, Venture Aero-Marine.

Finally he would like to acknowledge the tremendous assistance by David Rose of Jane's Yearbooks, by Erica Lock for typing the manuscript and to the production team, headed by Glynis Long, for their enthusiasm and hard work.

Grateful acknowledgement is also made for the use of extracts from the following papers and features;

The PHM-Surface Warfare Ship Technology Takes a Step Forward, Captain Joseph N Shrader, USN and Cdr Karl M Duff, USN.

SES Decision Pending, L Edgar Prina, Editor Emeritus, *Sea Power,* *November 1978*

Why PHM? Further Studies on Roles and Missions, J T S Coates, R G Merritt and T C Weston, Boeing Marine Systems, Seattle, Washington.

Transport in the Future; Things to Come, V S Molyarchuk, DSc, Mir Publishers, Moscow.

CONTRIBUTED PAPERS

A worldwide hovercraft appreciation

by Neil MacDonald, Market Research & Route Analyst,
Hovercraft Development Limited

(Based on a paper presented by the author to the United Kingdom Hovercraft Society)

Mention the word 'hovercraft' in a typical British railway carriage and there is a strong likelihood that most of the occupants will associate it with noise, skirts and day trips to the Isle of Wight or France! Despite this very few of the occupants are likely to have travelled by hovercraft. Carry out a similar exercise in German, Canadian or Japanese railway carriages and the response is likely to be zero!

Disappointing as these observations may be, they demonstrate the wide variation in knowledge of the hovercraft and show that despite having a better awareness than most of its existence, even the British public has rather less personal experience of travelling by hovercraft than one might expect. Once you look beyond Britain the position becomes even more obvious and there is no doubt that large areas of the world, particularly those that could make the most use of its versatile qualities, have only a slight awareness that the hovercraft exists at all! However, it is also necessary to realise that whereas the aircraft is approaching a time span of eighty years, the hovercraft is much younger. In fact the first man-carrying hovercraft, SR.N1 made its first flight only in June 1959, less than twenty years ago! What might we have expected from the aircraft industry twenty years after the Wright brothers' flight?

Indeed, some observers might comment that in many ways the aircraft industry was lucky in being 'blessed' with a major conflict (World War 1) which showed very clearly the role that even the early aircraft might play in warfare and this, in turn, provided some additional incentive for their development. There is little doubt that without such recognition of its capabilities the aircraft industry might have tried for many years to gain acceptance from governments the world over. The hovercraft, by comparison, has featured little in major conflicts. This might have resulted in its potential gaining less recognition than might have been the case if, for example, a full-scale conflict had occurred in the Far East which had necessitated the use of amphibious and high-speed hovercraft for assault or support duties. Hovercraft were employed in a minor role in the Viet-Nam affair, but probably due to the lack of a full appreciation of their capabilities and the unfamiliarity of the environment, were not a major influence on the activities there and their record would appear to have been unremarkable. Looking back on that event it is all too easy to see where the craft failed and how better use might have achieved a far greater reputation for hovercraft in the military sphere. Unfortunately, such hindsight does not offer much compensation and there are too many instances where one might have placed greater effort in certain directions knowing the eventual outcome or likely outcome of events such as Viet-Nam. Without becoming embroiled in this area, the same could probably be said of the Egypt-Israel conflict and the temptation is even greater to suggest that with the wider application of air cushion vehicles of different types the outcome of the affair might have been different. Interestingly, since the last conflict in that area the Egyptians have equipped with a handful of SR.N6 craft and the Israelis with two much smaller SH.2 Mk 5s. The growth of interest (which seems to be continuing) by Arab states in the use of hovercraft of the amphibious variety, might be interpreted by some specialists that the hovercraft is seen as a more influential *future* military force than in the past.

Quotes on hovercraft abound and it is sometimes difficult to refer to the vehicle without recourse to some comment made by an Admiral in the US Navy, of the Soviet Fleet or well-established advocates of the vehicle; I cannot profess to be any different and offer the following comments which have been made within my hearing: "The hovercraft is a solution looking for a problem", "the hovercraft is the best thing since sliced bread", "those who most need hovercraft are those who can least afford them". Reconciling these quotations is difficult and quite obviously will depend where one stands in such a debate. Perhaps the only way of getting at the facts is to look at the achievements to date of the industry and see whether these match the statements made about it!

A question which is frequently asked concerns the size of the world hovercraft industry. This can be answered in a number of ways. In terms of the total 'hovercraft population', figures suggest that there are probably between 2,000 and 3,000 hovercraft of various types in existence. These include about 400 large and medium-sized hovercraft and hoverplatforms. The remainder consist of privately-used craft of one or two seats. Another way is to calculate the turnover of the different companies. This is extremely difficult and cannot be accurately defined for some companies where the major effort is on military hovercraft.

There can be little doubt about the extent of Britain's influence on the world's view of hovercraft. As a country it has not only borne the brunt of development work in technical terms but also the equally complex and time-consuming tasks of defining its legal status, being neither ship nor aircraft. Even today its attitudes to hovercraft seem to be watched with interest by countries at a formative stage in the development of their own industry. The old adage about it being preferable to be second rather than first would seem to be especially applicable and thought-provoking.

Britain's service to the hovercraft can be viewed in different ways. There is, of course, that of providing the initial products from which customers from abroad gain their first operational experience of applying hovercraft to different tasks. Such sales, and the sales support or training schemes which accompany them, have earned this country many millions of pounds. My own estimate, based on constant pounds, suggests that the figure is probably in excess of £50 million. In addition, Britain would appear to supply 85 to 90% of the world's civil requirements with the exception of the Soviet Union. A very high proportion of military hovercraft also emanates from Britain or employs substantial technical expertise from British firms, which further strengthens the influence of British experience in this field. Additionally, some key components such as engines and skirts might continue to be supplied to hovercraft customers for a number of years after the delivery of the craft in the form of spares or replacements, and so bring in further earnings. Licensing agreements with overseas manufacturers whose craft or products employ patented design features, particularly relating to skirts, also continue to provide useful foreign currency earnings to Britain.

Next I should like to identify the main areas of hovercraft manufacture, research and development around the world. It is important to realise that although British-made products might currently comprise large proportions of the world's fleets, this position could change dramatically in future years if some of the overseas activities continue to expand and begin to offer competitively priced and technically superior designs.

Main centres of hovercraft (or ACV) production and research and development activities

United Kingdom
United States of America
USSR
Canada
Japan
France
China

The countries shown above indicate that interest in hovercraft is spread widely although some nations have a greater interest in possible military applications of the hovercraft than commercial production. This is particularly relevant in the case of the United States of America and the Soviet Union, where significant amounts of money are believed to be currently allocated to programmes of research and development leading to military designs. These activities will be discussed in greater detail at a later stage.

The ferry business

The first commercial hovercraft service began in Britain in July 1962 between Rhyl and Wallasey and lasted eight weeks. It used the VA.3 hovercraft made by Vickers and was intended to evaluate the craft in the passenger carrying role. A total of 3,760 fare-paying passengers was carried and some valuable lessons were learned.

Since then hovercraft have operated passenger carrying services in many areas of the world. A substantial number of the earlier services no longer exist and, perhaps with hindsight, should never have been operated. To take new hovercraft and try to employ them on highly competitive routes against well-proven displacement craft is not a wise thing to do, particularly if the craft happen to be first generation designs with problems still to be solved. None the less, this did happen and where these early services were set up overseas the problems were increased.

The present operators of commercial hovercraft services number about thirty and between them employ in the region of 264 craft. Many of these craft are operated on river networks in the Soviet Union where the sea state requirements are far less demanding than for more exposed areas of water such as the Solent.

Table 1

Commercial hovercraft (30 September 1978)

	No of craft
Bolivia	2
Brazil	4
France	3
Greece	1
Hong Kong	8
India	1
Japan	14
New Zealand	1
Nigeria	3
Philippines	3
Portugal	4
USSR	200+
United Kingdom	15
USA	1
Uruguay	1
Venezuela	3
World total	264+

This table serves to illustrate the spread of craft to a number of regions where hovercraft had not previously been used; the developing countries in

Africa, the Far East and South America have been quick to recognise the potential even if the craft which they have chosen cannot offer the fully amphibious capabilities generally associated with hovercraft.

Some of the more advanced nations have been unable to establish successful services for a combination of complex reasons. As a result we see that the USA, which might well have been expected to be at the forefront of their use, has negligible involvement whereas the Soviet Union has shot ahead. Other areas such as the People's Republic of China are displaying great interest in hovercraft of various types, rigid sidewall and fully amphibious, for use on their extensive river networks and coastal routes, although reliable information on the extent of their present activity suggests only one or two craft may exist in this role.

I do not intend to try to describe in detail any of the current hovercraft ferry operations. To attempt to do so would inevitably lead to this paper becoming much longer and covering ground which others have travelled before. However, some of the most significant should be identified with passing comments made about their status.

The first must be the cross-Channel operations of Hoverlloyd Ltd and British Rail Hovercraft Ltd (BR Seaspeed), the latter with the French National Railways (SNCF) as a partner. In what is widely accepted to be a very competitive market, the two companies have managed to generate traffic as well as capture business from existing ship ferries operated across the Straits of Dover.

Hoverlloyd has probably made the biggest impact: in 1977 it carried over 1·1 million passengers and 211,000 vehicles and is reported to have made profits of about £1·4 million during the year with its four SR.N4 Mk 2 craft. To reach these figures on a new route such as Ramsgate/Calais after only nine years is an amazing feat and one of which that operator is justly proud. High reliability for the craft has also been a major achievement.

Another impressive operation is that of the Hong Kong & Yaumati Ferry Co (HYF) which has a fleet of eight rigid sidewall Hovermarine 216 and 218 craft. These craft have established a fine reputation among the Hong Kong commuters and are employed in conjunction with HYF's other ferry craft which in 1977 carried an estimated 130 million passengers, probably the largest private ferry operation in the world. Hovercraft operations began in 1974 and the annual carryings by Hovermarine 216 and 218 craft are believed to be about 1·3 million passengers. Two more craft will be delivered to HYF in 1979, bringing the operation up to a total of ten hovercraft and making it the largest fleet of commercial hovercraft in use. A new route from Hong Kong to Canton, was started by HYF in November 1978, heralding further expansion of the fleet. Nigeria and the Philippines are other locations for successful use of rigid sidewall craft of the Hovermarine design and find parallels in South America. The future trends in selling these craft will, I am confident, be towards developing countries where the need for a flexible yet reliable water transport system exists. In some regions these requirements may be necessary to cope with the exploitation of the countries' tourist potential and for others their plans for new developments and townships.

Finally a few facts and figures on this topic. My own estimates suggest that since the first service began in 1962, somewhere in the region of 27 million people have travelled on hovercraft and each year about 7 million more passengers are carried as well as 300,000 vehicles. Neither of these figures includes carryings for Soviet hovercraft services since statistics from that country are difficult to verify.

The military potential

This is an extremely controversial area of hovercraft activity and one that can be traced back to the early days of the invention when Christopher Cockerell undertook his rounds of the different British government departments. Sales of hovercraft for military (or paralitary) applications constitute a high proportion of exports by British makers and there are indications that this trend will continue into the future.

The principal uses of hovercraft in the military role are broadly:

- Amphibious assault and logistics (AAL)
- Mine countermeasures (MCM)
- Anti-submarine warfare (ASW)
- Coastal patrol (CP)

Table 2

Principal military hovercraft

	No and type of craft
Egypt	3 SR.N6
France	2 N102
Iran	8 SR.N6
	6 BH.7
Israel	2 SH.2/5
Italy	1 SR.N6
Saudi Arabia	8 SR.N6
USSR	15+ Aist
	30+ Gus
United Kingdom	3 SR.N6
	1 BH.7
USA	2 LACV-30
	2 AALC Jeff
	2 SES-100

Compiling new information on military hovercraft activities without resorting to the use of unpublished material is rather difficult. The above table shows the main operators of military craft and the size of their respective fleets. In many ways it is supplemented by table 3 which lists the principal applications by countries' craft and role.

Table 3

	Principal role
Egypt	Coastal patrol and minelaying
France	ASW/Coastal patrol
Iran	Coastal patrol and amphibious assault
Israel	Logistic support
Italy	Coastal patrol
Saudi Arabia	Coastal patrol
USSR	Amphibious assault and coastal patrol
United Kingdom	Mine countermeasures trials
USA	Amphibious assault and anti-submarine warfare

In addition to the nations shown in these tables, military research and development activities are believed to be underway in the People's Republic of China and some Eastern Bloc countries. China has good reason to investigate the use of hovercraft. Its long coastline and reliance on major ports for much of its international trading means that minesweeping/minehunting hovercraft would be a logical use, together with hovercraft for river and coastal patrol duties. The Eastern Bloc has, for fairly obvious reasons, been closely concerned with development of the Soviet Aist and Gus.

Canada has also shown an interest in using fully amphibious hovercraft for defensive tasks and in 1978 the Canadian Armed Forces ordered from Air Vehicles a small AV Tiger hovercraft for evaluation. This craft will be delivered early in 1979. Three Pindair Skima 12 hovercraft are being operated in Oman for a variety of security duties and have been in use since autumn 1977. These activities are not included in tables 2 and 3.

Additional purchases of military hovercraft will be announced in the next year or so, and the prime candidates are countries in the Middle East and South America. These regions offer great opportunities and there is good reason to believe that British manufacturers, particularly the British Hovercraft Corporation, will be at the head of the field. BHC has already supplied the craft for Iran, Saudi Arabia, Egypt and Italy as well as for the British Ministry of Defence and has acquired an unrivalled knowledge of military applications of fully amphibious hovercraft.

The USA has long had plans for building large rigid sidewall Surface Effect Ships (SES) of between 2,000 and 5,000 tons. As a result of trials with two 100-ton SES test craft, the objectives of the programme have been refined and the current plan is to construct a prototype 3,000-ton SES (invariably referred to as the 3KSES). The detailed design work for such a craft has virtually been completed. If evaluation of the 3KSES proves encouraging the next step will be a 5,000-ton SES. One of the delays with this project has been securing approval for spending large amounts of money on this prototype; in December 1976 it was announced that Rohr Marine Inc had been awarded a contract worth US$159·9 million (then about £100 million) for the design of the 3KSES with the possibility of the firm securing a further contract valued at US$155·7 million (or £97 million) for the construction and testing of the 3KSES if it was decided to proceed. Over the past year or so the funding of the programme has been under scrutiny by different Congressional committees and reductions have been suggested. The present position is still rather unclear but approval of US$93 million (£49 million) for SES research and development in fiscal year 1979 appears to have been given. Other programmes of work are in progress in the USA related to amphibious assault and logistic support projects using fully amphibious hovercraft.

Soviet hovercraft activities have been the subject of much speculation over the years and evidence of the Soviet Union's using hovercraft for military tasks has appeared. Perhaps the most significant is the Soviet Union's largest hovercraft, Aist, which is believed to be deployed in Eastern Europe and the Baltic. This craft compares in size to the BHC SR.N4 Mk 2, with a length of about 150 feet and a beam of 60 feet. In terms of weight it is a good deal heavier: estimates place its loaded weight at 260 to 270 tons (compared with SR.N4 Mk 2's 200 tons). Reports suggest that fifteen or more craft have been built and they are capable of carrying tracked or wheeled vehicles (bow and stern loading doors are fitted) as well as troops. They would thus seem to be versatile additions to the Soviet Navy. Thirty or more of the smaller 27-ton Gus craft are also deployed.

Admiral Gorshkov of the Soviet Navy has said: "Construction of warships with dynamic principles of support (ie air cushion vehicles or SES) has already become practicable. Undoubtedly the appearance *en masse* of such warships in the composition of navies will increase their combat capabilities; the surface naval forces will be able to carry out combat missions successfully and acquire completely new qualities." As Admiral of the Fleet of the Soviet Union his comments are worth taking seriously.

Special-purpose uses

With its versatility and lack of restrictions, the hovercraft has quickly been assessed for different applications. These may range from coastguard duties in Pakistan to survey tasks in Belgium or airport crash/rescue in Canada. In fact, special uses of hovercraft cover a wide variety of jobs and offer opportunities for fully amphibious, rigid sidewall and industrial designs.

Since August 1968 when it was formed, the Canadian Coast Guard Hovercraft Unit has proved to be a major success. In nine years it carried out over 1,400 rescue missions which accounted for 10% of all search and rescue (SAR) missions off the west coast of Canada each year. In May 1977 the unit, which already had a British made SR.N5, took delivery of a larger BHC SR.N6 hovercraft enabling the unit to tackle a greater range of tasks and operate a 24-hour service. An important factor of the unit's work is the ability of the hovercraft to respond to SAR requests in only three minutes. Between January and September 1978, the unit had performed 948 rescue missions and the craft achieved some 1,500 hours utilisation each, per annum.

A similar role has been played by a single SR.N6 hovercraft at Mangere Airport in Auckland, New Zealand, since 1970. This hovercraft is operated by the NZ Department of Transport and provides fast access to aircraft that come down short of the runways and yachts which are stranded on mud-banks close to the airport.

The Belgian Ministry of Public Works employs a hovercraft of the rigid sidewall type for hydrographic surveys on the River Scheldt. This Hovermarine 216 hovercraft has been in operation since 1972 and allows the authorities to undertake surveys of areas faster than with conventional survey launches. Such a role could become important for developing countries where plans call for the development of new port or harbour facilities in areas that have been subject to preliminary surveys only. Even the British hydrographic authorities responsible for providing charts of our coastal waters might find the hovercraft (whether it is fully amphibious or not) eminently suitable for high-speed hydrographic surveys around our shores.

Another multi-purpose role performed by hovercraft was demonstrated in the Beaufort Sea and northern areas of Canada within the Arctic Circle between 1973 and 1977 and was halted only by decisions regarding the laying of a pipeline in this area and other non-hovercraft matters. Two SR.N6 hovercraft were used to transport personnel and equipment in support of oilfield operations. One craft was converted into a freighter and on one occasion it carried a single point load of 8 tons. The other passenger-carrying craft travelled over 50,000 miles within the Arctic Circle and once journeyed more than 100 miles in complete darkness with an outside temperature of minus 53 degrees Fahrenheit.

Icebreaking

There seem few more unlikely applications of the hovercraft than icebreaking. There are actually two methods which have been defined as low speed and high speed. For simplicity I shall refer here only to the low speed method, which depends on having an area of open water from which to start. This could, of course, be at the edge of a sheet of ice or a hole in the ice itself made by nature or the hovercraft. This method is also dependent on having a cushion pressure head that approximates to the thickness of the ice sheet. As the hovercraft (more likely it will be a hoverplatform fastened by cables to the bow of a ship) approaches the edge of the ice sheet, the air pressure generated under the craft (and contained within its skirt) depresses the water level beneath it relative to the surrounding surface by an amount that approximates to the air cushion head. Gradually, as the hovercraft moves onto the sheet of ice, the skirt rides over the ice but still maintains its sealing properties. The ice sheet penetrates the pressurised air zone where the depressed water level allows an air cavity to form between the underside of the ice and the water, which extends forward and around the advancing hovercraft, being fed by the cushion. The sheet of ice beneath the hovercraft (with the buoyant force of the water removed) in effect becomes a cantilever beam which eventually fails because of its own weight when the cantilevered section reaches a critical length. The overhanging section of ice then breaks off and the broken pieces drop into the water which is at a depressed level due to the cushion pressure.

Although rather difficult to explain, this phenomenon has been observed on several occasions and filmed from inside the cushion of different hovercraft. The greater the thickness of ice the higher the relative cushion pressure required. Although it had been known for some years that hovercraft, when operating over certain types of ice, could break it the full potential of this phenomenon had not been realised and remained unexploited until tests with the ACT.100 air cushion transporter in the winter of 1971/72. Now the matter has aroused great interest and the Canadian Government has been quick to identify the various areas of application and conduct trials with different sizes of hoverplatform and self-propelled hovercraft to evaluate their possible roles. The results of these tests have indicated that further development work needs to be undertaken but so far ice up to 5ft 4in (160cm) thick can be broken. It should also be mentioned that most of the trials conducted have been in fresh water and using relatively smooth ice. Trials over salt water and rough or rafted ice have still to be undertaken. Despite this limitation to existing knowledge, the future use of hovercraft icebreakers looks bright. Already similar trials have been started in the USA to evaluate such hoverplatforms for icebreaking duties on important inland waterways during winter when barge traffic carrying heating oil may be disrupted by iced-up rivers. Similarly, the Soviet Union has announced that it has also conducted trials with hovercraft icebreakers and that these might be employed in oil exploration.

Industrial applications

Although often regarded as the less glamorous uses of the hovercraft principle, the industrial applications contribute a great deal to the versatility of the technology. Whether it is moving large indivisible loads such as 150-ton electrical transformer units along unstrengthened roads or over bridges, providing an all-year cable ferry across a river in North America, or relocating 700-ton storage tanks several hundred yards, the principle may still be the same. Indeed the range is quite remarkable and growing all the time. It can include specially designed freight-carrying hoverplatforms which are towed or winched, smaller hoverpallets fitted with spraying equipment, and specially adapted hovertrailers which are linked together to provide a platform for a drilling platform for operations over marshland and swamp. The sale of special UBM recovery systems for crashed aircraft to Nigeria was a particular achievement. Once again the development of these has taken place in Britain and subsequently been applied to similar problems on almost every continent. Future applications offer greater mobility and scope for the civil engineer planning a port complex, refinery or power station. Farmers can also expect help with the possibility that in years to come the hovercraft principle might enable work to continue even when surface conditions prevent horses or cattle from venturing across inundated fields. Special air cushion supported spraying booms have already been developed.

Recreation

As with many important developments additional 'spin-offs' have been discovered which had not been fully appreciated in earlier years. This is certainly true of the use of light hovercraft (craft weighing less than 1,000kg empty and not used for reward). Since the early 1960s people all over the world have experimented with making their own small hovercraft—probably of one or two seats—using a collection of motorcycle engines and other components. Some proved themselves capable of producing original designs which offered satisfactory performance but most found the task too difficult and sought commercially-available craft or kits.

Today this sector of the hovercraft business is an extremely active one and throughout the world individuals are able to design, construct and operate their own craft. However, instead of reducing the interest in professionally-made products, this activity has spurred on many small companies in Britain, Canada, USA, France, Japan, Italy, Australia, New Zealand and other countries. The result is that, despite a fairly high failure rate, interest in commercially-produced craft offering one to four seats continues.

Of the many companies that have been involved in making such craft, Britain's Pindair Ltd remains the most impressive and successful. Since 1972 the company has built and sold large numbers of two-and four-seat craft and achieved sales in a wide variety of countries. These craft have been used for civil engineering jobs, light utility functions and as site personnel vehicles.

Hoverclubs have been set up in several countries to tap the interest in using small hovercraft for recreational activities and Britain's body, The Hoverclub of Great Britain, has been at the forefront of developments since the mid-1960s. Over 40 craft compete at its regular race meetings and its standards of construction and dissemination of technical information are unmatched.

What of the future?

Any summary of world hovercraft activity must leave out some items and give only passing mention to others. This has, inevitably, been the case with this paper. I can only hope that enough is aroused to suggest that the hovercraft industry is alive and well—but often undervalued! I know that many within the British industry would like to see greater injection of money from state sources and more encouragement from those areas of industry and shipping which could benefit most from hovercraft developments. The same comments could, I am sure, be echoed by other countries. Personally, I am in no position to forecast what the eventual outcome of these suggestions or hopes will be although I am confident that the hovercraft industry will be listed as a major technological development of the twentieth century.

World-wide potential applications of the hovercraft principle

Rec and LU: recreational and light utility
Ind: industrial
HT/P: hovertrailers/hoverplatforms
Tank: tank moving
Ice: ice breaking

	Passenger car ferry	Military	Special purpose	Freight	Port patrol	Rec and LU	Industrial
Afghanistan							HT?
Albania	x(Dalmatia)	x(coastal)					
Algeria	x	x		x(fruit)	x(Algiers)		tank
American Samoa	x						
Angola		x(river)		x(ore)	x(Luanda)		
Argentina	x(Buenos Aires)	x(coastal and river)		x(livestock)	x		HT/P
Australia	x(Sydney)	x		x(ore)	x(Sydney)	x	HT/P
Austria	x(river)	x(river)		x(timber)			HT/P
Bahamas	x(island)					x	
Bahrain	x(to Saudi Arabia)	x(patrol)			x		tank
Bangladesh		x	x(relief and survey)		x(Chittagong)		
Barbados	x(inter-island)					x	
Belgium	x(to UK)	x(coastal)	x(survey)	x	x(Antwerp)	x	tank
Belize	—	x(coastal)		x(fruit)			HP/T
Benin	x(tourist)						
Bermuda	x(tourist)				x(Hamilton)		
Bhutan	—						
Bolivia	x(Titicaca)			x(ore)			tank
Botswana				x(Zambezi)			HT/P
Brazil	x(Rio etc)	x(river and coastal)	x(survey river)	x(ore)	x(Rio)	x	tank
Brunei	—	x(coastal)					tank
Bulgaria	x(Black Sea)	x(coastal)				x	
Burma	x(Rangoon)	x(coastal and river)	x(survey)	x(timber)	x(Rangoon)		HT/P
Burundi	—	x(lake)					
Cameroon	x(tourist)			x			
Canada	x(BC etc)	x	x(ice)	x	x	x	tank
Cape Verde Islands	—	x			x		tank
Central African Empire	—						
Chad	—		x(relief and survey)				
Chile	—	x(coastal)		x(copper ore)	x(Valparaiso)		HT
China, People's Republic	x(river tourist)	x(coastal)	x(river survey)	x	x		HT/P
Colombia	x(tourist)	x(coastal)		x			HT/P
Comoro Islands	x(tourist)						
Congo	x(tourist)	x(patrol)	x(survey)	x(ore)			HT/P
Costa Rica	x(coastal tourist)		x(coast guard)				HT/P
Cuba	x(tourist)	x(patrol)					tank
Cyprus	x(tourist)						
Czechoslovakia	—						
Denmark	x	x	x(ice)		x(Copen-hagen)	x	tank
Djibouti		x(coastal)					
Dominican Republic	x(tourist)						
Ecuador	—	x(river)		x(bananas)			HT/P
Egypt	x	x(coastal)	x(survey)		x		HT/P
Equatorial Guinea	x						
Ethiopia	—	x(coastal)					
Fiji	x		x(survey)				
Finland	x	x	x(ice)		x	x	tank HT/P
France	x	x	x(survey)		x	x	tank
French Guiana	x	x(coastal)	x(survey)			x	HT/P
Gabon	x	x(coastal)		x			tank HT/P
Gambia	x	x	x(survey)				HT/P
Germany (East)	x	x	x(ice)		x		tank
Germany (West)	x	x	x(ice)		x(Hamburg)	x	tank
Ghana	x	x(river and coast)	x(survey and patrol)		x		HT/P
Gibraltar	x				x		tank
Gilbert Islands and Tuvalu	x(tourist)		x(survey)			x	
Greece	x	x	x(survey)		x		tank
Greenland	—	x	x(ice)			x	tank
Guam	x(tourist)	x					tank
Guatemala	—	x					tank
Guinea	x	x(river)	x(survey)				HT/P
Guyana	—	x(river and coast)					HT/P

	Passenger car ferry	Military	Special purpose	Freight	Port patrol	Rec and LU	Industrial
Haiti	x	x(coastal)					
Honduras	—	x					tank
Hong Kong	x	x	x(survey)		x	x	tank
Hungary	x(Danube)		x(river survey)			x	tank
Iceland	—						tank
India	x	x(coast and river)	x(relief and survey)	x	x		tank HT/P
Indonesia	x	x	x(survey)		x		HT/P
Iran	x(tourist)	x			x		tank
Iraq	x(tourist)	x	x(survey)		x		tank
Ireland	x				x	x	
Israel	—	x				x	tank
Italy	x	x			x	x	tank
Ivory Coast	x	x			x		tank
Jamaica	x				x	x	tank
Japan	x	x	x(survey)	x	x	x	tank
Kampuchea (Cambodia)	—	x					tank
Kenya	x		x(survey)		x(Mombasa)		tank
North Korea	—	x					tank
South Korea	x	x					HT/P
Kuwait	—	x	x(survey)		x		tank
Laos	—	x(river)					HT/P
Lebanon	x	x					tank
Lesotho	—						
Liberia	—	x			x(Monrovia)		HT/P
Libya	x	x(coastal)			x		tank
Macao	x				x		
Madagascar	x	x					tank
Malawi	x						
Malaysia	x	x	x(survey)	x	x	x	tank
Maldives	x						
Mali	x(tourist)		x(river survey)				HT/P
Malta	x					x	tank
Mariana Islands	x						
Martinique	x						
Mauritania	—						tank
Mauritius	x						
Mexico	x(tourist)	x			x(Vera Cruz)		tank
Monaco	x(tourist)					x	
Morocco	x	x(coastal)			x(Casablanca)		tank
Mozambique	—	x	x(survey)				tank
Netherlands	x	x			x(Rotterdam)	x	tank HT/P
New Caledonia	x						
New Hebrides	x						
New Zealand	x					x	tank
Nicaragua	x(tourist)	x					HT/P
Niger	—						HT/P
Nigeria	x	x	x(survey)		x		tank HT/P
Norway	x	x	x(ice)			x	tank
Oman	—	x			x		tank
Pakistan	x(tourist)	x	x(survey and relief)		x		HT/P
Panama	—	x	x(survey)				tank
Papua New Guinea	x		x(survey)			x	HT/P
Paraguay	x	x(river)					HT/P
Peru	—	x	x(survey)				tank
Philippines	x	x					HT/P
Poland	x	x	x(ice)				tank
Portugal	x	x			x	x	tank
Guinea-Bissau	—	x					tank
Puerto Rico	x						tank
Qatar	x	x			x(Doma)		tank
Romania	x(tourist)	x				x	tank
Rwanda	x(tourist)		x(survey)				HT/P
El Salvador	—	x					HT/P
Saudi Arabia	x(tourist)	x	x(survey)		x		tank
Senegal	x	x	x(survey)		x(Dakar)		HT/P
Seychelles	x(tourist)						
Sierra Leone	x	x			x		tank
Singapore	x				x	x	tank
Solomon Islands	x(tourist)			x(copra)			
Somalia	—	x					HT/P
South Africa	—	x	x(survey)	x(ore)	x	x	tank HT/P
Spain	x	x			x		tank
Sri Lanka	x(tourist)	x(coastal)					
Sudan	—	x	x(survey)				HT/P
Surinam	x	x					HT/P
Swaziland	—						HT/P

	Passenger car ferry	Military	Special purpose	Freight	Port patrol	Rec and LU	Industrial
Sweden	x	x	x(ice)		x(Gothenburg)	x	tank
Switzerland	—						tank
Syria	—	x					tank
Taiwan	x	x					tank
Tanzania	x	x			x	x	tank HT/P
Thailand	x	x	x(survey)				HT/P
Togo	—						HT/P
Tonga	x						
Trinidad & Tobago	x						tank
Tunisia	x		x(survey)		x		tank
Turkey	x	x			x		tank
Uganda	—						tank HT/P
USSR	x	x	x(ice)	x	x	x	tank HT/P
UAE	x	x	x(survey)		x		tank
USA	x	x	x(ice)	x	x	x	tank HT/P
Uruguay	x	x	x(survey)	x	x(Montevideo)		tank HT/P
Venezuela	x	x	x(personnel)	x	x		tank HT/P
Viet-Nam	—	x	x(survey)				HT/P
Virgin Islands	x						
Upper Volta	—						HT/P
North Yemen	—	x					tank
South Yemen	—	x			x(Aden)		tank
Yugoslavia	x	x			x		tank
Zaïre	x	x	x(survey)	x(ore)			tank HT/P
Zambia	—	x		x			tank HT/P

A Review of the Sidewall Hovercraft

by E G Tattersall, R & D Director, Hovermarine Transport Ltd

(The text of an informal talk to the United Kingdom Hovercraft Society on 20 September 1978)

The timing of this paper is appropriate in a number of ways. This is my twentieth year in hovercraft, mainly of the sidewall variety, and I sincerely hope that I shall have about another 20 years to contribute. Thus, in a way, this moment is a personal milestone and one of which I am proud. But it also provides an opportunity to look back over the years and see how the sidewall hovercraft concept came to be put into production and the current state of the art. I shall also mention my own thoughts concerning how I see the future for such craft.

Within what has been called the field of transportation, Hovermarine dominates a position where the operator can justify 30 to 50 knots in the small to medium size range. This speed range increases with size. Undoubtedly the more lift air which is used the more speed you have to employ to

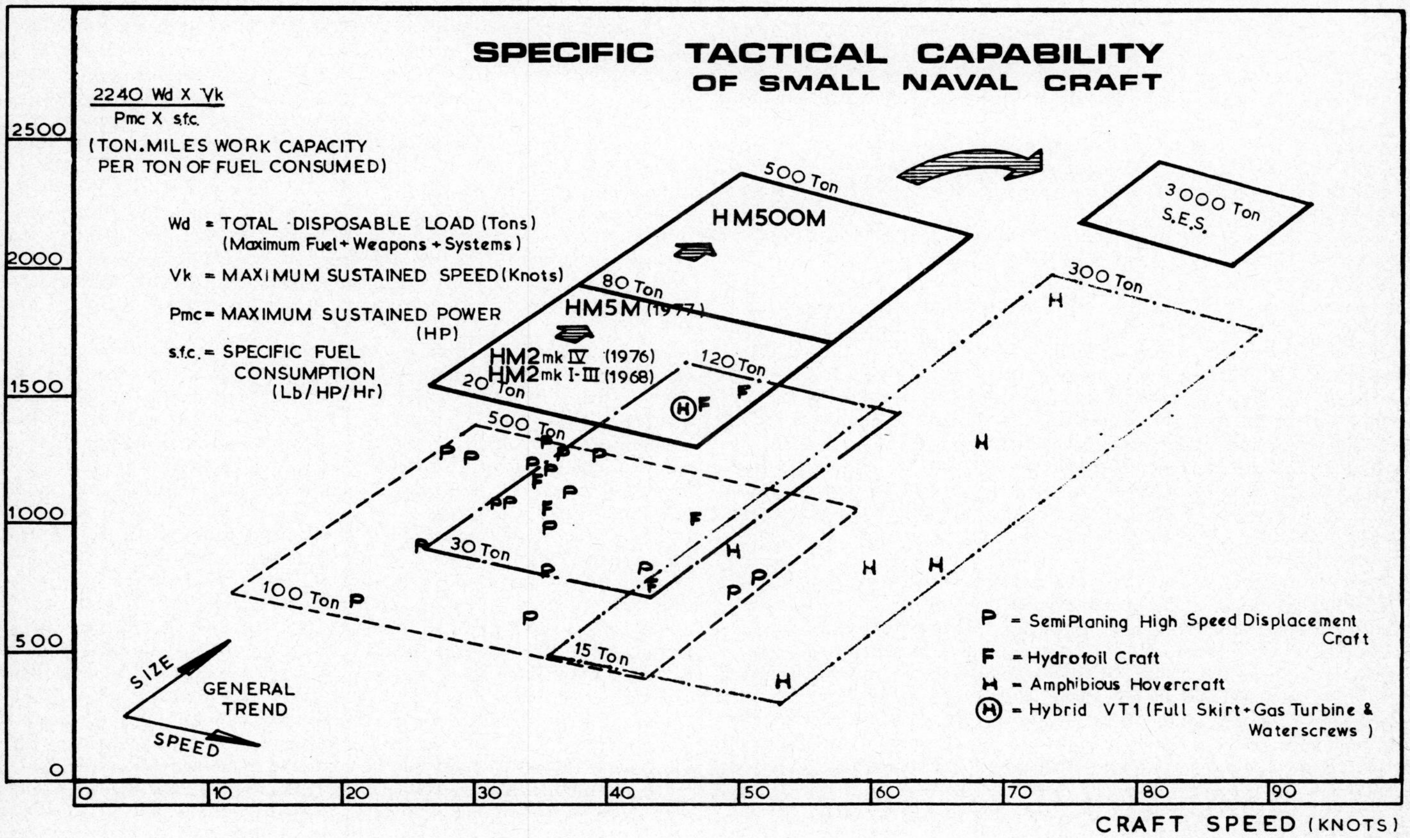

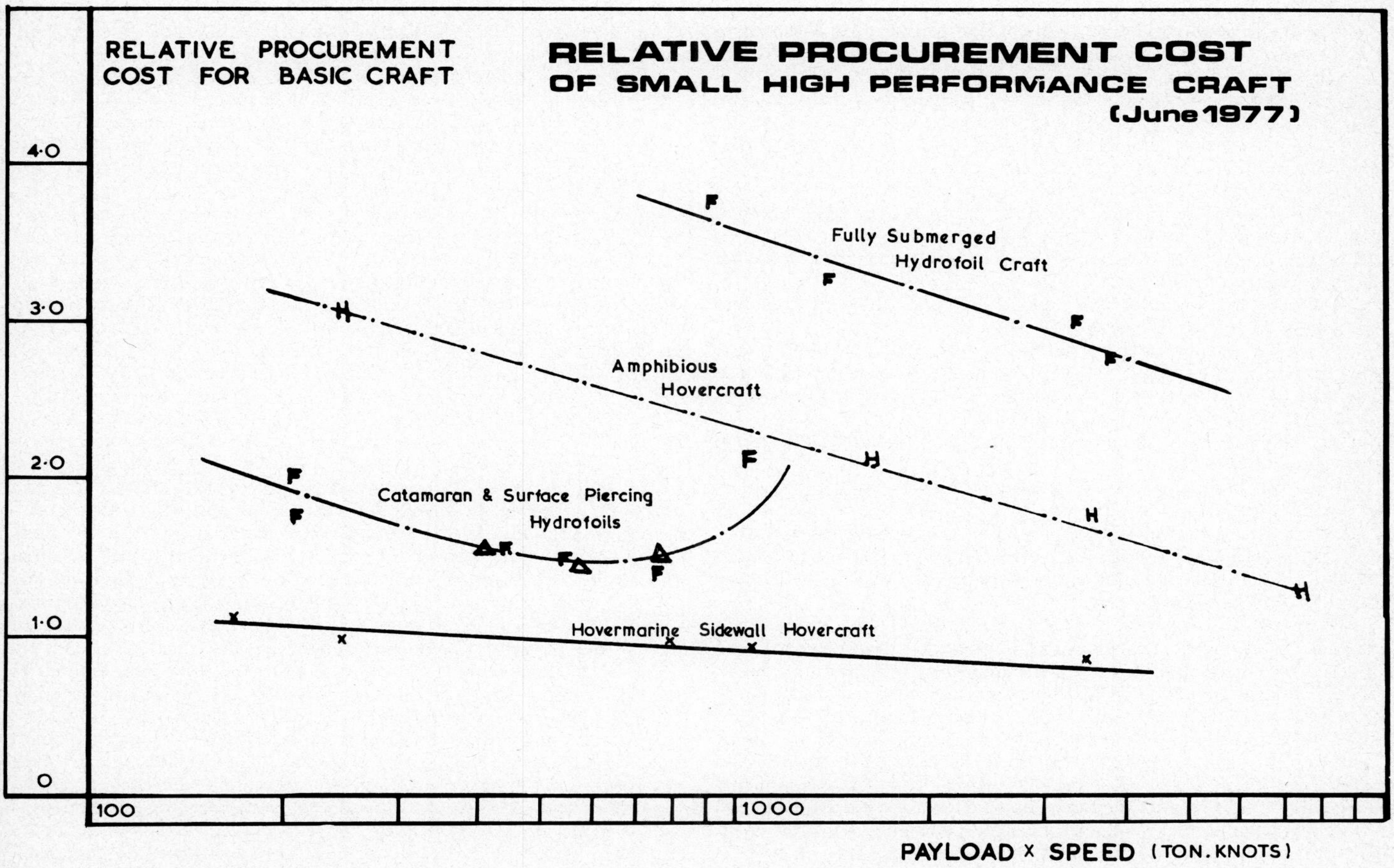

justify it. Displacement craft embodying no air cushion in the smaller sizes are reasonably efficient up to about 20 knots. The unique amphibious capability of the fully-skirted hovercraft requires up to about 50% of its power in lift and consequently has to be operated at higher speeds than a vessel requiring only 25% of its power for lift. However, speed for any role should be the result of combining sea state and hence size with traffic and frequency. On this basis we find a large proportion of the potential and identifiable market in the 30 to 50 knot speed bracket. It is for this reason that my own company is in business and it also explains how, by combining this with reasonable cost, we have been able to penetrate the market and prove so successful in selling our craft.

Without detracting from this important theme it is appropriate to look back to the origins of the sidewall concept. The earliest records of reducing the resistance of ships by bleeding air below the hull included the efforts of de Laval and Froude starting towards the end of the last century. Unfortunately they employed so little air that it formed bubbles rather than a steady flow and effectively increased the resistance of the models which they used.

Christopher Cockerell's first models around 1955 included a very basic sidewall configuration. He put side keels on a punt and fed air into the bow and showed that a significant reduction of drag was possible although unfortunately the amount of air used overcompensated for this. This work was undertaken before he invented the simple air curtain and long before flexible skirts.

I joined Sir Christopher in March 1959 being seconded from Saunders-Roe to Hovercraft Development Ltd (HDL). About six months after this Sir Christopher asked me to "Champion a somewhat unglamorous version of the hovercraft". This was to be a very basic platform with sidekeels and a small tin-roofed shed to contain the engines. It was to be water-propelled and was for carrying tea down the Brahmaputra River from the Assam Valley to Calcutta. The early sketches for this craft resembled some of the current civil engineering type projects except that our craft had to attain at least 20 to 25 knots. I must admit that initially my reaction was one of disappointment; after all, I had joined Christopher Cockerell to help him develop a craft with the unique capability of becoming amphibious. At that time we had even started to discover ways and means of providing lift power saving devices: recirculation systems, cascade foils, and on the horizon was the prospect of flexible skirts. These were going to halve the lift power of the simple jet system!

Shortly afterwards, Denny Bros of Dumbarton in Scotland expressed an interest in developing sidewall hovercraft. In many ways Dennys were a traditional shipbuilder although they placed a lot of emphasis on development. Their history included the Cutty Sark clipper, the first helicopter to rise under its own steam in the UK, a hydrofoil configuration during the war, a variable-pitch paddle wheel as well as their part in the Denny-Brown stabiliser. On the basis of the Indian enquiry for the tea transporter, the first manned model, D.1, was defined. This was a joint Denny/HDL venture and I was assigned as joint designer, with Hans Velpich and Hugh Orr from Dennys.

The D.1 craft was built within the existing skills and materials available from the shipyard: wood and steel. A very light central structure taking up to 80% of its 60 foot length was constructed in wood with very heavy steel fabricated airjet systems at each end. It was powered initially by a pair of 35bhp outboard motors and a couple of tiny Excelsior lift engines providing a very dubious 20hp at each end. The complete craft weighed about 5 tons and a cockpit provided spartan accommodation for a driver and up to three observers. Relative to its limited specification and the 12-inch hoverheight, this manned model behaved exceptionally well and encouraged Dennys and HDL to think of larger and faster craft for an identifiable ferry market requirement rather than the initial enquiry for an Indian tea freighter. D.1 was finally sent to HDL at Hythe for further testing and was equipped with a rudimentary skirt system. When powered with 50 hp outboard units the craft achieved speeds of more than 20 knots.

It is particularly interesting and relevant to look back and see what we learned from the D.1 project:

1: That you could limit the air input to the ends of a long craft and successfully lift it clear of the water.

2: We began to appreciate the sidewall wetted area varied with speed.

3: Theoretical assessments and experimental drag measurements gave reasonable correlation and some indication of reasonably low-wave drag profiles for the large length/beam ratio craft.

4: It provided a basic stability correlation: it did not require internal compartmentation.

5: It successfully applied open recirculation systems, to be superseded by the flexible skirt.

6: Seakeeping. It showed the need for a deeper cushion in proportion to its beam which further encouraged the development of skirt systems. It also emphasised the need for a different bow shape since the D.1 had a very rudimentary plough-shaped bow.

It gave me my first experience of a Press day! An odd thing to mention in essentially a technically inclined paper, but one that most engineers and particularly technical directors will appreciate. No matter how well planned Press days may be, it seems that they always include some element of drama; D.1's Press day was no exception. The craft was demonstrated in the Gare Loch off the Clyde Estuary and the press and other guests were all accommodated on a tug in the middle of the Loch. The idea was that we should make several Farnborough-style 'flypasts' with the craft at its phenomenal top speed of 15 to 17 knots! Without going into too much detail I might add that we found that, despite jammed rudder gear, we managed to satisfy both the natural curiosity of the journalists and the photogenic needs of their photographer colleagues.

Dennys were so encouraged with the prospects at that time that they decided to go further and embark on a private venture project to build a D.2. They formed a company called Denny Hovercraft Ltd and produced a specification for a craft able to carry about 70 passengers with a speed in excess of 20 knots. The craft in fact rarely exceeded 22 knots. Internally Dennys could not decide which material to use for construction of the craft. Initially they decided on grp (glass-reinforced plastic) but while tooling was under way they began work on a second wooden prototype; although this wooden prototype was completed first it proved to be grossly overweight. It employed in the early phases a semiflexible simple jet nozzle system with long diffusion ducts to minimise losses. It was driven by two Caterpillar D333 propulsion engines and a pair of D330 units, turbo-charged, for lift. In the early stages there were problems in getting the craft through hump which we diagnosed as being due to propeller design, the overweight problem and the then indeterminate shallow water characteristics. Eventually the craft reached speeds of about 22 knots and Dennys decided that they wished to measure the drag at full scale. (They had previously undertaken resistance trials on a full scale displacement craft named *The Lucy Ashton* by propelling it with jet engines over the measured mile at an amazing fuel consumption rate!) Dennys decided that D.2 was to be towed from the stern and the Royal Navy volunteered to provide *Brave Borderer*. Unfortunately in their enthusiasm they pulled the back off the wooden prototype which then began to sink. However, more successful and elegant expeditions were to befall the first grp prototype which made the then epic journey from Dumbarton to the Thames via the Caledonian Canal and the east coast. When it reached London it began an experimental service and demonstrated the potential of the craft to various civic dignitaries. A total of 2½ craft were built.

In 1962 things began to look bleak for Dennys: the ferry boat business was extremely slack and they had overspent on modernisation and building craft 'on spec.'. However, before their voluntary liquidation in 1963, HDL and Dennys completed a project study for a 150-ton version with a 40-ton payload capacity; HDL contributed model testing, an outline structural study in light alloy and an overall costing exercise for a proposed cross-Solent operation. The craft had a modest cushion depth of 4 feet and a maximum speed of 40 knots.

Around this period obvious interest was being expressed in the USA in various papers written by staff at the David Taylor Model Basin and the US Maritime Administration. Alan Ford put forward the notion of a large sidewall craft effectively riding on a captive or replenished bubble of air, talking of designs with large all-up weights and high-speed capabilities. Among some of these optimistic claims lay a lot of sense, and with suitable factoring and making assumptions that suitable skirts would be developed to meet the requirements, there seemed to me no basic reason why a captured air bubble in excess of 1,000 tons should not be built and operated in a naval environment. To see the sidewall concept suddenly thrust into the foreground with such claims startled a number of people in the 'amphibian lobby'. To see this in perspective it is necessary to realise that up to this time the sidewall hovercraft had only been publicised with the antics of the D.1 and D.2, whereas Westland and Vickers had both started work towards their SR.N4 and VA.4 craft of about 150 tons. With the claims for the sidewall concept coming from an authoritative body in the USA with the hint that millions of dollars might be spent on it, it was not something that could be ignored.

With the dissolution of Dennys there seemed to me to be less and less external enthusiasm to revive the sidewall theme in the UK but I felt that it was still worthwhile saving and developing. As a result I made sure that a nucleus of technical enthusiasts kept in contact, including some ex-Denny personnel and a few of us at HDL. The alternative, of course, would have been to emigrate to the USA with John Chaplin and Wilf Eggington (now senior personnel at Bell Aerospace Textron and Rohr Marine Inc respectively). Kindred spirits inevitably cross paths and after a short while we met a couple of people who were interested in the commercial development and exploitation of sidewall craft. After a few heart-searching sessions we decided to give sidewall hovercraft another lease of life and five of us put up an embarrassingly small amount of money and formed Hovermarine Ltd in September 1965. Obviously I had to take the plunge and I left the relative security of HDL and Christopher Cockerell gave me some kind, practical advice and assured me that he would help in whatever way he could.

The company's registered office was in the premises of an accountants' in the Strand in London and we worked from my spare bedroom at my home in Hythe, near Southampton. Up to this time the group had undertaken a design study on a small 26 passenger craft which was, in effect, HM.1 and was to be propelled by inboard/outboard units and would have had a hoverheight of about 2 feet. The same team contributed to the first small contract procured by Hovermarine from the (then) Ministry of Aviation. This was for a small sidewall craft to be used in a logistic application and was equipped with a retractable wheel system for climbing prepared slipways.

For the first 18 months, however, a large proportion of everybody's effort was directed towards attracting investment into the company.

During this period the team grew to about eight and we moved premises to a small office in Southampton. Our progress was somewhat thwarted by the fact that we had no manufacturing licence from HDL. HDL, in return, were reluctant to grant Hovermarine a licence when the company had such a meagre capital base. This problem was solved only when Czarnikow Ltd, the world's largest sugar brokers based in London, with encouragement from Miles Dawson, became industrial philanthropists and presented us with a cheque for £50,000. With this encouragement and a legitimate outlook we started on the design of HM.2. Very rapidly we drew together a team of engineers, sales staff and accountants and moved to more spacious offices in another part of Southampton. At this point we had no production premises and so the first HM.2 hull was built for us by Halmatic and we undertook the fitting out in an open-ended shed further up the River Itchen from our existing premises.

At the prototype pre-launch stage we thought that it would be worthwhile if the (then) Ministry of Technology bought the first HM.2 so that we could "de-bug" it before putting a lot of effort into selling it. The Ministry declined and told us "Come back when it works!". Eventually they bought the tenth HM.2.

The first HM.2 was launched in January 1968. We were all delighted (the unbelievers were relieved!) to see that it worked first time and, in fact, performed extremely well. How long it worked was, unfortunately, another matter and like all other participants in this business we learnt that the problems really start at the hardware stage. The first operational experience was after three months when the craft was put into service with BR Seaspeed on the busy Portsmouth/Ryde route across the Solent. We quickly identified the areas of the craft on which we had to concentrate our efforts: they were the propulsion transmission, particularly the gearbox, and the skirt system.

Considerable effort was put into getting these systems corrected. Some additional investment in the company was forthcoming from Wm Cory but when this ended we were forced to look elsewhere to attract a longer-term approach to the company's financial problems. It appeared impossible to get this support from the UK so we were forced to seek it overseas and luckily found a group of enthusiasts in the USA with some Texan money and considerable keenness to see the project go ahead. However, they were keen only to pick up the assets and these were duly transferred to the new company, Hovermarine Transport Ltd at the end of 1969. The parent

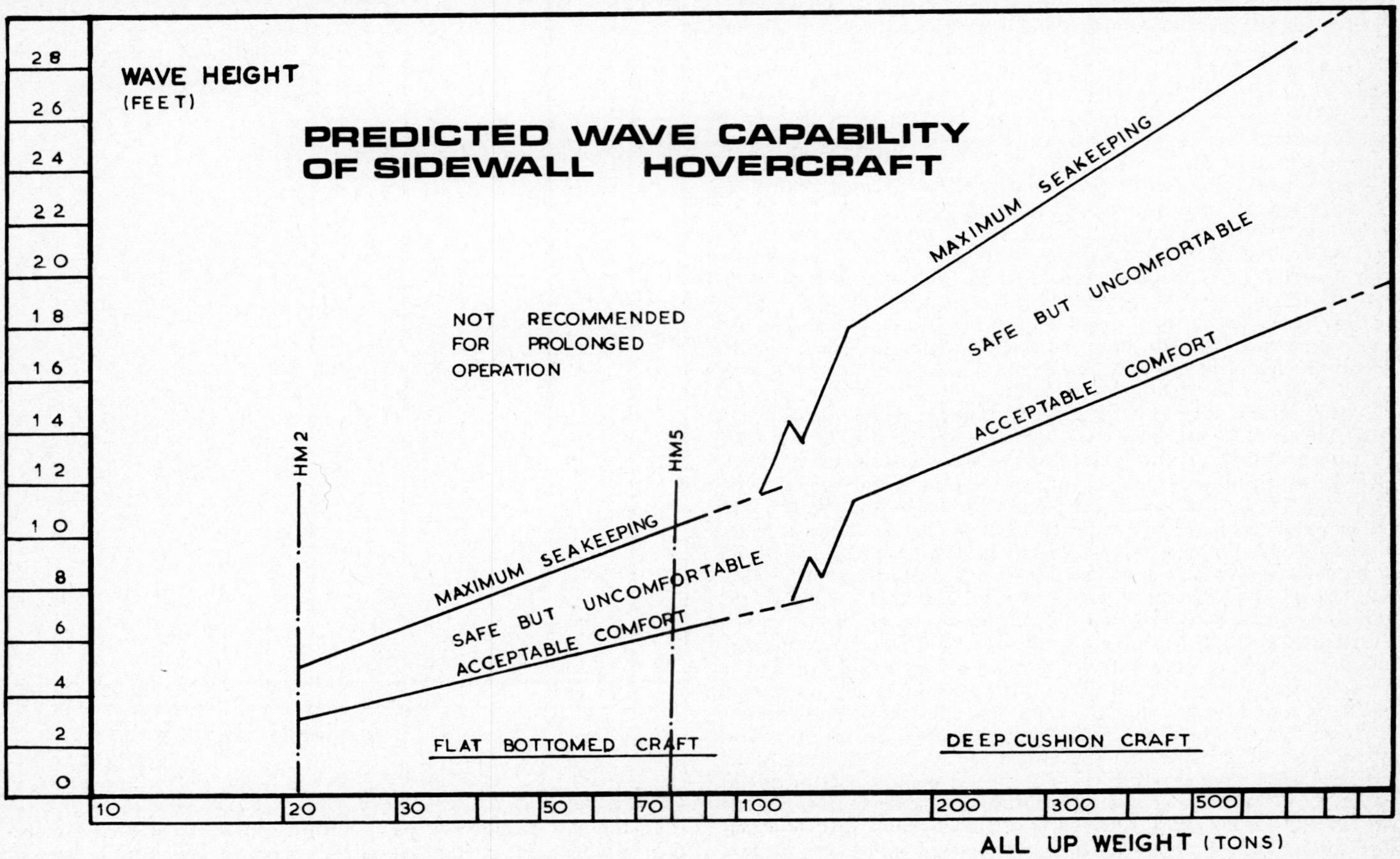

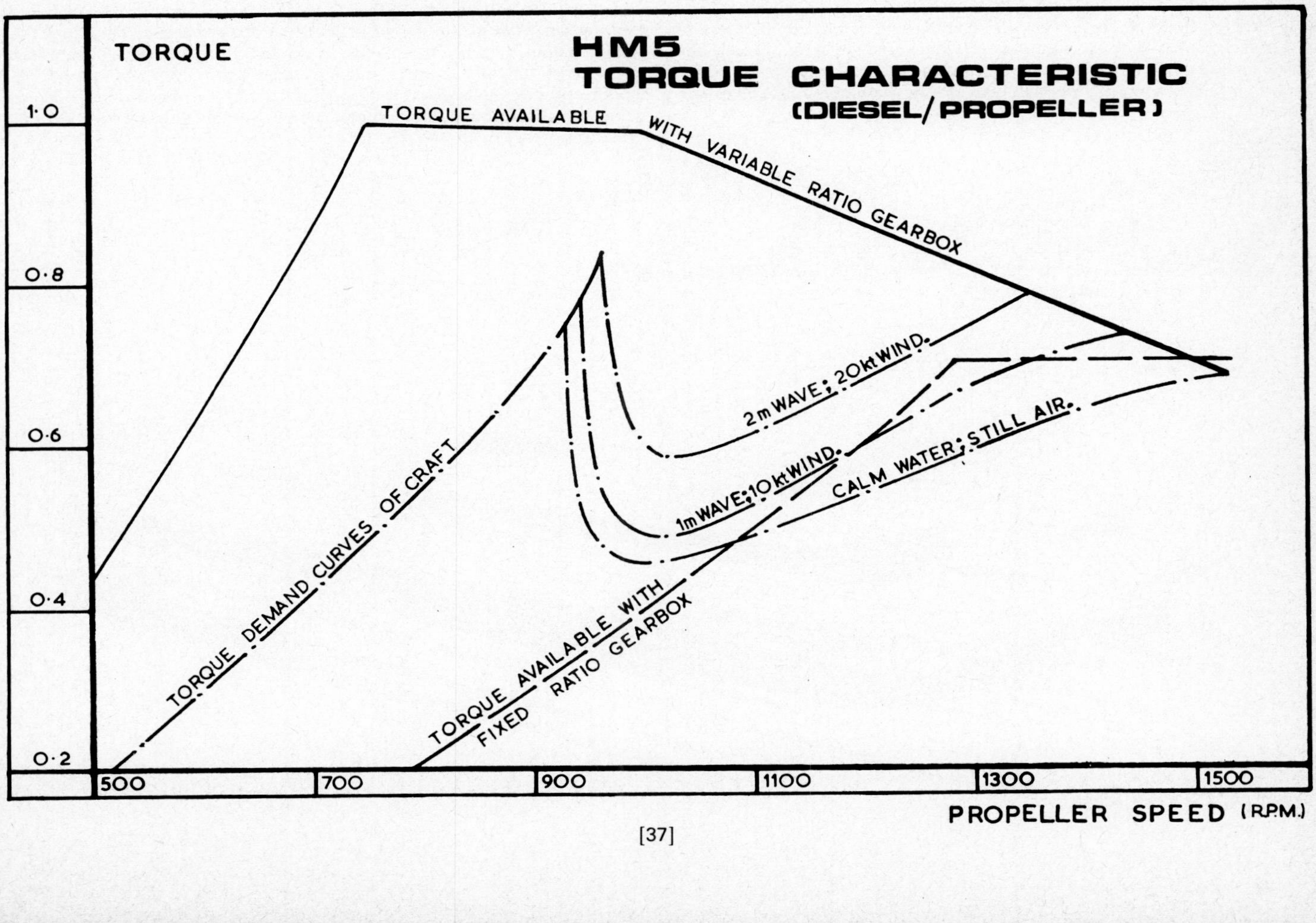

company in the USA, called Transportation Technology Inc, finally went public and in 1974 was re-named Hovermarine Corporation.

The first job of the new company was to revamp the HM.2 design to resolve remaining problems. This culminated in the HM.2 Mk 3 as it was to be designated, now known as the Hovermarine 216 design. Thirty-eight of these craft were built before the basic design was stretched by about 10 feet and became the HM.2 Mk 4 (or Hovermarine 218). The number now sold, including those under construction, is about 60. Sales have been concluded in more than 20 countries with the largest fleets being in Hong Kong, Portugal, the Philippines, Venezuela and Nigeria. The latest sales have included four craft for patrol duties in the port of Rotterdam, two fireboats for the City of Tacoma and three oil rig support versions for Venezuela. For the City of Tacoma in the state of Washington, USA, the craft has been further stretched to 70 feet (21 metres). In fact, the Rotterdam, Tacoma and recent Venezuelan orders reflect our company's policy of diversifying beyond the passenger ferry market and more and more we are aligning ourselves to marketing 'platforms' on which a multitude of different equipment can be installed. The ease with which new superstructure configurations can be fitted with a moulding method has certainly helped us and the physical stretch of the craft has also been facilitated by using this form of construction. As a passenger craft the 21-metre long version can accommodate about 110 people.

Apart from the HM.2 series, a new family of craft designated the HM.5 or Hovermarine 500 series was planned around 1973-74. Initially aimed at a ferryboat version for 150 passengers the craft was later increased in size to a basic capacity of 180 to 220 passengers depending on the layout selected. The basic HM.5 is 27 metres long but provision has been made for stretching the hull to 33 and 39 metres. The prototype 27-metre craft is at an advanced stage of construction with the hull being virtually complete and launching planned for late 1979. The craft's proportions allow it about double the cushion depth of the smaller HM.2 and it has a tapered sidewall with a fuller cross-section than HM.2.

Propulsion power for HM.5 is currently centred around the MTU 331 series and the total installed power is approximately 3,100hp of which 700 hp is available for lift. Other powerplant alternatives include the US General Motors' engine series. The high-speed diesel at this size is a relatively expensive unit but still considerably less than the comparable size gas-turbine, far less thirsty and cheaper to maintain. The disadvantage of the high-speed diesel is its poor low-speed torque capability and, to enhance this capability, a variable gear ratio box was commissioned from Vickers. This box will allow a range of ratios between 2:1 and 1·3:1 and allow the engine to operate 95% of the time at full rpm at varying loads.

Before the HM.5 tooling was produced, some 2000 or more separate tank test runs evolved the configuration. Differences from the HM.2 centred on the bow shape and the development of the spray strip along the sidewall which contributes significantly to the lower pitching characteristics of the craft in a reasonably high sea. The fan arrangement was also investigated at model scale and the characteristics of the main fan are such that under relatively calm conditions only 75% of the maximum power of the lift system is required to give optimum performance. The fan can also operate at a low slope on the pressure flow curve compatible with a high frequency small disturbance while in rough conditions full power will be used which at higher rpm will allow the fan to operate at a higher slope. The connection between fan slope characteristics and heave comfort was certainly established but we are the first to admit that this phenomenon at model scale and full scale on a dynamic basis is far from understood. Hovermarine is working on this problem at present together with other dynamic response investigations.

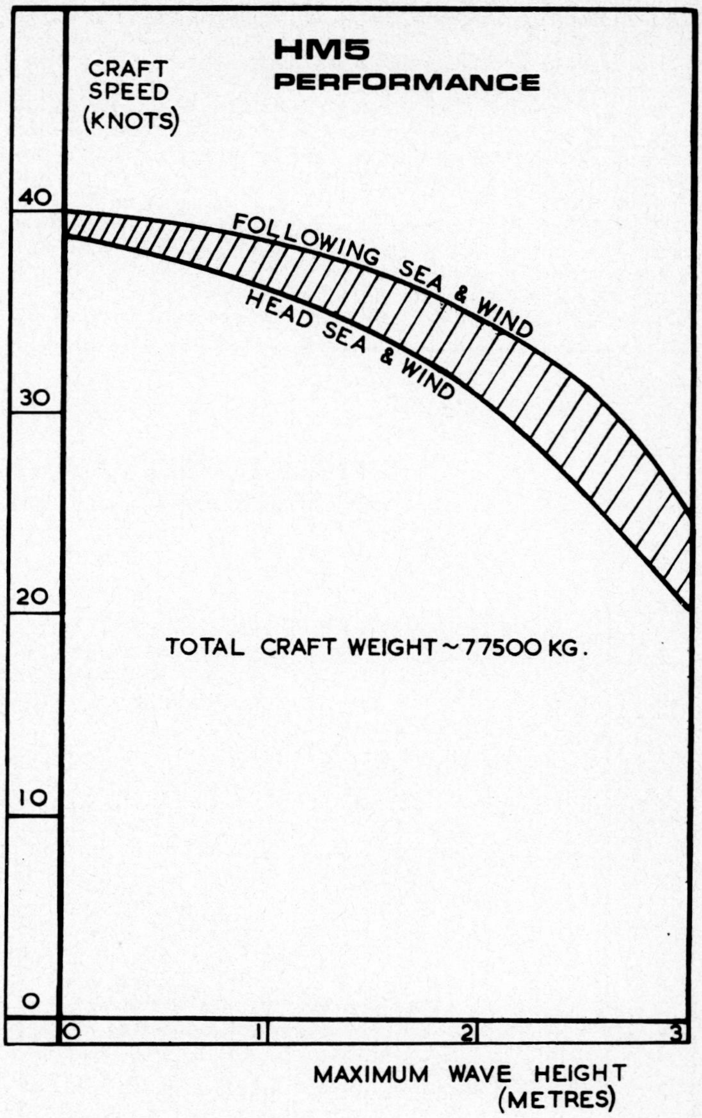

Among these the most noteworthy milestone has been the adaption of the inclined rudder configuration to a roll control system. This investigation was undertaken in conjunction with Marconi Avionics. A computer receives information from a rate gyro and feeds correction signals back into the rudder system. Trials on HM.2 have shown significant benefits in beam seas and this system will become a standard feature on HM.5 and an optional modification to the present HM.2. Other systems for pitch attenuation are being investigated, employing both passive and active systems. It is our

100-ton payload Hoverfreighter

general impression that having solved the roll and pitch problems, the heave may be considerably less and already there appears to be an indication of this during demonstration of the roll system.

In 1975 a joint venture company was set up in Japan called Hovermarine Pacific Co Ltd. This is the combination of Taiyo Fisheries, one of the largest deep sea fishing organisations in the world, Sasebo Heavy Industries, a US company Fairfield Maxwell and Hovermarine. Initially this unit has been formed to sell and manufacture HM.2 and HM.5 designs in Japan and its adjacent countries, but will go on to build larger craft such as our concept of the Hoverfreighter. These craft will generally be too large to export as deck cargo and since there is a natural market for them in Japan we are planning that the first of the line will be built at Sasebo. Tank tests under way at present are of a 300-ton version which will initially take the form of a car ferry. These craft differ from the high-performance sidewall designs in that the speed will be somewhat less in relation to their size and it is aimed at a much greater percentage payload factor. Such craft can be extrapolated up to vessels of several thousand tons all-up weight and might include transporters for perishable goods, coastal or inter-island container carriers and many other applications.

Another active development project is what we have termed the deep cushion type of craft. As a concept this is now some 12 years old, but only recently have sufficient resources been found to initiate serious research and development work. An initial attempt was made in 1968 (a test tank model being built but unfortunately was lost in a fire at a previous factory) but this was not re-started until the beginning of 1978.

To date British investment in the sidewall type of craft has been minimal; only 2% of the money afforded and contracted by the UK Government to the hovercraft industry has been allocated to the sidewall version. The progress of the craft, company and our part of the business has come in the main from private investment, both in the UK and from the USA with additional encumbent but helpful participation from other merchant bodies and from the National Research Development Corporation (NRDC). Inevitably research and development has been very restricted and as a result we have had to be very selective in attempting to get back from this effort information which we can directly apply to production craft.

The past twenty years or so have been undoubtedly, in many ways, a struggle; a struggle for recognition, a struggle for survival and a struggle for perspective! The struggle has not, in my view, ended and is not likely to do so in the foreseeable future. Large projects go out of the range of entrepreneurial interests, and governments and civil servants will make more decisions. Undoubtedly if the USA decides to proceed with its Surface Effect Ship programme, it will have a profound effect on the recognition of this species of craft. It will materialise and quickly put into perspective a craft which, at present, is only peeping over the horizon. It will allow many other operators, ferry companies and military interests, to draw a mental line between the HM.2 as the present smallest craft, to a very sizeable oceangoing craft and will suggest an appropriate size and speed for their own needs. However, the successful manufacturer will still have to provide the product at the right price to complete the solution to the equation.

I remain optimistic about the future and my company has a good grounding of hard-won experience to know that the essential ingredient—besides a basically good product—is the will to win through, and this comes from the people within the company, within the industry and probably many of the readers of this book.

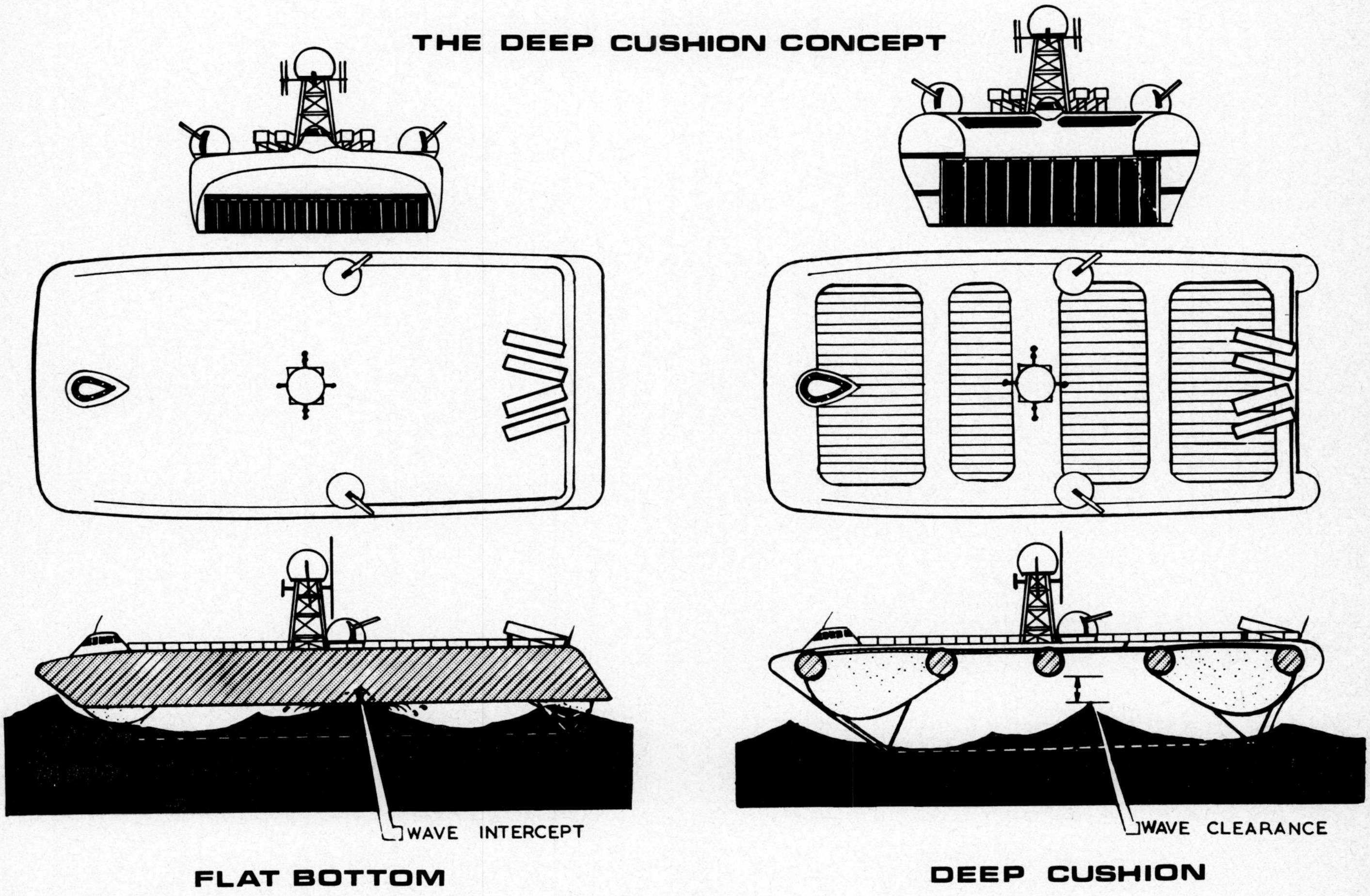

ACV MANUFACTURERS AND DESIGN GROUPS

ARGENTINA

BRUZZONE

Peru 327, Buenos Aires, Argentina
Officials:
Jorge O Bruzzone, *Executive Designer*
Larry Baqués, *Production Executive*

Jorge Oscar Bruzzone, an Argentinian aeronautical engineer, designed an amphibious craft, the Guaipo BMX-1, which was built and tested by the Argentine Navy. (Described in *Jane's Surface Skimmers 1971-72*).

Mr Bruzzone has experimented with ACVs for nearly 15 years. At present he is building, privately, a light two-seater and a three-seater. Preliminary details of his Yacare JOB-3 two-seat recreational craft and the Yacare II twelve-seater are given below.

YACARE JOB-3

The prototype of this fibreglass-hulled amphibious two-seater is undergoing trials. It has a maximum speed over water of 110km/h (68·5mph).

LIFT AND PROPULSION: Lift air is provided by a 1,200cc Volkswagen air-cooled, four-cylinder four-stroke automotive engine driving a 90cm (2ft 11½in) diameter centrifugal fan. Propulsive thrust is supplied by a 1,600cc Volkswagen automotive engine driving a 130cm (4ft 3in) diameter ducted, two-bladed propeller.

CONTROLS: Twin aerodynamic rudders control craft heading.

HULL: Moulded glass reinforced plastic structure.

ACCOMMODATION: Side-by-side seating for two in an open cockpit.

DIMENSIONS
Length: 4·4m (14ft 5¼in)
Beam: 2·4m (7ft 10½in)
Height: 1·2m (3ft 11¼in)

WEIGHTS
Normal empty: 270kg (595lb)
Normal all-up: 520kg (1,149lb)
Normal payload: 200kg (441lb)

PERFORMANCE
Max speed: 110km/h (68·5mph)
Vertical obstacle clearance: 0·3m (11¾in)

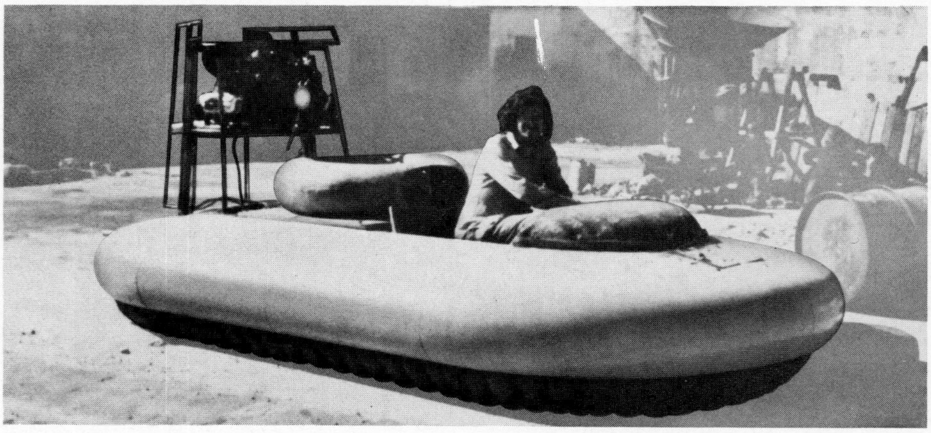

Prototype of the JOB-3 amphibious two-seater which has attained a speed of 110km/h (68·5mph) over water. Volkswagen air-cooled four-cylinder engines are employed for both lift and propulsion

YACARE II

The Yacare II is a single-engined fully amphibious ACV designed to carry payloads of up to 1,600kg (3,528lb) on its load deck in containers or modules. The passenger module seats 12.

LIFT AND PROPULSION: Integrated system powered by a single 300hp engine. This drives a centrifugal lift fan and a variable-pitch propeller for propulsion.

CONTROLS: Craft heading is controlled by twin aerodynamic rudders hinged to fins located at the rear of the propeller. Side located thrust ports aid low-speed manoeuvring.

HULL: Moulded glass reinforced plastic and aluminium structure.

ACCOMMODATION: The control cabin, forward, has seats for the two-to-three man crew. Passenger module seats twelve passengers.

DIMENSIONS
EXTERNAL
Length overall, power off: 11m (36ft 1in)
skirt inflated: 11m (36ft 1in)
Beam overall, power off: 6m (19ft 8in)
skirt inflated: 6m (19ft 8in)
Height overall on landing pads, power off: 3m (9ft 10in)
skirt inflated: 3·8m (12ft 6in)
Skirt depth: 0·8m (2ft 7½in)
INTERNAL
Control cabin max width: 2·3m (7ft 6½in)
floor area: 5·3m² (58ft²)
Passenger cabin, floor area: 8·74m² (93ft²)
Freight deck area: 21m² (226ft²)

WEIGHTS
Normal empty: 2,200kg (4,851lb)
Normal all-up: 3,500kg (7,717lb)
Normal payload: 1,300kg (2,866lb)
Max payload: 1,600kg (3,528lb)

PERFORMANCE
Max speed, calm water, max power: 60 knots
Max speed, calm water, max continuous power: 55 knots
Cruising speed, calm water: 40 knots
Max wave capability, scheduled runs: 1m (3ft 3in)

AUSTRALIA

NEOTERIC ENGINEERING AFFILIATES PTY LTD

Box 2438, GPO Melbourne 3001, Australia
Telephone: (03) 391 3639
Officials:
Christopher J Fitzgerald, *Managing Director*
Robert K Wilson *General Manager*
Alan Fitzgerald, *Company Accountant*

Neoteric Engineering Affiliates Pty Ltd specialises in the research and development of industrial and commercial ACV systems in addition to the design and marketing of small recreational hovercraft. A number of Neoteric's executives have been active in ACV research in Australia since 1960 and before forming the present company conducted a business under the name of Australian Air Cushion Vehicles Development.

The company is at present concentrating on marketing single and two-seat models of the Neova amphibious hovercraft, which are available in kit or ready-built form. A three-seat sports model, also available in a light utility configuration, is under development.

In 1975 Neoteric-USA Incorporated was established. This is now the corporate headquarters for the Neoteric Group of Companies and is based at the Fort Harrison Industrial Park, Terre Haute, Indiana 47804. Details of the Neova range of light hovercraft will be found in this edition under the entry for Neoteric-USA Inc.

The Neova is suited to production line manufacture and can be substantially scaled-up for increased load capacity.

International patents are pending and the company is seeking licensing agreements with overseas manufacturers.

Duck shooting from the Neoteric Neova II light hovercraft

STOLKRAFT PTY LTD

52 Hilltop Road, Clareville Beach, New South Wales 2107, Australia
Telephone: 918 3620
Cables: Stolkraft Sydney
Officials:
Leo D Stolk, *Managing Director/Designer*
Clive M Backhouse, *Chairman*
Rhodea Gladys Stolk, *Director/Company Secretary*
Consultant:
James Eken, Commercial Marine Design, 24 Thomas Street, Chatswood, New South Wales 2067, Australia
Overseas Representative:
United Kingdom
Richard M Jones, 61 Grayling Road, Stoke Newington, London N16, England

L D Stolk's Stolkraft concept is a new approach to the air-lubricated planing hull. His main objectives have been to overcome the basic pitch instability apparent in some earlier designs and to eliminate bow wash.

At speed an appreciable amount of aerodynamic lift is built up by a ram-air cushion at the bow, and this, combined with air fed through twin bow intakes and vented from a transverse step beneath the hull aft, creates a second ram-air cushion and lifts the craft in order to reduce frictional resistance.

A feature of the concept is the absence of trim variation. The craft rises bodily, parallel to the surface and has no tendency to porpoise. At speed it creates neither bow-wash nor hull spray outward. The aerodynamic lift is approximately 37%.

The hull design is applicable to a wide range of vessels from passenger ferries for inland waterways to seagoing craft.

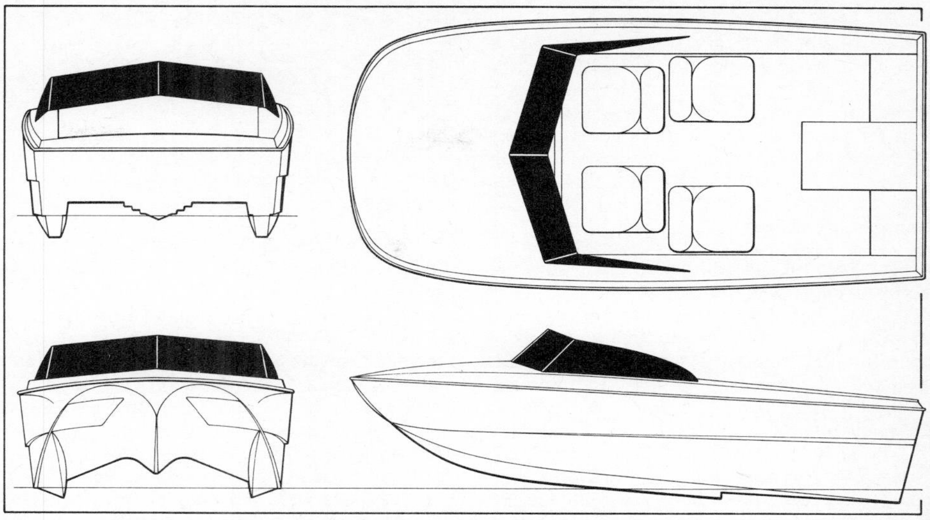

General arrangement of the Stolkraft Swift I fibreglass-hulled sports craft

INCEPTOR II SKI.16 Mk 1

The prototype of the company's first production runabout is the fibreglass-hulled Inceptor II SKI.16 Mk 1.

Location of the air intakes and the vented transverse step is seen in the accompanying drawing of the Stolkraft Swift I, the production model.

PROPULSION: A Volvo Aquamatic stern-drive of either 170 or 225hp, drives a water screw for propulsion. Alternatively twin outboards can be fitted. Fuel is carried in two 20-gallon tanks located amidships, port and starboard.

HULL: Stepped trimaran configuration. Moulded fibreglass construction with bulkheads in fibreglass-covered seaply. Craft has eight foam-filled airtight compartments for positive buoyancy.

ACCOMMODATION: Open cockpit for driver and six adults and up to two children.

DIMENSIONS
Length overall: 4·95m (16ft 3in)
Beam: 2·13m (7ft)
Width overall: 2·44m (8ft)
WEIGHTS
Normal load: 550kg (1,200lb)
Max load: 680kg (1,500lb)
PERFORMANCE
PROTOTYPE, INCEPTOR I
Max speed/load 600lb/170hp: 80km/h (50mph)

Prototype of Stolkraft's first production runabout, the Inceptor II. Power for this seven-seater is provided by a 170hp Volvo Aquamatic stern drive engine. Twin bow intakes feed pressurised air to a ventilated transverse step and thence to a second air cushion created beneath the hull aft

SWIFT I

Configuration of the Swift I is almost identical to that of the Inceptor II, except for the side hulls which have a 20% outward deadrise at the cushionborne waterline level, a feature designed to eliminate bow wash and inward hull spray. This particular model has been built with an eye to watersport applications—water-skiing, towing and racing.

PROPULSION: Waterscrew powered by either an inboard V drive or outboard engine. Alternatively, a ducted fan can be employed. Power output normally in the 75-150hp range, although more powerful engines can be installed for racing. Speed predicted for the Mk I, with a 75hp engine and a load of 204·1kg (450lb), is 35 knots. No estimate at this stage can be given for the higher hp range as research has not been completed at higher speed levels.

Stolkraft SKI.16 Mk 1 at speed demonstrating the absence of wave formation, bow wash and outward hull spray

HULL: Similar to Inceptor II.
DIMENSIONS
Length overall: 4·12m (13ft 6in)
Beam: 1·78m (5ft 10in)
Width overall: 1·93m (6ft 4in)
WEIGHTS
Normal load: 204·1kg (450lb)
Max load: 362·85kg (800lb)

24 METRE COMMUTER FERRY

Latest addition to the Stolkraft range is this 110-tonne passenger ferry, designed at the request of the Public Transport Commission of New South Wales for consideration and evaluation for fast commuter services across Sydney Harbour. One of the main attractions of the Stolkraft concept is the absence of wave formation in the wake and consequently the lack of erosion along the foreshores.

LIFT AND PROPULSION: Motive power is supplied by two marinised gas-turbines, each developing 3,500hp. Output is transmitted to two waterjets which discharge through area nozzles beneath the transom. Watertight bulkheads separate the engine room from the waterjet pumps. At 25 knots and upwards aerodynamic lift is built up by a ram-air cushion at the bow and this, combined with air fed through twin bow intakes and vented from a transverse step beneath the hull aft, creates a second ram-air cushion and raises the craft in order to reduce frictional resistance. Stability is inherent and a stable platform is provided.

Despite pitch and heave forces in choppy seas, extensive tests have shown that this type of craft can self-regulate its riding attitude. Recovery from wave-induced perturbation is rapid and smooth and optimum trim is resumed. Direction (yaw) and transverse (roll) stability is always maintained.

HULL: Hull and superstructure are in marine grade weldable aluminium alloy. Subdivisions are incorporated in accordance with international safety regulations for passenger ferries.
ACCOMMODATION: Passengers are accommodated in an aft saloon on the main deck, seating 166, and a forward saloon, on the main foredeck, seating 54. Thirty standing passengers can be accommodated on short runs, giving a total capacity of 250 passengers. The captain is accommodated in a raised wheelhouse located between the forward and main saloons. Access to the passenger cabins is via four doors (two port, two starboard) each 1·35m (4ft 5in) wide by 2·1m (6ft 10½in) high, sited on the main deck, and located to ensure an equal flow through both entrances. Entrance to the engine rooms is via hatches in the main deck aft of the main passenger saloon.

DIMENSIONS
Length overall: 24·45m (80ft 5½in)
Beam: 9·9m (32ft 6in)
Width overall: 11·1m (36ft 5in)
Deck length: 23·85m (78ft 3in)
width: 10·85m (35ft 7in)
Total deck area: 258m² (2,784ft²)
Passenger deck area: 189·3m² (2,140ft²)
Draft hullborne: 1·95m (5ft 5in)
Draft cushionborne at cruising speed: 90cm (3ft)

WEIGHTS
Empty: 68·25 tonnes
Operating: 93 tonnes
Normal operating: 110 tonnes

PERFORMANCE
Cruising speed, sea state 3: 35 knots
Max speed: 39 knots

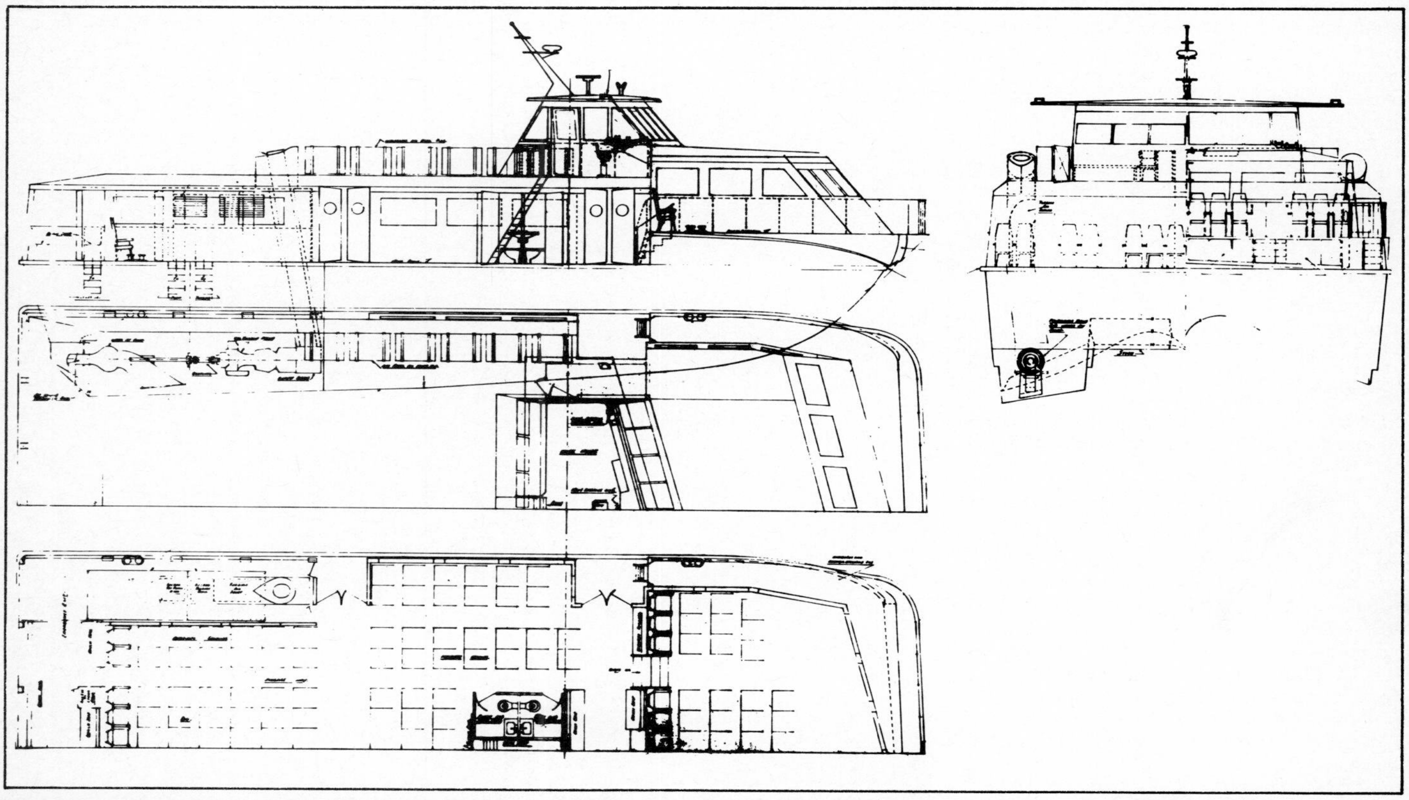

Stolkraft study for a 24 metre, 220-seat high-speed commuter ferry, prepared for the Public Transport Commission of New South Wales. Displacement of the craft fully loaded, would be 109 tonnes and its cruising speed, in sea state 3, would be 35 knots

TAYLORCRAFT TRANSPORT (DEVELOPMENT) PTY LTD

Parafield Airport, South Australia 5106, Australia
Telephone: 258 4944
Officials:
R V Taylor, *Managing Director*
J Taylor, *Director*
R J Lomman, *Director*
G Nimmo, *Director*
G A Barnes, *Director*

Taylorcraft has been active in ACV research and development since 1966. It is currently developing and marketing machines ranging from the Kartaire, a light single-seater for home builders, to a mixed-traffic sidewall craft designed to carry ten cars and up to 100 passengers.

Other additions to the company's range are the Islander IA for coastal medical work and the Islander IV freighter.

The Skimaire range is licensed to Fairey Australasia Pty Ltd by a holding company, Taylorcraft Transport Pty Ltd.

AIR-BOAT

This light alloy-hulled high-speed air-boat is intended for use in shallow or weed-choked rivers and lakes, or for operations in coastal and river waters in general. The planing hull is protected by skids on its bottom. Full-length guard rails and a propeller guard ensure safety when operating near overhanging trees.

The large deck and open cockpit area permit bulky loads to be carried. Seating is provided for four people.

PROPULSION: A GM 308 in³ V8 automotive engine drives via a gearbox a 1·82m (6ft) diameter propeller, giving the craft sufficient reserve power for riding over reeds and mud banks. A closed cooling system is employed to avoid blocked intakes in weed-choked waters.

CONTROLS: Stick-operated rudders and elevators control craft heading and trim.

DIMENSIONS
Length: 6·09m (20ft)
Beam: 2·43m (8ft)
Height: 2·28m (7ft 6in)
Draft: 152mm (6in) empty
101mm (4in) laden
38mm (1½in) planing

WEIGHTS
Empty: 453·59kg (1,000lb)
Payload: 453·59kg (1,000lb)
Fuel tank: 45·46 litre (10 gallon)
COST: A$ 6,250

KARTAIRE III

A lightweight, aluminium-hulled, single-seater, the Kartaire III is intended for recreational and light liaison duties. It is fully amphibious and capable of operating over light vegetation as well as over water, mudflats and sand.

LIFT AND PROPULSION: Lift power is supplied by a single 172cc Fuji two-stroke, driving a 609mm (2ft) diameter, six-bladed axial fan. The lift fan duct is of light alloy and is located behind the driver's seat to provide a clear load space at the front. Thrust is furnished by a second Fuji engine of the same type driving a six-bladed, fixed-pitch 609mm (2ft) diameter ducted fan. The thrust unit is carried on light alloy members above the rear of the hull and can be detached if required to simplify storage or transport.

CONTROLS: An aircraft type control column

operates twin aerodynamic rudders set in the thrust fan slipstream for directional control. The engines are fitted with pull starters and each engine has its own fuel tank.
HULL: Light aluminium alloy construction, riveted and caulked at the seams. Watertight buoyancy box amidship serves as the seat.
DIMENSIONS
HARD STRUCTURE
Length: 3·35m (11ft)
Beam: 1·82m (6ft)
Height: 1·37m (4ft 6in)
WEIGHTS
Empty: 72·57kg (160lb)
Gross: 158·75kg (350lb)
PERFORMANCE (with 77·1kg (170lb) driver only)
Still air speeds:
land: 72·42km/h (45mph)
water: 64·37km/h (40mph)
Hard structure clearance: 152mm (6in)
Gradient from standstill: 1 : 9
PRICE: A$1,250

KARTAIRE IV

The Kartaire IV is an ultra-light air cushion vehicle designed for use over water, mud flats and sand. It may be used as emergency transport in flooded areas or as a dinghy in sheltered waters. Its useful hard structure clearance allows it to operate over fairly rough surfaces.
LIFT AND PROPULSION: Lift power is supplied by a single Fuji 172cc two-stroke driving a 609mm (2ft) diameter six-bladed axial fan. Propulsive thrust is furnished by a similar engine, driving a six-bladed, fixed-pitch 609mm (2ft) diameter axial fan. The lift and thrust fan ducts are of alloy construction.
CONTROLS: Stick-operated rudder and throttle levers for lift and thrust engines. Both engines are fitted with pull starters.
HULL: The hull is a simple inflatable raft, from which is suspended a finger type skirt. All fabric parts are made from neoprene and hypalon-coated nylon. The hull side and end members are inflated by hand bellows. A light alloy frame with plug-in side stringers supports the two engines.
ACCOMMODATION: The open cockpit is 1·52m (5ft) long and 0·55m (1ft 10in) wide and is provided with a single inflated seat which is adjustable to ensure correct trim. Although designed as a single-seater, a passenger may be carried under overload conditions.
DIMENSIONS
Length, hard structure: 3·04m (10ft)
Beam: 1·52m (5ft)
Height: 1·37m (4ft 6in)
WEIGHTS
Empty: 45·35kg (100lb)
Gross: 127kg (280lb)
PERFORMANCE
STILL AIR
Max speed, over land: 72·42km/h (45mph)
over water: 64·37km/h (40mph)

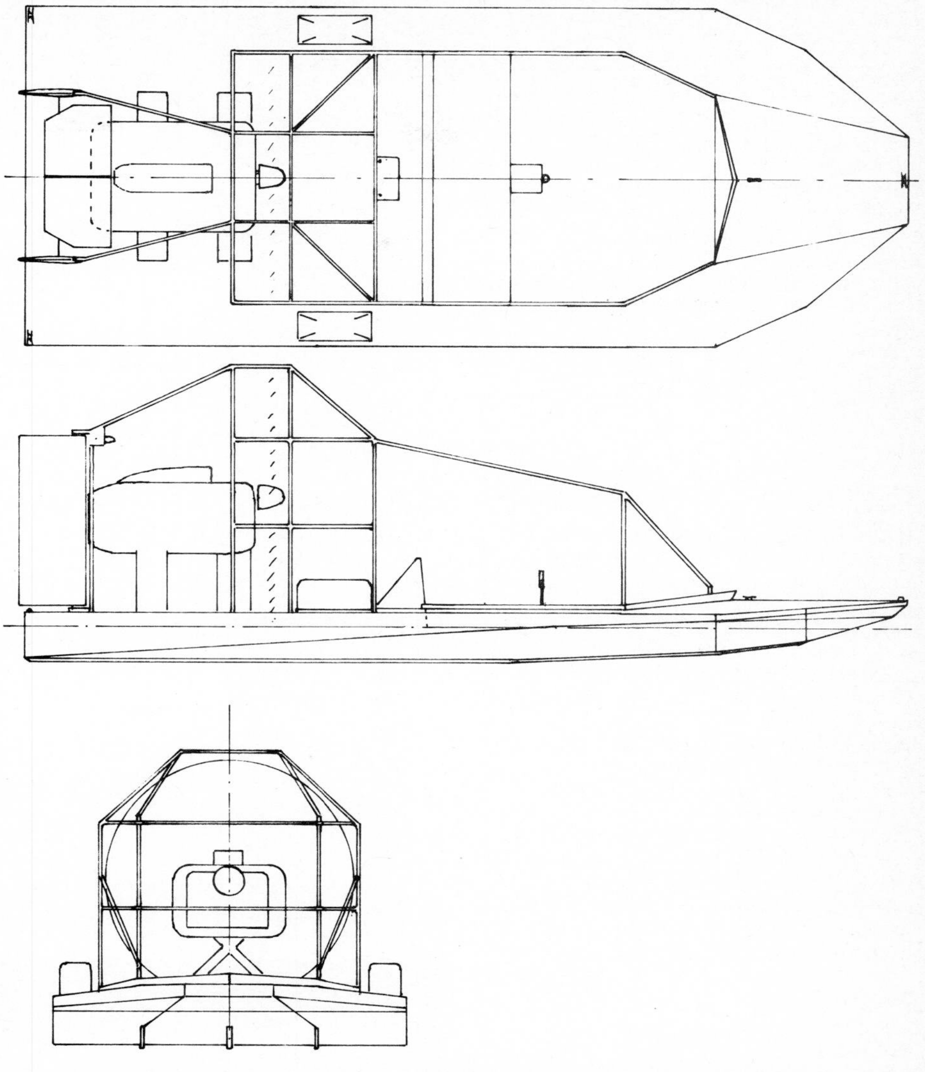

The Taylorcraft four-seater Air Boat, powered by a GM 308 V8 automotive engine and designed for use in shallow, weed-choked rivers

Kartaire III, an enlarged version of Kartaire I, powered by two 172cc engines. It will carry one adult and up to two children

SPORTAIRE I

An inflatable-hulled three-seater, the Sportaire was designed as a light recreational craft, but the large open cockpit makes it suitable for a number of utility roles ranging from skin-diving support to flood rescue and light patrol duties. Deflated and folded for transport or storage the Sportaire measures 1·8 × 1·2 × 1·2m (6 × 4 × 4ft). It can be carried by two people or towed behind a vehicle on a small trailer.
LIFT AND PROPULSION: Two ducted fans provide forward or reverse thrust while a third ducted fan is employed for lift. All three fans are driven by a single 30hp two-cylinder two-stroke engine, via belts. Cushion area is $11·78m^2$ ($127ft^2$); cushion pressure is 311 Pa ($6·5lb/ft^2$). Static thrust is 533N (120lb). Recommended fuel is 25 : 1 two-stroke mixture.
CONTROLS: Steering is by conventional wheel which controls twin aerodynamic rudders. Levers control thrust reversal mechanism.
HULL: Simple inflatable multi-compartment hull, from which is suspended a segmented skirt. Hull has built-in handgrips. A simple drainage system and a bow canopy are provided. The hull can be inflated by a car vacuum cleaner. Special bellows are provided to bring the hull up to its operating pressure of 2·5psi.
DIMENSIONS
Hull length, overall: 5·18m (17ft)
Hull beam, overall: 2·74m (9ft)
Height,
on landing pads: 1·06m (3ft 6in)
on cushion: 1·52m (5ft)
WEIGHTS
Empty: 127kg (280lb)
Payload: 158·9kg (350lb)
Driver and fuel: 86kg (190lb)
Gross: 363kg (800lb)
PERFORMANCE
CALM WATER
Cruising speed: 64·37km/h (40mph)
Range: 96km (60 miles)
Gradient: 1 in 6

Clearance height: 45cm (1ft 6in)
PRICE: On application

SPORTAIRE II

An aluminium-hulled three-seater, Sportaire II is intended for both light commercial and recreational use. Maximum speed is 65-70km/h (40-45mph).

LIFT AND PROPULSION: Lift is supplied by a 10hp Briggs and Stratton four-stroke engine driving an axial fan located ahead of the cockpit. Propulsive thrust is provided by a 45hp Cyuna 440cc two-stroke driving two ducted fans via belts. Both fans provide either forward or reverse thrust.

Fuel recommended is standard grade petrol and 50 : 1 two-stroke mixture.

CONTROLS: Twin stick type controls operate the air rudders and the thrust reversal mechanism. Throttle controls for the two engines are mounted on the sticks. Starter and shut-off switches are located in the cockpit. Other controls are located on the engines.

HULL: Built entirely in marine grade light alloy sheet. Basic structure is a 6in deep flat-bottomed buoyancy tank with a 45 degree deadrise to the skirt outer hinge line. Forward hull is checked in from above the skirt line to the windscreen.

ACCOMMODATION: Open cockpit with single bench seat, behind which is a 0·457 × 1·8m (1ft 6in × 6ft) well for light freight or equipment.

DIMENSIONS
Length overall, on cushion: 6·2m (20ft 4in)
off cushion: 5·9m (18ft)
Beam overall, on cushion: 3·05m (10ft)
off cushion: 2·4m (8ft)
Height overall, on cushion: 1·68m (5ft 6in)
off cushion: 1·37m (4ft 6in)

WEIGHTS
Empty: 285kg (630lb)
Payload: 3 × 77·1kg (3 × 170lb)
Driver and fuel: 86·2kg (190lb)
Gross: 603kg (1,330lb)

PERFORMANCE
Speed: 65-79km/h (40-45mph)
Gradient: 1 : 10
Range: approx 96km (60 miles)
Clearance: 305mm (12in) (hard structure)

SPORTAIRE IIIA

This new derivative of the Sportaire has a redesigned hull and elongated fan ducts. As with earlier craft in this series it is intended for both light commercial and recreational use.

LIFT AND PROPULSION: Lift is supplied by a 10hp Briggs and Stratton four-stroke engine driving an axial fan located ahead of the cockpit. Propulsive thrust is provided by a single 45hp Cyuna 440cc two-stroke driving two ducted fans via belts. Fuel recommended is standard grade petrol and 50:1 two-stroke mixture.

CONTROLS: Stick-operated rudders control craft direction.

HULL: Built in marine grade light alloy.

ACCOMMODATION: Open cockpit with single bench seat. Well for light freight or equipment behind.

DIMENSIONS
Length overall, on cushion: 4·52m (14ft 10in)
off cushion: 4·01m (13ft 2in)
Beam overall, on cushion: 2·74m (9ft)
off cushion: 2·23m (7ft 4in)
Height overall, on cushion: 1·21m (4ft)
off cushion: 0·91m (3ft)

WEIGHTS
Empty: 158·75kg (350lb)
Gross: 385·53kg (850lb)

PERFORMANCE: Not available at the time of going to press.

INTERCEPTAIRE

The Interceptaire is a two-seat sports craft intended for use on rivers and sheltered waters. The standard model is powered by a 45kW (60bhp) Volkswagen automotive engine, but with a more powerful engine of up to 68kW (90bhp), it will perform well as a three-seater.

LIFT AND PROPULSION: Integrated system

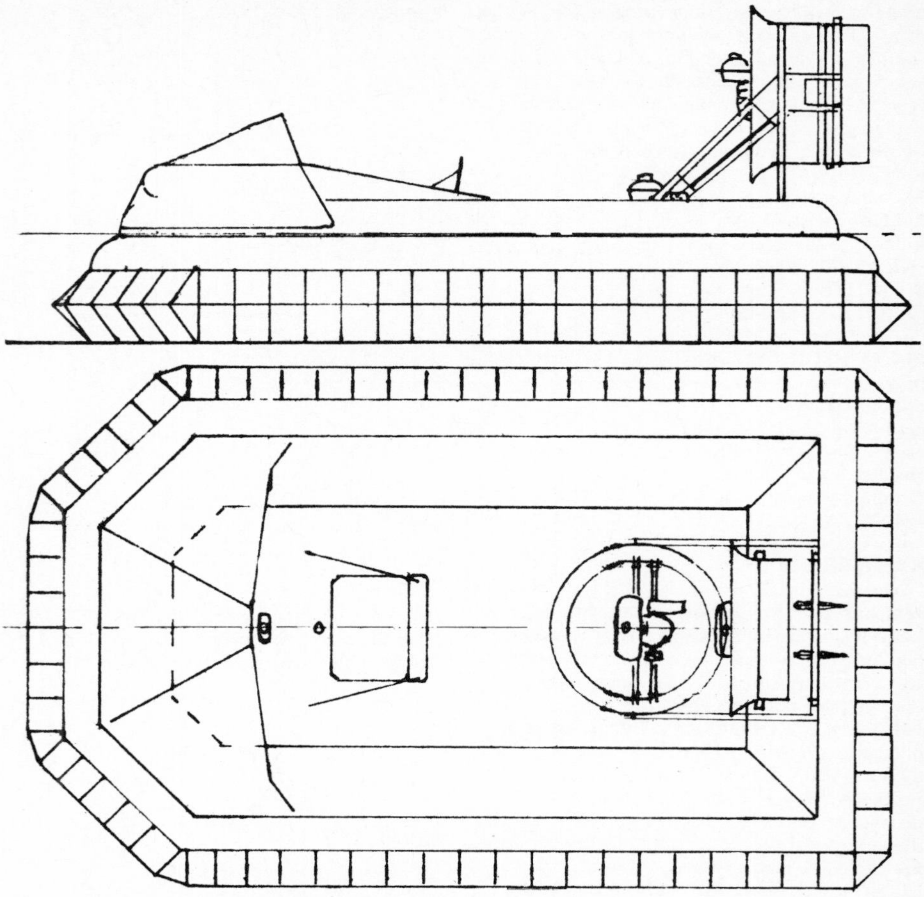

Taylorcraft Kartaire IV, a single-seater with an inflatable hull. Power is supplied by two 172cc Fuji two-strokes, one for lift and one for propulsion

Kartaire IV amphibious single-seater. Top speed over land is 72·42km/h (45mph)

Sportaire II aluminium-hulled three-seater for recreational and light commercial applications

powered by a single 45kW (60bhp) Volkswagen 1,600cc air-cooled automotive engine, located aft of the cockpit, and mounted on a steel frame which is bonded and bolted to the bottom of the hull. The fan is driven directly, avoiding the use of gears or belts.
CONTROLS: Centrally-mounted control stick operates flaps and valves in the duct outlets, enabling all the thrust air to be ejected aft, reversed for braking or applied differentially for turning. With the stick in the central position static hover can be maintained.
HULL: Monocoque construction in grp with reinforcing bulkheads.
ACCOMMODATION: Open cockpit, with bench-type seat for driver and up to two passengers.
DIMENSIONS
Length overall, on cushion: 5·25m (17ft 3in)
Beam overall, on cushion: 3·05m (10ft)
Height, on cushion: 1·03m (3ft 5in)
Draft, displacement: 229mm (9in)
WEIGHTS
Empty: 454kg (1,000lb)
Gross: 635kg (1,410lb)
PERFORMANCE
Cruising speed over land: 70km/h (45mph)
Cruising speed over water: 55km/h (35mph)
Hard structure clearance: 305mm (12in)
Range: 195km (120 miles)

PUFFAIRE II

This small, sturdily built utility vehicle is intended for operation over land, rivers and sheltered waters. It has an open cockpit with two seats and an open deck which can accommodate bulky loads of up to 453kg (1,000lb). Various alternative accommodation arrangements can be made, including the installation of a folding awning to protect both the crew and cargo, or a five-seat modular passenger cabin, which fits into the well deck immediately aft of the control cabin. A Trailaire VII ACV trailer unit (see company's entry in section covering ACV Trailers and Heavy Lift Systems) can be towed by the craft, increasing the payload capacity to two tons.
LIFT AND PROPULSION: Integrated system powered by a Ford 350 V8 water-cooled automotive engine developing 153kW (205hp) at 3,800rpm. Fuel is premium grade petrol. Mounted inboard, the engine drives two centrifugal fans through a torque convertor. Both fans are totally enclosed in ducts to eliminate any danger from rotating parts. A high thrust unit can be supplied for special applications.
CONTROLS: Directional control is effected by a skirt shift system and supplemented by differential use of airjet thrust. A single control column, on which is mounted the throttle lever, is located on the right hand side of the cockpit. This also controls reverse thrust.
SKIRT: 457mm (1ft 6in) high skirt with 100% segments. Fingers and groups of fingers are easily replaced when necessary.
DIMENSIONS
OVERALL
Length, on cushion: 6·7m (22ft)
hard structure: 5·8m (19ft)
Beam, on cushion: 4·27m (14ft)
hard structure: 2·49m (8ft 2in)
Height, on cushion: 2·13m (7ft)
hard structure: 1·69m (5ft 7in)
Draft afloat: 229mm (9in)
Cargo deck size: 2·13 × 1·83m (7ft × 6ft 3in)
WEIGHTS
Empty: 1,193kg (2,630lb)
Payload: 453kg (1,000lb)
Fuel and driver: 168kg (370lb)
Gross: 1,814kg (4,000lb)
PERFORMANCE
Max speed, over land: 70km/h (45mph)
over water: 55km/h (35mph)
Hump speed: 20km/h (12mph)
Max gradient: 1 : 6
Hard structure clearance: 457mm (1ft 6in)
Max wave height: 0·914m (3ft)
Range: 400km (250 miles)

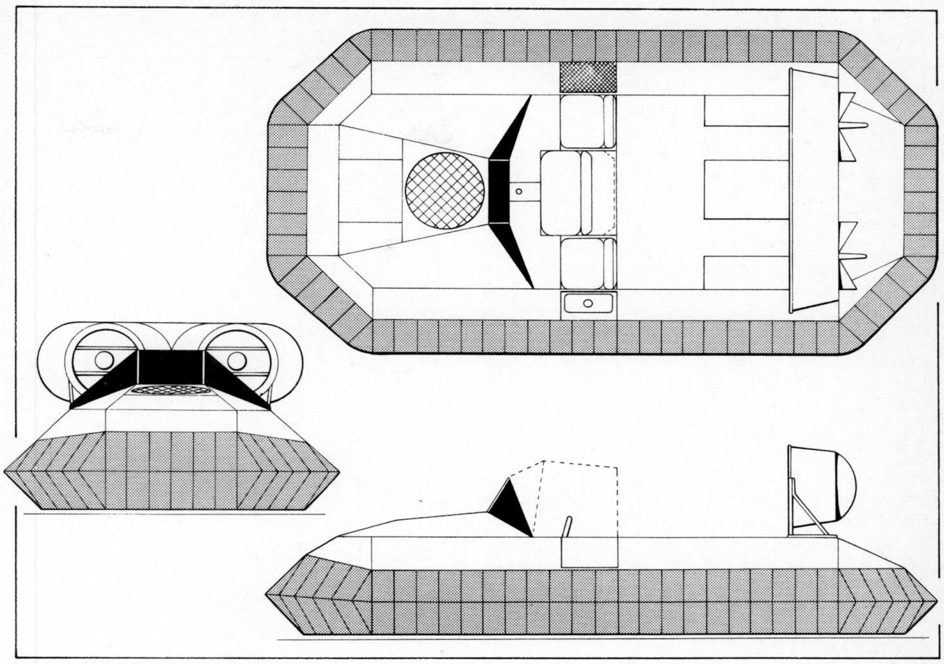

General arrangement of the Sportaire II

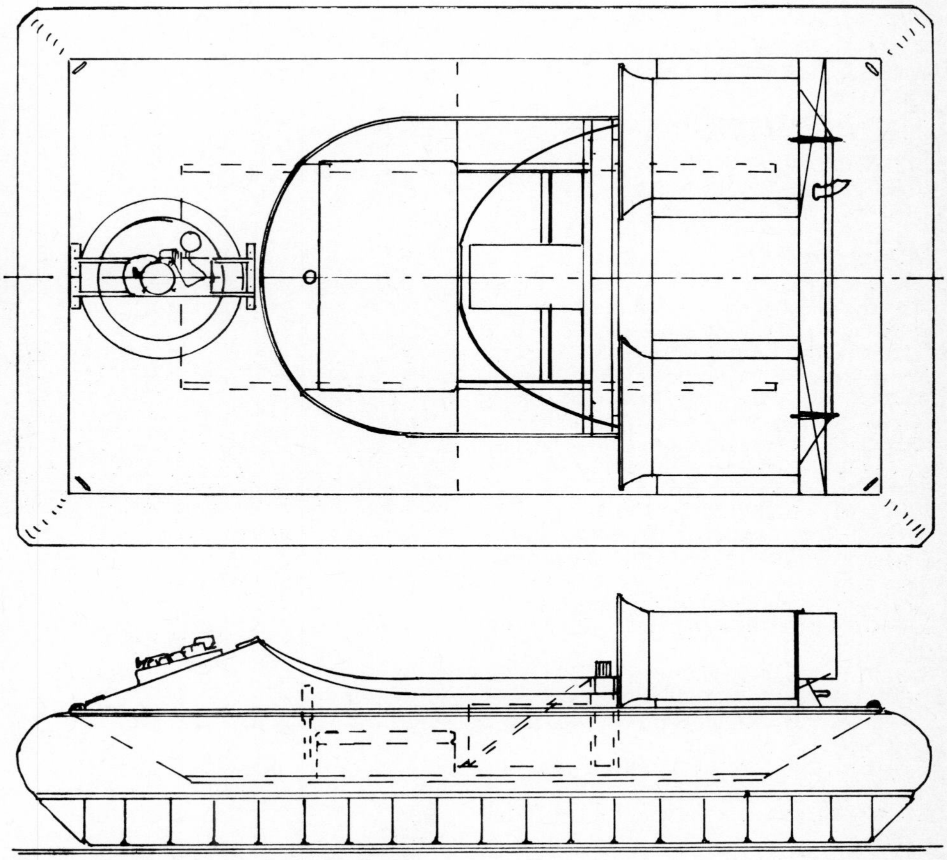

Sportaire IIIA light hovercraft

PUFFAIRE IIS

This new model of the Puffaire features a 1·82m (6ft) longer hull, enabling it to carry loads of greater bulk or a lengthened cabin module containing seats for 12 passengers. Compared with Puffaire II, Puffaire IIS has a payload capacity of 975kg (2,150lb), an increase of 521·6kg (1,150lb).

The overall load space measures 4·42 × 1·83m (14ft 7in × 6ft). Lift, propulsion and control arrangements are identical or similar to those of the Puffaire II.
DIMENSIONS
Length, hard structure: 9·24m (30ft 4in)
on cushion: 9·24m (30ft 4in)
Beam, central hull: 2·49m (8ft 2in)
Beam, sidebodies extended: 4·57m (15ft)
Height, on landing pads: 1·69m (5ft 2in)
cushionborne: 1·82m (6ft)
Draft, afloat: 229mm (9in)
Deck load space: 4·42 × 1·83m (14ft 7in × 6ft)
Deck loading height: 330mm (13in) with 508mm (20in) sill
WEIGHTS
Empty: 902kg (1,990lb)
Payload: 975kg (2,150lb)
Fuel and driver: 168kg (370lb)
Gross: 2,063kg (4,550lb)
PERFORMANCE
Speed over land: 70km/h (45mph)

Speed over water: 55km/h (35mph)
Hard structure clearance: 457mm (18in)
Max wave height: 1m (3ft)
Gradient: 1 in 8

MODEL 750/1

Taylorcraft's latest utility ACV is intended for a range of light commercial roles and is also suitable for search and rescue operations in sheltered and coastal waters.

LIFT AND PROPULSION: Cushion air is supplied by a single 95bhp Leyland 4·4 litre V8 automotive engine driving two 0·68m (2ft 3in) diameter centrifugal fans. Both fans are enclosed in ducts to eliminate any danger from rotating parts. Propulsive thrust is from a single 120hp Leyland 4·4 litre V8 engine aft driving a pylon-mounted 1·82m (6ft) diameter McCauley reversible-pitch propeller.

CONTROLS: Directional control is by twin aerodynamic rudders aft operating in the propeller slipstream. Braking and reversing is effected by reversed propeller pitch.

SKIRT: Bag and segment type with a high outer hinge line around the hull. A separate skirt blower gives variable response characteristics.

HULL: All metal construction with a foam sandwich buoyancy tank.

ACCOMMODATION: Enclosed cabin seating driver and one passenger.

DIMENSIONS
Length overall, on cushion: 9·75m (32ft)
Width overall, on cushion: 5·48m (18ft)
Height on cushion: 3·43m (11ft 3in)
Well deck area: 2·4 × 2·4m (8 × 8ft)

WEIGHTS
All-up: 2,023kg (4,460lb)
Payload: 450kg (992lb)

PERFORMANCE
Cruising speed: 72·42km/h (45mph)
Gradient: 1 in 8

MODEL 775A

This new multi-role ACV is available in two versions: Model A, which is intended for services on inland and sheltered waters and Model B, a more powerful variant, with greater clearance height, designed for operation under a wider range of sea and land conditions. The craft is suitable for light utility work, patrol duties, search and rescue and communications. Stretchers and rescue gear can be carried in the cabin instead of seated passengers.

LIFT AND PROPULSION: Integrated system powered by a Leyland 4·4 litre V8 light alloy automotive engine developing 130hp at 3,800 rpm. Output is transferred to a double 0·76m (2ft 6in) diameter centrifugal fan for cushion lift and to two 0·91m (3ft) diameter ducted axial fans for thrust.

SKIRT: Bag and segment type.

DIMENSIONS
Length overall: 8m (26ft 3in)
Beam overall: 4·34m (14ft 3in)
Cabin deck: 2·43 × 2·74 × 1·37m (8ft × 9ft × 4ft 6in)
Bench seat length: 2 × 1·82m (6ft), 1 × 0·91m (3ft)
Door sizes: 0·76m (2ft 6in) wide × 1·06m (3ft 6in) high

WEIGHTS
All-up: 1,905·08kg (4,200lb)
Payload: 589·64kg (1,300lb)

PERFORMANCE
Cruising speed: 69·2km/h (43mph)
Gradient: 1 in 8
Hard structure clearance, Model A: 406mm (1ft 4in)
Model B: 0·6m (2ft)

ISLANDAIRE SERIES

This is a new series of multi-purpose, amphibious ACVs, each of which is powered by four automotive engines. Passenger, freight, fast patrol and ambulance versions are projected. The passenger versions—the Islandaire I, II and III—vary in length only, the cabins being arranged to seat 15, 20 and 25 respectively. An ambulance version, with an 8ft wide cabin to accommodate four stretcher cases, is designated Islandaire IA, and a fast patrol version, with more powerful engines, is designated IIIM. The freight model is the Islandaire IV, with a cargo deck measuring 2·28 ×4·26m (7ft 6in × 14ft).

The Islandaire series is designed to comply with the British Hovercraft Safety Requirements and the Australian ACV Code. Construction is closely supervised by qualified personnel at all stages and is generally subject to survey requirements.

Though differing in size, superstructure and

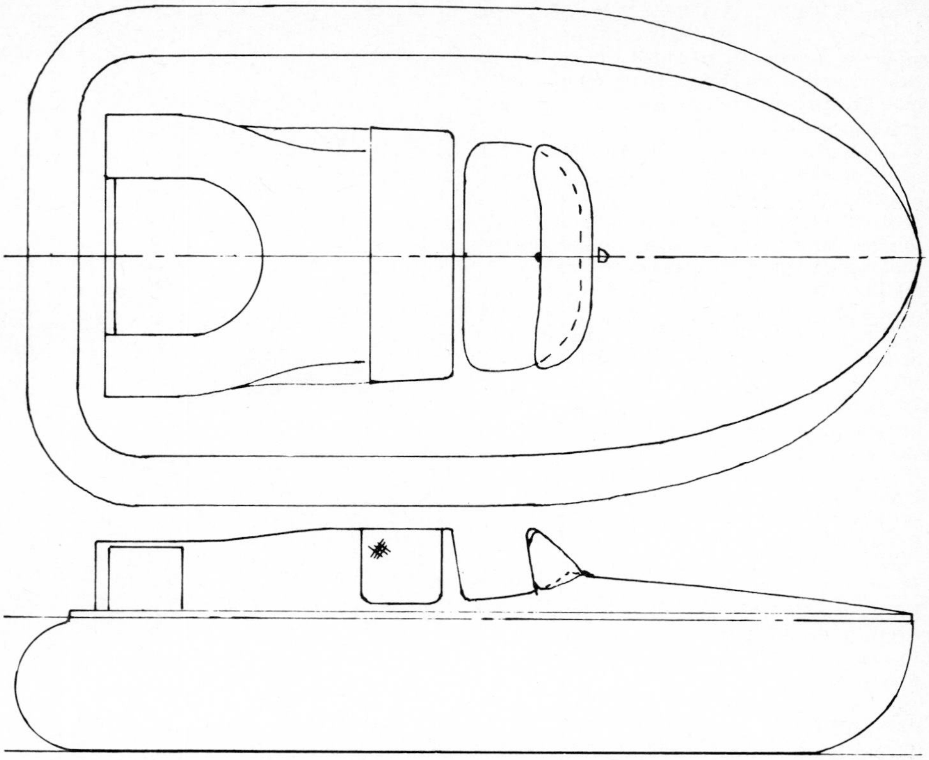

Interceptaire, a grp-hulled two-seater for use on rivers and sheltered waters. Power is supplied by a single 60bhp VW automotive engine

Puffaire II utility ACV during tests

Model of the Taylorcraft Puffaire II, showing the location of the centrifugal fans and load deck. The removable passenger module has five seats

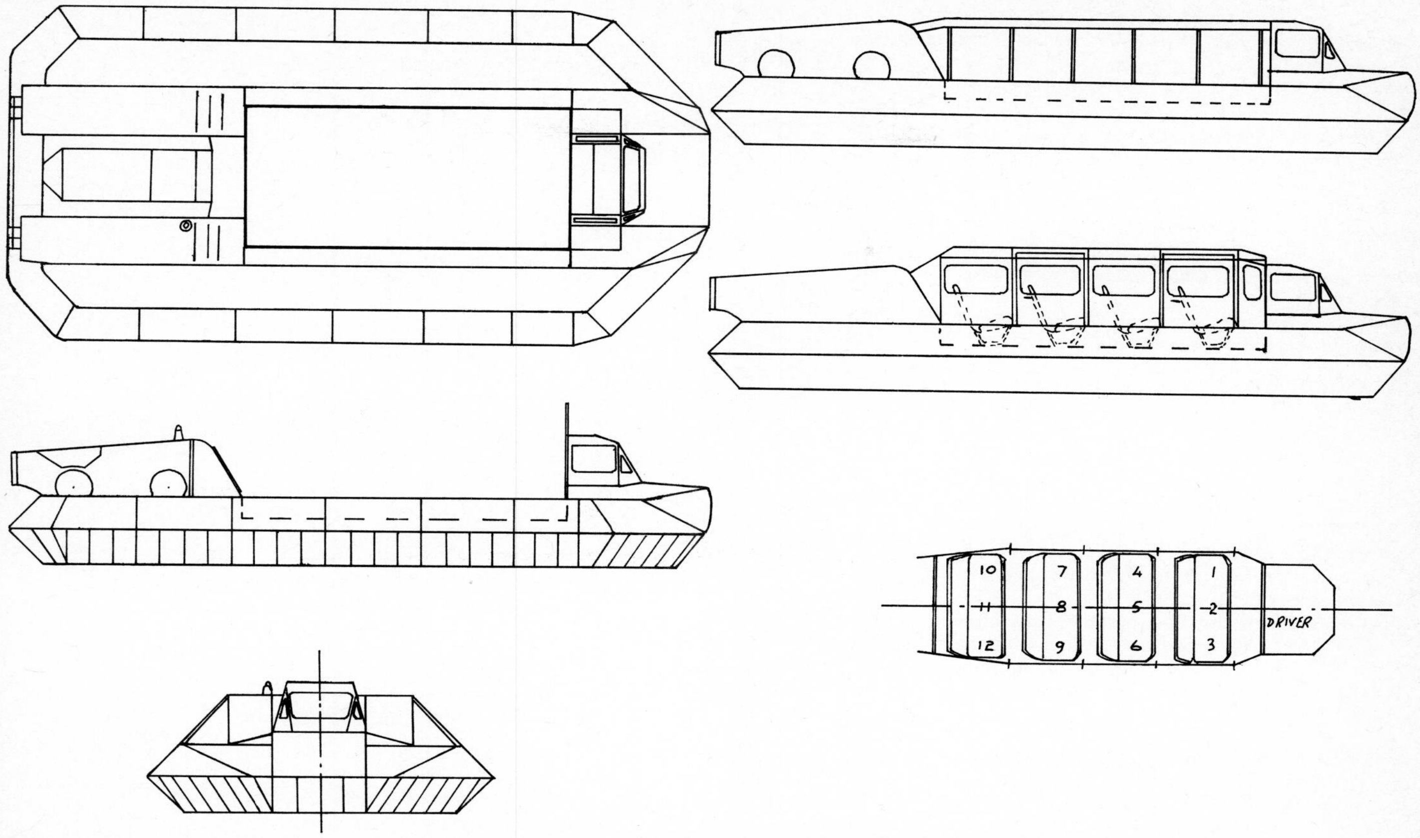

Stretched model of the Puffaire open-deck utility vehicle, the Puffaire IIS, with a payload capacity of 975kg (2,150lb)

equipment, vehicles in the Islandaire series are almost identical in terms of overall design. Dimensions, weights and performance figures are given at the end of this summary. The following characteristics apply to all designs:

LIFT AND PROPULSION: Cushion air is supplied by two V8 water-cooled automotive engines driving two 1016mm (3ft 4in) diameter centrifugal, double-intake fans through bevel gears. Propulsive thrust is furnished by two pylon-mounted V12 automotive engines, each driving a 1·82m (6ft) diameter reversible-pitch propeller through reduction gearboxes on the engine blocks. Lift and thrust engines have closed coolant systems and standard automotive radiators. The lift engines have flexible mountings to reduce interior noise.

CONTROLS: Directional control is effected by twin aerodynamic rudders operated by a rudder bar, differential propeller thrust and a plenum discharge system. The craft can be reversed into confined spaces and can be moved forward or turned without the use of its propellers.

HULL: The hull is divided into three longitudinal structures; the centre section, containing the accommodation, lift system, controls and main beams, and the two outer sections which serve as buoyancy tanks and extend the structure to the required width. Aluminium alloy is used throughout. Most frames, ribs and stringers are fabricated from alloy sheet to ensure lightness and strength. All parts are treated during assembly and exposed surfaces are finished in polyurethane paint. Foam-filled bottom sections and watertight compartments provide buoyancy.

SKIRT: Tapered bag and segment type skirt with a high outer hinge line around the hull. Skirt is fabricated in nylon neoprene with reinforced lower members. Nylon and corrosion resistant alloy fasteners are fitted. Skirt segments can be individually replaced for maintenance. Bag pressure is variable for maximum stability and anti-plough-in characteristics.

ACCOMMODATION: CREW CABIN: The control cabin is located in a raised position forward to provide the operating crew with a 360 degree view. Access to the forward deck for craft handling is provided by a hatch on the starboard side. A walkway and rail allow the cabin to be reached from a side boarding point. The rear of the control cabin is open to the main cabin, which is located amidships at a lower level. Forced air ventilation is provided.

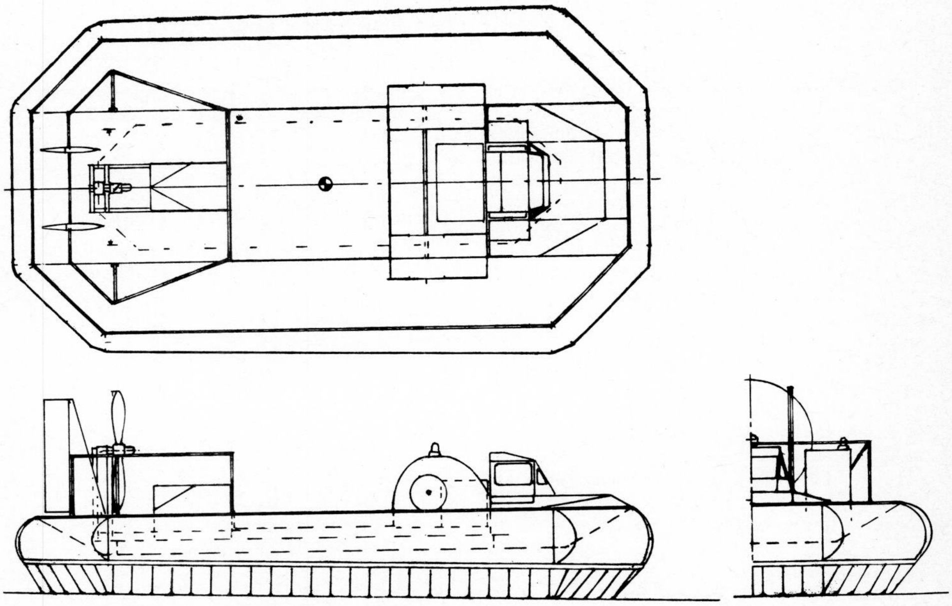

Taylorcraft Model 750/1 light commercial ACV powered by two Leyland V8 automotive engines

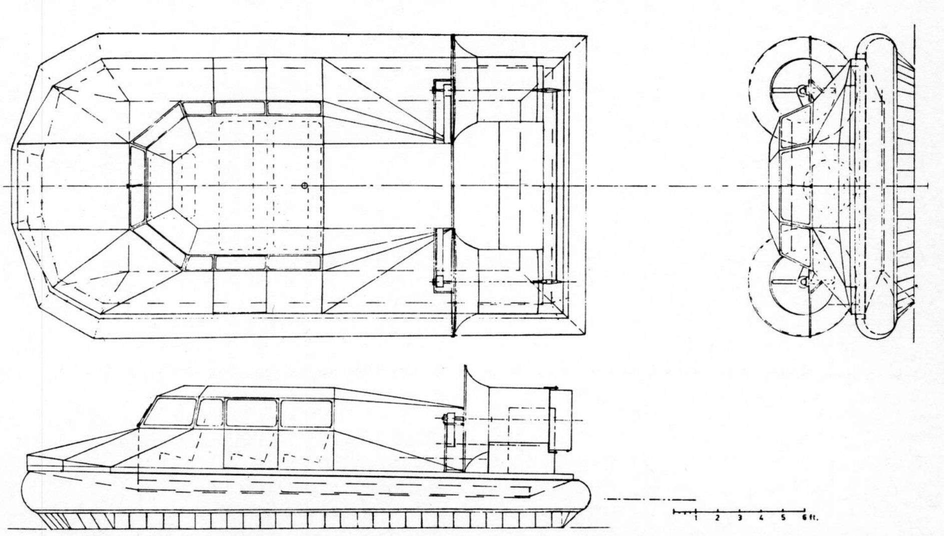

Taylorcraft Model 775A multi-role ACV, powered by a single 130hp Leyland V8 automotive engine. Payload is 590kg and the cruising speed is 69km/h

PASSENGER VERSIONS (ISLANDAIRE I, II AND III)

The Islandaire I, II and III vary only in length, the cabins being arranged to provide 15, 20 and 25 seats respectively.

Seats are arranged in rows of two and three with a central aisle. Space is provided at the rear of the cabin for toilet, galley and bar facilities. There is standing headroom in the cabin and the wide rear entry doors simplify access.

Emergency exits are provided in the cabin sides and space is available for rafts on the after deck.

Fire extinguisher stations are fitted at several points inside and outside the hull.

AMBULANCE FACILITIES (ISLANDAIRE IA)

The main cabin is 2·43m (8ft) wide at window level and 1·82m (6ft) high with 914mm (36in) wide doors. Bench seats each side of the central aisle will take a total of eight seated passengers or four stretcher cases. Space is provided for toilet and washing facilities. The attendant's seat is positioned to give access to both driver and passengers. An extendable gangway on the rear deck provides access to the cabin, whether the craft is on land or at a jetty. Space is available for the installation of any ambulance equipment required. Blanket lockers and stretchers are located beneath the seats.

FREIGHT VERSION (ISLANDAIRE IV)

The Islandaire IV has a freight deck measuring 2·28 × 4·26m (7ft 6in × 14ft) (enclosed by a tilt and canopy if required) and a two-seat control cabin. Loading is over the stern and down a ramp, with a side entry to the cabin. Loads may be laid fore and aft alongside the offset control cabin to a limit of 6·09m (20ft) in length.

FAST PATROL VERSION (ISLANDAIRE IIIM)

The combined control and main cabin area is available for rearrangement to suit specific military requirements. Providing the centre of gravity (vertical and horizontal) limitations are met, a variety of military weapons systems or other equipment can be carried within the gross weight of 4,989kg (11,000lb). The thrust engines are of larger cubic capacity and drive three-bladed propellers, allowing performance to be maintained at the increased weight.

SYSTEMS, ELECTRICAL: Normal automotive engine electrical systems are used, with a central fuel control and starting system. Power at 12V is available for navigation lights, radio, radar, cabin lights and auxiliary items from pairs of 45Ah batteries. All circuits are fused and warning lights are arranged so that they can be checked during starting procedures.

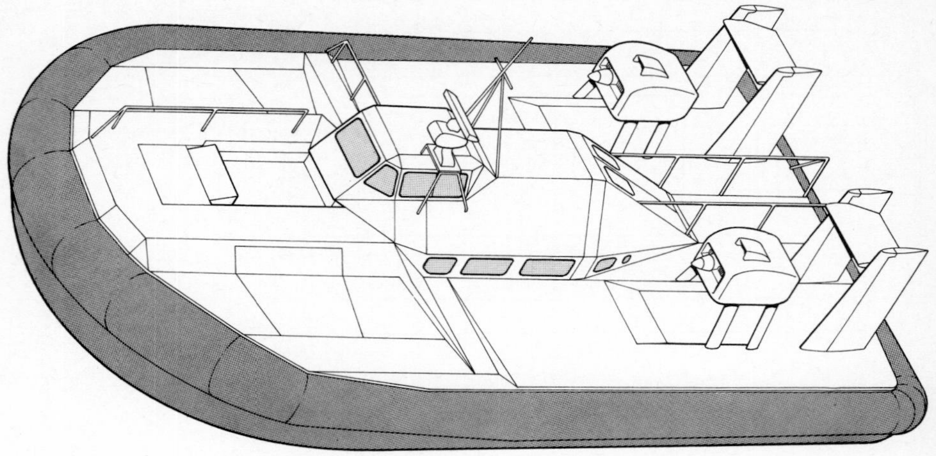
Islandaire IA ambulance and casualty evacuation craft

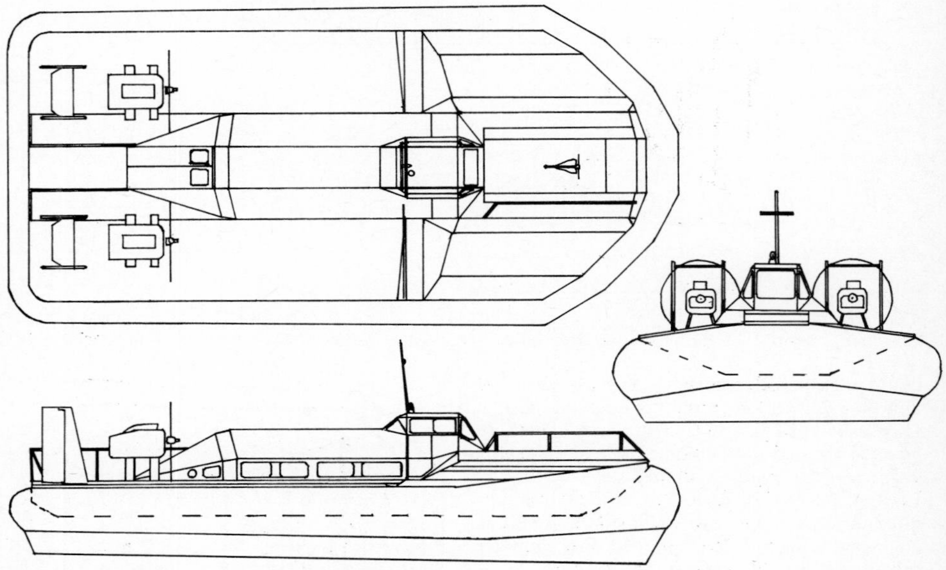
Islandaire II, twenty-seat, high-speed ferry

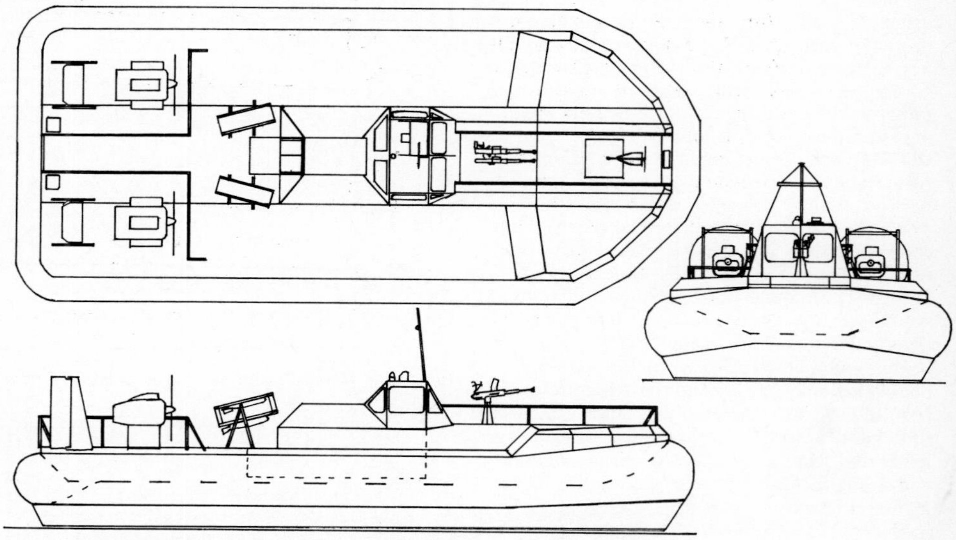
Fast patrol version of the Islandaire, the Islandaire IIIM

ISLANDAIRE I

DIMENSIONS

EXTERNAL

Length overall, on cushion: 12·95m (42ft 6in)
Width overall, on cushion: 7·31m (24ft)
Height (excluding mast) on cushion: 3·65m (12ft)
Hard structure clearance: 1·06m (3ft 6in)
Height on landing pads: 2·59m (8ft 6in)

INTERNAL

Main cabin (15 seats)
Length: 2·74m (9ft)
Width: 2·13m (7ft)
Height: 1·82m (6ft)
Control cabin (2 seats)
Length: 1·82m (6ft)
Width: 2·43m (8ft)
Height: 2·36m (7ft 9in)
Rear gangway and doors
Width: 0·914m (3ft)
Toilet and galley/bar at rear of cabin.

WEIGHTS

Gross: 4,535kg (10,000lb)
Fuel and payload: 1,904kg (4,200lb)
Max freight: 952kg (2,100lb)

PERFORMANCE

Cruising speed: 72·42km/h (45mph)
Max speed: 104·6km/h (65mph)
Fuel consumption: 113 litres/h (25 gallons/h) at cruising speed
Endurance: 5 hours at cruising speed
Gradient: 1 in 7·5, standing start
Bank/single step: 1·21m (4ft)
Wave height: 1·82-2·43m in long sea (6-8ft)
Isolated obstacle: 0·914m (3ft)

ISLANDAIRE IA AMBULANCE

DIMENSIONS

EXTERNAL

Length overall on cushion: 12·95m (42ft 6in)
Width overall on cushion: 7·31m (24ft)
Height (excluding mast) on cushion: 3·65m (12ft)
Hard structure clearance: 1·06m (3ft 6in)
Height on landing pads: 2·59m (8ft 6in)

INTERNAL

Main cabin (8 seats or 4 stretchers)
Length: 2·74m (9ft)
Width: 2·13m (7ft)
Height: 1·82m (6ft)
Control cabin (driver and attendant/deckhand)
Length: 1·82m (6ft)
Width: 2·43m (8ft)
Height: 2·36m (7ft 9in)
Rear gangway and doors
Width: 0·914m (3ft)

WEIGHTS
Gross: 4,082kg (9,000lb)
Fuel: 1,477·43 litres (2,500lb, 325 gallons)
Six persons: 453kg (1,000lb)
PERFORMANCE
Cruising speed: 72·42km/h (45mph)
Max speed: 104·6km/h (65mph)
Fuel consumption: 113 litres/h (25 gallons/h) at cruising speed
Endurance: 11 hours at cruising speed
Gradient: 1 in 7·5, standing start
Bank/single step: 1·21m (4ft)
Wave height: 1·82-2·43m (6-8ft) long sea
Isolated obstacle: 0·914m (3ft)

ISLANDAIRE II
DIMENSIONS
EXTERNAL
Length overall on cushion: 12·95m (46ft)
Width overall on cushion: 7·31m (24ft)
Height (excluding mast): 3·65m (12ft)
Hard structure clearance: 1·06m (3ft 6in)
Height on landing pads: 2·59m (8ft 6in)
INTERNAL
Main cabin (20 seats)
Length: 3·35m (11ft)
Width: 2·13m (7ft)
Height: 1·82m (6ft)
Control cabin (2 seats)
Length: 1·82m (6ft)
Width: 2·43m (8ft)
Height: 2·36m (7ft 9in)
Rear gangway and doors
Width: 0·914m (3ft)
Toilet and galley/bar at rear of cabin
Cabin layout—four rows of five seats facing forwards, centre aisle
WEIGHTS
Gross: 5,443kg (12,000lb)
Fuel and payload max: 2,076kg (4,600lb)
Max cabin freight: 1,270kg (2,800lb)
PERFORMANCE
Cruising speed: 72·42km/h (45mph)
Max speed: 104·6km/h (65mph)
Fuel consumption: 113 litres/h (25 gallons/h) at cruising speed
Endurance: 5 hours at cruising speed
Gradient: 1 in 7·5, standing start
Bank/single step: 1·21m (4ft)
Wave height: 1·82-2·43m (6-8ft) long sea
Isolated obstacle: 0·914m (3ft)

ISLANDAIRE III
DIMENSIONS
EXTERNAL
Length overall on cushion: 15·08m (49ft 6in)
Width overall on cushion: 7·31m (24ft)
Height (excluding mast): 3·65m (12ft)
Hard structure clearance: 1·06m (3ft 6in)
Height on landing pads: 2·59m (8ft 6in)
INTERNAL
Main cabin (25 seats)
Length: 5·18m (17ft)
Width: 2·13m (7ft)
Height: 1·82m (6ft)
Control cabin (2 seats)
Length: 1·82m (6ft)
Width: 2·43m (8ft)
Height: 2·36m (7ft 9in)
Rear gangway and doors
Width: 0·914m (3ft)
Toilet and galley/bar at rear of cabin
WEIGHTS
Gross: 7,257kg (16,000lb)
Fuel and payload: 2,730kg (6,020lb)
Max cabin freight: 1,586kg (3,500lb)
PERFORMANCE
Cruising speed: 72·42km/h (45mph)
Max speed: 104·6km/h (65mph)
Fuel consumption: 113 litres/h (25 gallons/h) at cruising speed
Endurance: 5 hours at cruising speed
Gradient: 1 in 7·5, standing start
Bank/single step: 1·21m (4ft)
Wave height: 1·82-2·43m (6-8ft) long sea
Isolated obstacle: 0·914m (3ft)

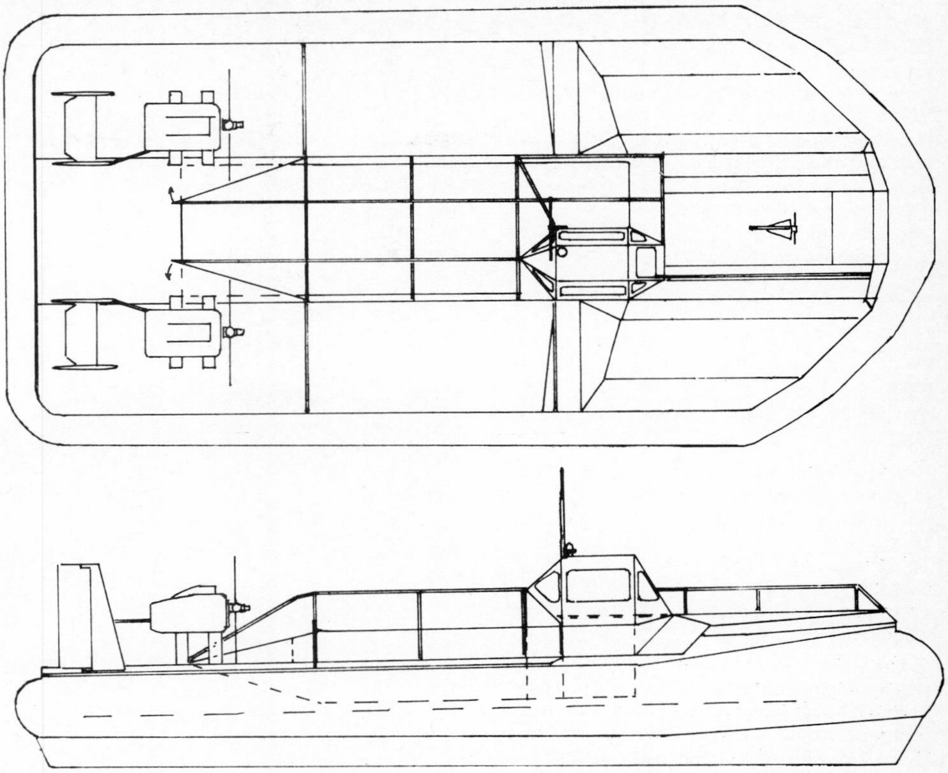

Freighter model of the Islandaire, the Islandaire IV. Loads up to 6·09m (20ft) long may be carried

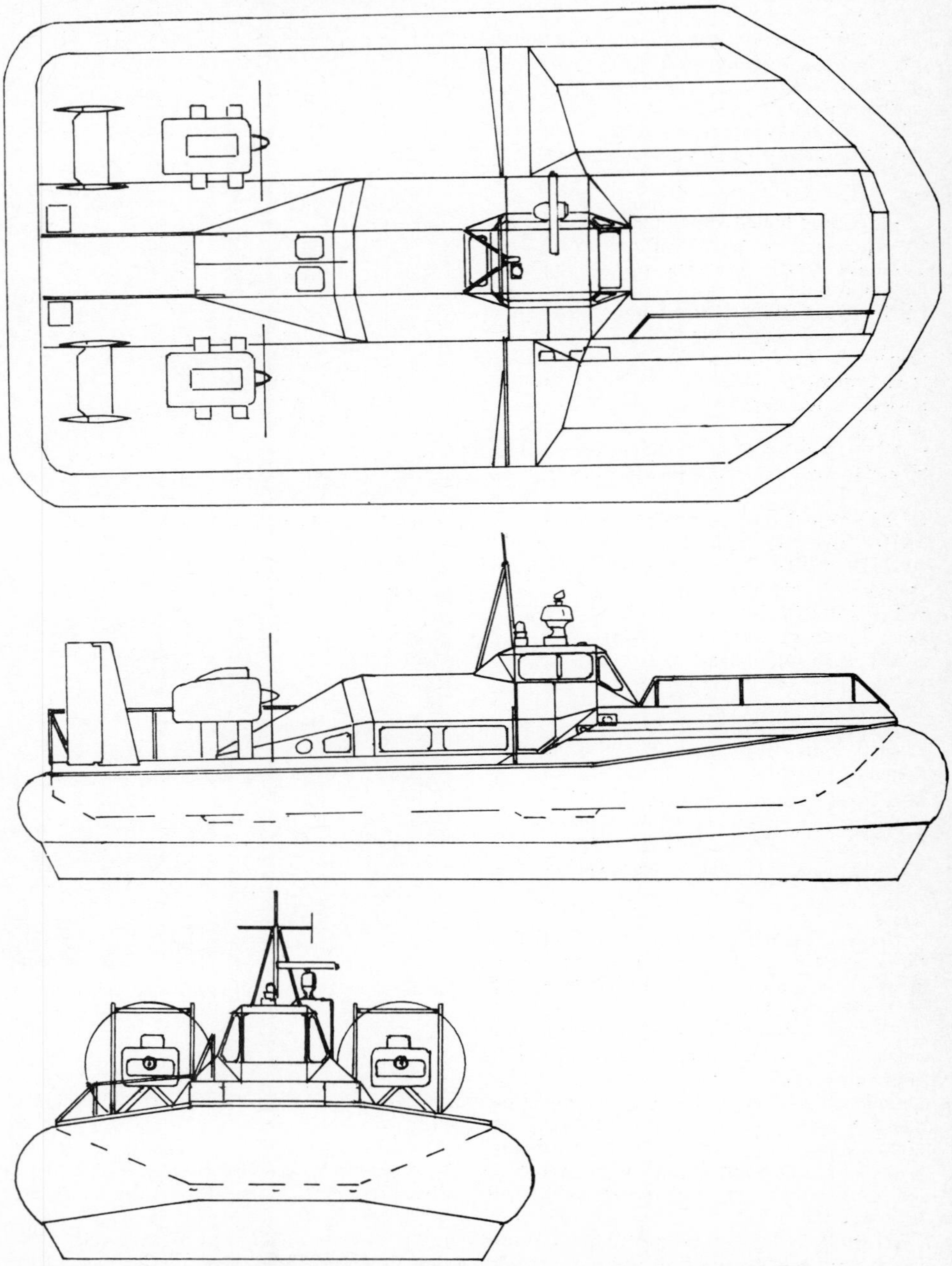

General arrangement of the Taylorcraft Islandaire I, fifteen-seat amphibious passenger ferry

ISLANDAIRE IV
DIMENSIONS
EXTERNAL
Length overall on cushion: 15·08m (49ft 6in)
Width overall on cushion: 7·31m (24ft)
Height (excluding mast): 3·65m (12ft)
Hard structure clearance: 1·06m (3ft 6in)
Height on landing pads: 2·59m (8ft 6in)
INTERNAL AND FREIGHT DECK
Control cabin
Length: 1·82m (6ft)
Width: 1·21m (4ft)
Height: 2·36m (7ft 9in)
Freight deck
Length: 4·26m (14ft)
Width: 2·13m (7ft)
Loads up to 6·09m (20ft) long may be carried subject to weight distribution requirements.
Freight area is half enclosed at 3ft height; remainder may be closed by canopy.
WEIGHTS
Gross: 6,087kg (13,420lb)
Fuel and payload: 2,730kg (6,020lb)
PERFORMANCE
Cruising speed: 72·42km/h (45mph)
Max speed: 104·6km/h (65mph)
Fuel consumption: 113 litres/h (25 gallons/h) at cruising speed
Endurance: 5 hours at cruising speed
Gradient: 1 in 7·5, standing start
Bank/single step: 1·21m (4ft)
Wave height: 1·82-2·43m (6-8ft) long sea
Isolated obstacle: 0·914m (3ft)

BRAZIL

Power for the VA is supplied by a single 50hp VW 1300 automotive engine which gives it a top speed over water of 70km/h (43·5mph)

FEI VA two-seat light sports ACV during trials

Model of FEI's VA-1 four-seat utility vehicle for operation over land, rivers and sheltered water

FEI
FACULTY OF INDUSTRIAL ENGINEERING

Research Vehicle Department (DEPV), Faculty of Industrial Engineering, São Bernado do Campo, Avenido Oreste Romano 112, São Paulo, Brazil
Telephone: 443 1155
Officials:
Eng Rigoberto Soler Gisbert, *Director of Vehicle Research*

The Vehicle Research Department of the FEI was founded in 1968. Its first major task was to conduct a full-scale investigation into Brazil's transport problems and its likely future requirements. An outcome of this was the design and construction by students and faculty of a 15·54m (51ft) long prototype of a tracked ACV, the TALAV.

Since then the Department, under the direction of Eng Rigoberto Soler Gisbert, has designed, built and tested a number of light amphibious ACVs, including the VA and the VA-1, which it is expected will be put into production by a Brazilian industrial concern.

VA

A glassfibre-hulled amphibious two-seater, the VA is powered by a single Volkswagen VW 1300 automotive engine and has a top speed of about 80km/h (50mph).
LIFT AND PROPULSION: Integrated system powered by a single 50hp VW 1300 automotive engine driving a ducted fan. Air from the fan feeds into the plenum below for lift and aft propulsion. Total fuel capacity is 30 litres (6·6 gallons).
CONTROLS: Single aerodynamic rudder, hinged to rear of fan duct, provides heading control.
HULL: Moulded grp structure.
SKIRT: Bag-type, 15cm (6in) deep.
ACCOMMODATION: Open cockpit with seating for two, side-by-side.
DIMENSIONS
Length, overall: 4·1m (13ft 5⅜in)
Beam: 2·1m (6ft 10⅝in)
Height: 1·5m (4ft 11in)
WEIGHTS
Empty: 400kg (882lb)
Loaded: 750kg (1,654lb)
PERFORMANCE
Max speed over land: 80km/h (50mph)
over water: 50km/h (31mph)
Max gradient, static conditions: 1 : 10
Vertical obstacle clearance: 15cm (6in)

VA-1

The VA-1 is designed for use in a variety of projects aimed at opening up and developing areas of the Amazon and traversing the swamps of the Mato Grosso.
LIFT AND PROPULSION: Cushion lift is provided by a single 40hp Volkswagen 1300 automotive engine driving twin fans located on the centre line, one each end of the open load deck. Thrust is supplied by two 90hp Volkswagen 2000 engines, each driving a ducted two-bladed propeller aft. Cushion area is 13·5m², and cushion pressure 11g/cm². Total fuel capacity is 100 litres (22 gallons).
CONTROLS: A single aerodynamic rudder provides directional control.
HULL: Moulded fibreglass.
SKIRT: Bag type flexible skirt, 25cm (10in) deep.
ACCOMMODATION: Enclosed cabin, forward, seats a driver and three passengers. Access is via two hinged doors, one port, one starboard.
DIMENSIONS
Length overall: 6·6m (21ft 7⅞in)
Beam: 3·05m (10ft 1⅛in)
Height: 2·35m (7ft 8½in)
WEIGHTS
Empty: 800kg (1,764lb)
Loaded: 1,500kg (3,308lb)
PERFORMANCE
Max speed, over water: 70km/h (43·5mph)
over land: 120km/h (74·5mph)
Max gradient, static conditions: 20%
Vertical obstacle clearance: 25cm (10in)

BULGARIA

OKRUJNAYE POLYTECHNIC
Plovdiv, Bulgaria

ICARUS II
Relatively little news has been forthcoming over the years on hovercraft activities in the smaller countries of the Eastern bloc. That interest is probably just as keen in these parts as it is in the West is indicated by the accompanying photograph. Described as "an automobile that rides on an air-cushion", Icarus II was designed and built by students of the Okrujnaye Polytechnic, Plovdiv, Bulgaria, under the guidance of Christel Christov.

The vehicle has been demonstrated extensively at exhibitions dedicated to the achievements of engineering students and is reported to have made an appearance in the Soviet Union.

Icarus II

CANADA

AIR CUSHION INDUSTRIES LTD
Head Office: Suite 206, 77 City Centre Drive, Mississauga, Ontario L5B 1M5, Canada
Telephone: (416) 270 8780
Works: Unit 3, 9 Lime Bank Road, Ottawa, Ontario, Canada
Mailing address: PO Box 660, Ontario K1G 3N3, Canada
Telephone: (613) 521 1647

AC 800
This is a new multi-purpose amphibious ACV designed to carry a driver and four passengers or up to 362·85kg (800lb) of freight. Built in reinforced high impact strength fibreglass, it is powered by a single V8 engine and cruises over ice and snow at 56·32km/h (35mph).

LIFT AND PROPULSION: Integrated system powered by a single 230hp water-cooled V8 engine. Mounted inboard, the engine drives two centrifugal-flow fans mounted at opposite ends of a transverse shaft. Both fans are enclosed in ducts to eliminate any danger from moving parts. Airflow is ducted beneath the craft for lift and via outlets aft for thrust. Fuel recommended is standard gasoline. Fuel capacity, 109·1 litres (24 imperial gallons).

CONTROLS: Craft heading is controlled by rudders in the airjet outlets aft.

AC 800 utility hovercraft built by Air Cushion Industries Ltd

HULL: Moulded fibreglass, with steel engine mounting and frame. Aluminium and stainless steel fittings. Buoyancy 150%.

DIMENSIONS
Length, overall: 5·79m (19ft)
Beam, overall: 3·5m (11ft 6in)
Beam, skirt deflated for trailering: 2·28m (7ft 6in)
Height, skirt inflated: 2·33m (7ft 8in)
on landing pads: 1·72m (5ft 8in)

WEIGHTS
Empty: 1,043·2kg (2,300lb)
Payload: 362·85kg (800lb)

PERFORMANCE
Cruising speed: 56·32km/h (35mph)
Hard structure clearance: 355mm (1ft 2in)

BELL AEROSPACE TEXTRON, CANADA
(A division of Textron Canada Ltd)

PO Box 160, Grand Bend, Ontario NOM 1TO, Canada
Telephone: (519) 238 2333
Officials:
William G Gisel, *President*
Norton C Willcox, *Vice President*
Joseph R Piselli, *Vice President*
James G Mills, *Managing Director*

In January 1971, Bell Aerospace Textron Canada acquired facilities at Grand Bend, Ontario, for the development and production of its Voyageur heavy haul ACV, and the smaller 17-ton Viking multi-duty craft.

The facilities at Grand Bend Airport include two buildings with a total of 3,350m² (30,000ft²) of floor space on a 21-hectare (52-acre) site.

The company has worked closely with the Canadian Department of Industry, Trade and Commerce in planning a programme which has led to the establishment in Canada of a commercially viable air cushion industry to meet the growing requirements for Coast Guard, remote area cargo hauling, high speed passenger ferry services and other specialised applications.

The first two 40-ton Voyageurs were built under a joint agreement between the company and the Canadian Department of Industry, Trade and Commerce. The prototype, Voyageur 001, differs from later craft insofar as it is fitted with two GE LM-100 engines, as opposed to the ST6T-75 Twin-Pac gas-turbines which are now standard.

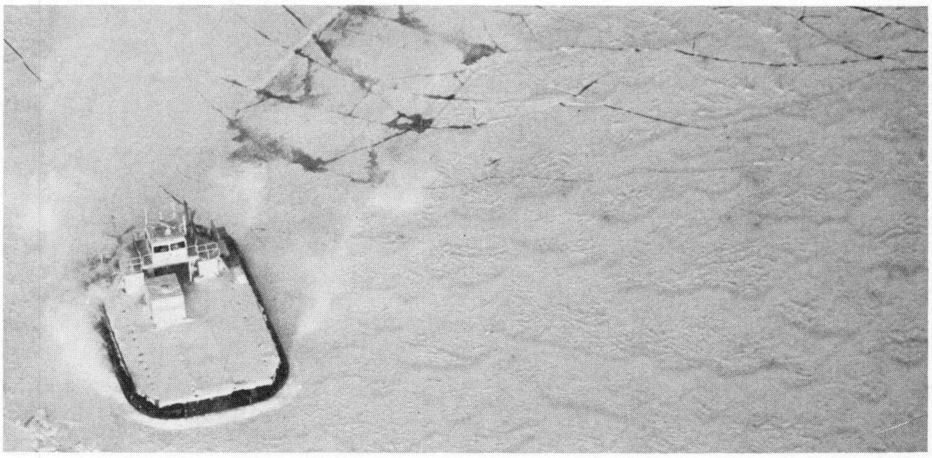

Voyageur 002, operated by the Canadian Coast Guard, breaking up a 3½-mile long ice jam on the Rivière des Prairies, north of Montreal. The craft was operated at a speed of 10 knots to create a series of trailing waves, one of which was allowed to precede the Voyageur into the ice pack, breaking the surface ice into pieces

The Voyageur features a basic flatbed hull of all-welded extruded marine aluminium that can be adapted to a variety of operational needs by adding the required equipment and superstructure.

Construction of Voyageur 001 started in March 1971. It began operational trials and certification testing in November 1971. Voyageurs have operated in the Canadian and American arctic regions on oil industry exploration logistics support. Voyageur 002 is owned and operated by the Canadian Coast Guard and since March 1975 has worked as an ACV icebreaker. Ice in excess of 1·01m (3ft 4in) thick has been successfully broken.

A stretched version of the Voyageur, the Model 7467 LACV-30, has been built to meet

US Army requirements for a high speed amphibious vehicle for LOTS (Logistics-Over-The-Shore) operations. The LACV-30 is intended to replace conventional vessels of the LARC-5 and LARC-15 types by 1980. Details will be found in the entry for Bell Aerospace Textron, USA.

MODEL 7380 VOYAGEUR

The Bell Model 7380 is a twin-engined fully amphibious hovercraft designed to haul payloads of up to 25 tons over arctic and other terrain at speeds up to 87km/h (54mph).

The 25-ton payload is equal to that of most transport aircraft engaged in regular supply operations in the north and other remote regions, including the C-130 Hercules. The Model 7380 therefore provides a direct transport link from the airstrips to settlements and operating bases for the movement of men, equipment and supplies.

The craft has been tested extensively by the Canadian Coast Guard and the US Army for a variety of high speed amphibious missions.

Modular construction is employed and the craft can be dismantled into easily handled units, plus skirts, for ease of transporting by road, rail or air.

Estimates indicate that ton-mile operating costs will be less than 25% of those experienced with heavy lift helicopters and 50% that of existing small ACVs.

By adding superstructure to the basic flatbed hull, the craft can be used for various alternative roles from a 140 seat passenger ferry to military weapons platform.

LIFT AND PROPULSION: Two 1,300hp Pratt & Whitney ST6T-75 Twin-Pac gas-turbines mounted aft, one each side of the roll-on/roll-off cargo deck, power the integrated lift/propulsion systems, which employ fans, propellers and transmissions similar to those of the Bell SK-5 and BHC SR.N6. Each engine has two separate gas-turbine sections which drive into a combining gearbox, providing twin-engine reliability for each integrated lift fan and propeller. The second gearbox employed in the Twin-Pac installation is a strengthened version of the integrated drive used in the SR.N5, developed by the SPECO Division of Kelsey-Hayes. The output of each engine is absorbed by a three-bladed Hamilton Standard 43D50 reversible-pitch propeller of 2·74m (9ft) diameter and by a 12-bladed 2·13m (7ft) diameter light alloy centrifugal lift fan. The fans deliver air to the cushion via a 1·21m (4ft) deep peripheral skirt which incorporates stability trunks. Air drawn by the engines first enters a Donaldson filter that traps and removes dust particles. It then passes through a fine knitmesh filter and into a Peerless Vane filter that gathers water droplets. Lift fans and propellers are linked mechanically and the power output of each engine can be apportioned between the propellers and lift fans allowing speed and hoverheight to be varied to suit prevailing operating conditions. The engines have multifuel capability and can be started in extremely low temperatures (−65°F). Two fuel tanks, each consisting of three interconnected bays containing flexible rubber cells, are built into the aft end of the port and starboard forward flotation boxes. Total fuel capacity is 15,000 litres (3,300 imperial gallons), sufficient for a range of approximately 550 nautical miles with a 15-ton payload. Types of fuel which may be used are kerosene, AVTUR, JETA, JP4, JP5 and Arctic diesel.

CONTROLS: Steering is by means of two aerodynamically-balanced rudders hinged to the rear of propeller, supplemented by the use of differential propeller pitch control. Side-located bow thrusters aid low-speed manoeuvring. All controls are located in the raised cab, which seats a crew of two plus four passengers. Propeller pitch controls are located on the starboard side of the operators seat, so that they can be operated by the right hand, while power can be controlled with the left hand. A conventional foot-operated control bar is provided for rudder actuation.

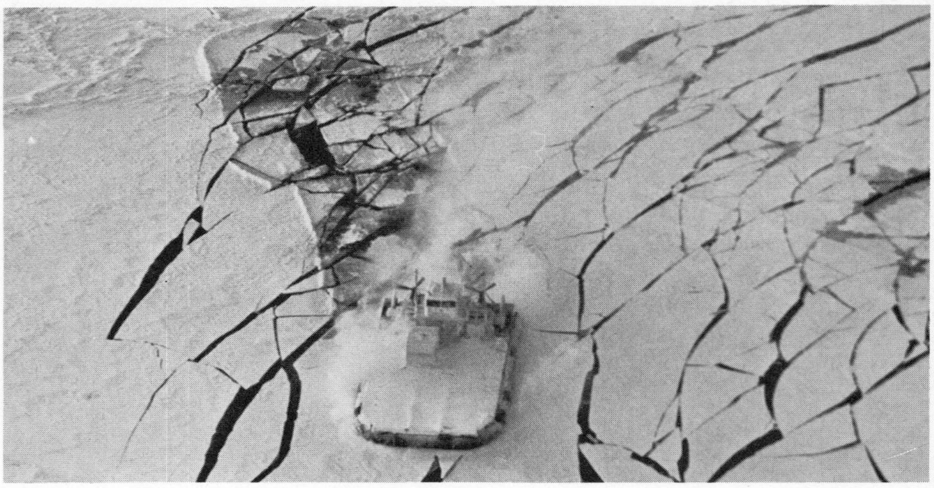

The Voyageur compressing and cracking the jammed ice into smaller segments. The gaps between the segments increase as they move downstream, carried by the river's three-knot current

Voyageur, in the foreground, accompanied by the Viking prototype during a patrol mission with the Canadian Coast Guard

HULL: Exceptionally rugged all-metal structure, fabricated in corrosion-resistant 6,000 series extruded aluminium alloys, with double wall skinning and multiple watertight compartments. The design of the modular structure incorporates hollow-core, thin-walled aluminium extrusions similar to those employed in the superstructures of commercial and naval ships. Use of this material, with extruded corners for constructing joints, produces a structural box of great strength and stiffness. The hull design is based on flat surfaces, thus eliminating the need for formed parts and simplifying repairs. The structural modules are welded using gas-shielded metal arc and gas-shielded tungsten arc processes.

The basic craft hard structure is broken down for transporting into twelve sections. These consist of three forward flotation boxes, two forward and two aft side decks, two power modules, an aft centre flotation box, a cabin support pedestal and the control cabin.

The three forward flotation boxes are almost identical in appearance and measure 12·19 × 2·43 × 0·952m (40ft × 8ft × 3ft 1½in). The port and starboard boxes each contain a fuel tank and a landing pad support structure.

The aft centre flotation box is of similar construction, but shorter in length. Scallops are formed in each side to prevent airflow blockage around the perimeter of the lift fans, which are contained in the power modules located on either side of the centre box. This module, together with the three forward boxes, forms the structural backbone of the craft. Loads from the side decks and power modules are transmitted into this primary structure.

The main deck is designed to accept loadings of up to 4,882kg/m² (1,000lb/ft²). Cargo tiedown-rings and craft handling gear are provided. Off-cushion, the cargo deck is sufficiently low to permit rapid loading and unloading from trucks and fork lifts.

The craft is completely amphibious and has a reserve buoyancy in excess of 100%.

SKIRT: 1·22m (4ft) deep neoprene nylon skirt developed from that of BHC SR.N6. 50% peripheral fingers. High attachment line at bow, similar to that employed on the BH.7. Airflow to the side and bow skirts is supplied through the duct formed by the side hulls. The transverse stability trunks are also supplied from the side hull airflow, via a duct built into the outboard forward flotation boxes immediately forward of the fuel tanks. The port and starboard rear trunks are supplied by rearward airflow from the respective fans. The longitudinal keel is fed by ducts leading from each fan forward to the centre of the aft centre flotation box, then downwards into the keel bag.

ACCOMMODATION: The control cabin is supported on a raised platform aft of the deck between the power modules. It is raised sufficiently to provide 1·93m (6ft 4in) of headroom for personnel or cargo and provides the operator with a 360 degree view. The unit is basically a modified 2·64 × 2·38m (8ft 8in × 7ft 10in) four-door truck cab. The operating crew of two are seated forward. The operator's position is on the starboard side, and the relief driver or radar operator is at the port position. The control console is located between the two seats and contains the control levers for the engines.

A full-width bench seat is located across the back of the cab, with access provided by the two rear doors. Seat belts are provided for four passengers. Cabin heating and window defrosting is provided by a dual heater, operating on vehicle fuel, and located at the forward end, beneath the port walkway to the control cabin. Electronically heated windows are also installed. Thermal insulation and double glazing are provided throughout the cab and this also attenuates engine noise.

Additional features provided in the cab design are structural provisions for roof mounted radar, air-conditioning and the provision of space in the control console for radio communications and navigation equipment.

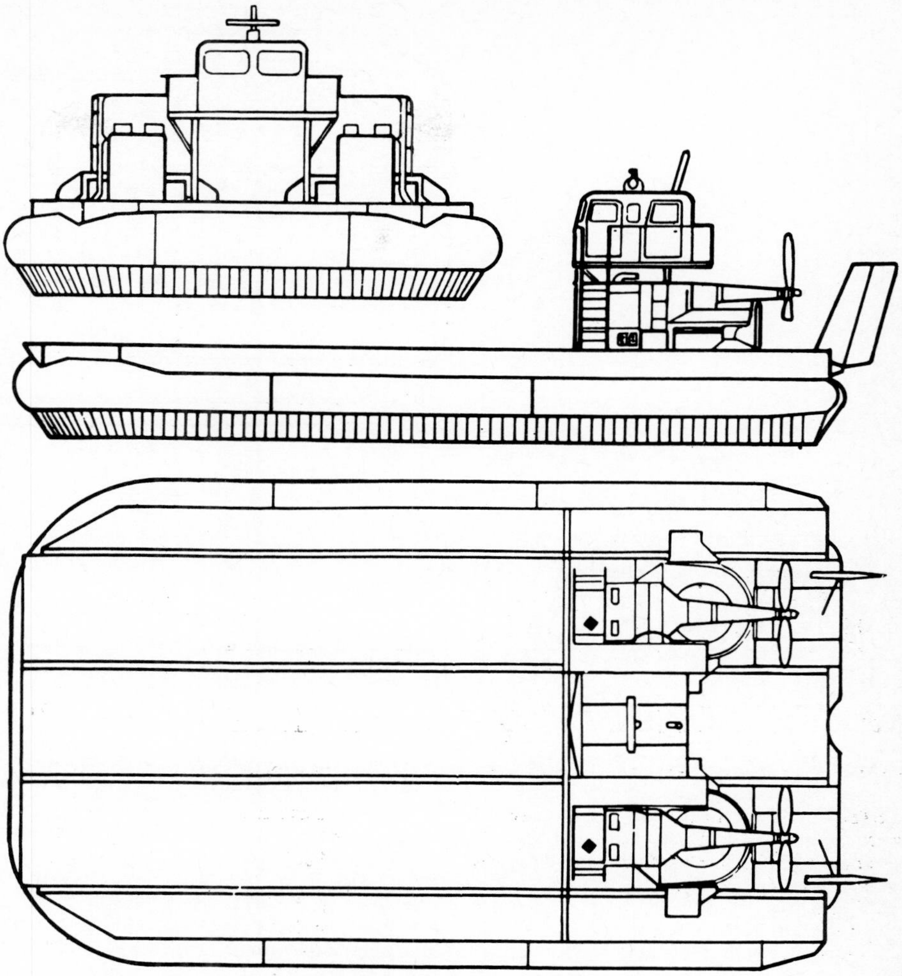

Bell Model 7380 Voyageur twin-engine utility hovercraft

Upper left and right: For two years, Voyageur 001 was operated by KAPS transport in the Mackenzie Delta region of Northern Canada on oil exploration logistics support missions. Typical loads were a caterpillar tractor and a Nodwell seismic driller weighing 46,000lb, a 3,300 imperial gallon fuel tank (filled) and miscellaneous items of earth moving equipment. **Bottom left:** Voyageur 004 hauls a cargo container from a freighter to ice-locked communities along the St Lawrence river in Quebec. **Bottom right:** Voyageur 003 carrying oil tanks to a drilling site in North Alaska

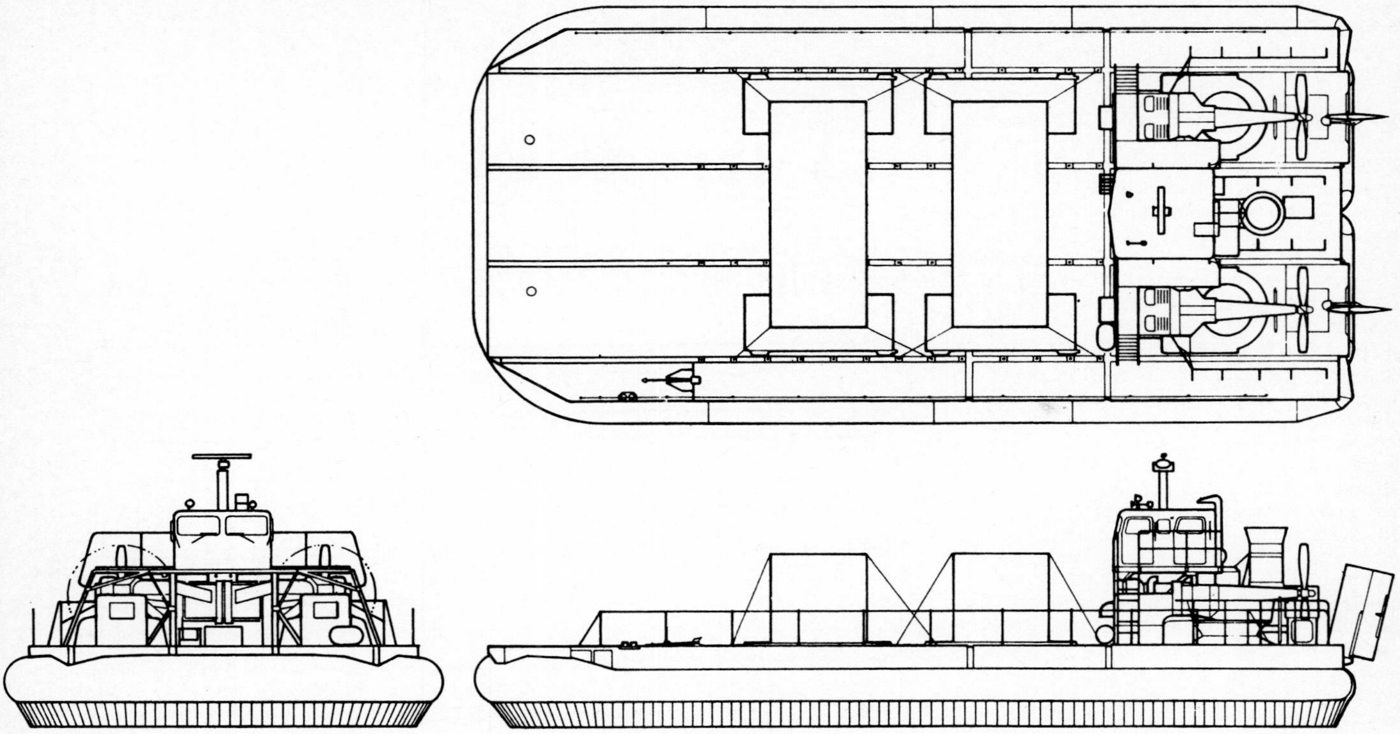

Bell AL-30, a commercial derivative of the US Army's LACV-30, intended for the rapid transfer of containers from ships to shore and other port cargo handling

SYSTEMS, ELECTRICAL: Four gearbox-driven brushless generators, each supplying 28V dc, and two 28V Nickel-Cadmium batteries.
External power: 28V dc.
DIMENSIONS
Length overall: 20m (65ft 8in)
Beam overall: 11·2m (36ft 8in)
Height overall, power on: 6·7m (22ft)
Height overall, power off: 5·74m (18ft 10in)
Height of cargo deck, power off: 1·17m (3ft 10in)
Skirt height: 1·22m (4ft)
Cushion area: 166m² (1,789ft²)
Cushion loading at 41,277kg (91,000lb): 248·92kg/m² (50·88lb/ft²)
Buoyancy reserve at 41,277kg (91,000lb): 125%
Cargo deck size: 12·19 × 9·75m (119m²) (40 × 32ft) (1,280ft²)
WEIGHTS
Basic, empty: 16,202kg (35,720lb)
Design gross: 40,823kg (90,000lb)
Max permissible gross: 41,277kg (91,000lb)
PERFORMANCE
Max speed over calm water, still air conditions, at a sea level standard day temperature of 15°C (59°F) with a 20-ton payload.
At 35,381kg (78,000lb) gross, 2,600shp: 87km/h (54mph)
Endurance at cruise power with 2,280 litres (600 US gallons) and 30-ton payload: 3 hours
Endurance can be extended to 10-13½ hours by trading off payload for fuel, with maximum fuel of 15,000 litres (3,300 imperial gallons) the payload will be in the region of 18 tons at the maximum permissible gross weight of 41,277kg (91,000lb).

BELL AL-30

A commercial derivative of the US Army's LACV-30, the Bell AL-30 amphibious lighter is intended for use in port cargo handling systems and is particularly suited to the rapid transfer of containers from ships to shore. Fully amphibious,

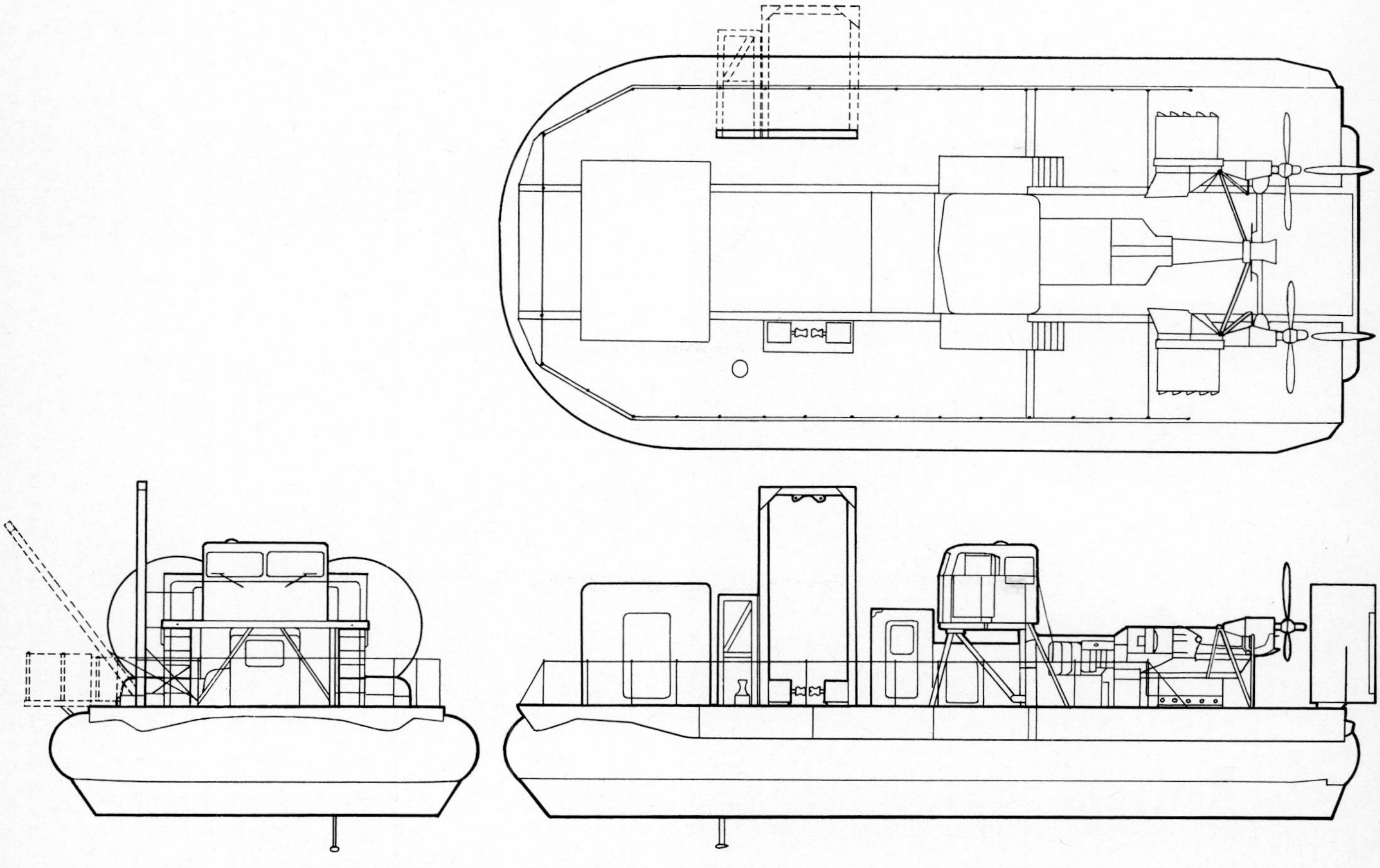

Provisional three-view drawing of the projected Bell Model 7505 stretched-Viking showing the A frame gantry, walkout platform and passenger and laboratory modules

it can carry a 30-ton payload, ranging from vehicles to break-bulk type cargo. In an integrated lighterage cargo transfer system the AL-30 can offload ships independently of existing berth and dock facilities and will permit the direct transfer of cargo from the ship into the transport system of the country, hence speeding its arrival at its final destination.
LIFT AND PROPULSION: Integrated system powered by two Pratt & Whitney ST67-76 gas-turbines mounted aft, one at each side of the raised control cabin. Each engine is rated at 1,800shp maximum and 1,400shp at normal output. The output of each is absorbed by a three-bladed Hamilton Standard variable-pitch propeller and a 2·13m (7ft) diameter, twelve-bladed, fixed pitch light aluminium alloy, centrifugal lift fan. Cushion pressure at maximum gross weight, 267kg/m² (54·7lb/ft²).
FUEL SYSTEM: Recommended fuel is standard aviation kerosene, Jet A1, JP4, JP5 or light diesel fuel oil. Main fuel usable capacity is 7,000kg (15,450lb) (2,272 US gallons). Fuel ballast/emergency fuel capacity, 4,695kg (10,350lb) (1,520 US gallons). Estimated fuel consumption during lighterage missions, 454kg/h (1,000lb/h) (147 US gallons/h).
SYSTEMS, ELECTRICAL: Starter generators: Four gearbox driven brushless, 28V dc, 200A each. Batteries: Two nickel cadmium, 28V dc, 40A each.
DIMENSIONS
Length overall, on cushion, without optional swing crane: 23·3m (76ft 3in)
Beam overall, skirt inflated: 11·2m (36ft 8in)
Height overall, on landing pads: 6·6m (21ft 6in)
Height overall, on cushion: 7·5m (24ft 8in)
Length, cargo deck: 15·7m (51ft 6in)
Width, cargo deck: 9·9m (32ft 6in)
Height, cargo deck, off cushion: 1·2m (3ft 11½in)
Cushion height: 1·22m (4ft)
WEIGHTS
Gross: 49,783kg (109,751lb)
PERFORMANCE
Max speed (calm water, zero wind, at 49,783kg (109,751lb) gross weight): 86·9km/h (54mph)
Cruising speed: 67·59km/h (42mph)

MODEL 7505 STRETCHED VIKING

Bell engineers have designed an improved version of the earlier Viking (see *Jane's Surface Skimmers 1978* and earlier editions) by stretching the hull. Development work on the new model is in hand. The following details apply to the baseline configuration, with the hull stretched by 3·35m (11ft) to 16·9m (55ft 6in).
DIMENSIONS
Length overall: 16·9m (55ft 6in)
Beam overall: 7·9m (26ft)
Height overall: 6·1m (20ft)
Cargo deck area: 102·2m² (1,100ft²)
Deck height, off cushion: 1·2m (3ft 11in)
WEIGHTS
Empty: 11,475kg (25,299lb)
Max permissible gross: 19,051kg (42,000lb)
PERFORMANCE
Calm water: 94km/h (58mph)
Continuous gradient capacity: 11 degrees
Ditch crossing width: 2·7m (9ft)
Endurance with max fuel: 10·5 hours
Max wave height: in excess of 1·8m (6ft)
Max range: 1,020km (550n miles)

HOVERJET INC

55 Glen Cameron Road, Unit 21, Thornhill, Ontario L3T 1P2, Canada
Telephone: (416) 881 0737
Officials:
Ralph Schneider, *President*
E De Asis, *Chief Engineer*
R Bittner, *Chief Technician*
Subsidiaries and Affiliated Companies:
Alpha Aerospace Corporation Ltd, Canadian Airships Development Corporation.

Hoverjet Inc is currently developing the HJ-1000, five-seat passenger and utility craft, the prototype of which completed its trials in April 1974, the Chinook, a lightweight single-seater, and the Rapier, a two-seater with a moulded grp hull. The company is engaged primarily in ACV research and development and undertakes contract design, consultancy and prototype construction for other companies. Ralph Schneider, formerly director of research and development at Hoverair Corporation and Airfloat Ltd, is responsible for Hoverjet's development and engineering programmes.

Hoverjet HJ-1000 workhorse hovercraft, designed for freight and passenger applications over marginal terrain. Power is supplied by three 42hp Kohler K440-2AS two-cycle aircooled engines, one for lift and two for propulsion. Normal cruising speed is 35mph depending on surface and wind conditions

HOVERJET HJ-1000

An amphibious "workhorse" designed to meet the needs of exploration parties, the HJ-1000 is of frp construction and carries a payload of up to 362·85kg (800lb). The vehicle can be modified to suit a variety of applications ranging from ambulance or rescue craft to water taxi and pilot boat. Power is provided by three 42hp Kohler engines.

The craft has been designed to permit transport by air, sea and road. It will fit into a transport aircraft with a 2·43m (8ft) door opening; it can be accommodated in a standard 2·43 × 2·43 × 6·09m (8 × 8 × 20ft) container for delivery by sea, or it can be loaded onto a 2·43 × 6·09m (8 × 20ft) boat trailer.
LIFT AND PROPULSION: Lift is supplied by a single 42hp Kohler K440-2AS two-cycle aircooled engine driving two 0·5m (1ft 8in) diameter ten-bladed aluminium fans mounted vertically at the opposite ends of a transverse shaft. Cushion pressure is 15·9lb/ft². Propulsive thrust is supplied by two duct-mounted, 42hp Kohler K440-2AS two-cycle aircooled engines, each driving a single 0·762m (2ft 6in) diameter ten-bladed axial fan. For manoeuvring and hullborne operation over water a 7hp outboard motor on a remotely-operated swing mount can be fitted as an optional extra. Fuel is carried in two 45·46 litre (10 gallon) tanks, one port, one starboard, each with a refuelling neck located on deck. Recommended fuel is two-cycle mix, 40 : 1.
CONTROLS: Craft heading is controlled by an aircraft type control stick which activates twin rudders at the rear of the thrust ducts via push-pull cables. Separate throttles are supplied for each engine, providing differential steering control. Complete engine instrumentation is provided.
HULL: Two-piece construction, comprising upper and lower bodies in colour impregnated fibreglass plastic on welded steel inner frame. Engine and fan mounts are of tubular, welded steel construction.
SKIRT: Segmented loop in laminated 16oz nylon/neoprene.
ACCOMMODATION: Driver sits forward and up to four passengers are accommodated in a wide cabin aft. Access is via a large door and roof opening on the port side. The passenger seats fold against the sides of the cabin to provide a cargo hold measuring 1·21 × 2·43 × 1·32m (4ft × 8ft × 4ft 4in). Safety equipment includes "pop-out" emergency exit windows, built-in buoyancy, a fire extinguisher and an electric bilge pump.
STANDARD EQUIPMENT: Electric starters, battery, navigation lights, flashing beacon, spotlight, horn, tie-up cleats and fire extinguishers.
OPTIONAL EQUIPMENT: Navigation lights, flashing beacon, spotlight, radio, lifejacket.
DIMENSIONS
EXTERNAL
Length, power off: 5·43m (17ft 10in)
skirt inflated: 5·74m (18ft 10in)
Beam, power off: 2·38m (7ft 10in)
skirt inflated: 2·69m (8ft 10in)
Height, power off: 1·77m (5ft 10in)
power on: 2·08m (6ft 10in)
Draft afloat: 101mm (4in)
INTERNAL
Main cabin
Length: 2·43m (8ft)
Max width: 1·21m (4ft)
Max height: 1·32m (4ft 4in)
Floor area: 3·01m² (32·5ft²)

PERFORMANCE
Normal cruising speed: 56·32km/h (35mph)
Vertical obstacle clearance: 330mm (1ft 1in)

CHINOOK

This is a lightweight amphibious single seater with a maximum payload capacity of about 147·41kg (325lb). Built in fibreglass reinforced plastics it is 3·42m (11ft 3in) long and sufficiently small and light to be transported on the roof of a family car.

Maximum speed over water is 48·28km/h (30mph).

LIFT AND PROPULSION: Cushion air is supplied by a 5hp Tecumseh two-cycle engine driving a 0·6m (2ft) diameter ten-bladed polypropylene fan. A 26hp Kohler 295-2AX, two-cycle engine drives a 0·6m (2ft) diameter, ten-bladed ducted polypropylene fan for thrust. Fuel capacity is 22 litres (5 imperial gallons). Fuel recommended gasoline and oil mixed: 30 to 1.

HULL: Moulded in fibreglass reinforced plastic.

SKIRT: Bag type in neoprene impregnated nylon.

ACCOMMODATION: Open cockpit with single seat for driver.

DIMENSIONS

OVERALL

Length: 3·42m (11ft 3in)

Beam: 1·52m (5ft)

Height: 1·09m (3ft 7in)

Hoverheight, hard structure to ground: 203mm (8in)

WEIGHTS

Normal empty: 129·26kg (285lb)

Maximum payload: 147·41kg (325lb)

PERFORMANCE (at normal operating weight)

Max speed, over calm water: 48·28km/h (30mph)

over land: up to 64·37km (40mph)

over ice and snow: up to 72·42km (45mph)

Still air range and endurance at cruising speed: 4·5-5 hours

Max gradient, static conditions: 20 degrees

Vertical obstacle clearance: 203mm (8in)

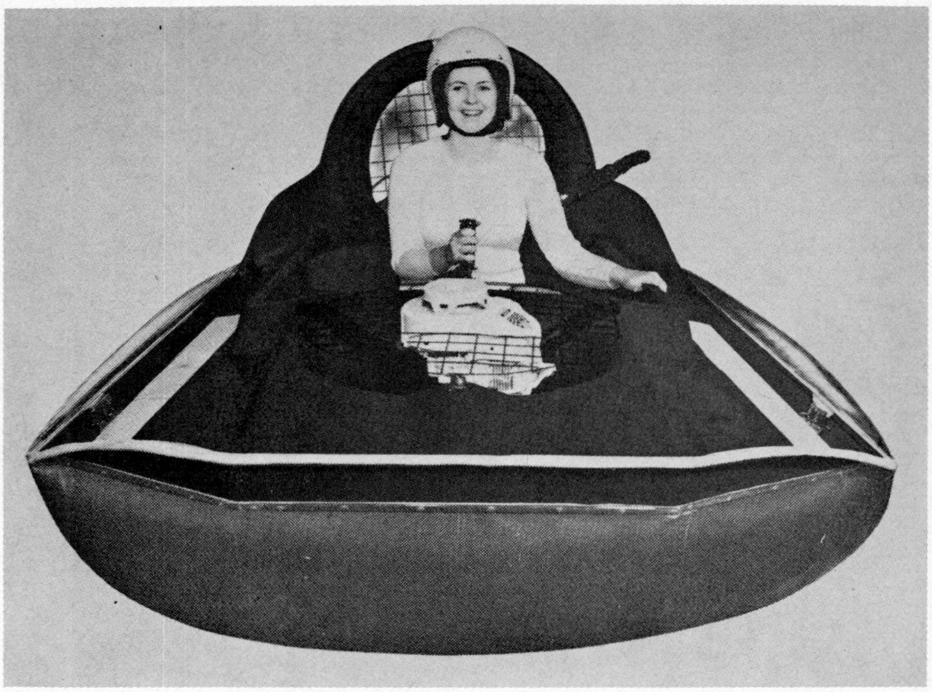

Hoverjet's light amphibious single-seater, the 48km/h (30mph) Chinook. The craft measures 3·42m (11ft 3in) by 1·52m (5ft) and can be carried on the roof of a family car

RAPIER

This fibreglass-hulled two-seater is designed for a range of recreational and light utility applications.

LIFT AND PROPULSION: A single-cylinder, two-cycle 12hp engine installed immediately ahead of the cockpit drives a 0·6m (2ft) diameter five-bladed polypropylene axial flow fan for lift. Thrust is supplied by a 42hp two-cylinder, two-cycle engine mounted aft and driving a single 0·76m (2ft 6in) diameter ducted fan. Thrust is 74·83kg (165lb). Both engines have mountings fabricated in industrial steel.

CONTROLS: Craft direction is controlled by a centrally-located control stick which operates a single aerodynamic rudder. A throttle lever is located on the control stick for the thrust engine.

HULL: Moulded fibreglass structure with reinforced landing skids.

SKIRT: Bag type in neoprene impregnated nylon.

ACCOMMODATION: Open cockpit with bench seat for driver and passenger side-by-side.

DIMENSIONS

Length, hard structure: 4·26m (14ft)

Beam, hard structure: 2·13m (7ft)

Height, hard structure: 1·52m (5ft)

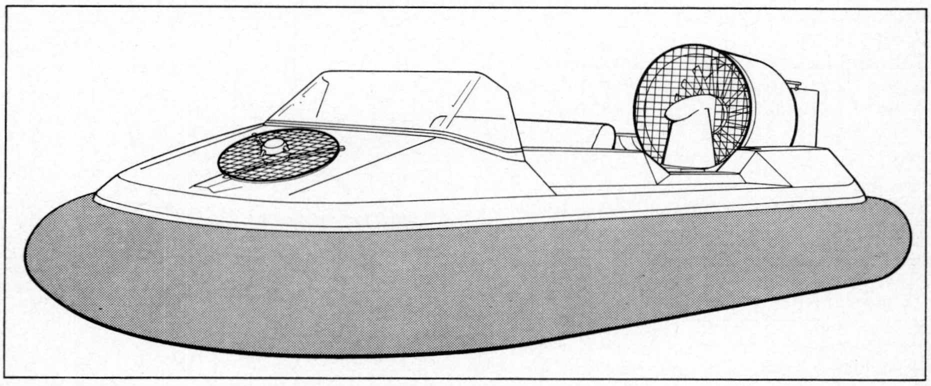

Hoverjet Rapier two-seat recreational and lightweight hovercraft

SPACE HOVERCRAFT LIMITED

Box 660, RR5 Ottawa KIG 3N3, Canada
Telephone: (613) 733 3296

ODYSSEY 700

This new fibreglass-hulled four seater has been designed as an all-terrain, all-season runabout. It is claimed to be quiet in operation and easy to control. The average person can learn to operate the craft over varied terrain in only six hours.

LIFT AND PROPULSION: Motive power is supplied by twin 58hp water-cooled engines, one driving the lift system, the other a ducted propeller aft. Fuel capacity is 68·18 litres (15 imperial gallons) and fuel consumption is 13·63 litres (3 gallons) per hour.

CONTROLS: Craft direction is controlled by three air rudder-vanes hinged at the aft end of the propeller duct. Reverse thrust system for braking is available as an optional extra.

HULL: Moulded glass fibre. Buoyancy 150% of all-up weight. Bilge blower fitted as standard.

ACCOMMODATION: Fully enclosed cabin for driver and three passengers or a 317kg (700lb) load when operated for freight carrying. Access to the cabin is via two gull-wing doors, port and starboard.

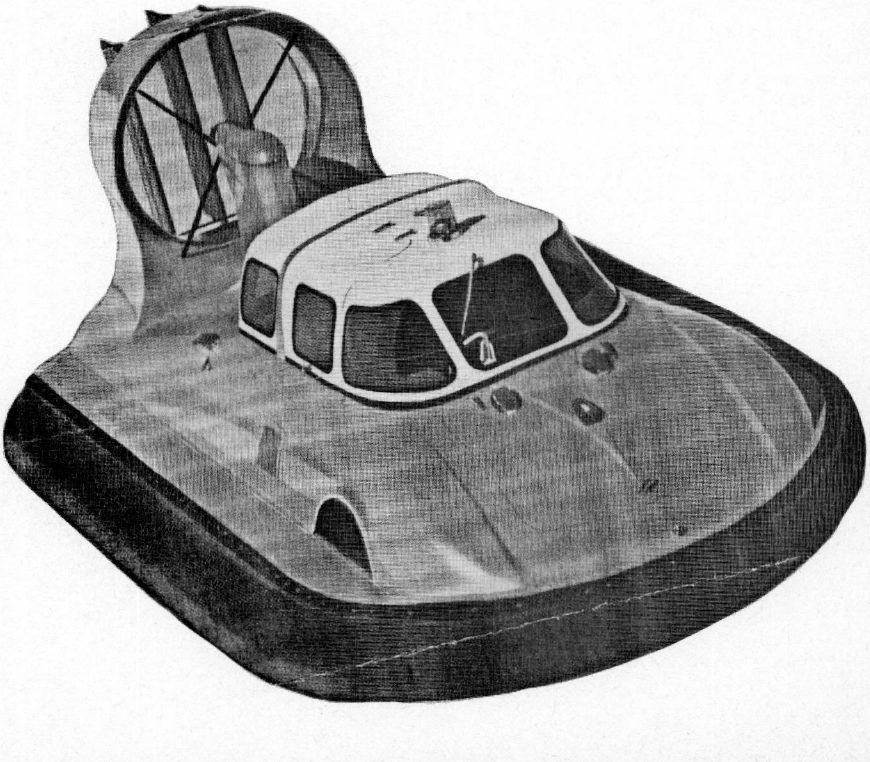

Odyssey 700 utility hovercraft designed for all-terrain and all-season operation.

DIMENSIONS
Length overall, on cushion: 5·74m (18ft 10in)
on landing pads: 5·43m (17ft 10in)
Width overall, on cushion: 3·4m (11ft 2in)
on landing pads: 2·28m (7ft 6in)
Height, on cushion: 2·38m (7ft 10in)
on landing pads: 2·08m (6ft 10in)
WEIGHTS
All-up weight: 680kg (1,500lb)
Payload: 317·5kg (700lb)
PERFORMANCE
Speed, depending on wind and surface conditions: 56-64km/h (35-40mph)
Vertical obstacle clearance: 304mm (1ft)

SUPERIOR HOVERCRAFT CORPORATION

Head Office: PO Box 1214, North Bay, Ontario P1B 8K4, Canada
Research and Evaluation Centre: Riverbend Road, North Bay, Ontario P1B 8K4, Canada
Telephone: (705) 472 7761
Officials:
H R Irving, *President*
A Robertson, *Vice President*
D J Murray, *Test and Demonstration Manager*

The first craft to be marketed by Superior Hovercraft Corporation is the Turbo Super Hover Mk 5, a 4-5 seat utility hovercraft designed to meet year-round climatic conditions in the Canadian North. Three prototypes have been built and are undergoing tests.

TURBO SUPER HOVER Mk 5

This new multiduty ACV has been designed for a variety of commercial and military applications in the more remote areas of North America and Canada. It carries a driver and up to four passengers or 453kg (1,000lb) of freight. Built in moulded high impact fibreglass, it is powered by a single 390hp V8 water-cooled engine and has a top speed over ice and snow of 35-40mph.

LIFT AND PROPULSION: Integrated system powered by a single 390hp V8 water-cooled engine with heat exchanger. Mounted inboard, the engine drives two axial-flow fans mounted at opposite ends of a transverse shaft. Both fans are enclosed in ducts to eliminate any danger from moving parts. Airflow is ducted beneath the craft for lift and via outlets aft for thrust. Fuel recommended is Hi-Test gasoline. Cushion area is 14·86m² (160ft²). Cushion pressure, 0·28kg/cm² (4psi).

CONTROLS: Craft heading is controlled by multiple rudders in the airjet outlets aft. Driving controls comprise a steering wheel, which actuates the rudders, an electric starter, automatic choke and a throttle lever for lift and thrust. Reverse thrust is applied for braking and stopping.

HULL: Moulded fibreglass and corrosion resistant aluminium construction. Buoyancy, 150%.

ACCOMMODATION: Access to the enclosed cabin is via twin gull-wing doors, one port and one starboard.

DIMENSIONS
Length overall: 5·79m (19ft)
Beam overall: 3·5m (11ft 6in)
Height, cushionborne: 2·33m (7ft 8in)
WEIGHTS
Empty: 1,310kg (2,890lb)
Payload, freight: 453kg (1,000lb)
Gross: 1,882kg (4,150lb)
PERFORMANCE
Max speed: 64·37km/h (40mph)
Range: 201-244km (125-150 miles)
Endurance: 4½ hours
Distance for emergency stopping: 15m (50ft)
Normal stopping distance: 45m (150ft)
Gradient capability: 8·7%
Craft can climb long 20% gradients and short 30% gradients, including river banks.

Driving position showing the steering wheel which actuates the rudders, controls and instruments

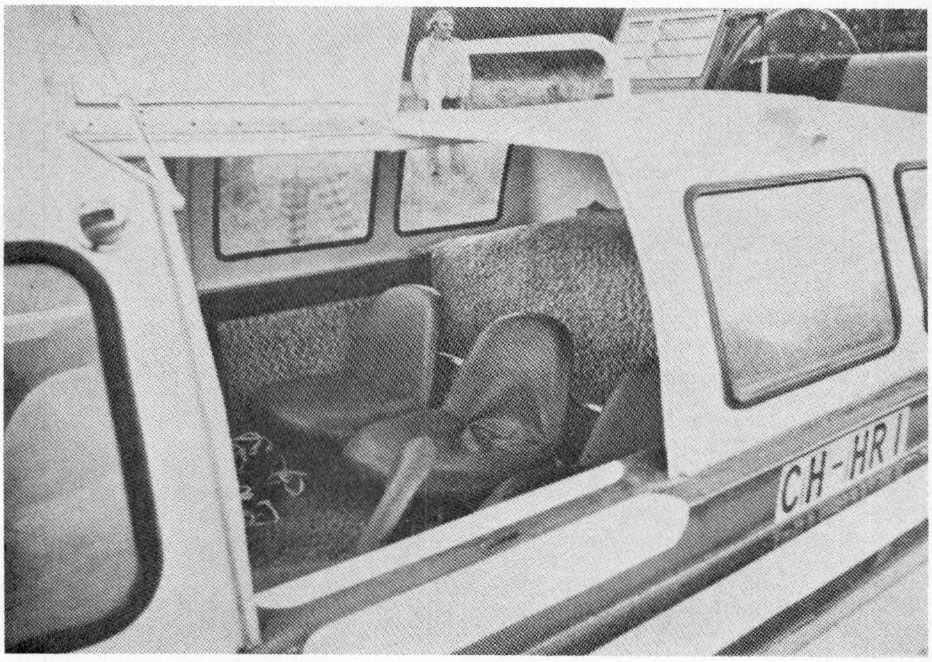

Cabin of the Turbo Super Hover looking aft

Aft view of the Turbo Super Hover Mk 5 showing the fan ducts and the multiple rudders in the airjet outlets

TRANSPORT CANADA
Air Cushion Vehicle Division

Tower A, Place de Ville, Ottawa, Ontario K1A 0N7, Canada
Officials:
T F Melhuish, *Chief ACV Division*

The Air Cushion Vehicle Division, Transport Canada, was established in 1968 as part of the Marine Administration. The Division is responsible to the Director Canadian Coast Guard Ship Safety Branch for all aspects of air cushion vehicle regulations. This includes the establishment of vehicle fitness standards, certification of pilots and maintenance engineers and registration of air cushion vehicles.

On the operations side, the Division has direct responsibility to the Director Canadian Coast Guard Fleet Systems Branch to advise and assist Coast Guard in its air cushion vehicle activities. Included in this is the use of air cushion technology for ice-breaking and the Division has been instrumental in developing this new air cushion technology.

The Canadian Coast Guard Air Cushion Vehicle Evaluation and Development Unit is also a responsibility of the ACV Division. There is also close collaboration with Transport Canada's Policy and Planning Branch, Surface Administration and the Transport Development Agency. The advice of the Division is constantly sought by other federal departments and provincial governments.

The division also participates actively on the National Research Council Associate Committee of Air Cushion Technology.

CHANNEL ISLANDS

T S GOOCH

La Genètière, Route Orange, St Brelada, Jersey, Channel Islands.
Telephone: Central (0534) 42980

T S Gooch has designed and built a number of lightweight air cushion vehicles, the latest of which is the J-5. In May 1969, his J-4 became the first home-built ACV to make a Channel crossing to France under its own power. The craft completed the 28·96km (18 mile) outward crossing from Gorey, Channel Islands, to Carteret in Brittany in 65 minutes and the return journey in 40 minutes.

The J-4 won first place in the Thames Hover Race in 1970 in the under 500cc class, and has since been acquired by Hovercraft Development Ltd for research and development applications. Details of the craft will be found in *Jane's Surface Skimmers 1976-77* and earlier editions.

Mr Gooch is now concentrating on the development of the J-5 four-seater with almost double the cushion area of the J-4.

Plans of the J-4 are available for amateur construction.

Bow-on view of the new Gooch J-5 showing the bow thrust ports and the 0·91m (3ft) wide sidewings which hinge upwards to reduce the overall beam for transport

One application foreseen for the J-5 is that of beach rescue craft. The cockpit, which can be enclosed by a plexiglas canopy, is large enough to accommodate a standard stretcher

J-5

This new four-seat recreational craft, a derivative of the J-4, is under development. The design may be made available either in plan or kit form.

At the time of going to press, the craft was partially dismantled and was being re-engined with a 1200cc VW engine. The two centrifugal impellers were being replaced with three multi-wing axial fans for easier construction.

LIFT AND PROPULSION: Motive power for the integrated lift/propulsion system is provided by a single 1200cc VW engine. Power is transmitted via a chain drive to two pairs of 0·58m (1ft 11in) diameter, double-entry centrifugal fans, mounted on a common shaft, with each pair located in a transverse duct aft of the cockpit. Air is drawn from both sides of each fan housing and expelled forward through the side bodies to pressurise the cushion, and aft through rectangular ducts for propulsion. Cushion pressure is about 10lb/ft^2. Air can also be ejected through thrust ports forward for braking and manoeuvring at low speeds. Two pedal-operated, aluminium braking/reverse buckets are fitted above each air-jet duct. Total fuel capacity is 45·56 litres (10 gallons) carried in tanks under the rear passenger seats on C/P.

CONTROLS: Heading is controlled by differential thrust and by twin sets of rudders operating in the air-jets.

ACCOMMODATION: Seats are provided for an operator and three passengers. The cockpit, which can be open or closed, is sufficiently large to accommodate a standard hospital stretcher should craft of this type be employed for beach rescue.

HULL: Wooden construction, similar to that employed for J-4. Structure consists primarily of 1in square spruce frame members glued and screwed to 4mm marine ply sheet. Hull base is in 6mm ply sheet. Buoyancy compartments are provided fore and aft. Fan intakes are in glassfibre and the braking buckets are in aluminium.

SKIRT: Loop-and-segment type in 4oz Briflon. The skirt is attached to the outer edges of the two 0·91m (3ft) wide ply sidewings which run the full length of the hull structure and hinge upwards to reduce the overall beam for transport.

UNDERCARRIAGE: Two retractable, independently sprung trailing wheels can be fitted. In the retracted position they can be employed as landing skids.

DIMENSIONS
Length overall, skirt inflated: 4·57m (15ft)
Beam overall, skirt inflated: 3·75m (12ft 4in)
sidewing folded: 1·87m (6ft 2in)
Height overall, skirt inflated: 1·37m (4ft 6in)

WEIGHTS
Empty: 185·96kg (410lb)

PERFORMANCE
Max speed, over water: about 35 knots
over land: 64·37km/h (40mph)

CHINA (People's Republic)

An ACV research and development programme has been underway in China since 1970. Much of the experimental work appears to have been undertaken at a shipyard in the Shanghai area which has constructed a small number of test craft, one of which is being operated from Chungking on a passenger ferry service. It is understood that this particular craft is fully amphibious, is powered by one aircraft piston-engine and operates at between 25 and 30 knots. The craft is constructed in aluminium and steel and the skirt is of simple bag type. Although the skirt has proved adequate for this craft it is clear that a great deal of development work has to be undertaken in this area of ACV technology before Chinese-designed amphibious ACVs can operate satisfactorily across open waters.

At present Chinese interest in amphibious craft is focused on vehicles in the N6 to BH.7 size range (approximately 10-55 tons). These are required for a variety of military and civil applications, including the operation of fast passenger ferry services over river networks with route distances of up to 240-320km (150-200 miles).

Little interest has been displayed in large craft in the 100-200-ton range but this is because the smaller craft present fewer problems when selecting power plants, in addition to which they can be built more easily by smaller shipyards.

Considerable interest is also centring on sidewall type ACVs with moulded grp hulls. Because relatively unskilled labour can be employed in the production of these craft they will almost certainly be introduced on a larger scale than craft with light metal hulls.

The photograph accompanying this entry shows an amphibious ACV passenger ferry, one of a number built by the Shanghai 708 Research Unit. Features include two radial aircraft engines, each driving a two-bladed propeller for thrust, and twin aerodynamic rudders for directional control. The hull is of the light alloy buoyancy type with a simple bag skirt suspended beneath. An elevator set above the twin fins aft provides pitch trim at cruising speed.

New ACV passenger ferry prototype built by a hovercraft research unit at Shanghai. Thrust is supplied by two aircraft-type radial engines driving two-bladed propellers. The skirt is of simple bag form. Craft direction is controlled by twin aerodynamic rudders and differential thrust

DENMARK

DANISH SKIMMERCRAFT

Fejö, Lolland, Denmark

Officials:

Frode Hansen, *Chairman*

Danish Skimmercraft, based on the island of Fejö, north of Lolland, is completing the prototype of a 16-seat amphibious hover ferry which has been designed primarily for services among the Danish islands. Development of the craft is supported by the Danish Ministry of the Environment which has made DKr 1·3 million available as part of an investigation programme into ACVs. On completion the prototype will undergo nine months of testing in Southern Denmark. If the trials prove successful, the regional authorities of Storstroms Amt, Funen and West Zealand, each of which is responsible for a number of islands, will jointly purchase a production craft from Fejö. A description based on preliminary press reports is given below.

FEJÖ SKIMMERCRAFT

This multi-duty ACV is designed to meet a variety of needs in Danish sea transportation, especially for short-distance coastal and inter-island traffic between small communities. One requirement is that it can, without modification, undertake missions by rescue corps, coastguards, police and customs, or assist the pilotage service. The prototype is designed to carry a driver and sixteen passengers, or up to 1,200kg (2,646lb) of freight.

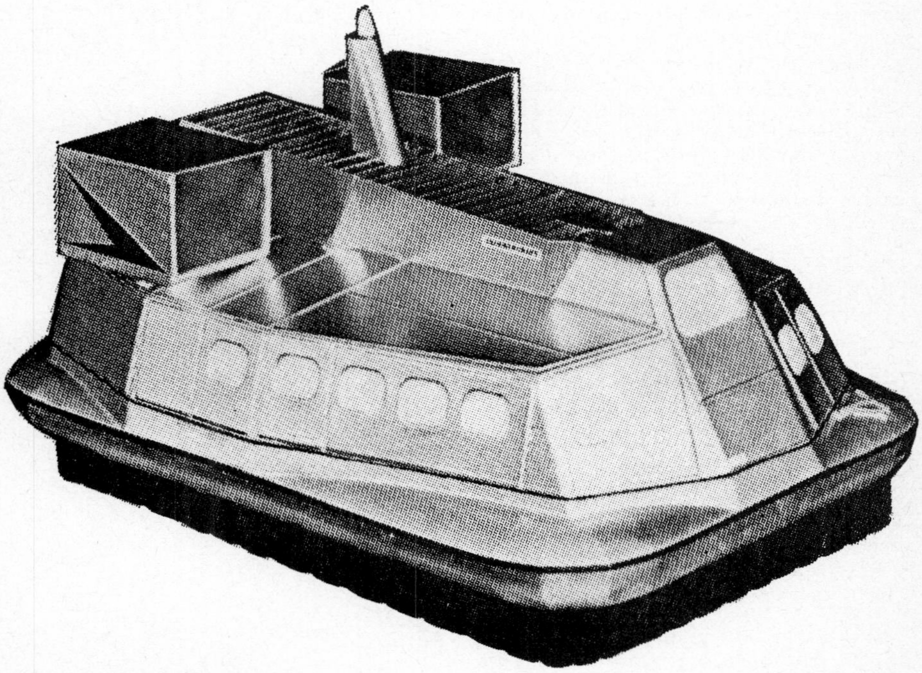

Model of the 16-seat inter-island hover ferry being built by Danish Skimmercraft on the island of Fejö

LIFT AND PROPULSION: Integrated system. Motive power is supplied by a lightweight diesel developing 750hp at 2,055rpm continuous. Output is transferred by V-belts to two sets of axial lift fans. Thrust air is expelled from two ducts mounted above the cabin superstructure aft. Both ducts rotate to control craft heading.

HULL: Welded aluminium construction. Double-bottom raft structure divided into compartments to form fuel, water ballast and buoyancy tanks.

SKIRT: Multiple bag system employing 52 replaceable skirt bags, each 0·5m (19·7in) in diameter and 0·75m (29·5in) high.

Bags are attached to the craft by a collar with a lock which permits rapid replacement of each bag unit without tools.

ACCOMMODATION: The passenger saloon, equipped to seat sixteen, is located ahead of the engine compartment. Access is via a hydraulically-operated sliding door forward, enabling the driver to ensure that tickets are issued to passengers on boarding. This door, which is located on the starboard side, is also used as an emergency exit. The driver sits in an elevated position forward, raising him above the saloon superstructure and giving him a view of 180 degrees. At the rear of the superstructure is a double door which allows light commercial vehicles either to be placed loaded aboard by fork lift or driven into the craft via ramps. The aft deck can also be equipped for search and rescue work or boarding at sea by pilots.

DIMENSIONS, WEIGHTS AND PERFORMANCE: Details not available at the time of going to press.

FINLAND

LUKKARILA

Lohtaja Commune, Kokkola, Gulf of Bothnia, Finland

Telephone: 968 57044

Jalmari Lukkarila, whose hobbies include seal hunting and building fibreglass boats, has developed a number of craft which can be operated across both sea, ice and water. His designs include a number of air boats driven by air propellers and wheeled drives. One employs a toothed wheel aft which bites into the sea ice for propulsive thrust. These vehicles have been used frequently on his hunting trips in the Gulf of Bothnia, some of which have lasted for several weeks. It was during one of these hunting vacations that he first became interested in air cushion vehicles.

Mr Lukkarila's first hovercraft was built in 1973 in conjunction with P Karhula and T Virkola. This machine had two 45hp VW 1600 industrial engines, one for lift and one for propulsion. A three-seater, it was used successfully across both ice and water until the owners sold it to a new owner in North Finland where it was destroyed in an accident. This occured when the driver failed to follow at high speed one of the curves in the meandering Kani river.

LUKKARILA TWO-SEATER

The latest air cushion vehicle designed by Jalmari Lukkarila is a fully amphibious two-seat runabout with an estimated speed of 50km/h (31mph) over water and 70-80km/h (43-50mph) across flat ice. The craft was first tested in 1976, since when a number of modifications have been introduced to improve its performance.

LIFT AND PROPULSION: Lift air is supplied by a 30hp Kohler engine driving an axial fan. For thrust the craft is fitted with a four-bladed propeller driven by a 30hp Sachs engine aft of the enclosed cabin.
CONTROLS, HULL: Details not available at the time of going to press.
DIMENSIONS
Length overall: 3·5m (11ft 6in)
Width overall: 2·7m (8ft 10¼in)
WEIGHTS
Empty: 250kg (551lb)
PERFORMANCE
Max speed over water: 50km/h (31mph)
over ice: 70-80km/h (43-50mph)

This 80km/h (50mph) two seater is the latest hovercraft to be built by Finnish designer Jalmari Lukkarila

PINTALIITÄJÄPALVELU (HOVERCRAFT SERVICE)

Paattistentie 141, SF-20360 Turku 36, Finland
Telephone: 921 472376
Officials:
Esko A Hietanen, *Director*
Ari Hietanen, *Director*

This company was formed in 1971 to design and manufacture light hovercraft capable of operation in extreme winter conditions in Finland when other forms of surface transport are either too expensive, too slow, or incapable of operation across wide expanses of snow and ice. The company's first product is the four-seat Amficat 4, of which only the prototype has been built so far. Since March 1975 this machine has been in continuous service as a high-speed amphibious taxi between Turku and the islands in the Turku archipelago.

The prototype has proved to be extremely reliable and economical and the service is expected to continue until two new craft come into service—the more powerful Amficat 4b, which is intended for series-production, and the larger Amficat 10, a ten-seater. The company is seeking a licensing agreement with a manufacturer prepared to undertake series production.

AMFICAT 4 PROTOTYPE

A light amphibious ACV powered by a single 45hp Volkswagen engine, the Amficat 4 is of wooden construction and seats a driver and three passengers. Directional control is good and by employing special speed brakes the craft is easily stopped and reversed.

An operating certificate has been granted by the Finnish Board of Navigation for running passenger services with the craft. Registered as the M/S Pinturi, and operated by Pintaliitäjäpalvelu, the craft began taxi runs in the Turku archipelago on 21 March 1975. Most of the operations have been undertaken during the spring and winter months when other forms of surface transport have proved either inoperable, because of ice or snow conditions, or too expensive. During the past four years the craft has visited over fifty different points in the archipelago. By early summer 1978, it had completed 11,000km (6,214 miles) in 1,300 operations and carried nearly 1,000 passengers.

LIFT AND PROPULSION: Integrated system powered by a single Volkswagen 1600 industrial engine developing 45hp at 3,200rpm. Power is absorbed by a single 600mm (23in) diameter centrifugal lift fan and a three-bladed grp propeller mounted forward in an NACA duct. Fuel is carried in two separate tanks, one forward and one amidship. Total fuel capacity is 90 litres (19·8 gallons). Recommended fuel is Super Grade gasoline.

CONTROLS: Craft heading is controlled by triple aerodynamic rudders operating in the propeller slipstream. Other controls include a speed brake, a reverse system and an electronically operated pitch trim system.

HULL: Wooden hull frame covered with marine quality ply. Integral buoyancy chambers. Structure designed for loads of up to 6g and for operation in moderate sea conditions.

Amficat 4, Finland's 30-knot amphibious hover-taxi which has completed 11,000km (6,214 miles) in 1,300 operations in the Turku archipelago since March 1975. Features include the ducted propeller for thrust, the novel cabin layout with the driver seated in a raised position aft, and the triple fins to control craft heading. A ten-seat derivative with a 160hp aero-engine is under construction.

SKIRT: Bag type, 0·41m deep, fabricated in pvc fabric.
ACCOMMODATION: Fully-enclosed cabin seating a driver and three passengers. Two passengers sit side-by-side at the front of the cabin with the third passenger and driver seated immediately behind in tandem. Cabin is both heated and ventilated. Entry is via two access doors on the left side. Emergency equipment includes life jackets, distress rockets and fire extinguishers.

SYSTEMS, ELECTRICAL: 500W alternator.
DIMENSIONS
EXTERNAL
Length overall, power off: 6m (19ft 8in)
skirt inflated: 5·9m (19ft 4in)
Beam overall, power off: 2·9m (9ft 6in)
skirt inflated: 3·1m (10ft 2in)
Height overall on landing pads, power off: 2·1m (6ft 11in)
skirt inflated: 2·5m (8ft 2in)
Draft afloat: 0·07m (3in)
Cushion area: 13m² (140ft²)
Skirt depth: 0·41m (1ft 4in)
INTERNAL
Cabin length: 2·4m (7ft 10in)
Max width: 1·15m (3ft 9in)
Max height: 1·48m (4ft 10in)
WEIGHTS
Normal empty: 650kg (1,433lb)
All-up weight: 900kg (1,984lb)
Normal payload: 250kg (551lb)
Max payload: 370kg (816lb)
PERFORMANCE
Max speed over calm water: 30 knots
Cruising speed: 26 knots
Turning circle diameter: 150m (164yds) on ice
100m (109yds) on water
Wave capability on scheduled runs: 0·6m (1ft 11in)
Max survival sea state: State 2
Still air range and endurance at cruising speed: 360km (223 miles)
Max gradient, static conditions: 1 in 7
Vertical obstacle clearance: 0·3m (12in)
PRICE: Approximate cost of craft fob FMk 120,000.

AMFICAT 4b

Almost identical to the Amficat prototype but with small improvements in the light of operating experience. Modifications include a more powerful engine and entry doors on both sides of the cabin. The craft is intended for series production.

AMFICAT 10

This is a high performance 10-seater based on the Amficat 4. Designed for both civil and military applications, it is powered by a 160hp aero engine. The prototype is under construction and is scheduled for completion in late 1979.

FRANCE

BERTIN & CIE

BP 3, 78370 Plaisir, France
Telephone: 056 25 00
Telex: 296231
Officials:
Fernand Chanrion, *President, Director General*
Michel Perineau, *Director General*
Georges Mordchelles-Regnier, *Director General*

Société Bertin & Cie has been engaged in developing the Bertin principle of separately fed multiple plenum chambers surrounded by flexible skirts since 1956. A research and design organisation, the company employs a staff of more than 500, mainly scientists and design engineers who are involved in many areas of industrial research, including air cushion techniques and applications.

Société de l'Aérotrain is responsible for the construction and development of Bertin tracked air cushion vehicles (Aérotrain) and SEDAM is responsible for developing the Naviplane and Terraplane vehicles. Designs based on the Bertin technique are described under the entries for these two companies in this volume.

The Bertin principle for air cushions has also led to numerous applications in the area of industrial handling and aeronautics. These applications, developed by Bertin, are described in the sections devoted to Air Cushion Applicators, Conveyors and Pallets; and Air Cushion Landing Systems.

GEORGES HENNEBUTTE

Société d'Exploitation et de Développement des Brevets Georges Hennebutte
Head Office: 43 avenue Foch, 64000 Biarritz, France
Works: 23 impasse Labordotte, 64000 Biarritz, France
Telephone: 24 22 40
Officials:
M Ellia, *Senior Director*
G Hennebutte, *Chief Executive*

Ets G Hennebutte was founded in 1955 to design and build inflatable dinghies. Its Espadon series of sports craft is used extensively by French lifeguard patrols and the French Navy.

The Espadon 422 is the only inflatable craft to have crossed the Etal Barrier.

Development of the Espadon to meet a range of special requirements led to the construction of a number of experimental craft, including one equipped with foils, one with hydroskis and a third with an inflatable parasol delta wing for aerodynamic lift. Several of these have been described and illustrated in earlier editions.

George Hennebutte's latest released craft is a further variant of the Espadon 422 inflatable sports craft equipped with hydroskis, wings and an air-propeller for thrust. A preliminary description of this new project, designated the Etel 422 Swordfish, will be found in the Hydrofoil section of this edition.

Z O ORLEY

21 rue Mademoiselle, 75015 Paris, France
Telephone: 828 29 49, 350 93 13

GLIDERCRAFT

Z O Orley and Ivan Labat have designed a range of lightweight recreational craft employing the glidercraft air cushion system invented by M Orley. The object of the system is to reduce the loss of cushion air by fully skirted vehicles when crossing uneven surfaces.

Beneath the hard structure of the glidercraft is an air cushion chamber in rubberised fabric, the base of which is divided into a number of small cell compartments.

Each cell is equipped at the lower end with a perforated shutter.

A short surface sensor protruding beneath each shutter is designed to open up, to deliver cushion air fully, whenever the cell encounters an obstacle rising above the general plane of the reaction surface, and reduce cushion air delivery when crossing a hollow.

A design study is being undertaken for a small commercial craft for operations in South America to carry twelve passengers and freight.

M Orley and his partner will build to order commercial and military prototypes employing his system for use over arctic and tropical terrain. Illustrations of a dynamic model incorporating the glider-craft air cushion system appears in *Jane's Surface Skimmers 1973-74* and earlier editions.

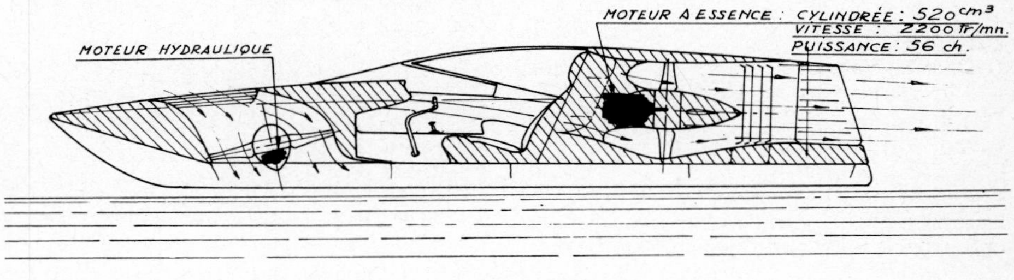

Inboard and outboard profiles of the two-seat Orley Escapade

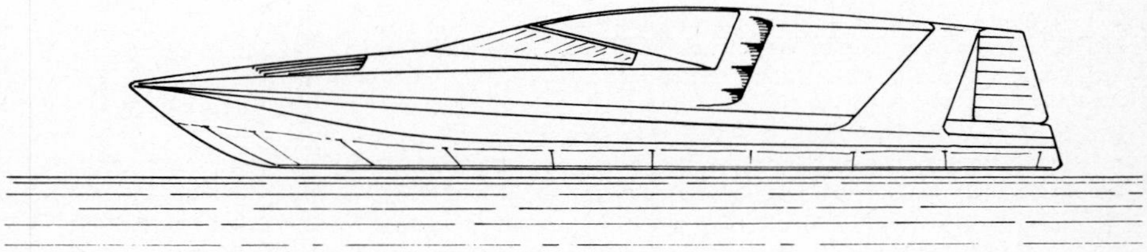

ESCAPADE

Recently M Orley and M Labat, who was a member of the N 500 design team, have projected a 100km/h (62mph) two-seater—the Escapade.

A feature of the design is the combination of a petrol engine for thrust and a hydraulic drive for the lift fan. This arrangement allows a continuous sharing of the power output between the lift and propulsion systems.

Aircraft-style seating and furnishing is provided for the driver and passenger.

DIMENSIONS
Length overall: 5·5m (18ft)
Hull beam: 2·7m (8ft 10¼in)
Folded width for transport: 1·9m (6ft 2¾in)
Height overall, on cushion: 1·15m (3ft 9¼in)

WEIGHTS
Craft with fuel: 240kg (529lb)

Loaded for operation on air cushion: 390kg (860lb)
Loaded for operation as hydroplane: 420kg (926lb)
PERFORMANCE
Max speed, calm water: 90km/h (55mph)
over land: 100km/h (62mph)
Cruising speed over calm water: 70km/h (43·5mph)
Max gradient static conditions: 15%
Vertical obstacle clearance: 0·3m (1ft)

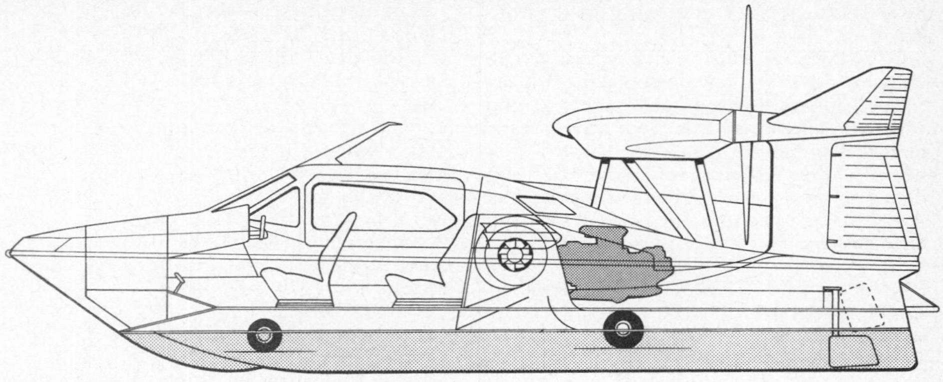

Projected four/five-seat amphibious ACV with retractable wheels and water rudder

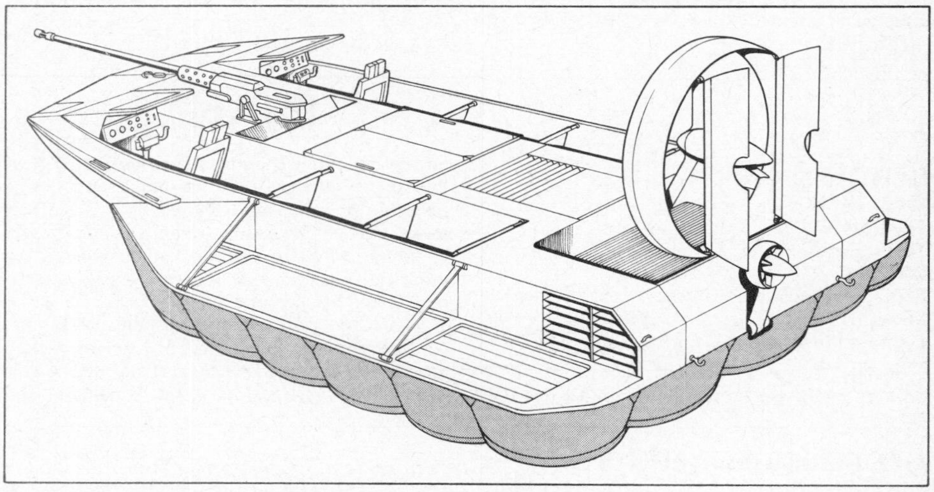

Armed reconnaissance ACV based on the Orley Glidercraft System

DUBIGEON-NORMANDIE SHIPYARDS

152 avenue Malakoff, 75116 Paris, France
Telephone: 501 71 43
Telex: 612921 F DUBINOR
Officials:
M Perreau, *Deputy General Manager*
A de Dampierre, *Sales Manager, Hovercraft*

SEDAM

Technical Office: 80 avenue de la Grande Armée, 75017 Paris, France
Telephone: 574 41 69
Telex: 290124 SEDAM PARIS
Officials:
P Guienne, *Technical Adviser*
R Anger, *Works Director*
G Herrouin, *Head of Technical Department*

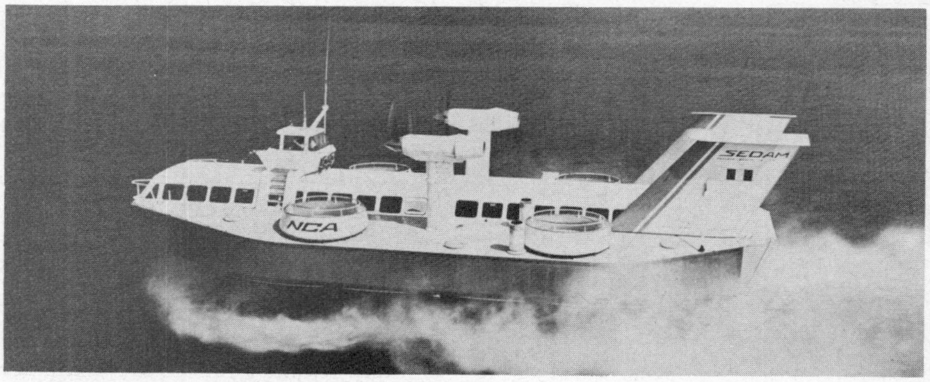

N 300 Naviplane, 90-seat passenger ferry

All technical and commercial activities of Société d'Etudes et de Développement des Aéroglisseurs Marins, Terrestres et Amphibies (SEDAM) have been taken over by Dubigeon-Normandie, the French shipbuilding concern, which will be responsible in future for the development and construction of all Naviplanes.

SEDAM was incorporated on 9 July 1965, to study, develop and test the Naviplane series of amphibious ACVs based on principles conceived by Bertin & Cie. In April 1968, the company was vested with similar responsibilities for the Terraplane wheeled ACVs based on identical principles. The company holds the exclusive world licence for Bertin patents involving both the Naviplane and Terraplane series.

In 1965 the 5-ton Naviplane BC 8 was completed, after which SEDAM built several small research craft, including the N 101, a quarter-scale manned research model of the 30-ton, 90-passenger N 300. Two N 300s were completed in the winter of 1967/68 and operated along the Côte d'Azur up to the summer of 1971. One has since been operated by the Department of Gironde as a passenger/car ferry across the Gironde estuary and is available for charter operation.

Following its reorganisation in late 1972, the company has been concentrating on three main objectives: the final design, construction and marketing of the 260 ton N 500 Naviplane series: incorporation of improvements on the N 300; and the introduction of a series of air cushion barges. Details of the latter are to be found in this edition in the section devoted to ACV Trailers and Heavy Lift Systems.

Two firm orders have been received for the N 500 from SNCF (French National Railways) for operation across the English Channel on the Boulogne-Dover route.

On 3 May 1977, N 500-01, named 'Côte d'Argent', was severely damaged by fire while minor skirt modifications were being undertaken and was subsequently 'written off'.

N 500-02 named 'Ingenieur Jean Bertin' made its first 'in service' flight on 5 July 1978 and has since been operating in conjunction with British Rail Hovercraft Ltd's Seaspeed service. The approval in principle for ordering N 500-03 was decided at an SNCF board meeting on 25 June 1978. In addition an option is understood to have been taken on N 500-04 and discussions have taken place with Hoverlloyd Limited which is considering ordering two N 500s for its cross-Channel car and passenger ferry service between Ramsgate and Calais.

Another of the company's current activities is the development of the N 300 Mk II, a fast patrol craft based on the N 300, but modified in the light of experience gained from the N 500. Major differences include the relocation of the wheelhouse and thrust propellers, and a redesigned hull and skirt system. Alternative military uses include coastal patrol, salvage, rescue and assault landing craft. A further variant of the N 300 is the N 304, an amphibious passenger ferry with alternative seating configurations for either 137 or 146 passengers.

The company is also undertaking feasibility studies for surface effect warships of 4-5,000 tons and more for the French Navy.

In July 1972, in response to an EEC request, SEDAM completed a study for a 4-5,000 tonnes mixed-traffic sidewall vessel propelled by water-jets.

NAVIPLANE N 300

A 27-ton multi-purpose transport for amphibious operation, the N 300 was the first full-scale vehicle in the Naviplane series designed for commercial use.

The first two N 300s were built at Biarritz at the Breguet factory and started tethered hovering and preliminary handling trials in December 1967. Afterwards they were transported by sea to the SEDAM test centre at l'Etang de Berre. In September 1968 N 300-01 and -02 went to Nice for a series of experimental services and tests conducted by the French armed services.

During the summer of 1970 the two craft operated a scheduled passenger service along the Côte d'Azur. One N 300 was later acquired by the Gironde Department for the operation of a passenger/car ferry service across the Gironde estuary between Blaye and Lamarque. The craft, which was operated by the Bordeaux Port Authority, carried up to four cars and 35 passengers per crossing. It operated 30 crossings per day, seven days a week.

The passenger version seats 90 in a lightweight cabin structure above the open deck.

LIFT AND PROPULSION: Motive power is provided by two Turboméca Turmo IIIN3 gas turbines located in separate engine rooms, port and starboard and drawing filtered air from plenum compartments behind the forward fan ducts. Each engine is coupled via a main gearbox located directly beneath each propeller pylon to a three-bladed Ratier-Figeac 3·6m (11ft 10in) diameter, variable and reversible pitch propeller and via a secondary gearbox to two 11-blade 1·9m (6ft 3in) diameter axial lift fans. The main gearboxes are cross-connected by a shaft so that in the event of one engine failing or malfunctioning the four fans and two propellers can all be driven by the remaining engine. The fans deliver air to eight individual Bertin skirts, each 2m (6ft 7in) deep and with a hemline diameter of 3·09m (10ft 2in). These are in turn surrounded by a single wrap-around skirt.

CONTROLS: The wheelhouse, which seats a captain and navigator, is located above a bridge spanning the foredeck to provide a 360 degree view. The main driving controls and the instrumentation are positioned in front of the port seat.

The wheel of a control column varies the pitch of the two propellers differentially and fore and aft movement of the column alters pitch collectively.

HULL: The hull is a raft-like structure built in marine corrosion resistant aluminium alloys. Main buoyancy compartments are beneath the freight deck. Fans and machinery are installed in separate structures on either side of the freight/passenger deck, port and starboard.

ACCOMMODATION: Aircraft-type seats are provided for 100-120 passengers. Baggage areas are provided in the centre of the passenger saloon, port and starboard, and at the rear of the saloon where there is also a dinghy stowage area. Access to the passenger compartment is by steps built into the bow and stern ramp/doors.

DIMENSIONS

Length overall: 24m (78ft 9in)
Beam: 10·5m (34ft 5in)
Height overall: 7·5m (24ft 7in)
Skirt depth: 2m (6ft 7in)
Cabin floor area: 80m² (861ft²)
Cushion area: 160m² (1,722ft²)

WEIGHTS

Basic: 14 tons
Passenger version: 100-120 passengers
Freight version: 13 tons
Normal all-up weight: 27 tons

PERFORMANCE

Max speed: 57-62 knots
Cruising speed: 44-50 knots
Endurance: 3 hours

NAVIPLANE N 300 Mk II

In June 1977, SEDAM announced that plans were under way for an improved model of the N 300, known as the N 300 Mk II. This is intended for a variety of military roles, from fast patrol to search and rescue and amphibious assault landing craft.

The chief differences between this craft and its predecessor lie in the resiting of the wheelhouse at the bow, the location of the two thrust propellers aft and the redesigned hull and skirt system.

The bow door has been removed and the entire bow has been redesigned for improved rough water performance. The stern ramp/door is retained. Gross weight will be 37 tonnes. A military version, powered by two 1,200kW Turboméca Turmo XII gas-turbines, is envisaged. Armament would comprise a SAMM fully automatic twin 30mm naval gun mount at the bow and a further SAMM automatic gun mount aft. Full air-conditioning would be installed in the living and working spaces of the tropicalised version.

DIMENSIONS

EXTERNAL

Length overall: 23m (75ft 6in)
Beam overall: 12·2m (40ft)
Height, on cushion to tips of fins: 8m (26ft 3in)

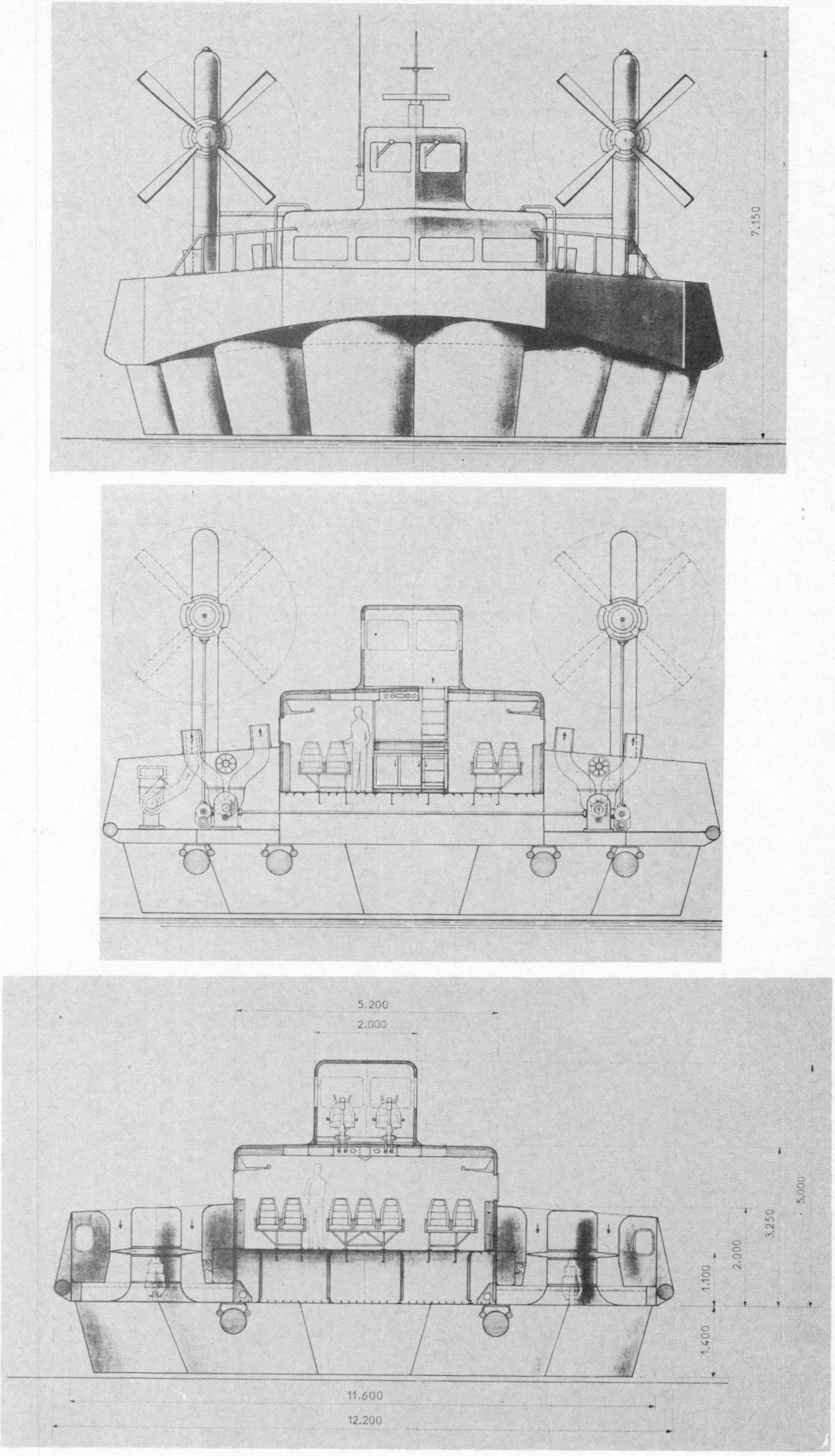

Bow-on views of the Dubigeon-Normandie/SEDAM N 304 passenger ferry

NAVIPLANE N 304

This new derivative of the N 300 is a fully amphibious passenger ferry with seats for 137-146 passengers. Chief external differences between the N 304 and its predecessor are the location of the two thrust propellers on fins aft of the passenger cabin, the resiting of the raised wheelhouse forward and the completely redesigned bow.

The bow ramp/door has been removed and the bow and bow skirt have been redesigned for improved rough weather performance. The loading ramp/door aft has been retained for passenger and crew access. The passenger cabin is fully air-conditioned and can be equipped with a refreshment bar.

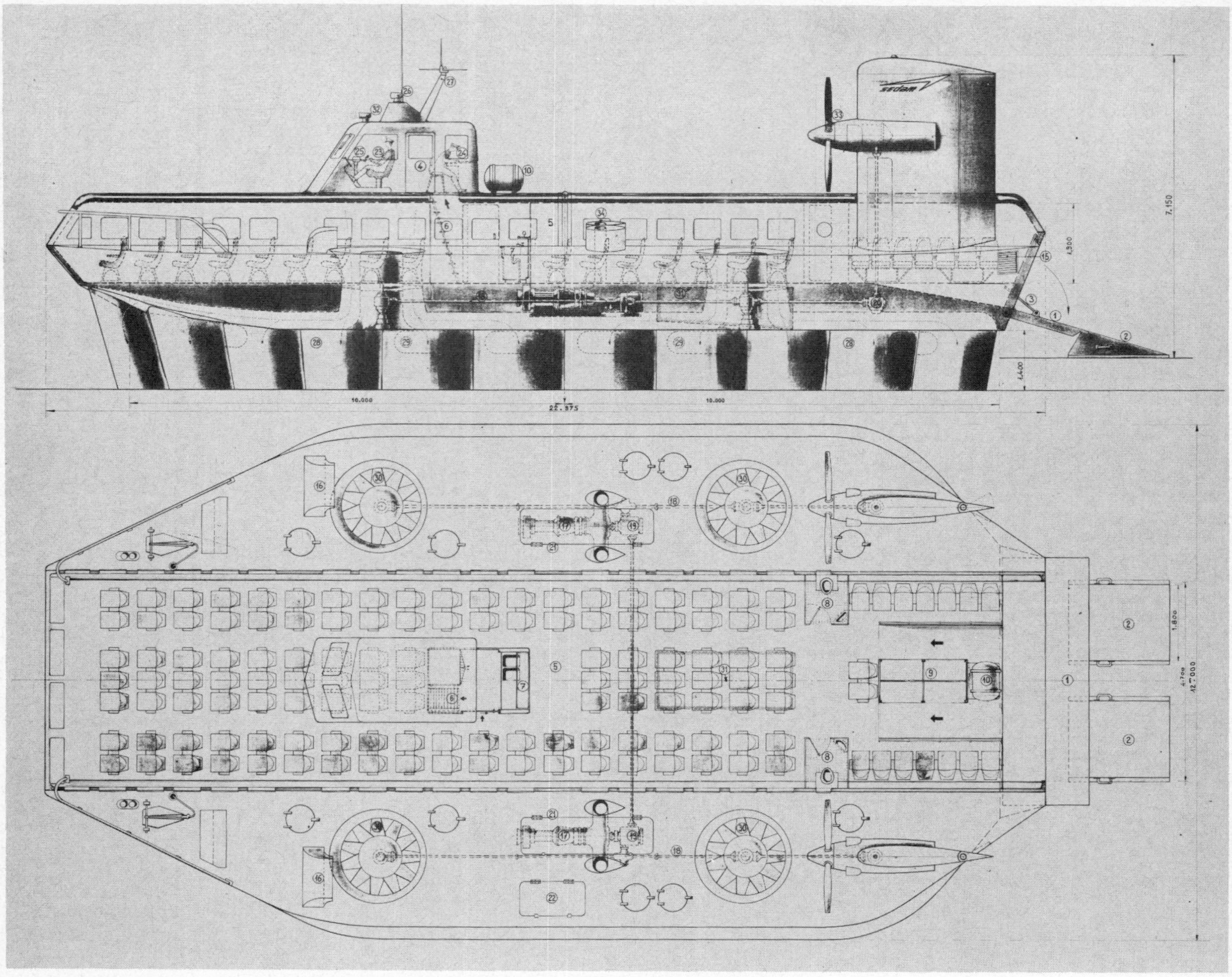

Inboard elevation and deck view of the Dubigeon-Normandie/SEDAM N 304 137-146 seat passenger ferry

Power is supplied by two 1,200kW Turboméca Turmo XII gas turbines.

DIMENSIONS

EXTERNAL

Length overall: 22·97m (75ft 4¼in)
Beam overall: 12m (39ft 5in)
Height on landing pads: 7·15m (23ft 5½in)

Details of weights and performance on application.

NAVIPLANE N 500

The N 500 is a 260-tonne, mixed-traffic hoverferry with a payload capacity of 85 tonnes and a maximum speed of 130km/h (70 knots) in calm conditions. The first two craft were built for SNCF (French National Railways) to operate under the Seaspeed banner on a service across the English Channel, between Boulogne and Dover, starting in 1978.

N 500-01 started trials on 19 April 1977 but on 3 May 1977 was severely damaged by fire during minor skirt repairs and the craft was subsequently 'written off'. N 500-02, 'Ingenieur Jean Bertin', began trials on the English Channel in November 1977 and made its first official 'in service' flight on 5 July 1978. The SNCF board took the decision in principle to order N 500-03 at a meeting on 25 June 1978. An option is also believed to have been taken on N 500-04. Discussions have also taken place between Dubigeon-Normandie Shipyards and Hoverlloyd Ltd which is considering ordering two N 500s for its Ramsgate-Calais route.

LIFT AND PROPULSION: Motive power is supplied by five Avco Lycoming TF40 marinised gas-turbines, two for lift and three for propulsion. Maximum output of the TF 40 is 3,000hp; maximum intermittent output is 3,400hp and maximum continuous is 3,200hp. Specific fuel consumption is 247 gallons/h. Each lift engine drives via a reduction system and bevel gear a 4m (13ft 1½in) diameter, 13-bladed, axial-flow fan of laminated construction. The fans, built by Ratier-Forest, are based on experience gained with the N 300 series, and the blades can be adjusted, when stopped, to suit flight conditions. Revolution speed is 900rpm and the tip speed is limited to 200 metres/second to avoid excessive noise. Each fan weighs 800kg (1,764lb) and their rated input power is 2,150kW.

Fan air intakes are located immediately aft of

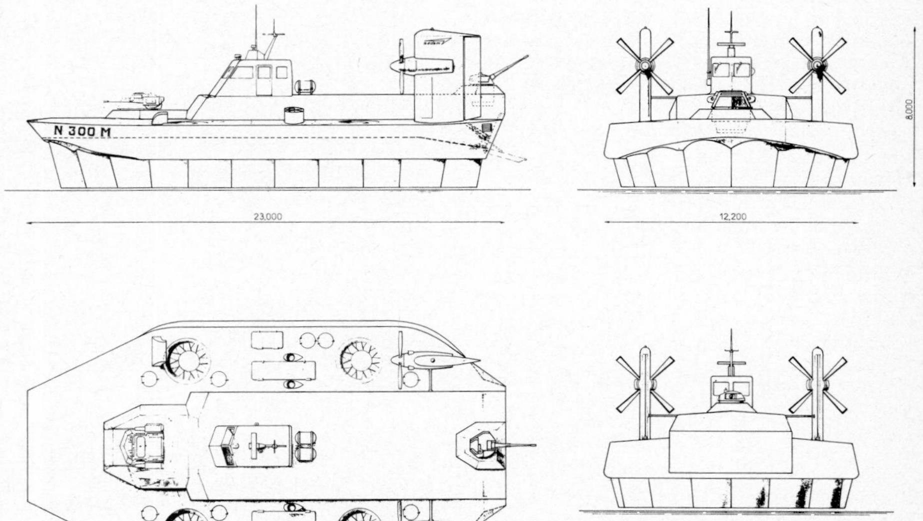

General arrangement of the N 300 Mk II fast patrol boat.

the wheelhouse, one each side of the longitudinal centreline. Cushion air is drawn into two wells reaching down through the passenger and car decks, into a plenum beneath the latter, from which it is fed to the multiple skirts. The flow of air to each group of skirts is controlled by air valves.

Both fans deliver air to a common plenum and in the event of either having to be shut down, the remaining unit has sufficient capacity to enable the craft to take-off and operate in waves up to 2·5m (8ft 3in) high.

Lift and propulsion systems are totally independent of each other in order to reduce gearing to a minimum. The three propulsion engines, each contained in a separate nacelle, are mounted on a horizontal stabiliser aft, where each TF40 drives a 6·3m (20ft 8in) diameter, four-bladed variable- and reversible-pitch propeller at a maximum rotation speed of 640rpm. Three reduction units reduce the nominal engine speed of 15,400rpm to 622rpm at the propeller. The second of these units is equipped with a brake to stop propeller rotation in case of engine failure. The propellers, designed and built by Hawker-Siddeley Dynamics, are similar to those used on the BH.7. The blades consist of a duralumin spar, forged and machine-finished, and covered with a glass fibre and epoxy resin shell to NACA Series 16 and 64 modified profiles. Tractive power is 15 tonnes at zero speed and 11·5 tonnes at 36 metres/second.

The horizontal stabiliser is designed to counteract pitching during take-off and create sufficient lift to compensate the tail-load moment induced by the aerodynamic forces acting on the craft.

CONTROLS: Craft directional control is provided by pedal-operated aerodynamic rudders and differential propeller pitch. In the event of either outboard propeller being stopped, yawing moment is compensated by the use of rudders. Pitch control is provided by elevators on the horizontal stabiliser, and fuel is transferred between forward and aft tanks to adjust fore and aft static trim.

HULL: Modular structure built in simple light alloy units. The main platform structure is made up of welded longitudinal and transverse girder boxes which also form buoyancy chambers. The main longitudinal box girder is the central lane for coaches and heavy vehicles. Beneath each car deck is a structure made up by welded trellis-type lateral beams. The main hull platform supports the box-like coach compartment on the longitudinal centreline and the two car decks, one each side of the coach deck. On land, off-cushion, the craft rests on small cylindrical inflated pads. Lifting jacks are employed to raise the craft off the ground for inspection and servicing. Both the forward and aft load door/ramps can accommodate three vehicles abreast for loading and offloading.

SKIRTS: Arrangement based on that adopted for the N 300. Planform of the N 500's hull is a rectangle, elongated at the bow by a semicircle. The skirt system comprises 48 identical skirts, each of 4m (13ft 1½in) diameter, arranged around the outer perimeter of the hull base in a continuous double ring. The skirts are in Tergal (Terylene) covered with synthetic rubber. Air is fed to the skirts in groups, giving a labyrinth effect. It is also fed into the central cushion area direct.

ACCOMMODATION: In the mixed-traffic version, passengers are accommodated in two saloons on two upper half-decks on either side of the box structure containing the coach passageway. The arrangement is claimed to give passengers greater safety, since they are on a different level from the vehicles; as well as greater comfort as their location is in the centre of the craft. Since their seats are sited above the spray they will also have a better view. The payload of 85 tonnes would comprise 400 passengers and 45 medium-sized cars, or 280 passengers, 10 cars and five coaches. The wheelhouse, located above the forward end of the longitudinal coach box, accommodates a crew of three—captain, co-pilot and radio operator/navigator. Access is via a

Impression of the SEDAM N 300 Mk II in fast patrol boat configuration with a SAMM 20mm twin naval mounting forward and a single 30mm mounting aft

Close-up of the N500-02 Ingenieur Jean Bertin showing the forward load door/ramp and the bow skirt system

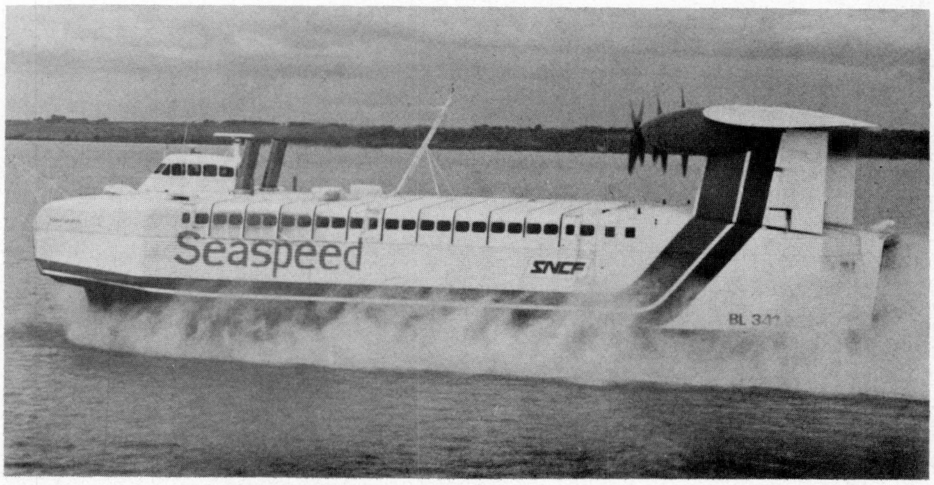

N 500-02, which made its first official flight 'in service' on 5 July 1978, operating under the Seaspeed banner on the Boulogne-Dover cross-Channel route

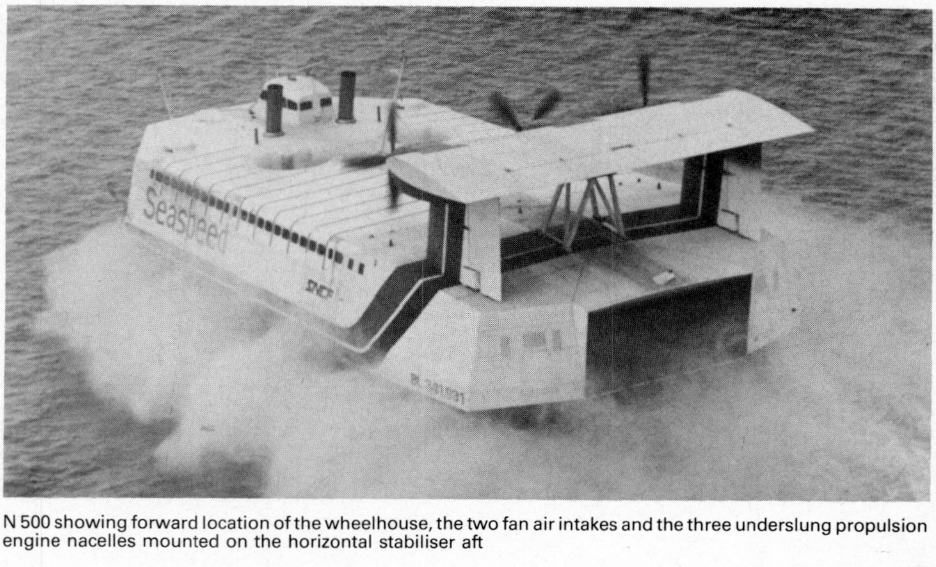

N 500 showing forward location of the wheelhouse, the two fan air intakes and the three underslung propulsion engine nacelles mounted on the horizontal stabiliser aft

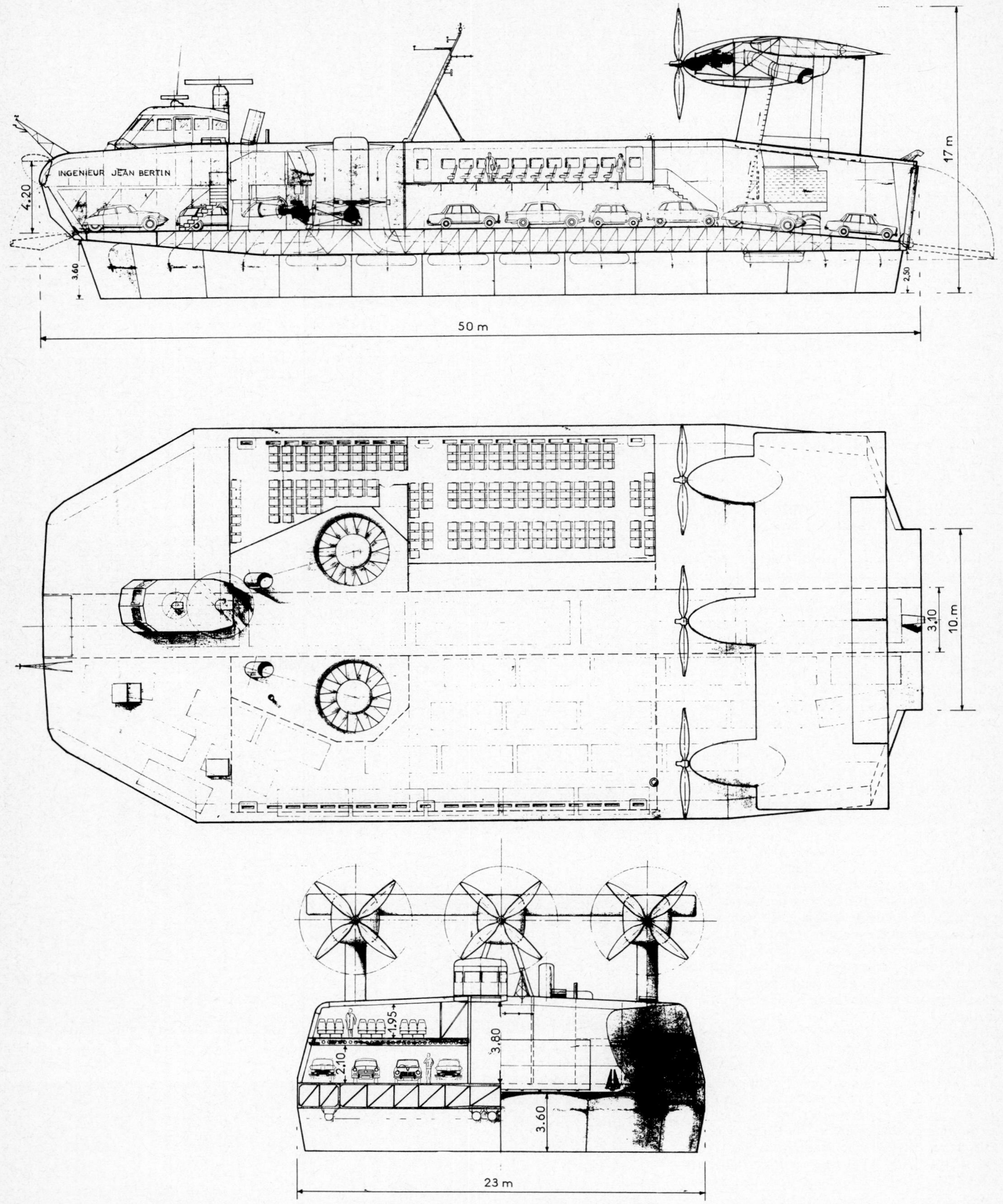

General arrangement of the N 500, powered by five 3,200hp Avco Lycoming TF 40 marinised gas-turbines, two for lift and three for propulsion

companionway at the base of the starboard lift engine compartment and a vertical ladder from the passenger saloon.

SYSTEMS, ELECTRICAL: Electrical supply is provided by two turbo-alternators, each comprising a Deutz T216 gas-turbine driving an Auxilec 1602 alternator.

NAVIGATION: Two Decca radars, one 10cm, one 3cm plus one gyro and one magnetic compass.

DIMENSIONS

EXTERNAL

Length overall: 50m (164ft 1in)
Beam overall: 23m (75ft 1½in)
Height overall, on cushion: 17m (55ft 9in)
Cushion length: 45m (147ft 8in)
Cushion beam: 22m (72ft 2in)

INTERNAL

Cargo deck length, inboard: 46m (150ft 11in)
Cargo deck width, inboard: 22m (72ft 2in)
Cargo deck area: 960m² (10,332ft²)

WEIGHTS

Empty: 155 tonnes
Fuel etc: 20 tonnes
Payload: 85 tonnes
Total gross: 260 tonnes

PERFORMANCE

Max speed, calm water: 75 knots, attainable in less than 200 seconds
Cruising speed, 1·5m (5ft) waves: 58 knots
Cruising speed, 2·5m (8ft) waves: 48 knots
Endurance over 2·5m (8ft) waves: 5 hours
Max wave height: 4m (13ft 2in)
Normal stopping distance from
70 knots: 1,000m (3,280ft)
emergency: 500m (1,640ft)
vertical acceleration: 0·15g

MN.2 RESEARCH CRAFT

While conducting design studies for the N 500, SEDAM made extensive use of data gathered from models. Wind tunnel tests were undertaken at the Eiffel research centre with a 1:50 scale model, and a 1:20 model was tested at the Carèsnes tank to measure aerodynamic and hydrodynamic resistance.

Two manned, dynamic research craft employed were the MN1 and the MN2. The former, a 1:9 scale, 6m (19ft 8in) long model was designed for testing the fans and multiple skirt system, while the latter was built for handling and manoeuvrability trials. In addition, a number of tests were conducted with scale model skirts, singly and in groups.

4-5,000 ton SES

A study for a 4,000-5,000 ton surface effect ship for the French Navy is being undertaken by SEDAM in conjunction with Société des Ateliers et Chantiers de Bretagne (ACB). The study has been requested by the Centre de Prospective et d'Evaluations (CPE) of the Ministry of Defence.

The configuration selected is known as the AQL, an abbreviation of the French term for sidewall craft—aéroglisseur à quilles latérales.

The studies are being undertaken at the Bassin des Carèsnes, Paris, with the aid of models equipped with rigid sidewalls integral to the hull structure and flexible seals fore and aft to contain the air cushion.

Several versions of the projected vessel are envisaged. An ASW variant appears to be high on the list of the French Navy's requirements. In ASW configuration, the craft would carry VDS and could also be fitted with auxiliary medium depth sonar enabling it to conduct attacks with its own weapons. In addition it could carry ASW

Control cabin of the N 500. Basic manning requirement is for a crew of three—captain, first officer and radio operator/navigator

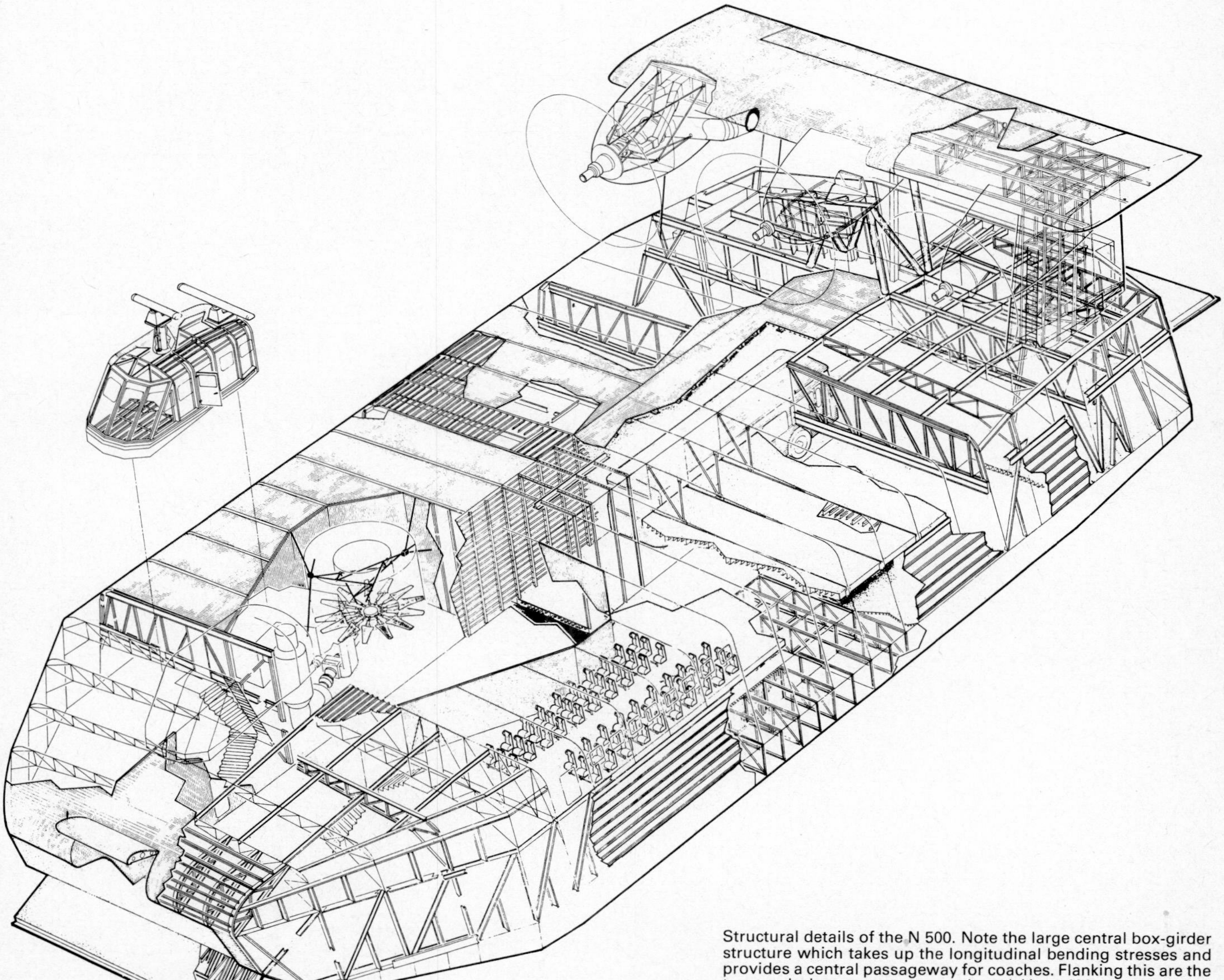

Structural details of the N 500. Note the large central box-girder structure which takes up the longitudinal bending stresses and provides a central passageway for coaches. Flanking this are the two car decks, one port, one starboard. Up to 400 passengers are accommodated in the two centrally-located saloons on the upper half-decks

helicopters on its aft deck which could locate distant targets and conduct attacks on their own.

All versions of the projected vessel would be equipped with defensive armament based on naval automatic guns, surface-to-air missiles and electronic warfare systems.

Long-range offensive patrols, the transport of helicopter-borne assault forces and escort destroyer are among the other applications foreseen.

PROPULSION: Various alternative methods of propulsion are being examined, including four hydrojets, four semi-submerged propellers and four turbofans. The power output necessary to operate the vessel is estimated as follows:
Operation hullborne: 110,500CV 84mW
Operation on air cushion: 190,000CV 140mW
Power to operate lift fans and generate cushion: 30,000CV 22mW
Electricity: 4,000-22,000CV 3-16mW

The specification below applies to the hydrojet-propelled variant.

DIMENSIONS
Length overall: 119·4m (392ft)
Beam overall: 47m (154ft)
Beam across sidewalls: 31m (98ft)
Width of each sidewall: 8m (26ft 3in)
Cushion length: 100m (328ft)
Cushion width: 37m (121ft)
Cushion height: 10m (32ft 9in)
Cushion area: 3,700m² (39,826ft²)

WEIGHTS
Empty: 2,900 tons
Fuel: 1,500 tons
Weapons and equipment: 600 tons
Total gross: 5,000 tons

PERFORMANCE
Max speed hullborne: 16 knots
Max speed on cushion in force 3 winds, wave height 1-1·5m: 60 knots
Max speed, force 3, wave height 3m: 55 knots
In waves higher than 5m, the vessel would operate in displacement condition.

Up to 400 passengers are accommodated in two saloons on two upper half-decks, one each side of the central box structure containing the coach passageway

Vehicles entering the N 500 via the rear load door/ramp. A large central box girder structure which takes up the longitudinal bending stresses provides a central passageway for coaches and other heavy vehicles

One of the configurations of a 5,000 ton SES for the French Navy being studied by Dubigeon-Normandie in conjunction with Société des Ateliers et Chantiers de Bretagne (ACB). Alternative propulsion systems under consideration include four turbofans, four hydrojets and four semi-submerged propellers

Dynamic model of the 4-5,000 ton SES undergoing tank tests at the Bassin des Carèsnes, Paris

TRANSFUTUR S.A.

9 rue Ambroise Thomas, 75009 Paris, France

First hovercraft to be built by this new Paris-based company is the Windlord, an amphibious grp-hulled four-seater powered by a 65cv Citroen automobile engine and capable of speeds of up to 35 knots. A preliminary description is given below.

WINDLORD

LIFT AND PROPULSION: Integrated system employing a single 65cv Citroen GS X 2 automobile engine which drives a single 1·25m (4ft 1in) diameter eight-bladed ducted propeller. The primary airflow is directed aft for propulsion while the secondary air flow is ducted into the plenum below for cushion lifts. Fuel consumption is 13·72 litres (3 gallons) per hour at maximum speed. Engine has two-stage anti-vibration mountings and is mounted in a sound insulated compartment.

CONTROLS: Craft heading is controlled by four rudders hinged to the rear of the propeller duct and activated by foot pedals. Conventional throttle control for engine. Full engine instrumentation is provided.

HULL: Double-skinned glass reinforced polyester structure filled with polyurethane. Buoyancy 1,350kg (2,976lb)

SKIRT: Loop and segment type in neoprene coated nylon.

ACCOMMODATION: Enclosed cabin seating for four.

Transfutur's grp-hulled four-seater, the Windlord *(Photo: Robert Trillo)*

ROAD TRANSPORTATION: A specially designed trailer unit, capable of being operated by one person, is available for towing the craft behind a car.

WEIGHTS

Payload: 350kg (772lb)

PERFORMANCE

Speed: 50 to 70 km/h (25 to 35 knots), depending on nature of terrain.

Range: 200km (124 miles)

Endurance: 4 hours

Vertical obstacle clearance: 30cm (11¾in)

GERMANY, FEDERAL REPUBLIC

RHEIN-FLUGZEUGBAU GmbH (RFB)

(Subsidiary of VFW-Fokker GmbH)

Head Office and Main Works: Flugplatz, Postfach 408, D-4050 Mönchengladbach, Federal Republic of Germany

Telephone: (02161) 662031

Telex: 08/52506

Other Works: Flughafen Köln-Bonn, Halle 6, D-5050 Porz-Wahn, Federal Republic of Germany and Flugplatz, D-2401 Lübeck-Blankensee, Federal Republic of Germany

Officials:

Dipl-Volkswirt Wolfgang Kutscher, *Executive Director*

Dipl-Ing Alfred Schneider, *Executive Director*

Founded in 1956, this company holds 100% of the stock of Sportavia-Pützer.

RFB is engaged in the development and construction of airframe structural components, with particular emphasis on wings and fuselages made entirely of glassfibre-reinforced resins. Research and design activities include studies for the Federal German Ministry of Defence.

RFB X-113 Am during a flight demonstration over the Wattenmeer

Current manufacturing programmes include series and individual production of aircraft components and assemblies made of light alloy, steel and glassfibre-reinforced resin for aircraft in quantity production, as well as spare parts and ground equipment. The company is also active in the fields of shelter and container construction.

Under contract to the German government, RFB services certain types of military aircraft, and provides target-towing flights and other services with special aircraft.

The X-113 Am Aerofoil Boat was built and tested under the scientific direction of the late Dr A M Lippisch. Flight tests of the 6-7 seat RFB X-114 have been successfully completed and after some hydrodynamic modifications a new series of tests will begin in the spring of 1979.

RFB (LIPPISCH) X-113 Am AEROFOIL BOAT

The Aerofoil Boat was conceived in the United States by Dr A M Lippisch. The first wing-in-ground-effect machine built to Lippisch designs was the Collins X-112, which was employed by Lippisch to examine the stability problems likely to be encountered in the design of larger machines of this type.

Since 1967 further development of the concept has been undertaken by RFB with government backing. The single-seat X-113 has been built as a test craft to provide data for the design of larger craft of the same type.

The X-113 Am underwent its first airworthiness test from Lake Constance in October 1970.

During the first series of tests, the craft demonstrated its operating ability on water as well as flight capability at very low altitudes. These tests were followed in the autumn of 1971 by a second series of trials during which performance measurements were taken. A cine camera built into the cockpit recorded instrument readings and a camera built into the lateral stabilisers took pictures of small threads on the upper wing surface for current flow analysis.

The earlier trials on Lake Constance were followed in November/December 1972 by a third series of tests in the North Sea in the Weser estuary area.

Apart from various performance measurements, the aim of these trials was to investigate the machine's capabilities in roughish weather conditions. Although the machine was originally designed for only a brief general demonstration on calm water, it proved capable of take-offs and landings in a moderate sea.

Remarkably good sea behaviour was shown from the outset. Take-offs and landings in wave heights of about 0·75m (2ft 6in) presented no problem. During the course of these tests, flights were made in the coastal region, and sometimes on the Wattenmeer, in wind forces of up to 25 knots, without any uncontrollable flying tendencies being observed in low-level flight.

The flight performance measurements gave a gliding angle of 1 : 30, which cannot be greatly improved by enlarging the machine. It is also of interest to note that the relatively thin outer laminate of the gfr wing sandwich, with a thickness of 0·4mm, stood up to the loads involved in taking off in a roughish sea and also remained watertight throughout the whole period of trials.

Towards the end of the trials, in order to reduce noise and give the airscrew better protection from spray, the machine was converted to pusher propulsion.

The company envisages a range of Aerofoil craft for a variety of civil and military purposes, from single-seat runabouts to cargo transporters with payloads of up to 10 tons. As transports they could be employed on coastal, inter-island and river services. Military variants could be used as assault craft, FPBs and ASW vessels.

Flight tests, including a series performed over rough water in the North Sea near Bremerhaven, have established that 50% less power is required in ground effect, enabling operations in excess of 50-ton-miles per gallon of fuel at speeds in the 90-180 knot range.

Underside of the X-113 Am, showing the anhedral reversed delta wing which overcomes the problem of pitch instability during the transition from surface effect to free-flight and back again

Above and below: The new 6-7 seat RFB X-114 Aerofoil Boat which began flight trials in April 1977. Powered by a 200hp Lycoming IO-360 driving an RFB ducted fan, the X-114 cruises in ground effect at 150km/h (93mph) and has a maximum range of 2,150km (1,336 miles). A retractable wheel undercarriage is fitted enabling the craft to operate from both land and water

RFB X-114 AEROFOIL BOAT

Evolved from the X-113, this 6-7-seater has a maximum take-off weight of 1,500kg and is fitted with a retractable wheel undercarriage, enabling it to operate from land or water.

Power is provided by a 200hp Lycoming IO-360 four-cylinder horizontally-opposed air-cooled engine driving a specially-designed Rhein-Flugzeugbau ducted fan. Range, with 100kg (220lb) of fuel is more than 1,000km (621 miles). Operational speed is 75-200km/h (46-124mph).

An initial trials programme was successfully completed in 1977. The X-114 is currently undergoing hydrodynamic modifications in preparation for a new series of tests beginning in the spring of 1979.

The vehicle is designed to operate over waves up to 1·5m (4ft 11in) in ground effect and can therefore be used without restriction during 80% of the year in the Baltic Sea area and 60% of the year in the North Sea. On days with high seas of more than 1·5m (4ft 11in) takeoff and landing takes place in waters near the coast. Flying is virtually unrestricted, providing due allowance is made for the loss in economy.

Fuel consumption costs, while flying in ground effect, are lower than those for cars. RFB states that its economics cannot be matched by any other form of transport aircraft.

Although built primarily as a research craft to extend the experience gained with the X-113 Am single-seater, Aerofoil Boats of the size of the X-114 are suitable for air-taxi work along coastlines, the supervision of restricted areas, patrol, customs and coastguard purposes and search-and-rescue missions.

Without any significant new research the construction of a vehicle with a takeoff weight of approximately 18,000kg is possible. On a vehicle of this size, the ratio of empty weight to takeoff weight is less than 50%.

DIMENSIONS
Length overall: 12·8m (42ft)
Wing span: 7m (22ft 11⅝in)
Height overall: 2·9m (9ft 6⅛in)

WEIGHTS
Max takeoff: 1,500kg (3,307lb)
Payload: 500kg (1,102lb)

PERFORMANCE
Max cruising speed: 200km/h (124mph)
Cruising speed in ground effect: 150km/h (93mph)
Max flight range: 2,150km (1,336 miles)

JAMAICA

CILMA HOLDINGS LTD

10 Glendon Drive, Kingston 10, Jamaica
Officials:
J Scarlett, *Managing Director*
C Scarlett, *Director*

Cilma Holdings Limited was formed in February 1976 to investigate the feasibility of hovercraft application in Jamaica. Areas to be investigated include recreational vehicles for the tourist industry, rapid transit ferry services and industrial and military applications.

CILMA V

First hovercraft to be designed and built in Jamaica, Cilma V is being employed as a test vehicle and also to undertake feasibility studies. The data provided will be used in determining the design of future production hovercraft.

LIFT AND PROPULSION: Lift air is provided by a 30hp, 1,200cc Volkswagen engine driving a 0·774m (2ft 6½in) diameter, 45 degree pitch multi-wing fan fitted directly to the crankshaft. Thrust is supplied by a 1,500cc 65hp Volkswagen engine, geared to a 2·28m (7ft 6in) diameter propeller fabricated from the main rotor of a Sikorsky helicopter. Chord of the propeller is 304mm (12in) and pitch 15 degrees. Maximum engine speed is 3,000rpm.

CONTROLS: Craft heading is controlled by twin aerodynamic rudders hinged to the tubular metal guard aft of the propeller. The control stick is connected to the rudders via a torsion rod running the length of the craft. Fore and aft movement of the control stick operates the throttle of the propulsion engine.

HULL: Wooden frame, with top and bottom skins of ¼in marine ply separated by stringers and ribs. All spaces within the hull are filled with polyurethane foam, which supplies buoyancy in the event of the marine ply skin being ruptured.

SKIRT: Bag type, in neoprene impregnated fabric.

ACCOMMODATION: Seats are provided for a driver and two passengers in an enclosed cabin. Access is via two gullwing doors, one on each side. Lifebelts are stored in the forward compartment. A 1½hp outboard engine, intended for emergency use, and anchors are stowed behind the seats. A fire-extinguisher is attached to the dashboard and safety belts are provided.

DIMENSIONS
Length: 3·04m (10ft)
Beam: 2·43m (8ft)
Height to prop tip, off cushion: 2·74m (9ft)
Height to prop tip, cushionborne: 3·04m (10ft)

WEIGHTS
Empty: 589·64kg (1,300lb)
Loaded: 816·42kg (1,800lb)

PERFORMANCE
Max speed, calm water: 120·7km/h (75mph)
Normal cruising speed: 80·46km/h (50mph)
Vertical obstacle clearance: 254mm (10in)

The Cilma V three-seater research craft during trials. Thrust is supplied by a 65hp Volkswagen engine driving a 2·28m (7ft 6in) diameter propeller fabricated from the main rotor of a Sikorsky helicopter

JAPAN

AOYAMA GAKUIN UNIVERSITY

LN 360

This combined ground effect machine and wheeled vehicle was developed jointly by the Traffic Engineering Department at Aoyama Gakuin University, under the direction of Eigi Tonokura and the Aerodynamics Laboratory at Nihon University, under the direction of Masahiro Mino.

The test vehicle illustrated, which has front wheel drive only, represents the first stage in the development of a vehicle with air cushion assist and a four-wheel drive. The objective is to design a plenum-type vehicle capable of operating over both rough tracks and unprepared terrain while carrying heavy loads.

DIMENSIONS
ACV CONVERSION
Length: 4·95m (16ft 3in)
Width: 1·70m (5ft 7in)
Height: 1·39m (4ft 6½in)
Cushion area: 3·92m² (42·19ft²)
Cushion length: 8·3m (27ft 3in)

WEIGHTS
All-up, with driver only: 580kg (1,280lb)

LIFT AND PROPULSION
Thrust engine: Honda N360E 354cc 31hp at 8,000rpm
Lift engine: (1) Yamaha YD-2 247cc 14·5hp at 6,100rpm two-cylinder, air-cooled, two cycle; (2) Daihatsu ZD305 305cc 12hp at 4,500rpm one-cylinder, air-cooled, two cycle.
Lift fan: 570mm (22½in) diameter, six-bladed axial fan. Weight 2·5kg (5½lb)
Tyre: Agricultural type tyre AL-3 (19 × 10,000-10) Ohtsu Tyre Co Ltd

Combined ground effect machine and wheeled vehicle under development at Aoyama Gakuin University, Japan. Designated LN 360, the vehicle has a plenum lift system powered by either a 14·5hp Yamaha YD-2 or 12hp Daihatsu ZD 305 petrol engine. The front wheels are fitted with agricultural tyres and are steered by a conventional steering wheel

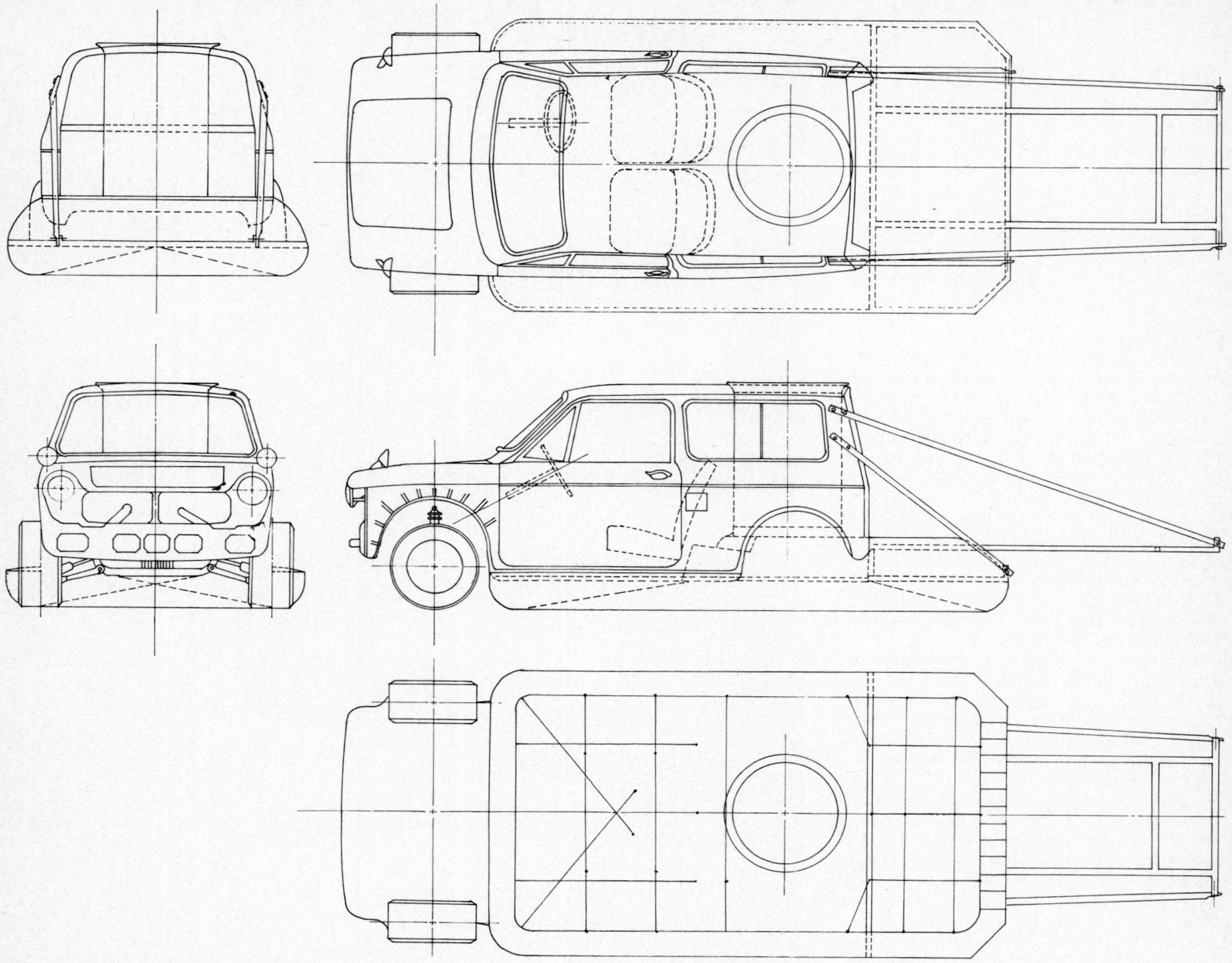

General arrangement of the LN 360 air cushion assist research vehicle developed jointly by Aoyama and Nihon Universities

ASHIKAGA INSTITUTE OF TECHNOLOGY

Mechanical Design Study Group, Institute of Technology, 268 Ohmae-cho, Ashikagishi 26326, Japan

Officials:

T Imamura, *Director*
E Sakai, *Director*
S Suzuku, *Director*

The Mechanical Design Study Group at the Ashikaga Institute of Technology is conducting an ACV research programme in conjunction with the Aerodynamics Section of the Physical Science Laboratory, Nihon University. It has recently taken over the Pastoral 1, constructed at Nihon University in 1970, and introduced various modifications. In its new form the craft is some 35% lighter, and has been redesignated Pastoral 2.

Pastoral single-seat research ACV

PASTORAL 2

This is a light amphibious single-seater employed to gather data for research and development projects. The modified craft has completed nearly five hours of tests over sand, grass and mud and has attained a speed of 98km/h (55mph).

LIFT AND PROPULSION: A single 8hp Fuji Heavy Industries two-cycle, single-cylinder air-cooled engine installed immediately aft of the cockpit drives a five-bladed 540mm (1ft 9¼in) diameter axial-flow fan for lift. Propulsion is supplied by a 36hp Toyota 2U-B four-cycle, two-cylinder engine driving a 1,200mm (3ft 11¼in) diameter two-bladed propeller.

CONTROLS: Twin aerodynamic rudders operated by a wheel in the cockpit control craft heading.

HULL: Moulded glassfibre, with inflatable fabric-reinforced neoprene sidebody/skirt.

DIMENSIONS

Length overall, skirt inflated: 4·2m (13ft 9½in)
Beam overall, skirt inflated: 1·8m (5ft 11in)
Height, skirt inflated: 1·55m (5ft 1in)

WEIGHTS

Normal all-up: 320kg (706lb)

PERFORMANCE

Max speed, over land: 90km/h (56mph)
over water: 60km/h (37mph)

FANBIRD HOVERCRAFT

Head Office: 4F Nakauchi Bld 1-7-6, Nihonbashi Chuo-ku, Tokyo 103, Japan
Telephone: (03) 278-0227

Officials:

Jiichiro Yokota, *Director*
Yoshimichi Kushida, *Director*

Consultant:

Masahiro Mino

Fanbird Shikoku Division

164-1 Samukawa-cho, Iyomishima-shi Ehime 799-04
Kazunori Takahashi, *Director*

Fanbird Kohchi Division

2490-11 Niida, Kohchi-shi Kohchiken 781-01
Arioshi Armitsu, *Director*

Fanbird Hovercraft was formed in May 1976. It is currently engaged in the design, development and manufacture of light hovercraft, which are available in plan and kit form to Japanese amateur hovercraft constructors. The company also publishes *The Light Hovercraft Handbook* and holds stocks of materials for homebuilders including fans, propellers, engines, ducts, completed skirts and skirt material, shafts, pulleys, belts, mounts,, wood for ribs and stringers and marine ply.

Design consultant to the company is Masahiro Mino, Senior Director of the Aerodynamics Department at Nihon University, which has been conducting an extensive ACV research programme for a number of years.

Abbreviated specifications of eight of the company's designs appear in the accompanying table.

"UHO" a 1·8m diameter saucer-shaped ACV designed by Fanbird Hovercraft. It can be purchased in either plan or kit form. A variety of engines can be fitted, from 4 to 8 hp

Fanbird FB24 Mosquito single-seat sports hovercraft

Fanbird FB26 Mini single-seat sports hovercraft

Fanbird FB32 single-seat sports runabout

Fanbird FB36 two-seat sports hovercraft

Type	*l × w* (*m*)	*l × w on Cushion* (*m*)	*Seats*	*Type*	*Engine Power* (*hp*)	*Empty Weight* (*kg*)	*Total* (*kg*)	*Max Speed* (*km/h*)	*Hover Gap* (*m*)	*Skirt Type*
UHO	1·8	2·3	1	—	4-8	60	120	20	0·25	Finger
FB24	2·4 × 1·2	2·6 × 1·6	1	L/P	8-15	60	120	30	0·18	Bag
FB26 Mini	2·6 × 1·6	2·8 × 2·0	1	L/P	12-20	80	145	40	0·2	Bag
FB26 Super Mini	2·6 × 1·6	2·8 × 2·0	1	L/P	20-30	100	170	45	0·2	Bag
FB32 Std	3·2 × 1·8	3·4 × 2·2	1	L/P	30-40	120	195	40	0·23	Bag
FB32 Sports	3·2 × 1·8	3·4 × 2·2	1	L + P	6-30	150	225	50	0·23	Bag
FB36 Sd	3·6 × 1·8	3·8 × 2·2	2	L + P	8-40	190	340	50	0·25	Bag
FB36 TD	3·6 × 1·8	3·8 × 2·2	2	L + P	15-65	220	390	65	0·25	Bag

Number of plans/number of craft sold by March 1978:
UHO 30/12; FB24 42/24; FB26 Mini 208/118; FB26 Supermini 32/11; FB32STD 202/113; FB32 Sports 251/123; FB36SD 108/58; FB36TD 38/20; Total 911/479

Fanbird FB32 in standard configuration. Maximum speed of this amphibious single-seater is 40km/h

Fanbird FB36 TD with twin ducted thrust fans powered by a single 65hp engine

FUN VEHICLE CO LTD

Nakauchi Building 3F, 1-7-6 Nihonbashi, Chuo-ku, Tokyo, Japan Z.C. 103
Telephone: (03) 278 0225

Officials:
Hiroshi Suzuki, *President*
Isao Ishii, *Managing Director*
Haruo Ota, *Design Director*
Yoshimichi Kushida, *Technical Director*
Kouji Mizauo, *Marketing Director*
Kazutoshi Okamato, *Marketing Service Director*
Masahiro Mino, *Consultant*
Yasuyo Minemura, *Secretary*

Fun Vehicle Co Ltd was founded in June 1977 to undertake the development, manufacture and marketing of sports and utility vehicles, with particular emphasis on hovercraft and air boats.

Its first product is the FV-10 Newpole, an amphibious single-seater with separate lift and propulsion systems. The company is selling this craft in Japan, throughout south-east Asia and in the USA. It is available as a kit, a kit with completed hull or as a finished craft, 'ready-to-fly'.

First production machine to be marketed by Fun Vehicle Co, the FV-10T Newpole amphibious single-seater

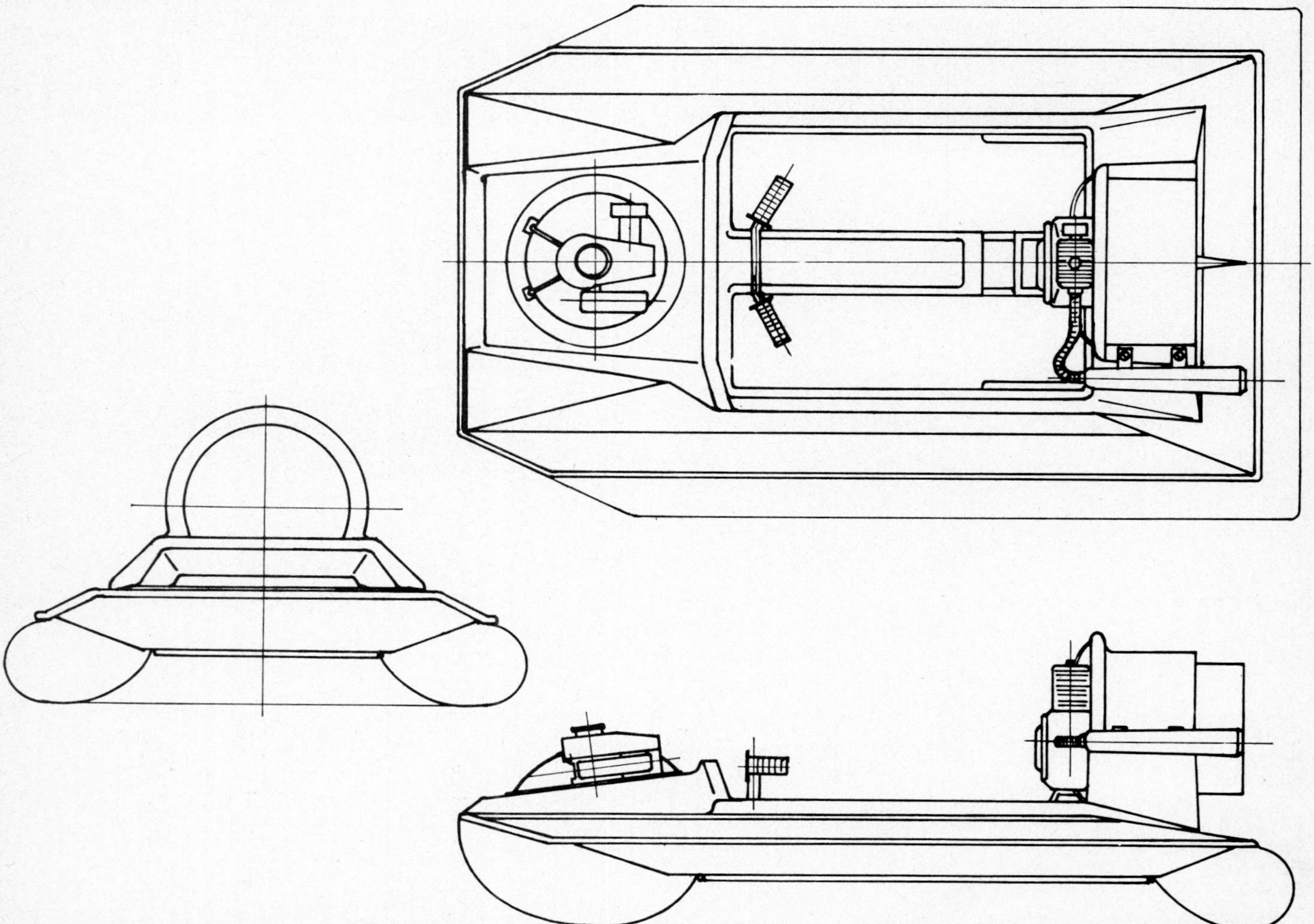

General arrangement of the FV-10T grp-hulled single-seater

FV-10 NEWPOLE

Development of this grp-hulled single-seater began in 1976 and six prototypes were built and tested before the craft was finally put into production in late 1977. Maximum speed across land and water is 50km/h (31·2mph).

LIFT AND PROPULSION: Lift is provided by a single Fuji EC-17D two-stroke, rated at 6·5hp at 5,000rpm and driving a 480mm (19in) five-bladed, 30 degree pitch ducted fan. Thrust is supplied by a single Kyoritsu KEC 225cc two-stroke, rated at 12·5hp at 5,500rpm, driving a 580mm (23in) diameter five-bladed, 30 degree pitch fan.

CONTROLS: Handlebar-operated air rudder mounted in the fan duct controls craft heading. Twist-grip throttle for propulsion engine on handlebar.

HULL: Complete hull structure is built in self-coloured glass-reinforced plastics. Polyurethane foam, contained in the underside of the hull, provides 200% buoyancy.

SKIRT SYSTEM: Simple bag skirt, fabricated in polyurethane-coated nylon fabric provides 0·19m (7½in) obstacle clearance.

ACCOMMODATION: Driver sits astride a central bench in an open cockpit.

DIMENSIONS

Length overall, on cushion: 3·09m (10ft 6in)
  on landing pads: 2·9m (9ft 6in)
Width overall, on cushion: 1·98m (6ft 6in)
  on landing pads: 1·6m (5ft 3in)
Height, on cushion: 1·09m (3ft 7in)
  on landing pads: 0·9m (3ft)

FV-10Ts under construction at Fun Vehicle's Isezaki factory

WEIGHTS

Empty: 140kg (308lb)
All-up: 210kg (463lb)

PERFORMANCE

Maximum speed, calm water: 50km/h (31·2mph)
Hard structure clearance: 0·19m (7½in)

HOVERMARINE PACIFIC CO, LTD

Head Office: Fuji Building 1-5-3, Yayesu, Chuo-ku, Tokyo, 103, Japan
Telephone: (03) 278 0821
Telex: 2228198
Works: c/o Sasebo Industries Co Ltd, Tategami-cho, Sasebo 857, Japan
Telephone: 0956-24-8391
Telex: 748219 (SSK J)

Officials:

T Nakabe, *President*
K Hishiya, *Senior Managing Director*
K Tsuru, *Junior Managing Director, Production and Design*
A Okiyoshi, *Customer Service Manager*
T Nakamae, *Marketing Manager*
K Hayashi, *Sales Manager*
M Tachiki, *Technical Manager*
K Ohono, *Production Manager*

Hovermarine Pacific is a joint venture by Hovermarine Corporation, Taiyo Fishery Co Ltd, Sasebo Heavy Industries Ltd, and Fairfield International Limited. Taiyo is the world's biggest fish processing company, with an annual sales revenue in excess of US$2,000 million and Sasebo is the world's tenth largest shipbuilder. Fairfield International is a private company with extensive interests in shipping. The company was established on 9 April 1976 with a capital of Y100,000,000.

The company's first craft, an 82-seat HM.2 Mk 4, was completed in 1978 at Hovermarine Pacific's factory at Saseko, on the Japanese island of Kyushu. The company is also undertaking the marketing of HM.5 in Korea. Future plans include the building of the 100-ton payload Hoverfreighter, a joint technical development with Hovermarine Transport Limited, and the HM.5. The Hoverfreighter, designated HM.100F, will have all of the characteristics of the basic Hovermarine designs and is intended to meet the need for heavy cargo transportation where limited harbour facilities exist and speed of movement is a primary requirement.

HM.100F has an all-up weight of 200 tons and a cruising speed of 25 knots. It will measure about 55·5m (182ft) long, 11·3m (36ft) wide and be 9m (29ft 6in) high. The floating draft is likely to be about 1·68m (5ft) and hovering draft of about 0·43m (1ft 3in).

Hovermarine is licensed by Hovercraft Development Ltd, an agency of the National Research Development Corporation, under various world-wide patents relating to air cushion technology. The licence excludes the Japanese market, and therefore Hovermarine products have not previously been available there. Hovermarine Pacific will be licensed directly to engage in this business.

Hovermarine Pacific Co Ltd, has constructed its first HM.2 Mk 4 at its plant at Sasebo on the island of Kyushu

Impression of the 100-ton payload Hoverfreighter being developed jointly by Hovermarine Transport Ltd, and Hovermarine Pacific Co Ltd

KANAZAWA INSTITUTE OF TECHNOLOGY

Hydrodynamic Laboratory, Department of Mechanical Engineering, Kanazawa Institute of Technology, Kanazawa South, Ishikawa 921, Japan

Officials:

Syoichi Fukumitsu
Yutaka Matsuyama

WATER SPIDER II

The Department of Mechanical Engineering, Kanazawa Institute of Technology, is conducting a research programme aimed at determining the performance potential of ACVs operating across snow-covered terrain. The programme is being conducted in conjunction with the Japanese National Ship Research Institute and Nihon University at Narashino.

In Japan the specific gravity of snow is between 0·1 and 0·5 and Kanazawa is an area which generally experiences heavy annual snowfalls. The Department of Mechanical Engineering at the Kanazawa Institute of Technology built its first hovercraft, the Water Spider I, in 1976. An improved model, the Water Spider II which is seen in the accompanying illustrations, was completed the following year.

LIFT AND PROPULSION: Lift is provided by a single 30hp two-cycle, twin-cylinder, air-cooled engine located ahead of the cockpit and driving a multi-bladed axial fan. Thrust is supplied by an identical engine driving a ducted axial fan aft.

CONTROLS: Craft direction is controlled by a single aerodynamic rudder hinged to the rear of the thrust fan duct and operated by a handlebar.

DIMENSIONS

Length overall: 3·9m (12ft 9½in)
Width overall: 2m (6ft 6¾in)
Height: 1·3m (4ft 3¼in)

Water Spider II research hovercraft operating across 457mm (1ft 6in) deep snow in Kanazawa

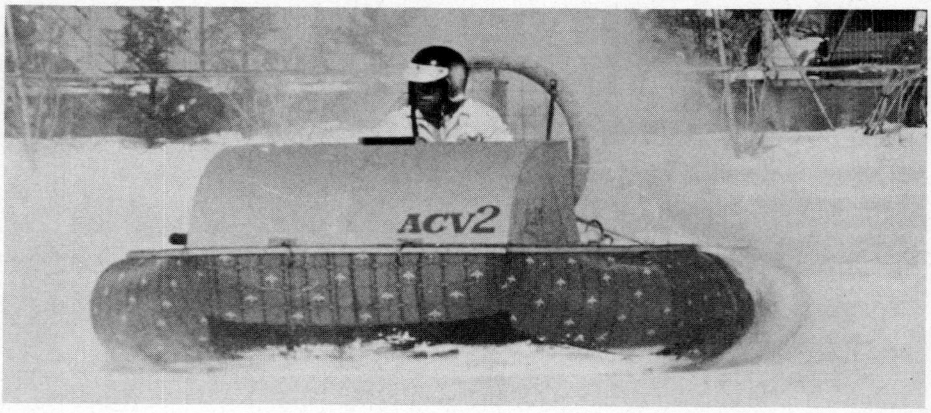

WEIGHTS

All-up: 310kg (684lb)

PERFORMANCE

Max speed, on land: 40km/h (25mph)
on water: 30km/h (19mph)

MITSUI ENGINEERING & SHIPBUILDING LTD

6-4, Tsukiji 5-chome, Chuo-ku, Tokyo 104, Japan

Telephone: 544-3451
Telex: J22821, J22924

Officials:

Isamu Yamashita, *President*
Jiro Komatsu, *Senior Managing Director*
Shoji Massaki, *Senior Managing Director*
Kazuo Hamano, *Senior Managing Director*
Kazuo Maeda, *Senior Managing Director*
Kazuo Nagai, *Managing Director*
Ryoji Kawazura, *Managing Director*
Tatsuhiko Ueno, *Managing Director*
Masahiko Irie, *Managing Director*
Hiromasa Kikuchi, *Managing Director*
Hideo Matsushima, *Managing Director*
Yoshio Ishitani, *Managing Director*
Koji Arase, *Managing Director*
Takeo Takayanagi, *Director*
Masataro Takami, *Director*
Tetsujiro Tomita, *Director*
Shunkichi Matsuoka, *Director*
Isshi Suenaga, *Director*
Fusao Hongo, *Director*
Kiichi Takano, *Director*
Niro Harano, *Director*
Fumio Makino, *Director*
Kazuhiko Ezaki, *Director*
Satoru Ohashi, *Director*
Shogo Saeki, *Director*
Kyoichi Kato, *Auditor*
Nobuo Yashima, *Auditor*
Yoshinori Takahashi, *Auditor*
Saburo Yanagi, *Auditor*
Takeshi Higuchi, *Auditor*
Masatomo Ishibashi, *Chief Engineer (Hovercraft), Ship and Ocean Project Headquarters*
Yoshio Yamashita, *Manager, Naval and Special Craft Sales Department*

Mitsui's Hovercraft Department was formed on 1 May 1964, following the signing of a licensing agreement in 1963 with Hovercraft Development Ltd and Vickers Ltd, whose ACV interests were later merged with those of British Hovercraft Corporation. In addition, the com-

Mitsui's MV-PP15 50-ton passenger ferry, powered by twin 1,950hp Avco Lycoming TF25 gas turbines. The craft seats 155 passengers and has a top speed of 65 knots. Seen in these photographs are the raised control cabin, the pylon mounted propellers, lift fan air intakes and the thrust ports beneath the passenger door entrances, port and starboard

pany was licensed by Westland SA in 1967, following the formation of BHC.

The company has built two 11-seat MV-PP1s, one of which has been supplied to the Thai Customs Department, 14 MV-PP5s and four MV-PP15s.

The MV-PP5 was put into production at the initial rate of four craft a year. In the summer of 1969 the craft was put into service by Meitetsu Kaijo Kankosen Co Ltd, between Gamagoori and Toba, Ise Bay.

Since October 1971 three MV-PP5s designated Hobby 1, 2 and 3 have been operated by Oita Hoverferry Co Ltd on a coastal route linking Oita airport with the cities of Oita and Beppu. The three craft complete a total of 16 round trips per day to link with flight schedules at the airport.

Other PP5 operators include Japanese National Railways (two craft), Kagoshima Airport Hovercraft Co Ltd (four craft), Yaeyama Kanko Ferry Co Ltd (one craft) and Nippon Hoverline (two craft). The MV-PP5 has now been joined in production by the bigger, 155-seat MV-PP15.

The company is also developing the MV-PP05, a five-seater, and has started the design of a 200-ton mixed-traffic ferry.

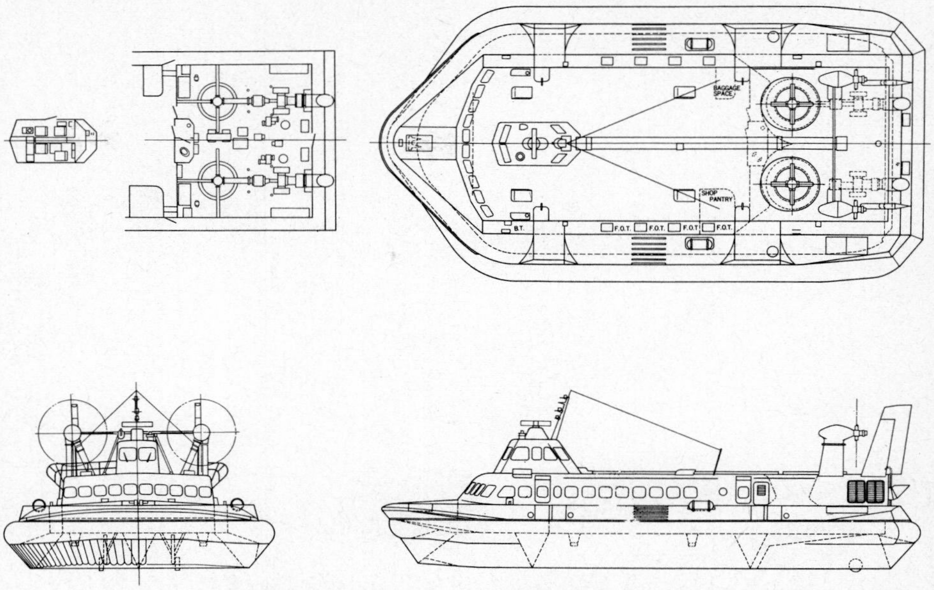

Mitsui MV-PP15 155-seat hoverferry. Twin Avco Lycoming TF25 gas-turbines power the integrated lift and propulsion system and give the craft a maximum speed of about 65 knots

MV-PP15

Developed from the earlier PP5, the Mitsui MV-PP15 is designed for high speed passenger ferry services on coastal and inland waterways. Accommodation is provided for 155 passengers and a crew of five.

Four craft of this type have been completed so far.

LIFT AND PROPULSION: Two Avco Lycoming TF25 gas-turbines, each with a maximum continuous output of 2,200hp at 15°C, drive the integrated lift/propulsion system. Each turbine drives a 2·3m (7ft 6in) diameter, 13-bladed centrifugal fan and a 3·2m (10ft 6in) diameter, four-bladed variable-pitch propeller. Power is transmitted via a main gearbox, propeller gearbox, fan gearbox and an auxiliary gearbox, all connected by shafting and flexible couplings. Auxiliary systems, such as hydraulic pumps for propeller pitch and lubricating oil pumps, are driven directly by auxiliary gears. Fuel is carried in two flexible tanks located immediately ahead of the lift fan assemblies. Total volume of the fuel tanks is 6m³ (21·2ft³).

CONTROLS: Twin aerodynamic rudders in the propeller slipstream and differential propeller pitch provide directional control. The rudders are operated hydraulically by a wheel from the commander's position. In addition, two retractable wheels, located aft, one each side of the main buoyancy tank, can be extended downwards into the water to prevent drift when turning and assist braking at high speeds. On land, the wheels assist manoeuvring and help to reduce skirt wear.

A thrust port air bleed system provides lateral control at slow speeds. Four ports are located beneath the passenger door entrances, port and starboard. A water ballast system is provided for longitudinal and transverse centre of gravity adjustment.

HULL: Construction is primarily in corrosion resistant aluminium alloy. The basic structure is the main buoyancy chamber which is divided into watertight sub-divisions for safety, and includes the fore and aft ballast tanks. Overall dimensions of the main buoyancy raft structure are 19·8m (64ft 10½in) long by 7·1m (23ft 3½in) wide by 0·7m (2ft 4in) high. Sidebodies of riveted construction are attached to the sides of the main buoyancy structure. The outer shell of the main buoyancy chamber, machinery deck space, the forward deck and passageways around the cabin interior, are all constructed in honeycomb panels with aluminium cores. The lift fan air intake, inner window frames and hood for the electric motor that rotates the radar scanner are in glassfibre reinforced plastics.

Six rubber-soled landing pads are fitted to the hull base, together with jacking pads. Four lifting eyes for hoisting the craft are provided in the buoyancy chamber.

SKIRT: 1·6m (5ft 3in) deep fingered-bag skirt of Mitsui design, fabricated in nylon-based sheet and coated both sides with synthetic rubber. Two transverse stability bags are included in the skirt system to minimise pitch and roll.

ACCOMMODATION: The passenger cabin, containing 155 seats, is located above the forward part of the main buoyancy chamber. The seats are arranged in three groups and divided by two longitudinal aisles. Seats in the two outer sections are arranged in rows of three abreast, and in the centre section, six abreast.

The four cabin entrance doors, two port, two starboard, are divided horizontally, the top section opening upwards and the lower section opening sideways. A lavatory, toilet unit, pantry and luggage room are provided aft, and a second luggage room is located forward. Lockers are sited close to the forward entrance doors. The control cabin is located above the passenger cabin superstructure and provides a 360 degree view. It is reached from the passenger saloon by a companion ladder. An emergency exit is provided on the starboard side.

The cabin has a total of four seats, one each for the commander and navigator, plus two spare ones of the flip-up type. The wheel for the air rudders, the two propeller pitch-control levers, instrument panel and switches are arranged on a console ahead of the commander; and the radio, fuel tank gauge, water ballast gauge and fire warning system are arranged ahead of the navigator.

On the cabin roof are the radar-scanner, mast for navigation lights, a siren and a searchlight.

SYSTEMS, ELECTRICAL: 28·5V dc. Two 9kW generators are driven directly by the main engines. One 24V 175Ah battery is employed for starting, and another for control. Both are located in the engine room and are charged by the generators when the main engines are operating. A shore-based power source is used for battery charging when the main engines are not in use.

RADIO/NAVIGATION: Equipment includes one 10in radar, compass, radio and one 22cm, 250W searchlight.

AIR CONDITIONING: Two Daikin RKA 1000R-PP15 air coolers, each with a capacity of 20,000 Kcal/h. Compressors are driven by belts from the auxiliary gearboxes and cooled air is supplied via air-conditioning ducts. Four ceiling ventilators are provided, each equipped with a 40W fan.

SAFETY: Remotely-controlled BCF or BTM fire extinguishers provided in the engine room. Portable extinguishers provided in the passenger cabin. Inflatable life boats, life jackets, automatic SOS signal transmitter and other equipment carried according to Japanese Ministry of Transport regulations.

DIMENSIONS

EXTERNAL

Length overall, on cushion: 26·4m (86ft 8in)
on landing pads: 25·09m (82ft 4in)
Beam overall, on cushion: 13·9m (45ft 7in)
on landing pads: 11·1m (36ft 5in)
Height, on cushion: 7·9m (25ft 11in)
on landing pads to tip of propeller blade: 6·9m (22ft 8in)
Skirt depth: 1·6m (5ft 3in)

INTERNAL

(Passenger cabin including toilet, pantry and locker rooms):
Length: 14·14m (46ft 5in)
Max breadth: 7·06m (23ft 2in)
Max height: 2·1m (6ft 11in)
Floor area: 93m² (1,001ft²)

WEIGHTS

All-up: about 50 tons

PERFORMANCE

Max speed: about 65 knots
Cruising speed: about 50 knots
Fuel consumption: about 280g/shp/h at 15°C
Endurance: about 4 hours

MV-PP5

Mitsui's first large hovercraft, the 50-seat MV-PP5, is a gas-turbine powered craft intended primarily for fast ferry services on Japanese coastal and inland waters.

LIFT AND PROPULSION: All machinery is located aft to reduce to a minimum the noise level in the passenger cabin. A single IHI IM-100 gas-turbine (licence-built General Electric LM100) with a maximum continuous rating of 1,050hp at 19,500rpm drives the integrated lift/propulsion system. Its output shaft passes first to the main gearbox from which shafts extend sideways and upwards to two three-bladed Hamilton/Sumitomo variable-pitch propulsion propellers of 2·59m (8ft 6in) diameter. A further shaft runs forward to the fan gearbox from which a drive shaft runs vertically downwards to a 2·27m (7ft 7in) 13-bladed lift fan mounted beneath the air intake immediately aft of the passenger saloon roof. The fan is constructed in aluminium alloy and the disc plate is a 40mm (1½in) thick honeycomb structure.

To prevent erosion from water spray the propeller blades are nickel plated.

Fuel is carried in two metal tanks, with a total capacity of 1,900 litres (416 gallons), located immediately ahead of the lift fan assembly.

CONTROLS: Twin aerodynamic rudders in the propeller slipstream and differential thrust from the propellers provide directional control. The rudders are controlled hydraulically from the commander's position. In addition two retractable water rods, located slightly aft of amidships

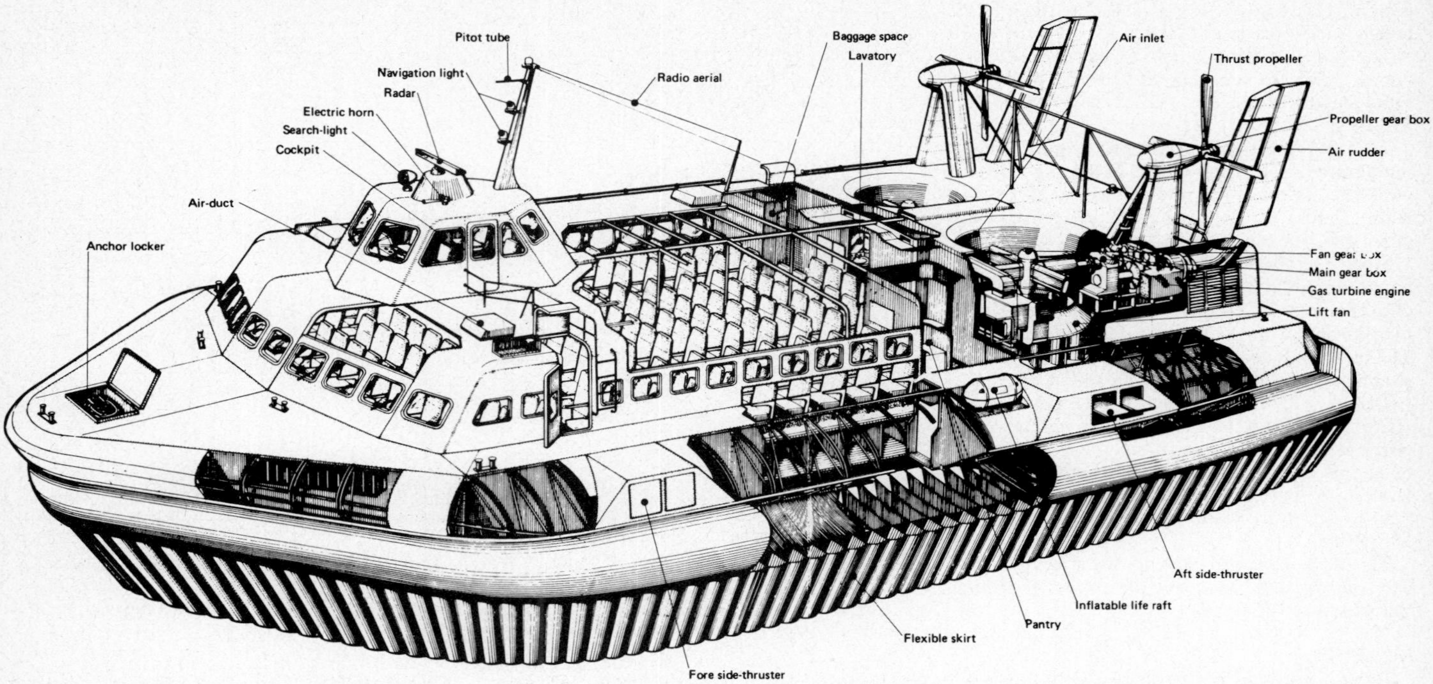

Cutaway of the Mitsui MV-PP15, showing the seating arrangements for the 155 passengers. Seats are arranged in three groups, divided by two longitudinal aisles. In the two outer sections they are arranged in rows of three abreast, and in the centre, six abreast

on each side of the main buoyancy tank, can be extended downwards to prevent drift when turning and these also assist braking at high speeds. The water rods are operated hydraulically by foot-pedals. When used in conjunction with the rudders, the turning radius is reduced to about a third of that taken when only air rudders are used.

A thrust-port air bleed system provides lateral control at slow speeds. The thrust ports are actuated by air extracted from the engine compressor and are located beneath the passenger door entrances, port and starboard.

HULL: Construction is primarily of high strength AA502 aluminium alloy suitably protected against the corrosive effects of sea water. The basic structure is the main buoyancy chamber which is divided into eight watertight subdivisions for safety, and includes fore and aft trimming tanks. Two further side body tanks, each divided into three watertight compartments, are attached to the sides of the main buoyancy

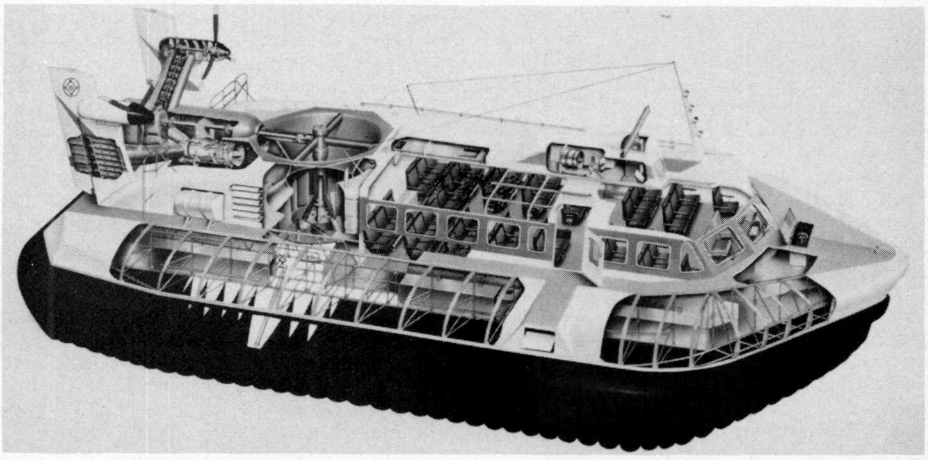

Internal arrangement of the MV-PP5 showing passenger accommodation and the gas-turbine powered lift/propulsion system aft of the cabin

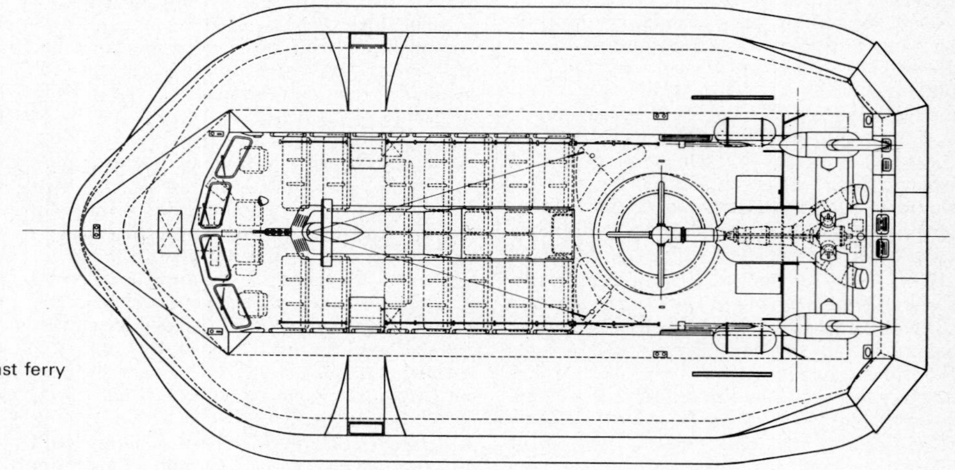

Mitsui MV-PP5 50-seat hovercraft, designed for fast ferry services on Japanese coastal and inland waters

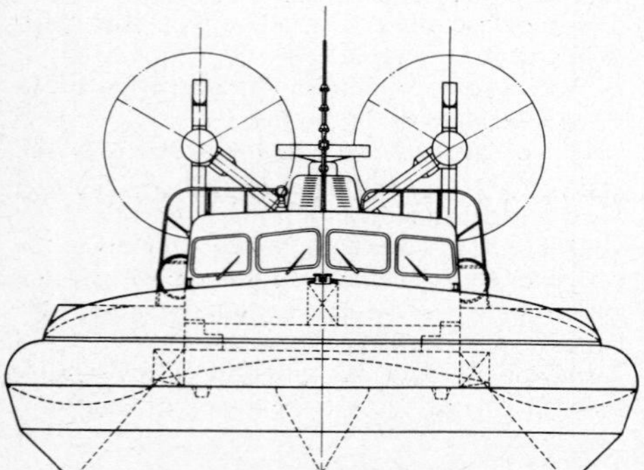

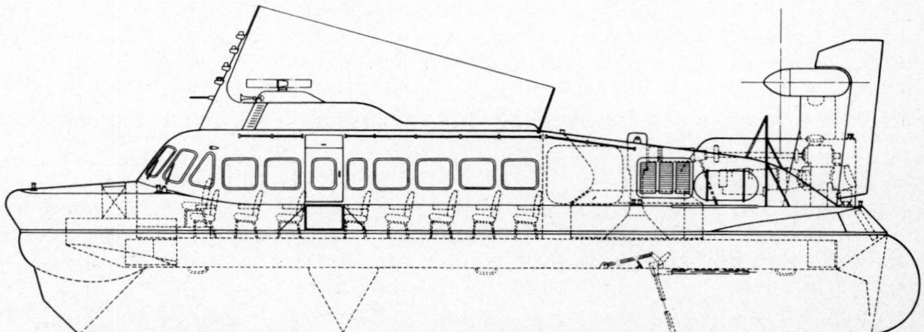

chamber. To facilitate shipment the side body tanks can be removed, reducing the width to 3·75mm (12ft 4in).

The outer shell of the main buoyancy chamber, the machinery deck space, the forward deck and the passage decks around the cabin exterior are all constructed in honeycomb panels with aluminium cores.

The lift fan air intake, radar cover, part of the air conditioning duct, and inside window frames are in glassfibre-reinforced plastic.

Design loads are as required by the Provisional British ACV Safety Regulations.

SKIRT: The flexible skirt was designed by Mitsui in the light of research conducted with aid of the RH-4 (MV-PP1 prototype). It is made of 0·8mm ($^1/_{32}$in) thick chloroprene-coated nylon sheet. A fringe of finger type nozzles is attached to the skirt base at the bow and on both sides. At the stern a D-section bag skirt is used to avoid scooping up water.

Two transverse and one longitudinal stability bags are fitted.

ACCOMMODATION: The passenger cabin is sited above the forward end of the main buoyancy chamber. Seats for the two crew members are on a raised platform at the front of the cabin. All controls, navigation and radio equipment are concentrated around the seats. The windows ahead are of reinforced tempered glass and have electric wipers.

The two cabin entrance doors are divided horizontally, the lower part opening sideways, the top part upwards. The standard seating arrangement is for 42 passengers but ten additional seats can be placed in the centre aisle.

In accordance with Japanese Ministry of Transport regulations a full range of safety equipment is carried, including two inflatable life rafts, 54 life jackets, one automatic manually activated fire extinguisher for the engine casing and two portable fire extinguishers in the cabin. Other standard equipment includes ship's navigation lights, marine horn, searchlight and mooring equipment, including an anchor. The twelve side windows can be used as emergency exits and are made of acrylic resin.

SYSTEMS, ELECTRICAL: Two 2 kW, 28·5V ac/dc generators driven by belts from the main gearbox. One 24V, 100Ah battery for engine starting.

HYDRAULIC/PNEUMATIC SYSTEMS: A 7kg/cm^2 (99·56lb/in^2) hydraulic system pressure for water rods and 4·7-7kg/cm^2 (56·8-99·5lb/in^2) pneumatic system for thrust port operation.

COMMUNICATIONS AND NAVIGATION: Equipment includes a radio and radar.

DIMENSIONS

EXTERNAL

Length overall: 16m (52ft 6in)
Beam overall: 8·6m (28ft 2in)
Height overall on landing pad: 4·4m (14ft 5in)
Skirt depth: 1·2m (3ft 11in)
Draft afloat: 0·2m (11in)
Cushion area: 88m^2 (741ft^2)

INTERNAL

Cabin:
Length: 7·1m (23ft 4in)
Max width: 3·8m (12ft 6in)
Max height: 1·9m (6ft 3in)
Floor area: 26m^2 (280ft^2)

MV-PP5 02 "Hakusho", which has been in service with Meitetsu Kaijo Kaukosen KK since September 1969

Doors:
Two 0·65 × 1·4m (2ft 1½in × 4ft 6in), one each side of cabin
Baggage-hold volume: 0·6m^3 (24ft^3)

WEIGHTS

Normal all-up: 14 tons
Normal payload: 5·5 tons

PERFORMANCE

Max speed, calm water: 102km/h (55 knots)
Cruising speed, calm water: 83km/h (45 knots)
Still air range and endurance at cruising speed of about 160n miles: 4 hours approx
Vertical obstacle clearance: 0·6m (2ft) approx

MV-PP1

The MV-PP1 is a small peripheral jet ACV built for river and coastal services and fitted with a flexible skirt. It seats a pilot and ten passengers and cruises at 40 knots.

Two craft of this type have been built to date—the prototype, which was completed in July 1964 and has been designated RH-4, and the first production model, the PP1-01.

The latter was sold to the Thai Customs Department, for service in the estuary of the Menam Chao Phya and adjacent waters, and has been named Customs Hovercraft 1. It has been in service with the Thai Customs Department since September 1967.

Details of construction weights, performance, etc will be found in *Jane's Surface Skimmers* for *1970-71* and earlier editions.

NAKAMURA SEISAKUSHO CO LTD

2-13 2-Chome, Tamagawa, Ota-ku, Tokyo 144, Japan
Telephone: (03) 759 2311
Cables: Gamecreator, Tokyo
Officials:
Masaya Nakamura, *President*
Hazime Yamauchi, *General Director*
Takeharu Daira, *Sales Director*
Tadashi Manabe, *Director*
Shigeru Yamada, *Director*
Tadanori Yanagidaira, *General Manager, NAMCO Group*
Tatuo Ichisi, *Sales Manager*
Hiromichi Kuroda, *Designer*
Noboru Horii, *Designer*
Fumio Tatumi, *Designer*

Nakamura Seisakusho Co of Tokyo is a leading Japanese manufacturer of amusement and recreational equipment. The company's first venture into the ACV field is a battery-powered single-seater, the Namco-1. Designed initially as an amusement novelty, the vehicle is now undergoing development as a hand-propelled pallet, capable of lifting loads of up to 120kg (265lb).

NAMCO-1

This novel, battery-powered single-seater is intended for amusement only and is designed for use over relatively smooth surfaces. A feature of the craft is the use of a diaphragm-type industrial air bearing system for lift.

A pedestrian-propelled pallet version has been built.

LIFT AND PROPULSION: Motive power is supplied by five Hitachi 12V 50Ah automobile storage batteries. Three of the batteries power three National 12V dc 0·125W blowers which operate at 19,000rpm to provide pressurised air to inflate the diaphragm, which is in 0·04in thick neoprene rubber. Air then passes through holes in the base of the diaphragm to form a continuous air film between the diaphragm and the surface beneath.

Thrust is supplied by two National 24V dc, 0·6 kW electric motors (powered by the remaining

two batteries) each driving a 0·6m (1ft 11in) diameter, five-bladed, 30 degree pitch Multiwing fan made by Yashima Kogyo. Total propulsive thrust available is 10kg (22·05lb).
CONTROL: Craft heading is controlled by differential use of the thrust fans. It can travel forward, backwards or sideways, or spin around on its own axis.
HULL: Hull of prototype is in steel plate with bumper in polyethylene. Production models will be in fibreglass with pneumatic bumpers.
DIMENSIONS
Height overall on landing pads, power off: 0·94m (3ft 1in)
Diaphragm inflated: 1m (3ft 3½in)
Diameter overall: 1·6m (5ft 3in)
Diameter of diaphragm: 1·2m (3ft 11in)
Cushion area: 0·95m² (11·02ft²)
WEIGHTS
Normal empty: 120kg (264·6lb)
Total battery: 60kg (137·3lb)

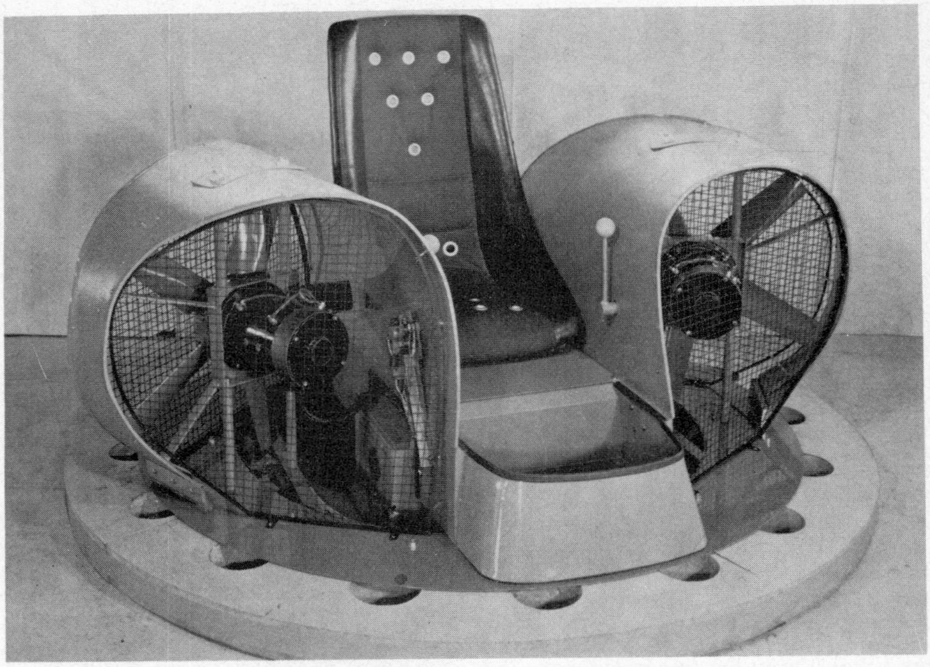

Nakamura Seisakusho's battery-powered Namco-1 amusement ACV is raised above its supporting surface on a diaphragm-type industrial air bearing

Side view of the Namco-1 amusement ACV

NIHON UNIVERSITY, NARASHINO

Aerodynamics Section, Nihon University at Narashino, 7-1591 Narashinodai, Funabashi, Chiba-Ken, Japan
Telephone: 0474 66 1111 4
Officials:
Masahiro Mino, *Senior Director*
Toyoaki Enda, *Director*

The Aerodynamics Section of the Physical Science Laboratory, Nihon University, is conducting an extensive ACV research programme, which includes the construction and test of four small experimental craft: the Pastoral light amphibious single-seater, the Mistral, propelled by either waterscrew or waterjet, the Floral, a two-seat sidewall craft and the N73.

An air boat, the Ripple, is employed as a "chase" craft to record on film the behaviour of these light ACVs over water.

Nihon University's ACV design group works in close co-operation with similar groups at the Institute of Technology, Ashikaga, and the University of Aoyama Gakuin. Pastoral, in modified form, is now being employed in a research programme conducted by the Institute of Technology, Ashikaga.

Floral 1, two-seater sidewall ACV, built by students of the Aerodynamics Section of Nihon University, Narashino, Japan

A new design, the LJ-10 Jimny, a combined ground effect machine and wheeled vehicle, has been completed by Nihon in conjunction with Aoyama Gakuin University.

FLORAL 1

This experimental two-seater was completed in February 1971, and was the first sidewall craft to be built in Japan. In calm water the performance has proved to be superior to that of standard displacement runabouts of similar size and output. The craft was reconstructed in 1972 when the twin outboard propulsion units were replaced by a single unit, and a new stern skirt and trim flaps were introduced. Instrumentation includes trim, roll angle and speed indicators and gauges for measuring pressure in the plenum chamber.

LIFT AND PROPULSION: Lift is provided by a single 8hp ZD-305 two-cycle single-cylinder air-cooled engine, located aft of the open cockpit and driving an F S Anderson 710-20-3L plastic fan. Propulsion is provided by a single Penta 550 outboard engine driving a waterscrew.

CONTROL: Engine/propeller unit turns for steering.

DIMENSIONS
Length overall: 5·2m (17ft 1in)
Beam overall: 1·8m (5ft 11in)
Height overall: 0·8m (2ft 7½in)

WEIGHTS
Normal gross: 540kg (1,191lb)

PERFORMANCE
Max speed over calm water: 62·7km/h (39mph)
Max speed, 0·4m (16in) waves: 52·1km/h (32mph)

MISTRAL 2

Developed jointly by Nihon University, Masahiro Mino and the Institute of Technology, Ashikaga, the Mistral 2 is an experimental waterscrew propelled single-seater derived from the SEA-NAC.

LIFT AND PROPULSION: A single 8hp Fuji ES-162DS- two-cycle single-cylinder air-cooled engine mounted immediately aft of the cockpit drives a 580mm (22⅞in) S11-03-FS03 five-bladed aluminium alloy fan for lift. Propulsion is supplied by either a 22hp Fuji KB-2 or 50hp Mercury 500 driving a waterscrew.

HULL: Moulded glassfibre, with inflated fabric-reinforced neoprene sidebody/skirt.

CONTROLS: Engine/propeller unit turns for steering.

DIMENSIONS
Length overall: 4·1m (13ft 5in)
Beam overall: 1·8m (5ft 11in)
Height overall: 1·09m (3ft 7in)

WEIGHTS
Normal gross: 310kg (664lb)

PERFORMANCE
Max speed over calm water: 67·5 km/h (42mph)
Max speed, 0·6m (2ft) waves: 45·5km/h (28mph)

LJ-10 JIMNY

Based on a reconditioned Suzuki Auto Co LN-360 Jimny—a jeep counterpart—this is a combined ground effect machine and wheeled vehicle, and can be driven like a car or truck. It was built by the Aerodynamics Section of Nihon University, headed by Masahiro Mino, in conjunction with the Traffic Engineering Dept, Aoyama Gakuin University, headed by Eiji Tonokura. The vehicle is designed for use over uneven ground, marshes, and other terrain which cannot be traversed by wheeled or tracked cars and trucks. During 1973 the craft successfully completed running tests over normal road surfaces, unprepared tracks and stretches of water.

LIFT AND PROPULSION: Motive power for the lift system is provided by a single 55hp Nissan A-10 988cc engine which drives two 595mm (23½in) diameter 10-bladed centrifugal fans mounted on a common shaft to the rear of the driving position. Air is drawn through two inward facing metal ducts and expelled downwards into a fingered-bag skirt system. The vehicle has a four-wheel drive system, powered by a Suzuki FB 395cc petrol engine developing 27hp at 6,000rpm. Heading is controlled by a normal steering wheel located ahead of the driver.

Mistral 2 single-seat research ACV

LJ-10 Jimny, a combined ground effect machine and wheeled vehicle. Designed for use over terrain normally impassable to wheeled or crawler-equipped tractors the vehicle comprises a Suzuki Auto Co LN-360 Jimny—a counterpart to the US Army's jeep—equipped with a sidebody to support the skirt system and two lift fan assemblies. Cushion air is supplied by a 55hp Nissan engine driving two 10-bladed centrifugal fans

N 73 amphibious runabout during trials. Built by the Aerodynamics Section, Nihon University, the craft has attained 90km/h (55mph) over water

DIMENSIONS
Length: 5·39m (17ft 8in)
Width: 3·44m (10ft 11in)
Height: 1·82m (5ft 11in)

WEIGHTS
All-up weight: 998kg (2,200lb)

PERFORMANCE
No details received

N 73

This experimental single-seater has attained 90km/h (55mph) over water and 60km/h (37mph) during trials over land.

LIFT AND PROPULSION: A single 13hp Daihatsu two-cycle, single-cylinder air-cooled engine immediately ahead of the cockpit drives a 560mm (22in) diameter Multiwing fan for lift. Propulsion is supplied by a 40hp Xenoav G44B two-cycle twin-cylinder engine driving a 1·2m (3ft 11¼in) diameter two-bladed propeller.
CONTROLS: Craft heading is controlled by twin aerodynamic rudders hinged to the rear of the propeller shroud and operated by a handlebar.
HULL: Moulded glassfibre with inflated fabric-reinforced neoprene sidebody/skirt.
DIMENSIONS
Length overall: 4·5m (14ft 9in)
Beam overall: 1·8m (5ft 10⅞in)
Height: 1·55m (5ft 1in)
WEIGHTS
Normal empty: 340kg (750lb)
Normal payload: 215kg (474lb)
PERFORMANCE
Max speed, over water: 90km/h (55mph)
over land: 60km/h (37mph)
Range: 150km (93·2 miles)

NETHERLANDS

MACHINEFABRIEK ENBE BV

Air Cushion Vehicle Design and Manufacturing Subsidiary:

BV LUCHTKUSSENVOERTUIGEN FABRIEK

Industrieterrein, Asperen, Netherlands
Telephone: 03451 2743/2744
Telex: ENBE NL 47864
Officials:
W A G v Burgeler, *Director, Shareholder BV Enbe*
N C Nap, *Director, Shareholder BV Enbe*
A H Nap, *Shareholder BV Enbe*

ENBE has built three light amphibious ACV prototypes, the B-1, B-2 and B-3, all designed by W A G v Burgeler.

Since 1 January 1974 the company has been the distributor in the Netherlands for the Air Vehicles AV2 light utility ACV.

NEW ZEALAND

HOVER VEHICLES (NZ) LTD

PO Box 10, Ohau, New Zealand
Telephone: 80792 LEVIN
Officials:
Roy Blake, *Director*
David Clemow, *Director*
Jim Pavitt, *Director*
Ron Wadman, *Director*
Brian Shaw, *Director*
Mel Douglas, *Director*
D Hammond Murray, *Managing Director*

Hover Vehicles (NZ) Ltd has been formed by a group of New Zealand pilots, engineers and businessmen in association with Roy Blake, winner of the "Hovernaut of the Year" title in the United Kingdom in 1968, who afterwards emigrated to New Zealand.

The company plans to build vehicles which can be employed either on light utility applications or as recreational craft. The first craft under development is the H.V.4, a 6·4m (21ft) long amphibious six-seater, the final design for which has been completed. Initial tests of the prototype began in May 1975, when speeds of up to 80·46km/h (50mph) were recorded over land. Good stability and handling qualities were observed.

It is envisaged that several pre-production models will be built before consideration is given to putting the craft into full-scale production.

Apart from the design and construction of the H.V.4 the company has built and tested its own variable- and reversible-pitch fibreglass airscrew which will be used for ACV propulsion.

Government financial assistance was provided for the first prototype. Preliminary details of the company's first craft are given below.

H.V.4

The prototype of this attractive six-seat recreational ACV is complete. It is intended as a quiet, easily controlled craft which can be driven by an "above average" car driver after two hours training. The craft can be towed on a trailer behind most six-cylinder cars.
LIFT AND PROPULSION: Power for the integrated lift/propulsion system is provided by a single 185hp Rover V8 automobile engine which drives a 914mm (3ft) diameter centrifugal lift fan and two 914mm (3ft) diameter variable-pitch shrouded airscrews.
ACCOMMODATION: Seats are provided for a driver and five passengers in a fully enclosed cabin.
DIMENSIONS
Length overall: 6·4m (21ft)
Beam overall: 3·04m (10ft)
Reduced for transport by road: 2·43m (8ft)
Ground clearance: 609mm (2ft)
WEIGHTS
Normal loaded: 1,360·77kg (3,000lb)
PERFORMANCE
Max speed: 80·46km/h (50mph)

During initial trials, Hover Vehicles' H.V.4 attained speeds of up to 80·46km/h (50mph) over land

Power is supplied by a single 185hp Rover V8 automobile engine which drives a 914mm (3ft) diameter centrifugal lift fan and two 914mm (3ft) diameter variable-pitch ducted propellers

Seats are provided for a driver and up to five passengers

TRINIDAD

COELACANTH GEMCO LTD

1 Richardson Street, Point Fortin, Trinidad
Telephone: Point Fortin 2439
Cables: Coelacanth, Trinidad
Officials:
Nigel Seale, *Director*
Kelvin Corbie, *Director*
R Varma, *Secretary*

Coelacanth Gemco Ltd, the first company to specialise in the design and construction of air cushion vehicles in the West Indies, has been granted Pioneer Status for the manufacture of hovercraft in Trinidad by the government-controlled Industrial Development Corporation. The company has obtained the approval of the Town and Country Planning Commission to construct an ACV factory and a hoverport at Guapo Beach, Trinidad. Guapo Bay and the neighbouring Antilles Bay will be used by the company for sea tests and a disused runway adjacent to the site will be used for overland tests.

The company also plans to build a two-mile long, 100ft wide ACV roadway between Guapo Beach and the Point Fortin Industrial Estate.

Meetings have been held with the Trinidad Government to negotiate a right-of-way over Government-owned land.

A freight operation is planned with ACVs taking aboard finished goods from the factories, and delivering them to Port of Spain, 40 minutes away at a speed of 60 knots.

Craft at present under development by the company are the Pluto, Jupiter, Venus, Arcturus and Mars, and a military ACV.

Progress is also being made with the development of a hover truck, with a payload of 3 tons, for carrying sugar cane from the Trinidad cane fields in wet weather.

PLUTO Mk I AND II

The Pluto is a two-seat test vehicle, built in marine ply, and designed to provide data for a sport and recreational craft which will be marketed under the same name.

The production prototype, which is based on the existing hull and designated Pluto Mk II is undergoing trials. A four-seat version, Pluto Mk III, is due to go into production.

Two and four-seat versions are planned. A standard feature of the production models will be a two-berth cabin and cooking facilities, which will allow the craft to be used for cruising to the northwest of Trinidad in the Gulf of Paria.

LIFT AND PROPULSION: Lift power on Pluto Mk II is supplied by two 6hp Briggs and Stratton motor-mower engines driving two Rotafoil fans. Thrust is supplied by two 250cc Velocettes driving two 0·685m (2ft 3in) diameter ducted Hordern-Richmond propellers at 5,000rpm.

DIMENSIONS

EXTERNAL

Length: 4·87m (16ft)
Width: 2·38m (7ft 10in)
Height: 1·82m (6ft)

WEIGHTS

Empty: 498·92kg (1,100lb)
Loaded two seat model: 680·35kg (1,500lb)

PERFORMANCE

Speed, over water: 35·4km/h (22mph)
over land (with one person): 62·76km/h (39mph)
Vertical obstacle clearance: 203mm (8in)

PLUTO Mk III

Developed from Pluto Mk II, Mk III is a four-seater runabout and yacht.

The production prototype was launched on 26 July 1975 at Point Fortin beach.

LIFT AND PROPULSION: Lift is provided by a single 20hp Sachs Wankel rotary engine driving two Rotafoil fans, and propulsion by two 250cc Velocettes driving two 0·685m (2ft 3in) diameter ducted Hordern Richmond propellers at 5,000rpm.

All series production craft will be powered by three Sachs Wankel engines—one for lift and two for propulsion. Fuel is carried in two standard marine power boat tanks, mounted amidships on the outer hull periphery.

Plans are being made to power a de luxe model with a 120hp engine driving a hydraulic pump which will, in turn, drive three hydraulic motors. Two of these will power the propulsion system and the third will power the lift system.

CONTROLS: Craft heading is controlled by twin rudders aft operating in the slipstreams of the two propellers. Thrust ports are fitted port and starboard, fore and aft, to provide additional control at slow speeds when approaching and leaving jetties.

HULL: First production craft will be in $^3/_{16}$in mahogany marine ply, with the bottom and sides sheathed to 152mm (6in) above the waterline in glassfibre.

ACCOMMODATION: The cabin accommodates a family of four—two adults and two children—and stores for an overnight stay. The seats are removable and can be used on the beach. On board the craft, the position of the seats can be altered if necessary to adjust craft trim. Built-in steps are provided on each side of the hull to simplify access to the craft after bathing. A hatch is provided aft for baggage items and stores and another forward to facilitate the handling of mooring lines and the anchor. The cabin windows, in $^3/_{16}$in plexiglass, slide rearwards in their frames for access to the cabin.

DIMENSIONS

EXTERNAL

Length: 5·48m (18ft)
Width: 2·38m (7ft 10in)
Height, inflated skirt: 1·82m (6ft)
Cushion depth: 381mm (1ft 3in)
Freeboard in displacement mode: 0·76m (2ft 6in)

Pluto Mk II, a manned test model of Coelacanth Gemco Pluto series, puts to sea for a test run off Point Fortin, Trinidad

Pluto III undergoing tests

Nigel Seale, designer of Pluto Mk III, stands at the side of the craft as it is put through static hovering trials in Coelacanth Gemco's workshop. Hatches in the cabin roof and at the bow enable mooring lines to be handled more easily

INTERNAL
Cabin floor area (total usable area): 3·71m² (40ft²)
WEIGHTS
Empty: 566·9kg (1,250lb)
Normal gross (4 passengers and 20 gallons of petrol): 884·5kg (1,950lb)
PERFORMANCE
Speed over water: 40·23 km/h (25mph)
over land: 64·37km/h (40mph)
PRICE: Estimated price, grp model £3,500 (West Indies $16,800).

VENUS

This craft has been designed principally for carrying oil company executives to and from wells in the Gulf of Paria, in Soldado and other areas in the West Indies. Ten- and fifteen-seat versions will be built, and like the Jupiter, the craft will be available in either amphibious form with a continuous skirt or as a rigid sidewall type with bow and stern skirts.

A manned scale model hull of the craft was completed in November 1968. This craft is also being used as a test bed for the two- and four-seat Pluto series.

JUPITER

A projected four-seat ACV runabout, Jupiter is designed around the basic hull of the company's Super Bee cabin cruiser, and will be available either as an amphibious craft, with a continuous peripheral skirt, or as a rigid sidewall type with bow and stern skirts.

Lift will be provided by a 75hp modified outboard driving two Rotafoil fans, and propulsive thrust by a 90hp modified outboard driving a reversible-pitch ducted propeller.

DIMENSIONS
Length: 5·48m (18ft)
Beam: 3·04m (10ft)
Height: 2·13m (7ft)
WEIGHTS
Including fuel: 1,275kg (2,810lb)
PERFORMANCE
Max speed (estimated): 50 knots

ARCTURUS

The Arcturus is a 35-seat amphibious ACV designed by Nigel Seale. Motive power for the lift and propulsion system will be supplied by high speed diesel generators driving Lear Siegler Electric Motors.

Work has started on a manned scale model but activity has been suspended temporarily while the company concentrates its resources on the development of the Pluto series.

MARS

Coelacanth Gemco's first military design is the 10·66m (35ft) long Mars, a 10-ton patrol craft designed to operate in sheltered waters. It will carry seven fully armed men. A manned scale model capable of testing hovering performance has been built.

Construction will be in grp, with aluminium extrusions and panels. Six Rotafoil fans will be employed in the integrated lift/propulsion system.

A feature of the craft will be the employment of stabilisers to reduce drift.

DIMENSIONS
Length: 10·66m (35ft)
Beam: 4·57m (15ft)
Height: 4·57m (15ft)
WEIGHTS
Normal all-up: 10 tons
PERFORMANCE
Cruising speed: 35 knots

UNION OF SOVIET SOCIALIST REPUBLICS

CENTRAL LABORATORY OF LIFESAVING TECHNOLOGY (CLST)

Moscow

Officials:
Yury Makarov, *Chief Engineer*
A V Gremyatskiy, *Designer*
Yevgeniy P Grunin, *Designer*
N L Ivanov, *Designer*
S Chernyavskiy
Y Gorbenko
V Shavrov, *Consultant*
A Baluyev, *Director of Flight Trials*

The Central Laboratory of Rescue Techniques (CLST), a division of OSVOD—the Rescue Organisation for Inland Waters—has designed a small aerodynamic ram-wing machine, capable of 120km/h (75mph), which will be used to answer distress calls on the Soviet lakes, rivers and canals. The vehicle, which is available in several versions, is the Eska—an abbreviation of Ekranolyetny Spasatyelny Kater-Amphibya (Surface-effect Amphibious Lifeboat). It has also been referred to as the Ekranolet and the Nizkolet (skimmer).

Apart from meeting emergency situations on waterways, the craft, which is amphibious, is capable of operating in deserts, tundra, arctic icefields and steppeland. Derivatives are to be employed as support vehicles for geologists, communications engineers and construction groups.

In Russian publications emphasis has been given to the potential value of such craft in opening up the mineral wealth of Siberia, the Soviet Far-east, Far-north and other virgin territories.

As with the X-113 Am and other machines of this type, the vehicle operates on the principle that by flying in close proximity to the ground, the so-called image flow reduces drag by about 70%. Whereas an average aircraft at normal flight altitude carries about 4kg (9lb) per hp of engine output, the wing-in-ground effect machine, on its dynamic air-cushion carries up to 20kg (44lb), an improvement of more than 400%. Weight efficiency of the craft (ratio of useful load to all-up weight) is 48·9%.

At angles of attack of 2-8 degrees near the ground, its lift is 40-45% greater than when flying out of ground effect. In addition the supporting surface hinders the vortex flow from the lower wing surface to the upper surface which decreases induction drag.

Control of the Eska is said to be easy and pilots require no special training. Within ground effect it is no more complicated to control than a car.

The design, which has been strongly influenced by the Lippisch "aerofoil boat" concept, employs an almost identical short span, low aspect ratio reversed delta wing with anhedral on the leading edge, dihedral tips and wing floats. A description of Eska-1 follows, together with illustrations of three other aerodynamic machines built at the CLST—the saucer-shaped E-120 single-seater; the AN-2E, which incorporates the fuselage, engine and cabin of the Antonov AN-2W seaplane, and a new two-seater powered by a 210hp Walter Minor engine.

One of the Ekranoplan's designers has been quoted as saying: "Craft of this type are destined to become, in the not-too-distant future, as popular as hydroplanes, hovercraft and helicopters."

Eska variant employed as a research craft by the Soviet Ministry of Inland Waterways. The replacement of wingtip floats by spring skids and the low-set tailplane suggest that the craft has a wheel undercarriage and is land based

Maximum effective flying height in ground effect is 0·3-1·5m (1ft-5ft). The vehicle, a two-seat aerodynamic ram-wing, is employed as an experimental, high-speed rescue and liaison craft on the Soviet Union's inland waterways

ESKA-1

Designed initially as an amphibious highspeed rescue craft for use on Soviet inland waterways, the Eska has been developed into a general utility vehicle with a wide range of applications in underdeveloped areas.

Eska-1 completed its first flight on 29 August 1973, over the Klyazminskoye reservoir, carrying a pilot, passenger and an additional load. It took off at 120km/h (74·5mph) after a run of 80-100m (260-300ft) and flew for several minutes at between 20-30m (60-90ft), before descending to make a low level pass across sandy spits and banks and forcing its way through the thickets and reeds of an islet. After climbing to avoid a launch coming to meet it, it landed and taxied out of the water onto a gently sloping bank.

The youthful design group responsible for the Eska-1 took two years to study world experience of ramwing and aerodynamic ram-wing construction, after which a series of small-scale models were built, followed by the construction and test of five different full-size craft.

Three prototypes similar to Eska-1 had been built by mid-February 1974. Two other models, one with fabric-covered flying surfaces and rear hull, the other a four seater, were reported under construction in March 1974. Variants with greater seating capacity and more powerful engines are being developed, also land-based non-amphibious models.

POWER PLANT: Single 30hp M-63 motorcycle engine, on tripod dorsal mounting aft of cockpit, drives via shafting a two-bladed fixed-pitch propeller.

CONSTRUCTION: Forward hull design based on that of two-seat sports boat. Corrosion resistant aluminium alloy construction employed for first three craft. Heavy fabric covering employed on wings inboard of tips and hull aft of crew compartment on one later model.

CONTROLS: Single aircraft-type control stick, incorporating engine throttle, located in the centre of the cockpit. Conventional foot-operated bar to control rudder.

ACCOMMODATION: Enclosed cabin for two, seated side-by-side. Access is via hinged hood. Initial arrangement is for rescuer/pilot, with one seat available for the person being rescued. Three and four seat models are under development.

DIMENSIONS
Wing span overall: 6·9m (22ft 5⅝in)
Length: 7·55m (24ft 7in)
Height: 2·5m (8ft 2½in)
Wing area: 13·85m² (148·13ft²)
Tail area: 3m² (32·4ft²)

WEIGHTS
All-up weight: 450kg (992lb)
Empty: 230kg (507lb)
Useful load: 220kg (485lb)
Weight efficiency: 48·879%

PERFORMANCE
Max speed with full load in ground effect: 122km/h (75·8mph)
Cruising speed: 110km/h (68·35mph)
Take-off speed: 55km/h (34·17mph)
Landing speed: 50-55km/h (31-34mph)
Take-off run from water: 80-100m (260-300ft)
Take-off run from snow: 50-60m (162-195ft)
Landing run on water (without braking parachute): 40m (131ft)
Most effective flying height in surface effect: 0·3-1·5m (1ft-4ft 11in)
Max altitude, with 50% load, for obstacle clearance: up to 50m (164ft)
Range with full fuel supply: 300-350km (186-217 miles)
Wing loading: 32·5kg/m² (6·67lb/ft²)
Power loading: 15kg/hp (33lb/hp)
Limiting weather conditions—can operate in force 5 winds.

The Eska-1 has been strongly influenced by the Lippisch "Aerofoil boat" concept, and employs an anhedral, reversed delta wing, dihedral tips and wing floats.

CLST ANTONOV An-2E

This adaptation of the well-known An-2 multi-duty 12-seat biplane was built in 1973 to the design of Y P Grunin. It incorporates several major components of the Russian-built floatplane version, the An-2W, including the forward fuselage, cabin and engine—a 1,000hp Shvetsov ASh-621R nine-cylinder radial air-cooled engine, driving a four-bladed variable-pitch metal propeller.

The craft is intended for a range of utility applications in addition to carrying passengers and freight. Like the new RFB X-114, currently undergoing trials in the German Federal Republic, the An-2E has a retractable wheeled undercarriage enabling it to operate from land as well as rivers, lakes and coastal waters.

DIMENSIONS
Span: 15·75m (51ft 8in)
Length: 18·65m (61ft 2in)
Height: 8·1m (26ft 7in)
Lift area: 94m² (1,011ft²)

WEIGHTS
All-up weight: 7,000kg (15,435lb)

PERFORMANCE
No details available at the time of going to press.

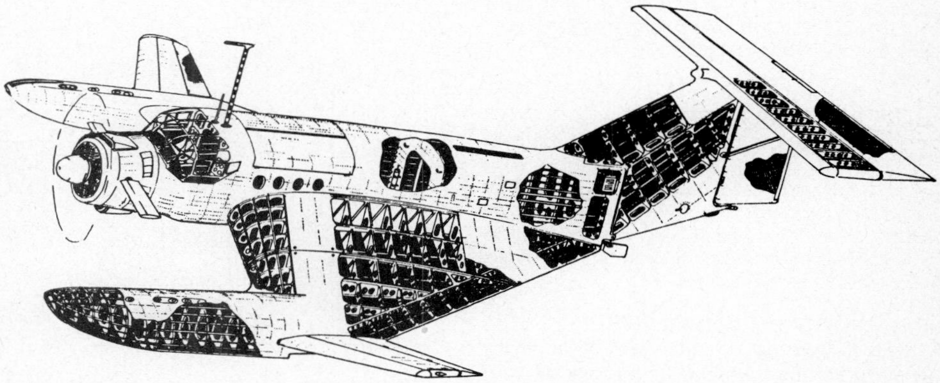
Cutaway of the CLST ekranoplan adaptation of the 12-seat Antonov An-2W floatplane

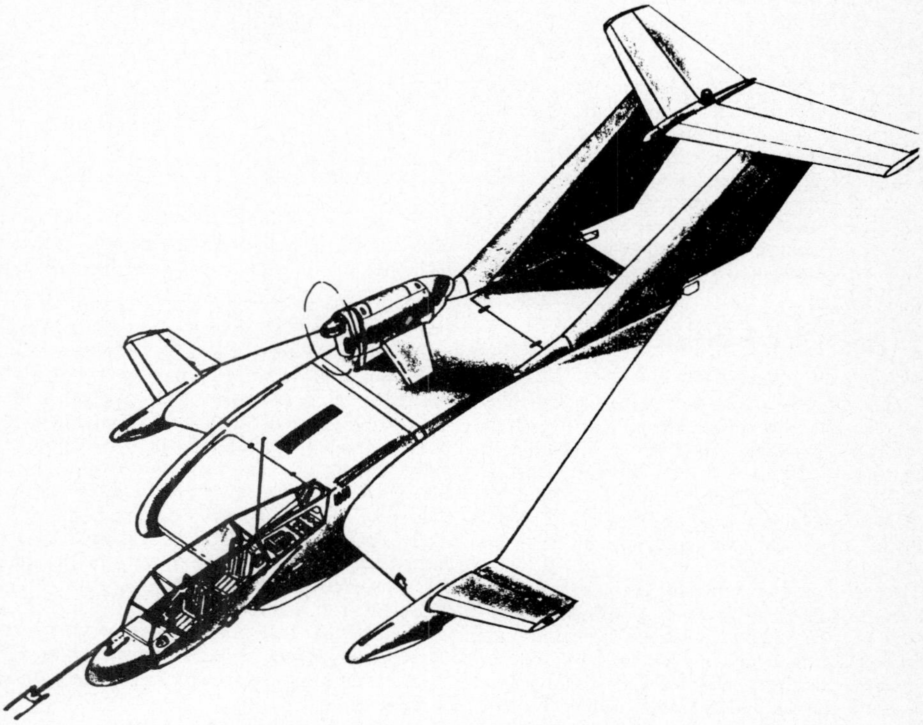
CLST ekranoplan two-seater employed for light liaison duties with the Soviet fishing fleet.

CLST TWO-SEATER

In 1974 the Central Laboratory of Lifesaving Technology developed a two-seater ekranoplan for light liaison duties with the Soviet fishing fleet. Visually the craft bears signs of having been influenced by the late Dr Alexander Lippisch's design studies for a 300-ton Aerofoil boat, a major departure from the Lippisch concept being the asymmetrically located cabin jutting ahead of the broad aerofoil-shaped hull on the port side. Reports suggest that in building the wings and hull extensive use was made of grp laminate reinforced with carbon fibres.

Power is supplied by a 210hp Walter Minor VI engine, of Czechoslovakian manufacture, and the craft has an all-up weight of 1,460kg (3,219lb).

Dynamic models were used to gather design data on stability, manoeuvrability and performance.

CLST ESKA EA-06

A developed version of Eska-1, believed to be a four seater, began its trials in September 1973, one month after Eska-1 made its first flight. Photographs of a radio-controlled model of the EA-06 indicate that its lines are similar to those of Eska-1, major differences being a wider cabin with a full-view windscreen and an aft fuselage angled upwards to support the fin and high-mounted tailplane well clear of the water.

The dynamically similar model was built to ¼ scale and had a wing span of 1·75m (5ft 9in). Power was supplied by a two-cylinder motor, developing 1·8hp at 12,500rpm, and driving a 300mm (11·81in) diameter laminated airscrew. Laminated balsawood construction was employed.

CLST EKRANOLET E-120

No technical details have been released concerning this novel, circular planform WIG single-seater. One of a number of experimental wing-in-ground-effect machines designed by the CLST, it was built in 1971. Its general features and propulsion arrangement can be seen in the accompanying photograph.

Ekranolet E-120, an experimental machine built by the CLST in 1971

PARAWING EKRANOPLANS

The originator of the idea of applying Rogallo-type flexible delta wings to light ekranoplans is Yevgeniy Grunin, one of the designers of the Eska-1. The parawing is well known for its outstanding aerodynamic qualities and stability and is convenient for transport and storage. Grunin, assisted by S Chernyavskiy and N Ivanov, fitted a flexible wing to the fuselage of the Czechoslovakian Let L-13J Blanik, a powered version of the well known two-seat, all-metal sailplane. Power is supplied by a 42hp Jawa M-150 piston-engine driving a 1·1m (3ft 7¼in) diameter Avia V210 propeller on a tripod mounting aft of the cockpit, an arrangement almost identical to that employed on Eska-1. Profiting from the encouraging results of the flight trials, the team has designed a number of small ekranoplan projects incorporating flexible wings, including a modified version of the An-2W, the floatplane version of the Antonov An-2, single-engine general-purpose biplane.

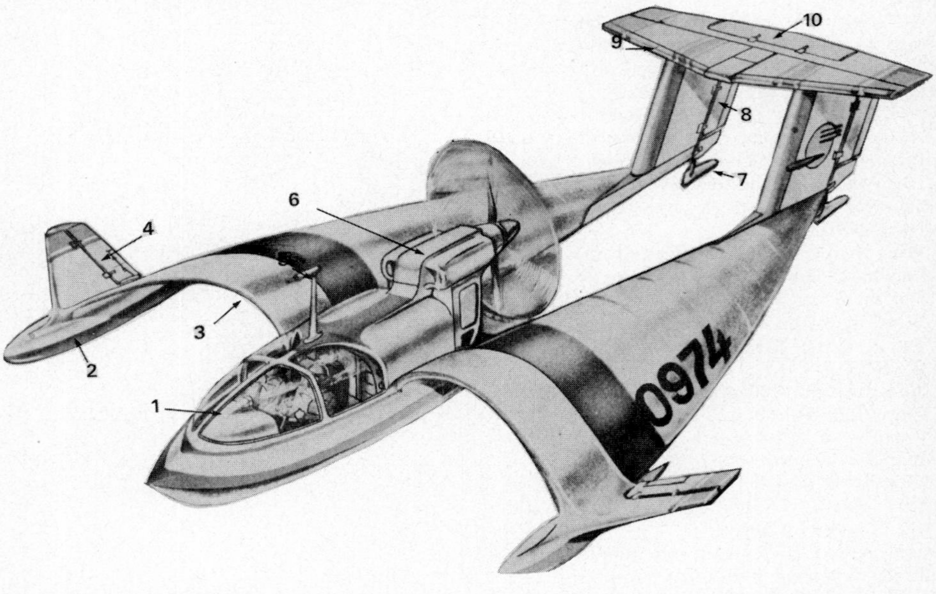

Twin-boom parawing ekranoplan concept. 1. cabin; 2. float; 3. split parawing; 4. aileron; 5. pressure head; 6. powerplant; 7. hydrodynamic rudder; 8. aerodynamic rudder; 10. elevator

KRASNOYE SORMOVO

Gorky

This shipyard began work in the ACV field by building a five-passenger air cushion river craft known as the Raduga in 1960-61. Since then it has built the Sormovich, a 30-ton peripheral jet ACV for 50 passengers, the Neva, a plenum-chambered type craft seating 38 and the Gorkovchanin, a 48-seat prototype sidewall craft for shallow, winding rivers.

A production version of the Gorkovchanin, the Zarnitsa, of which more than 100 have been built, is employed on almost all the river navigation lines of the Russian Federative Republic as well as on the rivers of the Ukrainian, Moldavian, Byelorussian and Kazakhstan Soviet Socialist Republics.

The design of an 80-seat rigid sidewall ferry, the Orion, was approved by the Soviet Ministry of Inland Waterways in 1970. Construction of the prototype began in 1972 and a trial operation was successfully undertaken in 1975. The craft is now in series production.

A third sidewall vessel is the Rassvet, designed to carry up to 80 passengers along local sea routes. Like Zarnitsa, the craft is able to run bow-on to flat sloping beaches and does not require piers or specially prepared moorings. The prototype, Chaika-1, is undergoing trials. Work is also in hand aimed at evolving a substantially bigger sidewall ACV ferry which has been given the name Turist (Tourist). This particular craft has a design speed of 36 knots and is intended for use along waterways of limited depth and unsuitable for hydrofoils. Two variants are projected, a 300-seat passenger ferry and a mixed-traffic model for 15 cars and 100-120 passengers.

Over the next four years work is expected to have been completed on a variety of sidewall ACV projects including the following:

1. A 120-150 seat river ferry
2. A passenger ferry for very shallow rivers
3. A freight vessel for both narrow and major rivers, including rivers with limited navigation seasons
4. A 120-150 seat seagoing craft
5. A high-speed mixed-traffic ferry for long distance routes

In 1969, prototypes of two fully skirted hovercraft made their debut: the Breeze, a light utility craft, and the Skate, a 50-seat passenger ferry with an all-up weight of 27 tons and a cruising speed of 57·5 mph. Military versions of the Skate, known in the West as Gus, are now in production for the Soviet naval marine infantry and army. Development of the Skate and its naval and army counterparts is believed to have been undertaken in conjunction with the Leningrad Institute of Marine Engineers, which is also thought to have been responsible for the design and construction of the Soviet Union's biggest skirted hovercraft, known in the West as Aist. About 12 to 15 are in service with the Soviet Navy as amphibious assault landing craft. Aist is generally similar in shape, size and performance to the BHC SR.N4.

The Sormovo yard is likely to have been responsible for building the world's largest air cushion vehicle — a wing-in-ground-effect machine capable of carrying 800-900 troops at speeds up to 300 knots. In 1972 it was announced that plans were in hand to build wing-in-ground effect machines capable of navigating rivers at a speed of about 250km/h (155mph). A number of these craft are understood to be in experimental service.

270-ton Naval ACV
Nato Code Name AIST

The first large amphibious hovercraft to be built in the Soviet Union, Aist is entering service in increasing numbers with the Soviet Navy. Reports suggest that about twelve to fifteen have been constructed to date. Built in Leningrad it is similar in appearance to the SR.N4 Mk II Mountbatten though giving the impression of being very much heavier than the British craft. It

Three-quarter view of Aist. Major differences between this craft and earlier variants lie in the increased length of the control cabin, the provision of two 30mm fully automatic AA cannon mounts at the bow and the lengthening of the two fins

is likely that the bare weight, equipped but no payload, crew or fuel is as much as 170 tons.

Several variants have been built and differ externally in fin height, overall length, superstructure detail and defensive armament.

Since delivery to the Soviet Navy, craft of this type have been employed largely as an amphibious assault landing and logistic supply craft, delivering mechanised infantry, self-propelled weapons, and main battle tanks to simulated beach-heads. Alternative military uses for amphibious craft of the Aist type would be mine countermeasures, ASW, and fast patrol.

LIFT AND PROPULSION: Integrated system with motive power supplied by two marinised gas-turbines, each of which is likely to be rated at 12-15,000hp. Each gas-turbine drives two 3·65m (12ft) diameter axial fans and two identical, pylon-mounted propellers, arranged in a facing pair, with the pusher propeller forward and the puller aft. The propellers, which are of the four-bladed variable- and reversible-pitch type are mounted so closely as to be virtually contraprops. Diameter of each propeller is thought to be about 5·79m (19ft). With this integrated arrangement, some seven gearboxes per side are probably required, in addition to an initial reduction gearbox. Cross-coupling, which could be carried within the 'T piece' at the end of the intake trunk, would require a further four.

Air for the main engines appears to be supplied by a curved spine-like trunk above the longitudinal centre line, about 60-70ft long and terminating in a T-piece running athwartships across the stern superstructure between the two fins.

Additional intakes appear to be sited in the sides of the superstructure towards the stern.

CONTROLS: Deflection of twin aerodynamic rudders aft, differential propeller pitch and the employment of fore and aft thrust ports provide steering control. All controls are located in a raised bridge located well forward on the superstructure.

HULL: Built mainly in welded marine corrosion resistant aluminium alloys. Structure appears to follow standard practice for large amphibious ACVs. The main hull is formed by a buoyancy raft based on a grid of longitudinal and transverse frames which form a number of flotation compartments. Two main longitudinal vertically stiffened bulkheads run the length of the craft separating the central load deck from the outer or side-structures, which contain the gas-turbines and their associated exhausts, lift fans, transmissions and auxiliary power systems.

Bow view showing the large control cabin, the bow ramp and the high attachment line of the bow skirt

Seen in this photograph are Aist's rear ramp, turbine tail pipes and twin skirt flaps. These could be sacrificial strips, since they are just below the tail pipes, rear bag feed ducts or possibly the rear ends of twin keels. Atop the main superstructure is the curved transverse component of the T-shaped duct system supplying air to the main engines

Seen in this photo are details of the propulsion system and the semi-circular guard rails around the intakes for two of the four axial-flow fans. The four pylon-mounted propellers are arranged in facing pairs, with the pusher propeller forward, the puller aft. Of four-bladed, variable and reversible pitch design they are mounted so closely as to be virtually contraprops. Diameter of each propeller is thought to be about 5·79m (19ft)

Aist showing the bow ramp, skirt, thrust ports, and two of the vertical drive shafts which transmit power to the upper gearboxes of the pylon-mounted propellers

A full width ramp is provided at the bow and a second at the stern, providing through loading facilities.

SKIRT: Fingered bag type in rubberised fabric. Features include a high bow skirt line to protect the bow loading door against wave impact.

SYSTEMS, WEAPONS: Two twin 30mm fully-automatic AA mountings controlled by Drum Tilt radar.

DIMENSIONS (Estimated)
Length overall, off cushion: 47·8m (156ft 10in)
Beam overall, off cushion: 17·5m (57ft 5in)
Height, control cabin: 1·98m (6ft 6in)
Length, control cabin: 10·5m (34ft 6in)
Width, bow ramp: 4·41m (14ft 6in)
Width, rear ramp: 4·87m (16ft)

WEIGHTS (Estimated)
Bare weight: 170 tons
Crew, fuel, AFVs or two main battle tanks: 90 tons
All-up weight: 260-270 tons

PERFORMANCE (Estimated)
Max speed: about 65-70 knots
Endurance: about 5 hours
Hard structure clearance when hovering: 1·2-1·5m (3ft 6in-4ft 11in)

BREEZE

This interesting light amphibious ACV has external features which are reminiscent of the Vickers VA-2 and VA-3.

It was developed by a design group led by German Koronatov, a graduate of the Leningrad Shipbuilding Institute and was completed in 1968. The craft was built to enable the problems of operating a lightweight hovercraft to be understood more clearly and to help assess its economic viability.

The design incorporates the cabin and propulsion system of the Kamov KA-30 Aerosled. Its basic dimensions were dictated partly by the requirement that it should be transportable by rail and trailer.

Trials began during the first half of 1969, during which speed and manoeuvrability tests were conducted over water, snow and ice. Instrumentation was installed in the passenger saloon. In calm water, against a 1-2 metre per second wind, the measured speed was 70km/h (43·5mph). In similar conditions across ice, the speed was 82km/h (57mph). During winter trials the craft operated over snow 50cm (1ft 8in) deep and shrubs 1m (3ft 3in) high. On the river Neva, when the ice was moving, Briz travelled at 60km/h (37mph) across the icefloes.

In August 1973, extensive trials were undertaken on the rivers and lakes of the Carolia Isthmus and on the basins of the Neva and Ladoga. Briz was transported on a trailer to the Burna estuary and made its way to the source. It also negotiated the Lozevsk rapids and continued on up the river Vuoks until it reached the famous waterfall. It negotiated this, also, then returned to the Burna estuary according to plan. During this endurance test, the craft successfully navigated blocked rivers, stony banks, rapids and raging torrents.

The next series of trials took place in a very busy shipping area, across Lake Lagoda to the Neva and thence back to Leningrad. During this phase, the Briz completed a distance of 1,000km (621 miles). According to the Soviet authorities, the experience gained with Briz confirmed that craft of this type may well have great economic potential.

LIFT AND PROPULSION: Thrust is provided by a 220hp AI-14RS radial piston engine, driving an AV-59 three-bladed metal, controllable and reversible-pitch propeller. Lift is supplied by two 33hp Moskvich MZMA-407 automobile engines mounted aft on the sidestructures, one port and one starboard, each driving a set of four 400mm diameter axial fans mounted on a cardan shaft. The fans are of welded light alloy construction. Cushion pressure is 150kg/m^2.

CONTROLS: Directional control over most of the speed range is provided by twin aerodynamic rudders operating in the slipstream. Low speed control is assisted by thrust ports fore and aft. Braking and reversing is achieved by reversed propeller pitch.

HULL: Riveted, buoyancy raft-type structure in corrosion resistant V84-4 light alloy. Engine mountings, strengthening members in the hull base and landing pads are in welded AIMg-5 alloy. Hull is divided by four transverse and two longitudinal bulkheads into eight watertight compartments for buoyancy.

SKIRT: Fingered bag type in rubberised fabric. Longitudinal keel and athwartship stability bags for pitch and roll stiffness. Skirt and fingers easily replaceable.

ACCOMMODATION: Fully enclosed cabin, seating operator and six passengers. If required, seating in the passenger saloon can be removed for transporting cargo.

SYSTEMS, ELECTRICAL: The thrust engine drives a 1·5kW, 27V dc generator, type GSK-1500. The lift engines drive a 0·2kW, 12V generator each. The circuitry enables the GSK-1500 to work in parallel with two GST 54 batteries connected in series.

DIMENSIONS
Length overall, cushionborne: 8·4m (27ft 6in)
Hull length: 7·8m (25ft 7in)
Beam overall: 4·1m (13ft 5in)
Height overall, cushionborne: 3m (9ft 10⅛in)
Draft, displacement condition: 0·3m (11¾in)
Skirt depth: 0·4m (1ft 3¾in)

WEIGHTS
All-up weight: 3,100kg (6,835lb)

PERFORMANCE
Max speed over land and water: 100km/h (62mph)

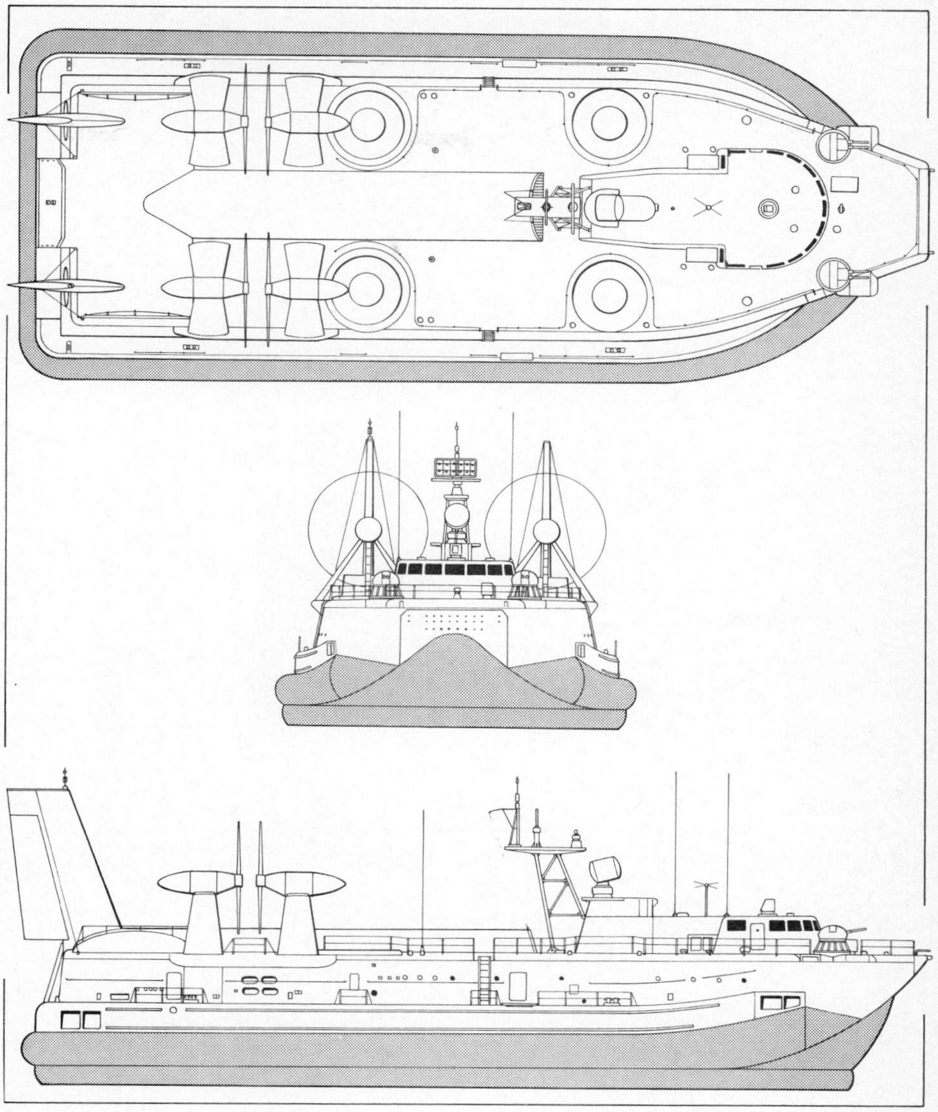

General arrangement of the Aist 220-ton amphibious ACV

Chayka-1 sidewall type ACV passenger ferry. The craft has an air-conditioned passenger saloon and will operate between resorts in the Crimea and Caucasus.

CHAYKA-1 (GULL-1)

This is the name given to the prototype Rassvet, 80-seat sidewall ACV ferry, designed for service in coastal areas with limited water depth. Details will be found in the entry for the Rassvet.

GORKOVCHANIN

The Gorkovchanin is a waterjet-propelled, 48-seat, rigid sidewall ACV, designed for water-bus services on secondary rivers with a guaranteed depth of 0·5m (1ft 8in). In view of the winding nature of these rivers, the craft operates at the relatively low speed of 30-35km/h (19-22mph). No marked reduction of speed is necessary in water up to 50cm (1ft 8in) deep.

The craft has been developed from a ten-seat scale model built at the experimental yard of the Institute of Water Transport Engineers at Gorky in 1963, and the pre-production prototype was completed in September 1968. Design was undertaken by a team at the Volgobaltsudoproekt special design office.

Preliminary trials were conducted in September and October 1968, and official trials were completed on the Sura river in May and June 1969. During speed tests over a measured mile with a full complement of passengers aboard, 36·6km/h (22·75mph) was attained. The main engine developed 265hp of which approximately 30hp was used to drive the centrifugal fan.

The craft has covered the journey from Gorky to Moscow (1,016km (622 miles)) and back in 31 and 27 running hours respectively at an average speed of approximately 35km/h (22mph) and has good manoeuvrability when running both ahead and astern. In 1970 the Gorkovchanin was succeeded in production by a developed version, the Zarnitsa.

LIFT AND PROPULSION: Integrated system powered by a 3D6H diesel engine rated at 250hp continuous. The engine is mounted aft and drives a 960mm (3ft 1¾in) diameter six-bladed centrifugal fan for lift, and a 410mm (1ft 4½in) diameter single stage water-jet rotor for propulsion. Fan air is taken directly from the engine compartment. Skirts of rubberised fabric are fitted fore and aft. The bow skirt of production craft is of segmented type. Cushion pressure is 180kg/m².

The waterjet intake duct is located 100mm (4in) below the displacement water level to prevent air entry, with a consequent reduction in the navigable draft.

CONTROLS: Vanes located in the waterjet stream provide directional control. Thrust reversal is achieved by the use of waterflow deflectors.

HULL: Similar in appearance to that of the Zarya, the hull is in riveted D16 corrosion resistant aluminium alloy. The hull bottom and sides have transverse frames and the sidewalls and superstructure top longitudinal frames. Thickness of plating on sides and bottom is 1·5mm (1/16in) (2·5mm (3/32in) in the bow section); and on the sidewalls 1mm (3/64in) (up to 5mm (13/64) in the bow section). Deck plates are 1mm (3/64in) thick and the top of the superstructure is in 0·8mm (1/32in) plating.

Acoustic and thermal insulation includes use of 100mm (4in) thick foam polystyrene sheeting.

ACCOMMODATION: Seats are provided for a crew of two, who are accommodated in a raised wheelhouse, and 28 passengers. Access to the passenger saloon, which is equipped with airliner-type seats, is through a single door located at the bow in the centre of the wheelhouse. The craft runs bow-on to flat sloping banks to embark and disembark passengers.

SYSTEMS, ELECTRICAL: One 1·2kW, 24V dc, engine-operated generator and batteries.

COMMUNICATIONS: Car radio in wheelhouse and speakers in passenger saloon.

DIMENSIONS
Length overall: 22·3m (73ft 2in)
Beam overall: 4·05m (13ft 3½in)
Hull beam: 3·85m (12ft 7⅝in)
Height of hull to top of wheelhouse: 3·3m (10ft 9⅞in)
Height of sidewalls: 0·45m (1ft 5¾in)
Draft afloat: 0·45m (2ft 1⅝in)
Draft cushionborne: 0·65m (1ft 4⅞in)

WEIGHTS
All-up weight with 48 passengers, crew and fuel: 14·3 tons

PERFORMANCE
Normal service speed: 30-35km/h (19-22mph)
Distance and time from full ahead to full astern: 60m (197ft) and 14 seconds

NAVAL RESEARCH HOVERCRAFT

A 15-ton experimental ACV has been employed by the Soviet Navy since 1967 to assess the potential of hovercraft for naval applications and investigate controllability and manoeuvrability. Lift is provided by a single 350hp radial aircraft engine driving a centrifugal fan and propulsion by two pylon-mounted radials of the same type driving controllable-pitch airscrews.

DIMENSIONS
Length: 21·33m (70ft)
Beam: 9·14m (30ft)

WEIGHTS
Displacement: 15 tons

PERFORMANCE
Max speed: 50 knots

The Breeze light amphibious ACV for ten passengers. Thrust is supplied by a radial aircraft engine driving a three-bladed airscrew, and lift by twin Moskvich 407 automotive engines, each driving a set of four centrifugal fans mounted in series on a common shaft. Fan air is drawn through fixed louvres

Passengers boarding the Breeze. To facilitate access to the cabin a panel is removed from the lift fan cowl ahead of the engine and a handrail and steps are slotted into position

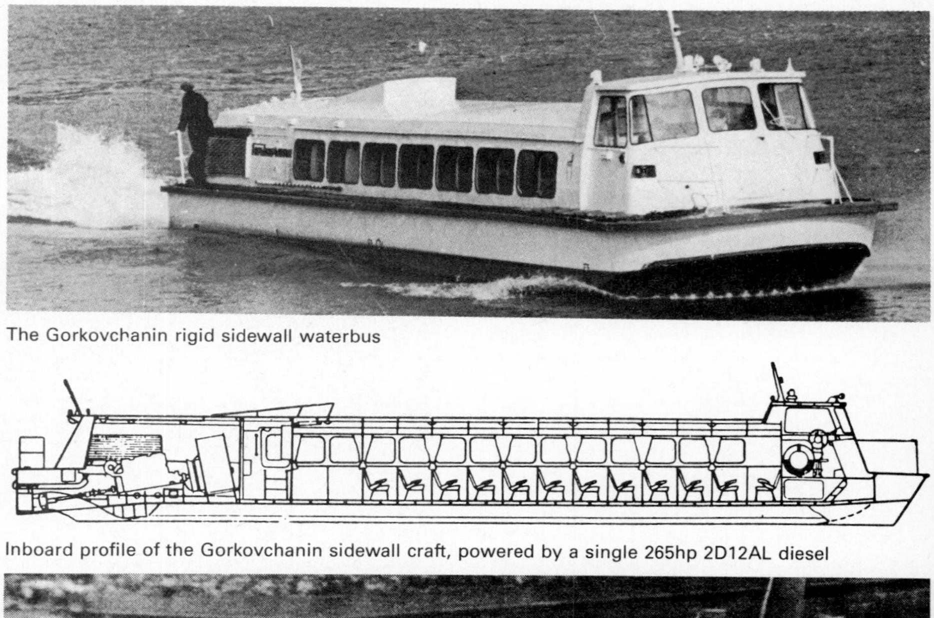
The Gorkovchanin rigid sidewall waterbus

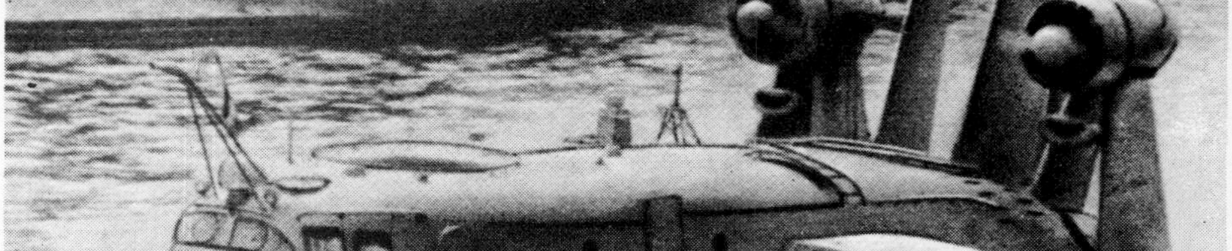
Inboard profile of the Gorkovchanin sidewall craft, powered by a single 265hp 2D12AL diesel

This 15-ton research craft has been employed by the Soviet Navy to assess the potential of the skirted air cushion vehicle for naval applications

LOGISTIC SUPPORT ACV
NATO Code Name "GUS"

It is thought that thirty to thirty-five of these 27-ton vehicles are in service.

The craft is a variant of the Skate, which was designed as a 50-seat amphibious passenger ferry, but which does not appear to have been put into production. Gus is now employed extensively by the Soviet Marine Infantry. During 1978 it was announced that the Soviet Navy's latest and largest amphibious landing ship, the Ivan Rogov, is capable of carrying three amphibious assault ACVs of the Gus type. Each of these craft can carry a fully-armed platoon onto a landing beach at speeds of up to 92km/h (57mph).

LIFT AND PROPULSION: Motive power is provided by three 780hp TVD 10 marine gas-turbines mounted aft. Two drive three-bladed variable and reversible-pitch propellers for thrust and the third drives an axial lift fan. Cushion air is drawn through a raised intake aft of the cabin superstructure.

CONTROLS: Craft direction is controlled by differential propeller pitch, twin aerodynamic rudders and forward and aft puff ports. Elevators provide pitch trim at cruising speed.

HULL: Hull and superstructure are in conventional corrosion-resistant marine light alloy. Basic structure comprises a central load-carrying platform which incorporates buoyancy tanks and outer sections to support the side ducts and skirt. The cabin, fuel tanks, lift fan bay engines and tail unit are mounted on the platform.

ACCOMMODATION: Up to fifty troops are accommodated in an air-conditioned cabin. Commander and navigator are seated in a raised wheelhouse.

DIMENSIONS

EXTERNAL

Length overall, power on: 21·33m (69ft 11½in)
Beam overall, power on: 7·3m (23ft 11⅜in)
Height to top of fin: 6·6m (21ft 8in)

WEIGHTS

Normal operating: 27 tons

PERFORMANCE

Cruising speed: 92·5km/h (57·5mph)
Normal cruising range: 370km (230 miles)

Gus assault landing craft of the Soviet Marine Infantry during a beach landing exercise. Note the large bellmouth intake for the lift fan amidship

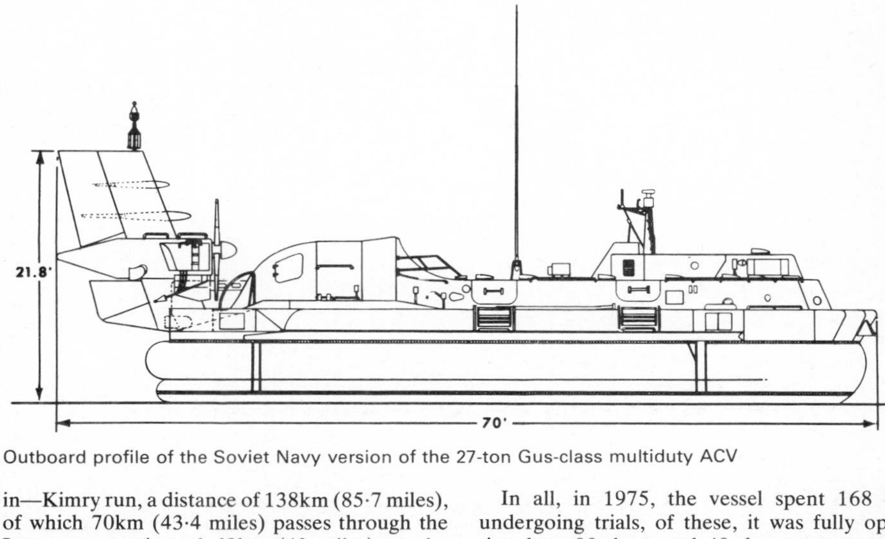

Outboard profile of the Soviet Navy version of the 27-ton Gus-class multiduty ACV

ORION-01

Design of the Orion, a rigid sidewall ACV with seats for 80 passengers, was approved in Moscow in the autumn of 1970. The prototype, built in Leningrad, began her trials in October 1973, and arrived at her port of registry, Kalinin, in late 1974, bearing the serial number 01.

The craft is intended for passenger ferry services along shallow rivers, tributaries and reservoirs, and is capable of landing and taking on passengers, bow-on from any flat sloping bank. It is both faster than the Zarnitsa and is less affected in terms of comfort and performance by choppy conditions. Cruising speed of the vessel, which is propelled by waterjets, is 53km/h (32·3mph). It belongs to the R class of the Soviet River Register.

Consideration is being given to the introduction of several variants, including a 'stretched' model seating 100 passengers on shorter routes, a mixed passenger/freight model, an all-freight model and an 'executive' version for carrying government officials.

Experimental operation of the Orion-01 was organised by the Port of Kalinin, Moscow River Transport, the initial run being Kalinin—1st May Factory, a distance of 99km (61·5 miles), of which 45km (28 miles) is on the Volga, 42km (26 miles) on the Ivanov reservoir and 12km (7·5 miles) on the shallow waters of the Soz. The experience of the first weeks of operation was that there was an insufficient flow of passengers on this particular route.

The vessel was then employed on public holidays only for carrying holiday makers and day trippers on such runs as Kalinin—Putlivo 31km (19 miles), Kalinin—Kokoshky 19km (12 miles) and Kalinin—Tarbasa 28km (17·3 miles), and subsequently on a regular schedule to Putlivo. Finally, Orion-01 was used on the Kalinin—Kimry run, a distance of 138km (85·7 miles), of which 70km (43·4 miles) passes through the Ivanov reservoir and 68km (42 miles) on the Volga.

In all, in 1975, the vessel spent 168 days undergoing trials, of these, it was fully operational on 90 days, and 49 days were spent on repairs or modifications or awaiting work to be undertaken. Time spent underway amounted to 493 hours, during which 7,800 passengers were carried.

Particular attention was paid to assessing the reliability of the skirt. The side sections of the lower part of the bow skirt were badly chafed and split due to contact with the skegs when coming onto the shore. Upper parts of the skirt were not damaged. Problems were also experienced with the aft skirt made from a balloon type fabric. Layers of rubber in the aft part of the segments peeled off; chafing was caused by securing washers and splitting was experienced in the vicinity of the fastenings.

In order to reduce the time spent on repairs, sections of the stern skirt were attached to removable frames. Later a new stern skirt was introduced, based on panels made from a 12mm (0·47in) thick conveyor belt. This enabled the stern draft, on cushion, to be reduced by 10cm (3⅞in) and the speed to be increased by 1·5km/h (⅞mph). It also improved the reliability of the craft. During the 200 hours underway from the time the skirt was fitted until the end of the vessel's trials, there was no damage.

It was considered that, in the main, the Orion met the requirements of the Soviet operators for the rapid transport of passengers on R Class rivers and reservoirs. The elimination of the defects revealed during the experimental operation will make it possible to improve the vessel's operational charcteristics and increase its reliability.

Series production of vessels of this type is being undertaken at the Sosnovska Shipbuilding Yard in Kirovskaya Oblast.

"Gus", the Soviet Union's 27-ton amphibious assault landing craft, is entering service in growing numbers with the Soviet Marine Infantry

ORION—Stopping and starting characteristics

	Shallow water	*Deep water*
Distance run by vessel from Full Ahead to Stop		
Metres	136	120
Time in seconds	67	40
Distance run by vessel from Full Ahead to Full Astern		
Metres	84	65
Time in seconds	23	20
Distance necessary for attainment of Full Speed from Stop		
Metres	250	330
Time in seconds	60	80

"Gus" is powered by three 780hp marinised gas-turbines and cruises at 93·34km/h (58mph). The operating crew appears to comprise a Commander, generally a Senior Lieutenant, First Officer, Flight Engineer and Navigator

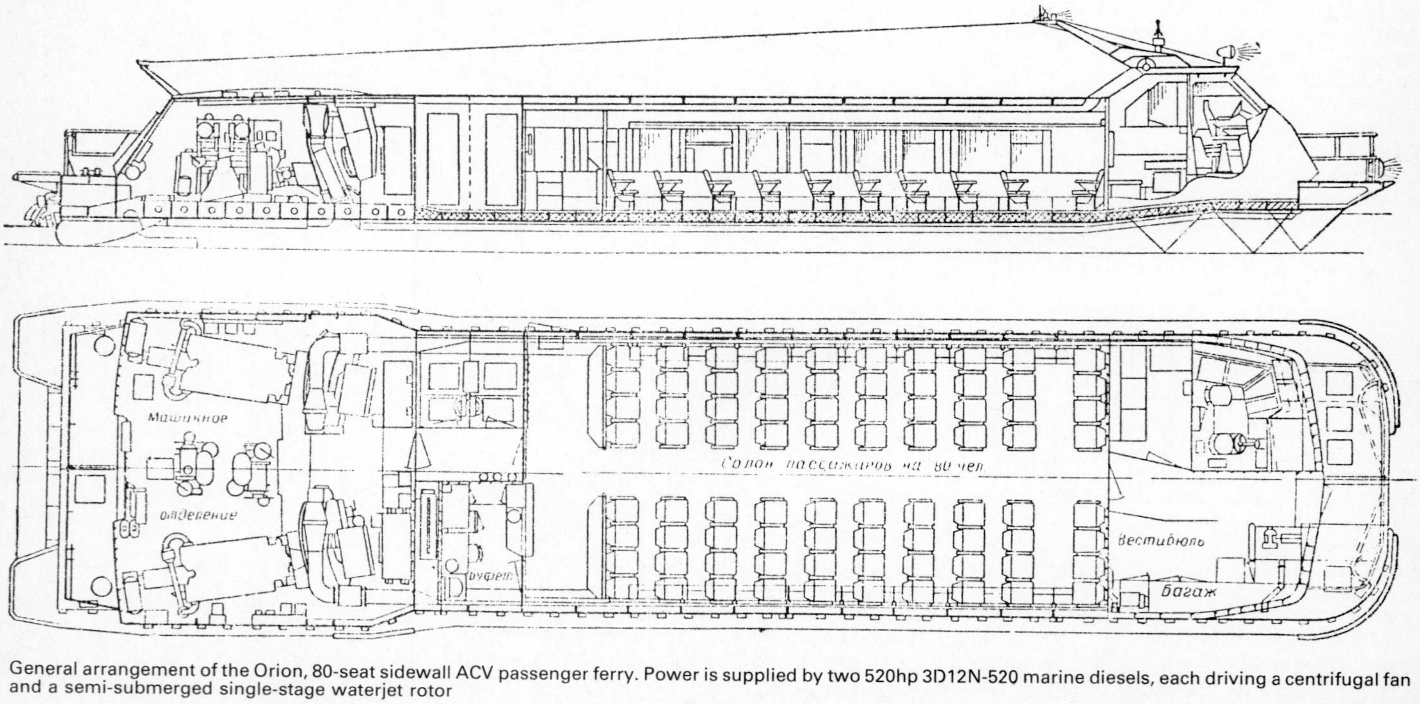

General arrangement of the Orion, 80-seat sidewall ACV passenger ferry. Power is supplied by two 520hp 3D12N-520 marine diesels, each driving a centrifugal fan and a semi-submerged single-stage waterjet rotor

LIFT AND PROPULSION: Integrated system powered by two 520hp 3D12N-520 diesels mounted in an engine room aft. Each engine drives a Type Ts 39—13 centrifugal fan for lift, and via a cardan shaft, a semi-submerged single-stage waterjet rotor for propulsion. Fan air is fed via ducts to the bow skirt, a transverse stability slot and to the fingered bag skirt aft. Casing of the waterjet system which is removable, forms the stern section of the vessel. In order to reduce vibration the waterjets are mounted on shock absorbers.

HULL: Similar in overall appearance to Zarya and Zarnitsa types. All-welded structure in AlMg-61 aluminium-magnesium alloy. Lateral framing employed throughout hull with the exception of the bow and stern decks, where longitudinal frames have been fitted. Superstructure and wheelhouse are of welded and riveted duralumin construction on longitudinal framing.

ACCOMMODATION: Seats are provided for the operating crew of 3, who are accommodated in a raised wheelhouse, a barman, two seamen and 80 passengers. At the aft end of the passenger saloon are two toilet/washbasin units and a bar. There is also an off-duty cabin for the crew. Access to the passenger saloon is via a single door at the bow, in the centre of the wheelhouse. A ram-air intake provides ventilation while the craft is underway. Stale air is drawn out by the lift fans aft.

CONTROLS: Rudders located aft of the waterjet inlets and two waterjet deflectors control craft direction. Rudder and flap movement is effected by cables.

SYSTEMS, ELECTRICAL: Two G-73Z engine-driven generators, linked with two sets of STK-18M batteries, provide 28V, 1,200W. One battery set is employed for engine starting, the other for supplying current for the ship's systems.

COMMUNICATIONS: Standard equipment comprises an R-809MZ radiotelephone, a Kama-3 UHF radio and an Unja cabin announcement system.

DIMENSIONS
Length overall: 25·8m (84ft 7¾in)
Beam overall: 6·5m (21ft 4in)
Height overall to mast top: 5·27m (17ft 3½in)
Height to top of wheelhouse: 3·97m (13ft 0¼in)
Draft, displacement condition, fully loaded: 0·84m (2ft 9⅛in)
Draft, displacement condition, empty: 0·76m (2ft 5⅞in)
Draft, cushionborne:
bow: 0·1m (4in)
stern: 0·5m (1ft 8in)

WEIGHTS
Loaded displacement: 34·7 tonnes
Light displacement: 20·7 tonnes

PERFORMANCE
Max speed: 60km/h (37·25mph)
Cruising speed, full load: 53km/h (33mph)
Max wave height on scheduled runs: 1·2m (4ft)
Range: 400km (249 miles)
Diameter of turn to port: 182m (597ft)
Time to complete turn with rudders at 33 degrees: 187 seconds

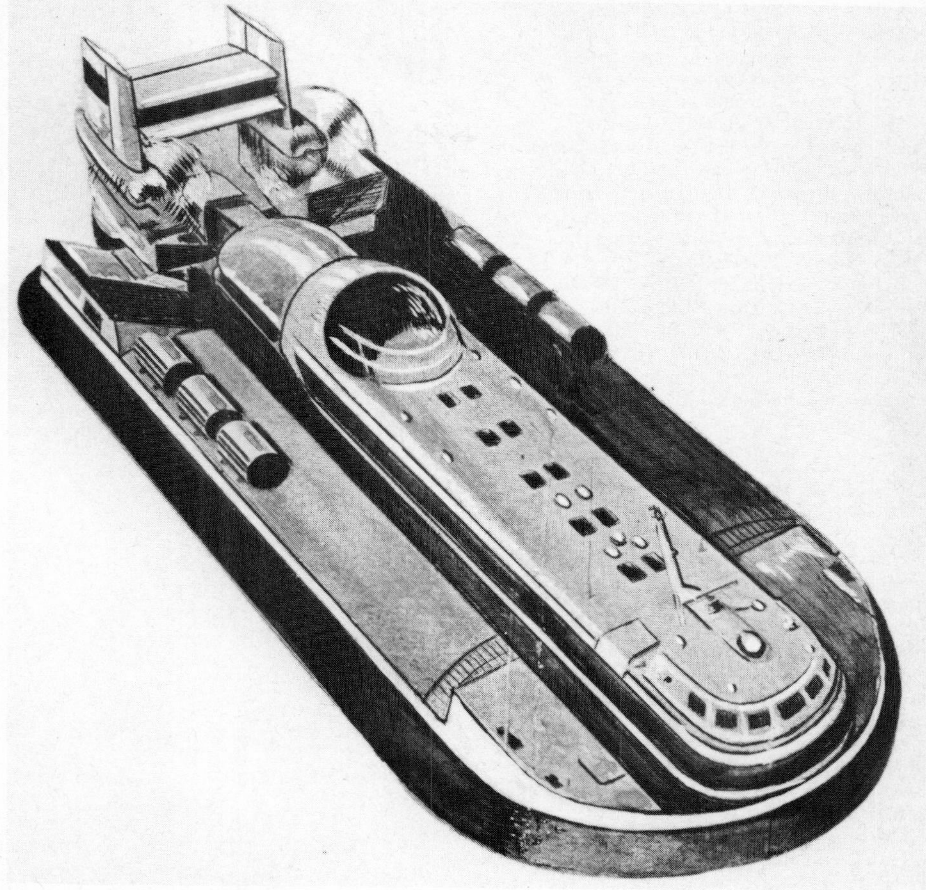
Impression of the Skate 50-seat amphibious hoverferry

Time taken from start of berthing procedure to completion: 1 min approx
Time taken to attain cruising speed from leaving berth: 2 min approx

EKRANOPLAN EXPERIMENTAL

A giant Soviet experimental wing-in-ground-effect machine, with a span of 40m (131ft 3in) and a length of nearly 122m (400ft), is undergoing tests on the Caspian Sea. Trials began in 1965 and are continuing in the company of proportionally smaller models.

The machine, which operates at heights of 7-14m (23-43ft) above the water, has a speed of about 300 knots. Power is supplied by eight marinised gas-turbines mounted above a stub wing forward, and two 'booster' turbines installed at the base of the dihedral tailplane aft. All ten engines are employed at take-off, when thrust has to be 2·5-35 times greater than that required to maintain cruising conditions in flight.

At take-off the thrust from the eight forward engines is deflected downwards to create additional cushion pressure beneath the wing. After take-off the jet exhaust is directed above the upper surface of the wing to create additional lift.

Western WIG specialists, commenting on the design have stated that it does not facilitate pitch stability during its transition from ground-effect to free flight and back again. Thus the machine is probably intended to fly only in close proximity to the surface. This means it may not be able to operate safely either in extremely turbulent weather conditions or in areas where it would encounter projections higher than 15·24m (50ft) above the surface.

Soviet experts maintain that craft of this type should be able to negotiate sand spits, shallows, marshes, ice, snow, relatively even and gently sloping banks and low obstacles. Low bridges have been mentioned. They are also stated to be sufficiently seaworthy to operate in rough seas. Wide employment of this type of vessel is foreseen, particularly in the Soviet Navy, which has suggested that they will be invaluable in amphibious operations.

Large numbers of troops could be carried to the selected landing zones with little regard to the condition of the sea, tidal currents, underwater obstacles and minefields, none of which would

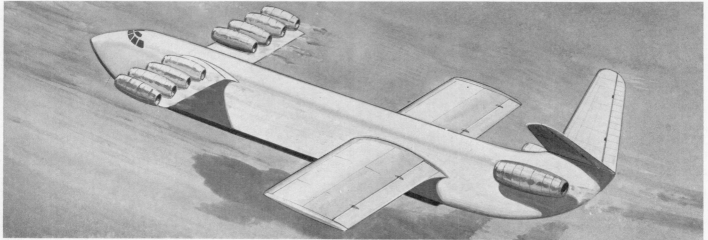

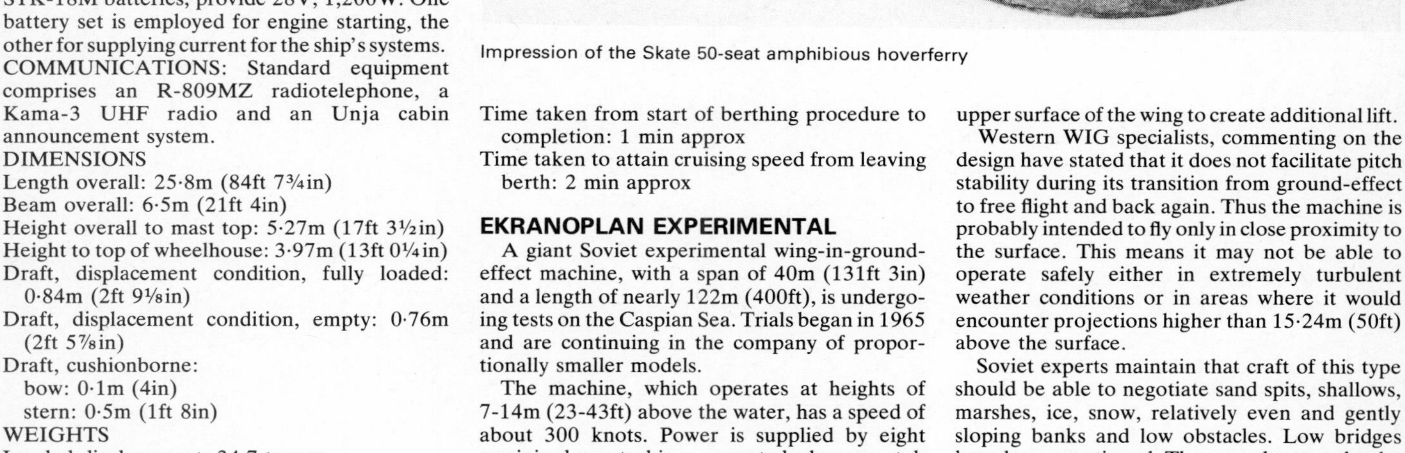
The giant Soviet ten-jet experimental Ekranoplan which is currently undergoing tests on the Caspian Sea

constitute a hazard.

Advantages in the battle zone will include high speed manoeuvring, and a considerable reduction in the time taken to undertake a mission compared with conventional landing craft.

The capacity of the WIG craft, Ekranoplan machines as they are known in the Soviet Union, will enable them to carry the biggest items of military equipment. Another application for this type of vehicle, according to its designers, is ASW patrol, where its considerable range and endurance will prove an advantage.

References have been made in Soviet technical publications to vehicles with chords of 30-40m (98ft 6in-131ft 2in) and speeds of 400 knots being under consideration. This suggests that research is being aimed at a number of alternative configurations including flying wings and delta wings.

Impression of a new catamaran-hulled Ekranoplan research craft now under development in the Soviet Union. Designed for high speed long distance passenger services along the main Soviet rivers, it rides on a dynamic air cushion formed between its wings and the supporting surface below. Seats are provided for forty passengers in each of the twin hulls. Top speed is likely to be between 150-200 knots

EKRANOPLAN RIVER BUSES

The Ministry of the River Fleet announced in April 1972 that it planned to build craft of the Ekranoplan (WIG) type "which will travel within several metres of a river surface at speeds of some 250km/h (155mph)".

It seems probable that in order to avoid navigation problems in busy river port areas these craft will be of smaller overall dimensions than the 40m (131ft 3in) span machine described earlier. Low aspect ratio wings are likely to be employed and it is possible that these early production craft are of 5-6 tons displacement. A number of these machines were reported to be in experimental service in 1973.

On Moscow television in July 1973, a programme commemorating Soviet Navy Day traced the progress of high speed water transportation and confirmed that Ekranoplanes are being developed in the Soviet Union. The craft were described by the commentator as "ground gliders", capable of operating over land, water, snow and ice. A small machine built in Odessa in the early 1960s was shown to viewers, together with a completely new research craft of much larger size.

The craft is of catamaran configuration and carries up to forty passengers in each of the two hulls. The crew and operating controls are accommodated in a central pod carried on the forward wing.

Thrust is provided by six marinised gasturbines mounted in pairs on the triple fins aft. Length of the craft is about 100ft.

The Raduga experimental air cushion vehicle

RADUGA

This experimental amphibious ACV was completed at the Krasnoye Sormovo shipyard in the summer of 1962 and is reported to have attained a speed of 100km/h (62mph) during trials.

Built originally as a peripheral jet type, it is now being used to develop control techniques, and provide amphibious experience and data on skirt design.

LIFT AND PROPULSION: The craft is powered by two 220hp air-cooled radial engines. One, mounted amidships, drives a 1·8m (5ft 11in) 12-bladed lift fan; the second, mounted on a pylon at the stern, drives a two-bladed propeller for propulsion. The fan delivers air to the cushion via a continuous peripheral skirt, the bow and side sections of which are of the fingered bag type.

CONTROLS: Directional control is provided by an aerodynamic rudder operating on the propeller slipstream.

HULL: Riveted aluminium construction.

ACCOMMODATION: The cabin seats five.

DIMENSIONS

Length: 9·4m (30ft 10in)

Beam: 4·12m (13ft 6in)

WEIGHTS

Operating weight: 3 tons

PERFORMANCE

Max speed: 120km/h (75mph)

Endurance: 3 hours

The Sormovich 50-seat passenger ferry

RASSVET (DAWN)

The Rassvet is designed for local sea routes of limited water depth and is an offshore counterpart to the Orion sidewall ACV. Plans call for the Rassvet to serve resort routes in the Crimea, the Caucasus, on the Caspian and in the Baltic, as well as on large lakes and reservoirs. Like the Orion and the Zarnitsa, its two predecessors, it can run bow-on to flat, sloping beaches to embark and disembark passengers.

Features include shallow draft, good manoeuvrability and seagoing qualities and simple construction.

The Rassvet prototype, named Chayka-1 (Gull-1) is at present undergoing trials. News of the existence of Chayka-1 was given in Moscow for the first time in December 1974 when it was reported that the vessel was the first of thirty of this type, all of which would be built at the Sosnovska Shipyard in Kirovskaya Oblast for the Black Sea Shipping Line. In January 1976 it was stated that the vessel was the first seagoing passenger ACV to be built in the Soviet Union.

LIFT AND PROPULSION: Lift is provided by a 150hp marinised lightweight diesel driving a single centrifugal fan. Propulsive thrust is supplied by twin 520hp diesel engines, each driving a waterjet. Fuel capacity, 1,800kg.

HULL: Aluminium construction, part welded, part riveted.

ACCOMMODATION: Up to eighty passengers are accommodated in an air-conditioned cabin in airliner-type seats. Captain and engineer are accommodated in an elevated wheelhouse, forward.

DIMENSIONS

Length overall: 26·5m (87ft)

Beam overall: 7·1m (23ft 3½in)

Height of sidewalls: 9·06m (29ft 8½in)

Draft off cushion: 1·24m (4ft)

Draft on cushion: 0·7m (2ft 4in)

WEIGHTS

Displacement full load: 45 tonnes

PERFORMANCE

Service speed: 25 knots

Max permissible wave height: 2m (6ft 6¾in)

Range: 400km (248 miles)

SORMOVICH

Launched in October 1965, the Sormovich is a 50-passenger ACV designed by Valeri Schoenberg, Chief Constructor of the Krasnoye Sormovo Shipyard, with the assistance of the N E Zhukovski Central Institute of Aerodynamics.

In general layout, the craft represents a "scale-up" of the configuration tested with the Raduga.

In 1970 the craft was equipped with a 4ft deep flexible skirt. Several experimental services have been operated with the craft. It is not yet in production, although orders are expected from the Ministry of the River Fleet.

TESTS: Rigorous acceptance trials included a special programme of runs between Gorky and Gorodets, Gorky and Lyskovo, Gorky and Vasilsursk, and also on the Gorky Reservoir.

These trials confirmed the craft's ability to operate across shoals, sandy spits and dykes, and run on to dry land for cargo handling and repairs.

In the air-cushion mode, her ability to maintain course up- and downwind is satisfactory, and controlled entirely by the rudders. In sidewinds, control is by combined rudder movement and differential propeller pitch. Steering during turns by rudders alone is unsatisfactory, the turning-circle diameter being 2,500-3,000m (2,734-3,280 yards) with substantial drift. Turning is improved if the manoeuvre is accomplished by varying propeller pitch. The distance from the inception of the manoeuvre to securing a 180 degree course then drops to 700-1,000m (765-1,093 yards) and the diameter of the subsequent turning circle falls to 150m (164 yards).

Collision avoidance manoeuvres with a floating object employing rudder deflection, showed that avoidance is feasible at a distance of not under 500m (546 yards). This distance can be reduced, however, if the manoeuvre is accomplished with variable propeller pitch. Successful undertaking of this manoeuvre depends largely on the skill of the operator.

In the air-cushion mode, while accelerating to 60-70km/h (37-43mph) and turning through 180 degrees in both directions, stability is adequate in any of the load conditions investigated, and passengers may move about freely.

In addition to the basic flight-trial programme, tests were made to check vehicle response to sudden splash-down in case of the emergency shutdown of the main engine while underway. The splash-down tests were conducted at various speeds and drift angles, and showed that the loads imposed are not excessive and that the passengers were not alarmed. In 1·2m (4ft) waves the craft operates at reduced speed, but steering control and satisfactory passenger comfort are maintained.

Since late 1970, Sormovich has been in experimental service with the Volga United Steamship Company.

While operating on the Gorky-Cheboksary run in light conditions and with passengers aboard during the 1971 season, various problem areas were identified. In particular, it was found necessary to improve the reliability of the airscrew and fan drive transmission; improve the design of the flexible-skirt and select a stronger material from which it can be manufactured; find ways of reducing engine noise and improve its operation and maintenance; render more effective the devices employed to reduce craft drift during highspeed turns; and raise the overall economic efficiency of the craft.

After modification, the vehicle returned to experimental service on the Gorky-Cheboksary-Gorky passenger run in 1972, with flights scheduled for daylight hours only, in winds not over 10-12m/s (32-39ft/s) and at speeds not above 80km/h (50mph). The route selected was generally beyond that negotiable by a conventional vessel, with depths not less than 0·5m (1ft 8in).

Two crew training flights and 42 passenger flights were undertaken during this particular service. Some 5,655 people were carried a total of 25,000km (15,534 miles).

However, experimental operation of the craft during the 1972 season was a financial loss. The economic viability of Sormovich, as in the previous season, was impaired by the craft being withdrawn from service to eliminate main transmission reduction gear defects and attend to various other repair and maintenance jobs.

A passenger survey indicated that noise levels in the rear of the saloon are acceptable, but high external noise levels are a nuisance to shore personnel and members of the public in the vicinity.

The Sormovich ACV passenger ferry, powered by a single 2,300hp Ivchenko AI-20K gas turbine

Experimental operation of the Sormovich has indicated the possibility of its being used on inland waterways.

During the 1972/73 off-season period, measures were being taken to eliminate the shortcomings revealed, replace the reduction gear, improve flexible-skirt nozzle elements, and undertake various other modifications found necessary. There are grounds for believing that these measures will make Sormovich into a viable economic proposition.

LIFT AND PROPULSION: All machinery is located aft behind a sound-proof bulkhead to keep down the noise level in the passenger compartments. A single 2,300hp Ivchenko AI-20K shaft-turbine, at the extreme stern, drives the integrated lift/propulsion system. Its output shaft passes first to a differential gearbox from which shafts extend sideways to the two four-blade ducted variable pitch propellers. A further shaft runs forward from the differential to a bevel gearbox from which a drive-shaft runs vertically upward to the 12-blade variable pitch lift-fan mounted under the intake on the rear of the roof of the vehicle. The gas-turbine operates on diesel fuel. Cushion area is 220m².

CONTROLS: Each propeller duct contains two hydraulically-actuated rudders, working in the slipstream.

HULL: Light alloy buoyancy type, with air feeding to the cushion through a peripheral slot. Fore and aft stability slots are located on each side parallel to and about 1·5m (5ft) inboard of the peripheral slot.

ACCOMMODATION: The crew compartment, forward, contains two seats and is separated from the main cabin by a partition containing a door. The front two rows of seats in the cabin are only four-abreast to facilitate entry through the forward door on each side. The remaining 42 seats are six-abreast, in three-chair units with centre aisle. Aft of the cabin is a wardrobe on the port side, with a buffet opposite on the starboard side. Then comes the main entry lobby, with a passenger door on the port side and service door opposite, followed by a toilet (port) and baggage hold (starboard).

An unusual feature of the Sormovich is that it is fitted with retractable wheels which can be lowered to avoid damage to the hull when the craft operates over uneven ice or rough country. The wheels are carried on lightly-sprung legs, enabling them to ride easily over obstructions.

The craft is equipped for navigation at night.

DIMENSIONS
Length: 29·2m (96ft)
Beam: 10m (32ft 9½in)
Height to top of hull, on cushion: 7m (22ft 11½in)

WEIGHTS
Normal loaded: 36·5 tonnes

PERFORMANCE
Max cruising speed: 120km/h (74·56mph)

ZARNITSA

Evolved from Gorkovchanin, the Zarnitsa is a 48-50 seat waterjet-propelled rigid sidewall ferry designed to operate on shallow rivers, some less than 0·7m (2ft 3in) deep. Series production is underway, and large numbers have been delivered.

The prototype was put into trial service on the Vyatka river, in the Kirov region, in the summer of 1972, and the first production models began operating on shallow, secondary rivers later in the year. During 1973-74, Zarnitsas entered service on tributaries of the Kama, Lena and Volga.

The Zarnitsa 48-50 seat waterjet-propelled rigid sidewall ferry for shallow rivers

Passenger saloon in the Zarnitsa, looking aft

More than 100 are currently employed on almost all the river navigation lines of the Russian Federative Republic as well as on the rivers of the Ukrainian, Moldavian, Byelorussian and Kazakhstan Soviet Socialist Republics.

LIFT AND PROPULSION, CONTROLS, HULL: Arrangements almost identical to those of the Gorkovchanin.

ACCOMMODATION: Seats are provided for two crew members, who are accommodated in the raised wheelhouse, forward, and 48-50 passengers. Access to the passenger saloon is via a single door located at the bow in the centre of the wheelhouse. The craft runs bow-on to flat sloping banks to embark and disembark passengers.

DIMENSIONS
Length: 22·3m (72ft 3in)
Beam: 3·85m (12ft 8in)
Skeg depth: 0·45m (1ft 6in)

WEIGHTS
Light displacement: 9 tonnes
All-up weight, with 48 passengers, crew and fuel: 15 tonnes

PERFORMANCE
Service speed: 33-35km/h (20-22mph)

The Zarnitsa, a derivative of the Gorkovchanin, is now in series production

Zaryas in series production at the Moscow Shipbuilding and Ship Repair Yard.

ZARYA (DAWN)

Experiments with high speed "aéroglisseur" (literally air skimmer) waterbuses, capable of negotiating the many shallow waterways in the Soviet Union, began in 1961.

The object was to develop a vessel for services on shallow waters, with depths of only 0·5m (20in), at speeds of at least 21·5 knots. The prototype Zarya, called the Opytnye-1 (experimental), was put into experimental operations on the river Msta in 1963. During trials the craft attained a speed of 42km/h (26mph) and proved to have a turning radius of 40-70m (44-76 yards). The craft runs bow-on to any flat, sloping bank to embark passengers.

Built with a strong aluminium alloy hull and equipped with a well protected waterjet, the craft is unharmed by floating logs, even when they are encountered at full speed.

Variants include models with a flat load deck in place of the passenger cabin superstructure amidships, and used as light freight vessels.

Zarya was designed by a team at the Central Design Office of the Ministry of the River Fleet, Gorky, working in conjunction with the Leningrad Water Transport Institute. Series production is under way at the Moscow Shipbuilding and Ship Repair Yard of the Ministry of the River Fleet.

Given the design prefix P83, Zarya conforms to Class P of the River Register of the USSR.

The latest model is distinguished by its trimaran bow configuration, which gives improved performance in waves and enables the craft to be routed on major waterways. Apart from the large number of Zaryas in service in the USSR, a number have been supplied to Czechoslovakia, Poland and the German Democratic Republic.

LIFT AND PROPULSION: Power is provided by a single M401A-1 four-stroke, watercooled, supercharged, 12-cylinder V-type diesel with a normal service output of 870-900hp at 1,450-1,500rpm and a maximum output of 1,000hp. It has a variable-speed governor and reversing clutch and drives a single 0·7m (2ft 2½in) diameter variable-pitch, four-bladed waterjet impeller.

The waterjet is of single-stage type, with a semi-submerged jet discharge. The impeller, which is made in brass, sucks in water through an intake duct which is covered by a protective grille. The discharged water flows around two balanced rudders which provide directional control. Two reversal shutters, interconnected by a rod and operated by cable shafting, are employed to reverse the craft or to reduce the waterjet thrust when variations in speed are necessary.

A localised ram-air cushion, introduced by an upswept nose and contained on either side by shallow skegs, lifts the bow clear of the water as the craft picks up speed. The airflow also provides air/foam lubrication for the remainder of the flat-bottomed hull.

CONTROLS: Irrespective of load, the radius of turn is between 30-50m (98-164ft) with the rudder put hard over at an angle of 30 degrees. This can be decreased if necessary by either throttling down the engine or closing the valves of the reversing system. At slow speed the craft is capable of pinwheeling. The time required to stop the vessel is 8-10 seconds, the coasting distance being between 50-60m (164-196ft). Manoeuvrability of the craft is such that it is able to navigate small winding rivers with waterways of 12-15m (39-49ft) wide with the radii of windings varying between 40-70m (131-229ft) without slowing down.

The vessel can easily pull into shore without landing facilities, providing the river bed slope is no steeper than 3 degrees. The time required for pulling in, embarking passengers, then leaving, averages 1·5 minutes. Steps to facilitate access are located at the bow, port and starboard, and lowered by a control in the wheelhouse.

HULL: Hull and superstructure are of all-welded aluminium alloy plate construction, the constituent parts being joined by argon-shielded arc welding. Framing is of mixed type, with transverse framing at the sides and the main longitudinal elements within the hull bottom. The outside shell and bottom plating is 5mm ($^{13}/_{64}$in) thick, except for the base at the bow where it is 6mm ($^{15}/_{64}$in) thick. The wheelhouse is in moulded glass-reinforced plastic. The waterjet duct and nozzle are in grade Cr3 steel and are riveted to the hull.

ACCOMMODATION: Three tranverse bulkheads and two recesses divide the hull into six compartments. Behind the forepeak and wheelhouse (frames 0-3) is the passenger cabin (frames 3-27) and aft of this is a compartment housing a small bar and toilet (frames 27-30). A soundproof cofferdam (frames 30-31) follows, aft of which is the engine room (frames 31-41) and steering compartment (frames 41 to stern). The raised wheelhouse, located at the bow, gives

Zarya is powered by a 1,000hp M401A-1 four-stroke turbocharged diesel driving a single-stage waterjet. Cruising speed is about 40km/h (25mph).

360 degree visibility. The latest export model of the Zarya seats 63 in the passenger cabin, plus another four, without luggage, in two recesses. On routes of up to 45 minute duration an additional 20 standing passengers can be carried. Life jackets for passengers are stowed in lockers in the baggage compartment and under seats at the rear of the cabin.

The crew off-duty room contains a sofa, table, wall-mounted cupboard, folding stool and a mirror. The toilet contains a wash basin, a bowl, mirror and soap tray.

The wheelhouse has rotating seats for the captain and engineer, two sun visors and there are two windscreen wipers.

Both the passenger cabin and wheelhouse are heated by warm air produced by hot water from the closed circuit main engine cooling system. Warm air is admitted into the passenger cabin and wheelhouse through a perforated chamber at the bulkhead. The engine room is heated by two 1·2kW electric heaters and the crew room by a 0·6kW electric heater. Windows of the wheelhouse and the wheelhouse itself are heated by a 330kW electric heater.

SYSTEMS, ELECTRICAL: Main engine driven 3kW, 28V dc generator, charges the storage batteries and meets the demands of 24V circuits while the vessel is underway. Four lead-acid batteries supply 24V for monitoring and alarm cir-

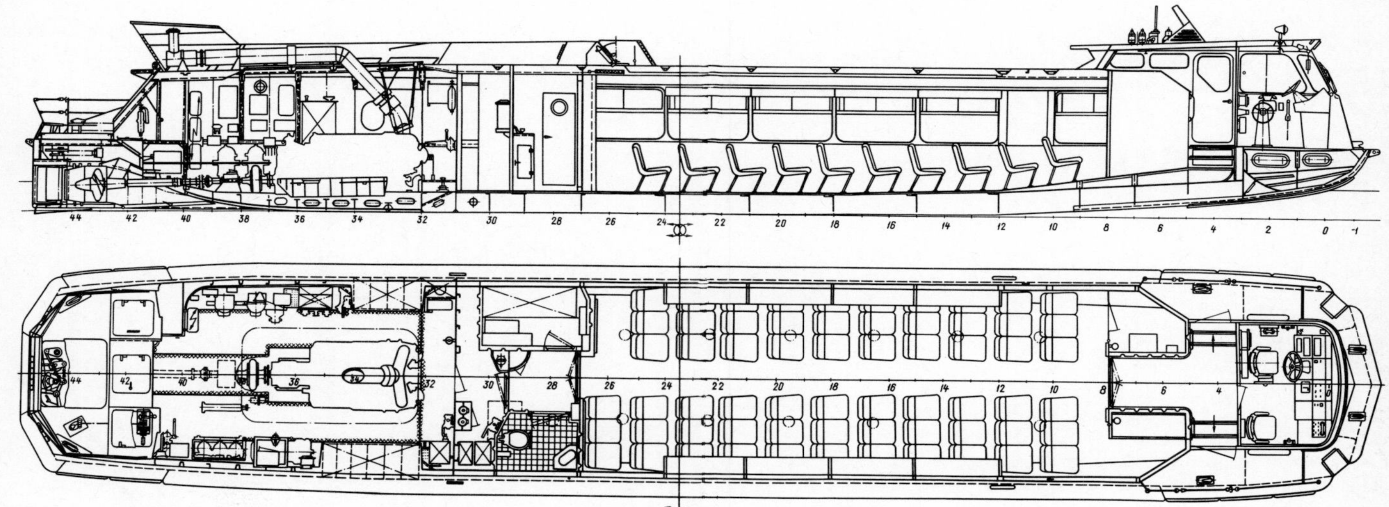

Inboard and outboard profiles and deck views of the latest export model of the Zarya waterjet-propelled passenger ferry

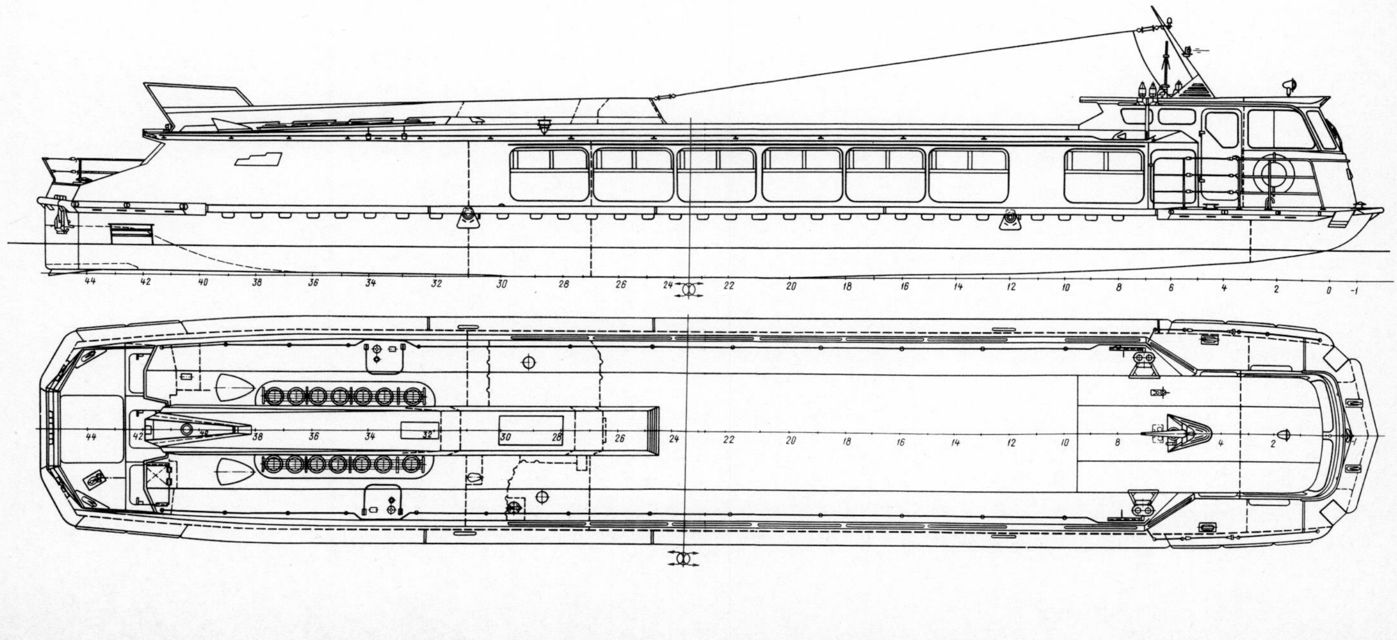

cuitry and starting the main engine.

Equipment supplied for charging the storage batteries, operating electric heater, engine room and service space heaters from a shore-based 220V source.

FIRE-FIGHTING: Two tanks containing fire-extinguishing compound and hoses for fighting an outbreak in the engine room. System can be brought into operation either from the engine room or from the wheelhouse. Engine room is also provided with two portable carbon dioxide fire extinguishers. Another of the same type is provided in the wheelhouse and two foam fire extinguishers are standard equipment in the main cabin.

FUEL: Craft is refuelled through a filling hose and a neck on the port side of the superstructure. Fuel is fed to the main engine from a service tank with a capacity of 4·13m³, sufficient to enable a vessel to cruise for 8 hours without refuelling. In addition, there is a 400 litre storage tank which contains a 2 hour reserve to be used in an emergency. The same tank supplies fuel to a water heater.

COMPRESSED AIR: Starting system for main engines comprising three 45 litre air-cylinders, valves (safety, shut-off, pressure reducing and starting) and piping. Pressure 150-75kgf/cm². Two cylinders in operation, one standby.

DIMENSIONS
Length overall: 23·9m (78ft 5in)
Beam overall: 4·13m (13ft 7in)
Freeboard up to undetachable parts at mean draft of 0·44m (1ft 5½in): 3·2m (10ft 6in)
Mean draft, light: 0·44m (1ft 5½in)
Mean draft, loaded: 0·55m (1ft 9½in)

WEIGHTS
Empty: 16·68 tonnes
Weight with 60 passengers, and stores for 8 hour trip: 24·78 tonnes
Maximum weight of cargo that can be stowed in luggage recesses: 1 tonne
Fuel capacity: 3·8 tonnes

Compared with earlier variants, this new model of the Zarya is distinguished by its trimaran bow, introduced for improved seakeeping. The new bow design allows the vessel to be routed into major waterways

PERFORMANCE
Speed (in channel of 0·8m depth): 45km/h (27·96mph)
Range: suitable for service distances of 150km (93 miles) and above
Endurance at cruising speed: 8 hours

MARIISKY POLYTECHNICAL INSTITUTE

Ioshka-Ola, USSR

Officials:
Stanislav F Kirkin, *Leader, Student Design Group*
Anatoli Loskutov, *Engineer*
Valeri Vedernikov, *Engineer*
Vladimir Akulov, *Engineer*

To meet the need for light personal modes of transport capable of operating under winter conditions in the virgin territories of the USSR, the student design group at the Mariisky Polytechnical Institute has developed a range of small ACVs and other vehicles capable of operation over snow, ice and—in the case of the amphibious models—over water. One of the group's first designs was the MPI-4, a "strap-on" system of air propulsion for individual skiers. Known as the "satchel aero-propelling unit" it comprised a 5hp Ural circular-saw engine, a 5-litre petrol tank and an 80cm diameter propeller rotating inside a protective circular duct. Under favourable conditions it propelled the wearer at up to 50km/h across snow or hard-frozen snow crust. This was followed by the MPI-6 air propelled snow motorcycle, capable of running across any kind of snow at speeds up to 65km/h. This vehicle was basically a lightweight motorcycle frame with a sprung, steerable main ski forward and a second main ski aligned with it, aft. An 18hp IZH-Planeta motorcycle engine driving a 1·2m diameter propeller was located behind its driving saddle.

Other concepts included a variety of aero-sledges, some with open cockpits and more sophisticated models with fully-enclosed and heated cabins. Two of the group's more recent designs are the MPI-15 and MPI-18, brief descriptions of which appear below.

MPI-15 CASPIAN

Derived from the MPI-10 snowmobile-

MPI-15 Caspian snowmobile amphibian

MPI-18 cross-country ACV, designed to carry passengers and freight

amphibian, this new design has undergone tests at the Chief Directorate of the Fishing Industry's seal-fishing posts on the Caspian sea and is being prepared for series production. A single-seater, the Caspian can move at speeds of up to 75km/h across snow, frozen snow, ice and water; traverse smaller ice hummocks and climb gradients of up to 20 degrees from a standing start and up to 50 degrees at speed. Power is supplied by a 25hp petrol engine driving a 2m diameter two-bladed propeller. The craft is capable of towing a trailer with a payload of up to 80kg.

MPI-18

Described as a snow glider-cum-amphibious air cushion vehicle, this 70km/h cross-country vehicle is designed to carry passengers or freight across snow, water and swamps. Air is fed into the cushion by a forward-mounted axial lift fan. Propulsive thrust is supplied by a rear-mounted petrol engine driving a two-bladed propeller. An aerodynamic rudder controls craft heading.

KHARKOV MOTOR TRANSPORT TECHNICAL SCHOOL

AERO-GLIDER

Built by V Kalekin, a teacher at Kharkov Motor Transport Technical School, this 5m long air-propelled sled has been in use since 1972, during which time it has travelled more than 15,000km, including long stretches of mountain rivers. According to its designer, it has performed particularly well during long-distance journeys over water.

DIMENSIONS
Length overall: 5m (16ft 5in)
Beam: 1·86m (6ft 1in)
WEIGHTS
Payload: 500kg (1,102lb)
Fuel capacity: 260 litres (57 gallons)
PERFORMANCE
Range: 1,000km (621 miles)

The Aero-Glider, a 5m long air-propelled sled built by V Kalekin of the Kharkov Motor Transport Technical School

OIIMF (ODESSA ENGINEERING INSTITUTE OF THE MERCHANT FLEET)

OIIMF-2

This is one of a number of experimental wing-in-ground-effect machines built at the institute by a group of students under the direction of Y Budnitskiy.

The craft is a single-seater with an all-up weight of 420-450kg (926-992lb) and a payload of 80-100kg (176-220lb). The wings, floats and hull are of semi-monocoque construction and built in duralumin.

Power is supplied by two 18hp aircooled motorcycle engines driving two 1·2m (3ft 11in) diameter two-bladed airscrews.

Special flaps have been designed to improve the starting characteristics of the craft by creating a static air cushion through the utilisation of the airscrew slipstream. The flaps are located between the wings and are secured by special shock absorption cables in the operating position at the moment of starting the craft. As speed increases so the flaps hinge upwards automatically.

Tests indicate that the flaps noticeably decrease the leakage of air from the high pressure area under the aft wing, thus increasing wing lift and unloading the floats.

A vertical tail assembly and flap are provided for steering and stabilisation. The flap on the aft wing is designed to balance the craft during starting and control it in pitch. The leading wing barely generates any lift at low speeds, therefore a pitching moment, obtained by deflecting the flap upwards, must be created during the initial period of its run in order to balance the craft. As speed increases and the forward wing comes into operation, the centre of pressure shifts forward, which requires a diving moment (deflection of the flap downward) in order to balance the craft.

Static stability in pitch is provided by constant contact of the aft section of the floats with the water surface and the corresponding stabilising effect of the forward wing.

The vehicle has good manoeuvrability, and the turning diameter, at a speed of 20mph is approximately 32ft.

DIMENSIONS
Length overall: 5m (16ft 5in)
Hull beam: 3·2m (10ft 6in)
Wing span: 2·8m (9ft 2¼in)
Chord, forward
lower wing: 1m (3ft 4in)
Chord:
upper wing: 3m (9ft 10in)

The OIIMF-2 single-seat wing-in-ground-effect research craft

The Skat on display in Moscow

UFA AVIATION INSTITUTE

An experimental circular planform ACV, the Skat, has been designed and built by students of the UFA Aviation Institute. The vehicle was displayed in 1970 in Moscow at the USSR National Economy Achievements Exhibition.

UNITED KINGDOM

AIRHOVER LTD

Hoverplane Works, Main Road, Arlesford, Colchester, Essex CO7 8DB, England
Telephone: 020 636 356
Officials:
R P Wingfield, *Managing Director*

Airhover Ltd is marketing the Aero Sabre Mk I and AS-2 light hovercraft—both open single- or two-seaters—and the more sophisticated Aero Sabre III high performance sports ACV.

Latest addition to the line is the Mk IV, a luxury four-seater with ducted fan propulsion.

AERO SABRE Mk I

The new Aero Sabre Mk I is a high performance amphibious light sports hovercraft. It is in production and is available either complete or in kit form.

LIFT AND PROPULSION: Power for the integrated lift/propulsion system is provided by a 10bhp Rowena engine, although a wide choice of alternative power plants is available ranging from a 6bhp or 13bhp Stihl to a 12hp Kyoritsu. The primary airflow from the eight-bladed axial-flow fan is ejected through a propulsive slot aft of the fan duct, and the secondary airflow, for the cushion, passes downwards into the plenum chamber.

CONTROLS: Throttle twist grip control, with dummy grip opposite and ignition cutout switch. Steering is by kinesthetic control (body movement). The manufacturer points out that as the performance is "very lively," experience at low speeds is desirable before attempting high speed runs.

HULL: Mixed aluminium, glassfibre and wooden construction. Basic hull structure is built from light alloy square section tubing with curved members in laminated wood. The nose fairing, tandem seat and fuel tank form a single unit. These and the streamlined duct aft are in moulded grp. The upper surface is covered with lightweight nylon, impregnated on both sides with pvc for tear resistance. Fuel tank is integral with glassfibre superstructure with filler neck aft of driver's seat. Fuel capacity is 9·09 litres (2 gallons).

SKIRT: Made in extra strong nylon fabric and reinforced with double skin of pvc. Skirt is in eleven segments and is stitched with rot-proofed thread. Skirt attachment rails provided.

ACCOMMODATION: Open motor-cycle type upholstered seating for one or two in tandem.

DIMENSIONS
Length: 2·74m (9ft)
Beam: 1·82m (6ft)
Height: 0·914m (3ft)

WEIGHTS
Unladen: 45·35kg (100lb)
Max payload: 181·43kg (400lb)

PERFORMANCE
Designed speed, land: 64·37km/h (40mph)
water: 40·23km/h (25mph)
Fuel consumption: 4·5 litres/hour (1 gallon/hour)
Obstacle clearance: 15·24cm (6in)

AERO SABRE AS-2

A modified version of the Mk 1, the AS-2 has been produced for Education Authorities and youth training organisations which include hovercraft design amongst their educational projects. Like the Mk 1 SP, which it replaces, it is available in kit form and can be constructed without recourse to complicated tools and equipment.

A number of alternative power plants can be installed, from a 10bhp, 210cc Rowena to any suitable twin-cylinder engine of about 22bhp, depending on the performance required. With 22hp installed the maximum speed in calm conditions is about 96 km/h (60mph).

On this model the fan duct, fin and rudder are of alloy reinforced glass reinforced plastics. The duct contains an adjustable "splitter" plate enabling the airflow fed into the cushion and ejected through the propulsive slot aft to be shared as required.

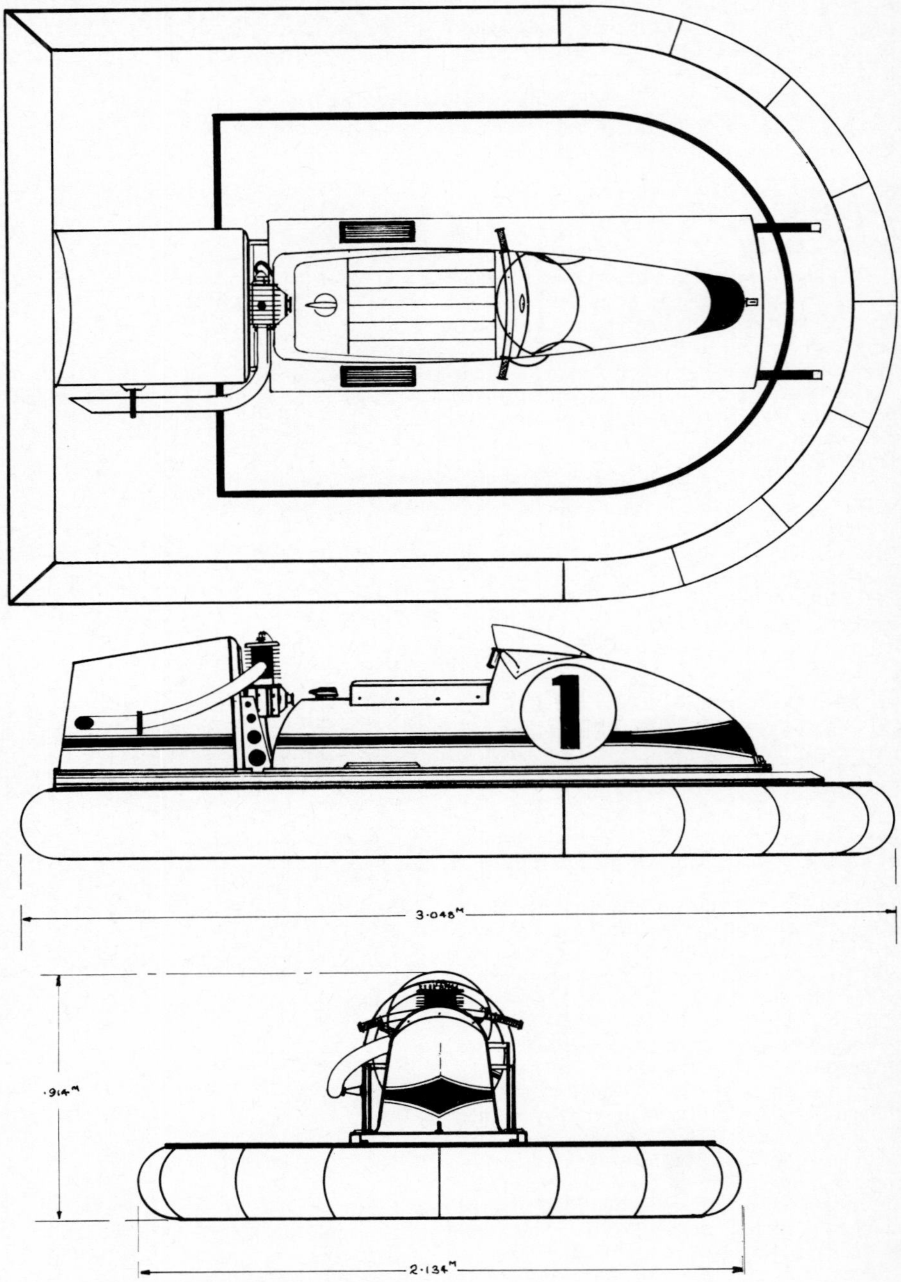

General arrangement of the Aero Sabre Mk I

The Aero Sabre Mk I SP, now available in partially assembled kit form for educational authorities for school educational projects including hovercraft theory.

DIMENSIONS
Length, overall: 4·57m (15ft)
Beam, on cushion: 2·43m (8ft)
Height to top of rudder: 1·37m (4ft 6in)
WEIGHTS
Empty: 80·73kg (178lb)
Load: 236·76kg (522lb)
PERFORMANCE
Max speed: up to 96·56km/h (60mph)
Vertical obstacle clearance: 0·22m (9in)

AERO SABRE Mk III

The prototype of this exceptionally elegant two-seater is undergoing tests. One of the aims of the designers has been to produce a high-performance light ACV which combines the lines of a racing aircraft with the comfort of a modern sports car. Various alternative layouts are available to suit commercial applications. Performance depends upon the power installed, but the designed maximum speed is 95·56km/h (60mph).

LIFT AND PROPULSION: The lift engine, a 20hp MAG type 1031 two-stroke is located forward of the cabin beneath a protective metal mesh panel and drives a 0·53m (1ft 9in) diameter fan with blades set at 30 degrees. Each blade is detachable to facilitate replacement. Located aft of the cabin, the propulsion engine, a 33hp MAG 2062-SRB twin cylinder two-stroke, drives a 0·914m (3ft) diameter two-bladed variable-pitch propeller. The entire thrust unit will be surrounded by a plated protective mesh guard. Both engines have electric starters.

CONTROLS: Heading is controlled by a single, swept back aerodynamic rudder operating in the propeller slipstream. Aircraft-type wheel, instrumentation, switches and throttles.

HULL: Built in high grade marine ply and incorporating three watertight buoyancy compartments. In the event of either one or two of these sustaining damage, the remaining compartments will keep the craft afloat. The superstructure, which includes the canopy, forward decking and air intake is a one-piece moulding in grp. Windows and windshields are in perspex. Cabin access is via two light alloy gull-wing doors which are raised electrically.

SKIRT: Conventional bag-type, 304mm (1ft) deep.

CABIN: Access is via gull-wing doors. Semi-reclining, upholstered seats are provided side-by-side for driver and passenger. Panels and pillars are finished in matching colours.

DIMENSIONS
Length, overall: 5·18m (17ft)
Beam, overall: 2·43m (8ft)
Height to top of rudder (on landing pads): 1·52m (5ft)
Skirt depth: 406mm (1ft 4in)
WEIGHTS
Unladen: 308·42kg (680lb)
Payload: 272·14kg (600lb)
PERFORMANCE
Max speed: 96·56km/h (60mph)
Obstacle clearance: 304mm (12in)

AERO SABRE Mk IV

Work on the prototype of this luxury four-seater is currently in progress.

One of the main objectives has been to provide a fast, amphibious vehicle suitable for business executives working in countries with a dry and dusty environment. Simplicity of construction and ease of maintenance are two of the design keynotes.

LIFT AND PROPULSION: Power for the integrated lift/propulsion system is provided by a single Rolls-Royce Continental aero-engine rated at 100hp. This drives a single 1·16m (3ft 10in) diameter, four-bladed ducted fan, the primary airflow from which is ejected through a propulsive slot aft, while the secondary airflow is ducted downwards into the plenum chamber for lift. Fuel is carried in two tanks of 35 litre (7·7 gallon) capacity.

The Aero Sabre Mk I high performance light sports ACV. The most recent model is fitted with a completely redesigned duct, illustrated in the accompanying three-view drawing

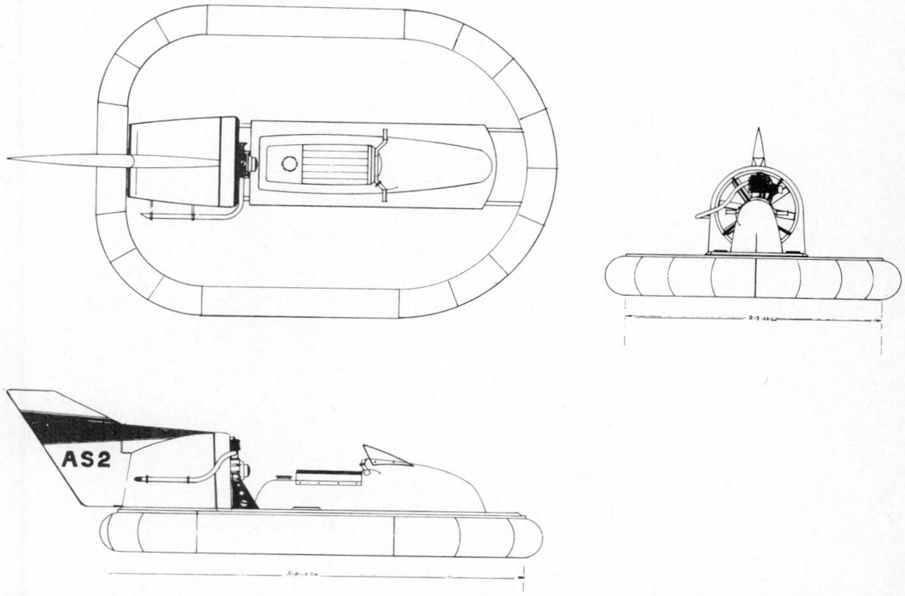

Three-view of the new Aero Sabre AS-2. Alloy brackets ahead of the fan air duct permit the installation of a wide choice of engines

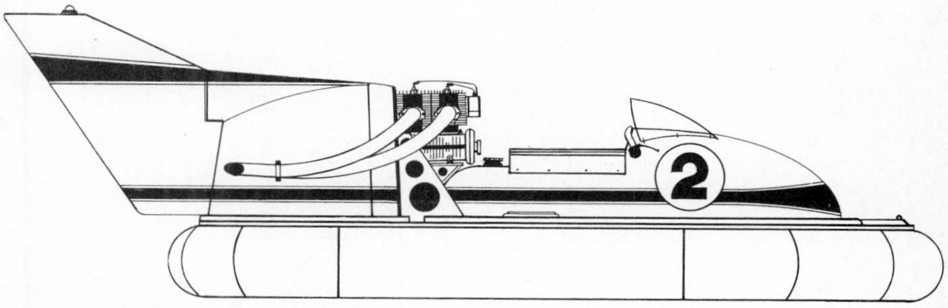

Elevation of the Aero Sabre AS-2 with a 22bhp twin-cylinder engine installed

Aero Sabre Mk III, a 96-56 km/h (60mph) amphibious two-seater, combines elegance and high performance with the comfort of a modern sports car

CONTROLS: Craft heading is controlled by triple rudders in the airjet outlet aft. The two outer units are uncoupled for braking and reverse thrust.
HULL: Mixed grp and light alloy construction.
ACCOMMODATION: Totally enclosed cabin fitted with four semi-reclining seats. Aircraft style instrumentation.
DIMENSIONS
Length: 6·4m (21ft)
Beam: 2·74m (9ft)
Height: 1·21m (4ft)
WEIGHTS
All-up: 521·5kg (1,150lb)
Payload: 294·82kg (650lb)

One-seventh scale model of the new Aero Sabre Mk IV four-seater. Power for the integrated lift/propulsion system is provided by a 100hp Rolls-Royce Continental aero-engine

AIR VEHICLES LIMITED

Head Office and Works: 1 Sun Hill, Cowes, Isle of Wight, England
Yard: Dinnis' Yard, High Street, Cowes, Isle of Wight, England
Telephone: 098 382 3194 and 4739
Telex: 86513 (Hoverwork, Ryde)
Officials:
P H Winter, MSc, *Director*
C D J Bland, *Director*
C B Eden, *Director*

Air Vehicles Ltd was founded in 1968 and has concentrated on the development of small commercial hovercraft and various systems, including skirts and ducted propellers, for larger craft.

The company's main product is the AV Tiger 8-10 seat hovercraft which now has increased hoverheight and the new AV Tiger S, with accommodation for 12-14 passengers. The first production Tiger has been supplied to the Canadian armed forces.

Air Vehicles Ltd is approved by the Civil Aviation Authority and undertakes design and manufacture of major modifications to larger craft. These have included flat-deck freight conversions for the SR.N5 and SR.N6 and power-assisted rudder packs for both types.

The company is now a leader in the design of low-speed ducted propeller systems and, following the success of the propeller duct fitted to an SR.N6, a smaller unit with integral controls was made for the AV Tiger. Two larger units have been supplied to the United States for a military hovercraft.

Several studies involving the use of hoverbarges have been completed particularly for ship-to-shore operation, and an on-site survey has recently been undertaken in Indonesia.

Air Vehicles Ltd designed and commissioned the first hoverbarge to operate on the Yukon River, the 'Yukon Princess'.

The company has a major interest in two SR.N5 craft, GH 2009 and GH 2041. These craft have both been on charter, GH 2009 in Australia and GH 2041 on the Wash in England.

SR.N5 modified by Air Vehicles

AV Tiger, an 8-10 seat light hovercraft powered by a 3·5 litre Rover V.8 petrol engine

AV TIGER

Developed from the AV2 series, the AV Tiger employs a similar hull with inflated sidebodies and skirt. The craft is offered with either a single Rover V.8 3·5 litre engine or an AMC 360in^3 engine at 300lb extra weight. The additional horsepower of the AMC engine permits the same payload to be carried with the same performance.

LIFT AND PROPULSION: Motive power for integrated lift/propulsion system is provided by a single 3·5 litre Rover V8 petrol engine, delivering 150 DIN at 4,600rpm. Engine output is transferred to a 12-bladed centrifugal lift fan and a 1·37m (4ft 6in) diameter, four-bladed, ducted propeller through a notched belt system. Normal fuel capacity is 145 litres (32 imperial gallons); overload, 225 litres (50 imperial gallons). An alternative engine, the AMC 360, is offered which delivers 220hp maximum at 4,000 rpm.

CONTROLS: Multiple rudder vanes hinged at the aft end of the propeller duct provide directional control. Elevators provide trim, and when raised fully, assist braking by reducing thrust by 75%.

HULL: Superstructure and all bulkheads are of marine grade aluminium sheet welded to form a strong rigid box structure. Side members are inflatable, giving additional buoyancy and protection for the craft when mooring. By deflating

the side members the vehicle can be trailed behind any large car or small truck. Built-in jacking system provided for loading.
ACCOMMODATION: Enclosed cabin for driver and up to nine passengers. Access via hinged doors, one port, one starboard. The driver's seat is forward right; the navigator's forward left. Adequate space is provided for the installation of a radar scope, radios and navigation equipment ahead of these positions.
SKIRT: Pressurised bag skirt with separate segments. The inflatable sides and skirt are attached to the craft with quick-release nylon fasteners. On the production Tiger the size of the inflatable sides has been increased, giving greater hoverheight and improved performance over land.
SYSTEMS, ELECTRICAL: 12V dc, negative earth, with engine driven 35A alternator and 60Ah battery.
DIMENSIONS
Length: 6·94m (22ft 9in)
Width, inflated: 3·85m (12ft 6in)
Transport width: 2·44m (8ft)
Height, static: 2·5m (8ft 3in)
Hoverheight: 50-55cm (20-22in)
8 place cabin: 3 × 1·8m (10 × 6ft)
WEIGHTS
ROVER ENGINE
Empty: 1,000kg (2,200lb)
Max: 1,680kg (3,700lb)
Disposable load: 680kg (1,500lb)
PERFORMANCE
ROVER ENGINE
Max speed: 65km/h (35 knots)
Cruise speed: 46km/h (25 knots)
Max conditions: 46km/h (25 knot) wind, 1m (3ft) sea
Speed in 46km/h (25 knot) wind: 37km/h (20 knots)
Gradient climbing: 1 : 7 (standing start)
Fuel consumption, cruise: 21 litres/h (4·6 imperial gallons/h)
Max: 45 litres/h (9·8 imperial gallons/h)

AV TIGER S

A 'stretched' model of the Tiger, the Tiger S has a lengthened cabin seating 12-14 persons. Power is supplied by an AMC 410 automotive engine delivering 260hp maximum at 4,000 rpm. Performance is comparable with that of the standard version. The chief differences lie in the dimensions, weights and fuel consumption.
DIMENSIONS
EXTERNAL
Length: 8·1m (26ft 2in)
Width, inflated: 3·85m (12ft 6in)
INTERNAL
Cabin length: 3·9m (12ft 9in)
Width: 1·8m (6ft)
WEIGHTS
Empty: 1,136kg (2,500lb)
Maximum: 2,090kg (4,400lb)
Disposable load: 954kg (2,100lb)
PERFORMANCE
Fuel consumption, cruising: 26 litres/h (5·6 imperial gallons/h)
Max: 71 litres/h (15·5 imperial gallons/h)

AV **Tiger** showing the four-bladed ducted propeller

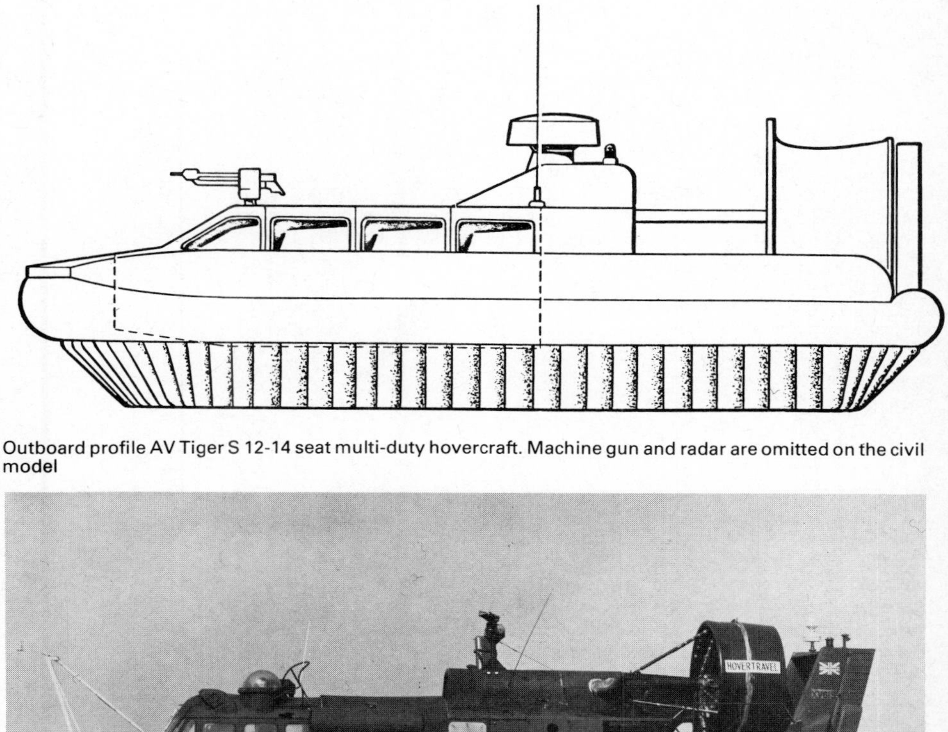
Outboard profile AV Tiger S 12-14 seat multi-duty hovercraft. Machine gun and radar are omitted on the civil model

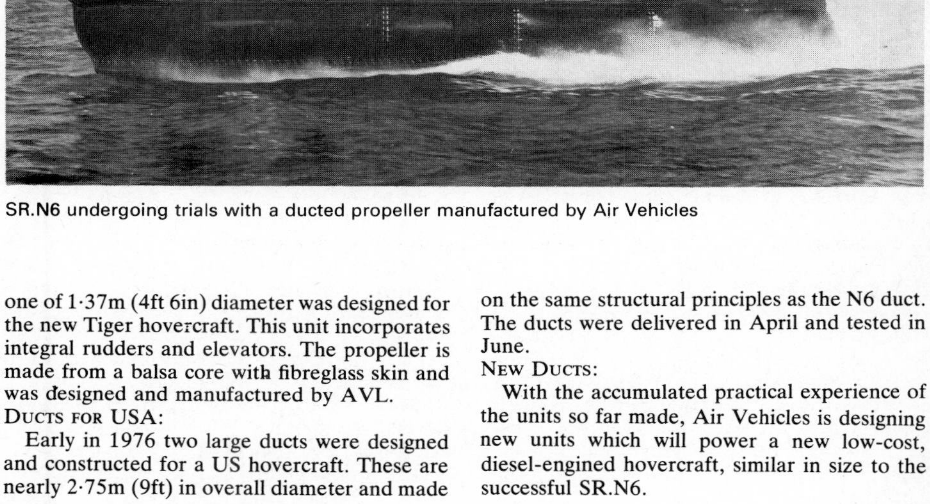

SR.N6 undergoing trials with a ducted propeller manufactured by Air Vehicles

DUCTED PROPELLERS

SR.N6:
The first ducted propeller unit designed for the N6 has proved capable of reducing noise by up to 12 dBA. During extensive trials, it was demonstrated that it would also augment static thrust, enabling the craft to negotiate steeper slopes. The propeller was that of the standard N6 but cropped to 2·08m (6ft 10in) diameter. The shape of the duct ensures that thrust is maintained at high angles of yaw. A set of integral rudders is being constructed which will give improved control over the standard N6 and dispense with the existing tail unit.
AV TIGER:
Following the success of the N6 duct, a smaller one of 1·37m (4ft 6in) diameter was designed for the new Tiger hovercraft. This unit incorporates integral rudders and elevators. The propeller is made from a balsa core with fibreglass skin and was designed and manufactured by AVL.
DUCTS FOR USA:
Early in 1976 two large ducts were designed and constructed for a US hovercraft. These are nearly 2·75m (9ft) in overall diameter and made on the same structural principles as the N6 duct. The ducts were delivered in April and tested in June.
NEW DUCTS:
With the accumulated practical experience of the units so far made, Air Vehicles is designing new units which will power a new low-cost, diesel-engined hovercraft, similar in size to the successful SR.N6.

BRITISH HOVERCRAFT CORPORATION

East Cowes, Isle of Wight, England
Telephone: 098 382 4101
Telex: 86190
Officials:
Sir Christopher Hartley, KCB, CBE, DFC, AFC, BA, *Chairman*
B D Blackwell, MA, BSc(Eng), CEng, FIMechE, FRAeS, FBIM, *Deputy Chairman*
R Stanton-Jones, MA, DCAe, CEng, AFRAeS, *Managing Director*
R L Wheeler, MSc, DIC, CEng, AFRAeS, *Technical Director*
J M George, BSc(Eng), DCAe, *Sales Director*
J McGarity, *Works Director*
T Bretherton, *Finance and Secretary*
W A Oppenheimer, FCA, *Director*
G S Hislop, PhD, BSc, ARCST, CEng, FIMechE, FRAeS, FRSA, *Director*

The British Hovercraft Corporation is the world's largest hovercraft manufacturer. It was formed in 1966 to concentrate the British hovercraft industry's major technical and other resources under a single management.

The corporation deals with a wide variety of applications of the air cushion principle, the emphasis being on the development and production of amphibious hovercraft. Other activities include the investigation of industrial applications of the air cushion principle.

The capital of the corporation is £5 million, which is wholly owned by Westland Aircraft Ltd.

BHC established the world's first full-scale hovercraft production line in 1964. Currently it is producing the 10-ton Winchester (SR.N6) Class craft, the 50-ton Wellington (BH.7) Class craft and the 200-300-ton Mountbatten (SR.N4) Class craft at East Cowes.

At present six Mountbatten Class craft are in service as passenger/car ferries on the Dover/Boulogne and Ramsgate/Calais routes; two with British Rail Hovercraft, and four with Hoverlloyd Ltd.

All four Hoverlloyd craft have been converted to Mk 2 standard, one of the Seaspeed craft has been converted from Mk 1 to Mk 3 (Super 4) standard and the remaining Seaspeed craft is currently undergoing conversion at BHC. It will be redelivered as a Super 4 in time for the 1979 summer season.

The first Super 4 craft, "The Princess Anne", was delivered to British Rail Hovercraft Limited's Seaspeed service on 6 April 1978 and entered service on the Dover-Boulogne-Calais routes on 9 July. During the first six weeks of operation the craft carried more than 100,000 passengers and over 12,000 vehicles. At 300 tons all-up weight Super 4 is the world's largest hovercraft. It has a payload of 418 passengers and 60 vehicles, a cruising speed of 55 knots and a maximum speed of 65 knots.

One BH.7 is in service with the Royal Navy's Naval Hovercraft Trials Unit and six have been delivered to the Imperial Iranian Navy.

Military and general duty variants of the Warden and Winchester Class hovercraft are now in service with the Naval Hovercraft Trials Unit, Imperial Iranian Navy, Italian Interservice Hovercraft Unit, Egyptian Navy and the Canadian and Saudi Arabian Coast Guard.

Winchesters have been employed since 1967 in trials and sales demonstrations in Africa, Canada, Denmark, Finland, India, South America and the Middle and Far East, logging well over 200,000 operating hours.

Commercial general purpose variants of the Warden and Winchester are in service with Solent Seaspeed Ltd, Department of Civil Aviation, New Zealand, Department of Transport, Canada, Hovertravel Ltd and Hoverwork Ltd. In recent years the Winchester has been used increasingly for general purpose roles including hydrographic and seismic survey, freighting and search and rescue duties.

British Rail Seaspeed's 300-ton Super 4 "The Princess Anne", the world's biggest hovercraft. A lengthened and refitted BHC SR.N4, the craft entered service on the Dover/Boulogne/Calais route on 9 July 1978. Seaspeed's second SR.N4, "The Princess Margaret", is undergoing similar conversion to Mk 3 standard and is expected to return to Dover in the spring of 1979.

Seaspeed's BHC Super 4, with its 16·76m (55ft) section amidships and widened superstructure, seen alongside Seaspeed's SR.N4 Mk 1, "The Princess Margaret", at the new Dover Hoverport before the craft was returned to Cowes for the 'stretching' operation

MOUNTBATTEN (SR.N4) CLASS Mk 2

The SR.N4 Mk 2 is a 200-ton passenger/car ferry designed for stage lengths of up to 184km (100n miles) on coastal water routes. It has an average service speed of 40-50 knots in waves up to 3·04m (10ft) in height and is able to operate in 3·7m (12ft) seas at a speed of about 20 knots.

LIFT AND PROPULSION: Power is supplied by four 3,400shp Rolls-Royce Marine Proteus free-turbine, turboshaft engines located in pairs at the rear of the craft on either side of the vehicle deck. Each has a maximum rating of 4,250shp, but usually operates at 3,400shp when cruising. Each engine is connected to one of four identical propeller/fan units, two forward and two aft. The propulsion propellers, made by Hawker Siddeley Dynamics, are of the four-bladed, variable and reversible pitch type 5·79m (19ft) in diameter. The lift fans, made by BHC, are of the 12-bladed centrifugal type, 3·5m (11ft 6in) in diameter.

Since the gear ratios between the engine, fan and propeller are fixed, the power distribution can be altered by varying the propeller pitch and hence changing the speed of the system, which accordingly alters the power absorbed by the fixed pitch fan. The power absorbed by the fan can be varied from almost zero shp (ie boating with minimum power) to 2,100shp, within the propeller and engine speed limitations. A typical division on maximum cruise power would be 2,000shp to the propeller and 1,150shp to the fan; the remaining 250shp can be accounted for by engine power fall-off due to the turbine rpm drop, transmission losses and auxiliary drives.

The drive shafts from the engine consist of flanged light-alloy tubes approximately 2·28m (7ft 6in) long supported by steady bearings and connected by self-aligning couplings. Shafting to the rear propeller/fan units is comparatively short, but to the forward units is approximately 18·27m (60ft).

The main gearbox of each unit comprises a spiral bevel reduction gear, with outputs at the top and bottom of the box to the vertical propeller and fan drive shafts respectively. The design of the vertical shafts and couplings is similar to the main transmission shafts, except that the shafts above the main gearbox are of steel instead of light alloy to transmit the much greater torque loads to the propeller. This gearbox is equipped with a power take-off for an auxiliary gearbox with drives for pressure and scavenge lubricating oil pumps, and also a hydraulic pump for the pylon and fin steering control.

The upper gearbox, mounted on top of the pylon, turns the propeller drive through 90 degrees and has a gear ratio of 1·16:1. This gearbox has its own self-contained lubricating system.

Engines and auxiliaries are readily accessible for maintenance from inside the craft, while engine, propellers, pylons and all gearboxes can be removed for overhaul without disturbing the main structure.

The fan rotates on a pintle which is attached to the main structure. The assembly may be detached and removed inboard onto the car deck without disturbing the major structure.

CONTROLS: The craft control system enables the thrust lines and pitch angles of the propellers to be varied either collectively or differentially. The fins and rudders move in step with the aft pylons. The pylons, fins and rudders move through ±35 degrees, ±30 degrees and ±40 degrees respectively. On Hoverlloyd's craft the rudders have been deleted and on Seaspeed's craft the rudders have been locked relative to the fins.

Demand signals for pylon and fin angles are transmitted from the commander's controls electrically. These are compared with the pylon or fin feed-back signals and the differences are then amplified to actuate the hydraulic jacks mounted at the base of the pylon or fin structure. Similar electro-hydraulic signalling and feed-back systems are used to control propeller pitches.

The commander's controls include a rudder bar which steers the craft by pivoting the propeller pylons differentially.

For example, if the right foot is moved forward, the forward pylons move clockwise, viewed from above, and the aft pylons and fins move anticlockwise, thus producing a turning movement to starboard. The foregoing applies with positive thrust on the propellers, but if negative thrust is applied, as in the case of using the propellers for braking, the pylons and fins are automatically turned to opposing angles, thus maintaining the turn. A wheel mounted on a control column enables the commander to move the pylons and fins in unison to produce a drift to either port or starboard as required. The control of the distribution of power between each propeller and fan is by propeller pitch lever. The pitch of all four propellers can be adjusted collectively over a limited range by a fore-and-aft movement of the control wheel.

HULL: Construction is primarily of high strength, aluminium-clad, aluminium alloy, suitably protected against the corrosive effects of sea water.

The basic structure is the buoyancy chamber, built around a grid of longitudinal and transversal frames, which form 24 watertight sub-divisions for safety. The design ensures that even a rip from end-to-end would not cause the craft to sink or overturn. The reserve buoyancy is 250%, the total available buoyancy amounting to more than 550 tons.

Top and bottom surfaces of the buoyancy chamber are formed by sandwich construction panels bolted onto the frames, the top surface being the vehicle deck. Panels covering the central 4·9m (16ft) section of the deck are reinforced to carry unladen coaches, or commercial vehicles up to 9 tons gross weight (maximum axle load 5,900kg (13,000lb)), while the remainder are designed solely to carry cars and light vehicles (maximum axle load 2,040kg (4,500lb)). An articulated loading ramp, 5·5m (18ft) wide, which can be lowered to ground level, is built into the bows, while doors extending the full width of the centre deck are provided at the aft end.

Similar grid construction is used on the elevated passenger-carrying decks and the roof, where the panels are supported by deep transverse and longitudinal frames. The buoyancy chamber is joined to the roof by longitudinal walls to form a stiff fore-and-aft structure. Lateral bending is taken mainly by the buoyancy tanks. All horizontal surfaces are of pre-fabricated sandwich panels with the exception of the roof, which is of skin and stringer panels.

Double curvature has been avoided other than in the region of the air intakes and bow. Each fan

Interior of the main starboard cabin amidships on the BHC Super 4, "The Princess Anne". Payload of the Super 4 is 54-60 cars and up to 418 passengers

Hoverlloyd's SR.N4 Mk 2 Swift, en route to Calais in Sea State 4

air intake is bifurcated and has an athwartships bulkhead at both front and rear, supporting a beam carrying the transmission main gearbox and the propeller pylon. The all-moving fins and rudders behind the aft pylons pivot on pintles just ahead of the rear bulkhead.

The fans deliver air to the cushion via a peripheral fingered bag skirt.

The material used for both bags and fingers is nylon, coated with neoprene and/or natural rubber, the fingers and cones being made from a heavier weight material than the trunks.

ACCOMMODATION: The basic manning requirement is for a commander, an engineer/radio operator and a radar operator/navigator. A seat is provided for a fourth crew member or a crew member in training. The remainder of the crew, ie those concerned with passenger service or car handling, are located in the main cabins. The arrangement may be modified to suit individual operator's requirements.

The control cabin is entered by either of two ways. The normal method, when the cars are arranged in four lanes, is by a hatch in the cabin floor, reached by a ladder from the car deck. When heavy vehicles are carried on the centre section, or if for some other reason the ladder has to be retracted, a door in the side of the port forward passenger cabin gives access to a ladder leading onto the main cabin roof. From the roof an entrance door gives access into the control cabin.

The craft currently in service carry 282 passengers and 37 cars.

The car deck occupies the large central area of the craft, with large stern doors and a bow ramp providing a drive-on/drive-off facility.

Separate side doors give access to the passenger cabins which flank the car deck. The outer cabins have large windows which extend over the full length of the craft. The control cabin is sited centrally and forward on top of the superstructure to give maximum view.

DIMENSIONS

EXTERNAL

Overall length: 39·68m (130ft 2in)

Overall beam: 23·77m (78ft)

Overall height on landing pads: 11·48m (37ft 8in)

Skirt depth: 2·44m (8ft)

INTERNAL

Passenger/vehicle floor area: 539m² (5,800ft²)

Vehicle deck headroom-centre line: 3·43m (11ft 3in)

Bow ramp door aperture size (height × width): 3·51 × 5·48m (11ft 6in × 18ft)

Stern door aperture size (height × width): 3·51 × 9·45m (11ft 6in × 31ft)

WEIGHTS

Normal gross: 200 tons

Fuel capacity: 20·456 litres (4,500 imperial gallons)

PERFORMANCE (at normal gross weight at 15°C)

Max waterspeed over calm water, zero wind (cont power rating): 70 knots

Average service waterspeed: 40-60 knots

Normal stopping distance from 50 knots: 480m (525 yards)

Endurance at max cont power on 2,800 imperial gallons: 2·5 hours

Negotiable gradient from standing start: 1 : 11

SR.N4 Mk 3 'SUPER 4'

The Super 4 differs from earlier Marks of the SR.N4 primarily in that it is 16·76m (55ft) longer, increasing the overall length to 56·38m (185ft) with a beam of 28·04m (92ft).

Modification of an SR.N4 Mk 1 to Super 4 standard necessitates adding a new 16·76m (55ft) section amidships, widening the existing superstructure and strengthening the original bow and stern halves to accept the increased stresses resulting from the 40% increase in length. The propeller pylons are raised to allow 6·4m (21ft) diameter propellers to be fitted, the transmission systems are realigned and four uprated 3,800shp Rolls-Royce Marine Proteus gas-turbines are installed.

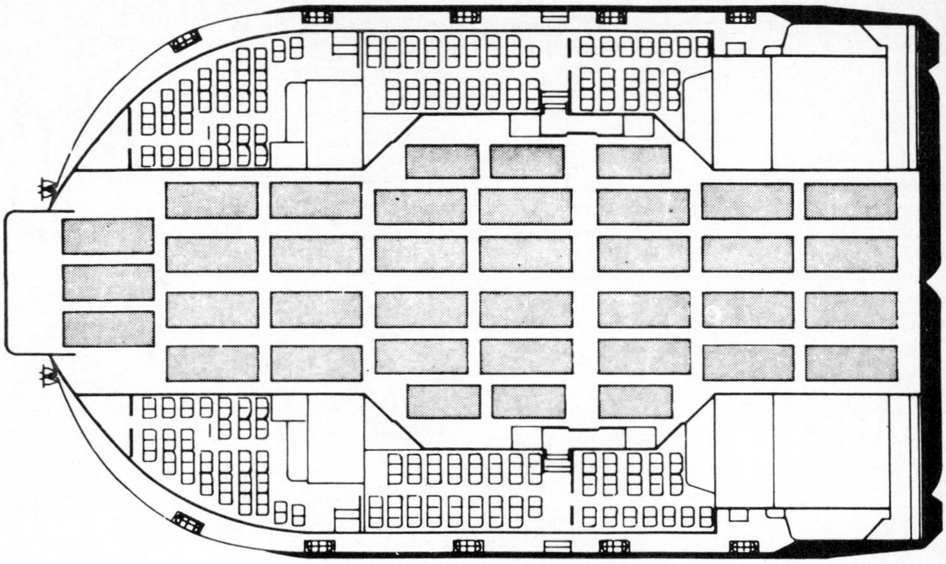

SR.N4 configuration with space for 37 vehicles and 282 passengers

"The Prince of Wales," the fourth 200-ton SR.N4 Mk 2 mixed-traffic hovercraft to be delivered to Hoverlloyd Limited. The craft began operation on the company's Ramsgate-Calais service on 18 June 1977, permitting the number of daily services in each direction to be increased to 27 in high summer. With the addition of the fourth craft, Hoverlloyd has the capacity to carry up to 15,000 passengers and 2,000 vehicles daily.

Coach being loaded via the 9·45m (31ft) wide stern doors

A more efficient low pressure ratio skirt system with larger fingers is fitted, giving a mean air cushion depth of 2·7m (9ft). Passenger cabin trim and seating have been completely revised and sound-proofing increased.

Compared with the SR.N4 Mk 1, the Super 4 has a 70% greater revenue earning capability, but costs only about 15% more to operate. The increased length and advanced skirt system give both a higher performance in adverse weather and greatly improved ride comfort for the passengers.

Craft handling and skirt behaviour have proved entirely satisfactory over the entire weight range from 212 to 300 tons in sea conditions up to Force 7. Measurements taken in the passenger cabins of acceleration forces show a three-fold improvement in ride comfort over the SR.N4 Mk 2. The uprated Rolls-Royce Proteus gas-turbines have been completely trouble-free and the new propellers have substantially reduced external noise when operating into and out of hovercraft terminals.

Super 4 has a payload of 418 passengers and 60 vehicles, a laden weight of 300 tons and a top speed in excess of 65 knots.

LIFT AND PROPULSION: Motive power is supplied by four Rolls-Royce Marine Proteus Type 15M/529 free-turbine turboshaft engines, located in pairs at the rear of the craft on either side of the vehicle deck. Each engine is rated at 3,800shp continuous under ISA conditions and is connected to one of four identical propeller/fan units, two forward and two aft. The propellers, made by Hawker Siddeley Dynamics, are of four-bladed, controllable-pitch type D258/485A/2. The lift fans, made by BHC, are of 12-bladed centrifugal type, 3·5m (11ft 6in) in diameter. Maximum fuel tankage, 28·45 tonnes; normal fuel allowing for ballast transfer, 18·29 tonnes.

AUXILIARY POWER: Two Lucas turboshaft engines driving 55kVA 200V, 400Hz Lucas alternators.

DIMENSIONS

Length overall: 56·38m (185ft)

Beam, hardstructure: 23·16m (76ft)

Height overall, on landing pads: 11·43m (37ft 6in)

Bow ramp door aperture size,

Height: 3·5m (11ft 6in)

Width: 5·48m (18ft)

Stern door aperture size,

Height: 3·51m (11ft 6in)

Width: 9·45m (31ft)

Car deck area: 631m² (6,790ft²)

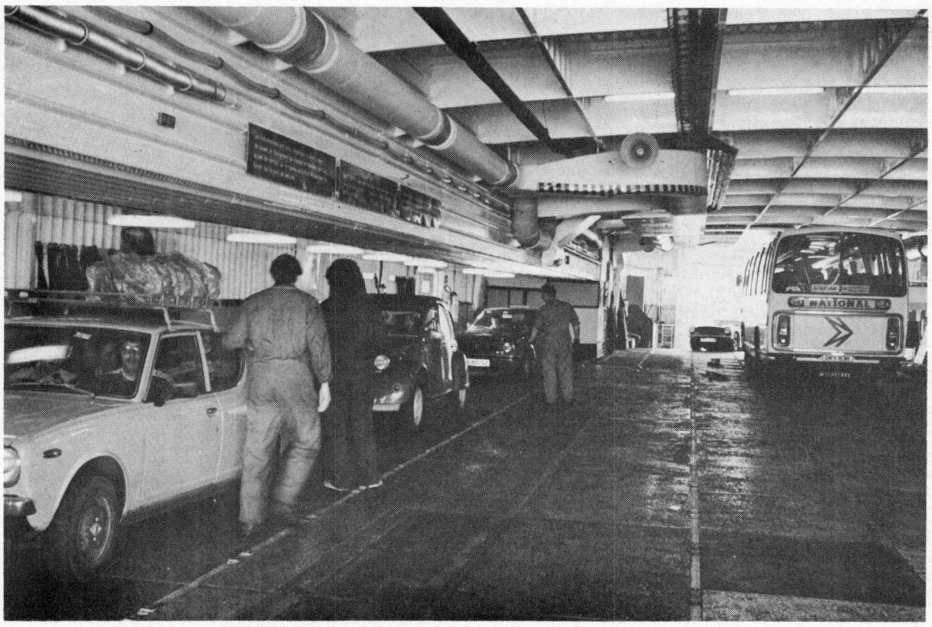

Panels covering the central 4·9m (16ft) of the vehicle decks are reinforced to carry unladen coaches or commercial vehicles of up to 9 tons gross weight while the remainder of the deck is designed solely to carry cars and light vehicles

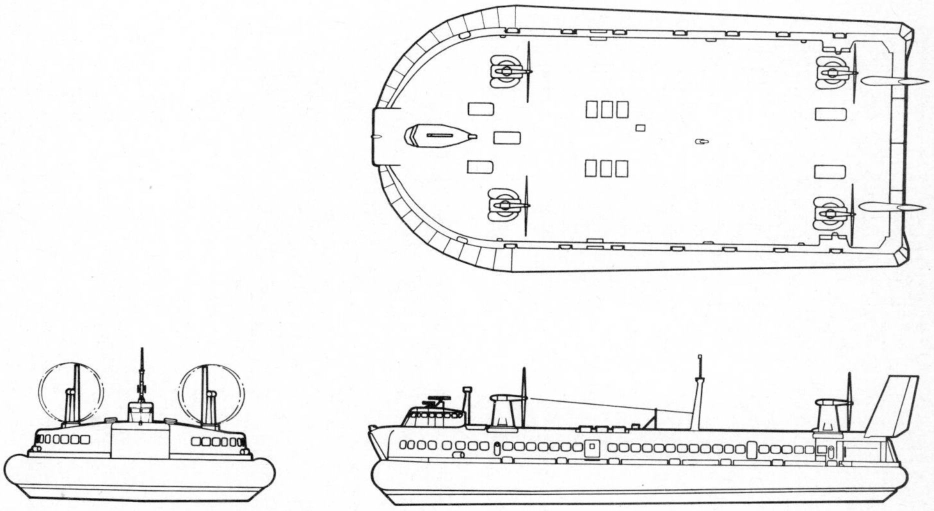

General arrangement of the SR.N4 Mk 3 'Super 4'

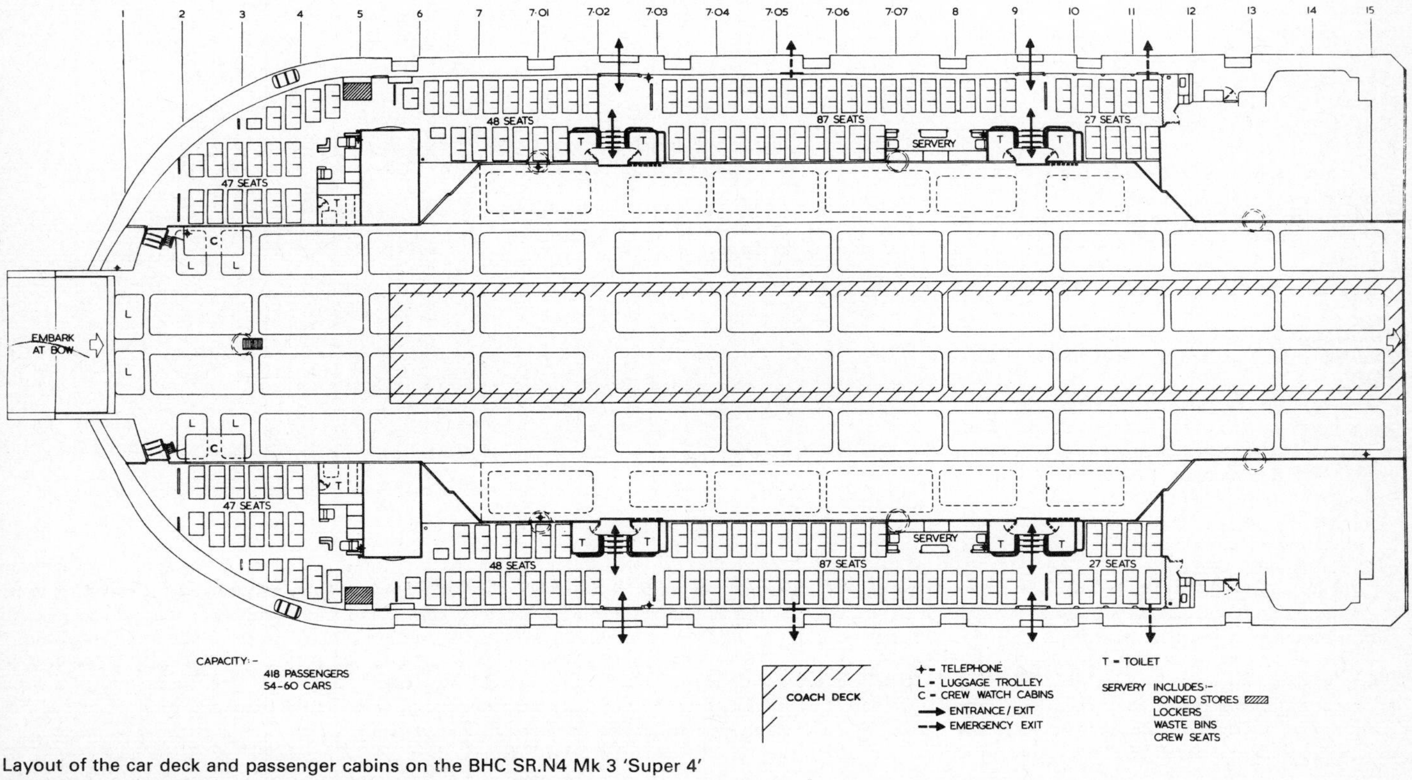

Layout of the car deck and passenger cabins on the BHC SR.N4 Mk 3 'Super 4'

Typical cruising speeds over water of the BHC Super 4 are 60-65 knots in calm seas, 50-55 knots in moderate seas and 35-45 knots in rough seas. Larger skirt fingers are fitted giving a mean air cushion depth of 2·7m (9ft). Accelerometer measurements in the passenger cabins show a three-fold improvement in ride comfort over the SR.N4 Mk 2

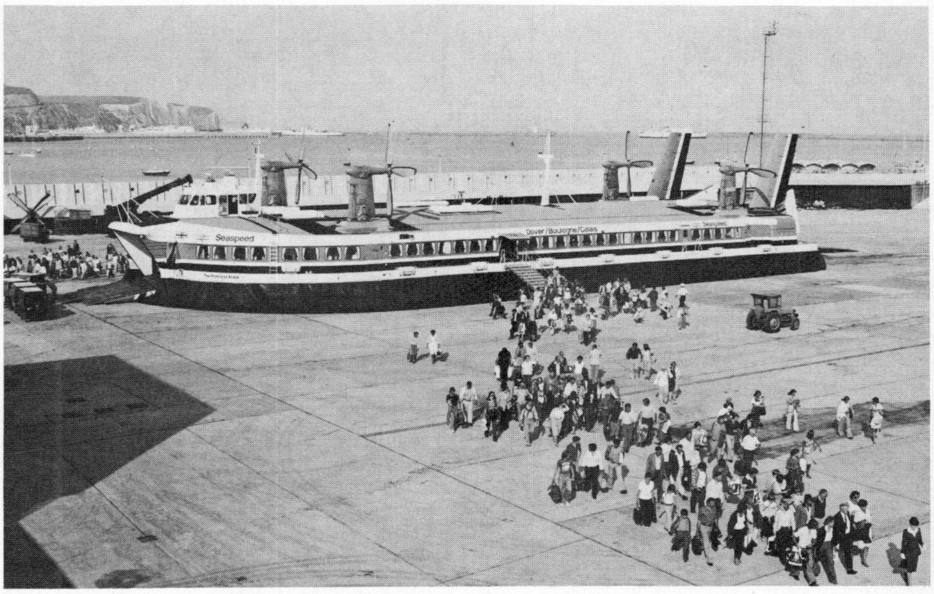

BHC's Super 4 has a payload of 418 passengers and up to 60 cars

One of three SR.N6s operated by the Royal Navy's Hovercraft Trials Unit, Lee-on-the-Solent. This particular variant is a Mk 2

WEIGHTS
Max laden: 300 tons
Max disposable load: 112 tons
Typical fuel load: 20 tons
Payload: 54-60 cars, 418 passengers
PERFORMANCE
Typical cruise waterspeeds:
Calm (2ft waves, 5 knots wind): 60-65 knots
Moderate (5ft waves, 20 knots wind): 50-55 knots
Rough (8ft waves, 27 knots wind): 35-45 knots
Endurance per ton of fuel: 0·23 hours

WINCHESTER (SR.N6) CLASS

Designed primarily as a fast ferry for operation in sheltered waters, the Winchester can accommodate either 38 passengers or 3 tons of freight.

Fully amphibious, it can operate from relatively unsophisticated bases above the high water mark, irrespective of tidal state.

Directional control is achieved by twin rudders and a thrust port system. Two manually actuated elevators provide pitch trim at cruising speed.

Winchesters have been in regular commercial service since 1965. Current operators include Hovertravel Ltd, Hoverwork Ltd and Solent Seaspeed. A further Winchester is in service with the Civil Aviation Department, Ministry of Transport, New Zealand, as a crash rescue craft at Auckland International Airport. Both the Winchester and its smaller, 7-ton predecessor, the SR.N5 (see *Jane's Surface Skimmers 1971-72* and earlier editions) are in service with the Canadian Coast Guard.

Military variants are in service with the Royal Navy's Hovercraft Trials Unit, the Imperial Iranian Navy, Italian Navy and the Saudi Arabian Frontier Force and Coast Guard.

LIFT AND PROPULSION: Power for the integrated lift/propulsion system is provided by a Rolls-Royce Marine Gnome gas-turbine with a maximum continuous rating at 15°C of 900shp. This drives a BHC 12-blade centrifugal 2·13m (7ft) diameter lift fan, and a Dowty Rotol four blade variable pitch 2·74m (9ft) diameter propeller for propulsion.

DIMENSIONS
EXTERNAL
Overall length: 14·8m (48ft 6in)
Overall beam, skirt inflated: 7·7m (25ft 4in)
Overall height on landing pads: 3·8m (12ft 6in)
Height hovering: 5m (16ft 6in)
Skirt depth: 1·22m (4ft)
INTERNAL
Cabin size (length × width): 6·62 × 2·34m (21ft 9in × 7ft 8in)
Cabin headroom-centre line: 1·83m (6ft)
Door aperture size (height × width): 1·75m × 0·99m (5ft 9in × 3ft 3in)
WEIGHTS
Normal gross: 10 tons
PERFORMANCE (at normal gross weight at 15°C)
Max water speed over calm water zero wind, (cont power rating): 96km/h (52 knots)
Average service waterspeed in sheltered coastal waters: 55·65km/h (30·35 knots)
Endurance at max continuous power rating on 265 imperial gallons of fuel: 3·6 hours

WINCHESTER (SR.N6) CLASS—PASSENGER FERRY/GENERAL PURPOSE

Since the SR.N6 first entered service as a passenger ferry in 1965, it has carried well over three million fare-paying passengers and is now firmly established in certain areas as an integral part of surface transport networks.

The popularity of these services subsequently led to the introduction of an SR.N6 with a larger carrying capacity, designated the SR.N6 Mk 1S. At 58ft in length, the Mk 1S is 10ft longer than the standard craft and can carry up to 58 passengers as opposed to 35-38 in the standard SR.N6.

Other modifications to this craft include additional baggage panniers, emergency exits and improved cabin ventilation. An additional bonus is a significant increase in ride comfort. To ensure that performance is maintained, the rating of the Rolls-Royce Marine Gnome gas turbine engine has been increased by 100shp to 1,000shp.

Two Mk 1S craft are in service with Solent Seaspeed Ltd, linking Cowes and Southampton, and one Mk 1S is in operation on the Ryde/Southsea route with Hovertravel Limited.

Apart from passenger services, commercial SR.N6s have also made successful inroads into other fields of operation in recent years and typical examples of such applications include freight-carrying, hydrographic/seismographic survey, offshore support operations, general communications, crash rescue and firefighting.

To undertake these duties, craft have been modified either with the fitting of specialised equipment or by structural alterations such as flat-decks.

WINCHESTER (SR.N6) CLASS—MILITARY

Currently, variants of the SR.N6 are in service with a number of the world's military and paramilitary forces on coastal defence and logistic support duties.

The SR.N6 Mk 2/3, for logistic support, features a roof loading hatch and strengthened side-decks for carrying long loads of up to ½ ton. Lightweight armour may be fitted to protect troops being carried in the cabin; the engine; and other vital systems. Defensive armament is provided by a roof-mounted light machine gun (7·62mm or 0·5in).

The craft can carry upwards of 20 fully-equipped troops or supply loads of up to 5 tons. A small auxiliary generator is installed to provide power when the main engine is stopped.

The SR.N6 Mk 4 for coastal defence duties may be fitted with 20mm cannon or short-range wire-guided surface/surface missiles. Communications equipment is concentrated behind the rear cabin bulkhead.

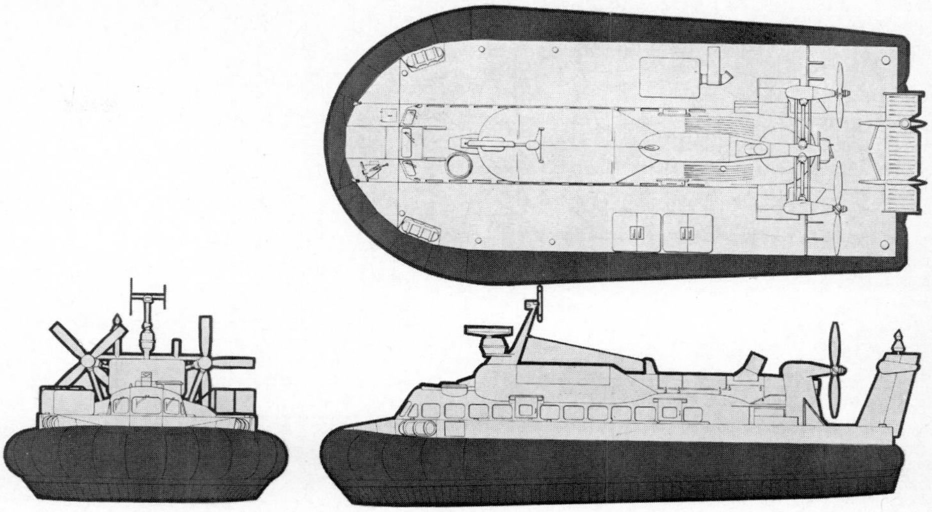

General arrangement of the SR.N6 Mk 6

SR.N6 Mk 6 GENERAL PURPOSE

The SR.N6 Mk 6 is the latest development in the successful Winchester series and represents significant steps forward in terms of increased payload, all-weather performance, and increased manoeuvrability, especially in high winds and at low speeds. There is also a significant reduction in the external noise level.

These advances have been achieved by the introduction of twin propellers for thrust, a more powerful engine, wider sidedecks and a redesigned skirt for better seakeeping capabilities. The tapered skirt, which is deeper at the bow than the stern, cushions the effect of operating over larger waves and surface obstacles and enables the craft to operate in winds of up to Beaufort Scale 8 and waves of up to 3·04m (10ft).

The craft, with its large cabin, can carry up to 55 passengers or between five and six tons of equipment. Various options are available including air-conditioning and VIP interior trim.

LIFT AND PROPULSION: Motive power is supplied by a single 1,125hp Rolls-Royce Marine Gnome GN 1301 gas-turbine driving a single 2·13m (7ft) diameter BHC lift fan and two 3·05m (10ft) diameter Dowty Rotol variable-pitch propellers. Maximum fuel capacity is 4,840 litres (1,065 imperial gallons).

DIMENSIONS

Length overall: 18·3m (60ft)

Beam overall: 8·5m (28ft)

Height overall, on landing pads: 5·6m (18ft 4in)
on cushion: 6·7m (22ft)

WEIGHTS

Max operating: 17,010kg (37,500lb)

PERFORMANCE

Max speed over calm water: 60 knots

Fuel consumption: 410 litres/h (90 imperial gallons/h)

One of two BH.7 Mk 4s operated by the Imperial Iranian Navy. The craft are employed on logistics duties and have bow loading doors

WELLINGTON (BH.7) CLASS

BH.7 is a 50-ton hovercraft which was designed specifically for naval and military roles. The prototype, designated BH.7 Mk 2, has been in service with the Royal Navy since 1970 where it has been evaluated in a number of roles including Fishery Protection, ASW and MCM work.

The second and third craft, designated Mk 4 and a further four Mk 5As, are all in service with the Imperial Iranian Navy.

LIFT AND PROPULSION: Power for the integrated lift propulsion system on the Mk 2 and Mk 4 is provided by a Rolls-Royce Marine Proteus 15M541 gas-turbine with a maximum rating at 23°C of 4,250shp. On the Mk 5A, a 15M549 is installed with a maximum rating of 4,250shp. In both types the engine drives, via a light alloy driveshaft and bevel drive gearbox, a BHC 12-blade, centrifugal 3·5m (11ft 6in) diameter lift fan and an HSD four-blade, variable-pitch pylon-mounted propeller. Propeller diameter on the Mk 4 is 5·79m (19ft) and 6·4m (21ft) on the Mk 2 and Mk 5A. Normal fuel capacity is up to 3,000 imperial gallons.

CONTROLS: Craft direction is controlled by swivelling the propeller pylon angle by a footpedal. Thrust ports are fitted at each quarter to assist directional control at low speed, and a hydraulically-operated skirt-shift system helps to bank the craft into turns, thereby reducing drift.

Fuel is transferred between forward and aft tanks via a ring main to adjust fore and aft trim.

HULL: Construction is mainly of corrosion resistant light alloy. Extensive use is made of components which were designed for the N4. The bow structure is a Plasticell base covered with glass fibre.

SKIRT: The fan delivers air to the cushion via a continuous peripheral fingered bag skirt made in neoprene coated nylon fabric. The skirt provides an air cushion depth of 1·68m (5ft 6in). The cushion is divided into four compartments by a full length longitudinal keel and by two transverse keels located slightly forward of amidships.

ACCOMMODATION: The raised control cabin, located slightly forward of amidships on the hull centre line, accommodates a crew of three, with the driver and navigator/radar operator in front and the third crew member behind. The driver sits on the right, with the throttle and propeller pitch control lever on his right, and the pylon angle footpedal and skirt-shift column in front.

The navigator, on the left, has a Decca radar display (Type 914 on the Mk 5) and compass in front and Decometers in an overhead panel.

The large main cabin area permits a variety of operational layouts. In a typical arrangement, the operations room is placed directly beneath the control cabin and contains communication, navigation, search and strike equipment and associated displays.

The craft has an endurance of up to 11 hours under cruise conditions but this can be extended considerably as it can stay 'on watch' without using the main engine.

Provision can be made for the crew to live aboard for several days.

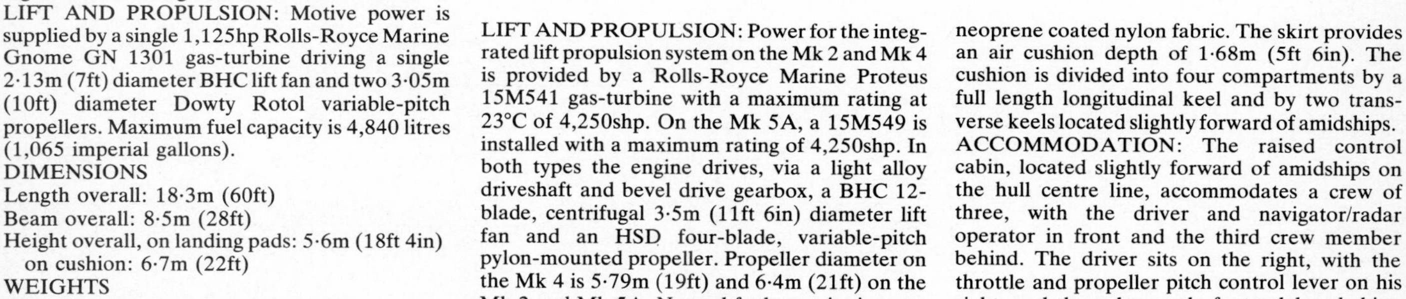

BHC's SR.N6 Mk 6 general purpose hovercraft, showing the twin-propeller arrangement and tapered skirt. Up to 55 passengers can be carried or between 5 and 6 tons of equipment.

SYSTEMS, ELECTRICAL: Two Rover IS/90 APUs provide via two 55kVA generators three-phase 400Hz ac at 200V for ac and dc supplies.
DIMENSIONS
EXTERNAL
Length overall: 23·9m (78ft 4in)
Beam overall: 13·8m (45ft 6in)
Overall height on landing pads: 10·36m (34ft)
Skirt depth: 1·67m (5ft 6in)
INTERNAL (Mk 4 only)
Bow door size: 4·18 × 2·2m (13ft 9in × 7ft 3in)
Headroom centre line: 2·38m (7ft 10in)
WEIGHTS
Normal gross: 50 tons
Payload: 14 tons
PERFORMANCE (at max operating weight at 15°C)
Max waterspeed over calm water (continuous power rating): 60 knots
Average water speed in 1·37m (4½ft) seas: 35·5 knots

WELLINGTON (BH.7) Mk 4 LOGISTIC SUPPORT

ACCOMMODATION: In this role, the main hold floor area of 56m² (600ft²) of the Mk 4 provides an unobstructed space suitable for loading wheeled vehicles, guns and military stores.

Two side cabins, filled with paratroop-type seats, can accommodate up to 60 troops and their equipment.

Access at the bow is through a "clamshell" door.

Machine guns can be fitted in gun rings on the roof on either side of the cabin and provision can be made for armour plating to protect personnel, the engine and vital electrical components.

SYSTEMS, ELECTRICAL: Two Rover IS/90 gas turbine APUs provide electrical power independently of the main engine.

TYPICAL MILITARY LOADS: 170 fully equipped troops or 3 field cars and trailers plus 60 troops or two armoured scout cars or up to 20 NATO pallets.

DIMENSIONS
EXTERNAL
Overall length: 23·85m (78ft 4in)
Overall beam: 13·8m (45ft 6in)
Overall height on landing pads: 10·06m (33ft)
INTERNAL
Main cabin floor area: 56m² (600ft²)
Main cabin headroom—centreline: 2·38m (7ft 10in)
Access door aperture (height × width): 2·2 × 4·2m (7ft 3in × 13ft 9in)
WEIGHTS
Normal gross: 45 tons
Fuel load at 45 tons all-up weight: 9 tons
Max fuel capacity: 12·5 tons
PERFORMANCE (at normal gross weight at 15°C)
Max waterspeed, calm water, zero wind, continuous power rating: 120 km/h (65 knots)
Rough waterspeed in 1·37m (4ft 6in) seas (depending on heading and wave length): 65-92km/h (35-50 knots)
Endurance at max continuous power rating with 9 tons of fuel (with 10% reserve): 8 hours

WELLINGTON (BH.7) Mk 5 COMBAT

Designed for coastal defence operations, the BH.7 Mk 5 carries medium-range surface/surface missiles, such as Exocet, on its sidedecks. Secondary armament consists of a twin 30mm surface/AA radar controlled mounting situated on the foredeck forward of the main centre cabin.

The main central cabin, employed on the BH.7 Mk 4 for load-carrying, is equipped as an operations and fire control room. Since it is fully amphibious, the BH.7 Mk 5 can be operated from relatively unprepared bases on beaches and can head directly towards its target on interception missions regardless of the tidal state and marginal terrain. Also, since none of its solid structure is immersed, it is invulnerable to underwater defences such as acoustic, magnetic and pressure mines and to attack by torpedoes.

A full range of electronic navigational aids permit the craft to operate by day or night ensuring 'round-the-clock' availability.

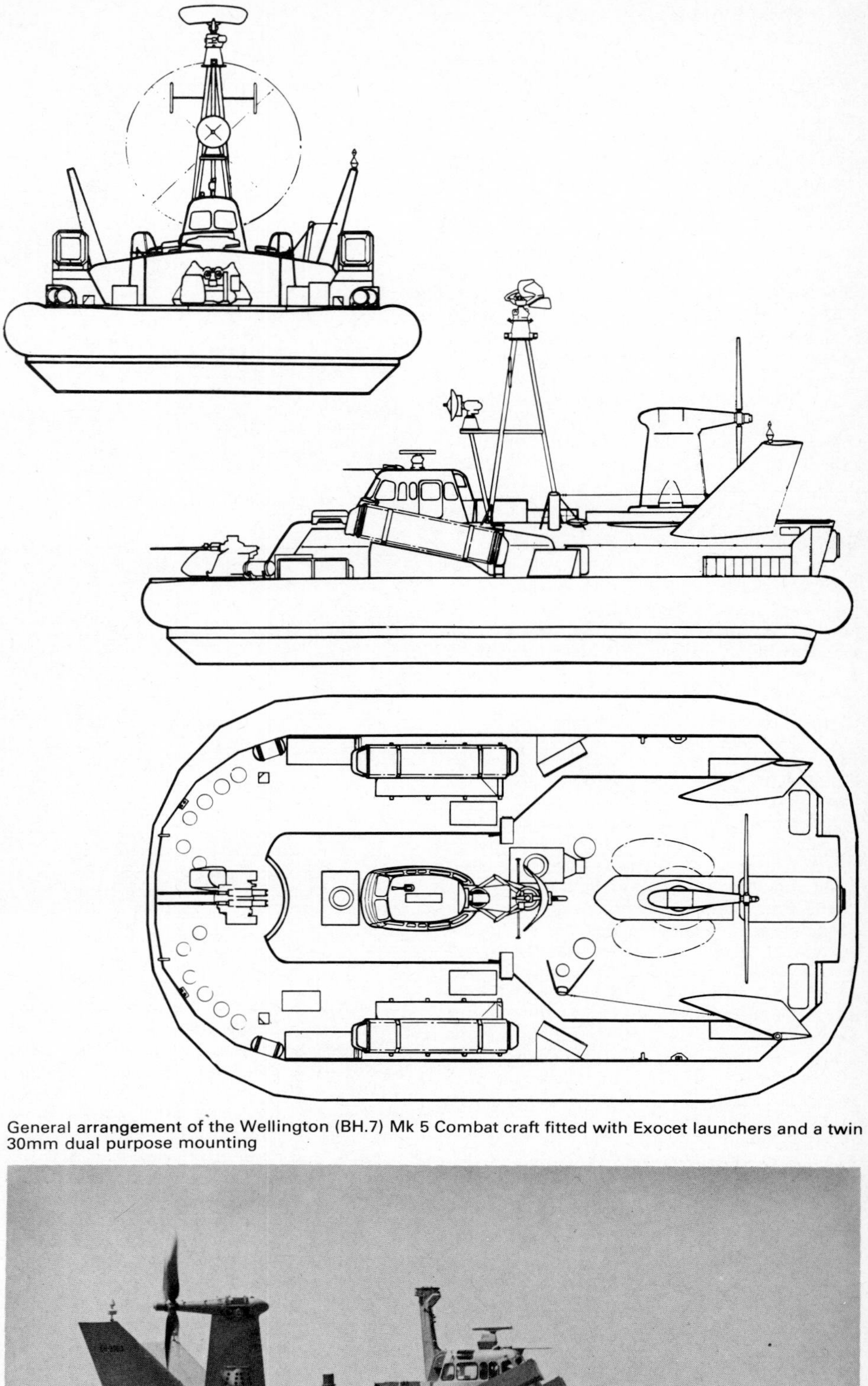

General arrangement of the Wellington (BH.7) Mk 5 Combat craft fitted with Exocet launchers and a twin 30mm dual purpose mounting

Wellington Mk 5A combat/logistic support craft. This particular variant carries medium range ship-to-ship missiles, such as Exocet, on its sidedecks and retains the bow loading door of the Mk 4

WELLINGTON (BH.7) Mk 5A COMBAT/LOGISTICS

Similar to the Mk 5 above, with the exception that the bow door is retained, giving the craft a dual fast attack/logistic capability. Secondary armament can consist of two roof-mounted single 20mm guns.

DIMENSIONS
Overall length: 23·9m (78ft 4in)
Overall beam: 13·9m (45ft 6in)
Overall height, on landing pads: 10·7m (34ft)
WEIGHTS
All-up weight: 55·88 tonnes (55 tons)
Capacity: Up to 5 persons and 7 ton weapon payload
PERFORMANCE
Max speed: 58 knots
Endurance: 8 hours
Long range endurance: 10 hours

BHC MINE CLEARANCE HOVERCRAFT

Minesweeping is one of the most hazardous of all naval activities. Clearance techniques in the past have been very much on a hit or miss basis with craft operating in pairs, one sweeping and the other hunting and destroying the released mines as they surfaced by rifle and machinegun fire. Since the precise location of each mine was unknown, it was not unusual for a released mine to surface in the path of or beneath the hull of the hunter craft.

In the USA in recent years, efforts to reduce the tremendous wastage in lives and craft led to the introduction of the Edo 105 and 106 foil-equipped catamaran minesweeping systems. These not only speed up the process of mine clearance, but since they are towed by helicopter, reduce very considerably the risks to the crews involved.

In the United Kingdom, the Ministry of Defence (Navy) has stated that as hovercraft normally operate clear of the water, they are less vulnerable to possible mine explosions than conventional vessels, and with mine countermeasures equipment they have a potential for this type of work.

The British Hovercraft Corporation has announced plans for both sweeper and hunter versions of the BH.7 and the SR.N4. Descriptions of these vessels are given below.

BH.7 Mk 5A MINESWEEPER

Among the advantages offered by the use of this type of fully amphibious hovercraft for MCM, as opposed to a displacement vessel are five times the transit speed; very low acoustic and magnetic underwater signatures; and virtual immunity to underwater explosions. Additionally, the craft can be used for crew rescue in mined waters. Since the craft is based on the standard BH.7 Mk 5A, and retains its bow loading door, it has logistic support capability when not being employed for minesweeping.

LIFT AND PROPULSION: Integrated lift/propulsion system powered by a single Rolls-Royce Marine Proteus 15M/549 gas-turbine with a continuous output at 15°C of 3,800hp at 10,000 turbine rpm. This drives via a light alloy drive shaft and bevel drive gearbox, a BHC 12-blade, centrifugal 3·5m (11ft 6in) diameter, lift fan and an HSD four-blade, variable-pitch 6·4m (21ft) diameter, pylon-mounted propeller.

ACCOMMODATION: Total crew complement is eight men. The raised control cabin accommodates a three-man operating crew, with the captain and navigator in front and the third crew member behind. An off-duty cabin is located immediately beneath, with bunks for four. Ahead of the off-duty cabin is a galley and aft, in the midship cabin, is the operations room with navigation, surface and under surface plotting tables, radar display and data processing equipment. The control cabin is air-conditioned and the rest areas are air-conditioned and soundproofed. Access from the off-duty cabin to the control cabin is via a ladder.

SYSTEMS, MCM EQUIPMENT: Minesweeping equipment, including winches and cable reels, are stowed on the side decks and sides of the superstructure forward. Equipment includes floats, depressors, otters and cutters, venturi acoustic sweeping gear, marker buoys and an inflatable dinghy.

SWEEP DEPLOYMENT: Sweeps are deployed from the port side deck and shackled to the primary tow cable which is permanently attached to the destabilising pulley running on the towing bridle.

DIMENSIONS

EXTERNAL

Length overall: 23·9m (78ft 4in)
Beam overall: 13·9m (45ft 6in)
Height overall, on cushion: 11·8m (38ft 8in)
on landing pads: 10·4m (34ft)

INTERNAL

Cabin headroom, on centreline: 2·4m (7ft 10in)
Bow door opening: 4·1 × 2·9m (13ft 9in × 7ft 3in)

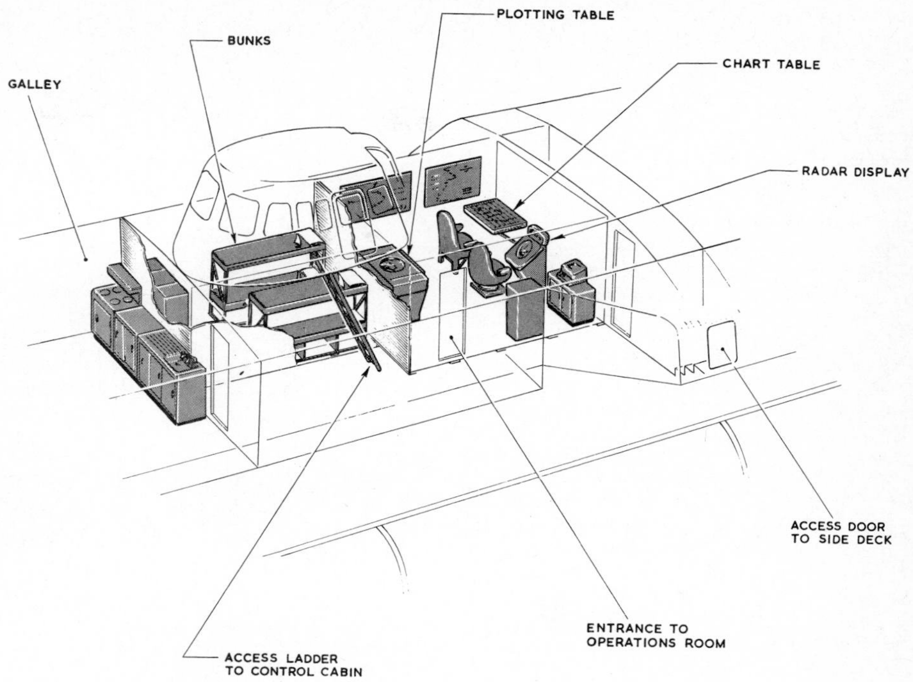

Interior layout of the BH.7 Mk 5A Minesweeper

The 200-ton SR.N4, Sir Christopher, accompanied by the 40-knot patrol craft, "Tenacity", during mine countermeasures trials with the Royal Navy off Portland in May 1976. During these trials the craft reached speeds in excess of 70 knots and covered the 167n miles from Portland back to Ramsgate at an average speed of 51·4 knots

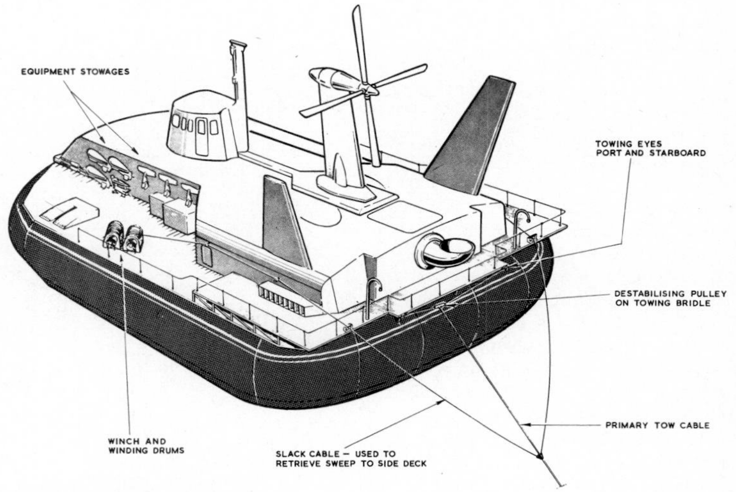

BH.7 Mk 5A equipped for Minesweeping

WEIGHTS
Starting all-up weight: 53 tons approx
Mean operating: 48 tons approx
MCM payload: 3 tons approx

PERFORMANCE
Cruising speed, knots:

Craft heading	Into wind	Beam wind
Calm water, still air	68	68
Significant wave height/wind speed		
4ft/6 knots	57	59
2ft/11 knots	47	52
3ft/15 knots	38	44

ENDURANCE: Total fuel consumption at max continuous power (includes both APUs): 1·16 tons/hour. Endurance on a nominal 10 ton fuel load: 8·6 hours.

Towing capability: a towing force of 3-5 tons is available at speeds of up to 10 knots in significant waveheights up to 3ft.

BH.7 Mk 5A MINE HUNTER

This version is identical in practically every respect to the mine sweeper model and can be reconfigured readily to sweeping duties or logistic support roles. It differs from the sweeper only in the mine disposal equipment carried.

SYSTEMS, MCM EQUIPMENT: A 20mm machine gun mount ahead of the control cabin is optional. Towed or dunking mine detection and classification sonars; remotely piloted mine disposal vehicles; sonar display units; recorders etc; navigation and communications gear.

DEPLOYMENT: Over the sidedecks via davits and swinging A frames. Towing lines are deployed and retrieved by winch and shackled to the primary tow cable which is permanently attached to the destabilising pulley running on the towing bridle.

PERFORMANCE

Cruising and towing speed: as for minesweeper

Endurance: in the case of a sonar being towed at a speed of 5 knots or less, but with the craft in full hover condition, the estimated fuel consumption (ton/hour) is:

Proteus: 0·677 ton/h (ISA conditions)

2 Rover APUs: 0·111 ton/h (assumed requirement)

Total: 0·778 ton/h

On a nominal 10 ton fuel-load, endurance would be 12·9 hours

SR.N4 Mk 4

The MCMH version of the SR.N4 is identical in most respects to the Mk 2 commercial craft but has a much larger fuel capacity. A high-speed self-jacking system which would allow the craft to be raised for skirt inspections and repairs on temporary landing sites can be installed if required. At its design maximum all-up weight of 220 tonnes it is capable of carrying up to 60 tonnes of role payload in addition to the fuel for a ten-hour mission.

The craft is able to undertake all the mine clearance tasks currently performed by conventional vessels such as a mine sweeper with wire or influence sweeps, or a mine hunter using towed sonar and mine disposal equipment. It can therefore operate either independently or as a unit of a mixed-craft MCM force.

The operations room, crew quarters and workshop can be accommodated in the twin side cabins or alternatively, on the central deck area forward of the winch positions. All major installations in the central area can be erected on palletised modules to facilitate changes of MCM equipment, and conversion for logistic support duties, enabling individual craft to perform any of the proposed MCM roles at short notice.

As with the standard craft, the SR.N4 MCMH has considerable development potential. Most of the future modifications which may be introduced to improve the efficiency of the civil versions will be applicable to the MCMH, including larger propellers, uprated engines and revised skirts. In particular its payload carrying capability could be increased by lengthening as is being undertaken for the Seaspeed craft.

All types of minesweeping gear used by conventional mine-sweepers—a wiresweep to cut the moorings of tethered mines or influence sweeps, magnetic and acoustic, to detonate influence mines—can be carried by the SR.N4. Additionally in the minehunting role it can tow sonars to locate mines which cannot normally be swept and carry the equipment to destroy them.

Trials with SR.N4 have shown that it maintains a track in winds of at least 20 knots to within a standard deviation of less than eight metres. In

The Royal Navy's BH.7 Mk 4 as modified by BHC for the mine countermeasures role, to enable the craft to play a more realistic part in naval exercises. In this particular configuration the craft embodies a bow door, sweep deck extension and a Sea Rider with davit to assist in deployment and recovery

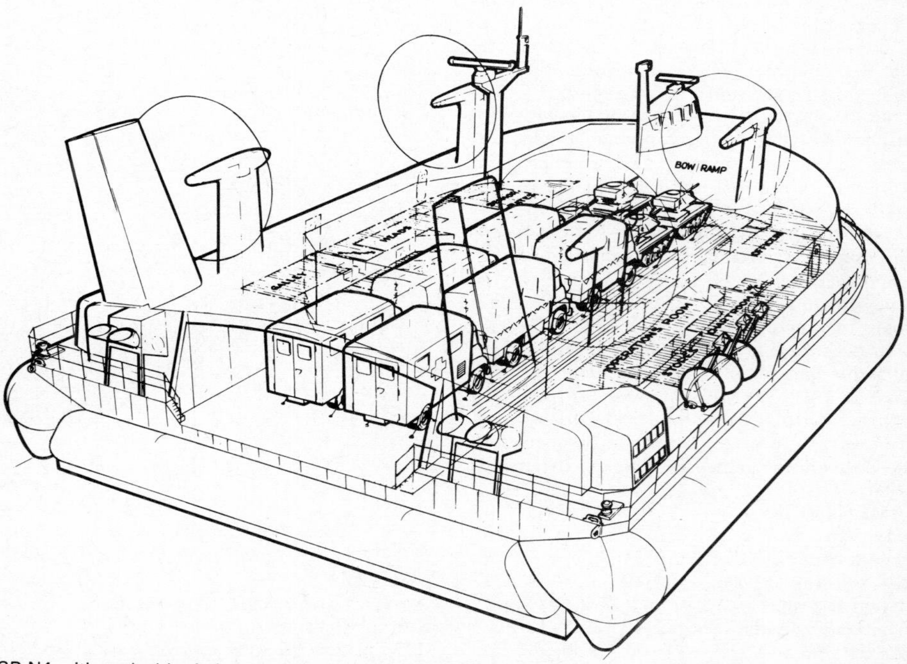

SR.N4 with typical logistic payload

the minehunting role, position accuracy as well as track keeping accuracy is required, since relocation may be necessary. These requirements can be met by the provision of two navigation modes. In the primary mode, position fixing could be derived from a high accuracy radio navigation aid. Secondary mode sensors could include a navigation radar with auto extraction, possibly by range-range measurement relative to short scope buoys. Decca Navigator could provide a further mode.

It is likely that the SR.N4 MCMH would have an integrated computer-based navigation and action information system. This would have inputs of heading from a gyro compass; velocities from a speed and drift sensor, probably a multi-beam doppler radar; position from Hi-fix 6, Decca Navigator and Inboard navigational radar; target position from a towed sonar.

The SR.N4 MCMH would operate from Forward Support Units (FSU) located in the general area of probable mining targets. One such unit could be the force headquarters, providing training facilities and co-ordinating mine clearance operations including, if necessary, those of conventional craft. In the event of a mining attack it may be desirable to establish an additional MCMH base closer to the area of operations. This could be in the form of a Mobile Advanced Base (MAB) able to support up to three craft for a period of 14 days. It is anticipated that MAB sites would be selected in advance of an attack but not necessarily prepared in any way.

Where the situation did not justify a MAB, fuel, sweep spares and crew could be readily transferred at a Temporary Replenishment Point (TRP) which need be no more than a suitable beach area having vehicular access.

It is envisaged that the MCMH force would be responsible for the establishment of any shore based navigation system such as Hi-fix which might be required for operation in particular areas.

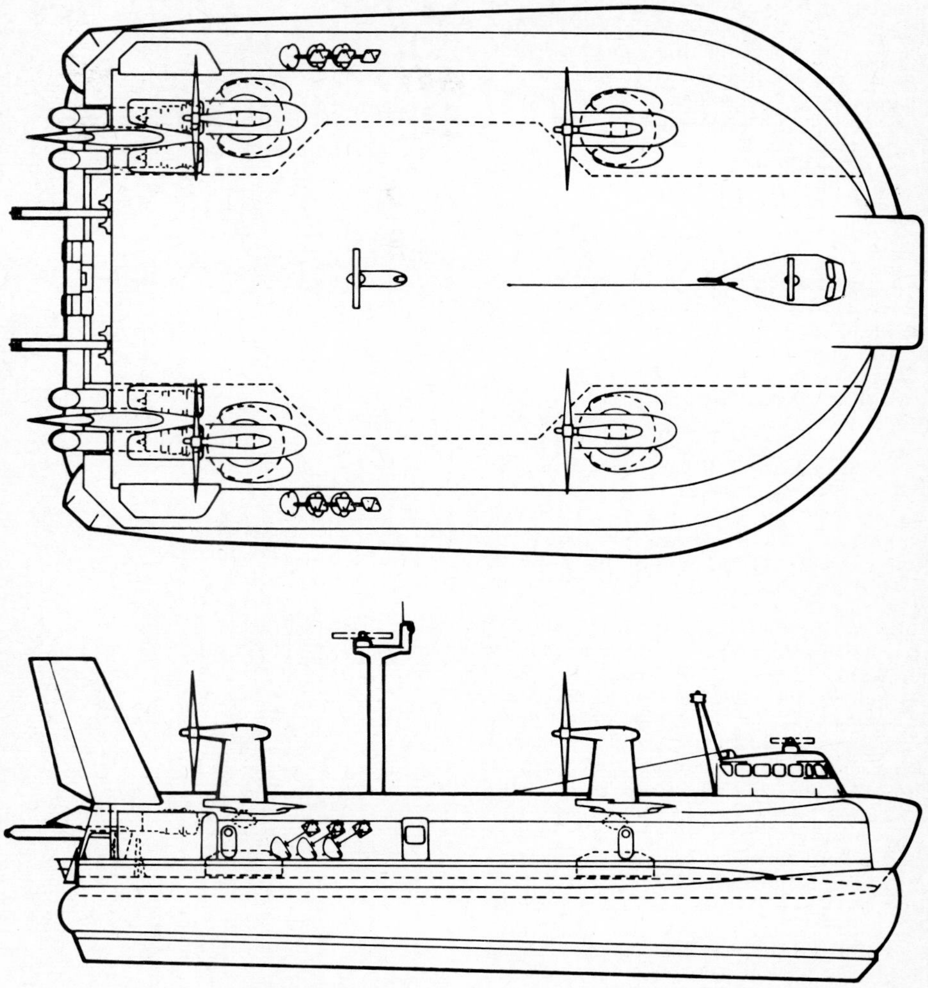

General arrangement of the SR.N4 MCMH, powered by four Rolls Royce Marine Proteus gas-turbines, each with a maximum rating of 3,170kW (4,250hp)

INFLUENCE SWEEPER

For operations against the various types of acoustic and magnetic mine the SR.N4 MCMH has sufficient carrying capacity and towing capability to operate existing influence sweeps such as the Osborn Acoustic and the MM Mk 2 Magnetic Loop.

These detonate the mines by reproducing the signature of the intended victim and are usually operated in combination. The relative immunity of the SR.N4 MCMH to underwater explosions gives it a marked advantage in this role.

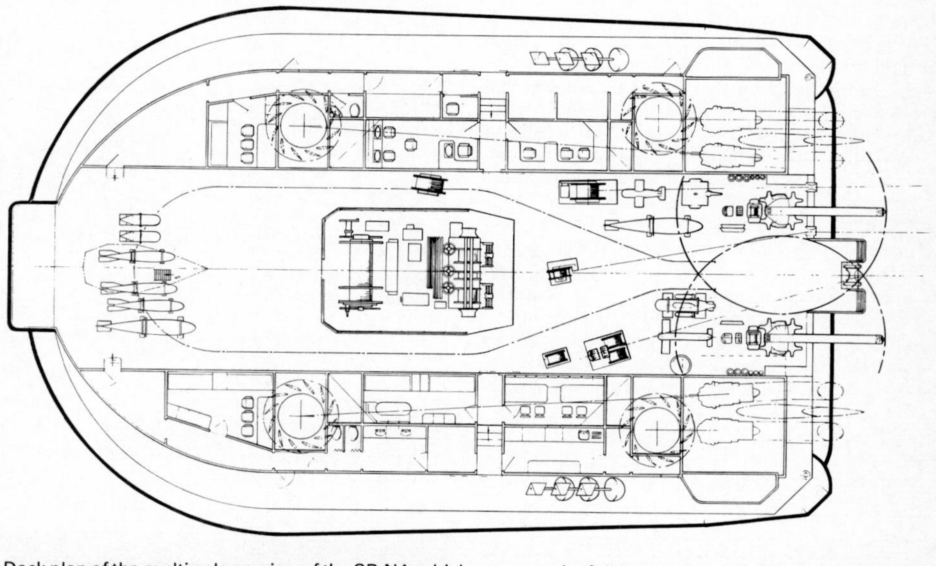

Deck plan of the multi-role version of the SR.N4, which can carry the full range of equipment associated with mine-sweeping, influence-sweeping and hunter disposal roles at the same time

WIRE SWEEPER

For mine sweeping operations against moored or tethered mines the SR.N4 MCMH can be fitted with the standard Wire Mk 3 Mod 2 Oropesa sweep and associated equipment as used by the Royal Navy Ton Class minesweepers and proposed for the Hunt Class MCMV's.

The winch has been redesigned for hovercraft use but if desired the standard Type B winch with modified drive arrangements could be accommodated without difficulty.

MOD (N)-sponsored trials with a simulated sweep have been conducted successfully in Coastal Code 5 and it is anticipated that sweeping could be carried out in more adverse conditions, but, as with conventional craft, the actual operating limits may be determined by the ability to stream and recover the sweep gear.

HUNTER/DISPOSAL CRAFT

Mines that cannot be swept using wire, acoustic and magnetic sweeps, such as pressure mines and those yet to be activated, are normally located using sonar devices and then destroyed by explosive charges.

For mine hunting the SR.N4 MCMH can be equipped with a pair of towed sidescan search sonars. Fitted with these the craft can carry out routine surveillance duties more rapidly than most conventional craft.

Relocation of the target can be achieved, if required, by using a dipped sonar and the mine disposal weapon can be delivered by a remotely piloted vehicle (RPC) such as the PAP.104 or the Sperry Catamaran. Alternatively the disposal charge may be placed in position from a manned Gemini dinghy.

MULTI-ROLE CRAFT

The SR.N4 MCMH can carry the full range of equipment associated with the mine sweeping, influence sweeping and hunter/disposal roles at the same time. There is adequate deck space for all the items to be stowed—the central through deck area is about 35m long by 10m wide—and the corresponding craft weight of 227·5 tonnes, which includes fuel for 11 hours endurance, is well within operational limits.

In practice the craft is unlikely to be required to carry all the equipment when operating in a specific role. Wire sweeping can be undertaken with the influence sweeping equipment on board since many components are common. The various mine hunting and disposal systems considered are sufficiently portable to be fitted at the Mobile Advanced Base when needed for specific tasks.

The characteristics of the standard SR.N4 are such that the craft can be adapted to other roles and in particular to those of fast attack craft and anti-submarine craft. As a fast attack craft a typical weapon fit could include at least four surface-to-surface missiles of Exocet or Harpoon type or similar, a 75mm Oto Melara gun and a twin 30mm gun mount for anti-aircraft defence, together with their associated sensors and control equipment. The anti-submarine version could carry upwards of 60 tonnes of equipment enabling it to operate in the hunter/killer role alone or in conjunction with other craft.

LOGISTIC SUPPORT

Should a situation develop which requires large numbers of troops and their equipment to be transported over water at high speed then the SR.N4 MCMH could, by removal of the bulk of the MCM equipment be converted for Logistic Support duties.

Typical loadings up to 90 tonnes:

a) 7 GS trucks; 250 troops
b) 1 battle tank; 2 light tanks; 6 1 tonne landrovers.
c) 4 light tanks; 2 laden trucks; 2 unladen trucks; 2 ambulances.

Operating around the clock over a 30n mile route in moderate conditions, the craft could, over a 24-hour period, transport approximately 1,500 tonnes of military personnel and equipment.

LIFT AND PROPULSION: Power is supplied by four Rolls-Royce Marine Proteus free turbine turboshaft engines located in pairs at the rear of the craft on either side of the working deck space. Each would operate at 3,800shp when cruising. Each engine is connected to one of four identical propeller/fan units, two forward, two aft. The propellers, made by Hawker Siddeley Dynamics, are of four-bladed, variable and reversible pitch type, 5·8m (19·03ft) in diameter. The lift fans, made by BHC, are of 12-bladed centrifugal type, 3·5m (11ft 6in) in diameter.

CONTROLS AND HULL: Similar to SR.N4 Mk 2.

ACCOMMODATION: Nominal crew complement is five officers, four senior ratings and six junior ratings. The operations room, crew accommodation and workshop can be fitted into the twin side cabins or alternatively within the central deck area forward of the winch positions. All major installations in the central deck area can be mounted on palletised modules to facilitate the changing over of MCM equipment and conversion to logistic support duties. Fuel for the craft is standard aviation kerosene DERD 2494 (AVTUR). Diesel fuel DEF.2404-4 may be used as an alternative. Capacity of the craft is 10 hours endurance + 10%, 47 tonnes.

SYSTEMS, ELECTRICAL: 2 × 55kVA alternators provide 200V three phase 400Hz power from APU. 28V dc power is provided by two TRUs supplied from 400Hz system. Batteries provide emergency power and APU starting.

PULSE GENERATOR: A gas turbine driven alternator unit provides 500kVA, three phase 400Hz power at voltages required for magnetic-loop sweeps.

DIMENSIONS

EXTERNAL

Overall length: 39·68m (130ft 2in)

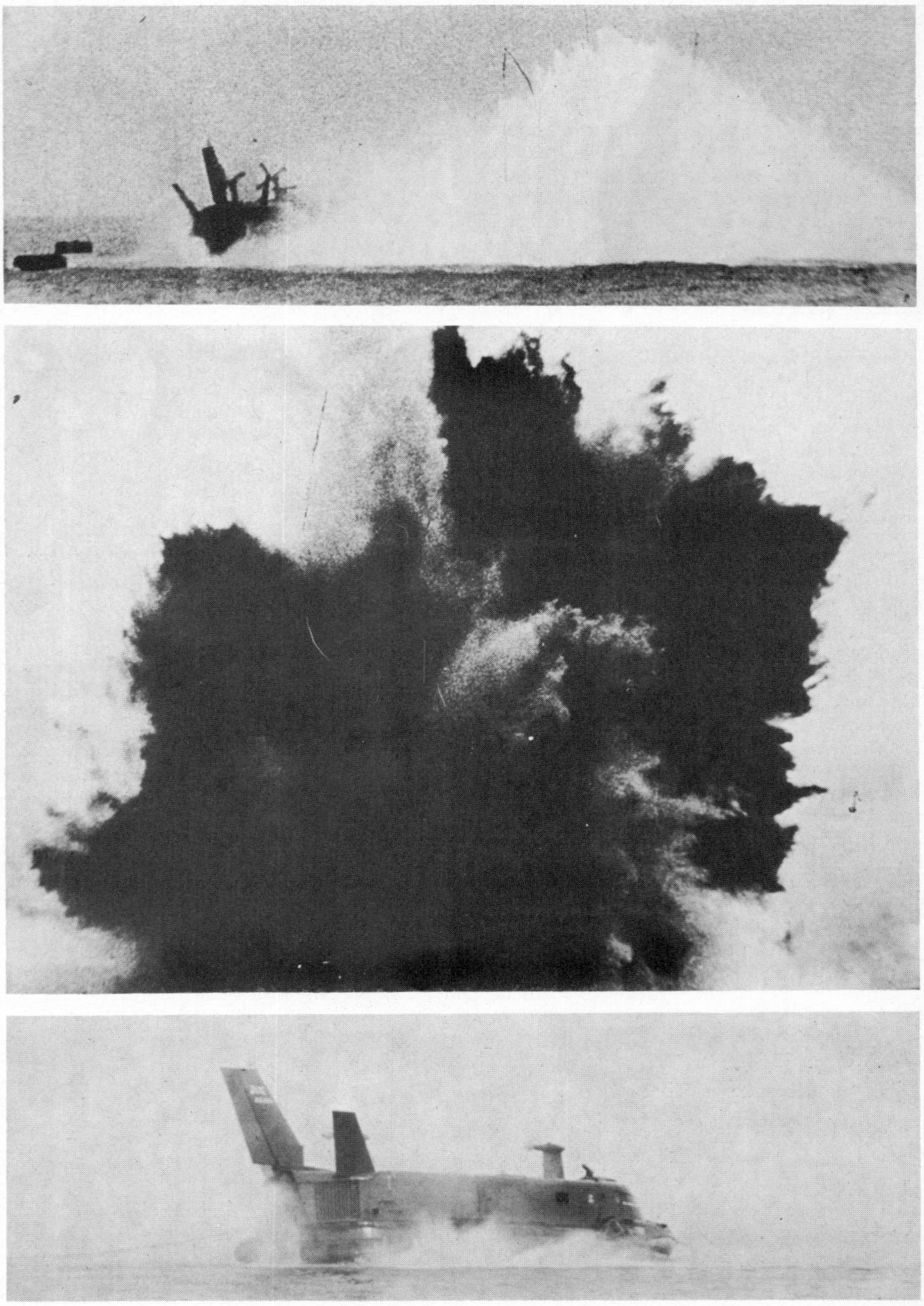

Underwater explosion tests being undertaken with the 35-tonne SR.N3 when operating with the Inter-Service Hovercraft Trials Unit

Top: The N.3, tethered, hovering, unmanned, within the shock dome of the charge
Centre: Rising plume of the explosion
Bottom: The N.3, after the explosion, damaged, but able to return to the base under its own power

Beam: 25·5m (83ft 8in)
Height (masthead): 17·2m (56ft 5in)
Sweepback, length: 24m (78ft 8⅞in)
beam: 10m (32ft 9¾in)

WEIGHTS

Basic: 113·5 tonnes
Normal max: 220 tonnes
Overload: 240 tonnes

CYCLONE HOVERCRAFT

8 Walton Road, Caldecotte, Milton Keynes, Buckinghamshire MK7 8AE, England
Telephone: 0908 64733
Officials:
N R Beale BSc, MSc, *Director*
P J Beale, *Director*

Cyclone Hovercraft has developed a plans, components and design service based upon the experience that won the British National Championships for five consecutive years.

Their latest enterprise is a simple single-engined hovercraft, plans of which are offered for home construction. This craft is designed around the new British-made "Breeza" axial fan, for which Cyclone has been appointed agent. "Breeza" fans employ adjustable pitch blades made from high strength glass-filled polypropylene.

Simple Cyclone, a single-engined light hovercraft employing a single ducted fan with adjustable pitch blades for its integrated lift and propulsion system (Photo: Nigel Beale)

THE SIMPLE CYCLONE

A single-engined design employing a single

ducted fan for its integrated lift and propulsion system, "Simple Cyclone" will carry one adult over water at speeds of up to 48·28km/h (30mph). Over smooth land its payload may be increased to two adults.

LIFT AND PROPULSION: A single Kyoritsu KEC 225cc two-stroke engine, rated at 12·5bhp at 5,550rpm, drives, via a toothed belt, a 23⅝in (600mm) diameter "Breeza" fan. The unit supplies air for both lift and thrust. Any suitable engine of between 10 and 25bhp may be used. The 4·5 litre (1 gallon) fuel tank gives a cruising endurance of more than one hour. A larger capacity tank may be fitted if desired.

CONTROLS: For the utmost simplicity, only two controls are provided, designed for single-handed operation. A lever control for the engine throttle is mounted on the control column which operates the twin rudders.

HULL: The hull is constructed from thin exterior grade plywood with wooden stringers. Polyurethane foam within the hull structure ensures adequate buoyancy. The fan duct unit is laminated from glass reinforced plastic.

SKIRT: The skirt fitted to the Simple Cyclone is a Cyclone-designed extended segment type employing an individual air feed through the hull to every segment.

DIMENSIONS
Length overall; 3m (9ft 11in)
Width overall: 1·83m (6ft)
Height at rest: 0·9m (2ft 11in)
Hard structure clearance: 180mm (7³⁄₃₂in)

WEIGHTS
Unladen: 80kg (176lb)
Normal payload: 90kg (198lb)

PERFORMANCE
Max speed over land or water: 48·28km/h (30mph)

Simple Cyclone at speed over water on Loch Lubraigh, Scotland. Maximum speed over land and water is 48·28km/h (30mph)

GP CONCESSIONAIRES LTD

Worton Hall, Worton Road, Isleworth, Middlesex TW7 6R, England
Telephone: 01-568 4711
Officials:
John Jobber, *Managing Director*

HOVER HAWK

This new four-seat utility ACV is intended primarily for survey and patrol duties although a variety of alternative applications are foreseen. Advanced orders for the craft have been received from Finland and Nigeria.

LIFT AND PROPULSION: Integrated system. A single Rotax two-stroke, two-cylinder, air-cooled engine drives via a belt a ducted fan aft. Propulsion air is expelled rearwards and lift air is ducted into the plenum below. Fuel capacity is 28 litres (6 imperial gallons). Fuel recommended 93 Octane.

CONTROLS: Single control column operates a single rudder hinged to the rear of the fan duct. Column incorporates a twist-grip throttle for the engine.

HULL: Moulded glass fibre reinforced plastics structure.

SKIRT: Fully-segmented type in neoprene-coated nylon.

ACCOMMODATION: Open cockpit with seating for driver and up to three passengers.

DIMENSIONS
Length overall: 4·04m (13ft 3in)
Width: 2·44m (8ft)
Height: 1·22m (4ft)

WEIGHTS
Empty: 200kg (441lb)
Payload: 249kg (549lb)

PERFORMANCE
Max speed: 64km/h (40mph)
Gradient capability: 1 in 7 from static hover
Obstacle clearance: 0·3m (12in)
Endurance, max: 5 hours

PRICE: £2,750 plus VAT. Car trailer for Hover Hawk, £135 plus VAT

Hover Hawk, a grp-hulled, four-seater designed for survey work and light patrol duties

HFL-SEAGLIDE LTD

PO Box 33, London N14 7NS, England
Telephone: 01-368 6013
Telex: 21879 IMP
Officials:
H F Lentge, *Managing Director*
R Bourn, *Director*
H V Lentge, *Director*

HFL-Seaglide Limited was formed in 1976 to build and market the Seabee series of aerodynamic ram-wings designed by Ronald Bourn. The company's first craft is a prototype three-seater with an overall length of 5·18m (17ft). The machine is based on data derived from an earlier delta wing prototype first flown in 1971. Among the range of designs projected by the company are a three-seat fast launch, an eight-seat water taxi or freight carrier and a 35-seat water bus or freighter.

SEABEE 3-SEATER

This novel grp-hulled three-seater was completed in 1972 and is undergoing development in three stages. During the first stage it was fitted with a converted 90hp General Motors flat six-cylinder air-cooled engine driving a four-bladed fixed-pitch wooden propeller optimised for 70 knots. For the second stage, this was replaced by a 130hp flat four-cylinder aero engine driving a two-bladed fixed-pitch propeller optimised for 120 knots. The third stage was reached in July 1976 when this engine was replaced by a 130hp Turboméca Artouste turbofan.

The vehicle has undergone both preliminary and advanced trials in ground effect, but no attempts to convert to free-flight and back had been made at the time of going to press.

POWER PLANT: 130hp four-cylinder horizontally-opposed Rolls-Royce 240A aero-engine driving a two-bladed de Havilland fixed-pitch propeller.

CONTROLS: Aircraft type, with yoke operating elevon on stabiliser, and foot-operated rudder bar linked to twin rudders.

HULL: Monocoque structure in moulded grp. Conventional hard chine design.

MAINPLANE: Wing tips in grp. Control surfaces in doped fabric. Spruce main spars. RAF 30 section with lift area of approximately 10m² (108ft²).

DIMENSIONS
Length, overall: 5·18m (16ft 11in)
Beam, overall: 4·57m (14ft 11in)
Height to top of stabiliser: 1·75m (5ft 9in)

The Seabee three-seat aerodynamic ram-wing prototype. Speeds of up to 112km/h (70mph) have been achieved in ground effect during tests

WEIGHTS
All-up weight with operator and one passenger: 502·1kg (1,107lb)

PERFORMANCE
130HP ROLLS-ROYCE 240A
Max speed (design): 120 knots
Craft can be operated at any desired speed between 2 and 100 knots
Take-off speed, depending upon payload and weather conditions: 35-40 knots

HOVERCRAFT DEVELOPMENT LTD

Head Office: Kingsgate House, 66-74 Victoria Street, London SW1E 6SL, England
Telephone: 01-828 3400
Telex: 23580
Officials:
T A Coombs, *Chairman*
D Anderson, *Director*
Prof W A Mair, *Director*
J E Rapson, *Director*
P N Randell, *Director*
B Bailey, *Secretary*
Technical Office: Forest Lodge West, Fawley Road, Hythe, Hampshire SO4 6ZZ, England
Telephone: 0703 843178

Hovercraft Development Ltd (HDL) was formed in January 1959 by the National Research Development Corporation (NRDC) to develop, promote and exploit the hovercraft invention. The company uses its large portfolio of patents as the basis of licensing agreements with the principal hovercraft manufacturers in the United Kingdom and overseas, and allows licensees access to work undertaken by its original Technical Group and the current Technical Office at Hythe. HDL may, in certain cases, provide financial backing to assist projects, such as the Hovermarine HM.5, the BHC SR.N4, Pindair Skima 12 and AVL Tiger.

The small technical team employed by the company makes assessments of new hovercraft designs and projects in addition to regional and route studies for proposed hovercraft operations. HDL's Technical Office at Hythe also provides a source of unbiased but informed technical information for government departments, official bodies, potential manufacturers, operators and backers of hovercraft enterprises.

HD.4 during overland tests of the HDL Balanced Skirt Shift System. Clearly visible is the degree of roll possible with this system

Currently, various programmes are being undertaken to evaluate new and improved control and cushion systems for hovercraft of all sizes. This work, together with other investigations, is aimed towards improving the control, skirt and propulsion aspects of modern hovercraft and assist the company's licensees to manufacture increasingly effective products for civil, military and industrial uses.

Patents held by the company largely result from the work undertaken by Christopher Cockerell and the HDL Technical Group, which investigated a wide range of marine, industrial and medical applications. The former Technical Group also operated three research hovercraft.

HDL SKIRT SHIFT SYSTEM

The HDL skirt shift system is designed to move the centre of pressure of the cushion without altering its area. Both straight side skirts are divided into two panels each of which can be moved in or out by a single cable which actuates an array of cranked skirt ties. By transferring the tension in each cable via a form of bell crank to the base of a joystick, diagonally opposite panels become balanced and the only loads felt in the stick are those due to friction. It is anticipated that for larger craft a hydraulic system will connect the bell cranks to the stick giving more freedom in the location of craft controls. When the stick is moved forward the front two panels are drawn in, while the rear panels are let out. The craft then pitches forward. The process is reversed for bow-up trim. Pushing the stick to the left shifts all four panels to the right, thus inducing the desired roll to the left.

The cp shift system was originally conceived to provide active pitch and roll control for craft having a high cg. Since then the system has shown itself capable of being operated sufficiently rapidly, due to its low inertia, to act as a "flying" control. It thus performs more effectively than a movable ballast system as well as showing a considerable weight saving. In addition it was found during the operation of HD.4 that potentially dangerous pitch oscillations caused by regular wave encounters could instantly be damped out by a single application of the pitch control.

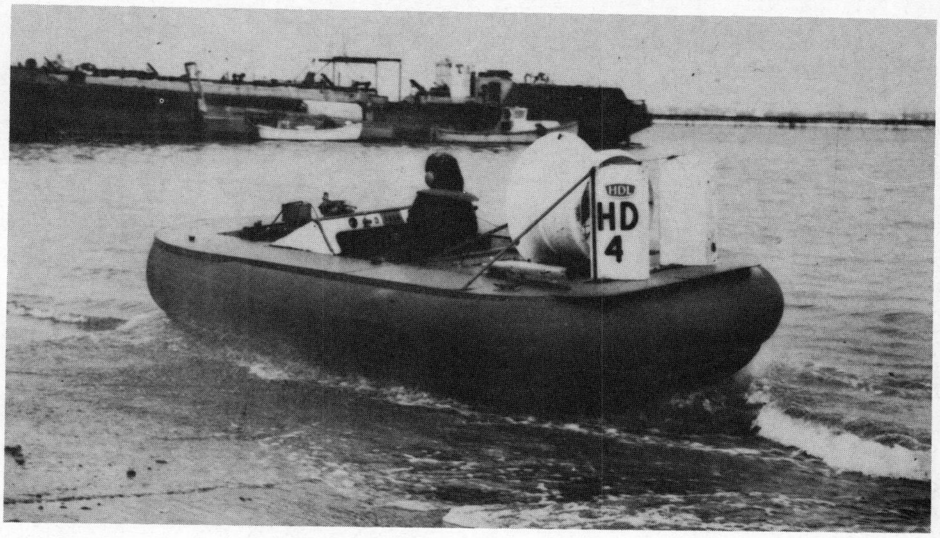

HD.4(b) during trials conducted along the shoreline at Hythe, Hampshire. The craft is seen with the new skirt fitted

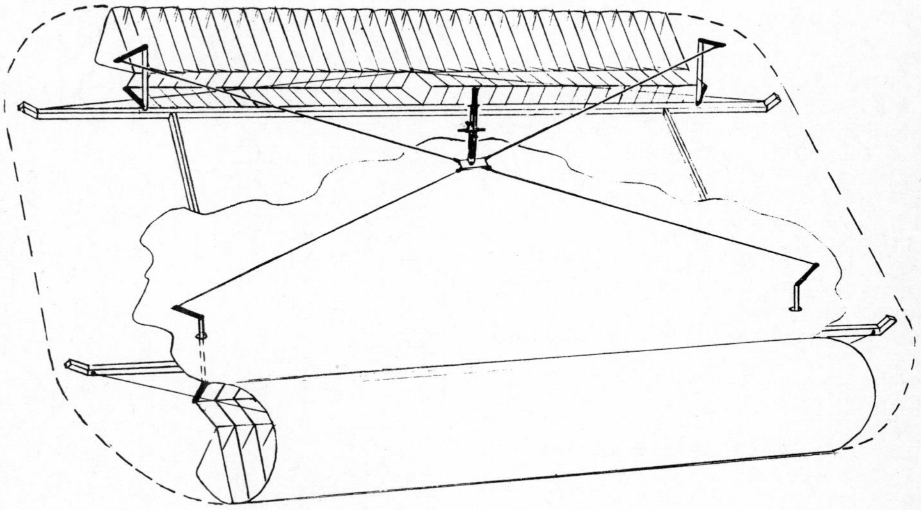
Schematic representation of HDL's Balanced Skirt Shift System as fitted to the HD.4 research hovercraft

HD.4(b)

This two-seat research craft has been used by HDL to test new and improved hovercraft control and cushion systems. The prototype, completed in July 1975, was employed to evaluate HDL's new centre-of-pressure shift system during the summer and autumn of 1976. Following the successful completion of these trials the craft was re-skirted prior to testing a number of devices concerned with cushion systems during the summer of 1977.

LIFT AND PROPULSION: Lift is supplied by a single 9bhp Villiers 8E 197cc engine, driving a 597mm (23½in) diameter Multi-wing ten-bladed axial fan with blades set at 30 degree pitch. Propulsion is provided by a single 12·5bhp Kyoritsu KEC 225cc engine, driving a single 584mm (23in) diameter, five-bladed, 30 degree pitch Breeza ducted fan. Fuel is carried in two 9·09 litre (2 gallon) tanks located one each side of the cockpit.

CONTROLS: Craft direction is controlled by twin vertical rudders operating in the fan slip-stream and an HDL balanced skirt shift system which can operate in pitch and roll.

HULL: Wooden construction with a framework in 25mm (1in) square spruce and 13mm (½in) square ramin, covered with 4mm and 1·5mm exterior-grade plywood sheets. Structure depth is 345mm (13½in). Planing surfaces of 35 degrees around the hull, reducing to 20 degrees on the bow centreline.

SKIRT: A single axial lift fan feeds air into the bow loop through 32 holes of 102mm (4in) diameter, arranged in a horse-shoe formation, extending back 1·5m (5ft) from the bow. Skirt is loop and segment type using lightweight material which is ultra-violet resistant. Cushion is uncompartmented.

Cushion pressure is 51kg/m² (10·55lb/ft²). Segments are 305mm (12in) long and have 137mm (5½in) pitch. Solid obstacle clearance is 292mm (11½in). Cushion depth is 340mm (13½in).

ACCOMMODATION: Open two-seat cockpit.

DIMENSIONS

Length overall, power off: 4·3m (14ft 1½in)
Beam overall, power off: 2m (6ft 6½in)
Height overall, power off: 1·1m (3ft 8in)
Height overall, hovering: 1·4m (4ft 7½in)

WEIGHTS

Normal all-up weight: 313kg (691lb)

HOVERMARINE TRANSPORT LIMITED

Hazel Wharf, Hazel Road, Woolston, Southampton SO2 7GB, England
Telephone: 0703 446831
Telex: 47141
Officials:
William A Zebedee (USA), *Chairman*
M R Richards, *Managing Director*
P Skov-Nielsen, *Sales Director*
E G Tattersall, *Research and Development Director*
P J Hill, *Customer Service Director*
E W Furnell, *Manufacturing Director*
J H Chapman, *Design Engineering Director*

Hovermarine Transport Limited, a subsidiary of Hovermarine Corporation, is a world leader in the design and construction of rigid sidewall (SES) hovercraft. The company has two plants located at Woolston in Southampton; one is a purpose-built factory providing 30,000ft² of floor area which is supplemented with internal balconies on which detail parts and sub-assemblies are fabricated. This unit has its own overhead gantry crane which, together with the full height main doors, permits the direct launching of craft on completion. This unit also has a controlled environment with special air conditioning that complies with the strict requirements of Lloyd's for grp hull construction. A second factory, acquired in the summer of 1978, is adjacent to the original factory and covers an area of seven acres, including a large fitting-out building.

The company is currently building craft of the Hovermarine 200 and 500 series. Hulls in the Hovermarine 200 series range in length from 16m (52ft) to 21m (70ft), and can be fitted out to accommodate a variety of different requirements including passenger ferry, survey craft, harbour patrol and coastguard configurations. In terms of passenger capacity, the three hulls in the 200 series offer from 60 to more than 100 seats. The 500 series also consists of three hull forms measuring from 27m (88ft) to 39m (130ft) in length. These craft can also be fitted out for civil, special duty and military specifications.

At the time of going to press, Hovermarine had completed 46 craft with a further 10 on order. Fleets have been delivered to Hong Kong, Portugal, the Philippines, Brazil, Venezuela and the Netherlands. The company's craft are also in operation in many other countries.

The company has under active development a 600 series Hoverfreighter project and a dynamic model of a car ferry version is being tank tested. During 1978 a deep cushion concept research and development programme was initiated.

HOVERMARINE 216 (HM.2 Mk III)

A rigid sidewall craft designed for ferry operations, the Hovermarine 216 carries 62-65 passengers or 4·8 tons of freight at speeds up to 35 knots. The craft has a reinforced plastic hull, and is powered by three marine diesel engines.

Its features include an extended bow skirt which permits operations in waves up to 1·6m (5ft), mixed-flow fans to provide improved cushion characteristics, a new propulsion transmission system, modified engine components and the provision of sound insulation in the cabin to reduce internal noise levels.

Hovermarine 216 (HM.2 Mk III) is type approved in the UK for Certificates of Construction and Performance and Hovercraft Safety Certificates issued by the Civil Aviation Authority, also for Operating Permits issued by the Department of Trade. In addition, the HM.2 has been certified by Lloyds Register of Shipping as a Class A1 Group 2 Air Cushion Vehicle. Fleets of HM.2s are operating in: Setubal, Portugal; Rio de Janeiro, Brazil; Hong Kong Harbour; Margarita, Venezuela; and Manila Bay, the Philippines. Elsewhere these craft are operating in Belgium, Bolivia, Brazil, France, India, Japan, USA and the United Kingdom.

The Hovermarine 216 is the shortest of the three hulls offered in the 200 series and can be built to order. Full details were given in *Jane's Surface Skimmers 1978* and earlier editions.

HM.2 Mk III general purpose sidewall craft equipped for hydrographic survey and operated on the River Scheldt by the Belgian Ministry of Public Works

HM.2 Mk III GENERAL PURPOSE CRAFT

The craft is equipped with a revised superstructure to suit a variety of roles from police and customs patrol to hydrographic survey, and search and rescue duties. For para-military roles, the craft can be equipped with a range of conventional automatic weapons.

DIMENSIONS

EXTERNAL

Length overall: 15·54m (51ft)
Beam overall: 6·09m (20ft)
Height above hovering water line to wheelhouse top: 3·25m (10ft 8in)
Draft hovering: 0·86m (2ft 10in)
Draft afloat: 1·47m (4ft 10in)

WEIGHTS

Max all-up weight (fully equipped): 19,300kg (42,500lb)
Normal disposable load: 5,830kg (12,300lb)

The passenger ferry version of the Hovermarine 218 can be fitted with either 92 utility seats or 84 aircraft type seats

HOVERMARINE 218

The Hovermarine 218 is a lengthened version of the 216 (previously known as the HM.2 Mk III) and retains many of the systems and design features of that craft.

It is 3·04m (10ft) longer than the 65 passenger 216 and provides capacity for up to 92 passengers. The 50% increase in payload has been achieved with only minimal increase in costs. The installation of two GM 8V92 marine diesels, each rated at 380bhp at 2,100rpm, provides a maximum service speed of 34 knots.

The craft hull is manufactured in glass reinforced plastic and is built to standards approved by a number of classification and certification authorities including Lloyds Register of Shipping, United States Coast Guard, the Hovercraft Division of the UK Civil Aviation Authority and the Marine Division of the Japanese Government.

The cabin area may be fitted with either 92 utility seats or 84 aircraft type seats. Five large tinted windows are fitted each side of the saloon. All craft are equipped with air-conditioning. Additional passenger aids include eight-track stereo and a public address system controlled from the stewardess's bay at the aft end. Toilet spaces are provided with an electric wc and vanity unit.

Interior of Hovermarine's No 1 plant, September 1978

DIMENSIONS

Length, overall: 18·29m (60ft)
Beam, overall: 6·1m (20ft)
Height, overall: 5·8m (19ft)
Hull depth, base to deck: 1·98m (6ft 6in)
Nominal freeboard: 0·91m (3ft)
Cabin beam: 4·88m (16ft)
Cabin length: 9·75m (32ft)
Draft floating, loaded: 1·69m (5ft 4½in)
Approx draft hovering, aft loaded: 1·06m (3ft 6in)

WEIGHTS

Normal payload: 84-92 passengers

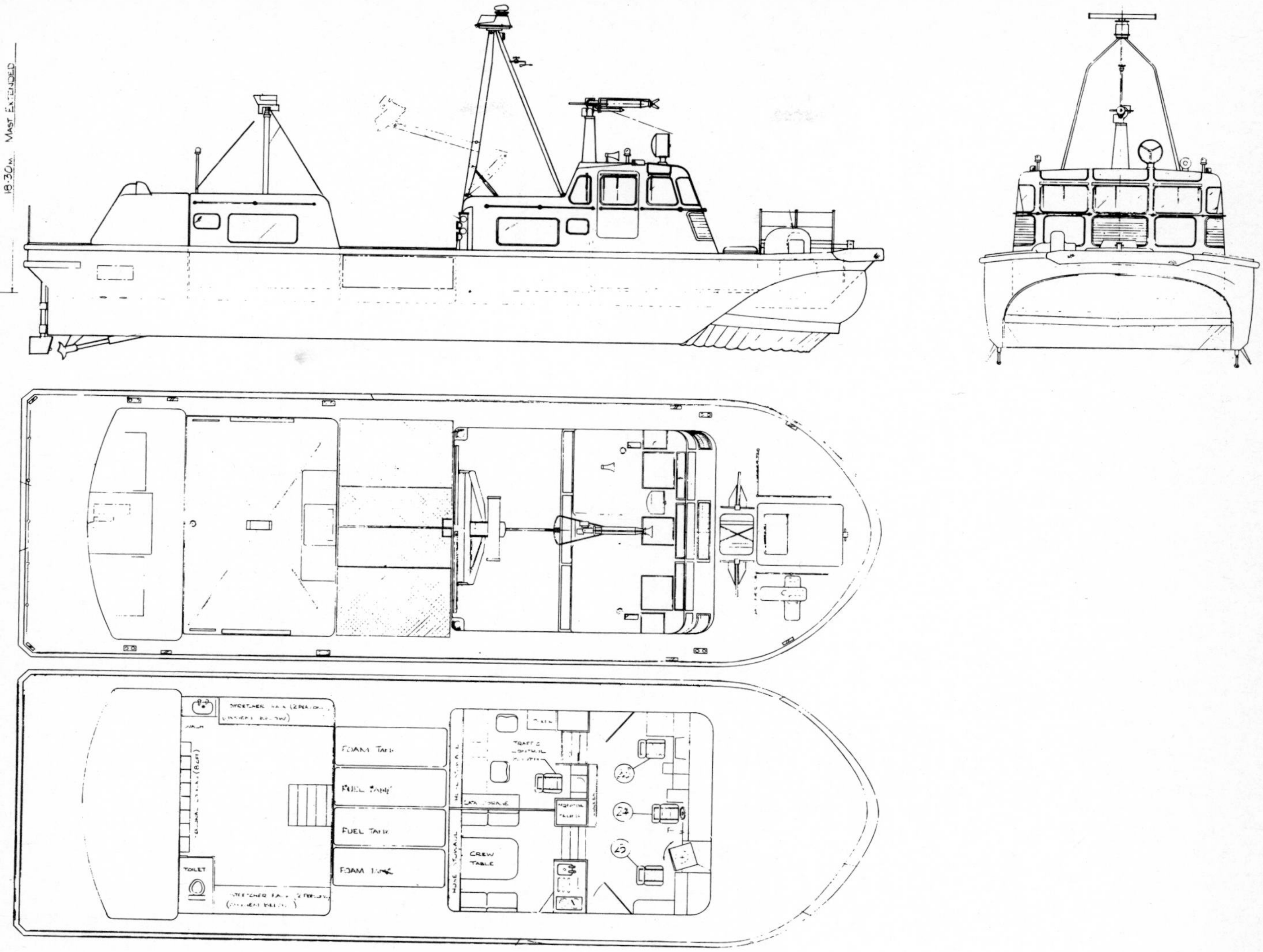

General arrangement of the Hovermarine 218 port patrol craft for the Rotterdam Port Authority

Nominal payload: 6,860kg (15,120lb)
Freight capacity: 7,350kg (7¼ tons)
Fuel tank capacity, standard: aft 635 litres (140 imperial gallons)
forward 182 litres (40 imperial gallons)
PERFORMANCE
Max service speed: 34 knots
Minimum endurance at max continuous rating: 4½ hours
Range at max speed: 250km (135n miles)

HOVERMARINE 218 PORT PATROL/FIREBOAT

In April 1978 Hovermarine Transport Ltd announced that the Rotterdam Port Authority had ordered four Hovermarine 218 Port Patrol craft in a contract valued at approximately Fl 11 million (£2·7 million). These are based on the standard 18m (60ft) long 218 hull, with provision for port monitoring and emergency services in two separate superstructure modules, and have closed circuit television cameras mounted on telescopic masts to enable them to scan ships' decks. They are due for delivery in the spring of 1979.

In addition to a GM 8V92 propulsion engine and single Cummins V504M lift unit, an auxiliary generating unit of the Mercedes Benz OM6 36 diesel type is fitted. The Mercedes engine drives a single 250V 50Hz single phase alternator.

EQUIPMENT: Firefighting equipment is fitted capable of delivering seawater, aspirated protein foam, high pressure fog, and dry powder. A remote-control monitor with foam and seawater nozzles has a range of 46m (151ft) and low rates of 2,270 litres/min (498 gallons/min) for water or water/foam mix, and 19,500 litres/min (4,179 gallons/min) for aspirated foam. The two deck hydrants can also be supplied with water or water/foam mix: each has four low pressure outlets and one high pressure outlet for fog generation. The craft also carries hoses, large quantities

Hovermarine 218 port patrol craft

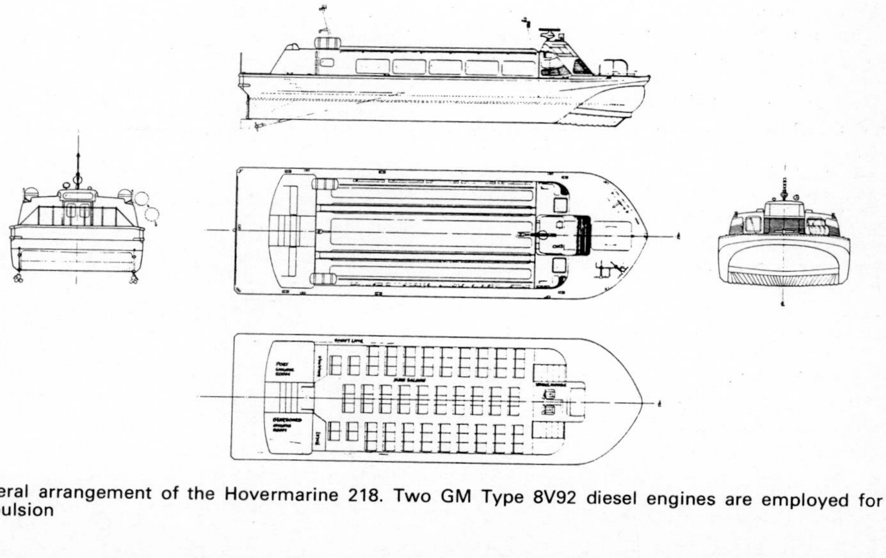

General arrangement of the Hovermarine 218. Two GM Type 8V92 diesel engines are employed for propulsion

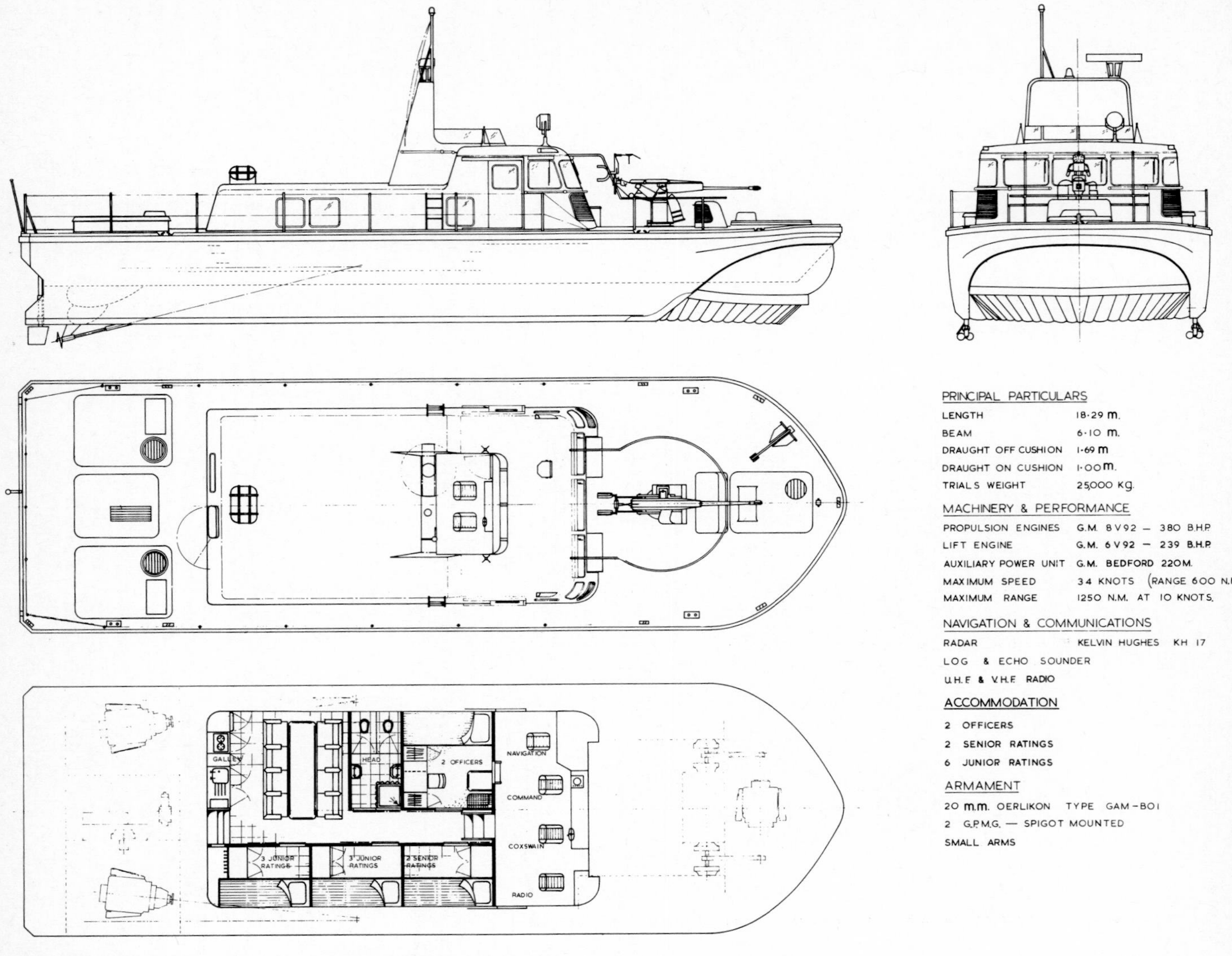

General arrangement of the Hovermarine 218 coastguard/patrol craft

of protein foam concentrate and a Graviner 100kg (220lb) portable dry powder firefighting system.

Hull and superstructure are protected by a waterskirt drenching system. Other ancillary equipment includes wind speed and direction meters, explosive gas detection apparatus, water temperature monitoring and compressed air breathing equipment. For surveillance and control, the craft is equipped with a Philips remote-control zoom lens closed-circuit television camera mounted on a 17m (55ft) telescopic mast; a 500W remote control searchlight and Decca 1214C radar with single scan and dual display. There is also a powerful loud-hailing system with facility for live and taped messages. Traffic guidance light-signalling systems are carried together with VHF radio.

To enable the craft to respond to emergencies requiring medical aid, it is equipped with racks for four stretchers, oxygen respiratory equipment and a resuscitation unit.

The craft, which also has a galley and crew room, can be operated on patrol by the commander and navigating officer, but for its full duties there are manning positions for a fire officer, traffic control officer, and a working crew of four.

DIMENSIONS
Length, overall: 18·29m (60ft)
Beam, overall: 6·1m (20ft)
Draft, hovering: 1·06m (3ft 6in)

PERFORMANCE
Speed, max: 34 knots
Range, at 30 knots: 610km (330n miles)

HOVERMARINE 221 MULTI-ROLE HARBOUR SERVICE CRAFT

The 221 is the largest of the Hovermarine 200 series hulls. In a multi-purpose harbour service

Hovermarine Transport Ltd's No 1 plant at Southampton. The roof of the company's No 2 plant is just visible behind

Hovermarine 218 passenger ferry undergoing trials on Southampton water

configuration it has been ordered by the City of Tacoma of Washington State, USA. Measuring 21m (70ft) in length, the craft will have a high pumping capability to enable it to cope with ship or harbour installation fires. The first of these craft is scheduled for delivery to the Tacoma authorities in July 1979 and the second approximately one year later. These craft will be equipped with a comprehensive range of firefighting, rescue and navigational and communications equipment.

Hovermarine 221 Tacoma Fireboat

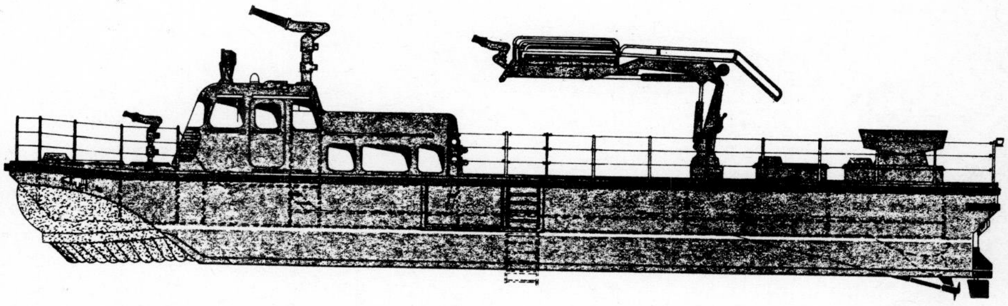

Outboard profile of the Hovermarine 221 harbour-service craft, as fitted out for the City of Tacoma Fire Department, Washington State, USA. The first of these craft is due to be delivered in July 1979.

HOVERMARINE 500 SERIES
HOVERMARINE 527

The world's largest sidewall-type hover ferry, the Hovermarine 527 is able to carry between 177 and 276 passengers at speeds of up to 40 knots. It has a maximum payload of 21,100kg and is designed to operate on coastal and inland waters in wave heights up to 3m (9ft 10in). A mixed-traffic variant for 140 passengers and 10 cars is projected.

The 527 complies with British Hovercraft Safety Requirements, the requirements of the Marine Division of the Department of Trade and Industry, United Kingdom, and Lloyds Register of Shipping, Air Cushion Vehicles 1970.

LIFT AND PROPULSION: All engines are marine diesels. All machinery is accommodated in two engine rooms, amidships, separated by a central passageway/stairway area. Each engine room contains one propulsion engine, one lift engine and one auxiliary propulsion unit. Power for the lift system is provided by two MAN type 10V 2530 MTE diesels, each developing 335hp at 2,300 rpm. Each drives via a gear box a lift fan to provide plenum air and, via a hydraulic pump and a hydraulic motor, a second fan to provide skirt inflation.

Propulsive power is provided by two MTU 12V TC331 diesels, each developing 1,200hp at 2,000rpm. Each incorporates a variable ratio gearbox and drives a single three-bladed propeller via transmission shafting inclined at 13 degrees. The propellers, which are outward rotating, operate at up to 1,540rpm.

All engines can be removed from the engine rooms after the removal of the detachable cowlings, via their lifting attachments, thus avoiding any interference with the passenger saloons.

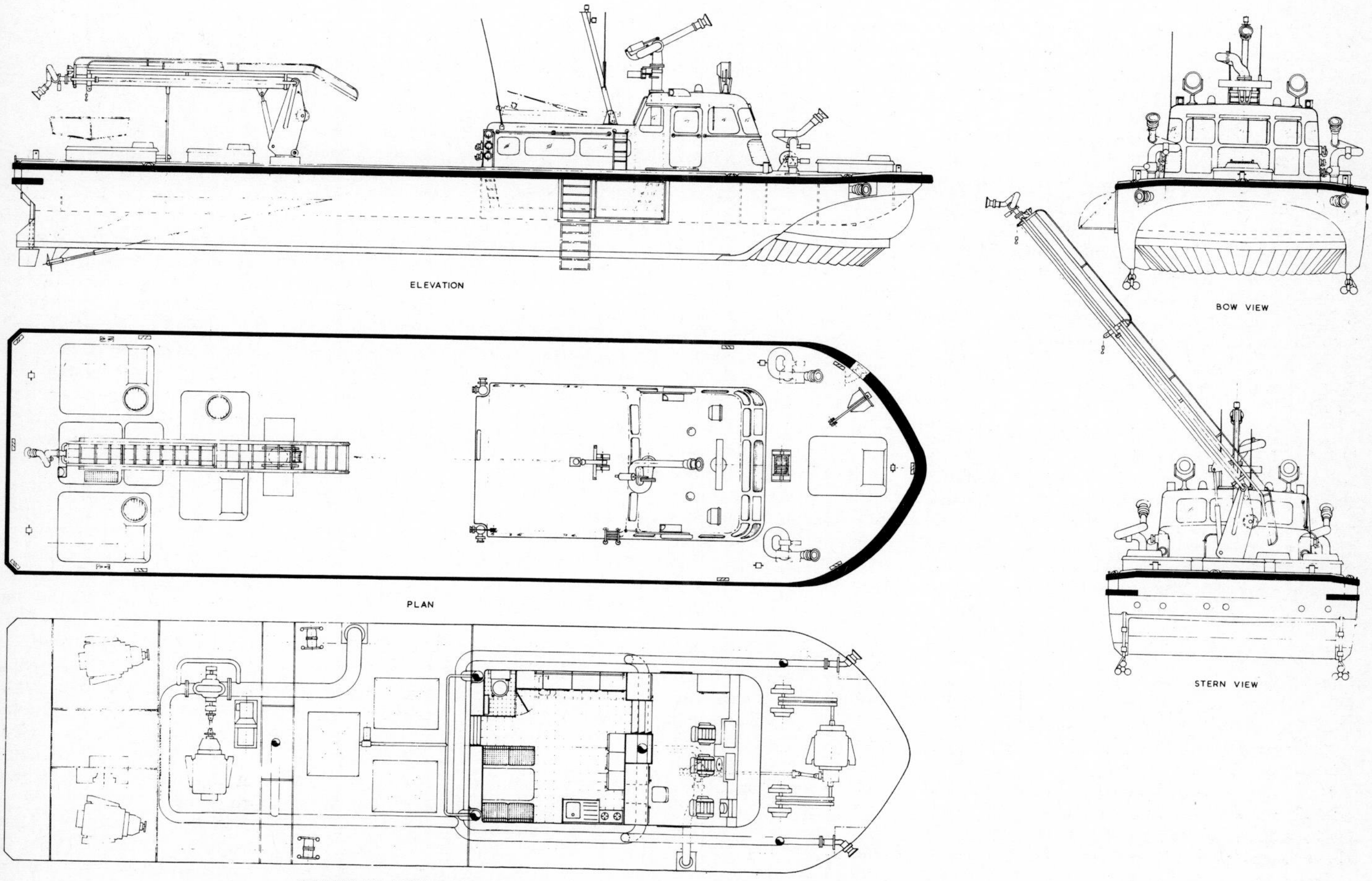

General arrangement of the Hovermarine 221 multi-purpose harbour craft

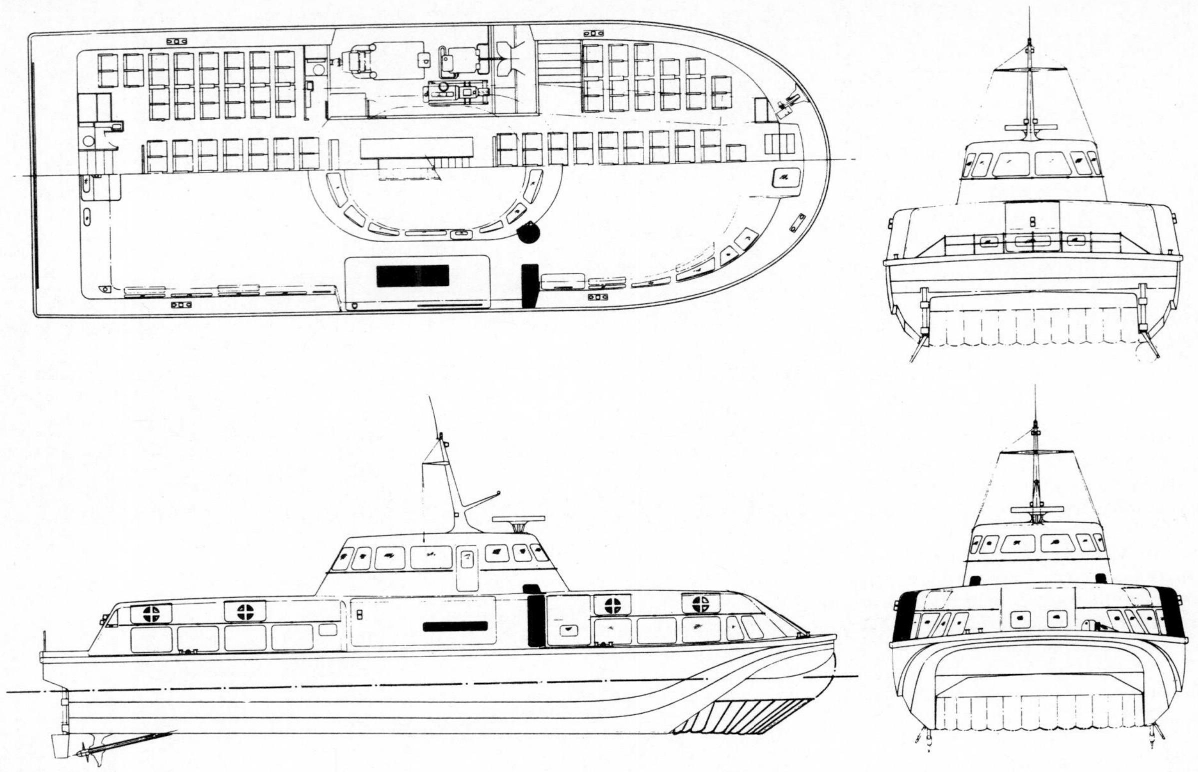

Hovermarine 527, 177-seat passenger ferry. Seating arrangements can be varied according to customer requirements. Up to 276 passengers can be accommodated. A mixed-traffic variant is planned with seats for 140 passengers and a vehicle deck for ten cars

Fuel is carried in four tanks, located in the transom bay, in-line athwartships. The two port tanks are inter-connected to form a single main tank, and the two starboard tanks are connected in a similar way. The port and starboard main tanks supply port and starboard engine rooms respectively. A ballast tank is fitted in each sidewall in the area of frame 15. Each tank, including ballast, has a fuel capacity of 993 litres and an expansion space of 24 litres. Fuel used is DIN 51/601, a marine gas oil to BS.2869 1957 class A. Filler points, with 86mm diameter necks, are located on the aft superstructure, port and starboard. Each refuelling point incorporates fuel contact repeater gauges and overflow warning lights which indicate when tanks are more than 90% full.

CONTROLS: Directional control is provided by power-operated twin water rudders. Additional control is provided by differential use of the water propellers. Transfer pumps fitted to ballast tanks provide trimming capability by movement of fuel between main tanks. All craft controls and instrumentation are concentrated in the wheelhouse, but certain instrumentation is duplicated in the engine rooms or at the refuelling points located on port and starboard aft superstructure.

SKIRT SYSTEM: The air cushion is retained between rigid longitudinal sidewalls and bow and stern flexible skirts. The main plenum chamber receives air from two fans driven by the lift engines via ducts located amidships port and starboard. Bow and stern skirt loops receive air from port and starboard fans driven hydraulically by lift engine gear box pumps. This air passes to the skirts via ducts forming part of the superstructure.

The bow skirt comprises two tailored loops of fabric suspended under the bow in 180 degree arcs, sidewall to sidewall. These are fabricated from neoprene rubber material reinforced with nylon, and joined at their lower edges to form an irregularly-shaped but inflatable compartment. When inflated, the degree of rigidity attained enables the loops to support an array of lower skirt segments, attached at the loop joint line, and also to absorb wave impact shock to a degree.

Twenty flexible single fabric segments attached to the loops are in contact with the water surface.

When inflated with the craft 'on cushion', an effective air seal is formed. Each segment is attached radially by a webbing loop and shackle to a central attachment flange on the hull underside. Four additional corner segments on each side are attached to the hull by ropes and shackles.

Two tailored loops of similar manufacture to the bow loops are suspended under the stern, sidewall to sidewall. The loops are joined at their lower edges to form a single inflatable compartment. When inflated, the degree of rigidity attained enables the loops to support 20 double fabric segments attached to the loop joint line. The forward-facing inner segment inflates with plenum air pressure to form a seal but is not in contact with the water surface. The aft-facing outer segment is in contact with the water surface and prevents scooping of water into the inner segment.

HULL: Single shell glass-reinforced plastics moulding with sub-moulding, frames, bulkheads and cabin sole panels bonded together. Materials used include expanded PVC foam, glassfibre, polyester resins, wood and aluminium alloy. Mechanical fasteners are used where necessary to augment strength. There are five watertight bulkheads. The wheelhouse/observation saloon is a single unit formed by a separate moulding in grp laminate, reinforced with Plasticell PVC foam/grp laminate sandwich, bonded and bolted into position on the superstructure and supported by the engine room bulkheads.

Each engine bearer is a welded structure of transverse and longitudinal members fabricated from hollow square-section aluminium tube 101·6 × 101·6 × 7·92mm thick. Each member rests upon a prepared frame, to which it is bonded by three to five layers of CSM glass fibre with polyester resin.

ACCOMMODATION: The prototype carries 177 passengers in aircraft-type seats in three air-conditioned saloons, 78 in the forward saloon, 84 in the aft saloon and 15 in the upper observation saloon. Alternative layouts accommodate up to 276 passengers.

The wheelhouse accommodates the commander, navigator and a third crew member. Two forward seats are provided for the commander (starboard seat) and navigator (port seat), separated by a central control console. The third crew member occupies a seat immediately aft of the console. The navigator's seat swivels for access to a chart table on his left. Instruments not included in the main array facing the crew seats are mounted in overhead panels. The main switchboard is located on the aft wheelhouse bulkhead. A window in the bulkhead between the door and the switchboard provides rearward visibility for the crew via the aft windows of the observation saloon. Access is via a stern door and doors in the port and starboard forward saloons. Two emergency exits are located in the rear cabin and two at the bow. Main forward and aft entrance doors and engine room doors incorporate a 'Door closed' indicator light and must be closed before departure. Fore and aft and upper saloon windows are all in Perspex and a proportion of window area is tinted to relieve sun glare. The forward windows of the wheelhouse are of laminated glass with provision for heating. Four toilet/washbasin units are provided, two located immediately aft of each engine room and two by the aft entrance stairway, one each side. A central luggage space, with 14m³ of stowage area is provided beneath the wheelhouse. The wheelhouse is reached from the main deck via a companionway, a door in the wheelhouse aft bulkhead providing access. Side doors in the wheelhouse provide access to the superstructure deck.

SYSTEMS, ELECTRICAL: Independent ac and dc systems, the latter providing power for safe craft return in the event of a total ac power failure. APU in each engine room incorporates one ac and one dc generator, normally on line. A third dc generator is driven by the port lift engine. The ac generators are Newage 20kVA 400V 0.8PF three-phase, four-wire 50Hz single bearing units. The APU dc generators are Delco Remy 28V 235A units. The port lift engine standby generator is an ac Delco 28V 65A dc unit. Each engine room contains a set of two 12V 128Ah batteries in series parallel, providing a total effective capacity of 24V 256Ah. A main switchboard is mounted on the wheelhouse aft bulkhead, containing ac and dc instrumentation, fuses and a common dc bus bar. A shore-based 230V single-phase 50Hz supply can be connected to the craft but can only be utilised when both ac generators are off live.

APUs: Two Perkins 6·354M marine diesels each with maximum intermittent rating of 115shp at 2,800rpm, drive the ac alternators, dc generators and compressors for the air-conditioning system.

NAVIGATION: Navigational instruments include a master magnetic compass, a Ritchie compass by the commander's station, a Redifon Sealand 30 VHF connected with the intercom system, a Kelvin Hughes Type 17/12 radar, complete with master compass stabilisation, and a Seascribe Seafarer echo sounder.

Subject to trials either an electromagnetic log or Doppler speed indicator will be fitted.

A variety of alternative or additional navigation aids can be installed to suit local legislation and route conditions.

COMMUNICATIONS: Standard equipment includes a VHF radio, an intercommunicating system, hailing system and a PA/entertainment system.

SAFETY: Safety equipment is in accordance with current CAA requirements and includes the following: seven 30-man liferafts, 190 inflatable life jackets, 4 lifebuoy and line-throwing apparatus.

DIMENSIONS

Length overall: 27·2m (89ft 3in)

Beam overall: 10·2m (33ft 5½in)

Freeboard, nominal: 1·1m (3ft 7¼in)

Height, waterline, hullborne, to wheelhouse top: 5·34m (17ft 6½in)

Draft, at nominal gross weight, measured from base of propeller stage

off cushion: 2·55m (8ft 4½in)

on cushion: 1·4m (4ft 7in)

WEIGHTS

Nominal gross (177 passengers, plus baggage and including fuel oil etc): 77,500kg (170,856lb)

Payload (177 passengers with airline type seats or 214 passengers with economy type seats with 5kg hand baggage): 17,700kg (38,846lb)

Max overload: 80,000kg (176,320lb)

PERFORMANCE

Max speed, still air, calm conditions: 40 knots

Cruising speed: 35 knots in conditions not exceeding 1m max wave height and 15 knot wind with 17,700kg payload, 78,000kg all-up weight

Range at cruising speed: 210n miles

Endurance at cruising speed: 6 hours minimum

HOVERMARINE 527 VARIANTS

In August 1977 Hovermarine announced that derivatives of the 527 were being developed for fast attack/patrol (527MA) and long-range surveillance (527MP). A further derivative, the 527MC, was announced in September 1978. Preliminary details are given below.

HOVERMARINE 527 MC

Latest design in the 27m (89ft) Hovermarine 527 series, the 527 MC is a high speed Coastguard/Rescue Craft with a maximum speed of 40 knots. At its cruising speed of 32 knots it has a range of 1,600n miles. Features of the design include a low noise profile, shallow draft and automatic roll stabilisation.

LIFT AND PROPULSION: All engines are marine diesels. Power for the lift system is furnished by a single 350hp MAN 10V 2530 MTE diesel. Propulsive power is supplied by two MTU 12V 331 diesels, each delivering 1,200hp at 2,000rpm. Each incorporates a variable-ratio gearbox and drives a single three-bladed water propeller via an inclined transmission shaft. Auxiliary power is provided by a Perkins 6·354m diesel.

CONTROLS: Craft heading is controlled by power-operated twin water rudders. Additional control is provided by differential use of the water propellers.

HULL: Constructed in moulded glass-reinforced plastics.

ACCOMMODATION: Designed to accommodate a crew of five, two officers and three ratings. A double cabin is provided for the officers and three-berth cabin for the ratings. There is also a first aid/detention room.

SYSTEMS, NAVIGATION AND COMMUNICATIONS: Radar, gyrocompass, log, echo sounder, HF, VHF and UHF radio.

ARMAMENT: Single 20mm Oerlikon GAM-BO1 naval mount on forward deck. Small arms.

Fibreglass hull of the Hovermarine 527 hoverferry under construction at the Hovermarine Transport Limited plant at Woolston, Southampton.

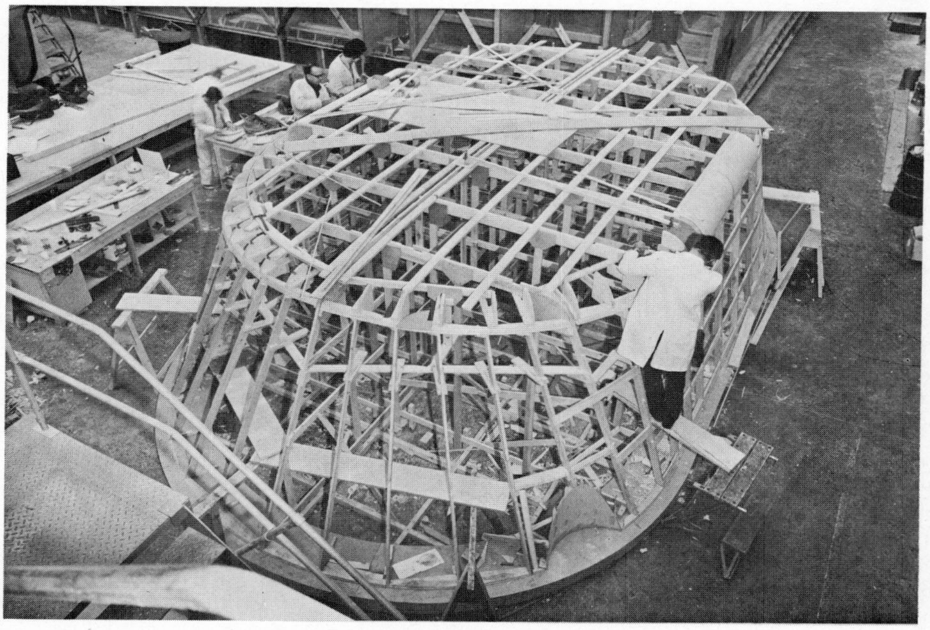

At work on the Hovermarine 527's wheelhouse and upper saloon.

Building the cabin superstructure of the Hovermarine 527

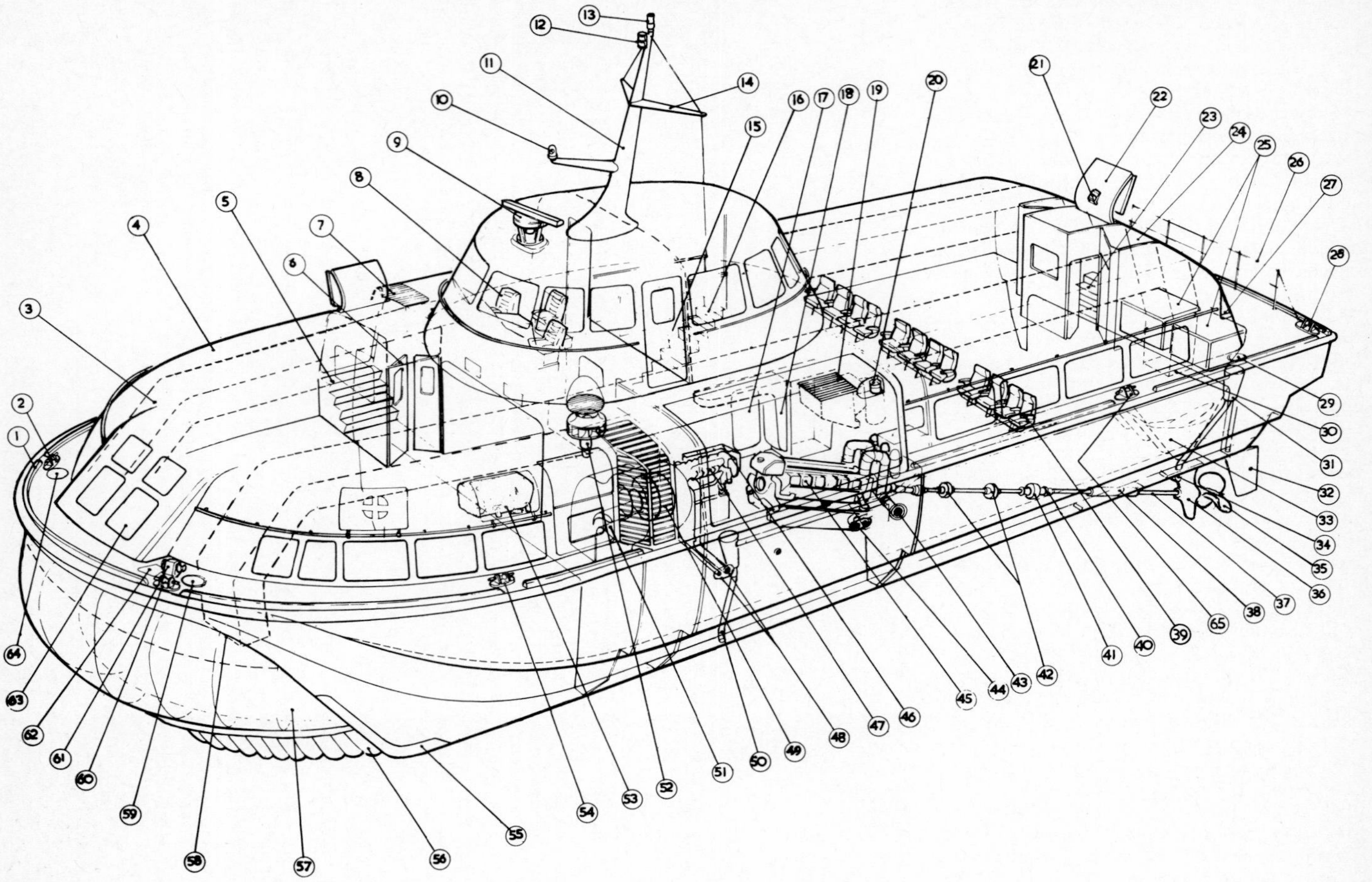

Hovermarine 527, 177-seat passenger ferry

1. Toe Rail; 2. Mooring Bitt; 3. Air Duct, Forward Skirt Loop Inflation; 4. Superstructure; 5. Forward Saloon Companionway; 6. Forward Saloon Companionway Doors; 7. Intake Grill, Starboard Lift Fan; 8. Commander's Seat; 9. Radar Scanner; 10. Flashing Hoverlight (Yellow); 11. Mast; 12. Masthead Light; 13. Anchor Light; 14. Crosstree; 15. Wheelhouse Door; 16. Stairway, Upper/Lower Decks; 17. Engine Room Door; 18. Air Conditioning Duct; 19. Engine Room Air Intake; 20. Navigation Light; 21. Stern Light; 22. Folding Hatch, Aft Companionway; 23. Aft Companionway; 24. Port Aft Toilet; 25. Fuel Tanks, Port; 26. Stern Rail; 27. Refuelling Point, Port; 28. Mooring Bitt; 29. Access Hatch, Port Aft Sea Water Strainer; 30. Air Duct, Aft Skirt Loop Inflation; 31. Sea Water Strainer; 32. Rudder; 33. Skirt Segment; 34. Aft Sea Water Intake; 35. Propeller; 36. 'P' Bracket/Skeg; 37. Propeller Shaft; 38. Shaft Log; 39. Passenger Seats, Aircraft Type; 40. Shaft Spacer and Coupling; 41. Thrust Bearing; 42. Shaft Bearing; 43. Exhaust, Propulsion Engine; 44. Sea Water Discharge; 45. Port Propulsion Engine; 46. Port Auxiliary Power Unit; 47. Port Lift Engine; 48. Exhausts, Lift Engine and Auxiliary Power Unit; 49. Lift Fan; 50. Forward Sea Water Intake; 51. Lift Fan Volute; 52. Skirt Loop Inflation Fan; 53. Liferaft Stowage in Soft Valise; 54. Mooring Bitt and Slinging Point; 55. Sidewall Impact Blade; 56. Skirt Segment; 57. Skirt Loop (Shown Inflated); 58. Air Duct, Forward Skirt Loop Inflation; 59. Chain Locker Access; 60. Mooring Bitt; 61. Winch (Electric); 62. Davit Mounting; 63. Forward Window and Emergency Exit; 64. Equipment Stowage Hatch; 65. Mooring Bitt and Slinging Point

DIMENSIONS
Length overall: 27·2m (89ft 3in)
Beam: 10·2m (33ft 5in)
Draft, off cushion: 2·55m (8ft 4in)
on cushion: 1·4m (4ft 7in)
WEIGHTS
Max gross: 82,000kg (180,000lb)
PERFORMANCE
Max speed: 40 knots
Cruising speed: 32 knots
Range: 2,965km (1,600n miles) at 32 knots
5,560km (3,000n miles) at 12 knots

HOVERMARINE 533 MA

At 110 tonnes, the Hovermarine 533 MA is one of the smallest missile-armed fast attack craft available. A typical weapons layout would be four Otomat missiles and a twin 35mm Oerlikon naval mount with a Marconi Sapphire fire control system. With a complement of twelve and two 1,200hp MTU 12V 331 diesels it has a top speed of 40 knots and a range of 1,350n miles. Cruising speed is 36 knots.

LIFT AND PROPULSION: All engines are marine diesels. Power for the lift system is furnished by a single 1,200hp MTU 12V 331 diesel. Propulsive power is supplied by two MTU 12V 331 diesels, each delivering 1,200hp at 2,000rpm. Each incorporates a variable-ratio gearbox and drives a single three-bladed water propeller via an inclined transmission shaft. Auxiliary power is supplied by Perkins 6·354m diesels.

CONTROLS: Craft heading is controlled by power-operated twin water rudders. Additional

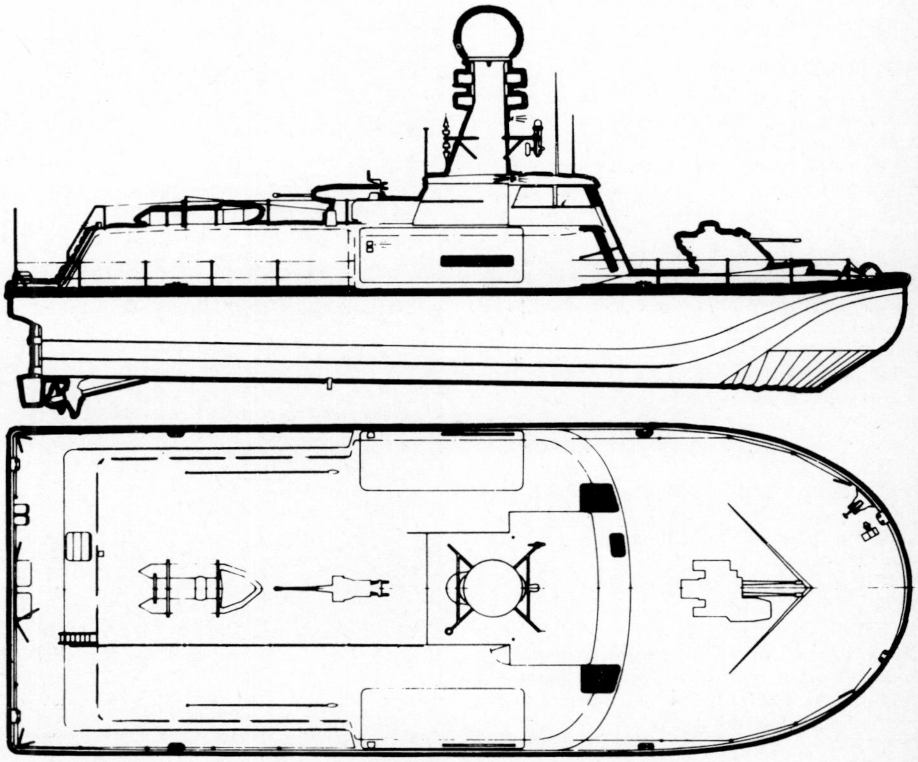

Hovermarine 527 long range patrol and surveillance craft

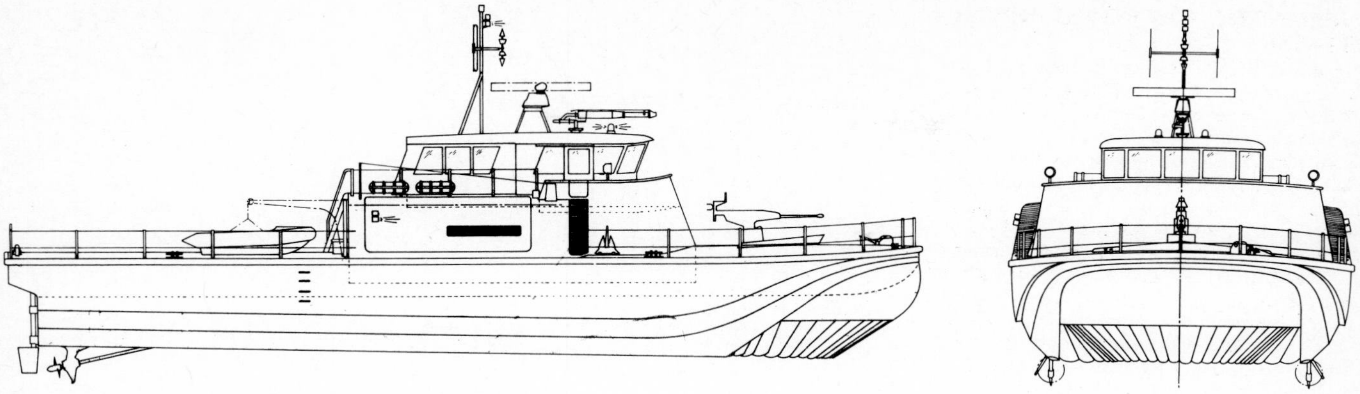

The Hovermarine 527 MC coastguard/rescue craft

control is provided by differential use of the water propellers.
HULL: Built in moulded glass-reinforced plastics.
ACCOMMODATION: Crew would normally comprise two officers and six junior ratings. Accommodation would include a double cabin and wardroom for the two officers and a six berth mess for ratings. There would also be a ratings dining hall and galley.
SYSTEMS, ARMAMENT: Four Otomat surface-to-surface missiles, one twin 35mm Oerlikon cannon with a Marconi Sapphire fire control system. Small arms.
NAVIGATION AND COMMUNICATIONS: Radar, gyrocompass, echo sounder, Decca Navigator or Loran C long range navigation equipment; Marconi S810 surveillance radar. HF, VHF and UHF radio.
ELECTRONIC WARFARE: Decca RDL, 1BC/5C/7C; IFF and chaff launchers.
BOATS: High speed inflatable dinghy, life raft.
DIMENSIONS
Length: 33·2m (109ft)
Beam: 10·2m (33ft 6in)
Draft, off cushion: 2·55m (8ft 4in)
on cushion: 1·4m (4ft 7in)
WEIGHTS
Max gross: 110,000kg (242,508lb)
PERFORMANCE
Max speed: 40 knots
Cruising speed: 36 knots
Range: 5,000km (2,700n miles) at 12 knots
2,500km (1,350n miles) at 36 knots

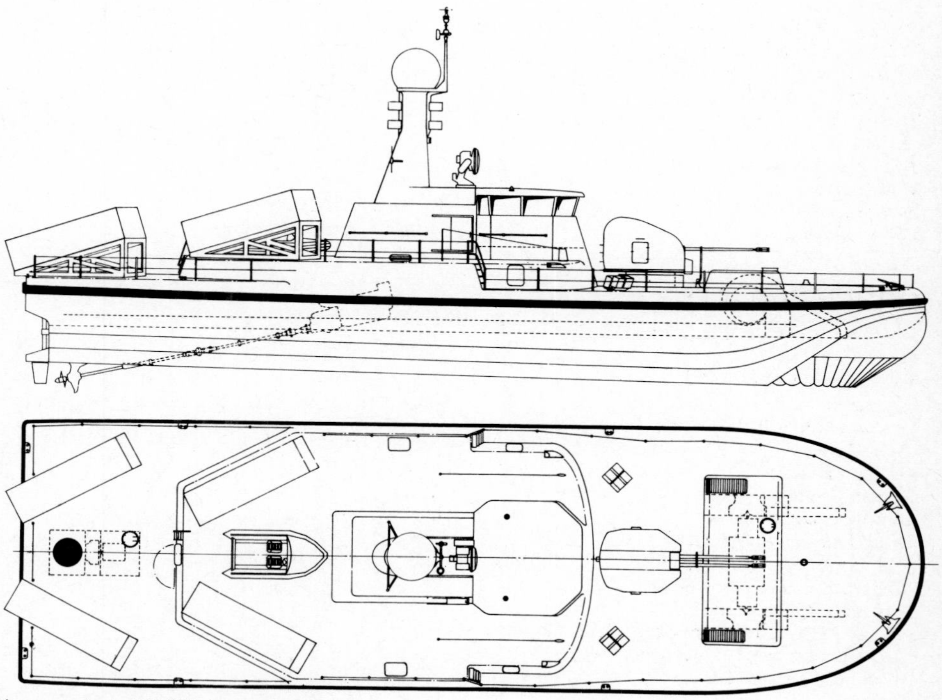

Hovermarine's 533 MA fast attack craft

HOVERMARINE 539 MP

The Hovermarine 539 MP patrol surveillance craft is designed to remain at sea for at least five days without replenishment. Maximum continuous speed is 38 knots while a cruising speed of 32 knots gives a range of 1,450 miles. Maximum range is 2,800 miles at 12 knots.
LIFT AND PROPULSION: All engines are marine diesels. Power for the lift system is furnished by a single 1,200hp MTU 12V 331 diesel. Propulsive power is supplied by two MTU 12V 331 diesels, each delivering 1,200hp at 2,000rpm. Each incorporates a variable-ratio gearbox and drives a single three-bladed water propeller via an inclined transmission shaft. Auxiliary power is provided by Perkins 6·354 diesels.
CONTROLS: Craft heading is controlled by power-operated twin water rudders. Additional control is provided by differential application of the water propellers.
HULL: Built in moulded glass-reinforced plastics.
ACCOMMODATION: Crew would normally comprise three officers, four senior ratings and six junior ratings. Accommodation would include three single cabins and a wardroom for the officers, a four-berth cabin plus an annex for the senior ratings, a galley, a six-berth mess and dining hall for the junior ratings.
SYSTEMS, ARMAMENT: One single 40mm Breda Compact twin mount linked with a Sea Archer fire control system.
NAVIGATION AND COMMUNICATIONS: Radar, gyrocompass, log, echo sounder, Decca Navigator or Loran C long range navigation equipment HF, VHF, UHF, MF/DF radio and Marconi S810 surveillance radar.
ELECTRONIC WARFARE: Decca RDL, 1BC/5C/7C; IFF and chaff launchers.
BOATS: High speed inflatable dinghy, life rafts.
DIMENSIONS
Length: 39·2m (128ft 6in)
Beam: 10·2m (33ft 5in)
Draft, off cushion: 2·55m (8ft 4in)
on cushion: 1·4m (4ft 7in)
WEIGHTS
Max gross: 130,000kg (286,600lb)
PERFORMANCE
Max speed: 38 knots
Cruising speed: 32 knots
Range: 5,190km (2,800n miles) at 12 knots
2,687km (1,450n miles) at 32 knots

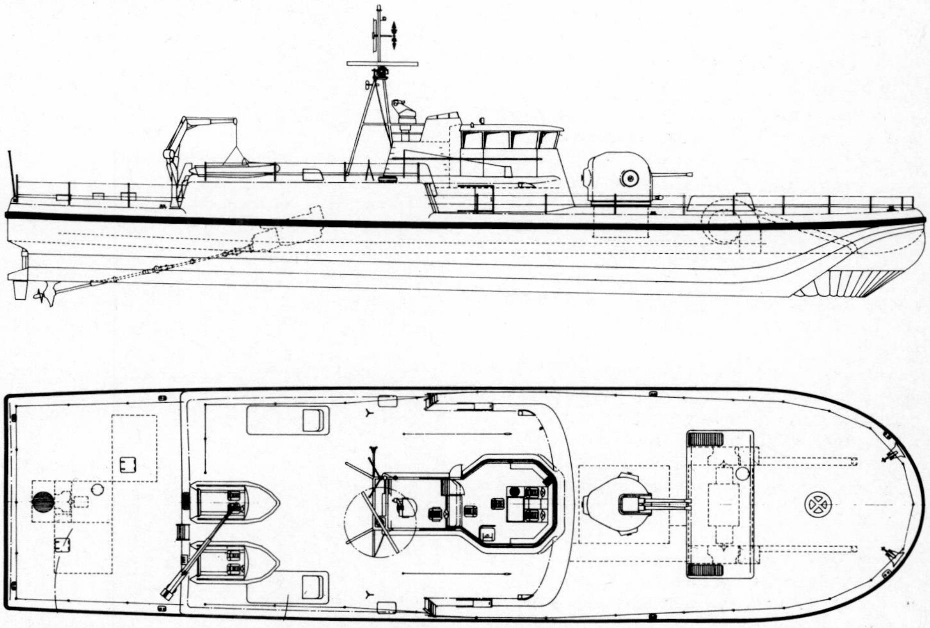

General arrangement of the Hovermarine 539 MP patrol surveillance craft

HOVERMARINE 600 SERIES HOVERFREIGHTER

Details of Hovermarine Transport Ltd's Hoverfreighter project were revealed in August 1977. Tank tests have now been conducted with a dynamic test model for a 35-knot, 309-ton car ferry version. This craft may be constructed in Japan by Hovermarine Pacific Ltd, at the Sasebo Yard.

The proposed car ferry will carry a payload of 149 tons, a typical load comprising 344 passengers, 33 private cars and 4 coaches. Provision has been made for the vehicles to be driven aboard the craft using either bow or stern loading doors. The craft structure will weigh about 106 tons, including two 3,750hp Paxman Valenta 18CM engines which would power the lift and propulsion systems. Total fuel load would be 14 tons.

DIMENSIONS
Length overall: 75m (246ft)
Beam overall: 14·5m (47ft)
Cushion length: 61m (200ft)
Cushion beam: 9m (29ft)
Cushion depth: 3·5m (11ft)
Max draft: 4m (13ft)

WEIGHTS
Payload: 149 tons
Structure: 106 tons
Machinery: 40 tons
Fuel: 14 tons
Total: 309 tons

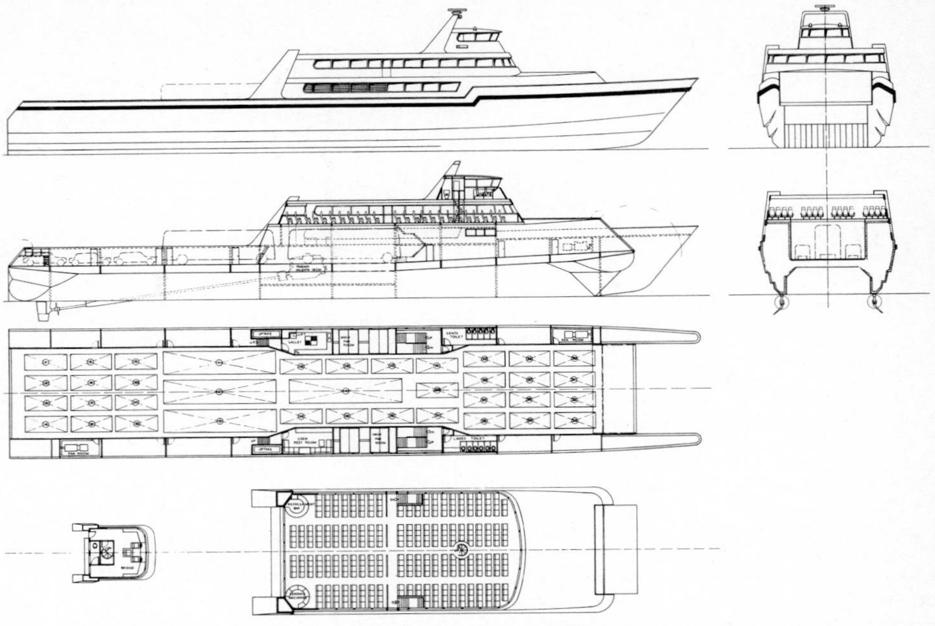

General arrangement of the 309-ton Hovermarine 600 series Hoverfreighter car ferry

PERFORMANCE
Cruising speed: 35 knots

HOVERSERVICES

24 Hazel Grove, Wallingford, Oxon OX10 0AT, England
Telephone: 0491 37455
Partners:
Graham Nutt
James Lyne
Graham Bran
William Baker
Overseas Distributors:
United States of America:
Hoverservices (USA), PO Box 12064, Shawnee Mission, Kansas 66212
Australia (Queensland):
Light Hovercraft Services, 148 Thornside Road, Thornside, Queensland 4158
Telephone: 207 2934
Australia (Western):
Hoverservices (Western Australia), PO Box N1136, Perth, Western Australia 6001
Ireland:
D O'Fahay, 581 Howeth Road, Raheny, Dublin 5

Hoverservices was formed in 1972 to market Scarab hovercraft plans and components. The company now offers a range of light hovercraft plans for the single-seat Scarab I and two-seat Scarab II, in addition to plans for other racing craft such as the Scarab III, Snoopy II and Eccles craft. All of these plans are marketed worldwide.

The company has a wide range of fans, grp ducts, skirt material and other components in stock and provides a complete engineering service.

The Scarab 10 range, two seat sports/racing and four seat cruising/utility craft, are also offered in grp and can be purchased as a kit or in a ready assembled form. All of these craft — including Scarab 10 — have been developed from an intensive programme of hovercraft racing over land and water.

SCARAB I (Plans)

This is a simple, lightweight craft, ideal for sheltered water operation. It uses low cost engines and is a useful craft for beginners. Many craft of this type have been selected for school or group hovercraft building projects. It seats one person.

LIFT AND PROPULSION: A single 3·5bhp Briggs & Stratton engine provides power to an axial lift fan of 482mm (19in) in diameter, fitted with Multi-wing blades. For thrust the craft employs a JLO 250cc 15bhp engine which drives a 609mm (24in) diameter ducted fan fitted with Multi-wing blades.

A Scarab 10 four-seat light hovercraft

Scarab 10 two-seater high performance sports/racing hovercraft

CONTROLS: There is a single rudder located in the thrust duct and movement of this control is achieved by a joystick located in the cockpit. A twist grip gives throttle control for the thrust engine and a simple lever controls the lift engine.
HULL: The hull is constructed using a triangulated plywood box technique upon a pine frame and finished with grp tape for extra strength. A full flow skirt of loop design is fitted to the craft.
ACCOMMODATION: A single seat is fitted in the open cockpit.
DIMENSIONS
Length: 3·05m (10ft)
Width: 1·68m (5ft 6in)
Hoverheight: 228mm (9in)
WEIGHTS
Empty: 72·57kg (160lb)
Normal payload: 90·72kg (200lb)
Normal all-up weight: 163·29kg (360lb)
PERFORMANCE
Over land or water the craft can achieve speeds of 40·2-48·2km/h (25-30mph)

Scarab II, a one or two seater with two ducted fans for thrust and a pressure fed extended segment skirt

SCARAB II (Plans)

Scarab II is a two seater light hovercraft designed for cruising in calm coastal or sheltered estuarial waters. With its larger size it will accept a variety of different engines for lift and propulsion functions.
LIFT AND PROPULSION: A typical lift engine for this craft would be a 5bhp Briggs & Stratton, driving a 558mm (22in) diameter axial lift fan fitted with Multi-wing blades. For propulsion the craft could use various powerplants up to 42bhp driving either 609mm (24in) or 762mm (30in) diameter ducted Multi-wing fans.
CONTROLS: Employs a single rudder positioned in the thrust duct which is activated by a joystick located in the open cockpit. A twist grip throttle is used for the thrust engine and a quadrant type lever for lift.
HULL: This is made from triangular plywood boxes upon a framework of pine with grp tape for additional strength for joints etc. A full flow loop skirt is fitted.
ACCOMMODATION: A driver and one passenger can be seated in the craft's open cockpit, sitting side by side.
DIMENSIONS
Length: 3·5m (11ft 6in)
Width: 1·83m (6ft)
Hoverheight: 228mm (9in)
WEIGHTS
Empty: 113·4kg (250lb)
Normal payload: 181·44kg (400lb) (two people)
All-up weight: 294·84kg (650lb)
PERFORMANCE
Over land and water Scarab II craft, with propulsion units of 35-42bhp, can achieve speeds of 48·28-56·32km/h (30-35mph)

SCARAB III

This is a very basic craft intended to be a lightweight racing hovercraft. It is based upon the Scarab I design and is fitted with a 42bhp propulsion engine.
LIFT AND PROPULSION: Lift air is supplied by a Rowena 225cc 8bhp engine which drives a 558mm (22in) diameter Multi-wing axial fan. For propulsion a 762mm (30in) diameter ducted Multi-wing fan is driven by a Hirth 440 engine rated at 42bhp.
CONTROLS: A pair of rudders are located in the propulsion duct and these are controlled by a simple joystick in the open cockpit. A twist grip throttle is used for the thrust engine and a quadrant lever for the lift engine.
HULL: A pine framework covered with a triangulated plywood box construction makes up the hull. Grp tape is used for extra strength on joints. A full flow loop skirt is fitted to the hull.
ACCOMMODATION: A seat in the craft's open cockpit is provided for one person.
DIMENSIONS
Length: 3·05m (10ft)
Width: 1·68m (5ft 6in)
Hoverheight: 228mm (9in)
WEIGHTS
Empty: 113·44kg (250lb)
Normal payload: 90·72kg (200lb)
All-up weight: 204·12kg (450lb)
PERFORMANCE
Over land and water the Scarab III is capable of achieving speeds of 72·42-80·49km/h (45-50mph)

SCARAB 10-2

(Available in kit or complete form)
This is a high performance two-seat sports/racing hovercraft with increased freeboard which gives it an improved standard of weather protection and comfort.
LIFT AND PROPULSION: A single 533mm (21in) diameter Multi-wing axial fan is driven by an 8bhp Rowena 225cc engine for lift. Two 609mm (24in) diameter Multi-wing ducted fans driven by a Hirth 440 engine of 42bhp are used for thrust. This unit gives a static thrust of about 72·57kg (160lb).
CONTROLS: A rudder is mounted in each of the thrust ducts.
HULL: The craft is made in moulded grp with polyurethane foam fill for buoyancy. It is fitted with a full flow loop skirt made from heavy duty nylon/PVC material.
ACCOMMODATION: Seating is provided for two persons in an open cockpit sitting in line.
DIMENSIONS
Length: 3·65m (12ft)
Width: 1·98m (6ft 5in)
Hoverheight: 254mm (10in)
WEIGHTS
Empty: 204·12kg (450lb)
Normal payload: 181·44kg (400lb) (two persons)
All-up weight: 385·55kg (850lb)
PERFORMANCE
This craft has a maximum speed over land and water of 80·46km/h (50mph) but cruises at speeds of 40·23-48·28km/h (25-30mph).

SCARAB 10-4 (Complete)

This is an extension of the Scarab 10-2 which utilises the same power units for lift and thrust. The craft's increased length and modified seating arrangements are the main differences between the two designs.
LIFT AND PROPULSION: A single 533mm (21in) diameter Multi-wing axial fan is driven by an 8bhp Rowena 225cc engine for lift. For thrust the craft is fitted with a pair of 609mm (24in) diameter ducted Multi-wing fans which are driven by a Hirth 440 engine rated at about 42bhp. This unit supplies a static thrust of about 72·57kg (160lb).
CONTROLS: A single rudder is mounted in each of the propulsion ducts.
HULL: This is grp moulded with polyurethane foam used for buoyancy within the hull. A full flow loop skirt fitted with individually fed segments is employed.
ACCOMMODATION: Seating is provided for four persons in an open cockpit.
DIMENSIONS
Length: 4·57m (15ft)
Width: 1·98m (6ft 5in)
Hoverheight: 254mm (10in)
WEIGHTS
Empty: 226·8kg (500lb)
Normal payload: 363·87kg (800lb) (four persons)
All-up weight: 590·67kg (1,300lb)
PERFORMANCE
Over land and water the Scarab 10-4 can achieve speeds of 40·23-48·28km/h (25-30mph)

SCARAB XI

This new sports craft is developed from the Scarab 10. The hull is built in foam-filled moulded grp. The skirt is of the pressurised segment type, and a modified thrust system is incorporated, with straightener vanes in the fan ducts.
LIFT AND PROPULSION: Cushion air is provided by a single 558mm (22in) Multi-wing fan driven by an 8hp Rowena lift engine. Thrust is provided by a 40hp Hirth engine driving two 609mm (24in) ducted Multi-wing fans. Each duct incorporates straightening vanes to give extra thrust. The unit gives a static thrust of about 190-200lb.

CONTROLS: Craft heading is controlled by a rudder fitted in each fan duct. Engine speeds are controlled by throttle levers.
HULL: One piece grp moulding. Polyurethane foam filling is used for buoyancy. The skirt is of the pressure fed extended segment type.
ACCOMMODATION: One to two seater. Open cockpit with tandem seating.
DIMENSIONS
Length: 3·35m (11ft)
Width: 1·98m (6ft 5in)
WEIGHTS
Empty: 147kg (325lb)
Payload: 181kg (400lb) (two persons)
All-up weight: 328kg (725lb)
PERFORMANCE
Max speed: approx 60mph over land and water

LIGHT HOVERCRAFT COMPANY

Felbridge Hotel & Investment Co Ltd, London Road, East Grinstead, Sussex, England
Telephone: 0342 24424
Officials:
L H F Gatward, *Proprietor*

Light Hovercraft Company has been active in the field of hoverpallets since 1969. It has entered the light sports ACV field with a fibreglass hulled variant of Nigel Beale's Cyclone, which won the British National Hovercraft Championships in 1971 and was joint winner of this event in 1972. In August 1972 a production Cyclone crossed the English Channel from Pegwell Bay hoverport to Calais, a total open sea distance of 56·32km (35 miles).

The company is now concentrating on the production of the two-seat Fantasy and the four-seat Phantom.

FANTASY

Light Hovercraft's latest design is the Fantasy, an amphibious two-seater with a top speed of 80km/h (40 knots). Separate lift and propulsion engines are employed, both of which are rubber-mounted to reduce vibration. Large silencers are fitted for quiet running.

The craft is sufficiently light to be carried by two people. It can be hovered onto a trailer for towing behind a car.

LIFT AND PROPULSION: Lift is provided by an 8hp engine driving a 482mm (1ft 7in) diameter Multi-wing fan. Aft of the passenger seat is a 42hp 640cc two-cycle engine driving a 762mm (2ft 6in) diameter ducted Multi-wing fan for propulsion. Fan ducts are covered by safety guards.

CONTROLS: A twin rudder hinged to the rear of the thrust fan provides directional control. A lever throttle operates the lift engine and a twistgrip throttle controls propulsion.

HULL: Foam-filled glassfibre hull. High freeboard and full planing surfaces.

SKIRT: Bag type skirt in polyurethane nylon, 0·41m (1ft 4in) deep.

ACCOMMODATION: Padded saddle seat with back rest, accommodates two.

DIMENSIONS
Length: 3·44m (11ft 4in)
Width: 1·86m (6ft 2in)

WEIGHTS
Empty: 160kg (350lb)
Payload: 200kg (400lb)

PERFORMANCE
Max speed: 40 knots
Endurance: 3 hours

Light Hovercraft Fantasy, two-seat amphibious sports craft

PHANTOM

This new fully amphibious sports/utility craft seats four persons in comfort or will carry up to 300kg (700lb) of cargo or equipment. Keynotes of the design are reliability, ease of maintenance and quiet operation. The ducted fans provide full thrust at low revolutions to maintain a low noise level. The craft is easily hovered onto a trailer for towing by a car.

LIFT AND PROPULSION: Integrated system powered by two fully enclosed 42hp 640cc two-cycle engines with electric starting. Each engine drives via a toothed belt a ducted axial fan, air from which is used for both lift and propulsion at a ratio of 1:3. Fuel capacity is 70 litres (15 gallons).

CONTROLS: Twin rudders hinged to the rear of each thrust duct control craft heading.

HULL: Foam-filled glassfibre structure. Buoyancy is 2,268kg (5,000lb).

SKIRT: 0·73m (2ft 5in) deep, fully-segmented skirt made in rot-proof fabric with an abrasive resistant coating.

ACCOMMODATION: Open cockpit seating a driver and up to three passengers. The cockpit is fitted with dual controls. Standard fittings include a wrap-around tinted perspex windscreen, a convertible hood for use in bad weather and two pairs of upholstered back-to-back seats that fold down to form a sunlounger or bed.

DIMENSIONS
Length overall: 4·8m (16ft)
Width: 2·9m (7ft 3in)
Height: 1·35m (4ft 6in)

WEIGHTS
All-up weight: 300kg (700lb)

PERFORMANCE
Max speed: 40 knots
Endurance: 6 hours
Hard structure clearance: 0·3m (1ft)

Light Hovercraft Phantom four-seater sports/utility craft, powered by two fully-enclosed 42hp two-cycle engines. Maximum speed is 40 knots

MISSIONARY AVIATION FELLOWSHIP

Ingles Yard, Jointon Road, Folkestone, Kent CT20 1RD, England
Telephone: 0303 59055
Officials:
S Sendall-King BSc, CEng, AFRAeS, FSLAET, *General Director*
David Stavely, *UK Director*
T J R Longley TEng, (CEI) AMRAeS, *Executive, Hovercraft Project*

The Missionary Aviation Fellowship is an international, interdenominational Christian organisation which operates a total of 75 light aircraft in support of missionary work in some of the world's more remote areas.

In the belief that a suitable hovercraft could make a valuable contribution to missionary work, MAF began the design of a craft to its own specification early in 1970. Design assistance was given voluntarily by several specialists in the field of hovercraft and aircraft engineering.

MAF's first craft was the Missionaire, a general purpose amphibious five-seater which was driven around the Isle of Wight with a 1,100lb payload in 2 hours 13 minutes. Block cruising speed was 27 knots and the total fuel consumption was only 2·7 gallons per hour. The organisation is now concentrating on the development of a six-seat machine, the River Rover.

MISSIONAIRE Mk I

This is a lightweight amphibious hovercraft powered by two Volkswagen engines. Although originally designed as a five-seater, the craft has a spacious cabin and has demonstrated its ability to carry seven adults over hump speed into a 12 knot headwind without any difficulty. Cruising speed over calm water is 35 knots. Details can be found in *Jane's Surface Skimmers 1978* and earlier editions.

RIVER ROVER

Designed as a river-borne counterpart to the Land Rover utility vehicle, River Rover is a sturdily constructed, six-seat cabin hovercraft which is being developed by MAF for service in many parts of the world where, potentially, small hovercraft can make a major contribution by providing transport and communications for small isolated communities.

MAF's studies indicated that the four main requirements for such a craft are:

Low cost, both of manufacture and operation;

Positive control characteristics, enabling the craft to follow safely the course of narrow, winding rivers with the minimum of sideways skidding;

Simple bolt-together unit construction, easy to repair and maintain yet sufficiently robust to guarantee a long and reliable service life;

An efficient and reliable skirt system, combining good wear resistance with ease of repair.

The River Rover is designed to embody all these features.

Following evaluation trials by the Royal Navy's Hovercraft Trials Unit at Lee-on-Solent, Hampshire, the craft has been chosen by the Joint Service Hovercraft Expedition to Nepal where it will be used to negotiate the Kali Gandaki river noted for its difficult rapids. Two River Rover Mark IIs are being built for the expedition and plans are also underway for its commercial production.

One interesting innovation is the provision of horizontally hinged elevators in the two thrust ducts to provide banking effect, craft trim and braking.

LIFT AND PROPULSION: Motive power is supplied by a single 80hp Renault R-16 automotive engine, This drives a 600mm (23·6in) diameter 10-bladed multi-wing lift fan, with blades at 30 degrees, and two 600mm (23·6in) five-bladed, adjustable-angle, Breeza thrust fans mounted on either side of the lift fan. Power is transmitted via three TBA timing belts, the lift fan drive incorporating a 1·67:1 speed reduction. All three fans are housed in a grp duct structure which channels the lift air through 90 degrees and then beneath the craft via the skirt bag. Fuel consumption at cruising speed is 11·25 litres/h (2·5 gallons/h)

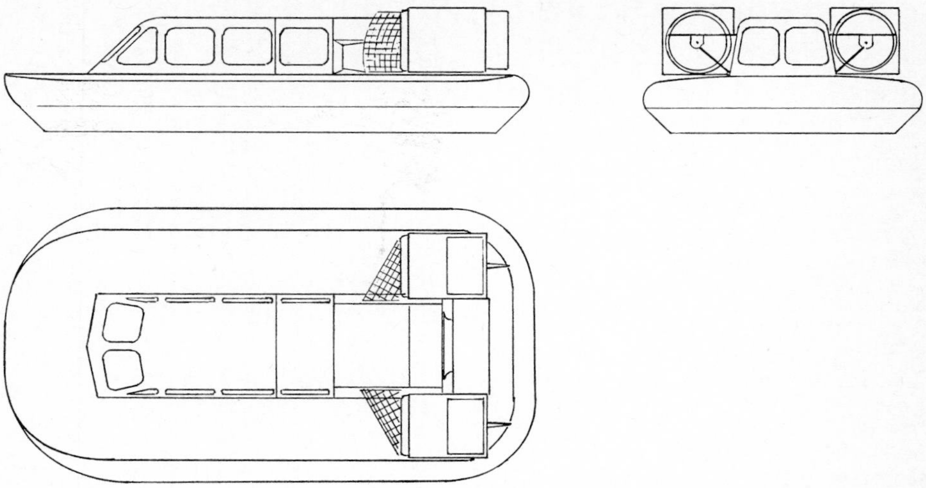

General arrangement of the Missionary Aviation Fellowship River Rover

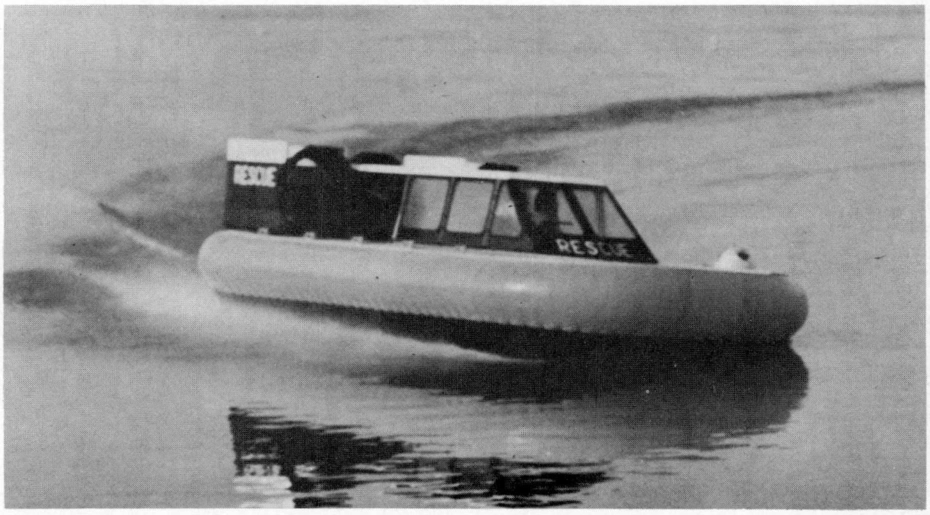

Missionary Aviation Fellowship's amphibious multi-duty six-seater, the River Rover. Powered by a single 80hp Renault R-16 automotive engine, the craft has a top speed of 56km/h (35mph). Horizontally-hinged elevons in the two thrust ducts provide banking effect, craft trim and braking

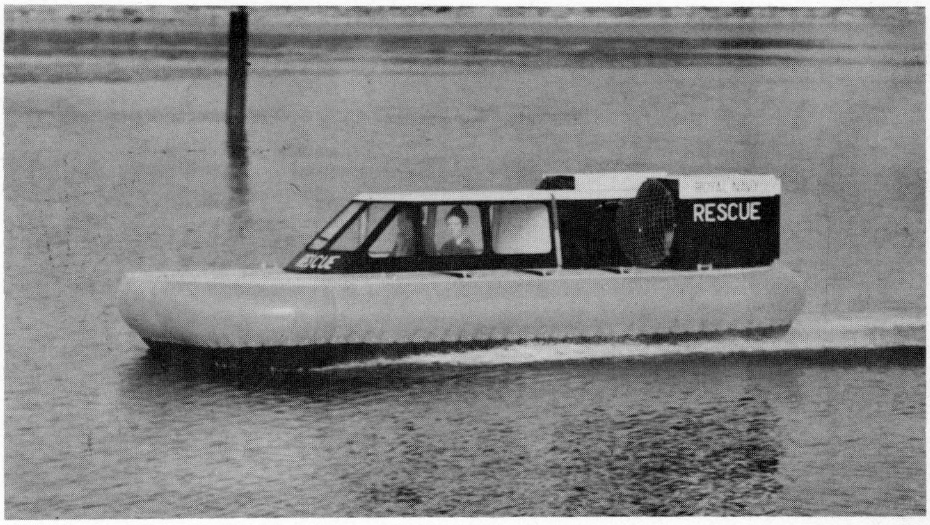

CONTROLS: Craft heading is controlled by two aerodynamic rudders, one hinged to the rear of each of the two thrust ducts. Additional control is provided by twin horizontally-pivoted elevons, one in each of the two square-sectioned ducts immediately aft of the fans. The elevons enable the craft to be banked into a turn (thereby reducing sideways skidding); provide craft trim and control thrust from the propulsion ducts. Movement of a joystick control rotates the elevons jointly or differentially. Employed together, craft trim is adjusted and when rotated fully braking is achieved. Used differentially they bank the craft prior to using the two rudders.

HULL: Aluminium alloy frame covered with ¼in marine grade plywood. Engine bay is decked in aluminium alloy sheet. Structure is bolted together for simplicity of breakdown and reassembly for transport. Engine bay is decked in aluminium alloy sheet and the sliding cabin canopy is in glass fibre.

SKIRT: HDL-type loop and segment skirt fabricated in Hypalon covered nylon fabric.

DIMENSIONS
Length on landing pads: 5·87m (19ft 3in)
Width on landing pads: 2·72m (8ft 11in)
Height on landing pads: 1·27m (4ft 2in)

WEIGHTS
Empty: 635kg (1,400lb)
All-up weight: 1,088kg (2,400lb)

PERFORMANCE
Max speed: 56km/h (35mph)
Cruising speed: 48km/h (30mph)

OSPREY HOVERCRAFT LTD

PO Box 34, Crawley, West Sussex RH10 4TF, England

Officials:

P V McCollum, *Director*
D McCollum, *Director*

This new light hovercraft company has been established by P V "Kip" McCollum, previously Technical Director of Surface Flight Ltd. The company is currently concentrating on the production of a range of four craft, Kestrel, Kestrel GT, Falcon and Cormorant.

CORMORANT

This new addition to the Osprey range originated as a one-off craft to meet a particular customer requirement. After trials it was decided to include the design in the standard range. The chief difference between the Cormorant and the Falcon is the departure from the integrated lift/propulsion system of the latter by the introduction of a separate lift engine and fan. This new arrangement has resulted in a craft with a greater payload capacity and generally increased all-round performance.

LIFT AND PROPULSION: A 15hp one-cylinder two-stroke engine mounted ahead of the cockpit drives a 560mm diameter (22in) polypropylene-bladed axial fan for lift. Thrust is furnished by a 40hp air-cooled twin-cylinder two-stroke driving a ducted 610mm (24in) polypropylene-bladed axial fan via a heavy duty toothed belt. Fuel capacity is 27 litres (6 imperial gallons). Consumption is 9-16 litres/h (2-3·5 gallons/h)

CONTROLS: Craft heading is controlled by twin aerodynamic rudders hinged to the rear of the thrust duct and operated by a handlebar.

HULL: Monocoque construction in self-coloured glass fibre. Preformed sealed polyurethane block at base of craft for buoyancy. Tools and spares compartment provided.

SKIRT: Segmented skirt fabricated in neoprene-coated nylon material.

DIMENSIONS
Length: 3·8m (12ft 6in)
Width: 1·83m (6ft)
Height: 1m (3ft 3in)

WEIGHTS
Empty: 218kg (480lb)
Normal payload: 182kg (400lb)
Max payload: 318kg (700lb)

PERFORMANCE
Max speed over land and water: 56 km/h plus (35mph plus)
Cruising speed: 32-40km/h (20-25mph)
Max continuous gradient, standing start: 1 in 8
Max short gradient, at speed: 1 in 4
Vertical hard obstacle clearance: 20cm (8in)

Osprey Hovercraft Ltd's Cormorant twin-engined runabout and light utility hovercraft

The Falcon two-seat recreational craft

Kestrel GT sports craft, powered by a 40hp air-cooled twin-cylinder two-stroke engine

FALCON

Though intended primarily as a two-seat recreational craft, the Falcon is also suitable for a variety of light commercial and utility roles. A keynote of the design is its simplicity. All maintenance can be undertaken by a competent mechanic or handyman.

Falcon is the fastest selling craft in the Osprey range. Some 50 per cent of those sold are being employed for utility purposes. Several have been purchased to act as standby emergency craft in tidal areas and one Falcon is employed in Scotland for harvesting 9·65km (6 miles) of salmon nets. This craft is in use twice daily and is often required to operate at night. One Falcon is being evaluated by the West German army.

A 'stretched' version, with a central driving position forward and a bench seat for two passengers aft, is in the planning stage. This arrangement will increase its ability to carry a larger payload when operating as a utility craft.

LIFT AND PROPULSION: Integrated system powered by a single 40hp air-cooled twin-cylinder two-stroke. This drives via a heavy duty toothed belt a 610mm (24in) diameter polypropylene-bladed ducted fan, air from which is used for both lift and propulsion. Fuel capacity is 27 litres (6 imperial gallons). Fuel recommended is 93 octane, oil mix 25 : 1. Consumption is 11-16 litres/h (2½-3½ gallons/h).

HULL: Monocoque construction in self-coloured glass fibre. All components and fasteners are made from marine quality material. Preformed sealed polyurethane block at base of craft for buoyancy. Tools and spares compartment provided.

SKIRT: Segmented skirt fabricated in neoprene-coated nylon material.

DIMENSIONS
Length: 3·8m (12ft 6in)
Beam: 1·83m (6ft)
Height: 1m (3ft 3in)

WEIGHTS
Empty: 172kg (380lb)
Normal payload: 164kg (360lb)
Max payload: 205kg (450lb)

PERFORMANCE
Cruising speed: 32-40km/h (20-25mph)
Max speed over land and water: 56km/h plus (35mph plus)
Max continuous gradient, standing start: 1 in 8
Max short gradient, at speed: 1 in 2 (45 degrees)
Vertical hard obstacle clearance: 20cm (8in)

KESTREL GT

Based on a standard Kestrel hull but fitted with the Falcon's engine and fan system, the Kestrel GT has been designed to meet the need of enthusiasts for a powerful lightweight hovercraft for sport and competitive racing. Due to its high power/weight ratio, it is particularly agile and can negotiate relatively steep slopes with comparative ease.

LIFT AND PROPULSION: Integrated system

powered by a single 40hp air-cooled twin-cylinder two-stroke. This drives, via a heavy duty toothed belt, a 610mm (24in) diameter polypropylene-bladed ducted fan, air from which is used for both lift and propulsion. Fuel capacity is 20·25 litres (4·5 imperial gallons). Fuel recommended is 93 octane, oil mix 25:1.
CONTROLS: Twin aerodynamic rudders, operated by a handlebar, control craft heading. Engine throttle mounted on handlebar.
HULL: Monocoque construction in self-coloured glass fibre. Preformed sealed polyurethane block at base of craft for buoyancy. Tools and spares compartment provided.
SKIRT: Fully segmented skirt fabricated in neoprene-coated nylon.
ACCOMMODATION: Open cockpit for driver.
DIMENSIONS
Length: 3·2m (10ft 6in)
Width: 1·83m (6ft)
Height: 1m (3ft 3in)
WEIGHTS
Empty: 164kg (360lb)
Normal payload: 113kg (250lb)
Max payload: 164kg (360lb)
PERFORMANCE
Max speed across land and water: 56km/h (35mph)
Cruising speed: 32-40km/h (20-25mph)
Max continuous gradient, standing start: 1 in 6
Max short gradient, at speed: 1 in 2 (45 degrees)
Vertical hard obstacle clearance: 20cm (8in)

KESTREL

Designed as a single-seater this fully-amphibious recreational craft has nevertheless operated many times on inland waterways with two aboard in force 5, gusting to force 6. Built on a base of solid foam it will not sink even if badly damaged.

Kestrel single seater powered by a single 24hp air-cooled two-stroke engine

LIFT AND PROPULSION: Integrated system with a single 24hp air-cooled twin-cylinder two-stroke driving one 610mm (24in) polypropylene-bladed ducted fan aft. Fuel capacity is 18 litres (4 imperial gallons). Recommended fuel, 93 octane/oil mix 25 : 1. Consumption, 6·75 to 9 litres/h (1½-2 gallons/h).
CONTROLS: Twin aerodynamic rudders controlled by handlebars. Engine throttle mounted on handlebars.
HULL: Self-coloured glass fibre structure based on a rigid foam block for strength and buoyancy. Built-in tools and spares compartment.
SKIRT: Segmented system fabricated in neoprene-coated nylon.

DIMENSIONS
Length: 3·2m (10ft 6in)
Beam: 1·83m (6ft)
Height: 1m (3ft 3in)
WEIGHTS
Empty: 127kg (280lb)
Normal payload: 113·5kg (250lb)
Max payload: 136kg (300lb)
PERFORMANCE
Cruising speed: 24-40km/h (15-25mph)
Max speed across land and water: 48km/h (30mph)
Max continuous gradient, standing start: 1 in 7
Max short gradient, at speed: 1 in 2 (45 degrees)
Vertical hard obstacle clearance: 20cm (8in)

PINDAIR LIMITED

Quay Lane, Hardway, Gosport, Hampshire PO12 4LS, England
Telephone: 070 17 87830
Officials:
M A Pinder, BSc, CEng, MIMechE, *Managing Director*
A M Pinder, *Director*
J Holland, FCA, *Director*
D R Robertson, *Consultant*
E W H Gifford, *Consultant*

Pindair Limited was formed in May 1972. It is currently engaged in the design, development, manufacture and sales of a range of inflatable hovercraft for private, commercial and military use as well as designing for outside manufacture ACV trailers of up to 10 tons payload. The company also supplies amateur hovercraft constructors in the United Kingdom with engines, fans, ducts, skirt materials and other specialised components.

Six amphibious models are currently in production and one model is at the prototype stage. Production capacity for the smaller models is currently ten per week and the larger models one per month.

The use of folding inflatable hulls for the Pindair Skima range offers a number of advantages including ease of transport and storage, low weight, and excellent buoyancy. Special attention has been paid to simplicity of maintenance and use of components with world-wide spares availability.

The smaller models are fitted with Valmet 160cc two-stroke engines coupled to ducted axial fans with replacement polypropylene blades. The larger models are fitted with four-stroke automotive engines.

Skima 1, low-cost single-seat inflatable hovercraft

Skima 2 during a demonstration run in the sea off Brighton

Skima 3s in a race during a Hoverclub meeting

Skima 4 four-seater travelling at speed over shallow water

SKIMA SPECIFICATIONS

Craft	Skima 1	Skima 2	Skima 3	Skima 4	Skima 6 (estimated)	Skima 12	Skima 18	Skima 25 (estimated)
Length	3·5m	3·25m	3·25m	4m	6·66m	7·77m	8·88m	9·99m
Width	1·7m	2m	2m	2m	2·5m	3·5m	3·5m	5m
Height off cushion	0·9m	1·2m	1·2m	1·2m	1·5m	2·3m	2·3m	2·5m
Unladen weight	50kg	90kg	125kg	160kg		990kg	1,500kg	2,000kg
Skirt	HDL	HDL	HDL	HDL	HDL	HDL	HDL	HDL
Skirt depth	15cm	15cm	15cm	20cm	30cm	50cm	50cm	75cm
Hard structure clearance	25cm	30cm	30cm	35cm	50cm	50cm	50cm	75cm
Folded dimensions	1 × 0·5 × 0·5m	1·15 × 1·52 × 0·6m	1·5 × 1·5 × 0·6m	1·22 × 1·52 × 0·6m		6·48 × 2·5 × 2·3m	7·59 × 2·5 × 2·3m	9·99 × 2·5 × 2·3m
Pack dimensions	1 × 0·5 × 0·5m	0·84 × 1·07 × 0·61m	0·84 × 1·07 × 0·84m	0·94 × 1·07 × 0·84m				
Engines	1 Valmet	2 Valmet	3 Valmet	3 Valmet		GM V8	GM V8	2 × GM V8
Fans—Lift	1 axial	1 axial	1 axial	1 axial	1 Centrifugal	1 Centrifugal	1 Centrifugal	2 Centrifugal
Thrust		1 axial	2 axial	2 axial	1 axial	1 axial	1 axial	2 axial
Total engine power hp	10	15	25	25	120	250	300	500

SKIMA PERFORMANCE DATA

Craft		Skima 1	Skima 2		Skima 3		Skima 4		Skima 6 (estimated)		Skima 12		Skima 18		Skima 25 (estimated)	
Payload	Units of 75kg or 1 person	1	1	2	1	3	2	4	3	6	6	12	9	18	12	25
Max speed	km/h	40	45	40	60	40	55	40	60	50	70	50	70	50	80	50
Max wind force	Beaufort	3	4	2	6	4	5	3	8	4	6	4	6	3	8	6
Fuel consumption	litre/h	4	7	7	9	9	9	9	25	25	25	25	30	30	50	50
Max range (standard tanks)	km	50	150	130	150	100	100	100	130	100	250	200	350	300	250	200
Max short slope	%	100	100	60	100	60	80	60	100	60	45	15	45	15	45	15
Max continuous slope	%	15	20	13	25	13	25	13	30	25	25	15	25	15	25	15

The Skima 12 has been developed with assistance from Hovercraft Development Limited. In all cases HDL segmented skirts are used.

Pindair hovercraft are in use in about 50 countries in all climatic conditions from equatorial heat to arctic cold. Prices generally compare with boats of similar payload and performance.

SKIMA 1

This has been designed as a low cost one-man hovercraft which can be stowed in the luggage compartment of most cars. It is light enough for portability by one man yet be capable of carrying one man on land or water in reasonable conditions. In 1972 three single-seat inflatable hovercraft designed by Pindair reached an altitude of 3,000m in the Himalayas by travelling along turbulent rivers.

SKIMA 2

This was the first craft marketed by the company. It is light enough to be carried by two people and can carry two people under reasonable conditions. It has separate lift and propulsion systems and can be folded to fit onto a car roof rack or into a small estate car.

The Skima 2 can be used as an amphibious yacht tender, runabout, for exploration or for class competition.

In 1977 a Skima 2 successfully completed a journey of over 300 miles on the partly unnavigable Brisbane river in Australia.

SKIMA 3

This is derived from a special version of the Skima 2 which has been raced successfully over a five year period in Hoverclub of Great Britain Championships, winning a number of open races and also speed, manoeuvrability and free style competitions outright.

Although capable of operating as a three-man hovercraft it is mainly used for two people or by one person in competitions.

SKIMA 4

During proving trials in 1973 this hovercraft covered the longest journey by a light hovercraft on inland and coastal waters. The Naval Hovercraft Trials Unit has recommended it as an alternative to the Gemini inflatable boat used by the British armed services, particularly in cases where its amphibious qualities would be an advantage.

Hardtop model of the Skima 12 operating in Portsmouth Harbour

Examples of the Skima 4 are in use in various parts of the world as amphibious transport for two people plus their equipment in most conditions or four people in good conditions. The rear seat is instantly removable for stowing freight or equipment. Users include missionaries, survey teams, pest research organisations, marine biology research groups, defence forces, and flood and beach rescue organisations.

SKIMA 6

A semi-inflatable hovercraft capable of carrying six persons, Skima 6 is at present under development. It is suitable as a personal transport as well as for police, military, rescue, pest control, freight, survey and exploration duties. It can be transported complete by road ready for use, or partly disassembled for shipment.

Either a folding hood or a hardtop can be fitted.

SKIMA 12

A semi-inflatable multi-role hovercraft, Skima 12 is capable of carrying up to 12 people or 1 tonne of freight. It combines features of an off-highway vehicle with those of a high-speed workboat. The Skima 12 is easily transported on a trailer with the inflatable cylindrical tube around the perimeter of the hull furled or detached and can be shipped in a standard 6 × 2·5 × 2·5m (19ft 8in × 8ft × 8ft) shipping container.

It can be built for a wide variety of applications, from police, coastguard, pilot and military uses, to pest control, flood relief, air crash rescue and

as a passenger ferry or ambulance.
LIFT AND PROPULSION: The engine, tooth-belt transmission, and ducted propulsor can be removed quickly for service or repair. Everything is easily accessible for maintenance.

The 5·7 litre GM V8 automobile engine is geared to run at relatively low speed for long life and low noise. The centrifugal aluminium lift fan and ducted four-blade propulsor are also designed to run at low speed to reduce noise and provide more than adequate air flow for good payload and performance.

The low cushion pressure, together with the HDL patented skirt system, generate a low spray pattern, allowing the Skima 12 to be operated with an open cockpit if desired. Individual skirt segments may be quickly replaced when they become worn or damaged without lifting the craft.
HULL: The aluminium hull is extremely strong and built with marine materials. It will not corrode or absorb water and if knocked will dent rather than fracture allowing repairs to be made at a convenient time. Separate compartments contain the accommodation, the engine and propulsor, the lift fan, rubber fuel bags, the trim system, batteries, safety equipment and stowage areas.
ACCOMMODATION: The standard craft has accommodation for 11 passengers and a driver. There are three bucket seats with the driver in the centre at the forward end of the cockpit with a U-shaped bench seat in the cabin. The bench seat is removable to provide a $5m^3$ load space. Various arrangements can be specified to provide cover for the accommodation. A cruiser-type folding hood with removable sides can be fitted, or a small cockpit cover or an insulated grp hard top with gull-wing doors. Additional equipment such as radio, radar, searchlights, heating and air conditioning can be incorporated. A trailer and lifting gear are available.

SKIMA 18

A stretched version of the proven Skima 12 capable of carrying 18 people or 1½ tonnes is available to special order.

SKIMA 25

This is a projected 25-seat, 2-tonne hovercraft incorporating two proven Skima 12 lift/thrust power units and many other components developed for Skima 12. Alternative layouts are envisaged including versions with a 25-passenger enclosed cabin, an open loadspace with bow ramp for vehicles or freight, firefighting and military configurations, and diesel engines.

Skima 12 military variant with folding hood operating in the Indian Ocean

Rescue model of the Skima 12, carrying sufficient self-inflatable life-rafts for most air crash situations

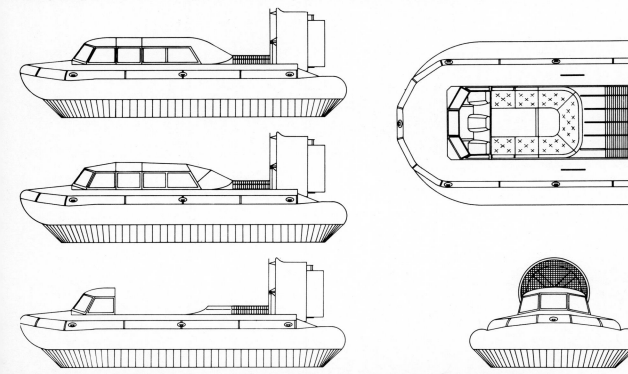

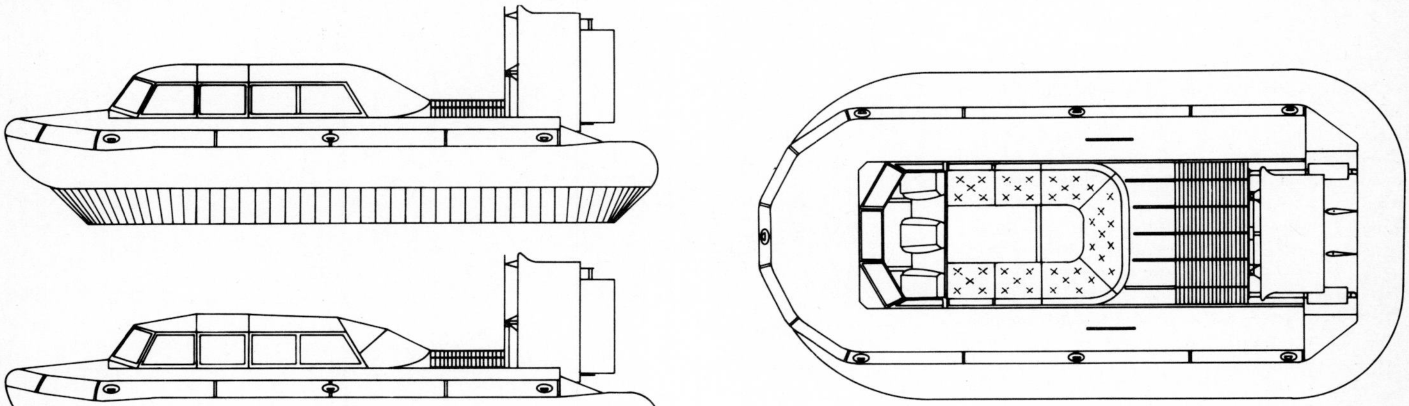
General arrangement of the Skima 12 with outboard elevations of the hardtop, folding hood and open-deck rescue versions

QUANTUM HOVERCRAFT LTD

Head Office: 31 West Street, Wimborne Minster, Dorset, England
Cables: 4M104 (QHL)
Works: 114 Magna Road, Bearwood, Bournemouth, Dorset, England
Telephone: 020 16 3940
Officials:
J R Raymond, *Secretary*
M Charman, *Director*
A G Field, *Director*
N V Charman, *Engineering Manager*

Formed in 1972, Quantum Hovercraft Ltd has been concentrating on the development of light amphibious passenger and utility craft. First vehicles to be marketed by the company are the Islesman 1000 six-seater, the Islesman 1500 nine-seater and the Islesman Utility. In 1978 the company announced that studies were being made for a Series 2 design which would offer improved payload and performance.

ISLESMAN 1000

This new glassfibre-hulled amphibious hovercraft is designed for a number of duties from six seat water-taxi to light transport and harbour inspection.

LIFT AND PROPULSION: Integrated system powered by a single Lotus 907 two-litre four-cylinder four-stroke aluminium engine rated at 155bhp at 6,500rpm. Cushion air is supplied by a 600mm (2ft) diameter 14-bladed Multi-wing axial-flow fan located at the rear of the craft behind the cabin. Cushion pressure is 22·25kg/m² (15lb/ft²). Thrust is supplied by two 600mm (2ft) diameter 14-bladed axial-flow fans of the same type mounted singly in two propulsion air ducts. Lift and propulsion fans are driven by the single engine via a hydraulic drive system developed by Volvo Hydraulics of Sweden. High pressure oil is piped to a manifold from whence it is diverted to the appropriate hydraulic fan motor by electric solenoid valves. Fuel is carried in four tanks, each with a capacity of 30 litres (8 gallons). Engine oil capacity is 9 pints; hydraulic capacity 56 litres (15 gallons). Engine access is via a large roof hatch and a removable panel in the cabin bulkheads.

CONTROLS: Craft heading is maintained by triple rudder vanes hinged at the rear of each of the propulsion ducts. Reverse thrust for braking is obtained by reversing the rotation of the propulsion fans through the hydraulic drive system, forcing the air forward. A fuel pumping system is used for longitudinal trim.

HULL: Prototype is of wooden construction. Hulls of production craft will be fabricated in coloured, fire retardent glass reinforced plastics. Sidestructure can be detached, bringing width to within 8ft for towing on roads.

SKIRT: 0·45m (18in) deep HDL loop and finger skirt fabricated in neoprene coated nylon fabric supplied by Leyland Rubber of Birmingham.

ACCOMMODATION: Basic version seats a driver and up to five passengers. Seats are secured by quick release fastenings that permit the interior to be cleared to carry stretchers, general cargoes and livestock. Full instrumentation is provided, including fan speed indicators. Access is via two large folding doors, one port and one starboard. Air conditioning can be fitted as an optional extra. Safety equipment includes electrically-operated fire detectors and extinguishing equipment.

SYSTEMS, ELECTRICAL: 12 and 24V systems. Engine driven 24V, 45A alternator.

DIMENSIONS

EXTERNAL

Length overall, power off: 6·12m (20ft 1in)
skirt inflated: 6·4m (21ft)
Beam overall, power off: 3·5m (11ft 5in)
skirt inflated: 4·26m (14ft)
Height overall, on landing pads: 1·5m (5ft)
skirt inflated: 1·92m (6ft 6in)
Draft afloat: 0·08m (3in)

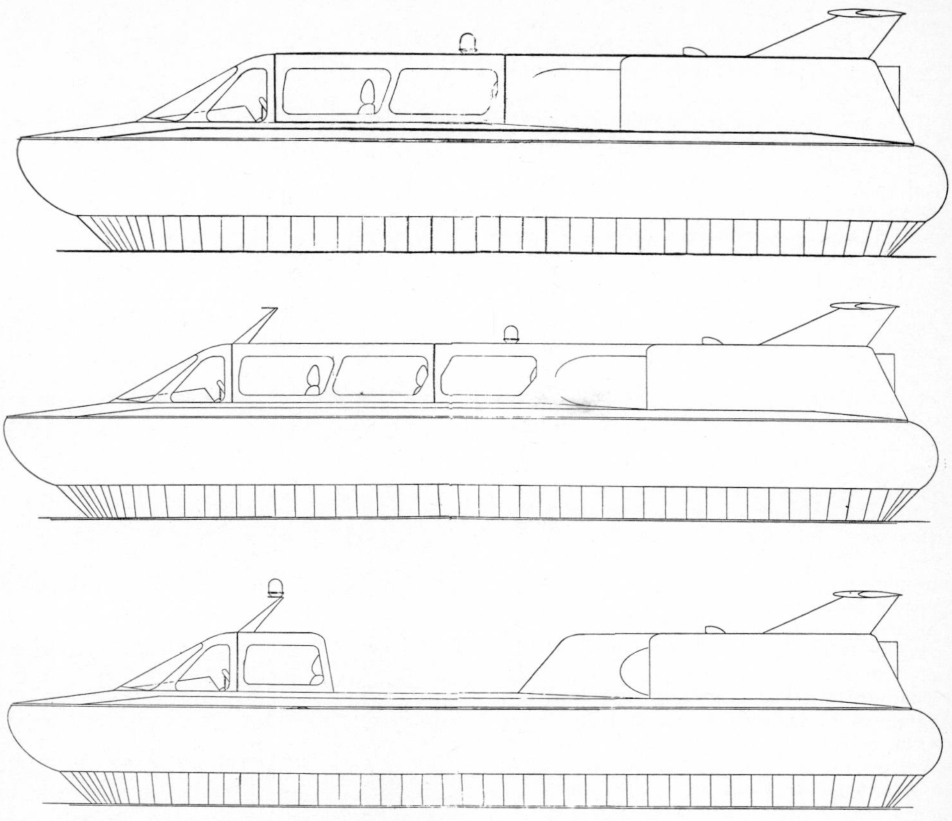

Outboard profiles of the Islesman 1000, **top**, the Islesman 1500, **centre** and **bottom**, the Utility model

Islesman loaded onto a trailer. Width, with sidebodies removed for towing, is 2·28m (7ft 6in)

Skirt depth, prototype: 0·48m (1ft 6in)

INTERNAL

Cabin length: 2·43m (8ft)
Max width: 1·45m (4ft 9in)
Max height: 1m (3ft 4in)
Floor area: 3·5m² (36·8ft²)

WEIGHTS

Normal empty: 680kg (1,500lb)
Normal gross: 1,134kg (2,500lb)
Normal payload: 454kg (1,000lb)

PERFORMANCE

Max speed, calm water, max power: 50 knots
Cruising speed, calm water: 35 knots
Max wave capacity: 1m (3ft)
Still air range and endurance at cruising speed: 400km (250 miles), 6 hours
Max gradient, static conditions: 1 : 8
Vertical obstacle clearance, prototype: 0·45m (1ft 6in)

PRICE: £30,000 ex-works UK

ROTORK MARINE LIMITED

Head Office: 51B High Street, Reigate, Surrey RH2 9AE, England
Telephone: 073 72 21121
Telex: 946764
Works: Lake Road, Hamworthy, Poole, Dorset, England
Telephone: 020 13 79419
Officials:
J J Fry, *Chairman*
A J C Percy, *Managing Director*
D T Smith, *Financial Manager*
S W Swierzy, *Sales Manager*
R J Kretschmer, *Engineering Manager*
S Marshall, *Production Manager*

Formed on 1 March 1966, Rotork Marine initially developed a simple marine-ply 8m planing hull which over the years became standardised and manufactured in grp. The range was extended from 8 to 12m five years ago and the Series 5, with a revised hull configuration was introduced in 1975. The boats are sold world wide and are in operation in over 50 countries and in service with 30 nations' defence forces. A key feature of the hull design is the use of air lubrication to reduce hydrodynamic drag. A ram-air cushion, contained by shallow side skegs, raises the bow clear of the water at speed. As the pressurised air flows aft it generates air/foam lubrication for the remainder of the hull, permitting speeds of up to 80·46km/h (50mph) to be achieved. The performance depends upon the payload, installed power and sea conditions. A wide choice of power plants is available, and cabin modules can be supplied for passenger and work crew accommodation. Bow loading ramps are fitted for ease of access and operation from beaches.

The company offers a series of fast assault craft and patrol boats, tactical personnel carriers and logistic support craft, together with a range of general purpose short haul passenger and vehicle ferries, 8m (25ft 3in) or 12m (39ft 4½in) in length.

ROTORK STW8 SEA TRUCK WORKBOAT

This is a heavy duty, multi-purpose workboat designed for high performance and low running costs. It can operate safely in only 304mm (1ft) of water and is equipped with a bow ramp to facilitate the loading of passengers, freight or light vehicles from beaches. The maximum payload is 3 tons.

POWER PLANT: Dependent upon payload and performance requirements and whether the craft is to be employed for sheltered water or open sea operation. Engines recommended are: Outboard: 135hp OMC OBMs, or 150 Mercury OBMs. These can be fitted as twin or triple installations. Inboard (diesel): 106hp Volvo AQD 32/270, installed as either single or twin installations. Supplied as standard with these units are the control console, and depending on the type of power unit, 223 litres (50 gallons) or 440 litres (100 gallons) fuel tanks in two fully isolated sections, together with fuel lines and built-in gauges.

HULL: Heavy duty glass fibre reinforced plastics. Buoyancy is provided by closed cell polyurethane foam of TD 1 type. The skegs are in prestressed cold drawn stainless steel tube. The ramp, which is manually operated, is in 25·4mm (1in) thick, polyurethane-coated marine ply. It is housed in a galvanised steel frame with galvanised steel capping, and is counter-balanced by a torsion bar.

ACCOMMODATION: As a workboat a grp covered aft control position can be fitted, together with extensions to provide adequate covered crew space and lockers.

SYSTEMS, ELECTRICAL: Heavy duty 12V batteries housed in acid-resistant reinforced plastic battery box mounted at deck level.

FUEL: Fuel is carried in one or more 50 or 100 gallon pannier type tanks.

SCUPPERS: Scuppers for the removal of deck water are located in the transom. Discharge capacity is 818·27 litres/min (180 gallons/min).

Rotork's SPV 512C 36-seat high-speed passenger ferry. A feature of the craft is its shallow draft which gives direct access to the shore

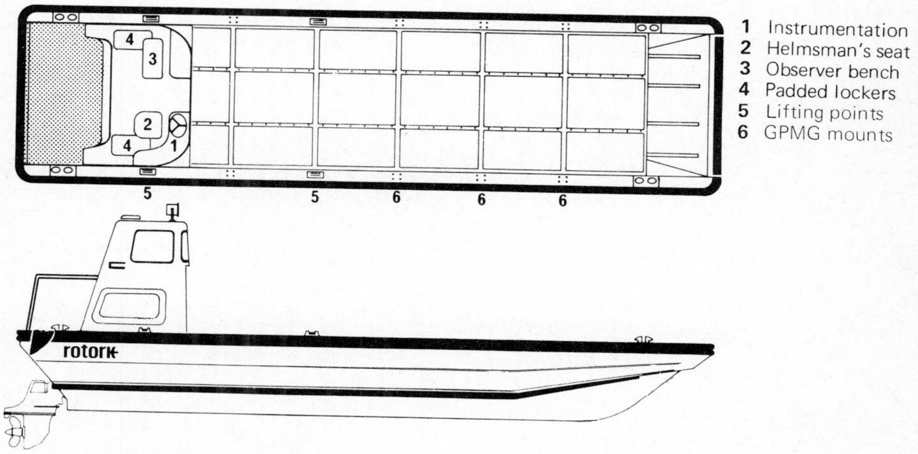

Elevation and deck plan of the LSC 512S logistic support craft. Built to carry a payload of 5 tons, it can exceed 30 knots in light conditions

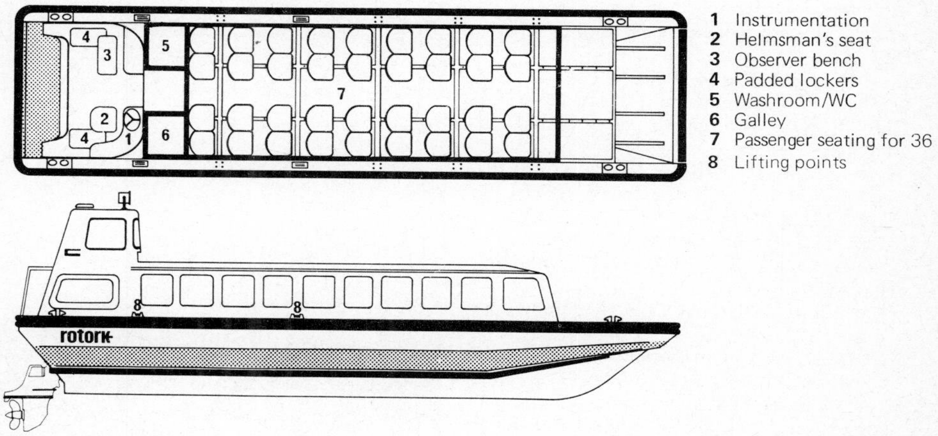

SPV 512C high speed passenger ferry, available with either twin diesel or gasoline engines driving propellers or waterjets

DIMENSIONS
Length, overall: 7·36m (24ft 2in)
Length, at waterline: 6·09m (20ft)
Beam: 2·74m (9ft 10in)
Freeboard, unladen, to deck level: 127mm (5in)
to top of bulwarks: 0·914m (3ft)
max load, to deck level: 50·8mm (2in)
to top of bulwarks: 838·2mm (2ft 9in)
Deck area (with outboard power): 15·81m² (170ft²)
Draft:
unladen, outboard drive up: 177·8mm (7in)
outboard drive down: 0·584m (1ft 11in)
max load, outboard drive up: 279mm (11in)
outboard drive down: 0·685m (2ft 3in)
WEIGHTS
Total: 1,545kg (3,400lb)
Max normal loading: 3,000kg (8,379lb)
PERFORMANCE (8m)
Performance varies with rig, type of load,

installed power and operating conditions. An approximate guide, based on the standard open deck-hull, is provided by the accompanying performance graph. This applies to the STW8 Sea Truck 8m workboat configuration.

ROTORK STW 12 SEA TRUCK

This 12m variant of the Sea Truck is available in two versions, the STW workboat and the FAC 12 fast assault craft. The latter variant can carry up to 50 men or 20 men with a Land Rover at speeds up to 25 knots. It can operate in only 177·8mm (7in) of water and can unload vehicles, personnel and supplies directly on to a beach.

HULL: Standard Rotork Sea Truck hull in glass fibre reinforced plastics. Reinforcement: E glass chopped strand mat. E glass woven roving. Silane finish. Buoyancy: Closed cell polyurethane foam. Deck has a non-slip bonded grit surface applied to a point load resisting composite structure. Chassis is of star frame type, integral with the hull structure. Fender frames are in hot-dip galvanised welded mild steel tube 101·6mm (4in) diameter. Rotating fender wheels are fitted as standard at bow and stern. A polyurethane coated and grit bonded 24·4mm (1in) thick marine plywood ramp is fitted at the bow. The ramp is opened and closed manually by galvanised mild steel levers.

FUEL: Fuel tanks are in welded mild steel. Type 1 tanks have a capacity of 220 litres (50 imperial gallons) and are in pannier form for bulwark mounting. Type 2 tanks have a capacity of 440 litres (100 imperial gallons) and are designed for athwartship mounting. Independent fuel lines and built-in gauges are provided.

ACCOMMODATION: A grp covered control position can be supplied together with an extension of the control position, providing additional crew space and lockers.

DIMENSIONS

Length overall: 11·27m (37ft)
  at waterline: 9·8m (32ft 2in)
Beam: 2·99m (9ft 10in)
Freeboards, unladen to deck level: 127mm (5in)
  unladen to top of bulwarks: 914·4mm (36in)
  with max load to deck level: 50·8mm (2in)
  with max load to top of bulwarks: 838·2mm (33in)
Height, of top rail from deck: 787·2mm (31in)
  of metacentre above centre of gravity: 5·51m (18ft 1in)
Deck area, overall: 30·85m² (287ft²)
Draft, unladen, outdrive up: 177·8mm (7in)
  unladen, outdrive down: 584·2mm (23in)
  max load, outdrive up: 279·4mm (11in)
  max load, outdrive down: 685·8mm (27in)

WEIGHTS

Less engine: 2,405kg (4,500lb)
Total integral foam buoyancy: 886kg (1,953lb)

PROPULSION (Alternative power plants and weights)

1 Two 135hp OMC OBMs: 282kg (620lb)
2 Two 150 Mercury OBMs: 282kg (620lb)
3 Three 135hp OMC OBMs: 424kg (932lb)
4 Three 150 Mercury OBMs: 424kg (932lb)
5 One 106hp Volvo AQD 32/270 inboard: 391kg (861lb)
6 Two 106hp Volvo AQD 32/270 inboards: 782kg (1,721lb)

PAYLOAD: Maximum normal loading in the 12m Sea Truck Workboat is 5,000kg (11,023lb). This figure is dependent on choice of optional equipment and propulsion system. Individual weights are as indicated.

See accompanying graph for approximate performance figures.

ROTORK SERIES 5 MULTI-DUTY CRAFT

Four versions of this new addition to the Rotork 12m range are now available: the PVF 512C personnel/vehicle ferry; the SPV 512C 36-seat passenger ferry; FPB 512S fast patrol boat and the LSC 512S logistic support craft.

The basic hull is constructed in heavy duty grp to British Admiralty specifications and is foam-filled, resulting in the craft being unsinkable,

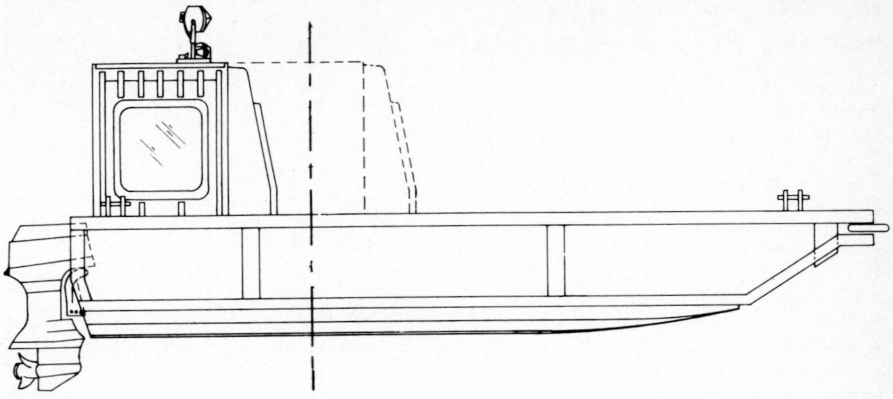

Rotork STW8 8m Sea Truck workboat

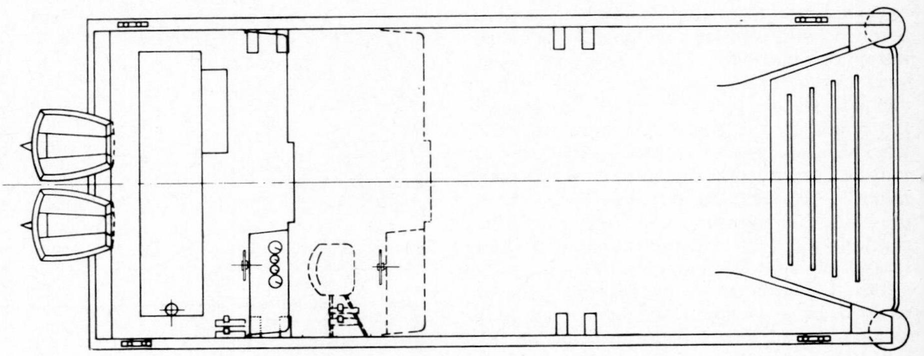

Rotork STW 512 workboat

Rotork CSB8, 8m combat support boat

even when fully laden. Extensive use is made of stainless steel, rubber, nylon and other non-corrodible materials for minimum maintenance.

The PVF 512C, which is designed for ferrying vehicles, cargo, livestock and passengers in areas where jetties and other landing facilities are not available, was conceived with international safety requirements in mind, enabling, where applicable, local authorities to issue certificates for the operation of these boats under varying conditions.

HULL: Glass reinforced plastic with non-slip bonded grit surface on deck. Superstructure in integrally coloured grp. Stainless steel rolled section gunwales. Full peripheral fendering at gunwale. Solid rubber strake at waterline. Black nylon full length skegs, additional beaching skegs at bow. Winch operated reinforced plastic loading ramp with non-slip surface. Scuppers for the removal of deck water located in transom. Fuel is carried in two 200 litre (44 imperial gallon) pannier tanks mounted on internal bulwarks.

ACCOMMODATION, BRIDGE: An all-weather grp cabin is provided aft above the gunwale level with a canvas dropscreen giving access to the quarterdeck. Door and steps give access to the welldeck. A seat is provided for the helmsman and a bench seat for two observers. Padded covers on two lockers provide additional seating for two. Standard bridge equipment includes navigation lights, searchlight, internal light, klaxon, windscreen wiper, rechargeable fire extinguishers (two) and bilge pump. Personnel accommodation varies according to type. On the SPV 512C it comprises a cabin on deck forward of the bridge, with access doors to the bridge and foredecks, a washroom/toilet unit, galley unit with sink, cooker and 20 gallon fresh water supply system and ferry seating for 36 passengers.

COMMUNICATIONS: Optional. Fully synthesised, 25W VHF radio transceiver, up to 56 channels. 55B-HF radio telephone.

NAVIGATION: Optional. Illuminated helmsman's compass. Short range radar (Decca 060, range 24n miles).

DIMENSIONS

Length, overall: 12·65m (41ft 6in)
Length, waterline: 10·75m (35ft 3in)
Beam, overall: 3·2m (10ft 6in)
Overall height, hull: 1·487m (4ft 10in)
with cabins: 2·501m (8ft 2in)
with flying bridge: 3·525m (11ft 7in)

Performance graph for Rotork 12 metre Sea Truck workboat

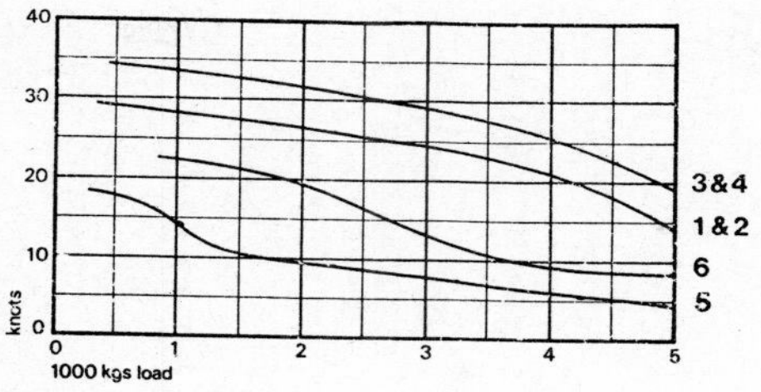

Propulsion
1 Two 135hp OMC OBMs 282kg (620lb)
2 Two 150 Mercury OBMs 282kg (620lb)
3 Three 135hp OMC OBMs 424kg (932lb)
4 Three 150 Mercury OBMs 424kg (932lb)
5 One 106hp Volvo AQD 32/270 inboard 391kg (861lb)
6 Two 106hp Volvo AQD 32/270 inboards 782kg (1,721lb)

Approximate performance graph for Rotork 8 metre Sea Truck

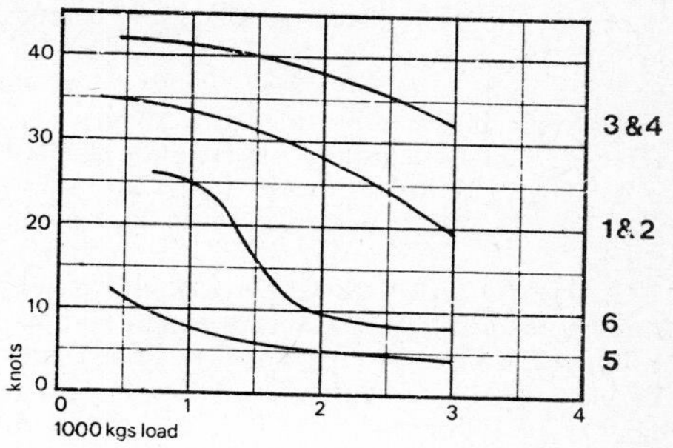

Payload: Maximum normal loading in the 8m Sea Truck Workboat is 3,000kg and that of the 12m STW12, 5,000kg. These figures are dependent on choice of optional equipment and propulsion system. Individual weights are as indicated.

Height of gunwale above deck: 1m (3ft 3in)
Deck area: 9 × 2·5m = 22·5m² (29ft 6in × 8ft 3in = 243ft²)

WEIGHTS

Unladen, less fuel, engines and superstructure: 2,370kg (5,225lb)
Max allowable displacement: 9,000kg (19,841lb)

FREEBOARDS

With max load to deck level: 52·5mm (2·07in)
With max load to gunwale: 1,052·5mm (41·4in)

DRAFT

Unladen: 268mm (10·55in)
With max load: 383mm (15·07in)

PROPULSION SYSTEMS AND PERFORMANCE

including full engine instrumentation, steering and throttle controls	Performance guide Speed in knots Light	50%	Laden	Weight Light kg	Max Payload kg	Draft laden mm drive up	down
1 × 200hp diesel/outdrive GM 6V.53 MN (naturally aspirated)	22·0	18·0	12·0	4694	4306	42	93
2 × 100hp diesel/outdrive GM 3·53 MN (naturally aspirated) Ford 254 cu in (turbocharged)	21·0	18·0	12·0	5143	3857	42	93
2 × 130hp diesel/outdrive GM 3·53 MTI (turbocharged & Intercooled) Ford 254 cu in (turbocharged & Intercooled)	24·0	20·5	14·0	5143	3857	42	93
2 × 150hp diesel/outdrive GM 3·53 MTI (A) (turbocharged & Intercooled)	26·0	22·0	19·5	5143	3857	42	93
2 × 200hp gasoline inboard/outboard OMC 235	31·0	26·0	22·5	4742	4258	42	83
2 × 130hp diesel/waterjet GM 3·53 MTI (turbocharged & Intercooled) Ford 254 cu in (turbocharged & Intercooled) coupled to heavy duty high thrust waterjet	19·0	16·0	11·0	5173	3827	42	42
2 × 150hp diesel/waterjet GM 3·53 MTI (A) (turbocharged & Intercooled) coupled to heavy duty high thrust waterjet	20·0	17·0	12·0	5173	3827	42	42
2 × 200hp gasoline/waterjet OMC 235, coupled to heavy duty high thrust waterjet	24·0	20·0	17·5	4930	4070	42	42

SURFACE CRAFT LTD

4 Rubastic Road, Brent Park Industrial Estate, Southall, Middlesex UB2 5LL, England

Officials:

R F King, *Director*
E A Revel
P E King, *Secretary*

NIMBUS Mk III

This inflatable two/three-seater is intended for leisure, commercial and para-military applications. It can be towed on a specially designed trailer fitted with a remotely controlled electric winch. Loading and unloading is a one-man operation which can be undertaken in a matter of minutes.

LIFT AND PROPULSION: Integrated system powered by a single 40bhp Rotax 635cc air-cooled twin-cylinder engine. The primary airflow from the two axial fans is ejected through a propulsion slot aft of the fan duct and the secondary

Nimbus, an 80km/h (50mph) two/three seater built by Surface Craft Ltd

flow, for the cushion, passes downwards into the plenum chamber. Fuel tank capacity 45 litres (10 imperial gallons). Fuel recommended, 90 octane, oil mix 25 : 1.
CONTROLS: Fourteen small rudder vanes in the propulsion slot control craft heading.
HULL: Main structure in colour-impregnated glass fibre. Twin neoprene buoyancy tubes integral with craft structure. Electric bilge pump fitted.
ACCOMMODATION: Open cockpit for two-three passengers, depending on weight and distribution. Access through forward sliding entry door.
DIMENSIONS
Length: 4·41m (14ft 6in)
Width: 2·13m (7ft 2in)
Height: 1·33m (4ft 5in)
WEIGHTS
Normal all-up weight: 498kg (1,100lb)
Max all-up weight: 590kg (1,300lb)
Empty: 362kg (800lb)
Normal payload: 136kg (300lb)
Max payload: 226kg (500lb)
PERFORMANCE
Max speed, land and water: up to 80km/h (50mph)
Cruising speed: 48-56km/h (30-35mph)
Range: 280km (175 miles)
Endurance: up to 5 hours
Max gradient: 40 degrees
Vertical hard structure clearance: 229mm (9in)

Nimbus Mk IV, a two-seat hovercraft for para-military use, with a light machine gun mounted forward of the open cockpit

NIMBUS Mk IV

This is a para-military version of the Mk III Nimbus with a modified windscreen and light machine gun mounting ahead of the open cockpit. Three Mk IV craft have been sold for coastguard duties in South Yemen.

NIMBUS Mk V

Introduced in 1978, this new model is very similar to the Mk III but has an improved power-to-weight ratio and therefore a generally enhanced performance.

SURFACE FLIGHT LIMITED

Unit 10, Holton Heath Industrial Estate, Poole, Dorset, England
Telephone: 0202 624284
Officials:
G R Nichol, *Director*
V M Nichol, *Director*

Surface Flight Limited is currently producing two low-cost amphibious two-seaters, the Sunrider and the Shamal. Although designed primarily for recreational use both craft are suitable for a range of light 'workhorse' roles from high-speed rescue and surveying inland waterways to harbour inspection.

SUNRIDER

The Sunrider is a popular glass fibre hulled two-seater, which has been exported to twelve different countries. Ruggedly constructed, it has a low noise level and has been operated at speeds in excess of 80 km/h (50mph).
LIFT AND PROPULSION: A 10bhp two-stroke single-cylinder engine located ahead of the open cockpit drives a seven-bladed fan for cushion lift. Thrust is supplied by a 38·5bhp two-cylinder two-stroke driving a ducted 20-bladed fan aft of the cockpit. Tank capacity, 28 litres (6 imperial gallons). Fuel recommended, 93 octane.
CONTROLS: Single control column operates twin rudders hinged to rear of fan duct. Column incorporates a twist-grip throttle for the lift engine. Electric starter provides for thrust engine. Recoil hand starter for lift engine. Engine speed control and propulsive thrust are regulated by foot-operated throttles on each side of the cockpit.
HULL: Moulded glass-reinforced plastics. Sides and bow reinforced by foam plastic beneath. Closed compartments along each side of craft packed with low density plastic foam for buoyancy.
SKIRT: Fully segmented skirt in neoprene-coated nylon. Replaceable segments.
ACCOMMODATION: Open cockpit with single bench-type seat for driver and passenger.
SYSTEMS, ELECTRICAL: Propulsion engine has 12V 100W charging circuit for the battery which supplies electric start and any optional extras such as lights and gauges.
DIMENSIONS
Length overall: 4m (13ft 2in)
Beam overall: 1·98m (6ft 6in)
Height: 1·11m (3ft 8in)
WEIGHTS
Empty: 250kg (540lb)
Payload: 190kg (420lb)

The Sunrider two-seater has been operated at speeds in excess of 80km/h (50mph)

Rear view of the Sunrider. Thrust is supplied by a 38bhp two-stroke with electric start

PERFORMANCE (calm conditions)
Max speed: in excess of 80km/h (50mph)
Normal cruising speed: 56km/h (35mph)
Endurance: 4 hours
Gradient capability: 1 in 8 from static hover
Obstacle clearance height: 23cm (9in)
PRICE: ex-factory £2,500

SHAMAL

Latest addition to the Surface Flight range, the Shamal is a simple, fast, lightweight recreational craft intended for the Middle Eastern and North American markets. Like Sunrider, however, it can be employed for a variety of light utility roles. Although based on the company's long experience with the Sunrider the Shamal displays several major differences. It has an integrated lift/propulsion system powered by a single engine, and, in the interests of both lightweight construction and ease of maintenance, it has only one-third of the total number of components required by its predecessor.
LIFT AND PROPULSION: Integrated system. A 38·5bhp 640cc twin-cylinder two-stroke, air-cooled engine drives via a belt a five-bladed, ducted fan. Propulsion air is expelled through stators aft and lift air is ducted into the plenum below.
CONTROLS: Single control column operates a single rudder hinged to the rear of the fan duct. Column incorporates a twist grip throttle for the engine.
HULL: Moulded glass-reinforced plastics structure. Sides and bow reinforced with plastic foam. Closed compartments along each side of craft packed with low density plastic foam for buoyancy.
SKIRT: Fully segmented type in neoprene-coated nylon.
ACCOMMODATION: Open cockpit with side-by-side contoured racing car type seats for driver and passenger.
DIMENSIONS
Length overall: 3·42m (11ft 3in)
Beam overall: 1·93m (6ft 5in)
Height overall: 1·21m (4ft)
WEIGHTS
Empty: 122·46kg (270lb)
Payload: 181·42kg (400lb)
PERFORMANCE (calm conditions)
Max speed: in excess of 80km/h (50mph)
Cruising speed: 56·32km/h (35mph)
Endurance: 4 hours
Gradient capability: 1 in 7 from static hover
Obstacle clearance height: 23cm (9in)
PRICE: ex-factory £1,750

Surface Flight Shamal, intended for the Middle Eastern and North American markets. Keynotes are light-weight construction and ease of maintenance. Maximum speed of this two-seater is in excess of 80km/h (50mph)

TROPIMERE LIMITED

Head Office: 17 Wigmore Street, London W1H 9LA, England
Telephone: 01-580 5816
Telex: 24637
Factory: Devonshire Road, Millom, Cumbria LA18 4JT, England
Telephone: 0567 2234-5

Tropimere Limited has re-established the production of the SH2-4 hovercraft at the former Sealand Hovercraft factory in Millom, Cumbria, and is also introducing a new ten passenger or 1 tonne payload amphibious hovercraft — the Dash 6 and a smaller six-seater, the Dash 7. Two SH2-4s have been delivered since the factory resumed work — one to the Spanish army and one to Abu Dhabi for oil rig support. SH2-4s are still available in limited numbers to meet customers' specification on a ten-week delivery schedule. The company offers a full factory warranty coupled with complete spares, service and driver training. It also offers spares, service and driver training to any organisation already operating Sealand Hovercraft.

DASH 6

The Dash 6 is the first of a new series of hovercraft designed to fill the gap between the light recreational machine and the large commercial hovercraft. Twin engines are fitted, providing adequate power to cope with difficult terrain and sea conditions and at the same time ensuring that the craft can return safely to base in the event of one engine failing.

Although the craft is currently being constructed to meet the requirement of Coast Guard operations, it is suitable for a wide range of alternative roles.
LIFT AND PROPULSION: Integrated system powered by two 150hp Mazda RX-2 Wankel rotary engines. Each engine drives a 1,092mm (3ft 7in) diameter propeller which provides lift and propulsion. Engines are cooled by a totally enclosed fresh water system and high efficiency radiators. Cooling air is drawn through the radiators by the propellers. Two explosion-proof fuel tanks are fitted providing sufficient capacity for eight hours endurance at cruise setting. Fuel is drawn through a stainless steel pipework to each engine via a filter and an electrical solenoid valve to the carburettor.
CONTROLS: Aerodynamic rudders aft of the propeller ducts provide heading control and elevators provide longitudinal trim. Additional trim is provided by two water tanks, one in the bow and one aft. Water is transferred from one tank to the other by electrical pumps.
HULL: Sandwich construction employing expanded PVC foam faced with glass-reinforced marine polyester. Built-in buoyancy compartments with additional buoyancy provided by sidebodies. Sidebodies can be removed from the main hull structure to reduce the overall width for road trailing.
SKIRT: 50/50 fingered bag type fabricated in PVC-coated nylon fabric.
ACCOMMODATION: In standard configuration the cabin is equipped with ten seats. Heating and air-conditioning is supplied. Seats can be removed to provide various mixed passenger/cargo layouts. Access is via a large gull-wing door on the starboard side. An emergency escape hatch is provided on the port side opposite. Ambulance, patrol/assault, coastguard, firefighting, and utility configurations are available to customers' requirements.
SYSTEMS, ELECTRICAL: 12V negative earth system, powered by two 12V-63A alternators. Power is stored in two 12V-65Ah batteries providing reserves of power for radar, radio, searchlights etc. Circuit breaker switches protect all essential services.

Tropimere Dash 6 ten-seat passenger ferry, powered by two 150hp Mazda RX-2 Wankel rotary engines

TRANSPORTATION: To enable the craft to be transported by road over long distances a six-wheeled undercarriage and towbar is provided with each craft, together with a lifting beam and slings to facilitate a total lift.
SAFETY EQUIPMENT: Each craft is supplied with the following: full navigation lighting to IMCO 1972 requirements; a life raft stowed in the bow compartment; life jackets; flares; anchor and fire extinguishers.
NAVIGATION AND COMMUNICATIONS: Radar and radio are optional extras and are fitted to customers' specifications.
DIMENSIONS
Length overall, power off: 8·24m (27ft)
on cushion: 8·9m (28ft 10in)
Beam overall, power off: 3·5m (11ft 6in)
on cushion: 5·8m (19ft)
Height overall, power off, excluding mast: 2·3m (7ft 6in)
on cushion: 3·6m (11ft 10in)
Draft afloat, static: 0·2m (8in)
Hard structure clearance: 0·46m (1ft 6in)
Cabin dimensions:
length: 4·1m (13ft 5in)
width: 2·1m (6ft 10in)
height: 1·4m (4ft 7in)
WEIGHTS
Max gross: 3,000kg (6,614lb)
Payload: 1,000kg (2,205lb)
PERFORMANCE
Max speed, calm water: 40 knots
Cruising speed: 30 knots
Still air endurance at cruising speed: 8 hours

DASH 7

This is a new single-engined light utility hovercraft designed to carry a driver and up to five passengers or a 0·6 tonne payload.
LIFT AND PROPULSION: Integrated system powered by a single 150hp Mazda RX-2 Wankel rotary engine. Power is transmitted to a 1,092mm (3ft 7in) diameter ducted fan which provides lift and propulsion. Cooling is provided by a totally enclosed fresh water system and high efficiency radiators. Two explosion-proof tanks are provided giving sufficient capacity for 6 hours endurance at cruise setting. Fuel is drawn through a stainless steel pipework via a filter and electrical solenoid valve to the carburettor.
CONTROLS: Aerodynamic rudders aft of the propeller duct provide heading control and elevators provide longitudinal trim. Additional trim is provided by two ballast tanks, one located in the bow, the other in the stern. Water is transferred from one tank to the other by electrical pumps.
HULL: Sandwich construction employing expanded PVC foam faced with glass-reinforced marine polyester. Built-in buoyancy compartments with additional buoyancy provided by

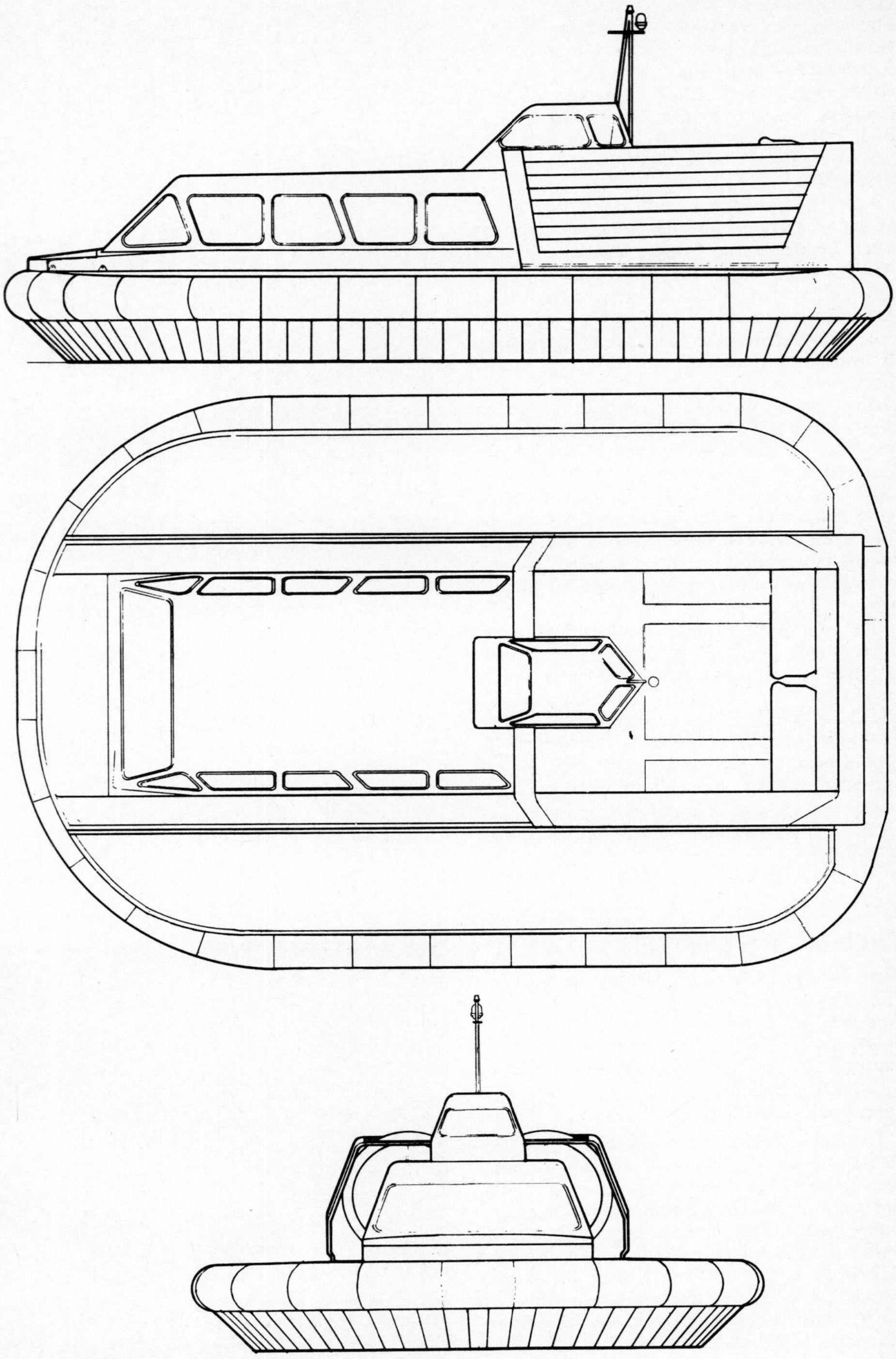

General arrangement of the Dash 6 multi-purpose hovercraft

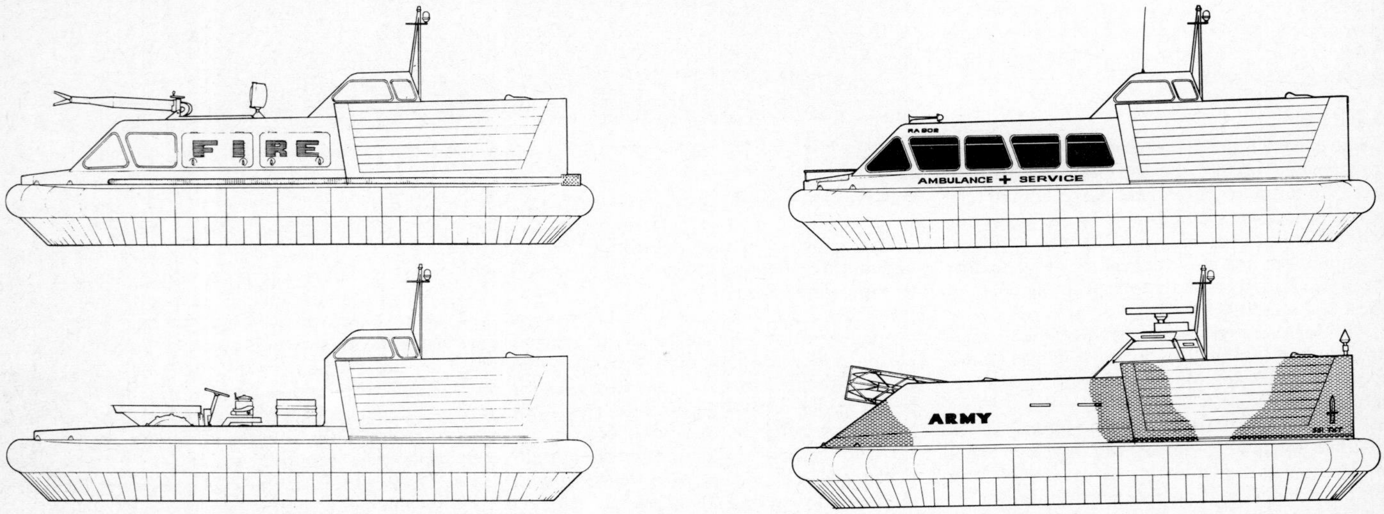

Top left: Tropimere Dash 6 in firefighting configuration: up to 200 gallons of foam-making chemical would be delivered by a roof-mounted monitor. Fitted with lockers for rescue equipment, liferafts for survivors and a searchlight
Bottom left: Utility version with flat deck for harbour or coastal engineering or light inter-island freight and supply carrying applications
Top right: High speed emergency craft for areas with poor communications. Fitted with four stretchers and attendant's seating, oxygen and resuscitation equipment
Bottom right: Patrol model equipped with surface to air missiles and a twin machine gun mount. Radar is fitted for night operation. Plastic armour and explosion-proof fuel tanks are available

sidebodies. Sidebodies can be removed from the main hull structure to reduce the overall width for road trailing.

SKIRT: 50/50 fingered bag type in PVC-coated nylon fabric.

ACCOMMODATION: In standard configuration the cabin is laid out as a 6-seater. Heating and air-conditioning is supplied. Removal of seats enables various passenger/layouts to be achieved. Access is via a large gull-wing door. An emergency escape hatch is located on the opposite side of the cabin.

SYSTEMS, ELECTRICAL: 12V negative earth electrical system, powered by one 12V-63A alternator. Power is stored in one 12V-65Ah battery, providing a reserve of power for radio, searchlights, pumps etc, when the engine is shut down.

NAVIGATION AND COMMUNICATIONS: Radio and radar are optional extras and are fitted to customer's specifications.

BILGE SYSTEM: Cabin is bilged by means of a hand bilge pump, the engine bay being bilged by an electrical pump.

SAFETY EQUIPMENT: Each craft is supplied with the following items: full navigation lighting to IMCO 1972 regulations; a life raft stowed in the bow compartment; life jackets; flares; anchor; fire extinguishers.

TRANSPORT: To permit the craft to be transported by road over long distances, a six-wheeled undercarriage and towbar is provided with each craft. A lifting beam and slings are also provided to facilitate a complete lift.

DIMENSIONS

EXTERNAL

Length overall, power off: 8·68m (28ft 6in)
 on cushion: 8·68m (28ft 6in)
Beam overall, sidebodies removed: 2·8m (9ft 2in)
 on cushion: 5·08m (16ft 8in)
Height overall, power off: 1·65m (5ft 5in)
 on cushion: 2·1m (6ft 10in)
Draft hullborne: 0·25m (10in)
Cushion area: 28·33m² (305ft²)
Hard structure clearance: 0·46m (1ft 6in)

INTERNAL

Cabin:
 length, max: 4·19m (13ft 9in)
 width, max: 1·55m (5ft 1in)
 height, max: 1·24m (4ft 1in)
 floor area: 5·2m² (56ft²)

WEIGHTS

Max gross: 2,600kg (5,732lb)
Payload: 600kg (1,323lb)

PERFORMANCE

Max speed, calm water: 40 knots
Cruising speed: 30 knots
Still endurance at cruising speed: 6 hours

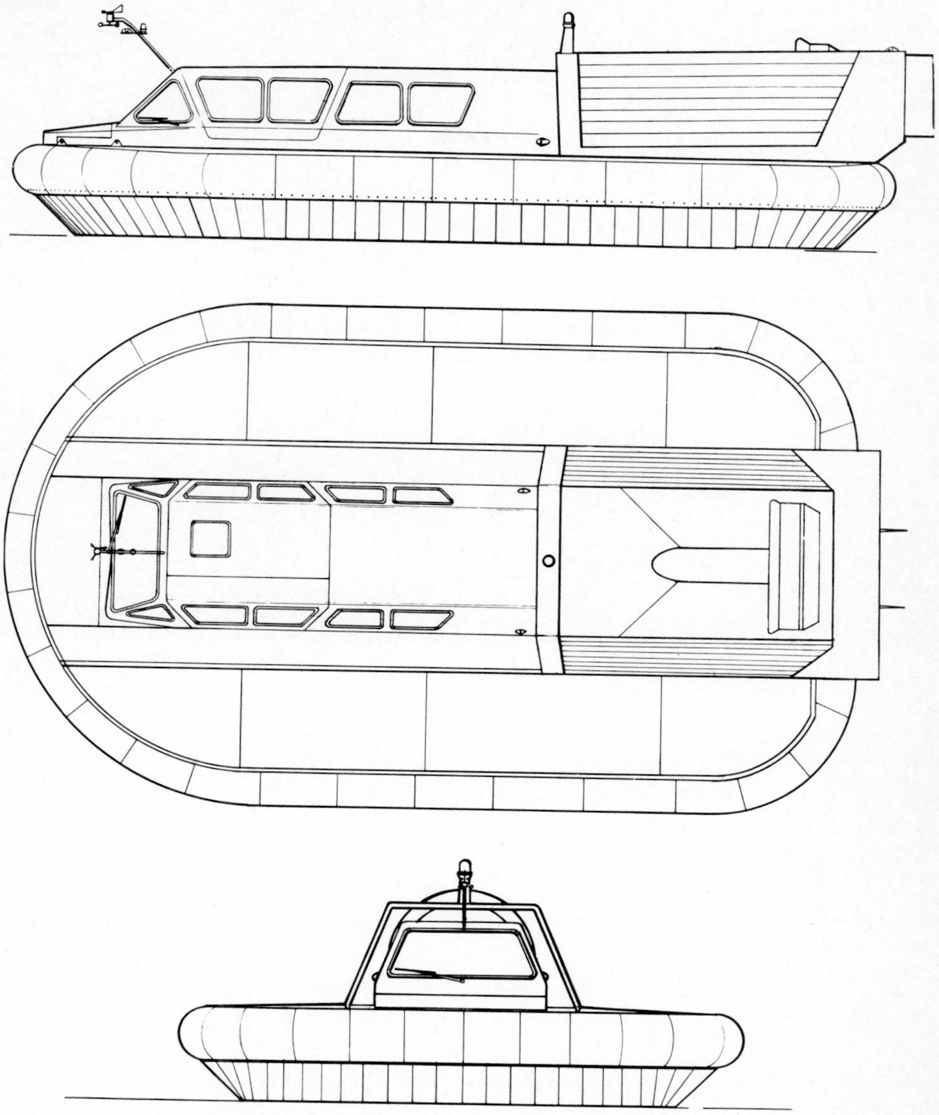

The Tropimere Dash 7, powered by a single 150hp Mazda RX-2 Wankel rotary engine

Tropimere's new six-seat utility craft, the Dash 7. Maximum speed over calm water is 40 knots

TROPIMERE SH2-4

The SH-2 is an attractive, amphibious six-seater designed for a variety of roles from water taxi and ambulance to patrol craft. Simplicity of operation and maintenance are keynotes of the design. Features include the use of a single 200hp Chrysler automotive engine and transmission to power lift and propulsion system, and the incorporation of hinged sidebodies to facilitate transport. Overall beam with sidebodies folded is 2·28m (7ft 6in). Trailer wheel units can be attached for towing along roads.

LIFT AND PROPULSION: Integrated system powered by a single 200hp Chrysler 440 CD V8 automotive engine. Cushion air is supplied by a 0·81m (2ft 8in) diameter cast aluminium fan driven via a clutch, shafting and a right-angled gearbox. Thrust is supplied by four 0·81m (2ft 8in) diameter, four-bladed Permali axial-flow fans, mounted in pairs on a common shaft in each of the two propulsion air ducts. Each pair is driven via a toothed belt by a pulley on the power take-off shaft, aft of the clutch assembly. Air for the lift fan, located at the end of the hull, is drawn through an intake located between the two propulsion duct outlets. From the fan it is fed via a bag to individual fingers. Cushion area is 22·29m² (240ft²) and cushion pressure is 17·9lb/ft². Engine, fans and transmission are built onto a steel sub-frame to form a single, easily removed unit.

Fuel is carried in two grp tanks located in the pannier sections, port and starboard, outboard of the main beams. Total capacity is 236·39 litres (52 imperial gallons). Refuelling points are provided at the centre of the craft, port and starboard. Fuel recommended is 95 octane. Oil capacity is 7·38 litres (13 pints).

CONTROLS: Directional control is maintained by twin aerodynamic rudder vanes hinged to the rear of each of the propulsion ducts. Reverse thrust for braking is obtained by opening out the paired rudder vanes in opposing directions to block the propulsion duct outlets, forcing the air through louvres. The craft can be steered by use of the braking system. An electrically-powered water ballast system is used for longitudinal trim.

HULL: Main members are of sandwich form, employing Airex pvc foam cores faced with grp polyester. Hinged sidebodies are grp laminate, beneath which are two sectional buoyancy bags, inflated via an air induction system, controlled from the cabin. Structure is stressed to withstand forward impact loads of up to 6g, roughly the equivalent to driving into 3ft waves at 43 knots.

SKIRT: 457mm (1ft 6in) deep 50% fingered bag type, fabricated in pvc-coated nylon.

Tropimere SH2-4 037 undergoing water trials before being delivered to Abu Dhabi for oil rig support operations

ACCOMMODATION: Basic version has 9-12 seats. The cabin is both heated and ventilated.
SYSTEMS, ELECTRICAL: 12V alternator. 45Ah battery.
COMMUNICATIONS AND NAVIGATION: Optional extras: Viking Princess ten-channel marine radio; Decca 050 radar; Type E2A compass.
ARMAMENT: 7·65mm machine gun and wire-guided missiles to order.

DIMENSIONS

EXTERNAL

Length overall, power off: 8m (26ft 3¼in)
power on: 8·6m (28ft 4¼in)
Beam overall, power off: 2·8m (7ft 7½in)
sidebodies and skirt inflated: 5·08m (16ft 8in)
Height overall on landing pads: 1·65m (5ft 5¾in)
overall, skirt inflated: 2·1m (7ft)
Draft afloat: 0·25m (10in)
Cushion area: $28{\cdot}33m^2$ ($305ft^2$)
Skirt depth: 0·46m (1ft 6in)

INTERNAL

Length: 4·19m (13ft 9in)
Max width: 1·55m (5ft 1in)
Max height: 1·24m (4ft 1in)
Floor area (excluding driver's seat area): approx $5{\cdot}2m^2$ ($56ft^2$)

WEIGHTS

Normal gross: 3,084kg (6,800lb)
Payload, including driver: 1,016kg (2,240lb)

PERFORMANCE

Max speed over calm water: 42 knots
Cruising speed: 25 knots
Turning circle diameter at 30 knots: 274m (900ft)
*Still air range and endurance at cruising speed: 241km (150 miles)
Vertical obstacle clearance: 0·46m (1ft 6in)

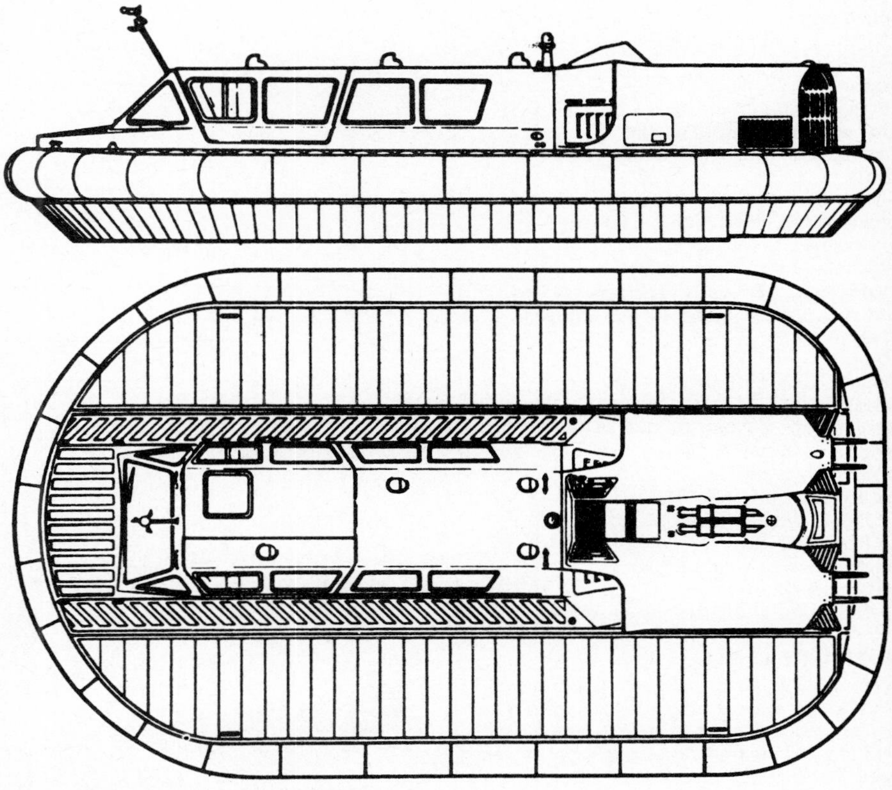

Tropimere SH2-4 amphibious six-seater

*With ferry fuel tanks range is increased to 483km (300 miles).

PRICE: Price and terms on application, according to specification.

VOSPER THORNYCROFT (UK) LIMITED

Paulsgrove, Portsmouth, Hants PO6 4QA, England
Telephone: 070 18 79481
Telex: 86115

Officials:

A E Bingham, BSc (Tech), MIMechE, MRAeS, *Chief Hovercraft Designer.*

Vosper Thornycroft (UK) Limited, a member of British Shipbuilders, continues the shipbuilding business originally established over a century ago by two separate companies, Vosper Limited and John I Thornycroft & Co Ltd. These well-known companies merged in 1966 and the organisation has continued the design and construction of warships from fast patrol boats to large frigates. The company was nationalised on the 1 July 1977 and is now part of British Shipbuilders.

The company's main activities embrace the design and construction of warships and hovercraft intended primarily for military purposes. Diversified engineering work is also undertaken including the design and manufacture of ship stabilisers and specialised electrical and electronic control equipment for marine and industrial use.

Vosper Thornycroft entered the hovercraft field in 1968. Shortly afterwards an order was received for VT 1, an 87-ton ferry. In 1973 the company announced details of the VT 2 military hovercraft, similar in size to VT 1 but with a completely different propulsion system. The prototype VT 1 was converted to become the prototype VT 2. These two craft are described below, together with a number of other hovercraft projects. The latest design, an 18 metre fast patrol hovercraft, was announced in June 1978.

18 METRE PATROL HOVERCRAFT

This new 18 metre design can be adapted to a number of different roles including coastal patrol, logistic support, coastguard and customs duties. In the logistic support role it is capable of carrying up to 35 troops with their equipment. Fire-fighting and rescue duties can also be undertaken by fitting bolt-on equipment to mountings on the hull structure. A gun of up to twin 30mm calibre can be mounted on a well deck forward. All-up weight of the craft is about 25 tonnes and under normal conditions it will carry a disposable load of about 9 tonnes. Maximum continuous speed for the craft is estimated at 60 knots in calm conditions. Range is about 600n miles at a speed of 50 knots.

LIFT AND PROPULSION: Integrated system powered by a single Avco Lycoming Super TF25 gas-turbine rated at 3,000shp maximum and 2,500shp continuous at 15°C. The gas-turbine is installed in an engine bay amidship and has easy access for servicing. Power is transmitted to a 3·2m (10ft 6in) diameter ducted controllable-pitch propeller aft, and via a vertical driveshaft, to a bevel drive gearbox beneath from which shafts extend sideways to drive four 1·2m (4ft) diameter lift fans, housed in pairs in two volutes, one on either side of the craft, outboard of the superstructure. The ducted propeller is designed for improved efficiency, noise reduction and to eliminate the risk of injury to anyone working alongside. An auxiliary power unit provides electrical supplies when the main engine is stopped.

CONTROLS: Vertical and horizontal control surfaces are fitted aft of the propeller duct.

HULL: Built in marine aluminium alloys.

SKIRT: Loop and segment skirt system, similar to that of VT 2, providing a cushion depth of more than 1·5m (5ft). This ensures good seakeeping for a craft of this size and enables it to clear substantial obstacles when manoeuvring ashore.

ACCOMMODATION: The arrangement of the craft includes a central superstructure with engine bay, the auxiliary machinery room and the crew's accommodation with bunks and galley. Above this is a control cabin, with pilot's and navigator's positions. The well deck forward provides space for the gun mounting and its operator, or, with suitable ramps, can be used to carry up to two Land Rovers or similar vehicles. Alternatively troops, in addition to the 35 who can be accommodated in the superstructure, can be transported in the well deck. Another option is a larger superstructure capable of accommodating more troops.

DIMENSIONS

Length overall: 18·4m (60ft 5in)

Width, hard structure: 9·3m (30ft 6in)

Height overall, on cushion: 6·2m (20ft 4in)

WEIGHTS

All-up weight: 25 tonnes

Disposable load, max: 9 tonnes

PERFORMANCE

Max continuous speed, calm conditions: 60 knots

Max range at 50 knots, calm conditions: 600n miles

VT 2

One of the largest military hovercraft yet built, VT 2 has an overall length of 30·1m (99ft) and an all-up weight of 100-105 tonnes, according to role. Developed from the earlier VT 1 passenger/car ferry, it incorporates the same basic hull structure and skirt system, but has a completely new propulsion system to permit higher speeds and fully amphibious operation.

A number of variants are available. In addition to a strike version, there is a logistic version for carrying troops, vehicles and guns; a multipurpose configuration combining both weapons and a logistic capability and a minecountermeasures variant.

The VT 2 prototype has been employed by the Royal Navy on mine-countermeasures trials, but it is at present being chartered by the Royal Navy to participate in exercises and trials mainly in the logistic support role.

In both 1977 and 1978 the craft was employed in the Whisky Galore exercises to land troops and vehicles from ships in and around Loch Ewe and the Outer Hebrides. In 1977 VT 2 returned to the Solent by way of the north of Scotland and Pentland Firth, so completing a circumnavigation of Britain in a passage time of 60 hours.

To extend the VT 2's overall capabilities before participating in exercises in 1978, VT 2-001 was modified under Ministry of Defence contract to permit palleted cargo to be handled for transport from ship-to-shore. Modifications included the fitting of a loading hatch in the superstructure roof and laying roller tracking on the deck below.

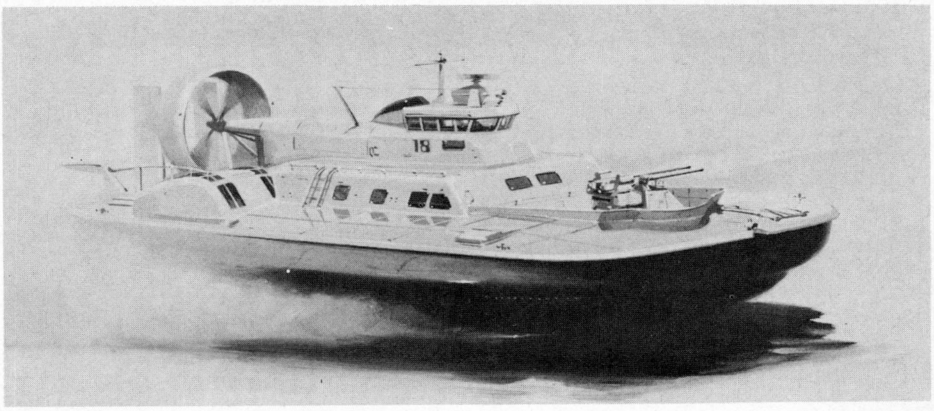

Impression of Vosper Thornycroft's new 25-ton 18 metre patrol hovercraft. Maximum continuous speed is estimated at 60 knots in calm conditions, with a range of about 600n miles at a speed of 50 knots

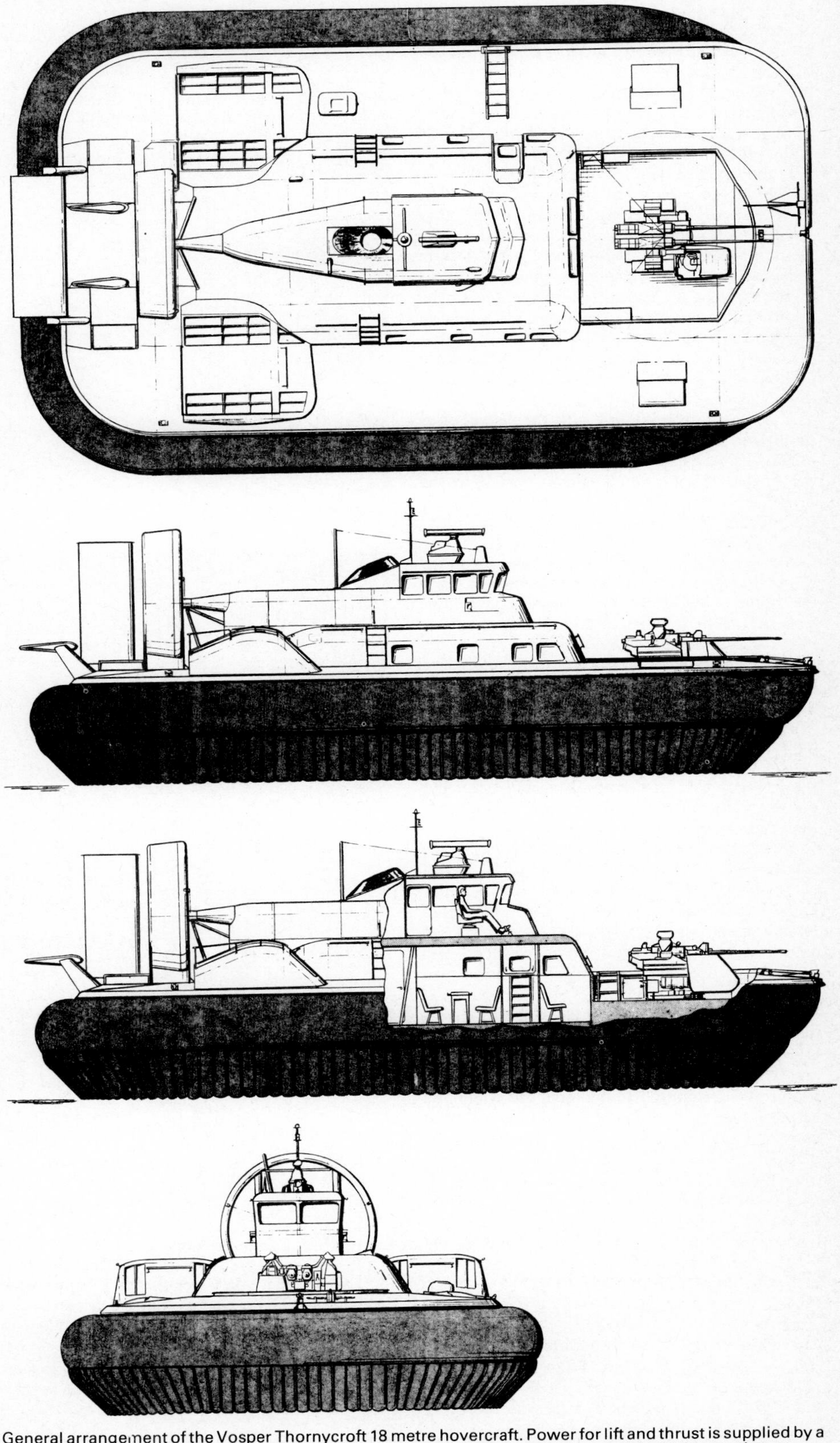

General arrangement of the Vosper Thornycroft 18 metre hovercraft. Power for lift and thrust is supplied by a single Avco Lycoming Super TF25 gas turbine rated at 3,000shp maximum and 2,500shp continuous

LIFT AND PROPULSION: Motive power for the integrated lift/propulsion system is supplied by two Rolls-Royce Proteus marine gas-turbines, rated at 4,500shp maximum and 3,800shp continuous. The two gas-turbines are installed in port and starboard engine rooms amidships and each powers two drive shafts via a David Brown gearbox. One shaft transmits power to a bank of four centrifugal lift fans, which absorbs about one third of the output, the other drives a ducted propulsion fan via an inclined shaft.

The two variable-pitch fans, each 4·1m (13ft 6in) in diameter, have seven blades and each rotates in a duct of streamline section. The blades are of foam-filled glass-reinforced plastics. Manufactured by Dowty Rotol Limited, they are the largest propulsion fans yet made. In comparison with air propellers, ducted fans offer increased efficiency and substantial reductions in noise levels. The noise reduction results from the low fan tip speed of 150m/sec (500ft/sec). Other advantages offered are reduced diameter for a given thrust and power, and less danger to crew working in their vicinity. The variation in pitch provides differential thrust for manoeuvring. Downstream of the fan blades are stator blades, sixteen in each duct, ensuring uniformity of thrust and of the directional control provided by rudders mounted at the aft ends of the ducts.

The ducted fans are mounted with their shaft axes at an angle to the horizontal of about 13½ degrees, avoiding the need for right-angle gearbox drives. This entails some slight loss in efficiency, but this is offset by savings in the losses in the right-angle boxes themselves and in the additional power for air cooling which would be needed for their lubricating oil.

Gas turbines, main gearboxes and lift fans are all housed in machinery spaces on either side of the craft outboard of the main longitudinal webs. The engines are mounted with their shaft axes parallel to those of the propulsion fans, so that normal gearing can be used for the 75% or so of the engine output which is transmitted to the propulsion fans. This arrangement also directs the turbine exhausts upwards, thereby simplifying the ductwork.

The remaining 25% of engine power is applied to the lift fans which are accommodated in separate compartments of the machinery spaces, two each side, with their axes horizontal. A vee-drive gear system effects the change in shaft axis at the output from the main gearbox to the lift fans. The fans draw air through grilled areas in the upper outboard part of the craft's superstructure amidships and discharge down to the cushion loop. A quantity of cushion air is diverted via a filtration system to remove salt and sand contamination to the Proteus gas turbine intakes, and a further quantity is ducted to bow thrusters for manoeuvring at low speeds.

CONTROLS: The pilot and engineer are accommodated atop the superstructure in a control cabin which has an all-round view. Rudder pedals provide steering via the control surfaces in the fan slipstream. Twin levers between pilot and engineer control fan pitch, and hence speed, and can be moved differentially to provide additional turning moments. To give close lateral control at low speeds a bow thruster is fitted. This consists of thwartships ducts forward, to which cushion air is supplied. Hydraulically-actuated doors direct air from the ducts to port or starboard as required, in response to movement of a combined selector control at the pilot's position. A ballast control enables craft trim to be adjusted by pumping reserve fuel, totalling 2 tonnes, from one compartment to another. This is done electrically by means of a switch. Engine throttle levers are available to both pilot and engineer. Communications are normally operated by the pilot. Full navigational and machinery instrumentation is provided.

HULL: Construction is mainly in marine aluminium alloys with bolted or riveted joints. The main structural elements are the buoyancy raft, of egg-box form, providing 26 watertight compartments and a buoyancy reserve of more than 100%, and two deep vertical webs, forming fore-and-aft bulkheads enclosing the central bay of the craft. On the underside of the buoyancy raft are three pads on which the craft is supported when at rest on dry land. A lighter shell structure attached to the periphery of the raft and the main longitudinal webs encloses accommodation and machinery spaces and the central bay. In logistic support configuration a door with loading ramp is provided at the bow, extending across the full width of the central bay. A door can be incorporated aft if through loading is required. The design allows substantial flexibility in the choice of superstructure arrangement to suit a wide variety of roles.

SKIRT: A peripheral skirt contains a 1·58m (5ft 6in) deep air cushion at a pressure of about 31mb (65lb/ft²). The cushion is in the form of a single undivided cell, the first time this configuration

Operational bases for the 60-knot plus VT 2 fast patrol hovercraft can be established on any gently sloping beach. Equipped with missiles, it carries an armament load comparable to that of a much larger conventional patrol boat. Armament would normally comprise two or four anti-ship missiles and either an Oto Melara 76mm general purpose automatic cannon or a Bofors 57mm cannon, together with their associated control equipment

VT 2-001 in logistic configuration operating from a Cornish beach while en route from Lee-on-the-Solent to Loch Ewe for Exercise Whisky Galore in 1977

has been used for a large hovercraft. It provides a comfortable ride in rough seas, and enables the craft to clear obstacles overland up to 1·1m (3ft 7in) high.

The skirt is made of nylon-reinforced neoprene and consists of two main parts, loop and segments. The loop forms a continuous duct around the periphery of the craft, contained between inner and outer bands of skirt material attached to the raft structure. The lift fans deliver air to the loop through apertures in the raft plating. The segments are attached to the lower edges of the loop, and consist of 157 sets of inner and outer scoop-shaped pieces. The inner segments direct air flow outwards and downwards into the outer segments, and have holes which allow a controlled proportion of the air flow to pass directly into the main cushion under the craft. The outer segments turn the airflow from the inner segments downwards and inwards.

The whole flexible skirt assembly is stabilised by cables connecting every junction between adjacent pairs of segments and the inner loop to the raft structure. The outer segments are the only ones subject to wear and are attached with special fasteners so that they can be changed in a few minutes with hand tools, without having to lift the craft. Quite severe damage to the skirt, the loss of 30% of segments or 15% of the loop for example, can be accepted without seriously effecting the manoeuvrability of the craft.

SYSTEMS, ELECTRICAL AND HYDRAULIC: Auxiliary machinery includes gas-turbine alternator sets for electrical supplies, a hydraulic system for the fan pitch control, loading ramp and door actuation, and bow thruster doors.

DIMENSIONS (Typical)
Length overall: 30·17m (99ft)
Width overall: 13·3m (43ft 6in)
Cushion height: 1·58m (5ft 6in)
Cushion pressure: 31mb (65lb/ft²)

WEIGHTS
All-up weight: 100-105 tonnes, according to role.

PERFORMANCE
The basic VT 2 hovercraft design provides a vehicle which can carry a load of up to 32 tonnes for 550km (300n miles) at speeds of more than 60 knots (111km/h, 69 mph) over sea, river shallows, shoals, mudflats, ice and snow. It can also travel over dry land reasonably free from obstructions. It is capable of operating in rough seas and accepting a substantial amount of damage.

VT 2—VARIANTS
LOGISTIC SUPPORT

Designed to carry a company of 130 fully-armed troops and their vehicles. The vehicle bay is approximately 21·33m (70ft) long, 5·02m (16ft 6in) wide and 2·89m (9ft 6in) high. It has a full-width bow ramp and door together with a 2·43m (8ft) wide stern ramp and door for the through loading and unloading of vehicles. The craft can carry payloads of 32 tons, together with fuel for five hours. Considerable overloading of the craft is acceptable at reduced performance so that with suitable deck and entrance ramp reinforcing a Chieftain battle tank could be carried. The vessel can be either shipped to a theatre of operations, or if required by a NATO country, it could be deployed to any point on the coastline of Europe or the Mediterranean under its own power. The longest "stage" would be from the United Kingdom to Gibraltar, a distance of approximately 1,100n miles. To allow an adequate reserve en route for rough seas the craft would carry an additional 10 tons of fuel, starting out at an all-up weight of 115 tons.

WEIGHTS
Operating: 62·5 tons
Payload: 32 tons
Fuel: 10·5 tons
Starting all-up weight: 105 tons

Impression of a VT 2 leaving a temporary base on a light patrol assignment

Troops landing from VT 2-001 during Exercise Whisky Galore

VT 2-001 demonstrating its amphibious capability by operating at speed along the shore line

MULTI-PURPOSE

This version is designed and equipped for the following role capabilities: light patrol, logistic support, firefighting, disaster relief and crash rescue. Normally these roles can be performed without adding to the basic equipment carried. The craft is also suitable for additional roles such as pollution control, radio interception and hydrographic survey. However these roles require extra equipment to be installed on board, in the form of palletised units which can be loaded into the centre bay. Although based on the VT 2, the multi-purpose craft differs from the logistic variant in several respects. The chief difference is in the design of the forward superstructure, where an extra deck level is provided, port and starboard, above the forward accommodation areas. This provides a location for a light gun to starboard (a 30mm twin Oerlikon mount is shown) and a fire-fighting monitor, hoses etc together with a Gemini inflatable to port. In addition, a new bow ramp is included which eliminates the need for an upward opening door and provides a clear field of fire for the gun. In the logistic role, trucks of up to about 4 tonnes may be carried and through loading is available for 1 tonne trucks. The rear door may also be used in such roles as crash rescue, pollution control and hydrographic survey when equipment must be deployed and recovered.

The control cabin is located amidships on the centreline for good all-round vision and is large enough to act as an operations centre. Lightweight machine-gun mountings are provided aft of the cabin, also a Saab-Scania TV tracking system for gunfire control.

Internal accommodation includes space for 70 personnel, plus 86 folding seats in the centre bay. Galley equipment is located in the forward port compartment, while to starboard sick bay equipment, including four convertible berths, is fitted. Two chemical toilet facilities are located aft.

WEIGHTS
Operating (including fixed equipment): 70·5 tons
Disposable load: 34·5 tons
Starting all-up weight: 105 tons

FAST MISSILE HOVERCRAFT

This version is equipped with two Otomat surface-to-surface missiles and an Oto Melara 76mm Compact gun. Other armament of similar weight can be fitted to meet individual specifications. Armament and crew weight is 23½ tons, and with 10½ tons of fuel the endurance is five hours or 300n miles at 60 knots. An additional 10½ tons of fuel for the overload case (giving a half fuel weight of 100 tons) results in a range of 600n miles.

WEIGHTS
Operating: 66 tons
Armament and crew: 23·5 tons
Fuel: 10·5 tons
Starting all-up weight: 100 tons

MINE COUNTERMEASURES

Extended trials have been undertaken by the Naval Hovercraft Trials Unit, Lee-on-the-Solent, which is primarily concerned with the development of hovercraft for mine-countermeasures duties. Interest in amphibious hovercraft for this application stems from its relative invulnerability to underwater explosions compared with displacement vessels, and their low magnetic and underwater noise signatures. The accompanying artist's impression shows one possible arrangement of a VT 2 for this particular role. As can be seen from the picture, the VT 2 is of suitable size for this work. The picture shows the sweepdeck space with sweepgear stowed. The gear illustrated is either in current use or readily available commercially.

The craft itself is a version of the multi-purpose design with an extended rear deck equipped with davits and MCM gear. The bow ramp is retained and this together with the use of containerised MCM equipment modules, allows some of the multi-role characteristics to be retained.

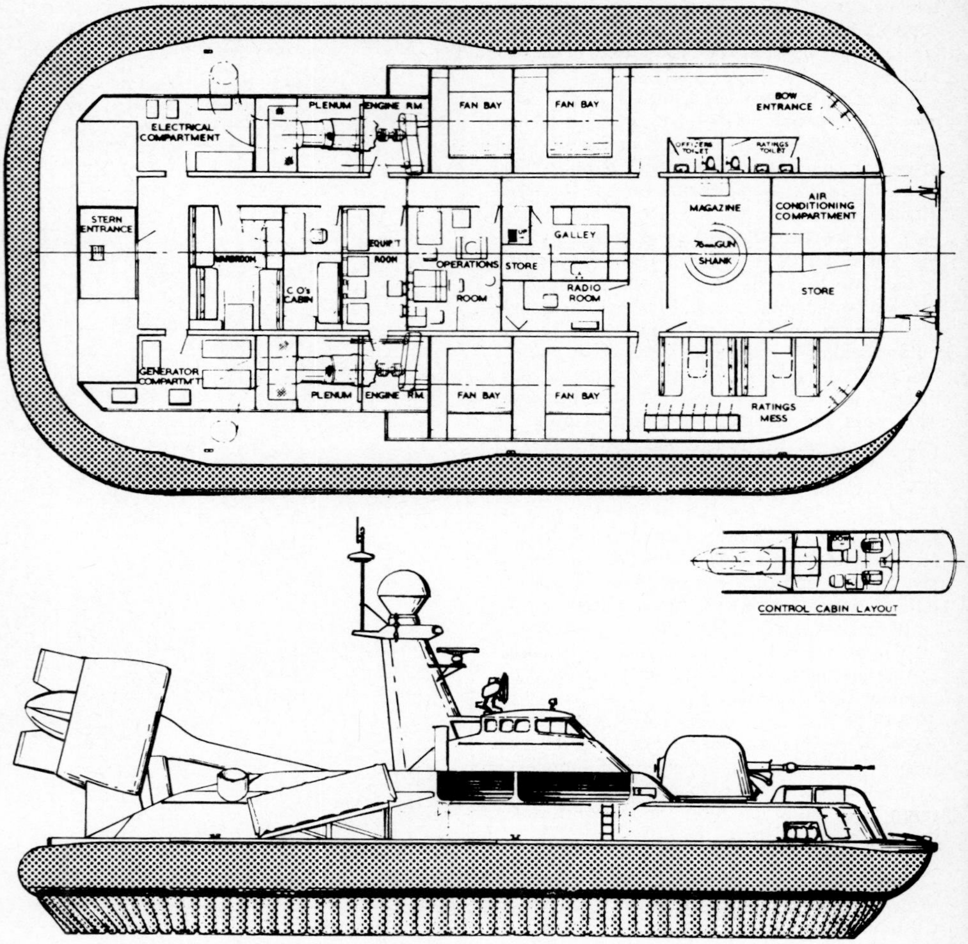

Outboard profile and deck plan of the VT 2 in fast missile hovercraft configuration. The craft illustrated is equipped with two Otomat surface-to-surface missiles and a 76mm Melara Compact gun

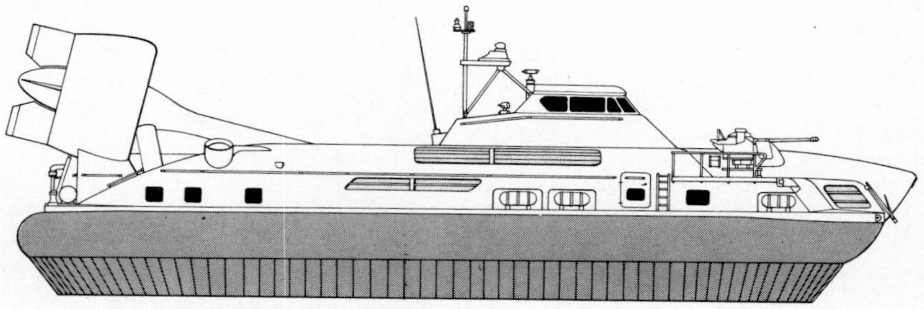
Outboard profile of the multi-purpose variant of the VT 2

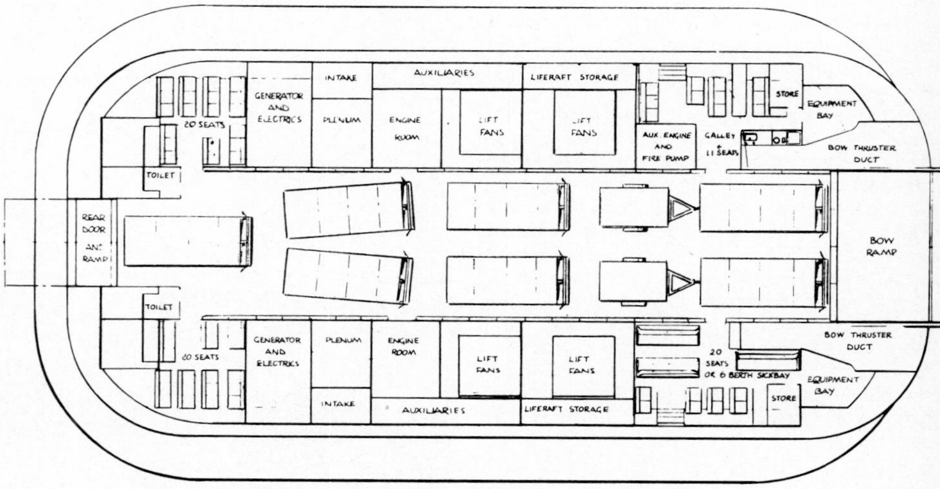

Deck plan of the VT 2 multi-purpose craft. Employed in the logistics role, a typical payload would comprise seven one-ton Land Rovers and two trailers

WEIGHTS
Operating: 69·3 tons
Disposable load: 35·7 tons
Starting all-up weight 105 tons

VT 1

Vosper Thornycroft's first hovercraft, the VT 1 is no longer in production. An 87-ton ACV designed for fast, low-cost passenger/car operation, it was built to the standards required by the British Civil Air Cushion Vehicle Safety Requirements. Cruising speed was 65-70km/h (35-38 knots) and it could operate in wave heights up to 3-3·7m (10-12ft). The VT 1 prototype underwent trials to evaluate its commercial viability and particularly its reliability and seakeeping, both in the English Channel and in the rough waters between the Channel Islands and the French coast. The first two all-passenger craft built by the company were operated in Scandinavian waters between Malmö, Sweden and Copenhagen, Denmark in 1972. Operationally, the two craft proved extremely successful. They carried more than 310,000 passengers and travelled more than 61,000 miles, with a mechanical reliability of 98·73%.

VT 1M

Before construction of VT 1 a 40% linear scale model designated VT 1 M was built for full evaluation of the design. Once this work was complete the craft was used for an extensive programme of development testing on the application of water-jet propulsion to hovercraft of this type.

OTHER PROJECTS

Among other project studies undertaken by the Vosper Thornycroft hovercraft design office has been one for a 500 ton ocean-going escort with helicopter landing pad and hangar and another for a 3,000 ton SES, mainly for ASW applications. The latter would be capable of a speed of 100 knots and a range of 2,800n miles and carry two helicopters or V/STOL aircraft.

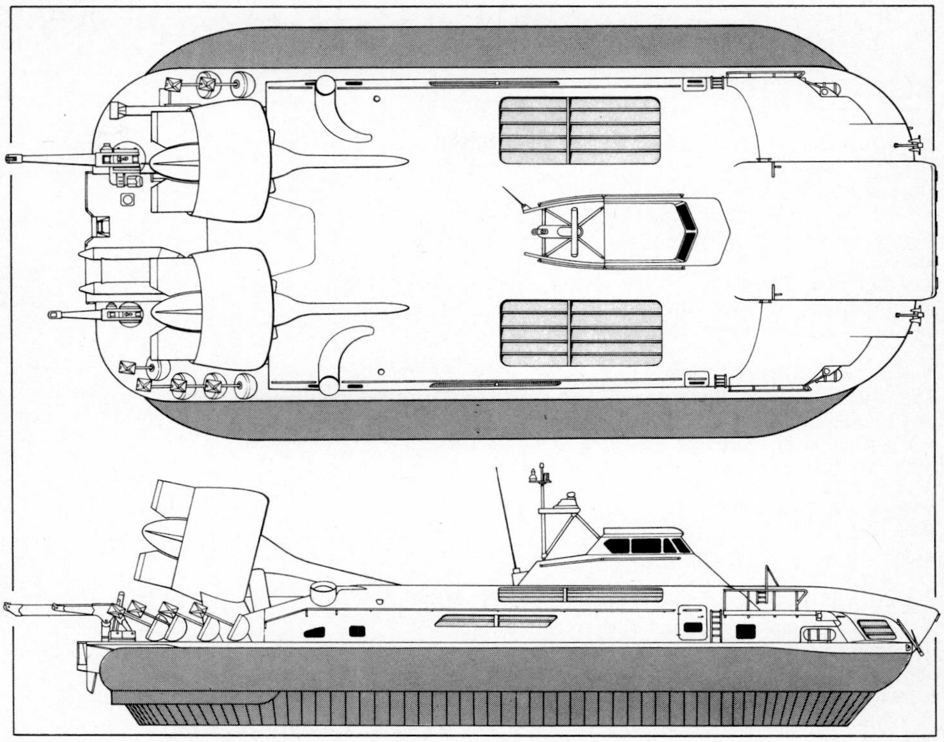

General arrangement of the VT 2 mine countermeasures craft

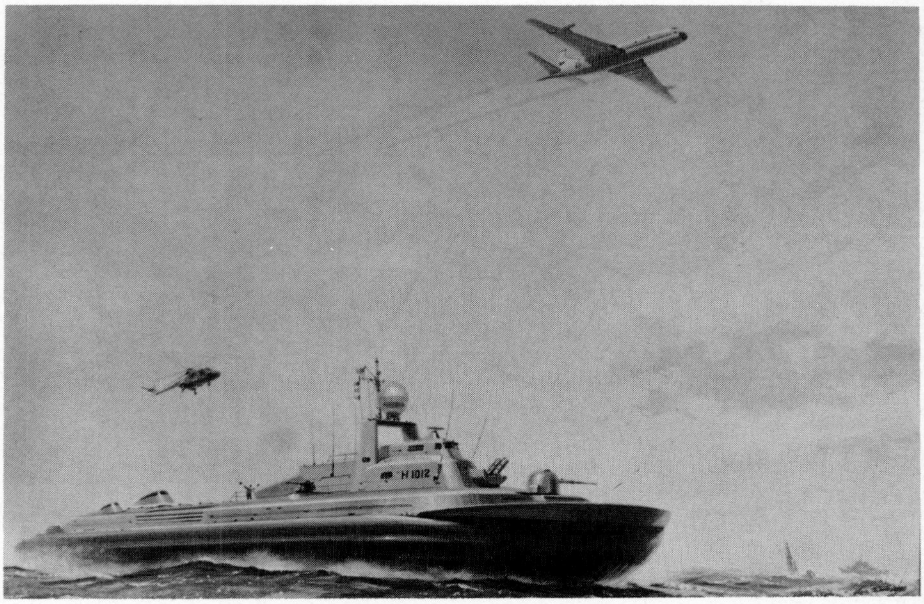

A 500-ton ocean-going escort designed by Vosper Thornycroft. A helicopter landing pad and hangar can be provided aft of the superstructure

Impression of a mine countermeasures craft based on the VT 2. Note the sweepgear on the rear deck extension

VT 2 preparing to tow. Note the protection to personnel afforded by the fan ducts and the ample deck space aft

UNITED STATES OF AMERICA

AEROJET-GENERAL CORPORATION

(Subsidiary of The General Tire and Rubber Co)

Corporate Office: 9100 East Flair Drive, El Monte, California 91734, USA
Telephone: (213) 572 6000
Officials:
J H Vollbrecht, *President*
Aerojet Liquid Rocket Company Office:
PO Box 13222, Sacramento, California 95813, USA
Telephone: (916) 355 1000
Officials:
R I Ramseier, *President*
AALC Operations Office:
6906 West Highway 98, Panama City, Florida 32407, USA
Telephone: (904) 234 3378
Officials:
E F Davison, *Vice President and General Manager*
F F Herman, *Manager, AALC Programme*

Aerojet-General began research and development programmes on both rigid sidewall and skirted amphibious air cushion configurations in June 1966. The company's research and development programmes include lift system development, skirt and structural materials investigations and development, sub-scale and full-scale dynamic model testing, test laboratory development and full-scale vehicle operation. In addition, Aerojet has conducted government and company funded design and application studies on many rigid sidewall and skirted air cushion vehicle designs for military, non-military government and commercial roles. Work is at present concentrated on a US Navy contract for the development and testing of the AALC JEFF(A) amphibious assault landing craft.

AALC JEFF (A)

In 1970, Aerojet-General was awarded a contract by US Naval Ship Systems Command for the preliminary design of an experimental 160-ton 50-knot amphibious assault landing craft. This was followed in March 1971 by a further contract for the detail design, construction and test of the craft, which is designated AALC JEFF(A). Construction of the hull was initiated by Todd Shipyards Corporation, Seattle, Washington, in 1974. Hull construction was completed in November 1976, when the craft was moved to Aerojet's facility in Tacoma, Washington for final outfitting and contractor's tests. The craft first hovered on

AALC Jeff (A) amphibious assault landing craft during lift fan testing

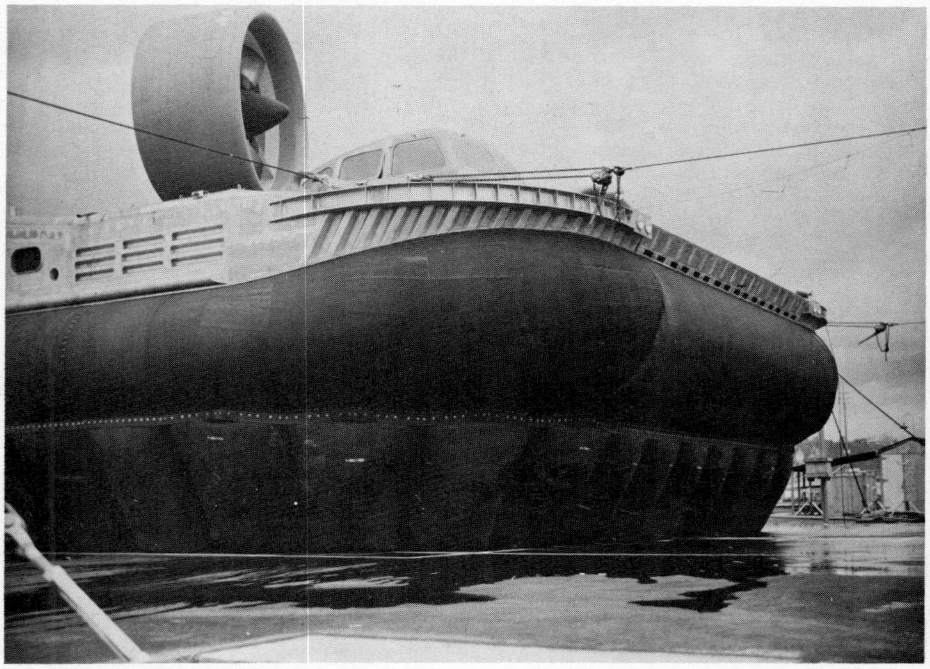

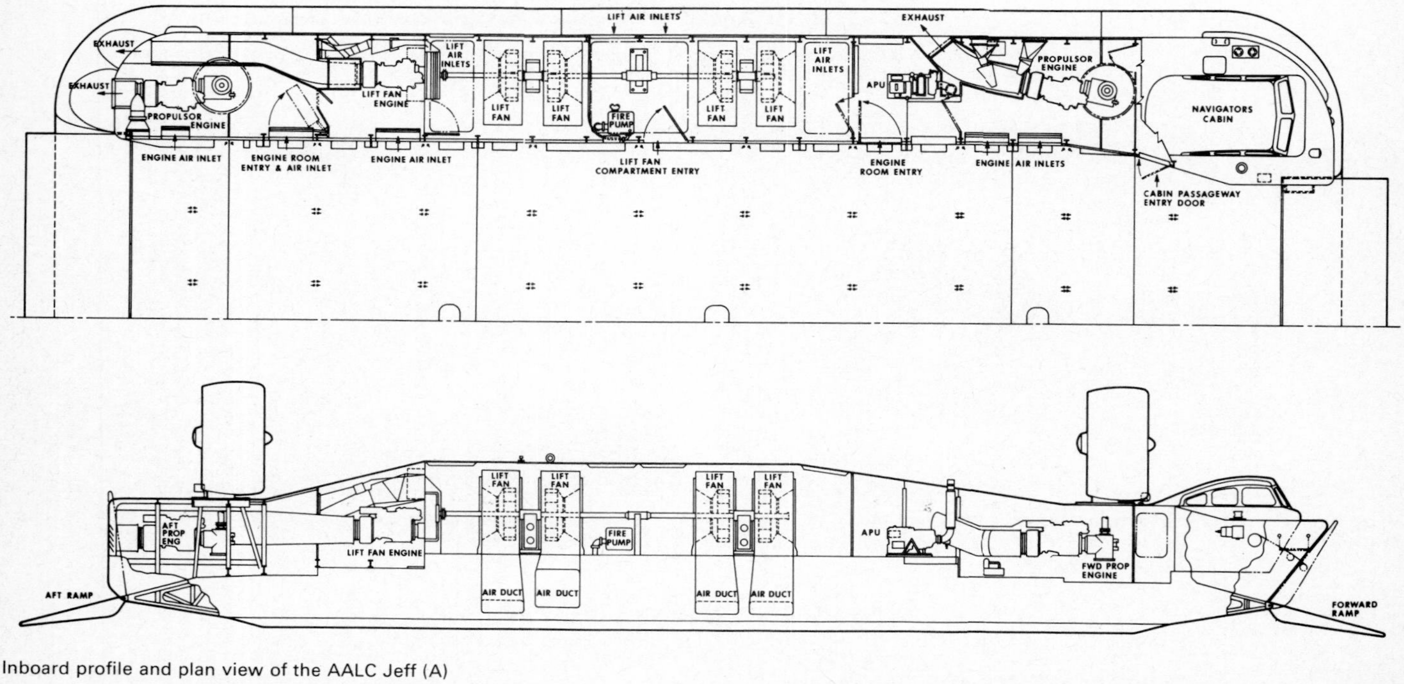

Inboard profile and plan view of the AALC Jeff (A)

15 April 1977. It was delivered to the US Navy's test facility in Panama City, Florida, in September 1977 for continuation of contractor tests and Navy trials.

The craft is designed to operate at a nominal speed of 50 knots in Sea State 2 and carry up to 75 tons in palletised supplies and/or equipment. It is designed primarily for use by the US Marine Corps, and will carry tanks, trucks, half-tracks and other equipment from an LPD, LSD or LHA support ship to a point inland.

To ensure adequate world-wide operational capability, the specification calls for operation in temperatures from 0°—100°F.

LIFT AND PROPULSION: Cushion lift is provided by two 3,750hp Avco Lycoming TF40 gas-turbines, one in each of the two sidestructures, driving two sets of four 1·21m (4ft) diameter fans through lightweight transmission and shafting connections.

Thrust is supplied by four 3,750hp Avco Lycoming TF40 gas-turbines each driving a 2·26m (7ft 5in) diameter pylon-mounted shrouded propeller, located above the side-structure, and outside the cargo deck area to provide free access and uninterrupted air flow. Each propeller pylon rotates to provide both propulsion and directional control.

HULL: Constructed in marine aluminium with maximum use of corrugated structures to minimise total craft weight. The main hull is formed by a buoyancy raft with port and starboard side structures. Each sidestructure contains three Avco Lycoming gas-turbines with associated air intakes, exhausts, shrouded propellers, lift fans, transmissions and auxiliary power systems.

The bottom and deck structures of the hull are joined by longitudinal and transverse bulkheads to form a number of watertight flotation compartments. The cargo deck area is 211·82m² (2,280ft²); the bow ramp opening width is 6·55m (21ft 6in) and the aft ramp width is 8·33m (27ft 4in).

SKIRT: 1·52m (5ft) deep "Pericell" loop and cell type.

ACCOMMODATION: Two air-conditioned and sound-insulated compartments, each seating three crew members or observers. Access to each compartment is via the cargo deck.

DIMENSIONS
Length overall, on cushion: 29·3m (96ft 1in)
on landing pads: 28·04m (92ft)
Beam overall, on cushion: 14·63m (48ft)
on landing pads: 13·41m (44ft)
Height overall, on cushion: 7·03m (23ft 1in)
on landing pads: 5·77m (18ft 11in)
Bow ramp opening width: 6·55m (21ft 6in)
Stern ramp opening width: 8·33m (27ft 4in)
Cargo deck area: 211·82m² (2,280ft²)

WEIGHTS
Gross: 156,991kg (340,000lb)
Empty: 81,697kg (180,000lb)
Fuel: 18,144kg (40,000lb)
Design payload: 54,431kg (120,000lb)
Design overload: 68,038kg (150,000lb)

PERFORMANCE
Design speed with design payload: 50 knots
Range at 50 knots: 200n miles
Max gradient, standing start: 11½%
Nominal obstacle clearance: 1·21m (4ft)

AIRCUSHION BOAT COMPANY INC

401 Alexander Avenue, Building 391, Tacoma, Washington 98421, USA
Telephone: (206) 272 3600
Officials:
W W Buckley, *President*
F C Gunter, *Vice President*

The Aircushion Boat Company is responsible for the development of the Airboat—a concept described by the company as an air-cushion-assisted catamaran. Vessels of this series of sidewall craft are based on conventional fibreglass hulls and employ water propeller or waterjet propulsion. Lift is supplied by an independent engine/fan system and flexible skirts are fitted fore and aft to contain the air cushion.

The company states that the cushion supports 75% of the loaded weight of the Airboats, and that as a result of the reduced drag the prototype uses 20% less fuel per mile. Another advantage is that when travelling at high speed, the air cushion softens the ride by preventing heavy slamming. Vessels of this type are being marketed by the company for a variety of applications including fast crew boats, water taxis, patrol boats, survey and sports fishing craft.

AIRBOAT III

Airboat III is employed as a development craft and began trials in Puget Sound in January 1974.

It has performed in short 1·21m (4ft) waves at speeds up to 35 knots without undue discomfort to the crew due to slamming. Another characteristic is that it generates very little wash when executing full speed runs on smooth water in protected waterways.

LIFT AND PROPULSION: Two 330 Chrysler petrol engines driving twin waterscrews propel the craft. A third engine powers a centrifugal fan for cushion lift.

HULL: Fine retardant foam and fibreglass sandwich construction.

DIMENSIONS
Length: 11·58m (38ft)
Beam: 4·11m (13ft 6in)

WEIGHTS
All-up weight: 7,257kg (16,000lb)
Normal payload: 1,360kg (3,000lb)

PERFORMANCE
Cruising speed: 35 knots
Max speed: 40 knots plus

Airboat III during trials on Puget Sound

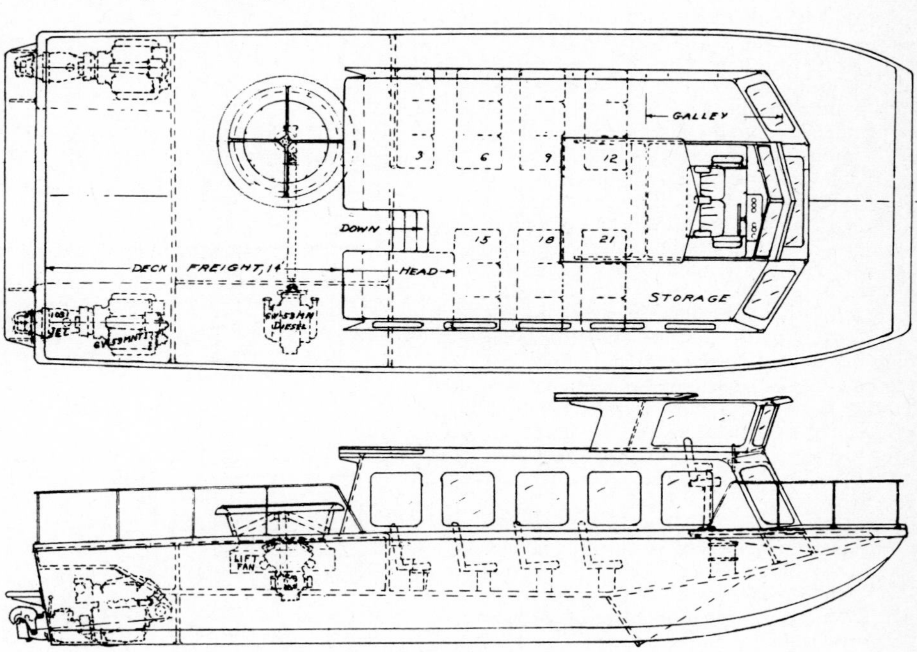

General arrangement of the waterjet-propelled 42ft Airboat

42FT AIRBOAT

The 12·8m (42ft) long Airboat is a high speed passenger ferry/freighter capable of operating in 1·37m (4ft 6in) waves. In passenger configuration seating is provided for 21 plus a crew of two.

A feature of the design is the extension of the bow well ahead of the air cushion. When rough water forces the bow down at speed the broad area forward of the cushion planes and raises the bow without slamming.

With the lift fan system off, the craft operates as a conventional displacement catamaran and has a top speed of 15 knots. With the lift system on, acceleration to the cruising speed of 30 knots is easily attained in ten boat lengths. In 2·4-3·04m (8-10ft) following seas a stable, near horizontal attitude is maintained while contouring swells and no tendency to broach or lose directional control is experienced.

LIFT AND PROPULSION: Motive power is supplied by three diesels, one for lift and two for propulsion. The lift engine drives a large low rpm centrifugal fan contained in a reinforced box which is an integral part of the hull structure. Power is transmitted via a clutch and Spicer shaft to a heavy duty, lightweight right-angle gearbox. Power delivered to the fan at cruise condition pressure and airflow is 180hp. Each of the propulsion engines is turbocharged and drives a waterjet. The standard fuel tank capacity is 300 gallons, providing a cruising range of more than 250 miles at 30 knots.

Marine propellers can be fitted to the vessel instead of waterjets if required. The powerplant remains the same, but the propulsion engines supply power through reversing gearboxes to shafts and marine propellers. Hydraulically operated twin rudders are mounted on the transom of each of the hulls. The propeller-driven version is capable of the same top speed, with slightly improved fuel economy.

HULL: Robust, fire-retardant foam and fibreglass sandwich structure, with unitised beam tying the catamaran hulls. High freeboard, wide buoyant hull and low profile for seaworthiness in rough seas and gale force winds.

ACCOMMODATION: In passenger/crew boat configuration, accommodation is provided for 21 seated passengers and a crew of two. The passenger saloon is completely enclosed with 1·98m (6ft 6in) high headroom throughout. The cabin contains a galley, head and large storage area. The bridge is elevated for 360 degree view and is located slightly aft of the bow. A sliding hard top provides upward visibility if required.

DIMENSIONS
Length: 12·8m (42ft)
Beam: 5·18m (17ft)
PERFORMANCE
Service speed: 30 knots
Max speed: in excess of 33 knots
Max speed, displacement condition: 15 knots
Fuel consumption at 30 knots: 154·56 litres/h (34 gallons/h)
Cruising range at 30 knots: over 402km (250 miles)

AIRBOAT IV

Work on this new addition to the Airboat range began in the summer of 1976. Like the Airboat III, the new vessel, a 16·7m (55ft) survey craft, is based on the concept of an air-cushion assisted catamaran hull on which a cabin and pilothouse have been built to suit customer requirements.

In the case of the Airboat IV, the cabin can be adapted to seat up to 40 passengers.

Maximum speed of the new craft, which will be propelled by water screws driven by two 550hp Cummins KTA 1150 diesels, will be about 35 knots.

LIFT AND PROPULSION: Cushion lift is provided by two 275hp Volvo Penta TAM D70CS, each driving twin 0·6m (2ft) diameter double-entry, centrifugal fans. Fan air is discharged directly through the wet deck, between the catamaran hulls, into the cushion. Motive power for the propulsion system is provided by either two 550hp Cummins KTA 1150 diesels or twin 800hp MTU 8V331 diesels. Each engine drives a 0·66m (2ft 2in) diameter Michigan bronze propeller via a reversing gearbox and an inclined shaft. Waterjets can be fitted to the vessel instead of marine propellers if required. Fuel is carried in four 2,272 litre (500 gallon) capacity integral fibreglass tanks, two in each hull. Refuelling points are located on the weatherdeck, two on each hull. Recommended fuel is grade 2 diesel.

CONTROLS: Hydraulically-operated twin rudders control craft heading on the propeller-driven variants. On models equipped with waterjets, craft direction is controlled by jet flow deflection.

HULL: Fabricated in Airex core, fibreglass sandwich laminate. Decks and top of pilothouse in balsa cored fibreglass. Bow shell plate designed to withstand slamming loads of up to 20 psi.

SKIRT: Patented inflated double-cylinder bags at bow and stern.

ACCOMMODATION: Operating crew comprising captain, navigator and deckhand are accommodated in a raised pilothouse forward. Up to 40 passengers can be accommodated in the main cabin, which is heated and ventilated. Air conditioning is optional. Passenger seats are of lightweight aircraft-type, with a central aisle between the seat rows. Entry doors are at the side of the deckhouse, one port, one starboard.

SYSTEMS, ELECTRICAL: 110V ac from diesel auxiliary generator. Shore power adaptor, plus 24V dc supply for engine starting, and 12V dc for navigation lights, etc.

APU: Onan diesel.

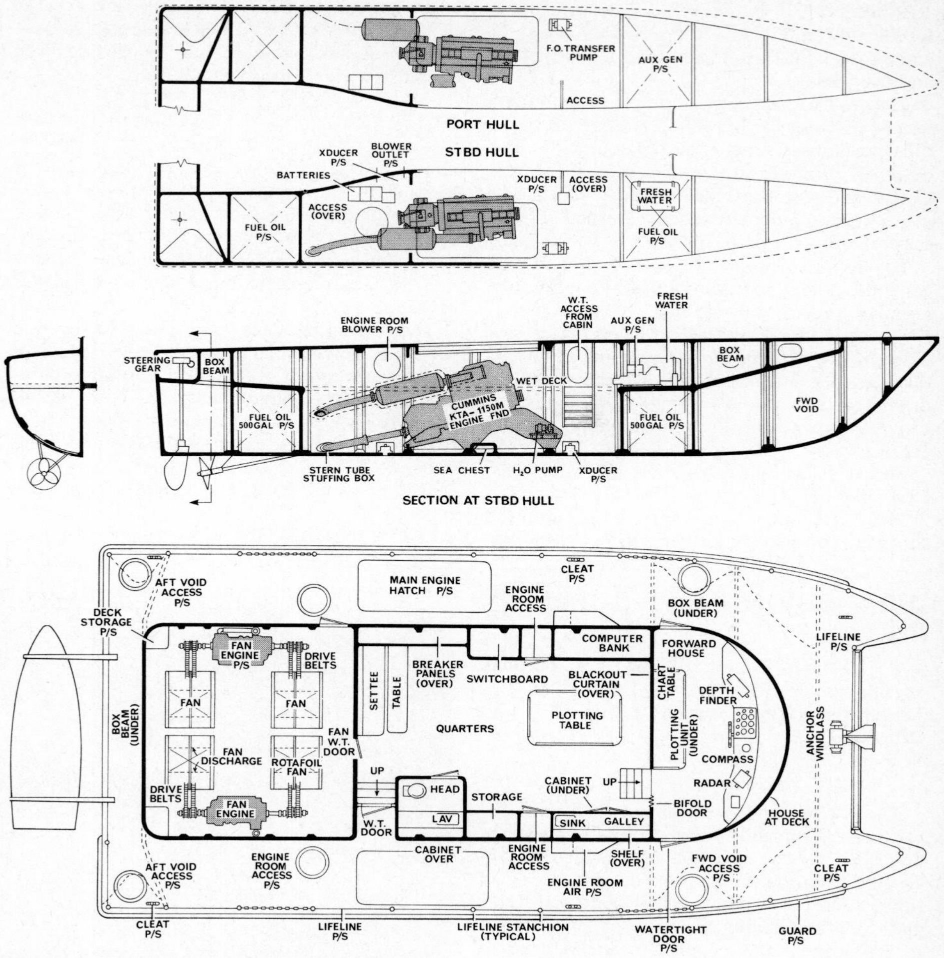

Inboard profile and deck plans of the Airboat IV

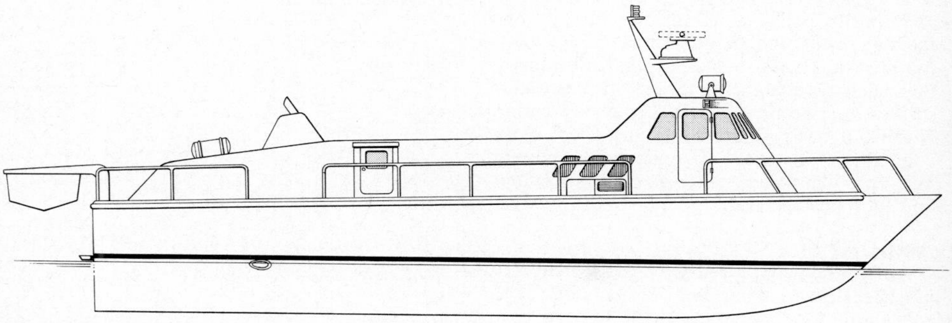

Outboard profile of the Airboat IV

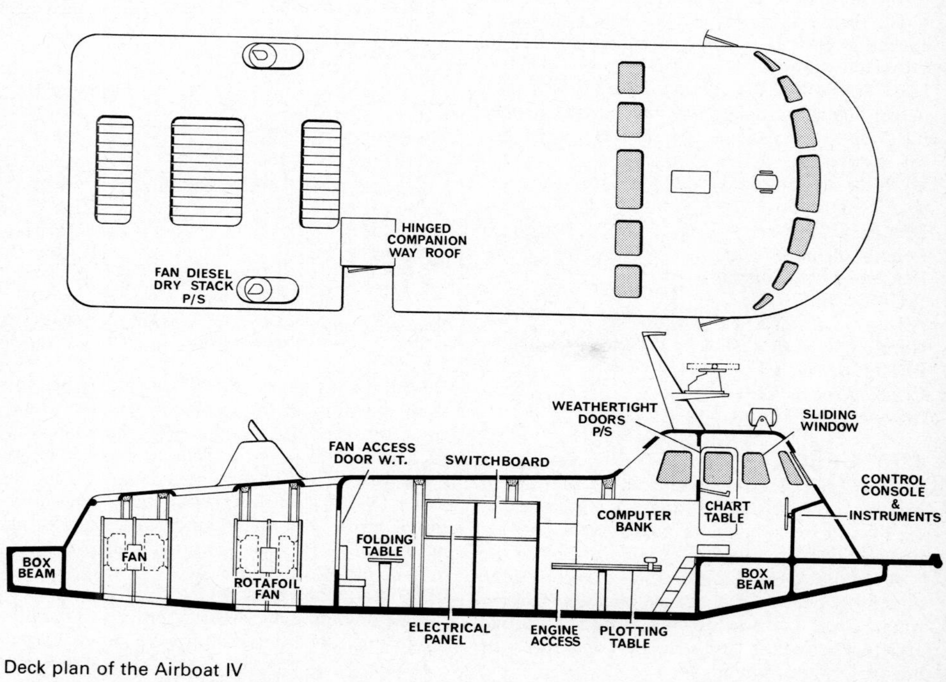

Deck plan of the Airboat IV

DIMENSIONS
EXTERNAL
Length overall, power off: 16·7m (55ft)
on cushion: 16·7m (55ft)
Beam overall, power off: 7·62m (25ft)
on cushion: 7·62m (25ft)
Height overall, displacement condition excluding mast: 3·65m (12ft)
on cushion: 3·9-4·2m (13-14ft)
Draft afloat, propellers: 1·82m (6ft)
waterjets: 1·06m (3ft 6in)
INTERNAL
Passenger Cabin
Length: 12·19m (40ft)
Max width: 4·57m (15ft)
Max height: 1·98m (6ft 6in)
Floor area: 55·74m² (600ft²)
Baggage holds: In cabin, plus weatherdeck storage locker.
WEIGHTS
Normal empty: 21,681·7kg (47,800lb)
Normal all-up weight: 29,483·48kg (65,000lb)
Normal payload: 2,177·2kg (4,800lb)
Max payload: 4,082kg (9,000lb)
PERFORMANCE
Max speed, calm water: 35 knots
Max speed, calm water, max continuous power: 30 knots
Cruising speed, calm water: 30 knots
Turning circle diameter at 30 knots: 3 boat lengths
Water speed in 4ft waves and 15 knot headwind: 30 knots
Max wave capability on scheduled runs: 1·82m (6ft)
Max survival sea state: 5
Still air range and endurance at cruising speed: 650n miles
PRICE: Approx price of craft, fob Tacoma USA—US$575,000. Base engines extra, depending on choice.
TERMS: Partial payment on signing contract, plus progress instalments.

AIR CUSHION SYSTEMS

Ensign, Raymond Enterprises, PO Box 2160, Rancho Palos Verdes, California 90274, USA
Telephone: (213) 377 8750
Officials:
Col Jacksel M Broughton USAF (Retd)

First craft to be introduced by this new ACV manufacturer is the AC-5 Beaver, an amphibious utility vehicle powered by three Avco Lycoming piston engines, and designed to carry payloads weighing up to 2,268kg (5,000lb) on its 19·5m² (210ft²) cargo deck. In the design stage is an enlarged version, the AC-44, powered by three 900hp lightweight diesels. The AC-44 is intended primarily as a heavy lift freighter or amphibious barge for the trans-shipment of loads in the 20-ton range.

AC-5 BEAVER

This new ACV "workhorse" has been designed to accomplish a wide variety of tasks requiring the movement of people and equipment in environments and weather conditions where wheeled vehicles, boats and helicopters cannot work effectively or efficiently. To ensure low maintenance costs and ease servicing in remote areas the craft is powered by three Avco Lycoming 10-360 engines which are identical to those employed in thousands of fixed-wing aircraft and helicopters used throughout the world. The three-bladed reversible-pitch thrust propellers are also standard items, with spares readily available "off-the-shelf".

A wide range of equipment and superstructure modules can be accommodated on the Beaver's flatbed hull which incorporates a number of tie-down points. An optional self-powered rotating extension boom crane can be fitted for loading and unloading. The deck height and open side areas simplify self-loading from trucks or by fork lift.

One of the major features of the craft is the simplicity with which it can be transported from one work site to another. It can be shipped over long distances by air or sea in a 12·19m (40ft) container after minor disassembly of its modular components, or it can be converted into a trailer by two men, ready for trailing behind a pick-up truck.

LIFT AND PROPULSION: A single Lycoming 10-360 AIB aero-engine drives a 1·52m (5ft) diameter six-bladed axial fan mounted in a vertical duct aft of the control cabin for lift. Thrust is furnished by two pylon-mounted Lycoming 10-360 aero-engines aft, each driving a ducted 1·57m (5ft 2in) diameter Hartzell Propeller Company three-bladed reversible-pitch aluminium propeller.

CONTROLS: Directional control is provided by six vertical vanes hinged to the rear of each propeller duct. At low speeds craft heading is controlled by a retractable nose wheel.

HULL: Welded aluminium space frame construction with riveted aluminium skin and plywood decking. Integral wash water and fuel tanks. Two outer 0·6m (2ft) wide sponsons running the full length of the craft each side, hinge upwards to reduce the overall width to 2·4m (8ft) for stowing into containers or towing by road.

SKIRT: Bag type skirt, with roll stabilisation subdivision, provides 0·6m (2ft) hard structure clearance.

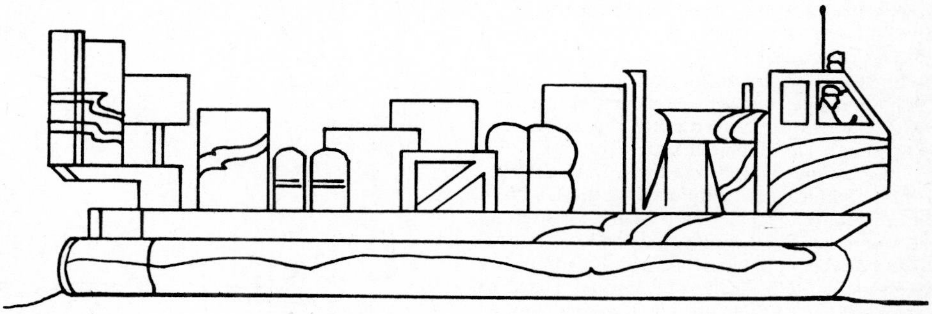

AC-5 Beaver amphibious ACV. Motive power is supplied by three Avco Lycoming 10-360 aero-engines, one for lift, two for propulsion. The Beaver can carry loads of up to 2,267kg (5,000lb). Maximum speed over calm water is 55 knots.

ACCOMMODATION: Fully enclosed cabin forward for driver. Optional extras include passenger modules with 12 and 16 seats.
DIMENSIONS
Length overall: 10·58m (34ft 9in)
Width overall: 4·21m (13ft 10in)
Hull width: 3·6m (11ft 10in)
Height overall, on cushion: 3·53m (11ft 7in)
on landing pads: 2·89m (9ft 6in)
Main load space, deck level: 3·55 × 4·01m (11ft 8in × 13ft 2in)
Main load area: 14·21m² (153ft²)
Side deck area: 4·64m² (50ft²)
WEIGHTS
Max gross: 5,125kg (11,300lb)
Empty: 2,540kg (5,600lb)
Max deck load: 2,267kg (5,000lb)
PERFORMANCE
Max operating speed, over smooth water at max gross weight: 55 knots
over rough water: 32 knots
over smooth ground and paved areas: 45 knots
over rough/rocky ground: 20 knots
Turning radius, tracking gear extended, over land: 3·65m (12ft) at 5 knots
4·57m (15ft) at 10 knots
Turning radius, tracking gear up, land and water:
6·09m (20ft) at 5 knots
12·19m (40ft) at 10 knots
24·38m (80ft) at 20 knots
60·96m (200ft) at 40 knots
Stopping distance, on cushion, hard ground from 40 knots: 48·76m (160ft)
smooth water: 36·57m (120ft)
Hard structure clearance height: 0·6m (2ft)
Max gradient, at sustained speed of 5 knots at 5,125kg (11,300lb) gross weight: 17%

AC-44

Currently in the design stage, the AC-44 is an enlarged version of the AC-5 with a load capacity of 20 tons. It will accept a 12·19 × 3 × 2·43m (40 × 10 × 8ft) cargo container directly from a ship and carry it across combinations of water and land to designated storage or delivery areas. Heavy cargo handling equipment will be carried on the craft.

The hull structure and skirt system will be similar to those of the AC-5, but because of the mass of the AC-44 and its payload, it will be fitted with a separate lateral control augmentation system which will take the form of a bow-mounted steering fan driven by the lift engine.

LIFT AND PROPULSION: Lift will be supplied by a single 900hp lightweight diesel driving two eight-bladed axial fans. Two 900hp diesels driving two 2·9m (9ft 6in) diameter three-bladed reversible-pitch propellers will provide thrust.
DIMENSIONS
Length overall: 26·21m (86ft)
Width overall: 8·23m (27ft)
Hull depth: 1·06m (3ft 6in)
Height, off cushion: 4·26m (14ft)
Skirt depth: 0·9m (3ft)
WEIGHTS
Empty: 14,061kg (31,000lb)
Payload and fuel: 20,865kg (46,000lb)
Gross: 34,926kg (77,000lb)
PERFORMANCE
Max operating speed, over land: 96·5km/h (60mph)
over water: 64·37km/h (40mph)
Fuel consumption: 306·61 litres/h (81 US gallons/h)

BELL AEROSPACE TEXTRON

Division of Textron Inc
New Orleans Office: PO Box 29307, New Orleans, Louisiana 70189, USA
Telephone: (504) 255 3311
Officials:
John J Kelly, *Vice President*
John B Chaplin, *Director of Engineering*
Roland Decrevel, *Project Manager*
Clarence L Forrest, *Director, Full-Scale Test and Project Manager, SES-100B*
Donald E Kenney, *Director of Administration*
Robert S Postle, *LC JEFF(B) Project Manager*

Bell Aerospace began its air cushion vehicle development programme in 1958. Craft built by the company range in size from the 18ft XHS3 to the 160-ton JEFF(B) which is undergoing sea trials.

The company has rights to manufacture and sell in the USA machines employing the hovercraft principle through a licensing arrangement with the British Hovercraft Corporation and Hovercraft Development Ltd.

In addition to importing seven BHC SR.N5s, three of which were employed by the US Navy and later by the US Coast Guard for use and evaluation, Bell built three SK-5 Model 7255s—the company's first production ACVs—to a US Army specification. The craft were airlifted to Vietnam, where they performed a variety of missions, including high speed troop/cargo transportation and patrol.

In January 1969 the US Surface Effect Ships Project Office awarded Bell a contract for the detailed design of a 100-ton surface effect ship test craft. Construction began in September 1969 and the preparation of the craft for trials began early in 1971. An extensive test and evaluation programme began in February 1972 on Lake Pontchartrain, Louisiana.

In May 1973 the SES-100B was transferred to the Naval Coastal Systems Laboratory at Panama City, Florida, for deep water and high sea state testing in the Gulf of Mexico. In January 1974 the company announced that the SES-100B had successfully completed the testing necessary to confirm and expand the technology necessary for the design of a 2,000-ton ocean-going surface effect ship.

In March 1971 the company was awarded a Phase II contract by the US Navy authorising it to start work on a programme covering the detail design, construction and test of an experimental 160-ton AALC (amphibious assault landing craft), designated LC JEFF(B).

Built at the NASA Michoud Assembly Facility, New Orleans, the craft was transferred to the Naval Coastal Systems Laboratory, Panama City, Florida, in early April 1977. A period of checking all systems was followed by contractor's tests in the Panama City area. The craft was then delivered to the US Navy's Experimental Trials Unit at Panama City for crew training and operational trials.

In July 1974 Bell was awarded a US $36 million contract to conduct an advanced development programme for a 2,000-ton, high-speed ocean-going, operational warship—the 2KSES. The 18-month contract awarded by the Naval Material Command covered the design, development and testing of full-scale subsystems and components including transmission, waterjet systems, lift fans and skirts, as well as a method of controlling the vessel's ride characteristics in a variety of sea states. In addition, the company continues to support surface effect ship development through studies in advanced systems in lift and propulsion.

In October 1977, it was announced that Bell had linked with Halter Marine, the New Orleans-based shipbuilders in a joint venture to develop and build a range of commercial surface effect ships.

Bell Aerospace Canada (see Canadian section) has built several prototypes of the Bell Model 7380 Voyageur heavy haul ACV, the second of which has been purchased by the Canadian Ministry of Transport for use by the Canadian Coast Guard. Production of additional Voyageurs is in hand. Two Voyageurs, designated 001 and 003, were transferred to the ACV/SES Test and Training Center, Panama City, in late 1975 for use in a training programme for US Army personnel.

The company also initiated a programme for the US Air Force that covers the design, development, installation and test of an air cushion landing system aboard a de Havilland XC-8A Buffalo transport aircraft. The first ACLS landing of the XC-8A took place at Wright-Patterson Air Force Base, Dayton, Ohio on 11 April 1975.

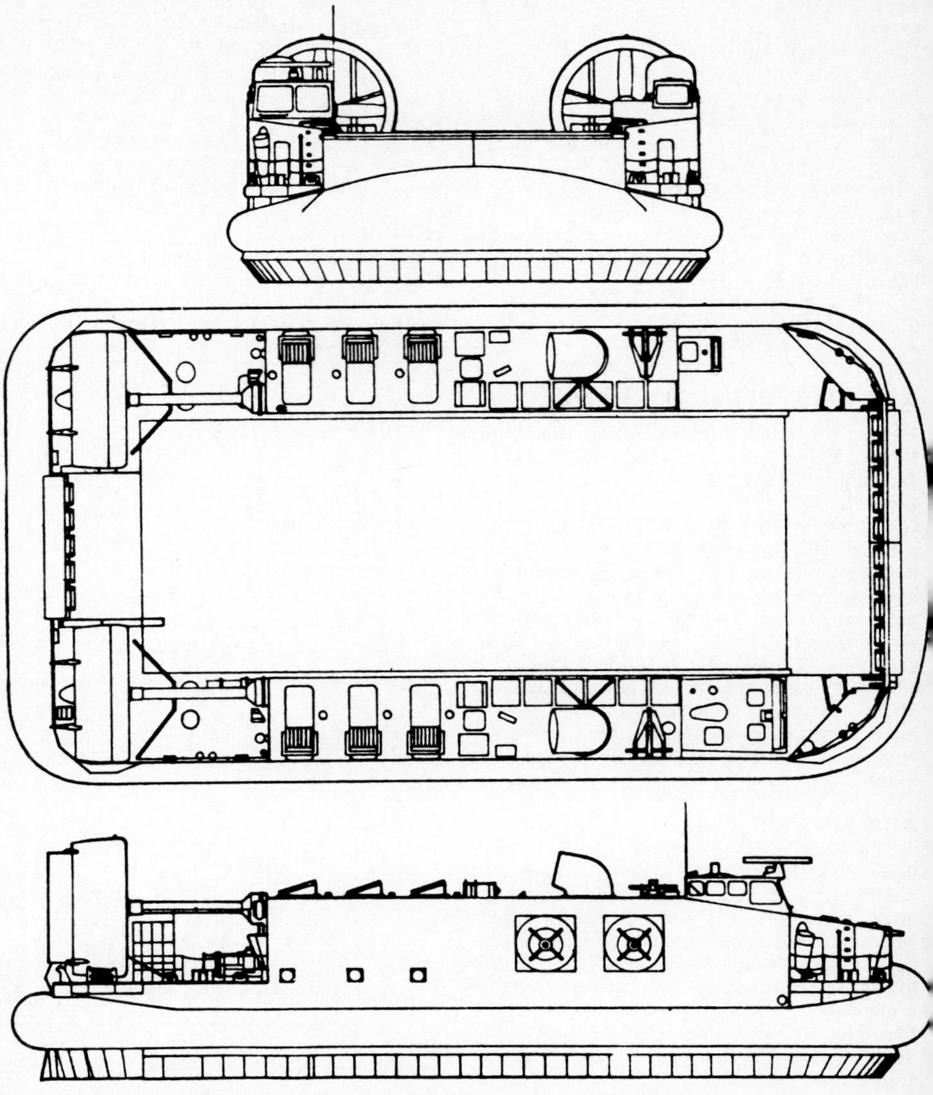

General arrangement of Bell's Amphibious Assault Landing Craft (AALC) JEFF (B). Power is supplied by six 2,800hp Avco Lycoming gas turbines driving four centrifugal impellers for lift and two four-bladed ducted propellers for thrust

SK-5 MODEL 7255

Details of the SK-5 Model 7255 and its predecessor, the Model 7232, will be found in *Jane's Surface Skimmers 1972-73* and earlier editions.

AALC JEFF(B)

In March 1971 US Naval Ship Systems Command awarded Bell's New Orleans Operations a contract for the detail design, construction and testing of an experimental 160-ton, 50-knot air cushion assault landing craft.

Two companies are developing ACV test craft to the 68,038kg (150,000lb) payload, 50-knot specification—Bell and Aerojet-General. The Bell project is designated LC JEFF(B). Both craft will operate from the well-decks of landing ships and also alongside cargo ships.

The Bell contract involves mathematical and scale model investigations, interface and support system design, subsystem and component testing and design and systems analysis.

The 160-ton Amphibious Assault Landing Craft LC JEFF(B) was completed in March 1977. It was transferred on 1 April 1977 to the US Naval Coastal Systems Laboratory, Panama City, Florida, for builder's trials. Overwater trials of JEFF(B) began on 16 December 1977 and by May 1978 it was halfway through its contractor's trials. The craft has been demonstrated at its design gross weight of 147,411kg (325,000lb) and has expanded its operating envelope to more than 40 knots. It has proved to be extremely stable and manoeuvrable. Data produced during those preliminary trials indicate that all the design performance goals will be attained. The craft was delivered to the US Navy's Experimental Trials Unit at Panama City for crew training, tests and operational trials in the autumn of 1978. Further information is to be found in the Addenda.

LC JEFF(B) is designed to operate at a nominal speed of 50 knots in Sea State 2, and accommodate 60 to 75 tons in palletised supplies and/or equipment, up to the size of the 60-ton US Army main battle tank. To ensure adequate world-wide operational capability, the specification calls for operation in temperatures from 0°-100°F and requires that the performance criteria can be met with a 25 knots headwind on a 100°F day.

LIFT AND PROPULSION: Motive power is supplied by six 2,800hp Avco Lycoming gas-turbines, driving four 1·52m (5ft) diameter double-entry centrifugal impellers for lift, and two four-bladed 3·58m (11ft 9in) diameter, Hamilton-Standard variable pitch, ducted propellers, for thrust. Fuel capacity is 29,094 litres (6,400 gallons).

CONTROLS: Deflection of two aerodynamic rudders hinged at the rear of the propeller duct exits, differential propeller pitch, and the deflection of bow thrusters atop the side structures provide steering control. All controls are located in a raised bridge located well forward on the starboard superstructure. The helmsman's platform is raised to provide 360 degree vision for the two helmsmen, who have within easy reach all the necessary controls, navigation equipment and instruments. A third seat is provided at this level for another crew member or wave commander. On a lower level in the bridge is an engineer's station with monitoring instrumentation and a radar operator/navigator station. The crew will normally comprise four operating personnel and two deck supervisors.

HULL: Overall structural dimensions of the craft, 24·38 × 13·1 × 5·79m (80 × 43 × 19ft), have been dictated by the well deck dimensions of the US Navy's LSDs (Landing Ships Dock) and LPDs (Amphibious Transport Dock).

The main hull is formed by a 1·37m (4ft 6in) deep buoyancy raft with port and starboard side structures. The main deck between the side structures forms the cargo deck, which is 20·11m long by 8·02m wide (66ft by 26ft 4in), and provides an unobstructed cargo area of 161·46m² (1,738ft²). A full width ramp is provided at the bow and a narrower ramp, capable of taking the main battle tank, at the stern.

The bottom and deck structures of the hull are separated by longitudinal and transverse bulkheads to form a buoyancy raft with a number of watertight flotation compartments. The craft fuel tanks and bilge system are contained within these compartments.

Plating at the bottom and side of the hull is stiffened by aluminium extrusions, and the main cargo deck is in mechanically fastened hollow truss-type core extrusions. The transverse bulkheads consist of sheet webs of aluminium alloy integrally-stiffened extrusions, with upper and lower bulkhead caps, also of aluminium extrusions.

The basic framing of the side-structures is aluminium back-to-back channels, which coincide with the transverse bulkheads and are spaced apart to straddle the hull bulkheads.

Each sidestructure contains three Avco Lycoming gas-turbines, and their associated air intakes, exhausts, lift fans, transmissions and auxiliary power system.

SKIRT: Peripheral bag and finger type, with a 1·52m (5ft) high cushion compartmented by longitudinal and transverse keels. The upper seal bag attachment hinge line is raised high over the bow ramp area and the vertical diaphragm contains non-return valves similar to those fitted to the SR.N4.

DIMENSIONS
Length overall: 26·43m (86ft 9in)
stowed: 24·38m (80ft)
Beam overall: 14·32m (47ft)
stowed: 13·1m (43ft)
Height: 7·16m (23ft 6in)
Cargo area: 160·71m² (1,738ft²)
Bow ramp width: 8·53m (28ft)
Stern ramp width: 4·41m (14ft 6in)
WEIGHTS
Normal gross: 149,688kg (330,000lb)
Normal payload: 54,431kg (120,000lb)
Overload payload: 68,038kg (150,000lb)
PERFORMANCE
Speed: 50 knots in sea state 2
Range: 200n miles
Max gradient continuous: 13%

SES-100B TEST CRAFT

SES-100B is the official designation for the 100-ton class sidehull surface effect ship (SES) test craft which has been built for the US Navy by Bell Aerospace at New Orleans.

It is part of a long-range programme by the US Navy to develop multi-thousand ton, ocean-going ships with speeds of 80 knots or higher.

This programme stems from research undertaken by the US Office of Naval Research in 1960, the US Navy Bureau of Ships (now the

JEFF(B) AALC hovering for the first time in October 1977 at the US Naval Coastal Systems Laboratory, Panama City, Florida

Overwater trials of JEFF(B) began in December 1977. This stern view shows the port and starboard propeller ducts and the two thrusters atop the sidestructures

Formal acceptance of JEFF(B) by the US Navy took place in the autumn of 1978. Fore and aft loading ramps are provided for the rapid on and off loading of troops, equipment and vehicles, including the 60-ton main battle tank

Naval Ship System Command) and the US Maritime Administration, which in 1961 sponsored the first programme for the development of a 100-ton SES, known as the Columbia.

Construction of the Bell SES began in August 1970. The vessel was launched on 22 July 1971 for hovering trials, and builder's trials, with the craft underway, began on 4 February 1972. A test and evaluation programme encompassing performance trials, stability and seakeeping characteristics, structural load investigations, habitability and operational data, and other pertinent data necessary for the development of high speed surface effect ships, was conducted in the New Orleans area and in the Gulf of Mexico where a variety of sea conditions were experienced.

In January 1974, Bell Aerospace announced that the SES-100B had successfully completed the testing necessary to confirm and expand the technology necessary for the design of a 2,000-ton ocean-going SES.

On 2 April 1977, the SES-100B achieved a new world speed record of 90·3 knots (104mph) on St Andrew Bay near Panama City.

The craft has operated at sustained speeds of more than 50 knots in Sea State 3 in the Gulf of Mexico, and has repeatedly demonstrated performance, stability, and habitability exceeding expectations.

It successfully launched an SM-1 (General Dynamics RIM 66B Standard MR) medium-range guided missile on 8 April 1976, while travelling at a speed of 60 knots (70mph) across the Gulf of Mexico. The solid rocket motor propelled the 16ft 6in missile straight upwards, it then pitched over in a westerly direction toward the target five nautical miles away. The missile's sensing device located the target and guided it to a hit.

Development of SES systems will result in the production of very high speed, multi-thousand ton ships for a variety of missions. Such development would make it possible for the US Navy to have a smaller but more effective fleet which would revolutionise naval warfare.

LIFT AND PROPULSION: Power is supplied to the lift system by three United Aircraft of Canada (UACL) ST6J-70 marine gas turbines. The engine/fan systems provide pressurised air to seals and cushion in both normal modes of operation and in the event of system failure. An important feature of the design has been to ensure the safety of ship and crew since the craft is designed to investigate the boundaries of ship operation at high speed in rough seas. The fans, constructed from marine aluminium, are of centrifugal design for ruggedness and stability of operation.

Power is supplied to the two marine propellers by three Pratt & Whitney FT 12A-6 marine gas turbines.

Auxiliary power for engine starting and emergency use is provided by a Solar T-62T-27 high speed turbine producing 100shp at 8,000rpm.

All engines are housed in engine rooms beneath the weather deck and take in air through appropriately placed demister screens to minimise sea water and spray ingestion.

The fuel system, which also serves as a ballast system, is integral with the sidehulls.

HULL: The SES-100B is a single, all-welded continuous structure, incorporating two catamaran-style sidehulls and is constructed from high-strength, corrosion-resistant marine aluminium alloy sheet and plate. The hull carries an integral deckhouse welded to the after portion of the weather deck. The deckhouse is so positioned to optimise the ride quality and habitability of the ship's complement of personnel while retaining good visibility from the command station.

The sidehulls, which virtually skim the surface of the water, provide basic stability to the craft and also seal the air cushion and prevent leakage along the port and starboard sides of the ship. The sealing of the air cushion is completed at the bow and stern by flexible fabric seals. The bow seal is of pressurised bag type with convoluted

The SES-100B set up a new world record speed of 90·3 knots (104 mph) on 2 April 1977. A US Navy crew operated the craft on its record breaking run which was made across an instrumented test range in St Andrew Bay, Florida. Its speed was recorded by tracking radar operated by US Navy personnel

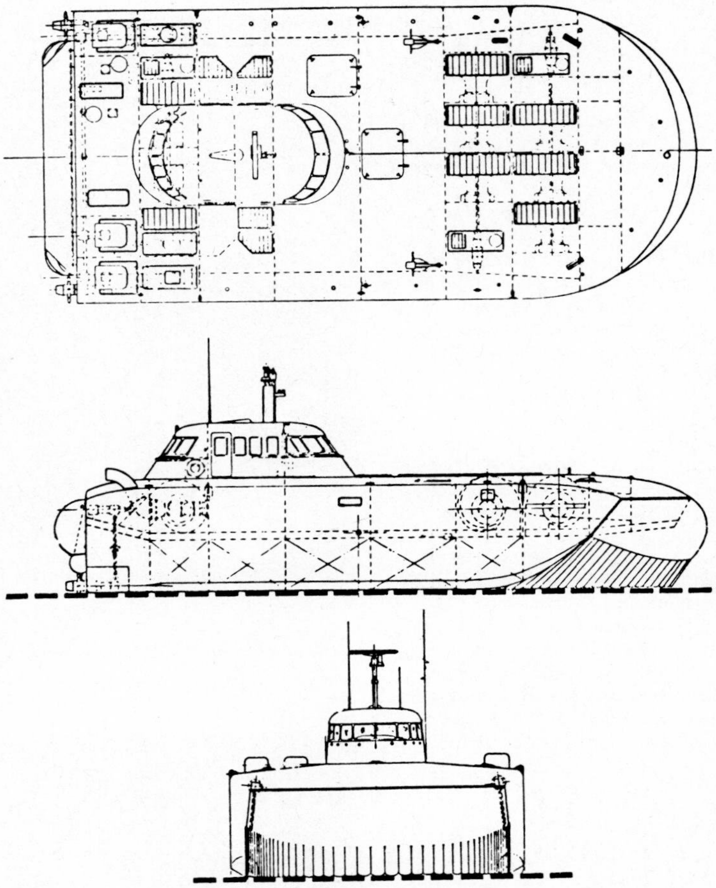

General arrangement of the Bell SES-100B 105-ton test craft

The SES-100B, 105-ton surface effect ship testcraft seen at speed in Sea State 3 in the Gulf of Mexico, off Panama City

fingers. The stern seal is of Bell design and capable of providing the necessary trim to the craft.
ACCOMMODATION: The deckhouse houses all controls necessary for the operation of the craft and accommodation for four test crew and six observers. It is capable of sustaining the crew and observers for greater than 24 hour missions in life support functions. Navigation and communication equipment for all-weather operation is included in the crew subsystem and housed in the deckhouse.
SYSTEMS, EMERGENCY: Safety equipment in the form of fire detection and extinguishing equipment, life rafts, warning lights, etc, meet the requirements of the US Coast Guard Rules of the Road, both International and Inland.

The characteristics of the SES-100B are as follows:

DIMENSIONS
Length overall: 23·68m (77ft 8½in)
Beam: 10·67m (35ft)
Height (top of radar): 8·2m (26ft 11in)
WEIGHTS
Normal gross: 105 tons
Normal payload: 10 tons
POWER PLANTS
Propulsion: 3 Pratt & Whitney FT 12A-6 marine gas turbines
Lift: 3 UACL ST6J-70 marine gas turbines
PERFORMANCE
Speed greater than 80 knots on calm water
PERSONNEL
Crew (test mission): 4
Observers: 6
MATERIALS
Hull and Appendages: Marine aluminium and titanium
Seals: Nitrile PVC Nylon

MODEL 7467 LACV-30

This stretched version of the Voyageur has been designed to meet the US Army's requirements for a high-speed amphibious vehicle for LOTS (Logistic-Over-The-Shore) operations.

The chief modifications are a 3·35m (11ft) lengthening of the deck ahead of the raised control cabin to facilitate the carriage of additional Milvan containers; the siting of a swing crane at the bow, also the provision of a surf fence and a bow loading ramp.

The LACV-30 is intended to replace conventional vessels of the LARC-5 and the LARC-15 types by 1980. It will provide the US Army with a rapid lift capability enabling it to move cargo and equipment over water, beaches, ice, snow and marginal areas. A range of military cargoes can be carried, from containers, wheeled and tracked vehicles, to engineering equipment, pallets, packs and barrels.

Endurance at cruising speed depends on the configuration/role in which the craft is used. For the drive-on cargo and Milvan cargo roles the craft can carry payloads of 30 tons with an endurance of two hours. In the self-unload Milvan cargo role the payload is reduced to 26·5 tons for the same endurance. Other configurations give endurance figures of between 5 hours and 9 hours 6 minutes with varying payloads.

Although intended primarily for use as a lighter in support of LOTS operations, the craft is also suitable for a number of secondary roles such as coastal, harbour and inland water inspection; patrol, search-and-rescue missions and medical evacuation.

Two pre-production craft have been sold to the US Army for evaluation as ship-to-shore lighters.
LIFT AND PROPULSION: Integrated system, powered by two Pratt and Whitney ST6T Twin-Pac gas-turbines mounted aft, one at each side of the raised control cabin. Each engine is rated at 1,800shp maximum and 1,400shp at normal output. The output of each is absorbed by a three-bladed Hamilton Standard 43D50-363 reversible-pitch propeller and a 2·13m (7ft) diameter, twelve-bladed, fixed-pitch light aluminium alloy, centrifugal lift fan.
FUEL: Recommended fuel is standard aviation kerosene-Jet A-1, JP4, JP5 or light diesel fuel oil.

The deckhouse is at the aft end of the weatherdeck and accommodates a four-man crew and up to six observers. The engines—three FT12A-6s for propulsion and three ST6J-70s for lift—are located beneath the weatherdeck. Air is drawn through demister screens to minimise seawater and spray ingestion

An SM-1 medium-range guided missile was successfully launched from the SES-100B while travelling at a speed of 60 knots across the Gulf of Mexico on 8 April 1976. Twenty seconds later the SM-1 hit its target, a surplus vessel positioned 10 miles off the Florida coast, on the test range of the Armament Development and Test Centre, Eglin Air Force Base, Florida

LACV-30-1 with a bow-mounted swing crane which gives the craft a self-discharge capability in areas where materials handling equipment is not available

Main usable fuel capacity is 9,419 litres (2,272 gallons). Fuel ballast/emergency fuel capacity 6,960 litres (1,531 gallons).

SYSTEMS, ELECTRICAL: Starter generators: four gearbox-driven, brushless, 28V dc, 200A each. Batteries: two nickel cadmium, 28A dc, 40Ah each.

DIMENSIONS

Length overall, on cushion: 23·3m (76ft 6in)
Beam overall, on cushion: 11·2m (36ft 8in)
Height overall, on cushion: 8·83m (29ft)
off cushion: 7·86m (25ft 9in)
Skirt height, nominal: 1·21m (4ft)
Height, cargo deck, off cushion: 1·16m (3ft 10in)
Cargo deck: 15·69 × 9·9m (51ft 6in × 32ft 6in)

WEIGHTS

Gross: 52,163kg (115,000lb)

PERFORMANCE (estimated)

Standard day, zero wind, calm water, at gross weight of 52,163kg (115,000lb):
Normal rating: 74km/h (46mph)
Max rating: 90km/h (56mph)
Estimated fuel consumption at cruising speed: 1,159 litres/h (255 gallons/h)

LACV-30-2 during tests conducted by the US Army at Fort Story, Virginia. For the drive-on cargo and Milvan container cargo roles the craft can carry a payload of 30 tons, with an endurance of two hours

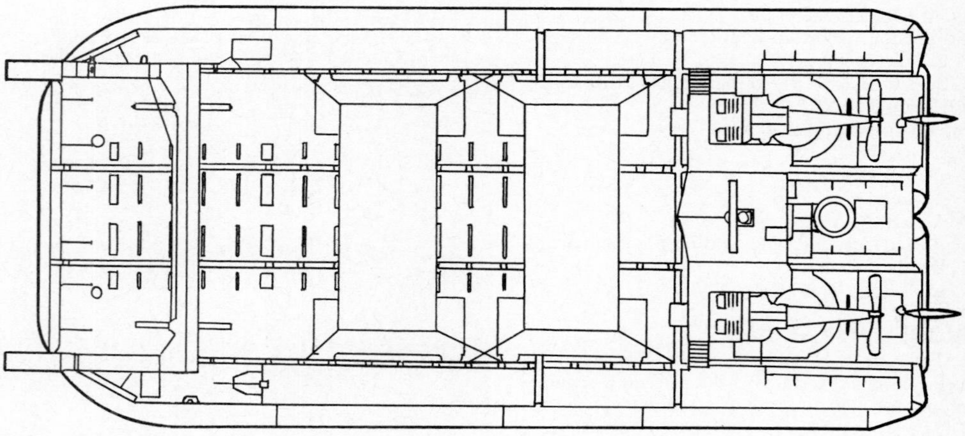

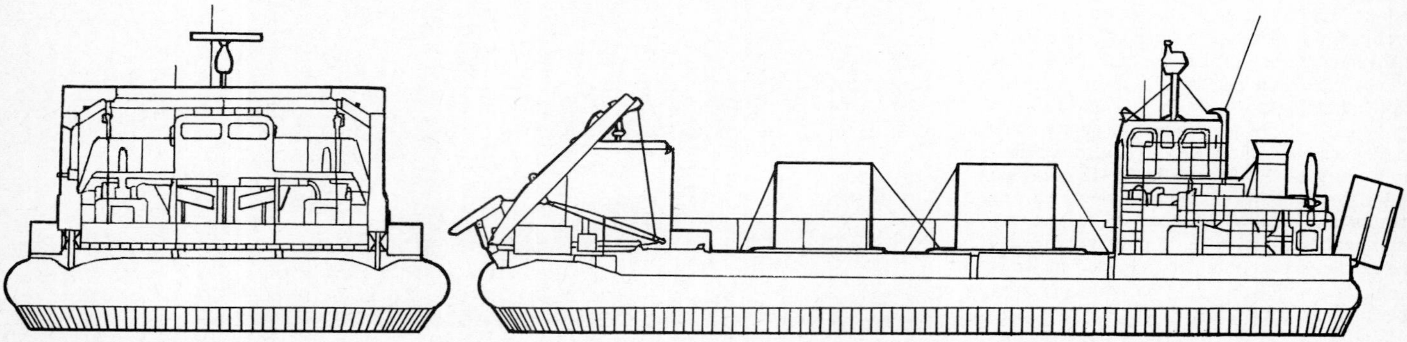

General arrangement of the Bell Model 7467 LACV-30, an amphibious lighter with a 30 ton payload. Two pre-production craft have been sold to the US Army

BELL-HALTER

PO Box 29211, New Orleans, Louisiana 70189, USA
Telephone: (504) 254 2862
Telex: Halmar/58-4200
Officials:
J J Kelly, *Manager*

Bell-Halter is a joint venture established in August 1977 by the Bell Aerospace Textron division of Textron Inc, and Halter Marine Services, Inc. It combines Bell's technical background in surface effect ships with Halter's 20 years experience as boatbuilders. Halter Marine is the world's largest builder of offshore supply vessels, more than 700 of which have been supplied for American and overseas use. Their hulls have been constructed in aluminium, steel and fibreglass. Halter has also built a large number of fast patrol boats for navies in the Middle East, South America and Far East.

Bell-Halter, the new joint-venture company, currently offers a range of sidewall ACVs (SES configuration) capable of speeds up to 60 knots and with overall lengths of up to 60·96m (200ft). These are currently available on normal commercial terms with performance assured and with warranties. Larger vessels, up to 121·92m (400ft) will be available in future. Bell-Halter is at present building a diesel powered 33·52m (110ft) SES which was launched on 31 October 1978.

BELL/HALTER 48 HYDROGRAPHIC SURVEY BOAT

The Bell-Halter 48 operates as a displacement catamaran at low speeds and as an air-cushion-assisted planing catamaran at high speeds. With the lift system shut down, speeds in excess of 24km/h (15mph) are possible, with the sidehulls supporting 100% of the weight through a combination of buoyancy and planing forces. The lift system can be employed at any speed to support part of the weight of the boat. At high speeds, up to 85% of the weight can be supported by the air cushion, with a resulting increase of lift-to-drag ratio from 5 to approximately 11. The maximum speed is thereby increased to 56·32km/h (35mph). Over the complete speed range, from 24 to 56km/h (15 to 35 mph) approximately, total power requirements, and hence fuel consumption, can be reduced by selecting the appropriate lift fan rpm settings.

LIFT AND PROPULSION: The lift system is powered by a single Detroit Diesel 4-53N rated at 105shp at 2,600rpm (85°F and 457m (500ft)). Propulsive thrust is supplied by twin Detroit Diesel Allison 8V92N marine diesels, each driving a propeller via a standard Allison M reduction gear with a ratio of 1·52:1. Fuel is carried in four tanks, each with a capacity of 1,325 litres (350 US gallons).

CONTROLS: Directional control is provided by twin water rudders aft, one on each sidehull, in addition to the differential use of propeller thrust for slow speed manoeuvring.

HULL: The hull primary structure is built throughout in welded marine aluminium alloy 5086. The structure is of catamaran configuration and consists of two sidehulls, separated by decks and the cabin structure. The sidehull shell plating varies between ⅛ and ¼in thick, depending on local pressures, and is stiffened by T-section longitudinals. Sidehull is maintained by frames and bulkheads that are spaced generally by 0·91-1·52m (3-5ft) and support the hull longitudinals.

Three watertight bulkheads are used in each sidehull and also across the centre section between the hulls. Two of these are located at the forward and aft ends of the cabin, and one is

forward of the helmsman's platform. The latter also forms a collision bulkhead. The bulkheads provide transverse bending and torsional continuity to the hull structure. There are also longitudinal watertight bulkheads running the full length of the craft aft of the collision bulkhead.
SKIRT: Flexible skirts are provided at the bow and stern. The bow seal consists of eight fingers, each approximately 3·96m (13ft) long, 0·6m (2ft) wide and 1·95m (6ft 6in) high. All fingers are identical.

The stern seal has a constant cross-section and consists of two inflated lobes of coated-fabric material, with horizontal diaphragms to sustain pressure loads. End caps, which bear partly on the sidehulls, contain the air at the ends of the seal. Five vertical diaphragms are set at intervals across the seal to maintain a flat lower surface in order to minimise water contact and drag. Principal dimensions of the stern seal are: length 2·13m (7ft) and height 1·21m (4ft). Each of the lobes has a radius of approximately 304mm (1ft).
ACCOMMODATION: The deckhouse structure contains the pilothouse, cabin and lift system housing. The pilothouse is located in the forward portion with the pilothouse deck slightly higher than the weather deck elevation. The main cabin deck is recessed below the weather deck between the sidehulls. Similarly, the main cabin profile is lower than the pilothouse to allow visibility directly aft through rear-facing pilothouse windows. Two interior stairways lead from the main cabin deck level; one to the pilothouse level and the other to the aft section of the weather deck. Provision has been made for a total complement of seven crew members and/or observers.
DIMENSIONS
EXTERNAL
Length overall: 14·63m (48ft)
Beam overall: 7·31m (24ft)
Height overall: 4·72m (15ft 6in)
Draft, max static: 1·6m (5ft 3in)
Skirt depth, bow: 1·82m (6ft)
stern: 1·21m (4ft)
Cushion area: 62·92m^2 (677ft^2)
INTERNAL
Length: 7·01m (23ft)
Max width: 3·65m (12ft)
Max height: 2·13m (7ft)
Floor area: 25·64m^2 (276ft^2)
WEIGHTS
Normal empty: 16·7 tons
Normal all-up weight: 18·7 tons
Normal gross: 22·3 tons
Normal payload: 2 tons
Max payload: 5·6 tons
PERFORMANCE
Max speed over calm water, max continuous power: 33 knots (29°C (85°F))
Cruising speed, calm water: 23 knots
Water speed in 1·22m (4ft) waves and 15 knot headwind: 24 knots
Still air range and endurance at cruising speed: 1,090n miles and 50 hours
Max speed, over calm water, hullborne at 18·7 long tons displacement: 17 knots
PRICE AND TERMS: On request

BELL-HALTER 85 (HIGH-SPEED PASSENGER AND CREW BOAT

This 85ft long diesel-powered, high-speed ferry is available in two configurations, 25-100 seat crew boat or 188 seat passenger ferry. The hull and machinery are identical in each case, the main difference being an increase in the length of the passenger cabin of the latter.
LIFT AND PROPULSION: Two Detroit Diesel Allison 8V92N diesels (or similar) each rated at 350hp supply power for the lift fans and electrical generators and two Detroit Diesel Allison 16V92TA diesels, rated at 860hp each, are installed for propulsion. Each lift engine drives a 36·5in diameter lift fan to provide airflow to the cushion and seals. Two fan air inlets are located in the aft section of the weatherdeck. Air is blown through two longitudinal ducts leading to the bow and stern seals. Intermediate openings are provided for cushion pressurisation. Cushion pressure is 341·77kg/m^2 (70lb/ft^2)

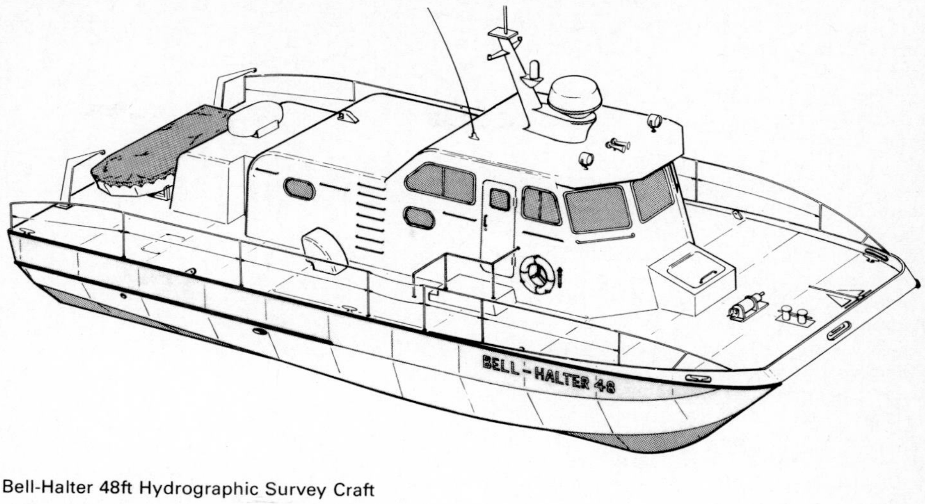

Bell-Halter 48ft Hydrographic Survey Craft

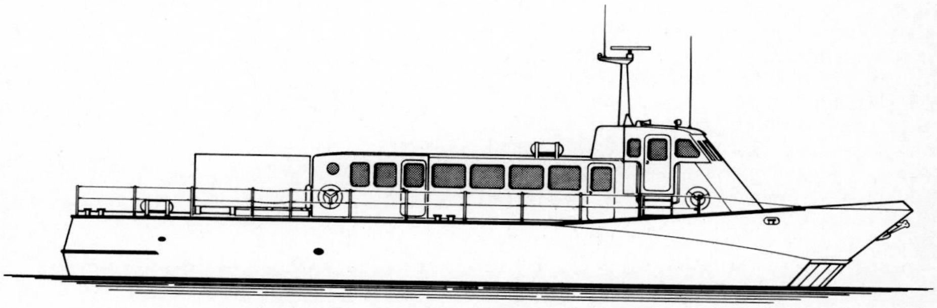
Bell-Halter 85ft high-speed passenger and crew boat.

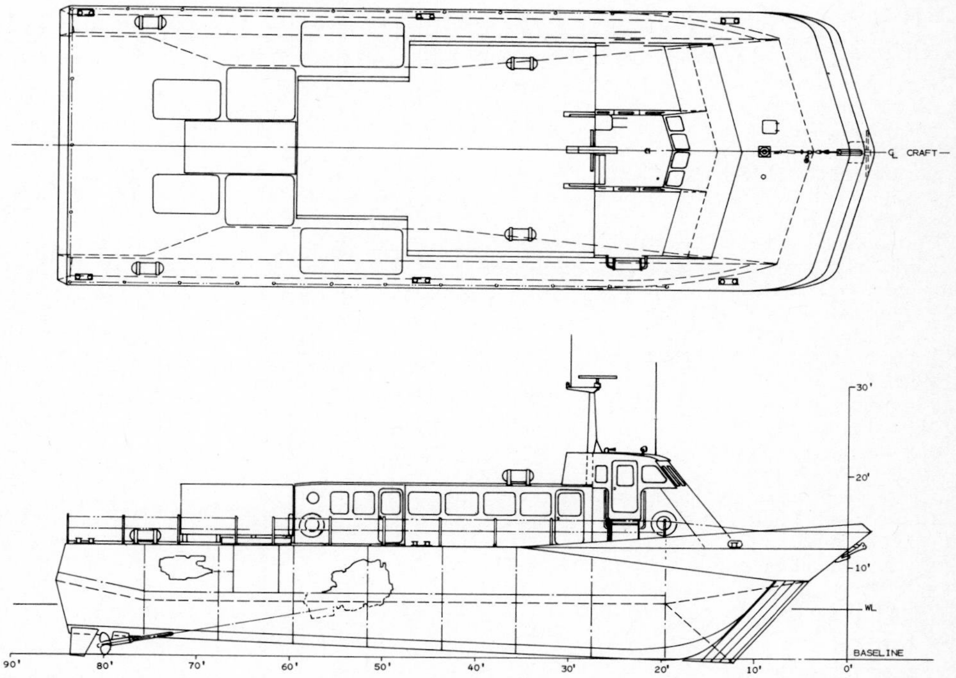

General arrangement, Bell-Halter 85ft high-speed passenger and crew boat

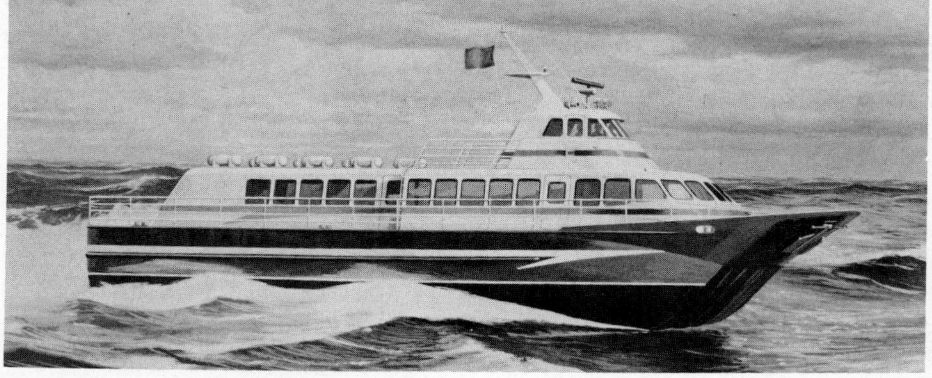
Bell-Halter 85ft, 188 seat passenger ferry

The two propulsion engines drive two 508mm (1ft 8in) diameter Michigan Wheel fixed-pitch, subcavitating propellers. Fuel is carried in four integral tanks built into the sidehulls. Total fuel capacity is 1,893 litres (500 US gallons). The lubricating system is an integral unit of the lift and propulsion engines and transmission systems. Fuel recommended is standard marine diesel. Refuelling points are located on the main deck on the port and starboard side of the deckhouse.

CONTROLS: Craft direction is controlled by twin rudders aft, one on each sidehull. Differential propeller thrust is employed for slow speed manoeuvring. The steering system is two-station hydraulic, operating with a rotary control valve which acts in conjunction with the steering wheel. Primary control is the hydraulic control system with a 762mm (30in) aluminium steering wheel located on the centre-line in the pilothouse. A second steering station is located on the upper deck, aft of the pilothouse. Mathers pneumatic engine controls are installed in the pilothouse and the upper deck stations.

HULL: The hull primary structure is built in welded marine aluminium alloy 5086.

SKIRT: The bow seal consists of twelve fingers, each of which is approximately 7·31m (24ft) long, 609mm (2ft) wide and 3·65m (12ft) high. All fingers are identical. The stern seal, which has a constant cross section consists of two inflated lobes of coated-fabric material, with horizontal diaphragms to sustain pressure loads. End caps, which bear partly on the side-hulls, contain the air at the ends of the seal. Five vertical diaphragms are set at intervals across the seal to maintain a reasonably flat lower surface in order to minimise water contact and drag. Principal dimensions are a fore and aft length of 2·74m (9ft) and a height of 1·22m (4ft). Each of the lobes has a radius of approximately 304mm (1ft).

ACCOMMODATION: Operating crew comprises a captain, first officer and four seamen. The work-boat version seats 25 to 100 passengers and the passenger ferry seats 188.

DIMENSIONS

EXTERNAL

Length overall: 25·99m (85ft)
Beam overall: 9·44m (31ft)
Height overall: 6·7m (22ft)
Cushion area: 155·6m^2 (1,675ft^2)
Skirt depth, bow: 1·56m (5ft)
stern: 1·21m (4ft)
Depth, moulded: 3·65m (12ft)
Draft, operational: 1·21m (4ft)
Draft, off cushion: 1·82m (6ft)

WEIGHTS

Normal empty: 47 tons
Normal gross: 60 tons
Normal payload: 13 tons

PERFORMANCE

Cruise speed, calm water: 33knots (29°C (85°F))
Cruise speed, 1·37m (4ft 6in) waves: 30 knots, (29°C (85°F))
Range and endurance in 1·22m (4ft) waves, 15 knot headwind: 200n miles and 7 hours

PRICE AND TERMS: Upon request

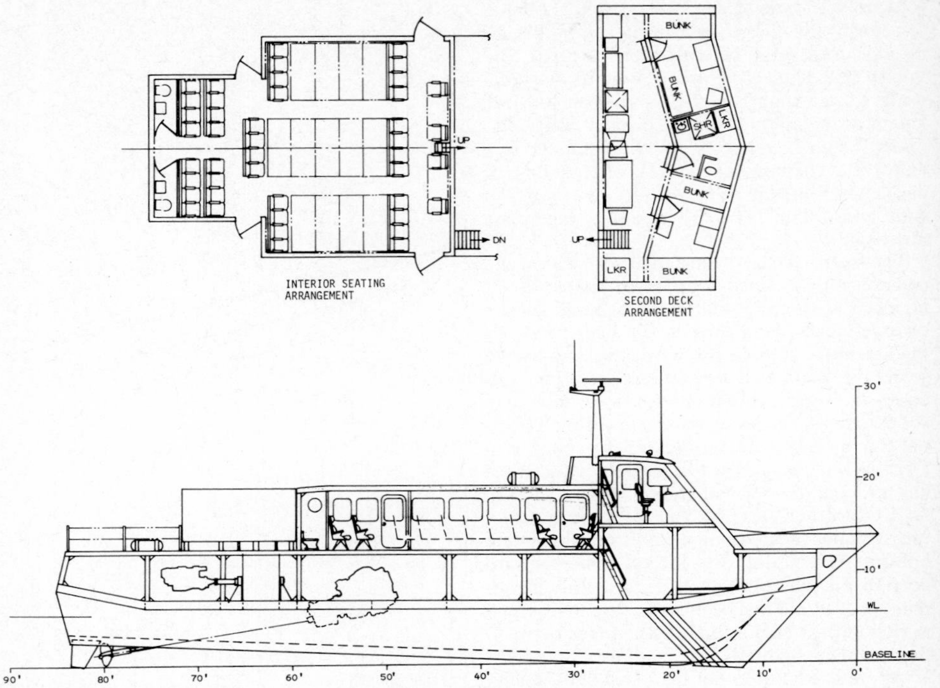

Bell-Halter 85ft passenger and crew boat. Inboard profile and deck plan.

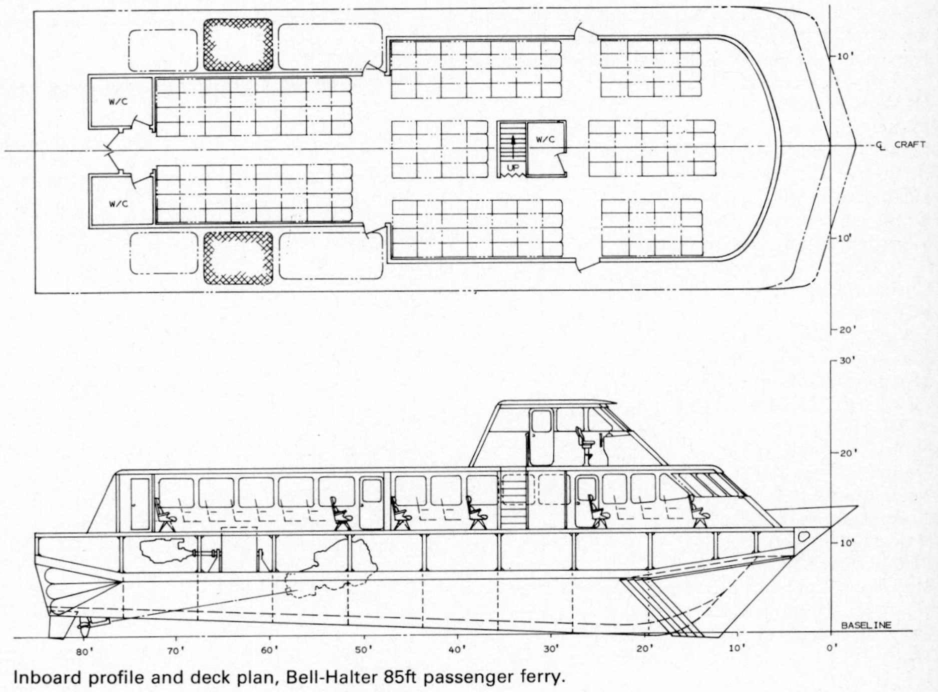

Inboard profile and deck plan, Bell-Halter 85ft passenger ferry.

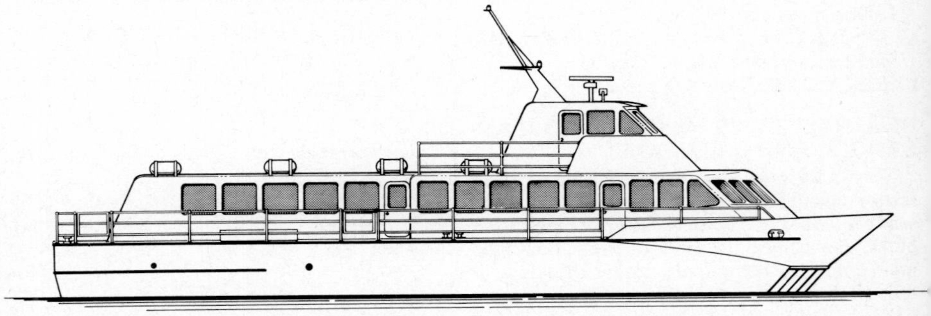

Outboard profile, Bell-Halter 85ft 188 seat passenger ferry

BELL-HALTER 110 DEMONSTRATION SES

Construction of this 110ft demonstration craft began in January 1978. The basic hull and machinery layout permits modification of the deckhouse and arrangement of the deck space to suit a number of alternative applications, from crew boat and 275-seat passenger ferry to fast patrol boat.

LIFT AND PROPULSION: Cushion lift is provided by two 445hp Detroit Diesel Allison 8V92TI diesels each driving identical high-pressure industrial fans constructed in aluminium. Fan air inlets are located in a housing aft of the deckhouse. Cushion air is discharged into two longitudinal ducts between the second deck and well deck. Half is released into the cushion for pressurisation, the remainder is programmed between the bow and stern seals.

Motive power for the propulsion system is supplied by two Detroit Diesel Allison 16V194TI diesels, each rated at 1,335hp at 1,900rpm for the crew boat version. Each engine drives a 0·83m (32in) diameter Gawn-Burrill propeller via a Raentjes marine reduction gearbox. One right-hand and one left-hand rotating propeller are used. Four integral fuel tanks within the sidehulls provide a total capacity of 11,735 litres (3,100 US gallons). Refuelling is accomplished through filters in the main deck and on the port and starboard sides. Oil is integral with the engines and gearboxes.

CONTROLS: Craft direction is controlled by twin rudders, one aft of each sidehull. Differential propeller thrust is employed for slow-speed manoeuvring. The steering system is activated hydraulically from the helm unit in the pilothouse.

HULL: The hull primary structure is built in welded marine aluminium alloy 5086. The structure is of catamaran configuration and consists of two sidehulls that are separated by decks and transverse bulkheads. The sidehull shell plating varies between ¼ and ½in depending on local pressures, and is stiffened by T-section longitudinals. The spacing of the longitudinals is 178mm (7in) on the bottom plating and 304mm (12in) on the side plating. Sidehull shape is maintained by bulkheads spaced generally at 2·44m (8ft) and providing support for the hull longitudinals. Bulkheads have ⅛in webs with T-section and flat bar stiffening and flat bar caps sized appropriately for each bulkhead.

Four of the bulkheads in each sidehull and also across the centre section between the hulls are watertight. Two are located at the forward and aft ends of the cabin, and one is forward of the deckhouse. The latter also forms a collision bulkhead. The bulkheads provide the transverse bending and torsional continuity to the hull structure.

The cabin superstructure consists of T-section frames fabricated from flat bars and spaced the same as the frames on the hull. T-stiffened plate is welded to the framing.

SKIRT: The bow seal consists of eight fingers, each of which is attached to the underside of the centre hull. All fingers are identical. The stern seal, which has a constant cross section, consists of three inflated lobes of coated-fabric material. Horizontal diaphragms sustain pressure loads acting on the lobes. End caps, which bear partly on the sidehulls, contain the air at the ends of the seal.

ACCOMMODATION: The deckhouse structure contains a pilothouse on the 01 level and passenger cabin on the main deck. The pilothouse contains the controls, navigation and communications systems. The main cabin arrangement provides lounge-type seating and has a wet snack bar for passengers. Toilet facilities are located aft.

The second deck contains staterooms for the crew, lounge seating for passengers, a galley, messroom and toilet facilities.

SYSTEMS, ELECTRICAL: AC and dc electrical systems provide electrical power. The prime system is a Detroit Diesel Allison diesel/generator set. The prime mover is rated at 86hp at 1800rpm. The electrical output is 60Hz at 1800rpm. The voltage is 208/240 three-phase with a 55kW rating.

DIMENSIONS

EXTERNAL

Length overall: 33·52m (110ft)
Beam overall: 11·88m (39ft)
Height, on cushion: 8·53m (28ft)
off cushion: 6·87m (22ft 7in)
Draft, on cushion: 1·37m (4ft 6in)
off cushion: 2·36m (7ft 9in)
Skirt depth, bow: 2·28m (7ft 6in)
stern: 1·52m (5ft)

INTERNAL

Control cabin
Length: 4·57m (15ft)
Max width: 3·35m (11ft)
Max height: 2·13m (7ft)
Passenger cabin
Length: 8·53m (28ft)
Max width: 9·14m (30ft)
Max height: 2·13m (7ft)
Floor area: 78·04m² (840ft²)

WEIGHTS

Normal empty: 80 tons
Normal all-up weight: 107 tons
Max: 138 tons
Normal payload: 18 tons
Max payload: 49 tons

PERFORMANCE

	Sea State 0	Sea State 3
Cruising speed,		
on cushion:	40 knots	33 knots
off cushion:	19 knots	15 knots

Range: 500n miles in sea state 3
PRICES AND TERMS: On request

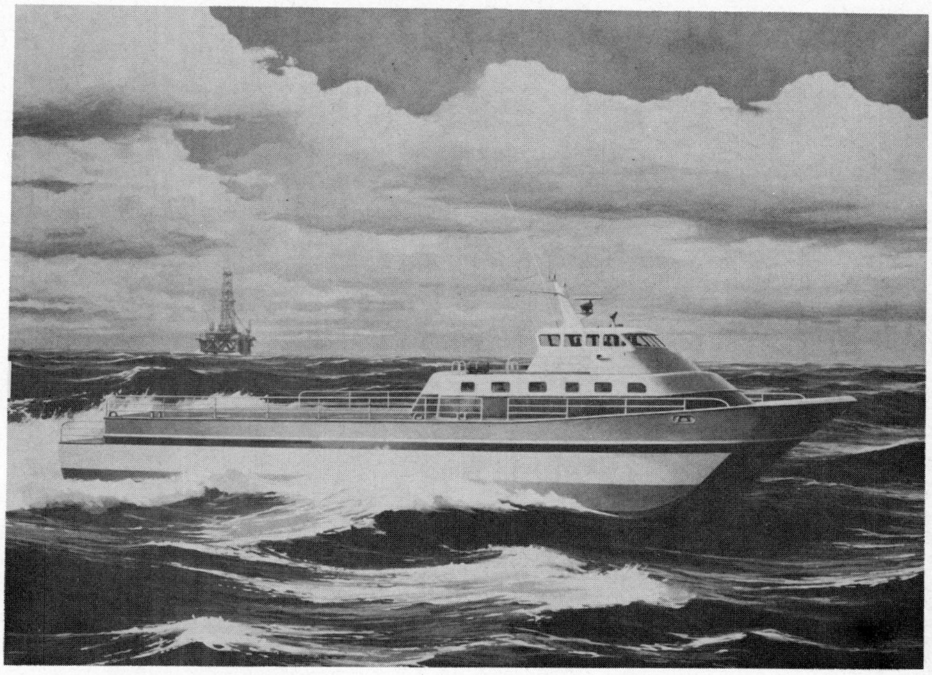

Bell-Halter 110ft demonstration SES

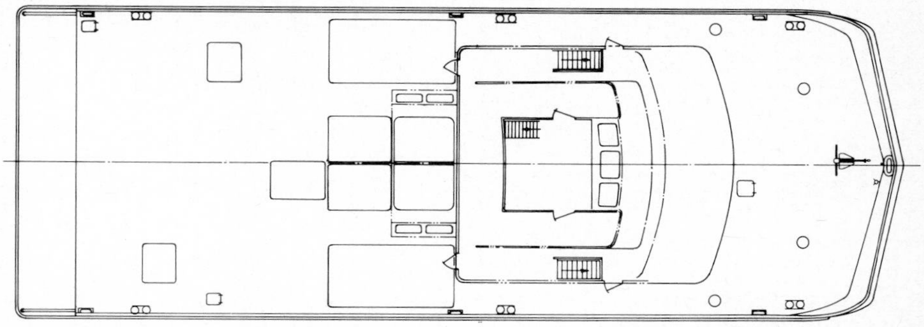

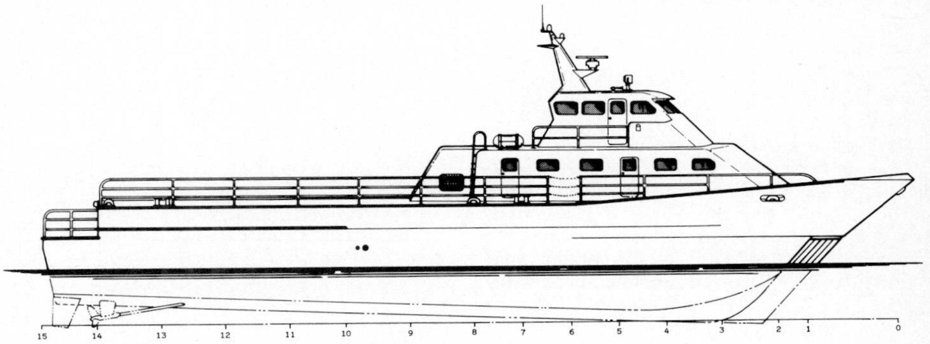

Outboard profile, Bell-Halter 110ft demonstration SES

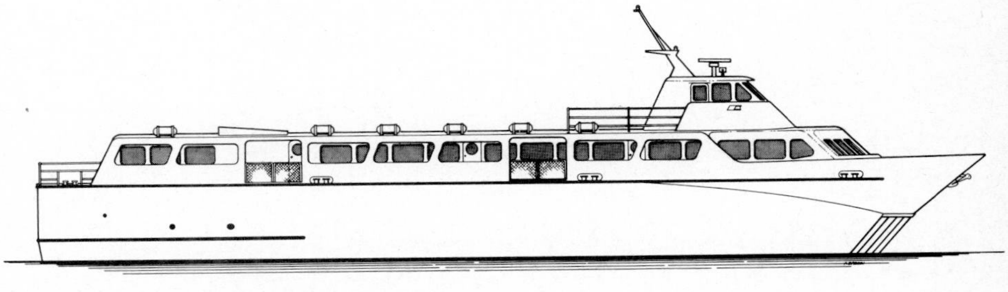

Outboard profile, Bell-Halter 133ft passenger ferry

BELL-HALTER 133 PASSENGER FERRY

A proposed "stretched" version of the 110ft demonstration craft, the Bell-Halter 133 is designed to carry 629 passengers or a payload of 45 tons. The propulsion engines are four Detroit Diesel Allison 16V149TI marine diesels rated at 1,335hp each, and driving two fixed-pitch, fully submerged propellers. The cruising speed is estimated at 40 knots in sea state 0 and 32 knots in sea state 3.

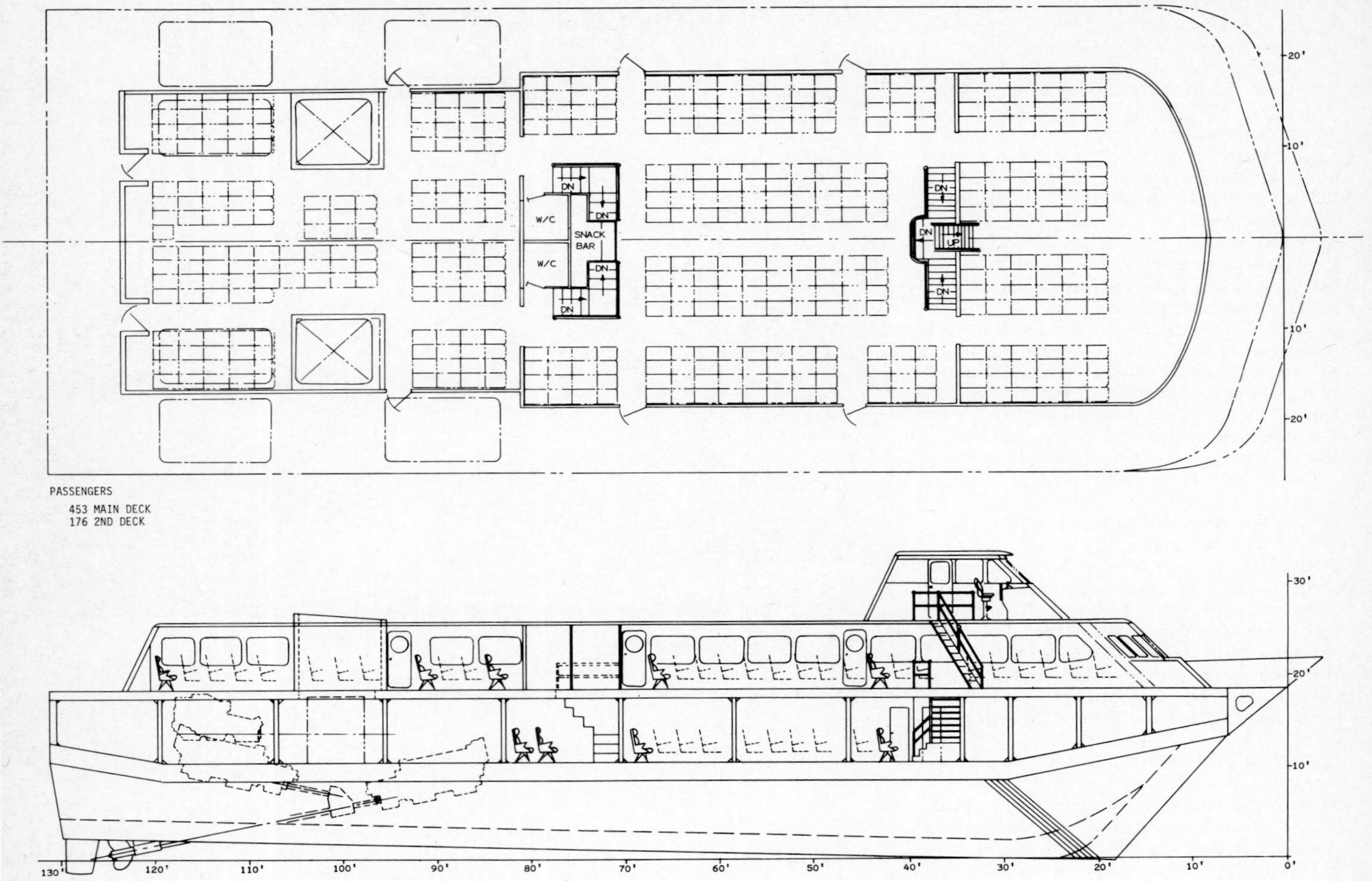

Inboard profile and deck plan, Bell-Halter 133ft passenger ferry

BELL-HALTER APB-47 ADVANCED PATROL BOAT

This 153ft (47m) patrol boat accommodates a wide variety of combat suites. Configurations have been prepared with gun, missile, and electronic systems to suit a number of alternative mission roles.

The propulsion system is a CODOG arrangement employing two Detroit Diesel Allison Model 570 gas-turbines, each rated at 6,400hp for high speed, and two MTU 16V532TC92 diesels for long endurance cruising conditions. The maximum speed is over 60 knots in calm water and over 30 knots in sea state 5. The estimated range is 2,780km (1,500n miles). Endurance capability is over 100 hours.

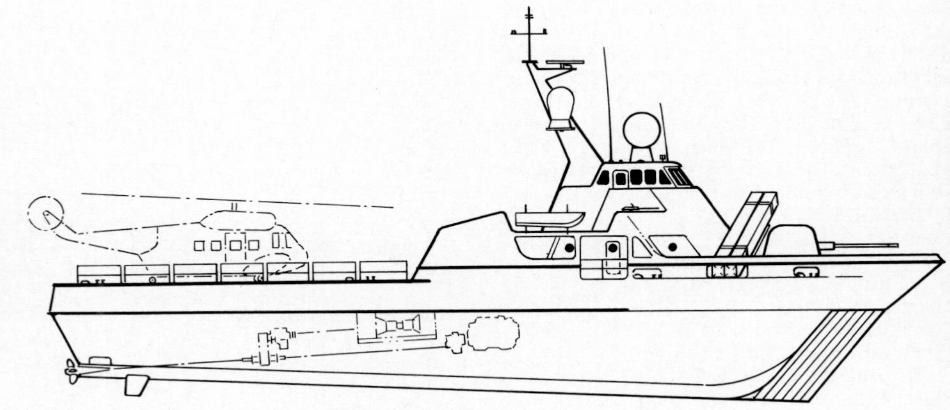

Outboard profile, Bell-Halter advanced patrol boat

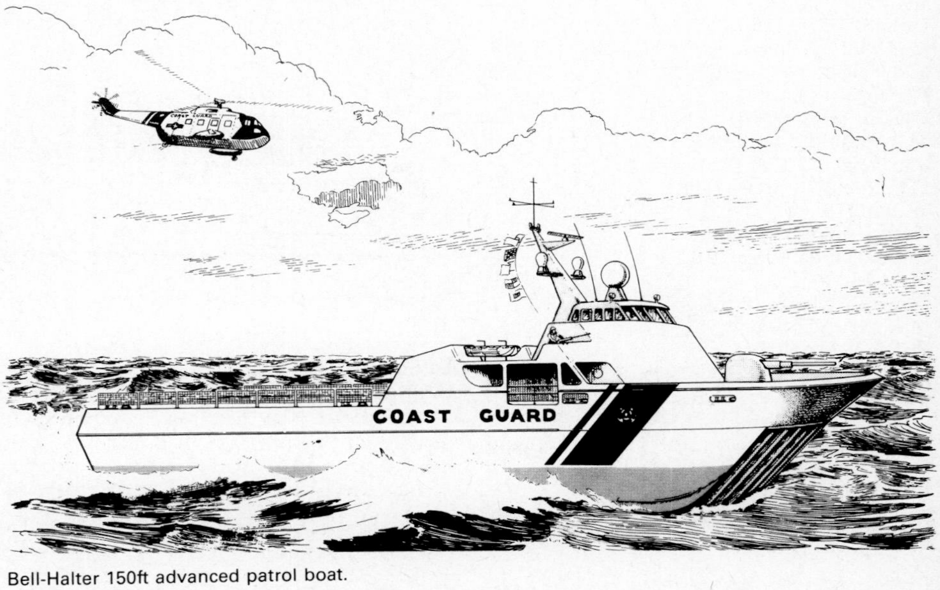

Bell-Halter 150ft advanced patrol boat.

BERTELSEN, INC

Head Office: 10526, West Cermak Road, Westchester, Illinois 60153, USA
Telephone: (312) 562 6170
Works: 113 Commercial Street, Neponset, Illinois 61345, USA
Officials:
William R Bertelsen, *Chairman of the Board, Vice-President and Director of Research*
William C Stein, *President and Treasurer*
Charles A Brady, *Secretary*

Dr William R Bertelsen, a general practitioner and talented engineer, was one of the first to build and drive an air cushion vehicle.

His interest was largely inspired by the difficulties he faced when trying to visit patients by car over icy roads. Having discovered that a helicopter would be too expensive to be a practical solution, he set to work to develop a vehicle that could be lifted free of the ground by air pumped beneath its base. Dr Bertelsen designed his first Aeromobile air cushion vehicle in 1950, and has since built and tested fourteen full-scale vehicles, ranging from simple plenum craft to ram-wings. One, the 18ft long Aeromobile 200-2, was a star exhibit at the US Government's Trade Fairs in Tokyo, Turin, Zagreb and New Delhi in 1961. First design to be marketed by the company is the Aeromobile 13, a four passenger amphibious communications and light utility ACV. The prototype was built in 1968 and trials are complete. A description of this model will be found in *Jane's Surface Skimmers 1972-73* and earlier editions. An Aeromobile system of rapid transit, based on the Aeromobile 13, is described in the section devoted to Tracked Skimmers in this edition.

Aeromobile 14 research platform employed by Bertelsen Manufacturing Co for the development of designs using single gimbal-mounted lift fan/propulsion units.

AEROMOBILE 14

Aeromobile 14 is a lightweight amphibious two or three-seater employing a single gimbal mounted lift fan/propulsion unit of similar design and construction to that introduced by Bertelsen on the Aeromobile 13.

The prototype was completed early in 1969 and trials ended in 1970.

LIFT PROPULSION AND CONTROLS: A single duct-mounted 55hp (740cc) JLO twin-cylinder engine driving a 914mm (36in) diameter eight-bladed axial-flow fan supplies lift, propulsion and control. The duct is spherical and gimbal-mounted at its centre so that it can be tilted and rotated as required in any direction. The discharge end of the duct faces a fitted aperture in the deck, from which air is fed into the cushion. When the fan shaft is vertical (no tilt), all the discharged air is fed into the cushion. By tilting the gimbal, the operator allows air from the fan to escape across the deck to provide thrust for propulsion and control.

Apart from the propulsion slipstream, there is no loss of lift air since the spherical duct fits closely into the deck aperture, and rotation of the sphere does not increase the air gap. Cushion pressure is 68·35 kg/m^2 (14lb/ft^2).

A simple mechanical linkage connected to handlebars enables the operator to tilt the fan duct fore-aft, right and left and make integrated movements. The only other controls are a throttle and a choke. Fuel is carried in a single 12 US gallon tank located in the deck structure at the centre of gravity, with a fuelling point in the centre deck. Recommended fuel is regular automotive gasoline mixed with two-cycle oil.

HULL: Moulded fibreglass with foam filling. Design load 500kg (1,100lb) gross weight.

SKIRT: Urethane nylon with conical exterior configuration. Depth 304mm (1ft).

ACCOMMODATION: Tandem seating for three, with operator forward with control handlebars.

SYSTEMS, ELECTRICAL: 12V alternator on engine for starting.

NAVIGATION: Magnetic compass.

DIMENSIONS
Length overall, power off: 3·96m (13ft)
skirt inflated: 3·96m (13ft)
Beam overall, power off: 2·13m (7ft)
skirt inflated: 2·13m (7ft)

Aeromobile 15, a 60-knot four-seater powered by a modified 125hp Mercury outboard. The vehicle is at present being employed as a test-bed for the gimbal-mounted lift/propulsion system. The photographs show the gimbal duct in neutral and in high forward tilt

Height overall on landing pads, power off: 0·914m (3ft)
skirt inflated: 1·21m (4ft)
Draft afloat: 101mm (4in)
hovering: 76mm (3in)
Cushion area: 5·57m^2 (60ft^2)
Skirt depth: 304mm (12in)
WEIGHTS
Normal empty: 317kg (700lb)
Normal all-up weight: 499kg (1,100lb)
Normal payload: 181kg (400lb)
Max payload: 226kg (500lb)
PERFORMANCE
Max speed over calm water: 80·46km/h (50mph)
Cruising speed, calm water: 64·37km/h (40mph)
Turning circle diameter at 30 knots: 30·4m (100ft)
Max wave capability: 0·914m (3ft)
Max survival sea state: 1·52m (5ft) waves
Still air range and endurance at cruising speed: 2½ hours
Max gradient, static conditions: 10%
Vertical obstacle clearance: 304mm (1ft)
PRICE: On request.

AEROMOBILE 15

Employing the same lift, propulsion and control system as the Aeromobile 14, the Aeromobile 15 is a light amphibious four-seater powered by a single 125hp Mercury outboard engine and capable of a speed of 60 knots over calm water.

The prototype is complete and development is continuing.

LIFT AND PROPULSION: A single duct-mounted 125hp Mercury outboard engine driving a 914mm (3ft) diameter, 16-bladed adjustable-pitch aluminium alloy fan, supplies lift, propulsion and control. The duct is spherical and gimbal-mounted at its centre so that it can be tilted and rotated in any direction. When the fan shaft is vertical, the total airflow is discharged into the cushion. By tilting the gimbal the operator allows air from the fan to escape across the stern to provide thrust for propulsion and control. At the maximum tilt angle of 90 degrees for maximum thrust only 30% of the fan air is delivered to the cushion.

Propulsion and/or control forces, including braking thrust, can be applied throughout 360 degrees from the stern by tilting the duct in the required direction.

The fan duct is controlled from the driver's position by servo system. The driver has a wheel on a control column. Turning the wheel tilts the duct sideways to produce yaw force, and fore-and-aft movement of the column tilts the duct fore-and-aft to produce forward propulsion or braking. Fuel is carried in one 18-gallon tank located on the cabin floor beneath the rear seat at the centre of gravity. The fuelling point is located on the left deck outside the cabin. Fuel is automotive gasoline with two-cycle oil.

HULL: Moulded fibreglass.

SKIRT: Urethane nylon fabric, 457mm (1ft 6in) deep.

ACCOMMODATION: Entry to the cabin is through a sliding canopy which moves from the windshield rearwards. Two bench type seats are fitted, one forward for the driver and one passenger, and one aft for two passengers. The cabin may be heated or air-conditioned if required. In emergencies the sliding canopy, windows and windshield may be kicked out.

SYSTEMS, ELECTRICAL: 12V alternator and 12V storage battery.

COMMUNICATIONS AND NAVIGATION: A magnetic compass is standard. Radio, radar and other navigation aids optional.

DIMENSIONS

EXTERNAL

Length overall, power off: 5·48m (18ft)
skirt inflated: 5·68m (18ft 8in)
Beam overall, power off: 2·43m (8ft)
skirt inflated: 2·99m (9ft 10in)
Height overall, on pads, power off: 1·32m (4ft 4in)
skirt inflated: 1·75m (5ft 9in)
Draft afloat: 139mm (5½in)
hovering: 101mm (4in)
Cushion area: 8·36m² (90ft²)
Skirt depth: 457mm (1ft 6in)

INTERNAL

Cabin
Length: 3·2m (10ft 6in)
Max width: 1·27m (4ft 2in)
Max height: 1·21m (4ft)
Floor area: 3·71m² (40ft²)
The sliding canopy opens 0·914m (3ft) rearwards from windshield.

WEIGHTS

Normal empty: 589·64kg (1,300lb)
Normal all-up weight: 952·5kg (2,100lb)
Normal payload: 317·5kg (700lb)
Max payload: 453·57kg (1,000lb)

PERFORMANCE (at normal operating weight, estimated)

Max speed over calm water, max power: 60 knots
Cruising speed, calm water: 50 knots
Turning circle at 30 knots: 152·4m (500ft)
Max wave capability: 914mm (3ft)
Max survival sea state: 1·52m (5ft) waves
Still air range and endurance at cruising speed: 3 hours
Max gradient, static conditions: 10%
Vertical obstacle clearance: 381mm (1ft 3in)

AEROMOBILE 16

Bertelsen Aeromobile 16 undergoing hovering tests. The 7·82m long craft is the company's biggest to date. Payload capacity is 680kg (1,500lb)

Interest in this new 7·82m (25ft 8in) long utility vehicle, the biggest to be constructed by Bertelsen so far, is being shown by potential customers throughout the United States and Canada. It employs a lift, propulsion and control system similar to that of the earlier Aeromobile 15. At the time of going to press the craft was being retrofitted with 1·01m (40in) diameter spun aluminium ducted fans powered by two 125hp Mercury outboard engines for increased thrust and efficiency. The ice-breaking capabilities of the A-16 were due to be demonstrated during the winter of 1978-79. The craft can operate on cushion with one engine only, the other being employed for full propulsion and steering. It is one of the few air cushion vehicles capable of sidehill operation.

LIFT AND PROPULSION: Power is supplied by two duct-mounted, 125hp, two-cycle Mercury outboard engines, each driving a 1·01m (40in) diameter axial fan fabricated in spun aluminium. Each duct is spherical and gimbal-mounted at its centre so that it can be tilted and rotated in any direction. When the fan shaft is vertical the total airflow is discharged into the cushion. By tilting the gimbal the operator allows air from the fan to escape across the stern to provide propulsive thrust.

The thrust force is instantly available throughout 360 degrees and, metered finely by degree of tilt, provides propulsion, braking or yaw torque. The maximum available force is equal to 100% of the propulsion force.

Fuel is carried in two 90 litre (24 US gallon) tanks, one behind the forward engine and one forward of the aft engine. Type of fuel recommended is regular automobile petrol. Fuelling points are located on deck above tanks.

HULL: Basic structure built in mild steel tubing. Designed to carry 680kg (1,500lb) payload. Total buoyancy 5,563kg (12,266lb).

ACCOMMODATION: Enclosed cabin with driver's seat forward and midship and rear bench seats behind, each seating three-four passengers. Access is via two entry doors, one each side. Seats are removable should the craft be required to undertake light utility roles. The cabin may be heated or air conditioned if required.

SYSTEMS, ELECTRICAL: Two 12V alternators and two 12V storage batteries.

DIMENSIONS

EXTERNAL

Length overall, power off: 7·44m (24ft 5in)
skirt inflated: 7·82m (25ft 8in)
Beam overall, power off: 4·31m (14ft 2in)
skirt inflated: 5·48m (18ft)
Structure width, power off, folded: 2·28m (7ft 6in)
Height overall, on landing pads: 1·72m (5ft 8in)
skirt inflated: 2·13m (7ft)
Cushion area: 24·15m² (260ft²)
Skirt depth: 406mm (1ft 4in)

INTERNAL

Cargo Bay
Length: 3·35m (11ft)
Max width: 1·82m (6ft)
Max depth: 0·68m (2ft 3in)
Deck area total: 27·78m² (299ft²)

WEIGHTS

Normal empty: 1,587kg (3,500lb)
Normal all-up weight: 2,267·96kg (5,000lb)
Normal payload: 680kg (1,500lb)

PERFORMANCE

Max speed, calm water, max power: 96·56km/h (60mph)
Cruising speed, calm water: 80·46km/h (50mph)
Turning circle diameter at 30 knots: 152·4m (500ft) estimated
Max wave capability: 1·21m (4ft)
Max survival sea state: 1·82m (6ft) waves
Still air endurance at cruising speed: 8 hours
Max gradient, static conditions: 10 degrees
Vertical obstacle clearance: 406mm (1ft 4in)

DOBSON PRODUCTS CO

2241 South Ritchey, Santa Ana, California 92705, USA
Telephone: (714) 557 2987
Officials:
Franklin A Dobson, *Director*

Dobson Products Co was formed by Franklin A Dobson in 1963 to develop and market small ACVs either in complete, factory built form, or as kits for private use. His first model, the Dobson Air Dart, won the first ACV race in Canberra in 1964. The company's Model F two-seater, has been described and illustrated in *Jane's Surface Skimmers 1973-74* and earlier editions.

The first Dobson craft designed for quantity production is the Model H, the latest test development of which is described here.

DOBSON AIR CAR, MODEL H

This is a simplified and slightly larger machine than the original Model H. It has more efficient lift and thrust systems together with simplified controls and a slightly lower structural weight. Originally this model had a fan and propeller mounted on the same shaft, but in its latest configuration the engine drives the fan through a separate shaft and gearbox. This arrangement allows a much lower cg as well as improved streamlining.

LIFT AND PROPULSION: A single engine is used for both lift and propulsion. The engine powers a four-bladed fan forward and a six-bladed, variable-pitch ducted fan aft.

CONTROLS: Lateral motion of a control stick operates twin rudders, while fore-and-aft motion controls the propeller pitch, forward for thrust, aft for braking. The control stick also incorporates a motorcycle type twist-grip throttle.

HULL AND SKIRT: Hinged floats are used for buoyancy and these also support a flexible skirt which gives about a 203mm (8in) obstacle clearance. With the floats hinged upwards or removed, the overall width is less than 1·21m (4ft).

DIMENSIONS
Length: 3·35m (11ft)
Width: 2·28m (7ft 6in)
Height: 1·29m (4ft 3in)
Folded width: 1·14m (3ft 8in)
Obstacle clearance: 203mm (8in)
Cushion area: 5·11m² (55ft²)

WEIGHTS
Empty: 104·32kg (230lb)
Tools and miscellaneous: 4·52kg (10lb)
Fuel (6¾ US gallons): 18·14kg (40lb)
Pilot: 72·57kg (160lb)
Passenger: 72·57kg (160lb)
Max gross: 272·14kg (600lb)

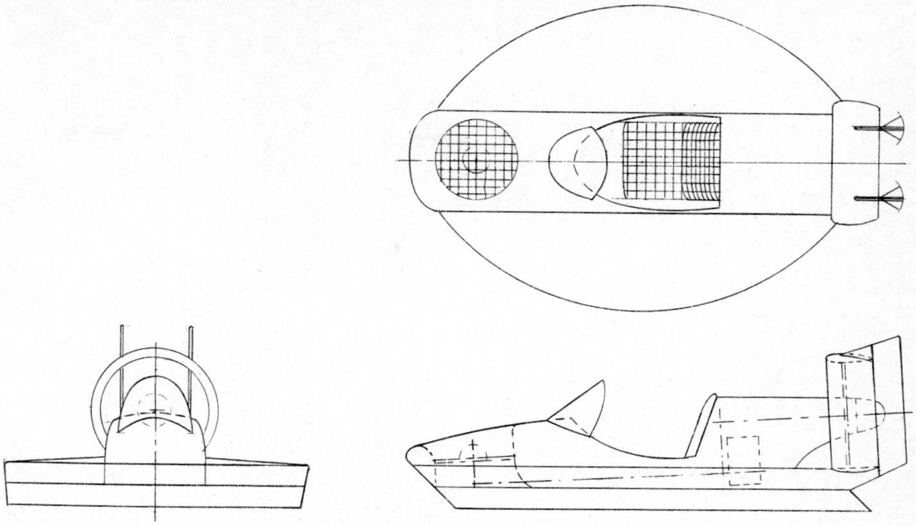
General arrangement of the Dobson Air Car Model H

EGLEN HOVERCRAFT INC

801 Poplar Street, Terre Haute, Indiana 47807, USA
Telephone: (812) 234 4307
Officials:
Jan Eglen, *President and General Manager*
Alfred Brames, *Secretary*
O Keith Owen Jr, *Treasurer*
Lewis R Poole, *Comptroller and Works Manager*
Woodrow S Nasser, *Director and Attorney*
Paul Ferreira, *Director Research*
George Kassis, *Director*
Jerry Chitwood, *Director*
Clarence Fauber, *Director*
Lionel Saunders, *Director of Production and Research*
Terry Moore, *Assistant Production Manager*
Middle East Representative: Al-Rodhan Trading & Contracting Est, PO Box 5020, Kuwait

Eglen Hovercraft Inc was chartered in August 1969, to design and manufacture recreational hovercraft and other air cushion devices. The company is at present concentrating on the production of the Hoverbug, an amphibious two-seater with a moulded plastic hull. The company is also producing the new Mk 2 model and four- and six-seat ACVs which incorporate a number of design improvements, including the employment of shock-mountings for both the lift and thrust engines. Another product, the Terrehover hoverplatform, is described in the section devoted to ACV Trailers and Heavy Lift Systems.

HOVERBUG Mk 2

A two-seat recreational ACV, the Hoverbug is powered by two Rockwell JLO engines and has a maximum speed of 48·28km/h (30mph) over water and 56km/h (35mph) overland. The standard version has an open cockpit, but a cabin top to form an enclosed cockpit is available as an optional extra.

The craft is available in either fully assembled or kit form.

LIFT AND PROPULSION: A 22hp Rockwell JLO-295 two-cycle engine, mounted immediately aft of the cockpit, drives a 609mm (2ft) diameter, 10-bladed Multiwing fan for lift. Thrust is supplied by a 25hp Rockwell JLO-395 driving a 914mm (3ft) diameter, Banks-Maxwell two-bladed propeller. Both lift and thrust engines on the Mk 2 model have shock-absorbing mountings, reducing the vibration transmitted to the hull by about 90%. Similar mountings are also employed to attach the thrust duct to the thrust engine frame, resulting in a longer life expectancy for the duct and the rudders, which are now mounted directly onto the duct. The propeller is of laminated hardwood, tipped in stainless steel. The company is currently investigating the use of a four-bladed propeller in order to reduce noise generation. A carburettor heat intake is required for running in snow or icy con-

A four-seater, developed from the Eglen Hoverbug, during trials

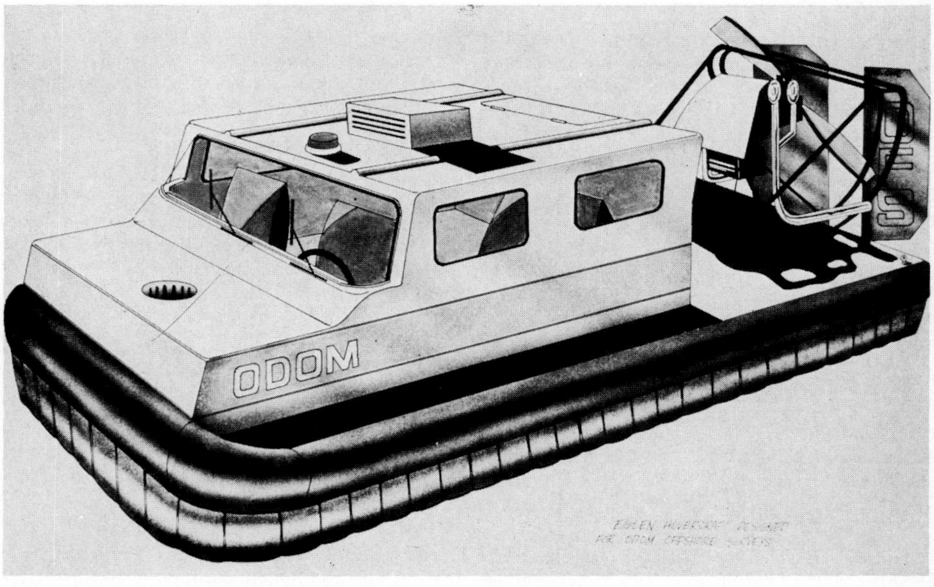

Impression of the new Eglen Hovercraft six-seat offshore survey and utility vehicle

ditions. Fuel capacity is 22·73 litres (5 gallons), representing about two hours running. Quick-release fittings to the fuel system facilitate maintenance.

CONTROLS: Directional control is provided by twin aerodynamic rudders hinged at the rear of the propeller duct and operating in the slip-stream. Cockpit controls comprise a steering wheel, two ignition switches, two throttles, two chokes, two emergency "kill" switches and a navigational lights switch.

HULL: High gloss, high impact plastic hull, formed by a thermovacuum moulding process developed by Hoosier Fibreglass Industries, Terre Haute, Indiana. Material used is Cycolac-brand ABS, supplied by the Marbon Division of Borg Warner Corporation. Hull side loading racks can be supplied as an optional extra. Two 152mm (6in) deep buoyancy chambers in the base of the hull are filled with foam plastic to provide 150% reserve buoyancy. Removable skids are fitted beneath.

SKIRT: Bag type, 304mm (1ft) deep, fabricated in neoprene-coated nylon. Skirt attachment system facilitates rapid removal and refitting.

ACCOMMODATION: Driver and passenger sit side-by-side in an open cockpit on a 1·21m (4ft) wide bench-type seat. Cockpit can be enclosed by a convertible top.

SYSTEMS, ELECTRICAL: 12V, 75W system for engine starting, instruments and navigation lights.

DIMENSIONS
Length overall, power on: 3·04m (10ft)
Beam overall, power on: 1·98m (6ft 6in)
Draft afloat: 152mm (6in)
Skirt depth: 304mm (1ft)
Cabin width: 1·21m (4ft)
WEIGHTS
Normal empty: 181kg (400lb)
Payload: 181kg (400lb)
PERFORMANCE
Max recommended speed, over water: 48·28km/h (30mph)
over land: 56·32km/h (35mph)
over ice: 64·37km/h (40mph)
Wave capability max: 457-609mm (1ft 6in-2ft)
Max gradient at all-up weight: 1 : 6
PRICE: Price of complete craft, fob Terre Haute: US $2,495
Price of standard kit: US$1,800

Eglen Hovercraft Hoverbug, a plastic-hulled two-seater powered by two Rockwell JLO engines. Speeds of up to 96·56km/h (60mph) have been attained by this craft over water with one person aboard

Hoverbug on a trailer prior to being used for spraying pesticides in a fumigation operation

OFFSHORE SURVEY SIX-SEATER

This new Eglen utility hovercraft is designed for a variety of duties including off-shore surveys. Of mixed wood and fibreglass construction, it carries a payload of 737kg (1,625lb) and cruises at 35 knots. Construction time is 4-6 months depending on optional equipment or special features required.

LIFT AND PROPULSION: Lift air is provided by a 90hp Continental PC-60 aero-engine driving a 609mm (24in) diameter Rotafoil fan. Cushion pressure is 83-92·77kg/m² (17-19lb/ft²). Thrust is supplied by a 100hp Lycoming air cooled piston engine driving a two-bladed Dobson reversible-pitch propeller.

CONTROLS: Craft heading is controlled by twin aerodynamic rudders hinged to the tubular metal guard aft of the propeller. Reversible and variable-pitch propeller provides braking and reverse thrust.

HULL: Wooden frame covered with fibreglass skin and finished with epoxy marine exterior paint. Cabin superstructure is in moulded fibreglass with 30oz Durasonic ¼in foam-backed sound proofing. Windows are of the "push out" type, in tinted plastic. Total fuel capacity is 55 gallons.

SKIRT: 355mm (14in) deep HDL type.

ACCOMMODATION: Seats provided for driver and five passengers. Optional items include seat belts, heating and air-conditioning and intercom system.

SYSTEMS, ELECTRICAL: 12V dc, with auxiliary outlets. Batteries: 2-12V, 72Ah capacity.

DIMENSIONS
Length: 7·31m (24ft)
Beam, on cushion: 3·04m (10ft)
Skirt depth: 355mm (1ft 2in)
Hover gap: 19mm (¾in)
WEIGHTS
Empty: 1,179·98kg (2,500lb)
Payload (including 400lb fuel): 737kg (1,625lb)
Overload capacity: 226·79kg (500lb)
Total in overload condition: 2,097·85kg (4,625lb)
PRICE: On request. Domestic orders: 50% payment with order, balance upon delivery. Overseas orders: irrevocable letter of credit for full price placed with American Fletcher National Bank in Indianapolis, Indiana.

GULF OVERSEAS ENGINEERING CORP

PO Box 204, New Iberia, Louisiana 70560, USA

Officials:

T E Sladek, *Vice President and General Manager*

Gulf Overseas Engineering Corporation has acquired the exclusive US design and manufacturing rights for the Secat surface effect catamaran from Teledyne Inc. The Secat was developed by Sewart Seacraft, a Teledyne company. With the acquisition of the design, Gulf also obtained the 12·19m (40ft) long prototype Secat built by Sewart.

In February 1976 Gulf announced that it had designed a 35·05m (115ft) version of the Secat, the Secat 115. This is an all-weather air-cushion supported catamaran designed specifically to meet the transportation needs of the offshore oil industry.

SECAT 115

In general layout this craft represents a "scale-up" of the configuration tested with the 12·19m (40ft) Secat built by Sewart Seacraft. Secat 115 is designed for a service speed of 29 knots in the open sea and to be capable of operating at full power in 3·65m (12ft) seas.

The afterdeck, which is 60ft long by 40ft wide, can accommodate a Bell 206B Jet Ranger helicopter.

Propulsion is by two marine propellers, powered by two 1,200hp marine diesels. The lift system will be powered by a single 600hp diesel engine.

The company states that at high speeds the manoeuvrability of the Secat will be comparable to that of a "well-performing crewboat". At low speeds the craft will be able to turn through 360 degrees in its own length.

DIMENSIONS
Length overall: 35·05m (115ft)
Beam overall: 12·8m (42ft)
WEIGHTS
Empty: 90 tons
Full load displacement: 140 tons
PERFORMANCE
Cruising speed: 29 knots

LOCKHEED-GEORGIA COMPANY

(A division of Lockheed Aircraft Corporation)

86 South Cobb Drive, Marietta, Georgia 30063, USA
Telephone: (404) 424 9411

A wing-in-ground-effect logistics transport weighing 1·4 million pounds was one of several naval advanced vehicle studies displayed in model form by Lockheed-Georgia Co, at the US Navy League Sea-Air-Space Exposition in April 1977. The company defined concepts for an air loiter vehicle, a sea loiter vehicle and a wing-in-ground-effect transport that could be developed in the 1980-2000 time period.

The studies were initiated in July 1976 under the direction of Capt Thomas Meeks, USN, Project Officer, Advanced Naval Vehicles Concepts Evaluation, and were completed under an eight-month $540,000 contract from the Naval Air Development Center.

Lockheed's WIG proposal was described as being a "seaplane capable of transporting large amounts of cargo over long distances." Its span is 32·91m (108ft) and its length 72·54m (238ft).

Features of interest include the mounting of the four turbofans forward so that the propulsion effect can be ducted beneath the wing to provide a cushion for lifting the vehicle at low speeds, and the attachment of end plates beneath the deep aerofoil section, low aspect-ratio wings to improve their aerodynamic characteristics.

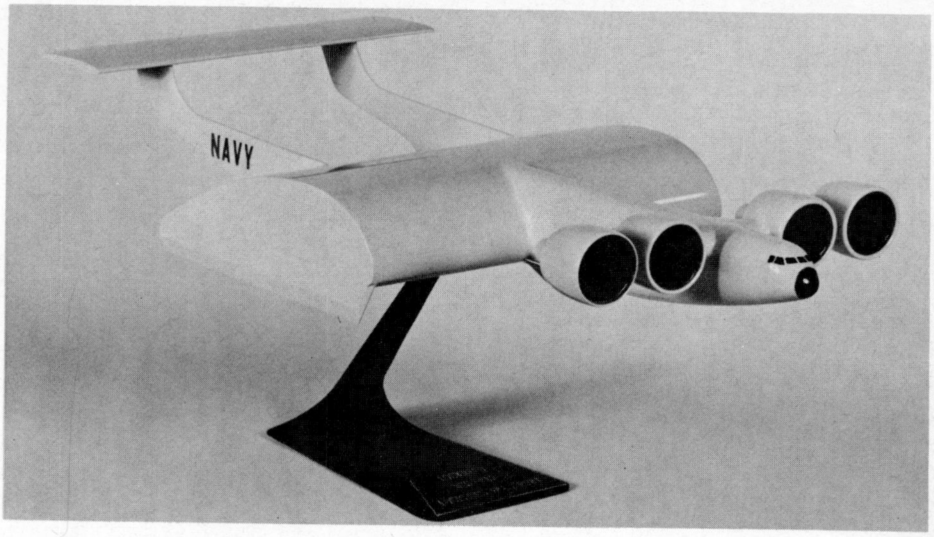

Model of Lockheed-Georgia's long-range WIG transport study for the US Navy's Advanced Naval Vehicles Concepts Evaluation Project

MARITIME DYNAMICS

1502 54th Avenue, East Tacoma, Washington 98401, USA
Telephones: (206) 759 1709; (206) 922 5233
Officials:
William C House, *President*

Maritime Dynamics is at present undertaking SEV data reduction, performance analysis and model testing for the US Navy. It is also developing a number of new ACV concepts.

NEOTERIC—USA—INCORPORATED

Fort Harrison Industrial Park, Terre Haute, Indiana 47804, USA
Telephone: (812) 466 2303
Officials:
Chris Fitzgerald, *President*
Cindy Lee, *Secretary*

Neoteric—USA—Incorporated was formed in 1975 by three of the founders of Neoteric Engineering Affiliates Pty Ltd, of Melbourne, Australia (see separate entry). The Neova range of single and two-seat ACVs, which is now being built and marketed by Neoteric USA, was first introduced by the Australian associate. The Neova, which is fully amphibious, is available in kit or ready-built form. The company welcomes enquiries from businesses wishing to manufacture the Neova range under licence.

NEOVA II

A highly-manoeuvrable light ACV, the Neova is an amphibious two-seater, intended primarily for recreational use. Neova II is supplied in kit form in four individual modules—base, machinery, ducts and controls and skirt. Individual components can also be supplied, enabling the home builder to assemble any part of the complete vehicle. The purchaser can therefore buy what is needed and make the rest himself to keep costs as low as possible.

The overall dimensions of the machine—2·13 × 4·27m (7 × 14ft)—allow it to be transported by road on a flat trailer.

LIFT AND PROPULSION: Integrated system powered by a single 46hp Volkswagen engine driving via a Getrag industrial gearbox and a simple chain drive transmission two axial fans. Airflow is ducted into the plenum for lift and two outlets aft for thrust. The power module, comprising engine, transmission and axial-flow fans is mounted on a rubber-seated platform, secured to the main hull by three bolts. It is totally enclosed and when operating is impossible to touch. A large hatch provides ready access to the engine and all components.

CONTROLS: Back and forward movement of a dual stick control column operates two thrust buckets which vary the power and the direction of the thrust. The column is pulled back for reverse

Latest version of the Neova II two-seater sports craft and runabout. Both the front cowl ahead of the cockpit and the protective grille above the engine and fans can be raised or removed to simplify access to the controls, battery and machinery

Forward and aft movement of a dual stick control column operates two thrust buckets which vary the power and direction of the thrust

thrust and moved ahead for forward thrust. Differential use of the two columns, with one stick forward and the other back, is used for changing craft direction. The aerodynamic rudders at the rear of the propulsion ducts are normally used only for small corrections in heading at cruising speeds.

HULL: Home-built models are of ply construction, with steel attachments at lifting and towing points. A two-seat fibreglass body assembly is available as an optional item. Skid pads on the underside protect the structure from damage by abrasion. An inflatable fender is attached to the periphery to prevent structural damage when travelling at low speeds. An integral siphon system prevents the collection of excessive water within the hull. Buoyancy is 150%. The skirt module is removable as a single unit.

ACCOMMODATION: Side-by-side seating for two. Safety features include a cockpit roll bar which is stressed to withstand three times the vehicle's weight. Models can be equipped with a detachable canopy on request.

DIMENSIONS
Length overall: 4·27m (14ft)
Beam overall: 2·13m (7ft)
Height overall, skirt inflated: 1·54m (5ft)

WEIGHTS
Normal all-up weight: 454kg (1,000lb)
Payload, maximum: 196kg (430lb)

PERFORMANCE
Cruising speed (at 75% power setting): 56km/h (35mph)
Max gradient from standing start: 1 : 10
Vertical obstacle clearance: 203mm (8in)
Endurance on full power: 1½ hours

PRICE
Neova II
Information pack US$5, plus $2 air mail overseas
Deluxe plan pack US$50, plus $4 air mail overseas, (free with complete kit purchase)
Complete kit, less engine $3,761·54
Fully assembled Neova II, US$8,000. Payment in either Australian or US dollars
Individual components and material sets available from either Melbourne, Australia or Terre Haute, USA.

Underside view of the Neova II's foam-filled glass fibre hull. Positive buoyancy is 680kg (1,500lb)

NORTH AMERICAN HOVERCRAFT COMPANY

One World Trade Centre, New York, NY 10048, USA
Telephone: (212) 775 1415
Officials:
George Daghar, *President*

North American Hovercraft Co is building the UK-designed AV Tiger in the United States under licence. Negotiations between the company and Air Vehicles Ltd of Cowes, Isle of Wight, were completed early in 1978. Air Vehicles Ltd supplied a number of components for the first five craft. Three of these were reported as being complete at the time of going to press.

Future production craft are likely to differ in certain aspects including the fitting of a US-built engine. Basic price is believed to be similar to that of the UK-built machine, about £30,000.

POWER BREEZE

8139 Matilija, Panorama City, California 91402, USA
Telephone: (213) 785 0197
Officials:
Dan W Henderson Jr, *President/Designer*

Power Breeze Air Cushion Vehicle Systems was founded originally to stimulate public interest in ACVs, and is currently selling plans to home builders for a small, easily assembled amphibious single-seater.

A set of plans costs US$5 and a ready made skirt costs US$35.

Total cost of construction in the USA, including ply for the hull, skirt material, metal tubing, propeller and engine is about US$400. Weight of the craft is 113kg (250lb) and the maximum speed is approximately 40·23km/h (25mph). The latest model of this circular platform single-seater folds to a width of 1·21m (4ft) to simplify storage and to permit it to be carried by a light truck or pick-up van.

A number of craft have been built to this design in the United States and Australia.

In addition to selling plans, the company is engaged in the sales of second-hand ACVs, and specialises in finding craft to meet the individual needs of its clients.

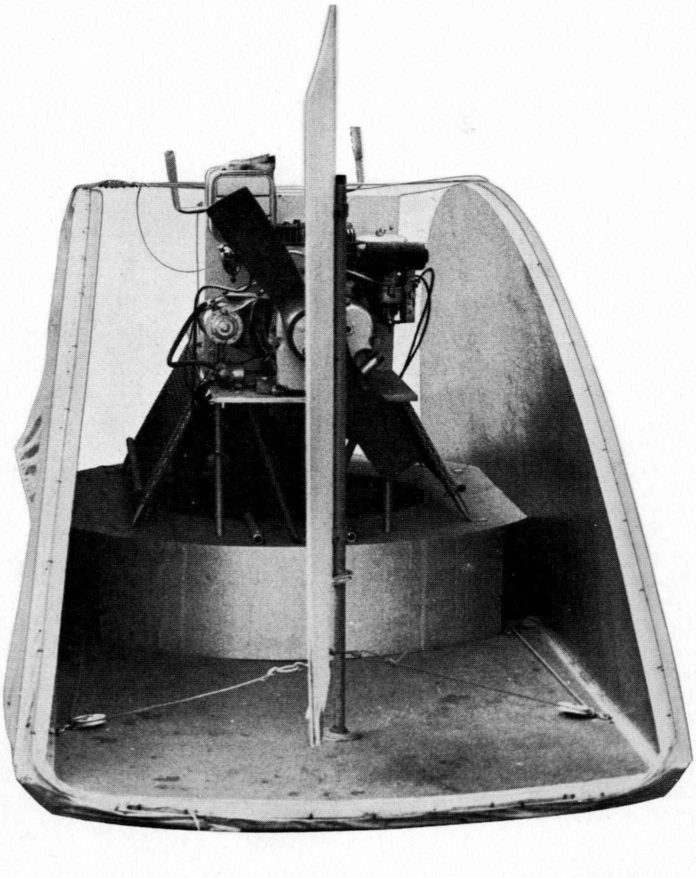

Power Breeze is marketing plans for this light, easily assembled amphibious single-seater

ROHR INDUSTRIES, INC

Head Office: Foot of H Street, PO Box 878, Chula Vista, California 92012, USA
Telephone: (714) 575 4111
TWX: (910) 322 1870
Officials:
Frederick W Garry, *Chairman of the Board and Chief Executive Officer*
Jerome J Filiciotto, *President and Chief Operating Officer*

ROHR MARINE, INC

(A Subsidiary of Rohr Industries, Inc)
Head Office: Foot of H Street, PO Box 2300, Chula Vista, California 92012, USA
Telephone: (714) 575 4100
TWX: (910) 322 1870
Officials:
Wilfred J Eggington, *President*
G Douglas McGhee, *Vice President, 3KSES Programme*
Darrell L Reed, *Chief Financial Officer*
Leon A Kranz, *Vice President, Administration*
Howard L Kubel, *Director, Planning*
F Patrick Burke, *Deputy Programme Manager, 3KSES*
Dario E DaPra, *Director, New Business Development*
Robert E Perry, *Director, Manufacturing*
Robert S Cramb, *Group Manager, Analysis*
Glenn F Guerin, *Group Manager, Procurement*
Thomas C Gurley, *Group Manager, Quality Assurance*
George G Halvorson, *Group Manager, Test and Evaluation*
John J Lansford, *Group Manager, Subsystems Development*
Charles M Lee, *Group Manager, Design*
Paul A West, *Director, Industrial Relations*
Jimmie Sober, *Manager, New Projects Planning*
Washington Office: 1660 L Street NW, Suite 505, Washington DC 20036, USA
Telephone: (202) 659 3255
Telex: 892793
Officials:
Ted Harmon, *Customer Liaison*

One of the world's leading producers of aircraft power packages and structures for three decades, Rohr Industries is a growing designer and builder of aerospace and marine systems. Founded in 1940, the company is based in Chula Vista, California. Its main plant occupies 130 acres of land, more than 2 million square feet of which comprises covered accommodation. Rohr currently has approximately 6,500 employees.

The company has 38 years of experience as a major subcontractor to the aerospace industry, supplying engine pods and other specialised structural components for commercial and military aircraft. Manufacturing facilities include machines, tooling, and precision welding equipment, which has been used extensively in the production of welded aluminium marine structures including boat hulls and offshore mooring systems for fuel transfer.

In 1972 Rohr joined with Litton Industries to begin work on preliminary design studies of a US Navy 2,000 ton Surface Effect Ship (SES) with ocean-going capability. While working on the design studies, Rohr continued its research and development programme, begun in 1970, on the XR-1, a Navy research test craft weighing approximately 20 tons. On completing preliminary design studies, a contract for the advanced development for the 2,000-ton concept was awarded to Rohr by the US Navy in July 1974. At this point the size of the ship concept was increased from 2,000 to 3,000 tons. Work completed under this contract covered advanced development of bow and stern seals; materials for seals and structures; lift fans; ride control devices to minimise vertical ship motions; waterjet pumps and reduction gearing. The proposed features were tested aboard the XR-1 and the SES-100A, one of the two 100-ton test craft built by the Navy to support the SES study programme. On completion of the design and development phase, a proposal was submitted to the US Navy for advanced work.

The XR-1, seen in D configuration, has a refined waterjet-propulsion system with a variable-geometry water inlet similar to that on the SES-100A

In December 1976. Rohr received a major contract from the US Navy for design, component verification testing and long-lead procurement for a 3,000-ton surface effect ship. Included in the contract is an option for the construction and trials of the ship.

Concurrently with the new contract, Rohr announced the formation and incorporation of a new wholly-owned subsidiary, Rohr Marine, Inc, formerly the SES Division, located at Chula Vista, California, which is dedicated to research, development and production of advanced marine systems with emphasis on the US Navy surface effect ship and other air cushion vehicle development programmes.

XR-1 TESTCRAFT

Built by the Naval Air Engineering Facility in 1963, the XR-1 was the first US Navy craft to demonstrate the captured air bubble principle. The initial configuration included a high length-to-beam ratio and air propulsors. Early tests of this craft contributed to the formulation of the Navy's SES development programme and led to the decision in 1966 to establish the SES project office.

In 1970, the XR-1 was equipped with waterjets, modified to low length-to-beam ratio and assigned to Rohr for further development and evaluation. Since then the craft has undergone a series of other modifications to evaluate new concepts in cushion seals, waterjet inlet systems, lift air distribution, craft structures, and associated developments in instrumentation, It was the first craft of its type to demonstrate flush and variable-geometry waterjet inlets, and to provide operational data on the performance of these concepts under sea state conditions where inlet broaching is induced.

In 1973, further modifications of the craft were undertaken, including the replacement of the earlier rigid, articulated seals with flexible, rubberised-fabric seals and the installation of a redesigned lift system to permit investigation of the effects of variations in lift air distribution. In addition, a structural test programme was undertaken, involving rebuilding the bow structure and incorporating instrumentation to permit measurement of structural loads due to slamming in heavy seas.

Although much smaller and less sophisticated than the SES-100A or SES-100B, the XR-1 has proved to be a versatile and relatively inexpensive research vehicle for investigating new SES concepts, and for verifying scaling techniques for application in the design of larger craft.

In October 1974, the XR-1 underwent further modification to demonstrate several subsystem innovations being developed under the 2KSES programme. These included a refined waterjet inlet system with a varible-geometry feature similar to that in the SES-100A; flexible, planing-type bow and stern seals designed for high durability; variable-flow lift fans as an alternative to the use of cushion venting for attenuating craft motion in a seaway; cushion vent valves for comparision with the variable-flow lift fans; a ride control electronic system to sense craft motion and control the lift fans and vent valves. Basic elements of the propulsion system and craft structure were retained in the new configuration which was designated XR-1D. Test results conducted by Rohr during 1975 confirmed the value of the new concepts and the data obtained is currently in use to support the development of the 3KSES.

In April 1976, the XR-1D was transferred to the US Navy Surface Effect Ship Test Facility at Patuxent River, Maryland where the Navy now operates the craft with Rohr support.

LIFT AND PROPULSION: Lift is supplied by three Aerojet Liquid Rocket Company variable output centrifugal fans with two pairs of heave attenuation valves. Cushion pressure at 35,000 cfm is 60 lb/ft². Two T53-L-7A Avco Lycoming gas turbines, driving two Pratt and Whitney Sea-jet 6-1A pumpjets, provide propulsion.

DIMENSIONS
Length overall: 15·3m (50ft)
Beam overall: 5·8m (19ft)

WEIGHTS
Operating displacement: 191·3kN (43,000lb)

PERFORMANCE
Max speed, calm water: 22·1m/s (43 knots)

SES-100A

The SES-100A was one of the two major testcraft vital to the 2,200 ton SES programme. It was designed and developed by Aerojet General Corporation under the sponsorship of the US Navy Surface Effect Ship Project Office and launched in 1971. Rohr Marine, Inc under contract to the US Navy, is currently modifying the existing SES-100A to verify the functional performance and structural integrity of the 3KSES-type seals. In addition, Rohr Marine has provided craft maintenance logistics, engineering, test planning and data handling support for the Navy's SES-100A test programme and will perform similar functions once the craft has been modified.

Upon completion of over two years of extensive contractor trials, the craft was transferred to the US Navy in July 1974. Under Navy direction, the pod waterjet propulsion system was modified to incorporate variable-geometry flush inlets. Subsequently, the craft was moved from the Tacoma, Washington, area to the Navy's Surface Effect Ship Test Facility (SESTF) at the Naval Air Station, Patuxent River, Maryland, where tests were continued, under Navy direction, until July 1977 when the craft was removed from service in order to complete the modifications. The craft will be redesignated SES-100A1 upon completion.

Primary technical objectives of the test programme to date, have been the thorough evaluation of the propulsion system, following installation of the variable area flush inlets (complete with "fences", which reduce air ingestion into the inlet) and measurement of the craft's ride quality characteristics. The SES-100A1 modification requires the installation of a new "square" bow structure, modified stern structure, new bow and stern planing seals and retraction mechanisms, modified air distribution system, and modification to many of the existing ship's auxiliary systems. Upon completion, the craft will be turned over to the Navy and the ensuing testing will be aimed at verifying the data utilized in the design development of 3KSES type seals.

LIFT AND PROPULSION: Motive power for the integrated lift/propulsion system is supplied by four TF-35 3,100shp Avco Lycoming gas turbines. The transmission system couples the gas turbines to two Aerojet General two-stage axial/centrifugal waterjet pumps and three axial-flow lift fans. Powerplant airflow is supplied through demisters from inlets located on the topside. The two waterjet pumps (port and starboard units) are installed on rail mounts that permit them to be removed through a port in the transom. The three axial-flow fans are located in compartments between the port and starboard engines. The four gas turbines can be employed in any combination to drive the lift/propulsion system.

The variable geometry waterjet inlets are illustrated in the accompanying sketch. To provide cavitation-free operation over a wide range of speeds, the throat area of the inlet diffuser is varied by means of a hydraulically actuated linkage connected to a flexible roof ramp. At low speeds, and while the craft is passing through the "hump" speed, the inlet is in the open position, and is progressively closed to maintain the correct water flow rate as the speed increases.

CONTROLS: At low speeds, directional control is provided by waterjet thrust vector and at high speed by movable skegs, port and starboard. The fuel and fuel-trim subsystem comprises four fuel storage tanks—two in each sidewall; a service tank and bow and stern trim tanks. Trim is adjusted by transferring fuel from tank to tank by means of the fuel transfer pumps.

HULL: The hull is welded aluminium. It is divided into compartments by transverse and longitudinal bulkheads. The cargo deck, bridge, and portions of the weatherdeck are glass-reinforced plastic.

ACCOMMODATION: The bridge, located on the centreline forward, is air-conditioned and sound-insulated. It accommodates five test crew members and six observers. Four other test crew members monitoring systems data acquisition are located below deck on the starboard side, outboard of the bridge.

SYSTEMS, ELECTRICAL: Power generation and distribution system supplies electrical and electronic operational equipment and the data acquisition subsystem (DAS). The primary purpose of the DAS is to measure selected testcraft performance parameters and record the resulting data on magnetic tape. The secondary purpose is to provide instantaneous data on display.

COMMUNICATIONS AND NAVIGATION: Standard marine radio is carried and radar is included for collision avoidance. A gyro compass is fitted.

HYDRAULIC SYSTEM: 3,000psig pressure and 100psig return pressure.

COMPRESSED AIR: Engine bleed air is used for stern seal spring pressurisation. Stored compressed air is used for stern seal spring pressurisation. Stored compressed air is used for turbine braking.

DIMENSIONS

Length overall: 24·3m (79ft 8in)

Beam overall: 12·7m (41ft 11in)

The SES-100A surface effect ship. Test planning, engineering services and data handling are among the services provided by Rohr under US Navy contract in support of the SES-100A test programme

Cutaway drawing of the SES-100A showing one of the two flush-mounted waterjet inlets and the new stabilising fins which replace the original pod-type inlet and fin assembly

Cushion area (designated static): 186m² (1,998ft²)

Height on cushion: 7·01m (23ft)

Draft to designed waterline: 2·1m (6ft 9¾in)

WEIGHTS

Light displacement, 10% fuel load: 91,400kg (90 tons)

Load displacement design: 101,600kg (100 tons)

PERFORMANCE

Designed max speed: 41·16m/s (80 knots)

3KSES (3,000-TON SURFACE EFFECT SHIP)

In 1972 the US Navy, through the Surface Effect Ships Project Office (SESPO), now PMS-304, initiated a programme to build a large ocean-going SES. The programme involved four competing contractors who each produced a conceptual design, of a 2,200-ton SES, together with plans for the subsequent detailed design, analyses, and major subsystems development and testing. These studies included requirements to define and integrate on-board combat systems and aircraft, and crew requirements in terms of accommodation, operation, and maintenance.

In 1974, a selection was made from the submitted designs and work was continued by two of the contractors on two competing concepts. Technology development was advanced in relation to bow and stern seals, material for seals and structures, lift fans, ride control devices, waterjet pumps and reduction gearing. In addition, the basic ship designs underwent refinement. During this period, an increase was made in the size of the ship, raising its fully loaded displacement from 2,200 tons to 3,000 tons.

Rohr Marine was awarded a contract in late 1976 for the detail design, sub-system verification testing, planning the construction, test and evaluation of the 3KSES and procurement of long-lead equipment for the construction phase. The contract includes an option for the US Navy to proceed with construction of the ship.

The ship, to be tested in the early 1980s is to validate not only air cushion performance advantages for a ship operating in an open ocean environment, but also to demonstrate the operational utility and benefits of that ship as an element of US Naval Forces. To this end, the ship will be equipped with selected weapon systems representative of a modern fleet frigate.

The 3KSES can be considered to have three distinct modes of operation. Firstly, as an on-cushion ship, in which mode it achieves its highest speed in a seaway. Secondly, as a partially cushion-borne vessel (wet deck positioned to be just above the significant wave height in the seaway), which can operate efficiently in the sub-hump and trans-harsh regimes through the suppression of secondary and tertiary hump drag phenomena. This mode of operation maximises the inherent speed stability of the SES for such operations. Thirdly, as a displacement craft, the mode best suited for navigating restricted channels, precise station-keeping control when deploying dipping sonars, and during harbour and dockside manoeuvring.

It is designed to integrate operationally with other US Navy ships, craft, shore commands and aircraft during test and evaluation deployments. It will use existing Navy logistic support together with certain special repair facilities ashore for seals, fans, and waterjet pumps. Provision is made for vertical replenishment (VERTREP) underway with the capability for rapid strike down of stores, provisions, and parts. It is also designed for underway alongside fuel connected replenishment (CONREP) and helicopter-inflight-refuelling (HIFR). Full maintenance support of embarked ASW helicopters is provided together with provision for the hangarage and fuelling of a V/STOL aircraft.

LIFT: Three variable geometry constant-speed centrifugal lift fans are located in each sidewall. Each sidewall group is driven by a General Electric LM 2500 gas-turbine via a reduction gear train. Pressurised air from the forward fans is ducted to the bow seal bag, then into the cushion; air from the centre fans is ducted directly into the cushion, while air from the rear fans enters the cushion via the stern seal bag. Air intakes are located in the weather deck. A feature of the design is the employment of variable-flow fan inlets in conjunction with cushion vent valves to provide a rapid response ride control system.

PROPULSION: Initially, power for the waterjet-propulsion system will be supplied by four General Electric LM2500 gas-turbines with growth space allotted for possible replacement by four marinised Pratt & Whitney FT9A-2A units when they become available. Two propulsion units are located in each sidewall, each comprising a gas turbine transmission, a two-stage Aerojet Liquid Rocket Co waterjet pump and nozzle.

A thin skeg beneath the bottom extremity of each sidewall prevents cushion air from flowing transversely beneath the sidewalls into the waterjet inlets and also limits the loss of cushion air as the ship passes over wave troughs.

SEALS: Forward and aft seals are inflated by the cushion air supply and employ a planing surface at their lower extremities to eliminate flagellation damage and minimise hydrodynamic drag. Both seals are retractable and can be raised or lowered independently to reduce drag while accelerating beyond "hump" speed in addition to controlling ship trim and the depth of the waterjet inlets throughout the speed range. Seals are normally fully retracted for hullborne manoeuvring.

CONTROL: Craft heading is controlled by vectoring the thrust nozzles and by differential thrust. Thrust reversers are provided on the two outboard nozzles for braking, stopping, backing and low speed manoeuvring.

HULL: All aluminium welded structure consisting of longitudinally stiffened plate supported by transverse web frames.

SYSTEMS, ELECTRICAL: Independent 60Hz and 400Hz subsystems, each powered by gas turbine generators (GTGs). Sets interconnected by a ring bus.

SHIP INTEGRATED CONTROL: Closed loop control for steering, propulsion, and lift systems. Automatic control of ride (lift fans and/or vent valve). Performance monitoring of auxiliary, electric plant, and distribution systems. Centralised ship damage control and integrated navigation and collision avoidance systems.

OUTFIT AND FURNISHINGS: Hull compartmentation, access and safety conforming to US Navy standards with generous habitability provisions.

AUXILIARIES:

HEATING, VENTILATING AND AIR CONDITIONING: 400Hz powered, vane axial fans, packaged condensing units, direct expansion cooling coils, variable volume air flow;

REFRIGERATION: Two 70Hz refrigeration plants;

FIREMAIN AND AUXILIARY SEAWATER: Open loop, horizontal 861·84kPa (125psi) system;

Impression of the Rohr 3KSES showing the bow cushion seal. The planing surface at its lower extremity is expected virtually to eliminate flagellation damage and minimise hydrodynamic drag

Weapons planned for 3KSES include two SH-3H helicopters or one AV-8B Harrier attack aircraft, Harpoon missiles and Mk 32 torpedoes. A Tactas towed array sonar with its deployment and retrieving system is located at the stern

Cutaway showing the machinery layout aboard the 3KSES. There are three constant-speed double-suction centrifugal fans in each sidewall. Wave-induced motions are reduced by combining variable fan inlets with cushion vent valves. Each sidewall also accommodates two waterjet-propulsion ducts. Area of the single water inlet beneath each sidewall is adjusted by a movable roof in the inlet duct

SCUPPER AND DECK DRAINS: Standard gravity drainage system utilising grp piping;
PLUMBING DRAINS (SOIL AND WASTE): Vacuum assisted collection discharged overboard or to holding tank;
MAIN DRAIN: Combines pumps and eductors for main machinery space dewatering and bilge water removal;
SECONDARY DRAIN: Seawater actuated eductors for miscellaneous drainage of spaces not served by main drain system;
POTABLE AND FRESH WATER: Standard shipboard system, operated to minimise storage;
COOLING WATER AND AUXILIARY FRESH WATER COOLING: Two systems (Freon and sea water cooled) are provided. Closed loop design meeting US Navy standards;
FUEL OIL: Provides for filling, storage transfer and purification of JP-5 fuel for ship use;
AVIATION FUEL: Two JP-5 fuel service tanks, filled from ships storage through filter coalescers for helicopter service;
COMPRESSED AIR: Low pressure air from engine bleed and high pressure air from 20·68mPa (3,000psig) compressor are provided;
NITROGEN: Charging system is capable of supplying 0·48 to 20·68mPa (70 to 3,000psig) of oil-free nitrogen;
FIRE EXTINGUISHING: High capacity AFFF, total flooding halon and high expansion foam;
HYDRAULIC: Closed 20·68mPa (3,000psig) system;
REPLENISHMENT AT SEA: VERTREP area, port/starboard alongside RAS for fuel, potable water stations, and vertical flow conveyor are provided;
ANCHORING: Utilizing one 4,000lb Danforth anchor and associated cable winch;
MOORING AND TOWING: Comprised of three capstans, as well as bits, chocks, and towing padeyes;
BOAT HANDLING AND STOWAGE: Six 25-man life rafts and an outboard motor driven, inflatable rescue craft and handling davit.

DIMENSIONS
Length overall: 81·15m (266ft 3in)
Max beam: 32·3m (106ft)
Wet deck height (above baseline—ABL): 5·49m (18ft)
Cushion area: 1,745·13m² (18,785ft²)
Effective cushion length: 67·36m (221ft)
Main deck height (ABL): 12·19m (40ft)
Hullborne design waterline (ABL): 6·2m (20ft 4in)
Max navigating draft: 9·36m (30ft 8in)
WEIGHTS
Full load displacement: 29·89 MN (3,000 tons)
PERFORMANCE
Max speed: approx 148·18km/h (80 knots)

SURFACE EFFECT SHIP ACQUISITION PROJECT

PO Box 34401, Bethesda, Maryland 20034, USA
Cables: SESPO c/o Naval Ship Research and Development Center, Bethesda, Maryland
Officials:
Captain Thomas M Barry, USN, *Project Manager*
Commander Jerome J Fee, USN, *Deputy Project Manager*

Through the design, construction and operation of several test craft, and an extensive technology programme, the US Navy Surface Effect Ship Acquisition Project can provide the Navy with large high-speed ships capable of performing numerous combat and support missions. In 1976 the US Navy selected Rohr Marine, Inc to design and build a 3,000-ton SES (3KSES). This ship is designed to operate at high-speed in open sea. Its transoceanic range will enable it to perform various missions and its substantial payload capacity permits the installation of an extensive weapons system. During the initial two-year test programme, the ship will demonstrate its open-sea capabilities, satisfactory operation of all systems, weapon system compatibility with the SES platform and military utility with a variety of equipment and throughout a wide range of environments. During this phase the ship will be dependent on standard US Navy support systems and practices to demonstrate the readiness with which an SES can be integrated into the fleet.

PRINCIPAL DATA:
Full load displacement (FLD): 3,000 tons
Length overall: 82·3m (270ft) approx
Beam overall: 32m (105ft) approx permits transit of Panama Canal
Wet deck height, on cushion: 5·48m (18ft) enables ship to operate in sea state 6
Cushion pressure FLD: 343kg/m² (275lb/ft²)
Propulsion engines: 4 FT9A-2
Lift engines: 2 LM-2500
Max speed: above 80 knots
For further details see the entry for Rohr Marine, Inc.

Test craft activities are directed primarily toward investigation of 3KSES type systems and subsystems. XR-1D and SES-100A both have systems representative of 3KSES installations and are engaged in tests and evaluations to bridge the gap between analysis, model tests and full scale installations. Midshipmen and officers are introduced to SES technology, operation and potential on the XR-5 at the US Naval Academy and the XR-3 at the Postgraduate School. SES-100B is temporarily inactive.

The XR-1D lift, seal and propulsion systems, similar to those being designed for the 3KSES, are being evaluated in a broad range of sea states

XR-1D STRUCTURAL LOADS TESTS

The XR-1D structural loads test programme was designed to provide two types of structural design information: slamming load pressures on the forward sloping wet deck (underside of the central hull) in the off-cushion condition with particular emphasis on a comparison between maximum localised point pressures and area-pressures in the fore-and-aft direction, and hull girder bending loads and shear reactions caused by wave slamming. There were four outstanding aspects to this SES test programme:
a. Hullborne operations were undertaken in high sea states with fully instrumented craft.
b. The XR-1D was equipped with pressure panels to measure design (distributed) rather than peak pressures.
c. Correlation was established between slamming loads and slamming pressure time histories.
d. Tests were of sufficient duration to measure design limit values without need for statistical extrapolation.

Test operations were conducted in Chesapeake Bay in relatively high sea states. The XR-1D operated at low speed, 2-3 knots in the displacement mode and at various headings. The most severe conditions encountered were waves up to eight feet high and wind gusts to 65 knots, corresponding to sea state 7 for the 3KSES. Although the craft was damaged, it returned under its own power to the Surface Effect Ship Test Facility. Following completion of repairs, the XR-1D was scheduled to continue the structural loads programme, but under less extreme conditions than previously.

XR-1D RIDE CONTROL SYSTEM TEST PROGRAMME

The 3KSES will have a Ride Control System (RCS) to attenuate vertical accelerations to within acceptable limits for habitability. This is accomplished by controlling valves which vent the cushion airflow overboard of variable geometry fans (controllable inlet blockage) or a combination of valve and fan control. Proper design and development of this control system is important to the overall 3KSES programme. RCS effectiveness significantly affects the capability of executing missions of extended duration and the usable range of speed/sea state operations. RCS power requirements can significantly affect range, payload and endurance. If designed to satisfy specific criteria, the RCS could potentially reduce structural loads and inlet broaching.

The XR-1D had been extensively modified to resemble a 3KSES design. Key aspects of the test craft's configuration pertinent to RCS testing include independent lift and propulsion systems, planing bow and stern seals, flush inlets and skegs, variable geometry lift fans, vent valves, RCS controller with built-in test equipment and PCM data system. The RCS test programme is intended to achieve four objectives:
a. Develop stable operation at full flow modulation capability (ie high gain) for simple control laws (pressure or acceleration).
b. Systematically evaluate RCS effectiveness in terms of ride quality improvement and power demands for various sea/speed conditions.
c. Correlate test results with predictive models used in the 3KSES RCS design and extrapolate significant results to 3KSES size.
d. Evaluate effectiveness of other control laws

proposed for the 3KSES RCS relative to effectiveness obtained with pressure or acceleration feedback.

XR-3

The XR-3 has been used for several years as a research "manned model" by students at the US Navy Postgraduate School, Monterey, California, and has served as a subject for numerous theses. The XR-3 is of special interest because of the resemblance of its stay-stiffened membrane two-dimensional seals to those in use on the SES-100A and those being designed for installation on the 3KSES.

Recent research has involved measurement of loads on the bow and stern seals and identification of their sources. Student programmes are concerned with optimisation of the XR-3 seal shapes and measurement upon seal loads of craft turns. Speed, heel, cushion pressure, craft weight and trim are some of the design parameters under study.

XR-5

The XR-5 testcraft was transferred in November 1977 from the Surface Effect Ship Test Facility to the US Naval Academy, Annapolis, Maryland. After the craft has been refurbished and modernised it will be used by midshipmen as a research vehicle for further development of high length/beam ratio surface effect ships. Direction and support will be provided by the Academy faculty and the Aviation and Surface Effects Department of the David Taylor Naval Ship R & D Center. One objective will be correlation of data generated in towing tanks on small models with that obtained from the XR-5. Other proposed subjects for student projects include: testing of new components such as seals and modified side hulls to improve operating and manoeuvring characteristics; development of a data base for projection into future SES designs; and study of acoustic phenomena, spray generating mechanism and behaviour, and man-machine interaction.

The XR-5 will operate both on the Severn River and Chesapeake Bay so that its characteristics can be determined throughout the full sea state/velocity range in which it is intended to function.

The craft and all test equipment will be operated by midshipmen, providing them with experience in SES performance, stability, control and handling qualities as well as in research and test procedures and analysis. This programme, together with use of the XR-3 at the Postgraduate School, will provide the Navy with a substantial number of officers who have technical and operational background in surface effect ships.

SES-100A FITTED WITH 3KSES-TYPE SEALS

The 3KSES will be equipped with bow and stern seals which have flexible, lightweight glass-reinforced-plastic "planers" in contact with the water surface. The planers are joined at their edges by flexible joints to form a compliant seal, developed with the expectation of achieving significant improvements over traditional "bag and finger" fabric seals. In combination with full length side hulls, these seals ensure positive pitch stability at all speeds and sea states. Their drag characteristics should prove comparable to or better than earlier seals. Most significantly, however, environmental testing has shown the grp planers to be highly resistant to the effects of water erosion at high speed.

Grp planing type seals have been operated successfully on the XR-1D testcraft and full scale grp planer elements were tested in a high-speed water environment test device at velocities of up to 90 knots. The next step in the seals development programme is to demonstrate this type of seal on a large scale.

The SES-100A was extensively modified to accept 3KSES type bow and stern seals tailored to SES-100A parameters and suitable for operations throughout the SES-100A envelope. Major alterations were:

The XR-3, the smallest operational SES, is in use at the US Navy Postgraduate School

The XR-5 is assigned to the US Naval Academy

SES-100B completed extensive high speed tests in the Gulf of Mexico before being transferred to the Surface Effect Ship Test Facility, Maryland. This propeller-driven testcraft has exceeded 90 knots; and in April 1976, while travelling at more than 60 knots launched a Standard 1 missile which struck a distant target

a. Structural modifications to the bow and stern centrebody and sidehulls to accommodate installation of 3KSES type planing seals and their retraction mechanisms.
b. Installation of bow and stern seals and retraction mechanisms.
c. Dedication of individual fans to the bow seal, stern seal and cushion by addition of bulkheads in the air plenum.
d. Modification and rerouting of air supply ducts to the bow seal and cushion. In connection with these changes, other internal modifications are required, such as relocation and re-arrangement of living quarters and the vibration test area.
e. Change in side hull dead rise to 45 degrees and decrease in blister ramp angle to duplicate more closely 3KSES lines. The modified sidewalls are essentially one-third scale models of the 3KSES sidewalls.

The excellent pitch stability of the new seals led to a sixth significant change, the removal of bow stabilisers and hydrofoils, conspicuous in photographs of this craft in earlier editions of *Jane's Surface Skimmers,* and substantial decrease in the area of the submerged stern stability fins. These changes further reduce hydrodynamic drag.

The basic purpose of the test programme is verification of the functional performance and structural integrity of 3KSES-type seals. Resultant design data and operating experience will have direct application in the detail design of 3KSES seals, and in refinement of loads and motions computer programmes and analysis procedures. The tests will also provide information on seal wear characteristics, demonstrate the resistance of the seal systems to damage propagation, and contribute to development of seal maintenance and repair concepts.

The SES-100A was placed in operation during March 1978 and within a few missions had attained 65 knots with significantly less propulsion power than required for the craft at the same speed in earlier configurations. The basic seals verification tests include a series of underway missions that progressively cover the scaled sea state range and, eventually, the full operating capability of the SES-100A. Data will be analysed in the time domains, and statistically for correlation with criteria being used in design of the 3KSES seals.

Additionally, tests will be required to check and adjust the craft's ride control system which has undergone major changes incidental to the conversion, including rearranged vent valves, modified air distribution ducting, and new control circuitry. It should be feasible to conduct a number of underway RCS tests concurrently with the seal tests.

Underway tests will then be expanded to cover higher sea states, first to the boundaries of the scaled 3KSES speed/sea state range and then to the limits of the testcraft's capabilities.

A maximum amount of underway operating time is required to evaluate seal reliability, maintainability and availability. 150 to 200 hours of on-cushion operation is desirable, subject to maintenance contingencies and other operating considerations. This amount of utilisation should help to disclose any significant problems with the seal design and manufacturing process, and provide a basis for confidence in the 3KSES seals concept.

ADVANCED DESIGN

The project's ultimate objective is development of SES technology to a high level of confidence and assist the introduction into the Navy of a class of SES escort ships of approximately 3,000 tons displacement, to be followed by design and construction of larger ships for additional missions. The designs of both the escort class and larger ships will be closely related and synchronised with the development, test and evaluation of the 3KSES.

SES-100A ashore. It has been modified by addition of 3KSES type bow and stern seals and changes in hull lines. Modifications were completed in January 1978

SES-100A performance was substantially improved following the major modifications described in this entry. It has attained 65 knots with significantly less propulsive power than required by earlier configurations

SES-100A entering the U-dock which supports the syncrolift platform

SKIMMERS INCORPORATED

PO Box 855, Severna Park, Maryland 21146, USA
Telephone: (301) 647 0526
Officials:
M W Beardsley, *President and General Manager*
H L Beardsley
W D Preston
Overseas Representative: United Kingdom: Airhover Ltd, St Osyth, Essex, England

Skimmers Inc was formed in April 1966 to produce plans and components for use by homebuilders in constructing the Fan-Jet Skimmer sport ACV. It is affiliated with the Beardsley Air Car Co.

During 1977 the company designed a small two-seat ACV and an experimental prototype is under construction.

FAN-JET SKIMMER

Fan-Jet Skimmer is one of the world's first practical solo sport ACVs. It was designed by Col Melville Beardsley, a former USAF technical officer, and one of the pioneers in ACV development in the USA.

The Fan-Jet Skimmer was designed to be the simplest and cheapest one-man ACV that could be devised. More than 40 craft of this type have been built to date.

LIFT AND PROPULSION: Power for the integrated lift/propulsion system is provided by a Chrysler two-cycle 6hp engine, driving a 457mm (18in) axial flow fan. The fan has a marine plywood hub with nine sheet metal formed blades. The primary air flow, used for direct thrust, is ejected through a propulsive slot control flap located aft of the fan duct. The area of the slot can be varied by a hinged flap controlled by a lever. This and the throttle lever and ignition switch are the only controls. The secondary air flow, for cushion lift, passes into a rearward plenum chamber.

CONTROLS: The craft is steered by kinesthetic control (body movement) which the designer feels is the ideal method of control for a craft of this size.

HULL: The main structural component is a tractor inner tube, giving 217·5kg (700lb) of buoyancy, around which is an aluminium framework of square tube, and L girders. The topside bow profile is in plywood. The structure is decked in vinyl-coated nylon fabric which is also used for the self-extending skirt system.

DIMENSIONS
Length overall: 2·9m (9ft 8in)
Beam overall: 1·8m (6ft 2in)
Height overall on landing pads: 0·9m (36in)
Skirt depth: 0·2m (9in)
Draft afloat: 0·12m (5in)
Cushion area: 4m² (44ft²)
WEIGHTS
Normal all-up weight: 113kg (250lb)
Normal payload (operating): 68kg (150lb)
Max payload: 397kg (180lb) approx
PERFORMANCE
Max speed, calm water: 29km/h (18mph)
Cruising speed, calm water: 29km/h (18mph)
Max wave capability: approx 153mm (6in)
Still air range: approx 56km (35miles)
Max gradient, static conditions: 5 degrees approx
Vertical obstacle clearance: 127mm (5in)

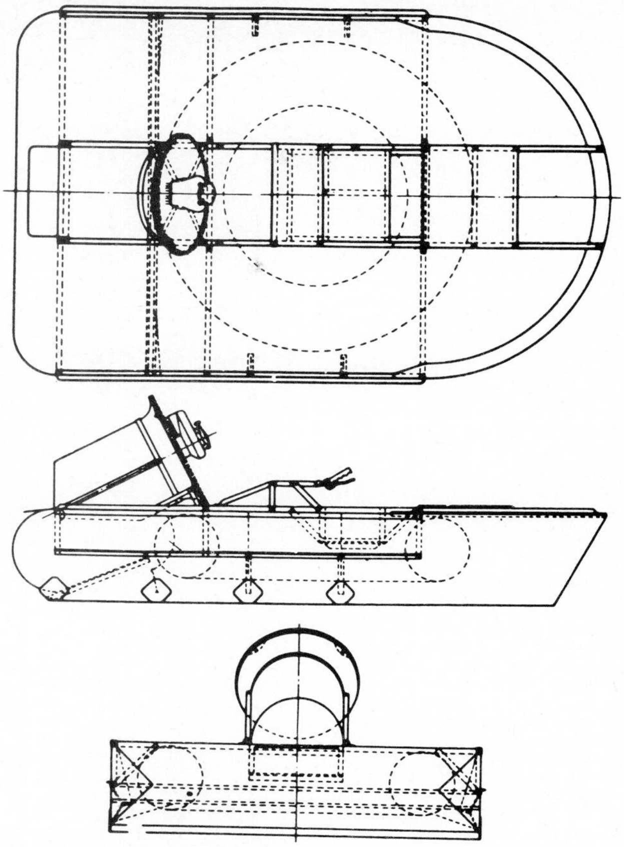
The Fan-Jet Skimmer, designed by Melville Beardsley

For full over-the-hump performance with an operator weighing more than 79·4kg (175lb) the installation of two power plants is recommended each identical with the standard single power unit. With an operator weighing up to 102kg (225lb) the speed of the twin is approximately 20% greater than the standard single engine.

With the overall length of the twin-engine model increased to 3·4m (11ft 2in), it will carry a useful load of 160kg (350lb) at maximum speeds of approximately 56·33km/h (35mph) over smooth land and 35·4km/h (22mph) over calm water.

PRICE: USA, fob Severna Park, Maryland: US$1,200 for complete vehicle, US $595 for kit. Terms of payment, 50% down.

UNITED STATES HOVERCRAFT MANUFACTURING CO INC

Box 1191, Lynwood, Washington 98036, USA
Telephone: (206) 743 3669
Cables: Hoverco, Box 1191, USA 98036
Officials:
Gerald W Crisman, *President*
A J Doug Nunally, *Vice President*
Michael S Curtis, *Secretary*
William D Crisman, *Financial Adviser*

Formed originally in 1961 as Gemco Incorporated, United States Hovercraft Manufacturing Co has built a number of light and ultra-light craft, including the first hovercraft to cross the Mississippi. The company is at present concentrating on the production of a two-seater, the 6300 Hoverbird, a six-seater—the Model 5501 Eagle—and a light utility variant, the model 5502 Crane. In the planning stage are two larger vehicles, the Alaskan, an amphibious utility craft with a payload capacity of 10-12 tons and the Pioneer, a 30-seat passenger ferry.

MODEL 5501 EAGLE

The prototype of this glassfibre-hulled six-seater completed its trials in 1974. Hulls for both the Eagle and a light utility version, the model 5502 Crane, are being built by the Tacoma Boatbuilding Co, of Tacoma, Washington, in conjunction with Rienell Boats.

The Eagle, a glass fibre-hulled six-seater

LIFT AND PROPULSION: Cushion air is supplied by a 46hp Volkswagen automobile engine driving a stainless multibladed fan. Thrust is provided by a 96hp Volkswagen engine driving a Hartzell variable and reversible-pitch propeller. Total fuel capacity is 151·5 litres (40 US gallons).

CONTROLS: Deflection of triple rudder vanes mounted at the aft end of the propeller duct, together with thrust ports, forward and aft, provide heading control. Reverse propeller pitch employed for braking.
HULL: Moulded fibreglass structure with honeycomb aluminium reinforcement at stress points. Buoyancy boxes filled with expanded polyurethane.
SKIRT: Simple bag type in Hypalon material.
ACCOMMODATION: Fully enclosed cabin for driver and five passengers. Access is via two centrally-placed gull-wing doors, one port, one starboard. Air-conditioning optional.
SYSTEMS, ELECTRICAL: 12V for starting and services.
DIMENSIONS:
Length overall: 6·4m (21ft)
Beam overall: 3·35m (11ft)
Height overall, on cushion: 2·74m (9ft)
off cushion: 2·13m (7ft)
Cabin: 2·13 × 1·83m (7 × 6ft)
WEIGHTS
Empty: 635kg (1,400lb)
All-up weight: 1,125kg (2,700lb)
Disposable load: 499kg (1,100lb)
PERFORMANCE
Max speed: in excess of 60 knots
Endurance: 4 hours
Normal range: 386km (240 miles)
Stopping distance: 106·68m (350ft)
Obstacle clearance: 609mm (2ft)
Max wave capability: 0·914-1·22m (3-4ft)

A multi-purpose variant of the Eagle, the Crane, with a well deck aft of a three-seat cabin

MODEL 5502 CRANE

This multi-duty version is almost identical to the Model 5501 Eagle apart from the provision of a well deck immediately aft of its cabin. The Crane's cabin measures 1·22 × 1·83m (4 × 6ft) and seats three, with the driver in the central position. Access to the cabin is via a gull wing door at the rear, leading from the well deck.

Machinery arrangement, dimensions, weight and performance are similar to those of the Eagle.

MODEL 6300 HOVERBIRD

The latest American light hovercraft to be put into series production, the Hoverbird is a fibreglass-hulled utility two-seater with twin ducted thrust fans. Preliminary details were received as this edition went to press. The company reports that forty have been ordered for use in Alaska and fifty-five in the rest of the USA. Price per craft "ready-to-fly" is slightly below US $4,000.
LIFT AND PROPULSION: Cushion air is supplied by a 28hp Kohler engine mounted ahead of the cockpit and driving a multibladed fan. Thrust is furnished by a single 46hp Volkswagen automotive engine driving via a belt transmission two ducted fans aft.
HULL: Moulded fibreglass structure.

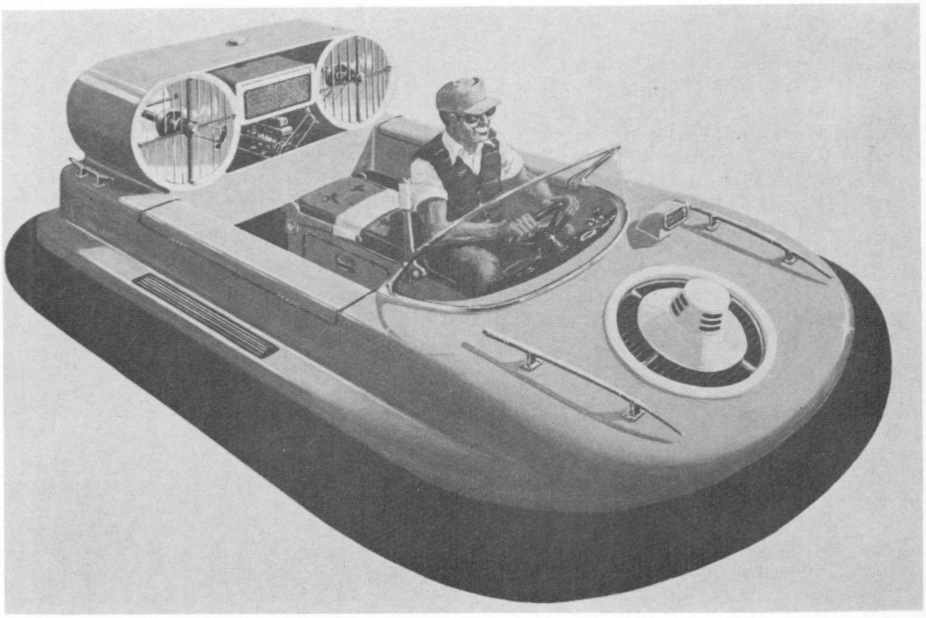
The Hoverbird amphibious two-seater

SKIRT: A simple bag skirt is standard. A segmented skirt can be supplied if required.
ACCOMMODATION: Open cockpit with tandem seating for driver and one passenger. Fold-down seat backs provided for comfort and safety.
DIMENSIONS
Length overall: 3·65m (12ft)
Width: 2·13m (7ft)
Height, on cushion: 1·49m (4ft 11in)
on landing pads: 1·21m (4ft)

UNIVERSAL HOVERCRAFT

1204 3rd Street, Box 281, Cordova, Illinois 61242, USA
Telephone: (309) 654 2588
Officials:
R J Windt, *Director*

Formed in 1969, this company has designed and built 30 different sports and utility ACV prototypes, ranging from an ultra-light single-seater to a seven-seater powered by a 200hp automotive engine. Plans for some of these designs are available to home builders. It has recently developed three new single-engined amphibious craft—a 3·65m (12ft) two-seater, a 3·96m (13ft) four-seater and a 5·48m (18ft) six-seater.

Work has also been undertaken on air cushion vehicles propelled by waterjets, outboard motors and sails.

UH-10C

This single-seat amphibious runabout was one of the company's earliest designs. Construction of the prototype was completed in November

UH-10C, an amphibious single-seater powered by single 10hp McCulloch 101 two-cycle engine

1969. The vehicle, which is of wooden construction, attains 43·45km/h (27mph) over land and 35·4km/h (22mph) over water.
LIFT AND PROPULSION: Integrated system employing a single 10hp McCulloch 101A or 101B two-cycle engine, which drives a 0·53m (1ft 9in) diameter, 12-bladed centrifugal fan mounted vertically on a shaft inside a transverse duct. Air is drawn by the fan from each end of the duct. Propulsion air is expelled through an outlet nozzle aft and lift air is ducted into a plenum below. Maximum thrust is 14·51kg (32lb).
CONTROLS: Multiple rudders in the thrust air outlet provide directional control.
HULL: Frame is built from fir ribs and stringers and covered with ⅛in ply.
ACCOMMODATION: Open cockpit with seat for driver. Craft will carry one person or a load of up to 79·35kg (170lb) over water, and up to 102·05kg (225lb) over land.
DIMENSIONS
Length: 3·14m (10ft 4in)
Beam: 1·82m (6ft)
Height, off cushion: 0·76m (2ft 6in)
WEIGHTS
Empty: 61·23kg (135lb)
Normal loaded: 140·14kg (310lb)
Max loaded: 163·28kg (360lb)
PERFORMANCE
Max speed over land: 48·28km/h (30mph)
over water: 40·23km/h (25mph)
Max gradient: 10%
PRICE: Complete set of plans for homebuilding, US$6.

UH-11S

An ultra-light runabout of wooden construction, the UH-11S seats two and has a top speed of 56·32km/h (35mph).
LIFT AND PROPULSION: Integrated system employing a single JLO two-cycle, 230cc engine, which drives a 0·61m (2ft) diameter, four-bladed fan for lift and a 1·21m (4ft) two-bladed fan for propulsion. Power is transmitted to the lift fan direct and to the propulsion fan through a reduction ratio belt drive.

8 or 10hp lawnmower engines with vertical shafts and aluminium cases may also be used to power the UH-11S.
CONTROLS: Large single rudder hinged to the rear of the propeller guard, provides directional control.
HULL: Structure built with fir ribs and stringers and covered in 3·17mm (⅛in) plywood.
ACCOMMODATION: Enclosed cabin with tandem seating for driver and passenger.
DIMENSIONS
Length: 3·48m (11ft 6in)
Width: 1·65m (5ft 6in)
Height, off cushion: 1·37m (4ft 6in)
WEIGHTS
Empty: 79kg (175lb)
Normal payload: 102kg (225lb)
Max payload: 147kg (325lb)
PERFORMANCE
Max speed, over land: 56·32km/h (35mph)
over water: 48·28km/h (30mph)
Max gradient: 16%
PRICE: Complete plans US$12.

UH-11T

Design keynotes of this new Universal two-seater are ease of construction and simplicity of operation. Constructed entirely in wood it can be powered by a wide selection of either new or used lawnmower engines in a range of outputs.
LIFT AND PROPULSION: A single 3·5hp Briggs and Stratton vertical shaft lawnmower engine drives a 0·6m (2ft) diameter, 12in pitch, four-bladed wooden fan for lift. Thrust is supplied by a 5hp Briggs and Stratton horizontal shaft lawnmower engine driving a 0·91m (3ft) diameter, 16in pitch propeller. Should higher output engines of 8 to 10hp be employed, a 1·06m (3ft 6in) diameter propeller is fitted. Total fuel capacity is 6·15 litres (1·5 US gallons).
CONTROLS: Triple aerodynamic rudders hinged to the rear of the propeller guard provide heading control.

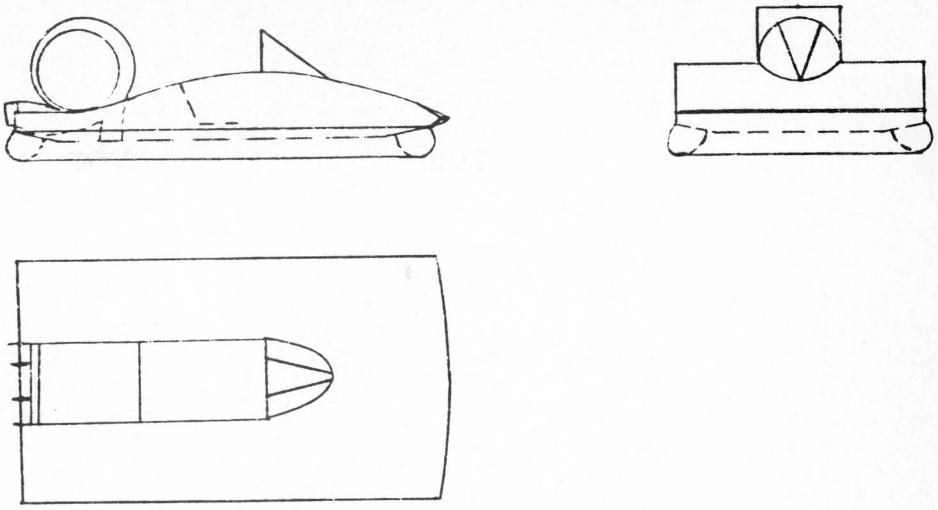

General arrangement of the UH-10 light ACV runabout

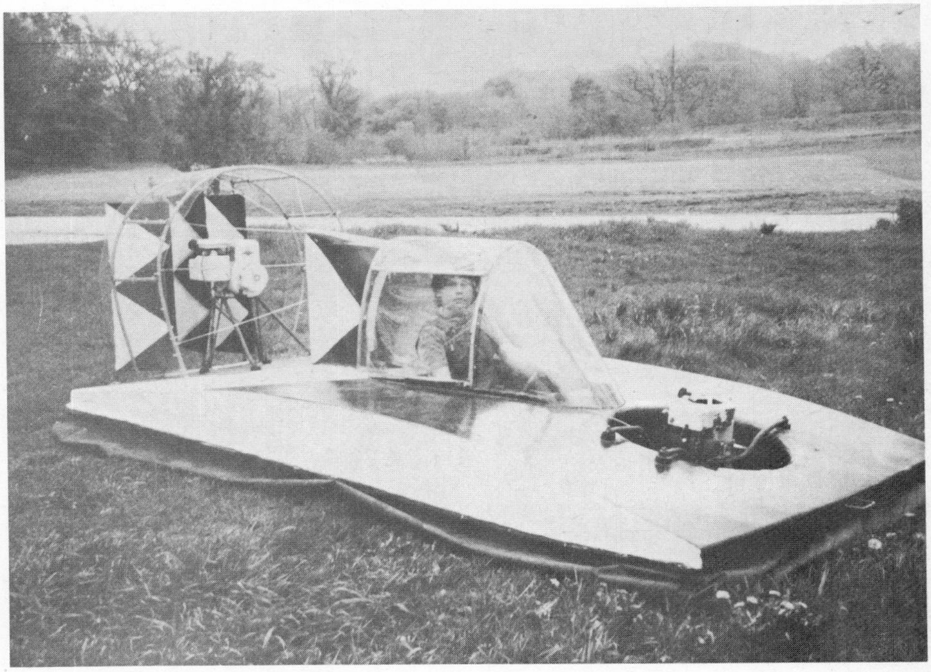

UH-11T two-seat amphibious runabout

UH-11, a two-seater powered by a single 230cc JLO two-cycle engine

HULL: Construction is of fir or pine ribs and stringers covered with an ⅛in plywood skin. Structure is designed to withstand the impact of a plough-in on choppy water at 64·37km/h (40mph).
SKIRT: 177mm (7in) high, 304mm (12in) diameter bag skirt fabricated in 16oz/yd neoprene coated nylon.
ACCOMMODATION: Enclosed cabin seating a driver and one passenger in tandem.
DIMENSIONS
EXTERNAL
Length overall, power off: 3·6m (11ft 10in)
Beam overall, power off: 1·67m (5ft 6in)
Cushion area: 5·11m² (55ft²)
Skirt depth: 177mm (7in)

INTERNAL
Cabin length: 0·91m (3ft)
Max width: 0·6m (2ft)
WEIGHTS
Normal empty: 113·39kg (250lb)
Normal all-up weight: 204·1kg (450lb)
Normal payload: 90·71kg (200lb)
Max payload: 113·39kg (250lb)
PERFORMANCE
Max speed over calm water with 5hp engine: 40·23km/h (25mph)
Max wave capability: 228mm (9in) chop
Max gradient static conditions, 204kg (450lb) gross weight and 5hp engine: 8%
Vertical obstacle clearance: 152mm (6in)
PRICE: Plans US $12

UH-12S

This lightweight two-seater is capable of carrying two adults and their camping or fishing equipment at up to 56·32km/h (35mph) over water.
LIFT AND PROPULSION: A single JLO 340 or 440 engine drives the lift fan and the thrust propeller via a V-belt system. The 0·61m (2ft) diameter fan turns at a maximum of 3,500rpm, while the 1·21m (4ft) diameter thrust propeller turns at 2,200rpm at full throttle.
CONTROLS: Three aerodynamic rudders behind the propeller provide directional control.
HULL: Construction is of fir ribs and stringers and ⅛in plywood covering. Fibreglass applied to all joints and edges.
ACCOMMODATION: Tandem arrangement with passenger seated behind driver on a sliding seat.
DIMENSIONS
Length: 3·91m (12ft 10in)
Width: 1·82m (6ft)
Height: 1·52m (5ft)
WEIGHTS
Empty: 147kg (325lb)
Normal payload: 158·75kg (350lb)
Max payload: 204·1kg (450lb)
PERFORMANCE
Max speed, over land: 72·42km/h (45mph)
over water: 56·32km/h (35mph)
Gradient at 450lb gross weight: 23%
PRICE: US$15.

UH-12T

This amphibious two-seater is based on the company's original prototype which was built early in 1969. The new hull is easier to build and provides automatic pitch control. As thrust is increased, the aerofoil-shaped hull generates more lift, offsetting the pitching moment caused by thrust. The height of the centre of thrust has also been reduced.
LIFT AND PROPULSION: Motive power for the lift system is provided by 133cc Chrysler two-cycle petrol engine which drives a 0·66m (2ft 2in) diameter four-bladed fan at 4,500rpm. About five per cent of the cushion air is employed to inflate the bag-type skirt. Thrust is provided by a 25hp JLO 395 two-cycle engine driving a 0·914m (3ft) diameter two-bladed propeller.
CONTROLS: Directional control is provided by a single aerodynamic rudder.
HULL: Mixed wood and fibreglass construction. Structure comprises fir ribs and stringers covered with ⅛in plywood. Cockpit floor and other highly stressed areas strengthened with fibreglass.
ACCOMMODATION: Single bench seat for driver and one passenger. Cockpit canopy can be fitted for use in cold weather.
DIMENSIONS
Length overall: 3·81m (12ft 6in)
Beam overall: 1·82m (6ft)
WEIGHTS
Empty: 124·73kg (275lb)
All-up weight: 272·14kg (600lb)
PERFORMANCE
Max speed, over land: 72·5km/h (45mph)
over water: 64·37km/h (40mph)
Max gradient: 26%
PRICE: Plans US$15 per set.

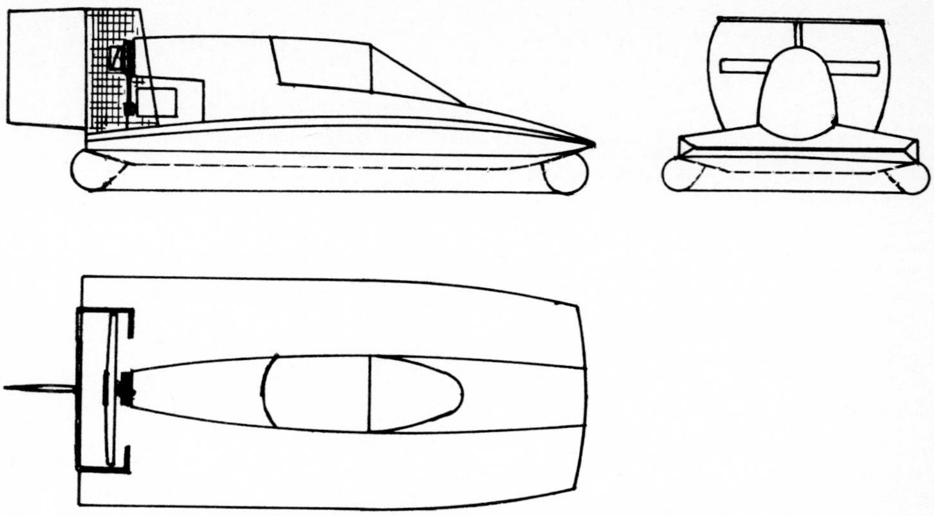

UH-12S a lightweight two-seater for two adults and their camping or fishing equipment

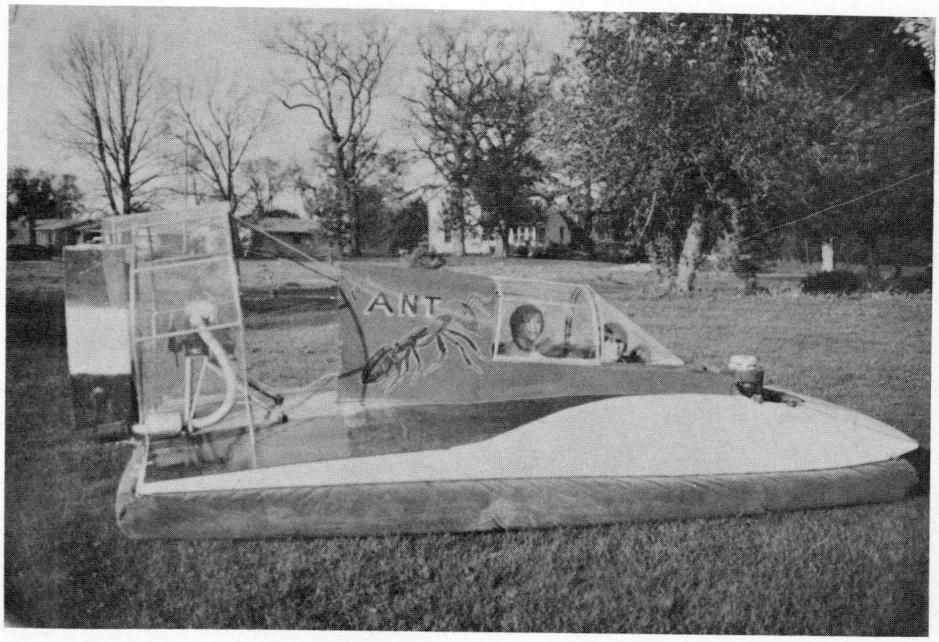

A new 2-3 seater for homebuilders, the UH-12T2 employs two standard lawnmower engines for lift and propulsion

UH-12T2

The latest 2-3 seater to be designed by Universal Hovercraft for the homebuilder, this easily constructed craft is powered by standard lawnmower engines. The low rpm of these engines ensures quiet operation and a long engine life. Construction costs range from US$200 - US$500, depending on the quality of the engines and the materials used.
LIFT AND PROPULSION: Lift is supplied by a 5hp Briggs and Stratton engine driving a 0·6m (24in) diameter, 14in pitch four-bladed wooden fan at 3,000rpm. Maximum cushion pressure is 11lb/ft². Thrust is provided by a 10hp Briggs and Stratton engine driving a 1·06m (42in) diameter, 40cm (16in) pitch two-bladed propeller aft. Total fuel capacity is 6·15 litres (1½ US gallons).
CONTROLS: Triple rudders hinged to the rear of the propeller guard control craft handling.
HULL: Wooden structure built from pine ribs and struts and covered with ⅛in plywood skin. The structure is designed to survive a 64km/h (40mph) plough-in in choppy water.
SKIRT: 177mm (7in) deep, 304mm (12in) diameter bag skirt, fabricated in 16oz/yd² neoprene-coated nylon.
ACCOMMODATION: Enclosed cabin seating driver and up to two passengers on a movable tandem seat.
DIMENSIONS
EXTERNAL
Length overall, power off: 3·93m (12ft 11in)
Beam overall, power off: 1·82m (6ft)
Beam overall, skirt inflated: 2·03m (6ft 8in)
Cushion area: 6·03m² (65ft²)
Skirt depth: 177mm (7in)
INTERNAL
Cabin length: 1·21m (4ft)
Max width: 0·6m (2ft)
WEIGHTS
Normal empty: 136·07kg (300lb)
Normal gross: 272·14kg (600lb)
Normal payload: 136·07kg (300lb)
Max payload: 181·44kg (400lb)
PERFORMANCE
Max speed, calm water: 56·32km/h (35mph)
Max wave capacity: 304mm (12in) chop
Max gradient, static conditions: 12 degrees at 600lb
Vertical obstacle clearance: 152mm (6in)
PRICE: Plans US$15

UH-13SA

The prototype of this craft was built in 1974 from 25mm (1in) thick urethane foam fibreglass laminate. This type of construction proved too difficult for the home builder and so the craft was redesigned for wooden construction. An integrated lift/propulsion system is employed. Once engine speed is above idling the correct amount of lift is automatically maintained throughout the entire engine speed range by a patented system.
LIFT AND PROPULSION: Motive power is provided by a single JLO 440 driving a 0·63m (2ft

1in) diameter four-bladed lift fan and a 1·21m (4ft) diameter propeller via a V-belt reduction drive.
CONTROLS: Craft heading is controlled by twin rudders behind the propeller.
HULL: Construction is similar to that of UH-12T.
ACCOMMODATION: Two adults and two children can be carried in two bench-type seats.
DIMENSIONS
Length: 4·21m (13ft 10in)
Width: 1·98m (6ft 6in)
WEIGHTS
Empty: 181·42kg (400lb)
Normal payload: 181·42kg (400lb)
Max payload: 272·14kg (600lb)
PERFORMANCE
Max speed, over land, snow, ice: 96·56km/h (60mph)
over water: 80·46km/h (50mph)
Max gradient: 26%
PRICE: Complete plans, US$9. Full-scale outline US$3 extra

UH-14B

An amphibious four-seater, the UH-14B has a maximum payload capacity of over 362·85kg (800lb). Employment of a large slow-turning propeller for thrust permits high-speed cruising while generating very little noise.
LIFT AND PROPULSION: A JLO 230 two-cycle engine turns a four-bladed fan for lift. Alternatively, an 8hp vertical shaft lawnmower engine may be used for lift. Thrust is supplied by a JLO 440 two-cycle engine driving a 1·21m (4ft) diameter propeller through a V-belt speed reduction system.
CONTROLS: Heading is controlled by multiple aerodynamic rudders aft of the propeller.
HULL: Construction is of fir or pine ribs and stringers, which are covered with ⅛in plywood.
DIMENSIONS
Length: 4·52m (14ft 10in)
Width: 2·13m (7ft)
Height off cushion: 1·52m (5ft)
WEIGHTS
Empty: 204kg (450lb)
Normal payload: 226·78kg (500lb)
Max payload: 362·85kg (800lb)
PERFORMANCE
Max speed, over land, snow, ice: 96·56km/h (60 mph)
over water: 88·51km/h (55mph)
Max gradient at 650lb gross weight: 28%
PRICE: Complete plans US$14. Full-scale outline US$5.

UH-14T

The UH-14T is a utility two-seater with a cargo hold aft of its bench-type seat. This space may also be used for a rearward facing seat. Total payload capacity is 317·5kg (700lb).
LIFT AND PROPULSION: Lift air is supplied by an 8hp lawnmower engine or a JLO 230cc engine driving a four-bladed 0·66m (2ft 2in) diameter fan. A JLO 440 engine driving a 0·914m (3ft) diameter two-bladed propeller provides thrust.
CONTROLS: Large aerodynamic rudder at rear of propellers controls craft heading.
HULL: Construction is similar to that of the UH-12T.
DIMENSIONS
Length: 4·26m (14ft)
Width: 1·98m (6ft 6in)
Height off cushion: 1·22m (4ft)
WEIGHTS
Empty: 181·42kg (400lb)
Normal payload: 226·78kg (500lb)
Max payload: 317·5kg (700lb)
PERFORMANCE
Max speed, over land, snow, ice: 88·51km/h (55mph)
over water: 72·42km/h (45mph)
Max gradient at 272·14kg (600lb) gross weight: 22%
PRICE: Complete plans, US$14. Full-scale outline, $4.

Structure of the UH-13SA is built in fir or pine ribs and stringers, covered with ⅛in plywood. Top speed over land is 96·56km/h (60mph)

UH-12S, a 72·5km/h (45mph) amphibious two-seater, powered by a single 440cc JLO two-cycle petrol engine

UH-14B, a four-seater with a maximum payload capacity of 362·85kg (800lb)

UH-14T utility two-seater with a total payload capacity of 317·5kg (700lb)

UH-17S

Construction of the prototype UH-17S, which has an integrated lift/propulsion system powered by either a Volkswagen or Corvair engine of 50-140hp, was completed in May 1970. The craft, which seats a driver and up to three passengers, is said to be extremely quiet and control is precise. It is capable of towing water or snow skier, sleds or ski boards.

LIFT AND PROPULSION: A single 75hp Corvair automobile engine drives a 1·06m (3ft 6in) diameter centrifugal fan mounted vertically on a shaft inside a transverse duct. Air is drawn by the fan from each end of the duct. Propulsion air is expelled through outlets at the stern and lift air is ducted into a plenum below. The fan feeds air into the cushion at 240ft³/s and provides 150lb thrust.

ACCOMMODATION: Enclosed cabin seating driver and up to three passengers on two bench-type seats.

DIMENSIONS
Length: 5·43m (17ft 10in)
Beam: 2·41m (7ft 11in)

WEIGHTS
Empty: 430·89kg (950lb)
Normal loaded: 725·71kg (1,600lb)
Max loaded: 861·78kg (1,900lb)

PERFORMANCE
Max speed, over land: 67·59km/h (42mph)
over water: 56-64km/h (35-40mph)
Continuous gradient at 1,200lb: 12%

UH-18S

This was the first hovercraft to complete the journey from Los Angeles to San Diego, a distance of 169·98km (105 miles) across open seas. It accommodates up to seven persons on three bench-type seats. Normal payload is 1,200lb. An automatic lift system similar to that used on the UH-13S is employed to simplify driving, improve reliability and decrease maintenance costs.

LIFT AND PROPULSION: Motive power is supplied by a single Corvair automotive engine, rated at 90hp at 3,600rpm, driving a 0·914m (3ft) diameter four-bladed fan for lift via the automatic lift system, and a 1·87m (6ft 2in) diameter two-bladed propeller through a V-belt speed reduction system. The lift fan turns at a constant 2,400rpm while the propeller turns 1,700rpm at full throttle.

Range of engines which can be used on this craft includes any air-cooled engine from 60-150hp and any four to six cylinder water cooled unit weighing under 181·42kg (400lb).

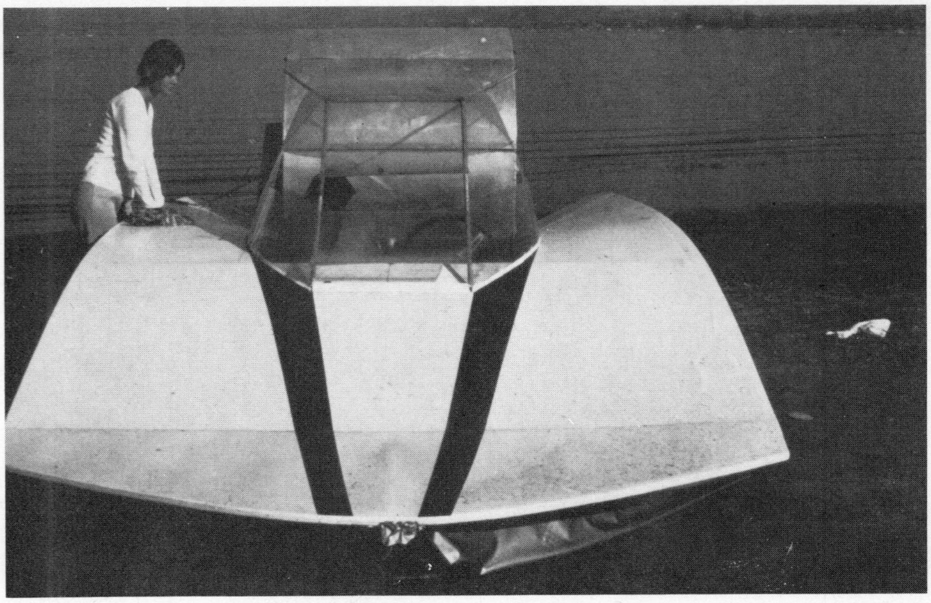

A feature of the UH-17S is the integrated lift/propulsion system powered by a 75hp Corvair automobile engine

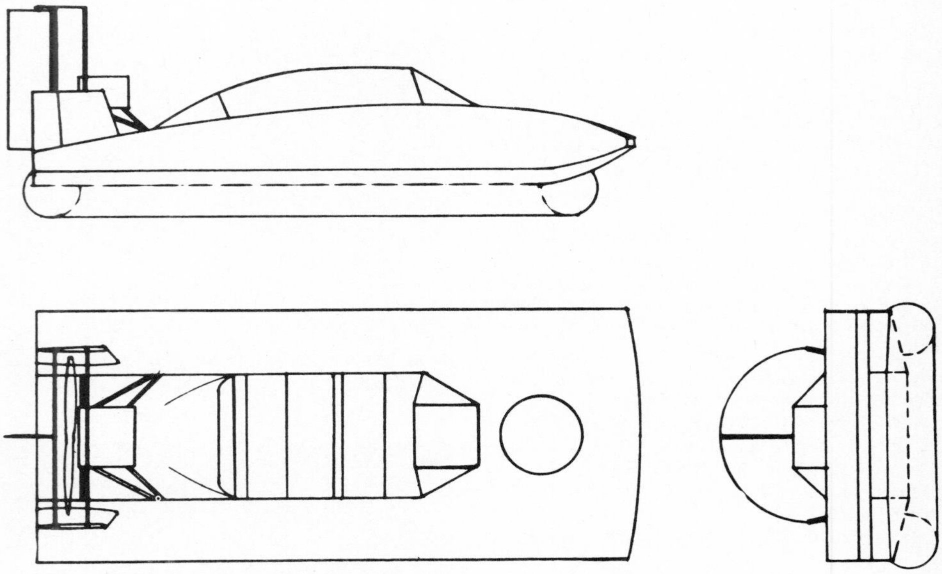

Universal Hovercraft UH-18T, a six seater of mixed wood and grp construction. Propulsive thrust is supplied by an 85hp Corvair engine driving a 1·52m (5ft) diameter two-bladed propeller

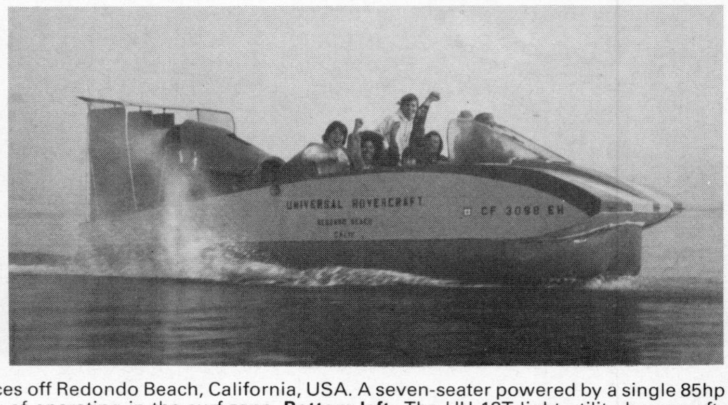

Top left and right and bottom right: Universal Hovercraft UH-18S showing its paces off Redondo Beach, California, USA. A seven-seater powered by a single 85hp Corvair automotive engine, it can tow two water-skiers at a time and is capable of operating in the surf zone. **Bottom left:** The UH-18T light utility hovercraft

CONTROLS: Heading is controlled by triple aerodynamic rudders located behind the propeller.
HULL: Construction is similar to that of the UH-18T.
DIMENSIONS
Length: 5·63m (18ft 6in)
Width: 2·43m (8ft)
Height: 1·82m (6ft)
WEIGHTS
Empty: 498·92kg (1,100lb)
Normal payload: 544·28kg (1,200lb)
Max payload: 635kg (1,400lb)
PERFORMANCE
Max speed, over land, snow, ice: 104·6km/h (65mph)
over water: 88·51km/h (55mph)
Max gradient: 30%
PRICE: Complete plans, US$21. Full-scale outline $5.

UH-18T

The prototype of this amphibious six-seater was built in 1971 and has accumulated over 400 operating hours, mainly on open seas.

It was the first hovercraft to visit Catalina island, 41·84km (26 miles) off the coast of California. It has also been employed extensively for water and snow skiing.

The aerofoil shaped hull is similar to that of the UH-12T and UH-14T.

LIFT AND PROPULSION: Lift is provided by a 25hp JLO 395 two-cycle engine driving a 762mm (2ft 6in) diameter four-bladed fan at 3,200rpm. About 5% of the air is employed to inflate the bag skirt. Propulsive thrust is supplied by an 85hp Corvair automobile engine driving a 1·52m (5ft) diameter two-bladed propeller at up to 2,800rpm.
CONTROLS: Craft heading is controlled by a single rudder operating in the propeller slipstream and two auxiliary rudders hinged to the rear of twin fins, one each side of the propeller guard. All three rudders are operated by a steering wheel. Separate throttles provided for lift and thrust engines.
HULL: Mixed wood and grp construction. Hull frame is built from fir ribs and stringers and covered with ¼in plywood. Highly stressed areas covered with glass fibre.
SKIRT: 0·46m (1ft 6in) diameter bag skirt, providing 0·304m (1ft) vertical clearance.
ACCOMMODATION: Driver and up to five passengers seated on two three-place bench seats. Cabin can be enclosed by canopy in cold weather.
DIMENSIONS
Length: 5·56m (18ft 3in)
Beam: 2·43m (8ft)
Height, off cushion: 1·82m (6ft)
on cushion: 2·13m (7ft)
WEIGHTS
Empty: 453·57kg (1,000lb)
Normal loaded: 907·14kg (2,000lb)
Max loaded: 1,088kg (2,400lb)
PERFORMANCE
Max speed, over land: 104·6km/h (65mph)
over water: 88·5km/h (55mph)
Max gradient: 30%
PRICE: Complete set of plans for homebuilding, US$25, including full-scale outline.

UNIVERSAL 15-SEATER

Universal Hovercraft is completing a 15-seat craft to be powered by a 350in³ V8 automobile engine. The vehicle will be 7·92m (26ft) long by 3·65m (12ft) wide. Ribs and stringers are in fir and pine and the structure is covered with a ¼in plywood skin. The craft was expected to complete its first run during the autumn of 1978. Plans for home builders will be available in June 1979 at US$45 per set.

VENTURE AERO-MARINE

Box 5273, Akron, Ohio 44313, USA
Telephone: (216) 836 8794
Officials:
Paul W Esterle, *Proprietor*

Venture Aero-Marine is a major supplier of kits for homebuilt hovercraft in the United States. It will also supply partially or fully assembled hovercraft, cushion built, to order and offers a wide range of components from engine mountings and fan ducts to skirts and steering systems.

In response to a demand from young enthusiasts who cannot afford full-scale craft, the company offers a line of five radio-controlled and free flight model hovercraft kits.

In addition the company publishes 'The Hoverlog', a comprehensive annual catalogue of sports hovercraft and accessories, currently in its sixth edition.

A Universal Hovercraft UH-18SF built for a client by Venture Aero-Marine. On the right is HA.5-002 which is being restored by the company

WATER RESEARCH COMPANY

3003 North Central Avenue, Suite 600, Phoenix, Arizona 85012, USA
Telephone: (602) 265 7722
Officials:
Richard R Greer, *President*

The Water Research Company was formed in 1972 to consolidate activities surrounding the patents held or applied for by Richard R Greer relating to various aspects of water-borne vehicles. The company has subsequently prepared conceptual studies on a class of winged surface effect vessels (WSEV) intended to fill a variety of US Navy and commercial freight applications. The conclusions of this study were published in *Naval Engineer's Journal,* April 1974, and further comprehensive conclusions also setting forth energy savings and use of alternate fuels were published in *Jane's Surface Skimmers 1975-76.* Present efforts are directed to providing assistance in related research activities and further research studies.

WINDCRAFT M & M INC

1526 Laskey Road, Toledo, Ohio 43612, USA
Officials:
Mike Clare, *President*
Don Collier, *Production Manager, Chief Test Driver*

Windcraft M & M Inc, is one of the few companies in North America involved in the quantity production of "ready-to-fly" sports hovercraft. Production is at present concentrated on the Hurricane, a one-two seat amphibious craft powered by a modified snowmobile engine and capable of 80km/h (35mph) over sand and snow. Hurricane is registered by the US Coast Guard as a Class A boat.

HURRICANE

In 1970 one of these moulded fibreglass sportscraft was the winner of the first national hovercraft race to be staged in the United States. Easy to operate, it is intended primarily to familiarise enthusiasts with the concept of air riding and is one of the fastest-selling, ready-built sports hovercraft in the world.

LIFT AND PROPULSION: Integrated system powered by a single 52hp Zenoah G44BW two-cylinder two-stroke liquid-cooled engine. The engine drives via a toothed belt a 53cm (30in) diameter Windcraft 30 axial lift/thrust fan. Airflow is ducted into the plenum for lift and via two outlets aft for thrust. Maximum static thrust is 34·47kg (76lb) at 3,900rpm.
CONTROLS: Heading is controlled by a single aerodynamic rudder at the base of the fin aft and operated by a handlebar.
HULL: Moulded fibreglass structure comprising top and bottom shells bonded together.
SKIRT: Bag type.
ACCOMMODATION: Open cockpit for up to two seated in tandem.
DIMENSIONS
Length overall: 3·6m (11ft 10in)
Width: 1·75m (5ft 9in)
Height: 1·7m (5ft 7in)
WEIGHTS
Basic: 165·55kg (365lb)
Gross: 360·58kg (795lb)
PERFORMANCE
Max speed, over ice: 80·46km/h (50mph)
short grass: 48·2km/h (30mph)
snow/sand: 56·32km/h (35mph)
water: 48·28km/h (30mph)

Windcraft Hurricane light sports ACV

ACV OPERATORS

BELGIUM
MINISTRY OF WORKS
Antwerp, Belgium

CRAFT OPERATED
HM.2 Mk III 315 "Kallo". Employed as River Scheldt survey craft.

BOLIVIA
HOVERMARINE TRANSPORT TITIKAKA LTD
La Paz, Bolivia

This company operates two specially furnished 30-seater versions of the sidewall HM.2 Mk III hovercraft on Lake Titicaca, between Tiquina Huatajata in Bolivia and Puno, Peru. Lake Titicaca is at an altitude of over 12,500ft above sea level.

BRAZIL
AEROBARCOS DO BRASIL TRANSTOR
This company operates three HM.2 Mk III sidewall hovercraft on a 3n mile route between communities and business areas in the Bay of Guanabara, Rio de Janeiro.

CRAFT OPERATED
HM.2 321 "Gavea"
HM.2 322 "Gragoata"
HM.2 323 "Guarativa"

CANADA
ALBERTA TRANSPORTATION
CRAFT OPERATED
HL-104 vehicle ferry at LaCrete, Alberta

CANADIAN COAST GUARD HOVERCRAFT UNITS
Headquarters: Transport Canada, Canadian Coast Guard, Fleet Systems Branch, Tower A, Place de Ville, Ottawa, Ontario K1A ON5, Canada
Unit Addresses: Canadian Coast Guard Hovercraft Unit, PO Box 23068, AMF Int'l Airport, Vancouver, British Columbia V7N 1T9, Canada
Telephone: (604) 273-2556
Canadian Coast Guard ACV Development and Evaluation Unit, Transport Canada, 850 Nuns Island Boulevard, Nuns Island, Montreal, Quebec H3E 1H2, Canada
Telephone: (514) 283-5841
Administration: Vancouver Unit: Regional Director, Canadian Coast Guard, PO Box 10060, Pacific Centre, 700 West Georgia Street, Vancouver, British Columbia V7Y 1E1, Canada
Montreal Unit: Director, Fleet Systems, Canadian Coast Guard, Transport Canada, Tower A, Place de Ville, Ottawa, Ontario K1A 0N7, Canada

The Canadian Coast Guard Hovercraft Unit in Vancouver was formed on 5 August 1968, to evaluate the use of hovercraft in search and rescue and other Coast Guard duties.

In May 1977, the unit took delivery of a new SR.N6 hovercraft, serial No 039 to boost the search and rescue capabilities.

OPERATIONS: The normal area of patrol is the Straits of Georgia and Gulf Islands — an area of approximately 500 square miles. The unit is often called upon outside this area on search and rescue missions.

The average patrol distance is 80 miles.

Since 1 April 1969, the unit has carried out well over 1,500 SAR missions, directly involving some 5,000 persons. These include marine, aircraft distress and mercy missions. The unit is now manned on a 24-hour basis in order to respond to the large number of incidents occurring in the area.

Other operations included the checking, servicing and repairing of marine navigational aids within the patrol area, transporting men and materials for aids construction and the laying of underground cables in marshy terrain; aircraft accident inspection; water pollution investigation; carriage of Inspectors for spot safety checks of tugs; working with police departments; exercises with the Canadian Armed Forces vessels; training and familiarisation of selected Government personnel, and experimental work with other Government agencies.

EQUIPMENT: One SR.N5 serial No 021, and one SR.N6 No 039, modified to Coast Guard requirements.

Equipment includes navigation and communications equipment, such as radar, HF and VHF direction finder, HF/MF, VHF/FM and VHF/AM radiotelephone, two Nightsun 65 million candle power searchlights, 2 × 6 man inflatable liferafts, 2 × 100 gallon auxiliary fuel tanks (extending endurance to 9 hours at maximum power), stretchers, first aid kit, fire-fighting equipment, towing gear and other SAR equipment.

In January 1974, the CCG took delivery of a refurbished Voyageur 002. This forms the equipment of her Development and Evaluation Unit, whose current task is to evaluate the vehicle in various CCG roles. In order to carry out this evaluation, the Unit may operate in different areas of Canada. For the past three years, it has been based in Montreal.

Of particular significance has been the development of icebreaking techniques using this vehicle, and as result of the past three winters' evaluation, the CCG Voyageur is now accepted as an operational unit for icebreaking in the Montreal area. Ice up to 76cm (30in) thick can be broken at the rate of 2·25km² (1 square mile) per hour, in any water depth, and many rivers have been cleared of ice jams to relieve serious flood threats. In some cases, the jams have been up to 4·75m (16ft) thick.

One Bell Aerospace Voyageur Serial No 002, registration CH-CGA, equipped with all the navigation and communications equipment required for safe operation in her area of work. This craft can carry a portable crew module to enable her crew to stay aboard overnight, if necessary.

SR.N6 operated by the Canadian Coast Guard for search and rescue

Voyageur 002 employed by the Canadian Coast Guard as an operational icebreaking unit in the Montreal area

DEPARTMENT OF ENVIRONMENT AND NATIONAL RESEARCH COUNCIL
CRAFT OPERATED
Towed trailers and air cushion assist transporters undergoing evaluation in logging and heavy transport.

NORTHERN TRANSPORTATION COMPANY LIMITED
Operations Office: 9945-108 Street, Edmonton, Alberta T5K 2G9, Canada
Telephone: (403) 423-9201
Telex: 037-2480
Officials:
S D Cameron, *Chairman of the Board*
L R Montpetit, *President*
W B Hunter, *Vice President Operations*
P L P Macdonnell, *Director*
John H Parker, *Director*
Arthur Kroeger, *Director*
Julien Béliveau, *Director*
Murray Watts, *Director*

A B Caywood, *Director*
Bert W Mead, *Director of Air Cushion Vehicle Operations*

Northern Transportation Company Limited (NTCL) is a wholly-owned subsidiary of Eldorado Nuclear Limited and was formed in 1931. It is Canada's largest Western Arctic marine transportation operator—and serves approximately 4,800 miles of water routes throughout the Mackenzie River Basin and the Western Arctic. The fleet includes three ocean-going ships, 28 diesel tugs, 163 all-steel dual purpose barges with varied capacities up to 1,500 tons, four thruster barges and the fleet has a reported capability of some 750,000 tons of cargo in any one season.

To supplement its Marine, Trucking and Aviation Divisions, NTCL operates two BHC SR.N6 vehicles in the Mackenzie Delta and Beaufort Sea area in support of oil industry activities.

One craft, CH-NTA-031 is a standard passenger version and at the end of the 1975 season had completed in excess of 50,000 miles, all within the Arctic circle. The second machine, CH-NTB, has been modified to enable rapid conversion from passenger to flat-deck configuration.

In flat-deck configuration, a standard payload is approximately 12,000lb, plus four passengers. Its passenger capacity when not converted is 26. Both machines have VHF/AM, VHF/FM, HFSSB, emergency locators, radio compass and radio telephone. A wide variety of support equipment necessitated by the extreme cold is fitted, including dual cabin heating systems. In May 1978 the company announced that it had temporarily suspended ACV operations, due to the lack of oil exploration and development activity in the North.

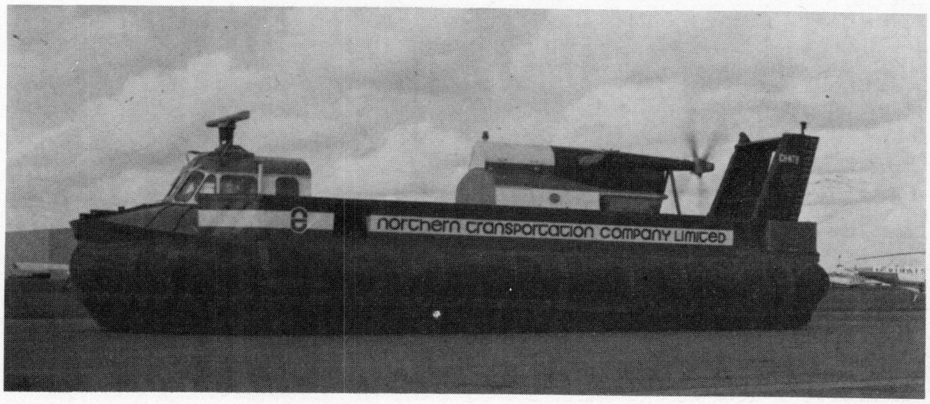

CH-NTB-030, a flat-deck version of the SR.N6, employed by the Northern Transportation Company in the Mackenzie Delta and Beaufort Sea areas in support of oil industry activities

CH-NTA Serno 031, a standard passenger version of the SR.N6 with reinforced extended side decks, carrying two container type mobile workshops

ST LAWRENCE SEAWAY AUTHORITY

CRAFT OPERATED
HL-301 icebreaker platform at Montreal.

EGYPT
EGYPTIAN NAVY

Alexandria, Egypt

In 1975 the Egyptian Navy purchased three refurbished SR.N6 hovercraft for coastal defence patrols along the Egyptian coastline. Negotiations for three BH.7 hovercraft for similar duties are in progress with BHC.

CRAFT OPERATED
SR.N6 016
SR.N6 032
SR.N6 034

FINLAND
PINTALIITÄJÄPALVELU (HOVERCRAFT SERVICE)

Paattistentie 141, SF-20360 Turku 36, Finland

CRAFT OPERATED
Amficat 4, M/S Pinturi
Route(s): Year-round taxi service to islands in the Turku archipelago. Licensed by Finnish Board of Navigation for passenger services. 11,000km (6,214 miles) completed by early summer 1978 in 1,300 operations.

FRANCE
FRENCH NAVY

Toulon, France

CRAFT OPERATED
2 × N.102

FRENCH RAILWAYS (SNCF)

Operating in conjunction with British Rail Hovercraft Ltd, SNCF began operating the N.500-02 "Ingénieur Jean Bertin" under the Seaspeed banner on 5 July 1978. SNCF also holds an option on a second craft. N.500-02 operates on both the Boulogne-Dover and Calais-Dover services. Various difficulties experienced in the operation of the N.500 in the initial stages are expected to be remedied by the time the craft returns to cross-channel operations in the spring of 1979.

LANGUEDOC-ROUSSILLON REGIONAL DEVELOPMENT BOARD

Montpellier and Perpignan, France

CRAFT OPERATED
2 × N.102

GREECE
HELLENIC HOVERCRAFT LINES ("HOVERLINES")

Piraeus, Greece

Executive:
A N Vomvoyiannis, *Managing Director*

CRAFT OPERATED
HM.2 Mk III 304 "Natouro 2"
Route(s): Piraeus-Hydra-Spetsai-Porto Heli

HONG KONG
HONG KONG AND YAUMATI FERRY CO LTD

This company, which is the biggest operator of passenger ferry hovercraft in the world, has a fleet of eight HM.2s, with a further two on order.

CRAFT OPERATED
HM.2-326 (Mk III) (HYF-101)
327 (Mk III) (HYF-102)
328 (Mk III) (HYF-103)
329 (Mk III) (HYF-104)
HM.2-435 (Mk IV) (HYF-105)
443 (Mk IV) (HYF-106)
445 (Mk IV) (HYF-107)
446 (Mk IV) (HYF-108)
447 (Mk IV) (HYF-109)
448 (Mk IV) (HYF-110)

The latter two craft are on order and due for delivery in early 1979. As of 17 November 1978 a service was opened between Hong Kong and Canton (PRC) using two Hovermarine HM.2 Mk IV craft. It is anticipated that up to five HM.2 Mk IV craft will be employed on this route. The company has received a licence to operate this service for up to five years.

INDIA
CITY AND INDUSTRIAL DEVELOPMENT CORP OF MAHARASHTRA LTD

Nirmal, 2nd Floor, Nariman Point, Bombay 40001, India
Telephone: 294515 (9 lines)
Telegrams: CITWIN
Officials:
M N Palwankar, *Manager, Town Services*

CRAFT OPERATED
HM.2 Mk III 214 "Jalapriya"
Route(s): Between Greater Bombay and New Bombay, linking Apollo Bunder and Ferry Wharf with Uran and Elephanta.

IRAN
IMPERIAL IRANIAN NAVY

Hovercraft base: Khosrowabad, Iran

Eight BHC Winchesters are being operated by the Imperial Iranian Navy on logistics duties and coastal patrol.

Also in service with the IIN are six BH.7 hovercraft. The first two craft, BH.7 Mk 4s, are operated in the logistic support role. The remaining four are Mk 5s. The Mk 5 is a multi-role craft and is designed to carry surface-surface, surface-air missiles on its side decks.

CRAFT OPERATED:
SR.N6 040 (IIN 01) Mark 4
SR.N6 041 (IIN 02) Mark 4
SR.N6 042 (IIN 03) Mark 3
SR.N6 043 (IIN 04) Mark 3
SR.N6 044 (IIN 05) Mark 4
SR.N6 045 (IIN 06) Mark 4
SR.N6 046 (IIN 07) Mark 4
SR.N6 047 (IIN 08) Mark 4
BH.7 002 (IIN 101) Mk 4
BH.7 003 (IIN 102) Mk 4
BH.7 004 (IIN 103) Mk 5

BH.7 005 (IIN 104) Mk 5
BH.7 006 (IIN 105) Mk 5
BH.7 007 (IIN 106) Mk 5

ISRAEL
ISRAELI NAVY

The Israeli Navy has two SH.2 Mk 5 nine-seater hovercraft for use as support craft.

ITALY
ITALIAN INTERFORCE UNIT

Ancona, Italy

CRAFT OPERATED
SR N6 036 (HC 9801)

JAPAN
BIWAKO KISEN CO LTD

CRAFT OPERATED
HM.2Mk III 63P
Route(s): Hamaohotsu-Biwako Ohohashi (15km)

JAPANESE NATIONAL RAILWAYS

Kokutetsu Building, 6—5 Marunouchi 1-chome, Chiyoda-ku, Tokyo, Japan

A service between Uno in Okayama Prefecture and Takamatsu in Kagawa Prefecture was inaugurated in November 1972, using MV-PP5-07, named "Kamome" (Sea Gull). Route distance is 20km; journey time 23 minutes. Craft has an annual utilisation of 1,800 hours.

KYUSHU YUSEN CO LTD

CRAFT OPERATED
HM.2 Mk IV 93P
Route(s): Hakata-Iki Island (73km). Opened 8 July 1978.

MEITETSU KAIJO KANKOSEN K K

99-1 Shin-myiazaka-cho, Atsuta-ku, Nagoya, Japan

Began regular services across the Mikawa and Ise Bays between Gamagori and Toba in September 1969 with an intermediate stop at Nishin. The craft employed is MV-PP5 14, Angel 3. Craft operates three routes: Gamagoori to Nishiura, Nishiura to Isako, 28km (30mins), and Toba, 23·2km (20mins). Annual utilisation, 300 hours for two months only each year.

NIPPON KAI KANKO FERRY CO LTD

This company began operating two PP15s, PP15-01 Cygnus and PP15-02 Cygnus No 1, in April 1978. These craft, one of which is used as a reserve, operate for six months each year (April to October) with an annual utilisation of about 1,500 hours per craft.
Route(s): Manao-Ogi, 150km (2 hours 15 mins); Ogi Suzu, 105km (1 hour 25 mins); Suzu-Manao, 60km (50 mins).

OITA HOVERFERRY CO LTD

1-14-1 Nishi-shinchi, Oita, Japan

Oita operates four MV-PP5s, 03, 04, 06 and 10 named Hakucho 3, Hobby 1 and 3, and Angel 2. Two craft are normally operated with two in reserve.
Route(s): Oita Airport to Oita City, 29km (24 mins), Oita Airport to Beppu City, 31km (26 mins), Oita City to Beppu City, 12km (10 mins). Annual utilisation, about 1,500 hours per craft.

YAEYAMA KANKO FERRY K K

No 1 Aza-ohkawa, Ishigaki, Okinawa, Japan

Delivered to her owners in the spring of 1972, MV-PP5 08—"Koryu"—operates a service linking Ishigaki with Taketomi, 6·5km (5 mins); Ishigaki to Obama, 19km (15 mins); Ishigaki to Kuroshima, 18·5km (20 mins); Ohara to Obama, 28km (20 mins); Ohara to Kuroshima, 14·5km (10 mins). Annual utilisation, about 1,800 hours.

Two of the four Mitsui MV-PP5 hovercraft operated by Oita Hoverferry Co Ltd between Oita Airport, Oita and Beppu cities

NETHERLANDS
ROTTERDAM PORT AUTHORITY

In April 1978 it was announced that the Rotterdam Port Authority had ordered four Hovermarine 218 Port Patrol Craft in a contract valued at approximately Fl 11 million (£1·7 million). The craft, which have the serial numbers 449, 450, 451 and 452, are based on the standard 18m (60ft) long 218 hull, with provision for port monitoring and emergency services in two separate superstructure modules. Each craft will have a closed circuit television camera mounted on a telescopic mast to enable on-watch personnel to scan ships' deck. The craft are due to be delivered in the spring of 1979.

NEW ZEALAND
DEPARTMENT OF CIVIL AVIATION

The New Zealand Department of Civil Aviation is operating one SR.N6 Winchester for crash rescue services at Mangere Airport, Auckland.
CRAFT OPERATED
SR.N6 014 "Whakatopa"

NORTH SHORE FERRIES

HM.2 319, "Whakatere", is operated by this company between Waiheke Island and Auckland, North Island. Service began in March 1978.

NIGERIA
PIPELINE CONTRACTORS INCORPORATED

CRAFT OPERATED
Sealand SH.2 007. The operator of this craft is an oil exploration company and the craft assists in this activity.

FEDERAL MINISTRY OF TRANSPORT (IND)

19th Floor, Western House, Broad Street, Lagos, Nigeria

This company operates a high-frequency passenger ferry service between Calabar and Oron, across the Calabar river, from 7 am to 7 pm daily. Distance, 15n miles. Load factor, 73-90%.
CRAFT OPERATED
Two HM.2 Mk IVs and one HM.2 Mk III.

PAKISTAN

The Pakistan Coast Guard authority has purchased two SH.2 five or six seat craft for patrol and interception duties.
CRAFT EMPLOYED
SH.2 009
SH.2 010

PHILIPPINES
BATAAN-MANILA FERRY SERVICES CO

Manila, Philippines

This company, which also owns a Raketa hydrofoil, has three HM.2 Mk III sidewall hovercraft for passenger ferry service between central Manila and the Island of Corregidor. Services to other parts of Manila Bay are also offered.
CRAFT OPERATED:
HM.2-320
332
336

PORTUGAL
SOCIEDADE TURISTICA PONTA DO ADOXE SARL

Avenida Casal Ribeiro 46-6, Lisbon, Portugal
CRAFT OPERATED
HM.2 Mk III 301 "Torralta"
HM.2 Mk III 308 "Soltroia"
HM.2 Mk III 316 "Troiamar"
HM.2 Mk III 318 "Troiano"
Route(s): Setubal-Troia/Sesimbra

SAUDI ARABIA
SAUDI ARABIAN COASTAL AND FRONTIER GUARD

Ministry of the Interior, Airport Road, Riyadh, Saudi Arabia

The Saudi Arabian Coastal and Frontier Guard operates a number of SR.N6 Winchesters on patrol, contraband control, search and rescue and liaison duties. The craft are attached to bases at Jeddah and Aziziyah on the east and west coasts. Negotiations are in progress for the supply of craft of larger capacity than the existing SR.N6s.
CRAFT OPERATED
SR.N6 038
SR.N6 048
SR.N6 049
SR.N6 050
SR.N6 051
SR.N6 052
SR.N6 053
SR.N6 054

UNION OF SOVIET SOCIALIST REPUBLICS
MINISTRY OF THE RIVER FLEET

The 50-seat Sormovich ACV has been operating experimental services on the Volga and Oka rivers and a derivative is expected to go into production. The most widely used commercial ACV at present is the 48-50 seat Zarnitsa sidewall craft, one hundred of which have been introduced into service since 1970. This is being followed into production by the enlarged, 80-seat Orion and the Chaika-1, thirty of which are being built at Sosnovska for the Black Sea Shipping Line.

Well over one hundred Zarya air-lubricated hull craft have been completed and many of these are in service on shallow rivers in the eastern areas of the Soviet Union. Wing-in-ground-effect machines are being developed for high-speed ferry services along the main rivers. These are described as being capable of travelling within several metres of the river surface at speeds of some 250km/h (155mph).

SOVIET ARMY

A military version of the Skate 50-seat fast ferry is in service with the Soviet Army.

SOVIET NAVY

Several experimental ACVs are being evaluated by the Soviet Navy, and a military version of the Skate which bears the Nato codename "Gus", is entering service in growing numbers with the Soviet marine infantry as an assault landing craft. Largest craft in service is the 220-ton "Aist", similar in many respects to the SR.N4 Mountbatten and employed to carry tanks and mechanised infantry. Some fifteen have been built and a number are in service in the eastern Baltic.

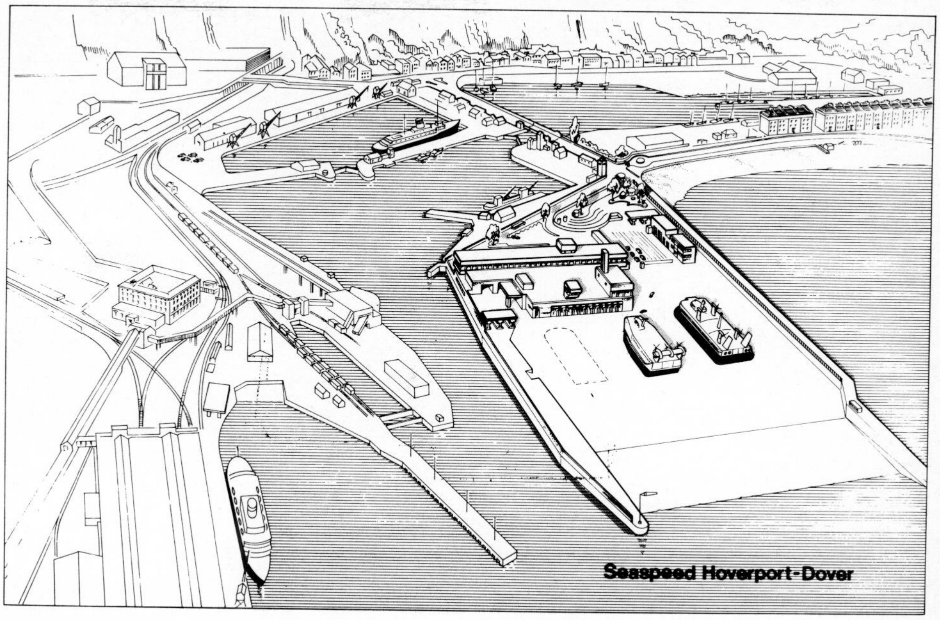

Above and below: British Rail's new hovercraft terminal, Western Docks, Dover

UNITED KINGDOM

BRITISH RAIL HOVERCRAFT LIMITED

(Seaspeed Hovercraft)

Head Office: Royal London House, 22/25 Finsbury Square, London EC2P 2BQ, England
Telephone: 01-628 3050
Telex: 883339
Representation Overseas: SNCF, Armement Naval, 3 rue Ambroise, Paré, 75010 Paris, France
Dover Route Headquarters: Seaspeed Hoverport, Western Docks, Dover, England
Telephone: 0304 203574
Telex: 965079
Reservations: Maybrook House, Queens Gardens, Dover CT1Y 9UH, England
Telephone: 01-606 3681
Telex: 96158
Officials:
J M Bosworth, CBE, *Chairman*
J M Lefeaux, *Managing Director*
D D Kirby, *Director*
A J Tame, *Marketing Director*
P A Yerbury, *Chief Engineer*
D H C. Sumner, *Finance Manager*
Captain D Meredith, *Operations Manager*

British Rail Hovercraft Ltd, a wholly-owned subsidiary of British Railways Board, was formed in March 1966 and launched its first commercial service in July 1966, between Southampton and Cowes. The cross-channel service for passengers and cars between specially constructed hovercraft terminals at Dover and Boulogne began in August 1968 using an SR.N4 "The Princess Margaret". A year later the service was augmented by the introduction of a sister craft. "The Princess Anne" and in October 1970 a service was initiated between Dover and Calais.

During 1978 the first of the two stretched SR.N4 Mk III craft came into operation. "The Princess Anne", formerly a Mk 1 craft has had a 55ft midships section inserted at the British Hovercraft Corporation's factory at Cowes, Isle of Wight. Now the largest hovercraft in the world, it is driven by four uprated Marine Proteus gas turbine engines of 3,800shp, each driving a fan unit and a 6·4m (21ft) propeller. Craft motion is considerably less than that experienced on the standard N4, and operating limitations have been extended to cope with wave conditions 2ft higher. Passenger comfort has also been improved by incorporating the car deck cabins into large, outward facing passenger decks. The finish and trim in these widened compartments has been completely re-designed, with new overhead ventilation, underseat heating, improved hand luggage storage and lighting. A new and improved skirt design with lower pressure ratio featuring deeper fingers and increased air cushion depth at the bow has improved passenger comfort and will result in faster crossing times in adverse weather. Completion of the 'stretching' of Seaspeed's second N4, "The Princess Margaret", will be completed by the summer of 1979.

A new era in cross-Channel hovercraft operations began in July 1978 when Seaspeed took delivery of the French-built SEDAM N.500-02. The craft, operated by SNCF (French Railways) flies under the Seaspeed banner. When British Rail's SR.N4 "The Princess Margaret" rejoins the fleet in 1979 after being 'stretched, Seaspeed's three jumbo hovercraft will provide an annual total carrying capacity for three million passengers and 400,000 vehicles. To accommodate this increased traffic of two stretched SR.N4s and one French SEDAM N.500 craft, a new purpose built terminal complex was opened in 1978, situated on 15 acres of reclaimed land between the Prince of Wales Pier and the North Pier in Western Docks, Dover. Completely independent of the conventional ferry operations it contains its own passport control and immigration services. Designed on an airport style principle, passengers arrive via a landscaped terminal approach and enter a spacious arrival concourse. Facilities include duty and tax free shops, licenced bars, cafeterias and a nursing mothers room. Motorists check into a multi-lane arrival area with space for 178 cars.

DEPARTMENT OF INDUSTRY

CRAFT OPERATED
HM.2 Mk III 310 (GH 2051)

Operated by the National Maritime Institute as a support craft for marine trials and operations. The HM.2 is based on the Lymington River.

HOVERLLOYD LIMITED

Ramsgate Office: International Hoverport, Sandwich Road, Ramsgate, Kent, England
Telephone: 0843 54881/55555, 4999481
Telex: 96323
Registered and Head Office: Board of Chief Executive, Sales Administration, 49 Charles Street, London W1X 8AE, England
Telephone: 01-493 5525
Telex: 262374
Officials:
Ingemar Blennow, *(Swedish), Chairman*
James A Hodgson, *Deputy Chairman and Managing Director*
James W Clement, *Director*
Folke Kristensen, *(Swedish) Director*
Howard V Archdeacon, *Associate Director*
Robert H Harvey, *Associate Director*
Emrys Jones, *Associate Director*
Andrew Ramsay, *Associate Director*
David Wise, *Associate Director*

Hoverlloyd was formed by two shipping companies, Swedish Lloyd and Swedish American Line (now both members of the Broström group) to operate a cross-Channel car and passenger ferry service between Ramsgate and Calais. The company operates four BHC SR.N4 Mk II widened Mountbattens.

The crossing between Ramsgate and Calais takes 40 minutes and there are up to twenty-seven return trips a day in summer and a minimum of four a day in winter. On 1 May 1969, the company opened coach/hovercraft/coach services between London and Paris. This service takes eight hours. There are up to five daily departures during summer and two during winter.

On 1 April 1974, Hoverlloyd opened coach/hovercraft/coach services between London/Kortrijk and Brussels. The service takes seven hours to Brussels. There are up to four daily services in the summer peak and a daily departure is maintained year-round.

Passengers are able to buy tickets from travel agents, or by making a booking direct from Hoverlloyd ticket office, 8 Berkeley Square, London W1 and at any Hoverlloyd terminal. Those travelling with a car pay only for their car, according to its length. The car charge covers the driver and up to four passengers. For vehicles there are four tariffs; 'A', 'B', 'C' and 'D'. 'A' tariff is more expensive and is applied in peak hours during summer, in either direction, according to a detailed traffic analysis, 'B' and 'C' tariffs are cheaper and account for the balance of the departures listed for the summer. The 'D' tariff applies throughout the year on selected flights.

The tariffs have been designed to encourage a balance in the origin of cross-Channel traffic, and to spread the daily peaks of traffic.

The company's hoverport covers 12½ acres below the cliffs at the north end of Pegwell Bay, Ramsgate. The site is raised 8ft above the level of the beach, so that operations are not affected by tides. It consists of a group of long low buildings running parallel to the cliffs. Between the buildings and the cliffs is a car park and the car reception area which is joined to the main Ramsgate-Sandwich road by an access road built up the cliff face.

In front of the building is a large square concrete apron with a semi-circular ramp extending at one end. The SR.N4 makes the most convenient approach, parks on the apron in front of the building while it loads and unloads, then departs from the most suitable point.

These buildings contain the main passenger and car terminal area which includes the inspection halls for customs and immigration, duty free shops, cafe, bar, restaurant, banks and other passenger facilities. Next to this area are the administrative offices.

CRAFT OPERATED:
SR.N4 002 GH 2004 "Swift"
SR.N4 003 GH 2005 "Sure"
SR.N4 005 GH 2008 "Sir Christopher"
SR.N4 006 GH 2054 "Prince of Wales"

HOVERTRAVEL LIMITED

Head Office: 12 Lind Street, Ryde, Isle of Wight, England
Telephone: 0983 65181
Telex: 86513-Hoverwork
Terminal Offices: Quay Road, Ryde, Isle of Wight (Tel: 0983 65241); Clarence Pier, Southsea (Tel: 29988)

Officials
E W H Gifford, *Chairman*
D R Robertson, *Director*
C D J Bland, *Chief Executive and Managing Director*
J Gaggero, *Director*
J M Youens, *Director*
A C Smith, *Director*
R G Clarke, *Director and General Manager*
G Palin, *Company Secretary*

Hovertravel Limited is a £120,000 company which was formed in 1965 to operate two SR.N6 Winchester hovercraft across the Solent between Ryde, Isle of Wight and Southsea and Gosport. The Gosport route was discontinued some years ago but the company has for the past three years assumed responsibility for the operation of the Cowes to Southampton hovercraft ferry service under the name Solent Seaspeed.

Swift, one of four BHC SR.N4 Mk II widened Mountbattens operated by Hoverlloyd between Ramsgate and Calais

Journey time is approximately 7 minutes on the Ryde to Southsea route and 20 minutes between Cowes and Southampton. Approximately 620,000 passengers are carried each year on both routes together with many tons of parcel packages. By September 1978 the total number of passengers carried exceeded 5 million.

The combined fleet operated by Hovertravel, Hoverwork and Solent Seaspeed, which during 1978 completed an estimated 8,000 hours of operation, includes:

3 SR.N6 Winchester Class Mk1S hovercraft GH2035, GH2014, GH2015; 3 SR.N6 Winchester Class Mk1 hovercraft GH2010, GH2012, GH2013; 1 SR.N6 Winchester Class Mk1 freighter GH2011.

SOME TYPICAL HOVERWORK OPERATIONS

Year	*Location*	*Type of Operation*	*Type of Terrain*
1969	Holland—the Waddenzee	Seismic survey	Shallow water, tidal area with large expanses of sand banks at low water
1969/70	Abu Dhabi	Seismic survey	Very shallow water combined with coral reefs
1970	Bahrain	Gravity survey	Shallow water and operations over coral reefs
1970	Holland—the Waddenzee	Seismic survey	Shallow water, tidal area with large expanses of sand banks at low water
1970	Tunisia—Sfax	Seismic survey	Very shallow water
1970	Algiers	Passengers	Transport from Algiers Port to Fair site including half a mile down a specially prepared road
1971	Bahrain	Seismic survey	Shallow water and operations over coral reefs
1971	Saudi Arabia—Red Sea	Seismic survey	Very shallow water combined with coral reefs
1971	Holland—the Waddanzee	Seismic survey	Shallow water, tidal area with large expanses of sand banks at low water
1971	Holland—Dollard Bay	Service drilling rig	Shallow water, tidal area. 3 miles of sand to cross at low water
1971	Arctic Circle	Logistics	In leads of pack ice over shallow water including plateau of rock with depths from 0·5 to 6 feet
1971	England—North Sea Haisbro & Leman Banks	Seismic survey	Very shallow water in places, moving sand banks with various tidal streams. Total area strewn with wrecks rendering it unsafe and impractical to use boats
1972	Tunisia—Sfax	Seismic survey	Very shallow water and shoreline land work
1972	North West Territories, Canada	Seismic survey	Shallow water, ice
1972	UK—The Wash	Logistics	Mud, shallow water
1973	UK—Maplin Sands	Geological survey for London's third airport	Tidal sands, shallow water
1974 through '75 to '76	Saudi Arabia	Seismic survey	Shallow water, reefs, uncharted areas
1975	Australia—Thursday Island	Casualty evacuation and general transport	Shallow water and reefs. No conventional docking facilities
1975	UK—The Wash	Transportation of men and materials	Tidal areas half mud half water
1976	UK	Seismic survey	Tidal area of Liverpool Bay and Blackpool
1976	Algiers	Passengers	Transport from Algiers Port to Fair Site including half a mile down a specially prepared road
1977	United Arab Emirates	Seismic survey	Very shallow water combined with coral reefs and sand bars
1978	United Arab Emirates	Seismic survey	Very shallow water combined with coral reefs and sand bars

HOVERWORK LIMITED

(Wholly owned subsidiary of Hovertravel Limited)

12 Lind Street, Ryde, Isle of Wight, England
Telephone: 0983 65181
Telex: 86513
Officials:
C D J Bland, *Managing Director*
D R Robertson, *Director*
E W H Gifford, *Director*
A C Smith, *Director*
R G Clarke, *Director*

Hoverwork Limited is a subsidiary of Hovertravel Limited and was formed in 1966. The company provides crew training and charter facilities for all available types of ACVs, thus bridging the gap between the operators and manufacturers.

The company has trained over 50 hovercraft captains and has received some 40 charter contracts, including film sequences and the operation of the SR.N6 craft for mineral surveys all over the world. The company operated the hovercraft passenger service during Expo' 67 at Montreal and a service at the 1970 and 1976 Algiers Expositions.

Hoverwork is the largest international operator of hovercraft, having access to Hovertravel's 38-seater SR.N6. Hoverwork has undertaken operations in areas from the Arctic to the equator. These have included logistics operations in the northern part of Svalbard and in equatorial parts of South America. To date Hoverwork has operated in the following areas: Canada, South America, Mexico, Brunei, Netherlands, Bahrain, Kuwait, the Trucial States, Saudi Arabia, Algeria, Tunisia, English North Sea, Spitzbergen and Australia.

During 1977, the company conducted operations in the United Arab Emirates.

INTERNATIONAL HOVERSERVICES LIMITED

Head Office: 138 Rownhams Lane, North Baddesley, Southampton, Hampshire SO5 9LT, England
Telephone: 0703 732588
Registered Office: 6 Rockstone Place, Southampton, Hampshire SO1 2EP, England
Operating Base: No 28 Berth, Old Docks, Southampton, Hampshire, England
Telephone: 0703 23068
Officials:
Lieutenant-Commander M D Dawson, RN MNI, *Chairman & Joint Managing Director*
Captain A S Hands, MRIN MNI, *Chief Executive & Joint Managing Director*
G W Black, *Director*
L R Colquhoun, DFC, GM, DFM, *Director*
Commander J R B Montanaro, RN, *Director*
Mrs E Hands, *Secretary & Alternate Director*

International Hoverservices Limited began operations in July 1970, between Bournemouth and Swanage, and since then has operated various scheduled and charter services in the Solent and Poole Bay areas. Since June 1971 the company has provided craft for a daily industrial commuter service for Vosper Shipbuilding Limited between Cowes, Isle of Wight, and its shipyard in Southampton. For the last three seasons the company has provided a craft on charter to Hovercross Limited, Jersey, Channel Islands for a summer service during the high water period between Gorey (Jersey) and Cartaret (France).

The company has provided training and personnel for Hovercross (France) Limited and its associated company, Hoverazur of Nice.

The company can provide craft for charter and a consultancy and training service for prospective operators.

CRAFT OPERATED
HM.2 Mark III, Nos 303, 305 & 312

NAVAL HOVERCRAFT TRIALS UNIT

HMS Daedalus, Lee-on-the-Solent, Hampshire PO13 9NY, England
Telephone: 0705 550143

An SR.N6 of the Royal Navy's Naval Hovercraft Trials Unit, (NHTU) accompanied by the unit's BH.7 Mk IV, which now incorporates a sweep deck on the port side

Commanding Officer: Commander P B Reynolds, OBE, RN

The Naval Hovercraft Trials Unit has been evaluating hovercraft in naval roles since 1975. The trials have been concerned mainly with mine countermeasures and amphibious assault and logistics.

Mine countermeasures trials are largely complete and the Ministry of Defence is now debating the future of hovercraft in this role. The NHTU has undertaken numerous trials in the amphibious assault and logistics role. Several exercises have also been completed assessing the feasibility of using hovercraft in support of amphibious operations. During 1977-78 the unit also evaluated the Vosper VT2-001.

CRAFT OPERATED
SR.N6 XV 859
SR.N6 XV 615
SR.N6 XV 617
BH.7 XW 255—modified to Mk IV version embodying bow door, sweep deck and Sea Rider with davit.

SOLENT SEASPEED

British Rail Hovercraft Ltd ceased to operate the Cowes/Southampton Hovercraft service on 1 May 1976 and Hovertravel Ltd, trading as Solent Seaspeed, commenced operating this route on 2 May 1976 using two SR.N6 Mk 1S hovercraft GH.2014 and GH.2015.

UNITED STATES OF AMERICA

COMMONWEALTH OF MASSACHUSETTS

Boston, Massachusetts, USA

After refurbishing, the first US-built Hovermarine HM.2 Mk3 sidewall hovercraft, 3001, has been sold to the Commonwealth of Massachusetts and is now based at Boston. The craft will be used by Boston municipal authorities for the evaluation of routes in the Boston area.

SURFACE EFFECT SHIP ACQUISITION PROJECT

PO Box 34401, Bethesda, Maryland 20034, USA

The Naval Air Station, Patuxent River, Maryland, is the site of the Surface Effect Ship Test Facility. A boat house, 'syncrolift' drydock and other SES-related support facilities provide the US Navy with an installation for the operation, test and evaluation of the SES-100A and B as well as other smaller test craft.

CITY OF TACOMA

The first of two Hovermarine 221 multi-role harbour service craft is to be delivered to the City of Tacoma, Washington State in July 1979. Based on a Hovermarine 200 series hull, it will be equipped with a wide range of firefighting, rescue, navigational and communications equipment. It is designed to cope with both ship and harbour installation fires. Confirmation of the order for the second craft will be placed on the acceptance of the first craft.

UNITED STATES ARMY

In 1972, a Bell SK-5 Model 7255 of the US Army's Cold Region Research Laboratory, Hanover, New Hampshire, was operated in Alaska for extended tests over varying arctic terrain and waterways. In early 1973, the SK-5 was shipped to the US Army's Weapons Command, St Louis, Missouri, for continued operations. In July 1976, the Bell LACV-30-001 was undergoing builder's trials at Fort Story, Virginia, and 002 was under test at Aberdeen Proving Ground, Maryland.

The Bell Viking underwent tests by the US Army Cold Regions Research and Engineering Laboratories at Toronto Island Airport in the autumn of 1975.

URUGUAY

BELT SA

A service was started in 1978 between Colonia, Uruguay and Buenos Aires, Argentina, a distance of about 30n miles across the River Plate. The craft is HM.2 Mk IV 442 and the company holds an option on a second craft.

VENEZUELA

TURISMO MARGARITA CA

This operator has a fleet of three HM.2 hovercraft which are used on services between the Isla de Margarita and Puerto la Cruz on the Venezuelan mainland. The HM.2 takes two hours for the 55 mile long journey.

CRAFT OPERATED
HM.2 325 "Kenndy"
HM.2 330 "Kenna"
HM.2 331 "Kelly"

ZAIRE

SOCIETE MINIERE DE BAKWANGA

Mbujimayi, R C Lulubourg 10,424, Zaire
CRAFT OPERATED
CC.7 002

ACV TRAILERS
AND
HEAVY LIFT SYSTEMS

AUSTRALIA

TAYLORCRAFT TRANSPORT (DEVELOPMENT) PTY LTD

Parafield Airport, South Australia 5106, Australia
Telephone: (08) 258 4944
Officials:
R V Taylor, *Director*
J Taylor, *Director*
R J Lommon, *Director*
G Nimmo, *Director*
G A Barnes, *Director*

Taylorcraft has recently introduced its Liftaire skirt system for lifting and moving bulky loads and the Trailaire range of ACV trailers with load capacities from 1¼ to 10 tons.

LIFTAIRE SYSTEM

Taylorcraft Liftaire industrial skirt system was employed for the first time at the Swan Brewery, Canning Vale, Perth, Australia early in 1977, when it was used to move 22 stainless steel holding tanks 150m (164yds) from the point of their construction to their final operating position. Each tank weighs about 30 tonnes and has a capacity of about two million cans of beer.

After the on-site fabrication of each tank a one-piece skirt was wrapped around the base and sealed by air pressure. Air was then blown into the tank which floated about 5cm above the floor, permitting it to be moved with relatively little effort.

Cushion pressures of up to 634·72kg/m² (130lb/ft²) of base area can be accommodated by this system which requires minimal fixing to its load. It is thus ideal for moving tanks and other vessels, transportable buildings, damaged aircraft and other bulky or fragile loads.

Once the load is lifted it may be winched or towed over almost any reasonable level surface. Movement on slopes is feasible but requires special precautions as do movements involving loads with a high centre of gravity or asymmetric weight distribution. Very low pulling forces are required on the level and there is complete control for positioning.

The skirt system is easily attached to and detached from most loads, making it ideal for situations where a number of loads are to be moved and for use where space is restricted.

Quotations are given for any task and are usually made in four parts:

1. skirt system: this may be purchased outright or leased for an operation;
2. air system: a blower unit and its controls are mounted on a trailer and designed to match the load. This may be leased, if a suitable unit is available, or designed and built for a specific task;
3. setting up (first operation only): this involves attendance at the site and return fares from Adelaide, together with freight costs involved;
4. local assistance: a compressor or air line, winch(es), towing vehicle and/or tackle and unskilled labour will be required at the site.

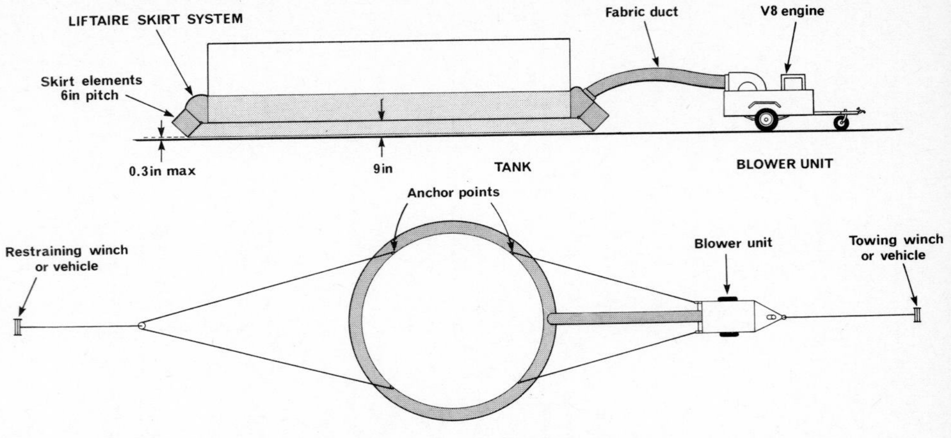

Diagram showing a typical application of the Liftaire industrial skirt system

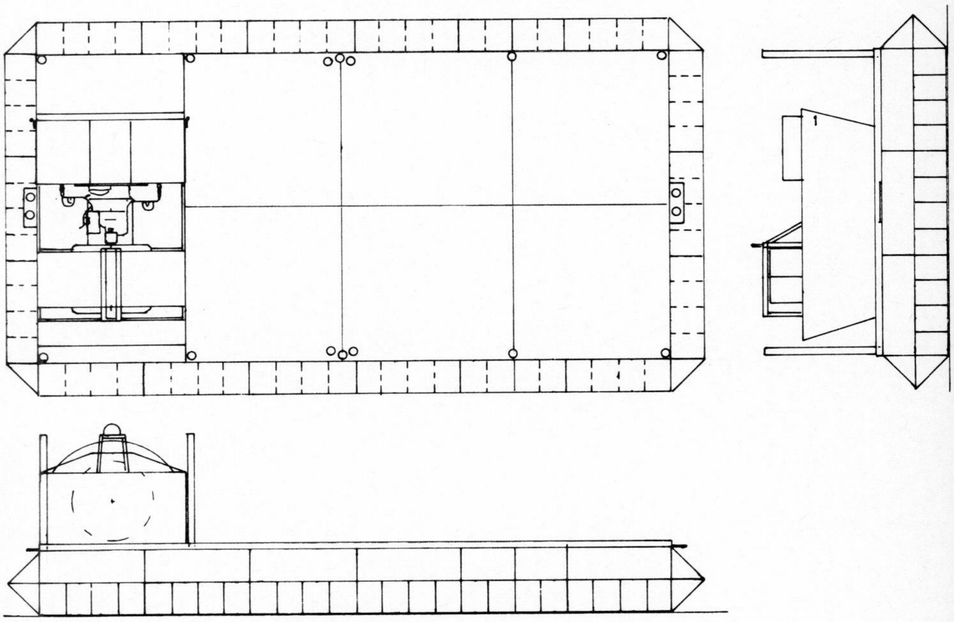
Trailaire II two-ton capacity air cushion trailer

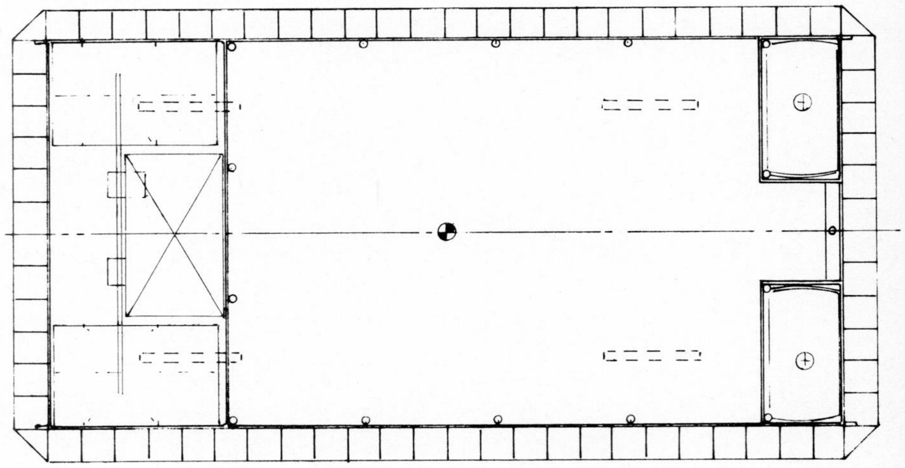
Trailaire IV

TRAILAIRE II

The basic unit is a 2·43 × 4·87m (8 × 16ft) platform capable of lifting 2 tons on its 2·43 × 3·65m (8 × 12ft) deck.

Units may be coupled together to give load platforms of 24 × 8ft; 16 × 12ft (4 tons payload) or 16 × 24ft (8 tons) or spaced to carry long loads, such as pipes. They can be towed by light vehicles or winched over land. Over water an outboard motor or a pump unit may be used for propulsion.

Space alongside the lift engine allows an operator to ride on the platform clear of the load space. Sockets around the platform edge are provided to accept posts to fence-in the load area.

Ground clearance of the standard unit is 10in but greater clearance can be provided if required. For amphibious operation buoyancy tanks can be fitted, though the standard unit can be operated over water as long as lift power is maintained.

POWER PLANT: GM 308 with 12 V generator, electric starter and 44A battery.
FAN: Double intake 0·83m (33in) centrifugal driven through reduction gears, via torque converter.
DIMENSIONS
SINGLE UNIT
Length overall cushion-borne: 5·38m (17ft 8in)
Width overall cushion-borne: 2·94m (9ft 8in)
Height of deck, hard structure: 254mm (10in)
Height overall, cushion-borne: 508mm (20in)
Height of lift unit, on pads: 1·21m (4ft)
cushion-borne: 1·47m (4ft 10in)
Load space: 3·75 × 2·43m (12ft 4in × 8ft)
Fence height (posts): 0·914m (3ft)
WEIGHTS
Empty: 630·46kg (1,390lb)
Gross: 2,721·55kg (6,000lb)

TRAILAIRE IV

This is a general purpose load-carrying platform for amphibious operation. Over water payload 2·5 tons.

Power is supplied by a single GMH 350 cu in V8 automotive engine driving two DWDI 0·68m (2ft 3in) centrifugal fans at 2,300 rpm via a clutch and 1·5 : 1 reduction. Electric battery for starting. Flashproof exhaust fan for engine compartment operates automatically before engine can be started. Close cooling system with automotive type radiator. 12 V pump for ballast system. 90 litres (20 gallons) fuel tank.

DIMENSIONS
Length (hard structure): 7·31m (24ft)
Width (hard structure): 3·65m (12ft)
Height off cushion, load deck: 355mm (14in)
Hard structure clearance: 304mm (12in)
Load space: 3·65 × 4·87m (12 × 16ft)

WEIGHTS
Empty: 3,628kg (8,000lb)
Gross: 6,350kg (14,000lb)
Overwater payload: 2½ tons
BALLAST: 907kg (2,000lb) maximum in forward tanks.
BUOYANCY: 6,803kg (15,000lb) without raised sides.

PERFORMANCE
Wave height, max: 1·21m (4ft)
Step: 304mm (12in)
Endurance: 2-3 hours

TRAILAIRE VI

Trailaire VI is designed for heavy duty applications and has a payload capacity of 10 tons. Two versions are available, a fully amphibious version and a non-buoyant version which can cross water only with the power on.

Power is supplied by a 200hp Ford V8 automotive engine driving two 0·68m (2ft 3in) centrifugal fans mounted in twin intakes aft.

Drawbar pull at the gross weight of 17 tons is 362·85kg (800lb).

DIMENSIONS
Length (excluding drawbar): 11·12m (36ft 6in)
Beam, hard structure: 3·65m (12ft)
amphibious version: 3·96m (13ft)
sidebodies version: 2·43m (8ft)
Hard structure clearance: 304mm (12in)
Loading height: 355mm (14in)

WEIGHTS
Gross: 17 tons
Empty: 7 tons

PERFORMANCE
Endurance: 4 hours

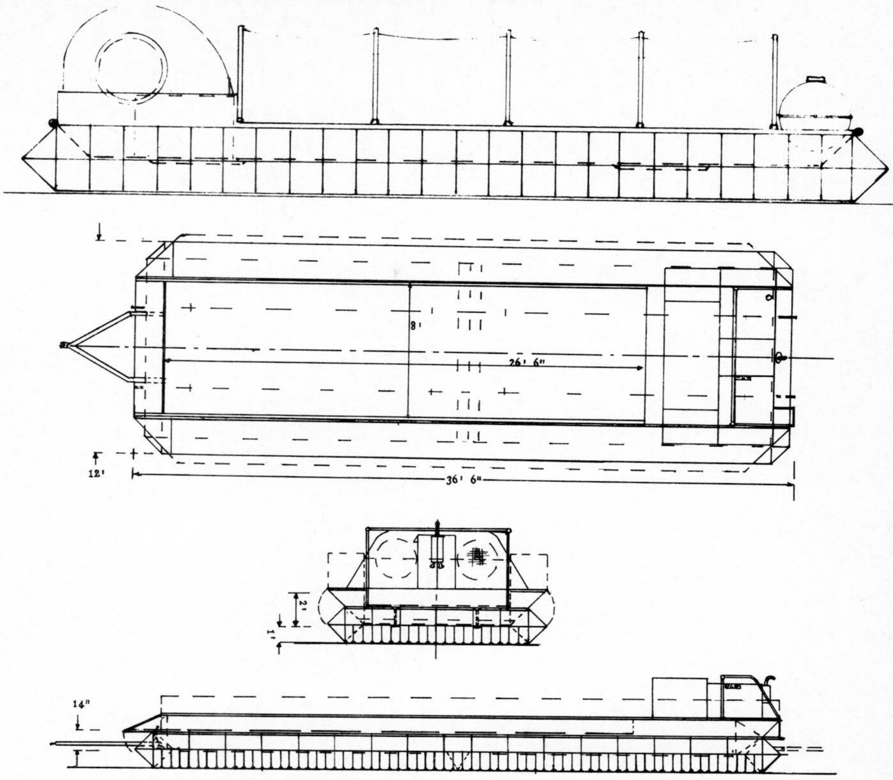

Trailaire VI, ten-ton capacity air-cushion trailer, available in fully amphibious and non-buoyant versions

CANADA

HOVERLIFT SYSTEMS LTD

6814U—6th Street SE, Calgary, Alberta T2H 2K4, Canada
Telephone: (403) 253 5239
Telex: 03-821682

Officials:
R D Hunt, P Eng, *President*
D M Simmons, P Eng, *Executive Vice President*
R W Dyke, *Vice President, Engineering*
C H Harcourt, *Manager, New Projects*
R F Mamini, *Production Manager*
G M Parkes, *Operations Manager*

Hoverlift Systems Ltd is a member of the Simmons Group of Companies. The group's main interest is the exploitation of mineral resources, and its entry into the field of industrial air cushion vehicles was through a requirement to mount oil drilling equipment onto an air cushion vehicle to extend its potential mobility during the summer. The company has diversified its product line to include heavy load amphibious transporters, both towed and self-propelled, icebreakers, and the conversion of awkward loads to an air cushion transportation mode. The company has also developed a range of modular construction transporters under the name Hoverflex. Using a series of common structural, power plant and skirt modules, transporters can be assembled at remote sites in sizes ranging from 43 tonnes (94,000lb) to 200 tonnes (442,000lb) load capacity.

Hoverlift HL-104 La Crete hoverferry, Pioneer 1, operated by Alberta Transportation on the Peace River, Northern Alberta

HOVERLIFT HL-101—Rubber Duck

Rubber Duck is a fully amphibious air cushion ferry or ship-to-shore lighter designed and built by oilfield personnel for operation in the Canadian North. The hull is an exceptionally rugged all-metal structure of welded steel construction.

Payload capacity is 20,000lb (9 tons) with 30% reserve buoyancy over water and 30,000lb (13·5 tons) over land at a maximum of 58mb (0·85psi) ground pressure.

For ease of transport the vehicle's side decks fold to permit loading on one live-roll oilfield trailer without crane. It can also be loaded on the C-130 Hercules, one of the transport aircraft engaged in regular supply operations in the Canadian North and other remote regions.

The prototype platform was produced during the latter part of 1975 and was used on river crossings throughout the winter of 1975-76, including the freeze-up period in early winter and the break-up period in the spring. The object was to establish the feasibility of an all-season air cushion ferry, and to obtain fundamental performance data for use in future designs. During the trials, the craft was fully instrumented, and continuous performance data was monitored by members of Alberta Research Council.

LIFT: Motive power is supplied by a single 197hp Caterpillar 3208, or equivalent Detroit diesel engine, driving a Joy Industrial steel fan, or equivalent, through a direct coupling.
PROPULSION: Cable and on-board winch or towed by tractor.
HULL: Welded steel structure.
SKIRT: 229mm (9in) pitch segmented skirt in hot-bonded natural rubber/nylon material. Spray skirt in neoprene nylon material. Skirt segments capable of routine operation across newly broken ice ledges; may be replaced individually from deck if necessary.
DIMENSIONS
Length overall: 12m (39ft 4in)
Width overall: 5·7m (18ft 10in)
Load deck length, centre deck: 8·5m (28ft)
side decks: 11m (36ft)
Load deck width: 5·5m (18ft 2in)
PERFORMANCE: Speeds and gradients within winch or tractor capability.

HOVERLIFT HL-104

As a direct result of the trials with HL-101 a contract was awarded by Alberta Transportation for the design and production of an ACV ferry to be operated at La Crete on the Peace River in Northern Alberta.

Following the design concept of HL-101, the hull of the ferry is constructed in road transportable sections which are pin-jointed together on site. This feature provides a convenient method of transport to the operational location, and the potential for removal to another site if traffic requirements change.

Another feature of the craft is its mode of operation. Due to a number of local conditions, including ice in the river, fast currents and steep banks on either side, the ferry moves in a broadside mode and climbs out of the river on both sides for loading and unloading from approach roads parallel to the river banks.

This feature allows shallower gradients on the approach roads, and a run-off escape route at the other end of the load deck in case of vehicle brake failure or iced-up decks. It also ensures that, during the break-up period when a considerable quantity of broken ice is coming down the river, there is no build-up of broken ice on the upstream side of the ferry during unloading or when waiting for traffic.

The ferry is winch propelled, using two bull-wheel winches hydraulically driven through variable displacement pumps mounted on the front end of the crankshaft of the lift engines.

The ferry is capable of continuing operation at lower speeds in the event of single engine failure. Operational trials and some service operations were carried out during the autumn and winter of 1977, and it has already demonstrated its capability of maintaining a ferry service when no other means of crossing was available, over both thin ice and rotting ice, and considerable water level changes.

LIFT: Motive power is provided by two Caterpillar 3408 diesel engines, each driving a fan and a variable displacement hydraulic pump. New York Blower Series 40 centrifugal fans are provided, driven through automatic centrifugal clutches.
PROPULSION: Two Timberland Equipment bull-wheel winches provide a variable speed drive along 1in diameter cables. The winches are driven by Sunstrand hydraulic motors.
HULL: The hull is an all welded steel fabrication constructed in three sections which are pin jointed together. Separate buoyancy compartments are provided to give a buoyancy reserve of 50% under fully loaded conditions.
SUPERSTRUCTURE: The control cabin and engine rooms are of fibreglass construction, and the general layout has been designed so the ferry can be operated by one man if necessary.
SKIRT: Segmented skirt in natural rubber/nylon material fabricated by hot-bonding. Segment depth from underside of hull, 0·91m (3ft). Each segment is individually mounted on light alloy bars for ease of changing.
DIMENSIONS
Length overall: 20·19m (66ft 3in)

Hoverlift HL-301 air-cushion icebreaker secured to the bow of a small harbour tug. Its hinged side sections permit it to be transported by road from one operating site to the next

Width overall: 11m (36ft 1in)
Load deck length: 20·02m (65ft 8in)
Load deck width: 4·88m (16ft)
Depth of hull: 1·37m (4ft 6in)
Trucking width of centre section: 3·66m (12ft)
Trucking width of side sections: 3·76m (12ft 4in)
PERFORMANCE
Payload: 45 tonnes (100,000lb)
Max speed over water: 2·68m/s (8·8ft/s)
Max gradient capability: 8–10% (1 in 12–1 in 10)
ALTERNATIVES: To accommodate various customer requirements the configuration of the craft may easily be "stretched" by the addition of appropriate structural and skirt sections.

HOVERLIFT HL-105

The HL-105, the first stretched version of the HL-104, is under construction for the Province of British Columbia, Ministry of Highways and Public Works. It will cross the Fort Nelson river near Fort Nelson in British Columbia. In this case it has been "stretched" in width by 4·73m (12ft 6in) by the addition of a second identical central hull section. This gives a potential payload of about 75 tonnes, although not all this increase may be used in this application. It was expected to enter service late in the summer of 1978.
SPECIFICATION
Generally as for HL-104, with the following modifications:
Engines: General Motors Detroit Diesel 12V-71
Width overall: 14·82m (48ft 7in)
Load deck width: 8·67m (28ft 6in)
Payload: 75 tonnes (165,000lb)

HOVERLIFT HL-301

Based on HL-101, the HL-301 has a heavier hull and increased power to adapt it for icebreaking duties. The hinged side sections are retained to enable the craft to be transported rapidly from one operational site to another by road when required.

In operation, the platform is designed to be winched to ice anchors or to be secured to the bow of a smaller harbour tug or similar craft.

It is intended for icebreaking in harbours and other congested areas where manoeuvring space is limited. The first production platform is in operation with St Lawrence Seaway Authority, where it has been used on the bow of a 20m (65ft) tug, breaking ice up to 0·6m (24in) thick.
SPECIFICATION
Generally as for HL-101, with the following modifications:
Engine: General Motors Detroit Diesel type 8V71.
Fan: New York Blower Series 40 centrifugal.

HOVERLIFT HL-302

HL-302 is an icebreaker bow with a configuration to fit a range of Canadian Coast Guard icebreakers. The design contract was awarded to Hoverlift Systems Ltd by the Department of Supply and Services in April 1977 and it is intended that construction will be completed in time for the 1978-79 icebreaking season. The platform is capable of hovering independently of the parent ship and when attached to the bow of the ship the cushion is sealed to the bow.
LIFT: Two diesel engine power units each of 600–750kW (800–1,000bhp) driving centrifugal fans.
HULL: Steel fabrication with built-in buoyancy reserve.
SKIRT: Segmented skirt system with individually mounted segments capable of being changed at sea. Segment depth 2·3m (7ft 6in).
DIMENSIONS
Length: 21m (70ft)
Beam: 21m (70ft)
Hull depth: 3m (10ft)
Cushion depth: 2m (6ft 6in)
WEIGHT (design operating): 272 tonnes (600,000lb)

HOVERLIFT 200 SERIES

This series comprises a number of self-propelled units, using other than air propulsion. Full-size development programmes, covering amphibious and land propulsion methods, are being undertaken with the aid of HL-101.

HOVERLIFT 400 HOVERFLEX SERIES

The Hoverflex amphibious barge range comprises 15 modular transporter designs, ranging from 43 to 200 tonnes load capacity. They are assembled from appropriate groupings of three different lift power modules, five different hull modules and one basic skirt. Alternative propulsion modules will be available, using winches, wheels, water propellers or air propellers. Alternatively, the unit can be notched to the bow of a ship as an icebreaker. All the modules are easily transported by truck, so that on-site assembly is possible for all sizes. Assembled Hoverflex transporters can be increased or decreased in size to suit changing needs.

Custom designs can extend the payload capability to over 500 tonnes without sacrificing the advantages of the modular concept.

SKIRT MANUFACTURE AND DEVELOPMENT

The company has built a hot bonding assembly facility for making a very wide range of skirt sizes. Development work has been undertaken on conventional segments, special units for icebreaker bow seals, special "add-on" skirt systems for converting various structures to an air cushion transportation mode, and spray suppressing skirts. Very efficient spray skirts have been developed for the company's product range, and an effective spray skirt has been supplied for the Voyageur hovercraft. The company is able to undertake design, development and manufacture of skirt systems and associated devices.

CONSULTANCY

In addition to the product range mentioned above, Hoverlift Systems Ltd can offer an all-Canadian Consultancy Service on all aspects of the industrial application of the air cushion principle by personnel who have had more than twelve years practical experience of design and operation.

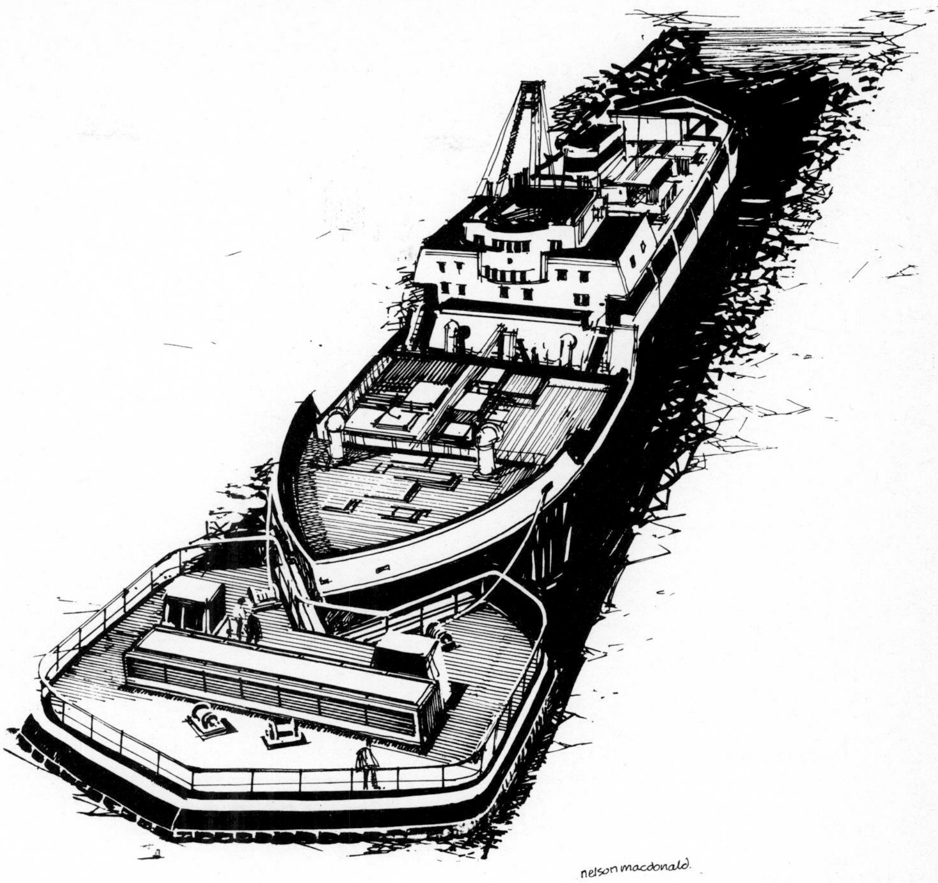

HL-302 ACV icebreaking platform

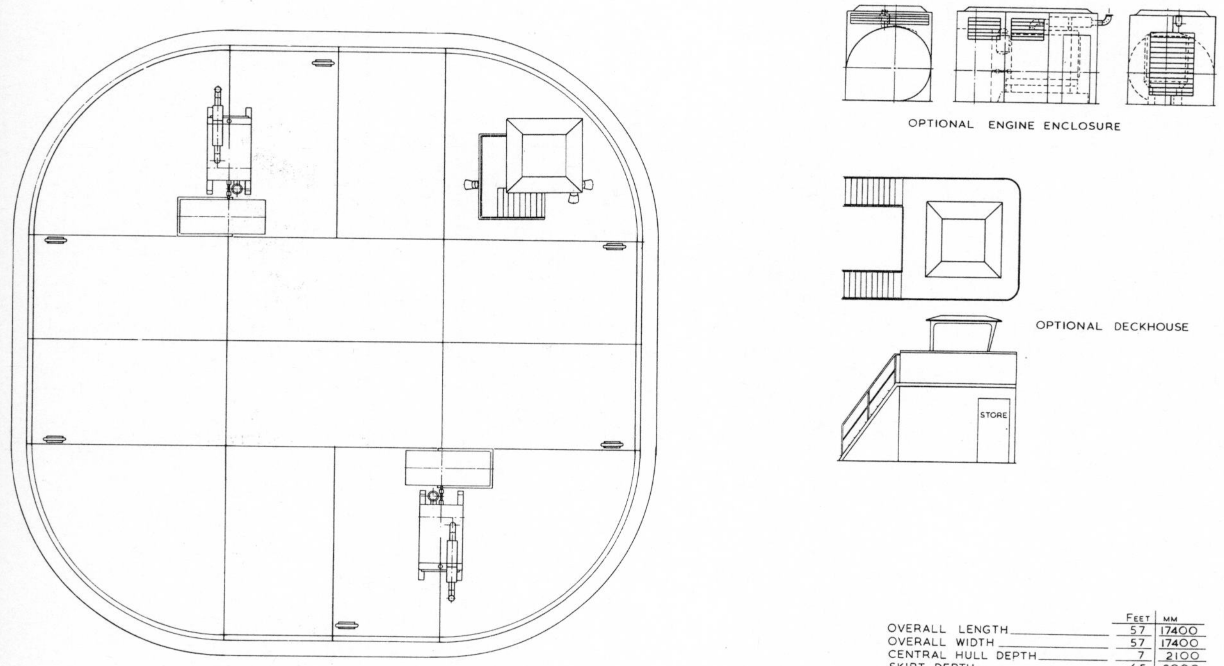

	FEET	MM
OVERALL LENGTH	57	17400
OVERALL WIDTH	57	17400
CENTRAL HULL DEPTH	7	2100
SKIRT DEPTH	6·5	2000
CLEAR CENTRAL ROADWAY	20	6100

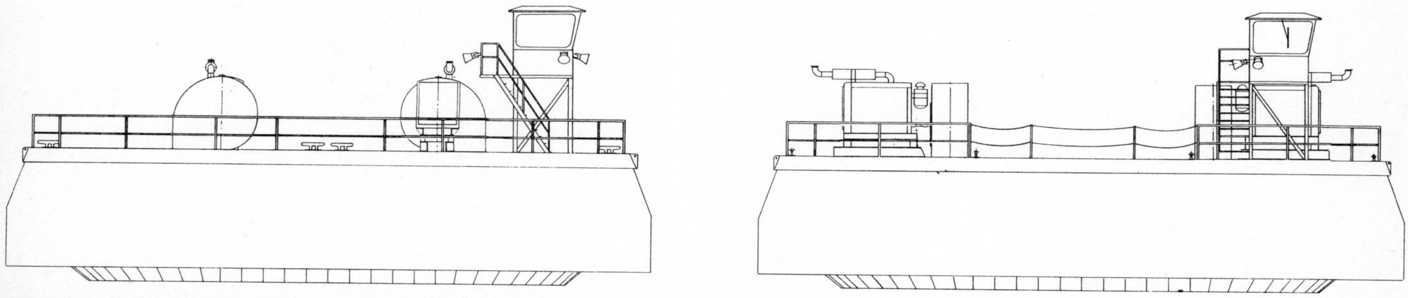

Outboard elevations and plan of a Hoverflex 400 amphibious barge with a 43 tonne load capacity

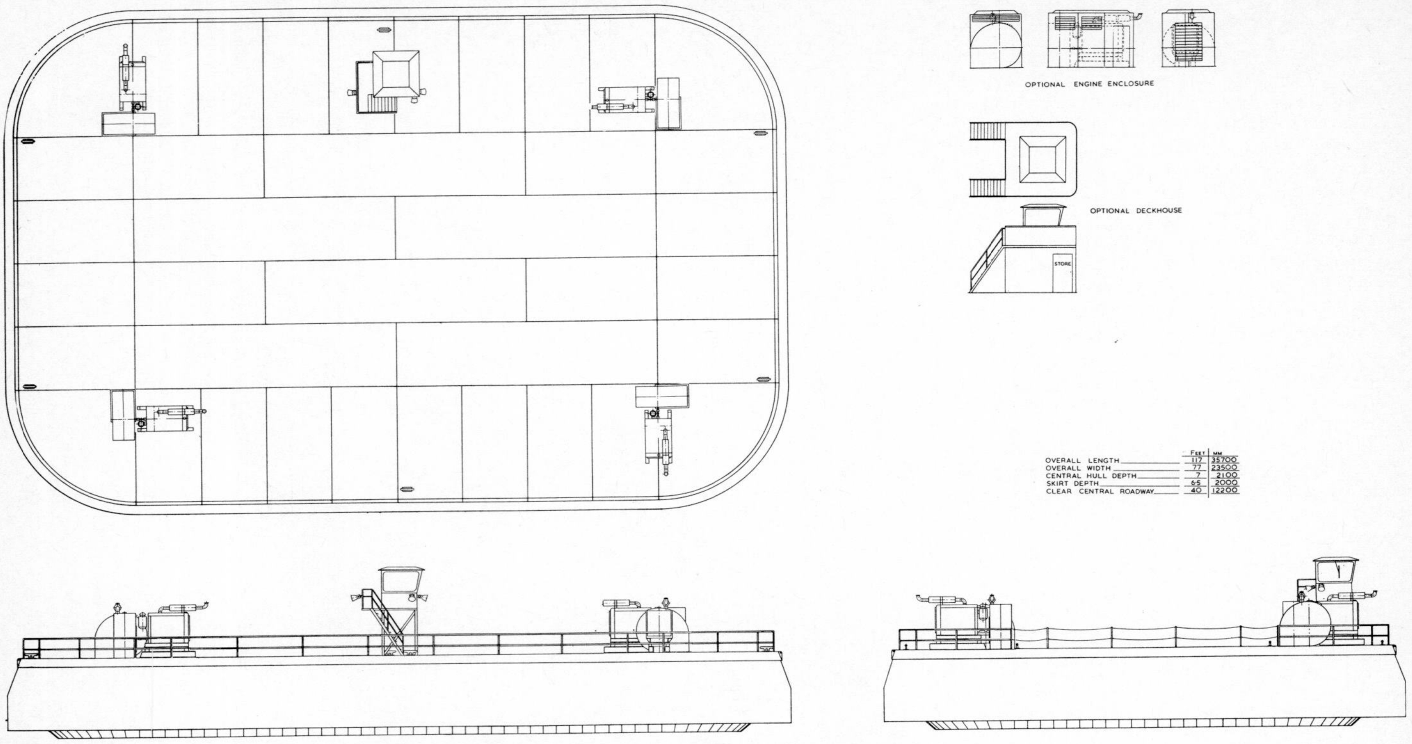

	Feet	mm
OVERALL LENGTH	117	35700
OVERALL WIDTH	77	23500
CENTRAL HULL DEPTH	7	2100
SKIRT DEPTH	6·5	2000
CLEAR CENTRAL ROADWAY	40	12200

Largest member of the Hoverflex 400 series is this 200 tonne capacity modular transporter design

FRANCE

DUBIGEON-NORMANDIE/ SEDAM

152 avenue Malakoff, 75116 Paris, France
Telephone: 380 17 69
Telex: 29 124 Paris

SEDAM is developing a range of amphibious barges to offload cargo ships in ports which, because of the vast growth of sea transport, have become almost permanently congested.

This congestion is forcing large numbers of vessels to queue up to be unloaded, and sometimes necessitates a wait of 30-100 days. Such delays, because of the high cost of demurrage and insurance, frequently lead to an increase of 50% to 100% in freighting charges.

SEDAM is proposing the use of its Amphibarges to unload the vessels and carry their cargo to warehouses close to the port, but clear of the main areas of congestion. Their amphibious capability would enable them to make the transition from water to land and carry their loads up to the warehouses where conventional fork lift trucks, mobile cranes and other freight handling equipment would be employed for offloading.

The manufacture of components for the Amphibarges could take place in the countries in which they are to be used. This would not only permit the customer to make considerable savings in transport costs, but also create a source of local employment.

AMPHIBARGES

LIFT: Four marinised diesel-engines, mounted one each side of the load deck, forward and aft, each drive a single centrifugal fan to feed air to the multiple skirt system. The skirts, made of terylene based material, are secured in position by quick-fasteners to facilitate repair and replacement. Skirt life is about 1,000 hours.

HULL: Modular craft structure comprising a number of cylindrical buoyancy tanks laid side-by-side longitudinally. Surmounting the buoyancy tanks are supports for the deck and below it are fastenings for the multiple skirt system and landing pads. At the bow and stern half-cylinders are employed as strengtheners against impacts incurred during towing or pushing. Surface of the deck is in diamond head plating. In the loading area the deck is strengthened by longitudinal and transverse girders. Railings are optional.

Impressions of a 100 ton capacity Amphibarge for both commercial and military use

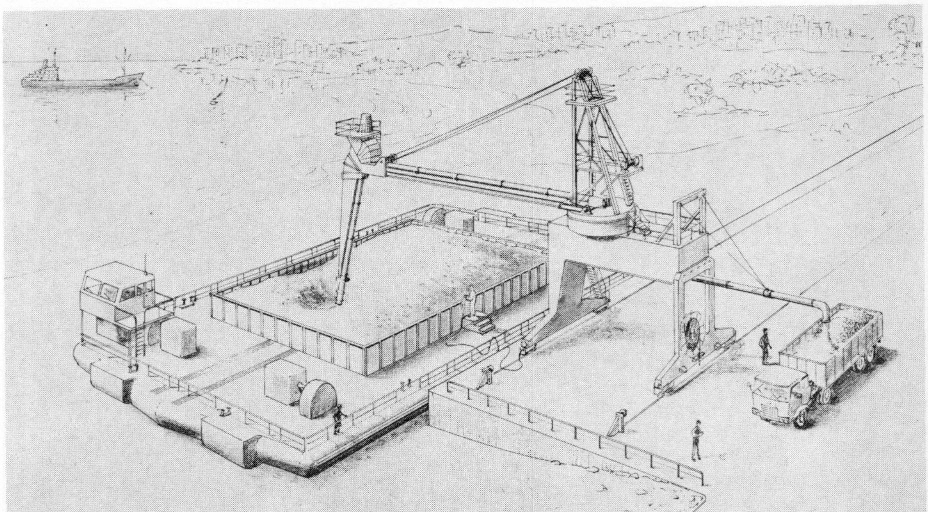

PROPULSION OVER WATER: Among alternative methods of water propulsion are tugs and outboard motors. Points for the installation of two outboard engines are provided aft. Speed with

outboard engines of suitable output will be about 5 knots.

OVER LAND: Drag overland is approximately 1% of the total weight when operating over a flat surface with no wind. Towing can be by a wheeled vehicle or a tractor with caterpillar tracks. Alternatively, one or more winches can be installed aboard, enabling the craft to pull itself overland to a fixed point by a cable.

CONTROLS: The operator's position and all necessary controls are in a raised bridge above the engine compartment on the starboard side. Crew would normally comprise an operator, engineer and seaman.

CARGO HANDLING: Optional roller track can be fitted for handling heavy vehicles. Express rollers are available for loading and positioning containers. Removable tank can be provided for handling bulk goods.

OPERATING PROCEDURE:

1 Cargo is off-loaded directly into the amphibarge by the ship's derricks (20 to 60 tons/h according to cargo):
2 the self-propelled amphibarge reaches the shore;
3 the amphibarge is lifted and pulled to the warehouse by minimal towing force (winch or tractor);
4 goods are unloaded by local means (cranes, forklifts, etc).

Particulars of the A50, A100 and A200 Amphibarges, with payloads capacities of 50, 100 and 200 tonnes, respectively, are given below:

DIMENSIONS	A50	A100	A200
Length	22m	35m	35m
Width	12m	18m	19m
Loading deck area	220m²	500m²	500m²
Height on rest	2m	2m	2·5m
Max load	1·8 tonnes/m²	1·8 tonnes/m²	1·8 tonnes/m²
Floatability volume	220m²	500m²	735m²
Weight when empty	55 tonnes	130 tonnes	155 tonnes
POWER			
Lift	4 × 300hp	4 × 500hp	4 × 500hp
Propulsion	2 × 100hp	2 × 200hp	2 × 300hp
Generator	20kVA	20kVA	20kVA
PERFORMANCES			
Payload	50 tonnes	100 tonnes	200 tonnes
Tolerable overload	10 tonnes	20 tonnes	none
Max wave height	1m	1m	1m
Speed (calm water)	5 knots	5 knots	5 knots
Recommended max gradient	3%	3%	3%
Land speed	5km/h	5km/h	5km/h
Fuel consumption:			
Lift	250kg/h	401kg/h	442kg/h
Propulsion	35kg/h	61kg/h	102kg/h

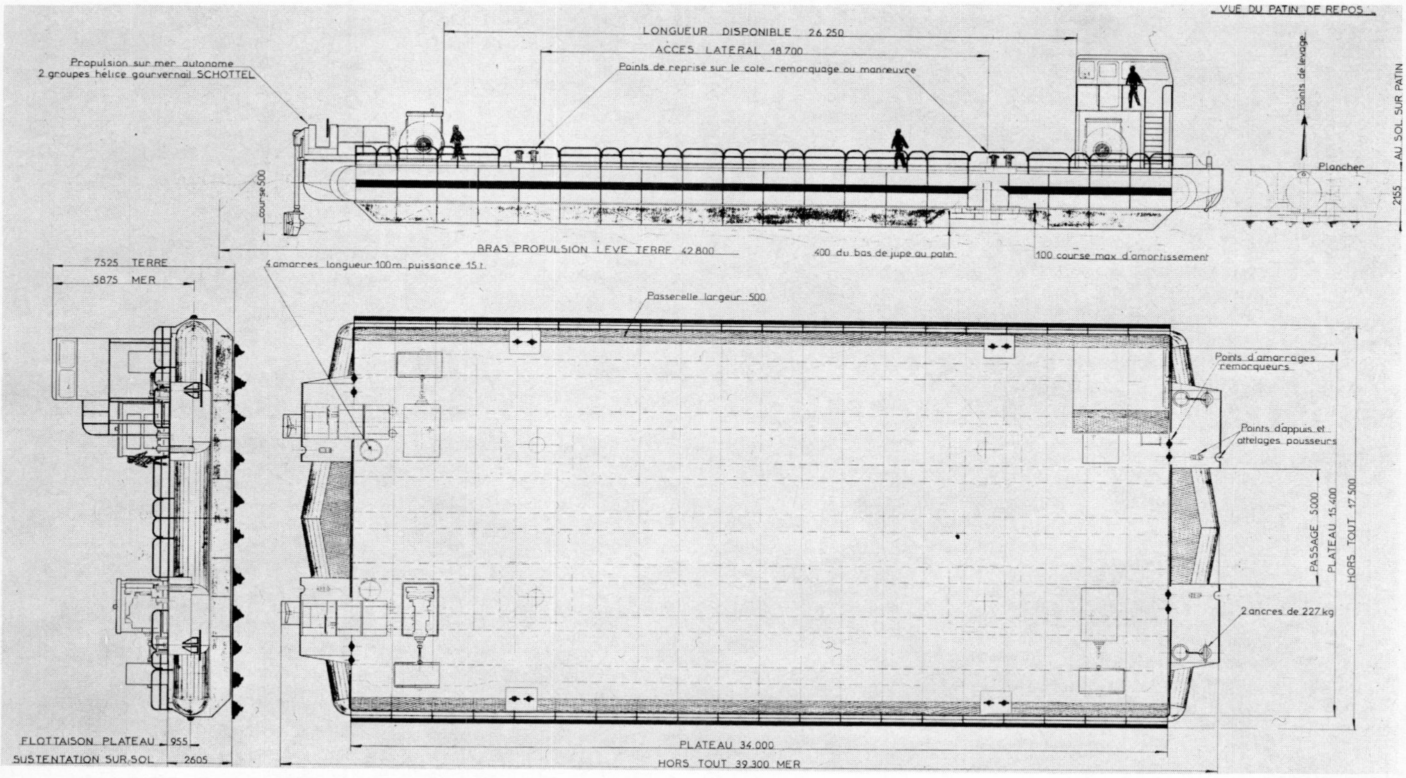

General arrangement of a Sedam 100 ton capacity Amphibarge. Power for the lift fans could be supplied by four 500hp marinised diesels. Two 100hp diesels driving water-propellers through Schottel drives give a water speed of 5 knots. The outboard propellers are raised at the point where the land towing system takes over

JAPAN

MITSUI ENGINEERING & SHIPBUILDING

6-4 Tsukiji 5-chome, Chuo-ku, Tokyo, Japan

Mitsui has designed a 310-ton hoverbarge for use in either deep or shallow waters. A feature of the craft, designated SEP-1, is the provision of jack-up legs, similar to those employed on some offshore oil rigs. This facility enables the craft to be located above test or survey sites in shallow waters or in areas of marsh or tundra.

UNION OF SOVIET SOCIALIST REPUBLICS

ALL-UNION OIL MACHINERY RESEARCH INSTITUTE, WEST SIBERIA (VNII neftmash)

Tyumen, USSR

Officials:

A V Vladimirskii, *Director*

V A Shibanov, *Head of Air Cushion Vehicle Department*

Air cushion platforms with load capacities of up to 200 tons have been under development in the West Siberian lowlands since 1965. Some 80% of the gas and petroleum sites in this area are located amidst almost impassable swamps, salt marshes, taiga and stretches of water.

In the Tyumensk area, where deep wells are being drilled, more than 200 tons of support equipment are required at each site in addition to between 130-180 tons of drilling gear. In 1965, a group of ACV engineers and designers headed by V A Shibanov left the Urals for Tyumen to apply their efforts to the design of a hoverplatform capable of carrying a complete oil rig across tundra and taiga, and also to the design and construction of an all-terrain vehicle capable of towing the drilling rig, on hover, to the drilling sites.

Small scale models were employed by the group during the development stages, and several attempts were made before a completely satisfactory design was conceived.

The most successful arrangement—the BU-75-VP—is illustrated. It comprises a rectangular, all-metal buoyancy raft (the load carrying member), with side structures to carry a bag-type skirt. A derrick, derived from a standard BU-75 drilling rig, was mounted on the central raft, and the drilling pump, generally delivered to sites separately, was also installed on board. Apart from specialist items of oil drilling gear, the platform is equipped with lift fans and drilling engines which serve a dual purpose by driving the lift fans when the platform is changing location.

Two tractors are normally required to tow the platform in a fully loaded condition.

Transport and routeing problems are now greatly simplified as the need to detour virtually impassable lakes, marshes, and snow or water-filled ravines no longer arises. The rig has been employed in oilfields at Shaimskoye, Urai and Samotlor.

Two more multi-ton cargo-carrying ACV platforms have been completed at the Tyumen Ship Repair yard. One new platform, which was put into service in 1974, has a load capacity of 200 tons.

A more recent design has been undergoing tests at the Strezhevoye workings at Alexandrov field in the Tomsk region. Large ACV rigs with a capacity of several thousand tons are under development.

BU-75-VP

DIMENSIONS
Length: 30m (98ft 5in)
Width: 20m (65ft 7in)
WEIGHT: All-up: 170 tonnes
PERFORMANCE: Speed (depending on towing vehicle): about 9·65km/h (6mph)

ACV TRAILERS

Three ACV trailers are being developed by the organisation—a 6-ton platform; the PVP-40 with a cargo capacity of 40 tonnes and a larger derivative with a capacity of 60 tonnes. The PVP-40 has been undergoing state acceptance trials in Surgut and the Soviet far north and if put into production will be employed in the construction of oil installations and pipelines, by geological surveys and on drainage and irrigation schemes.

The PVP-40 is powered by a single diesel engine driving two centrifugal fans. Its 60-ton counterpart is powered by a single gas-turbine driving twin axial-flow fans. Discs or wheels fitted to swinging arms at the rear provide directional control when reversing. "Trains" of ACV trailers can be employed to carry heavy loads and a further development is an articulated trailer, several times the length of platforms like the PVP-40, with one tractor forward and another at the rear.

ACV TRACTORS

Towing requirements for the rigs and ACV trailers built in Tyumen were met at first by conventional GTT amphibious crawler tractors. Since these were unable to cope with very soft terrain, development of a true multi-terrain tractor was undertaken, and this led to the construction of the Tyumen I. This was the first of a completely new ACV type with combined crawler propulsion and air cushion lift. The first model, now relegated to Tyumen's ACV museum, carried a 2-tonne load at speeds up to 40km/h (25mph) in off-road conditions. It is described as a broad, squat vehicle on long nar-

PVP-40 air cushion trailer undergoing field tests. The trailer, which has a load capacity of 40 tons, is designed for carrying heavy, single-piece cargoes and machines, drilling and oil-production equipment in the difficult and marshy terrain of Russia's northern regions

BU-75-VP oil rig, the first in the world to be mounted on an air cushion platform

Rear view of the PVP-40 air cushion trailer showing the unusual arrangement of varied length segments of the bag skirt

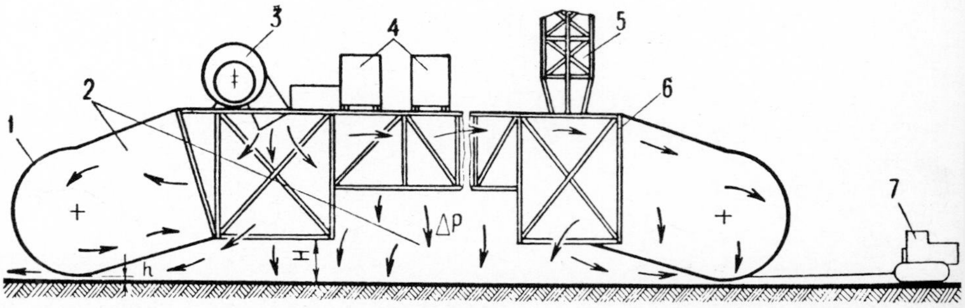

Diagram of a typical Soviet-designed ACV oil rig platform

1. flexible bag skirt;
2. air cushion;
3. fan;
4. drilling rig engines (employed to drive fans during moves);
5. derrick;
6. drilling rig base;
7. tractor;
h air gap;
H hard structure clearance.

row caterpillar tracks, with a flexible skirt between its crawlers. The second was the MVP-2 which was upgraded soon afterwards to the MVP-3 5-tonne capacity model. The MVP-3 uses extremely narrow crawler tracks for propulsion, steering and support on hard surfaces. As with the Bertin Terraplane series of wheel-assisted ACVs, the weight transfer to the crawler track is variable according to the nature of the terrain being crossed and the gradient. It is said to be capable of 80·46km/h (50mph) over swamps with 1·01m (40in) high hummocks and cruises at 48·28km/h (30mph). At the time of its first demonstration to the Soviet press in July 1974, it had completed 96·5km (60 miles) over Siberian swamps.

Operation of the vehicle appears to be relatively simple. Main controls are an accelerator for the single engine, which has an automatic clutch, and two standard tracked vehicle steering levers which skid-steer through the differential use of the tracks.

A 6-ton capacity air cushion trailer towed by a 5-ton capacity MVP-3 combined ACV/crawler tractor. Both vehicles have been developed by the West Siberian Branch of the All-Union Oil Machinery Research Institute

The policy at Tyumen is to standardise on composite crawler ACV systems rather than air propeller or endless-screw type propulsion.

UNITED KINGDOM

AIR CUSHION EQUIPMENT (1976) LTD

15/35 Randolph Street, Shirley, Southampton, Hampshire SO1 3HD, England
Telephone: 0703 776468
Telex: 477537
Officials:
J D Hake, *Chairman*
R J Howling, *Director*
L A Hopkins, *Director*
R C Gilbert, *General Manager*
R R Henvest, *Works Manager*

Air Cushion Equipment (1976) Ltd is involved in the design, development and manufacture of air and water cushion systems. Main products are air and water skirts for hovercraft and the industrial application and the 'Water Skate' heavy load carrying module system.

A service offered on a world-wide basis is the movement of heavy loads using either air or water cushions. The best known of the services offered by this company is the design and production of equipment used for moving oil storage tanks, of which 96 had been moved by the autumn of 1978.

The technology and skirt types developed by the company are based on the original work carried out by Hovercraft Development Ltd and developed to suit the special requirement and specification of the client.

Much research and development has been undertaken into the behaviour of skirt systems under widely varying operating conditions and the company has skirt systems operating in the Middle East and for ice-breaking in the Arctic.

Cushion pressures investigations range from the low pressure amphibious hovercraft requirement through to 225psi achieved during the development of the "Water Skate" system.

The company accepts contracts for all aspects of air cushion engineering and manufacturing.

LOW PRESSURE AIR SYSTEMS

Design services are offered in the application of the hover principle utilising low-pressure air (2psi and below) for the movement of heavy and awkward loads over unprepared ground. This embraces air cushion systems engineering and the design and manufacture of skirts.

THE "WATER SKATE" LOAD-CARRYING PALLET AND HIGH PRESSURE WATER SYSTEMS

The "Water Skate" load-carrying pallet uses water as the cushion fluid and has been tested up to 225psi. Modular in application the total system can be used in multiples of the required number of three sizes of pallet of 5, 35 and 100 tonnes capacity. The equipment uses normal contractors' pumps to give water at the required pressure and flow. One pump can feed several modules via a control manifold and console. The manifold can

Four AA Water Skate modules were used to move this 240-tonne grain barge from the point where it was fabricated to its launching position

Twenty-one Type AA Water Skate Modules were employed to launch this 1,800-tonne capacity deck cargo barge. The launching ramps comprised five 150ft temporary tracks of compacted limestone overlaid with steel sheet

be used to vary the pressures to each module thus eliminating the necessity to present equipment symmetrically about the centre of gravity. The pressure gauges can be calibrated in weight giving the operator the ability to weigh a bulky structure and to identify the centre of gravity to verify practical readings against calculation.

The areas of use for this product are diverse but include the movement of oil rig jacket structures and deck modules, concrete caissons, transformers, ship sections and hulls, plant and machinery, bridge sections and the launching of structures, ships and boats.

The high pressure water cushion system is offered to those companies who require a low cost system of dense and large load movement. The principle is similar to that of the modular skirt system and tank moving system but uses a water feed system similar to that used for the "Water Skate" modules.

Note: *the word "Water Skate" is a trade mark of ACE Ltd.*

This 700-ton oil storage tank is the largest ever moved by Air Cushion Equipment's hover flotation method. The operation was undertaken at Pauillac for Shell France. While the tank was being moved, the roof was floated on a second cushion of air to reduce both the possibility of damage to the roof and the pressure differential developed across the bottom of the tank

TANK MOVING

Tank moving, using an air cushion for support, has now become a well established procedure. The method offers many advantages over the older conventional forms of movement such as water flotation, mechanical skidding, cranes or bogies. Route preparation is kept to a minimum and it is seldom necessary to reinforce the tank. A tank move can usually be completed in about seven to ten days, depending on the size of the tank and the distance to be moved. Once the skirt has been assembled on the tank and the tank has been lifted from its foundation, the distance that it can be moved is infinite and only requires the provision of an appropriate means of propulsion and a clearway of adequate width. With all other methods movement is normally limited to comparatively short distances, or the time for the move becomes very extended.

As air is ducted from the fan to the cushion area it percolates through the tank foundation until sufficient pressure is built up to lift the tank. No jacking is required. Once on cushion the tank can be towed or winched to its new location. The air cushion system allows omnidirectional mobility, hence to change direction or rotate the tank about its vertical axis requires only the application of towing forces in the appropriate direction. Location to dimensional tolerances of ± 2in can easily be obtained. The towing force required is usually in the order of 1% of the weight of the tank.

Tanks of all types can be moved on air including those with floating, fixed and column supported roofs and welded or riveted construction. The illustration shows a 700-tonne floating roof tank being moved in Pauillac for Shell France. This is the largest tank moved on air to date and on this occasion an added innovation was used, floating the roof on a second cushion of air during the move. This not only reduces the possibility of damage to the roof but also reduces the pressure differential developed across the bottom of the tank.

Tank moving on air cushion is undertaken by licensed contractors as follows:

UK, Western Europe and Arabian Gulf (part)—Mears Construction Ltd

Canada and USA—Hover Systems Inc

Southern Africa—National Process Industries Pty

Japan—Nippon Kensan Co

BRITISH HOVERCRAFT CORPORATION

Osborne, East Cowes, Isle of Wight, England

Officials:

See ACV Section

AIR CUSHION HEAVY LOAD TRANSPORTER (AIR CUSHION EQUIPMENT SERIES I)

The development of this equipment was prompted initially by the Central Electricity Generating Board, which is constantly faced with route-planning problems caused by the high weights of laden transporters.

Transformer units now going into service weigh between 155 and 250 tons and 400-ton units are in prospect. On occasion the CEGB has been involved in the heavy expense of strengthening and even rebuilding bridges to accept these loads when no alternative route has been available.

The use of air cushion equipment, however, provides a practical and economic alternative. By providing an air cushion under the centre section of an existing transporter it is possible to support a high proportion of its gross weight. Distributing the gross load over the whole length of the transporter reduces the bending moments and sheer force imposed on bridges so that these heavy transformers can be transported without risk over existing bridges.

The investigation into and development of this air cushion transporter has been supported by the CEGB with the co-operation of the Ministry of Transport and the road haulage companies that operate the transporters.

A CEGB heavy load transporter

The transporter illustrated has a length of 27·4m (90ft) and a maximum width of 5·13m (16ft 10in). The payload is normally supported between two bogies each of which may have up to 48 wheels.

The skirt containing the air cushion is an easily handled unit which is fitted under the load and side beams of the trailer. Any spaces between the load and trailer frame are 'timbered-in' to take the upward thrust.

This type of skirt system can be built to suit any size of transporter and the one illustrated measures 9·57 × 4·26m (32 × 14ft). It is constructed largely of nylon/neoprene sheet extending across the underside of the load platform and formed into a bellows around its periphery. To the bottom of the bellows is attached a series of plates, each about 0·3m (1ft) long, which make contact with the road surface. Thus the only escape route for air from the cushion is through the small gap formed between the plates and the ground by the roughness of the surface.

Any general unevenness of the surface, such as the camber of a road or the hump of a bridge, causes the bellows of the 'skirt' to flex so that the plates can remain in contact with the road.

The cushion was designed for a 155-ton lift, when the cushion pressure reaches 5·4psi. At this pressure, when moving over the roughest road surfaces, the volume of air escaping from underneath the shoes is approximately 373·5m³/min (13,200ft³/min) (free air volume flow).

The power to maintain the air cushion is provided by four Rolls-Royce B81SV petrol engines delivering 235hp (gross) at 4,000rpm. Each engine drives, through a gearbox, its own centrifugal compressor, with engine, gearbox and compressor mounted together on a steel underbed as a complete working unit. The four units supplying the power are built onto a road vehicle chassis. This vehicle, which also contains stowage space for the folded cushion container, is attached to the rear of the transporter train whenever it is required for a bridge crossing. It is connected to the air cushion through four 1ft diameter air ducts, each connected to a power unit. The ducts are connected by sections of flexible hose to allow for relative movement between the vehicles.

The first commercial load carried by the transporter was a 155-ton transformer for delivery to the Central Electricity Generating Board's sub-station at Legacy, near Wrexham, from the AEI Transformer Division Works at Wythenshawe, Manchester. The route involved crossing the Felin Puleston Bridge which, under normal circumstances, was incapable of withstanding the combined weight of the transporter and the transformer. By using the air cushion to relieve the load on the transporter's wheels the stress on the bridge was reduced by about 70 tons.

Four 200hp Noel Penny gas-turbines are mounted together as a module on the swan neck of the heavy load trailer

Had a conventional transporter been used the bridge would have had to be strengthened at a cost equal to about half the cost of developing and equipping the transporter.

Optimum relief is obtained by taking up about one-third of the gross load in the skirt and transferring this proportion from the bogies to a position under the piece being carried. Current requirements are for re-distribution of between 85 tons and 125 tons of the gross load in this manner and to date over 870 bridges have been crossed using the air cushion with savings in bridge strengthening costs estimated to be well in excess of £2 million.

Future movements of larger plants are likely to call for relief up to 200 tons. Recognising this potential requirement and also the fact that the existing equipment has already had a considerable part of its operating life the Board decided in 1973 to order a second set of equipment, designated Series II, which would cover all present and anticipated future requirements whilst allowing the Series I equipment to be held for back up and stand by duties. The latter has become particularly important in view of the substantial increase in air cushion assisted movements recently.

Series II equipment incorporates new features and design improvements made in the light of operating experience with the original system; main differences being centred around the air supply units.

Air is supplied by four 200hp gas turbines running on diesel fuel and each directly coupled to an axial compressor to give an output potential up to 7·3psi with a 20% increase in air capability. The gas turbines, supplied by Noel Penny Turbines Ltd are mounted together on a module on the swan necks of the heavy load trailer. The swan necks also carry the control cabin, fuel tanks, batteries, and battery charger so that no separate air supply vehicle is required. The trailer can now operate as a single unit when the air cushion is in situ. The need for flexible air duct sections is avoided, also the loss of time in connecting or disconnecting flexible sections and replacing the rear tractor by the blower vehicle as is required for Series I equipment.

Since becoming operational the transporter has assisted in the movement of more than 40 pieces of heavy electrical plans to the CEGB's power stations and transmission sub-stations and in conjunction with the movement of plant destined for export. During these movements the equipment has been used to give loading relief at 1,000 bridges that would otherwise have needed to be strengthened or rebuilt at an estimated cost of more than £3 million.

The Series II equipment is now in full commercial service. Similar equipment is available on a world-wide hire basis to other users. The line diagram below indicates the differences in layout between the Series I and Series II equipment.

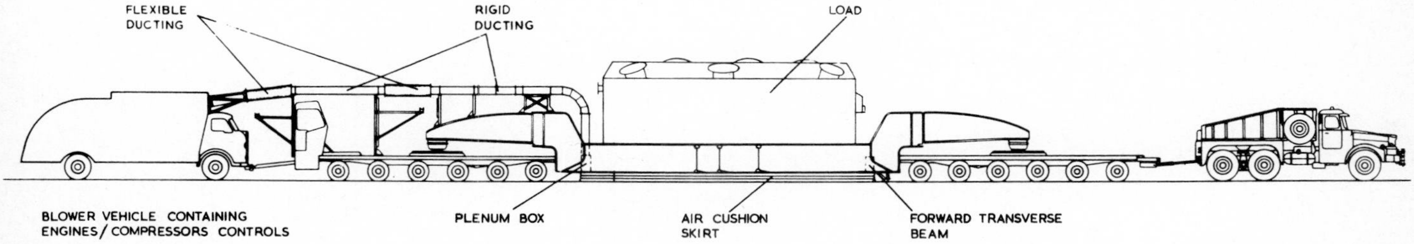

SERIES I ARRANGEMENT

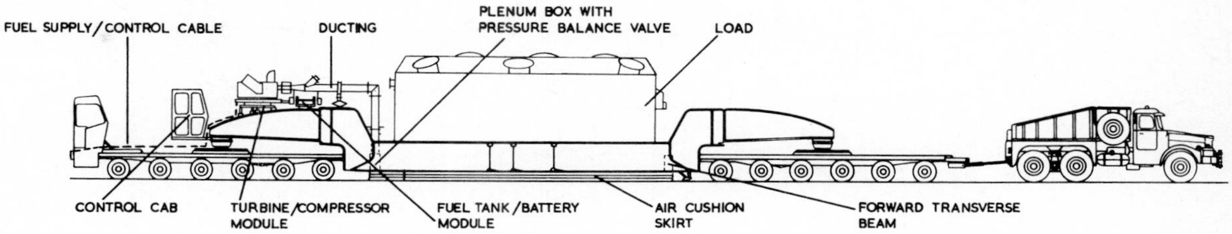

SERIES II ARRANGEMENT

UBM HOVER SYSTEMS

Lower William Street, Northam, Southampton, Hampshire SO9 2DN, England
Telephone: 0703 34366
Telex: 47106 Hovertrail Soton

Officials:
F Brooksbank, *Chairman*
A Haikney, *Managing Director*
L Beavis, *Director*
I R Bristow, *Director*

UBM Hover Systems is a division of UBM Engineering Limited, a subsidiary of the UBM Group. It was founded to specialise in the development, construction and marketing of two ranges of hover equipment, aircraft recovery systems and industrial/agricultural hoverplatforms of various types.

AIRCRAFT RECOVERY SYSTEMS

The new Mark III Aircraft Recovery System is the result of more than eight years research by

Recovering a Fokker F.28 with a UBM Hover Systems Aircraft Recovery System. The aircraft sustained no secondary damage during recovery

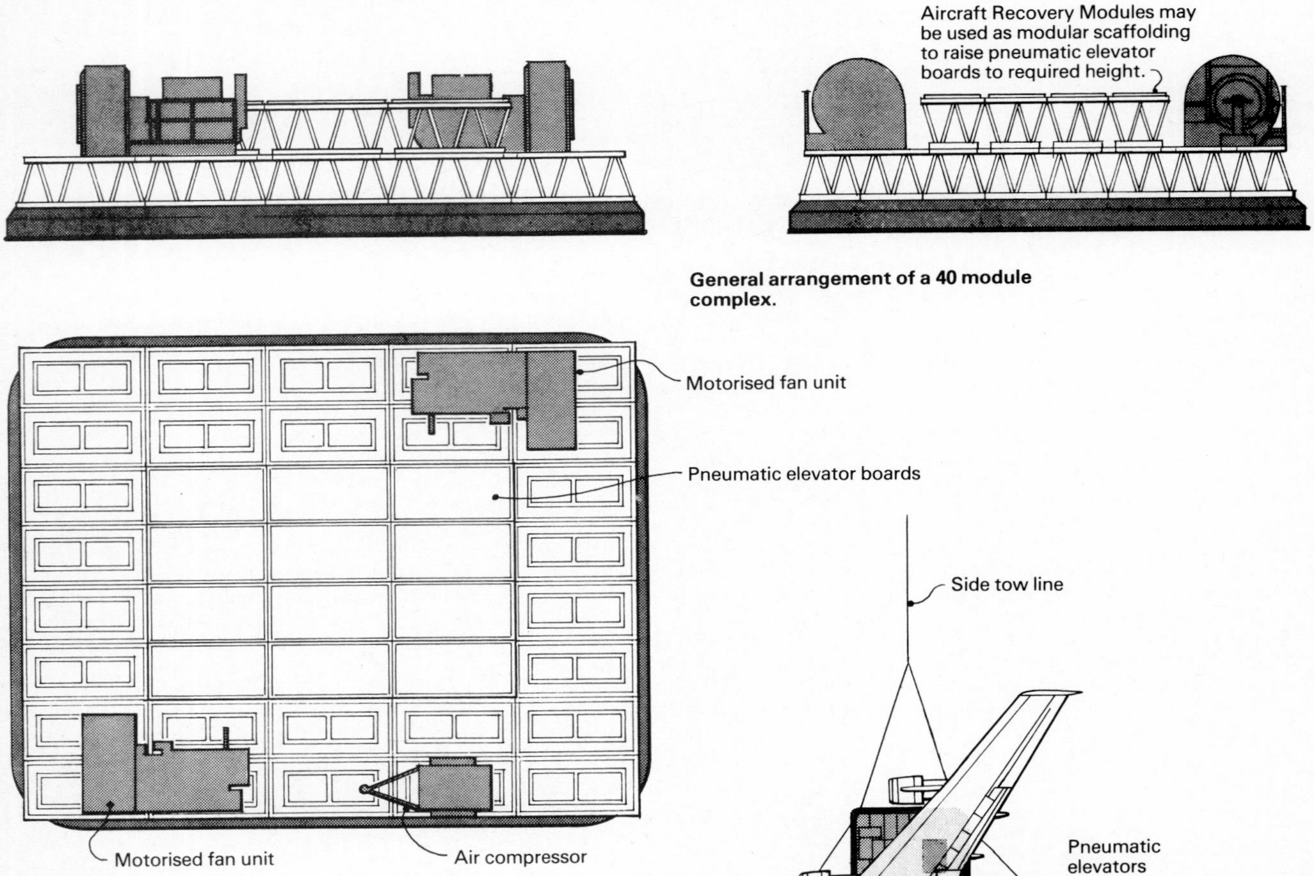

General arrangement of a 40 module complex.

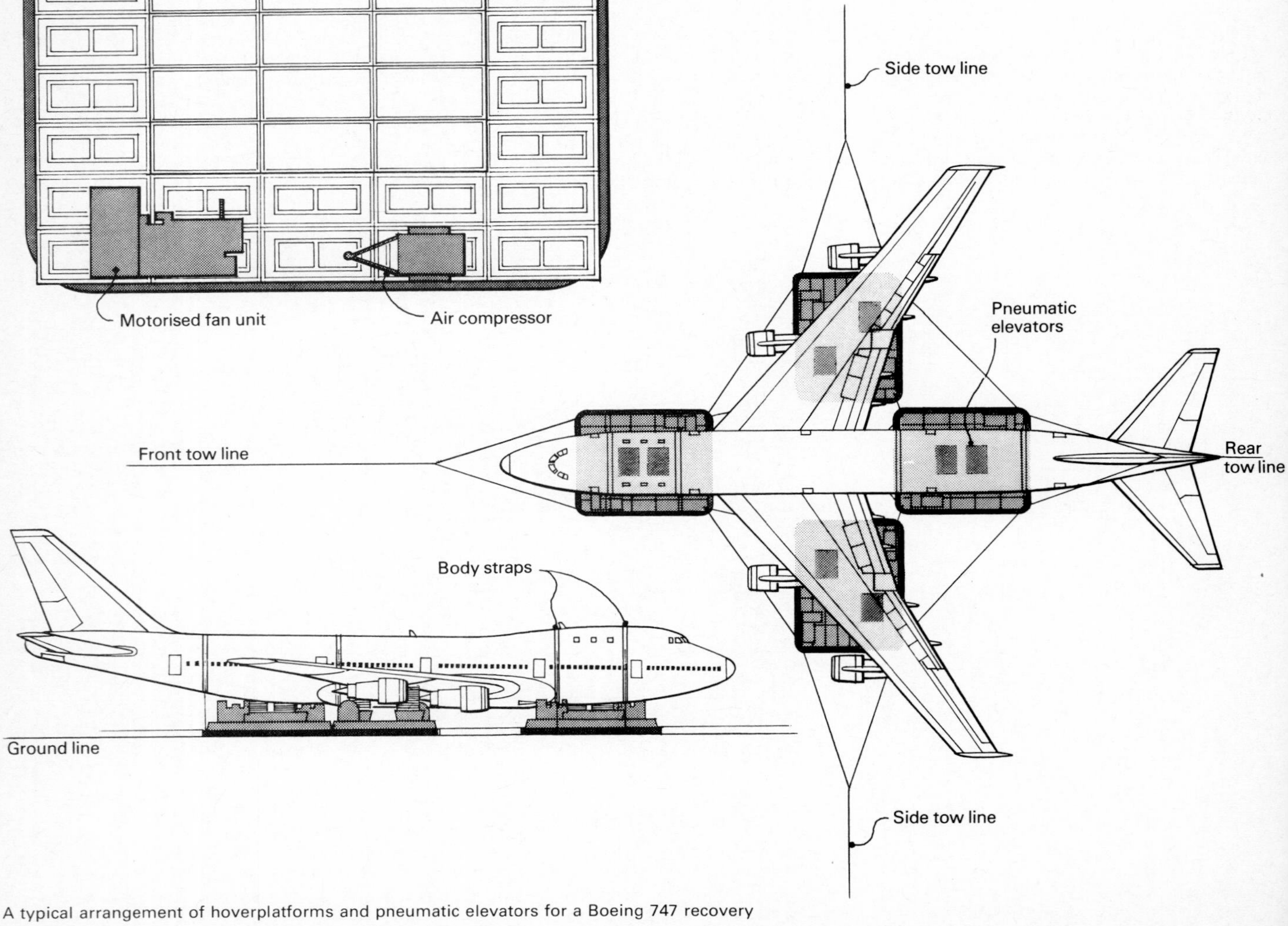

A typical arrangement of hoverplatforms and pneumatic elevators for a Boeing 747 recovery

UBM into low cost methods of recovering disabled aircraft and satisfies in full the requirements formulated in consultation with airline bodies, air forces and airport authorities. The system overcomes the considerable difficulties involved in recovering wide-bodied aircraft, eliminates much unnecessary handling and with a normal air cushion pressure of less than 1 psi, has the capability of hovering across all types of terrain, leaving the ground surface undisturbed, regardless of the load being carried.

Built on a modular system, the Mk III Aircraft Recovery System is completely air-transportable, making it readily available to almost any airfield in the world. Each standard Aircraft Recovery Module weighs only 190kg, may be handled by four men and nest-packed for air transport. Linked together these modules form the main structure of the platforms, 15 modules being needed to move 15,000kg (33,000lb), four sets of 40 modules to move a 747 airliner and a maximum system capacity of 227,000kg (500,000lb).

Following the very successful recovery in 1977 at Kano, Nigeria, of a Fokker F28 using a UBM Mk II Aircraft Recovery System, the Nigerian Civil Aviation Authority has purchased the more versatile Mk III system, delivery being taken in March 1978.

Impression of a hover rice harvester at work

INDUSTRIAL AND AGRICULTURAL HOVER PLATFORMS

These platforms are designed to transport a wide variety of heavy loads over terrain which is impassable for conventional wheeled or tracked vehicles under load. They may be used for widely varying applications from civil engineering, pipe- or cable-laying, forestry work, geological and mineral surveying, to agricultural, conservation or drainage schemes.

The basic structure is a rigid steel platform with a strong welded subframe, to which a hover skirt is attached. The lift power is supplied by a centrifugal fan driven by a petrol or diesel engine mounted on the platform. Special wheels fitted to swinging arms at the rear of the platform give directional control on side slopes and when reversing. Hover height of the platforms varies according to design and size.

Individual units of up to 100 tons capacity are available and awkward loads with high centres of gravity may be transported by linking together two platforms of the same type. Platforms of this type have been sold in the United Kingdom, Europe, Africa, Middle East, Asia, North and South America and Australia.

Both the aircraft recovery systems and industrial platforms may be either towed or winched. The ground bearing pressure of the air cushion system is usually less than 1 psi, and the towing force required is very low. For operation in extremely marshy conditions fully-tracked low ground pressure tractors are the most suitable towing vehicles.

An industrial hover platform loaded with six 12·19 m (40ft) by 0·68m (3ft) diameter pipes crossing soft sand

The rice harvester is another example of hover platforms designed by UBM Engineering to meet specific needs. The harvester itself is a readily available unit mounted on a self-propelled tracked hoverplatform, with a normal air cushion pressure of less than 1 psi, enabling it to move freely across the very soft surfaces of rice paddy fields.

The unit is capable of harvesting both rice and rice-straw at a very high rate and, when used in conjunction with small hover platforms as collection vehicles, can substantially reduce the harvest time. It is claimed that the use of this vehicle will make second and third harvests possible.

MACKLEY-ACE LIMITED

Funtley Road, Funtley, Fareham, Hampshire PO16 7XA, England
Telephone: 032 92 85541
Telex: 86518 MACHOV G
Officials:
D G W Turner, *Managing Director*
J R Mackley, *Chairman*
F R Mackley, C Eng, FICE, *Director*
A Truslar, *Secretary*
M J Fripp, *Director*

Mackley-Ace Limited, a wholly owned subsidiary of J T Mackley & Co Ltd, has specialised in the design and construction of air cushion supported platforms for use in many facets of industry. It has helped to build the world's first hover dredger, has built a range of modular platforms and has also built the world's largest hover transporter which has a payload capacity of 250 tons. In addition the company has constructed two 160-ton hover transporters to cross the River Yukon in Alaska.

It is now studying amphibious platforms of greater payload capacities capable of moving giant petrochemical modules.

The company has recently introduced a simple self-propulsion system for its hover platforms. It has also developed a new system for laying submarine cables which simplifies un-reeling the cable.

In 1977 Mackace moved to a 12-acre site near Fareham where it is constructing a research and development centre. Regular demonstrations are held to permit visitors to see hoverplatforms operate over land and water.

250 TON ACT

Sea Pearl, the world's largest hover transporter, was launched during 1974 and now operates in the Persian Gulf.

It was used initially to carry pre-fabricated sections of a liquid natural gas plant for a distance of about 110 miles. It allowed components to be transported from the fabrication area across rocks and sand to the sea, and then across the sea and directly onto the selected site without having to change the mode of transport for each sector of the journey.

Sea Pearl can be towed by crawler tractors on land and by tug at sea.

LIFT SYSTEM: Cushion lift is supplied by two 890hp MWM TBD 602 V12 diesels, each driving a 1·39m (4ft 7in) diameter Alldays Peacock 1,400 BA DIDW centrifugal fan. Each fan delivers 3,823m^3 (135,000ft^3) of air per minute, giving a cushion pressure of 0·7kg/m^2 (1psi).

SKIRT: 1·21m (4ft) deep, open segment type, with double segments aft and an anti-spray flap.

BALLAST: A seawater ballast system is fitted to permit the craft to be employed as a ship-to-shore transporter.

DECK EQUIPMENT: Two 10-ton hydraulic winches are fitted at the bow for loading plant components. Twin hydraulic capstans are located amidships for use during mooring, manoeuvring and anchoring.

ACCOMMODATION: Elevated bridge and quarters for a five-man crew.

DIMENSIONS
Length overall: 54·86m (180ft)
Beam overall: 24·38m (80ft)
Length, load deck: 48·16m (158ft)
Beam, load deck: 15·85m (52ft)
Height on cushion: 9·94m (32ft 8½in)

Sea Pearl, the world's biggest hover transporter, in operation in the Persian Gulf

Two 160-ton payload hoverplatforms employed as chain ferries to carry vehicles and equipment across the Yukon river

Height off cushion: 8·72m (28ft 8½in)
WEIGHTS
All-up: 750 tons
Payload: 250 tons
PERFORMANCE, FULLY LOADED: Calm water, towing force of 15 tons, 7 knots. In 2·74m (9ft) high by 76·2m (250ft) long waves, 3 knots.

160 TON AIR CUSHION FERRY

Following experiments conducted in November 1974, Mackace was awarded contracts to build two cable-drawn hoverferries, which operated across the River Yukon in Alaska. Named the Yukon Princess I and Yukon Princess II, the platforms were used to carry vehicles and equipment across the River Yukon whether frozen solid, breaking up, liquid or just covered with thin ice. During this contract it was observed that the hover ferries broke up ice up to one metre thick. The hover platforms were based on a modular float raft with special Mackley-Ace skirt frames attached to the periphery. The cushion system gave a hover height of 48in when fully laden. The two craft were carrying up to 2,000 tons of cargo across the Yukon daily.

LIFT SYSTEM: Two 700hp GM Detroit diesel engines designed to operate in temperatures of −57°C (−60°F). Each engine drives an Alldays Peacock 1,100 BA DIDW centrifugal fan, each of which delivers 2,605m³ (92,000ft³) of air per minute, giving a cushion pressure of 0·7kg/m² (1psi).

SKIRT: 5ft deep segmented skirt with spray skirt.

WINCHING SYSTEM: Two winches were employed to tow the craft backwards and forwards across the 1,500m (5,000ft) crossing.

ACCOMMODATION: Heated cabin for the crew and an elevated bridge.

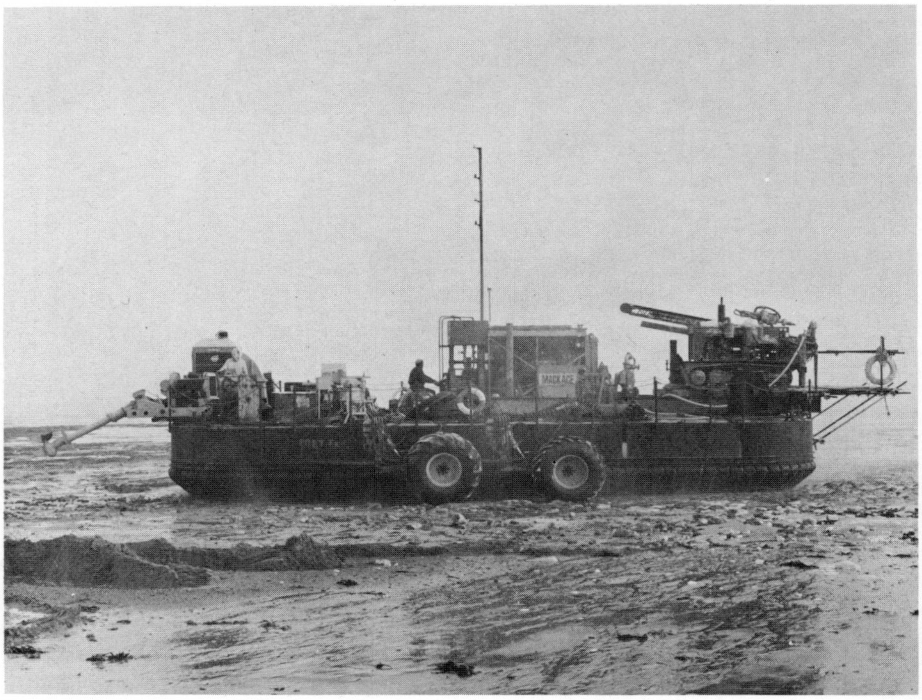

A Mackace self-propelled hover platform during an off-shore application

YUKON PRINCESS I

DIMENSIONS
Length overall: 38·7m (127ft)
Beam overall: 25·7m (84ft 6in)
Length of load deck: 29·9m (98ft 3in)
Beam of load deck: 17m (56ft)
Height on cushion: 7·62m (25ft)
Height off cushion: 6·1m (20ft)
WEIGHTS
All-up: 375·9 tonnes (370 tons)
Payload: 162·6 tonnes (160 tons)

YUKON PRINCESS II

DIMENSIONS
Length overall: 38·5m (126ft 6in)
Beam overall: 24·8m (81ft 6in)
Length of load deck: 29·8m (97ft 9in)
Beam of load deck: 16·1m (53ft)
Height on cushion: 7·62m (25ft)
Height off cushion: 6·1m (20ft)
WEIGHTS
All-up: 418·6 tonnes (412 tons)
Payload: 162·6 tonnes (160 tons)

A 30-ton Mackace hover platform for Jordan

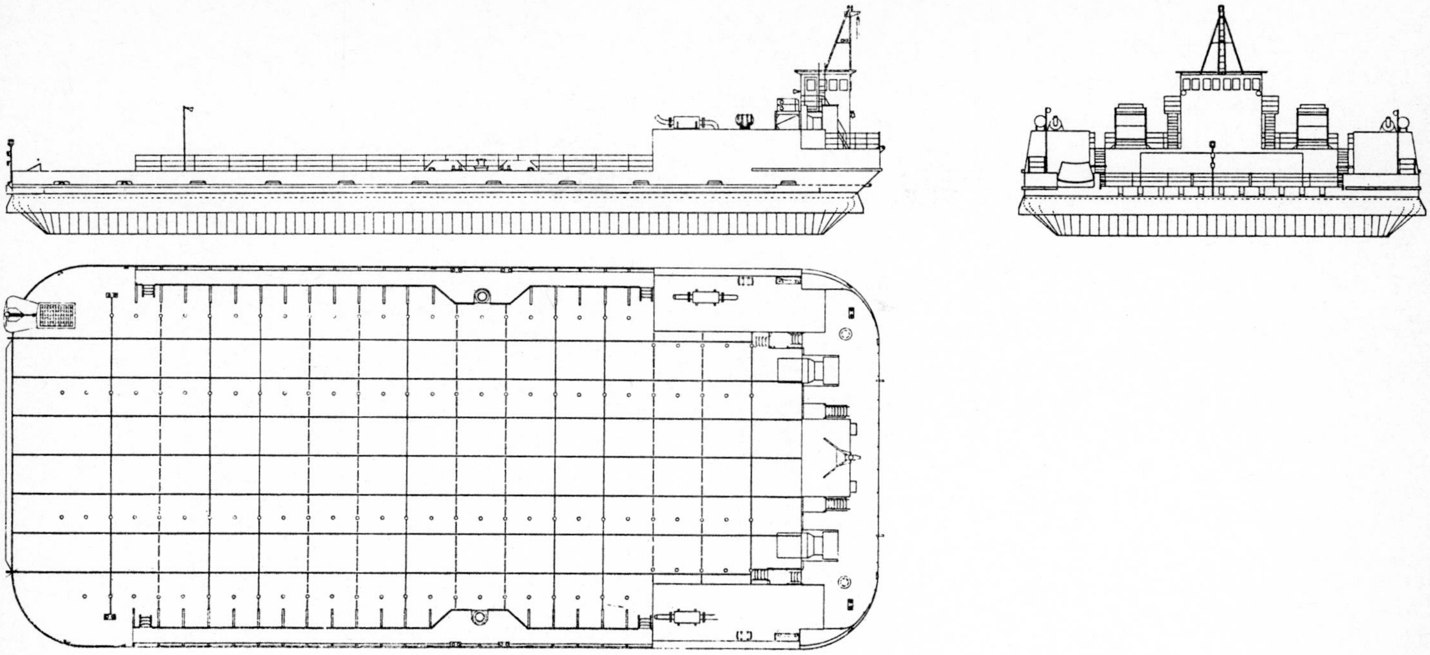

General arrangement of the 250-ton payload capacity Mackley-Ace hover transporter

HOVER PLATFORMS

Mackley Ace modular hoverplatforms range in payload capacity from 15 to 150 tons. Based on the standard Uniflote pontoon, each platform can be expanded or contracted to suit particular requirements.

Specially fabricated skirt frames are cantilevered off the sides of the Uniflote pontoons. The neoprene-coated nylon weave skirt is attached beneath the frames to protect it against accidental damage.

Each frame has its own skirt segment attached and is quickly replaced if damaged. The self-contained power packs driving the lift system are also mounted on the skirt frames, leaving the deck area clear. Contract labour can handle and assemble the platforms on site.

PROPULSION: The platforms can be self-propelled up to 150 tonnes; alternatively they can be winched or towed. Outboard motors can be employed for marine propulsion.

The overland self-propulsion system is based on hydraulically-operated driving wheels. Combined with the hover system, the driving wheels allow the hover platform complete freedom of movement over any terrain, independent of towing equipment.

CUSTOM-BUILT PLATFORMS

Purpose-built hover platforms can be designed and built from 15 to 1,000 tons, depending on the customer's requirements and proposed operating conditions. These can be built on-site or in nearby fabrication facilities using local labour and materials under supervision of Mackace engineers.

SPIN TANK

This was developed in response to a request for a simplified cable-laying system. The Mackley-Ace Spin Tank system of cable laying employs a cushion of low pressure water and simple skirt to support a cable drum on a vertical axis, thus eliminating problems with cable snatch, reel sagging and over-feed. The system has been tested at Mackley-Ace's test facilities.

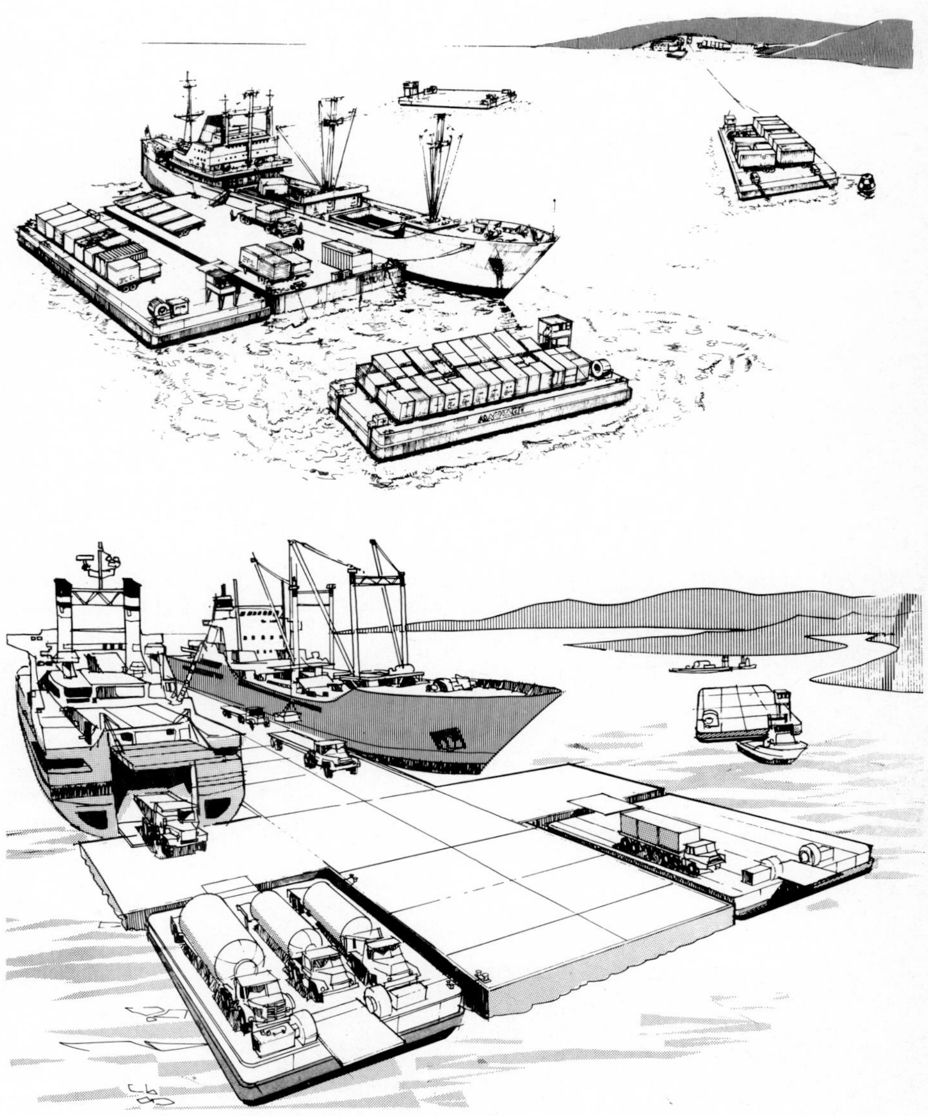

Two proposed ship-to-shore systems employing Mackace transporters

HOVER MODULES FOR PETROCHEMICAL PLANT

In March 1977 Mackace Hover Systems announced that it is able to offer large hover modules of up to 5,000-ton capacity for petrochemical plants.

The concept is to build the petrochem modules on a giant 400 × 200ft modular steel grid. Once completed a Mackace hover system is attached to the periphery and the module is hovered from the fabrication bay into the sea where its air cushion carries it above a ballasted sea-going barge. The barge is deballasted, the module comes off hover and is made fast to the barge ready for a normal sea tow to the installation site.

On arrival the barge is ballasted to water level so that the module can hover off. It then hovers to the exact installation site (towed or winched by conventional means) where, once in position, the air power is switched off and the module sits on its prepared foundation. The Mackace hover system is removed for re-use and the grid (already with services fitted) is filled with concrete to make a permanent base.

This simple concept reduces the need for heavy lifting gear and site work is restricted to the assembly of modules to form the complete plant.

The key feature of this concept is its simplicity. A petrochem module can be assembled by usual contracting labour in an established fabrication facility and the self-contained skirt frames are fixed to the platform module by mechanical couplings which are re-usable.

The actual number of skirt frames needed depends on the number of modules to be towed to site, the duration of the voyage and the rate of delivery required. Mackace has been involved in the petrochem and construction industry for some years, supplying hover platforms and large hover transporters to overcome transportation and logistics problems in geographically hostile areas.

The result of this experience is a range of hover transporters capable of operating with maximum reliability in any climate. Their independence from ports, docks, tides or ground and sea conditions make the hover transporters one of the few machines which can work literally round-the-clock in any conditions.

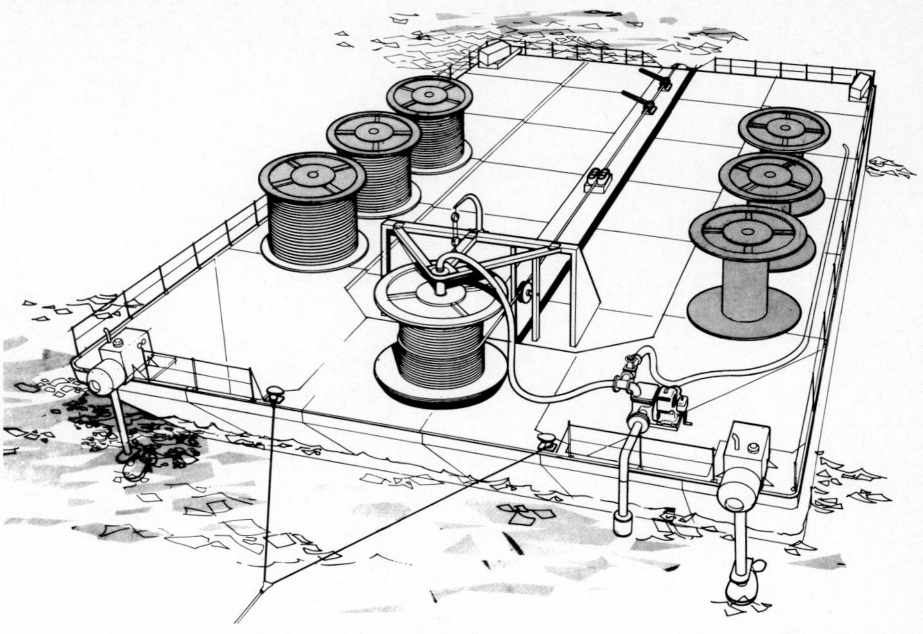
The spin tank system of cable laying, developed by Mackley-Ace, employs a cushion of low pressure water and a skirt to support a cable driven on a vertical axis, thereby eliminating problems of overfeed, reel sagging and cable snatch

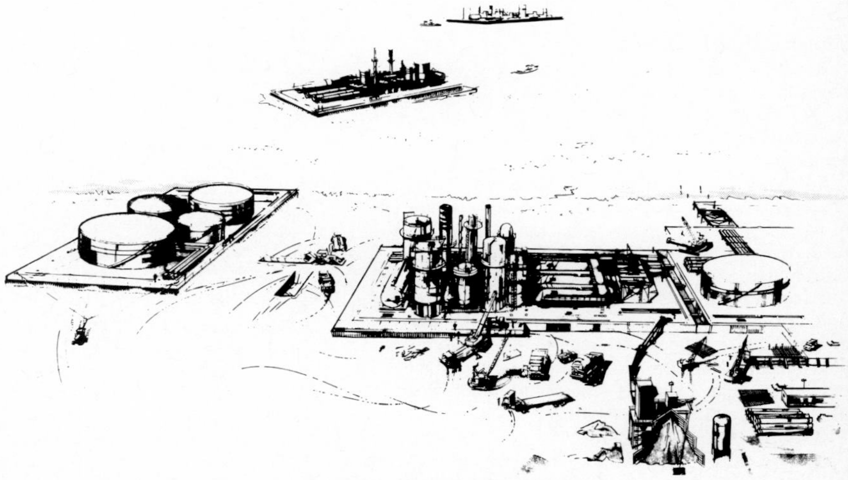
Impression of a Mackace petrochemical plant module. The module would be built on a 400 × 200ft modular steel grid. Once completed, a Mackace hover system would be attached to the periphery. The module would then be hovered from the fabrication bay into the sea where its air cushion would carry it onto the top of a ballasted sea going barge

MEARS CONSTRUCTION LIMITED

Dorcan House, Dorcan Way, Swindon, Wiltshire SN3 3TS, England
Telephone: 0793 40111
Telex: 449824 (G)
Air Cushion Division:
515 Upper Elmers End Road, Eden Park, Beckenham, Kent BR3 3SH, England
Telephone: 01-658 3711
Officials:
R W Bale, BSc CEng FICE, *Managing Director*
D R Eales, *Director in Charge, Air Cushion Division*
P F Morgan, *Manager, Air Cushion Division*

Mears Construction Limited holds the franchise for Air Cushion Equipment (1976) Ltd's system of tank moving throughout the United Kingdom, Western Europe and the Middle East.

Tanks moved by the company range in size between 48m diameter, 700 tonnes weight; 68m diameter, 530 tonnes weight and 6m diameter, 7 tonnes weight. A 700-tonne tank was relocated by Mears Construction Ltd for Shell Française at their refinery near Bordeaux.

The equipment consists of a segmented skirt system, diesel driven air supply fans and interconnecting ducting, all of which can be readily shipped to any location in the above areas.

Site surveys are undertaken by a Mears engineer in conjunction with an appointed associate company, in countries outside the United Kingdom, which provide non-specialist plant and equipment for the move. Mears provide the lift equipment.

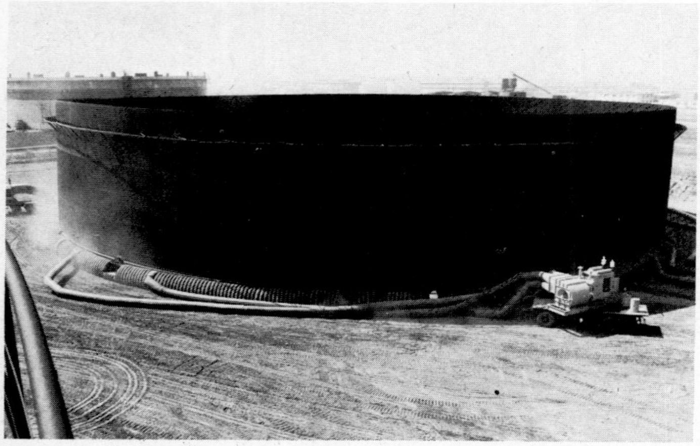

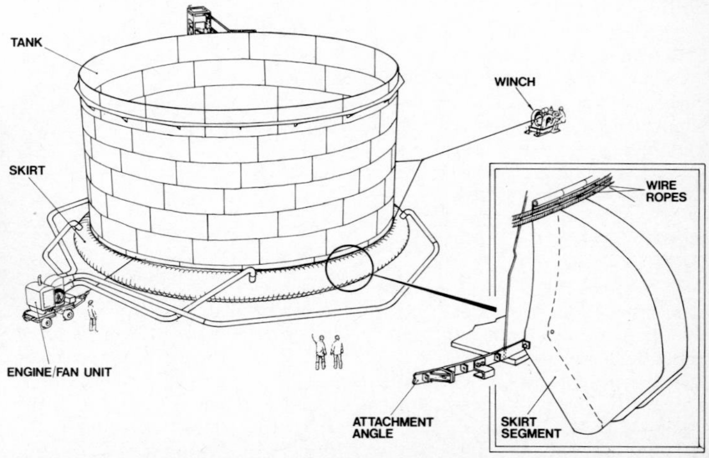

A 68m diameter tank, weighing 530 tonnes relocated for Stanic at the company's refinery in Livorno, Italy. The technique employed by Mears Construction Limited is shown in the accompanying diagram

PINDAIR LIMITED

Quay Lane, Hardway, Gosport, Hampshire PO12 4LJ, England
Telephone: 070 17 87830
Officials:
M A Pinder, BSc, CEng, MIMechE, *Managing Director*
A M Pinder, *Director*
John Holland FCA, *Director*

See ACV Section for company background.

Pindair is currently engaged in design studies for several customers requiring rigid and folding hovertrailers of up to 10-tonne capacity. The company welcomes inquiries for specific applications.

RIGID HOVERTRAILERS

Designed for manufacture by Pindair or the customer. Features include low cost, light weight and robust construction.

INFLATABLE HOVERTRAILERS

Designed for manufacture by Pindair. Fully transportable. A 2-tonne version will carry a Land Rover yet is designed to be carried inside a Land Rover. Particularly suitable for military, relief and rescue applications.

VOSPER THORNYCROFT (UK) LTD

Vosper House, Southampton Road, Paulsgrove, Portsmouth, England
Telephone: 070 18 79481
Telex: 86115
Officials:
See main entry in ACV Section

Vosper Thornycroft released preliminary details of its hoverbarge in May 1976.

The Vosper Thornycroft hoverbarge is designed to carry cargo between ship and shore where there are no conventional port facilities. Hoverbarges can operate over land and water, carrying goods between a ship anchored off any shelving beach and a simple warehouse nearby where they can be unloaded by mobile cranes or fork-lift trucks and transferred to an existing road or railway. When a particular loading or unloading operation has been completed in one place, a hoverbarge operation can be transferred almost in its entirety to another location if desired.

The hoverbarge will have its own fans to maintain an air cushion, with outboard propeller units for propulsion over water. In shallow water it would be connected to an endless cable system to haul it up through the surf and on to a hard area of beach from which it would be towed by a tractor to the unloading point. Vosper Thornycroft hoverbarges would be comparatively slow and simple craft, with relatively modest power units.

Impression of a Vosper Thornycroft hoverbarge facility in operation

UNITED STATES OF AMERICA

ARCTIC ENGINEERS AND CONSTRUCTORS

1770 St James Place, Suite 106, Houston, Texas 77056, USA
Telephone: (713) 626 9773
Telex: 762587
Officials:
R G Longaker, *General Manager*
M R Bade, *Operations Manager*
Associated Companies:
Arctic Systems, Calgary, Alberta and Ottawa, Ontario, Canada

Arctic Engineers and Constructors, a wholly-owned subsidiary of Global Marine Inc of Los Angeles, was formed to create a company with the capability and experience to offer a complete construction and drilling service to the petroleum industry in the Arctic.

Prior to the formation of Arctic Engineers and Constructors, engineers of the parent company had conducted an extensive environment, design, equipment and engineering study of the problems involved in the search for and production of petroleum in the Arctic. The study's objective was to analyse and define the operational problems encountered both onshore and offshore. It included analyses of climate, ice properties and distribution, land and air transport vehicles, drilling and construction, transportable arctic housing, and past and present arctic drilling operations.

It was concluded that air cushion transporters, used on a year-round basis, would offer substantial economic and technical advantages in arctic drilling, construction, and transportation.

The company's air cushion transporters are designed to transport heavy equipment and as a foundation support for drilling and construction equipment. The transporters are non-self-propelled and of simple robust construction for ease of operation and maintenance. The company designs air cushion transporters to suit specific operations. It owns and operates the transporters under contract to its clients.

ACT-100 air cushion transporter

Apart from its activities in the development and exploitation of air cushion transporters, the company has also developed a unique ice breaking attachment for conventional ships. By linking a VIBAC craft (Vehicle, Ice-Breaking, Air Cushion) to the bow of a conventional ship, the ship's ice passage ability is greatly enhanced.

A further development is the company's Pneumatically Induced Pitching System (PIPS) which significantly improves a vessels's icebreaking ability by inducing large amplitude pitching at the natural frequency of a given hull.

The company is licensed by Hovercraft Development Ltd.

ACT-100

Construction of the prototype ACT-100 was completed in April 1971. The craft is essentially an ACV barge designed to transport 100-ton payloads throughout the year across Arctic tundra, muskeg and marsh without unduly disturbing the soil and vegetation. It will also traverse offshore ice and open water.

Five months of testing under arctic winter conditions on the Great Slave Lake at Yellowknife during 1971-72 demonstrated that the craft is able to operate in temperatures of −45·6°C (−50°F) without difficulty. It proved extremely stable and manoeuvrable when travelling over level terrain, slopes, water, and over varying thicknesses of ice. It also showed unusual ice-breaking ability in thicknesses up to 660mm (26in) and had no difficulty in traversing broken ice.

The Canadian Ministry of Transport employed the ACT-100 under contract to investigate the feasibility of operating air cushion ferries in the Mackenzie River highway system. Initial trials were conducted at Tuktoyaktuk, NWT, in

November 1972. The craft was towed 322km (200 miles) up the Mackenzie for final ferry trials at Arctic Red River in June 1973.

In December 1973 the ACT-100 was employed by Imperial Oil Ltd to transport drill rig supplies and equipment from Langley Island to Adgo Island. Adgo is an expendable artificial island constructed by Imperial in the Beaufort Sea to support an exploratory drilling operation. The ACT-100 carried loads of up to 99·8 tons over ice, broken ice, and water.

LIFT: Cushion air is supplied by two 640hp Caterpillar D-348 diesel engines driving two 1·37m (4ft 6¼in) diameter Joy 5425 NOL steel centrifugal fans. Air is fed directly into the cushion without ducting. Cushion pressure is 144lb/ft². Diesel is contained in a single 500 US gallon integral tank in the main hull amidships.
CONTROLS: Towing cables to pull vehicle and wheels beneath centre of hull. A liquid ballast is provided for trim.
HULL: Box-type hull in A537 low temperature alloy steel. Hull is designed to support a 100-ton payload.
SKIRT: 1·52m (5ft) deep fully segmented skirt in rubber-coated nylon.
CREW: Control cabin accommodates one operator and assistant. A third member of the operating crew is the towing vehicle operator.
ACCOMMODATION: A "habitat" unit, with complete camp facilities for 35-40 men and storage facilities, can be mounted on the hull.

SYSTEMS: 110/220 V, 60 cycle 30kW generator for lighting, control and pumping.
COMMUNICATIONS: None permanently installed.
DIMENSIONS
Length,
power off: 23·71m (75ft 3⅜in)
skirt inflated: 24·15m (79ft 3in)
Beam overall,
power off: 17·38m (57ft 0⅜in)
skirt inflated: 18·59m (61ft)
Height overall,
power off: 1·98m (6ft 6in)
skirt inflated: 3·2m (10ft 6in)
Draft afloat: 1·04m (3ft 5in)
Cushion area: 308·068m² (3,316ft²)
Skirt depth: 1·52m (5ft)
CONTROL CABIN
Length: 2·43m (8ft)
Max width: 2·74m (9ft)
Max height: 2·43m (8ft)
Floor area: 6·89m² (72ft²)
FREIGHT HOLDS: Open deck, with tankage available beneath.
WEIGHTS
Normal empty: 150 US tons
Normal all-up: 250 US tons
Normal payload: 100 US tons
Max payload: 130 US tons
PERFORMANCE (at normal operating weight):
Speed (dependent on tow vehicle): 9·65km/h (6mph) plus
Still air range and endurance at cruising speed: 12 hours at average speed of 9·65km/h (6mph) = 115·87km (72miles)
Vertical obstacle clearance: 1·21m (4ft)

ADS

The company's latest vehicle—the ADS (Arctic Drilling System) combines a large air cushion barge with modern offshore drilling equipment and an ice-melting positioning system. It is designed for arctic offshore use.

The system offers two important advantages: (1) the complete drilling system can move between locations at any time during the summer or winter, and (2) the unit can remain over the well bore in ice moving at moderate speeds.

The three basic components of the ADS are:

(1) a large 70·4 × 43·7 × 4·5m (231 × 143·5 × 15ft) self-contained, shallow-draft aluminium drilling hull.

ACT-100 air cushion transporter

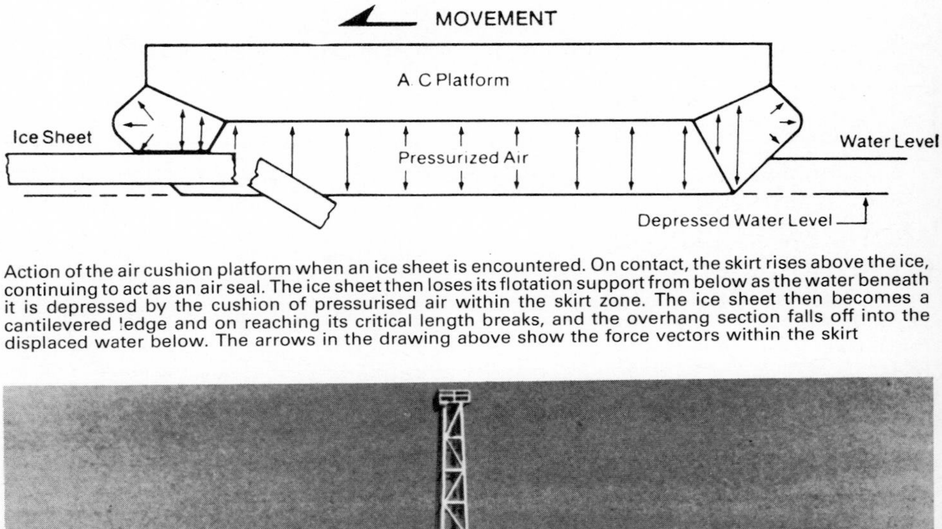

Action of the air cushion platform when an ice sheet is encountered. On contact, the skirt rises above the ice, continuing to act as an air seal. The ice sheet then loses its flotation support from below as the water beneath it is depressed by the cushion of pressurised air within the skirt zone. The ice sheet then becomes a cantilevered ledge and on reaching its critical length breaks, and the overhang section falls off into the displaced water below. The arrows in the drawing above show the force vectors within the skirt

Impression of the 3,840-ton ADS, designed to carry a complete offshore drilling system

(2) an air-cushion system capable of lifting the hull—complete with drilling, crew, and drilling expendables—2·59m (8ft 6in) above the surface.

(3) an external hull heating system capable of

melting a ledge of ice moving from any direction at a rate of 4·57m (15ft) per day, using waste heat from three 1,300hp Caterpillar D-399 diesel engines.

LIFT: A 4,000kW common-bus ac power generating system, with silicon-controlled rectifiers, supplies power to the drilling equipment and lift fan drive motors. The system comprises five 800kW, 1,200rpm ac generators, driven by five Caterpillar D-399, series B diesel engines, each delivering 1,300hp at 1,200rpm. Because the unit will not hover while drilling, the power system will serve a dual purpose. It will be used to drive the drilling equipment when located above a well bore, and the lift fans when moving to a new location.

The fans deliver a maximum pressure of 1·78psig. For normal rig moves the maximum cushion pressure will be used only in an emergency.

SKIRTS: 2·59m (8ft 6in) deep, fully-segmented HDL-type skirt in nylon rubber.

PROPULSION: Moving the ADS during the winter season will be accomplished by onboard mooring winches and logistic support vehicles. The support vehicles will pull out approximately 914·4m (3,000ft) of 44·45mm (1¾in) wire line for each of two modified National 4204-E winches mounted on the bow of the drilling hull. The support vehicles will act as dead men while the winches are taking up the line and pulling the ADS forward.

The support vehicles will have special design features to lock onto the ice sheet and resist the estimated 68,038·86kg (150,000lb) maximum lifting force. Winches on-board, powered by GE 752dc motors, will provide a winching speed of 6·43km/h (4mph). An overall average moving velocity of 1·6-3·21km/h (1-2mph) providing a 38·62–77·24km (24–48 mile) rig move in one day is anticipated.

It is expected that icebreaker workboats will permit the ADS to be towed through moderately thick ice during the winter season.

LOGISTIC SUPPORT: Candidate vehicles include ice-breaking workboats; self-propelled, 25-ton Voyageur hovercraft; large payload air-cushion barges; conventional barges frozen-in near the drilling locations; fixed-wing aircraft; tracked vehicles and large rubber-tyred vehicles. The selection will be determined by specific condition, economics, availability and other operator requirements.

HULL HEATING SYSTEM: An external heating system on the hull will permit the vessel to remain over the well bore in ice moving at moderate speed.

A four-point mooring system, with ice anchors attached to the ice sheet, allows tension to be pulled on appropriate anchor lines opposing the direction of motion of the ice sheet. This action forces the hot side of the hull to bear against the encroaching ice face. Sufficient heat transfer to the ice sheet melts the ice at a rate equal to the ice sheet motion.

It is anticipated that motion of land-fast ice will be random, and with anchor placement 1,000ft or more away from the drilling unit, resetting of the anchor spread should not be necessary. However, the ice anchors can be reset.

It is only necessary to melt a ledge of ice equivalent to the draft of the hull and the side or sides exposed to ice motion. If the ice thickness exceeds the hull draft, an auxiliary ice removal system is used below the centre well so that the total projected area of the centre well is open through the ice sheet. Deployment of this system is necessary for riser and guidelines protection and for BOP retrieval when necessary.

This drilling well provides communication between the water below the ice sheet and the "lake" in which the ADS is floating while drilling. This makes the unit buoyant without its weight being transferred to the ice sheet below the barge gull.

The primary hull-heating system uses waste heat recovered from three of the five available D-399 Caterpillar engines during normal drilling operations. Sufficient BTUs are available from this source to melt a volume of sea ice moving toward a corner of the hull at 15ft per day and exposing the drilling draft area of one side and one end of the hull to ice motion.

A considerable amount of research and development was committed to the ice-melting system. Both model and full scale studies were conducted to learn the mechanism of heat transfer and fluid flow between the hull and ice sheet and to establish heat input requirements for different velocities. These studies confirmed the mathematical model and proved the validity of the concept.

CONTROLS AND SYSTEMS: A central drilling control room is provided for the well-control personnel. Instrumentation will be installed to provide data on mud weight, mud pump pressure and flow rates, casing pressure, pit level, bit weight, rotary torque, rate of penetration and other critical drilling details. All remote BOP and choke line controls will be housed in the centre.

The design also features a large bulk mud, cement storage and handling system. The bulk storage system will accommodate 6,060ft³ of mud and 3,140ft³ of cement. A pneumatic bulk-handling system permits rapid material transfer.

ACCOMMODATION: A totally enclosed and heated working environment will help maintain maximum crew efficiency, even during the coldest arctic weather. Modern crew quarters for 70 men and a large helipad are included.

A preliminary specification for the 3,840-ton ADS is given below.

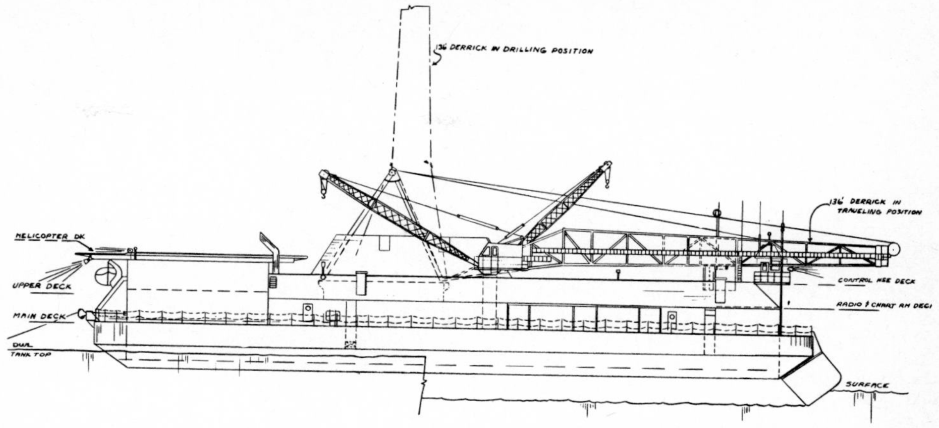

Profile of the 70·4m (231ft) long, 3,840-ton air cushion arctic offshore drilling system (ADS), showing the derrick in travelling and drilling position, the control house and helipad.

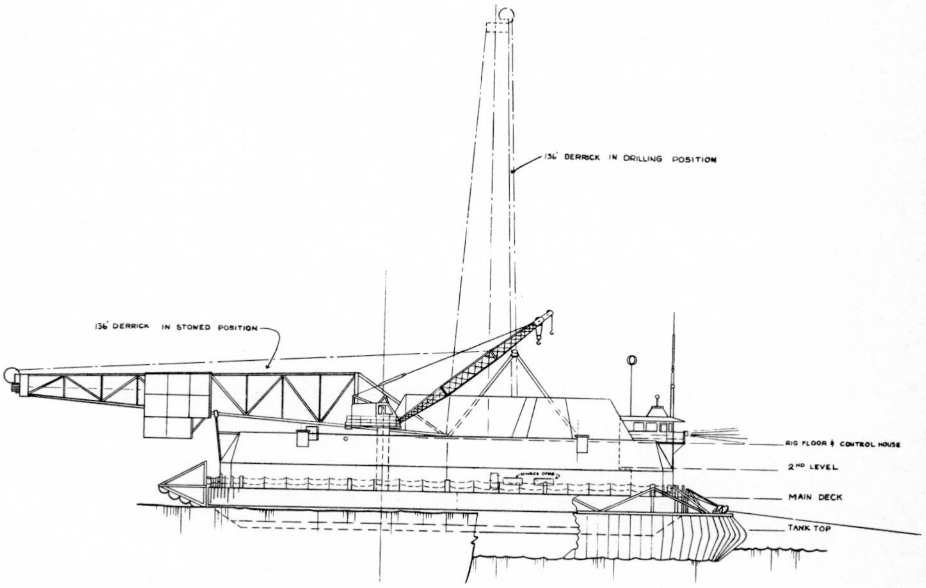

A smaller version of the ADS with a length of 46·93m (154ft). Height of the derrick in drilling position would be 41·45m (136ft) measured above the upper deck

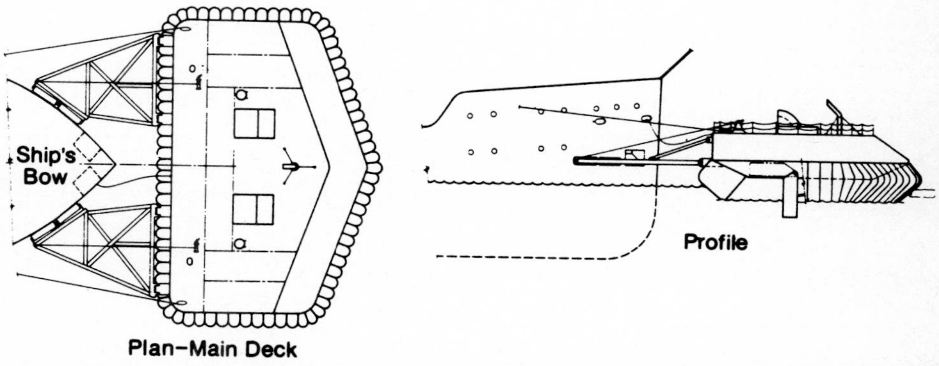

An early VIBAC air-cushion ice-breaker concept designed for attachment to conventional ships travelling through Arctic waters. The unit was an outcome of experience with the ACT-100 on the Great Slave Lake, where it continuously broke ice as thick as 0·685m (27in)

DIMENSIONS
Length: 70·4m (231ft)
Beam: 43·7m (143ft 6in)
Depth of hull: 4·5m (15ft)
WEIGHTS AND CAPACITIES
Gross weight: 3,840 long tons
Casing: 360 long tons
5in drilling pipe: 12,000ft
Reserve mud: 2,357bbl
Active mud: 746bbl
Bulk mud: 6,060ft³
Bulk cement: 3,140ft³
Stacked materials: 17,556ft³
Drill water: 10,695bbl
Potable water: 746bbl
Fuel oil: 3,731bbl
Lubricating oil: 1,500 gallons
Total complement: 70 persons

Design of the ADS is 95% complete. The unit, with a gross weight of 3,840 long tons, is designed to operate in land-fast ice in water depths from 0-183m (0-600ft) during the 7-8 month arctic winter season and in water depths of 9·14-183m (30-600ft) during the open-water summer season. The ADS is designed to operate in nearshore conditions in the Beaufort Sea at the Mackenzie Delta, the Alaskan North Slope, and the inter-island areas of the Canadian Arctic Islands. It could be used in any arctic land-fast ice areas including the continental shelves of Greenland and Siberia.

ICEATER-I

The icebreaking characteristics of the ACT-100 led to the development of a new vehicle designed specifically to aid the passage of a conventional ship through ice-bound waters.

The craft, known as the VIBAC (Vehicle, Ice-Breaking, Air Cushion) system, is attached to the bow of the ship as soon as it enters an ice-field. Close visual observation and films have revealed what happens when the air cushion platform approaches an ice sheet, and how the air cushion ice-breaking phenomenon takes place.

On making contact with the ice sheet the skirt rises up over the ice while continuing to maintain its air seal. The ice-sheet then penetrates the zone of pressurised air beneath the craft, where the water level within the skirt area is depressed to a lower level than the bottom of the ice layer. The ice has now become a cantilevered ledge without water support beneath. When the cantilevered section reaches its critical length, failure occurs and the overhanging section breaks off and falls into the depressed water below.

A plough-like deflector attached to the VIBAC unit will thrust the ice aside as the vessel progresses through the ice sheet.

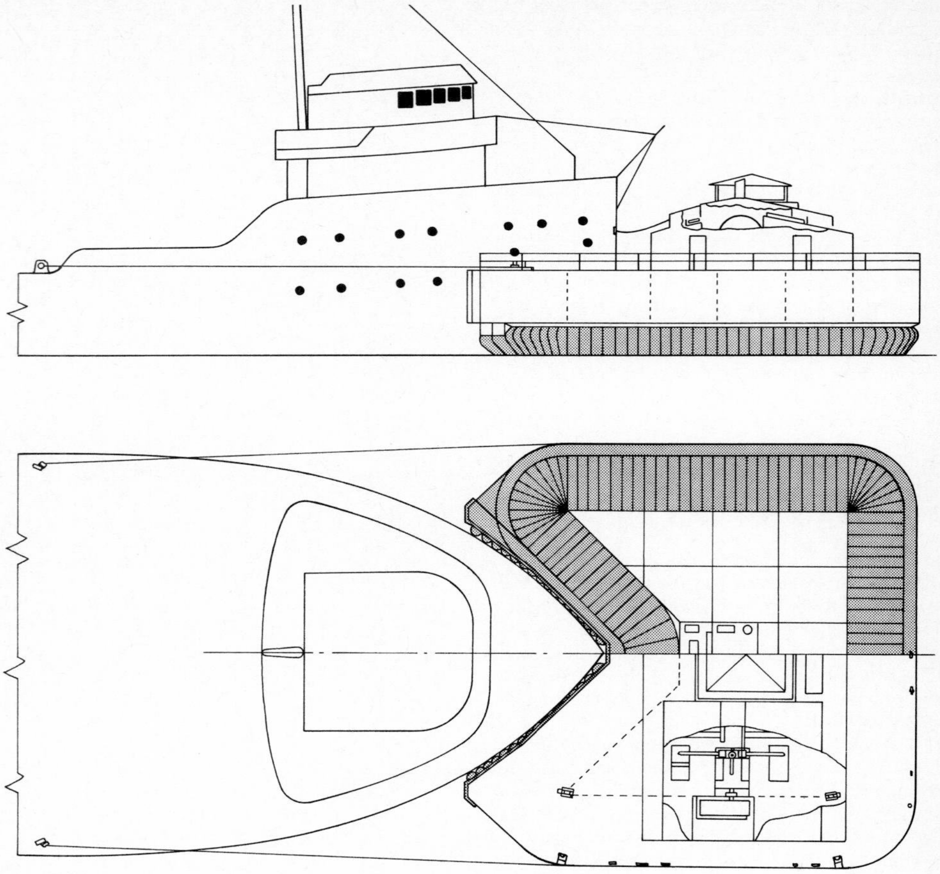

Iceater-I—general arrangement

ASL Iceater-I has now operated with four different vessels:-

	Length	Beam	Displacement	Horsepower
Thunder Cape, harbour tug	32m (105ft) CCG	8·11m (26ft 7in)	600 tons	1,440shp
CCGS Alexander Henry	57·91m (190ft)	13·2m (43ft 6in)	2,240tons	3,550shp
CCGS Griffon	65·22m (214ft)	14·93m (49ft)	2,793tons	4,250shp
MV Imperial St Clair	122·49m (415ft)	22·55m (74ft)	16,450 tons	6,500 shp

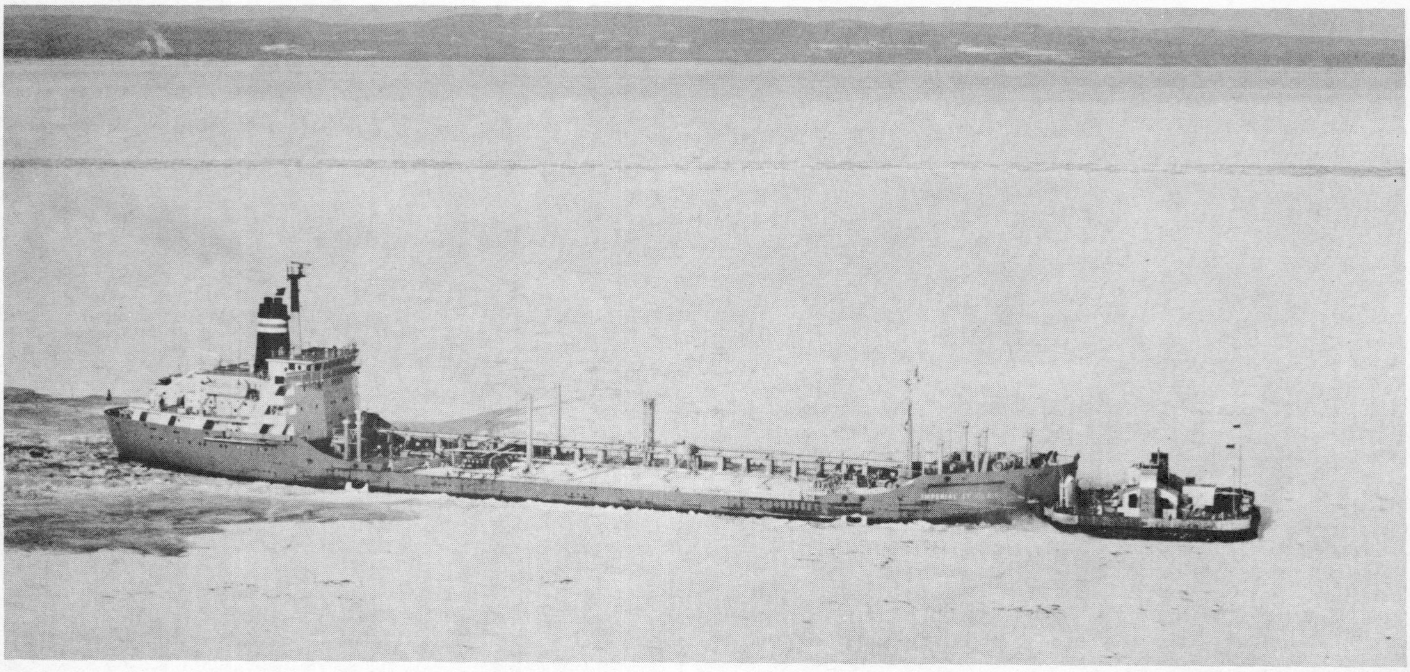

Iceater-I coupled with the 16,450 ton MV Imperial St. Clair. With the ice-breaker platform attached, the cleared track is straighter and wider than that created by conventional ice-breaking techniques and the ship is more manoeuvrable

Under the sponsorship of Transport Canada, the ACT-100 was modified into an icebreaking system and named Iceater I. It was first demonstrated during the 1975-76 winter season at Thunder Bay, Ontario. Scoring an impressive first in the history of ice breaking and transiting, it maintained continuous headway through ice up to 0·812m (32in) thick at speeds up to 9 knots.

A 14ft-deep 'V' notch was cut into the stern of the ACT-100 to accommodate the bow of the CCGV Alexander Henry. The Thunder Bay tests began on 15 January 1976 in temperatures of −30°C. They continued for 3½ months, with the Alexander Henry and Iceater I coupled together as a single unit.

Maximum speed of the ice-breaking operations undertaken so far has been 9 knots in 431mm (17in) thick ice and the maximum thickness of ice broken continuously has been 0·812m (32in). Channel clearing has been significantly simplified and speeded-up by the system and it has been found that because of the method employed and its configuration, Iceater can work alongside locks, piers, docks and other vessels without fear of damage.

The soft coupling method employed has proved both simple and effective and accommodates the differential motions of the two craft without transference. Port and starboard aft air tugger winch lines are passed to the pusher vessel from the Iceater and made fast to port and starboard nylon ship's lines forward of amidships. The Iceater then winches into operating position with the bow of the pusher vessel set firmly into the 'V' notch. Ship's port and starboard snubber lines are then connected to the Iceater's stern bollards to complete the coupling.

LIFT: Air pressure is generated by two Caterpillar D-348 diesels, each directly coupled to a 1·37m (4ft 6in) Joy A-1670 Airfoil centrifugal fan. Each engine develops 440hp at 1,850rpm. The fans develop 170,000ft³/min air flow within the plenum at a nominal pressure of about one psi, or 29in water pressure gauge. Consequently, water below the ice sheet is depressed by an equal amount 29in (0·73m).

HULL: Box type structure in ASTM A537 low temperature alloy steel.

SKIRT: 1·52m (5ft) deep fully segmented skirt in natural rubber coated on nylon fabric, 99 oz/yd² gauge 126.

GENERATOR: Single Perkins/Bemac II, 30kW

BALLAST PUMP: 10hp Viking, 200gallons/min

DIMENSIONS

Length: 23·77m (78ft)

Beam: 17·37m (57ft)

Height (on landing pads):

to main deck: 1·21m (4ft)

WEIGHTS

Light: 190 tons (including 980 US gallons (7,000lb) fuel and 3,239 US gallons (28,700lb) liquid ballast)

Gross: 270 tons

A notch plug has been built to fit the 14ft-deep 'V' cutout in the stern of Iceater-I to accommodate a ship's bow. The purpose of the plug is threefold: to permit the Iceater to be pushed by a flat bow tug; to further break up ice cusps in the after end of the plenum, and to divert broken ice outboard as far and as quickly as possible. The plug was designed and built in the winter of 1977-78 and the two photos show it being raised from lowered to stowed position

ICEATER II

DIMENSIONS

Length: 24·08m (79ft)

Beam: 23·16m (76ft)

Hull depth: 3·05m (10ft)

Hover height: 1·67m (5ft 6in)

WEIGHTS

Full load displacement: 325 tons

EGLEN HOVERCRAFT INC

801 Poplar Street, Terre Haute, Indiana 47807, USA

Telephone: (812) 234 4307

TERREHOVER

Eglen Hovercraft Inc has designed and built a variety of hover platforms, in order to investigate possible agricultural applications. Particular attention is being given to its use for transporting heavy loads, including fertiliser tanks, over wet and muddy fields which cannot be negotiated by conventional farm equipment.

Recently the company has been developing a tomato bin-carrying harvester platform and a cranberry sprayer. It has also built a hovertractor.

The prototype Terrehover is built in wood and measures 4·87m (16ft) long by 2·43m (8ft) wide.

The prototype Eglen Terrehover, a 4·87m (16ft) long hover platform, designed for carrying agricultural equipment over wet and muddy terrain. Production models will be self-propelled, with the operator seated in an enclosed cabin

Air is put under pressure by two 0·6m (2ft) diameter axial-flow fans, driven by two JLO Rockwell L395 two-cycle engines. An HDL type segmented skirt is used and the hoverheight is 228mm (9in).

Although designed originally to lift 907·18kg (2,000lb) the platform has successfully lifted 1,814·37kg (4,000lb), and has applied fertiliser in conditions normally considered too severe for conventional fertilising equipment. The prototype is towed by another vehicle with low pressure tyres, but the production version will be self-propelled with the operator housed in a cab mounted on the platform. Two centrifugal fans, powered by a small diesel engine, will be used and the engine will also drive a hydraulic pump which will power a hydrostatic motor for propulsion.

The vehicle will be capable of highway operation, riding on wheels which will be retracted while in the hovering mode.

A joint development programme is being undertaken with an internationally-known agricultural equipment company.

TIGER MACKACE HOVER SYSTEMS

222S Riverside Plaza, Chicago, Illinois 60606, USA
Telephone: (312) 648 4100
Telex: 253546

Officials:
Thomas V Murphy, *Director*
J T Mackley, *Director*
D G W Turner, *Director*
Michael J Gray, *Director*
Judith Jordan, *Director of Marketing*
T G W Turner
Max Fripp

TM 160 HOVER TRANSPORTER

The Trans Alaska Pipeline, the costliest construction project ever undertaken by private industry, necessitated crossing the Yukon River throughout the year.

Crossings had to be undertaken in temperatures varying from 90 degrees above zero with a river current in excess of 6 mph, to temperatures of 65 degrees below zero with winds in excess of 50 mph.

Due to the nature of this project Tiger Equipment & Services Ltd suggested a company who are designers and contractors of numerous hover transporters. Mackley Ace Alyeska Pipeline Service Co accepted the possibility of modifying Mackley Ace transporters to the Yukon River requirements. A contract was negotiated with Tiger Equipment & Services Ltd who then, in a joint venture with Mackace Hover Systems, undertook the design and construction of the first two air cushion transporter ferry systems.

The initial problem of establishing crossing points was resolved by selecting sites the minimum distance from the projected pipeline route. The south debarkation area is on the tip of Carlos Island while the north side is within five miles of the main artery which supplies the northern sector of the pipeline.

The system had to be capable of operating when the "ice bridge" consisting of reinforced layers of ice capable of supporting traffic crossing the river during winter months, was no longer operable. The time allowed to complete the system was fourteen weeks.

Criteria based on the quantity of supplies necessary to support the work schedule called for two ACTs capable of delivering a payload of 160 tons every 30 minutes. The design of the ACTs had to be sufficiently flexible to permit operation in arctic winters and mild summers, while adjusting to the conditions brought about by the unpredictable Yukon River. The design of the skirt system was especially demanding since the ACT's would be required to hover over solid irregular ice, land, water and any combination of these. The system would also be subjected to floating ice, dislodged trees, and other types of debris during the spring thaw.

Two Tiger Mackace hover transporters ferrying trucks across the Yukon

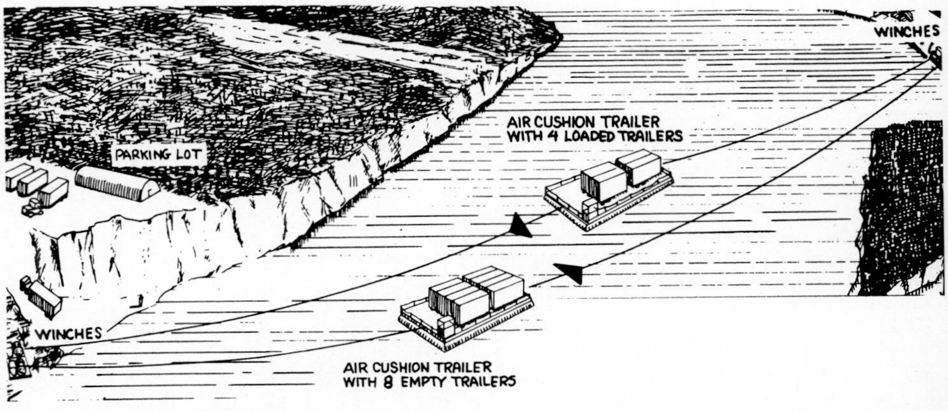

Schematic showing the operation of the two Tiger Mackace TM 160 hover transporters across the Yukon

Crew of the TM 160 normally comprises one engineer and one deckhand.

LIFT AND PROPULSION: Motive power for the lift system is provided by two Detroit Diesel Model 16V 71T diesels, each developing 700hp at 2,100rpm at 85°F. Each engine transmits power to a single squirrel cage, industrial ventilator type centrifugal fan which operates at 1,780rpm. Volume flow is 133,000cfm and static pressure 28in swg. Fuel is carried in two tanks each with a capacity of 500 US gallons, located in the engine/fan mountings.

Propulsion is by cable. Two double drum winches are located on the north bank of the Yukon and a tail pulley system is located on the south bank. Cable guides are fitted on both craft and stationary guides are mounted ahead of the winches. Total length of cable strung across the Yukon is 42,800ft.

To adjust to the rise and fall of the waterline, mobile loading ramps have been constructed. The ramps have the capacity to handle single-bearing loads in excess of 160 tons.

DIMENSIONS
Length: 39·47m (129ft 6in)
Beam: 25·75m (84ft 6in)
Hull depth: 1·22m (4ft)
Deck loading space: 29·57 × 15·85m (97 × 52ft)

WEIGHTS
Gross operating: 392 tonnes (865,000lb)

PERFORMANCE
Max operating speed: 8 knots
Max wave capability: 1·83m (6ft)
Max gradient, static conditions: 8 degree
Vertical obstacle clearance: 1·22m (4ft)
PRICE: US$ 1·8 million. Lease or cash sale.

AIR CUSHION
LANDING SYSTEMS

FRANCE

SOCIETE BERTIN & CIE

BP 3, 78370 Plaisir, France
Telephone: 462 25 00
Telex: 692471
Officials:
Fernand Chanrion, *President, Director General*
Michel Perineau, *Director General*
Georges Mordchelles-Regnier, *Director General*

Bertin & Cie has developed an air cushion landing system based on the company's technique of separately-fed multiple plenum chambers.

ATTERROGLISSEUR

The Atterroglisseur is an air cushion drop platform for damping both vertically and horizontally the landing of heavy loads dropped by parachute. The system comprises a platform carrying the load and an air cushion system which includes inflatable balloons fitted on the underside of the platform, a light tray at the base of the balloons, and flexible skirts beneath the tray connected to the balloons.

While in the aircraft, the complete air cushion system is tightly packed beneath the platform and secured in position by a plate. When the platform is dropped, the securing plate detaches itself automatically and both the flexible skirts and the balloons inflate.

On landing the balloons deflate first, thus feeding the skirts continuously. It is only when the balloons are empty that the skirts slowly collapse to bring the platform to a standstill.

AIRCRAFT LANDING SYSTEM

The same basic system but incorporating air generators is being developed as an air cushion landing system for heavy cargo aircraft and wing-in-ground-effect machines, providing them with multi-terrain landing and take-off capability.

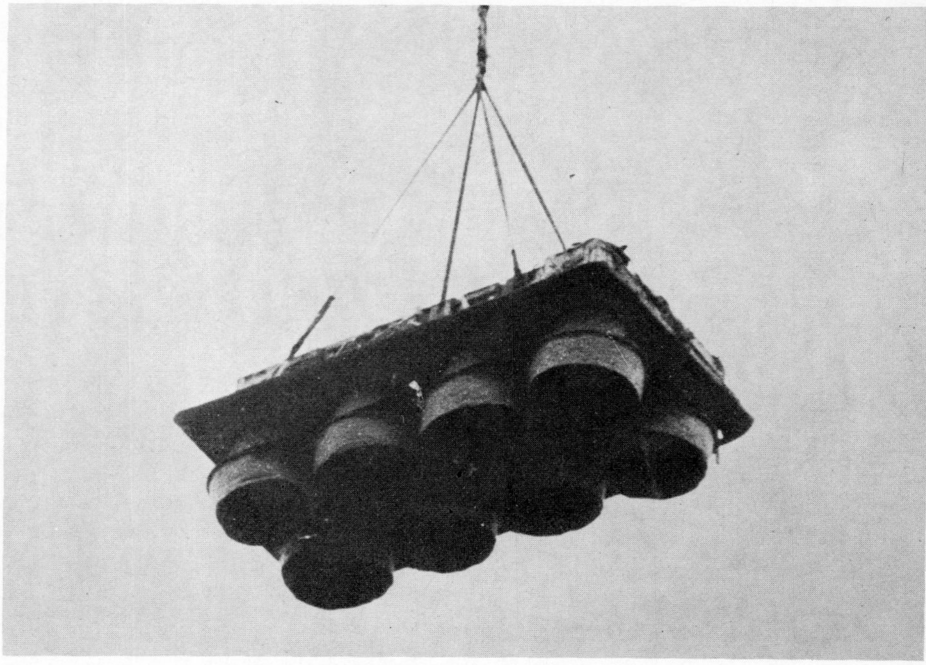

Bertin Atterroglisseur in action. The system is designed to prevent loads dropped by parachute from turning over on hitting the ground. As the loaded platform lands, balloons beneath it cushion the impact as they deflate. Air from the balloons is then fed below into a series of multiple skirts, inflating them and creating an air cushion. This allows the platform to skim the terrain in the dropping zone while the parachutes settle, thus reducing the possibility of the platform and load overturning. When the balloons are finally deflated, the skirts collapse and friction brings the platform to a standstill

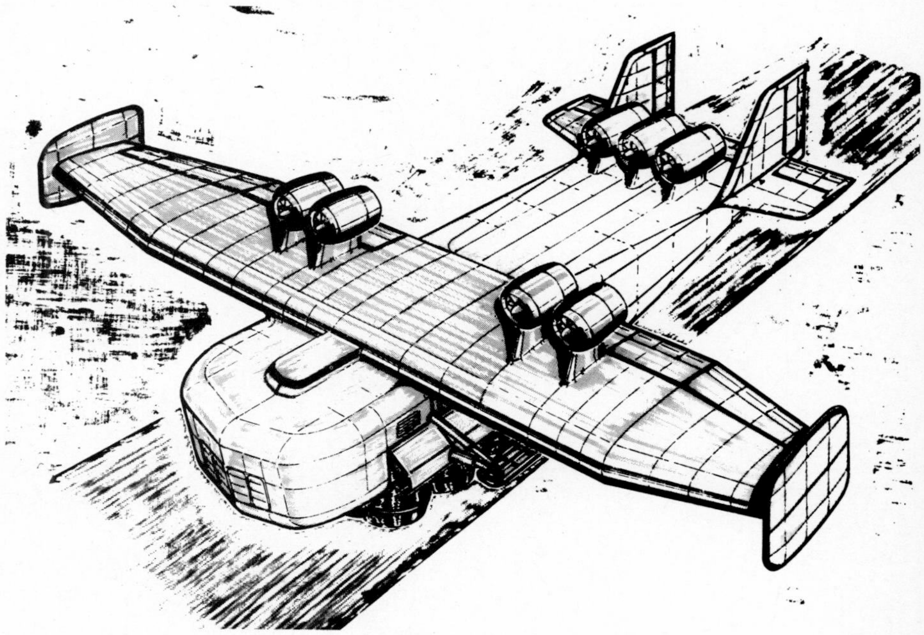

Bertin air cushion landing employed on a giant cargo carrying wing-in-ground-effect machine, providing multi-terrain landing and take-off capability

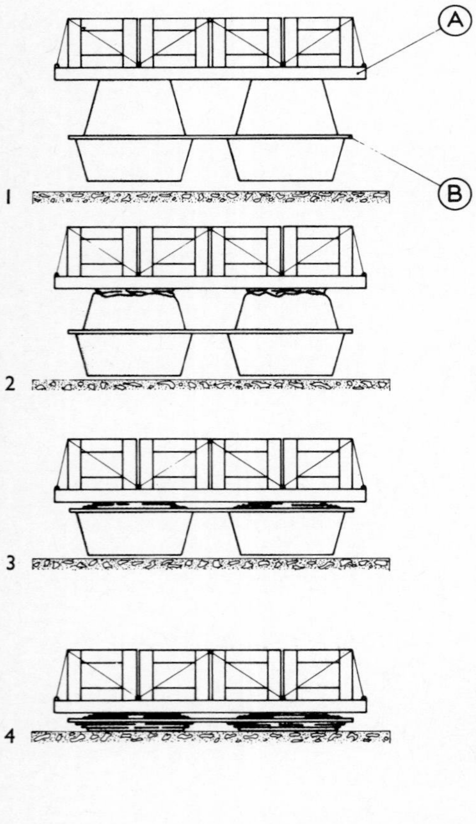

Four phases during an air drop employing an Atterroglisseur skirted platform: 1 during descent, balloons above the multi-skirt cells are fully inflated; 2 on hitting the ground the balloons are gradually crushed and eject air below to inflate the skirts; 3 balloons are deflated and collapse; 4 skirts are flattened and increased friction through surface contact brings the platform to a halt.
The platform comprises: A The load platform with balloons fitted below and B a light tray, to which the lower ends of the balloons are secured. The multi-cell skirts are hung beneath the tray

UNION OF SOVIET SOCIALIST REPUBLICS

BARTINI

Robert Oros di Bartini, a Soviet aircraft designer of Italian birth, has indicated that air cushion landing systems are under development in the Soviet Union, and will possibly replace conventional wheeled undercarriages on a number of aircraft type machines by the end of the century.

His Stal-6, of 1933, was the first in the Soviet Union to be equipped with a completely retractable undercarriage.

Bartini is former head of the group of designers at the Scientific Research Institute of the Civil Air Fleet. His Stal-7 was shown at the Fifteenth Paris Aviation Salon and achieved a world speed record in 1939. He worked with Lavochkin and Myasishchev on fighter development and his later designs include the ER-2 long-range night bomber. In recent years he has participated in the development of VTOL aircraft.

During the summer of 1970-71 an initial test programme employing a towed ACLS test rig was undertaken at Molodezhnaya Station, Antarctica, during the Sixteenth Soviet Antarctic Expedition. The air cushion test rig, which was towed behind a GAZ-47 oversnow truck, took the form of a small air cushion trailer.

Tests included runs over a series of courses, including slopes, and surfaces with natural irregularities. Performance over a variety of surfaces was studied, including powdered snow, ice and compacted ice.

Soviet ACLS test rig undergoing trial runs during the Sixteenth Soviet Antarctic Expedition

It was later stated that the rig was operated successfully over terrain from which ski-equipped aircraft could neither take-off nor land. Another advantage was that the skirt did not freeze to the surface, a not infrequent problem with conventional, ski-equipped aircraft.

Stage two of the tests involved mounting sensors employed on the ACLS rig on one of the expedition's IL-14s equipped with skis.

Take-offs, landings and taxiing were performed, mainly under extreme conditions of wind, temperatures and surface states, and the data recorded was compared with the rig results.

Instrumentation was provided on the test rig to record vertical and angular accelerations plus pressures in the air-cushion plenum.

UNITED STATES OF AMERICA

BELL AEROSPACE TEXTRON

Division of Textron Inc.

Head Office: Buffalo, New York 14240, USA

Telephone: (716) 297 1000

Officials:

See ACV Section

The air cushion landing system was designed by Bell to replace wheels, skis, or floats on any size or type of aircraft, with a single system combining the functional capabilities of them all. In addition its overall weight and cost is less than that of a combination of conventional systems.

This application of the air cushion principles is an outgrowth of work in the field of air cushion vehicles. The system minimises airstrip requirements and enables aircraft to take-off and land on unprepared surfaces, in open fields, on open water, ice, snow, marsh, sand or dirt. Factors contributing to this feasibility are the very low pressure in the bag supporting the aircraft, the elimination of friction because of the air jets, and the increased area of contact during braking.

It has proved to be an ideal gear for crosswind take-off and landing.

The first aircraft to be fitted with ACLS was a Lake LA-4 light amphibian converted by Bell. In November 1970 Bell was awarded a USAF contract to install similar equipment on a de Havilland CC-115 Buffalo.

The aircraft, so modified, was redesignated XC-8A and delivered to the US Air Force in November 1973.

ACLS-EQUIPPED LA-4

Preliminary tests were undertaken with the converted LA-4 amphibian which performed its first take-off and landing on 4 August 1967.

The LA-4 ACLS consists primarily of a doughnut-shaped trunk inflated to a thickness of approximately 0·6m (2ft) by an axial fan. The fan, powered by a separate engine, forces air down into the trunk. This flow of air escapes through hundreds of small jet nozzles on the underside, providing a cushion of air upon which the aircraft floats. The trunk is fabricated from multiple layers of stretch nylon cloth for strength, layered with natural rubber for elasticity and coated with neoprene for environmental stability. When deflated during flight its elasticity

The de Havilland XC-8A landing on grass at the Wright-Patterson Air Force Base

Equipped with an air cushion landing system, the XC-8A can operate from a range of surfaces including rough ground, marshland, ice, snow, water and grass. Floats are mounted beneath each wing for operation from water. Fibreglass spring skids beneath the floats prevent the machine from rolling excessively while taxiing

ensures that it retracts tightly against the underside of the hull.

At touchdown, six brake skids on the underside of the trunk are brought into contact with the landing surface by pneumatic pillows. When fully inflated for maximum braking, these pillows are each slightly larger than a basketball. For parking on land or water a lightweight internal bladder seals the air jets, thus supporting the aircraft at rest or providing buoyancy to keep it afloat indefinitely.

DIMENSIONS

AIRCRAFT

Wing span: 11·58m (38ft)
Overall length: 5·59m (24ft 11in)
Gross wing area: 15·79m^2 (170ft^2)

AIR CUSHION

Length: 4·87m (16ft)
Width: 1·16m (3ft 10in)
Area: 4·18m^2 (45ft^2)

LOADINGS

Wing loading: 73·24kg/m^2 (15lb/ft^2)
Air cushion pressure: 268·53kg/m^2 (55lb/ft^2)

WEIGHTS

Gross operating: 1,113·92kg (2,500lb)
Air cushion system: 117kg (258lb)

POWER PLANTS

Propulsion engine rating:
Lycoming Model 0 360 01A, 180bhp
Air cushion engine rating:
Modified McCulloch Model 4318F (driving 2-stage axial fan), 90bhp

PERFORMANCE

Cruising speed: 201km/h (125mph)
Stalling speed: 86·9km/h (54mph)
Take-off run: 198·12m (650ft)
Landing run: 144·78m (475ft)

ACLS-EQUIPPED XC-8A BUFFALO

The XC-8A was a joint United States/Canadian programme to adapt the ACLS for military transport aircraft. This would allow such aircraft to operate from a variety of surfaces, including rough fields, soft soils, swamps, water, ice and snow.

A de Havilland Canada XC-8A Buffalo STOL military transport aircraft was loaned by the Canadian Department of National Defence, as the testbed aircraft for this programme.

Bell Aerospace Textron designed and fabricated the air cushion system and was responsible for overall programme integration, funded by the US Air Force.

De Havilland Aircraft of Canada Ltd modified the XC-8A testbed aircraft to take the ACLS installation, and United Aircraft of Canada Ltd was responsible for development and flight qualifications of the air cushion auxiliary power system. The Canadian Government funded the work of these two latter companies.

Taxi tests and an initial take-off on the ACLS were completed in March 1975. The first ACLS landing of the XC-8A took place at Wright-Patterson Air Force Base, Dayton, Ohio on 11 April 1975. During the subsequent US Air Force test programme over 70 take-offs and landings were made in varying conditions, in about 85 hours of operation, with 250 inflations of the ACLS trunk. This included take-offs and landings on concrete runways, grass and snow, with taxi tests over craters and operations in temperatures down to —29°C (–20°F).

ACLS employs a layer of air instead of wheels as the ground contacting medium. The system's trunk, a large flat sheet, becoming inner-tube-like when inflated, encircles the underside of the fuselage, and, on inflation, provides an air duct and seal for the air cushion.

The underside of the rubberised trunk is perforated with thousands of vent holes through which air exhausts forming the air cushion.

Air cushion brakes are also part of the system. Six skids on the bottom operate when the pilot applies the aircraft brakes. The braking action pushes the skids, of tyre tread-type materials, against the ground and ventilates the air cushion cavity. This stops the aircraft. Stopping distance

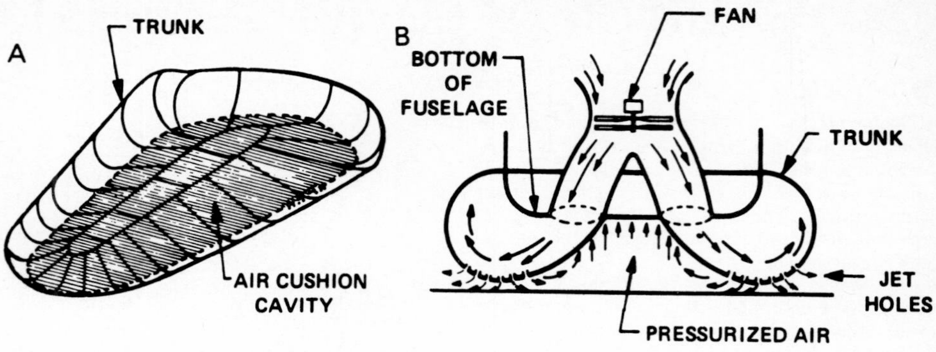

ACLS PRINCIPLE
A Function of the inflated trunk, left, is to contain the pressurised air in the air cushion cavity. This cushion of air supports the weight of the craft
B Air continuously forced through the jet holes pressurises the air cushion cavity, and also provides air bearing lubrication between the trunk and its supporting surface

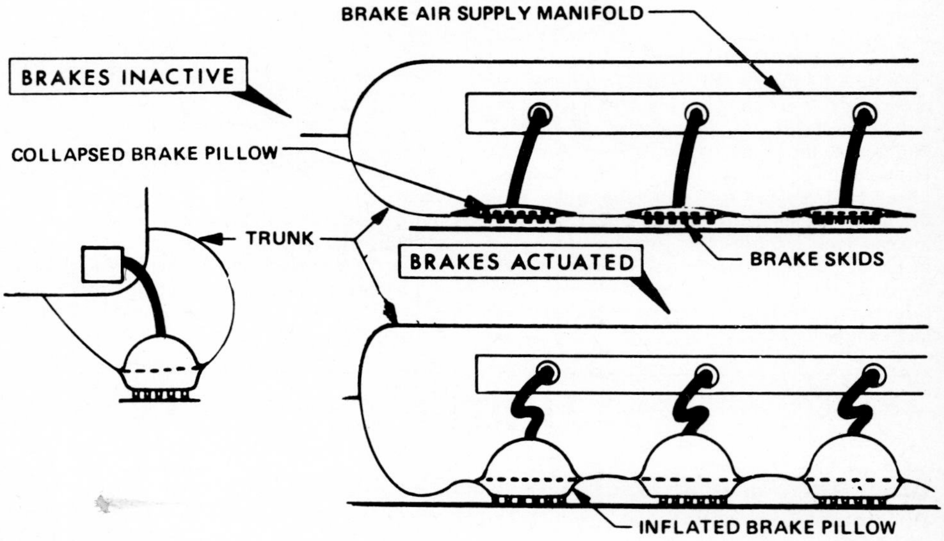

BRAKE SYSTEM
Inflation of the brake pillow of the ACLS-equipped plane brings multiple brake skids into ground contact, drawing the aircraft to a halt

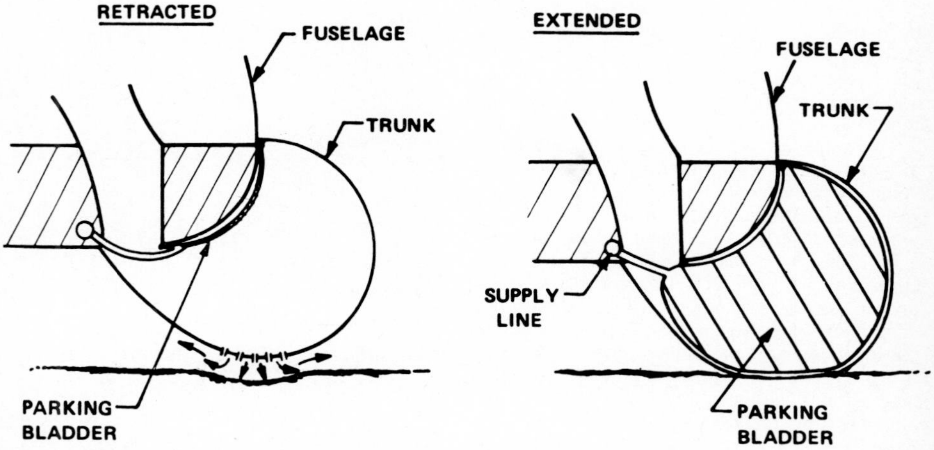

PARKING SYSTEM
A separate bladder within the rubberised air cushion trunk is inflated to support the weight of the aircraft when parked

is comparable to that of conventional wheel and brake landing systems.

Cushionborne control is accomplished by using differential thrust, forward and reverse from the propulsion engines. This involved modification of the standard propellers which was performed by Hamilton Standard Division of United Technologies.

Balancer floats are mounted on struts beneath each wing for operation on and from water. Beneath the floats are fibreglass spring skids to prevent excessive roll and protect the propellers while taxiing over land.

XC-8A BUFFALO

DIMENSIONS

AIRCRAFT

Wing span: 29·26m (96ft)
Overall length: 23·57m (77ft 4in)
Gross wing area: 22·63m^2 (945ft^2)

AIR CUSHION

Length: 10·25m (32ft 2in)
Width: 4·26m (14ft)
Area: 21·18m^2 (228ft^2)

LOADINGS

Wing loading: 211·8kg/m^2 (43·4lb/ft^2)
Air cushion pressure: 830kg/m^2 (170lb/ft^2)

WEIGHTS

Gross operating: 18,597kg (41,000lb)
Air cushion system: 1,006·92kg (2,220lb)

POWER PLANT

PROPULSION ENGINES

Two General Electric Model CT64-820-1, rated at 3,055eshp

AIR CUSHION ENGINES
Two United Aircraft of Canada ST6F-70, rated at 800bhp

PERFORMANCE
Cruising speed at 10,000ft: 230 knots TAS
Stalling speed, 40 degree flap at 39,000lb: 66 knots
Take-off run on level surface: 344·42m (1,130ft)
to 15·24m (50ft) from level surface: 500m (1,640ft)
Landing run from 15·24m (50ft) on level surface: 344·42m (1,130ft)
on level surface: 200m (650ft)

ACLS APPLICATION CONTRACTS

Bell has also studied the feasibility of using an ACLS on Space Shuttle vehicles and an Advanced Technology Transport under NASA contract, a high-performance fighter under US Navy contract, and has designed an ACLS for a Remotely Piloted Vehicle—the Australian Jindivik—under a US Air Force contract. In 1978 Bell began conducting application studies for the National Aeronautics and Space Administration (NASA). These studies are aimed at defining optimum integrated designs which are not constrained by retrofit as in the earlier studies. The NASA studies range from small general aviation applications up to very large cargo aircraft of one million pounds and more all-up weight.

TRACKED SKIMMERS

BRAZIL

FEI
FACULTY OF INDUSTRIAL ENGINEERING

Research Vehicle Department (DEPV), Faculty of Industrial Engineering, São Bernado do Campo, Avenido Oreste Romano 112, São Paulo, Brazil
Telephone: 443 1155
Officials:
Rigoberto Soler Gisbert, *Director of Vehicle Research*

The Vehicle Research Department of the FEI, founded in 1968, has designed a number of small air cushion vehicles, one of which is about to be put into production.

The Department's first and most ambitious project to date has been the design and construction of the TALAV tracked air cushion vehicle, development of which is being supported by the Ministry for Industry and Commerce through FUNAT—a government fund for sponsoring new technological developments.

The prototype, an all-metal vehicle propelled by twin Marbore VIs, and seating 20 passengers, displays several novel features, including the siting of the main passenger access door at the front. The whole of the front section moves forward telescopically to provide space for entry and exit. This arrangement facilitates the loading of freight when necessary, and should an emergency stop occur when carrying passengers on a narrow elevated guideway, walking out through the front will be far safer than through the sides, say the designers.

It is also stated that passenger handling will be simplified at termini, where the vehicles can be drawn up side-by-side without the need to devote valuable space for platforms.

The main application foreseen for vehicles of this type is that of city centre to suburbs or city centre to airport links.

To enable construction to be undertaken without difficulty in developing areas where manpower is available, the structure is based on easily-handled sub-assemblies and standard panels of aluminium honeycomb.

The design team is at present concentrating on the development of an efficient yet economical approach to the construction of guideways.

LIFT AND PROPULSION: Cushion air is delivered by fans powered by a 70hp engine. Cushion pressure, 195·3kg/m² (40lb/ft²), cushion area 301·93m² (3,250ft²). Two 900lb st Turboméca Marbore VI gas-turbines supply propulsive thrust.

DIMENSIONS
EXTERNAL
Length: 15·54m (51ft)
Width: 2·26m (7ft 5in)
Height: 2·87m (9ft 5in)

Prototype of the FEI, 20-seat TALAV tracked air cushion vehicle. Designed to cruise at 321·86km/h (200mph), the vehicle is powered by twin Turboméca Marbore VI gas-turbines

INTERNAL
Internal height, passenger saloon: 2·13m (7ft)
WEIGHTS
Empty: 2,948·35kg (6,500lb)
Loaded: 5,896·7kg (13,000lb)
PERFORMANCE
Cruising speed: 321·86km/h (200mph)

FRANCE

SOCIÉTÉ DE L'AÉROTRAIN

Tour Anjou, 33 quai National, 92806 Puteaux, France
Telephone: 776 43 34
Telex: 610385 Bertrin Putau
Officials:
Jean Gautier, *Chairman*
Benjamin Salmon, *Director General*

Originally named "Société d'Etudes de l'Aérotrain", this company was formed on 15 April 1965 to develop a high speed transportation system based on air cushion support and guidance principles conceived by Bertin & Cie.

Jean Bertin, Chairman of the company from 1971 until he died, prematurely, on 21 December 1975, was known as the father of the Aérotrain. His name will remain attached to a number of outstanding inventions in the air cushion field and in many others, including aeronautics.

The Aérotrain has completed its experimental phase as far as the air cushion technique is concerned. The 01 half-scale prototype, after nearly three years of test runs at speeds up to 346km/h (215mph), has successfully attained its phased design requirements, namely the verification of dynamic behaviour, the development of integrated suspension systems, and the accumulation

The Aérotrain 01, a research vehicle built for tests up to and above 250 mph on the No I track at Gometz

of data for the design and costing of full-scale operational vehicles.

The 02 half-scale prototype has undergone similar tests in order to produce data for vehicles operating at speeds above 322km/h (200mph). A speed of 423·26km/h (263mph) was attained by the vehicle in January 1969.

There are three families of Aérotrain systems, Interurban, with speeds of 280-400km/h (115-250mph); Suburban, with speeds of 160-200km/h (100-125mph) and the new Tridim system, designed for speeds of up to 80km/h (50mph) as the distance between suburban stations generally ranges between several hundred yards and one or two miles.

The speeds selected will be based on economic considerations. Suburban systems will cover a variety of routes from city centres to airports and city centres to satellite towns and suburban areas. The size, speed and control system of each vehicle will be decided according to the route.

Current studies are aimed primarily at developing associated techniques including propulsion modes for the various speeds and environments, controls, signals and stations.

A mathematical model has been developed in order to computerise the various parameters for both families of applications. This enables operating costs to be obtained, in an optimised form, for given traffic requirements.

Two full-scale vehicles, the 80-seat Orleans inter-city Aérotrain and the 40-44 seat suburban Aérotrain have undergone extensive trials. During trials between 1969 and 1971, the 80-seat 1-80 "Orleans" Aérotrain has completed more than 700 hours of operation on its 18km (11·2 mile) track north of Orleans, carrying more than 10,000 people at a speed of 260km/h (160mph). In January 1973, the vehicle was taken to the UTA maintenance facility at Le Bourget airport where it was equipped with a 15,000lb st JT8D-11 turbofan, permitting its speed to be studied in the 360-400km/h (220-250mph) range.

In November 1973, a speed of 400km/h (250mph) was attained and by May 1974, 150 hours of operation had been logged in this configuration, during which 2,000 professionally interested passengers had been carried.

All these programmes, completed or under way, represent a financial development effort of roughly US $22 million. The French Government extended its support at every stage by means of various loans, subsidies and orders.

In November 1969, the company formed a US subsidiary, Aérotrain Systems Inc, to build and market Aérotrains in the United States and Mexico. Initially this company was jointly held by Rohr Industries Inc, Bertin et Cie and Société de l'Aérotrain. Since 1976, it has been held by the two latter. A 60-seat, 140mph, LIM-propelled prototype was completed in December 1972 and was successfully tested in 1975-76 on an experimental line built at the US Department of Transport centre at Pueblo, California.

In 1971, another subsidiary was formed, Aérotrain Scandinavia AB, in which the Salén Group has a 50% interest. A third company, formed in Brazil with the support of four French banks, is Aérotrain Systemas de Transporte.

In December 1973 an agreement was signed between Bertin & Cie, Aérotrain, Spie-Batignolles, Jeumont-Schneider, SGTE MTE and Francorail-MTE to co-operate with the promotion and operation of Aérotrain systems and various aspects of production of French projects.

Turntables are installed at each end of the present Aérotrain test track, but they will not be used normally on operational lines. In service Aérotrains will be able to manoeuvre independently on the flat floor surfaces of stations

The Aérotrain 02, a research vehicle built for tests up to and above 250 mph on the No I track at Gometz

The I-80HV Aérotrain with its turbofan thrust unit

EXPERIMENTAL AEROTRAIN AEROTRAIN 01

An experimental, half-scale prototype, this vehicle was operated along a test track 6·7km (4·2 miles) long. The track has an inverted T cross section, the vertical portion being 55cm (1ft 10in) high and the horizontal base 1·8m (5ft 11in) wide. A turntable is fitted at each end.

The vehicle is of light alloy construction. The slender body has seats at the front for six people, and an engine compartment at the rear. Lift and guidance are provided by two centrifugal fans, driven by two 50hp Renault Gordini motor car engines, linked by a shaft. The fans supply air to the guidance and lift cushions at a pressure of about 25g/cm^2 (0·35lb/in^2), the maximum airflow being 10m^3/s (350ft^3/s). Propulsion is provided by a 260hp Continental aero-engine, mounted at the top of a 1·2m (3ft 11in) tail pylon and driving a reversible-pitch propeller, which is also used for normal braking. There are brake pads at the rear of the vehicle which grip the vertical track section like a disc brake.

The first test run on the track was made on 29 December 1965. The prototype was intended to evaluate and demonstrate the Aérotrain principle on a small scale, and was developed with the active support of the French Government and French Railways.

Although the vehicle was designed for a maximum speed of 200km/h (125mph) tests have been undertaken at higher speeds with the help of booster rockets to supplement the propulsive airscrew. In December 1967, the vehicle reached the top speed of 345km/h (215mph) several times with a jet engine assisted by two booster rockets.

DIMENSIONS
Length, overall: 10m (32ft 10in)
Width, overall: 2m (6ft 7in)
Height, overall: 3·7m (12ft 2in)

Aérotrain guideway track beams can be adjusted at the pylon heads in the event of ground subsidence

Height to top of body: 1·6m (5ft 3in)
WEIGHTS
Basic: 2,500kg (5,500lb)
PERFORMANCE
Cruising speed: 200km/h (125mph)
Top speed: 303km/h (188mph)

EXPERIMENTAL AEROTRAIN 02

Aérotrain 02 is an experimental half-scale pro-

The prefabricated concrete beams of the Orleans track have a minimum ground clearance of 4·87m (16ft). This allows the track to be constructed across roads and agricultural land without causing obstruction. *(Photo: P M Lambermont)*

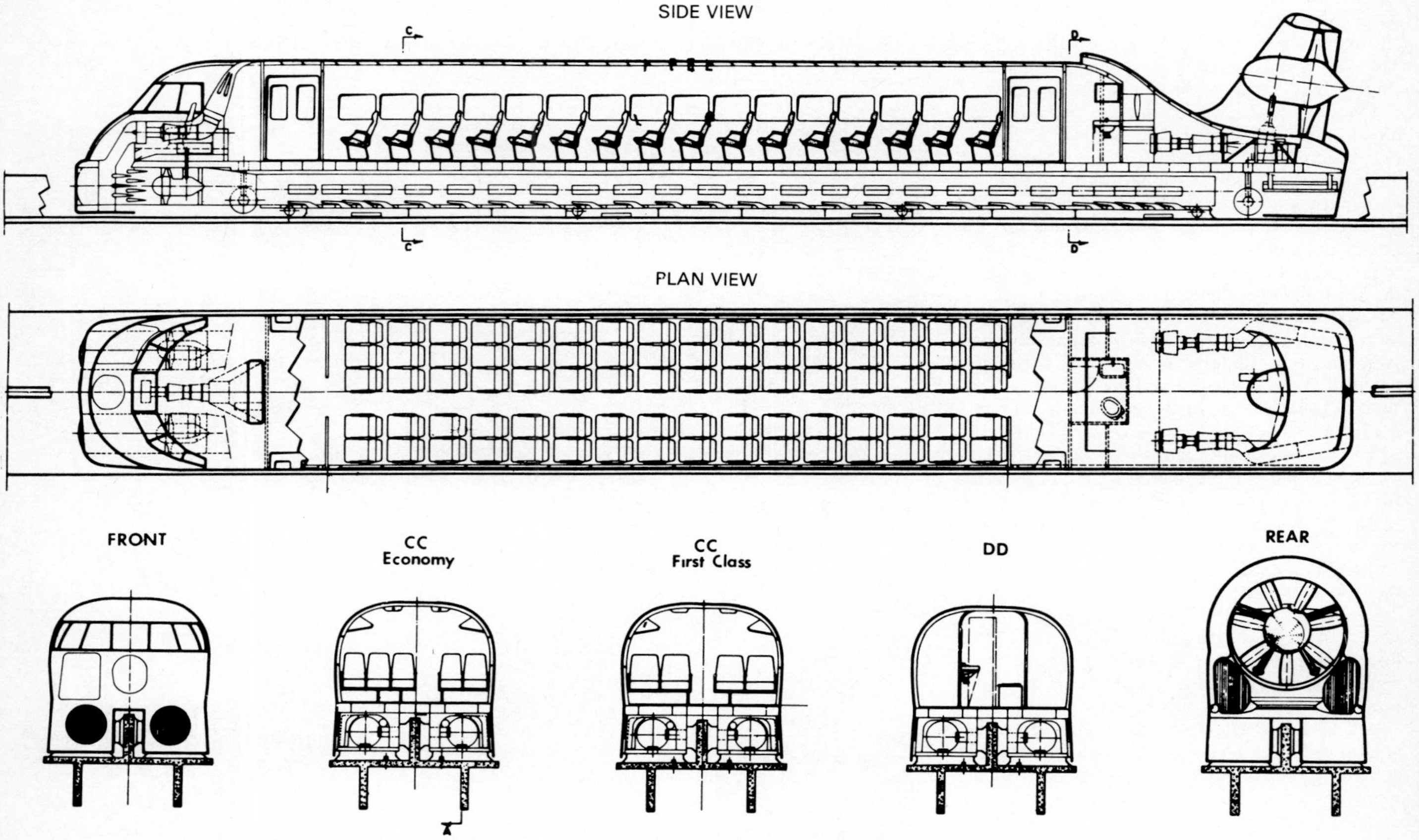

The Aérotrain I-80—a typical Aérotrain configuration for medium-range inter-city traffic, carrying 80 passengers at a cruising speed of 180mph and a top speed of 190mph

totype designed for high speed tests on the track at Gometz used by the first prototype.

Due to the track's relatively short length, a more powerful thrust engine, a Pratt & Whitney JT 12, is installed in order to maintain high speeds over a distance of 2km (1·3 miles) for performance measurements.

During its first series of test runs, the Aérotrain 02 attained 378km/h,(235mph). A booster rocket was then added, and a series of tests followed, culminating in a record speed of 422km/h (263mph) being attained. The average speed recorded over the 2-3 mile track was 411km/h (255mph).

The air cushions for lift and guidance are provided by fans driven by a Turboméca Palouste gas-turbine. At high speed, the dynamic pressure is sufficient to feed the air cushions.

The internal space has been devoted in the main to test instrumentation. Seats are provided only for the pilot and a test engineer.

Aérotrains 01 and 02 were both equipped with propulsion engines which were readily available from the aviation market and capable of giving high speed on a short test track. Operational vehicles use quieter power arrangements.

FULL-SCALE AEROTRAIN I-80 ORLEANS INTERCITY PROJECT

This medium range inter-city vehicle (the Orleans-Paris line will be 113km (70 miles) long) was designed originally with airscrew propulsion for speeds up to 300km/h (186·41mph), but has now been equipped with a silenced turbofan engine which has increased its speed to 400km/h (250mph). The vehicle carries 80 passengers, in airline comfort, in an air-conditioned and sound-proofed cabin.

The lift and guidance air cushions are fed by two axial fans driven by a 400hp Turboméca Astazou gas turbine. At high speeds, they will be fed by dynamic intake pressure.

On the original model thrust was supplied by a shrouded propeller, driven independently by two 1,300hp Turmo III gas turbines.

In January 1973, the vehicle was taken to the UTA maintenance facility at Le Bourget, where it was fitted with a 15,000lb thrust Pratt & Whitney JT8D-11 turbofan, which permitted the systematic study of the I-80 and its components at speeds in the 354-426km/h (220-250mph) range.

Hydraulically retractable tyred wheels are incorporated to help to achieve silent operation near and in stations, and also to assist in manoeuvring and switching the vehicle on station floors. The vertical rail of the inverted T track is unnecessary at low speeds.

A very low empty-weight-to- payload ratio has been possible because of the lack of concentrated loads inherent in the vehicle. This permits the use of lightweight supporting structures—tracks and stations.

Vehicles will not be coupled, so that very high frequency services can be maintained throughout the day. With headways as low as one minute, simple or articulated vehicles offer a range of capacities which largely cope with the peaks of traffic expected in known inter-city lines.

Two articulated cars with seats for up to 160 passengers and luxury models with a wider aisle and reduced seating capacity are being considered in feasibility studies being undertaken for several projected routes.

DIMENSIONS
Length, overall: 30·5m (101ft 8in)
Length, at track level: 27·75m (92ft 6in)
Width: 3·2m (10ft 8in)
Height at fan jet air intake: 5·1m (17ft)
WEIGHTS
Gross: 24 tonnes
PERFORMANCE
Test speed range: 354-426km/h (220-250mph)

THE GUIDEWAY

The first leg of the future Orleans to Paris line—a track 18·5km (11·5 miles) long—was completed in July 1969. It includes turntables at both ends and a central platform for manoeuvring and switching.

In mid-1973 the French Government confirmed that the line is to be completed in due course, but did not announce details.

The track has been designed for a service speed of 402km/h (250mph). It is mounted on pylons along the entire route. The prefabricated concrete beams, of 20m (67ft) span, have a minimum ground clearance of 4·9m (16ft). This allows the track to be constructed across roads and cultivated land.

Due to the low stresses produced by the Aérotrain vehicles it has been possible to design a lightweight elevated track structure, which is less expensive than an equivalent ground track. Local ground subsidence, which may occur during the first years after erection, will be countered by adjusting the pylon heads. This will be limited to a simple jacking operation using built-in devices in the pylon structure.

The radii of curves and gradient angles will depend upon the accelerations admissible without causing discomfort to passengers. Banking can be provided if necessary. Banking of 7% is in fact incorporated in three curves in the Orleans track. The radius requirements are therefore the same as for other guided systems of transport for similar speeds. The advantage of the Aérotrain track is that there are no gradient limitations and it can therefore be constructed with a much smaller number of curves.

TESTS

Speed, acceleration and braking characteristics have confirmed expectations, and the riding comfort has proved to be highly satisfactory. Under all operating conditions, including propeller reverse braking, negotiating curves and in cross winds of 50km/h (31mph), the average accelerations were less than 0·6m/s² at all times, with values of 0·3 to 0·5m/s² during normal cruising conditions.

Since the interior noise level in the passenger compartment is between 75 and 78 dBA, it is possible to converse in normal tones. A level of 70-72 dBA will be reached on series production vehicles.

External noise, 90-95 dBA at 60m (65yds) compares favourably to that of a modern electric train, with a much shorter duration.

During the 850 hours of operation there was no breakdown which caused the vehicle to stop on the guideway, with the exception of a single incident involving hydraulic circuits to the propeller, which were repaired in less than an hour. Only three items, other than the air cushions, have necessitated a major repair since the vehicle was put on the guideway. The air cushions have been completely trouble-free.

The third phase of the test programme consisted of an endurance, or accelerated service test involving 200 hours of running time. Thirty-six operating days were utilised and a daily average of six hours continuous operation were completed. The cruising speed established was 250km/h (154·33mph). Since this involved acceleration and deceleration between 0 and 250km/h (154·33mph) every six minutes, a commercial operation of 1,000-2,000 hours or 200,000-400,000km in terms of wear on the vehicle was simulated. The rate of air cushion lip wear experienced indicates a useful lip life of 40,000 to 50,000km and a practically negligible cost factor of 0·001 to 0·002 francs per passenger/kilometre.

It is to be noted that cultivation has been resumed around and underneath the guideway which, in sharp contrast with the high permanent way maintenance costs experienced by the railways, has required no maintenance whatsoever since it was built.

HIGH SPEED I-80 HV "ORLEANS" AEROTRAIN

In November 1973, the I-80 "Orleans" Aérotrain began a series of tests with a new propulsion system. The two Turmo III gas-turbines, which powered a shrouded propeller, were replaced by a 15,000lb thrust Pratt & Whitney JT8D-11 turbofan, fitted with a sound supressor system designed by Bertin & Cie. The ride characteristics remained outstanding at speeds up to 416km/h (260mph) in spite of the size of the new propulsion unit which resulted in the vehicle being 4 tons over weight.

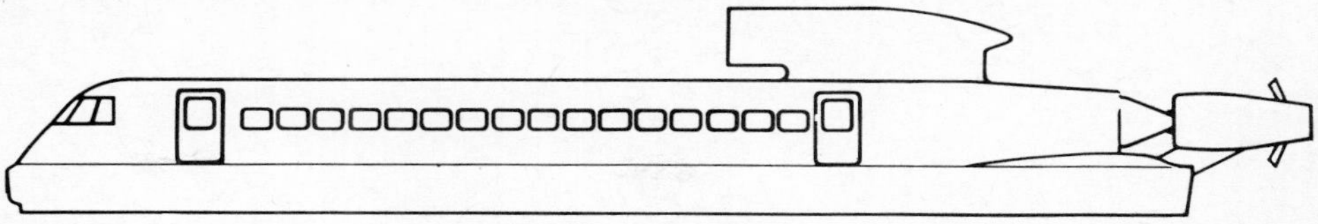

Side view showing the revised configuration of the I-80HV Aérotrain with its new turbofan thrust unit

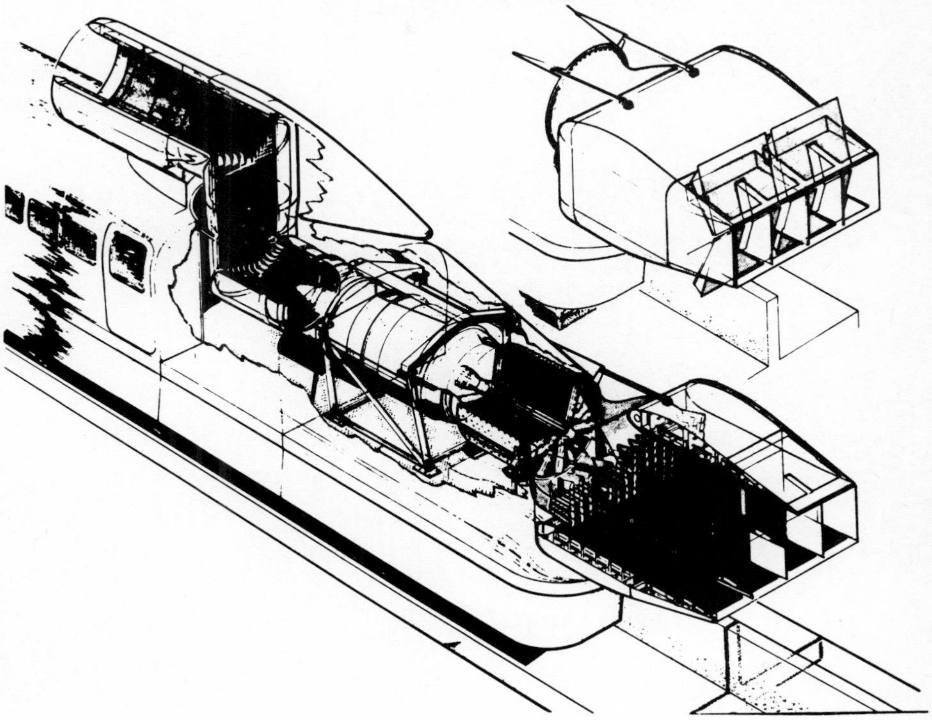

The I-80HV Orleans Aérotrain after being fitted with a 15,000lb thrust Pratt & Whitney JT8D-11 turbofan, which has permitted the behaviour of the vehicle's systems to be studied at speeds of 380-430km/h (220-270mph). Considerable attention has been given to sound attenuation. As seen in the cutaway drawing, the air intake has been designed for the maximum effectiveness, and a special high dilution ejection system suppresses the noise of the exhaust gases

The compressors and air feeders remained unchanged.

On 5 March 1974, the vehicle attained 430km/h (270mph), with an average speed (in each direction) of 418km/h (263mph) over a distance of 1·86 miles. The sound insulation has been extremely effective, resulting in a noise level 2dBA lower than the original propulsion system.

In 1976, the Orleans vehicle was still in use for demonstrations. By May 1976 it had completed 925 hours of operation including 212 hours with its JT8D-11 turbofan. During this time it has carried 13,500 passengers, 3,280 of whom have been carried at speeds in excess of 400km/h (250mph).

SUBURBAN AEROTRAIN AEROTRAIN S-44

The prototype 40-44 passenger suburban vehicle is equipped with a linear induction motor. The vehicle underwent trials at Gometz between 1969 and 1972, where its 3km (1·9 mile) test track runs parallel to that used by the Aérotrain 01 and 02 experimental vehicles. During its test programme the vehicle was operated at speeds up to 170km/h (105mph). The S-44 is currently undergoing modification as part of the company's development programme for the new 24km (15 mile) La Défense—Cergy line.

The power for the two axial lift fans is provided by a 525hp GM Chevrolet V8 car engine. Practically silent operation is achieved since there is no noise of rolling wheels. No vibration is communicated to the track structure which can therefore be erected in urban areas without fear of any noise disturbing local communities, even if steel is used for the longer spans of the guideway.

This vehicle is equipped with an electrical linear motor developed by the Société Le Moteur Linéaire (Merlin & Gerin Group). It provides a thrust of 18,000N at 137km/h (85mph) and has been currently operated at speeds above 160km/h (100mph).

Electric current is collected from the threephase 1,000V power line set alongside the track.

Braking performance is particularly efficient. During normal operation braking is obtained either by dephasing the linear motor supply (or in the case of failure of this supply by feeding it with dc current from the battery), or by a hydraulic braking system equipped with friction pads which grip the vertical portion of the track.

The passenger cabin is divided into four ten-seat compartments, each provided with two doors. An additional half-compartment forward can accommodate four passengers seated on folding seats.

Automatic doors are provided on both sides of each passenger compartment which will help to reduce stopping time. The coupling of several of these vehicles will be possible, but this should only be necessary at peak hours for heavy commuter traffic.

The seating arrangement is optional; each of the various layouts is optimised to provide the maximum possible space for passengers.

DIMENSIONS
Length: 14·4m (47ft)
Beam: 2·75m (9ft 4in)
Height: 3·1m (10ft 2in)
WEIGHTS
Loaded, linear motor: 11,500kg (25,000lb)
automotive version: 10,000kg (22,000lb)
PERFORMANCE
Cruising speed: 180km/h (113mph)

A lower speed system is being designed for urban lines with stations only ½ mile apart.

THE GUIDEWAY

In this programme the track is at ground level.

Prototype of the 40-44 seat suburban Aérotrain seen on its 3km (1·9 miles) test track at Gometz

The horizontal support is an asphalt carpet and the upright is an aluminium beam which is used for both guiding the vehicle and as an induction rail for the linear motor. A 3km (1·9 mile) long track has been constructed at the company's base at Gometz.

Operational suburban lines will generally be supported on pylons in order to leave the ground free. The use of an elevated track will reduce the construction time and avoid costly tunnelling on many sections of urban/suburban projects.

PROJECT STUDIES

Société de l'Aérotrain has conducted detailed studies of a dozen projects. The technical and operational characteristics of the vehicles may substantially differ from those of the two prototypes, particularly as regards capacity and cruising speed.

The mathematical model, which has enabled the company to examine technico-economical optimisation procedures, an approach to operations, station design, and baggage handling has produced data based on a number of projected situations. The two major fields which are being investigated are inter-city services and suburban links, mainly between city centres and airports.

Suburban links require, in some cases, a higher capacity than the one provided by the Gometz-type vehicle. Capacity can be increased by widening the vehicles, or coupling them, to provide an hourly capacity of around 10,000 passengers each way.

Projects of an almost urban nature are also being investigated with the Tridim version.

CERGY-PONTOISE—LA DEFENSE SUBURBAN AEROTRAIN

A decision was taken by the French government in July 1971 to build an Aérotrain rapid transit line from the new business centre of La Défense, just outside Paris, to the new town of Cergy-Pontoise. The line was due to be opened early in 1979. Although the contract for its construction was signed on 21 June 1974, it was cancelled the following month by a new French government which introduced sweeping cutbacks in public expenditure to counter inflation.

Artist's impression of the Cergy-Défense suburban Aérotrain

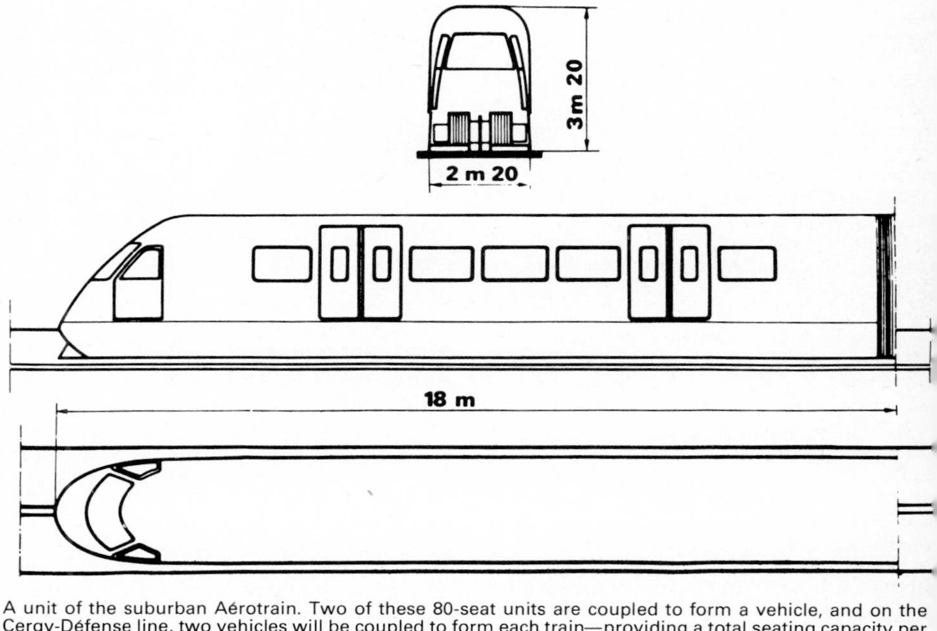

A unit of the suburban Aérotrain. Two of these 80-seat units are coupled to form a vehicle, and on the Cergy-Défense line, two vehicles will be coupled to form each train—providing a total seating capacity per train of 320 passengers

A three-phase powerline alongside the track at ground level provides electric current for the linear motor

The travel time between Cergy-Pontoise and La Défense with this system would have been less than ten minutes. The line was intended to connect with the new express metro linking La Défense with Etoile, and the Opéra, the journey times being four and seven minutes respectively.

Cergy-Pontoise had a population of 200,000 in 1975 and will have between 350,000 and 400,000 by the year 2000. A satellite town of the capital, it is about 30km west of Paris.

TRACK: The length of the route is 24km (15 miles).

The track will be elevated for most of the distance, providing a clearance of 5m (16ft) above ground. Supporting pylons will be 20-25m (66-83ft) apart. The track itself will be 5·3m (17ft 8in) wide and will be double. Each side will have an aluminium alloy vertical centre rail providing both guidance for the vehicles and the secondary, or induction element, for the linear motor. Electric power is supplied by wayside rails carrying 1,500V dc.

The horizontal radii of curves are kept above 1,200m to allow a high cruising speed. The steepest slope is 6% and occurs when climbing a cliff after a crossing of the Seine.

The Aérotrain vehicle to be used on this service will be supported and guided by air cushions, and propelled by a linear induction motor.

The vehicles will each comprise two units, and on the Cergy-Défense line a train will consist of two coupled vehicles.

SUPPORT AND GUIDANCE: Each unit has its own air cushion guidance and support systems, air for which is put under pressure by electrically driven fans.

PROPULSION: Each unit will be equipped with a linear induction motor of variable voltage and frequency which will be regulated by on-board power-control equipment.

BRAKING: Two systems will be employed.

Another line for the first commercial operation is being selected. One possibility is in the Marseilles area, with a section linking the suburbs of the city with Marignane airport and Aix-en-Provence, and extensions to the industrial complexes and new cities under construction around Etang de Berre.

TRIDIM URBAN TRANSPORTATION SYSTEM

The Tridim system has been designed to solve the transportation problem in urban areas or suburbs where the distance between stations ranges from a few kilometres down to several hundred metres.

It is believed that the solution to this problem lies in an overhead transportation system adapted to passenger flows ranging from a few thousand to 10-15,000 per hour and offering appreciable comfort, speed and frequency. To transport 6,000 passengers per hour, trains of three vehicles of 50 seats each every 90 seconds will be sufficient. If a larger module is adopted, 20,000 passengers can be carried hourly.

The Tridim system is designed to meet these requirements through the use of an air cushion for suspension and a flexible rack-and-pinion system, rubber-tyred traction-wheels, or linear induction motor for propulsion.

It consists of small-size self-powered air cushion vehicles moving on a lightweight overhead track.

The capacity of each vehicle can be between four and 100 seats according to customer requirements. The required capacity can be obtained by varying the width and the length of the vehicles or grouping any number of vehicles to form a train. Since June 1973, a four to six seat prototype vehicle has been under test at a research centre of the French National Electricity Company (EDF) located at Les Renardières, near Fontainebleau, on a 305m (1,000ft) track which includes a straight section, grades, curves and points.

Characteristics of this vehicle are as follows:
Loaded weight: 1·2 tons
Nominal propulsion power: 15kW
Lifting power: 4kW
Max speed: 50km/h (31mph)
Max slope: 20%
Power supply: cc 160V
Number of air cushions: 8
Air pressure: 900kg/m² (184·33lb/ft²)

The Tridim vehicle is built on a modular basis, with additional modules being added as required to provide the desired capacity.

In the case of the type VM 1 (designed for a specific client), the passengers are transported in modules measuring approximately 10ft by 6ft and equipped with nine seats placed along the longitudinal walls. There is also room for a maximum of four standing passengers, which brings the rush-hour capacity to 13 passengers for each module, ie 52 per vehicle, 36 of whom are seated (the vehicle consists of four modules).

The Rohr-built Aérotrain, constructed under a US Department of Transportation contract. The vehicle, which is 94ft long, with 60 seats, is designed to US specification. In May 1976 it attained a speed of 230km/h (144mph) a world record for a LIM-propelled, all-electric TACV

A four-seat Tridim urban transport vehicle on its "switchback" test track

Propulsion and lift are obtained from electric energy collected from a "third" rail (direct-current power supply).

The vehicle is guided by a low metal rail fixed on the track in line with the vehicle axis. This is the inverted-T track fundamental to the Aérotrain technique. Besides its guidance function, this rail carries the propulsion rack and keeps the vehicle retained on the track, which makes overturning impossible in the event of incident or abnormal operating conditions.

LIFT: The basic advantages of employing the air-cushion principle are: suspension of concentrated loads and shocks, hence possibility of a lightweight vehicle structure on the one hand, and of the overhead track on the other; the absence of rolling noise and vibration; vehicle maintenance drastically reduced, and virtually non-existent for the track; and finally low total cost of the transportation system due to the simplicity and the light weight of the track.

The air cushion system requires a power supply of only 4 to 5hp per supported metric ton. This is expected to be reduced to the order of 2hp per metric ton. The air cushion supply is operated by sound-insulated electric fans.

PROPULSION: In the case of the VM 1 the vehicle is propelled by a patented rack-and-pinion system. But alternative methods include rubber-tyred traction wheels acting on the centre guidance rail or linear induction motor, according to requirements. The former consists of a dual rack fixed on the guiding rail and two pinions carried by the vehicles and driven by electric propulsion motors. It allows operation on tracks with steep slopes and maintains acceleration and braking performance in any weather including conditions of snow and ice.

The ability to climb steep slopes enables the stations to be built at street level or at the level of another transportation system for ease of transfer.

OVERHEAD TRACK: The system is intended primarily for an overhead track but it can also be used at ground level or as an underground system. In the case of an overhead track, the viaduct can be made of metal or of reinforced concrete, the choice between the two materials being dictated mainly by the line layout.

This consists of pylons supporting beams of 20-30m (66-100ft) span carrying the guideway which has a width of about 2·23m (7ft 4in) for single track or 4·72m (15ft 6in) for dual track in the case of the VM 1 system. The track itself consists mainly of the guiding rail with its rack.

The absence of concentrated loads, either static or dynamic, allows the use of a light viaduct, which leads to less cost.

As an example, with metal construction, a dual track viaduct weighs approximately 590 kg/m (1,300lb/m) (VM 1).

VM 1 SPECIFICATION

The system can be adapted to client specification.

Capacity of the VM 1 is 52 passengers, 36 of whom are seated.

Aérotrain Tridim urban transport vehicle

DIMENSIONS
Length: 16·26m (53ft 4in)
Width: 1·93m (6ft 4in)
Height: 2·59m (8ft 6in)
WEIGHTS
Empty: 5,900kg (13,000lb)
Loaded: 9,900kg (21,800lb)
PERFORMANCE
Nominal speed: 64-80km/h (40-50mph)
Max speed: 30-104km/h (50-65mph)
Average acceleration between 0 and 40mph: 0·12g
Emergency deceleration: 0·2g
Allowable slope at 40mph: 3%
Max allowable slope at reduced speed: 15% to 25%
Minimum turning radius: 24·4m (80ft) approx
MOTOR POWER
for propulsion: 150kW approx
for cushion: 35kW
OVERHEAD TRACK
Span: 20-30m (66-100ft) for normal span
Height above ground: 4·88m (16ft) on average
Width of track, single track: 2·23m (7ft 4in)
dual track: 4·72m (15ft 4in)
Electrical power supply by conductor rail

URBA

Compagnie d'Energetique Linéaire mb

5 rue Monge, 92000 Vanves, France
Telephone: 644 33 22
Officials:
J Rechou, *Manager, Marketing and Licensing*

The URBA mass transport system, invented in 1966 by Maurice Barthalon, aims at providing a means of urban transport which combines absence of noise, vibration and atmospheric pollution with low capital and maintenance costs and a high degree of flexibility of installation and operation. The vehicle, which may operate singly or in trains, is suspended from its track by an air lift system in which the pressure is sub-atmospheric, and propulsion is by electric linear induction motors. The cabin of the vehicle is suspended from a number of Dynavac air bogies which run within an elevated track, the section of which is like a flattened, inverted U, with inward facing flanges on the bottom edges of the sides, on which the air bogies sit when at rest. The Dynavac air bogies house the lift fans which draw air from the space between the track and the top of the bogie, so producing a pressure difference which causes the air bogie to lift off the track flanges.

Special sealing arrangements provide a controlled leak into the lift chamber which decreases as the weight of the vehicle increases, so increasing the pressure difference. The air bogies therefore remain in a stable, floating condition without being in contact with the track.

Lateral guidance is provided by similar but smaller Dynavac cushions between the sides of the bogie and the sides of the track. The air bogies also house the linear induction motors which react with a reactor rail projecting downwards from the centre of the track. This effectively divides the lift chamber into two independent halves, thus providing a degree of roll control. The suspension between the cabin and the air bogie acts as a secondary suspension system (the air cushion being the primary) and provides for articulation of the air bogies so that the vehicle can take curves of small radius.

In order to carry the development of URBA

Impression of a single-track URBA 30 line, with supporting columns located in the centre of a highway

from a vehicle to a fully integrated public transport system, the Société d'Etudes de l'URBA (SETURBA) has been formed by the Caisse des Dépôts et Consignation, the Entreprise Bouygues and the Gazocéan-Technigaz Group.

The registered office of the Society is at 4 place Raoul Dautry, Paris 15, France.

SETURBA has accelerated the application of URBA by confirming, technically and economically, the best means of applying this new method of transport and has prepared the constitution of a new company charged with the industrial and commercial development of the URBA system.

A technical and financial appraisal of URBA, undertaken by the SETURBA study group, proved favourable, and this has led to the establishment of Société de l'URBA (SU), supported by former associates of SETURBA.

URBA has been specially designed to satisfy the transport needs of medium-size towns of 200,000 to 1,000,000 inhabitants, and the suburbs of large cities.

The prototype URBA 4, and later two URBA 8s coupled together, were demonstrated at Lyon during 1968. The prototype has been in daily use for almost four years at the Ecole Centrale of Lyon, where research and development has been supported by DGRST, DATAR, ANVAR and the Ministry of Transport. To date it has carried 30,000 visitors. The computer analysis of its dynamic behaviour has confirmed its stability, its comfort and its ability to take small radius curves.

Several international assessments, including a searching study by Eurofinance, consider URBA as one of the most promising of the new means of transport for the years 1970 to 1990. A certain number of towns in France and abroad, including Rouen, Bordeaux and Montpellier, and three different lines located on the outskirts of Paris, have been studied. A special study has also been undertaken for the new business centre of La Défense, on the western side of Paris. These bring out the favourable capital and operating costs which should place the price per passenger per kilometre of URBA at a level comparable with that of the bus today.

The URBA 4 prototype seats 6-12 passengers and has a cruising speed of 80km/h (50mph)

URBA 20, a light urban transport vehicle with a service speed of 72km/h (45mph) and seating 20 passengers

URBA 8

A prototype urban and suburban monorail, URBA 8 is an improved version of the URBA 4, with three linear motors instead of two, and seats for eight passengers. Two URBA 8s were demonstrated at Lyon on 4 December 1968, on a 79m (87yd) track. They operated singly and coupled, with acceleration and deceleration in the range 0·25 to 0·35g (with 0·5g deceleration in an emergency) and at speeds up to 48·28km/h (30mph). It consists of a rectangular-framed cabin seating up to eight passengers and suspended from three Dynavac air bogies running in an experimental 80m (260ft) track.

PROPULSION: Propulsion and normal braking is by three linear motors of 25kW, weighing 80kg (176lb) and providing a thrust of 100kg (220lb) at starting, 30kg (66lb) at normal service speed. Supply is from 380V, three-phase, 50Hz mains. The motor is the first to be designed as an industrial unit for vehicle propulsion.

CABIN: The cabin is rectangular and measures 4·5m (14ft 10in) long, 1·6m (5ft 3in) wide and 1·2m (4ft) high. It is built from 4cm square section tube and diecast corners of a type normally used for the framework of holiday bungalows.

The floor is of light alloy and the sides are perspex. Suspension between the cabin and the three air bogies is by rubber cord springs and hydraulic automobile shock absorbers.

Tests have demonstrated that the air bogie concept is suitable for sharp curves, can climb steep slopes and provides good acceleration and braking. It cannot be derailed.

URBA 20

An enlarged version of the URBA 4, this model will seat 20 passengers in a cylindrical cabin and have a top speed of 72km/h (45mph). More efficient lift fans will be employed on this model which will require a total of 12kW for lift power. All-up weight will be 4,750kg (10,470lb).

URBA 30

This is the first model designed to go into service as a public transport system and will seat 30 passengers in rows, three abreast. The initial design will have five special, lightweight automatic doors on one side. Overall dimensions of the cabin will be: length 9m (29ft 6in), width 1·9m (6ft 3in), height 2m (6ft 7in) overall, loaded weight 5·3 tons. Propulsion will be by linear motors.

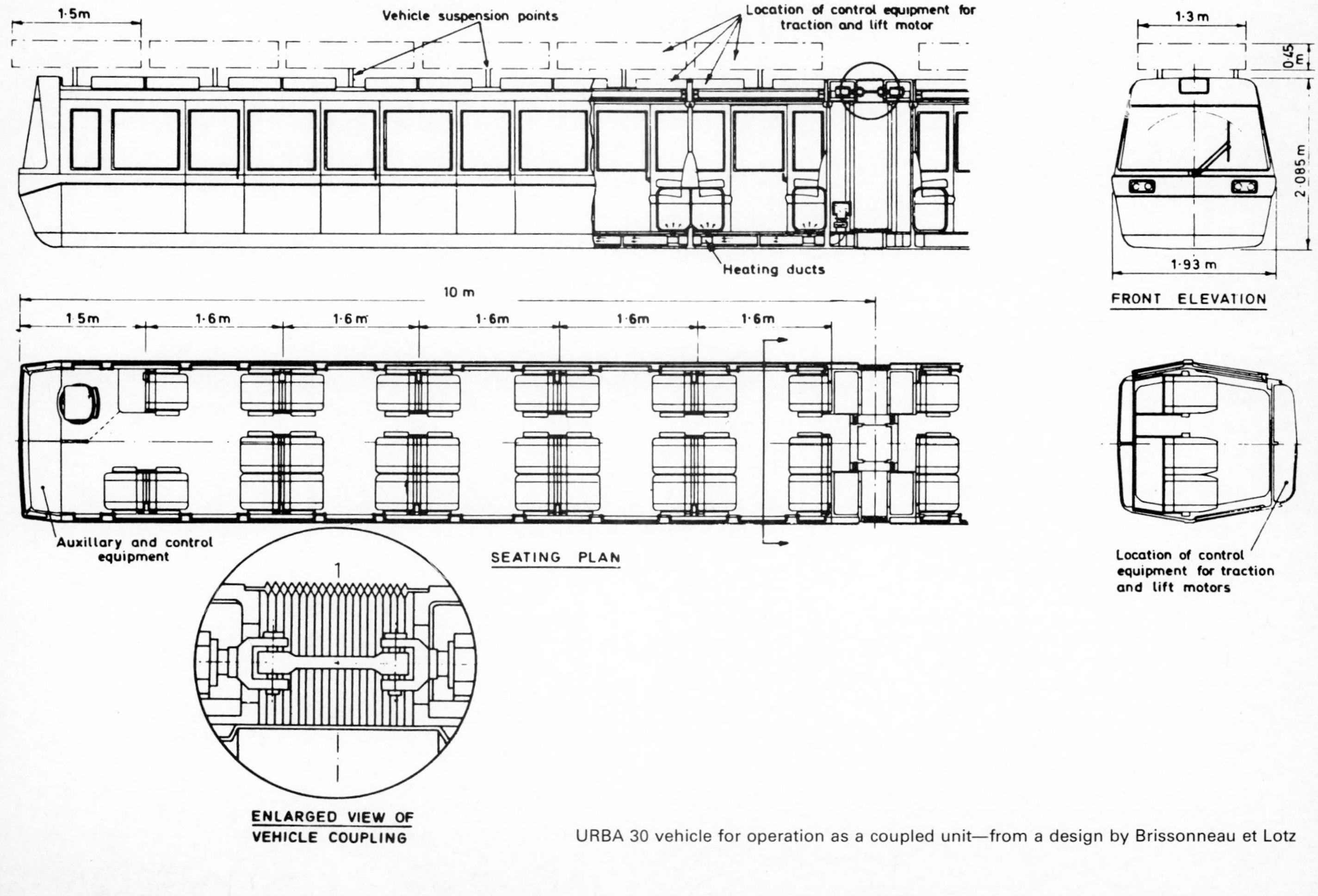

URBA 30 vehicle for operation as a coupled unit—from a design by Brissonneau et Lotz

GERMANY, FEDERAL REPUBLIC

TRANSRAPID-EMS

Gesellschaft für elektromagnetische Schnellverkehrssysteme (Joint Venture Group Krauss-Maffei and MBB)

Steinsdorfstr 13, D-8000 Munich 22, Federal Republic of Germany
Telephone: (089) 22 66 94/22 73 40
Telex: 529463 trmue

In April 1974 it was announced that Krauss-Maffei (KM) and Messerschmitt-Bölkow-Blohm (MBB) are to develop jointly a high-speed transportation system.

As agreed with the Federal Minister of Research and Technology, the corporate managements of both companies have decided to conduct their future development activities for a track-guided high-speed transportation system—started in the late sixties—on a joint basis.

In 1971 both companies presented to the public the world's first large-scale test vehicles supported, guided, and driven by magnetic fields. In the meantime extensive testing performed on test rigs and test tracks at München-Allach and Ottobrunn has demonstrated that contact-free magnetic suspension using controlled electromagnets can be achieved and is practical for high-speed ground transportation systems.

Both companies, using different approaches, arrived at very similar research results.

The chief objective of the joint venture group is to develop a uniform high-speed transportation system for Europe for economic long-haul passenger and freight transportation. To achieve this aim, international links, such as co-operation with DAF Netherlands began in 1973, and plans for the formation of an international management corporation for high-speed transportation are under way.

Research work is being financed by the Federal Minister of Research and Technology as well as by funds from the two companies.

On 19 February 1976, 401·3km/h (249mph) was attained by the Komet research vehicle, a world record for Maglev vehicles.

TRACK

The track for a rapid transit system based on the principle of magnetic suspension and guidance would consist of the supporting concrete pylons and beams, the ferromagnetic support and guidance rails, the secondary part of the linear motor, and the power rails.

In order to ensure the safe operation of a rapid transit system on the one hand, and not to endanger the environment by its operation on the other, the track will be supported on pylons spaced approximately 16m (52ft 6in) apart with the elevation (clearance) of the track being at least 4·5m (14ft 9in). This eliminates to a large extent, the need for special structures at intersections with roads, rail tracks, etc.

A fast and reliable switching system for traffic diverging from and merging with the main line is necessary for smooth and safe operation of a rapid transit system.

Experiments with an electromagnetic switch with no moving parts revealed that special devices were needed on board which added weight and increased aerodynamic drag. Currently, a mechanical switch is being developed.

PRINCIPLE OF MAGNETIC LEVITATION

In the selected principle of magnetic attraction, the vehicles are supported and guided by controlled electromagnets along armature rails fastened to the guideway. Sensors continuously measure the air gap between the vehicle magnets and the armature rails (10-20mm). The data measured is transmitted to the control unit which controls the attractive forces of the magnets and thus keeps the vehicle in a hovering condition.

In addition to the development of the magnetic levitation and guidance system, vehicle development also includes other components, such as linear motor propulsion energy transfer, vehicle frame, braking, emergency gliding and safety systems. The design of cost-saving, elevated guideways and planning of the necessary stationary facilities, such as stations, power supply, etc are of equal significance for the overall system.

Knowledge and experience gained and substantiated through extensive testing on various

Rotary test track to study the operational behaviour of synchronous linear machines (SLIM)

First full-scale test vehicle to employ magnetic suspension guidance and propulsion was MBB's basic experimental craft. Weighing 5·6 tonnes and 7m (23ft) in length, it has reached 100km/h (62mph) on a 700m (760yd) track

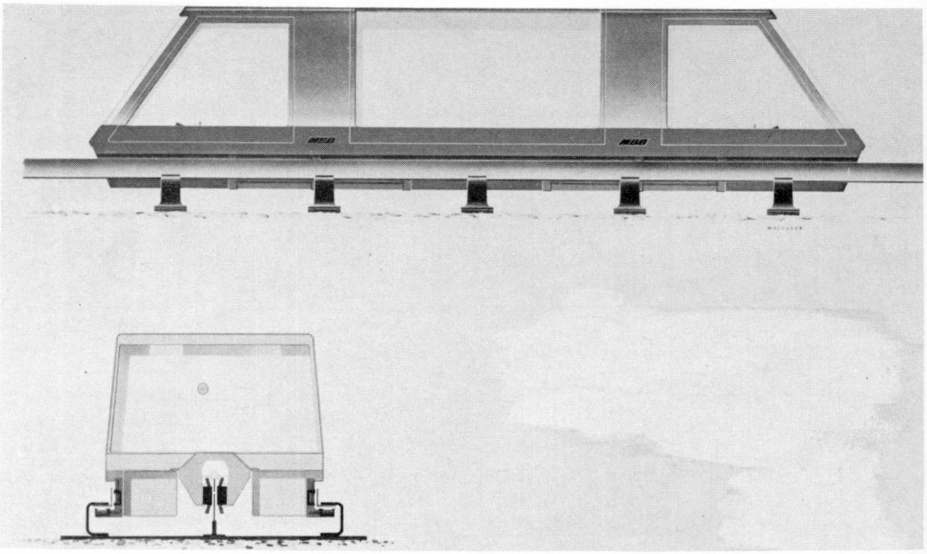

test stands formed the basis for the construction of experimental vehicles and test tracks in Ottobrunn, München-Allach and Manching.

TEST STANDS

Static, dynamic and rotating magnet test stands were built for the purpose of defining and optimising magnets for the levitation and guidance system and various control techniques. Support force losses and braking forces on magnets as a result of eddy current effects at high speeds can be measured and power transmission methods tested on rotation test stands. Switching tests with magnetically levitated vehicles are performed on switch test stands. Linear motor test stands are used to determine thrust and lateral forces on single- and double-sided linear motors and to measure temperature, current and voltage.

BASIC VEHICLE

MBB began work on the vehicle and the test track in July 1970. On 4 February 1971, the first suspension tests of the experimental vehicle took place in the test laboratory. On 2 April 1971, the first test runs were made on MBB's special test track.

On 5 May 1971, the experimental vehicle was presented to the public for the first time in the presence of the Federal Minister for Educational Science and the Federal Minister for Transportation.

It demonstrated the feasibility of magnetic suspension and guidance with linear motor propulsion, and provides information on those parameters not covered during simulation of the system, and development of the components.

Weighing 5·6 tonnes and with a length of 7m (23ft), it has an asynchronous linear motor with 200kW nominal power which is capable of accelerating the vehicle on the 700m (766yd) test track to a speed of 100km/h (62mph).

Four controlled suspension magnets and two guidance magnets on each side of the vehicle lift it and guide it during operation with a nominal air gap of 14mm (½in) between the magnets and the rails.

TRANSRAPID 02 RESEARCH VEHICLE

In October 1971 Krauss-Maffei started operating an experimental 12m (39ft 4in) long vehicle on a 930m (1,017yd) test track. It reached a maximum speed of 164km/h (101·9mph). A novel power pick-up system ensures troublefree transmission of electric energy at high speeds. A secondary suspension system with pneumatic shock absorbers and and vibration dampers constitutes the link between the vehicle superstructure and the hovering chassis.

Guideway and vehicle concepts provide realistic test data. The test results obtained so far have revealed that the system requirements can be fulfilled without difficulty.

TRACK
Length: 930m (1,017yds)
Radius of curvature: 800m (875yds)
EXPERIMENTAL VEHICLE
Length: 11·7m (38ft 4½in)
Width: 2·9m (9ft 6in)
Height above track surface: 2·05m (6ft 8¾in)
Number of seats: 10
Weight: approx 11 Mp
Payload: 4 Mp
Design speed of vehicle: approx 350km/h (220mph)
PROPULSION BY LINEAR INDUCTION MOTOR
Thrust (transient): approx 3·2 Mp
Present vehicle speed (due to short track length): approx 160km/h (100mph)
Synchronous speed LIM at 50Hz: approx 180km/h (112mph)
SERVICE BRAKES
Brake retardation by LIM: approx 2·5m/s²
by jaw brake: approx 8·5m/s²
by friction brake: approx 8m/s²
ELECTROMAGNETIC SUPPORT AND GUIDANCE SYSTEM
Specific carrying capacity: approx 800kp/m magnet length (25mm air gap)

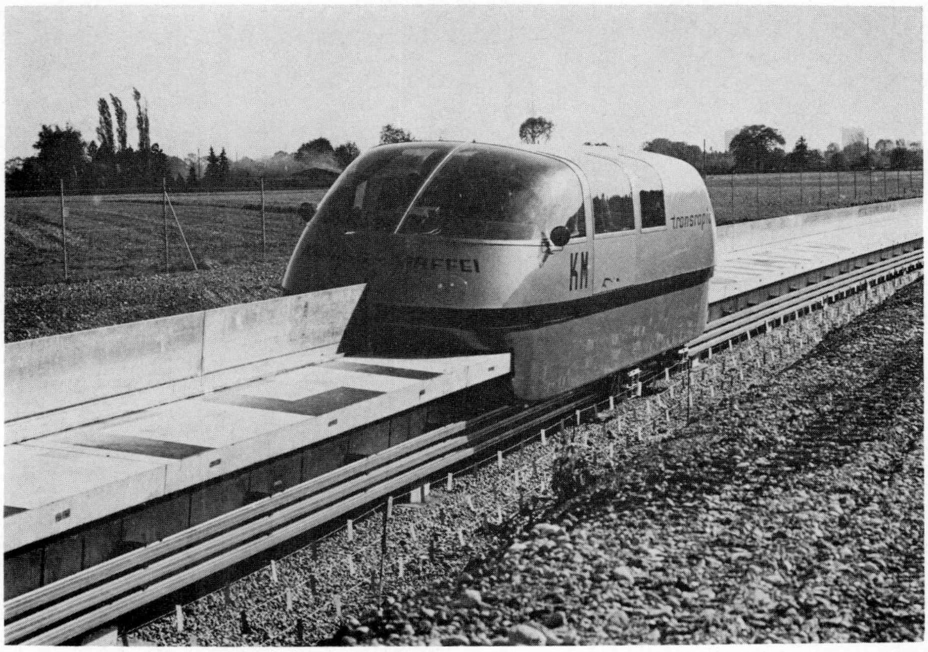

Krauss-Maffei's Transrapid research vehicle in 02 configuration, with magnetic support, guidance and propulsion systems

Transrapid's 03 research craft permitted a full systems comparison between magnetic and air cushion techniques, using the same vehicle specifications and the same track under completely identical operating conditions

Air gap: 10-25mm (½-1in)
POWER SUPPLY
Support and guidance system: Voltage 380V three-phase current, 50Hz
Power: 32kW

TRANSRAPID 03 RESEARCH VEHICLE

In October 1971, the company started operating a dual-purpose test facility which allows a comprehensive system comparison between magnetic cushion and air cushion techniques using the same vehicle specifications and the same track with completely identical operating conditions. Vehicles and track have been designed for a maximum speed of approximately 140km/h (87mph). The track length is 930m (1,017yds) allowing the attainment of a speed of about 160km/h (100mph), which has already been reached with the magnetic cushion vehicle. This experimental system provides realistic information since it subjects the support, guidance and propulsion system to extreme loads both during straight runs and cornering.

Transrapid 03 is the basic Transrapid 8-ton research vehicle adapted for tests as a tracked air cushion vehicle. The payload of two tons and overall dimensions are identical to those of the vehicle in its earlier configuration. The programme, which is supported by the Federal Ministry of Research and Technology, is enabling the TACV and Maglev concepts to be compared under identical conditions for the first time.

Tests with air cushion support began at the end of 1972 and finished in 1973.

As a TACV, the vehicle is supported and guided by a total of 14 air cushion pads. Six, each with a cushion area of 3m² (32·29ft²), support the vehicle on its elevated concrete guideway, and eight, mounted in pairs, each of about 1m² (10·76ft²) cushion area, provide lateral guidance along the LIM reaction rail. The air cushion lift system is of plenum type and each pad has a rubber skirt. Cushion air is supplied by a two-stage compressor.

The vehicle is propelled by a French-made LIM system, which accelerates the vehicle to 145km/h (90mph) on its 930m (1,017yd) guideway.

Comparisons covered the following areas: vehicle dynamics; weight; load tolerances; vertical air gap tolerances; specific power requirements for support and guidance; effects on the environment (noise level); reliability; life; reaction to weather influences; maximum speed; aerodynamic drag; investment, operating and maintenance costs.

Results of the comparison showed that magnetic levitation technology is superior.

TRACK
Length: 930m (1,017yds)
Radius of curvature: 800m (875yds)

EXPERIMENTAL VEHICLE
Length: 11·7m (38ft 4½in)
Width: 2·9m (9ft 6in)
Height above track surface: 2·05m (6ft 8½in)
Number of seats: 10
Weight: 9,600kg (21,200lb)
Design speed of vehicle: approx 140km/h (87mph)

PROPULSION BY LINEAR INDUCTION MOTOR
Thrust (transient): approx 2·9 Mp
Vehicle speed (due to short track length): approx 160km/h (100mph)
Synchronous speed LIM at 50Hz: approx 180km/h (112mph)

SERVICE BRAKES
Brake retardation by LIM: approx 2·3m/s²
by jaw brake: approx 8·5m/s²
by friction brake: approx 8m/s²

POWER SUPPLY
Support and guidance system: 380V three-phase current, 50Hz
Power: 235kW
LIM: Voltage 1·7 KV three-phase current, 50 Hz
Output: 3mVA

MAGNET TEST VEHICLE

Operation of the magnet test vehicle started on the Ottobrunn test track in 1972. The vehicle consists of a platform supported and guided by wheels and accelerated by a hot water rocket.

It was used to test magnets and acceleration sensors at different speed levels up to 225km/h (140mph). The components were tested in conjunction with an instrumented test rail mounted in the guideway.

TECHNICAL DATA
Vehicle length: 3·6m (11ft 9¾in)
width: 2·5m (8ft 2¾in)
Starting weight: 1,300kg (2,866lb)
Max speed: 225km/h (140mph)
Propulsion, type: hot water rocket
Guideway, length: 660m (722yds)

COMPONENT TEST VEHICLE KOMET

The Komet is an unmanned, magnetically levitated and guided vehicle with a mounting rack for testing components at speeds up to 400 km/h. This mounting rack allows the installation of magnets, linear motors and power pick-ups of various designs, which can be tested in combination with instrumented rails, which can also be easily replaced. The test data is transmitted to a fixed receiving station via a telemetry system. The Komet is accelerated by means of a thrust sled equipped with up to six hot-water rockets in order to achieve the desired high speeds on only 1,300m length of test track.

TECHNICAL DATA
Component Test Vehicle:
length: 8·5m (27ft 11in)
width: 2·5m (8ft 2½in)
height: 1·7m (5ft 7in)
weight (without instrumented components): 8,800kg (19,400lb)
max speed: 400km/h (250mph)
Thrust sled:
length: 5m (16ft 5in)
width: 2·5m (8ft 2½in)
height: 1·5m (4ft 11in)
starting weight: 7,500kg (16,534lb)
Guideway:
track gauge: 2·2m (7ft 2½in)
length: 1,300m (1,422yds)
including acceleration section: 300m (328yds)
test section: 300m (328yds)
deceleration and safety section: 700m (766yds)

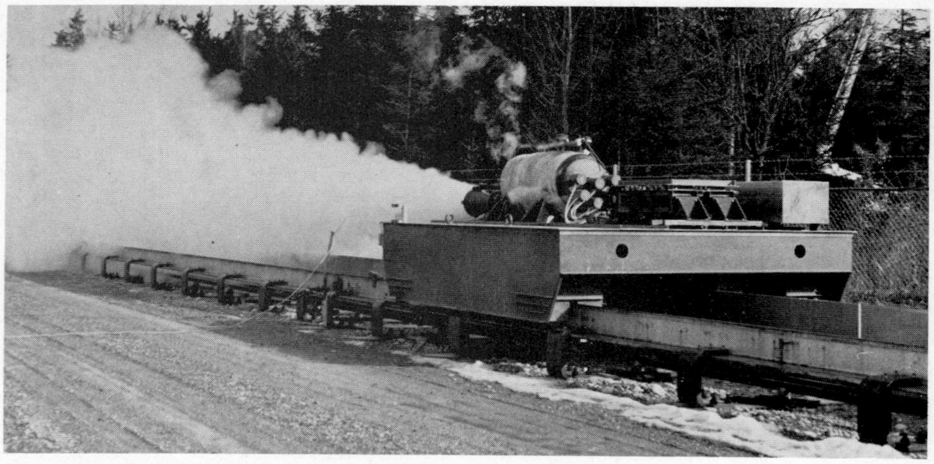

The MBB hot-water rocket-driven test carrier on its track at Ottobrunn

The Komet, an unmanned magnetically-guided and levitated component-test vehicle established a world record for Maglev vehicles on 19 February 1976 when it attained 401·3km/h on its 1,300m guideway

Transrapid 04, the world's largest passenger vehicle employing magnetic levitation and a linear induction motor for propulsion

TRANSRAPID 04

The Transrapid 04 is the largest passenger-carrying magnetically levitated and LIM-propelled experimental vehicle to date.

The elevated guideway, with curves of different radii, represents a further development on the way to future applications. Different design principles and materials, such as concrete and steel, were used in order to test various alternatives. For the first time, a LIM reaction rail was mounted horizontally on the guideway beam.

The 2,400m (1½mile) test track allows the testing of different system components under realistic conditions and at higher speeds. The results of the test programme will be the basis for the definition of future test vehicles and large-scale test facilities.

TECHNICAL DATA
Vehicle, length: 15m (49ft 2½in)
width: 3·4m (11ft 2in)
height: 2·8m (9ft 2in)
weight: 16,500kg (36,376lb)
max speed: 250km/h (155mph)
propulsion: asynchronous linear motor
max thrust: 50,000 N
Guideway:
track gauge: 3·2m (10ft 6in)

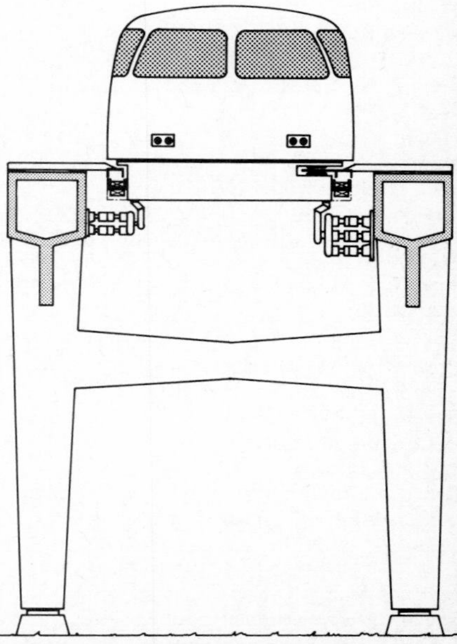

Elevated track employed for the Transrapid 04

length: 2,400m (1½ miles)
radii of curvature: 800-3,100m (875-3,390yds)
span: 17-20m (55ft 8in-65ft 7in)
max guideway inclination: ±11 degrees

TRANSRAPID 05

Transrapid-EMS (Krauss-Maffei and Messerschmitt-Bölkow-Blohm) has been awarded a contract from the German Federal Ministry of Research and Technology to build together with Thyssen Henschel Company a demonstration facility for a magnetically levitated transportation system. Site of this demonstration project will be the International Transportation Exposition, IVA 79, in Hamburg.

Transrapid-EMS has the responsibility for building the 26m long, two-section vehicle which has seats for 86 passengers. This will be the fifth maglev vehicle to be constructed by the Krauss-Maffei, MBB, and Transrapid-EMS consortium. The levitation and guidance system will have four bogies with individually spring-suspended electromagnets using a decentral, hierarchial control system.

A synchronous, iron-backed linear short secondary motor serves as propulsion unit. With this version of a linear motor the primary coils are mounted in the track while the levitation magnets serve as its secondary.

Within the joint programme, Thyssen Henschel and the Braunschweig Technical University are responsible for the guideway (length approximately 1000m), the track-mounted primary of the motor and other stationary installations. Sponsored and financed by the Federal Ministry of Research and Technology, the chief aim of the project is to demonstrate to a broad public the advanced state of development of the high-speed maglev system in Germany.

TECHNICAL DATA
Train (2 Sections)
Length: 26m (85ft 3in)
Width: 3·1m (10ft 2in)
Height: 2·7m (8ft 10in)
Capacity: 86 passengers
Total weight: 36 tonnes
Max speed: 80km/h (50mph)
Propulsion: Synchronous Linear Motor (SLIM)

Transrapid 05 maglev train which is being built for the IVA '79 International Transportation Exhibition in Hamburg

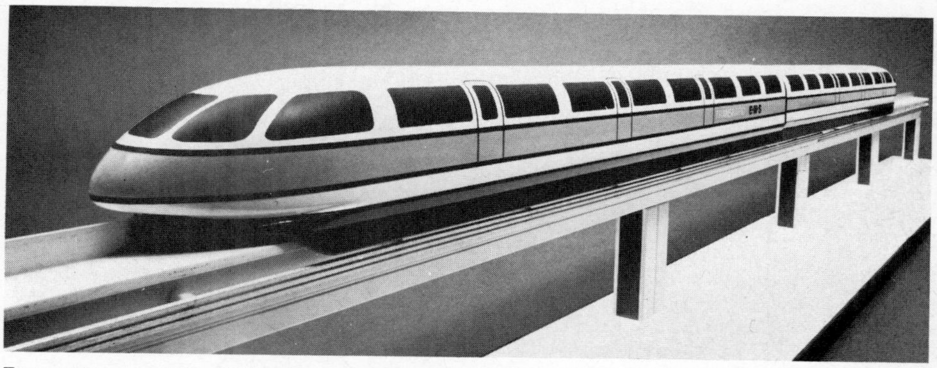

Transrapid concept for a 400km/h prototype train for 240 passengers. The first section of the train will be tested at the government operated test facility for transport technology near Augsburg from 1980 onwards. Vehicles of similar design will first be applied to less densely populated areas or to connect them with major airports

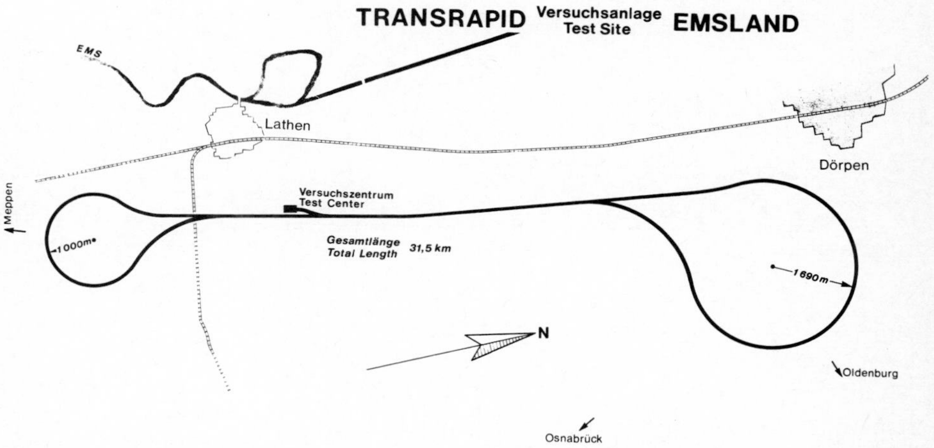

TRANSRAPID 06

The Federal Ministry of Research and Technology has agreed to build a 31km (19¼mile) test track in the Emsland district in northern Germany. The facility will be constructed in several steps, tests with the Transrapid 06 commencing in 1980-81. The train will consist of two sections and will be designed for speeds up to 400km/h (250 mph).

Development and construction of the vehicle and the test facility will be a joint effort by the West German companies already engaged in research and development in the maglev field.

TECHNICAL DATA
Train: 2 sections
Total length: 52m (170ft)
Width: 3·6m (11ft 8½in)
Height: 3·8m (12ft 6in)
Capacity (total): 134 seats
Total weight: 125 tonnes
Max speed: 400km/h (250 mph)
Propulsion: Synchronous linear motor

TRANSRAPID 07

A concept for a high speed, short haul, maglev system has been developed for connecting two cities or an airport to a city (airport link).

TECHNICAL DATA
Train: 2 or 4 sections
Length, per section: 32m (105ft)
the first 2 sections: 64m (210ft)
the second 2 sections: 124m (407ft)
Width: 3·6m (11ft 8½in)
Height: 3·85-4·15m (12ft 8in-13ft 7in)
Weight per section: 80 tonnes
Total weight: 320 tonnes
Max speed: 250-350km/h (155-220mph)
Propulsion: Synchronous/asynchronous linear motor

TRANSRAPID 08

This is a concept for a 400km/h prototype train for 240 passengers. The first section of the train will be tested at the government operated test facility for transport technology near Augsburg from 1980 onwards. Vehicles of similar design will first be applied to less densely populated areas or to connect them with major airports.

TECHNICAL DATA
Train: two sections
Length: 64m (210ft)
Width: 4·2m (13ft 9in)
Height: 4m (13ft 1in)
Capacity: 240 passengers
Payload: 24 tonnes
Weight of train: 170 tonnes
Max speed: 400km/h (250mph)
Propulsion: asynchronous linear motor

AEG-BBC-SIEMENS

Froebelstr 19-25, D-8520 Erlangen, Federal Republic of Germany
Telephone: (09131) 72 24 57
Telex: 629871

Officials:
Dipl-Ing A Lichtenberg, *Project Leader*

Three West German electrical engineering companies, AEG-Telefunken, BBC and Siemens, have been working together since 1972 on the development of a new type of high performance railway for future transcontinental transport. Magnetic levitation vehicles are intended to operate as track-bound land transport at speeds of between 400 and 500 km/h, to fill the gap between conventional railway and air travel. The three companies have combined to form the Magnetic Levitation Project Group in Erlangen. The entire project is receiving the support of the Federal Ministry for Research and Technology.

The electrodynamic levitation system makes use of self-stabilising repelling forces between the magnet system in the vehicle and the reaction rails in the track. The system also successfully incorporates futuristic technology, ie superconducting magnet coils which make it possible to produce very strong magnetic fields and thereby obtain levitation heights of 100 to 200mm, which are ideal for safe operation at high speeds. The magnetic fields can be maintained without any external power being supplied to the vehicle. This is possible because electricity flows almost entirely without losses at temperatures approaching absolute zero (−273°C). The magnet coils must therefore be energised and short-circuited while superconductive and the extremely low temperature must subsequently be maintained. Linde AG, of Munich, has developed the necessary cryogenic equipment.

Practical tests in the electrodynamic levitation project are being conducted in Erlangen. A circular test track 280m in diameter has been built on a site of 80,000m². In contrast to straight tracks, a circuit may be used for tests of any required duration. The test track is made up of U-shaped prefabricated concrete sections each 6m long, inclined inwards at an angle of 45 degrees and supported by a total of 144 columns. Almost 10,000 tons of concrete went into its construction.

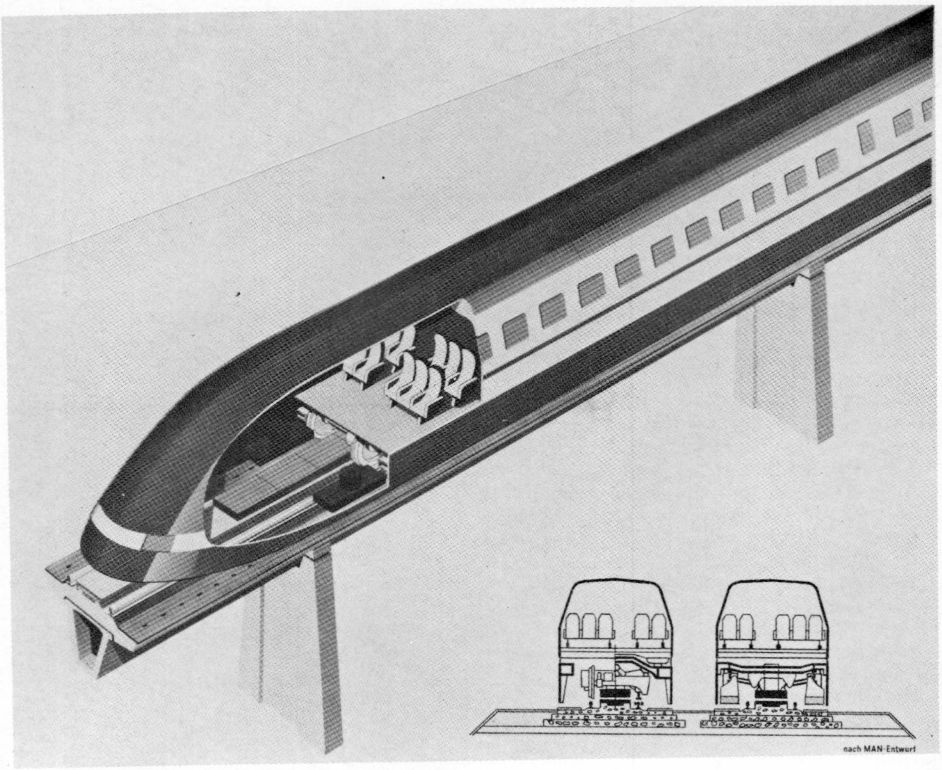

Passenger vehicle for services at speeds of 300-500km/h

Test vehicle EET 01 (Erlanger Erprobungsträger) was built by MAN in Nuremberg. It is 12m long, 4m wide and weighs 17 tonnes. During preliminary trials to test all the various components, the vehicle ran on 16 wheels fitted with pneumatic tyres. These wheels are also used for take-off and landing purposes, since the vehicle cannot levitate until it is under way.

LEVITATION AT 50KM/H

The interaction of the components has been progressively tested up to attainment of the levitation state and has proved entirely satisfactory. Trials have involved the power transmission system, which comprises six conductor rails beside the track, a current collector on the vehicle, and the electric propulsion system rated at 1200kW maximum. The latter comprises one thyristor converter, the 3,200kg linear motor and the superconducting magnets. The magnets weigh approximately 500kg and are carried in two magnet frames, together with the two on-board cryogenic plants. The vehicle rises about 10cm above the track from 50km/h onwards.

A different propulsion system will be tested at the next stage of development. This will enable the payload ratio of the vehicle to be substantially improved before it goes into service. An additional advantage is that it will no longer be necessary to transmit power from the track to the vehicle. At present equipped with a linear induction motor (short stator), the EET 01 vehicle will later be fitted with an ironless linear synchronous motor. With this new propulsion principle, the vehicle carries the superconducting magnets (excitation element) while the track is fitted with

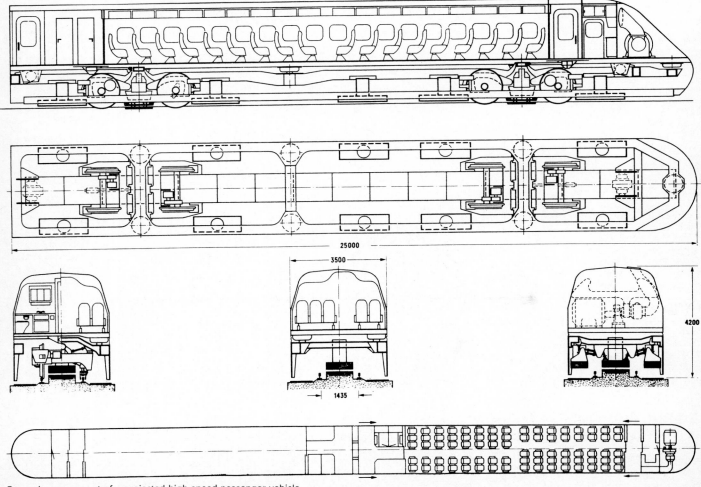

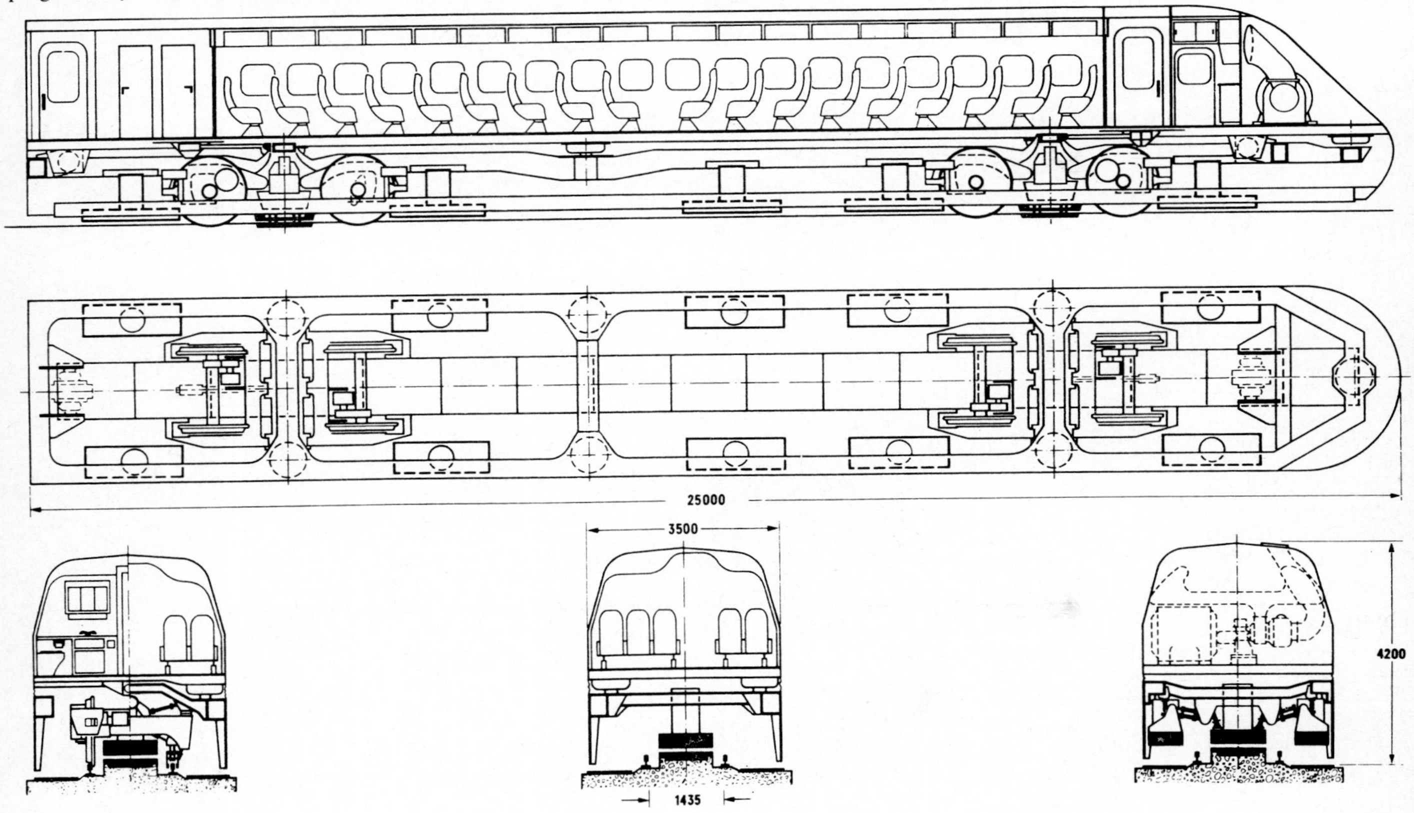

General arrangement of a projected high speed passenger vehicle

a three-phase winding (long stator). The magnetic circuit in the latter remains open, and therefore no iron yoke is required.

At present under construction in the main hall of the Erlangen test facility is a rotary test rig which will be used to check the design calculations for the new drive system. It consists of a revolving drum 6m in diameter which carries the three-phase winding. A test vehicle magnet with forced helium cooling is used as the excitation element.

To assure a high standard of passenger comfort on electrodynamic levitation vehicles, normally conducting coils will later be fitted under the superconducting magnets. In conjunction with a system, these extra coils enable vibrations to be damped in a simple and straightforward manner. Preliminary experiments relating to this type of damping system are being carried out in the same hall on another test rig equipped with a newly developed immersion-cooled superconducting magnet. This damping equipment will later undergo trials in the EET 01 vehicle.

Test vehicle EET 01 (Erlanger Erprobungsträger) built by MAN in Nuremburg for the Magnetic Levitation Project Group, formed by AEG-Telefunken, Brown-Boveri and Siemens

RAILWAY NETWORK INCLUDED IN PLANNING

The Magnetic Levitation Project Group has already drafted plans for passenger transport at speeds of 400 to 500km/h using vehicles powered by linear synchronous motors and weighing approximately 120 tonnes. These vehicles would be equipped with take-off and landing gear with dimensions compatible to conventional railway tracks. Conventional rolling stock carrying heavy goods loads could thus be hauled along the new tracks by linear-motor-powered tractive units, although not at the high speeds possible with the specially designed passenger trains.

Optimism prevails among the Magnetic Levitation Project Group. The results already obtained from their development work represent an important step towards the long-distance transport of the future.

CHARACTERISTICS

LEVITATION: by electrodynamic repulsion.
PROPULSION: by ironless linear synchronous motors (active track principle).
POWER TRANSMISSION: absolutely contactless.
VEHICLES: designed for high speeds (400 to 500km/h).
TRACK: The vehicles are intended to run on their own special tracks, but in urban areas will use conventional tracks, and passenger and goods stations (compatibility with wheel-on-rail system).

TRACK: Special ground-level or raised tracks for high speeds, conventional tracks for lower speeds (less than 150km/h).
SPEEDS: Up to 500km/h (levitated) for passenger transport; 150 to 200km/h (rolling) for goods transport.
VEHICLES: Passenger transport by motor trains comprising multiple sections each with seats for 100 passengers; goods transport using tractive units with linear synchronous motors hauling goods wagons from conventional wheel-on-rail rolling stock.
PROPULSION: Three-phase winding in track; superconducting excitation magnets on board the motor trains and tractive units.
NOISE: Aerodynamic noise only.

TECHNICAL DATA

PASSENGER VEHICLE
Number of coupled sections: 2
Length: 50m (164ft)
Width: 3·5m (11ft 6in)
Height of reaction rail: 4·2m (13ft 9in)
Minimum required clearance,
to propulsion magnet: 100mm (4in)
to levitation magnet: 170mm (6¾in)
Weight: 132 tonnes
Number of seats: 180
Payload: 18 tonnes
Payload factor: 13·6%
Max speed: 500km/h (310mph)
Aerodynamic drag: 55kN
Magnetic drag: 35kN
Propulsion power: 12mW
Auxiliary power requirement: 1mW
Specific primary power requirement: 150Wh/P·km

ITALY

PALERMO UNIVERSITY

Aeronautical Institute, University of Palermo, Viale delle Scienze, 90128 Palermo, Italy
Telephone: 42 27 48; 42 71 72; 22 74 39

The Institute is engaged in research in the field of magnetic levitation, the application of studies undertaken in conventional railway transportation and the development of a new type of marine air cushion vehicle.

JAPAN

JAPAN AIR LINES

General Secretary's Office, Overall Development Committee, Japan Air Lines, Tokyo Building, 73 Marunouchi 2-chome, Chiyoda-ku, Tokyo 100, Japan
Telephone: Tokyo (03) 284-2391
Officials:
Akira Hayashi, *Deputy General Secretary's Office, Overall Development Committee*

Japan Air Lines has completed a number of successful test runs with a manned dynamic model of a high speed train which is powered by linear induction motors and suspended above metal rails on a magnetic cushion. The vehicle, known as the High Speed Surface Transport (HSST) is being developed to provide air travellers with rapid ground transportation between cities and airports.

DEVELOPMENT PROGRAMME

The proposed development programme being conducted by JAL is as follows:

Phase 1: Basic study (by JAL only)—Design and construction of JAL HSST 01 — 1973-75.

Phase 2: Testing of LIM and JAL HSST 01 (JAL only) 1976.

Phase 3: The design and construction of HSST-02—1977. Testing of ride quality and secondary suspension—1978. Up to this stage, JAL's role is purely confined to the development of the HSST's technology. Beyond this stage, further development would have to be handled by a new organisation, such as a Government-backed Corporation, including private investors.

Phase 4: Construction and testing of pre-production prototype. Full size production vehicle, 1978-79. Introduction into commercial operation, 1980.

Japan Air Line's primary role is in the development of the HSST technology. This includes testing JAL HSST 01 at 300km/h with rocket-assisted thrust which is considered as its optimum operating speed.

JAL-HSST-01

The HSST test vehicle, now undergoing tests at a site in Higashi-Ogishima, Kawasaki, operates on a magnetic cushion which enables it to float above a metal track.

Propulsion is provided by a linear induction motor. The craft and all its electrical and mechanical components, including the magnets and linear induction motor, were designed and constructed by JAL engineers at the airline's engineering centre at Haneda Airport, Tokyo. JAL's test vehicle is 4·2m (13ft 9in) long, 2·6m (8ft 6in) wide and 1·1m (3ft 7in) high. Modifications undertaken during its development include the fitting of wings in order to increase its aerodynamic stability.

This test vehicle succeeded in attaining 307·8km/h (191¼mph) on 14 February 1978.

The next stage in the project was marked by the introduction of a new vehicle, HSST-02, which was designed and constructed in 1977. It seats up to 8 passengers and 1 operator, and is 6·84m (22ft 5in) long, 2m (6ft 6½in) wide and 1·75m (5ft 9in) high.

First demonstration flights of the HSST-02 were held successfully on 9 May 1978.

The full-size production vehicle will be capable of carrying up to 120 passengers at a speed of 300km/h (186mph). These vehicles will be able to operate singly or in trains.

Also projected is another type of vehicle which will operate at medium speeds (150-200km/h (93-124mph)) and lower speeds (60-120km/h (37-75mph)) and will be capable of carrying 40-80 passengers.

One of JAL's first objectives is to operate an HSST system between Haneda Airport, Tokyo and the new Tokyo International Airport at Narita, via central Tokyo. At the proposed operational speed it would be possible to travel from central Tokyo to Haneda (17km) in 4 minutes and to Narita (65km) in 14 minutes. Other proposals include an HSST link between Chitose Airport and Sapporo, in Hokkaido.

JAL has been developing its HSST system since 1971 and anticipates that the HSST could be introduced commercially by 1980, if full approval is given soon. Among the advantages claimed for the concept is that it will be pollution-free, will consume several times less energy than conventional railway systems and will be almost noiseless.

LINEAR INDUCTION MOTOR

Motive power is supplied by a linear induction motor, located in the centre of the vehicle. Power for the motor is picked up from a power supply rail by a carbon shoe, attached to the HSST itself.

The inboard motor reacts against an aluminium coated iron reaction plate, fixed to the central portion of the track.

Maximum thrust: 340kg
Power: three-phase electric current, variable voltage/variable frequency (VVVF)
Maximum electric power: 200kVA
Voltage: 0-600V
Frequency: 0-350Hz

Power is collected from a 'third-rail' which runs alongside the track. A carbon shoe, attached to the HSST maintains contact with the rail.

The reaction plate consists of an aluminium coated iron plate, which extends along the surface of the test track.

MAGNETIC CUSHION

There are two types of magnetic forces — attractive and repulsive — which can be used to develop a magnetic cushion. Attractive power is the simplest to use for it can be induced by normal conductivity. This means that it can be operated at normal temperatures, there is no need for wheels and in case of failure it has a safety advantage over repulsive power. The vehicle would simply attach itself to the rails.

Repulsive power can only be induced under super-conductivity. This needs very lower temperatures for efficient operation and therefore very heavy cooling equipment is necessary. It also needs a rail and wheel system to support it while it

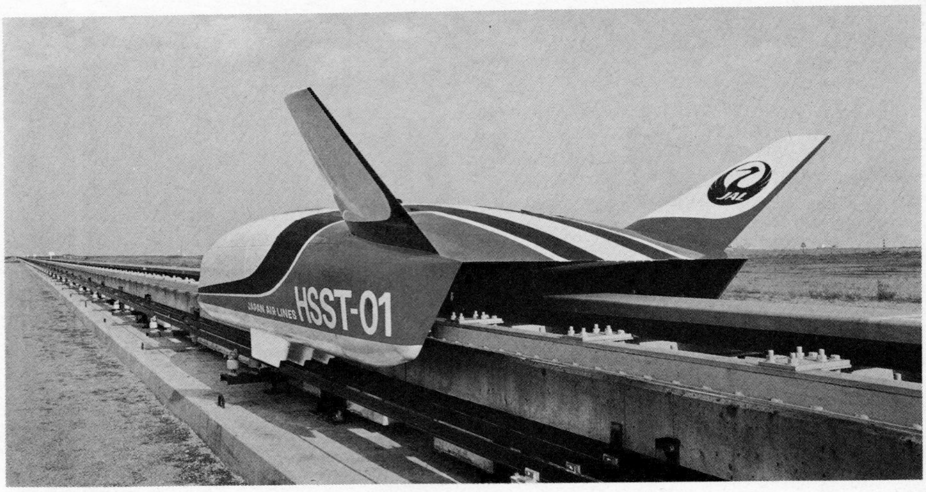

JAL's HSST-01 test craft on its 200m test track at Showa-Machi, Kanazawa-ku, Yokohama. High speed testing is currently undertaken on a 1,300m test track at Kawasaki.

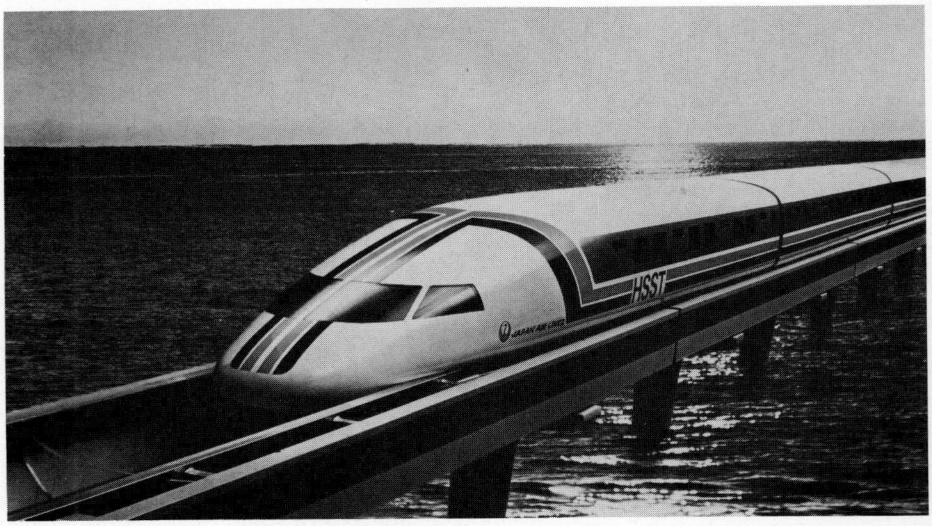

Impression of JAL's commercial HSST. Each car of the train depicted is between 18 and 22m long and will seat up to 120 passengers

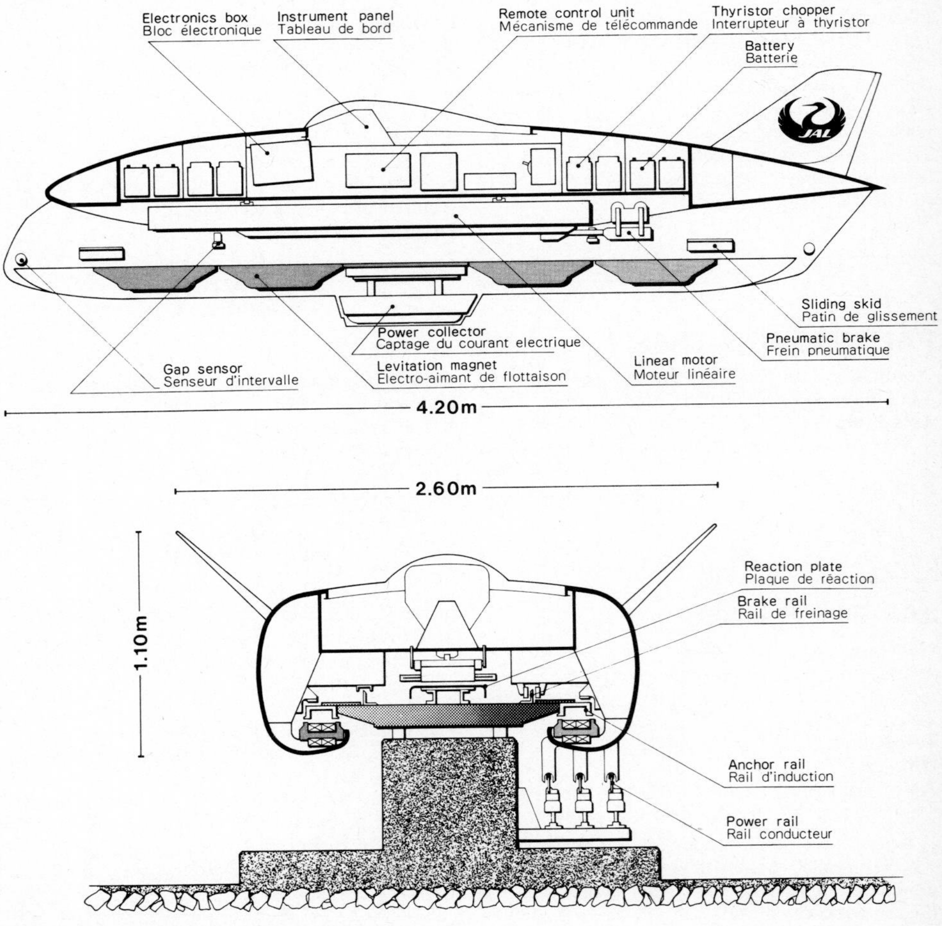

General arrangement of the HSST-01 test craft

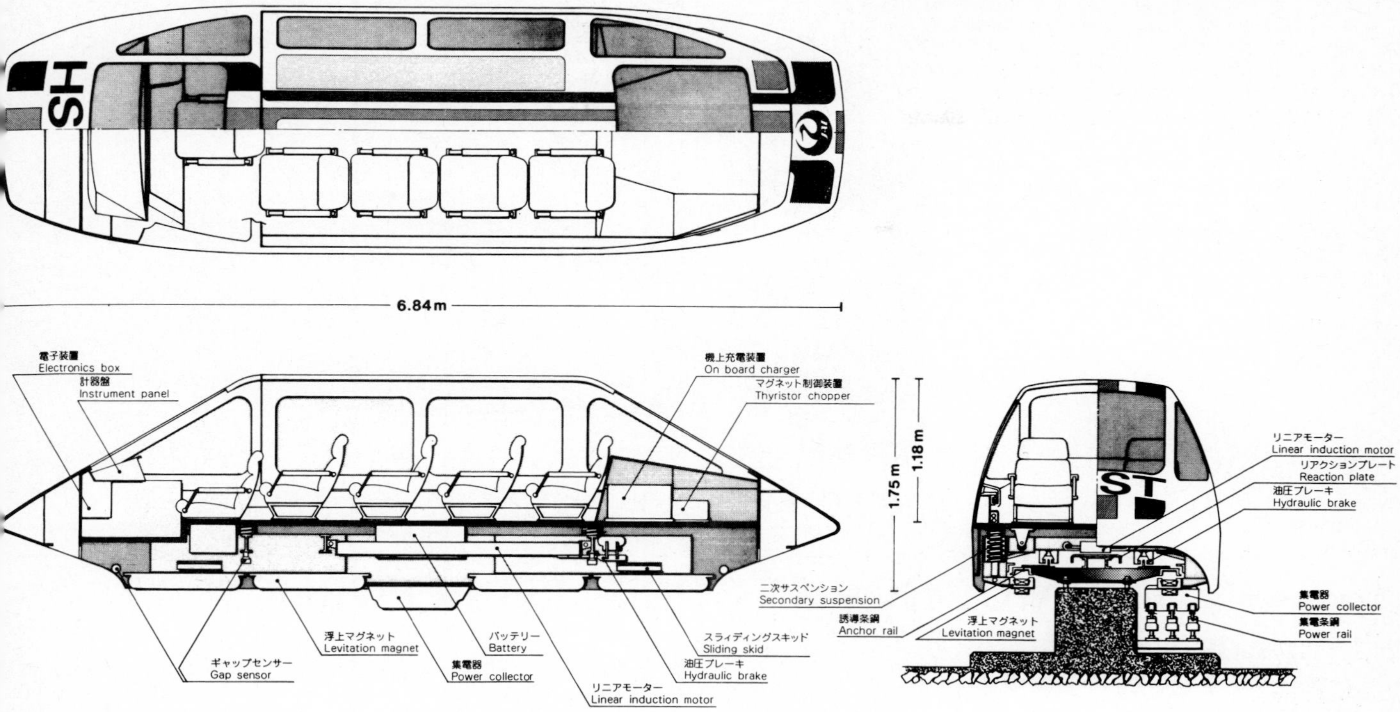

:xternal and seating arrangements of the HSST-02 test vehicle

s building up speed and would therefore have a ıigher gross weight. Should the system fail, the vehicle could be thrown off tracks by the action of polar repulsion.

On HSST-01 the magnetic cushion is created by the action of eight inboard electro-magnets. There are four on each side of the body, fixed to the 'wrap round' sections of the bodywork. The magnets are attracted to iron channels, one on each side of the track on the underneath section. They are prevented from actually making contact with the iron channels by an electronic sensing device which controls the gap between the magnets and the iron channels. This sensor is set to maintain the gap at 10mm. Inboard batteries provide the electricity to operate the magnets.

HSST-02

JAL's second test vehicle is designed to operate at speeds up to 100km/h (62mph) on a 1·3km (1,420yd) track. Seats are provided for an operator and up to eight passengers. The body is of semi-monocoque light alloy construction. Secondary suspension is provided between the body shell and the electromagnets of the levitation system.

LEVITATION SYSTEM: Power for the attractive magnet levitation system is supplied by 120V batteries which receive boosting current from a power rail located alongside the track. The power rail, which also feeds the linear motor, supplies the levitation system with three-phase AC current. The gap between the vehicle and the track is 10mm.

PROPULSION SYSTEM: A single-sided linear induction motor is employed. Maximum thrust is 300kg. Power supplied for propulsion is three-phase variable-frequency, variable-voltage from 0-120 Hz. Maximum power is 200kW at 0-600V.

BRAKING SYSTEM: Linear motor dynamic brake, also hydraulic brake.

TEST TRACK LENGTH: 1300m (1,420yds)

DIMENSIONS

Length overall: 6·84m (22ft 5in)

Width: 2m (6ft 6½in)

Height: 1·75m (5ft 9in)

WEIGHTS

Empty: 1,800kg (3,968lb)

Loaded, driver and seven passengers: 2,255kg (4,970lb)

PERFORMANCE

Max speed for test purposes on 1·3km (1,420yds) track: 100km/h (62mph)

COMMERCIAL HSST

JAL's proposed commercial HSST will have a body similar in shape to the Douglas DC-8 jet airliner with similar interior styling. The minimum train would comprise two cars, each seating 112 passengers, but multiple trains could be easily assembled by coupling up cars as necessary.

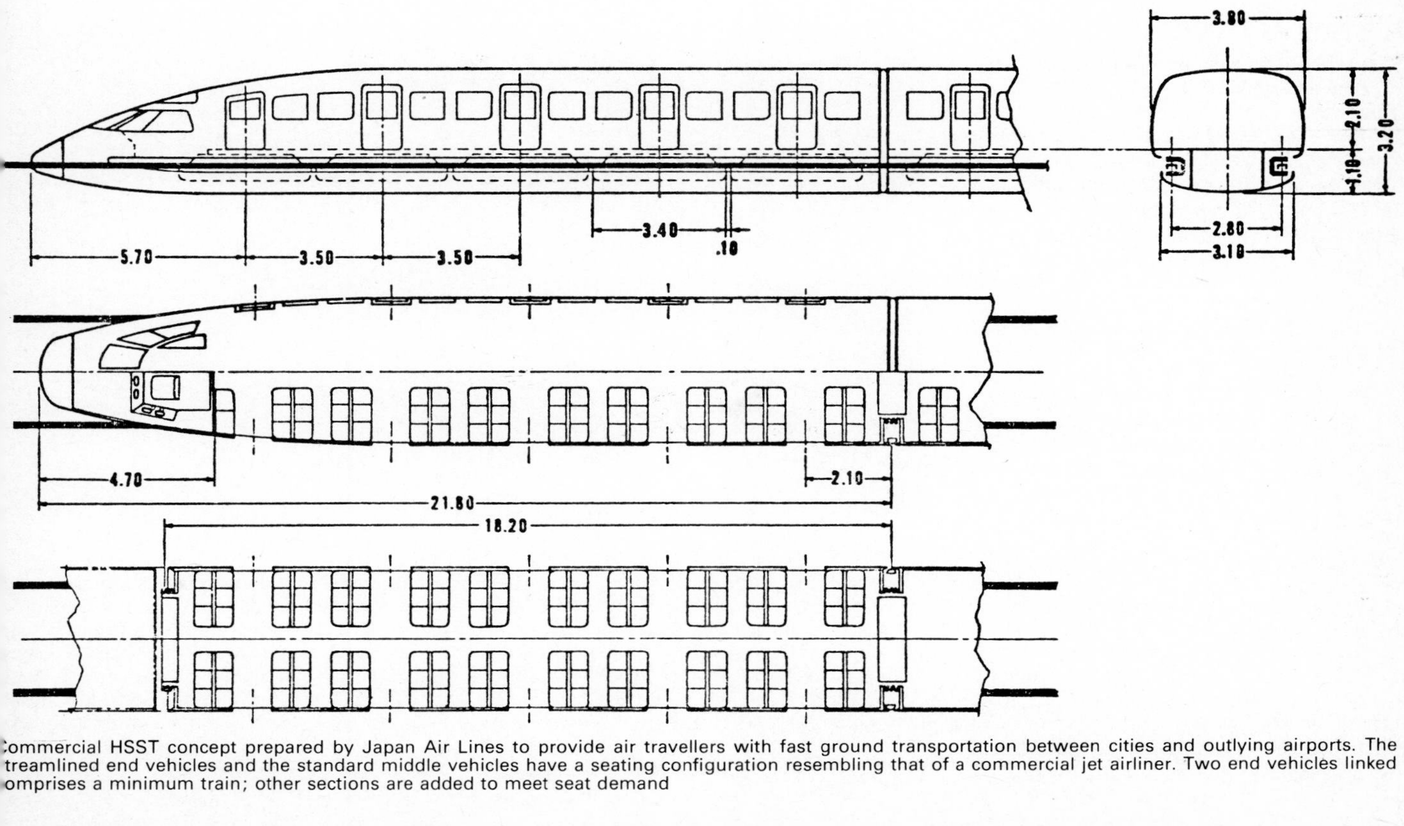

:ommercial HSST concept prepared by Japan Air Lines to provide air travellers with fast ground transportation between cities and outlying airports. The treamlined end vehicles and the standard middle vehicles have a seating configuration resembling that of a commercial jet airliner. Two end vehicles linked omprises a minimum train; other sections are added to meet seat demand

Cruising speed would be about 300km/h (186mph) and the standard acceleration 0·1g, approximately the same as a standard electric train. Power used at cruising speed would be in the region of 5kW per passenger. Levitation and propulsion arrangements would be the same as those for the HSST-01.

DIMENSIONS

Length forward (streamlined) car: 21·8m (71ft 6in)

Standard car: 18·2m (59ft 9in)

Width: 3·8m (12ft 6in)

Height: 3·2m (10ft 6in)

Seats forward car: 112

standard car: 120

Seating eight passengers and an operator, the HSST-02 is designed for speeds of up to 100km/h on a 1·3km test track

UNION OF SOVIET SOCIALIST REPUBLICS

INSTITUTE OF DIESEL LOCOMOTIVE ENGINEERING, MOSCOW

The design of tracked skimmers started in Moscow during the five-year plan period 1971-75. Professor Alexander Zolotarsky announced in May 1972 that the technical and economic assessment of TACV systems was being undertaken at the Institute of Diesel Locomotive Engineering at its research establishment near Moscow.

It appeared from his statement that the first vehicles were to be powered by gas-turbines and would operate on concrete tracks. Construction of prototype vehicles capable of speeds in excess of 300km/h (186mph) was due to start "in the nearest future". Professor Zolotarsky foresaw the use of TACVs to link densely populated industrial centres and resort areas where conventional railways are usually overloaded. They could also be operated successfully in the marshy areas of Siberia and in the North, as well as in permafrost areas.

Research undertaken jointly by the VNII Wagonbuilders, the Design Bureau for Aviation Research of AS Yakovlev and the Kalinim Wagon Factory led to the construction of a high-speed, jet-propelled research locomotive, the VNIIVOS-KOROST, preliminary details of which were released in 1971.

Thrust for the vehicle, which was designed to travel on wheels on a conventional track at speeds up to 250km/h (155mph) was provided by two Ivchenko AI-25 turbofans of the type employed on the YAK-40 airliner, and normally rated at 1,500kg (3,300lb st). These are sited above the cabin of the locomotive.

Data gathered from the Korost was employed in the design of primary and secondary suspensions systems, magnetic rail disc and air brakes and other features.

Full scale facilities for research into trains powered by linear induction motors have also been provided at a new transport research centre, a few miles from Kiev, capital of the Ukraine. It is intended to make a thorough investigation of the possibilities opened up by modern technology, including propulsion systems and original methods of suspension including air and magnetic cushions.

In 1978 it was announced in Moscow that construction of a track for the world's first operational magnetically levitated vehicles will begin at Alma Ata in 1979. The new system will lift the vehicles a few centimetres above the track and drive them by linear motors.

The first phase of the construction will be a 13km (8mile) commuter section within the city, to be followed later by a 65km (40mile) extension outside the city, providing fast access to a recreation complex at Kapchagai.

One of the aims of the Soviet railway authority is to provide maglev trains capable of speeds of 300-500km/h (186-310mph) suitable for rapid transportations of long-distance, commuter and airport services.

UNITED STATES OF AMERICA

BERTELSEN INC

Head Office: 9999 Roosevelt Road, Westchester, Illinois 60153, USA
Telephone: (312) 681 5606
Works: 113 Commercial Street, Neponset, Illinois 61345, USA

Dr William R Bertelsen, Director of Research, Bertelsen Inc, has proposed the use of a vehicle based on the twin-gimbal Aeromobile 13 for a tracked skimmer system. It is described in US Patent No 3,845,716 issued on 5 November 1974.

Dr Bertelsen suggests that the system, based on the use of ACVs in simple, graded earth grooves, would be ideal for mass transportation in developing countries where no large investments have been made in roads, railways or airlines. The fuel can be petroleum in oil-rich areas or hydrogen in depleted or polluted areas. Whereas in densely populated countries new rights of way will inevitably be elevated or underground, there should be little difficulty in obtaining rights for the guideways in developing countries. In large countries with relatively empty interiors, the low-cost surface groove will be ideal.

Current or abandoned railway rights-of-way can be used for the Bertelsen Aeromobile-Aeroduct system, since rail gradients are acceptable to the Aeromobile. Hills can be climbed by the use of steps on which the vehicle is on the level or slightly inclined uphill most of the time. It climbs simply by lifting its mass in ground effect up each step, each of which would be slightly lower than its skirt height. Relatively low propulsive power is neccessary to climb a hill in this manner and no increase in lift power is necessary.

Impression of a tracked air cushion vehicle, based on the Bertelsen Aeromobile 13, in its guideway system

The Aeromobile vehicles employed for the system would be fully automated. Journey data would be fed into an onboard mini-computer and the vehicles would follow the route through signals emitted at junction points. A tape could guide the car across the country with a sleeping or reading driver. Dr Bertelsen states that the car would move from low-to-high speed lanes automatically and remain in high-speed lanes until the signals at junctions told it to move down into a slower lane before turning off. This process would be repeated automatically until the car left the automatic guideway system.

THE AERODUCT SYSTEM

The air cushion vehicle, so unquestionably superior for off-road and amphibious transport of heavy loads, can also carry loads just as trucks and trains do, on rights-of-way. However, the right-of-way for the ACV will be different. It should be wider due to modern loads and because the length and width of the base of the vehicle determines the lift area and the total ACV hauling capacity. The ACV right-of-way should be semi-circular in cross section or a cylindrical tube to provide guidance and yaw stabilisation of the frictionless craft. There should be steps up and down grades to facilitate grade climbing and descent by frictionless but massive craft.

The system has the attributes of being frictionless; it has a high speed; provides a very soft, shockless, self-damped ride; offers a heavy load carrying capacity; and a low ground pressure which renders it amphibious.

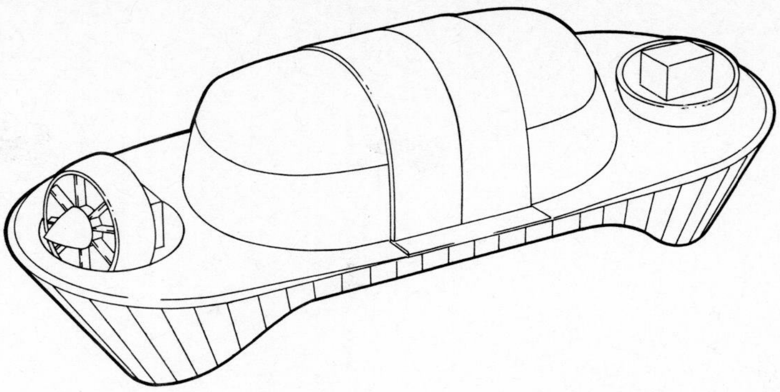

Impression of a tracked air cushion vehicle based on the Bertelsen Aeromobile 13

Because the ACV is frictionless, a cylindrical groove provides perfect guidance for high speed translation longitudinally down the track. It also allows the craft to centrifugate up the wall on a curve, which obviates side forces on passengers or loads.

The low ground pressure makes the right-of-way very inexpensive to built and maintain. Whether of sodded or lightly paved earth, ploughed, ice-coated snow or in the form of a sheet metal tube or groove, all are far less expensive than the high pressure of conventional roads or railways (30 to 100psi in tyres, up to 10,000psi on rails).

The groove (or tube) can be located on, along, next to, above, or below existing roads or rails, requiring no further acquisition, and will not interfere with existing road drainage. The new ACV modality can be compatible with all existing surface transport. It will cost far less per mile to built and maintain than its conventional counterpart.

Adaptation of ACVs and Aeroducts to massive loads of 100,000lb or more per vehicle is easily possible, and adaptation of the vehicle beds to flat surface for loading, unloading, storing, staging, servicing, etc, is also possible. The loaded "trailers" may be moved singly or in trains down the hollow path at high speed. Tractors or pushers for these loads would have similar adaptability to flat or semi-cylindrical surfaces. The tractors would probably be powered by turbine-driven gimbal fans, capable of full manoeuvrability with 100% of propulsive force available for forward thrust, braking, lateral force, or for steering torque. Only a gimbal type of handling vehicle or 'tug' could manage the 100,000lb AVCs on 'flat' surfaces and against winds and gusts. Crawlers or tyre wheel tractors could attempt the flat surface handling of the massive carriers, but experience shows that paving becomes necessary for repeated traverse of ground by any land vehicle. However, grass is often adequate for ACVs. The air cushion 'tug' will be irreplaceable in the sodded or otherwise lightly prepared mileages of grooves between important shipping centres, with, for example, grain elevators, mines, stockyards, factories, cities, forests, oil and gas fields.

The system is designed to be all-inclusive, providing every type of transport need, from personal transit, 'mass' transit, taxis, police, fire and emergency service, mail, freight, parcel, grocery and milk delivery to refuse pickup.

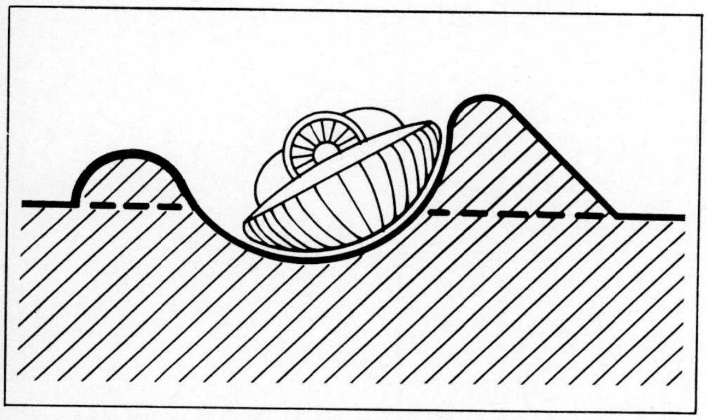

Aeromobile shown in graded groove at speed in left curve

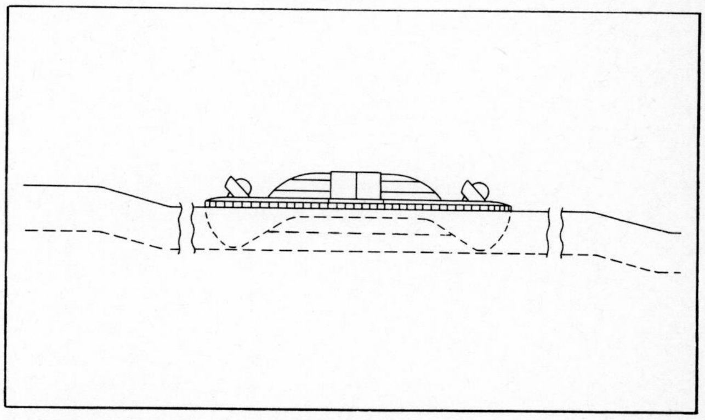

Side view, stepped aeroduct for grade climb and descent

AIR CUSHION APPLICATORS, CONVEYORS AND PALLETS

AUSTRALIA

FLOMAT (AUST) PTY LTD

12 Krestine Place, Mona Vale, New South Wales 2103, Australia

Flomat (Aust) Pty is a licensee of Jetstream Systems Co of Hayward, California. Details of the conveyor system built by the company can be found under the entry for Jetstream Systems Company, USA.

FRANCE

SOCIÉTÉ BERTIN & CIE

Head Office and Works: BP 3, 78370 Plaisir, France
Telephone: 056 25 00
Telex: 696231
Officials:
Fernand Chanrion, *President Director General*
Michel Perineau, *Director General*
Georges Mordchelles-Regnier, *Director General*

Air Cushion Handling Division
Centre d'Essais Aérotrain, Gometz la Ville, 91400 Orsay, France
Telephone: 592 03 18
Telex: 60 090
Officials:
M Croix-Marie, *Head of Air Cushion Department*

Research on ground effect and air cushion principle applications has been undertaken by Bertin et Cie since 1956. The company developed the original technique of separately fed plenum chambers surrounded by flexible skirts—see entries for SEDAM (ACVs) and Société de l'Aérotrain (Tracked Skimmers). The same basic technology is being applied extensively to industrial materials handling.

In the past, developments in this field have mainly covered special applications. A stage has now been reached where standard equipment can be made available for a large number of handling applications.

Bertin has now made available standard components and, according to the type of problem to be solved, offers clients 'do-it-yourself-kits', plus advice, technological assistance or full design services.

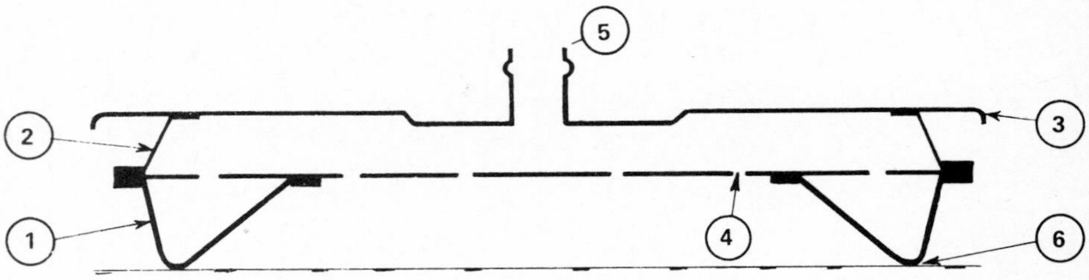

Basic configuration and components of a Bertin circular cushion

Standard Bertin circular cushion

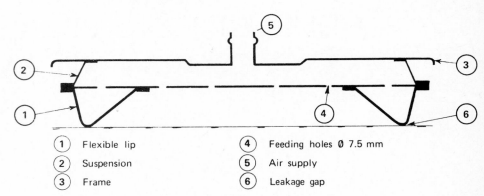

Bertin metal air cushion skids for use over very even surfaces.

Standard do-it-yourself kits

These are available in the following configurations:

Circular Cushions

These form the basis of the handling platforms. Their positioning and number is determined by function, the weight and nature of the loads (height, position of centre of gravity etc).

Three cushions at least must be employed to ensure stability.

The cushions can be fitted on to a chassis with spring fastenings.

The flexible lips will not suffer wear under normal conditions but are interchangeable in cases of accidental damage.

Circular cushions are produced as standard units in three sizes: Ø 300, Ø 450, Ø 600.

General characteristics are given in the accompanying table.

Standard Modules

Standard modules, complete with chassis, and based on one of the four types of standard circular cushions available (see table) are available in two models:

—quick assembly modules which can be assembled at will to form platforms in a variety of sizes
—independent pads ready to be inserted beneath loads which have a rigid, flat underside.

Lifting capacity of these modules is comparable to that of the corresponding circular cushion.

Honeycomb Cushions

Honeycomb cushions are available in three standard sizes. Fully stable, these cushions allow full use of the load-bearing surface for lift. In addition they are very thin but can bear very heavy loads when at rest.

These cushions employ inflatable joints to seal off adjacent square cells which are fed separately through vents from a single plenum. The plenum itself is fed from any suitable compressed air source.

Rigid Air Cushions

Metal air cushion skids are available in the range of Bertin industrial materials handling equipment. These can be used across even surfaces and operate without surface contact on an air film a few hundredths of a millimetre deep. Applications include a 3,000kg payload platform for feeding a press mounted on seven 200mm diameter skids. This unit can withstand a pressure of 26,000kg when at rest beneath the press.

Water Cushions

Circular water cushions are available for very heavy loads. Power required for lift with water cushions is 20 to 30 times less than with standard air cushions.

Machinery handling in factories

Major applications of Bertin air cushions to solve machinery and material handling problems within factories, listed in past issues of *Jane's Surface Skimmers,* include:
air film cushion sheer tables (1966);
air cushion platforms to install 40,000lb machinery units within factory buildings (1966);
air cushion chassis for moving machinery (1968);
air cushion conveyors adapted to specific loads (1969);
air film conveyors for the transfer of soft or tacky sheet material (1970);
loading platform for lorries (1970);

cast mould press feeding platform on air cushions (1971);
transfer of 12-ton spinning mills on air cushions (1972);
permanent air cushion platforms for the transfer of 5-ton diesel engine cooling units from the assembly line to the dispatching area (1972);
air cushion platforms for precise positioning of metal blanks under a magnetic unstacking unit (1973);
permanent air cushion platforms fitted under 30-ton profiling machines facilitating the use of alternative machines along a production line (1973);
50-ton capacity platform to introduce loads within an X-ray control room through staggered protection walls (1974);
air cushion turntable for 50-ton loads of glassware (1974);
space-saving air cushion system to rotate railway trucks along their assembly line (1975);
shipyard air cushion platforms to facilitate positioning of large hull sections (1976);
metal sheet handling platforms and two-tier mobile lifting table for transfers in stores (1976).

Aid to shipbuilding

One of the major European shipyards has adopted Bertin air cushion units to facilitate the positioning of hull sections.

The air cushion platforms are built to carry large sections, weighing 100 tons and measuring 25 × 15m (82 × 49 ft), and place them in the precise position for assembly. Each platform is fitted with four circular cushions and incorporates one pneumatic jack and four hydraulic jacks, which in turn support a top working surface covered in a film of oil. Once the hull sections have been introduced to the point of assembly, they are raised first by the pneumatic jack, then the hydraulic ones to reach the exact position for fixing. The oil film is used for the final lateral positioning.

Twelve units of this type have been built by Bertin. The employment of circular cushions in conjunction with pneumatic suspension assists operations on the undulating floor surfaces of dry docks.

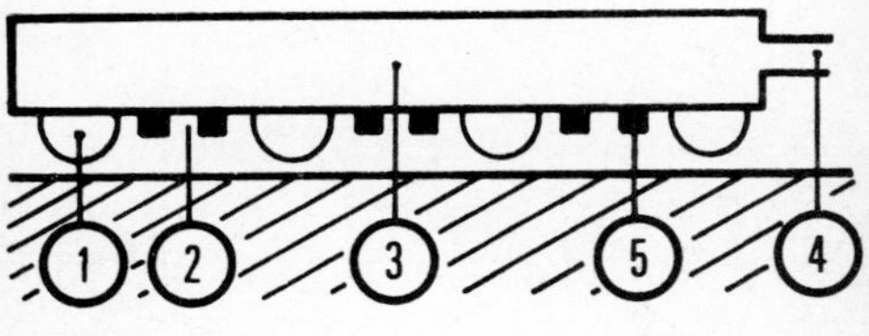

1 *joint*
2 *aperture*
3 *chamber*
4 *air supply*
5 *resting pads*

Diagram showing the basic structure of the Bertin honeycomb air cushion pallets

Circular Cushions

Type	Ø 300	Ø 450R	Ø 600	Ø 600R
Overall diameter	0·364m	0·54m	0·68m	0·68m
Height (at rest)	0·035m	0·05m	0·05m	0·05m
(under pressure)	0·045m	0·07m	0·075m	0·075m
	±5mm	±5mm	±5mm	±5mm
Weight	5·5kg	8·5kg	14kg	15kg
Lift area	0·07m²	0·16m²	0·28m²	0·28m²
Load capacity	500kg	1,200kg	2,500kg	4,000kg

Special cushions are available for higher load capacities

Honeycomb Cushions

	Type 1	Type 2	Type 3
Length × width	626 × 329mm	416 × 768mm	590 × 590mm
Height (at rest)	22mm	32mm	30mm
Lift area	0·162m²	0·250m²	0·250m²
Load capacity	1,000kg	1,700kg	3,000kg

Bertin air cushion platform in use on the Renault R14 assembly line

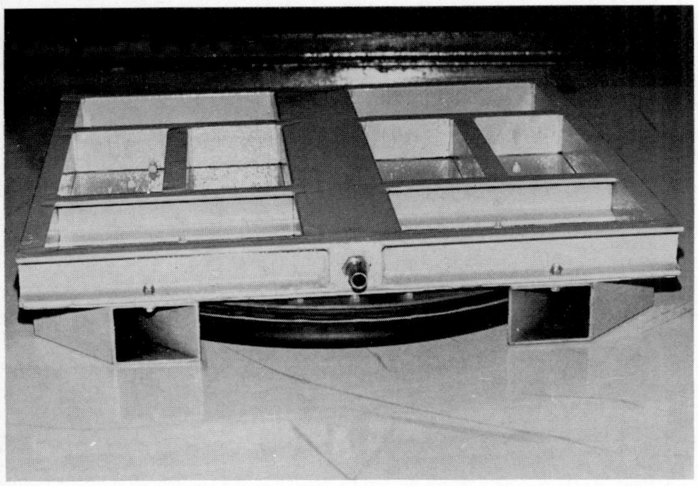

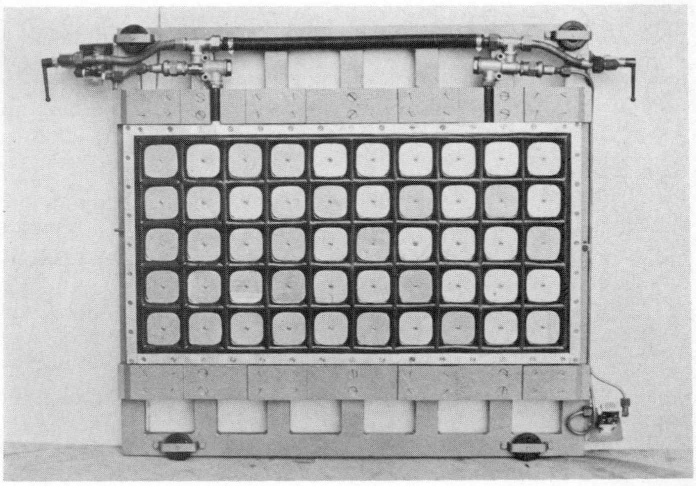

Left: Bertin standard module in the form of an independent pad, ready to be inserted beneath a load with a rigid, flat, underside. **Right**: Bertin honeycomb cushion for heavy loads

Metal sheet handling platform

A handling platform to facilitate feeding metal sheet to a work post has been produced for CEM at Le Havre, France.

The problem was to bring from an outdoor storage yard cases loaded with 2×8m thick metal sheets to feed cutting units within a workshop.

The cases have been equipped with ten Type 600 Bertin circular cushions and are capable of carrying 20 tonnes of metal sheet in one move.

The cushion air feed has been calculated so as to allow the loads to vary both in weight and centring, so that no special care is required when loading the cases.

Two-tier mobile lifting table

A mobile lifting table for placing sheet materials in a multi-level storage rack has been built for CEM, a company based at Le Havre.

The lower chassis, supported by eight Type 450 circular air cushions, is used to move the loaded table, weighing up to 6 tons, from the loading area to the storage racks. A six-cushion platform, which supports the actual load on the table, enables the material to be placed in position and elevated to the correct level. Once the material is in place, the modular air cushion platform is withdrawn onto the main lift table.

Renault assembly line

Bertin air cushion platforms have recently been adopted to facilitate the positioning and assembly of components at the Renault plant in France for the R14 design.

Building sites

Most industrial air cushion platforms require an even ground surface for satisfactory operation. Bertin platforms, with special cushions, are now in use on building sites to position heavy ceiling structures. They have proved capable of operating over relatively uneven temporary floor surfaces.

Fixture for the precise positioning of heavy parts for machining and the eventual movement of the machined components

Turntables for off-centre loads

Air cushion turntables are now a standard type of equipment, but turntables used to feed components to work posts along an assembly line are frequently required to carry off-centre loads. Bertin has recently evolved air cushion turntables employing rigid metal air pads for this purpose.

Left: Air cushion turntable for off-centred loads. **Right:** Platform for positioning ceiling structures

ETABLISSEMENTS NEU

BP 28, 59013 Lille, France

Etablissements NEU is a licensee of Jetstream Systems Co of Hayward, California, USA. Details of the conveyor system built by the company can be found under the entry for Jetstream Systems Company, USA.

GERMANY, FEDERAL REPUBLIC

HELMUT FRANK BLECHVERARBEITUNG

Laufdorferstrasse, D-6331 Bonbaden, Federal Republic of Germany.

This company is a licensee of Jetstream Systems Company of Hayward, California, USA. Details of the conveyor system built by the company can be found under the entry for Jetstream Systems Company, USA.

JAPAN

EBARA MANUFACTURING COMPANY

11 Haneda Asahi-cho, Ota-ku, Tokyo, Japan.

Ebara Manufacturing Company is a licensee of Jetstream Systems Company of Hayward, California, USA. Details of the conveyor system built by the company can be found under the entry for Jetstream Systems Company, USA.

TRINIDAD

COELACANTH GEMCO LTD

1 Richardson Street, Point Fortin, Trinidad
Officials:
Nigel Seale, *Director*
Kelvin Corbie, *Director*
R Varma, *Secretary*

Coelacanth Gemco Ltd, the first company to specialise in the design and construction of air cushion vehicles in the West Indies, has developed a hover conveyor system and a hover pallet.

The pallet, measuring 0·91×1·22m (3×4ft), is capable of lifting and moving 453·59kg (1,000lb) while operated by one man and great potential is seen for the use of these units within Trinidad factories.

The hover-conveyor system is designed in modules of 3·05m and 4·57m (10ft and 15ft), enabling a system of any length to be devised to suit changing production line requirements.

Coelacanth Gemco is also working on a self-contained unit, powered by a 100hp diesel engine driving a 0·91m (36in) eight-blade axial fan at 2,500rpm to produce 849·5m³ (30,000ft³) of air per minute at 6in wg pressure.

This will be used in the movement of oil company tanks between various locations. Multiples of this unit will enable tanks of any size to be moved after attaching the skirt system.

A Coelacanth hoverpallet employed in a workshop to move air-conditioning equipment. This particular model lifts loads up to 453·592kg (1,000lb). Other models, operating on factory air supplies of 5·62kg/cm² (80psi), will carry loads of up to 15·24 tonnes (15 tons). The model seen above operates on either 115 or 230V ac

UNION OF SOVIET SOCIALIST REPUBLICS

LENINGRAD INSTITUTE OF ENGINEERING AND CONSTRUCTION

Leningrad, USSR

An air cushion vibrating platform designed to improve the rate of setting and uniformity of concrete has been designed and built by the Leningrad Institute of Engineering and Construction. It oscillates vertically, horizontally and diagonally.

The idea of employing an air cushion in constructing vibrating platforms for the production of prefabricated reinforced concrete was proposed and introduced by technologists in the Byelorussian Ministry of Construction.

Conventional vibrating platforms require considerable quantities of metal in their construction and costly foundations, the weight of which can be 18-20 times the load capacity of the platform. The concentrated dynamic loads frequently lead to the breakdown of the platform's framework, and during operation the vibration and noise cause severe discomfort to plant personnel.

The operating principle of vibrating platforms using air cushions is as follows. Beneath the vibrating platform, which is a framework with a metal bottom, air is fed by a fan to form an air cushion between the foundation and the bottom of the vibrating platform. As a result, the vibrating platform (along with a form filled with mixed concrete) is lifted into the air. The vibrating system is then switched on and the mixture is allowed to set under the influence of vertical oscillations with an amplitude of 0·3–1mm. To limit power expenditure, the cushion forms a closed system with an elastic apron. The pressure in the air cushion is 600-800kg/m² with a lift of 6-10 tons.

These platforms have a load capacity of 2–3 tons. They do not require special concrete foundations and are mounted on a sandy base 100–150mm thick. The power consumption of existing mass-produced platforms with load capacities of 4, 6 and 8 tons are 14, 20 and 40 kW, respectively, in contrast to 10, 14 and 28 kW for air cushion vibrating platforms. Use is made of the ability of an air cushion to distribute pressure evenly over the entire reaction surface, and of its outstanding shock absorbing qualities.

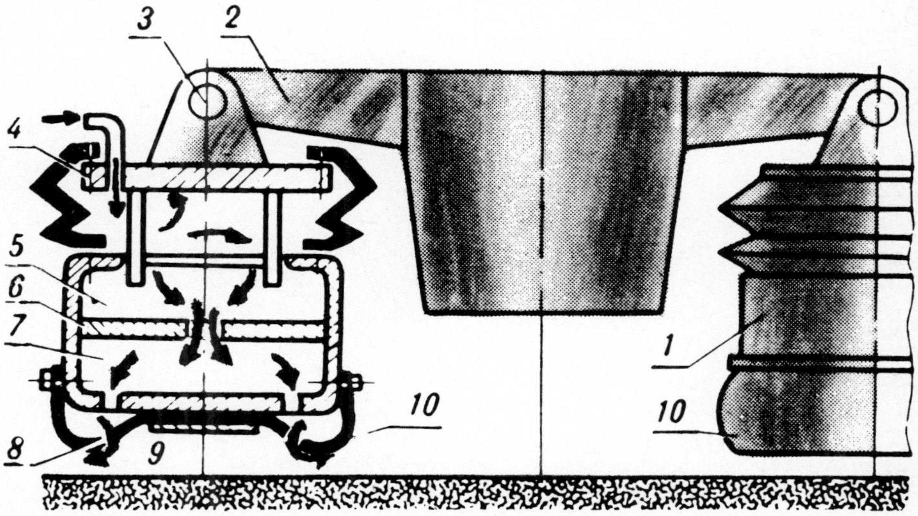

Diagram showing operation of the Novocherkaask Polytechnic air pads and handling platform

NOVOCHERKAASK POLYTECHNIC

The Novocherkaask Polytechnic has developed a series of air pads and platforms capable of supporting loads of up to 12·5 tonnes. The air supply is from a compressor or the factory air supply.

A platform with a load capacity of 40–80 tonnes is in the design stage and a feature is an automatic load relief should the air supply be cut off.

A diagram showing the system evolved at the Polytechnic accompanies this entry. It comprises two or more compressed air pads (1) which are generally rectangular in shape, and two connecting supports for the load or load platform (2). The supports are connected to the air pads by articulated joints (3) and rest on compressed air jacks (4). Air is fed into the pads through a regulator and enters the chamber of the compressed air jack (5). It then passes through the baffle plates (6) which ensure a constant differential in pressure between the cushion air plenums and the compressed air jack chamber. Cushion air enters the plenum (7) and then escapes through the discharge nozzle (8) into the recess (9) between the flexible seals and the supporting surface.

The system has undergone extensive tests and it is thought likely that it will have wide application in Soviet industry, particularly in the movement of machines and material stocks in warehouses.

UNITED KINGDOM

AIRMATIC ENGINEERING (UK) LTD

King Street, Sileby, Loughborough, Leicestershire LE12 7LZ, England
Telephone: 050 981 2816

Officials:
R D Owen, *Managing Director*
P Lucas, *Marketing Manager*

This company is manufacturing and marketing the Pneu-Move air bearing systems for manual movement of loads of up to approximately 10 tonnes.

TURNTABLES AND WORK TRANSFER SYSTEMS

Both turntables and linear systems can be stopped and effectively locked in any position by turning off the compressed air supply. At this point the metal bearing pads settle onto their tracks, resulting in a firm, robust working surface, sturdy enough for high precision work, as in the optics industry, for example.

Another advantage of Pneu-Move systems is that they are self-cleaning, exhaust air being constantly expelled onto the bearing track. They are also extremely adaptable: the control valves may be automatic, remote, foot or hand operated, to meet individual requirements.

Turntables are available in a range of sizes, either free-standing or flush floor fitted, with a machined surface, checker plate, 'T' slots or other arrangements by request. Linear systems are normally designed to suit the particular applications.

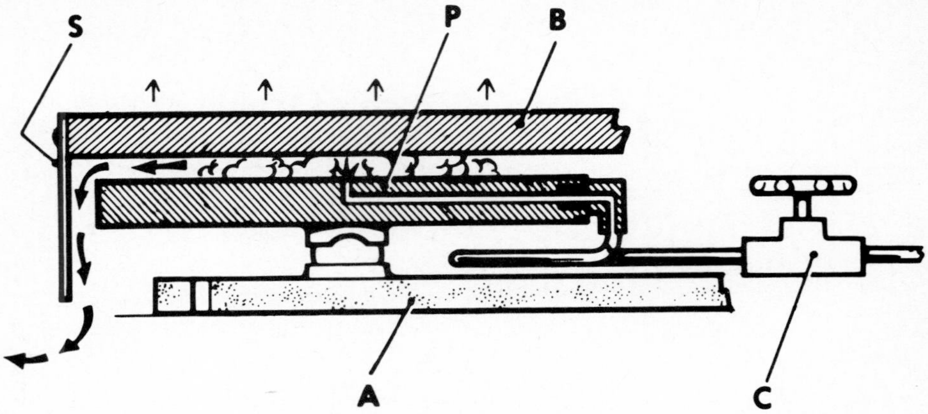

Method of turntable operation. Air suply valve 'C; is opened to allow compressed air to pass through the flotation pads 'P'. The pressure lifts turntable top 'B' on a cushion of compressed air to permit rotation. Exhaust air is expelled sideways, thus preventing any ingress of dirt. When the new position is reached, the air supply is closed, allowing the table top to settle onto bearing pads 'P'.
Pneu-Move turntables consist of a base plate 'A' with fixed air-flotation bearing pads 'P' (usually three), on which rests the rotating table top 'B'. The latter has a protective skirt 'S'. Each pad is connected to a common air-line supply through operating valve 'C'.

Pneu-Move Work Transfer System uses air flotation to provide rapid movement of heavy work-pieces between three drilling machines, saving time and reducing operator fatigue.

AIR CUSHION EQUIPMENT (1976) LTD

15-35 Randolph Street, Shirley, Southampton, Hampshire S01 3HD, England
Telephone: 0703 776468
Telex: 477537

Officials:
J D Hake, *Chairman*
R J Howling, *Director*
L A Hopkins, *Director*
R C Gilbert, *General Manager*
R R Henvest, *Works Manager*

ACE "WATER SKATE" LOAD-CARRYING PALLET

Two sizes of pallet are available: Module A, with 35 tonne maximum capacity at 6 bar and Module AA, with 100 tonne maximum capacity at 6 bar. Both have a rise height of 75mm and use water as the cushion fluid.

Due to the modular concept of the system, loads of many thousands of tonnes can be moved by the selection of the numbers of pallets used. A simple flexible skirt system retains water under pressure while still allowing sufficient water to escape to lubricate the surface between the skirt

Water Skate system being employed to move a French-built locomotive aboard a roll-on, roll-off cargo vessel for shipment to America.

Type AA pallets were used to launch this 300 tonne diving platform

Module size

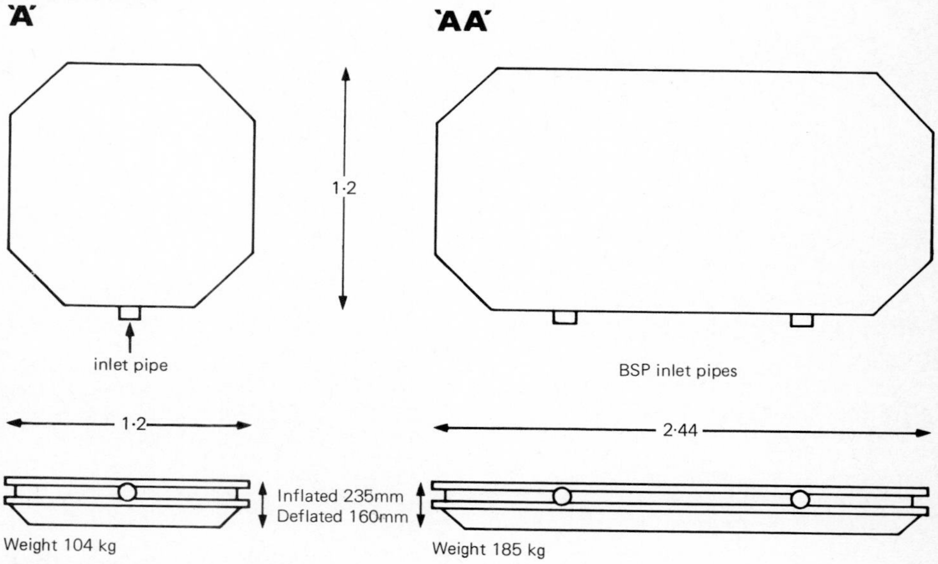

Lift pressure ratio

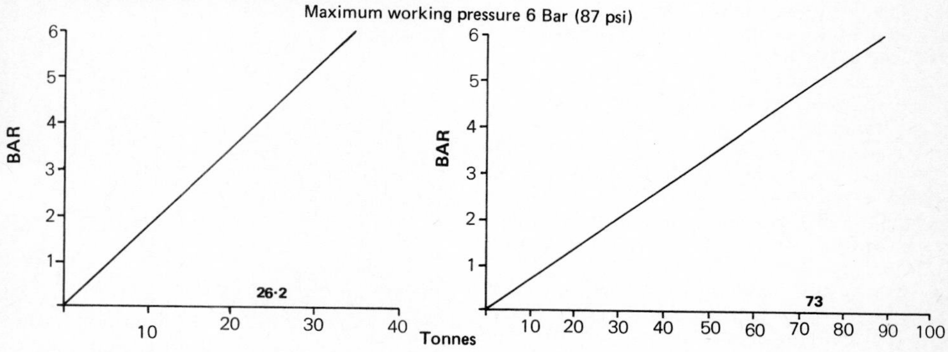

The Skate is a low cost lifting and manoeuvring pad using water under pressure from a standard commercial water pump. The two types shown here have a maximum lift of 35 tonnes and 100 tonnes respectively, and can be employed in a multi-modular system to suit individual requirements

and the ground. For movement of heavy loads on sloping surfaces a restraining line is recommended.

The type of flexible seal used in the pallet facilitates the lifting and movement of a load without the use of complex hydraulic jacking systems or heavy cranes. The equipment will operate over any surface from rough concrete to compacted soil with the minimum of ground preparation and the use of supplementary sheeting.

Water is usually provided via water pumps and distributed through normal flexible hoses. Each pallet is controlled by a standard gate valve. When the valve is opened water is supplied to the pallet and the lift of 75mm is achieved.

The load is normally moved by towing, winching or a combination of both. The drag coefficient, which is very low, especially when using a running sheet, is generally between 2-3% of the total weight.

The heaviest load movement to date using the AA modules was a 10,000 tonne capacity barge destined for operation in the North Sea, weighing 1,800 tonnes. Twenty-one AA modules were arranged in five lines and operated along five temporary tracks over a beach to the low water line. Water was supplied in two stages via two delivery pumps feeding a four pump system giving the required operating pressure of six bar.

One of the most difficult moves attempted to date was the loading of a railway locomotive into a roll-on, roll-off cargo vessel. The lack of head room in the ship and the requirement for a single load moving system to move the locomotive from the rail track into the ship, then from the ship to the new location and rail track, presented problems with equipment specification. The Water Skate system, however, gave the solution enabling the locomotive to be jacked from and onto the trackway while maintaining a low profile for entry between decks.

Another unusual marine loading took place when a 320-tonne Link Span Bridge, destined for a cross-channel ferry service, was loaded onto a sea-going barge which carried it to Boulogne. Other marine associated work included the slipway launching of a 240-tonne grain barge and a 180-tonne trawler.

On land, Water Skate operations have ranged from moving six oil production modules of 400 tonnes average weight destined for the North Sea, to the transfer of a dockside crane from one rail track to another.

The Water Skate is operated under licence from Air Cushion Equipment Limited by Lifting Services International, a division of Taylor Woodrow Construction Limited, except in North America, where Hover Systems Inc, of Media, Philadelphia, is the agent.

The equipment is normally hired by the client, who is also given technical assistance, although contract movements are also undertaken. Companies also have the option of purchasing Water Skate equipment for operation by their own personnel.

MINI WATER SKATE

To meet a growing demand from industrial users with heavy or dense 'problem' loads, Lifting Services International have introduced a Mini "Water Skate" load bearing module. Working at a water pressure of 6 bar each module will lift 10 tonnes and on smooth concrete will use 100 litres of water per minute.

The skates can be used in multiples of three or more to form a load movement system to suit individual applications and, because they are omni-directional, heavy loads can be manoeuvred in confined spaces. Force needed to move a load is approximately 2 to 5% of the deadweight.

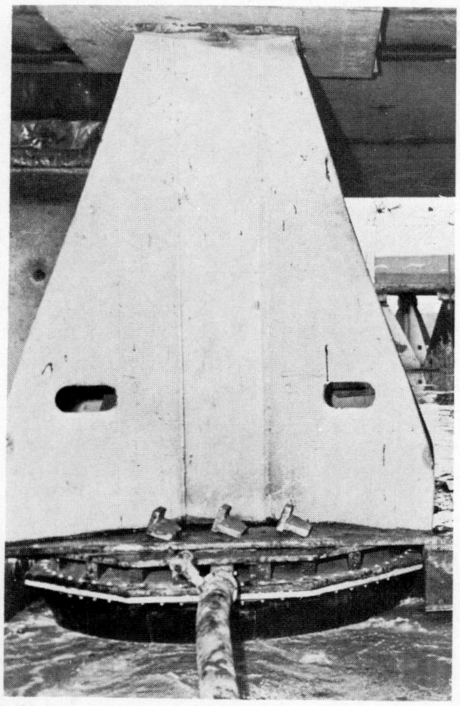

Close-up of a Water Skate load-carrying pallet in position below a ship section

Six type A pallets were employed to move and locate ship sections weighing 65-110 tonnes in a French dry dock

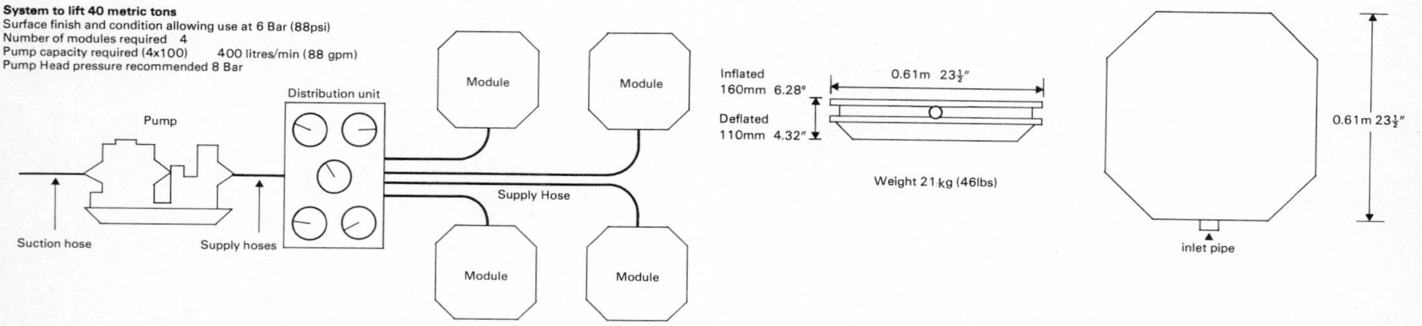

Example of Mini Water Skate module system

APPLIED TECHNOLOGY COMPANY LTD

Gatehouse 802A, Purley Way, Croydon, Surrey CR0 4RS, England
Telephone: 01-680 0871
Telex: 917392
Officials:
M Fitzcharles, *General Manager*
B Mitchell, *Sales Manager*

Applied Technology, one of the Hunting Group of companies, is the exclusive agent in the United Kingdom and Ireland for fluid film load-handling products based on Aero-Go (USA) fluid film Aero-Casters (air and water film bearings). The company offers standard, off-the-shelf equipment and systems as well as full design and manufacturing facilities for specially engineered applications.

The standard equipment available ranges from building block Aero-Caster Load Modules in load capacity sizes from 230kg (500lb) to 36,000kg (40 tons), lightweight aluminium pallets, heavy duty steel pallets, air-powered tractive drives and a variety of accessories.

Equipment and systems are supplied to operate from factory compressed air. For outdoor and special applications water or similar fluids can be used.

The equipment is most commonly powered from a factory's existing compressed air system, running costs are low and equipment maintenance is minimal due to the operating nature of the equipment. Load movement on near-frictionless fluid film systems further reduces floor wear or damage often experienced with wheeled equipment.

Industrial applications throughout the United Kingdom vary from the precision alignment of torpedo sections, crane bay transfer of loads, mobile omni-directional cranes, relocation of machinery, transformers, aircraft and paper rolls, to the movement of diesel engines through assembly. Actual load weights and sizes range from 100lb to 450 tons and from a few inches in length to 50ft long.

An Aero-Caster system produced by Applied Technology is employed by Hawker Siddeley Aviation for the movement of Nimrod aircraft at their Woodford factory.

One example of the application of heavy load fluid film equipment, is an Aero-Caster system produced by Applied Technology for Hawker Siddeley Aviation for moving the Nimrod aircraft during production at their Woodford factory. This air film movement system saved the expense of a new hangar to accommodate more production. The system permitted the movement of partially finished aircraft at a fixed angle between roof supports allowing sub-assemblies to be moved sideways across the hangar to a new parallel production line putting into use more of the existing building's space. Now two aircraft are assembled in a formerly unused area. Three air film pallets are placed beneath an aircraft's undercarriage. Locater pins in the pallets lock into a guide track fitted in the floor surface, thus providing precise load guidance. A conventional aircraft tug tows the floating load 150ft in 15-20ft, clearing it safely through limited space between roof support pillars by only a few feet which would have been an impossible task for any other wheeled or overhead handling equipment.

BRITISH HOVERCRAFT CORPORATION

East Cowes, Isle of Wight, England
Officials:
See ACV section

FLOATALOAD (1 Ton)

The 1-ton Floataload hoverpallet consists of a load-carrying, steel and plywood sandwich platform with four easily removable rubber diaphragm assemblies underneath. Air is supplied through a 1in BSP connector and control valve.

Designed for moving loads of up to 1 ton on smooth floors, the hoverpallet can also be used in conjunction with standard fork lift trucks, pallets and stillages, which can easily be modified for this purpose. Single man operation of the loaded pallet is easily effected.

Loads may be placed directly on to the platform of the Floataload hoverpallet, but a simple bridge system allowing the units to be slid under the load is more economical. When this is done the centre of pressure should be approximately under the centre of the load.

Operation is by opening the control valve until the load is airborne. The load can then be pushed, pulled or spun with minimum effort, the valve being closed and Floataload withdrawn when the load reaches the required position.

Floataload will operate satisfactorily over any smooth non-porous surface. Sheet metal, linoleum, vinyl, sealed concrete, plywood, smooth asphalt, and similar surfaces are all suitable.

DIMENSIONS
Max length: 1·16m (3ft 10in)
Width: 0·78m (2ft 7in)

AIR PRESSURE
For 45·3kg (100lb) load: 0·21kgf/cm² (3psi)
For 453·5kg (1,000lb) load: 0·42kgf/cm² (6psi)
¾in BSP connection, 1 ton load: 0·56kgf/m² (8psi)

HOVERPADS

BHC Hoverpads are simply fitted beneath a load carrying platform and connected by air-line via a control valve to the factory mains. Two sizes of hoverpad are currently available, 38cm and 66cm diameter (15in and 26in). These can be used in multiples to move loads in the range of 500-10,000kg (0·5-10 tons). Air consumption is dependent on the load and the smoothness of the floor surface. Typically, a 1,000kg (1 ton) load can be floated with 1m³/min (40ft³/min) air supply from a 6 bar (80psi) compressed air line.

Manoeuvring a 6-ton Rolls-Royce RB.211 gas-turbine from a Boeing 747 of British Airways into a maintenance bay. Four pads can be fitted beneath almost any load carrying platform to handle loads ranging from 0·5 to 10 tons

Coupling a diesel engine with a test cell dynamometer with the aid of BHC Hoverpads at the Leyland Vehicle's engine test plant

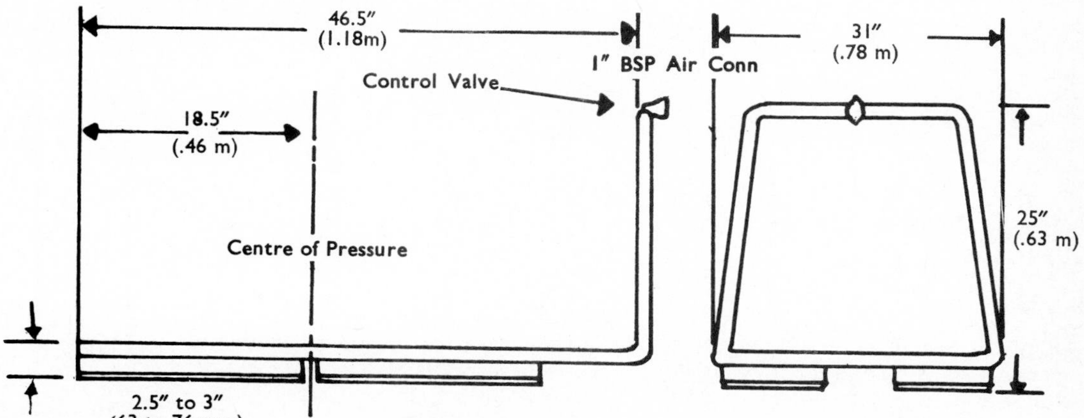

BHC 1 ton Floataload hoverpallet

LIGHT HOVERCRAFT COMPANY

Felbridge Hotel & Investment Co Ltd, London Road, East Grinstead, Sussex, England
Telephone: 0342 24424
Officials:
Lindsay H F Gatward, *Proprietor*

This company markets a pedestrian-controlled hoverpallet which has a payload capacity of 152kg (336lb).

Lift power is provided by an 8hp Briggs & Stratton petrol engine which drives a plastic/alloy axial fan mounted beneath a close mesh safety guard. Since the power unit is of the lawn mower type, the general noise level is low.

The pallet which is built in glass fibre can be used over a wide range of unprepared surfaces including snow, ice, mud, water, grass, swamp and sand. Ploughed fields with ridges of up to 152mm (6in) can be traversed with a reduced payload. The over-water and swamp applications are restricted by the amount the operator is prepared to become immersed, or the degree by which his ability to control the vehicle is impaired. Machines can be winched across areas of deep water. Working under these conditions, however, applications such as wildfowling, reed collection, slurry control and insect spraying in swamp areas are possible.

Two directional wheels are fitted and these can be adjusted or removed according to the degree of directional control or ground contact pressure required.

A clip-on spraying unit, manufactured by E Allman & Co Ltd, Birdham Road, Chichester, Sussex, has been developed for use in conjunction with the pallet.

Skirt is of HDL segmented type in nylon-coated polyurethane. Depth is 127mm (5in).

SPECIFICATIONS
Length (with handle): 2·89m (9ft 6in)
Width: 1·21m (4ft)
Height (with handle): 0·91m (3ft)
Weight (approx): 72·57kg (160lb)
Skirt depth: 127mm (5in)
Fuel capacity: 3·4 litres (6 pints)
Engine: 4-cycle (319cc)
Endurance (approx): 2 h/gallon
Payload: 152kg (336lb)
Payload area: 2·6m² (28ft²)

Light Hovercraft Co's hoverpallets can be used over a wide variety of unprepared surfaces including agricultural land. A clip-on attachment can be supplied for crop-spraying

Assembled hoverpallets ready for despatch. The plastic/alloy axial lift fan is mounted beneath a close mesh safety guard

One of the applications for which the hoverpallet has proved ideal is that of snow removal. Its payload capacity is 152kg (336lb)

LING SYSTEMS LTD

Unit 8, Station Road, Gamlingay Sandy, Bedfordshire SG19 3HG, England
Telephone: 0767 50101
Telex: 826439
Officials:
P J Long, *Joint Managing and Sales and Technical Director*
J R Arscott, *Joint Managing and Sales and Technical Director*
A J Cousins, *General Manager, Design and Works*

European Distributors
Denmark: ABC Hansen Comp A/S, Copenhagen
Netherlands: Miller Holding MIJ, Amsterdam

Ling Systems Ltd is the exclusive licensee in the United Kingdom, Ireland, and the Netherlands for the Jetstream air cushion conveyor system. Equipment is in use to handle a wide range of scrap materials—metal, paper, board and plastic, also many types of unit loads—boxes, both full and empty; plastic bottles; cap closures; can ends and pressed and moulded parts.

ROLAIR SYSTEMS (UK) LTD

Penta House, Basingstoke Road, Reading, Berkshire RG2 0HS, England
Telephone: 0734 82551
Telex: 848122 Garagco Reading
Officials:
B H Wright, RD, BSc, BCom, CEng, MIEE, *Chairman and Managing Director*
D L Campbell, MC, *Director*
M F Dowding, CBE, MA, CEng, MIMechE, *Director*
N F Haycock, CEng, MIEE, *Director*
R H Lacey, CEng, MIMechE, *Director*
Lord Macpherson of Drumochter, JP, *Director*
A A A Stammers, MIMechE, *Director*

Rolair Systems (UK) Ltd has an exclusive licence from Rolair Systems Inc, of Santa Barbara, California, USA, for the manufacture and sale of air film equipment for the transport of heavy industrial loads. Their range of equipment working off the shop air supply includes ST bearings which may be used in sets of four or more (individual ST bearing capacities range from ½ ton to 26½ tons); standard steel transporters incorporating four bearings with capacities from 1 ton to 107 tons which may be used separately or in combination for heavier loads. Also available are battery operated steel transporters with in-built air blowers which may be used where no air supply is available or in controlled environments where outside air cannot be used. A standard range of air film turntables with capacities up to 62 tons is available.

Existing applications of Rolair equipment in the United Kingdom range from unit loads of less than one ton to over one thousand tons. Applications include generator and transformer movements, ship section transporters, omni-mobile cranes on air bearings and standard transporters for interbay movement, steel ladle transfer cars, turntables incorporated into machine tools or used in paint booths and fettling shops, movements of machine tools, oil rig modules, printing machinery, heavy diesel engines. Rolair transporters can also be used to form a production line for heavy equipment.

United Kingdom customers include BP Chemicals, Brush Electricals, CEGB, GEC, Hawker Siddeley Group, IBM, ICI, Kodak, Rolls-Royce, Short Brothers & Harland, Sunderland Shipbuilders and Westland Helicopters.

An unloaded Rolair 24R4 transporter (10½ ton capacity) and a loaded Rolair 40B6 transporter (18 ton capacity) with an air-drive motor and fixed control handle fitted

Part of a 600 tonne Rolair movement system supplied to GEC Power Transformers, Stafford, for transformer handling

UNITED STATES OF AMERICA

AERO-GO, INC

5800 Corson Avenue South, Seattle, Washington 98108, USA
Telephone: (206) 763 9380
Telex: 320058
Officials:
Frank M Cohee, *President*
Kenneth G Wood, *Vice President*
William A Shannon, *Vice President*
Terry M Baker, *European Manager*

Associated companies:

Aero-Go Luft-Und Wasserkissentechnik GmbH
Nuelehweg 3, Postfach 1241, D-5340 Bad Honnef, Federal Republic of Germany
Goran Fredriksson, *General Manager*

Aero-Go Scandinavia AB
Energigatan 3A, S-721 38 Västerås, Sweden
Åke Hedman, *General Manager*

Applied Technology Co Ltd
Gatehouse 802A, Purley Way, Croydon, Surrey CR0 4RS, England
M Fitzcharles, *General Manager*

Avio-Diepen BV
Vliegeld Ypenburg, ZH 2109 Rijswijk, Netherlands
R de Rooij, *Director*

M Claessens
Kloosterstraat 107, B-2070 Ekeren, Belgium
R Metzelaar, *Sales Manager*

Dr Hans Kraus Ges mbH & Co KG
A-9210 Portschach, Austria
G Sandhofer, *Sales Manager*

International Marketing Services
22 rue de Vintmille, 75009 Paris, France
M Pioline, *Manager*

Pfingstweid AG
Box 761, Pfingstweidstrasse 31A, CH-8022 Zurich, Switzerland
B Maechler, *Director*

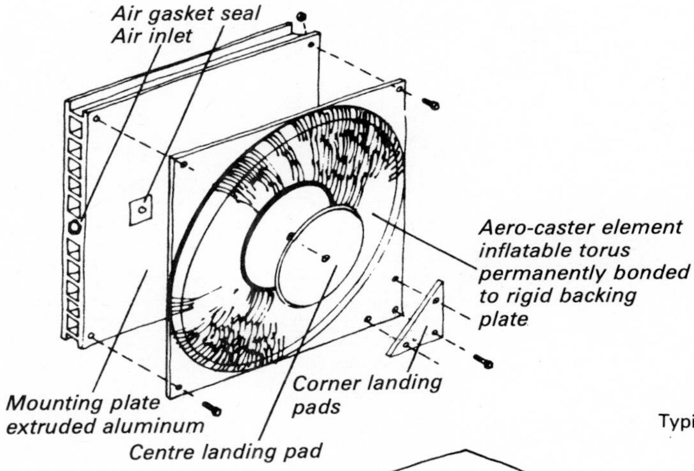

Typical Aero-Caster assembly

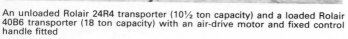

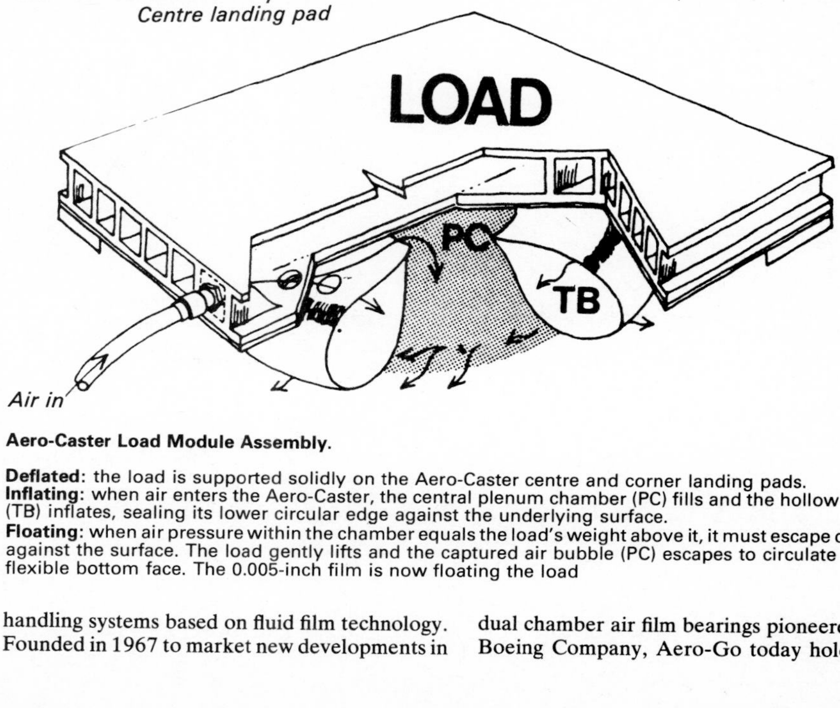

Aero-Caster Load Module Assembly.

Deflated: the load is supported solidly on the Aero-Caster centre and corner landing pads.
Inflating: when air enters the Aero-Caster, the central plenum chamber (PC) fills and the hollow torus bag (TB) inflates, sealing its lower circular edge against the underlying surface.
Floating: when air pressure within the chamber equals the load's weight above it, it must escape downward against the surface. The load gently lifts and the captured air bubble (PC) escapes to circulate under the flexible bottom face. The 0.005-inch film is now floating the load

Aero-Go, Inc manufactures fluid film load movement equipment and systems for general industrial applications. It provides a broad range of standard equipment complemented by the capability to supply complete complex materials handling systems based on fluid film technology. Founded in 1967 to market new developments in dual chamber air film bearings pioneered by the Boeing Company, Aero-Go today holds exclusive rights to extensive developments in the industry.

The basic principle of all Aero-Go Fluid Film Systems is shown in the cut-away illustration. Supporting heavy loads and simultaneously providing nearly zero friction and omni-directional movement is inherent in these systems. This results in low initial cost and low operating cost as the source of compressed air is normally the existing factory air system.

AERO-CASTER LOAD MODULES

The air film Aero-Caster is manufactured in eight sizes ranging from 30·5cm (12in) diameter, with a 454kg (1,000lb) lift capacity, to 121·9cm (48in) diameter with a 36,300kg (80,000lb) capacity. Individual load modules are used in sets of three or more of one size, and are normally slipped beneath a load in a triangular or square pattern with the centre of gravity of the load placed over the pattern's geometric centre.

Within the rated limit of each caster's lift capacity, a load is lifted in direct proportion to the air pressure applied. A 53·3cm (21in) unit with a face area of 1,808cm² (280in²) will lift 3,182kg (7,000lb) maximum at 1·76kg/cm² (25psi). Four model K21Ns will therefore float loads up to 12,700kg (28,000lb) maximum at an air pressure of 1·76kg/cm² (25psi).

Load module systems are available complete with interconnecting hose manifolds, air-regulation control console and fittings as required by a customer. They are a popular rigging tool for the movement of loads between crane bays, into tight storage areas, or installing new machinery into a plant.

The heaviest load was moved on air film in September 1977 at Beynes near Paris, France. A new 2,000 tonne concrete boxbridge was moved 34m (112ft) into a precise location under an overhead railway line in half an hour. Two truck winches pulled the load floating on 54 units of the 121·9cm (48in) load module size. The National French Railways (SNCF) has been using them to install bridges throughout France since March 1976.

AERO-PALLETS

Load-moving platforms can be supplied with built-in Aero-Casters. Lightweight aluminium extrusion or structural steel construction is employed when loads are over 18,150kg (40,000lb). Accessories include internal or detachable air motor drives to simplify large load movement and guidance by a single operator.

AERO-PLANKS

When the loads to be carried are long or are likely to vary in weight, as do the industrial air-conditioners at Trane Co's plant in Wisconsin, a set of two or more planks are placed beneath their base, spaced to meet the requirements of the changing load.

The company also manufactures air-driven platform trucks, Aero-Trucks, Aero-Turntables and machine-tool holding bedplates movable on air film.

"WATER FILM" AERO-CASTERS

In 1971 Aero-Go introduced "Water Film" casters which convey high-tonnage loads on water film. A number are in use at several major shipyards and offshore oil-drilling platform docks. To date, the largest ship constructed with the use of Aero-Caster load modules is a 3,400-ton ferry, built by Vancouver Shipyards Co, Canada.

The largest and heaviest single load yet moved on a water film system is a new 4,000-ton grandstand section added to the outdoor sports stadium in Denver, Colorado in spring 1977.

Seating 23,000 people, the three-tiered section is 163m (535ft) long by 60m (200ft) deep by 42m (135ft) high. It will be moved backwards or forwards 44m (145ft) several times per year to change the central playing field area for football, baseball, soccer and other outdoor events.

A total of 163 Model 48NHDW water film Aero-Casters are located in clusters of from two to four units each, under the section's support framing at 47 different lift points. The casters move over fourteen 2m (6ft) wide sealed-concrete runways with built-in drains. Water recirculates to the system from a 60,000 gallon storage tank. The thrust of hydraulic ram employed to push the grandstand into position i approximately 3,628kg (8,000lb).

In September 1977 the French Railways (SNCF) used high pressure air casters to lift and float a 2,000 tonne concrete bridge from its construction position to its final location. Fifty-four air casters were used to lift the bridge 76 mm (3 in). Small truck winches easily moved the load into precise location

One person moves 2,721kg (6,000lb) paper rolls loaded on Aero-Pallets with ease from storage and into exact location between the lifting arms of the printing presses at the Brown Co's plant in Michigan

In late 1974 Brown & Root activated a fluid film transport system capable of lifting and floating 2,000 ton dri rig platform structures. This water film system incorporates water elevators that evenly distribute load between the multiple legs of platform structures as these structures are moved from land to barges. Move are powered and controlled by rubber tyred vehicles. Sixteen water film transporters incorporating 32 heav duty water Aero-Casters lift and float loads up to 2,000 tons. A 100hp diesel driven water pump takes 303 litres (800 gallons) of water per minute to work this system.

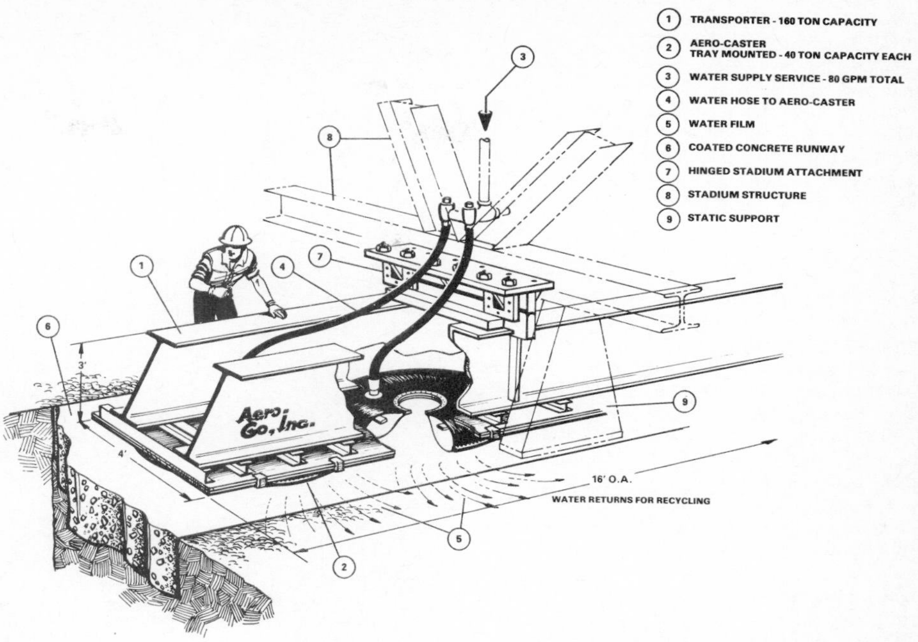

Typical lifting point beneath the grandstand at Denver

JETSTREAM SYSTEMS COMPANY

3486 Investment Boulevard, PO Box 4177, Hayward, California 94545, USA
Telephone: (415) 785 9360
Officials:
Stanley Lenox, *President*
Warren P Landon, *Vice President, Marketing*
Eugene S Batter, *Vice President, Operations*
John W Darrah, *Technical Vice President*

Jetstream Systems Company holds the world-wide rights for Jetstream air film conveyors and processing equipment.

Jetstream uses low-pressure air delivered to a plenum by a fan or fans and introduced to the conveyor surface through various types of orifices along the full length of the conveyor to maintain a film of air flowing close to the conveyor surface. This air film both lifts and moves the objects being conveyed. It conveys packages of various types; small items which must be kept properly oriented; scrap metal, plastic, and paper; and granular materials.

The air can be heated or cooled to condition the product while it is being conveyed. A rectangular fluid bed utilising the air film principle is available where longer retention times are required.

The system provides constant controlled power around curves and up inclines including vertical faces. Entry points and spurs, inputs and outputs, can be added easily anywhere along the conveyor. Maintenance and wear are greatly reduced because no moving parts are in contact with the product. Objects can be accumulated on the conveyor with very low back-pressure since they are riding on an air film and no belts or chains are dragged across the bottom.

POWER SUPPLY: Pressure of air necessary: $^{1}/_{10}$in water gauge to ½psi. Air ducting and centrifugal fans are generally fitted as an integral part of the conveyor.

CONVEYOR SYSTEM: Units are designed to suit product. The length can run to 1,000ft or more and the width from 1in to 10ft or more as necessary.

ROLAIR SYSTEMS, INC

PO Box 30363, Santa Barbara, California 93105, USA
Telephone: (805) 968 1536
Telex: 658 433
Officials:
R B Kieding, *President*
R E Burdick, *Vice President*
H W Huthsing, *Vice President*
L Morley, *Vice President*
R A Adams, *Secretary/Treasurer*
C A Bunton, *Director*
R E Burdick, *Director*
V L Cunningham, *Director*
H A Fritzche, *Director*
R B Kieding, *Director*
F Pendexter, *Director*
Licensees:
Rolair Systems (UK) Ltd, United Kingdom
Compagnie Française des Convoyeurs, France
Marubeni Corporation, Japan

Rolair Systems Inc manufactures a range of equipment making use of compliant air bearings for moving heavy or large loads. Key personnel with the company were engaged in the same field with General Motors between 1962 and 1968. The company was incorporated in 1968 as Transocean Air Systems Corporation. In 1971 its name was changed to Rolair Systems Inc.

The company's products include standard catalogue items and unlimited custom-engineered systems. Government, military and industrial use of Rolair air film systems is world-wide. Systems now operating range in weight handling capacities up to 14 million pounds.

The basic compliant air bearing device comprises a membrane holding compressed air which conforms to the floor. Controlled escape of this air in a thin layer between membrane and floor forms a frictionless air film which 'floats' the load, enabling it to be moved in any horizontal direction by a force only one-thousandth of the weight of the load. Air pressure is self-regulating according to the bearing size and its load. Typically a 2ft diameter bearing will lift 4,000lb; four 2ft bearings will carry a truck.

Several typical applications are described below.

Complete Rolair-assisted turntable assembly for offloading containerised cargo. In this photograph the turntable pier/platform is being rotated by two men.

PORTABLE PIERS FOR OFFLOADING CONTAINERISED CARGO

The Civil Engineering Laboratory, Naval Construction Battalion Center, Port Hueneme, California, USA has successfully designed a transportable pier/platform for over-the-shore offloading of containerised barge-ships and roll-on, roll-off supply vessels for the US Department of Defense. The pier/platform had to be able to accommodate two-way traffic comprised initially of 35 by 8ft trucks and with the capability to cope with 40 by 8ft trucks. In addition, in order to keep pier width to a minimum, it was necessary to install turntables for truck turnaround. Turntables would permit piers to be kept to two-lane widths rather than eight-lane widths which would be necessary if truck backing was required in turnaround.

All requirements have been fully satisfied by the development of a totally portable, two-lane, modular causeway. Each module measures 90 by 21ft. Truck turnaround is accomplished utilising Rolair air film components under a specially designed turntable.

Turntables are made up of 12 to 34in diameter Rolair ST Bearings. The bearings are mounted to deck beams in an inverted position and operate against the steel plate underside of the turntable rotating platen. This allows the load to be lifted and rotated while the bearings remain in a fixed position. The turntable structure is 48ft long, weighs 16 tons and can support a load of 22 tons. Two men can easily rotate fully loaded turntables manually, or one man can rotate it using a power drive conversion.

Causeways utilising Rolair turntables have been fully tested and accepted by the Navy as the solution to the problem of developing portable, quick-erection, over-the-shore piers for container offloading.

After rotation the container truck faces out over the water at the end of the causeway ready to drive aboard a containerised bargeship or roll-on, roll-off ferry. The turntables also permit piers to be kept to two-lane width rather than eight-lane width which would be necessary if truck backing was required in a turnaround

AIR BEARINGS AID SHIP STORAGE

A programme for reverse ship storage and upkeep for the US Navy has resulted in over $1 million savings in both money and man hours.

The US Navy's ship repairing facility on Guam operates a reserve craft branch, responsible for the security, maintenance and upkeep of out-of-service-in-reserve Navy vessels. The problem was to store effectively and protect ten 300-ton YFUs, a landing-craft type vessel, against Guam's hostile tropical environmental elements, including typhoons.

In this first application of its kind the problem was solved by utilising four Rolair air film transporters. The 120-ton capacity transporters, each equipped with four air bearings, enabled the craft to be floated on dry land to a "high and dry" area, safe from the problems inherent in water storage.

Experiments had been made previously, using heavy equipment and grease on steel plate, but it took four days and 714 man hours to store one YFU. With air film transporters, two a day can be positioned, requiring 76 man hours each, using very little in the way of equipment.

Manoeuvrability was another problem solved with air film transporters. The air film transporters allowed the manoeuvring of the craft in any direction with little difficulty.

The air film transporters, topped with interfacing keel or bilge blocks, are positioned under the YFU after the craft is lifted onto the dock from the water by two floating cranes. A 100 × 400ft steel-trowelled concrete slab is provided at the dockside for storage. Two lift trucks are used to tow and manoeuvre the craft to their storage position.

After trying both compressed air and water as the fluid for the air bearings, water was determined to be the best fluid for this particular operation. Rolair supplied transporters with both air and water inlets so either could be used.

To remove the air film transporters, a second set of keel or bilge blocks, 6½ft high was built-up between the concrete slab and the hull. Then, using wedges, the hull was raised a few inches so that the transporters could be simply moved. The 6½ft block height was chosen to permit personnel and vehicle access under the hulls for periodic hull inspection.

Securely-anchored, protected bay storage is the normal storage procedure practised by the Navy for other than small boats. It was recognised that there are a number of economic disadvantages with this method. For example, there is the need for cathodic hull protection; periodic dry-docking for barnacle removal; expensive electronic flooding alarm surveillance as well as regular visual waterline checks by each watch. In addition costly anchors ($3,000 each) are lost from time to time during the typhoon season.

Rolair air film transporters with keel or bilge blocks being "floated" beneath a crane-supported YFU

A fully "floated" 300-ton YFU landing craft being moved to its storage location on Rolair transporters by tw low-horsepower forklift trucks

It is estimated that the ten YFUs stored at SRF Guam by the "high and dry" method have saved the Navy $100,000 per craft to date, an amount continually increasing due to the reduced inspe tion necessary.

VARIABLE-PLAN SPORTS STADIUM

Rolair air bearings will be used to vary the seating configurations of a new 28,000-seat stadium under construction in Honolulu.

The stadium comprises four 7,000-seat sections and the air bearings will be employed to rotate each through a 45 degree arc to provide ideal seating patterns for either football or baseball games.

Located under each of the four stadium sections will be 26 Rolair transporters, each incorporating four air-bearings. These will be inflated by three main air compressors, each with a capacity of 1,250cfm. The sections will be moved by a system of lightweight hydraulic jacks. A rail guideline will prevent the sections drifting when 20-knot Pacific tradewinds are blowing. Each stadium section has a fixed pivot point and it is estimated that only 20 minutes will be required to move each one through its 45 degree arc—a total distance of 53·34m (173ft).

In baseball configuration the stadium will have an open double "horseshoe" look. For football the four sideline sections will be moved inward to form straight sidelines with the spectators on the 50 yard line only 12·19m (40ft) from the sideline, and only 7·62m (25ft) away from the goal line.

Ramps connecting the stadium sections extend and retract on air film with each move.

AUTOMATIC MODULAR HOME PRODUCTION LINE

Rolair has designed and installed a fully-automated air film walking beam conveyor system which moves factory built home modules simultaneously through eighteen assembly stations several times an hour.

The system can handle modules with lengths of up to 18·28m (60ft) and widths up to 4·26m (14ft).

ASSEMBLY LINE FOR CRAWLER TRACTORS

One of the most advanced air film systems in operation today is in use at the Caterpillar Tractor plant at Gosselies, Belgium, where an automatic assembly line has been installed by Rolair for Model 225 Excavators.

The first line for these vehicles was installed at the company's plant at Aurora, Illinois, USA. Experience with the Aurora plant has led to certain improvements on the Gosselies plant. For example, air tools are used throughout the line, allowing the air-powered transporters to serve as the air supply for the tools. This enables assemblers to connect their tools at the start of the assembly and leave them connected throughout the line.

The assembly operation begins on a 175ft-long section of track immediately preceding the air pallet area. There, drive assemblies are built on manually-propelled transfer carts.

First, the tractor's two planetary gears are aligned on a stationary fixture. A housing is then lifted into position by an overhead crane. After the housing has been connected to the axles, the unit is lifted onto a transfer cart. Small components are then added to the housing as the cart is moved to the end of the track. The sub-assembly and cart now weighs about 18,000lb and requires two men to push it. At this point the sub-assembly is lifted by the overhead crane and positioned on one of the air pallets. Now one man can easily move the 9-ton load.

Components are brought to the air pallet line on flat-bed trucks and lifted by crane onto the pallets. Workers climb portable step ladders to perform the necessary welding and bolting operations. The same air source that supplies the pallets is used to power air-articulated assembly tools.

Each transporter has a 45ft hose mounted on a retractable reel. Air hose connectors are installed below the surface every 25ft along the assembly line. This allows the transporter 90ft of travel before changing air connectors.

When air is fed into the system, each bearing

Air film is used to rearrange four massive 7,000-seat stadium sections at the Aloha Stadium, on the island of Oahau, Hawaii, about 3 miles from Honolulu. The movable grandstands enable the basic stadium shape to be changed easily to provide the best accommodation for both those taking part in the events and the spectators. Built and installed by Rolair Systems Inc, the air film system swings four of the 147ft high stadium sections a distance of some 200ft through a 40 degree arc to provide ideal seating patterns for football, baseball, soccer and special events. Moving time for each section takes less than 30 minutes. The three photographs above show the three main configurations: **Top:** oval configuration for football; **Centre:** double horseshoe for baseball: **Bottom:** open configuration for special events

diaphragm inflates, traps a shallow bubble of air and lifts the load slightly off the floor. Controlled leakage around the edge of the bearings creates a lubricating layer of air between the transporter and floor. Friction is practically eliminated and the transporter can be moved with a minimum of force.

A master clock controls the complete assembly line. Magnetic sensors are located on the bottom of the transporters, and utilising a series of electromagnets embedded every 10ft along the assembly line floor, the transporter can be directed to move from station to station. The electromagnets are normally energised. When the control clock de-energises a specific electromagnet, the sensor on the transporter opens, providing an air supply to the air bearing, causing the transporter to advance toward the next energised electromagnet. Since each electromagnet is individually controlled, the air transporter can be moved any distance along the line.

At the same time as the air system is activated, two guide wheels automatically lock onto a V-type floor rail and guide the transporter down the assembly line. As a safety factor a 25-second delay is provided between air activation and initial machine movement, allowing ample time for assemblers to move from the path of the transporter.

Although the major portion of the line is automatic, some manual movement remains. At the end of the line, where the assembly floor is wide enough for two machines on transporters to operate side-by-side, excavators undergo flushing and computer testing of the hydraulic system. Advancing from the assembly line, the transporter's guide wheels are retracted and two men simply 'float' the 20-ton load into the test area.

With the air film transporter system, Caterpillar feels that the assembly line can be easily altered. It can be lengthened over a weekend simply by laying more concrete. A turn can be added the same way, and if the line has to be shortened, the section no longer required is simply abandoned. A relocation can be effected by simply picking up the whole system and setting it down on a new strip of concrete.

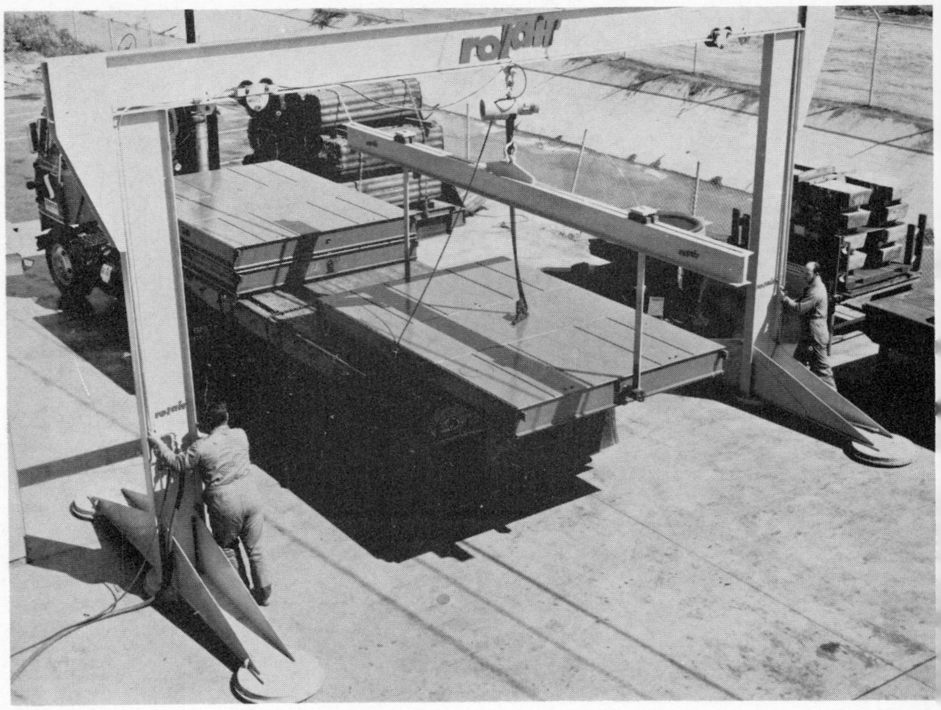

A gantry-type Omni-Mobile crane delivering a 1,814·37kg (4,000lb) load from the production line onto a flatbed truck.

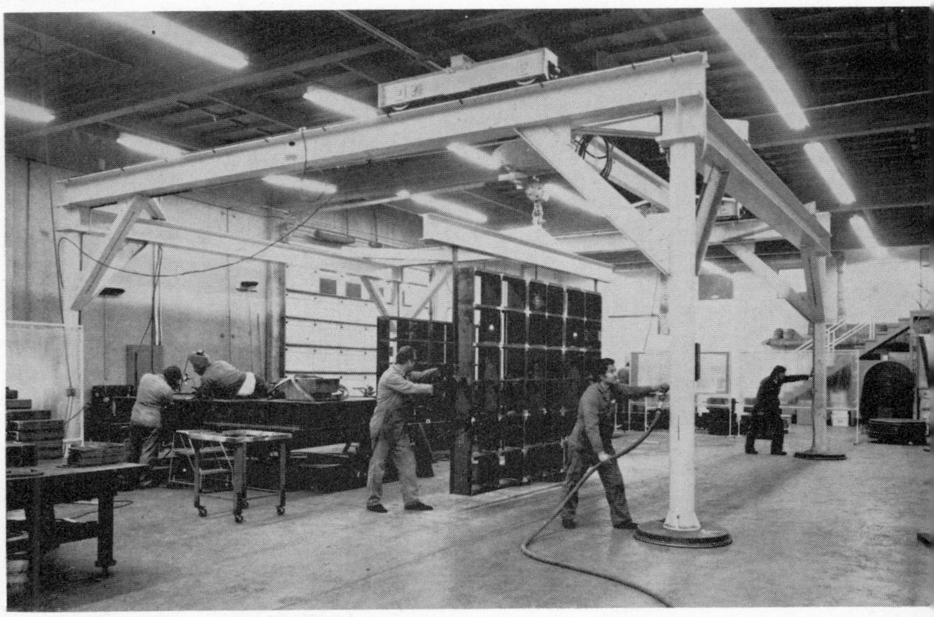
An Omni-Mobile crane of the travelling bridge type. Because of its omnidirectional movement, the crane can be moved around obstacles.

AIRCRAFT GROUND TESTING INSTALLATION

An air flotation system has been installed by Vought to allow quicker positioning of each plane for testing operational equipment. The system uses an air film and replaces hand-operated tripod-type jacks. It has provided not only a saving in time, but a safer environment for testing. Twelve Corsair II light attack aircraft can be closely positioned within a single hangar.

Three air bearings, connected directly to a T-shaped dolly, make up the casters for each of six "sets" of bearings in use in the hangar. Their design is such that they easily handle the 19,000lb aircraft. On-off air valves for the bearings are operated quickly by a single employee. The bearings have their own stabilising chamber, eliminating any throttling of incoming air. Inlet air pressure is supplied at 75psi from standard 1in plant lines.

MOVING STEEL PRESSURE VESSELS

Pressure vessels for refineries, nuclear generators and the chemical industry represent one of the most difficult types of material handling problems for their manufacturers. The vessels are massive, bulky and hard to handle.

At Kobe Steel's plant in Takasago, Japan, the problem of transporting 1,000-ton pressure vessels from the assembly floor to the X-ray facility for weld examination was solved by the use of four 250-ton capacity air transporters. The transporters, based on designs by Rolair Systems are manufactured by its Japanese licensee, Marubeni Corporation.

In the Kobe Steel plant, overhead cranes are used for loading and unloading the 1,000ft long pressure vessel fabrication line. The task of transporting the vessels between the fabrication line and the weld X-ray building, some hundreds of feet away for safety reasons, had been assigned to multi-axle, heavy-duty flatbed trucks at a round-trip cost of approximately $10,000 and a frequency of as much as twice a day. The new system, while representing a six-figure investment, provided Kobe Steel with an economical solution that is expected to pay for itself within the first year with ease.

The Rolair transporters are completely air-operated, using existing shop air supplies. Located underneath each 10in-high structural steel transporter are eight disc-like air bearings which are specially compounded elastomeric compliant diaphragms.

When air is applied to the system through flexible hoses connected to the shop air supply, the bearings inflate. Controlled leakage creates a lubricating layer of air between the bearings and the floor. Friction is completely eliminated and the transporter can easily be moved in any horizontal direction by means of a built-in air motor drive system.

Each 250-ton capacity transporter contains four air motor drives mounted in tandem on opposite axes. By selective activation of the drives, the load can be moved as the operator wishes, including a full 360 degree turn around the load's vertical axis.

Wall-mounted retractable hoses permit easy movement between the fabrication line and the X-ray building at slow walking speeds. The system is designed for one-man operation for loads up to 500 tons. Two operators, one for each pair of transporters, are required for heavier loads, with maximum system capacity at 1,000 tons.

Once in position, the load is lowered gently to the floor by simply shutting off the air supply. With this ability of frictionless movement, a 1 : 1,000 force : load ratio results which means simple lightweight air motors can move the unwieldy pressure vessels very easily and to precise positioning.

SPACE SHUTTLE SOLID ROCKET BOOSTERS

The use of air film movement systems in the production and operation of the solid rocket boosters (SRB) for the US Space Shuttle Programme represents an unmatched in-depth integration of air film into production. Air film equipment is used from the first phase of production to recovery and remanufacture.

Primary solid rocket booster elements are the

motor, which includes the case, propellant, igniter and nozzle; forward and aft structures; and separation, recovery, electrical and thrust vector control sub-systems. Each booster is 45·41m (149ft) long and 3·65m (12ft) in diameter, weighs approximately 1,293,000lb and produces 2,900,00lb static thrust.

The solid rocket motor, the primary component of the booster, contains 1,100,000lb of solid propellant. The motor is built in four casting segments: a forward segment, two centre segments, and the aft segment. To these segments the nozzle assembly is added. Each of the casting segments is manufactured independently and transported, together with the nozzle exit cone assembly, to the launch site, where they are assembled.

For the first time rocket motors will be routinely recovered and re-used. When the spent boosters are separated from the shuttle vehicle external tank they will descend to the ocean by parachutes. Towed back to the Kennedy Space Centre (or later to Vandenberg Air Force Base), the boosters are disassembled and the motors returned to the manufacturer, Thiokol Corporation. Residue is washed from the case segments, which are then refurbished, re-insulated and again loaded with propellant. Each case segment is designed to be used 20 times over. Some parts of the nozzle, igniter hardware, and the safe and arming devices will also be refurbished and re-used.

Rolair Systems, Inc, designed and built the air film equipment for Thiokol Corporation.

Production cycle: Use of air film begins at sub-contractor level and spans through the production steps at Thiokol's Utah-based Wasatch Division to NASA's operations at Marshal Space Flight Centre and Kennedy Space Centre.

For example, Standard Tool and Die Company uses Rolair bearings to position 22-ton mandrels during machining operations. The mandrels are used in casting the solid rocket fuel into the proper shape within the casting segment. What is unique about Standard Tool and Die's application of air film is that the air bearings remain with air-on for over 24 hours continuously to provide friction-free precision alignment during machining.

Utility handling equipment: Air film utility handling equipment is used throughout Thiokol. Examples include a standard air film transporter for handling such parts as nozzle flexible bearings to specially designed dollies to handle case segments weighing up to 11,000lb throughout the plant with ease.

Shot blast turntable: New segments are grit-blasted at one of Thiokol's sub-contractors, Rohr. As a part of the refurbishment after recovery, expended case segments are processed through grit blasting before painting and reprocessing. Rolair provided an air film turntable for this operation. The turntable rotates on inverted air bearings and has a low height and very few moving parts for high reliability. The turntable drive system is synchronised with the automatic grit-blasting equipment to avoid damage to the case segments.

Painting turntable: 32ft long casting segments are lowered into a pit by crane onto an air film turntable for automatic painting inside and out. Since the painting equipment moves only up and down, the rotational drive system of the Rolair turntable is designed for highly accurate and repeatable control to ensure uniform application of paint. The drives are hydraulic with a digital readout to indicate speed accurately.

Empty case handling and rotation: When the case segments are joined into casting segments the innovation of the air film system becomes pronounced. At this stage 3·65m (12ft) diameter cylinders, 9·75m (32ft) long and weighing up to approximately 25 tons must be manoeuvred throughout the plant. But, more important, they must be rotated around the horizontal axis of the cylinder as insulation and other components are added to the evolution of the solid rocket booster.

For movement over the floor in confined quarters Rolair designed a drive system with umbilical operator control. The operator first selects the mode of movement by a dial selector on the control. Then the left thumb depresses a dead-man protected button to actuate the air bearings, and the right thumb causes the drive mode selected to be activated. The release of either thumb causes

1,000-ton pressure vessel at the Kobe Steel Works, Takasago, Japan, being transported from the assembly floor to the company's weld X-ray facility on four 250-ton capacity Rolair air bearings

US Space Shuttle with boosters

movement to cease automatically.

As insulation and other components are added to the casting segments horizontal rotation is necessary. To accomplish this curved air bearings were perfected which conform to the perimeter of the 3·65m (12ft) diameter casting segments.

For rotation the same umbilical control selector switch is positioned to either clockwise, counter-clockwise, or free float. The same thumb-operated actuators implement the desired motion.

Air-bearing usage in the case processing areas has provided for very efficient usage of the existing floor space and enables these large space shuttle segments to be moved between work stations with minimum effort. The ability to rotate these large hardware items during various process operations without additional tooling has enabled a very streamlined process to be established.

180-ton loaded case handling and rotation: Before incorporation of the solid rocket fuel itself the empty casting segment weighs about 70,000lb. It is then moved horizontally to the casting pits on a special designed trailer, installed vertically into the casting pits and cast with approximately 290,000lb of solid fuel.

A tractor-trailer transporter 139ft long, 14ft wide and with a capacity of 200 tons arrives at the casting pit. On arrival the centre deck of the trailer is lowered to the ground by built-in jacks and the 58-wheeled front and rear wheeled jeep dollies are unhitched from the centre deck and moved away. The centre deck weighs 55,000lb and moves over the ground on twelve air bearings. In addition, thirty curved air bearings are shaped to support the solid rocket motor segments when loaded with propellant.

Using a similar but higher capacity drive and control system than the unloaded case dollies, the centre deck and empty casting segment are floated across a temporarily covered crane rail and into a 200-ton capacity breakover fixture. The breakdown raises the empty centre deck in preparation to receive a loaded socket motor segment.

A vertical loaded segment lifting beam attached to a 200-ton capacity gantry crane removes the loaded segment from the casting pit and places it onto the breakover fixture. The breakover process is reversed, the air bearings float the total system weighing approximately 200 tons back across the temporary crane rail covers and into position to hook to the tractor-trailer transporter.

When the loaded case segment and centre deck are re-united with the 58-wheeled trailer they are moved by road to the next manufacturing operation. At each location, the centre deck is again lowered and over-the-ground and rotation motion is accomplished using air film.

Air bearings have simplified the entire handling of loaded segments. The tractor-trailer transporter length prohibited it from being positioned between the casting pits, where the segment could be handled with the 200-ton gantry crane. Other methods considered for moving the segment to the crane, such as a rail system, exceeded the allotted budget for facility modification and re-arrangement. Air bearings require only a level concrete pad thick enough to withstand the total load and bridges for crossing over the gantry rails.

At other assembly buildings where crane capacity is limited to that required for tooling there was no other way to handle the segments short of expensive building modifications to provide drive through capabilities. Now, it is simply a matter of driving straight to the front of the building, lowering and disconnecting the air bearing dolly from the transporter, and floating it into the building.

Static test firing: Some of the completed motor segments are joined into a solid rocket motor (SRM) for test firing at Thiokol. An SRM consists of four segments, incorporates 1,100,000 million lb of solid propellant and produces 2,900,000lb st at sea level.

Rolair equipment is used to join the four segments horizontally to install the SRM into a massive static test stand for horizontal firing. Using a

This Rolair air film system dolly enables an operator to position 3·65m wide casting segments for the space shuttle solid rocket motor with a remote control device. A casting segment, one of which is seen in the background, can also be rotated horizontally on curved air bearings that cradle the segment on the dolly

Centre deck of this tractor-trailer transporter moves across the ground on 12 air bearings. A vertical loaded segment lifting beam attached to a 200-ton capacity gantry removes the loaded segment from the casting pit and places it onto the breakover fixture

Rolair equipment is used to join the four segments of a solid rocket motor horizontally before installing it in a huge static test stand for horizontal firing

A pair of Rolair Air Beams can handle weights up to 240,000lb

combination of hydraulics and air film the Rolair equipment permits adjustment on six axes to a tolerance of ±1/64in. The space shuttle joining equipment is a modification of earlier equipment built to join the Saturn V moon rocket which first put US astronauts on the moon.

Rolair is working with NASA, United Technology Corporation and other contractors "downstream" of the actual SRM production. At the launch area at Kennedy Space Center air film turntables, dollies, disassembly fixtures and other systems will be used to set up the SRBs for flight as well as recover and refurbish them after flight.

MOVEMENT OF GAS COMPRESSION MODULES

Southwest Industries Division of Ingersoll-Rand Co had the problem of moving a pair of gas compression modules in preparation for barge loading at Port of Iberia, Louisiana. Each module measured 40×60ft× 3 storeys high. Module No 1 weighed 370 tons and Module No 2 300 tons. An additional problem was an uneven surface over which the modules had to be moved.

The problem was solved utilising Rolair air bearings positioned under the modules after they had been jacked up. "Flooring" surface was made passable using sheet metal overlays. When air was introduced to the bearings, the modules were floated on a thin cushion of air allowing a small tractor to turn the massive loads 90 degrees and move them to the water's edge.

The use of Rolair air bearings, in addition to allowing relatively easy positioning of these massive units, also resulted in an estimated saving of 1½ weeks of time over conventional moving methods with the total time to accomplish two separate moves along the same path was three days. Actual movement of modules with the air film system took three to four hours.

Gas compression modules are used to conserve natural gas and eliminate the air pollution that results from flaring unused gas. The modules extract natural gas from a well, scrub (ie, clean) it, compress it and force the compressed gas back down the hole to maintain well pressure.

370-ton gas compression module being moved in preparation for barge loading, Port Iberia, Louisiana

Rolair LT lightweight air bearing with the air bearing housing built in structural aluminium

AIR BEAMS

A new, simple and low-cost material handling tool is the Rolair Air Beam which uses workshop air piped into compliant air bearings housed within tubular steel beams. Designed primarily for in-plant rigging and frequent large load movement assignments, Air Beams are available with lifting capacities from 4 to 120 tons. Cost comparisons against conventional moving methods show that Air Beams are lower in initial investment and operating costs.

LIGHTWEIGHT AIR BEARINGS

Named "LT" Air Bearings, these are primarily designed for medium duty and for circumstances under which one man might have to position bearings under load and move an entire load by himself. This has been accomplished by constructing the air bearing housing in structural aluminium which offers the additional benefit of reducing the cost of the complete bearing since aluminium is less expensive than structural steel.

Weight capabilities of a single bearing unit range from 500 to 2,000kg (1,000 to 4,000lb).

HYDROFOILS

CANADA

DE HAVILLAND AIRCRAFT COMPANY OF CANADA, LIMITED

Downsview, Ontario M3Y 1Y5, Canada
Telephone: (416) 633 7310
Telex: 22128

Officials:
D N Kendall, *Chairman*
R Bannock, *President and Chief Executive Officer*
P Genest, *Director*
D G A McLean, *Director*
J W McLoughlan, *Director*
G F Osbaldeston, *Director*
A M Guérin, *Director*
D B Annan, *Senior Vice President*
W T Heaslip, *Vice President, Special Projects*
R D Hiscocks, *Vice President, Engineering*
F A Johnson, *Vice President, Customer Support*
S B Kerr, *Vice President, Finance*
J A Timmins, *Vice President, Marketing and Sales*
F H Buller, *Chief Engineer, Product Design*
J P Uffen, *Chief Engineer, Research and Technology*
S Morita, *Hydrofoil Project Manager*

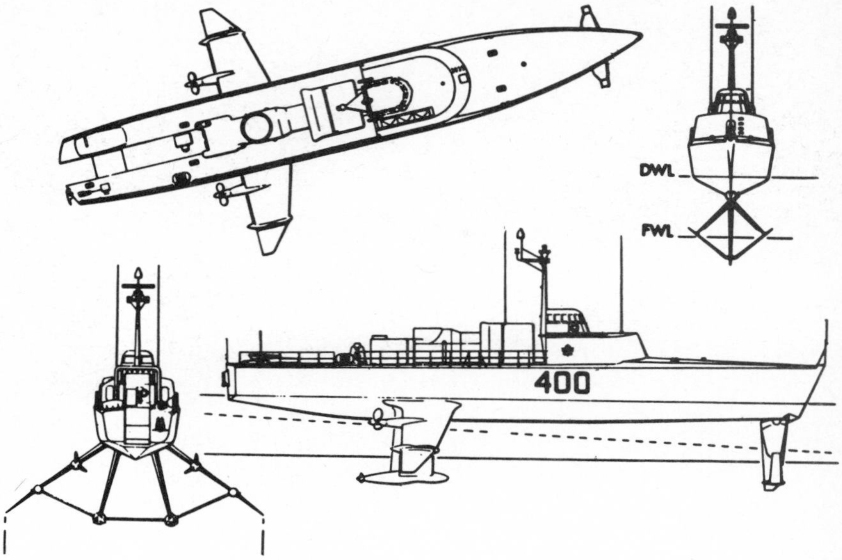

De Havilland FHE-400 ocean-going ASW warship

In early 1961 the Canadian Department of Defense contracted de Havilland Aircraft of Canada Ltd for a feasibility and engineering study based on the NRE ASW hydrofoil report. The company's recommendations were approved in April 1963 and led to the construction of the FHE-400 fast hydrofoil escort warship. The programme had two fundamental objectives: (a) to establish in practice the feasibility of an ocean-going hydrofoil of the proposed size and characteristics (b) to evaluate the prototype as an ASW system.

FHE-400 was commissioned as HMCS Bras d'Or in Halifax and was tested in brief displacement mode trials in September 1968. The foilborne transmission was fitted during the winter of 1968 and the first foilborne trial took place on 9 April 1969. The craft attained a speed of 63 knots during calm water trials in July 1969. Rough water trials during the winter of 1971 culminated in a 2,500 mile "shake down" cruise from Halifax to Bermuda and Norfolk, Virginia.

Foilborne trials were conducted in 3·04–4·57m (10–15ft) waves (sea state 5) at speeds in excess of 40 knots. Hullborne trials were conducted in higher sea states.

While objective (a), to confirm operations feasibility in open ocean conditions, was met, objective (b), ASW system operation, was suspended because of a change in Canadian defence priorities, requiring priority attention to territorial and coastal surveillance. The craft was therefore put into store, although research in this field continued. Reports suggest that the craft is to be reactivated. In the meantime the company reports that wide interest is being shown in a smaller and similar design—the DHC-MP (Maritime Patrol) 100 which will have the same seakeeping capability. Possible civil applications include oil-rig resupply, coastguard work and fisheries patrol.

During sea trials, the FHE-400 reached a foilborne speed of 62 knots. Capable of all-weather operation, the vessel has a maximum take-off displacement of 235 tons

FHE-400

FOILS: The foil system is a canard configuration of the surface-piercing type and non-retractable. The steerable bow foil is supercavitating and designed for good response in a seaway. The subcavitating main foil carries 90% of the static weight and is a combination of surface-piercing and submerged foils. The centre high speed foil section is protected from ventilation by the struts and the dihedral foils have full-chord fences to inhibit ventilation. Anhedral foils provide reserve lift at take-off and their tips provide roll restoring forces at foilborne speeds. All foil elements are in welded 18% nickel maraging sheet steel and forgings.

The struts are a compromise to provide the optimum fin effect in yaw in conjunction with the steerable bow foil.

HULL: Hull and superstructure are fabricated from ALCAN D54S, and extensive use is made of large extrusions with integral stringers for the plating.

A crew of 20 is carried, comprising 8 officers and 12 men. In order to maintain crew alertness at all times, comfortable crew quarters and good messing facilities were considered essential features. Both were intensively studied by the Institute of Aviation Medicine. The study included the testing of crew bunks on a motion simulator at NCR Ottawa, and the use of a simulator to assess crew efficiency under foilborne conditions.

POWER PLANT: Continuous search for a useful period demands economical operation in any sea state at displacement speeds and the ability to attack at high speeds. For this reason there are two propulsion systems—the foilborne marinised gas-turbine, a 22,000shp Pratt & Whitney FT4A-2, and a 2,000bhp Davey-Paxman 16YJCM diesel engine for hullborne power.

The FT4A-2, a marine version of the shaft-turbine engine developed from the JT4 and 5 gas turbine, is enclosed by a protective cowling aft of the bridge.

Shaft power is transmitted to the inboard gearbox directly aft of the engine exhaust elbow and is then transmitted via dual shafts through each of the two inner struts to the outboard gearboxes in the streamlined pods at the intersection of the struts and foils. The dual shafts are combined at the outboard gearboxes into a single drive then taken through an over-running clutch to each of the two 1·22m (4ft) diameter fixed-pitch supercavitating propellers.

A governor prevents overspeed if the propellers leave the water in rough seas.

The Paxman Ventura 16YJCM diesel-engine is sited in the engine room, on the ship's centreline. Power is transmitted to the variable pitch hullborne propellers through a dual output gearbox and thence through shafts to gearboxes located in the pods.

The KMW controllable-pitch displacement propellers of 2·13m (7ft) diameter are novel, since they are feathered when the craft is foilborne so as to minimise the appendage drag penalty. Slow speed manoeuvring is effected by control of individual propeller pitch settings.

CONTROLS: Diesel power, propeller pitch, main gas turbine speed and individual displacement propeller pitch are all normally controlled by lever from the bridge. Dual wheels are provided to steer the bow foil which acts as the rudder for both foilborne and displacement operation. It is also adjustable to rake enabling the best angle of attack to be selected for foilborne or hullborne operation. An engineer's console is located in the operation room and starting and stopping of all engines is undertaken from this position. Engine and propeller pitch controls duplicating those on the bridge are provided on the console.

Turns are fully or partially coordinated, depending on speed, by the variable incidence anhedral tips. The tips are also coupled to an auto-pilot and act as stabilisers to supplement the foil system's inherent roll resistance.

AUXILIARY POWER: An auxiliary gas-turbine, a United Aircraft of Canada ST6A-53 rated at 390hp continuous at 2,100rpm is used to power electric generators, hydraulic pumps and a salt-water pump. It can also be used to increase the available displacement propulsion power and for emergency propulsion power at reduced speed.

EMERGENCY POWER: The emergency power unit is an AiResearch GTCP-85-291 shaft-coupled turbine rated at 190hp continuous. In the event of the auxiliary gas turbine becoming unserviceable or being in use for the displacement propulsion, this tubine will power the ship's system. Alternatively bleed air may be drawn from the compressor for main turbine starting.

DIMENSIONS

EXTERNAL

Length overall, hull: 45·9m (151ft)
Length waterline, hull: 44m (147ft)
Hull beam: 6·5m (21ft 6in)
Width across foils: 20m (66ft)
Draft afloat: 7·16m (23ft 6in)
Freeboard, forward: 3·3m (11ft)

WEIGHTS

Gross tonnage (normal): 212 tons
Light displacement: 165 tons
Max take-off displacement: 235 tons
Useful load (fuel, crew and military load): over 70 tons

PERFORMANCE

Max speed, foilborne: 50 knots rough water, 60 knots calm water
Cruising speed, hullborne: over 12 knots
Sea state capability: Sea State 5, significant wave height 3·04m (10ft)

DHC-MP-100

De Havilland Canada's latest hydrofoil design is the DHC-MP-100, a multi-duty vessel of 104 tons displacement and a maximum speed of 50 knots. Twin gas-turbines power the foilborne propulsion system instead of the single turbine employed in the FHE-400, the foil system has been simplified, and although the craft is smaller than its predecessor the same outstanding sea-keeping performance is maintained.

A worldwide market survey has been undertaken to determine the needs of potential customers outside Canada and reports indicate that considerable interest is being shown in the craft particularly for the following applications: oil rig re-supply, coastguard patrol, search and rescue, customs and excise, gunboat, missilecraft and ASW patrol.

In general the configuration and construction follows that of the FHE-400.

FOILS: Canard, surface-piercing configuration with approximately 90% of the weight carried by the main foil and 10% by the bow foil. The bow foil is of diamond shape and acts as the rudder for both foilborne and hullborne operations. The main foil, of trapeze configuration combines a fully submerged central section with dihedral surfaces outboard.

POWER PLANT, FOILBORNE: Foilborne propulsion is supplied by two 3,100shp gas-turbines each driving a fixed-pitch supercavitating three-bladed propeller. Power is transmitted via dual shafts through each of the two inner foil struts to gearboxes at the intersections of the struts and foils.

Among the engines likely to be specified are the Rolls Royce Marine Proteus, the Marine Tyne and the Avco Lycoming TF 40.

POWER PLANT, HULLBORNE: Hullborne propulsion is supplied by two 400hp diesels driving two two-bladed propellers through outdrive units.

HMCS Bras d'Or during calm water trials

Data for the basic craft and the main variants are given below.

DHC-MP-100 GENERAL PURPOSE

In this configuration, the craft can be equipped for coastguard, search and rescue, fisheries and environmental patrol, customs and excise duties and oil rig re-supply.

DIMENSIONS

EXTERNAL

Length: 36m (118ft 1in)
Beam: 6·4m (21ft)
Width across main foil: 15·5m (50ft 9¾in)
Draft hullborne: 5·33m (17ft 5⅞in)
Freeboard, hullborne: 2·44m (8ft)

WEIGHTS

Crew and supplies: 2,930kg (6,460lb)
Roll equipment and fuel: 26,800kg (59,084lb)
Total payload: 29,730kg (65,540lb)
Basic: 75,740kg (167,000lb)
Displacement: 105,470kg (104 tons)

PERFORMANCE

Max speed, estimated: 90km/h (50 knots)
Range, 18,000kg fuel capacity
at 18·5km/h (10 knots): 3,500km (1,910n miles)
at 74km/h (40 knots): 1,180km (642n miles)
27,000kg fuel capacity
at 18·5km/h (10 knots): 5,250km (2,865n miles)
at 74km/h (40 knots): 1,770km (963n miles)

GUNBOAT

For coastal patrol, interdiction or for escorting larger ships or convoys, a 57mm Bofors gun can be fitted. For self-defence a Vulcan gun is mounted on the afterdeck. Other armament installations can be fitted within weight and centre of gravity limits.

Overload fuel will extend the range in displacement condition to a maximum of 4,600km (2,500n miles). In the maximum overload condition take-off may be restricted to moderate sea states.

The foil system stabilises the vessel and gives it the seakeeping characteristics of a ship of 1,000/1,500 tons, thus improving accuracy of shot and crew performance for a craft of this size.

DIMENSIONS

As for basic craft

WEIGHTS

Crew and supplies: 2,930kg (6,460lb)
Bofors gun and ammunition: 7,140kg (15,740lb)
Vulcan gun system: 1,540kg (3,395lb)
Fuel: 18,150kg (40,000lb)
Total payload: 29,760kg (65,600lb)
Basic: 75,740kg (167,000lb)
Displacement: 105,500kg (104 tons)

PERFORMANCE

Range at 18·5km/h: 3,500km (1,910n miles)
Range at 74km/h: 1,180km (642n miles)

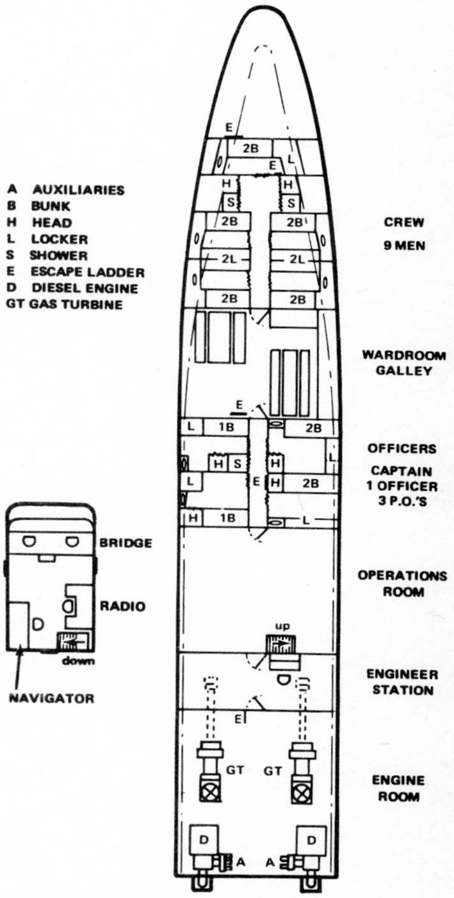

Typical accommodation arrangement on a patrol escort version of the MP-100 hydrofoil

MISSILECRAFT

To complement the gunboat role, the MP-100 may be fitted with missiles like the Harpoon and Exocet. The fire control system is located in the large operations room.

For self-defence a Vulcan gun system is mounted aft between the missile containers. An alternative arrangement is the mounting of the gun on the foredeck and its detection system above the bridge.

DIMENSIONS

As for basic craft

WEIGHTS

Crew and supplies: 2,930kg (6,460lb)
Missile system: 4,530kg (10,000lb)
Vulcan gun system: 1,540kg (3,395lb)
Fuel: 20,400kg (44,974lb)
Total payload: 29,400kg (64,816lb)
Basic: 75,740kg (167,000lb)
Displacement: 105,140kg (103·5 tons)

PERFORMANCE
Range at 18·5km/h: 3,960km (2,150n miles)
Range at 74km/h: 1,340km (723n miles)

ASW PATROL CRAFT

The craft can cruise at convoy speed on its displacement propulsion units while using variable-depth sonar to search for submarines. On making contact it can attack at high speed.

Lightweight VDS gear is installed. This has a low-drag body and cable and can be towed at over 55km/h (30 knots). The system is of modular construction and can be quickly installed or removed. Torpedoes can be mounted in multiple tubes. Sonar and fire-control systems are fitted in the operations room. A Vulcan gun can be mounted on the foredeck with sensors above the bridge.

DIMENSIONS
As for basic craft
WEIGHTS
Crew and supplies: 2,930kg (6,460lb)
VDS gear: 5,080kg (11,200lb)
Torpedoes: 3,035kg (6,700lb)
Vulcan gun: 1,540kg (3,395lb)
Fire control: 4,080kg (9,000lb)
Fuel: 15,860kg (35,000lb)
Total payload: 32,525kg (71,700lb)
Basic: 75,740kg (167,000lb)
Displacement: 108,265kg (106·8 tons)
PERFORMANCE
Range at 18·5km/h: 3,150km (1,710n miles)
Range at 74km/h: 1,040km (565n miles)

A multi-duty hydrofoil of 104 tons displacement, the DHC-MP-100 is available in a variety of configurations, three of which are depicted above:
Top: Equipped as a fast patrol boat or convoy escort, a 57mm Bofors automatic gun is mounted on the foredeck and for self-defence, a Vulcan gun package is mounted on the afterdeck.
Centre: Operated as a missile equipped patrol craft, the MP-100 would carry two launchers aft—Harpoon and Exocet missiles are two choices—and for self-defence, a Vulcan gun pack is mounted aft between the missiles. An alternative arrangement would be to mount the gun on the foredeck and its detection gear above the bridge
Bottom: An ASW version equipped with lightweight VDS gear and torpedoes mounted in multiple tubes. Full sonar and fire-control systems are provided in the operations room

WATER SPYDER MARINE LTD

157 Richard Clark Drive, Downsview, Ontario M3M 1V6, Canada
Telephone: (416) 244 5404

Officials:
J F Lstiburek, *President*
G A Leask, *Secretary/Treasurer*
A Lstiburek, *Vice President*
L Civiera, *Sales Manager*
J F Lstiburek, *Designer*

Water Spyder Marine Ltd is a wholly-owned Canadian company operating under charter issued by the Government of the Province of Ontario. It produces three fibreglass-hulled sports hydrofoils which are available either ready-built or in kit form.

WATER SPYDER 1-A

The Water Spyder 1-A is a single-seat sports hydrofoil powered by a long-shaft outboard of 10-25hp.

FOILS: The foil system comprises a split W-type surface-piercing main foil supporting 98% of the load, and an adjustable outrigged trim tab which supports the remaining 2%.
HULL: Two-piece fibreglass reinforced plastic construction, foam-filled for flotation. Standard fittings and regulation running lights.
ACCOMMODATION: Single fibreglass seat.
POWER PLANT: Any suitable outboard engine of 10–25hp (Mercury, Evinrude or Chrysler) with long shaft.

CONTROLS: Controls include joy-stick and rudder pedals.
DIMENSIONS
Length overall, hull: 1·828m (6ft)
Beam overall, foils retracted: 1·219m (4ft)
Beam overall, foils extended: 2·133m (7ft)
WEIGHTS
Empty: 36·24kg (80lb)
PERFORMANCE
Max speed: 64·37km/h (40mph)
Max permissible wave height in foilborne condition: 457·2mm (1ft 6in)
Turning radius at cruising speed: approx 3·04m (10ft)
PRICE: Standard craft and terms of payment, US$1,000; terms, cash. Delivery, three weeks approximately from date of order, fob Toronto.

WATER SPYDER 2-B

The Water Spyder 2-B is a two-seat sports hydrofoil powered by a long-shaft outboard of 20-35hp.
FOILS: The foil system comprises a split W-type surface-piercing main foil supporting 98% of the load and an adjustable outrigged trim tab which supports the remaining 2%.
HULL: This is a two-piece (deck and hull) moulded fibreglass structure and incorporates buoyancy chambers. Standard fittings include a curved Perspex windshield and regulation running lights, fore and aft.
ACCOMMODATION: The craft seats two in comfortably upholstered seats. Foils and the trim tab assembly are adjustable from inside the cockpit.
POWER PLANT: Any suitable outboard engine of 20-35hp (Mercury 200L or 350L Chrysler Evinrude) with long-shaft extension.
CONTROLS: Controls include steering wheel with adjustable friction damper and trim tab control.
DIMENSIONS
Length overall, hull: 3·6m (12ft)
Beam overall, foils retracted: 1·6m (5ft 4in)
Beam overall, foils extended: 2·2m (7ft 4in)
WEIGHTS
Empty: 99·7kg (220lb)
PERFORMANCE
Max speed: up to 64km/h (40mph)
Max permissible wave height in foilborne mode: 457·2mm (1ft 6in)
Turning radius at cruising speed: 3m (10ft) approximately
PRICE: Standard craft and terms of payment, US$1,600; terms, cash. Delivery, three weeks from date of order, fob Toronto.

WATER SPYDER 6-A

An enlarged version of the Water Spyder 2. Model 6-A is a six-seat family pleasure hydrofoil boat, with a two-piece moulded fibreglass hull.
The seats, located immediately over the main foil, are arranged in two rows of three abreast, one row facing forward, the other aft.
Power is supplied by a long-shaft outboard motor of 60-115hp.
DIMENSIONS
Length overall, hull: 5·79m (19ft)
Beam overall, foils retracted: 2·5m (8ft 3in)
Beam overall, foils extended: 3·96m (13ft)
Height overall, foils retracted: 1·37m (4ft 6in)
Floor area: 2·78m² (30ft²)
WEIGHTS
Gross tonnage: 1 ton approx
Empty: 444kg (980lb)

PERFORMANCE
Max speed: 56-64km/h (35-40mph)
Cruising speed: 51km/h (32mph)
Max permissible wave height in foilborne mode: 0·76m (2ft 6in)
Turning radius at cruising speed: 6·09m (20ft)
PRICE: Standard craft and terms of payment, US$3,500; terms, cash. Delivery, three weeks from date of order, fob Toronto.

Water Spyder 6-A is a six-seat hydrofoil. The main foil, trim-tab support and engine fold upward so the craft can be floated on and off a trailer

CHINA (People's Republic)

HUTANG SHIPYARD

Shanghai, People's Republic of China
Hydrofoil torpedo boats of the Hu Chwan (White Swan) Class have been under construction at the Hutang Shipyard since about 1966. Some 70 are in service with the navy of the People's Republic of China and another 32 have been lent or leased to the Albanian navy, six to Pakistan and three to Romania.
Seven others, of a slightly modified design, have been built in Romania since 1973.

HU CHWAN (WHITE SWAN)

FOILS: The foil system comprises a bow subfoil to facilitate take-off and a main foil of trapeze or shallow V configuration set back approximately one-third of the hull length from the bow. At high speed in relatively calm conditions the greater part of the hull is raised clear of the water. The main foil and struts retract upwards when the craft is required to cruise in displacement condition.
HULL: High speed V-bottom hull in seawater resistant light alloy.
POWER PLANT: Three 1,100hp M-50 type watercooled, supercharged 12-cylinder V-type diesels, each driving their own inclined propeller shaft.
ARMAMENT: Two 21in torpedo tubes, plus four 12·7mm machine guns in two twin mountings.
DIMENSIONS (approximate)
Length overall: 21·33m (70ft)
Beam overall: 5·02m (16ft 6in)
Hull beam: 3·96m (13ft)
WEIGHTS
Displacement full load: 45 tons
PERFORMANCE
Max speed foilborne calm conditions: 55 knots
Range: 500n miles approx

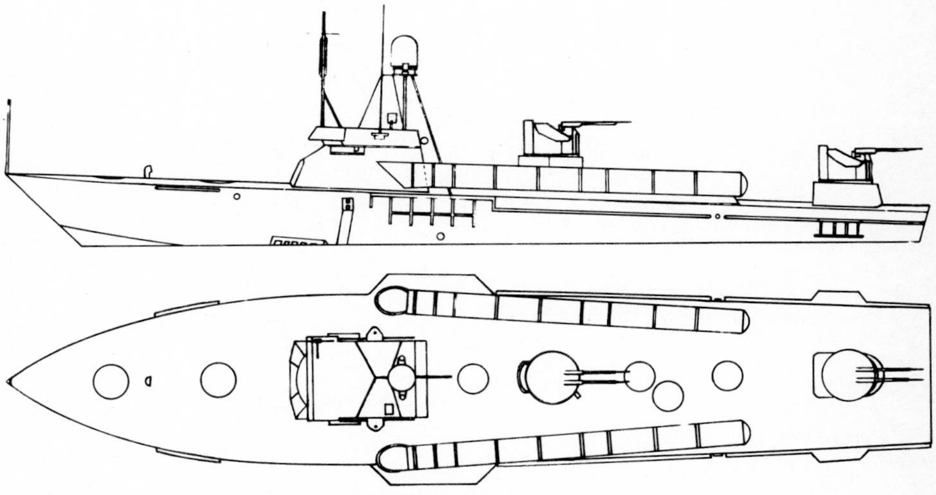

General arrangement of the Hu Chwan torpedo/fast attack hydrofoil of the Chinese Navy

One of six Hu Chwan-class torpedo/fast attack craft built by the Hutang Shipyard, Shanghai, and supplied to the Pakistan Navy

FRANCE

GEORGES HENNEBUTTE

Société d'Exploitation et de Développement des Brevets Georges Hennebutte

Head Office: 43 avenue Foch, 64000 Biarritz, France
Works: 23 impasse Labordotte, 64200 Biarritz, France
Telephone: 24 03 70
Telex: 22128

Officials:
G Hennebutte, *President, Director General*

Ets G Hennebutte was founded in 1955 to design and build inflatable dinghies. Its Espadon series of sports craft is employed by lifeguard patrols in France and elsewhere in the world and also by the French Navy.

Development of the Espadon to meet a range of special requirements had led to the construction of a number of experimental craft, including one with an inflatable parasol delta wing and another with a Lippisch type wing for aerodynamic lift while operating in ground effect. Preliminary descriptions of these craft have appeared in *Jane's Surface Skimmers 1977-78* and earlier editions.

In another approach hydroskis have been fitted to the Etel 422 Swordfish, a winged version of which is currently under construction.

Hennebutte Etel 422 Swordfish equipped with hydroskis. A winged variant is under construction

ETEL 422 SWORDFISH

This new variant of the Etel 422 employs the same basic inflatable hull but is equipped with hydroskis, wings and a ducted fan. The Etel 422 is the only inflatable craft to have crossed the Etel barrier, a feat accomplished during a severe storm in 1967. The accompanying photograph shows an earlier experimental version of the Etel 422 equipped with hydroskis and a marine outboard engine driving a water propeller. A speed of 112km/h (70mph) was achieved during trials.

LIFT AND PROPULSION: Aerodynamic lift at cruising speed and above is provided by a wing. Thrust is supplied by an RFB SG85 fan-thrust pod, combining a 50hp Wankel air-cooled rotary engine with a three-bladed, ducted propeller.

HULL: Catamaran type hull with rigid central frame and inflatable, nylon coated neoprene outer sections.

ACCOMMODATION: Open cockpit for driver.

DIMENSIONS
Length overall: 4·22m (13ft 10in)
Beam overall: 2·5m (8ft 2in)

SOCIETE NATIONALE INDUSTRIELLE AEROSPACE

Head Office: 36 boulevard de Montmorency, 75781 Paris (2) Cedex 16, France
Telephone: 224 84 00; 525 57 75
Telex: AISPA 62059F
Works: BP13, 13722 Marignane, France
Telephone: (91) 89 90 22

In 1966 the Direction des Recherches et Moyens d'Essais (Directorate of Research and Test Facilities) initiated a basic hydrofoil design and research programme with the object of building a prototype hydrofoil ferry with a displacement of 55 tons and a speed of 50 knots.

The companies and organisations co-operating in this programme are: Aérospatiale, project leader; STCAN, the hull test centre; several French government laboratories of the DTCN; Alsthom—Technique des Fluides—and Constructions Mécaniques de Normandie.

The main headings of the programme are:
hydrodynamics (foils, struts and hull);
foil hydroelasticity data and flutter phenomenon;
automatic pilot;
material technology relative to foils, struts and hull.

The design and research programme is nearly complete and the results will be processed and refined using a 4-ton submerged foil test craft, the H.890, designed by Aérospatiale.

The craft, which was launched on 16 June 1972, is employed in a comprehensive test programme which is under the control of Aérospatiale and DTCN, a French government agency.

In addition to the SA 800 55-ton hydrofoil ferry, preliminary designs have been completed for a missile-carrying 118-ton hydrofoil combat vessel, the H.851, and a commercial variant, intended for mixed-traffic ferry services. The latest project is a 174 tonne missilecraft with a speed of 54 knots and capable of operating in Force 5 weather at 50 knots. Armament would comprise four Exocet missiles and one rapid-fire automatic cannon.

The H.890 4-ton submerged foil test vehicle is being employed by Aérospatiale to develop automatic control systems and gather data for the design of larger vessels. It has attained 52 knots during high-speed runs

Impression of the Aérospatiale H.851 missile-equipped combat hydrofoil, being developed in conjunction with the French Navy

H.890

This 4·5-tonne seagoing test vehicle is being employed to gather data for foil systems and accelerate the development of autopilot systems for large hydrofoils.

The combination of catamaran hull and pure jet propulsion allows the foils to be arranged in either conventional configuration—two foils forward and one aft—or canard configuration, with one foil forward and two aft.

The vessel was developed and built under contract to the French government agency DTCN by Aérospatiale's Helicopter Division in conjunction with Constructions Mécaniques de Normandie and Alsthom—Techniques des Fluides—of Grenoble. It has been undergoing tests on the Etang de Berre since it was launched on 16 June 1972. A speed of 52 knots has been reached during trials.

FOILS: Fully submerged system with facilities for changing from conventional (aeroplane) to canard configuration as required. In aeroplane configuration about 70% of the weight is supported by the twin bow foils, which are attached to the port and starboard pontoons, and 30% by the single tail foil, mounted on the central hull section aft.

The stern foil rotates for steering and all three struts are fixed (non-retractable). Lift variation of the three foils is achieved by an autopilot sys-

tem, developed by Aérospatiale and SFENA, which varies the incidence angles of all three foils. During the first series of tests the foils were tested in conventional configuration. During the second series the canard configuration was adopted.
HULL: Catamaran type, constructed in corrosion-resistant light alloys. Central hull, which incorporates control cabin, engine bay and test instrumentation, is flanked by two stepped pontoons.
ACCOMMODATION: Seating is provided for two, pilot and test observer.
POWER PLANT: Twin 480 daN Turboméca Marbore VIc gas-turbines, mounted in the central hull structure aft of the cabin, power the craft when foilborne. Hullborne propulsion is supplied by a 20hp Sachs 370 engine driving via a hydraulic transmission a folding-blade Maucour waterscrew located at the top of the aft foil strut. The waterscrew rotates through ±90 degrees for steering.
DIMENSIONS
Length, overall: 10·66m (34ft 11½in)
Length, waterline: 9·3m (30ft 6in)
Beam, overall: 3·9m (12ft 9½in)
Draft, afloat: 1·72m (5ft 8in)
Draft, foilborne: 0·37m (1ft 3in)
WEIGHTS
Normal take-off: 4·5 tonnes
PERFORMANCE
Cruising speed, foilborne, calm conditions: 50 knots
Cruising speed, hullborne, calm conditions: 6 knots
Craft is designed to cross waves up to 0·8m (2ft 8in) high without contouring.

H.851

The H.851 is a preliminary design for a missile-equipped combat hydrofoil capable of all-weather operation. Initially it will have a displacement of 120 tonnes (118 tons) and cruise at 45 knots, but later models, with increased power, are expected to attain nearly 60 knots.
FOILS: Fully submerged canard arrangement with about 80% of the weight supported by the twin aft foils and 20% by the bow foil. The bow foil strut, which rotates for steering, retracts forwards and upwards ahead of the stem, and the two aft struts rotate rearwards and upwards. The strut locking system is designed to dampen shocks resulting from encounters with floating wreckage. Struts and foils have NACA Series 16 profiles.
Lift variation is achieved by an Aérospatiale autopilot system which varies the incidence angles of all three foils. Trailing-edge flaps on the foils augment lift during take-off.
HULL: Constructed in marine corrosion-resistant aluminium alloys.
POWER PLANT: Foilborne propulsion is supplied by a single 5,200kW SNECMA THS 2000 gas-turbine driving two SOGREAH water pumps, one at the base of each foil strut, via mechanical right-angle drives. Hullborne propulsion is provided by a single 770kW diesel engine driving a single variable-pitch propeller.
ACCOMMODATION: Berthing, galley and toilet arrangements for crew of 21.
ARMAMENT: Four Exocet MM 38 missiles and one 40mm Bofors rapid-firing cannon.
DIMENSIONS
Length, overall: 35m (114ft 10in)
Beam, overall: 15m (49ft 2½in)
Draft, hullborne, foils lowered: 8·3m (27ft 3in)
Draft, foilborne: 1·8m (5ft 11in)
WEIGHTS
Displacement, full load: 117 tonnes (115 tons)
PERFORMANCE
Max speed, calm conditions: 48 knots
Cruising speed, calm conditions: 45 knots
Cruising speed, sea state 5: 45 knots
Range and endurance, at 45 knots, calm conditions: 1,300n miles or 29 hours
at 45 knots, sea state 5: 1,165n miles or 25 hours
hullborne at 13 knots: 2,130n miles or 163 hours

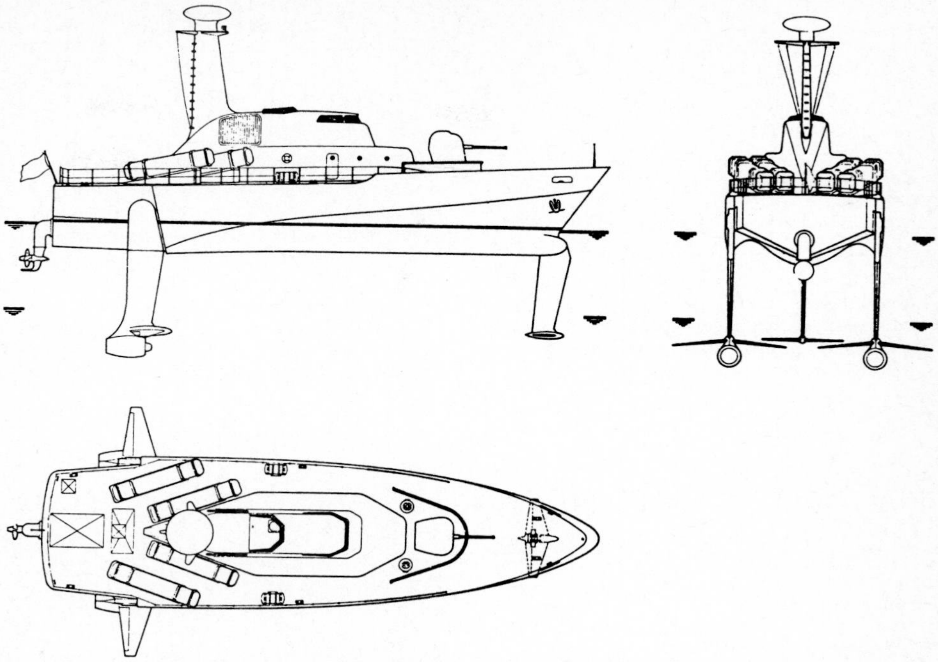

The H.851, 48-knot naval hydrofoil powered by a single SNECMA THS 2000 gas-turbine driving two SOGREAH water pumps

Artist's impression of the SNIA SA 800 waterjet-propelled hydrofoil ferry

SA 800

The SA 800 is a design study for a mixed-traffic hydrofoil powered by two Turmo IIIC turbines driving a waterjet propulsion unit. Conventional marine light alloy construction is employed and the craft will have incidence-controlled, fully-submerged foils operated by a sonic/electronic sensing system.
A number of variants of the basic design are being studied for alternative applications, including prospecting, marine research, coastal surveillance and naval patrol. Trials conducted with dynamic models have been successful and are continuing. Preliminary design studies are now complete.
FOILS: The foil system is fully submerged and of 'aeroplane' configuration. All three foil struts retract hydraulically completely clear of the water. An SNIAS sonic autopilot system controls the incidence angle of the two bow foils and adjustable control flaps on the rear foils.
HULL: The hull is of conventional marine corrosion-resistant aluminium alloys. Features include a deep V bow, designed to minimise structural loading due to wave impact, and a flat W section aft for good directional control when hullborne.
POWER PLANT: Foilborne propulsion is supplied by two 1,300shp Turboméca Turmo IIIC gas-turbines driving a SOGREAH waterjet propulsion unit mounted at the base of the aft foil strut.
Output from the transmission shafts of the two turbines, which are mounted end-to-end, intakes outwards, athwart the stern, passes first to a main bevel drive gearbox, then to a drive shaft which extends downwards through the aft foil strut to a waterjet pump gearbox located in a nacelle beneath the aft foil. Air for the turbines is introduced through intakes at the top of the cabin aft. Filters are fitted to the intakes to prevent the ingestion of water or salt spray into the gas-turbine. There is a separate hullborne propulsion system, with a 400hp diesel driving twin water propellers beneath the transom.
ACCOMMODATION: The elevated wheelhouse forward of the passenger compartment seats the captain and engineer. All instrumentation is located so that it can be easily monitored. Navigation and collision avoidance radar is fitted. Accommodation is on two decks, each arranged with three seats abreast on either side of a central aisle. As a passenger ferry the craft will seat 200—116 on the upper deck and 84 on the lower; and in mixed traffic configuration it will carry 8-10 cars on the upper deck with the lower deck seating capacity remaining at 84. Cars are loaded via rear door/ramps. Baggage holds are provided forward of both upper and lower saloons.
DIMENSIONS
Length overall: 26·88m (88ft)
Max beam, deck: 5·4m (18ft)
WEIGHTS
Displacement, fully loaded: 56 tonnes (55 tons)
Payload (200 passengers with luggage or 84 passengers with luggage and 8-10 cars): 18,300kg (40,300lb)
PERFORMANCE
Max speed, calm conditions: 55 knots
Cruising speed: 50 knots
Cruising speed, sea state 5: 48 knots
Range, at 50 knots, calm sea: 250n miles
at 48 knots, sea state 5: 200n miles
Craft is designed to platform over 3m (10ft) high waves, crest to trough, and contour 4m (13ft) high waves.

ISRAEL

ISRAEL SHIPYARDS LIMITED

POB 1282, Haifa 31000, Israel
Telephone: 749111
Telex: 45132 YARD IL
Cables: Israyard
Officials:
D Yallon, *Company Secretary*

Israel has for some time been negotiating with the United States government for the purchase of four Flagstaff multi-duty naval hydrofoils from Grumman Aerospace Corporation, together with the acquisition of a licence for the series production of these craft in Israel. It is understood that once the immediate needs of the Israeli Navy have been met, Israeli-built craft would be made available for export.

In 1976 it was revealed that the Israeli Navy was anxious to start building missile armed hydrofoils of about 100 tons displacement in conjunction with a US boatbuilder. It was suggested that the craft the Israeli Navy had in mind was a variant of the Grumman Flagstaff with a 4,250hp Allison 50LK20A gas-turbine.

In the early autumn of 1977 it was announced by the US government that agreement had been reached on the joint development of hydrofoils by the two countries and Grumman Aerospace Corporation stated it had "received its first order for the Flagstaff from an overseas client". Later the Corporation confirmed that the country concerned is Israel.

Construction of the vessel will almost certainly be undertaken by Israel Shipyards Limited, Haifa, which is currently building the 415-ton Reshef (Flash) missile boat for the Israeli and overseas navies.

Details of the Flagstaff will be found in this section in the entry for Grumman Aerospace Corporation, USA.

ITALY

CANTIERI NAVALI RIUNITI (CNR)

(Fincantieri Group)
Via Cipro 11, 16129 Genoa, Italy
Telephone: 59951
Telex: 27168 CANT GE
Officials:
Enrico Bocchini, *Chairman and Managing Director*
Antonio Fiori, *General Manager*
Sergio Castagnoli, *Commercial Director*
Pasquale Teodorani, *Project Director*
Francesco Cao, *Project Director*

Cantieri Navali Riuniti, SpA, has taken over the interests of Alinavi which was formed in 1964 to develop, manufacture and market advanced military marine systems.

Under the terms of a licensing agreement, CNR has access to Boeing technology in the field of military fully-submerged foil hydrofoil craft.

In October 1970, the company was awarded a contract by the Italian Navy for the design and construction of the P 420 Sparviero Class hydrofoil missilecraft. This is an improved version of the Boeing PGH-2 Tucumcari. The first vessel, given the design name Swordfish, was delivered to the Italian Navy in July 1974. An order for a further six of this type was placed by the Italian Navy in February 1976.

Turning radius of the Swordfish at 40 knots is less than 125m (137yds)

Swordfish hullborne with foils retracted. Continuous speed, hullborne, is 8 knots

SWORDFISH

The Swordfish missile-launching hydrofoil gunboat displaces a maximum of 64 tonnes and is designed for both offensive and defensive missions. Its combination of speed, firepower, and all-weather capability is unique in a ship of this class.

The vessel has fully-submerged foils arranged in canard configuration and an automatic control system. A gas-turbine powered waterjet system provides foilborne propulsion and a diesel-driven propeller outdrive provides hullborne propulsion. A typical crew comprises two officers and eight enlisted men.

FOILS: Fully-submerged canard arrangement, with approximately one-third of the dynamic lift provided by the bow foil and two-thirds by the two aft foils. The aft foils retract sideways and the bow hydrofoil retracts forwards into a recess in the bow. Bow doors preserve the hull lines when the forward hydrofoil is either fully extended or retracted. Foils and struts are built in corrosion-resistant stainless steel.

Anhedral is incorporated in the aft foils to enhance the directional stability of the craft at shallow foil depths. In addition, the anhedral assures positive roll control by eliminating tip broaching during rough water manoeuvres.

CONTROLS: Automatic system incorporating two aircraft-type gyros, one to sense pitch and roll and the other to sense yaw, plus three accelerometers to sense vertical movements (heave) of the craft. An ultrasonic height sensor is used to detect and maintain flying height above the water surface. Information from the sensors is sent to a hermetically-sealed solid-state computer, which calculates movement of the control surfaces necessary to maintain boat stability, and/or pre-selected flying height, and sends appropriate commands to the servo-mechanisms that control flap movement.

Foilborne steering: Helm commanded automatic control system controls hydraulic servo-actuated hydrofoil flaps and steerable forward hydrofoil strut to produce coordinated (banked) turns in design sea conditions.

Hullborne steering: Helm commanded steerable outdrive unit. Helm-driven potentiometer sends signals to a servo-valve controlling steering hydraulic motor. Manual emergency hullborne steering is provided on the aft deck.

HULL: Both hull and superstructure are built entirely in corrosion-resistant aluminium, the hull being welded and the superstructure riveted and welded.

BERTHING: Two fixed berths in the compartment under the bridge, plus eight folding berths in the forward crew space. One toilet and one sink. A folding table with benches in the forward crew space.

POWERPLANT, FOILBORNE: Power for the waterjet is supplied by one Rolls-Royce Proteus 15M/553 gas-turbine. At the customer's option the craft may be fitted with the "sprint" model of this gas-turbine, which incorporates water injection. The "sprint" model ("wet") develops 5,000shp maximum versus the 4,500shp of the normal ("dry") Proteus. Adoption of the "sprint" model permits take-off at higher displacements and therefore, more fuel and/or military payload to be carried. It also provides better craft performance in very high sea states, particularly in conditions of high ambient temperatures. The respective performance characteristics of the Swordfish equipped with 'dry' and 'wet' models of the Proteus are shown in the accompanying performance table.

Engine output is transferred to a single double-volute, double-suction, two impeller centrifugal pump, rated at 28,000 US gallons/min at 1,560rpm and absorbing approximately 4,700shp (4,766 CV). Water is taken in through inlets on the nose of each aft foil at the foil/strut intersection and passes up through the hollow interiors of the struts to the hull, where it is ducted to the pump. From the pump, the water is discharged through twin, fixed-area nozzles located beneath the hull under the pump.

POWERPLANT, HULLBORNE: A General Motors 6V-53 diesel engine, rated at 160shp (162 CV) at 2,600rpm, powers a Schottel-Werft SRP-100 steerable propeller outdrive unit, which is mounted on the centreline of the transom. The unit is retractable and rotates through 360 degrees. Propeller is fixed-pitch. Power is delivered to the outdrive at about 1,700rpm.

FUEL: Fuel oil is NATO 76, carried in three tanks located amidships and integral with the hull, side keelson and platform deck. Total capacity is about 14,550 litres (3,850 gallons).

Fuel oil system: Two primary 208V 400Hz 26·5 litres/min (7 gallons/min) submerged pumps and two standby 28V dc 26·5 litres/min (7 gallons/min) external pumps. The dc pump is started automatically by a pressure switch in the fuel supply line if ac pump power is lost.

Craft may be refuelled through main deck connection at dock or at sea. The fuel tanks are equipped with fuel level indicators and vents.

AUXILIARY SYSTEMS:

Hydraulics: Two independent systems: foilborne and ship service. Systems pressure, 3,000psi. Systems fluid, MIL-H-5606.

Foilborne system: normal and standby 21·8 gallons/min pumps serve hydraulic control system.

Ship service system: normal and standby 32·5 gallons/min pumps serve other uses including hydrofoil retracting and locking, bow door, hullborne outdrive retraction and steering, foilborne turbine starting, foilborne turbine exhaust door, cannon loading, and the fixed saltwater fire pump.

ELECTRICAL:

Turbine generator sets: At customer's option, either two or three identical sets, one installed in forward machinery space, the other(s) in the aft machinery space.

Each set consists of a Solar T-62 T-32 gas turbine engine capable of developing a maximum output of 150shp (152 CV) under standard conditions and driving a General Electric 208V 400Hz three-phase alternator rated at 75 kVA, a 30V dc starter-generator with 200A generating capacity, and one hydraulic pump for ship service and hullborne steering.

Starting battery sets: One 24V, 34Ah capacity starting battery is provided for the hullborne diesel engine and for each solar turbogenerator set.

Emergency battery set: Two additional 24V batteries in parallel provide 68Ah capacity to power in emergency conditions, radios, intercommunications system and navigation lights.

Shore power: Craft requires up to 30 kVA of 200V three-phase four wire 400Hz power.

Intercommunication system: The system consists of one station in each space and three external stations, allowing complete craft machinery and weapons coordination.

Every station is a control unit and has a reversible loudspeaker with press-to-talk switch.

Main station is equipped with radio operation access control.

Emergency announcements can be made to all stations simultaneously.

Selective communications are available between any two or more stations.

Navigation horn: One electrically operated horn mounted on forward top of deckhouse.

Signal searchlight: One portable incandescent signal searchlight mounted on the deckhouse canopy.

Depth sounder: Transducer on the hull bottom 152mm (6in) above the keel and a recorder at the navigation station measure and record water depth from echo soundings. Recorder may be set for sounding depths of 0-38·6, 38·6-86·9, 77·2-125·4, 0-115·8, 96·5-212, 193-309 metres (0-20, 20-45, 40-65, 0-60, 50-110, 100-160 fathoms).

First of the Italian Navy's missile equipped hydrofoil gunboats during foilborne firing tests of its 76mm Oto Melara cannon. Given the design name Swordfish, the craft is the first of the P420 Sparviero Class

PARAMETER	Without water injection		With water injection	
	15°C/ 59°F	22°C/ 80°F	15°C/ 59°F	22°C/ 80°F
Displacement (tonnes)	62·5	60	64	64
Military payload (tonnes)	11·7	11·7	14	14
Fuel (tonnes)	9·4	6·9	9·4	9·4
Max foilborne intermittent speed in calm sea (knots)	50	48	50	48
Max foilborne continuous speed in calm sea (knots)	45	43	45	43
Max foilborne continuous speed in Sea State 4 (knots)	41	39	41	39
Hullborne continuous speed (knots)	8	8	8	8
Foilborne range at max continuous speed (n miles)	400	300	400	400
Hullborne range (n miles)	1,050	920	1,150	1,050
Turning radius at 40 knots	less than 125 metres			
Foilborne stability: max vertical acceleration	0-25g (rms) in Sea State 4			
Hullborne stability with foils up	stable in 50 knot wind			
Hullborne stability with foils down	stable in 70 knot wind			
Endurance	5 days			

The Swordfish, the first missile-launching hydrofoil vessel to be built for the Italian Navy

Recorder contains electronic circuits and a two-speed mechanism with a stylus which burns a black mark on moving chart paper. A white line mode of recorder operation eliminates false traces below the true bottom line on the chart and allows detection of small objects close to the bottom and an indication of hard or soft composition of the sea bottom.

Navigation set: The shipboard navigation system (ShipNav) automatically performs, independently of all external aids, precise dead reckoning navigation for both foilborne and hullborne operations. It continuously computes and displays the craft's current position, true heading, true course, and true speed. Actual position is displayed digitally on counters in latitude and longitude coordinates and pictorially on standard charts having local coordinate information. Indicators display true heading, course, and speed.

Speed log: Hull rodmeter, foil rodmeter, rodmeter selector switch and calibration unit, transmitter and remote indicator set measures craft hullborne or foilborne speed, computes the distance travelled and displays both at the navigation station and helm.

IFF system: The system consists of an IFF/ATC transponder (APX 72) and an IFF interrogator coupled to the radar.

Navigation and search radar: SMA Model 3RM7-250B radar performs navigation and search operations with master indicator, rayplot with variable range marker (VRN) bearing control unit and remote indicator.

Set operates in "X" band and is tunable from 9,345 MHz to 9,405 MHz. Set has two different transmitters and it is possible to select the proper one by a RF switch unit. Peak power output is 7kW for navigation purposes and 250kW for search purposes.

Performance includes a minimum range less than 182m (200yds), range discrimination better than 10m (11yds), azimuth discrimination less than 1·2 degrees and maximum range of 40n miles.

HF-SSB radio system AN/ARC-102: The AN/ARC-102 uses the Collins 618T/3 HF single-sideband transceiver for long range voice, CW, data or compatible AM communication in the 2,000 through 29,999 MHz frequency range. It is automatically tuned in 28,000 1-kHz channel increments by means of an operator's remote control unit. The operating frequency is indicated directly in a digital-type presentation. Nominal transmit power is 400W pep. in SSB or 125W in compatible AM. The system is tuned through the antenna coupler Collins 490T-1 to a helical monoplane antenna.

UHF radio system AN/ARC-109: Two identical units are provided. The AN/ARC-109 transceiver has two separate receivers: a main tunable receiver and a guard receiver. Common circuit design is maintained in the two receivers. Each receiver uses a carrier-to-noise ratio squelch system. Receiver selectivity is ±22 kHz at —6 dB and ±45 kHz at —60 dB.

The 20-channel present memory in the frequency control utilises a magnetic core storage system with solid-state drivers and interrogators.

DAMAGE CONTROL:

Bilge pumps: Pumps are mounted in the bilge of each water-tight compartment and controlled from the engineer's station.

Freon flooding systems: Two 24kg (53lb) freon FE1301 (CBR F_3) storage cylinders are provided in the engineer's compartment. One 2·27kg (5lb) freon cylinder is piped to Proteus turbine shroud. Systems manually controlled by engineer.

Portable fire extinguishers: A 1kg (2lb) dry chemical extinguisher is mounted in each of the seven manned compartments.

VENTILATION AND CONDITIONING: Unit air conditioners (6 units) are distributed throughout the manned spaces to provide heating and cooling.

ARMAMENT: A typical military payload consists of:

- one dual purpose 76mm automatic OTO Melara gun and ammunition
- two fixed missile launchers and two ship-to-ship missiles, eg Sea Killers, OTOMAT or Exocet
- gunfire and missile launch control system(s)
- other military electronics, eg ECM

A variety of other payloads may be accommodated according to customer needs.

DIMENSIONS

Length overall: 22·95m (75ft 4in)
Length overall, foils retracted: 24·6m (80ft 7in)
Width across foils: 10·8m (35ft 4in)
Deck beam, max: 7m (23ft)

WEIGHTS

Max displacement: 64 tonnes

PERFORMANCE

Exact craft performance characteristics depend upon the choice of foilborne gas turbine by the customer and operating conditions which, in turn, can affect the quantity of fuel carried. Performance figures shown below, therefore, are representative:

Foilborne intermittent speed in calm water: 50 knots
Foilborne continuous speed in calm water: 45 knots
Foilborne continuous speed in Sea State 4: 38–40 knots
Hullborne continuous speed, foils down: 7·6 knots
Foilborne range at max continuous speed: up to 400n miles
Hullborne range: up to 1,150n miles
Turning radius at max foilborne continuous speed: less than 125m (410ft)
Endurance: 5 days

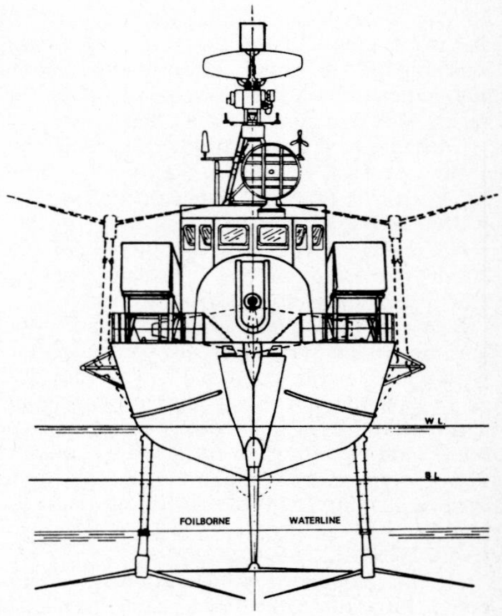

1 Forward hydrofoil retracted
2 OTO Melara 76mm cannon
3 Fire control radar
4 Vertical ladder
5 Main mast
6 Anemometer
7 Antenna
8 Navigation and search radar
9 Antenna
10 Antenna
11 Surface-to-surface missile launchers (P/S)
12 Ensign staff
13 Turbine exhaust: foilborne propulsion

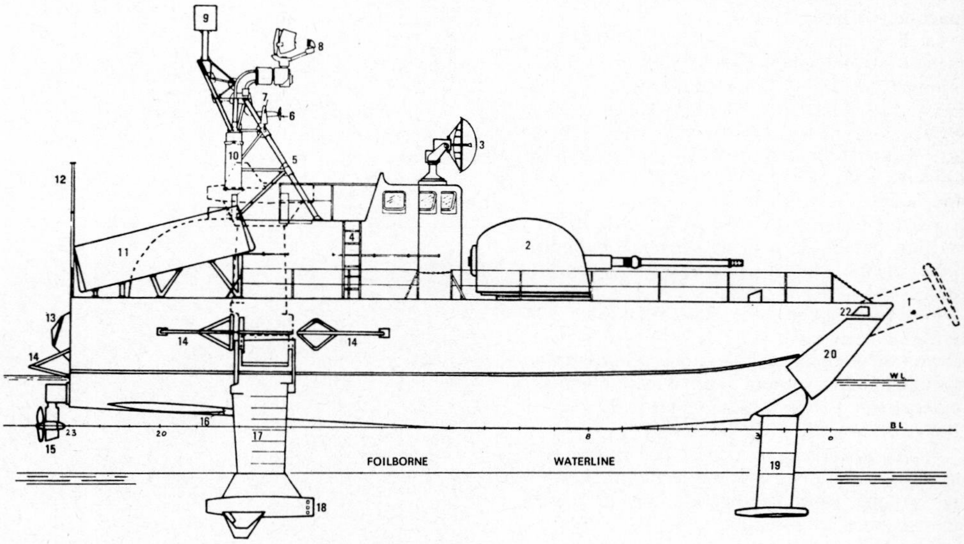

14 Guards
15 Propeller outdrive: hullborne propulsion
16 Waterjet nozzle (P/S)
17 Aft hydrofoil extended (P/S)
18 Water inlet (P/S): foilborne propulsion
19 Forward hydrofoil extended
20 Bow doors (P/S)
21 Watertight hatches
22 Height sensors: automatic control system (P/S)
23 Optical putter-on
24 Starboard gyrocompass readout
25 Port gyrocompass readout

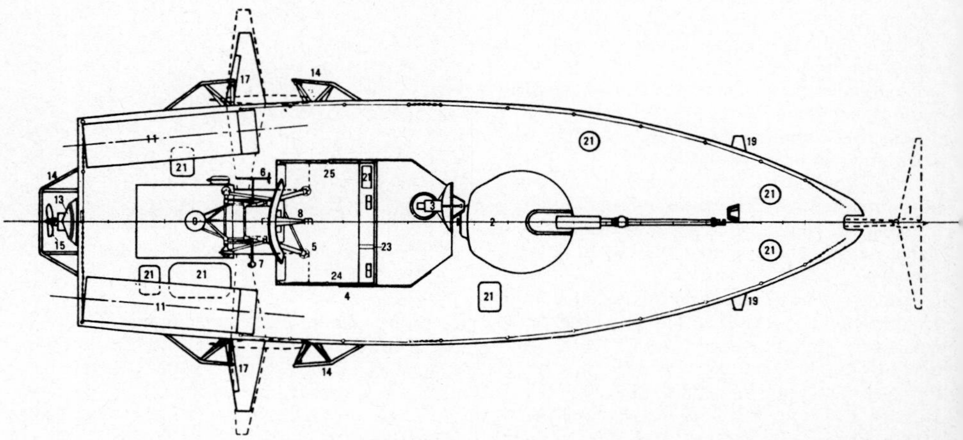

1 Helm/main control console
2 Helm station (starboard)
Conning station (port)
3 Combat Operations Centre, (COC) door
4 Companionway ladders
5 COC electric power distribution panel
6 Combat Operations Centre electronics (speed log, radios, etc)
7 Air intake forward machinery room
8 Demister panels for combustion air
9 Aft machinery room
10 Gas turbine engine: foilborne propulsion
11 Forward machinery room
12 Pump drive coupling
13 Waterjet pump
14 Waterjet nozzle (P/S)
15 Main electrical switchboard
16 Main electrical power distribution panel
17 Engineer's console
18 Engineer's station
19 Fuel oil tanks (3)
20 Void
21 Electric hot plate
22 Refrigerator

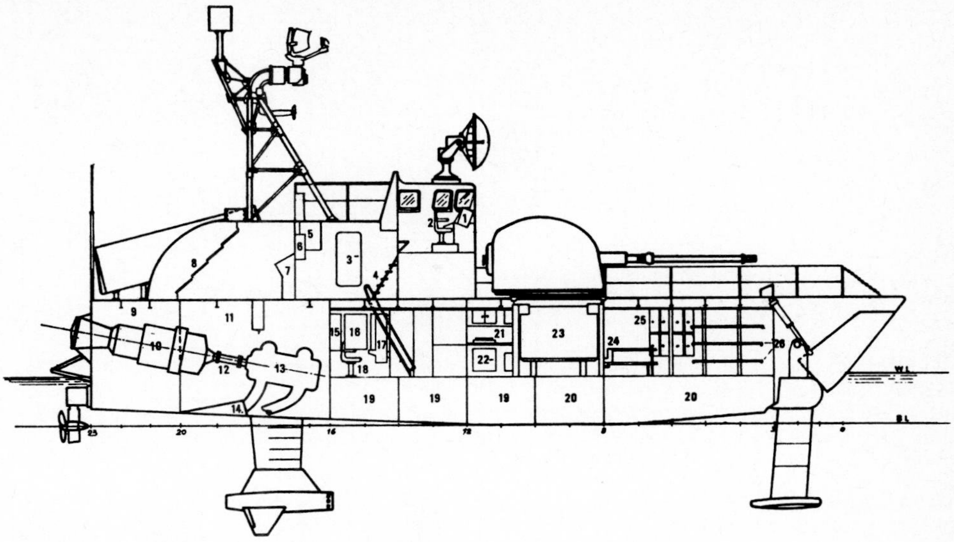

23 Cannon revolving feeding magazine
24 Folding mess table with benches (2)
25 Crew lockers (8)
26 Crew berths (8)
27 Rope locker (P/S)
28 Forward hydrofoil retraction well
29 Watertight doors
30 Galley stores locker
31 Lavatory
32 Sink
33 Officers' stateroom
34 Turbine generator set
35 Diesel engine: hullborne propulsion
36 Search and navigation radar electronics
37 Fire control radar components
38 Fire control radar computer
39 Gyrocompass and Stable element
40 Electronic equipment
41 Automatic control system
42 Electronic equipment bay (unmanned)
43 Water closet

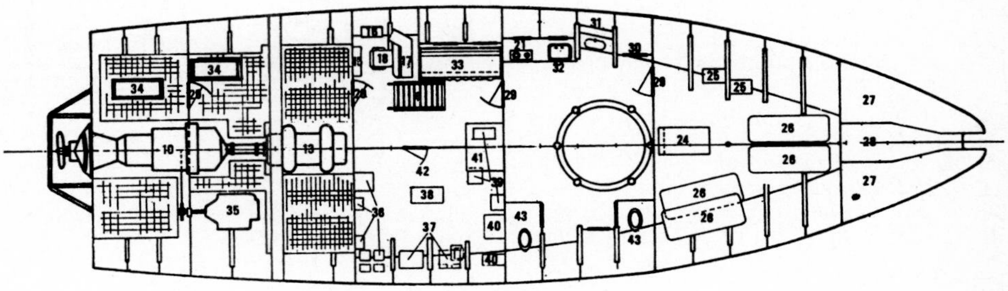

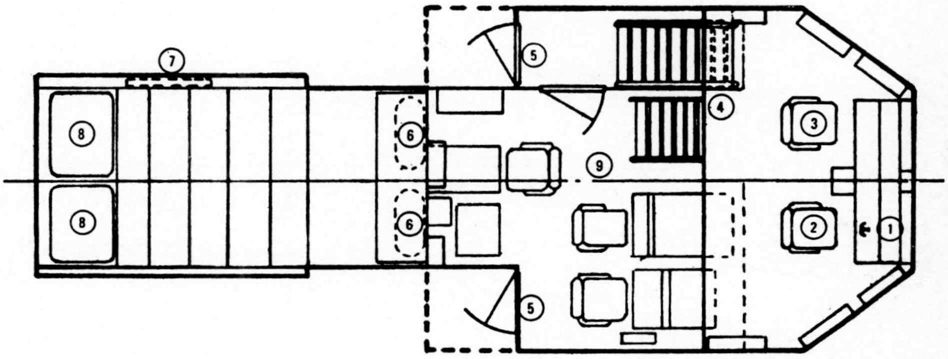

1 Helm/main control console
2 Helm station
3 Conning station
4 Companionway ladders
5 Watertight doors (P/S)
6 Air-inlet plenums: forward machinery room (P/S)
7 Exhaust duct
8 Machinery combustion air inlets
9 Combat operations centre

CANTIERE NAVALTECNICA SpA

Via S Raineri 22, 98100 Messina, Italy
Telephone: (090) 774862
Telex: 98030 Rodrikez

Officials:

Cav Del Lavoro Carlo Rodriquez, *President*
Dott Ing Leopoldo Rodriquez, *Executive Vice President and General Manager*
Dott Ing Giovanni Falzea, *Production Manager*

Cantiere Navaltecnica SpA, formerly known as Leopoldo Rodriquez Shipyard, was the first in the world to produce hydrofoils in series, and is now the biggest hydrofoil builder outside the Soviet Union. On the initiative of the company's president, Carlo Rodriquez, the Aliscafi Shipping Company was established in Sicily to operate the world's first scheduled seagoing hydrofoil service in August 1956 between Sicily and the Italian mainland.

The service was operated by the first Rodriquez-built Supramar PT 20, Freccia del Sole. Cutting down the port-to-port time from Messina to Reggio di Calabria to one-quarter of that of conventional ferry boats, and completing 22 daily crossings, the craft soon proved its commercial viability. With a seating capacity of 75 passengers the PT 20 has carried between 800-900 passengers a day and has conveyed a record number of some 31,000 in a single month.

The prototype PT 20, a 27-ton craft for 75 passengers, was built by Rodriquez in 1955 and the first PT 50, a 63-ton craft for 140 passengers, was completed by the yard in 1958.

Freccia delle Magnolie, a 71-seat Navaltecnica RHS 70 hydrofoil passenger ferry operated by Ministero di Trasporti on Lake Maggiore

By the end of July 1977, the company had built and delivered more than 130 hydrofoils. The new RHS models, the only craft now built by the company, are fitted on request with a Hamilton Standard electronic stability augmentation system.

At the time of going to press, the company had under construction two RHS 140s, one RHS 150 and five RHS 160s. Construction of the company's first RHS 200 began in 1978.

Apart from these standard designs, the company offers a number of variants, including the M 100, M 150 and M 200 fast patrol craft, the M 300 and 600 fast strike craft and the RHS Hydroil series of mixed passenger/freight hydrofoils, based on the RHS 70, 140 and 160, but adapted for servicing offshore drilling platforms.

RHS 70

This is a 32-ton coastal passenger ferry with seats for 71 passengers. Power is supplied by a single 1,350hp MTU diesel and the cruising speed is 32·4 knots.

FOILS: Surface-piercing type in partly hollow welded steel. During operation the angle of the bow foil can be adjusted within narrow limits from the steering position by means of a hydraulic ram operating on a foil support across the hull.

HULL: V-bottom hull of riveted light metal alloy construction. Watertight compartments are provided below the passenger decks and in other parts of the hull.

POWER PLANT: A single MTU MB 12V493 Ty 71 diesel, developing 1,350hp at 1,500rpm, drives a three-bladed bronze aluminium propeller through a Zahnradfabrik W 800 H 20 gearbox.

ACCOMMODATION: 44 passengers are accommodated in the forward cabin, 19 in the rear compartment and 8 aft of the pilot's position, above the engine room, in the elevated wheelhouse. A w/c washbasin unit is provided in

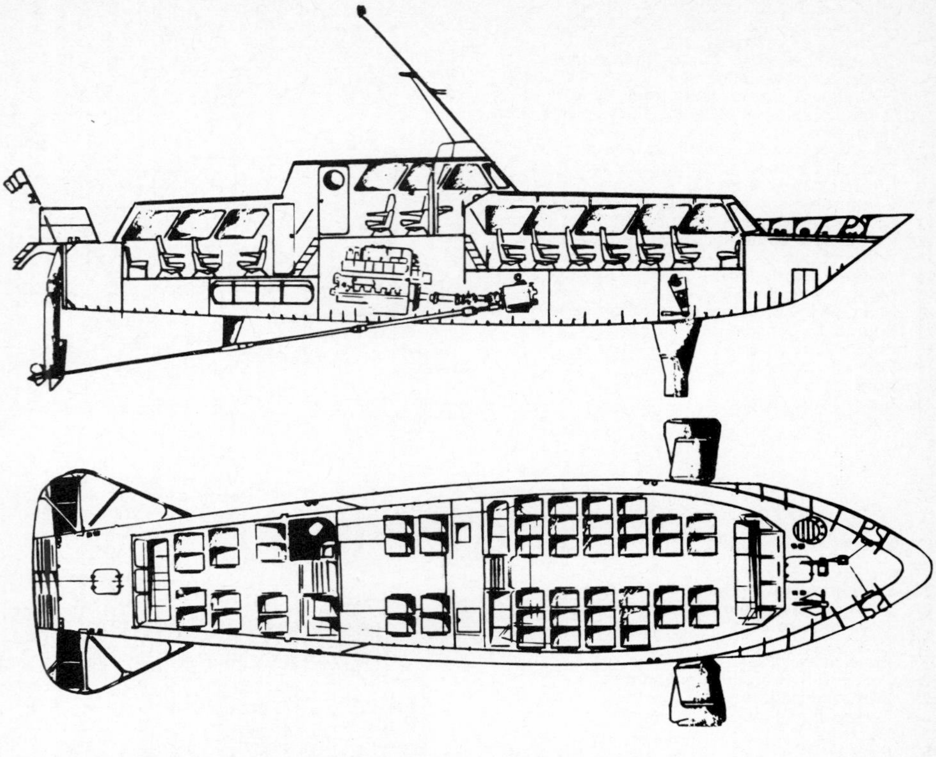

General arrangement of the RHS 70, 71-seat hydrofoil passenger ferry. Power is supplied by a single 1,350hp MTU MB 12V493 Ty 71 diesel

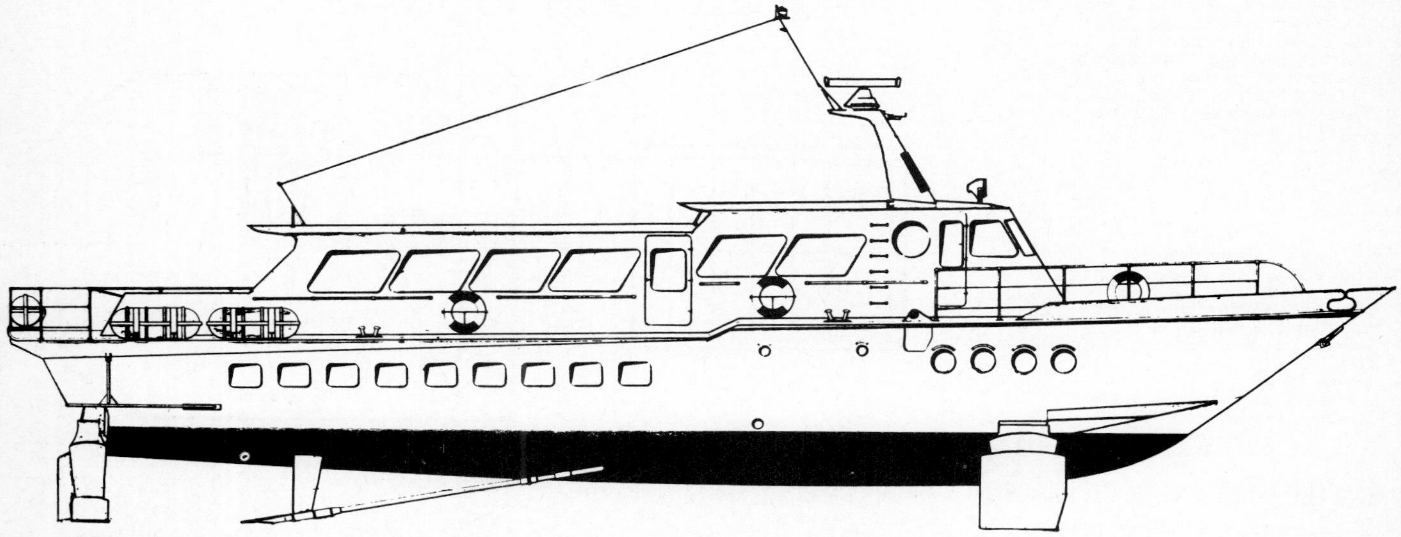

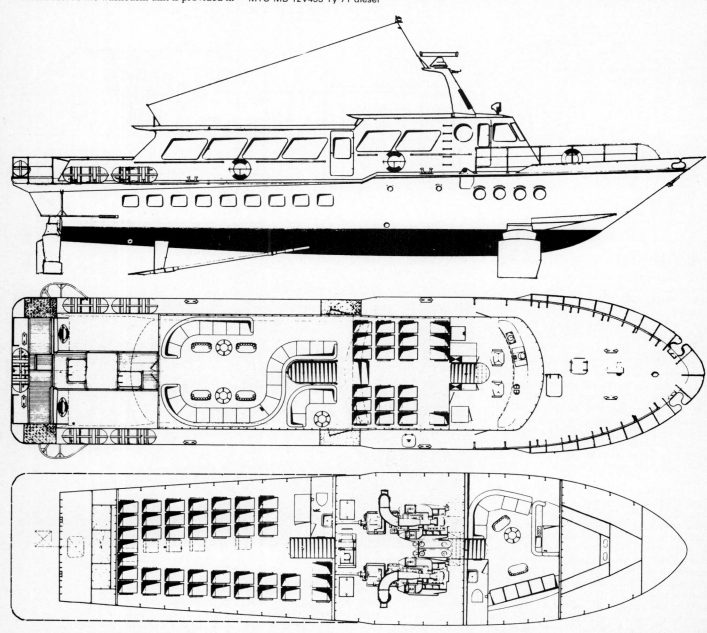

Outboard profile and deck plans of the RHS 110 54-ton hydrofoil passenger ferry

the aft passenger compartments. Emergency exits are provided in each passenger compartment.
SYSTEMS, ELECTRICAL: 24V generator driven by the main engine; batteries with a capacity of 350Ah.
HYDRAULICS: 120kg/cm^3 pressure hydraulic system for rudder and bow foil incidence control.
DIMENSIONS
Length overall: 22m (72ft 2in)
Width across foils: 7·4m (24ft 3in)
Draft hullborne: 2·7m (8ft 10in)
Draft foilborne: 1·15m (3ft 9in)
WEIGHTS
Displacement fully loaded: 31·5 tons
Useful load: 6 tons
PERFORMANCE
Cruising speed, half loaded: 32·4 knots
Max speed, half loaded: 36·5 knots

RHS 110, a 110-seat passenger ferry equipped with a Hamilton Standard stability augmentation system

RHS 110

A 54-ton hydrofoil ferry, the RHS 110 is designed to carry a maximum of 110 passengers over routes of up to 485·7km (300 miles) at a cruising speed of 37 knots.
FOILS: Surface-piercing type, in partly hollow welded steel. Hydraulically operated flaps, attached to the trailing edges of the bow and rear foils, are adjusted automatically by a Hamilton Standard stability augmentation system for the damping of heave, pitch and roll motions. The rear foil is rigidly attached to the transom, its incidence angle being determined during tests.
HULL: V-bottom of high-tensile riveted light metal alloy construction, using Peraluman plates and Anticorrodal profiles. The upper deck plates are in 3·5mm (0·137in) thick Peraluman. Removable deck sections permit the lifting out and replacement of the main engines. The superstructure which has a removable roof is in 2mm (0·078in) thick Peraluman plates, with L and C profile sections. Watertight compartments are provided below the passenger decks and other parts of the hull.
POWERPLANT: Power is supplied by two 12-cylinder supercharged MTU MB 12V493 Ty 71 diesels, each with a maximum output of 1,350hp at 1,500rpm. Engine output is transferred to two three-bladed bronze-aluminium propellers through Zahnradfabrik W 800 H20 gearboxes. Each propeller shaft is 90mm (3·5in) in diameter and supported at three points by seawater lubricated rubber bearings. Steel fuel tanks with a total capacity of 3,600 litres (792 gallons) are located aft of the engine room.
ACCOMMODATION: The wheelhouse/observation deck saloon seats 58, and the lower aft saloon seats 39. Additional passengers are accommodated in the lower forward saloon, which contains a bar.

In the wheelhouse, the pilot's position is on the port side, together with the radar screen. A second seat is provided for the chief engineer. Passenger seats are of lightweight aircraft type, floors are covered with woollen carpets and the walls and ceilings are clad in vinyl. Two toilets are provided, one in each of the lower saloons.
SYSTEMS, ELECTRICAL: Engine driven generators supply 220V, 50Hz, three-phase ac. Two groups of batteries for 24V dc circuit.
HYDRAULICS: Steering, variation of the foil flaps and the anchor windlass operation are all accomplished hydraulically from the wheelhouse. Plant comprises two Bosch pumps installed on the main engines and conveying oil from a 60 litre (13 gallon) tank under pressure to the control cylinders of the rudder, foil flaps and anchor windlass.
FIREFIGHTING: Fixed CO_2 plant for the main engine room, portable CO_2 and foam fire extinguishers of 3kg (7lb) and 10 litres (2 gallon) capacity in the saloons, and one water fire fighting plant.
DIMENSIONS
EXTERNAL
Length overall: 25·6m (84ft)
Width across foils: 9·2m (30ft 2¼in)
Deck beam, max: 5·95m (19ft 2in)
Draft hullborne: 3·3m (10ft 9⅞in)
Draft foilborne: 1·25m (4ft 1in)

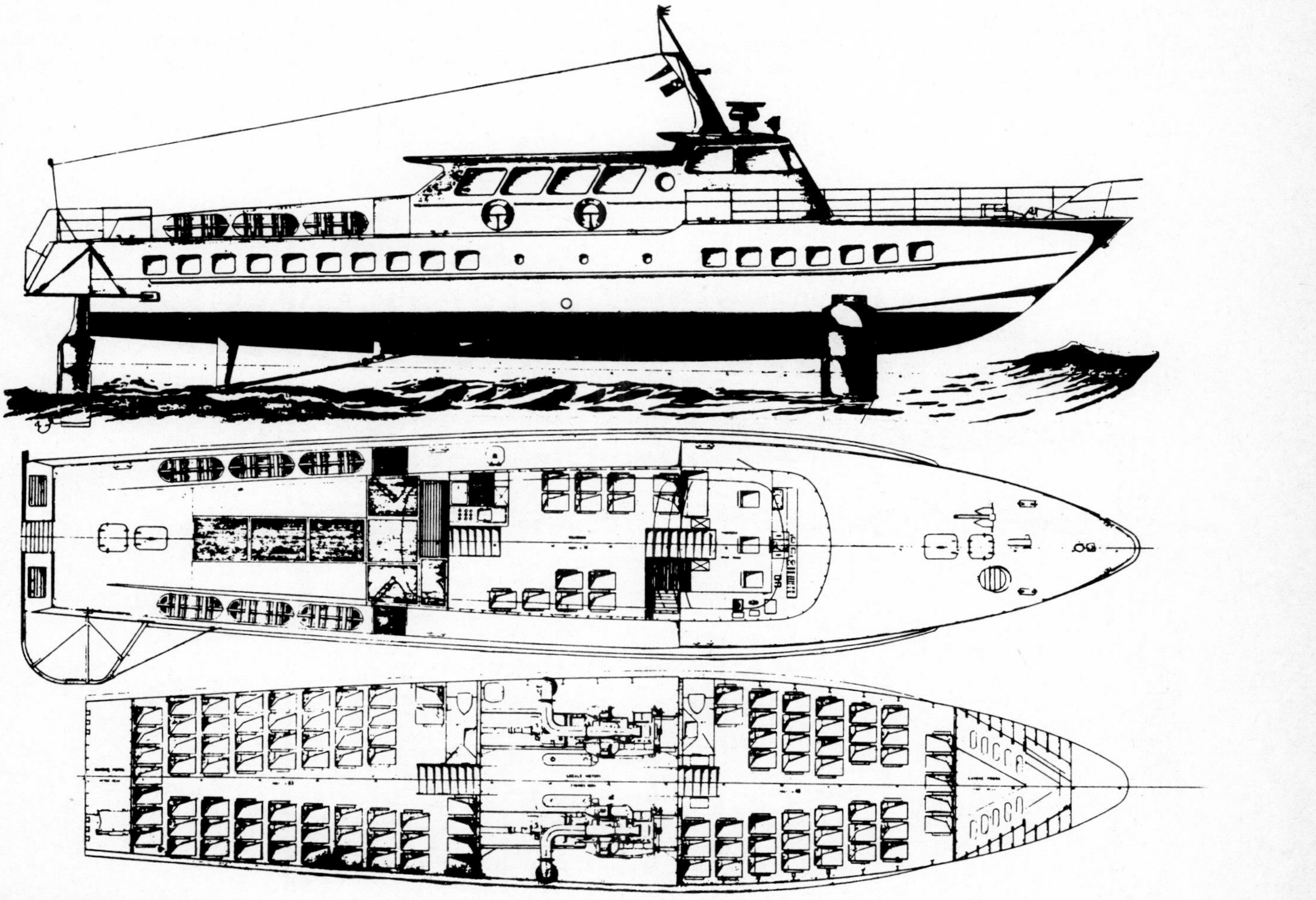

RHS 140, 125-140-seat passenger ferry

WEIGHTS
Displacement, fully loaded: 54 tons
PERFORMANCE
Max speed: 40 knots
Cruising speed: 37 knots
Range: 485·7km (300 miles)

RHS 140

This 65-ton hydrofoil passenger ferry seats 125-140 passengers and has a cruising speed of 32·5 knots.
FOILS: Surface-piercing V foils of hollow welded steel construction. Lift of the bow foil can be modified by hydraulically-operated trailing-edge flaps.
HULL: Riveted light metal alloy design framed on longitudinal and transverse formers.
ACCOMMODATION: 125-140 passengers seated in three saloons. The belvedere saloon, on the main deck above the engine room, can be equipped with a bar. W/C washbasin units can be installed in the forward and aft saloons.
POWER PLANT: Power is provided by two MTU 12V493 Ty 71 12-cylinder supercharged engines, each developing 1,350hp at 1,500 rpm. Engine output is transmitted to two, three-bladed 700mm diameter bronze propellers through Zahnradfabrik gearboxes.
SYSTEMS, ELECTRICAL: Two engine-driven generators supply 24V dc. Two battery sets each with 350Ah capacity.
HYDRAULICS: Steering and variation of foil flap incidence is accomplished hydraulically from the wheelhouse. Plant comprises two Bosch pumps installed on the main engines and conveying oil from a 70 litre (15·4 gallon) tank under pressure to the control cylinders of the rudder and foil flaps.
FIREFIGHTING: Fixed CO_2 plant for the engine room; portable CO_2 and foam fire extinguishers in the saloons. Water intake connected to bilge pump for fire hose connection in emergency.
DIMENSIONS
Length overall: 28·7m (94ft 1½in)
Width across foils: 10·72m (35ft 2¼in)
Draft hullborne: 3·5m (11ft 5¾in)
Draft foilborne: 1·5m (4ft 11in)
WEIGHTS
Displacement, fully loaded: 65 tons

Fabricia, an RHS 140 operated by Toremar on a passenger service between Livorno/Porto Ferraio and Piombino

Carrying capacity, including 3 tons bunker, and 5 tons fresh water, lubricating oil and hydraulic system oil: 12·5 tons
PERFORMANCE
Max speed, half load: 36 knots
Cruising speed: 32·5 knots
Range at cruising speed: 550km (340 miles)

RHS 160

One of the latest additions to the Navaltecnica range is the RHS 160, an 85-ton passenger ferry with seats for 160–200 passengers and a cruising speed of 36 knots.
FOILS: Surface-piercing W foils of hollow welded steel construction. Craft in this series feature a bow rudder for improved manoeuvrability in congested waters. The bow rudder works simultaneously with the aft rudders. Hydraulically-operated flaps, attached to the trailing edges of the bow and rear foils, are adjusted automatically by a Hamilton Standard electronic stability augmentation system, for the damping of heave, pitch and roll motions in heavy seas.
HULL: Riveted light metal alloy longitudinal structure, welded in parts using inert gas. The hull shape of the RHS 160 is similar to the RHS 140 series. In the manufacture of the hull, plates of aluminium and magnesium alloy of 4·4% are used whilst angle bars are of a high-resistant aluminium, magnesium and silicon alloy.
ACCOMMODATION: 160-200 passengers seated in three saloons. 57 passengers are accommodated in the forward cabin, 57 in the rear compartment and 46 in the belvedere. Forward and aft saloons and belvedere have a toilet, each provided with w/c washbasin units and the usual toilet accessories.
POWER PLANT: Power is provided by two supercharged MTU MB 12V 652 TB 71 4-stroke diesel engines each with a maximum output of 1,950hp at 1,460rpm under normal operating conditions. Engine starting is accomplished by compressed air starters. Engine output is transmitted to two, three-bladed bronze propellers through two Zahnradfabrik 900 HS 15 gearboxes.
SYSTEMS, ELECTRICAL: Two 35kVA generating sets, 220V, 60Hz, three-phase. Three insulated cables for ventilation, air-conditioning and power. Two insulated cables for lighting, sockets and other appliances, 24V dc for emergency lighting, auxiliary engine starting and servocontrol. A battery for radio telephone supply is installed on the upper deck. Provision for battery recharge from ac line foreseen.

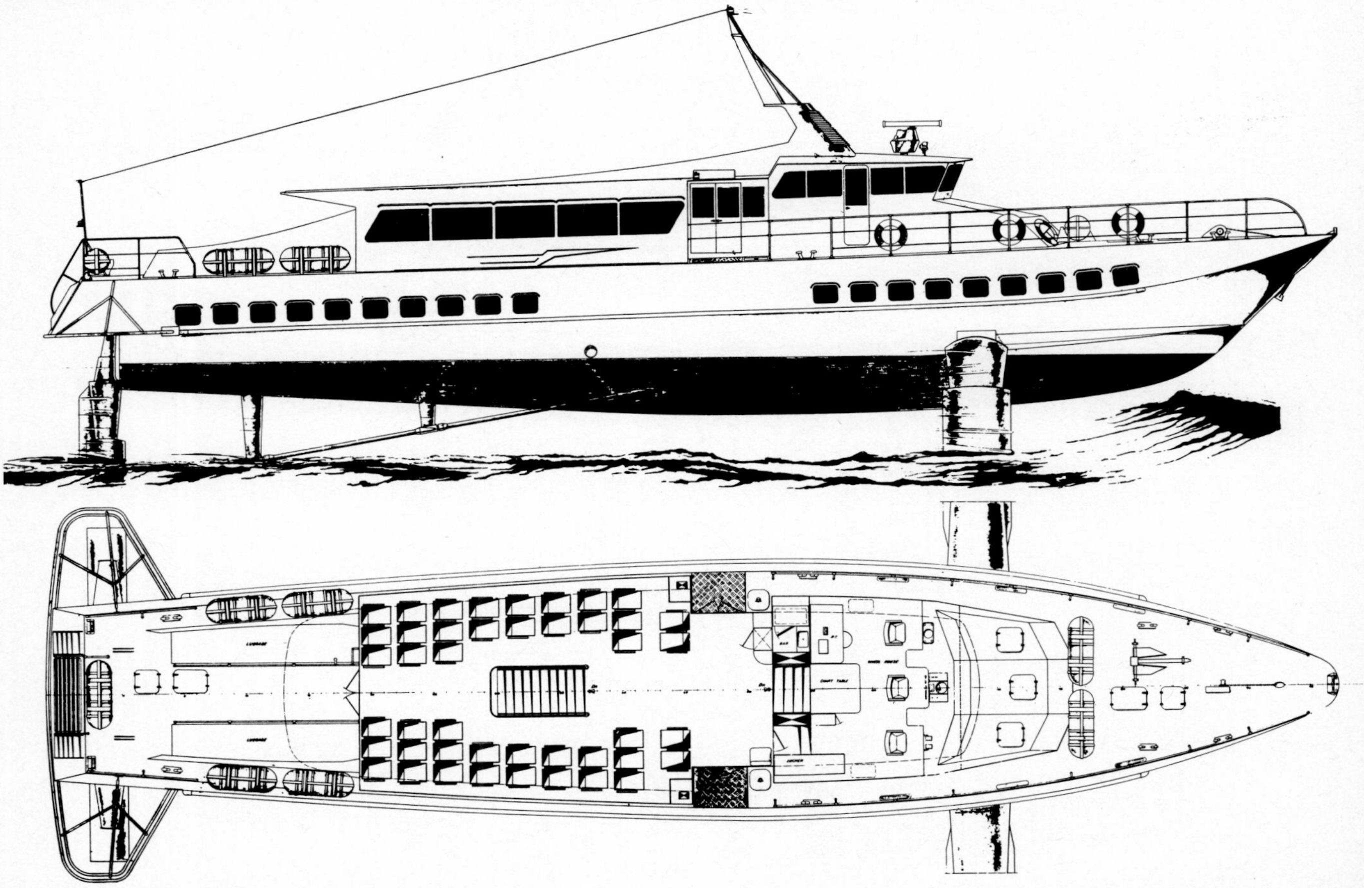
Outboard profile and upper deck plan of the RHS 160

HYDRAULICS: Steering is accomplished hydraulically from the wheelhouse. Plant comprises a Bosch pump installed on the main engines and conveying oil from a 45 litre (10 gallon) tank under pressure to the control cylinders of the rudder and anchor windlass, whilst a second hydraulic pump, which is also installed on the main engines, conveys oil under pressure to the flap control cylinders.

FIREFIGHTING: Fixed CO_2 plant of four CO_2 bottles of about 20kg each for the engine room and fuel tank space; portable extinguishers in various parts of the craft. Water intake connected to fire pump for fire connection in emergency.

DIMENSIONS

Length overall: 30·95m (101ft 6in)
Width across foils: 12·6m (41ft 4in)
Draft hullborne: 3·7m (12ft 6in)
Draft foilborne: 1·35m (4ft 6in)

WEIGHTS

Displacement, fully loaded: 85 tons
Payload, passengers and luggage: 13·5 tons

PERFORMANCE

Speed, max: 39 knots
Speed, cruising: 36 knots
Cruising, range: 483km (300 miles)

RHS 200

Construction of this 115-ton, 200–262 seat fast ferry began in 1978. Power will be provided by two supercharged MTU MB 16V TB 71 4-stroke diesel engines. The designed cruising speed is 37·5 knots.

FOILS: Surface-piercing V foils of hollow welded construction. Hydraulically-operated flaps are fitted to the trailing edge of the bow foil to balance out longitudinal load shifting, assist take-off and adjust the flying height. The craft can also be equipped with the Hamilton Standard electronic stability augmentation system, which employs sensors and servomechanisms to automatically position flaps on the bow and stern foils for the damping of heave, pitch and roll motions in heavy seas.

HULL: V-bottom hull of high tensile riveted light metal alloy construction, employing Peraluman plates and Anticorrodal frames. The rake of the stem is in galvanised steel.

ACCOMMODATION: Seats can be provided for up to 262 passengers, according to the route served. There are three main passenger saloons and a bar. The standard seating arrangement

The Navaltecnica RHS 160, an 85-ton passenger ferry with seats for 160-180 passengers and a cruising speed of 36 knots.

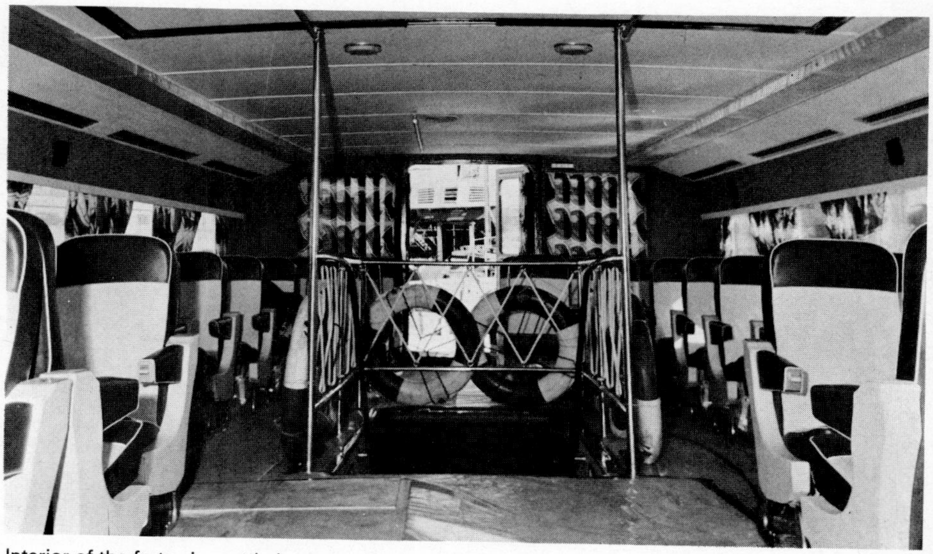

Interior of the forty-six seat belvedere cabin on the RHS 160

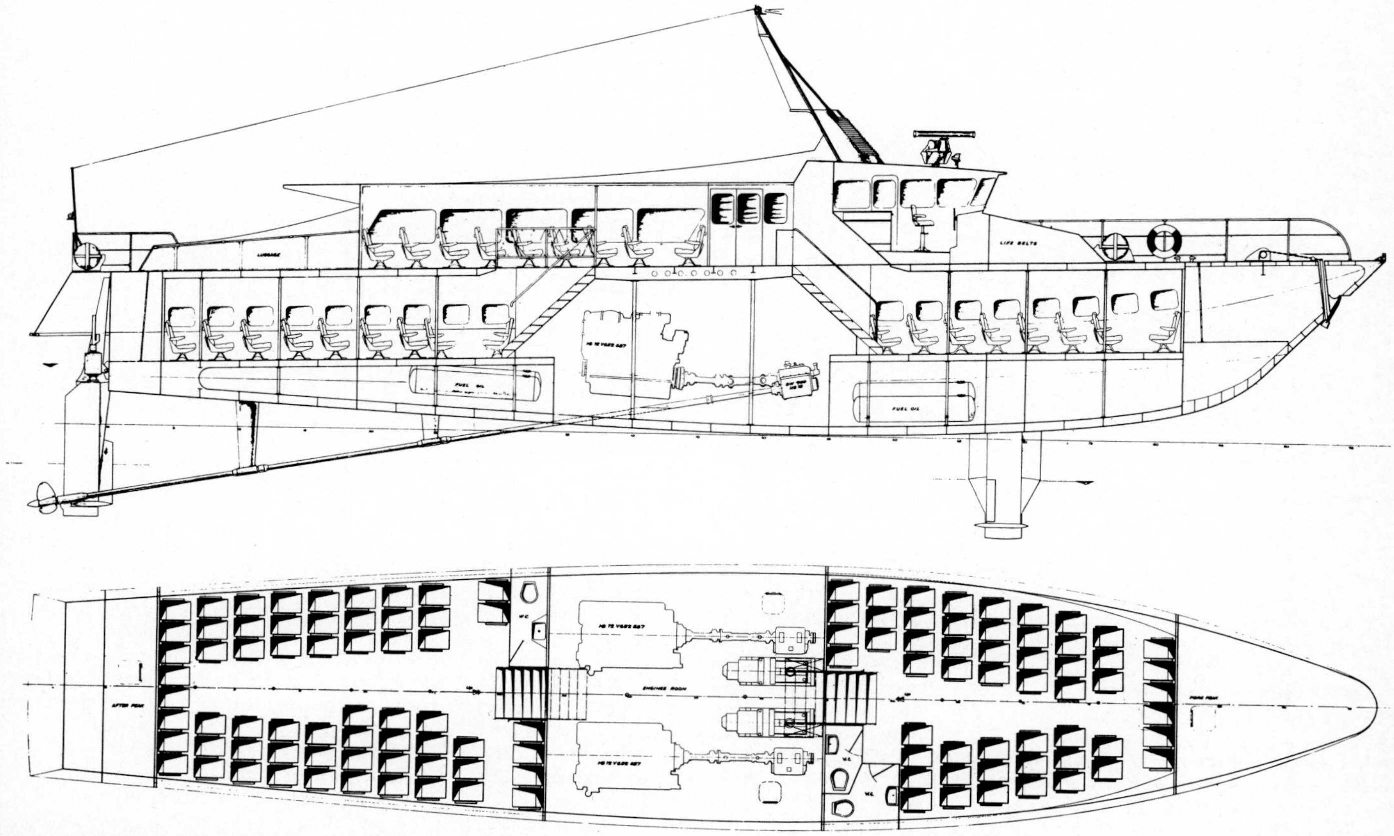

Inboard profile and lower deck plan of the RHS 160

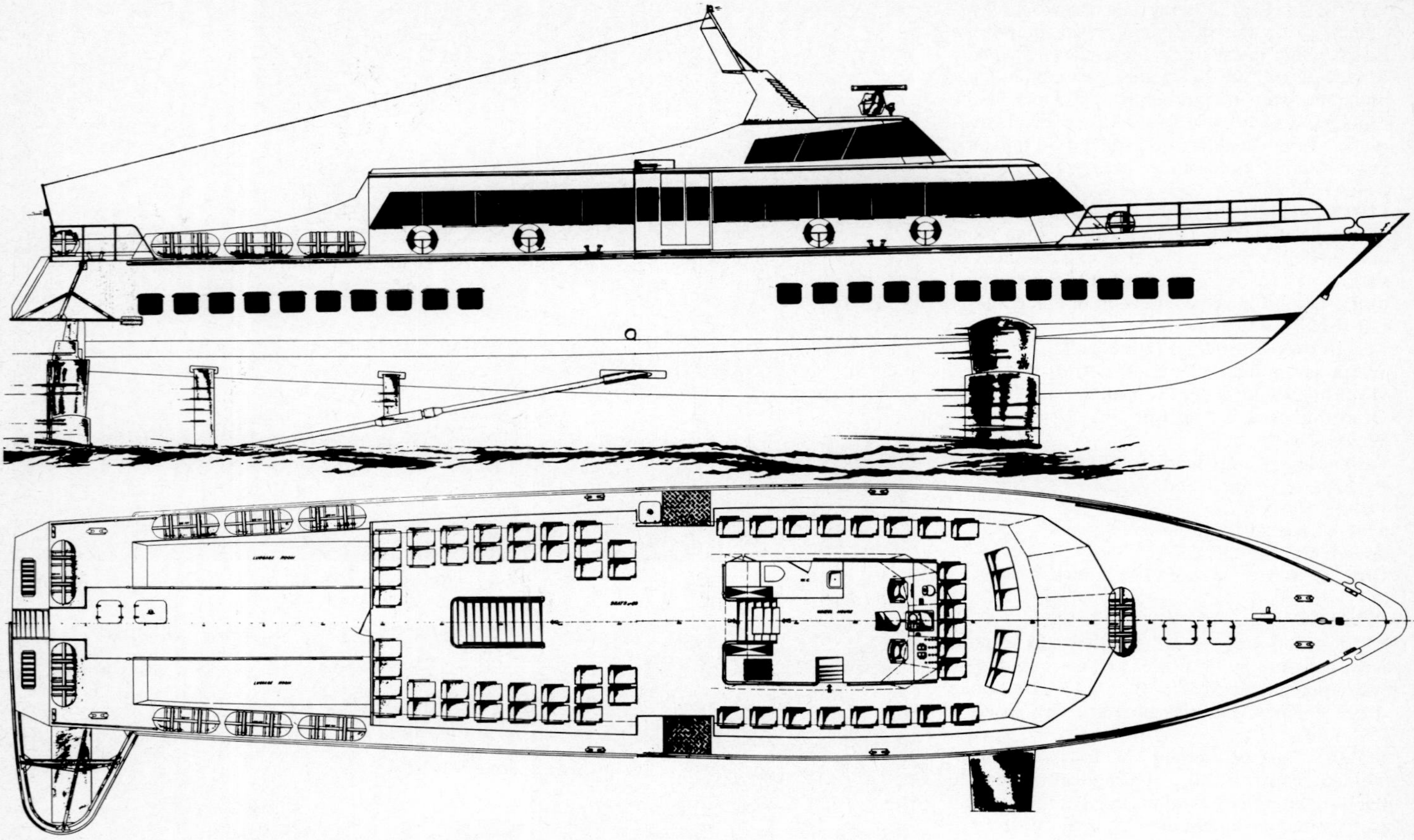

Outboard profile and main deck arrangement of the RHS 200, 115-ton hydrofoil ferry

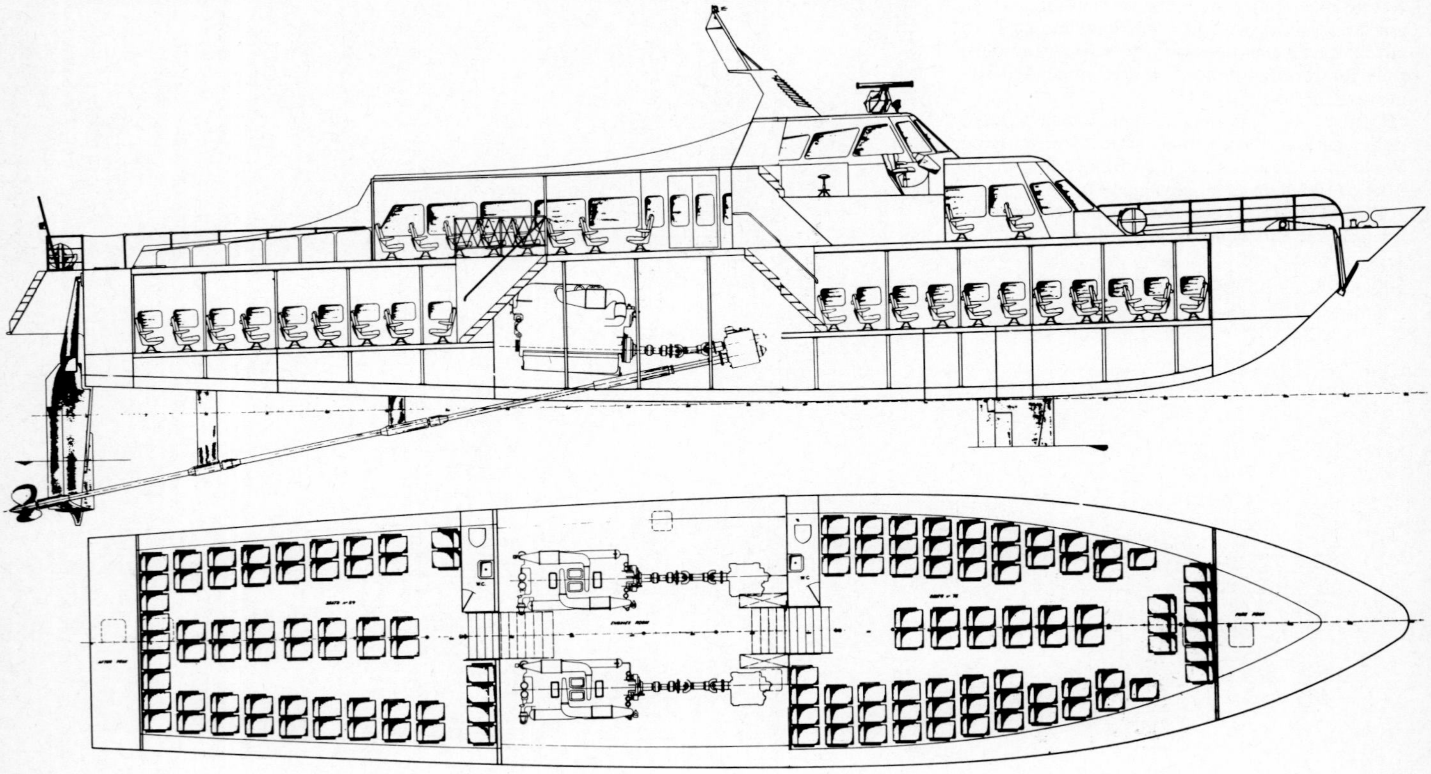

Inboard profile and lower deck arrangement of the RHS 200

allows for 60 in the main deck saloon, 75 in the aft lower saloon and 51 in the bow passenger saloon. Seating is normally four abreast in two lines with a central aisle. The bar, at the forward end of the wheelhouse belvedere superstructure, has either an 8-place sofa or 19 seats.

The wheelhouse, which is raised to provide a 360 degree view, is reached from the main deck belvedere saloon by a short companionway. Controls and instrumentation are attached to a panel on the forward bulkhead which extends the width of the wheelhouse. In the centre is the steering control and gyro-compass, on the starboard side are controls for the two engines, gearboxes and controllable-pitch propellers, and on the port side is the radar. Seats are provided for the captain, chief engineer and first mate. At the aft of the wheelhouse is a radio-telephone and a chart table.

POWER PLANT: Motive power is supplied by two supercharged MTU MB 16V 652 TB 71 4-stroke diesel engines, each with a maximum output of 2,415hp at 1,485rpm under normal operating conditions. Engine output is transferred to two supercavitating, controllable-pitch propellers.

SYSTEMS, ELECTRICAL: Two generating sets. One 220V, three-phase ac, for all consumer services, the second for charging 24V battery sets and operating fire-fighting and hydraulic pumps. Power distribution panel in wheelhouse for navigation light circuits, cabin lighting, radar, RDF, gyro compass and emergency circuits.

FIREFIGHTING: Fixed CO_2 self-contained automatic systems for power plant and fuel tank spaces, plus portable extinguishers for cabins and holds.

DIMENSIONS

Length overall: 35·5m (116ft 5⅝in)
Width across foils: 14·2m (46ft 6⅞in)
Draft hullborne: 4·32m (14ft 2⅛in)
Draft foilborne: 1·62m (5ft 3¾in)

WEIGHTS
Displacement fully loaded: 115 tons
PERFORMANCE
Cruising speed: 37·5 knots
Max speed: 41 knots
Cruising range: 275n miles

RHS ALIYACHT

A luxury hydrofoil yacht of light alloy construction, the RHS Aliyacht is derived from the RHS 110 passenger ferry. It is powered by two 1,350hp MTU MB 12V493 Ty 71 diesel engines and has a cruising speed of 38 knots.

The craft is equipped with the Hamilton Standard electronic stability augmentation system, which is designed to provide a smoother ride in heavy seas. The system uses sensors and servo-mechanisms to position foil flaps automatically for the maximum damping of heave, pitch and roll motions.

FOILS: Bow and rear foils are of surface-piercing type, and constructed in partly hollow welded steel. Two hydraulically-operated flaps, attached to the trailing edges of the bow foil, are adjusted automatically by the stabilisation system for the damping of heave, pitch and roll motions. The rear foil is rigidly attached to the transom, its incidence angle being determined during tests.

HULL: The V-bottom hull is of high-tensile riveted light metal alloy construction, using Peraluman (aluminium and magnesium alloy) plates and Anticorrodal (aluminium, magnesium and silicon alloy) profiles. The rake of the stem is in 3·5mm (0·137in) thick galvanised steel. The superstructure is constructed in 2mm (0·078in) Peraluman plate, and the roof is detachable to facilitate the removal and replacement of the main engines.

ACCOMMODATION: Main deck accommodation comprises the wheelhouse and radio cabin, a comfortably furnished saloon and a galley. The saloon can be fitted with two four-seat sofas, armchairs, tea-table, a metal table with four chairs, and a bar. Below deck, from aft peak forward, is a large cabin for the owner, with its own bathroom and small private drawing room; two double cabins for guests with adjacent WC/washbasin/shower units, and beyond the engines, a cabin for the captain and engineer, and two single cabins for guests.

The wheelhouse is reached via a companion-way from the saloon and is connected by a door with the upper deck. The pilot's position, controls and instruments are on the port side, together with the radar screen.

POWER PLANT: Power is supplied by two supercharged 12-cylinder MTU MB 12V 439 Ty 71 diesels, each rated at 1,350hp at 1,500rpm. Engine output is transferred to two three-bladed bronze-aluminium propellers through Zahnrad-fabrik BW 800 H20 gearboxes.

SYSTEMS, ELECTRICAL: Two 10kW, 220V, three-phase ONAN generating sets, coupled to batteries, provide 24V dc for engine starting, instruments, lighting, radio, etc.

DIMENSIONS
EXTERNAL
Length overall: 24·5m (78ft 9in)
Beam overall: 6·1m (20ft)
Hull beam: 5·85m (19ft 2¼in)
Draft hullborne: 2·95m (9ft 8⅛in)
Draft foilborne: 1·25m (4ft 1¼in)
WEIGHTS
Displacement, loaded: 52 tons
PERFORMANCE
Max speed: 41 knots
Cruising speed: 38 knots
Range: 644km (400 miles)

RHS HYDROILS

These are derivatives of RHS passenger-carrying hydrofoils, and are designed to ferry personnel, materials and equipment between offshore oil rigs and shore bases. Vessels in the series feature an open cargo deck aft of the bridge superstructure instead of an aft passenger saloon. The three main types are the RHS 70, the RHS 140, and the RHS 160 Hydroil.

RHS 70 HYDROIL

The first of the new series of RHS 70 Hydroil offshore drilling platform supply vessels has been built for ENI Oil Corporation, which is employing the craft in the Adriatic. A mixed passenger/cargo version of the RHS 70 passenger ferry, this variant has an open cargo deck aft of the bridge superstructure in place of the Caribe's main passenger cabin. Dimensions of the cargo deck are: length 7·5m (24ft 7in); width 3·5m (11ft 6in) and height 1·05m (3ft 5in).

FOILS: Bow and rear foils are of surface-piercing V configuration, with about 66% of the weight supported by the bow foil and 34% by the rear foil. Each foil, together with its struts and horizontal supporting tube, forms a rigid framework which facilitates the exchange of the foil structure. The foils are of hollow-ribbed construction and fabricated from medium Asera steel. The forward foil can be tilted within narrow limits by means of a hydraulic ram acting on the foil strut supporting tube. The angle of attack can therefore be adjusted during operation to assist take-off and counteract the effect of large variations in loading.

HULL: The hull is of riveted light metal alloy (Peraluman) and framed on a combination of longitudinal and transverse formers. Watertight compartments are provided in the bow and stern, and a double-bottom runs from immediately aft of the engine room, beneath the full length of the cargo deck, to the after peak. Contained within the double-bottom are six cylindrical aluminium fuel tanks with a total capacity of 2,250 litres (495 gallons). Access to the fore and aft compartments is via removable deck hatches. The deck is of 5mm (0·196in) Peraluman, suitably reinforced to withstand heavily concentrated loads. Two 125mm (4·9in) diameter scuppers are provided aft for rapid drainage. Heavy rubber fenders are provided at the bow and stern.

ACCOMMODATION: The craft has a crew of two, and seats up to 12 passengers in a comfortably appointed saloon, immediately aft of the wheelhouse. Passengers have a choice of six

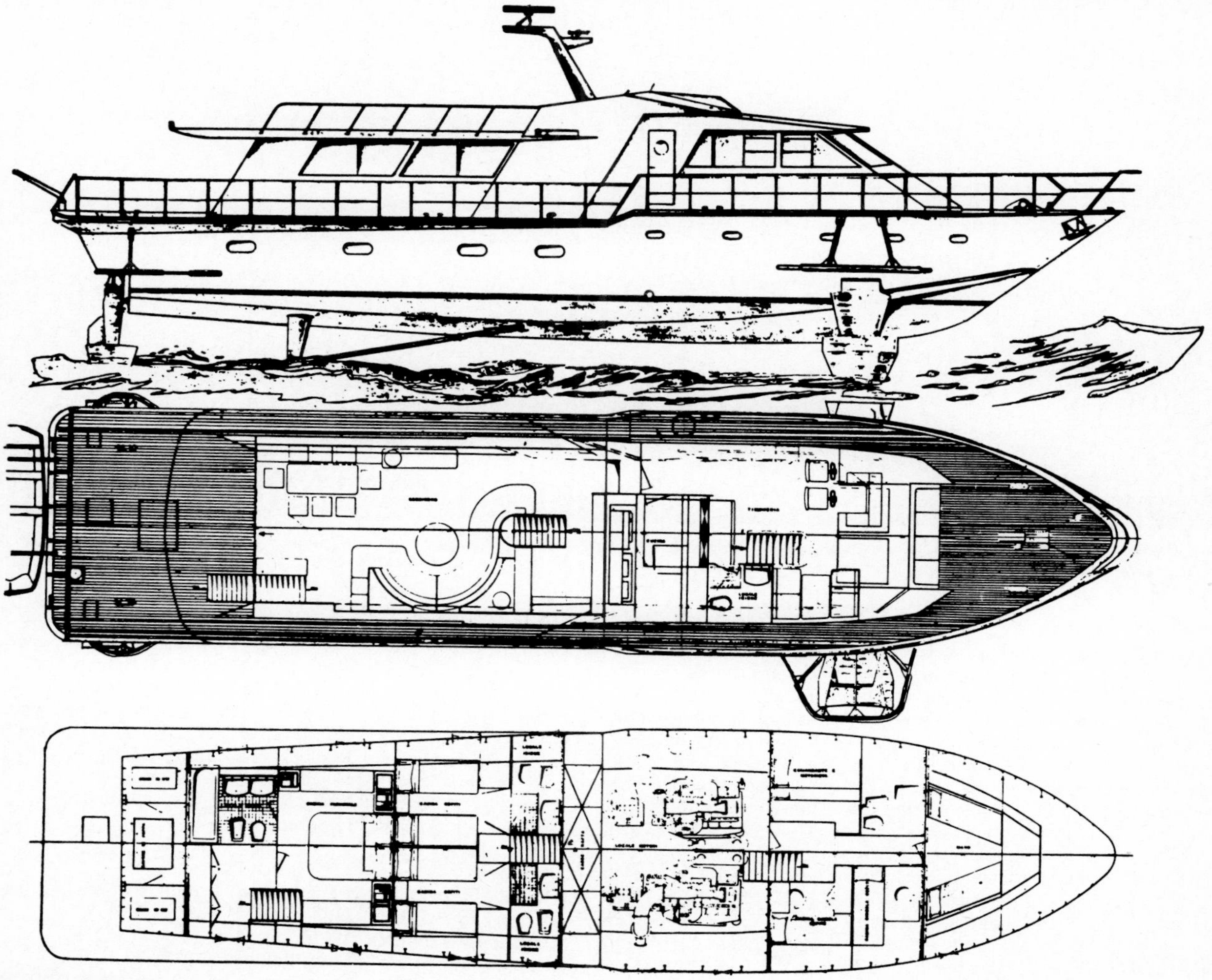

The Rodriquez RHS Aliyacht

The Rodriquez RHS Aliyacht, powered by two MTU diesels each rated at 1,350hp. Cruising speed is 38 knots and the range 400 miles

Porto Corsini, first of the RHS 70 Hydroil 33-ton off-shore drilling platform supply vessels. The craft has been built for ENI, the Italian oil company and is seen operating from one of the company's drilling platforms. Loads of up to 3 tons can be carried on the open cargo deck aft of the bridge structure. Cruising speed with normal payload is 32 knots

armchairs and two, three-place settees, one of which converts into a bed for transporting sick or injured personnel. All seats are equipped with safety belts. Aft of the saloon is a fully equipped galley, with refrigerator, a gas cooker with two gas rings, cupboards, plate rack and sink unit. Two folding wooden tables permit up to eight passengers to take meals at one sitting. A toilet/washbasin unit is provided opposite the galley on the port side. The engine room, wheelhouse and passenger saloon are fully heated and ventilated. A full range of safety equipment is carried including inflatable rafts and lifebelts for each passenger and crew member.

POWER PLANT: Power is supplied by a 12-cylinder supercharged MTU 12V493 Ty 71 with a maximum output of 1,350hp at 1,500rpm. Engine output is transferred to a three-bladed 700mm (27·5in) bronze-aluminium propeller through a Zahnradfabrik BW 800 H20 gearbox. The propeller shaft is 90mm (3·5in) in diameter, and supported at three points by seawater lubricated rubber bearings. In an emergency, hullborne propulsion is provided by a 105hp Mercedes OM 352 diesel with a Mercruiser Z-drive. The engine is installed in the aft peak and propels the craft at about 5 knots.

SYSTEMS, ELECTRICAL: 220V 50Hz three-phase ac, 24V dc; provision for 220V 50Hz three-phase shore supply. The dc supply is from a 24V generator driven by the main engine and feeding a 235Ah battery. AC supply is derived from a four-stroke Onan diesel generator set, located in the engine room.

HYDRAULICS: One Bosch Hy/ZFR 1/16 AR 101 for steering and bow foil incidence control.

COMMUNICATIONS AND NAVIGATION: Radio: VHF radio-telephone to customers' requirements.

Radar: Decca, Raytheon etc, to customers' requirements.

DIMENSIONS

Length overall, hull: 20·95m (68ft 9in)
Hull beam: 5·06m (16ft 7in)
Width over foils: 7·4m (24ft 3in)
Draft hullborne: 2·7m (8ft 10in)
Draft foilborne: 1·14m (3ft 9in)

WEIGHTS
Max take-off displacement: 33·12 tons
Max load on open cargo-deck: 3 tons
PERFORMANCE (with normal payload)
Cruising speed: 32 knots
Range: 480km (300 miles)

RHS 140 HYDROIL

The second in the Navaltecnica Hydroil range is a mixed passenger/cargo version of the 65-ton RHS 140. As with the smaller RHS 70 Hydroil, the main passenger saloon is replaced by a large open cargo deck for loads up to 6 tons. The deck is 9·5m (31ft 2in) long, 4·8m (15ft 9in) wide and 1·19m (3ft 11in) high.

The craft will carry a crew of two and up to 14 passengers. Two variants are available, one equipped with seats for 23 passengers and with a cargo capacity of 5 tons and the other with seats for 60 passengers and a cargo capacity of 3 tons. Power will be supplied by two 12-cylinder supercharged MTU 12V493 Ty 71 engines, each with a maximum output of 1,350hp.

DIMENSIONS
Length overall, hull: 28·5m (93ft 6in)
Hull beam: 6·1m (20ft)
Width over foils: 10·72m (35ft 2in)
Draft hullborne: 3·5m (11ft 6in)
Draft foilborne: 1·5m (4ft 11in)
WEIGHTS
Normal take-off displacement: 64 tons
PERFORMANCE
Cruising speed: 32-34 knots
Range at cruising speed: 480km (300 miles)

RHS 160 HYDROIL

Latest addition to Navaltecnica's range of offshore oil rig support vessels, the RHS 160 features an open cargo deck aft of the bridge superstructure and additional fuel and water tanks in the place of the lower aft passenger saloons. The vessel carries a crew of 5 and 42 passengers, plus 10 tons of cargo, at a cruising speed of 35 knots.

FOILS: Surface-piercing W foils of hollow welded steel construction. Craft in this series feature bow and aft rudders, both of which operate simultaneously. Hydraulically-operated flaps, attached to the trailing edges of the bow and rear foils are adjusted automatically by a Hamilton Standard electronic stability augmentation system, for the damping of heave, pitch and roll motions in heavy seas.

HULL: V-bottom hull of high tensile riveted light metal alloy construction. In the manufacture of the hull, plates of aluminium and magnesium alloy of 4·4% are used, whilst angle bars are of a high resistant aluminium, magnesium and silicon alloy. Inert gas welding (Argon) is used for strengthening beams, web frames, keelsons and stringers. Steel and rubber fenders are fitted aft and in the sides of the main deck to protect the foils from damage when docking.

ACCOMMODATION: Passengers are accommodated in a forward saloon, seating 37, and the upper belvedere saloon, seating 5. The seats, designed for maximum comfort, have arms and each is provided with an ash tray and magazine holder. The toilet, finished in Formica or similar laminate, is provided with a w/c basin and normal accessories.

Crew members are accommodated in two cabins forward, that on the starboard being provided with two berths and a locker, while the port cabin has three berths and lockers. The wheelhouse is located well forward and has seats for the master in the centre, chief engineer on the starboard side and radar operator on the port side. All steering and other controls are located in the wheelhouse, including a circuit control panel for the navigation lights, craft lighting, radar, gyro-compass and various other electrical consumer and emergency circuits.

POWER PLANT: Power is provided by two supercharged MTU MB 12V TB 71 4-stroke diesel engines, each with a maximum output of 1,950hp at 1,460rpm. Engine starting is accomplished by compressed air starters. Output is transmitted to two three-bladed bronze propellers through two Zahnradfabrik 900 HS 15 gearboxes.

SYSTEMS, ELECTRICAL: Two 35kVA gen-

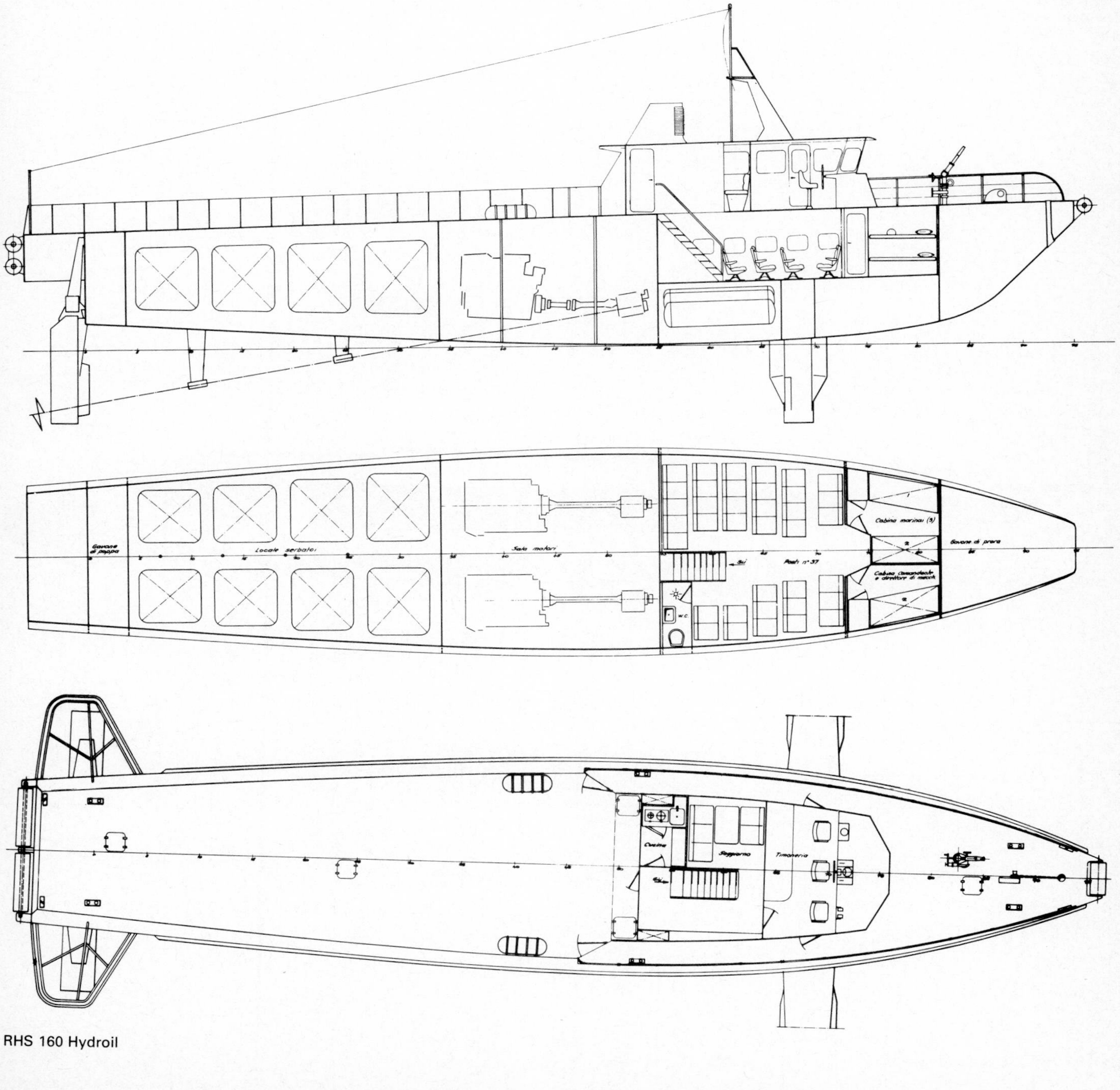

RHS 160 Hydroil

erating sets, 220V, 50Hz, three-phase for ventilation and air-conditioning; 220V, 50Hz, single-phase, for lighting and other appliances; 24V dc for auxiliary lighting, engine starting and servocontrol.

HYDRAULICS: Steering is accomplished hydraulically from the wheelhouse. Plant comprises a Bosch pump installed on one of the main engines and conveying oil under pressure from a 45 litre (10 gallon) tank to the control cylinders of the rudder and anchor windlass, whilst a second hydraulic pump, which is installed on the other main engine, conveys oil under pressure to the flap control cylinders.

The two systems are interchangeable and equipped with safety valves, manometers and micronic filters.

FIREFIGHTING: Fixed CO_2 plant for engine room and fuel tank space; portable appliances include two 6kg powder extinguishers and one 5kg CO_2 extinguisher in the engine room; two 10 litre water extinguishers in the passenger saloons and one 6kg powder extinguisher in the wheelhouse.

Two water extinguishing systems are provided, one driven by the main engine and the other by a motor driven pump. The system can supply a monitor on the upper deck at the bow and two fire hose water outlets located amidships on the upper deck. A dual-purpose water/foam nozzle can be supplied on request.

DIMENSIONS

Length overall: 31·3m (103ft)

Moulded beam: 6·2m (20ft $4\frac{1}{8}$in)

Width across foils: 12·6m (41ft 4in)

Draft hullborne: 3·7m (12ft 6in)

Draft foilborne: 1·35m (4ft 6in)

WEIGHTS

Displacement, fully loaded: 85 tons

PERFORMANCE

Cruising speed: 35 knots

Cruising range: 322km (200 miles)

M-RHS 150 SEARCH AND RESCUE CRAFT

This new variant of the well-known RHS 140 is a multi-purpose rescue craft equipped for a full range of S & R duties, including fire-fighting and wreck marking. It has a top speed of 36 knots and can operate in heavy seas at a considerable distance from its shore base. A Merryweather dual-purpose water/foam monitor is located on the foredeck and an 8·5m daughter boat is carried on the upper deck aft.

A sick bay is provided and can be fitted out to accommodate 30 to 40 survivors.

A feature of the design is the filling of the double bottom with expanded polystyrene to provide sufficient buoyancy to make it unsinkable, even with the watertight compartments flooded.

FOILS: Surface-piercing W foils of hollow welded steel construction. Foil lift is varied by flaps operated by an electronic/hydraulic system developed by Cantiere Navaltecnica in conjunction with Hamilton Standard. Under calm sea conditions, the flaps can be operated manually.

HULL: Riveted light metal alloy design framed on longitudinal and transverse formers. Areas of the attachment points of the bow and rear foils are reinforced with steel. Steel is also used for the rake of the stem, the stern tube for the propeller shaft and the propeller shaft attachment.

ACCOMMODATION: Berths, lockers and living accommodation provided for a crew of eleven, comprising the captain, two officers, two petty officers and six seamen. Seats are provided in the wheelhouse for an operating crew of three. A "flying bridge" with a duplicated set of instruments and controls, provides improved visibility during search operations. A ten-berth sick bay, complete with a small office for the doctor is provided aft. A large roof hatch is provided in the sick bay through which stretcher casualties can be lowered. If required, the sick bay can be fitted out to accommodate 30–40 survivors.

POWER PLANT: Power is provided by two MTU 12V 331 TC 82 12-cylinder supercharged diesel engines, each developing 1,430hp at 2,340rpm. Engine output is transmitted to two three-bladed, 700mm diameter bronze propellers through Zahnradfabrik gearboxes.

SYSTEMS, ELECTRICAL: Two engine-driven generators of 24V dc supply essential services and emergency lights. An ac system, powered by a generator set, supplies lighting and all other on board consumers. Two battery sets are provided for starting the main engines and generators.

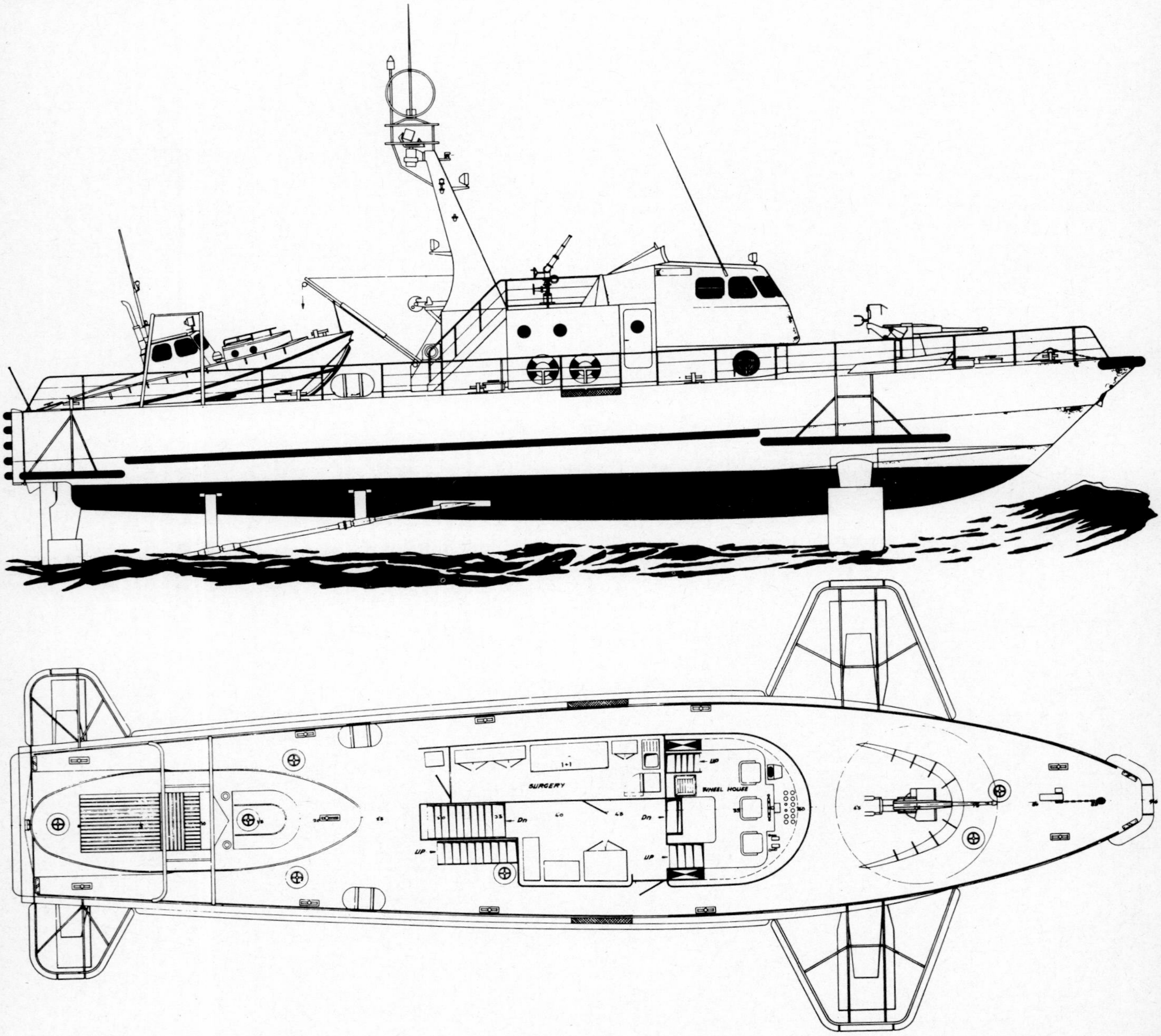

M-RHS 150 Search and Rescue craft

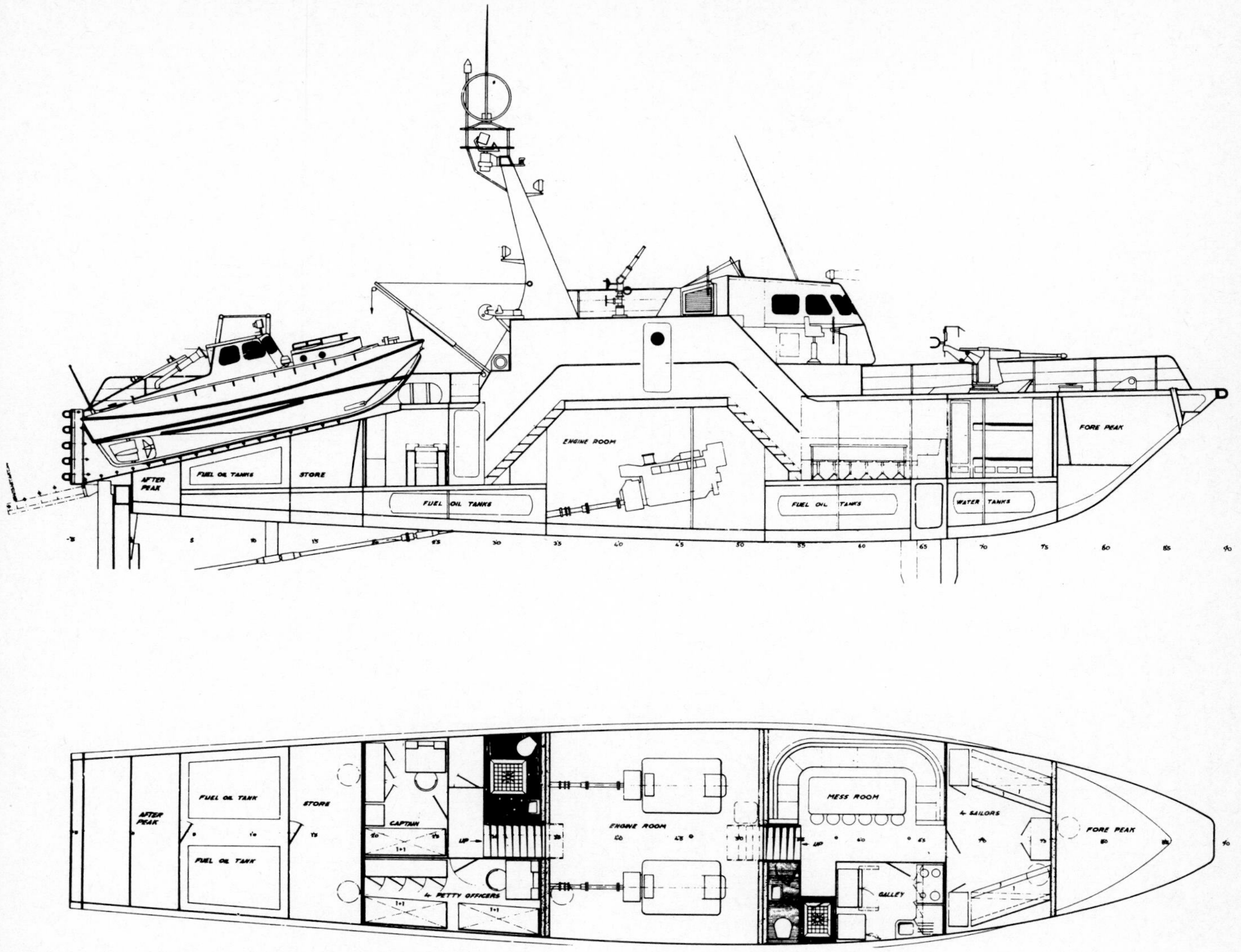

Inboard profile and deck plan of the M-RHS 150 Search and Rescue craft

HYDRAULICS: Steering and variation of foil flap incidence is accomplished hydraulically from the wheelhouse. Plant comprises two Bosch pumps installed on the main engines and conveying oil from a tank under pressure to the control cylinders of the rudder and foil flaps.
AIR CONDITIONING: Provided on request.
FIREFIGHTING: Fixed CO_2 plant for the engine room and fuel oil bays; portable CO_2 and foam fire extinguishers at various parts of the craft. One Merryweather dual purpose foam/water monitor.
DIMENSIONS
Length overall: 28·7m (94ft 1½in)
Width across foils: 10·9m (35ft 9in)
Draft hullborne: 3·15m (10ft 4in)
Draft foilborne: 1·2m (3ft 11in)
WEIGHTS
Displacement, fully loaded: 65 tonnes (64 tons)
PERFORMANCE
Max speed: 36 knots
Cruising speed: 32·5 knots
Endurance at cruising speed: 18 hours, 600 miles
Endurance at low speed: 50 hours, 600 miles
Cruising range: 1,110km (600 miles)

M-RHS 150 PATROL CRAFT

The patrol variant of the M-RHS 150 is designed for fisheries law enforcement missions, patrolling and customs operations against ships offshore. It has a similar specification to the Search and Rescue variant but a fully loaded displacement of only 64 tonnes. Accommodation is provided for a crew of twelve, comprising the captain, three officers, four petty officers and four seamen.

M PATROL CRAFT

Derived from RHS passenger vessels, the M series craft are designed for coast guard and anti-contraband patrol. Suitably armed, they can undertake various naval duties, ranging from patrol to minelaying. The armament shown in the accompanying drawings can be augmented or substituted by sea-to-air and sea-to-sea missiles according to requirements.

M 100

The M 100 is similar in design and performance to the two PAT 20 patrol hydrofoils built by Rodriquez for the Philippine Navy.
FOILS: Bow and rear foils are surface piercing V configuration and identical to those of the standard RHS 70. About 59% of the total weight is borne by the bow foil and 41% by the rear foil. The foils are of hollow ribbed construction and made from medium Asera steel.

Total foil area is 10·4m² (112ft²). The angle of incidence of the forward foil can be varied during flight by means of a hydraulic ram acting on the foil strut supporting tube.
HULL: The hull is of riveted light alloy construction with Peraluman (aluminium and magnesium alloy) plates and Anticorrodal (aluminium, magnesium and silicon alloy) profiles.
ACCOMMODATION: The crew comprises a captain, two officers and eight NCOs and ratings. The pilot's position is on the left of the wheelhouse, with the principal instrumentation; and the radar operator sits on the right with the auxiliary instrumentation. The pilot is provided with an intercom system connecting him with the officers' cabin, engine room and crew cabin. The internal space has been divided as follows:
(a) the forward or bow room, subdivided into two cabins, one for the captain, the other for two officers, and including a w/c with washstand and a storeroom with a refrigerator.
(b) the stern room, with eight berths for the NCOs and ratings, a w/c with washstand and a galley equipped with a gas stove and an electric refrigerator.
(c) the deck room, aft of the wheelhouse, with tilting sofa and table for R/T equipment.
Air conditioning is installed in the captain's and officers' quarters.
POWER PLANT: Power is supplied by a supercharged 12-cylinder MTU 12V493 Ty 71 with a max continuous output of 1,350hp at 1,500rpm. Engine output is transferred to a three-bladed bronze aluminium propeller through a Zahnradfabrik BW 800/S reversible gear. Fuel (total capacity 2,800kg) is carried in ten cylindrical aluminium tanks located in the double bottom beneath the bow room and the stern room. Dynamic and reserve oil tanks in the engine room give a total oil capacity of 120kg. An auxiliary engine can be fitted in the stern for emergency operation.
ARMAMENT AND SEARCH EQUIPMENT: Single 12·7mm machine-gun mounted above well position in bow, and two searchlights or one 8cm Oerlikon 3Z8DLa rocket launcher.
SYSTEMS, ELECTRICAL: 220V, 10kW, diesel generator with batteries. Supplies instruments, radio and radar and external and internal lights, navigation lights and searchlights.
HYDRAULICS: 120kg/cm² pressure hydraulic system for steering and varying forward foil incidence angle.
APU: Onan engine for air conditioning when requested.
DIMENSIONS
Length overall, hull: 20·89m (68ft 6in)
Hull beam: 4·79m (15ft 8¾in)

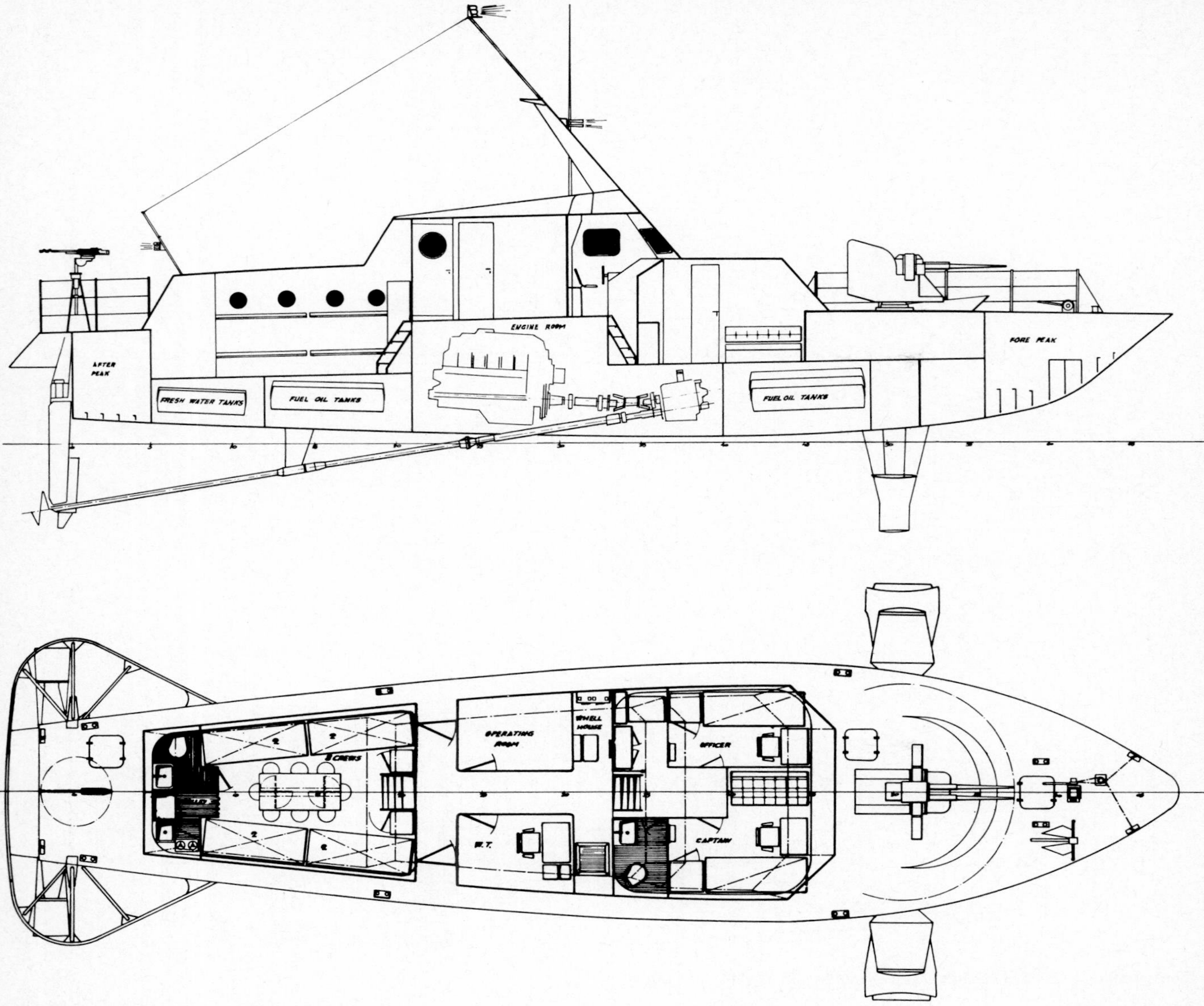

Inboard profile and deck plan of the M 100 fast patrol craft

Beam overall: 7·4m (24ft 4in)
Draft hullborne: 2·76m (9ft 1in)
Draft foilborne: 1·2m (4ft)
Height overall,
hullborne: 6·44m (21ft)
foilborne: 8m (26ft 3in)
WEIGHTS
Net tonnage: 28 tons
Light displacement: 26 tons
Max take-off displacement: 32·5 tons
Useful load: 7·6 tons
Max useful load: 8·1 tons
PERFORMANCE
Max speed foilborne: 38 knots
Max speed hullborne: 13 knots
Cruising speed foilborne: 34 knots
Cruising speed hullborne: 12 knots
Max permissible sea state, foilborne: Force 4
Designed range at cruising speed: 869km (540 miles)
Number of seconds and distance to take-off: 20 seconds, 100m (328ft)
Number of seconds and distance to stop craft: 12 seconds, 50m (164ft)
Fuel consumption at cruising speed: 145kg/h (320lb/h)
Fuel consumption at max speed: 180kg/h (397lb/h)

M 150

This is the fast patrol boat version of the RHS 110 passenger ferry. Modifications include a revised cabin superstructure with an upper bridge; the installation of 8 Sistel Sea Killer medium-range missiles and a 20mm Hispano-Suiza twin-mounting, and the provision of fuel tanks of additional capacity increasing the operating range to 347·96km (560 miles).
FOILS, HULL, POWERPLANT: Arrangements similar to those of the RHS 110.
ACCOMMODATION: Berths provided for eight officers and non-commissioned officers and eight ratings.
DIMENSIONS
Length overall: 25·4m (83ft 2in)
Beam overall: 8·4m (27ft 6¾in)
Height of hull structure: 2·85m (9ft 4in)
Draft foilborne: 1·25m (4ft 1in)
Draft hullborne, fully loaded: 3m (9ft 10in)
WEIGHTS
Displacement, empty: 36 tons
Displacement, loaded: 50 tons
PERFORMANCE
Max speed: 41 knots
Cruising speed: 38 knots
Cruising range: 896km (560 miles)

M 200

Derived from the RHS 140 passenger ferry this fast patrol variant can be armed with a 40mm Breda-Bofors twin naval mounting and one 8cm Oerlikon 2Z8DLa rocket launcher, and has a maximum speed of 37 knots. Above the wheelhouse is an open bridge with duplicate steering, engine controls and instrumentation.
WEIGHTS
Displacement loaded: 64 tons
Displacement empty: 50 tons
PERFORMANCE
Max speed foilborne: 37 knots
Cruising speed: 34 knots
Minimum foilborne speed: 23·3 knots
Range: 1,127km (736 miles)

M 300 AND 600 FAST STRIKE CRAFT

The 85-ton M 300 and 125-ton M 600 are two hydrofoil missilecraft designed to augment the existing range of Navaltecnica fast patrol boats.

Though differing in size, the two craft are almost identical in terms of overall design, construction and internal arrangements. Both are equipped with the SAS stability augmentation system, which stabilises the vessels in bad weather, and the Breda-Bofors twin 40mm/L 70 or similar rapid-fire cannon. In addition the M 300 will carry two Otomat or similar missile launchers and the M 600 will carry four.

Power for the M 300 is provided by two 1,950hp MTU 12V 652 TB 71 diesels, while the M 600 has two MTU 16V 652 TB 71 diesels each rated at 2,600hp. Maximum speed of both craft is in excess of 38 knots.

Dimensions, weights and performance figures are given at the end of the summary. The following characteristics apply to both designs.
FOILS: Surface-piercing W foils of hollow welded steel. Craft in this series have a bow rudder for improved manoeuvrability. The bow rudder works simultaneously with the aft rudders to provide fully co-ordinated turns. Hydraulically-operated flaps, attached to the trailing edges of the bow and rear foils are adjusted automatically by an SAS electronic stability augmentation system for the damping of heave, pitch and roll motions in heavy seas.
HULL AND SUPERSTRUCTURE: V-bottom hull of high tensile riveted light metal alloy construction. Argon gas welding employed on strengthened beams, web frames, keelsons and stringers. Basic hull structure is longitudinal; forepeak and after peak are transverse type struc-

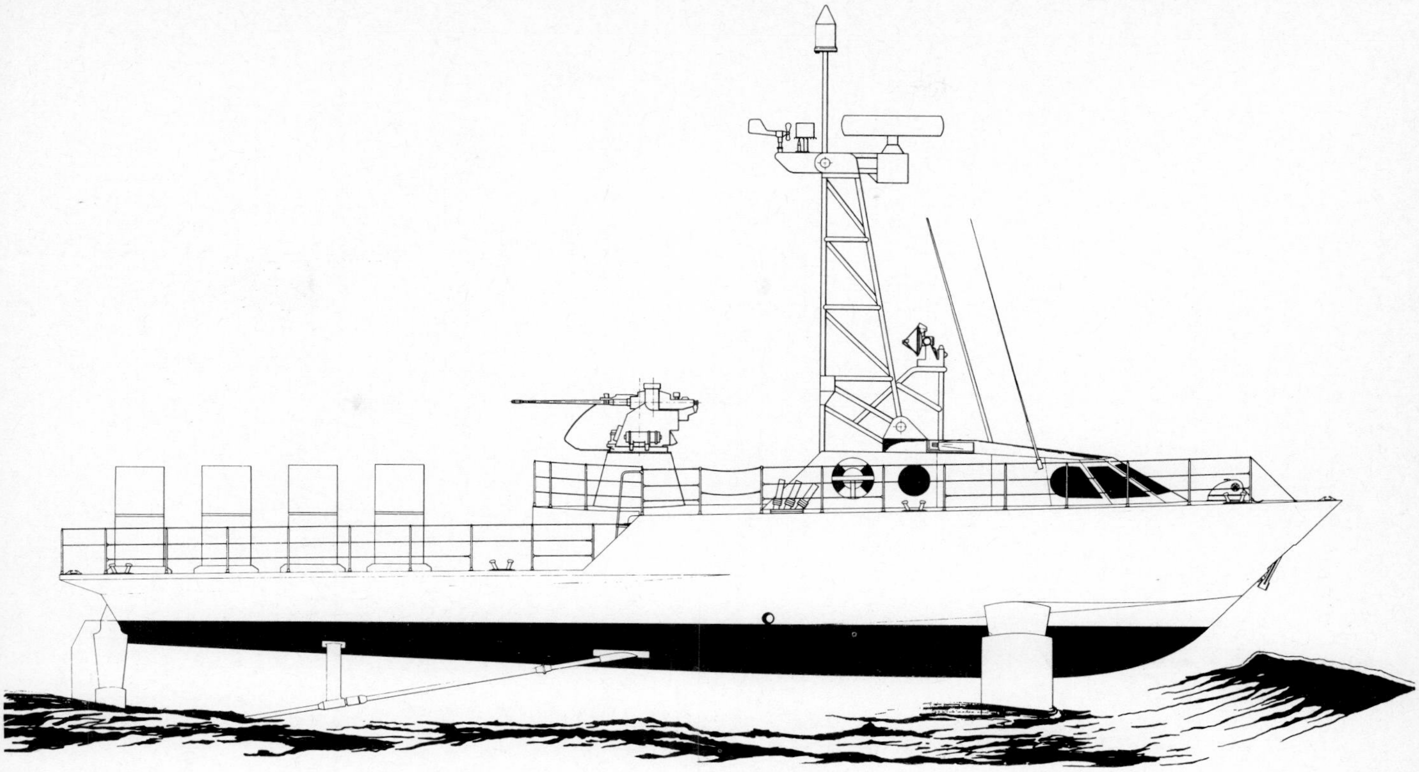

Outboard profile and deck views of the M 150, fast patrol variant of the RHS 110

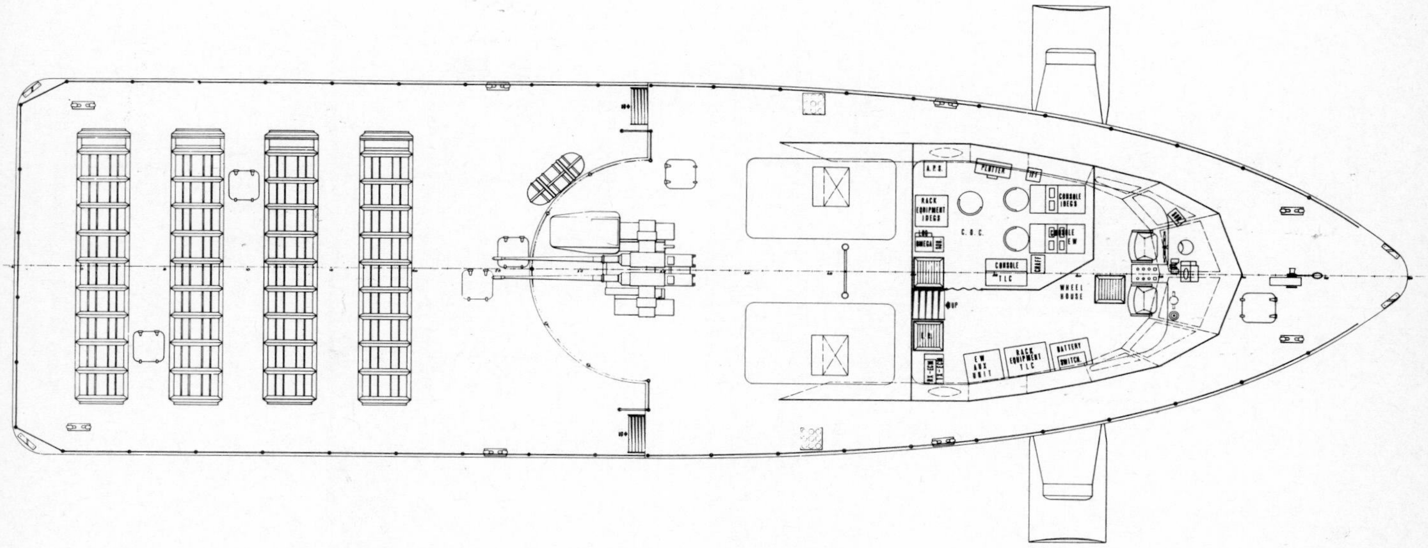

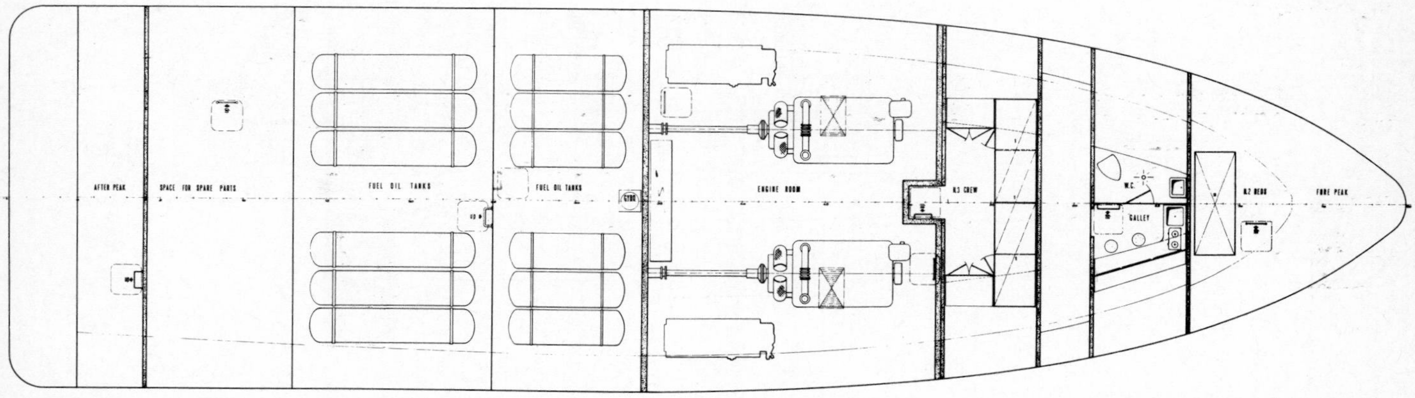

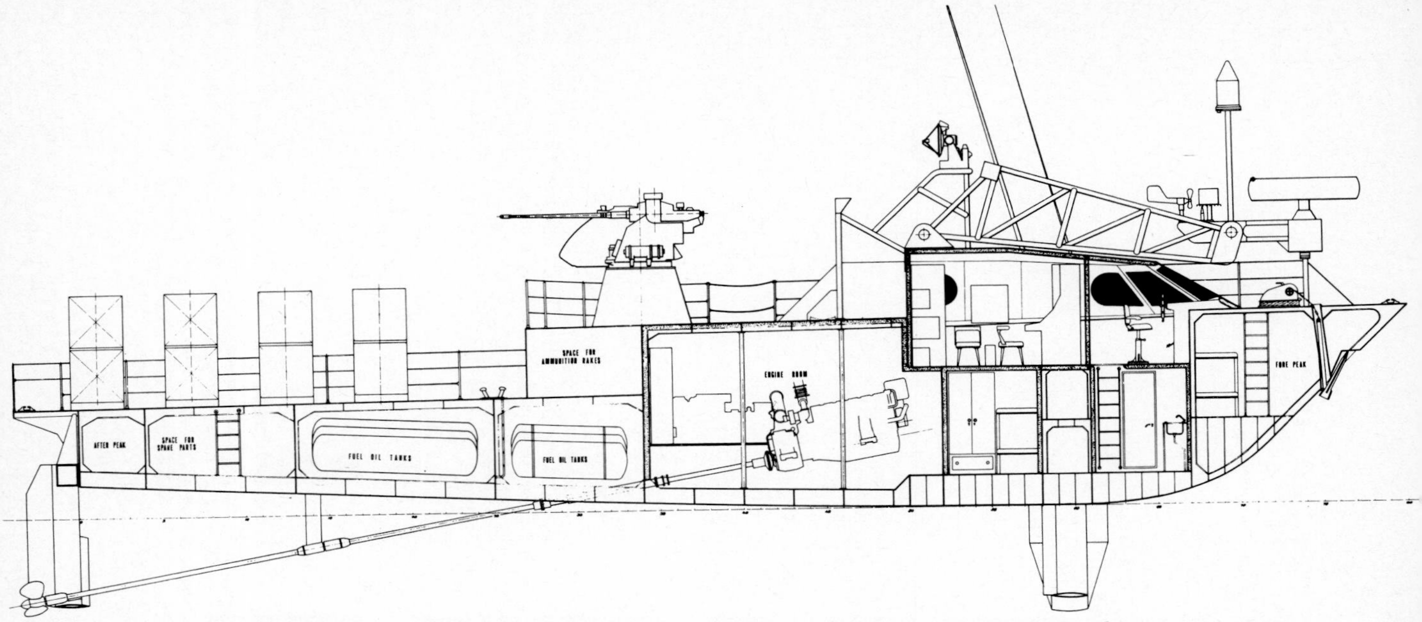

M 150, fast patrol boat variant of the RHS 110 passenger ferry

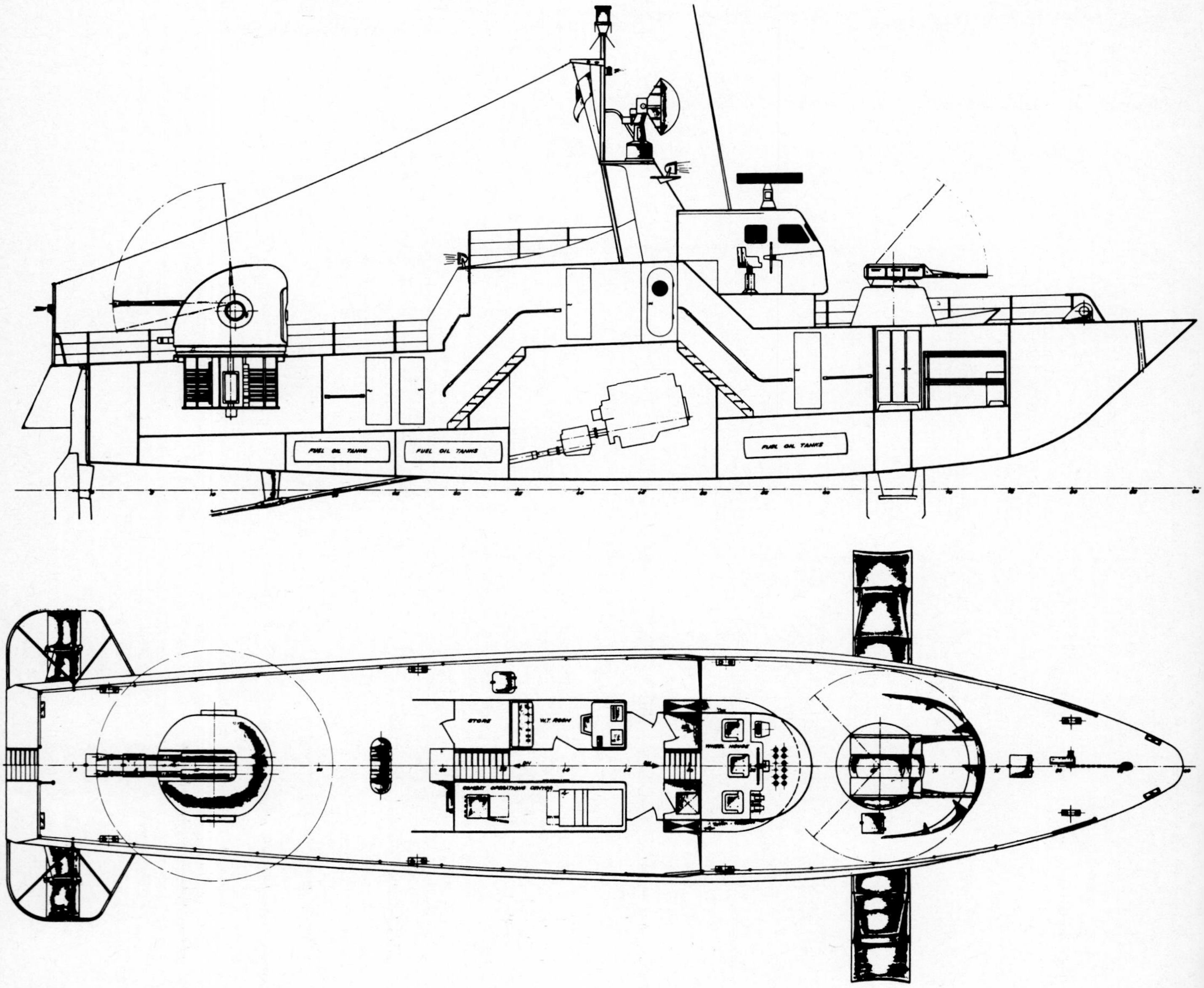

General arrangement of the M 200

tures. Steel is employed for the stern, fore and aft foil attachment points, propeller struts and foils. Cadmium plated rivets are used for jointing steel and light alloy components. Side plating ranges in thickness from 3·5–5mm; the upper deck varies from 3–4mm and plating on the stem and stern platforms is 2mm thick.

The superstructure is built on transverse frames with stanchions and beams every 300mm.

ACCOMMODATION: Berths, living and working accommodation and full w/c washroom facilities for total complement of 12, including commissioned and non-commissioned officers and ratings. The wheelhouse, all living spaces and fire control room are air-conditioned. Ventilation system provided for the engine room.

PROPULSION

M 300

Two MTU 12V 652 TB 71 4-stroke diesels, each delivering 1,950hp at 1,460rpm.

M 600

Two MTU 16V 652 TB 71 4-stroke diesels, each delivering 2,600hp at 1,460rpm.

On both designs engine output is transferred via a short intermediate shaft, universal joint and Zahnradfabrik 900 HS 15 gearboxes to two hollow, stainless steel propeller shafts operating two, three-bladed bronze-aluminium propellers. The drive shafts are supported by brackets and on the aft foils by rubber bearings lubricated by the water coolant system.

Stainless steel controllable-pitch propellers are available as an alternative to the fixed-pitch bronze-aluminium type.

FUEL OIL: Diesel fuel oil is carried in fibreglass-reinforced, welded aluminium tanks located in the double bottom. All tanks are connected to a service tank from which oil is delivered to the injection pumps. Each engine has two suction and two engine pumps. Before reaching the injection pumps, fuel is fed through two filters in parallel, with replaceable filter elements, and water drain cocks. Injection excess fuel is piped back to the service tank.

Tanks are refuelled through necks on the main deck, each equipped with air vents and fuel level calibrated in kilograms and gallons.

Mafius 150, fast patrol boat variant of the RHS 110 passenger ferry

SYSTEMS: Two systems are installed, each pressurised by a gear pump installed on one of the main engines. The first is used for the steering system and anchor winch, the second supplies the cylinder operating the lift control flaps and the bow rudder. The two systems are interchangeable and equipped with safety valves, manometers and micronic filters. Hydraulic pressure is also used for operating the weapons systems.

DRAINAGE AND FIRE CONTROL: Bilge pumps, operated by the main engines, can empty

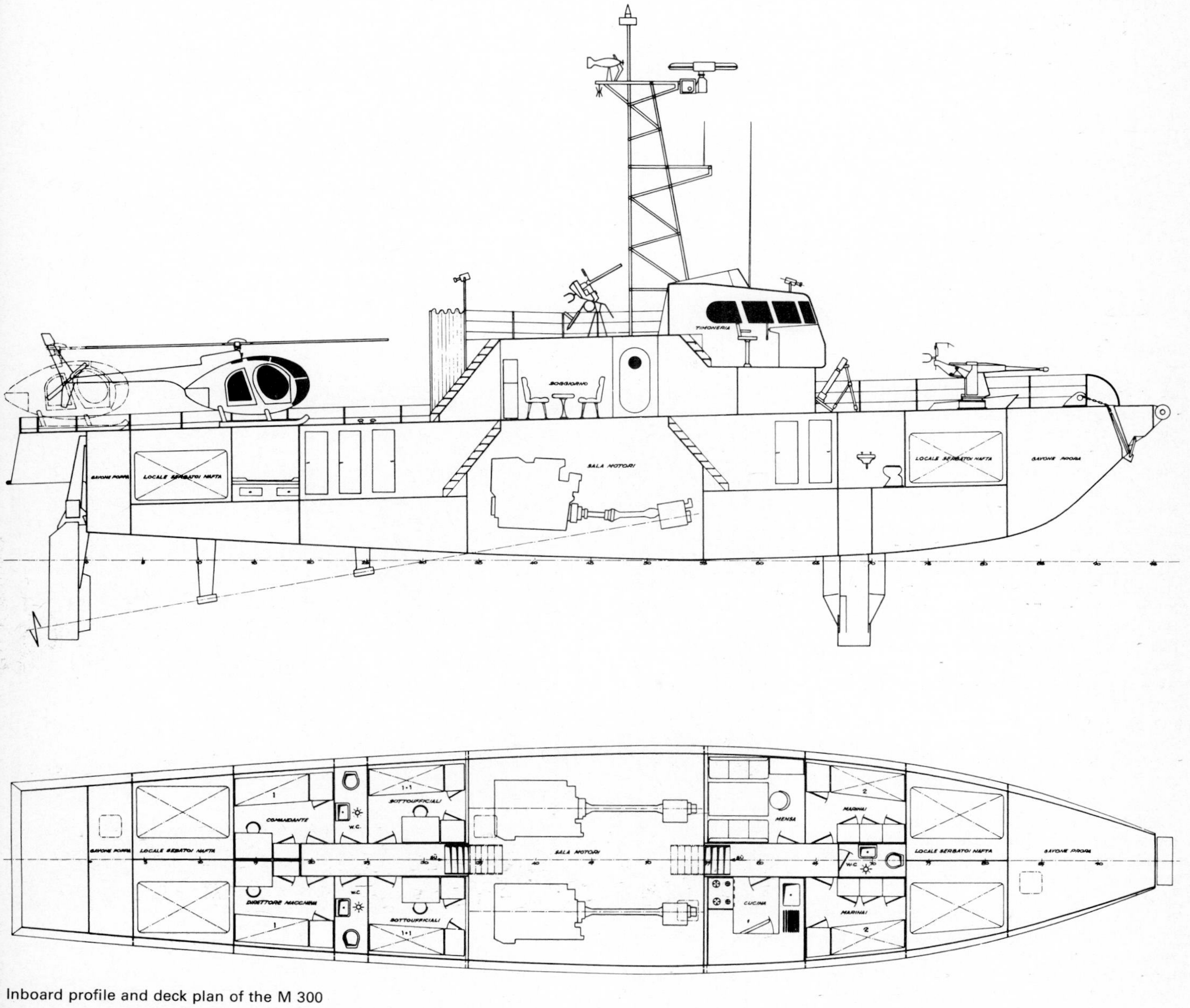

Inboard profile and deck plan of the M 300

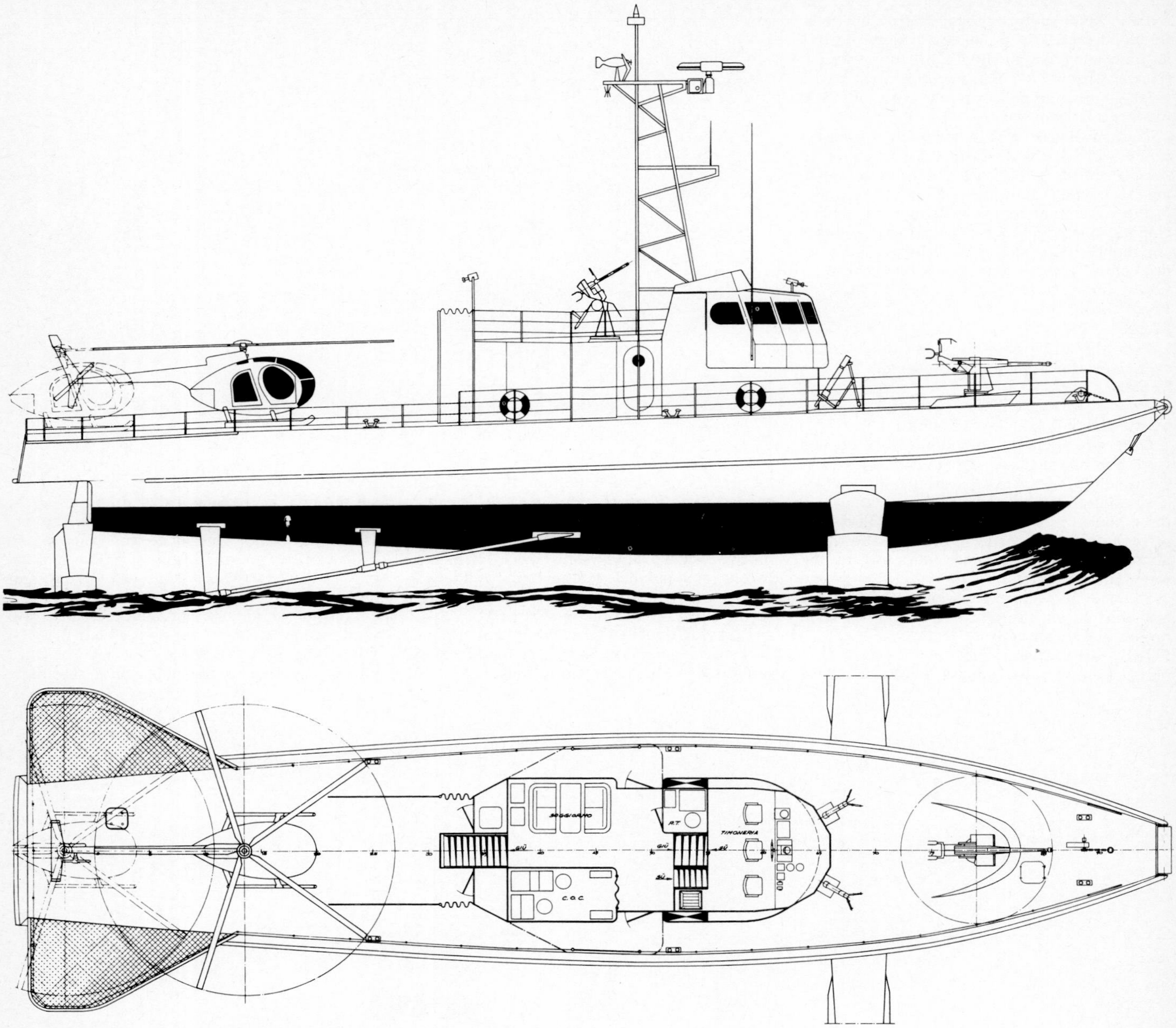

Outboard profile and deck plan of the M 300

water from any compartment. Drain valves can be operated from both the engine room or from the deck. One pump can also supply water for fire hoses located on the amidship and aft sections of the vessels, port and starboard.

CO_2 system installed for fuel bays and engine room. Portable dry chemical and foam extinguishers also fitted.

ELECTRICAL: Two systems, dc and ac. 24V dc system operates navigation lights, radio and starts auxiliary engines. AC system, for all the other requirements, comprises two diesel generating sets delivering 70kVA, 220V, three-phase 50Hz. Meters for monitoring voltage, amperage, frequency and power of ac systems are on main switchboard, located in engine room, from which isolated or parallel operation of the two alternators is controlled. Also on board are circuit breaker and switches for the transformer when the craft is connected to shore power, and distributing panels for the power and lighting system.

SAFETY: The presence of smoke, fire and high temperatures in various parts of the craft, as well as the malfunctioning of machinery, auxiliary systems and hydraulics automatically sets off an electric alarm.

NAVIGATION AND COMMUNICATIONS: The craft are equipped with all navigation lights as well as an electrically operated horn and signal lights. Communications and navigation systems (radio, Decca Navigator and Flight Log etc) are fitted to the customers' requirements and are therefore considered optional equipment.

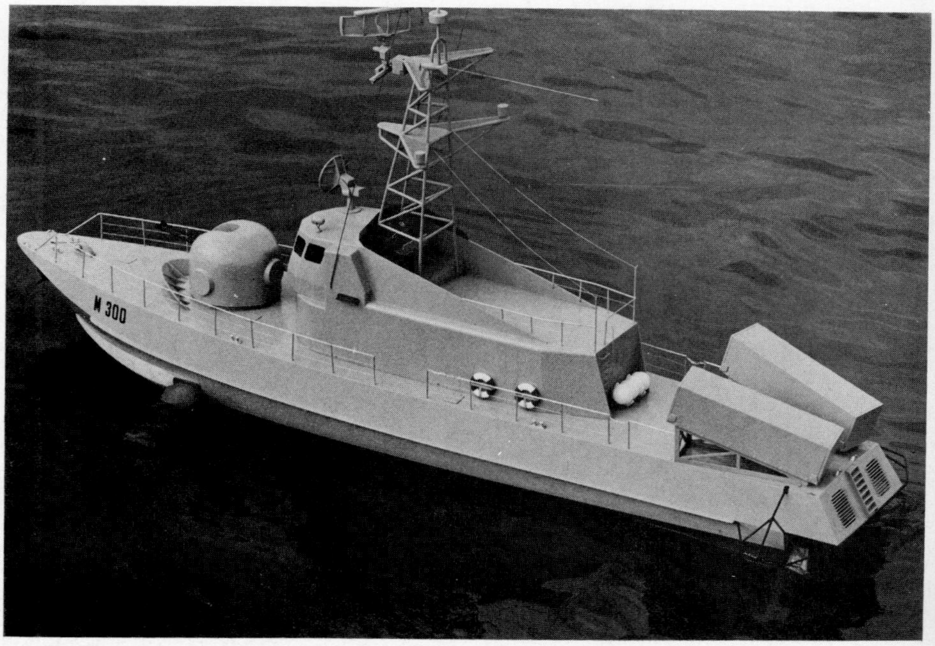

Dynamic model of the M 300

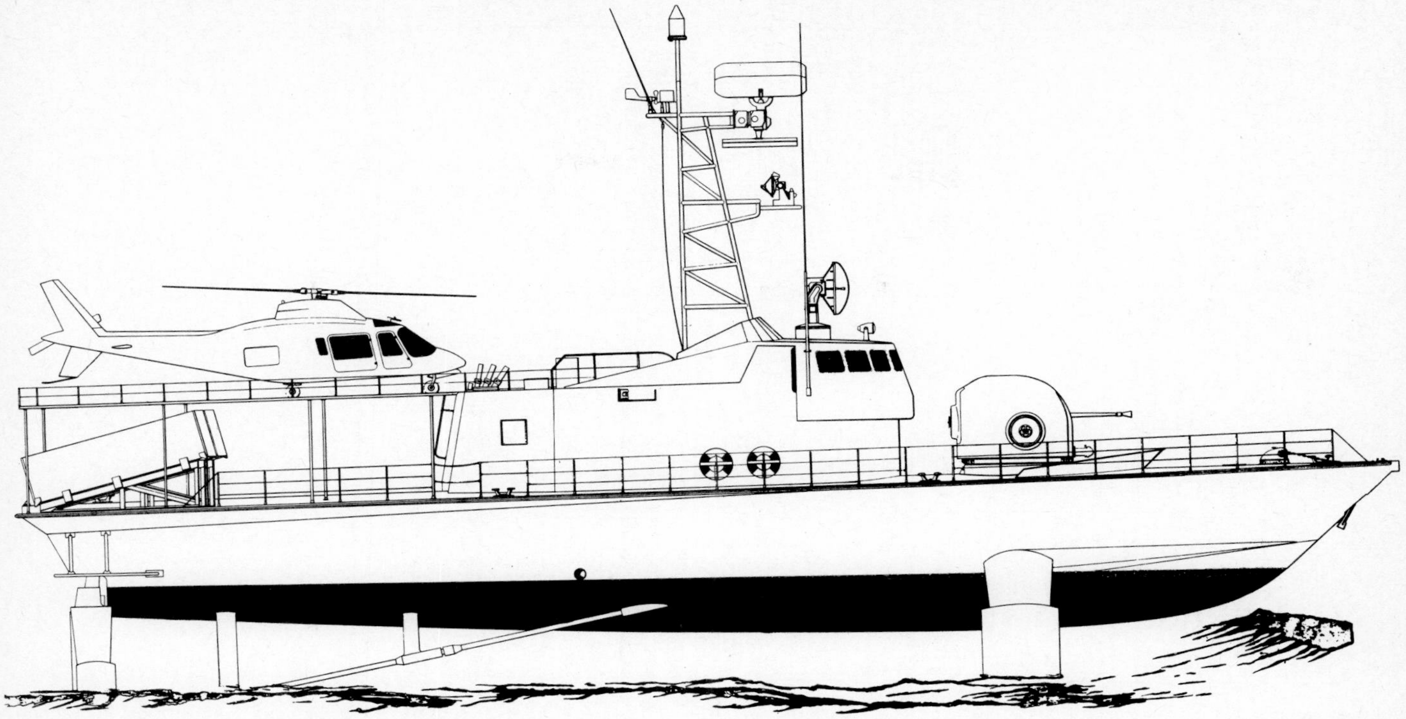

Outboard and inboard profile of the M 600 fast strike missile craft

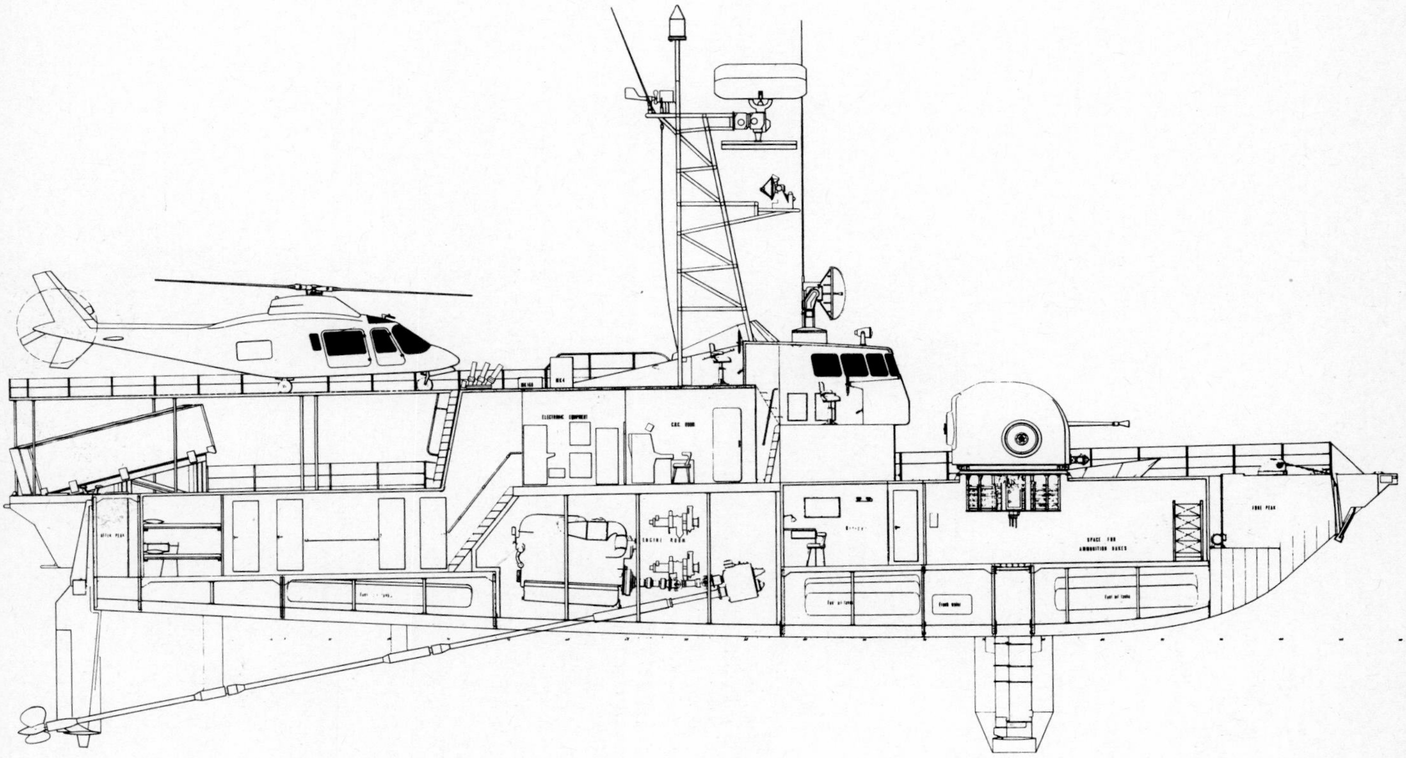

M 300
DIMENSIONS
Length, overall: 30·95m (101ft 6in)
Length, waterline: 26·25m (86ft 1in)
Beam, moulded: 6·2m (20ft 4in)
Beam, across foils: 12·5m (41ft 4in)
Draft, hullborne: 3·7m (12ft 1in)
Draft, foilborne: 1·4m (4ft 7in)
WEIGHTS
Displacement: 85 tonnes (83·66 tons)
Military payload: 15 tonnes (14·76 tons)
Liquids, fuel oil and water: 11·7 tonnes (11·52 tons)
PERFORMANCE
Max speed: in excess of 68·5km/h (37 knots)
Cruising speed: 66·5km/h (36 knots)
Cruising range: 925km (500n miles)

M 600
DIMENSIONS
Length, overall: 35m (114ft 9in)
Length, waterline: 30·1m (98ft 9in)
Beam, moulded: 7m (23ft)
Beam, across foils: 14·4m (47ft 3in)
Draft, hullborne: 4·55m (14ft 11in)
Draft, foilborne: 2·15m (7ft)
WEIGHTS
Displacement: 125 tonnes
Military payload: 21·45 tonnes
Liquids—oil, fuel, water: 16·3 tonnes
PERFORMANCE
Max speed: 70·5km/h (38 knots)
Cruising speed: 68·5km/h (37 knots)
Cruising range: 925km (500n miles)

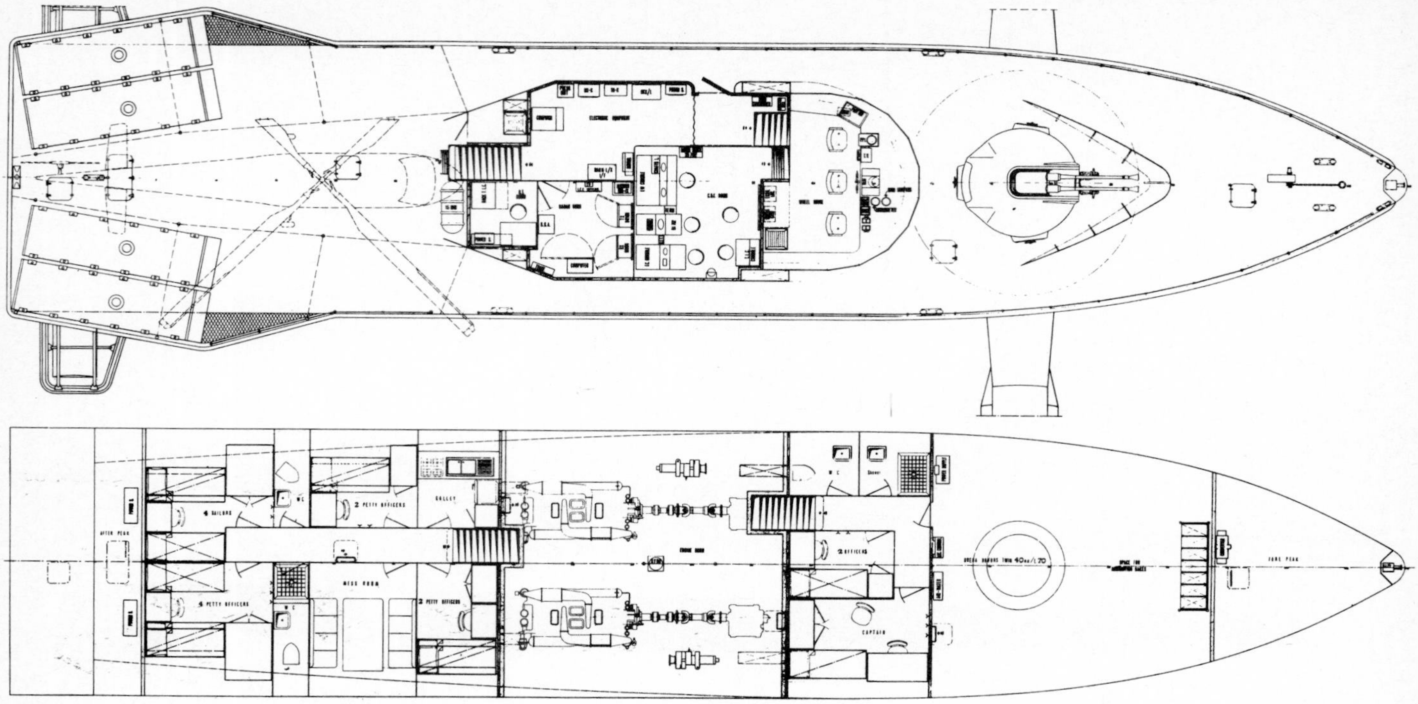

This version of the M 600 has a helicopter landing pad above the missile launchers aft. A Breda-Bofors twin 40mm L70 or similar dual-purpose rapid-fire cannon is mounted forward

Dynamic model of the M 600 undergoing tests

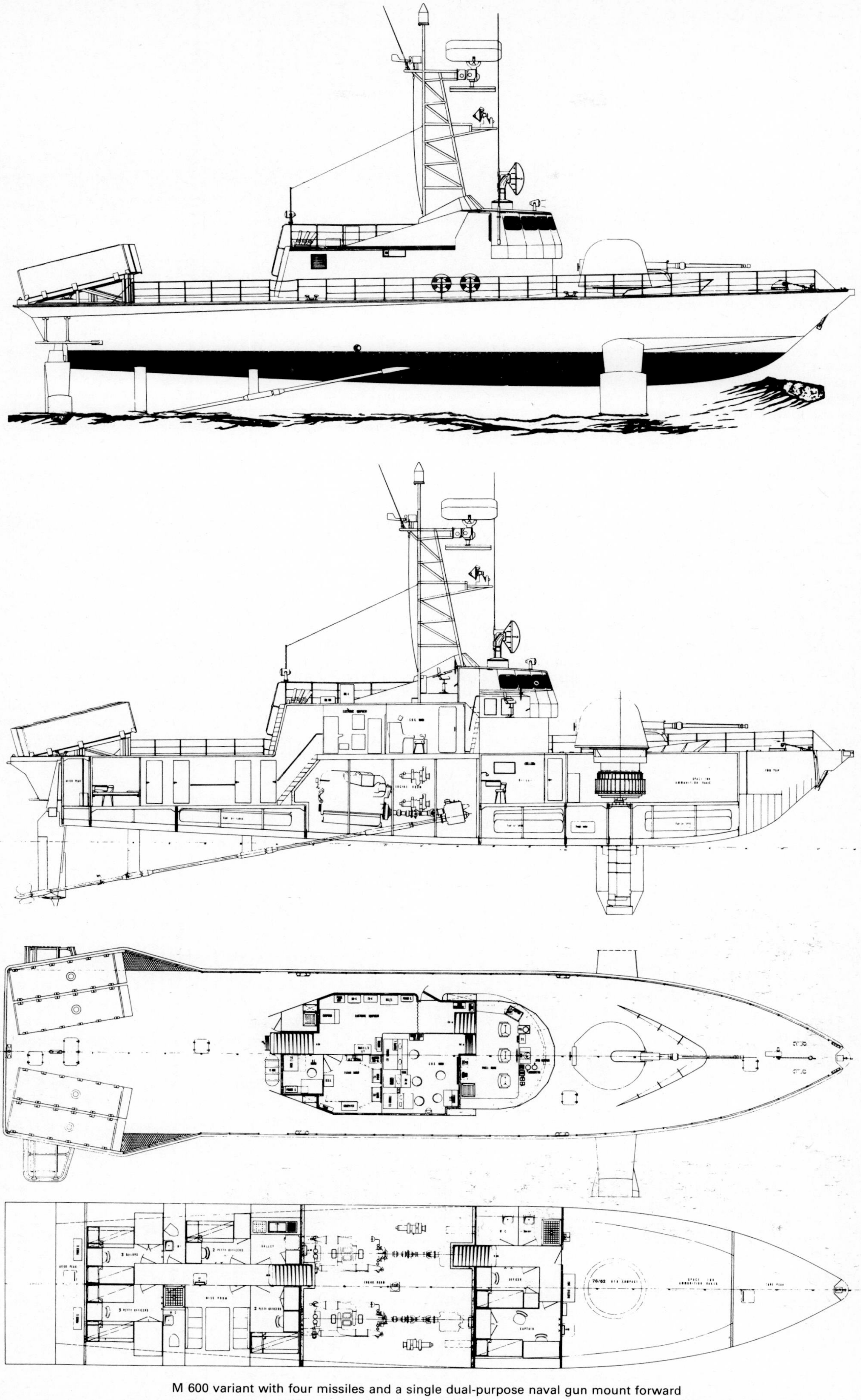

M 600 variant with four missiles and a single dual-purpose naval gun mount forward

SEAFLIGHT SpA Cantiere Navale

Villagio Torre Faro, 98019 Messina, Italy
Telephone: 81 25 79
Officials:
Dr Filippo M Laudini, *President and General Manager*
Dott Ing Emanuele Midolo, *Technical Manager*

In August 1976 fresh support for Seaflight was introduced by a new Italian financial group. Dr Filippo M Laudini, the new President and General Manager, has stated that it is the group's intention to give fresh impetus to the design and construction of hydrofoils and to their marketing on a world-wide basis.

The L90 will be the first production craft of the re-structured company. The prototype, launched in 1973, has been employed on the principal routes of the Tirrenian Seas. In the summer of 1973 it operated a service between Italy and Sardinia.

One of the company's latest projects is a 180-seat passenger ferry which will employ a completely new foil system. It is the intention of the new management to put stronger emphasis on the design and construction of hydrofoils for military applications in future.

Construction of the company's yard on the beach at Torre Faro, began in 1962, and the Seaflight P46 prototype, the C44, was launched in January 1965. The company has since built eight 30-seat P46s and seven H57s, the latter being a larger and more powerful development of the P46, seating 60 passengers, and one L90.

In July 1977 the company announced that it had sold an H57 to Crillon Tours Ltda of La Paz, Bolivia, which will employ the craft on scheduled services across Lake Titicaca.

Description of the P46 and military variants of this craft and the H57 appeared in *Jane's Surface Skimmers 1972-73* and earlier editions.

Seaflight's L90 prototype

SEAFLIGHT L90

The L90, latest passenger ferry hydrofoil in the Seaflight series, seats 118-123 passengers and cruises at 35 knots. The prototype, which was launched in 1973, was built under the supervision of Registro Italiano Navale.

FOILS: The foil system is of aeroplane configuration with surface-piercing bow and rear foils. Approximately 60% of the load is supported by the bow foil and 40% by the rear foil.

The bow foil, of W type, is attached to a supporting tube inside the hull by a central and two lateral struts. The foil pivots around the axis of the supporting tube between positions of maximum and minimum incidence.

The lift and drag generated by the foil tends to rotate it backwards, particularly during take-off and in rough seas, but this movement is opposed by a spring attached to an arm on the foil assembly shaft. The system is designed to produce the same amount of lift, whether the speed varies or the foil's submerged surface varies in a wave crest or cavity.

Foils, struts and the supporting tube are fabricated in steel. Four shear points are provided, two inside the hull at the attachment points of the support tube arm and the automatic incidence control system, and two externally, at the point of attachment of the two subfoils to the central strut. In the event of damage, the affected foils and their supporting structure can be quickly and easily repaired.

The rear foil combines a horizontal submerged centre section with inclined surface-piercing areas. It is attached to the hull by two struts and the two rudder supports and the angle of incidence is fixed.

HULL: Riveted light alloy construction is employed throughout. The structure is of the transverse type with frames spaced 300mm (1ft) apart. Full-length longitudinal members reinforce the hull bottom and the decks and run from stem to stern. All plates and sections are specially treated by the company for added protection against corrosion. Braking load of the plates is 30·35kg/mm^2. The hull is designed for two compartment sub-division and will remain afloat with any two adjacent compartments flooded.

ACCOMMODATION: The standard version accommodates a crew of 3–4 and 118–123 passengers, who are seated in three large saloons. Entry is through one of two side doors, one port, one starboard, in the central saloon, which provides access via a companionway to the aft saloon, the forward saloon and the wheelhouses. There are two w/c washbasin units in the aft saloon and one in the forward saloon.

The pilot's position, instruments and controls are on the starboard side of the wheelhouse and there is a crew member's observation position on the port side. Access to the engine room is from the wheelhouse via a watertight hatch.

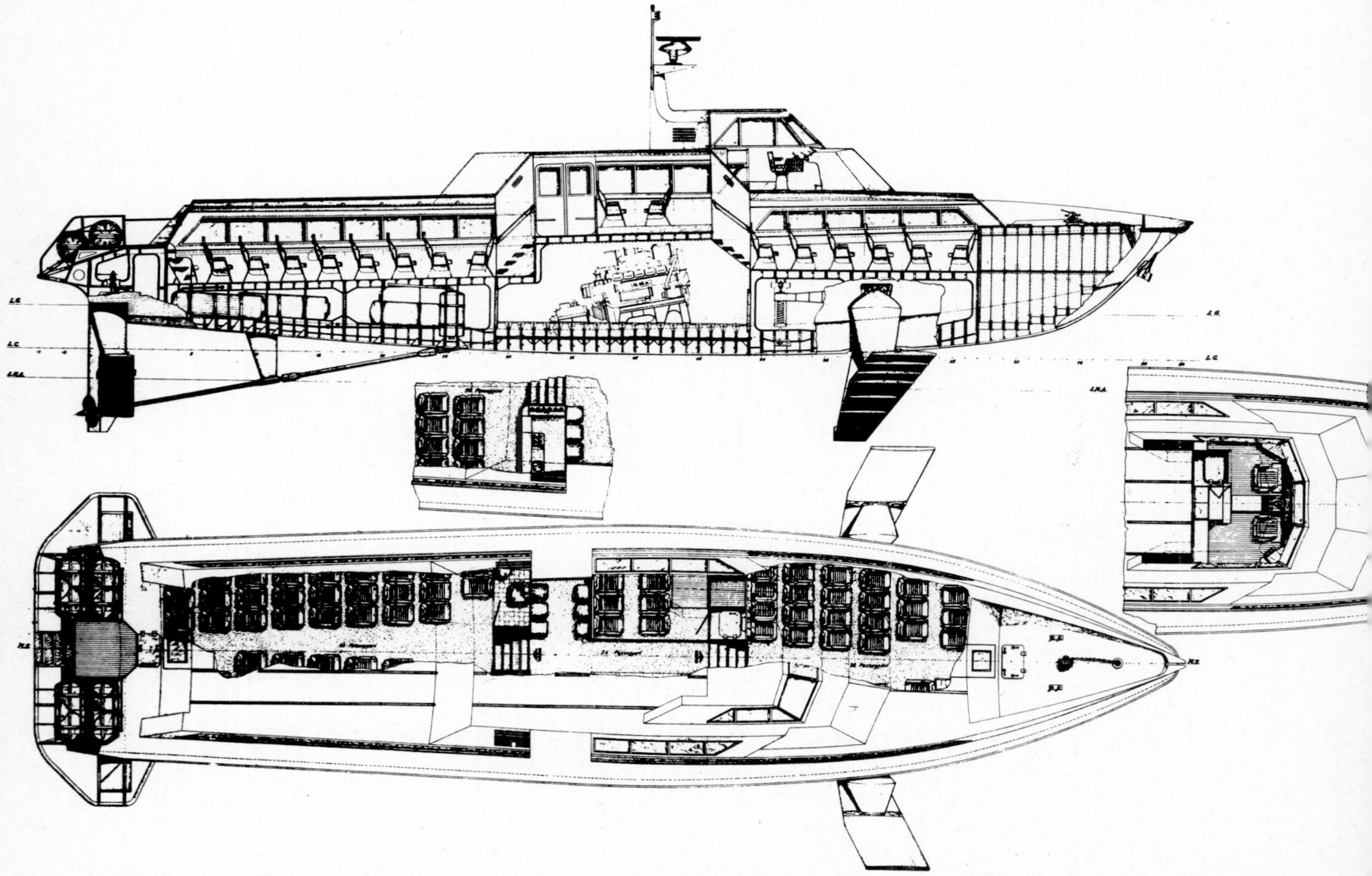
Inboard profile and plan view of the Seaflight L90 passenger ferry hydrofoil. Power is supplied by two 1,100hp MB 820 dc diesels

POWER PLANT: Power is supplied by two supercharged 12-cylinder Mercedes-Maybach MB 820 dc diesels, each with a maximum continuous output of 1,100shp at 1,400rpm. Engine output is transferred to two high tensile bronze propellers through Zahnradfabrik BW 800/s reversible gears.
SYSTEMS, ELECTRICAL: Two engine driven generators coupled to two battery sets provide 24V dc for engine starting, instruments, lighting, radio, etc. Separate diesel ac generating plant can be installed if required.
COMMUNICATIONS AND NAVIGATION: Ship-shore VHF and radar to customer's requirements.
DIMENSIONS
EXTERNAL
Length, overall: 27·34m (89ft 4in)
Length, waterline, hull: 22·7m (74ft 6in)
Draft, hullborne: 3·07m (10ft 1in)
Draft, foilborne: 1·25m (4ft 1¼in)
Hull beam: 6·04m (19ft 9¾in)
Width across foils: 10m (32ft 9¾in)
Freeboard: 1·35m (5ft 5in)
Height overall: 8m (26ft 3in)
INTERNAL
Aft passenger saloon compartment, including w/c,
Length: 8·7m (28ft 6½in)
Max width: 4·7m (15ft 5in)
Max height: 1·95m (6ft 5in)
Floor area: 37m² (398ft²)
Volume: 70m³ (2,472ft³)
Main deck saloon, excluding wheelhouse,
Length: 5·1m (16ft 8¾in)
Max width: 4·8m (15ft 9in)
Max height: 1·95m (6ft 5in)
Floor area: 24m² (258ft²)
Volume: 45m³ (1,589ft³)
Wheelhouse,
Length: 1·9m (6ft 2¾in)
Width: 3m (9ft 10in)
Height: 1·9m (6ft 2¾in)
Area: 6m² (64ft²)
Volume: 12m³ (423ft³)
WEIGHTS
Light displacement: 45 tons
Max take-off displacement: 59·5 tons
Deadweight (including fuel, water, passengers, crew): 14 tons
Payload: 10 tons
PERFORMANCE
Cruising speed foilborne: 32·4–35 knots
Max wave height in foilborne mode: 1·6m (5ft 3in)
Range at cruising speed: 500km (310 miles)
Turning radius at cruising speed: 300m (984ft)
Take-off distance: 200m (654ft)
Take-off time: 30 seconds
Stopping distance: 80m (261ft)
Stopping time: 10 seconds
Fuel consumption at cruising speed: 300kg/h (661lb/h)

JAPAN

HITACHI SHIPBUILDING & ENGINEERING CO LTD

Head Office: 47 Edobori 1-chome, Nishi-ku, Osaka, Japan
Telephone: Osaka 443 8051
Telex: J 63376
Works: 1 Mizue-cho, Kawasaki-ku, Kawasaki, Kanagawa Pref, Japan
Telephone: Kawasaki 288 1111
Officials:
Takao Nagata, *President*
Nobuo Inoue, *Executive Vice President, General Manager of Shipbuilding Division (Sales Director)*
Giichi Miyashita, *Manager of Kanagawa Shipyard*

Hitachi, the Supramar licensee in Japan, has been building PT 3, PT 20 and PT 50 hydrofoils since 1961. The majority of these have been built for fast passenger ferry services across the Japanese Inland Sea, cutting across deep bays which road vehicles might take two to three hours to drive round, and out to offshore islands. Other PT 20s and 50s have been exported to Hong Kong and Australia for ferry services.

Specifications of the PT 3, PT 20 and PT 50 will be found under Supramar (Switzerland). The Hitachi-built craft are identical apart from minor items.

In the spring of 1974, the company completed the first PT 50 Mk II to be built at its Kawasaki yard. The vessel Hikari 2, is powered by two licence-built MTU MB 820Db diesels, seats 123 passengers and cruises at 33 knots. It was delivered to its owner, Setonaikai Kisen Co Ltd, of Hiroshima City in March 1975.

Hitachi has constructed twenty-five PT 50s and fourteen PT 20s.

A special military hydrofoil, based on the Schertel-Sachsenburg foil system, and designated PT 32, has been designed by the company and two are in service with the Philippine Navy.

First PT 50 Mk II to be completed is the Hikari 2, built by Hitachi Shipbuilding & Engineering Co at its Kawasaki yard for Setonaikai Kisen Co Ltd. The vessel, which carries 123 passengers and a crew of seven, is employed on the route Hiroshima-Imabari

The second and third Hitachi-built PT 50 Mk IIs, operated by Arimura Line

POLAND

GDANSK SHIP RESEARCH INSTITUTE

Technical University, Gdansk, Poland
Telephone: 414712

Research on problems connected with hydrofoil design and construction has been conducted by the Department of Theoretical Naval Architecture at Gdansk Technical University since 1956.

Experience with various dynamic test models led to the construction of the K-3 four-seat runabout which, powered by an FSC Lublin converted auto-engine, has a top speed of 50km/h (27 knots).

In 1961 the Department was invited by the Central Board of Inland Navigation and United Inland Shipping and River Shipyards Gdansk, to design a hydrofoil passenger ferry for service in the Firth of Szczecin. Designated ZRYW-1 the craft seats 76 passengers and cruises at 35 knots. It was completed in 1965.

During 1966 the Ship Research Institute designed two hydrofoil sports craft, the WS-4 Amor and the WS-6 Eros. The prototypes were completed in 1967 and both types were put into series production during 1972.

In 1971, a catamaran-hulled research hydrofoil, the Badacz II, was built for the Ship Hydrodynamics Division of the Institute. The vessel is employed to tow models of ACVs and hydrofoils in coastal waters and provide data and performance measurements. It is also being employed to test new propulsion systems.

The largest hydrofoil craft to be designed by the Institute is a 300-ton passenger/car ferry.

Details of the ZRYW-1, Amor, Eros and Badacz II can be found in *Jane's Surface Skimmers 1974-75* and earlier editions.

ROMANIA

The Romanian navy is operating ten Chinese-designed Hu Chwan (White Swan)-class hydrofoil torpedo boats. The first three were shipped from the Hutang Shipyard, Shanghai, complete, while the remaining seven have been constructed locally under a building programme started in 1973.

Although the Romanian craft are identical outwardly in most respects to the imported models, there are minor differences in defensive armament and superstructure design.

FOILS: System comprises a bow subfoil to stabilise pitch and facilitate take-off and a main foil of trapeze or shallow V configuration set back approximately one-third of the hull length from the bow. At high speed in relatively calm conditions the greater part of the forward hull is raised clear of the water. The mainfoil and struts retract upwards when the craft is required to cruise in displacement conditions.

HULL: High speed V-bottom hull in seawater resistant light alloy.

POWER PLANT: Reported to be two 1,100hp M50 or M401 watercooled, supercharged 12 cylinder, V-type diesels, each driving its own inclined propeller shaft.

ARMAMENT: Two 21in torpedo tubes, plus four 14·5mm cannon in two twin mounts.

DIMENSIONS (Approx)
Length overall: 21·33m (70ft)
Beam overall: 5·02m (16ft 6in)
Hull beam: 3·96m (13ft)

WEIGHTS
Displacement full load: 45 tons

PERFORMANCE
Max speed foilborne,
calm conditions: 55 knots
Range: 926km (500n miles) approx

A Romanian-built hydrofoil torpedo boat of the Chinese designed Hu Chwan class *(Jane's Fighting Ships)*

SINGAPORE

VOSPER PRIVATE LIMITED

Mailing Address: PO Box 95, Singapore 1
Telephone: 4467144
Telex: RS 21219 AB: VOSPER
Cables: Vosper Singapore
Administration/Works: 200 Tanjong Rhu, Singapore 15
Officials:
Sir John Rix, MBE, *Chairman*
A A C Griffith, OBE, *Director*
Yeoh Ghim Seng, BBM JP, *Director*
Chua Boon Peng, *Director*
R G Bennett, CMG, *Director*
P Du Cane, *Managing Director*
C F Campbell, *Sales and Commercial Director*
S N Houghton, *Financial Director*
Poul Bakmand, *General Sales Manager*

Vosper Private Limited, the Singapore-based subsidiary of Vosper Limited, is the sole builder in South-east Asia of the Supramar range of hydrofoils. The company has a building licence agreement with Supramar AG of Lucerne, Switzerland and the prototype PTS 75 Mk III has been built at the Portchester shipyard for Far East Hydrofoils, Hong Kong.

Vosper Private Limited is building PT 20s and PT 50s and marketing them in the Far East. This is the first time any Singapore shipyard has built hydrofoils.

The vessels under construction are mainly for export. They will be used for high speed passenger transport, logistic support and patrol duties. Details of the designs are given in this section under Supramar AG, Switzerland.

A Supramar PT 20B Mk II built by Vosper Private Ltd at its Singapore yard

SWITZERLAND

SUPRAMAR AG

Ausserfeld 5, CH-6362 Stansstad, Switzerland
Telephone: (041) 61 31 94
Officials:
Hussain Najadi, *Chairman*
Baron Hanns von Schertel, *Director, Research and Development*
Martin Furrer, *Board Member*
Heinrad Schnueriger, *Board Member*
Dipl Ing Eugen Schatté, *Research and Development*
Dipl Ing Georg Chvojka, *Technical Adviser for Hull Design, Machinery and Foils*

Supramar was founded in Switzerland in 1952 to develop on a commercial basis the hydrofoil system introduced by the Schertel-Sachsenberg Hydrofoil Syndicate and its licensee, the Gebruder Sachsenberg Shipyard.

The co-operation between the companies started in 1937 and led to the development of the VS6, a 17-ton hydrofoil, which in 1941 attained 47·5 knots, and the VS8, an 80-ton supply hydrofoil completed in 1943 which attained 41 knots. The inherently stable, rigid V-foil system used on these and subsequent Supramar vessels, stems from experimental work undertaken by Baron Hanns von Schertel between 1927-1937.

In May 1953, a Supramar PT 10, 32-passenger hydrofoil began the world's first regular passenger hydrofoil service on Lake Maggiore, between Switzerland and Italy. In August 1956, the first Rodriquez-built Supramar PT 20 opened a service across the Straits of Messina and became the first hydrofoil to be licensed by a marine classification authority for carrying passengers at sea.

Established originally as a research and design office, Supramar has recently been reorganised and will produce hydrofoils of its own design at shipyards independently of the arrangements with its licensees.

The Marketing Department provides, in addition to its normal marketing functions, a consultancy service covering financing, leasing and operating.

Supramar employs a staff of highly qualified scientists and engineers specialising in hydrodynamics, marine engineering, foil design, propulsion and shipyard production. In addition to building its own hydrofoils it licenses other shipyards to produce its hydrofoil designs.

Supramar hydrofoils being built by these companies are referred to elsewhere in this section under the respective company headings.

The latest Supramar design is the PTS 75 Mk III, a development of the PT 50 with increased engine power and full air stabilisation. The prototype was constructed by Vosper Thornycroft at the company's Portchester yard and delivered to Hong Kong in late 1974. The second vessel of this type was completed in early 1976 by Supramar's licensee in Hong Kong. The company has also completed designs for a modernised PT 50 which is available as the PT 50 Mk II. A new version of the PTS 150 Mk II is operating between Miami and the Bahamas. This is the PTS 150 Mk III, a second generation craft with improved performance and greater passenger comfort.

The company is also developing a fully submerged foil system with air stabilisation. First craft to use this system is the Supramar ST 3A, a 4·9-ton experimental boat built under a US Navy contract. During tests in the Mediterranean it demonstrated promising stability and seakeeping qualities and reached a speed of 54·5 knots. Military and para-military versions of all Supramar commercial hydrofoils are now available. In addition Supramar has completed the design of a patrol boat hydrofoil which meets the tactical requirements of the NATO navies. The vessel, the MT 250G, has an operational displacement of 250 tons and a maximum intermittent speed of 60 knots.

Supramar's latest hydrofoil concept is the CT 70, a hydrofoil catamaran designed especially for use in shallow waters where draft limitations preclude the use of conventional hydrofoil craft.

A Supramar PT 20 built by Hitachi Shipbuilding & Engineering Co Ltd

PT 20 Mk II

The PT 20 Mk II, a 27-ton boat for 72 passengers, is considered by Supramar to be the smallest size hydrofoil suitable for passenger-carrying coastal services. The first of this very successful series was built by the Rodriquez shipyard at Messina in 1955 and since then nearly 70 PT 20s of various types have been built in Sicily, Japan, Netherlands and Norway. The design has been approved by almost every classification society. Fast patrol boat variants are also available.

FOILS: Foils are of standard Schertel-Sachsenberg, surface-piercing type, with 58% of the load supported by the bow foil and the remaining 42% by the rear foil. Submerged foil area in foilborne condition is 5·5m². Together with the struts and a horizontal guide, each foil forms a uniform framework which facilitates the exchange of the foil elements. The medium steel foils are of partly hollow, welded construction. The angle of incidence of the bow foil can be adjusted within narrow limits from the steering stand by means of a hydraulic ram operating on a foil support across the hull. To counteract the effects of large variations in passenger load and to ensure optimum behaviour in sea waves the angle of attack can be adjusted during operation.

HULL: The hull has a V-bottom with an externally added step riveted into place. Frames, bulkheads, foundations, superstructure and all internal construction is in corrosion-proof light alloy. Platings are of AlMg 5 and the frames, bars and other members are made in AlMgSi. Watertight compartments are provided below the passenger decks and in other parts of the hull.

POWER PLANT: Power is supplied by a super-

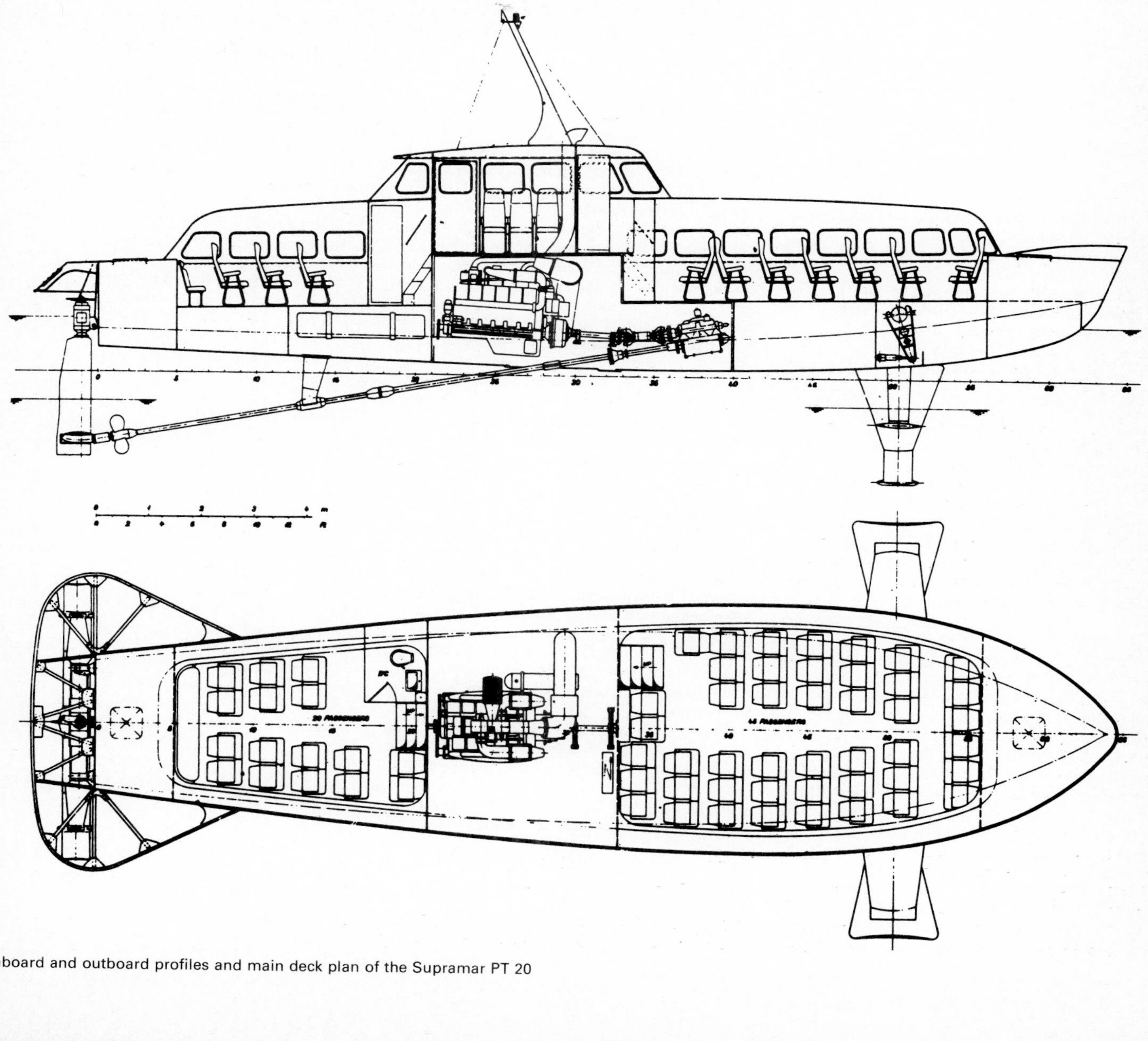
Inboard and outboard profiles and main deck plan of the Supramar PT 20

charged, 12-cylinder MTU 12V 493 Ty 70 diesel with an exhaust turbo-compressor. Maximum continuous output is 1,100hp at 1,400rpm. A BW 800/HS 20 reversible gear, developed by Zahnradfabrik Friedrichshafen AG, is placed between the engine and the drive shaft.
ACCOMMODATION: The boat is controlled entirely from the bridge which is located above the engine room. Forty-six passengers are accommodated in the forward cabin, twenty in the rear compartment and six aft of the pilot's stand in the elevated wheelhouse. There is an emergency exit in each passenger compartment, and the craft is equipped with an inflatable life raft and life belts for each person. A crew of four is carried.
SYSTEMS, ELECTRICAL: 24V generator driven by the main engine: batteries with a capacity of approx 250Ah.
HYDRAULICS: 120kg/cm² pressure hydraulic system for rudder and bow foil incidence control.
COMMUNICATIONS AND NAVIGATION: VHF ship-shore radio is supplied as standard equipment. Radar is optional.
DIMENSIONS
EXTERNAL
Length overall, hull: 20·75m (68ft 1in)
Length over deck: 19·95m (67ft 6in)
Hull beam, max: 4·99m (16ft 4in)
Width across foils: 8·07m (26ft 5in)
Draft hullborne: 3·08m (10ft 1in)
Draft foilborne: 1·4m (4ft 7in)
INTERNAL
Aft cabin (including w/c): 13·5m² (145ft²)
Volume: 27m³ (954ft³)
Forward cabin: 26m² (280ft²)
Volume: 50m³ (1,766ft³)
Main deck level (including wheelhouse): 12m² (129ft²)
Volume: 24m³ (847ft³)
WEIGHTS
Gross tonnage: approx 56 tons
Max take-off displacement: 32 tons
Light displacement: 25 tons
Deadweight (including fuel, oil, water, passengers, baggage and crew): 7 tons
Payload: 5·4 tons
PERFORMANCE (with normal payload)
Cruising speed, foilborne: 63km/h (34 knots)
Max permissible wave height in foilborne mode: 1·29m (4ft 3in)
Designed range at cruising speed: 400km (216 miles)
Turning radius: 130m approx (427ft)
Take-off distance: 150m approx (493ft)
Take-off time: 25 seconds
Stopping distance: 70m (230ft)
Fuel consumption at cruising speed: 150kg/h (330lb/h)
SEA TEST: Prototype tests were undertaken in the Mediterranean in every kind of sea condition, and further tests have taken place off Japan. Acceleration measurements have shown maximum values below 0·5g when accelerometer had been fitted above the bow foil. Maximum lateral acceleration was 0·32g. Measurements were made in wave heights of approximately 1·2–1·5m. These are the maximum measurements obtained and subsequent tests have seldom equalled these figures.

PT 20B Mk II

In this model of the PT 20, the engine room and bridge are arranged in the foreship. This improves the pilot's vision in waters likely to have an influx of driftwood and provides a large main passenger cabin with seats for 55 and an upper deck cabin with seating for 16 passengers.

The layout of this craft has been based on experience gained with the Supramar PT 27 which was designed for servicing the offshore drilling platforms on Lake Maracaibo. This design has been slightly modified to meet the requirements of passenger services.
FOILS: The foil design is similar to that of the PT 20 Mk II. About 66% of the total weight is borne by the bow foil and 34% by the rear foil. Submerged foil area in foilborne condition is 6·2m².

A Supramar PT 20B

The forward foil can be tilted within narrow limits by means of a hydraulic ram acting on the foil strut supporting tube. The angle of attack can therefore be adjusted during operation to assist take-off and to counteract the effect of large variations in passenger loads.
HULL: This is of riveted light metal alloy design and framed on a combination of longitudinal and transverse formers. Watertight compartments are provided below the passenger decks and in other parts of the hull, and some are filled with foam-type plastic.
POWER PLANT: Power is supplied by a supercharged 12-cylinder MTU 12V 493 Ty 70 diesel with a maximum continuous output of 1,100hp at 1,400rpm. Average time between major overhauls is approximately 10,000 hours. Engine output is transferred to a three-bladed 700mm diameter bronze subcavitating propeller through a BW 800/H 20 reversible gear made by Zahnradfabrik. The propeller shaft is supported at three points by seawater lubricated rubber bearings.
ACCOMMODATION: The PT 20B Mk II has a crew of four and seats 71 passengers. The main passenger compartment seats 55, and the small cabin behind the pilot's stand seats a further 16. Access to the main compartment is through either of two doors, located port and starboard, to the rear of the wheelhouse. An emergency exit is provided at the rear of the main passenger compartment.

The PT 20B Mk II can also be delivered with fully integrated air conditioning equipment. The total passenger capacity will then be reduced to 69.

A full range of safety equipment is carried, including inflatable rafts and lifebelts for each passenger and crew member.
SYSTEMS, ELECTRICAL: 24V generator driven by the main engine, batteries with a capacity of approximately 250Ah.
HYDRAULICS: 120kg/cm² pressure hydraulic system for operating rudder and bow foil angle of incidence control.
COMMUNICATIONS AND NAVIGATION: A VHF ship-shore radio is supplied as standard equipment. Radar is an optional extra.
DIMENSIONS
EXTERNAL
Length overall, hull: 20·85m (68ft 5in)
Length over deck: 19·5m (64ft)
Hull beam, max: 5·16m (16ft 11in)
Width over foils: 8·6m (28ft 3in)
Draft hullborne: 3m (9ft 10in)
Draft foilborne: 1·3m (4ft 3in)
INTERNAL
Main passenger compartment (including w/c):
Length: 9·3m (30ft 7in)
Width: 3·8m (12ft 6in)
Height: 2m (6ft 7in)
Floor area: 22·1m² (237ft²)
Volume: 44m³ (1,553ft³)
WEIGHTS
Gross tonnage: 50 tons approx
Max take-off displacement: 32·5 tons
Light displacement: 25·4 tons
Deadweight (including fuel, oil, water, passengers, luggage, crew): 7·5 tons
Payload: 5·8 tons
PERFORMANCE (with normal payload)
Cruising speed: 63km/h (34 knots)
Max permissible wave height in foilborne mode: 1·29m (4ft 3in)
Turning radius: approx 130m (426ft)
Take-off distance: approx 150m (492ft)
Take-off time: approx 30 seconds
Stopping distance: approx 70m (231ft)
Stopping time: approx 10 seconds
Fuel consumption at cruising speed: 150kg/h (330lb/h)

PTL 28

The PTL 28 is derived from the PT 27 utility and oil rig supply vessel, three of which have been in service for more than ten years with the Shell Oil Company on Lake Maracaibo, Venezuela.

Features of the new craft include facilities for

A Supramar PTL 28 employed by Shell for servicing offshore oil platforms on Lake Maracaibo, Venezuela

loading across the bow as well as the stern, twin rudders for improved manoeuvrability, and a variety of structural and mechanical modifications to simplify and reduce maintenance. The Schottel drive now has only two bevel gears, the hull is of welded construction, and the foil and propeller mounting arrangements have been redesigned to facilitate servicing. All components of a non-essential nature have been omitted.

Normally seats are provided for 54, but the number of passengers can be increased if the range is reduced. The weather deck above the engine room is available for cargo; heavy loads are compensated by a reduction in passenger capacity. A cargo compartment can be made available at the rear of the passenger cabin (up to frame 17), a typical load being 1,825kg (4,023lb) of cargo combined with 33 passengers.

FOILS: Schertel-Sachsenberg surface-piercing system similar to that of the PT 20 Mk II. Bow foil of hollow welded stainless steel. Foil, vertical struts, inclined fins and horizontal supporting tube form a framed structure which can easily be detached when necessary. The complete assembly divides into two to facilitate transport. Once the angle of incidence is adjusted no further alteration is necessary.

The rear foil is similar to the bow foil in type and construction. The complete system is mounted on its bearings at the transom by four bolts.

HULL: Constructed in seawater-resistant light metal alloy, the V-bottomed hull is of hard chine type and framed longitudinally. All joints are welded. Hoist fittings are provided to facilitate maintenance.

POWER PLANT: Power is supplied by a 12-cylinder MTU 12V493 Ty 70 diesel, rated at 1,000hp at 1,400rpm continuous and 1,350hp at 1,500rpm maximum.

Engine output is transferred to a three-bladed bronze propeller through a Zahnradfabrik BW 800 H20 reverse gearbox. Hullborne propulsion is provided by a 150hp diesel engine directly coupled to a Schottel Z-drive unit which can be rotated through 360 degrees. During take-off and when foilborne, the lower bevel gear and hullborne propeller are retracted hydraulically into a recess in the hull bottom.

ACCOMMODATION: The PTL 28 has a crew of three and seats 54 passengers in a single saloon aft of the engine room. The bridge is located forward and provides a 360 degree view. The captain's seat, together with the operating controls and instrumentation, is located on the hull centreline.

DIMENSIONS

EXTERNAL

Length overall, hull: 20·75m (68ft 1in)
Length over deck: 19·95m (67ft 6in)
Hull beam, max: 4·99m (16ft 4in)
Width over foils: 8m (26ft 3in)
Draft hullborne: 2·95m (9ft 8in)
Draft foilborne: 1·5m (4ft 11in)

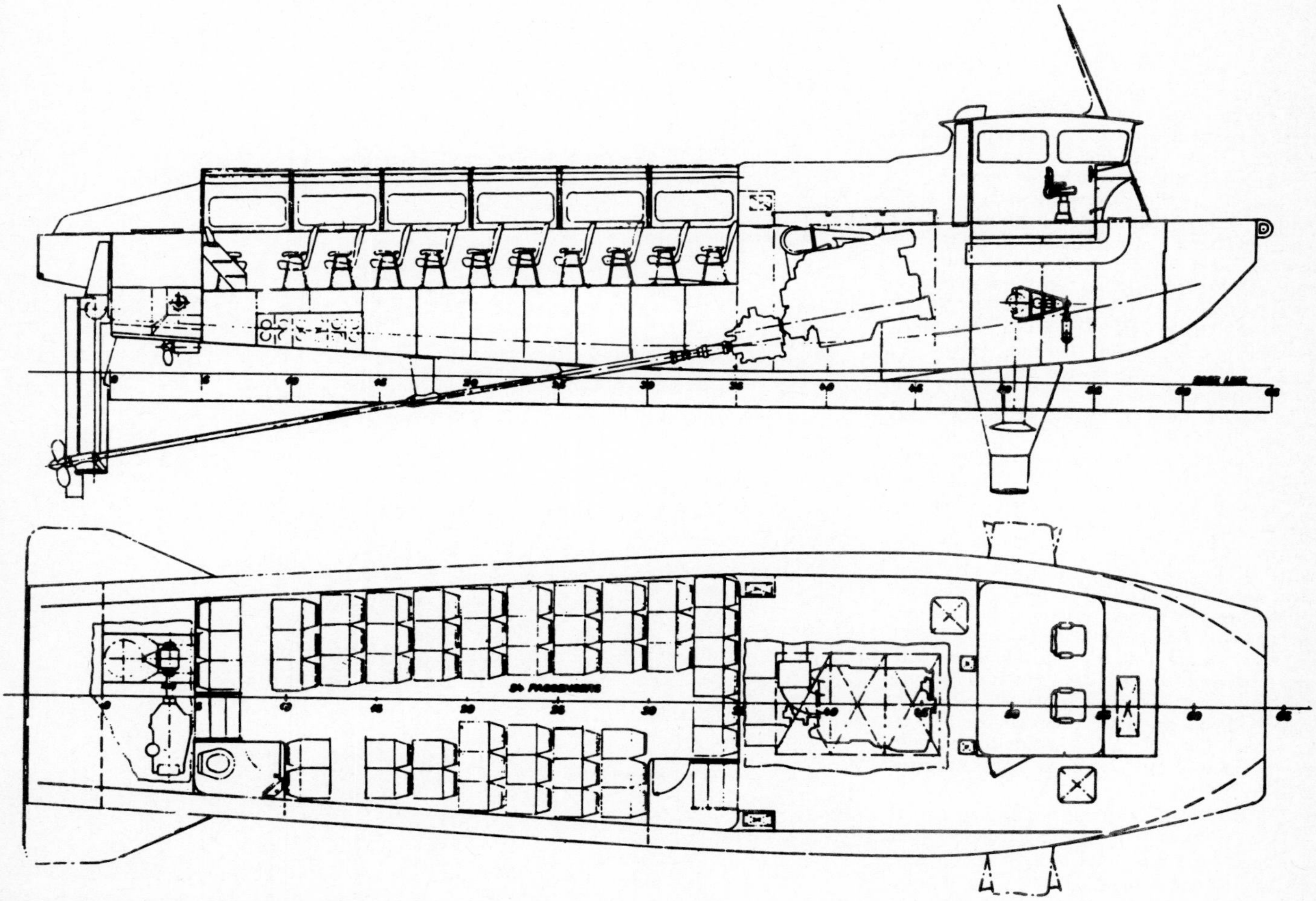

Inboard profile and passenger deck plan of the Supramar PTL 28 utility craft and supply vessel

WEIGHTS
Displacement fully loaded: 28 tonnes (27·56 tons)
Disposable load: 5·6 tonnes (5·51 tons)
Light displacement: 22·4 tonnes (22·05 tons)
PERFORMANCE
Speed max: 72km/h (39 knots)
Speed cruising: 65km/h (35 knots)
Range: 260km (140n miles) approx

PT 50 Mk II

The successful and profitable operation of the PT 20 led to the development of the PT 50, a 63-ton hydrofoil passenger ferry designed for offshore and inter-island services. The prototype was completed early in 1958, and more than 30 are operating regular passenger services in areas ranging from the Baltic and Mediterranean to the Japanese Inland Sea.

The craft has been approved by almost every Classification Society including Registro Italiano Navale, Germanischer Lloyd, Det Norske Veritas, American Bureau of Shipping and the Japanese Ministry of Transport. The requirements of the SOLAS 1960 convention for international traffic can be met by the type if required.

FOILS: Both rear and forward foils are rigidly attached to the hull but the lift of the forward foil can be modified by hydraulically operated flaps, which are fitted to assist take-off and turning, and for making slight course corrections and adjustment of the flying height. The foils are of hollow construction using fine grain and MSt 52-3 steel throughout. Foils in stainless steel construction are optional.

The bow foil comprises the following elements:
two fins, forming connecting links between the foil and the supporting structure which is riveted to the hull;
the hydrofoil, which (according to its foil section characteristics) generates the lift and, with the stern foil, provides transverse stability in foilborne conditions;
two struts, which transmit the main lift loads to the supporting structure.

The rear foil system comprises the following elements:
the hydrofoil, which generates the lift;
two side struts;
a single rudder which transmits the lift to the supporting structure.

For improved passenger comfort the PT 50 Mk II can be provided with a roll stabiliser on the bow foil. The system, including the motion sensing device, has been developed by Supramar.

HULL: Of hard chine construction, the hull is of partly riveted, partly welded light metal alloy design and framed on longitudinal and transverse formers. Steel is used only for highly stressed parts such as the foil fittings, and the shaft brackets and exits.

ACCOMMODATION: The PT 50 Mk II is available in three interior configurations:
1. For 111 passengers including bar and catering facilities.
2. Standard version, with seats for 122 passengers.
3. Commuter version, seating 136 passengers.

The crew varies from 6-8 members, depending mainly on local regulations.

Passenger seats are of lightweight aircraft type and the centre aisle between the seat rows has a clear width of 76cm (30in). Ceilings are covered with lightweight plastic material and the walls, including web frames, are clad in luxury plywood or artificial wood. Toilets are provided in the rear and forward passenger spaces. Floors in the passenger compartments are provided with thick carpets. Each passenger compartment has an emergency exit. Inflatable life rafts and lifebelts are provided for 110% of the passenger and crew capacity.

POWER PLANT: The craft is powered by two MTU 12V 331 TC 71 turbocharged diesels, each developing 1,100hp at 2,140rpm continuous. Engine output is transmitted to two three-bladed 700mm diameter bronze propellers through two inclined stainless steel propeller shafts, each sup-

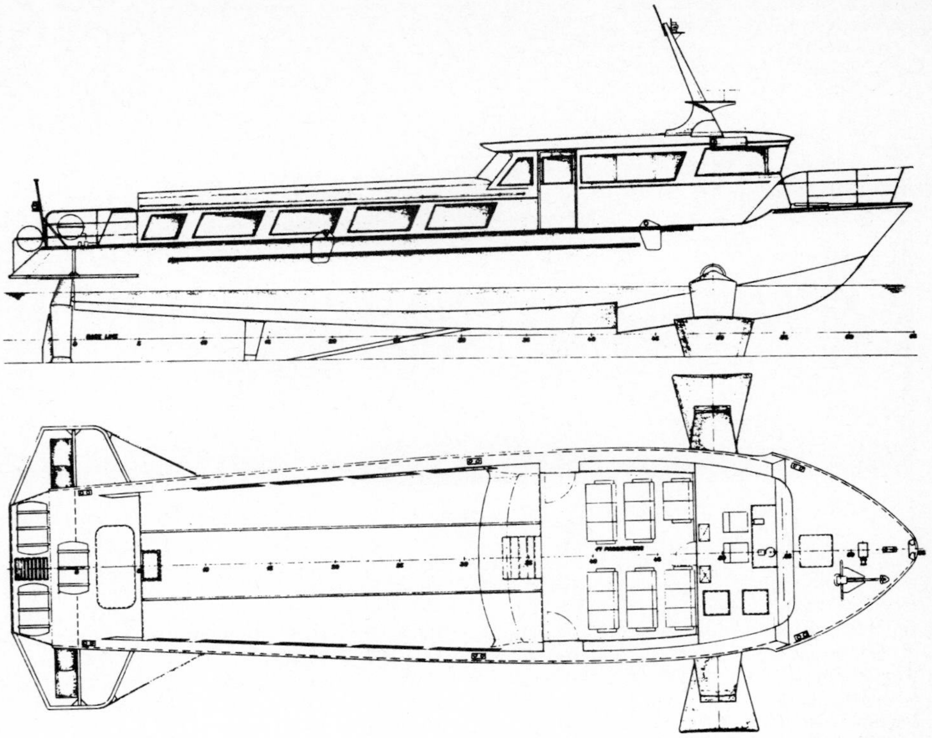

Outboard profile and plan and inboard profile and passenger deck of the Supramar PT 20B Mk II

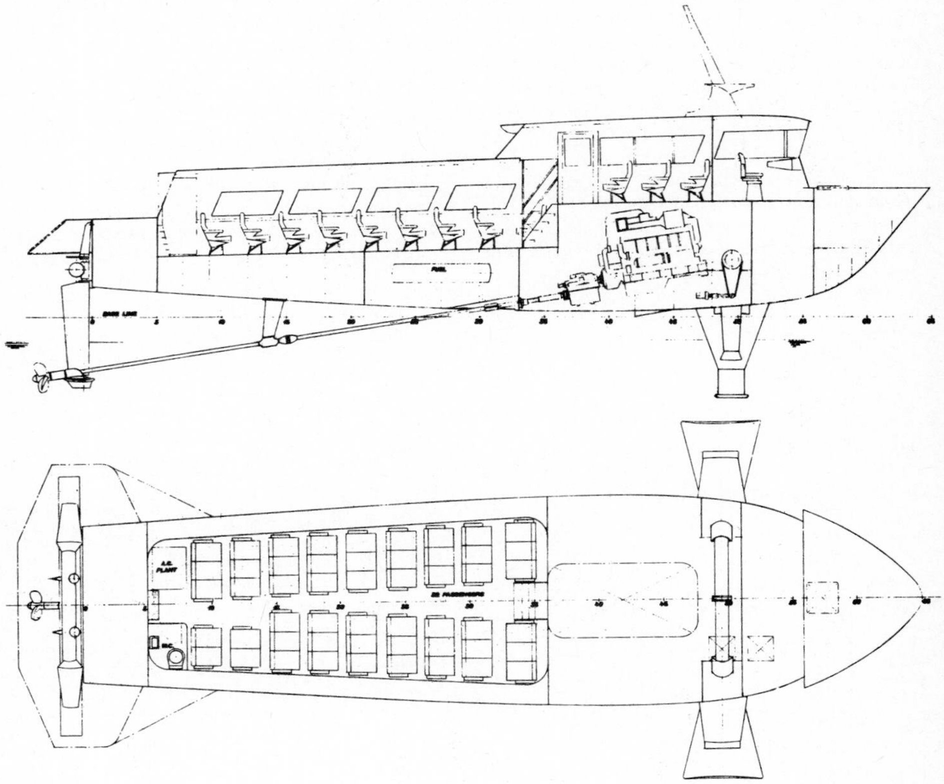

Guia, a Hitachi-built PT 50 which has been in regular service with Far East Hydrofoil Co Ltd, on the 36km Hong Kong-Macao route for more than 10 years

ported at four points by seawater lubricated runner bearings. Reverse and reduction gear with built-in thrust is manufactured by Zahnradfabrik Friedrichshafen, Germany. The reverse clutches are solenoid-operated from the bridge.

Eight cylindrical fuel tanks with a total capacity of 3,650 litres are located in the aft peak and below the tank deck. Oil capacity is 320 litres.

SYSTEMS, ELECTRICAL: Engine driven generator; 24V battery set.

HYDRAULICS: 120kg/cm² pressure hydraulic system for operating twin rudders and front foil flaps.

AIR CONDITIONING: Air conditioning can be provided as optional equipment.

COMMUNICATIONS AND NAVIGATION: Standard equipment includes UHF and VHF radio telephone. Radar and Decca Navigator is optional.

DIMENSIONS

EXTERNAL

Length overall: 27·75m (91ft)
Length over deck: 26·4m (86ft 7in)
Hull beam max: 5·84m (19ft 2in)
Beam over deck: 5·46m (17ft 11in)
Width over foils: 10·8m (35ft 5in)
Draft hullborne: 3·55m (11ft 8in)
Draft foilborne: 1·55m (5ft 1in)

INTERNAL

Aft passenger compartment (including w/c):
  Length: 9m (29ft 7in)
  Width: 4·9m (16ft)
  Height: 2m (6ft 7in)
  Floor area: 44·1m² (474ft²)
  Volume: 88m³ (3,108ft³)
Forward passenger compartment (including w/c):
  Length: 7·1m (23ft 3½in)
  Width: 5·4m (17ft 9in)
  Height: 2m (6ft 7in)
  Floor area: 37·3m² (412ft²)
  Volume: 67·6m³ (2,703ft³)
Main deck foyer:
  Length: 3·9m (12ft 9½in)
  Width: 4m (13ft 1½in)
  Height: 2m (6ft 7in)
  Floor area: 15m² (161ft²)
  Volume: 57·6m³ (2,030ft³)

WEIGHTS

Max take-off displacement: 63·3 tons
Light displacement: 49·3 tons
Deadweight (including fuel, oil, water, passengers, baggage and crew): 14 tons
Payload: 9·5 tons

PERFORMANCE (with normal payload)

Max speed foilborne: 67·5km/h (36·5 knots)
Cruising speed foilborne: 63km/h (34 knots)
Range: 600km (325n miles)
Turning radius: 470m (1,542ft)
Take-off distance: 250m (819ft)
Take-off time: 35 seconds
Stopping distance: 80m (264ft)
Time to stop craft: 10 seconds
Fuel consumption at cruising speed: 300kg/h (710lb/h)

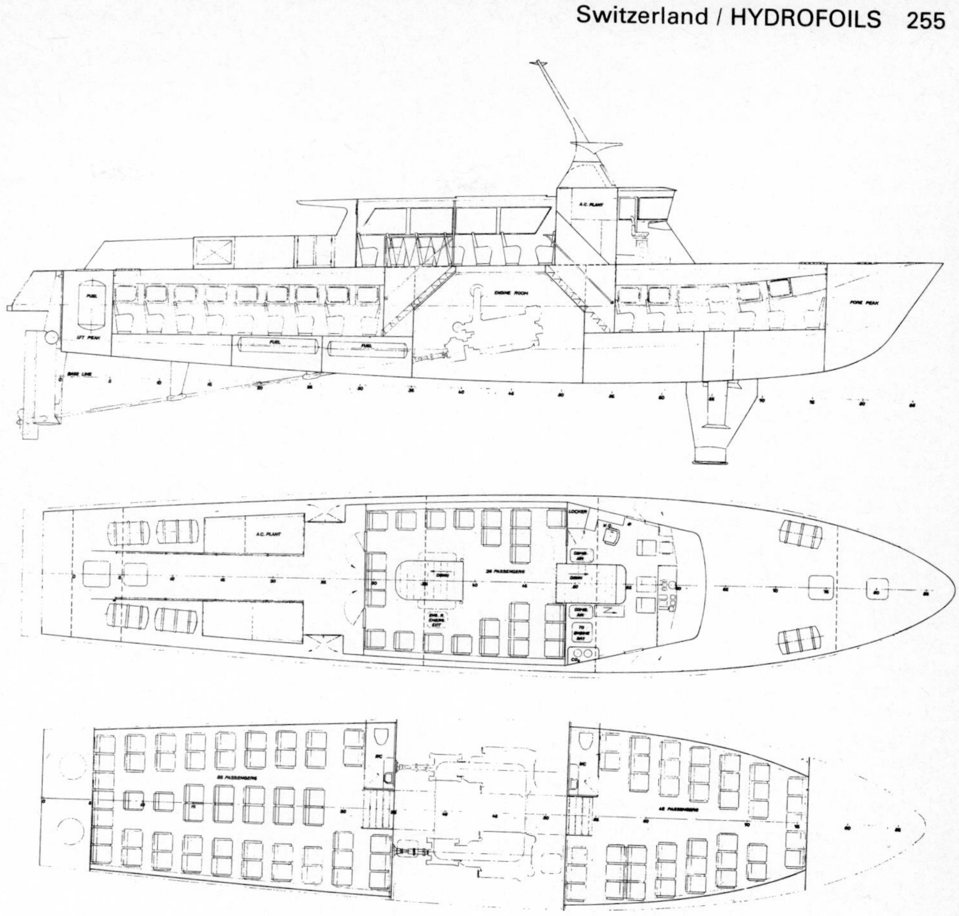

Inboard and outboard profile and main deck plan of the Supramar PT 50 Mk II

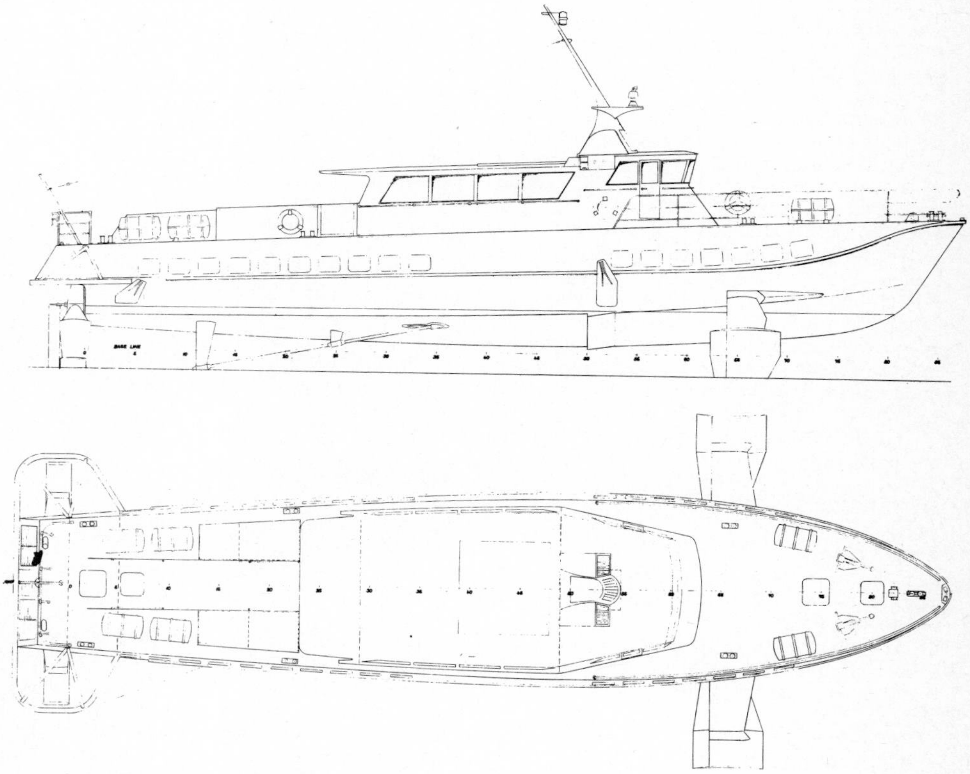

PTS 75 Mk III

The Supramar PTS 75 Mk III is an advanced derivative of the PT 50. It seats up to 160 passengers and is designed for higher speed, improved seaworthiness and greater riding comfort. By increasing the specific PT 50 engine power of 43hp/ton to 50hp/ton a top speed of about 38 knots is obtained with the vessel fully loaded, and sufficient power is provided for operation in tropical waters.

An improved Schertel-Supramar air stabilisation system is fitted, and this, combined with a new W-foil configuration, considerably reduces rolling, pitching and vertical accelerations. The vessel can operate foilborne in waves up to 1·82m (6ft) in height with full power.

The prototype was completed at the Vosper Thornycroft, Paulsgrove, Portsmouth yard in May 1974. The second craft of this type was completed in early 1976 by Supramar's licensee in Hong Kong, Supramar Pacific Shipbuilding Co Ltd.

FOILS: The foil configuration is surface-piercing and incorporates the Schertel-Supramar air stabilisation system. The bow foil assembly forms a rigid framework which facilitates the exchange of the foil structure. The foil is of hollow steel construction. It has three supporting struts, one on the centre line and one on either side. These are bolted to welded steel suspension points on the keel and chine respectively. Hydraulically operated flaps are fitted to the trailing edges to assist take-off, facilitate course corrections and provide automatic stabilisation when low frequency disturbances are encountered.

The rear foil is of surface-piercing Schertel-Supramar type and attached to the transom. Method of construction is the same as that employed for the bow foil. The complete assembly—foil, rudder sternpost, rudder, and two inclined struts—forms a rigid frame unit which is attached or detached as necessary. The aftermost propeller bearings are attached to the foil, the propellers being sited aft of the foil.

HULL: Hard chine type, constructed in partly riveted, partly welded corrosion resistant light metal alloy. A longitudinal frame system is employed, with transverse frames 900mm apart. Steel is used only for highly stressed parts such as the foil fittings and shaft exits. A new hull construction method is being employed for this design. The hull is built in the inverted position and

turned upright after the plating is completed.
ACCOMMODATION: Depending on operating requirements, between 130 and 160 passengers can be accommodated in three saloons. In the standard version airliner type seats are provided for 135 passengers, 19 in the upper aft saloon, 61 in the lower aft saloon and 55 in the lower forward saloon.

Ceilings are covered with lightweight plastic material, walls including web frames, are clad in luxury ply or artificial wood, and the floors are provided with thick carpets.

Three toilets are installed on the upper deck, within easy reach of all three saloons.

Passengers board the craft through wide side doors on the upper deck opening to a central foyer from which companionways lead to the lower passenger saloons. A promenade deck is available aft of the upper saloon and can be reached by passengers from the lower saloons via the foyer. Sufficient space for luggage is provided in the foyer. The upper aft saloon can be modified into a small dining room, if required, reducing the passenger capacity by 19.

All passenger saloons have emergency exits. A lifebelt is stowed beneath each seat and most of the inflatable life rafts are stowed aft and on the forward main deck.
POWER PLANT: Power is supplied by two 12-cylinder, MTU MB12 V652 SB70 supercharged diesels, each with a normal continuous output of 1,650hp at 1,380rpm, and 1,950hp at 1,460rpm maximum. Under tropical conditions normal continuous rating is 1,590hp at 1,380rpm and 1,810hp at 1,460rpm maximum. Engine output is transferred to two 950mm (3ft 1⅜in) diameter three-bladed bronze propellers through a Zahnradfabrik BW 900 HS 15 reversible gearbox, which is hydraulically operated and remotely controlled from the wheelhouse. The propeller shafts are in stainless steel and supported at four points by seawater lubricated rubber bearings. Fuel is carried in integral tanks beneath the lower deck in the bottom compartments.
SYSTEMS, ELECTRICAL: Two 37kVA water-cooled 60Hz diesel-driven 380V generators installed in the engine room. An emergency generator of similar capacity is provided at main deck level.
HYDRAULICS: 120kg/cm² pressure hydraulic system for operating all hydraulic driven consumers.
AIR CONDITIONING: An air conditioning system is provided. Capacity is sufficient for adequate temperature and humidity conditions in all passenger saloons and on the bridge when operating the craft in tropical conditions.
COMMUNICATIONS AND NAVIGATION: UHF radio, VHF radio-telephone and magnetic compass are standard. Radar, Decca Navigator and gyro compass to customer's requirements.
DIMENSIONS
EXTERNAL
Length overall, hull: 30m (98ft 6in)
Length overall, deck: 29·2m (96ft)
Hull beam max: 5·8m (19ft 1in)
Width across foils: 11·6m (38ft 1in)
Draft hullborne: 4m (13ft 1in)
Draft foilborne: 1·96m (6ft)
INTERNAL (standard version)
Aft lower saloon
Length: 9m (29ft 6in)
Width: 4·6m (15ft 1in)
Height: 2·15m (7ft 1in)
Floor area: 42m² (452ft²)
Volume: 92m³ (3,249ft³)
Forward lower saloon
Length: 8·1m (26ft 7in)
Width:4·7m (15ft 5in)
Height: 2·15m (7ft 1in)
Floor area: 37m² (398ft²)
Volume: 82m³ (2,896ft³)
Upper aft saloon
Length: 4·5m (14ft 9in)
Width: 4·2m (13ft 9in)
Height: 2·1m (6ft 11in)
Floor area: 18m² (193ft²)
Volume: 38m³ (1,342ft³)

The second Supramar PTS 75 Mk III to be ordered by Far East Hydrofoil Co for the Hong Kong-Macao service. The vessel was built in Hong Kong by Supramar Pacific Shipbuilding Co Ltd

Foyer
Length: 5·1m (16ft 9in)
Width: 4·2m (13ft 9in)
Height: 2·1m (6ft 11in)
Floor area: 20m² (215ft²)
Volume: 42m³ (1,483ft³)
WEIGHTS
Max take-off displacement: 85 tons
Light displacement: 68·5 tons
Disposable load (including fuel, oil, water, passengers, luggage and crew): 16·5 tons
PERFORMANCE (with normal payload)
Cruising speed: 66·5km/h (36 knots)
Max speed: 72·5km/h (39 knots)
Range: 333km (180n miles)
Turning radius approx: 700m (2,350ft)
Take-off distance approx: 500m (1,600ft)
Take-off time approx: 50 seconds
Stopping distance approx: 100m (330ft)
Time to stop craft approx: 20 seconds
Fuel consumption at cruising speed: approx 600 kg/h (1,323lb/h)

SUPRAMAR PT 100

A variant of the PTS 75 Mk III is the PT 100, designed especially for short-haul commuter routes and accommodating 200 passengers.

Main dimensions and characteristics are identical to those of the PTS 75 Mk III. The layout is shown in the accompanying general arrangement drawing.

SUPRAMAR PTS 150 Mk II

The Supramar PTS 150 Mk II carries 250 passengers and is the world's largest seagoing hydrofoil. The vessels fulfil SOLAS requirements, and have been built under the supervision of Det Norske Veritas, which has granted the class designation IA2-Hydrofoil-K.
FOILS: The foil configuration is a combined surface-piercing and submerged system. The bow foil, which provides the necessary static transverse stability, is of the Schertel-Sachsenberg surface-piercing V design and carries 60% of the load. The rear foil, which bears about 40% is of the submerged, Schertel-Supramar air-stabilised type. In foilborne conditions the boat is inherently stable.

Hydraulically-actuated flaps are fitted at the trailing edges of the bow foil to assist take-off and adjust the flying height.

The rear foil is fully submerged.

Air stabilisation is fitted to the rear foil which gives the necessary transverse and longitudinal stability and improves passenger comfort under heavy sea conditions. Separate port and starboard systems are installed to stabilise rolling and pitching.

The system feeds air from the free atmosphere through air exits to the foil upper surface (the low pressure region) decreasing the lift. The amount to lift is varied by the quantity of air admitted, this being controlled by a valve actuated by signals from a damped pendulum and a rate gyro. The stabilising moment is produced by decreasing the available air volume for the more submerged side and increasing that of the less submerged one.

The rear foil includes the lift-generating sections, rudders and the rear suspension structure which serves as a connecting element with the hull. Struts for the aftermost propeller bearings are also attached to the rear foil, the propellers being sited beneath the foil. The complete assembly is a framed structure which can easily be detached from the transom. The angle of attack of the rear foil can be controlled hydraulically both during take-off and when foilborne.

The surface-piercing bow foil is provided with air exits on the upper surface (the low pressure region) in order to vary lift and control pitch and heave motions by the quantity of air admitted. This is released by a valve which is actuated by amplified signals taken from a vertical accelerometer and a rate sensor.

Front and rear foil are of hollow construction and by the extensive use of welding, the number of connecting parts requiring screws, bolts or similar means of attachment is reduced to a minimum.
HULL: Partly riveted and partly welded construction and a system of longitudinal and transverse frames has been adopted. It has fairly high deadrise and hard chine sections for performance as a planing hull and for structural impacts in a seaway while foilborne. A step is provided to facilitate take-off. While the main or structure deck is continuous from bow to stern, the lower deck is interrupted by the engine room, sited amidships. The superstructure, which is also longitudinally and transversally framed, is not included in the load bearing structure. Several expansion joints have therefore been provided.
ACCOMMODATION: The PTS 150 Mk II carries 250 passengers in four saloons, two on the main deck and two on the lower deck. The forward compartment main deck seats 48, and the aft compartment 110. On the lower deck the forward compartment seats 40 and the aft compartment 52.

Passengers board the craft through double doors to the single centralised foyer, from which doors and companion ladders lead to the respective passenger saloons on the upper and lower decks.

Provision is made for all passengers to be served in their seats with cold meals and drinks.

Passenger seats are of lightweight aircraft type. Floors and ceilings are covered with lightweight plastic materials and the walls are clad in luxury plywood. Each passenger saloon has fitted car-

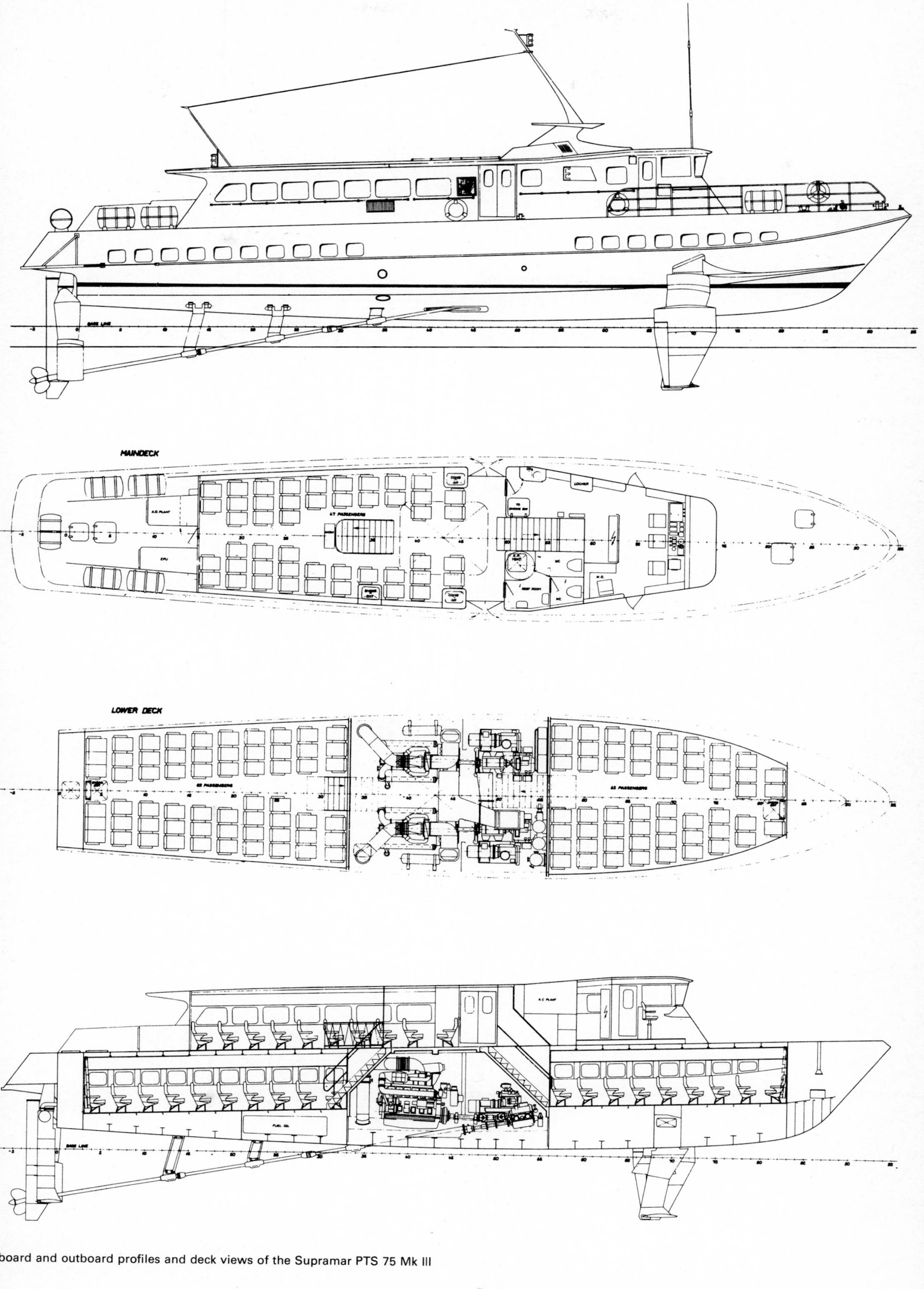

Inboard and outboard profiles and deck views of the Supramar PTS 75 Mk III

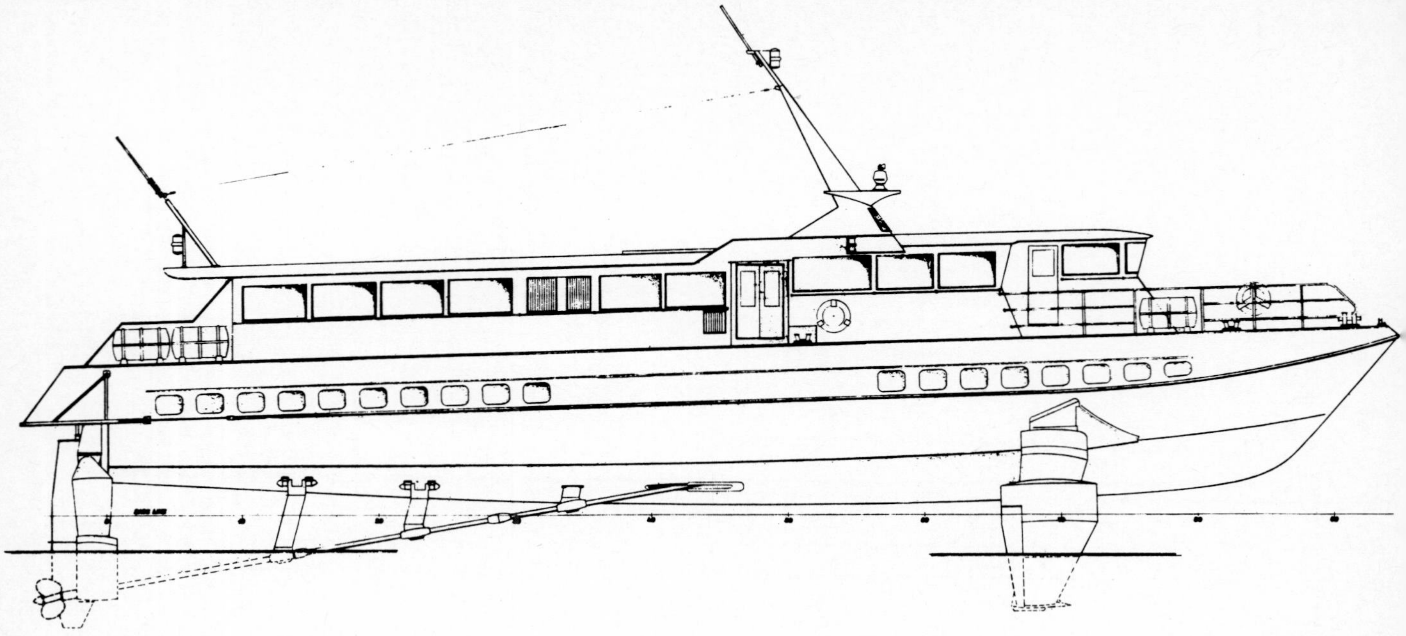

Outboard profile of the Supramar PT 100

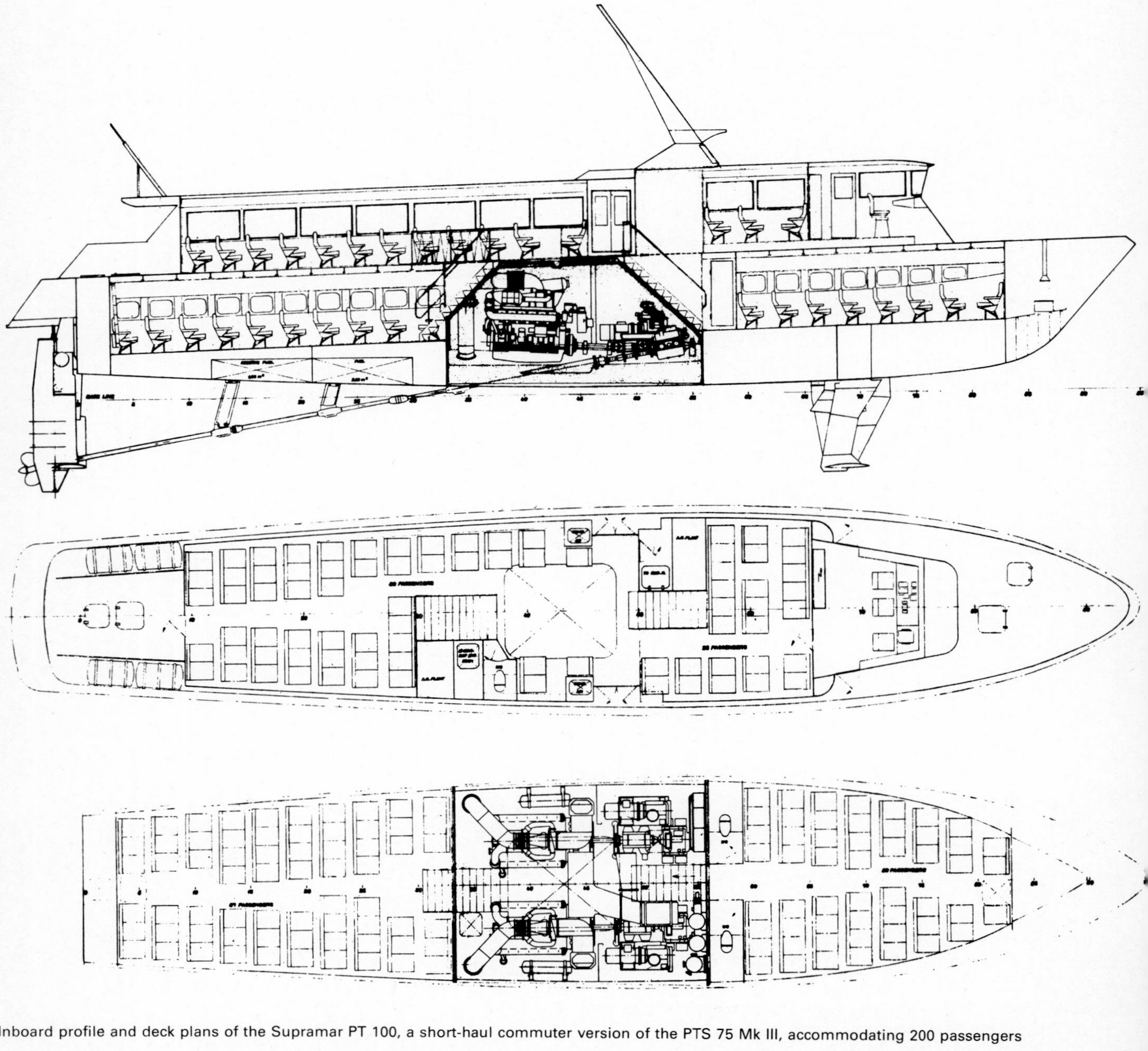

Inboard profile and deck plans of the Supramar PT 100, a short-haul commuter version of the PTS 75 Mk III, accommodating 200 passengers

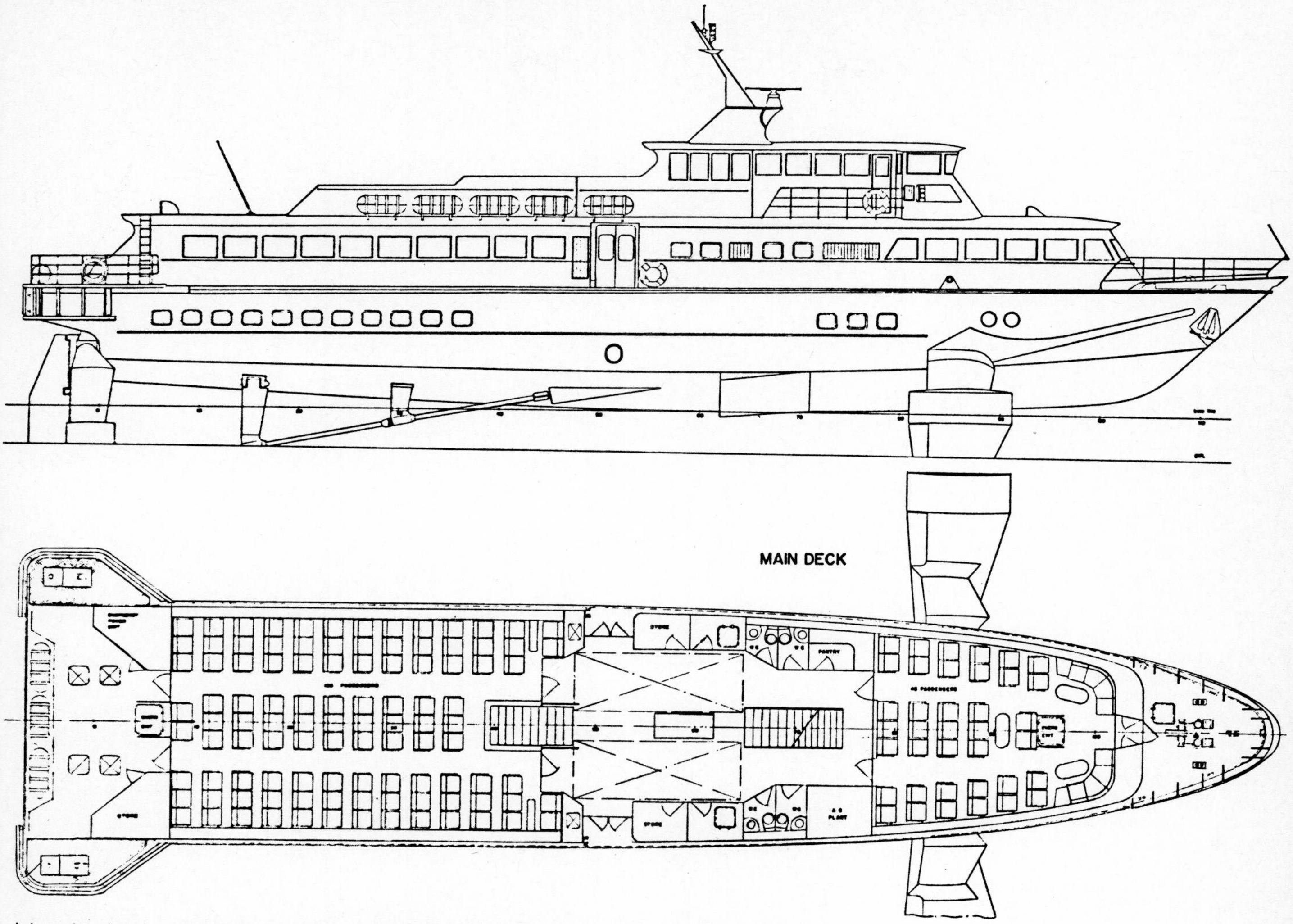

Inboard and outboard profiles, main deck and lower deck arrangements of the PT 150 Mk III

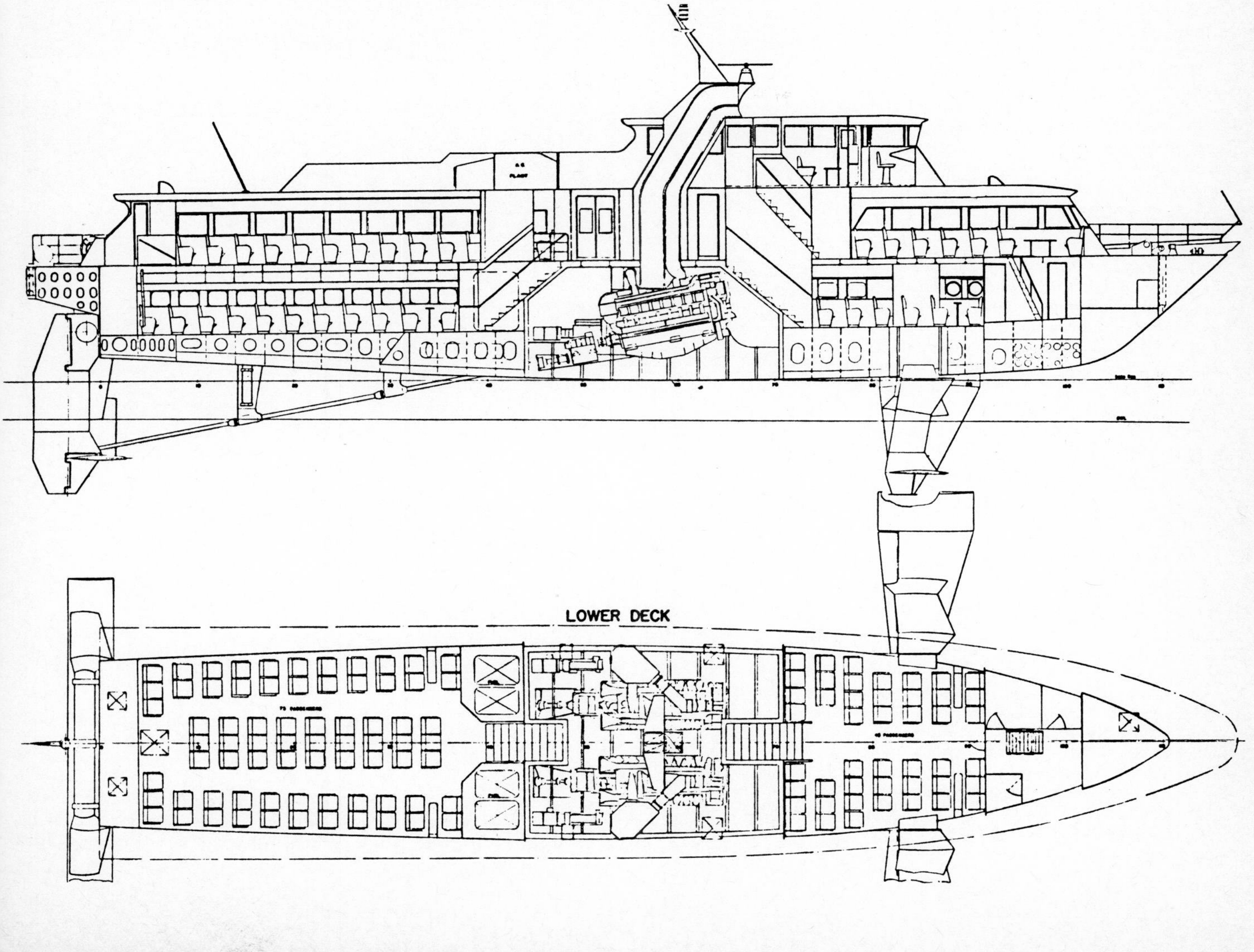

pets. Each room has an independent ventilation unit. Six toilets are provided.

The bridge, which is on a separate level above the main deck, slightly forward of midships, is reached by a companion ladder at the aft of the forward passenger compartment. All passenger saloons have emergency exits.

The craft carries 12 inflatable RFD liferafts (for 110% of the classified number of passengers and crew) which are stowed along both sides of the superstructure deck, and on the aft maindeck. Lifebelts are arranged beneath the seats.

POWER PLANT: Power is supplied by two 20-cylinder MTU MD 20V 538 TB8 supercharged and intercooled diesels each rated at 3,400hp continuous. To improve torque characteristics during take-off two engine-mounted Maybach torque converters are provided.

Reverse and reduction gears are of the lightweight Zahnradfabrik BW 1500HS22 hydraulically-operated type, and incorporate the propeller thrust bearings. They have three shafts and two gear trains, one of which has an idler. The output shafts rotate either in the same direction as the input shaft or the opposite direction, depending on the gear through which power is directed. Selection is by pneumo-hydraulic double-plate clutches on the input shafts. A mechanical lock-up is provided so that the gear can transmit full torque in the event of clutch slip while in service. This takes the form of a dog clutch which is effective in one direction, and can only be engaged in the "stop" condition. The gearboxes each have integral oil pumps for lubrication and clutch operation.

The angle between the engine crankshaft and the parallel shaft of the gearbox is accommodated by a cardan shaft with universal joints. The converter gear main shaft bearings, as well as those on the reverse gear primary shaft, are proportioned in such a way as to resist the forces and couples imposed by the cardan shaft universal joints. As a protection against accidents the cardan shaft is installed within a substantial removable tunnel.

SYSTEMS, ELECTRICAL: The total electrical system is supplied by three diesel generators with an output of 65 kVA each, one of them being an emergency generator installed on the upper deck.

In the event of an electrical failure the emergency generator is switched on automatically. The engines are started by fresh air and are fresh-water cooled. The following systems are supplied by the electrical plant. For power and permanently installed heating and cooling equipment: 380V rotary current, 50Hz. For light, pockets and instrumentation: 220V ac, 50Hz. For remote control and monitoring: 24V ac.

HYDRAULICS: Steering, variation of the front foil flap angle and the angle of attack of the rear foil are all operated hydraulically. Each system has its own circuit which is monitored by a pressure controlled pilot lamp.

CONTROLS: Starting, manoeuvring and operation of the craft is controlled from the bridge, but in cases of emergency the main engines may be controlled from the engine room.

The two main engines are each controlled by an operating lever designed for singlehanded control. Propeller reversal is also by means of these levers, the reverse gear being actuated by pneumatic remote control between bridge and main engines.

To start the boat both operating levers must be put in the "full ahead" position simultaneously. The engine mounted torque converter gear is actuated automatically. Foilborne speed can be regulated by fine adjusting of the operating levers. No other control devices are necessary for the main engines.

Levers for variation of the front foil flap angle and the angle of attack of the rear foil are actuated only before and after starting. During foilborne operation these can be used for trim compensation. All instrumentation and monitoring equipment is installed on the bridge.

AIR CONDITIONING: The vessel is equipped with air conditioning and heating plant which guarantees a room temperature of between 20 and 25°C, dependent on the relative humidity. Air rate is 25m³/h/person.

Interior of the PT 150 DC showing the forward saloon on the upper deck

The aft saloon on the upper deck of the PT 150 DC seen from the rear

A PT 150D operating in the Baltic

COMMUNICATION AND NAVIGATION: Standard navigation equipment includes a gyro master compass with transformers, rectifiers and one multiple steering repeater positioned ahead of the helmsman, Loran or Decca Navigator and radar.

Communications equipment includes radio telephone equipment for normal and emergency use.

DIMENSIONS

EXTERNAL

Length overall, hull: 37·9m (124ft 3in)
Length overall, deck: 37·1m (121ft 10in)
Hull beam, max: 7·5m (24ft 7in)
Deck beam, max: 7·4m (24ft 3in)
Width across foils: 16m (52ft 5in)
Draft hullborne: 5·5m (18ft)
Draft foilborne: 2·6m (8ft 6in)

WEIGHTS

Displacement, fully loaded: 165 tons
Disposable load (payload plus consumable stores): 23 tons
Passenger capacity: 250

PERFORMANCE

Cruising speed at 6,880hp: 67·5km/h (36·5 knots)
Range: 400km (250n miles)
Max permissible wave height in foilborne mode at full power (head seas) for passenger acceptability: 3m (10ft)

SUPRAMAR PTS 150 MK III

An improved version of the PTS 150 Mk II, the Mk III is fitted with an advanced surface-piercing

foil system which, compared with that of the Mk II, reduces hydrodynamic resistance by about 20%. Other features include the fitting of more powerful, supercharged diesels, raising the cruising speed to about 40 knots and the use of an improved stabilization system which enhances seakeeping capability and increases passenger comfort.
POWER PLANT: Two MTU 16V 956 TB82 supercharged diesels, each rated at 3,800hp continuous. Reverse and reduction gears are of lightweight Zahnradfabrik BW 1500 type.
DIMENSIONS: As for PTS 150 Mk II
WEIGHTS
Displacement, fully loaded: 175 tons
Disposable load: 36 tons
Passenger capacity: 270
PERFORMANCE
Cruising speed: 40 knots
Range: 250n miles
Max permissible wave height, foilborne, full power: head sea 3m (10ft)
Max permissible wave height foilborne at reduced speed: 3·5m (11ft 6in)

ST 3A FULLY SUBMERGED FOIL RESEARCH CRAFT

In 1965 the US Navy awarded Supramar a contract for the construction and testing of a five-ton research craft with fully submerged air stabilised foils. The objectives of the tests were the investigation of the effectiveness and reliability of the Schertel-Supramar air stabilisation system under a variety of wave conditions.
FOIL SYSTEM: The craft was fitted with two fully submerged bow foils and one fully submerged rear foil. The load distribution was 62% on the bow foils and 38% on rear foil. A rudder flap was attached to the end of the rear foil strut.
AIR FEED SYSTEM: Lift variation was achieved without movable foil parts. Each foil has two air ducts with outlets on the suction side. Air was drawn through these apertures from the free atmosphere via the foil suspension tube and the hollow struts. Air valves, controlled by sensors, governed the quantity of air admitted to the respective ducts.
CONTROLS: The signals of a depth sensor, a rate gyro and damped pendulum were added and amplified. The pneumatic follow-up amplifier drew its propulsion power from the subpressure which was produced at a suction opening at the strut near the foil. The amplifier output was connected with the air valve. The depth sensor probed the submergence depth digitally by means of suction orifices at the front struts. No motor-driven power source was required for the control system which, as well as the air feed system for lift variation of the foils, was designed for simplicity and reliability.
HULL: The hull, of hard chine construction, was basically that of a standard Supramar ST 3, modified to accommodate the new foil system, gas-turbine and test equipment. To facilitate take-off, a step was provided and a ram wedge was fastened to the stern bottom. The hull clearance (tip of step to water surface) of only 36cm (1ft 2½in) was due to the requirement that an existing ST 3 hull, with an inclined propeller shaft, was to be used for the tests.
POWER PLANT: The craft was powered by a single 1,000hp GE 7 LM100 PG 102 gas-turbine. Engine output was transferred to a 0·38m (1ft 3in) diameter S-C bronze propeller through a reduction gear, a V-drive and an inclined stainless steel shaft. A 35hp Mercury outboard was installed on the port side of the transom to provide auxiliary propulsion. To feed the stabilisation gyros a 6hp gasoline engine was installed in the forepeak and coupled to a three-phase ac generator.
DIMENSIONS
Length overall, hull: 10·32m (33ft 10in)
Width over foils: 3·6m (11ft 10in)
Width over hull: 2·7m (8ft 10in)
Draft hullborne: 1·55m (5ft 1in)
Draft foilborne (front foil): 0·5m (1ft 7½in)
Hull clearance: 0·36m (1ft 2½in)
WEIGHTS
Displacement: 4·9 tons

Supramar ST 3A

PERFORMANCE
Max measured test speed: 101km/h (54·5 knots)
Max speed (design): 104km/h (56 knots)
Take-off time: 14·5 seconds
Stopping distance: 50-5 knots: 120m (390ft)
Turning radius at 40 knots: 230m (750ft)
SEA TEST: Sea trials along the Mediterranean coast revealed that the craft, despite a small hull clearance, was capable of taking waves 0·9–1·2m (3–4ft) high, and with a minimum length of about 30·4–36·4m (100–120ft), at 45 knots in all courses from head to beam seas, partially contouring. In waves over 1·2m (4ft) the hull periodically touched wave crests, which was accompanied by a marked speed reduction (very high Froude number) during water contacting. In a following sea, and in all courses up to about 60 degrees to a following sea, foilborne operation was limited to 0·76m (2ft 6in) waves due to the control system, which at that time had no heave sensor. At a wave height of 0·91m (3ft) (a tenth of boat length), vertical accelerations of only 0·08g had been measured, which compares very favourably with the sea test results of other craft with fully submerged foils.

NAVAL HYDROFOILS

Derived from Supramar's range of commercial vessels, this new range of military hydrofoils is designed for naval defence duties, coast guard and anti-contraband patrol.

SUPRAMAR PAT 20

This military version of the Supramar PT 20B Mk II is in service with several navies for patrolling coastal and sheltered waters. It has good seakeeping capabilities for a craft of this size.
FOILS: Schertel-Sachsenberg surface-piercing type in structural steel.
POWER PLANT: The main propulsion engine is an MTU Type 331 12-cylinder, four-stroke diesel, developing 1,430hp maximum intermittent and 1,300hp continuous. Engine output is transferred to a three-bladed propeller via an inclined shaft.
HULL: Riveted seawater-resistant light metal alloy structure.
ARMAMENT: Two 40mm Bofors L/70 automatic guns, one forward, one aft. Ammunition stored in compartments beneath.
DIMENSIONS
Length overall: 21·75m (71ft 4in)
Width over foils: 8·6m (28ft 2in)
Draft hullborne: 3·1m (10ft 2in)
Draft foilborne: 1·4m (4ft 7in)
WEIGHTS
Displacement loaded: 31 tons
Disposable load (fuel, consumable stores, crew, provisions, armament and ammunition): 6·3 tons
PERFORMANCE
Cruising speed: 35 knots
Range: 536km (300n miles)

PAT 70

The PAT 70 is similar in design and construction to the PT 50 Mk II.
FOILS: Bow and rear foils are of surface-piercing V configuration and fabricated in structural steel.
HULL: Riveted light alloy construction.
POWER PLANT: Power is provided by two MTU MB 12V 652 12-cylinder four-stroke diesels, each rated at 1,725hp continuous and 1,950hp maximum intermittent. Engine output is transferred to two three-bladed propellers via twin inclined propeller shafts.
ARMAMENT: A typical weapon fit would comprise two 40mm Bofors L/70 automatic mounts, one forward, one aft.
DIMENSIONS
Length overall: 29·5m (96ft 9in)
Width over foils: 10·7m (35ft 1in)
Draft hullborne: 3·8m (12ft 6in)
Draft foilborne: 1·7m (5ft 7in)
WEIGHTS
Displacement loaded: 69 tons
Disposable load (fuel, consumable stores, crew, provisions, armament and ammunition): 14 tons
PERFORMANCE
Cruising speed: 39 knots
Range: 536km (300n miles)
Max permissible wave height foilborne: 1·8m (6ft) wave

NAT 85

Derived from the PTS 75 Mk III passenger ferry, this fast patrol boat variant is armed with a 40mm Breda Bofors twin naval mounting and Otomat guided missiles.
FOILS: Surface-piercing configuration, incorporating the Schertel-Supramar air stabilisation system.
HULL: Hard chine type, constructed in partly riveted, partly welded corrosion resistant light alloy.
POWER PLANT: Power is supplied by two MTU MB 16V 652 16-cylinder 4-stroke diesels, each rated at 2,300hp continuous and 2,610hp maximum. Engine output is transferred to two three-bladed propellers through a Zahnradfabrik reversible gearbox.
ARMAMENT: Anti-Ship Missiles: Two Otomat Mk I missile launchers aft. Guns: 40mm Breda Bofors L/70 twin naval mounting on the foredeck, ahead of the superstructure.
ELECTRONICS: Thomson-CSF Canopus C fire control system.
DIMENSIONS
Length overall: 30·4m (99ft 9in)
Width over foils: 12m (39ft 4in)
Draft hullborne: 4·3m (14ft 1in)
Draft foilborne: 2·3m (7ft 6in)
WEIGHTS
Displacement loaded: 85 tons
Disposable load (fuel, consumable stores, crew provisions, armament and ammunition): 16 tons
PERFORMANCE
Cruising speed: 42 knots

Range: 741km (400n miles)
Max permissible wave height: 2·3m (7ft 6in) waves

NAT 90

Based on the PTS 75 Mk III, this alternative fast strike missilecraft variant has waterjet propulsion and fully retracting foils. It is intended for operations in areas where the hullborne draft would be too deep for satisfactory navigation, particularly in sheltered waters. The foils are retracted hydraulically above the waterline.

FOILS: Surface-piercing V configuration. Bow foil is "split" to permit the two halves to swivel upwards hydraulically. The aft foil assembly is built as a single unit and comprises the foils, a central rudder/water strut, to which the rudder flap is attached, and two side struts.

HULL: Hull and superstructure in combined riveted and welded seawater resistant light metal. All compartments are air-conditioned, including the bridge.

POWER PLANT: Power for the waterjet propulsion system is supplied by two MTU MB 16V 652 16-cylinder, four-stroke diesels, each rated at 2,300hp continuous and 2,610hp maximum intermittent. Each is connected to a Rocketdyne Powerjet 18 single-stage, axial-flow waterjet. During foilborne operation water enters through an inlet located at the forward lower end of the aft centre foil strut. When the craft is operating in hullborne mode, with foils retracted, water enters the propulsion system through an inlet located in the bottom of the hull. Hullborne speed (foils retracted), with a single Powerjet 18 in use is 15 knots, with both Powerjets in use, 25 knots.

ARMAMENT: A typical weapons fit would be one Breda/Bofors L/70 twin 40mm mounting forward of the superstructure and two Exocet missile launchers aft.

DIMENSIONS
Length overall: 29·9m (98ft 1in)
Width across foils: 11·8m (38ft 8in)
Draft hullborne: 4·1m (13ft 5in)
Draft hullborne, foils retracted: 1·3m (4ft 3in)
Draft foilborne: 1·9m (6ft 3in)

WEIGHTS
Displacement loaded: 85 tons
Disposable load (fuel, consumable stores, crew, provisions, armament and ammunition): 15 tons

PERFORMANCE
Max cruising speed: 39 knots
Range: 741km (400n miles)
Max permissible wave height: 2·3m (7ft 6in) waves

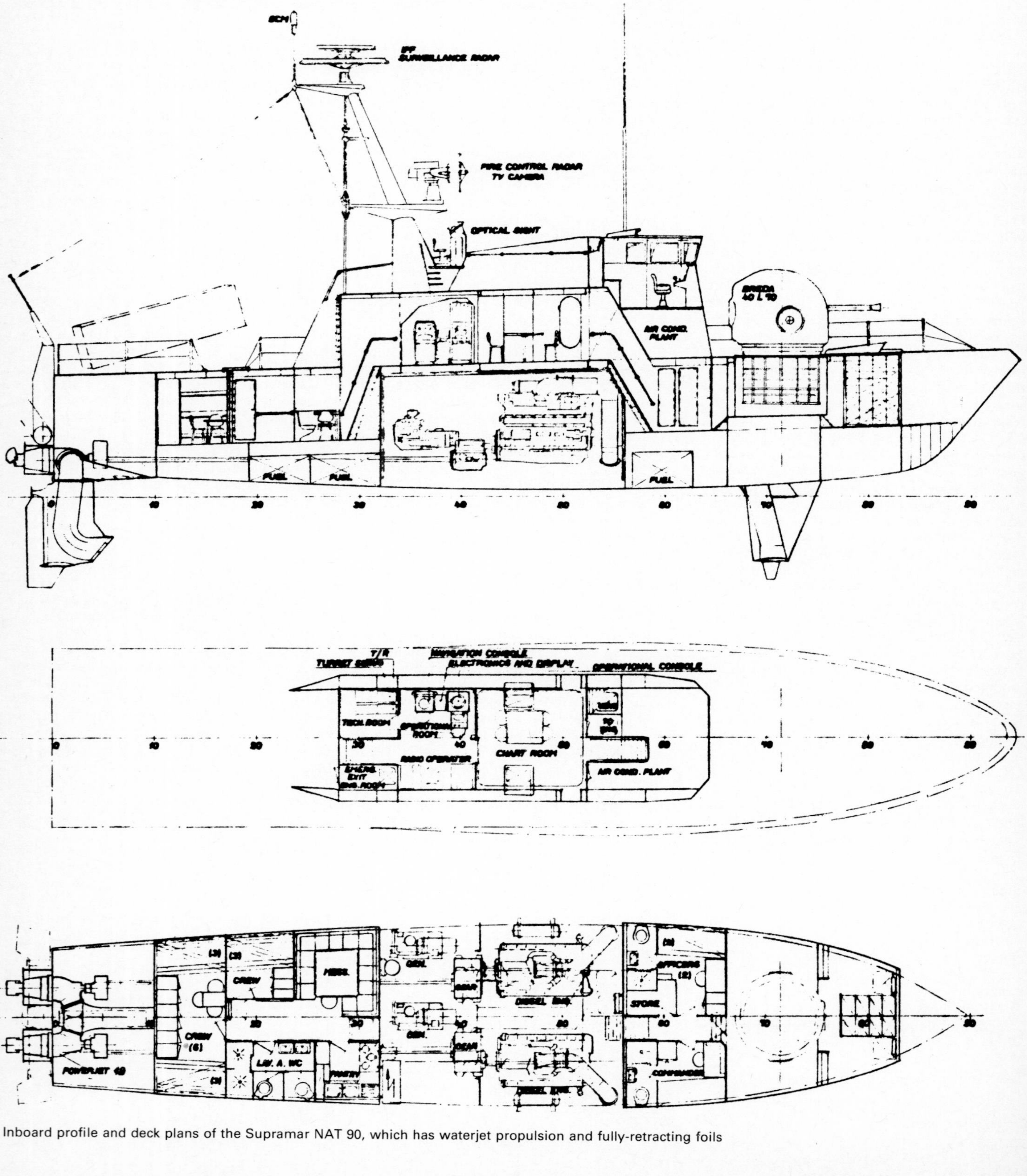

Inboard profile and deck plans of the Supramar NAT 90, which has waterjet propulsion and fully-retracting foils

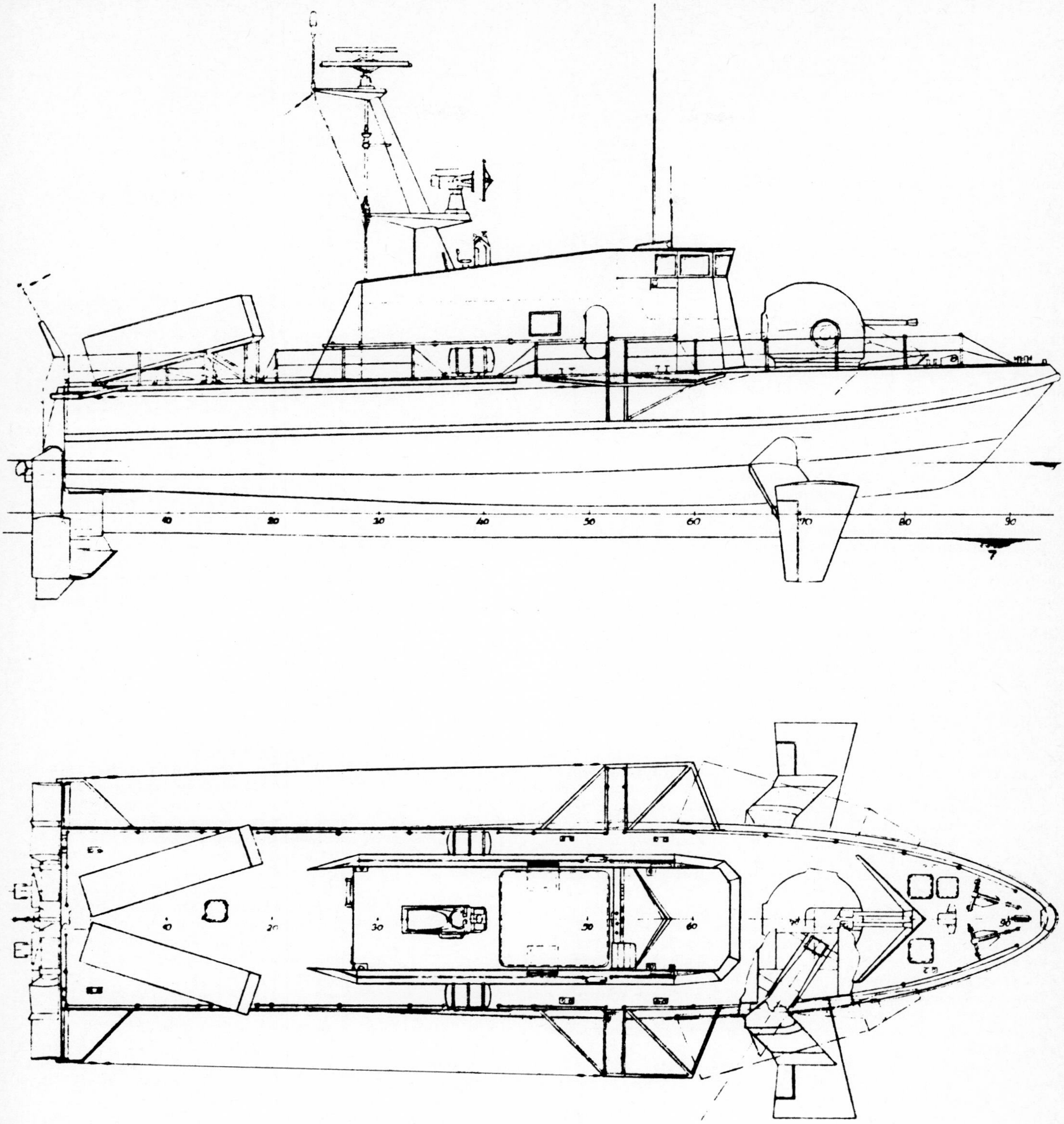

Outboard elevations and weatherdeck plan of the Supramar NAT 90 fast strike missilecraft

NAT 190

NAT 190 is the designation given to the military version of the Supramar PTS 150 Mk III. As a fast strike craft its main armament would comprise two 40mm Bofors L/70 automatic twin mounts and three Exocet MM 38 missile launchers.

FOILS: Fixed surface-piercing foils of Schertel-Supramar air stabilised type. In the event of the air stabilisation system failing, the craft is able to continue operating in foilborne mode although foil submergence would be increased moderately.

POWER PLANT: Foilborne propulsion is supplied by two MTU 16V 956 TB 82 16-cylinder diesels each driving a three-bladed propeller via an inclined shaft. Each engine is rated at 3,800hp continuous at 27°C.

ARMAMENT: Typical weapons fit would comprise two 40mm Bofors L/70 automatic dual purpose guns, one forward and one aft and three Exocet MM 38 anti-ship missile launchers.

ELECTRONICS: Thomson-CSF Vega-Pollux tactical information unit and fire control system.

DIMENSIONS

Length overall: 37·9m (124ft 4in)

Width over foils: 16·6m (54ft 6in)

Draft hullborne: 5m (16ft 5in)

Draft foilborne: 2·1m (6ft 11in)

WEIGHTS

Displacement loaded: 180 tons

Disposable load (fuel, consumable stores, crew, provisions, armament and ammunition): 40 tons

PERFORMANCE

Cruising speed: 39 knots

Foilborne range: 1,072km (600n miles) at 36 knots

Hullborne range: 1,850km (1,000n miles) at 10 knots

Endurance at sea: 3-5 days

Max permissible wave height: 2·8m (9ft) waves at reduced speed: 3·5m (11ft 6in) waves

SUPRAMAR MT 250

This is a design concept for a 250-tonne patrol boat hydrofoil which meets the tactical requirements established by the West German and other NATO navies. It conforms to the fast patrol boat standards of the West German Navy and has a maximum intermittent speed of 60 knots.

Main dimensions of the vessel are similar to those of the Swedish Spica class, Vosper Tenacity, Israeli Sa'ar class and the West German Type 148. It is designed for all-weather operation in the western Baltic, the Skagerrak and other areas with similar operational conditions.

Foilborne propulsion is supplied by gas-turbine powered waterjets. The foil system is of fully-submerged type employing the Schertel-Supramar air stabilisation system.

As a significant part of the total operating time will be in the hullborne mode, a separate hullborne propulsion plant is provided which guarantees adequate speed in the two hullborne modes: foils retracted and foils extended.

FOILS: Canard system with a single fully submerged bow foil and two fully submerged rear foils. The foils are of welded hollow shell construction in stainless steel. All three are retracted clear of the waterline hydraulically. The design avoids the use of hinged doors or panels to raise the bow foil.

CONTROLS: The stabilisation system is a combined automatic control process employing flaps for damping low frequency motions and air-control for high frequency motions. Roll stabilisation is effected by air control of the outer rear foil and the rear foil struts, also by the operation of flaps on the outer rear foil.

Pitch and heave are controlled by flaps on the bow foil and flaps in the centre section of the aft foil.

The stabilisation system consists of four units: the sensors, a computer (for automatic flight control), a command unit and the transactuators.

HULL: Hull and superstructure is of partly riveted, partly welded seawater-resistant light metal alloy. There are seven watertight transverse bulkheads.

INTERNAL LAYOUT/ACCOMMODATION: Accommodation and operations rooms are located almost entirely below deck leaving a relatively large free deck area. Crew would normally comprise twenty one, officers and ratings. Operating and control rooms are all fully air-conditioned. Minelaying equipment, conforming to NATO standards, can be installed as an alternative to missile launchers. Stand-by-space is available for a substantial number of Mk 55 mines. There are three officers' cabins and two crew rooms, two toilets with wash basins, one pantry, store rooms, operating and control rooms for ship and machinery. The control and operations rooms have direct access to the bridge and the radio room. All facilities are provided for an intended sea endurance of three to five days.

POWER PLANT, FOILBORNE: The main propulsion plant consists of a slightly modified version of the Rolls-Royce Marine Olympus TM 3, with the following ratings:

performance: 25,350ps
power turbine speed: 5,450rpm
spec fuel consumption: 0·219kg/PSh
ambient air temperature: 15°C

This comprises an Olympus gas-generator and a single-stage long-life power unit mounted on a common base. The forward end of the gas-generator mates with the air-intake plenum chamber, which has a cascaded bend to give an undisturbed airflow to the engine intake. Flexible joints are applied to the faces of the air-intake and exhaust system to allow relative movement between the module and the ship's uptakes and downtakes. At the engine ratings given, estimated time between overhaul for the gas-generator is 2,000 hours.

A Metastream M 4000 elastic coupling of approximately 1,500mm length connects the power turbine output shaft with an Allen epicycle gear box. The latter is flanged directly to a Rocketdyne Powerjet 46 pump. The Allen gear box has a reduction ratio of approx 1:5·5.

The Rocketdyne Powerjet 46 pump has twin side water intakes and is rigidly mounted to the ship's structure. It transmits thrust via three points.

AUXILIARY PROPULSION PLANT: The auxiliary propulsion plant comprises two 8-cylinder MTU 8V 331 TC 71 diesel engines driving via REINTJES WAV 500 A reverse and reduction gears and inclined propeller shafts two variable-pitch KAMEWA propellers. The propellers are arranged in a duct at the transom.

The MTU 8V 331 TC 71 diesel has the following ratings and characteristics:

output continuous: 750 PS at 2,055rpm
output intermittent: 815 PS at 2,120rpm
number of cylinders: 8 in V form

ARMAMENT: Optional, but can comprise surface-to-surface missiles of Exocet, Otomat or similar types or OTO Compact gun mount and additional 20mm anti-aircraft guns. Provision has been made for various types of combat systems including Vega II-53 or Mini-Combat-System WM 28.

The Supramar MT 250 fast patrol boat for all-weather operation. Main powerplant is a Marine Olympus TM3

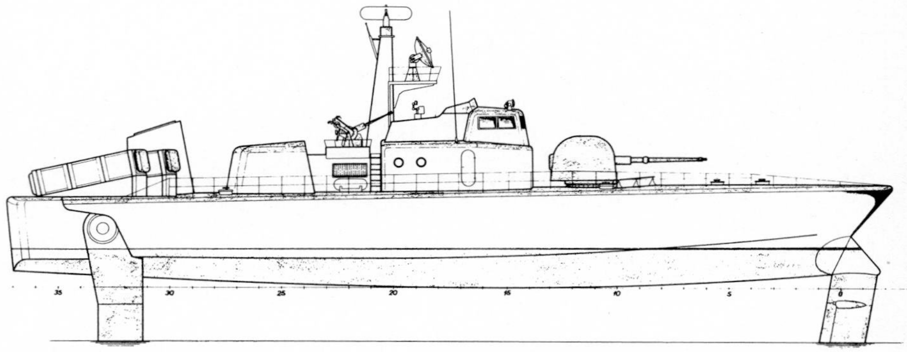

DIMENSIONS
Length overall, foils extended: 43·7m (143ft 4in)
Beam max over deck: 9·4m (30ft 9in)
Max width over foils: 15·8m (51ft 11in)
Draft foilborne: 3·35m (11ft)
Draft hullborne,
with foils extended: 6·95m (22ft 9in)
with foils retracted: 2·2m (7ft 2in)

WEIGHTS
Operational displacement: 250 tonnes

PERFORMANCE
Speed max continuous,
foilborne: 55 knots
hullborne, foils retracted: 13 knots
hullborne, foils extended: 9·5 knots
Range,
at max continuous speed foilborne: 741km (400n miles)
at max continuous speed hullborne, foils extended: 3,340km (1,800n miles)
at max continuous speed hullborne, foils down: 2,400km (1,300n miles)
Max permissible sea state, foilborne: 3·6m (12ft) waves

SUPRAMAR MT 80

The MT 80 is designed for operation in coastal waters. A fully submerged retractable foil system enables it to operate under adverse weather conditions. It can be equipped with a variety of weapons and control systems.

The hull and superstructure are of combined riveted and welded light metal alloy construction. The foils are of high tensile structural steel. The main propulsion system consists of one Rolls-Royce Proteus gas turbine driving either a water-jet pump, or a propeller via a double bevel gear arrangement. The armament and weapon control system is optional.

DIMENSIONS
Length overall: 29m (95ft 2in)
Beam max: 5·8m (19ft)
Width over foils: 8·9m (29ft 2in)
Draft hullborne, foils extended: 4·4m (15ft 5in)
foils retracted: 1·5m (4ft 11in)
Draft foilborne: 2·1m (6ft 10 in)

WEIGHTS
Displacement: 85 tons

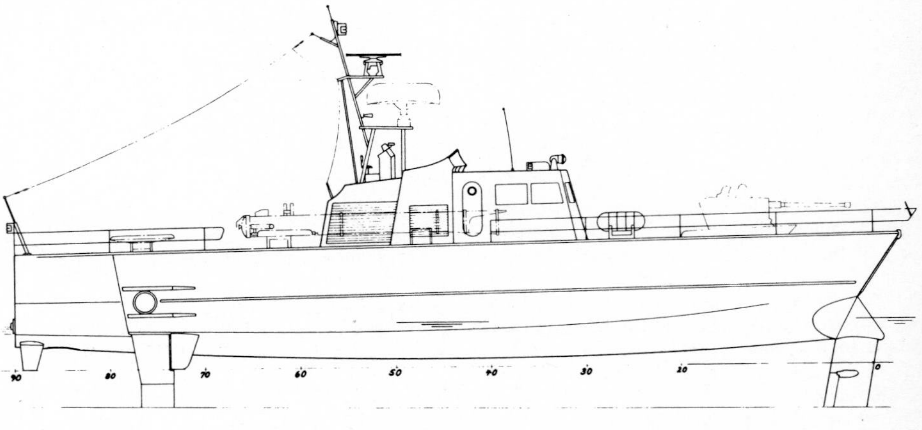

Outboard profile of the Supramar MT 80, 80-tonne hydrofoil for patrol duties in coastal waters. The foilborne propulsion system comprises a single Rolls-Royce Marine Proteus driving a waterjet pump or a propeller via a double-bevel drive

PERFORMANCE
Speed: 53 knots
Range: 741km (400n miles)
Crew: 8–12
Sea endurance: 3 days
Max permissible sea state, foilborne: 2·7m (9ft) waves

SUPRAMAR 500-SEAT PASSENGER FERRY

In August 1972, Supramar revealed that it is undertaking studies for the design of a 500-seat passenger ferry.

SUPRAMAR CT 70 CATAMARAN HYDROFOIL

The Supramar hydrofoil catamaran has been designed especially for operation in shallow and sheltered waters, where draft limitations preclude the use of conventional hydrofoil craft. Berthing is possible at any existing pontoon or quay facility without adaption, as the foils are well within the hull beam and thereby fully protected against damage while drawing alongside.

One of the major applications foreseen for this new class of hydrofoil is that of fast water bus on urban passenger services. Other likely roles include those of oil-rig support vessel, leisure craft and water sports, especially fishing.

About 80-90% of the lift is produced by the foils, and the remainder by the partly immersed hull planing surfaces forward, which also provides stability. The arrangement permits the placing of the foils below the water surface at a depth generally free of floating debris.

In the case of partial foil ventilation, the planing surfaces prevent high angles of list and also impede deep immersion in the waves of a following sea. In cases where retractable foils are required a simple method of retraction can be incorporated.

Because of the uncomplicated nature of the concept and the ease of foil retraction, it is felt that it could be successfully applied to outboard craft.

FOILS: System comprises two Supramar type foils arranged in tandem. The bow foil is located at frame 60 and the rear foil at frame 6.

When foilborne 65% of the weight is supported by the bow foil and the side keels while the remaining 35% is supported by the rear foil. Flying height is adjusted by hydraulically-operated flaps on the bow foil. Foils are in St 52-3 high tensile structural steel.

HULL: The hull, which is of hard chine construction, comprises two side hulls and one central hull. Its design is based on experience gained from the construction of a wide variety of hydrofoil craft.

All members included in the longitudinal strength of the vessel, such as longitudinals, shell and deck plating, are of riveted construction. Transverse members, including web frames and bulkheads, are welded, but the connections with main deck, side and bottom shell, are riveted.

POWERPLANT: Motive power is provided by two MTU 331 type 12-cylinder four-stroke diesel engines, each rated at 1,100ps continuous and 1,300ps maximum intermittent. Each drives a propeller via an inclined shaft. The engines are rated for 45°C air intake temperature and 32°C seawater temperature.

ACCOMMODATION: Total seating capacity is for 159 to 166 passengers. There is one large saloon only. Major obstructions, like staircases, have been avoided. Windows are in safety glass and tinted anti-sun grey. On the standard version passenger seats are each fitted with arm rests, an ashtray and a number plate. Four toilets are located in the aft of the saloon each fully-equipped with WCs, washbasins, mirrors and towels.

On the short-haul model the passenger seats are more simple and only two toilets are provided. There are three luggage compartments, one adjacent to the embarkation doors leading to the passenger saloon, and two at the aft of the saloon.

DIMENSIONS
Length overall: 28m (91ft 10in)
Beam, max moulded: 9·3m (30ft 6in)
Draft hullborne: 1·8m (5ft 11in)
Draft foilborne: 1m (3ft 3in)

WEIGHTS
Displacement, fully loaded: 68·5 tonnes (67·45 tons)
Displacement, unloaded: 51·7 tonnes (60·9 tons)
Disposable load: 16·8 tonnes (16·56 tons)
Payload: 13·6 tonnes (13·4 tons)
Driving fuel and crew: 3·2 tonnes (3·15 tons)
Number of seated passengers: between 159 and 165

PERFORMANCE
Max speed, foilborne: about 61·5km/h (33 knots)
Cruising speed, foilborne: about 57·5km/h (31 knots)

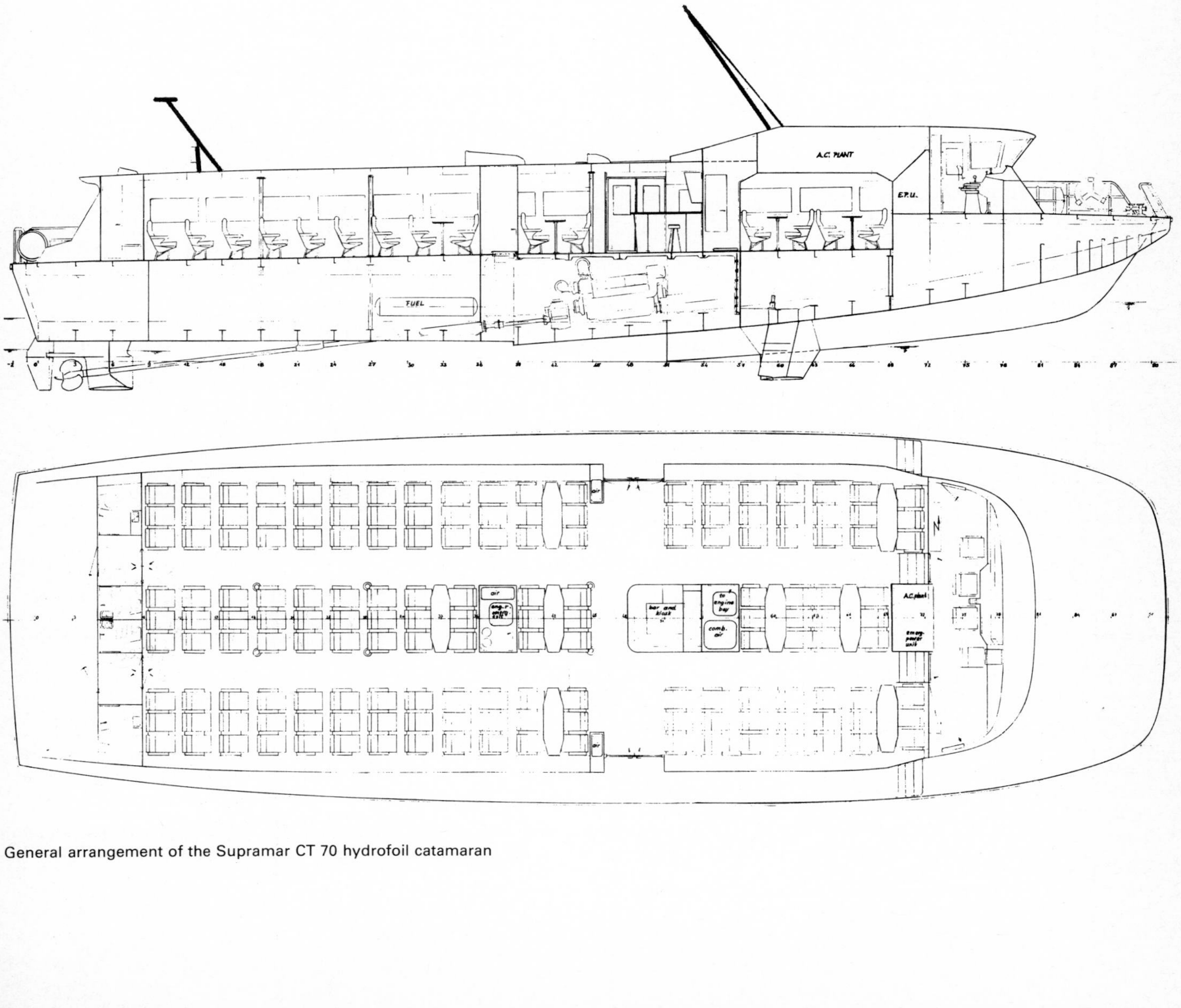

General arrangement of the Supramar CT 70 hydrofoil catamaran

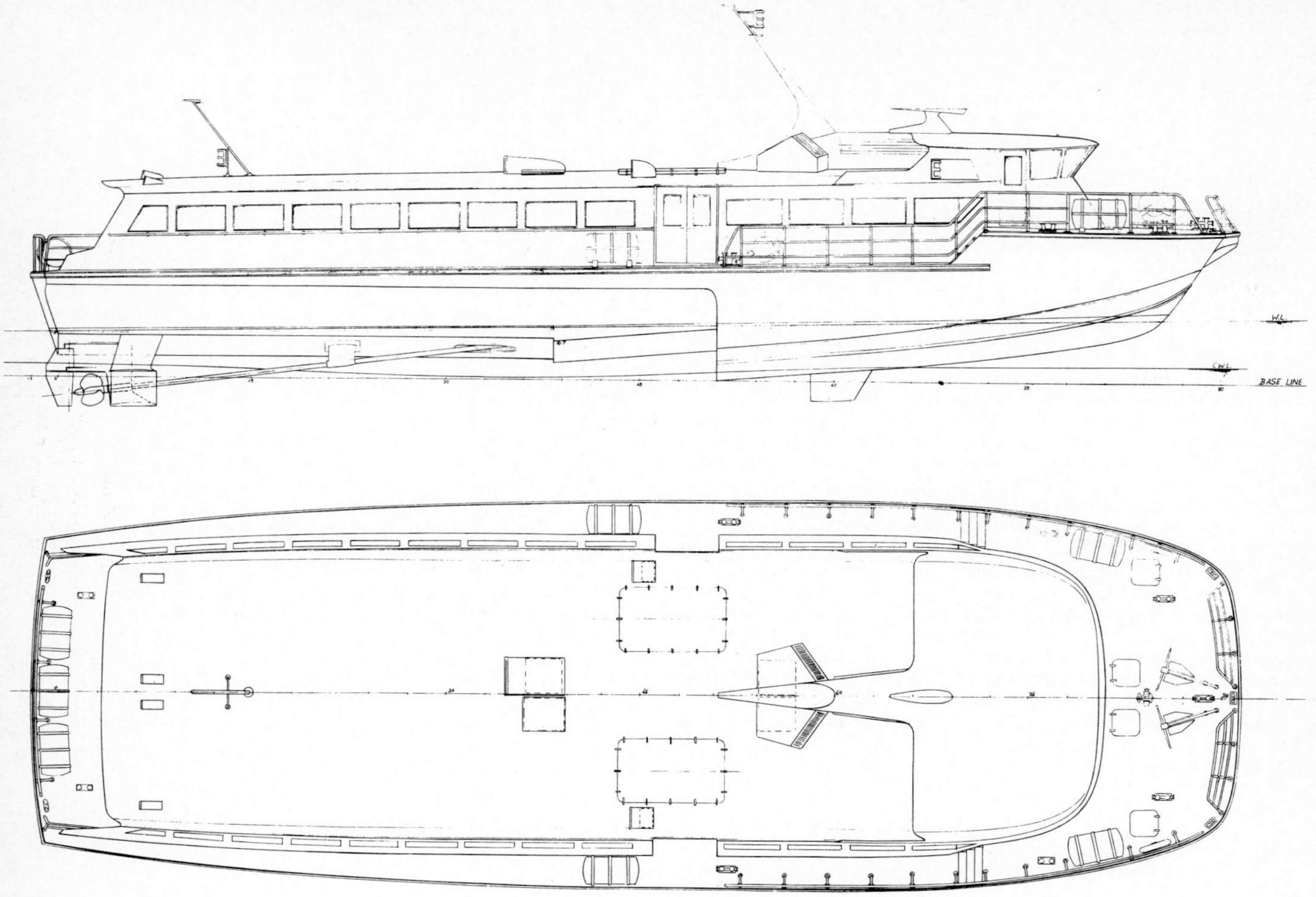

Supramar CT 70 hydrofoil catamaran

UNION OF SOVIET SOCIALIST REPUBLICS

KRASNOYE SORMOVO SHIPYARD

Head Office and Works: Gorki, USSR
Officials:
M Yuriev, *Shipyard Director*
Dr Rostilav Yergenievich Alexeyev, *Head of the Central Design Bureau for Hydrofoil Vessels*
Ivan Yerlykin, *Chief Hydrofoil Designer*
Export Enquiries: V/O Sudoimport, 5 Ul. Kalyaevskaya, Moscow K-6, USSR
Telephone: 251-60-37, 251-05-05, 251-03-85
Telex: 272
UK Representative: Umo Plant Ltd, Blackhorse Road, Letchworth, Hertfordshire SG6 1HR, England
Telephone: 046 26 71411/6
Telex: 825247

Krasnoye Sormovo is one of the oldest established shipyards in the Soviet Union. In addition to building displacement craft of many kinds for the Soviet River Fleet, the yard constructs the world's widest range of passenger hydrofoils, many of which are equipped with the Alexeyev shallow draft submerged foil system. Dr Alexeyev started work at the end of 1945 on the design of his foil system which had to be suitable for operation on smooth, but open and shallow rivers and canals. He succeeded in making use of the immersion depth effect, or surface effect, for stabilising the foil immersion in calm waters by the use of small lift coefficients.

The system comprises two main horizontal lifting surfaces, one forward and one aft, with little or no dihedral, each carrying approximately half the weight of the vessel. A submerged foil loses lift gradually as it approaches the surface from a submergence of about one chord. This effect prevents the submerged foils from rising completely to the surface. Means therefore had to be provided to assist take-off and prevent the vessel from sinking back to the displacement condition. The answer lay in the provision of planing sub-foils of small aspect ratio in the vicinity of the forward struts arranged so that when they are touching the water surface the main foils are submerged approximately to a depth of one chord.

The approach embodies characteristics of the Grunberg principle of inherent angle of attack variation, comprising a "wing" and a stabiliser system. When the Alexeyev foils drop below the shallow draft zone, the craft converts momentarily to the Grunberg mode of operation, duplicating its configuration. The otherwise inactive sub-foils, coming into contact with the water surface become the Grunberg stabilisers, cause the foils to climb up into the shallow draft zone where they resume normal operation in the Alexeyev mode.

The foils have good riding characteristics on inland waters and in sheltered waters.

The system was first tested on a small launch powered by a 77bhp converted car engine. Three more small craft were built to prove the idea, then work began on the yard's first multi-seat passenger craft, the Raketa, the first of which was launched in June 1957.

The yard also co-operates with the Leningrad Water Transport Institute in the development of seagoing craft with fully submerged V-type and trapeze-type surface-piercing foils, similar in configuration to those of the Schertel-Sachsenberg system. Craft employing V or trapeze foils are generally described as being of the Strela-type, Strela being the first operational Soviet design to use trapeze foils. Seating 92 passengers, the vessel is powered by two M-50 diesels and, visually speaking, is a cross between the PT 20 and the PT 50, though smaller than the latter. A military derivative, the Pchela (Bee) is currently employed by the Soviet frontier police for coastal patrol in the Baltic, Black Sea, Caspian and other sea areas.

The first hydrofoil vessels to enter service with the Soviet Navy were the 75-ton P 8-class, wooden-hulled torpedo boats which were equipped with bow foils and gas-turbine boost. These have now been retired.

Included in this entry are photographs of a hydrofoil fast patrol boat based on the Osa missile-firing FPB hull and given the NATO code name *Turya.* Like the earlier P 8-class and the highly successful Chinese Hu Chwan-class, the new craft has a bow foil only. Powered by three 4,330hp diesels it has a top speed of about 45 knots under calm conditions. Further military hydrofoil designs are under development, one of which is a 330-tonne fast strike craft, known to NATO by the code name Sarancha and the other a 400-tonne fast patrol boat known as Babochka. The Sarancha, armed with four SS-N-9 missiles and capable of speeds in excess of 50 knots, is currently undergoing trials with the Soviet Navy in the Baltic.

With an overall length of 50m (164ft) and an all-up weight of 400 tonnes, Babochka is the biggest military hydrofoil in operational service anywhere in the world today.

Among new Soviet passenger hydrofoils either in production or being prepared for series production at yards on the Baltic and Black Sea, are the gas-turbine powered, 98-105 seat Typhoon passenger ferry, the first Soviet production craft to have a fully submerged foil system, the Voskhod, a 71-seat Raketa replacement, the Albatros,

Largest operational hydrofoil warship in the world is this new 400-ton Soviet fast patrol craft which has recently been given the NATO codename Babochka (Butterfly). Babochka is thought to be powered by three gas-turbines of approximately the same size and power as the Rolls-Royce Marine Olympus, giving a total output of around 75,000shp

a Kometa derivative with seats for 150 passengers, stability augmentation and a speed in excess of 50 knots, and the waterjet-propelled, 250-seat, 45-50 knot, Cyclone. The Typhoon, which was built in Leningrad, has been undergoing operational trials carrying fare-paying passengers between Leningrad and Telinna, a journey time of 4½ hours.

Substantial numbers of Soviet hydrofoils—especially Kometas, Meteors, Raketas, Voskhods and Volgas—are being exported. Countries in which they are being operated include Austria, Bulgaria, Czechoslovakia, Finland, Yugoslavia, Italy, Iran, France, Cyprus, Greece, East Germany, Morocco, Spain, West Germany, Poland, Romania, the United Kingdom and the Philippines.

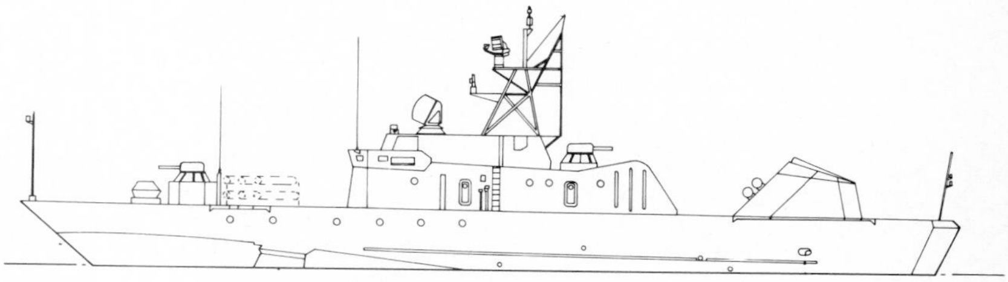

Outboard profile of Babochka showing the defensive armament, radar and electronic array. The foil system appears to be of conventional type with surface-piercing bow foils

Stern view of Babochka showing the three angled turbine exhaust ducts aft and the large air intakes at the aft end of the deckhouse. Note the top of the strut for what appears to be a fixed surface-piercing bow foil

ALBATROS

The prototype of this 150-seat Kometa derivative is due to be launched at the Poti shipyard on the Black Sea early in 1979. Two newly-designed 1,500hp diesels will give the craft a top speed in excess of 50 knots.

Among the various innovations introduced by the Central Hydrofoil Design Bureau are a new foil system with automatic lift control, the use of new materials in the hull structure and a more rational cabin layout, allowing the seating capacity to be increased by more than 40%. The engine room is located aft, as on the Voskhod.

Overall dimensions remain exactly the same as those of the Kometa-M.

BABOCHKA

The world's biggest and most powerful operational hydrofoil warship, this unexpected new addition to Soviet sea power is designed for anti-submarine warfare. Motive power for its foilborne propulsion system appears to comprise three gas-turbines, each comparable in size to the Rolls Royce Marine Olympus, providing a total output of 75,000shp.

Combustion air for the three gas-turbines appears to be fed through a large inlet occupying the aft end of the deckhouse. Exhaust discharge to atmosphere is via three angled funnels on the aft deck. Judging from its size, the craft is almost certainly intended for operation on the open seas. If propeller driven, either vee or Z-drives are likely to have been employed so as to provide as great a clearance height as possible.

FOILS: Thought to be of conventional surface-piercing V configuration, with an automatic sonic/electronic control system operating trailing edge flaps on each foil.

ARMAMENT: Two 30mm L/65 twin mounts for AA defence, activated by a Bass Tilt fire control radar, and ASW torpedoes in two triple mounts located immediately ahead of the superstructure between the deckhouse and the forward 30mm mount. Electronic equipment includes High Pole B IFF, Square Head and Peel Cone radar.

DIMENSIONS

Length overall: 50m (164ft)

WEIGHTS

Normal take-off displacement: about 400 tons

PERFORMANCE

Max speed foilborne: in excess of 50 knots

SARANCHA

The forerunner of a new class of extremely formidable fast strike missile craft, the 330-tonne Sarancha is one of the world's biggest naval hydrofoils. Designed and built in Leningrad, the craft is armed with four SS-N-9 anti-ship missiles, a ship-to-air missile system of a new concept, and a twin 23mm rapid fire cannon. The foil system is fully retractable to simplify slipping and docking. Autostabilisation equipment is fitted as well as an autopilot and the latest navigation, target detection and fire control systems.

Operational evaluation trials with the Soviet Navy began in the Eastern Baltic in mid 1977. Sarancha is the NATO Code Name for the vessel, but it has been referred to by the alternative name Tarakan.

FOILS: Combined surface-piercing and submerged system. The bow foil, which provides the necessary transverse stability is of split-V surface-piercing type and carries about 60% of

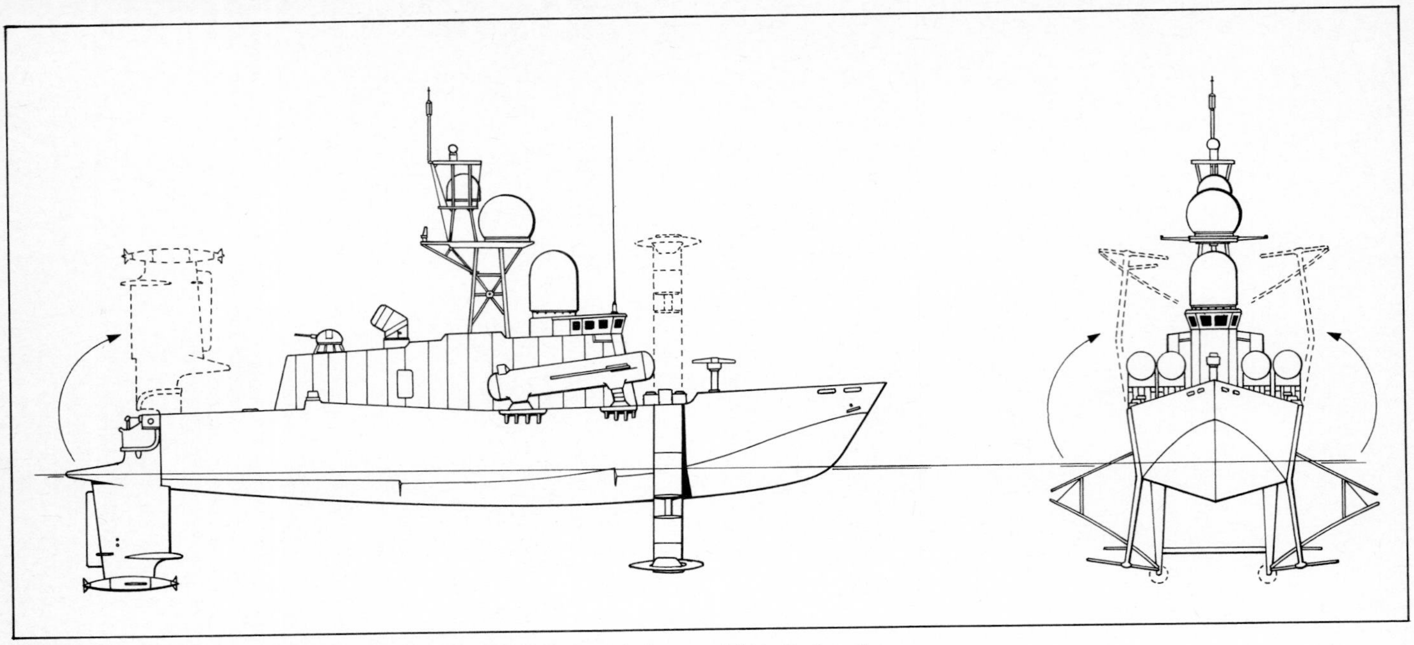

Provisional elevation and bow-on view of the 330-tonne Sarancha missile-armed fast attack craft

the load and the single fully submerged rear foil supports the remaining 40%. The rear foil is supported by two vertical struts, each of which carries a twin propeller pod assembly at its base. The struts also carry the vertical shafts and second bevel gears of the Z-drive systems which transmit power from the gas-turbines in the hull to the propellers. A sonic/electronic autopilot system controls lift by operating trailing edge flaps on each foil. Forward and aft flaps operate differentially to provide pitch variation and height control. Aft flaps operate differentially to provide roll control for changes in direction. Single rudders, which act individually for port or starboard turns, are fitted to the trailing edges of the aft foil struts. All three foil/strut units retract completely clear of the water, the two elements of the 'split V' bow foil sideways and the aft foil rearwards and upwards.

POWER PLANT: Foilborne power is believed to be provided by two marinised gas-turbines. Power is transmitted to the two propellers at the base of each strut through two sets of bevel gears and two vertical shafts to the nacelle. The central compartment of this contains the lower reduction gear which transmits power from the vertical shafts to the propeller shafts. The power transmission system is thought to have been derived from that employed on the Typhoon commercial hydrofoil, also built in Leningrad.

ARMAMENT: Four SS-N-9 anti-ship missiles on four lightweight launchers amidship, one twin SA-N-4 surface-to-air missile launcher on forward deck and one twin 23mm rapid fire AA cannon aft. The SS-N-9s are activated by a Band Stand radar, the SA-N-4 launcher is controlled by a Fish Bowl radar and the twin 23mm cannon has a Bass Tilt fire control. The craft also carries a High Pole aerial for the IFF installation, ECM/ECCM equipment and Square Head naval radar.

DIMENSIONS

Length overall: 45m (147ft 8in)
Width, foils extended: 23m (75ft 6in)
Hull beam: 10m (32ft 9½in)
Draft hullborne, foils retracted: 2m (6ft 7in)

WEIGHTS

Estimated normal take-off displacement: 330 tonnes

PERFORMANCE

Max speed foilborne: 50 knots plus

VOSKHOD-2

Designers of the Voskhod, which is gradually replacing craft of the 22-year-old Raketa series, have drawn on engineering experience gained with the Raketa, and also the more sophisticated Meteor and Kometa.

Among the basic requirements were that the Raketa's general characteristics should be preserved; foilborne operation should be possible in 1m (3ft 3in) high waves, with a 3% safety factor; accommodation should be acceptable from health and safety viewpoints; noise levels should be significantly reduced, and that the maximum use should be made of standard mechanical, electrical and other components and fittings proven on the Raketa.

In fact, the end product bears little resemblance to its predecessor. In the visual sense, the Voskhod is more akin to a scaled-down Kometa with its engine room aft, replacing the rear passenger saloon.

Among the many design improvements to attract operators in the Soviet bloc countries and elsewhere are the following:

1. Employment of a vee-drive transmission, giving greater mean calm water clearance height aft, thereby reducing hydrodynamic drag under certain load conditions.

2. Provision of alternative embarkation points to facilitate passenger handling. Bow embarkation platforms are incorporated for loading from low level pontoons, and a stern embarkation area is located above the engine room, for loading from high landing stages.

3. Raising the number of seated passengers from 64 to 71 for more profitable operation on medium distance services.

4. Generous additional soundproofing, including cowlings on the engine and reduction gear, and the provision of sound absorbing material in the engine room on the deckhead, sides and forward bulkhead.

5. Provision for the future replacement of the M 401A diesel by a 2,000shp M 415 diesel.

6. Fitting of a variable-pitch, six-bladed propeller for improved handling and operating characteristics.

In June 1974, Voshkhod 2-01 was put into service on the route Gorky-Kineshma, across the vast Gorky reservoir which cannot be navigated by the Raketa because of its limited seaworthiness. It continued in service until the end of the 1974 navigation season. During this time it was demonstrated that its operating and technical performance was significantly superior to that of the Raketa.

Experience accumulated during this experimental service indicated the need for a number of minor modifications which have been incorporated in the first series of production craft.

At the time of its inception, it was announced that the Voskhod would be available in a number of versions to suit a variety of local navigation and traffic requirements. Voskhod-3 will be powered by a gas-turbine.

The vessel is designed for high-speed passenger ferry services during daylight hours on rivers, reservoirs, lakes and sheltered waters. It meets the requirements of Soviet River Register Class 'O' with the following wave restrictions (3% safety margin): foilborne, 1·3m (4ft 3in); hullborne, 2m (6ft 7in).

The passenger saloons are heated and provided with natural and induced ventilation. Full air-conditioning can be installed in craft required for service in tropical conditions. The crew comprises a captain, engineer, motorman and barman.

FOILS: Fixed foil system, comprising one bow foil with a pitch stability sub-foil immediately behind, one aft foil, plus an amidship foil to facilitate take-off. Bow and amidship foils appear to be of shallow V configuration and each has four vertical struts. The fully submerged stern foil has two side struts and is supported in the centre by the end bracket of the propeller shaft. The surface and lower parts of the foil struts and stabiliser are in Cr18Ni9Ti stainless steel, while the upper parts of the struts and stabiliser and also the amidship foil are in AlMg-61 plate alloy.

HULL: Similar in shape to that of the Kometa and earlier models of the Sormovo hydrofoil series, with a wedge-shaped bow, raked stem and spoon-shaped stern. A single step is provided to facilitate take-off. In fabricating the basic structure, which is largely in AlMg-61 aluminium magnesium alloy, extensive use has been made of arc and spot welding. The hull is framed on longitudinal and transverse formers. Below the deck it is divided into eight watertight compartments by transverse bulkheads. It will remain afloat with any one compartment or the machinery space flooded. Access to the forepeak, which houses the anchor capstan, is via the forward passenger saloon, and then through a rectangular hatch on the forecastle. Aft of the main passenger saloon is an area split into three compartments by two longitudinal bulkheads. The lower central space contains the reduction gear and vee-drive, the starboard compartment contains the sanitary tank and the port compartment forms part of the double-bottom. Entrance to the engine compartment is via a door on the port side of the main deck. An emergency exit is provided on the starboard aft.

POWER PLANT: Power is supplied by a single M-401A four-stroke water-cooled, supercharged 12-cylinder V-type diesel, delivering a normal service output of 1,000hp at 1,550rpm. The engine which has a variable-speed governor and a reversing clutch, is sited aft with its shaft inclined at 9 degrees. Output is transferred via a flexible coupling to a single six-bladed variable-pitch propeller via an R-21 vee-drive gearbox.

Guaranteed service life of the engine before the first overhaul is 3,000 hours. The engine room is insulated with fire-retardent, heat and sound-insulating materials. Perforated aluminium alloy sheet is laid over the insulating materials.

CONTROLS: Single semi-balanced rudder in AlMg plate provides directional control. Operation of the engine, rudder, reverse gear and fuel supply is effected hydraulically from the wheelhouse.

ACCOMMODATION: Voskhod-2 carries a three-man operating crew, comprising captain, engineer and motorman plus a barman. Embarkation platforms sited immediately below the wheelhouse provide access for both passengers and crew. Passengers can be embarked from both sides and from the stern.

The captain and engineer are accommodated in a raised wheelhouse located between the forward and main saloon. Main engine controls are located in both the wheelhouse and the engine room.

Passengers are accommodated in two saloons, a forward compartment seating 17 and a main saloon seating 54. The main saloon has three exits, two forward, leading to the embarkation platforms and one aft leading to the stern embarkation area. Between the two saloons, on the starboard side, is a crew rest cabin. The saloons are fitted with upholstered seats, racks for small hand luggage and pegs for coats. Spacing between seats is 900mm and the central aisle is 800mm wide.

At the rear of the main saloon is a small buffet and bar, and aft of the main saloon, at the foot of the rear embarkation steps are two WC/wash-basin units.

SYSTEMS, ELECTRICAL: Power supply is 24-27V dc. A 3kW generator is attached to the engine and supplies 27·5V while the craft is operating. Four 12V storage batteries, each of 180Ah capacity and connected in series-parallel to form a single bank, supply power during short stops. An auxiliary circuit can be connected to shore systems for 220V, single-phase, 50Hz ac supply.

FIREFIGHTING: Four carbon dioxide and four foam fire extinguishers for the passenger saloons and wheelhouse. Remote-controlled system employing "3·5" compound in the engine room.

Voskhod-2, the latest hydrofoil passenger ferry to enter service on Soviet inland waterways

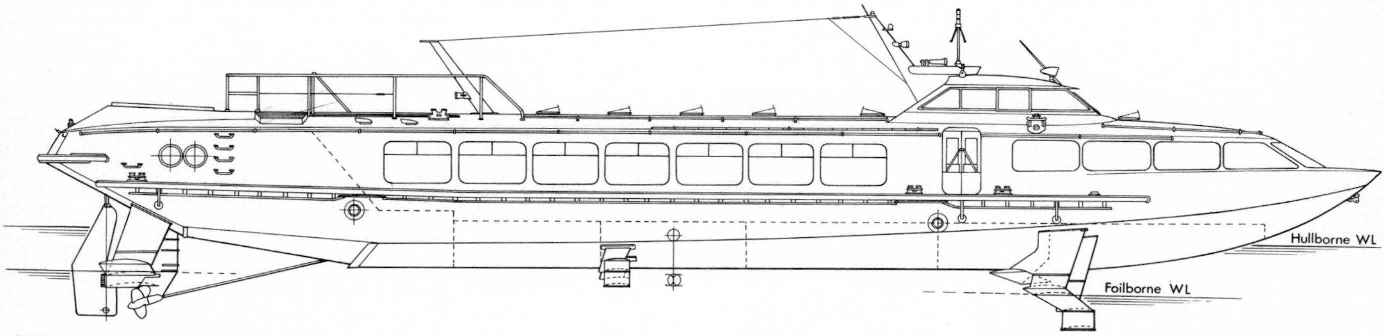

Voskhod-2, outboard profile

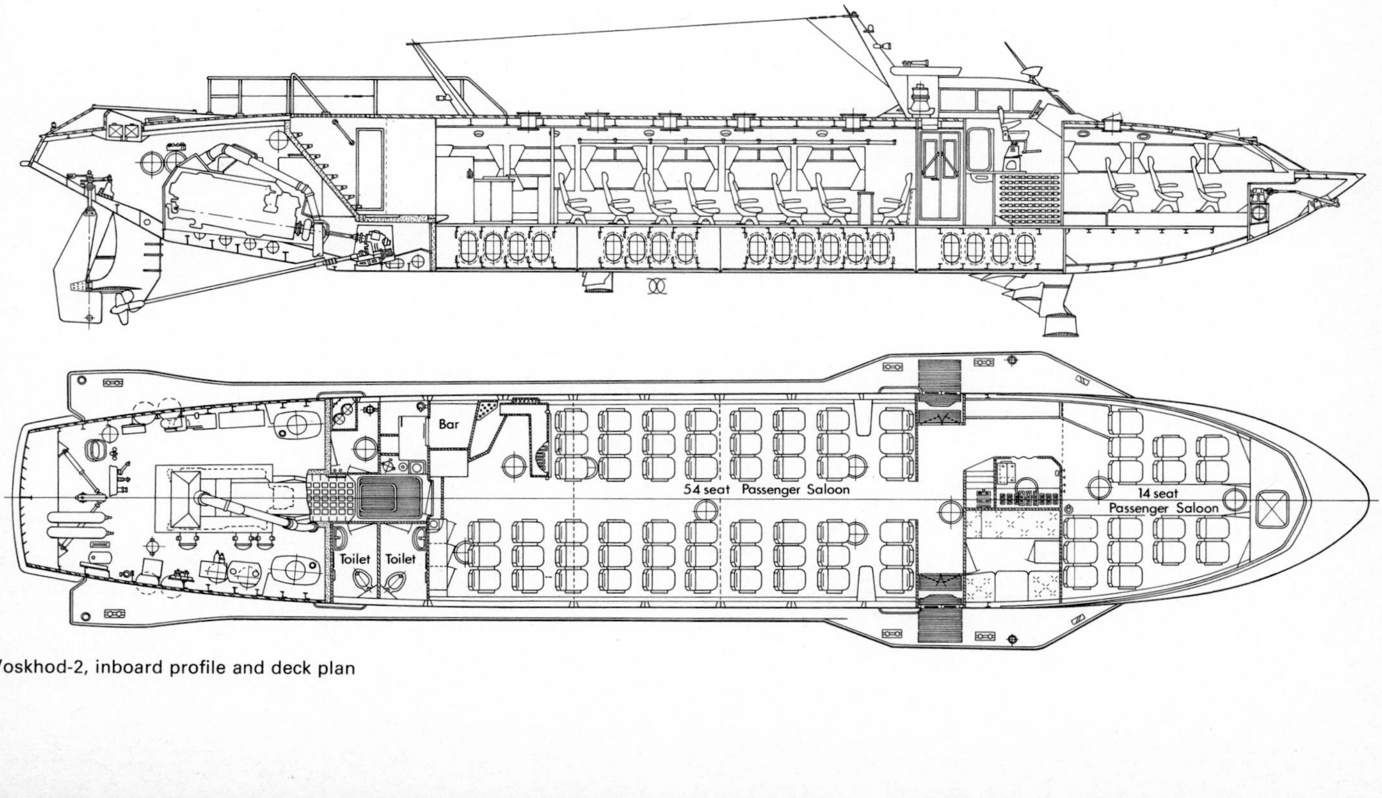

Voskhod-2, inboard profile and deck plan

HEATING AND VENTILATION: Heating in the saloons is provided by pipes circulating water from the internal cooling circuit of the engine. Ventilation is both natural, using the dynamic pressure of the approaching air flow, and induced, by means of electric fans.

During the spring and autumn, the temperature of the ventilating air can be heated up to 21°C.

DRINKING WATER: Hot and cold water supplies. An electric boiler supplies hot water for washbasins and the small kitchen behind the snackbar. Drinking water tank has a capacity of 138 litres.

BILGE WATER: System designed for bilge water removal by shore-based facilities or service vessels.

ANCHOR: Matrosov system, weighing 35kg (77lb), attached to an anchor cable 8·4mm (⅓in) in diameter and 80m (262ft) long, and operated by hand winch in the forepeak.

DIMENSIONS

EXTERNAL

Length overall: 27·6m (90ft 7in)
Hull length: 26·3m (86ft 3½in)
Beam overall: 6·2m (20ft 4in)
Height above mean water level, foilborne, including mast: 5·7m (18ft 8in)
Draft hullborne: 2m (6ft 6¾in)
Draft foilborne: 1·1m (3ft 7¼in)

INTERNAL

Deck area: 105m^2 (1,130ft^2)
Deck area per passenger: 1·48m^2 (15·35ft^2)

WEIGHTS

Displacement, fully loaded: 28 tonnes
Light displacement: 20 tonnes
Passengers per displacement tonne: 2·55
Payload, passengers and buffet/bar equipment: 5·9 tonnes
Payload/displacement ratio: 21·2%

PERFORMANCE

Max speed, calm water, wind not in excess of force 3,
at 1,550rpm (1,000hp): 64km/h (39·76mph)
at 1,450rpm: 60km/h (37·28mph)
Turning circle diameter
hullborne: 106m (348ft)
foilborne: 380m (1,246ft)
Range, based on normal fuel supply of 1,400kg: 500km (310·68 miles)
Max wave height, with 3% safety margin
hullborne: 2m (6ft 7in)
foilborne: 1·3m (4ft 3in)

TURYA

Latest hydrofoil to enter service in numbers with the Soviet Navy is a diesel-powered torpedo-boat with a displacement of 230 tons. The vessel, which is based on the well-proven Osa missile-firing FPB hull, is equipped with a fixed, surface-piercing V or trapeze foil set back approximately one-third of the hull length from the bow. At 20-23 knots in relatively calm conditions, the foil system generates sufficient lift to raise the greater part of the hull clear of the water, providing a "sprint" speed of 40-45 knots.

In addition to improving the maximum speed, the foils reduce the vessel's wave impact response, thus enhancing its performance as a weapon platform.

The installation of a pocket-size, variable-depth sonar on the transom suggests that the primary duty of Turya is anti-submarine patrol. The main armament appears to comprise four 21in single AS torpedo tubes similar to those mounted on the Shershen class fast attack craft, a forward 25mm twin mount and a twin 57mm AA mount aft.

The craft entered service in 1973 and a series production programme is under way, involving more than one yard in Western Russia and one in the Soviet Far East. Output is estimated at between four and five units per year and about thirty are in service.

FOILS: Single main foil of trapeze configuration set back one-third of hull length from bow. Raises greater part of hull bottom clear of the water in calm conditions at speed of about 20 knots depending on sea conditions and loading.

Turya foilborne. This 230-ton hydrofoil-assisted fast patrol craft is in production at more than one yard in Western Russia and one in the Soviet Far East

'Sprint' speed of the Turya, the primary duty of which appears to be anti-submarine patrol, is about 40-45 knots

Similar system employed earlier on Soviet P 8 class, now retired, and on the highly successful Chinese Hu Chwan class.

HULL: Standard Osa hull, welded steel construction.

POWER PLANT: Three Type 56 CLNSP 16/17 high performance diesels, each developing 5,000hp and driving variable-pitch propellers through inclined shafts.

SYSTEMS, RADAR: Pot Drum and Drum Tilt.

DIMENSIONS

Length: 39·3m (128ft 11in)
Beam: 25·1m (82ft)
Draft: 1·8m (5ft 11in)

WEIGHTS

Max loaded displacement: 230 tons
Normal displacement: 200 tons

PERFORMANCE

Max speed foilborne: 40-45 knots

TYPHOON

The Typhoon, a gas-turbine powered fast ferry for 98-105 passengers, is the first production craft with automatically controlled fully-submerged foils to be built in the Soviet Union.

The prototype, constructed in Leningrad, was launched after preliminary fitting out on 12 December 1969. It is designed to operate at a service speed of 40-42 knots under calm conditions and 38 knots in sea state 4. The craft is at present undergoing trials. Phase 1 of the test programme covered the foil system, the gas-turbine power plant, hull design and mechanical and other systems and during Phase 2, which was undertaken during 1972 and 1973, the vessel was put into passenger service to permit technical assessments to be made under commercial operating conditions.

It is stated that in waves of up to 2m (6ft 6in) high, not more than 10% of the 40-42 knot service speed is lost. Under these conditions, the Typhoon can complete the journey from Leningrad to Tallina, the Estonian capital, in 4½ hours.

Ten new inventions have found application in the design and the prototype has been awarded a certificate by the State Inventions and Discoveries Committee.

Late in 1975, it was announced that the Typhoon was to enter production at a shipyard on the Baltic as part of the shipbuilding programme for the period 1976-1980.

FOILS: Fully submerged system of conventional configuration with 77% of the weight borne by the bow foil and 23% by the stern foil. The bow foil is supported by four vertical struts which are tapered from top to bottom. The two outboard struts are supported by auxiliary fins which provide additional stability during the transition from displacement to foilborne mode. Twin rudders are fitted at the trailing edges of the aft foil struts. The foils are built in OCr17Ni7Al high strength stainless steel. A sonic/electronic autopilot system controls four flaps on the bow foil and two on the stern foil. The total weight of the autopilot system, including all electronic components, assemblies, drive mechanisms and cables is less than 600kg (1,320lb). The system stabilises the craft from take-off to touchdown in heave and all three axes—pitch, roll and yaw. It is programmed to govern the angle of trim, the c of g position in relation to speed and see that the craft makes coordinated banked turns according to speed and sea state. Overriding manual control can be introduced if necessary.

Two independent electro-hydraulic-drive systems are installed to actuate the flaps. Each has two pumps, one connected to the reduction gear of the main engine, the other to its turbo-compressor. Fluid reaches the actuating mechanisms under a pressure of $150kg/cm^2$. Should one of the mains leading to the actuating mechanisms become unserviceable the second is connected. The failure of one bow or one stern

The Typhoon, first gas-turbine powered passenger craft with fully-submerged foils to be built in the Soviet Union. Designed to operate at 36-45 knots, it seats 98-105 passengers. **Top left**: The basic similarity of the Typhoon's spoon shaped hull to that of the Kometa-M and other Sormovo designs is apparant. **Top right**: Typhoon during take off. Glass doors lead from the saloon into the vestibule and onto the promenade deck visible in this photo. **Bottom left**: View aft from the air-conditioned passenger saloon which can be equipped with 98-105 airliner-type seats. From the vestibule at the far end there are entrances to the baggage compartment, wheelhouse and WC/washbasin units. **Bottom right**: Captain B V Gromov, centre, at the helm, who has been responsible for handling the Typhoon during her trials programme with his engineer, G V Shikhurin

flap in conditions up to sea state 4 does not reduce the stability of the vessel.

HULL: Similar in shape to that of the Kometa and earlier models in the Sormovo hydrofoil series, with a wedge-shaped bow, raked stem and spoon-shaped stern. There are two steps beneath the hull to facilitate take-off. The hull is of riveted construction and built in high strength aluminium magnesium alloy V-48TL. Longitudinal and transverse framing is employed with a spacing of 500mm (19·68in) in the hull and 1,000mm (39·37in) in the superstructure. By locating the wheelhouse aft of amidships, it has been possible to reduce the length of the control system cables while preserving good all-round vision.

Beneath the passenger saloon superstructure the hull is divided by transverse bulkheads into nine watertight compartments in which are accommodated the fuel tanks, diesel generators, gas turbines and diesel for hullborne propulsion. A watertight door is installed in the bulkhead separating the diesel generator and gas-turbine compartment. The craft is designed to remain afloat should any two adjacent compartments become flooded.

POWER PLANT: Foilborne power is supplied by two 1,750hp Ivchenko AI-23C-1 marine gas-turbines, each driving a single 0·68m (2ft 3in) diameter three-bladed propeller at 2,200rpm cruising. The gas-turbines are started by starter generators from batteries and exhaust gases are expelled through an extension aft of the transom to prevent the craft from becoming covered with smoke or fumes.

Power from the main engines is transmitted to each propeller via a K-1700 Z-drive column, which is bolted to the transom. The drive shaft of each turbine is connected to the shaft of the upper reduction gear of the Z-drive. Power is transmitted via two sets of bevel gears and two vertical shafts to a nacelle which is divided into three compartments. The central compartment contains the lower reduction gear which transmits power from the two vertical shafts to the propeller shaft.

The stern foil is welded to the casing of the nacelle's bow compartment which contains the stern foil flap actuating mechanism.

Hullborne propulsion is supplied by a 165hp

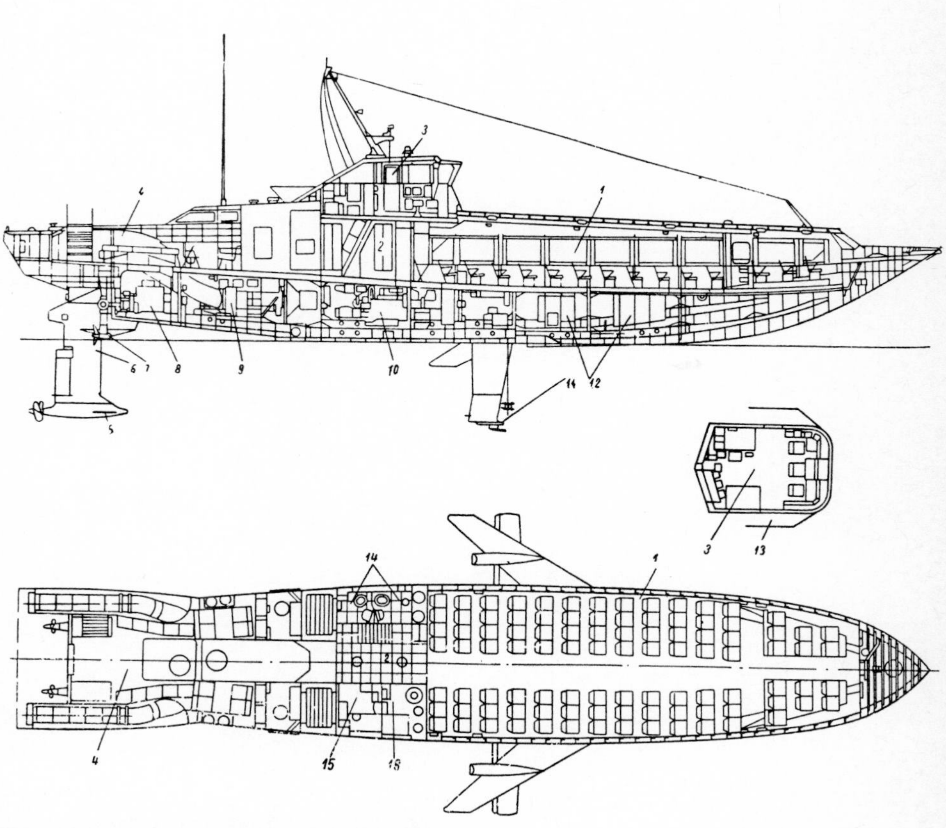

Inboard profile and passenger deck plan of the Typhoon:
1, passenger saloon; 2, vestibule; 3, wheelhouse; 4, promenade deck; 5, stern foil; 6, Z-drive foilborne transmission; 7, Z-drive hullborne transmission; 8, 165hp diesel; 9, AI-23C-I gas-turbines; 10, diesel generators; 11, bow foil; 12, fuel tanks; 13, bridge; 14, lavatories; 15, bar; 16, baggage compartment

6ChSP13/14 low-speed diesel driving two four-bladed propellers through KP-150 right-angle drives, which rotate for steering and retract upwards when the craft is foilborne. The columns are steered either from the central control console in the wheelhouse or from a portable control panel which can be operated from any part of the vessel.

ACCOMMODATION: The vessel carries an operating crew of four—captain, engineer, radio operator/electrician and a seaman. Passengers are accommodated in an air-conditioned saloon equipped with 98-105 airliner-type seats. Glass doors lead from the saloon into the vestibule and onto the promenade deck. From the vestibule there is an entrance to the baggage compartment, wheelhouse and WC/wash basin units. The panels along the sides of the saloon are covered in non-inflammable laminated plastic and above with Pavinol imitation leather glued onto plywood. The deckhead is covered with Pavinol on a wooden frame. A special vibration-absorbing covering has been applied to the bulkhead facing the turbine compartment.

Rafts type PSN-10 are stored in containers along the sides of the vessel. These can be launched onto the water either by manual or automatic control from the wheelhouse. Lifebelts and lifejackets are carried aboard the vessel.

SYSTEMS, ELECTRICAL: Two 22kW generators and eight batteries type 6STK-180. Main electrical equipment operates on 400Hz ac current. Shore supply is effected through a transformer.

NAVIGATOR: Gyro course indicator, magnetic compass, hydraulic log and anti-collision radar.

COMMUNICATION: Ship-ship, ship-shore transceiver operating on R/T and W/T, also emergency radio.

DIMENSIONS
Length overall: 31·4m (103ft 2¼in)
Width across foils: 10m (32ft 9¾in)
Hull beam: 5·6m (18ft 4½in)
Hull draft, displacement mode: 1·3m (4ft 3⅛in)
Draft, hullborne, including foils: 4·1m (13ft 5⅜in)
Mean draft foilborne: 1·1-1·3m (3ft 7in-4ft 3in)
Distance of bow foil below hull base line: 2·8m (9ft 2in)

WEIGHTS
Normal loaded displacement: 65 tons

PERFORMANCE
Max speed: 45 knots
Service speed: 40-42 knots
Hullborne speed: 5 knots
Max permissible sea state: designed to maintain a cruising speed of 38 knots in sea state 4

SEA TESTS

In sea state 4, vertical acceleration measured in the bows was reported to be at all times less than 0·5g. At the same time it was stated that angles of pitch and roll are around 0·75 degrees. In sea state 4, one bow flap and one stern flap out of action have not adversely affected stability.

BUREVESTNIK

First Soviet gas-turbine hydrofoil to be designed for series production, the Burevestnik has two 2,700hp marinised aircraft gas turbines driving two two-stage waterjets. The prototype was launched in April 1964 and it was intended to build two models; one for medium-range, non-stop inter-city services, seats 130 passengers, the other, for suburban services, seats 150.

There is a four-man crew, comprising captain, engineer, motorman and a seaman.

After extensive trials and modifications, the prototype Burevestnik began operating on the Gorky-Kuibyshev route, about 700km (435 miles), on 26 April 1968. It is understood that the vessel has not yet entered production.

FOILS: There are two main foils and a midship stabiliser foil, all built in titanium alloy. Each is square-tipped and slightly wedge-shaped in planform. The foils are secured to the hull by struts and brackets. Each foil strut is welded to the upper surface of the foils, then bolted to the brackets. Upper and lower ends of the struts are connected by flanges. As with other craft employing the Alexeyev system, the foil incidence can be adjusted when necessary by the insertion of wedges between the flanges and the foils when the craft is in dock.

HULL: Hull and superstructure are built in aluminium-magnesium alloy. The hull is of all-welded construction and framed on longitudinal and transverse formers.

ACCOMMODATION: The prototype has two air-conditioned saloons with airliner-style seating for a total of 150 passengers. The well-glazed forward saloon seats 38, and the aft saloon 112. The saloons are decorated with pastel shade panels and soundproofed with glass fibre insulation. The engine room is at the stern and separated from the saloon by a sound-proof double bulkhead.

POWER PLANT: Motive power is supplied by two 2,700shp Ivchenko marinised gas-turbines, adapted from those of the IL-18 airliner. These operate on either kerosene or light diesel fuel and have a consumption of 300 gallons per hour. Sufficient fuel can be carried to operate non-stop over a range of 500km (270n miles). The shaft of each of the two double suction centrifugal pumps for the waterjets is connected with the shaft of one of the turbines by means of a flexible coupling, via a reduction gear.

Auxiliary power is supplied by two 100hp turbo-generators, used for starting the main engines and generating the electrical supply when the craft is operating.

CONTROLS: Four rudders adjacent to the waterjet streams provide directional control. Reversing is achieved by applying deflectors to reverse the waterflow. The waterjets themselves are fixed and cannot be rotated.

Operation of the turbines, waterjets, rudders and deflectors is all effected from the wheelhouse by electro-hydraulic control.

SYSTEMS, ELECTRICAL: Two 12kW 28·5V generators mounted on each of the main engines supply power when the craft is operating. Two 14kW 28·5V generators driven by the auxiliary turbines supply power when the craft is at rest or when the 12kW generators are inoperative. Eight acid storage batteries are connected in series to give 24V supply power during short stops.

HYDRAULICS: $170kg/cm^2$ pressure hydraulic system for operating rudders, hydro-reversal unit and anchor.

COMMUNICATIONS: A radio transmitter/receiver with r/t and w/t facilities is installed in the wheelhouse for ship-shore and inter-ship communications on SW and MW bands. A public announcement system is fitted in the passenger saloons and a two-way crew communications sys-

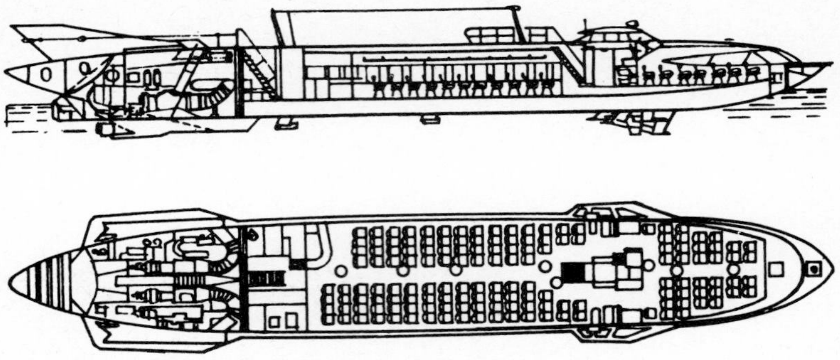

Inboard profile and deck view of the waterjet-propelled Burevestnik, powered by two 2,700hp Ivchenko AI-20 gas-turbines

Burevestnik prototype during trials on the Volga

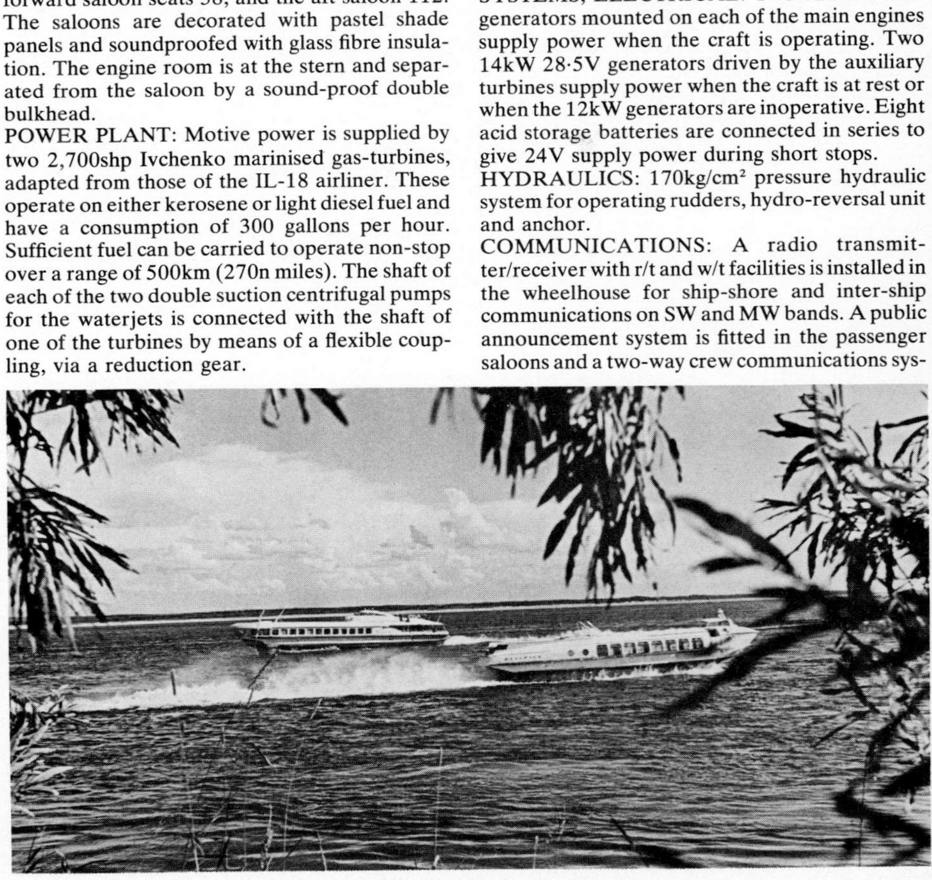

A Raketa, left, and a Byelorus, right, pass one another on the River Lena

tem is installed in the wheelhouse, engine room, anchor, gear compartment and mooring stations.

DIMENSIONS
Overall length: 43·3m (142ft)
Hull beam: 6m (19ft 8¼in)
Width across foils: 7·4m (24ft 3½in)
Draft hullborne: 2m (6ft 7in)
Draft foilborne: 0·4m (1ft 4in)

WEIGHTS
Light displacement: 41 tons
Full load displacement (max): 67 tons
Max fuel load: 11·5 tons

PERFORMANCE
Cruising speed: 93km/h (50 knots)
Range: 500km (310 miles)
Max wave height at reduced speed: 1-1·2m (3ft 3in-4ft)
Max wave height at full speed: 0·6m (2ft)
Speed astern: 6-9km/h (4-6mph)
Stop to full speed and distance: 95-100 seconds, 1,100m (1,203yds)
Stopping time from full speed and distance: 25 seconds, 360m (394yds)

BYELORUS

This craft was developed from the Raketa via the Chaika for fast passenger services on winding rivers less than 1m (3ft) deep and too shallow for vessels of the standard type.

In 1965 it was put into series production at the river shipyard at Gomel, in Byelorussia.

FOILS: The shallow draft submerged foil system consists of one bow foil and one rear foil.

HULL: Hull and superstructure are built in aluminium magnesium alloy. The hull is of all-welded construction and the superstructure is both riveted and welded.

ACCOMMODATION: The craft seats 40 passengers in aircraft-type seats, although the prototype seated only 30.

POWER PLANT: Power is supplied by an M-50 F-3 or M-400 diesel rated at 950hp maximum and with a normal service output of 600hp. The wheelhouse is fitted with an electro hydraulic remote control system for the engine and fuel supply.

DIMENSIONS
Length overall: 18·55m (60ft 6in)
Hull beam: 4·64m (15ft 2in)
Height overall: 4·23m (13ft 11in)
Draft foilborne: 0·3m (1ft)
Draft hullborne: 0·9m (2ft 11in)

WEIGHTS
Light displacement: 9·6 tons
Take-off displacement: 14·5 tons

PERFORMANCE
Cruising speed: 60km/h (34 knots)

CHAIKA

An experimental 30-passenger craft, Chaika is used as a test bed for the development of diesel-operated waterjet systems. It was designed initially as a 30 passenger waterbus for shallow rivers but was found to be unsuitable for negotiating sharp river bends at high speed. However, craft of this type are reported as being in limited service on the Danube.

In June 1971 it was announced that the craft had been employed in the development of super-ventilated V and trapeze foils for a speed range exceeding 50-80 knots.

HULL: Hull and superstructure are built in aluminium magnesium alloy.

POWER PLANT: An M-50 diesel, developing 1,200hp, drives a two-stage waterjet.

CONTROLS: Rudders adjacent to the water stream govern the flow of the ejected water for directional control.

DIMENSIONS
Length overall: 26·3m (86ft 3in)
Hull beam: 3·8m (12ft 6in)
Draft hullborne: 1·2m (3ft 10in)
Draft foilborne: 0·3m (1ft)

WEIGHTS
Displacement loaded: 14·3 tons

PERFORMANCE
Cruising speed, foilborne: 86km/h (46·5 knots)

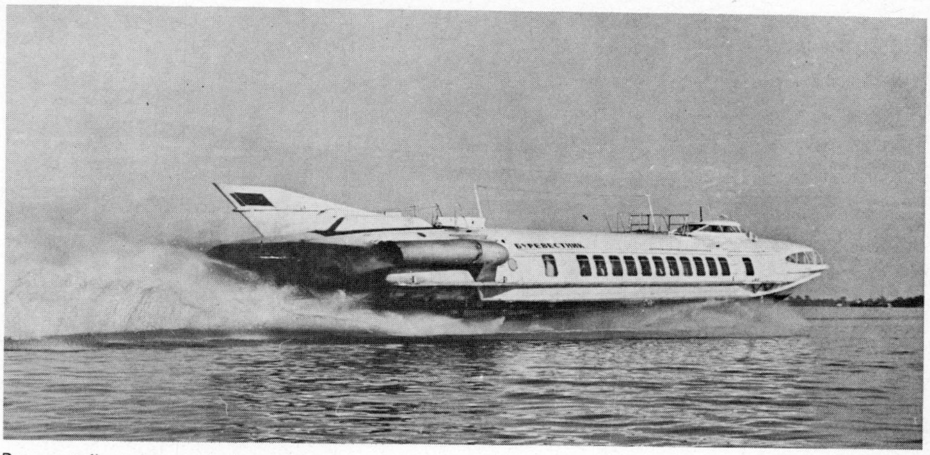

Burevestnik prototype during trials

Byelorus, a 30-45 seat hydrofoil for fast ferry services on shallow waters, seen on the Karakum Canal, Turkmenia. Powered by a 735hp M-50 diesel driving a waterjet, the craft cruises at 60km/h (34 knots)

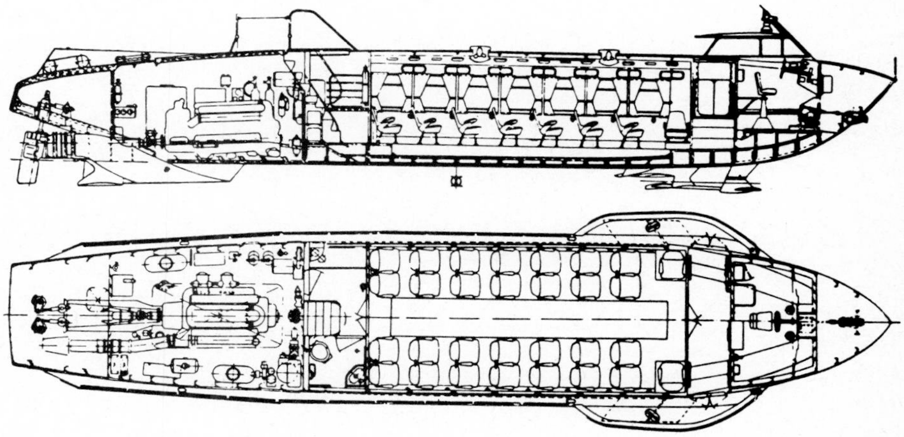

Profile and deck plan of the waterjet-propelled Byelorus, a ferry for fast passenger services on winding rivers less than 3ft 3in deep

Chaika, an experimental 30-passenger craft powered by a diesel-driven waterjet

CYCLONE

An enlarged, double-deck derivative of the Kometa, the Cyclone seats 250 passengers and is propelled by waterjets driven by two 5,000hp gas-turbines, making it the most powerful Soviet commercial hydrofoil to date. Maximum speed is 45-50 knots and the cruising speed is 42 knots.

It was announced in 1976 that, on completion

Outboard profile of the 140-ton Cyclone, a waterjet-propelled 250-seat hydrofoil ferry with accommodation on two decks. Design cruising speed is 42 knots

of trials, the vessel will be put into series production at the Poti shipyard, on the Black Sea. Export models are planned. It is probable that these will be fitted with imported gas-turbines and waterjet systems.

The craft complies with the requirements of Class KM 2MA2 of the USSR Passenger Register. It also meets fully all the specified conditions of the Stability Specifications, USSR Shipping Register. It is designed to operate foilborne in waves up to 3m (9ft 10in) high regardless of wave direction, and can operate hullborne in conditions up to sea state 5. Foilborne range, fully-loaded, is 300n miles.

FOILS: Surface-piercing system of conventional configuration comprising two main foils, one at the bow and one at the stern; an amidship foil to assist take-off, a pitch stability sub-foil immediately aft of the bow foil, and the associated struts by which the foils are attached to the hull. A sonic/electronic autopilot system controls lift by operating trailing edge flaps on the central section of the bow foil and at both ends of the stern foil. Flap angles are variable in flight and provide a variation in the lift generated by the bow foil of ±35% and ±85% by the stern foil. The foil flaps are adjusted automatically to dampen heave, pitch, roll and yaw motions in heavy seas. A rudder is fitted to the central bow foil strut for improved manoeuvrability in congested waters. Main and stability foils are of welded construction. Bow and stern foil surfaces, flap tie-rods, the lower ends of the bow and stern foil struts, and the central bow foil strut are built in steel alloy. The amidship foil and struts, pitch stability foil and the upper sections of the bow and stern foil struts are in aluminium-magnesium alloy.

HULL: Twin-deck structure. All-welded construction, similar to that employed on Kometa series. Extensive use is made of pressed panels and rolled aluminium-magnesium alloy strip. Hull is framed on longitudinal and transverse formers. Below the main deck the hull is subdivided by 11 watertight bulkheads into 12 compartments. The craft will remain afloat with any two adjacent compartments flooded up to a total length of 9m—or 21 per cent of the craft's overall length. To retard corrosion below the waterline, magnesium protectors are provided.

POWER PLANT: Power for the waterjet propulsion system is supplied by two marinised gas-turbines, each rated at 5,000hp maximum and 4,500hp continuous. Each unit has a gas-discharge device and the reduction gear rate of rotation at the power take-off shaft is 950rpm. The shafts of both gas-turbines are each connected via flange couplings to the reduction gear of an axial-flow waterjet pump, each of the two pumps receiving water from a common intake. Fuel consumption per horsepower at continuous rating is 225g/h. Oil consumption of each gas-turbine is 1·5kg/h and that of the reduction gear is 0·5kg/h. The service life of each gas-turbine is 10,000 hours before the first overhaul.

ACCOMMODATION: Standard model is designed to carry a crew of 6 and 250 seated passengers. Three saloons are provided on the main deck—a 46-seat bow saloon, a 66-seat amidships saloon and a 74-seat aft saloon—and a further 64 are seated in an upper saloon on the top deck. A separate cabin is provided for the crew. Facilities include a luggage locker, a three-sided refreshment bar, a smaller bar and a promenade deck. Passenger saloons are fully air-conditioned and equipped with airliner-type seats arranged three abreast (32) and two abreast (77). Extensive use is made of heat, sound and vibration absorbing and insulation materials. Decks and serving spaces are overlaid with deep pile carpets. Captain and navigator are accommodated in a raised wheelhouse providing a 360 degree view. A remote control console in the wheelhouse is equipped with the necessary controls and instrumentation for the main and auxiliary engines, the autopilot system, manual steering and fire-fighting.

SYSTEMS, ELECTRICAL: APU drives two 14kW turbogenerators for 28·5V dc service and a 75kW diesel-generator set supplies alternating current at 230V and 50Hz. Two-wire, group-bus type distribution system.

HYDRAULICS: Three separate systems, the first for control of reversing gear, rudder and anchor winch; the second for control of the main engines and water jet nozzles and the third for flap control.

COMMUNICATIONS: R/T simplex/duplex single-band transceiver operating on 18 pre-selected frequencies in the 1·6-8·8 MHz band and transmitting distress signals on 2,182 kHz and 3,023·5 kHz; VHF R/T transceiver operating on seven channels in the 156·3-156·8 MHz band; portable lifeboat type radio, and a PA system.

NAVIGATION: Navigational radar, course indicating system with a steering repeater which automatically provides the course to be steered and transmits data to the repeater, magnetic compass, a log and an automatic steering and stabilisation system.

SAFETY EQUIPMENT: Ten 26-seat inflatable life rafts with provision for the automatic release of five (one side) at a time.

DIMENSIONS
Length overall: 49·9m (163ft 9in)
Width across foils: 13·2m (43ft 6in)
Hull beam: 8m (26ft 3in)
Height above water:
  foilborne (with folded mast): 9m (29ft 6½in)
  hullborne: 6·4m (21ft)
Draft foilborne: 1·9m (6ft 3in)
  hullborne: 4·5m (14ft 9in)

WEIGHTS
Loaded displacement: 140 tonnes
Light displacement: 96·4 tonnes
Deadweight: 43·6 tonnes

PERFORMANCE
Max speed, foilborne: 45-50 knots
Cruising speed, foilborne: 42 knots
Endurance: 8 hours
Max wave height,
  foilborne: 3m (9ft 10in)
  hullborne: sea state 5
Range: 300n miles

KOMETA

Derived from the earlier Meteor, the Kometa is the first seagoing hydrofoil to be built in the Soviet Union. The prototype, seating 100 passengers, made its maiden voyage on the Black Sea in the summer of 1961, after which it was employed on various passenger routes on an experimental basis. Operating experience accumulated on these services led to the introduction of various modifications before the craft was put into series production.

Kometas are built mainly at Gorki and Poti, one of the Black Sea yards.

Kometa operators outside the Soviet Union include Inex-Nautical Touring, Split, Yugoslavia; Empresa Nacional de Cabotage, Cuba; Archille Onorato, Naples, Italy; and Transportes Touristiques Intercontinentaux, Morocco. Other vessels of this type have been supplied to Iran, Romania, Poland, Turkey, Greece, Bulgaria and the German Democratic Republic. Export orders totalled 52 by early 1978.

Export orders have mainly been for the Kometa-M, which was introduced in 1968. Two distinguishing features of this model are the employment of new diesel engines, with increased operating hours between overhauls, and a completely revised surface-piercing foil system, with a trapeze bow foil instead of the former Alexeyev shallow draft submerged type.

A fully tropicalised and air-conditioned version is now in production and this is designated Kometa-MT.

The present standard production Kometa-M seats 116-120. Because of the additional weight of the Kometa-MT's air-conditioning system and other refinements, the seating capacity is reduced in the interest of passenger comfort to 102.

Official designation of the Kometa in the USSR is Hydrofoil Type 342. The craft meets the requirements of the Rules of the Register of Shipping of the USSR and is constructed to Hydrofoil Class KM ★ 2 11 Passenger Class under the Register's technical supervision. IMCO recommendations on fire safety are now being taken into account and non-flammable basalt fibres are being employed for sound and heat insulation and the engine room is clad with titanium plating. The craft is designed to operate during daylight hours on coastal routes up to 81km (50 miles) from ports of refuge under moderate climate conditions.

The standard craft has proved to be exceptionally robust and has a good, all-round performance. On one charter, a Kometa-M covered 5,310km (3,300 miles) by sea and river in 127 hours. It can operate foilborne in waves up to 1·7m (5ft 7in) high and travel hullborne in waves up to 3·6m (11ft 10in).

One of the features of the latest models is the relocation of the engine room aft to reduce the noise in the passenger saloons and the employment of a vee-drive instead of the existing inclined shaft. The arrangement is expected to be similar to that on the Voskhod-2. The revised deck configuration allows more seats to be fitted. These modifications are also incorporated in the recently announced Kometa derivative, the Albatros, which will be fitted with two 1,500hp engines. In future, development of the Kometa and Albatros is likely to continue in parallel.

FOILS: Employment of a surface-piercing trapeze-type bow foil provides the Kometa-M with improved seakeeping capability in waves. The foil system comprises a bow foil, aft foil, and two auxiliaries, one (termed "stabiliser") located above the bow foil for pitch stability, the other sited amidship near the longitudinal centre of gravity to assist take-off. The foils are connected to the hull by struts and brackets. Middle and side struts of the bow foil are of the split type. The lower and upper components of each strut are connected by flanges and bolts. The upper sections are connected to the hull by the same means.

The bow and stern foils are of hollow welded stainless steel construction. The midship and pitch stability foils and the upper components of the foil struts are in aluminium-magnesium alloy.

HULL: Similar in shape to that of the earlier Meteor, the hull has a wedge-shaped bow, raked stem and a spoon-shaped stern. Hull and superstructure are built in AlMg-61 and AlM-6g alloys. Hull and superstructure are of all-welded construction using contact and argon arc welding. The hull is framed on longitudinal and transverse formers, the spacing throughout the length of the hull is 500mm and in the superstructure 1,000mm.

Below the freeboard deck, the hull is divided by watertight bulkheads into thirteen compartments, which include the engine room, fuel compartments, and those containing the firefighting system, tiller gear and fuel transfer pump.

ACCOMMODATION: The Kometa MT seats 102 passengers. It carries a six-man operating crew, comprising captain, engineer, motorman, radio-operator, seaman, and one barman. Embarkation platforms sited immediately below the wheelhouse provide access for both passengers and crew.

The captain and engineer are accommodated in a raised wheelhouse located between the forward and main saloons, and equipped with two seats, a folding stool, chart table, sun shield and a locker for signal flags. The wheelhouse also contains a radar display and radio communications equipment.

Main engine controls are installed in both the wheelhouse and engine room.

Passengers are accommodated in three compartments, a forward saloon seating 22, and central and aft saloons seating 54 and 26 respectively. The central saloon has three exits, two forward, leading to the embarkation platforms and one aft, leading to the promenade deck. This is located in the space above the engine room and is partially covered with a removable metallic awning.

In the current production model of the Kometa M, the forward saloon seats 24, the central saloon seats 56 and the aft saloon 36.

To the starboard side is a crew's off-duty cabin, hydraulic system pump room, bar store and bar, and to the port are two toilets, boiler room, battery room and fire extinguishing equipment.

The aft saloon has two exits, one forward leading to the promenade deck, the other aft, leading to the weather deck, which is used for embarking and disembarking when the vessel is moored by the stern.

Floors of the passenger saloons, crew's cabins, bar and wheelhouse are covered in coloured linoleum and the deckhead in the passenger saloons, as well as bulkheads and the sides above the lower edge of the windows, are finished in light coloured pavinol. Panels of the saloons beneath the windows are covered with plastic.

Passenger saloons are fitted with upholstered

Right (top to bottom): The Kometa is built keel-up to take the stress off the hull. Argon-shielded electric arc welding is employed to give the joints extra strength. All welds are checked closely with gamma-ray flaw detectors. **Left:** A new Kometa for the export market nears completion at the Poti shipyard

chairs, racks for small hand luggage and pegs for clothing. The middle and aft saloons have niches for hand luggage and the former is fitted with cradles for babies. The bar is fully equipped with glass washers, an ice safe, an automatic Freon compressor, electric stove, etc.

SAFETY EQUIPMENT: A full range of lifesaving equipment is carried including five inflatable life rafts, each for 25 persons, 135 life jackets, and four circular life belts with life lines and self-igniting buoyant lights. Life rafts are located two on the forward sponsons and two on the aft sponsons . When thrown into the water the life rafts inflate automatically. Life jackets are stowed under the seats in all saloons, and the circular life belts are stowed on the embarkation and promenade platforms. Kometas for export are provided with life jackets on the basis of 25 persons per raft.

FIREFIGHTING EQUIPMENT: An independent fluid fire fighting system is provided for the engine room and fuel bay. An automatic light and sound system signals a fire outbreak. The fire fighting system is put into operation manually from the control deck above the engine room door. Boat spaces are equipped with hand-operated foam and CO_2 fire extinguishers, felt cloths and fire axes.

POWER PLANT: Power is supplied by two M-401A water-cooled, supercharged 12-cylinder V-type diesels, each with a normal service output of 1,000hp at 1,550rpm and a maximum output of 1,100hp at 1,600rpm. Guaranteed service life of each engine before first overhaul is 2,500 hours. Each engine drives via a reverse gear its own inclined shaft and the twin propellers are contra-rotating. The shafts are of steel and are parallel to the craft. Guaranteed service life of the M-401A before each overhaul is 2,500 hours.

The propellers are of three-bladed design and made of brass.

Main engine controls and gauges are installed in both the wheelhouse and the engine room. A diesel-generator-compressor-pump unit is provided for charging starter air bottles; supplying electric power when at rest; warming the main engines in cold weather and pumping warm air beneath the deck to dry the bilges.

Diesel oil tanks with a total capacity of 3,000kg (6,612lb) for the main engines and the auxiliary unit are located in the afterpeak. Two lubricating oil service tanks and one storage tank located at the fore bulkhead of the engine room have a total capacity of 250kg (551lb). Diesel and lubricating oil capacity is sufficient to ensure a range of 370km (230 miles).

CONTROLS: The wheelhouse is equipped with an electro hydraulic remote control system for the engine reverse gear and fuel supply, fuel monitoring equipment, including electric speed counters, pressure gauges, lubricating and fuel oil gauges. The boat is equipped with a single, solid aluminium magnesium alloy balanced rudder, which is controlled through a hydraulic steering system or a hand-operated hydraulic drive. In an emergency, the rudder may be operated by a hand tiller. Maximum rudder angle is 35 degrees in hullborne conditions and 5·6 degrees foilborne. In the event of the steering gear failing the craft can be manoueuvred by differential use of the main engines, the rudder being locked on the centre line. The vessel can be pinwheeled in hullborne condition by setting one engine slow ahead, the other slow astern and turning the rudder hard over.

SYSTEMS, ELECTRICAL: Power supply is 24V dc. A 1kW dc generator is attached to each of the two engines and these supply power while the craft is operating. A 5·6kW generator is included in the auxiliary unit and supplies power when the craft is at rest. It can also be used when under way for supplying the heating plant or when the 1kW generators are inoperative. Four 12V acid storage batteries, each of 180Ah capacity and connected in series to provide 24V, supply power during short stops.

HYDRAULICS: The hydraulic system for controlling the main engines and reverse gear consists of control cylinders located in the wheelhouse, power cylinders located on the engines, a filler tank, pipe lines and fittings.

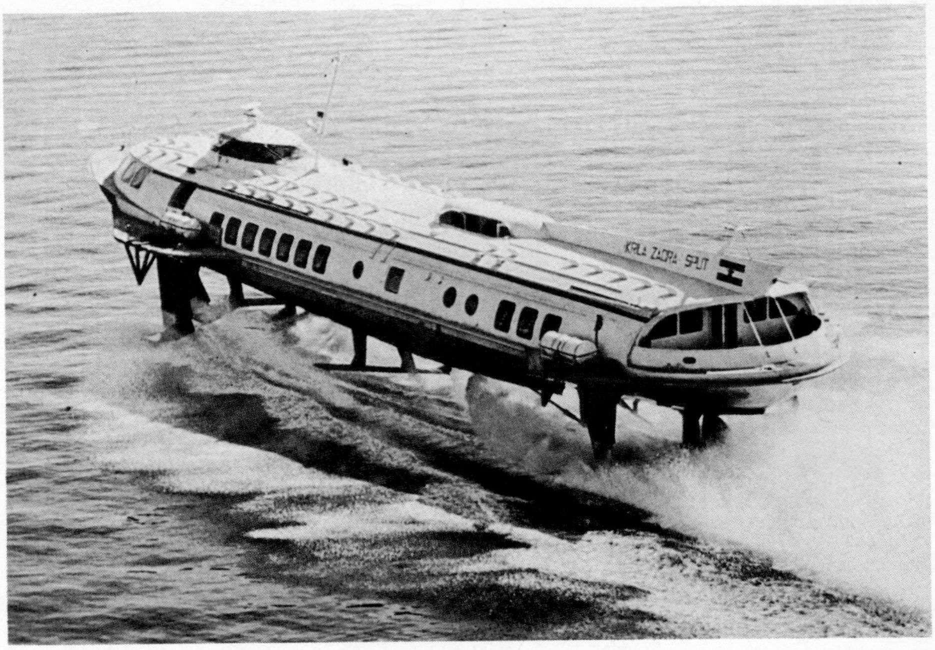

A Kometa-M of Inex-Nautical Touring, Split, Yugoslavia. The vessel, which has a service speed of 32 knots, operates a coastal service on the Adriatic between Krila, Zadar and Split

ANCHORS: The craft is equipped with two Matrosov anchors—a main anchor weighing 75kg (165lb) and a spare anchor weighing 50kg (110lb). The main anchor is raised by means of an electric winch located in the forepeak. The cable of the spare anchor can be heaved in manually and is wound over a drum fitted with a hand brake.

COMMUNICATIONS: A radio transmitter/receiver with r/t and w/t facilities is installed in the wheelhouse for ship-shore and inter-ship communications on SW and MW bands. A portable emergency radio and automatic distress signal transmitter are also installed in the wheelhouse. A broadcast system is fitted in the passenger saloons and a two-way crew communications system is installed in the wheelhouse, engine room, anchor gear compartment and mooring stations.

NAVIGATION: The following navigation aids are standard: a gyro compass, magnetic compass (reserve) and log.

KOMETA-M

DIMENSIONS
Length overall: 35·1m (115ft 2in)
Beam overall: 11m (36ft 1in)
Height, foilborne from waterline to tip of mast: 9·6m (31ft 6in)
Draft, hullborne: 3·6m (11ft 9¾in)
Draft, foilborne: 1·7m (5ft 6⅞in)
WEIGHTS
Light displacement: 44·5 tonnes
Fully loaded displacement: 60 tonnes
Gross register tonnage: 142·1 gross tonnes
PERFORMANCE
Max speed, intermittent: 66·8km/h (36 knots)
Cruising speed: 58km/h (32 knots)
Fuel consumption: 180g/bhp/h
Oil consumption: 5g/bhp/h
Max sea state: Speed of the Kometa-M at full load displacement in sea states 0-2 and wind conditions up to force 3 is 32 knots. Under the worst permissible conditions under which the craft is able to navigate (sea state 5, wind force 6) it will operate hullborne at 10-12 knots. Sea states up to 4 and wind conditions up to force 5 are considered normal for Kometa operation.

KOMETA-MT

DIMENSIONS
Length overall: 35·1m (115ft 2in)
Beam: 11m (36ft 1in)
Height, foilborne, waterline to tip of mast: 9·2m (30ft 2¼in)
Draft, hullborne: 3·6m (11ft 9¾in)
Draft, foilborne: 1·7m (5ft 6⅞in)
WEIGHTS
Light displacement: 45 tonnes
Fully loaded displacement: 58·9 tonnes
PERFORMANCE
Max speed: 61km/h (34 knots)
Service speed: 58km/h (32 knots)
Fuel consumption: 182g/bhp/h
Oil consumption: 58g/bhp/h
Range: 240km

Development of the Kometa is continuing. Current research is aimed at the introduction of a stability augmentation system employing either control flaps on the bow foil or air stabilisation on the stern foil and struts; the reduction of labour involved in construction; the introduction of design improvements through the use of grp and sandwich construction; noise reduction in the saloons and the extension of the cruising range.

METEOR

Dr Alexeyev's Meteor made its maiden voyage from Gorki to Moscow in the summer of 1960, bringing high performance and unprecedented comfort to the river boat scene, and setting the pattern for a family of later designs.

The craft is intended for use in daylight hours on local and medium-range routes of up to 600km (373 miles) in length. It meets the requirements of Class O, experimental type, on the Register of River Shipping in the USSR.

Accommodation is provided for a crew of five and 116 passengers. Cruising speed at the full load displacement of 54·3 tonnes across calm water and in winds of up to Beaufort force 3 is about 65km/h (35 knots).

Outside the Soviet Union Meteors are operated today in Bulgaria, Yugoslavia, Hungary and Poland.

FOILS: The foil arrangement comprises a bow foil and a stern foil, with the struts of the bow system carrying two additional planing subfoils. The foils are attached to the struts, which are of split type, by flanges and bolts. The foils are in stainless steel, and the subfoils in aluminium magnesium alloy. The foil incidence can be adjusted when necessary by the insertion of wedges between the flanges and the foils when the vessel is in dock.

HULL: With the exception of the small exposed areas fore and aft, the Meteor's hull and superstructure are built as an integral unit. The hull is framed on longitudinal and transverse formers and both hull and superstructure are of riveted

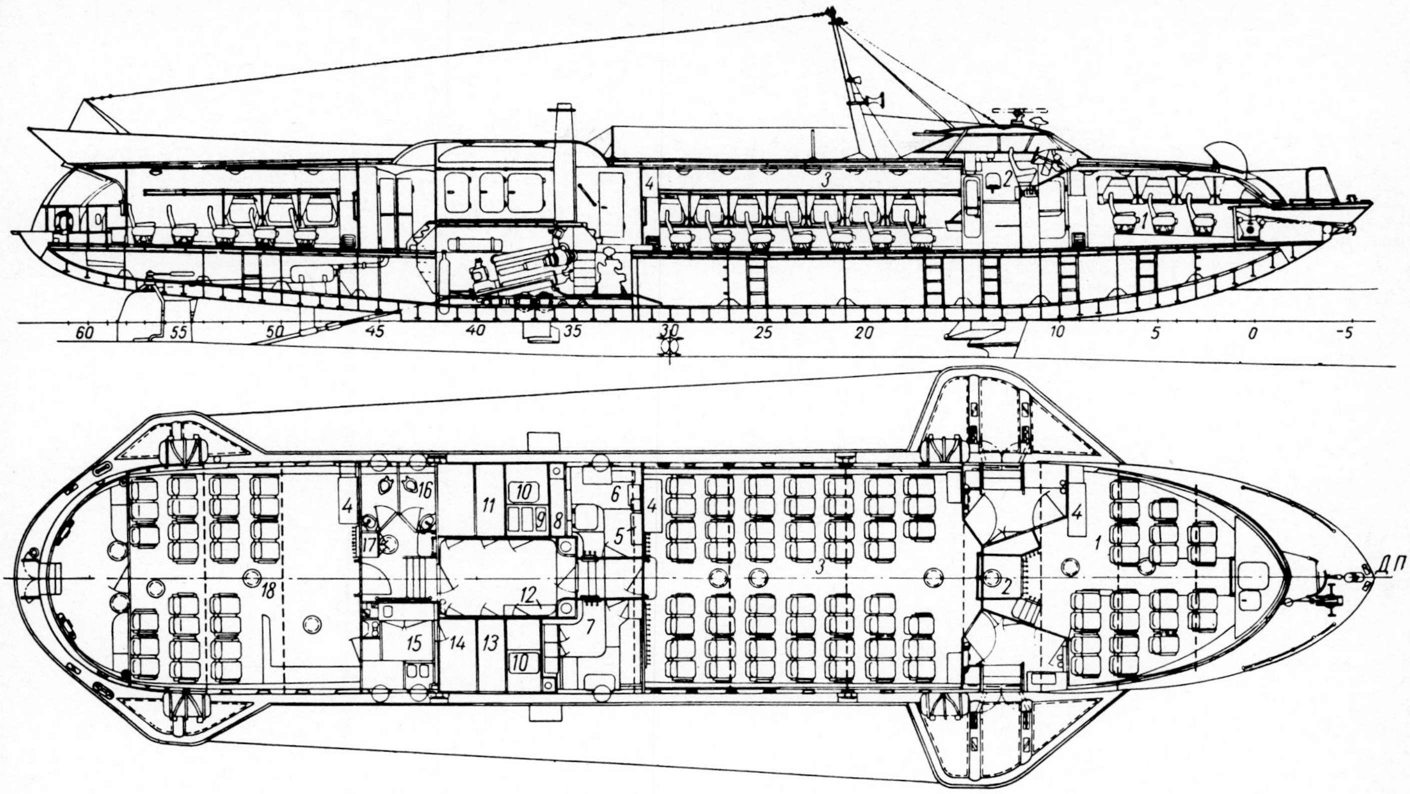

Internal arrangement of the Kometa-MT, designed for tropical operation. 1, 22-seat forward passenger saloon; 2, wheelhouse; 3, 54-seat main passenger saloon; 6, control position; 7, duty cabin; 8, liquid fire extinguisher bay; 9, battery room; 10, engine room; 11, boiler room; 12, installation point for portable radio; 13, store; 14, provision store; 15, bar; 16, WC/washbasin units; 17, boatswain's store; 18, 26-seat aft passenger saloon

duralumin construction with welded steel members. Below the main deck the hull is sub-divided longitudinally into eight compartments by seven bulkheads. Access to the compartments is via hatches in the main deck. The craft will remain afloat in the event of any two adjacent compartments forward of amidship flooding or any one compartment aft of midship. Frame spacing in the hull is about 500mm while that in the superstructure is 1,000mm.

POWER PLANT: Power is supplied by two M-50 12-cylinder, four-stroke, supercharged, water-cooled diesels with reversing clutches. Each engine has a normal service output of 1,000hp at 1,700rpm and a maximum output of 1,100hp at 1,800rpm. Specific consumption at rated output g/bhp/h is not more than 193, and oil, not more than 6. Guaranteed overhaul life is 1,000 hours. Each engine drives its own inclined propeller shaft through a reverse clutch. Propeller shafts are in steel and the propellers, which are five-bladed, are in brass. The drives are contra-rotating.

Refuelling is effected via filler necks on each side of the hull. Fuel is carried in six tanks located in the engine room. Total fuel capacity is 3,200kg. Lubricating oil, total capacity 370 litres, is carried in two service tanks and a storage tank located on the forward bulkhead in the engine room. Fuel and lubricating oil is sufficient for a cruising range, foilborne, of not less than 600km (373 miles).

AUXILIARY UNIT: 12hp diesel for generating electrical power when the craft is at its moorings, warming the main engines in cold weather and operating drainage pump.

CONTROLS: Control of the engines, reverse gear and fuel supply is effected remotely from the wheelhouse with the aid of a hydraulic system comprising transmitter cylinders in the wheelhouse, and actuators on the engine. The engines can also be controlled from the engine room.

Craft heading is controlled by two balanced rudders, the blades of which are in solid aluminium magnesium alloy. The rudders are operated hydraulically from the wheelhouse, the rudder angle being checked by an electric indicator in the wheelhouse. In an emergency, with the craft in hullborne conditions, the rudder is put over with the aid of a detachable hand tiller fitted to the rudder stock.

The Meteor is powered by two 12-cylinder M-50 diesels, each with a normal service output of 908hp. Ahead of the central fin is a removable metallic awning above the promenade deck

At low speed the craft is capable of turning in its own length by pinwheeling—employing both engines with equal power in opposite directions—one ahead, the other astern.

Minimum diameter of the turning circle is approximately 250m (819ft) with the engines running at low speed (700-750rpm) and with the rudder put through an angle of 35 degrees. Turning circle diameter when operating foilborne with the rudder at an angle of 10 degrees is approximately 750m (2,460ft).

The vessel takes-off for foilborne flight in 120-140 seconds, ie within a distance of 25-28 lengths of her hull.

Landing run, with engines reversed, ranges from 1·5 to 2 hull lengths, while the braking distance without reversing the engines is within 3-4 lengths of the hull.

ACCOMMODATION: Passengers are accommodated in three compartments, a forward saloon seating 26, and central and aft saloons seating 46 and 44 passengers respectively. The central saloon has three exits, two forward leading to the embarkation platforms and one aft leading to the promenade deck above the engine room. On the port side of the central saloon, aft, is a small buffet/bar. Beneath the wheelhouse is a duty crew room and a luggage compartment which opens into the forward saloon.

The aft saloon has two exits, one leading to the promenade deck above the engine room and one to the weather deck aft. Forward and aft on both sides of the craft are sponsons to protect the foil systems during mooring. The forward pair are used as embarkation and disembarkation platforms.

SYSTEMS, ELECTRICAL: 24-28·5V dc from the vessel's power supply or 220V ac, 50Hz, from shore-to-ship supply sources.

RADIO: Ship-to-shore radio telephone operating on any of ten pre-selected fixed frequencies. Also passenger announcement system and crew intercom.

NAVIGATION: Magnetic compass.

COMPRESSED AIR: System comprises two air storage bottles, each of 40-litre capacity, used for starting the main engines, operating emergency

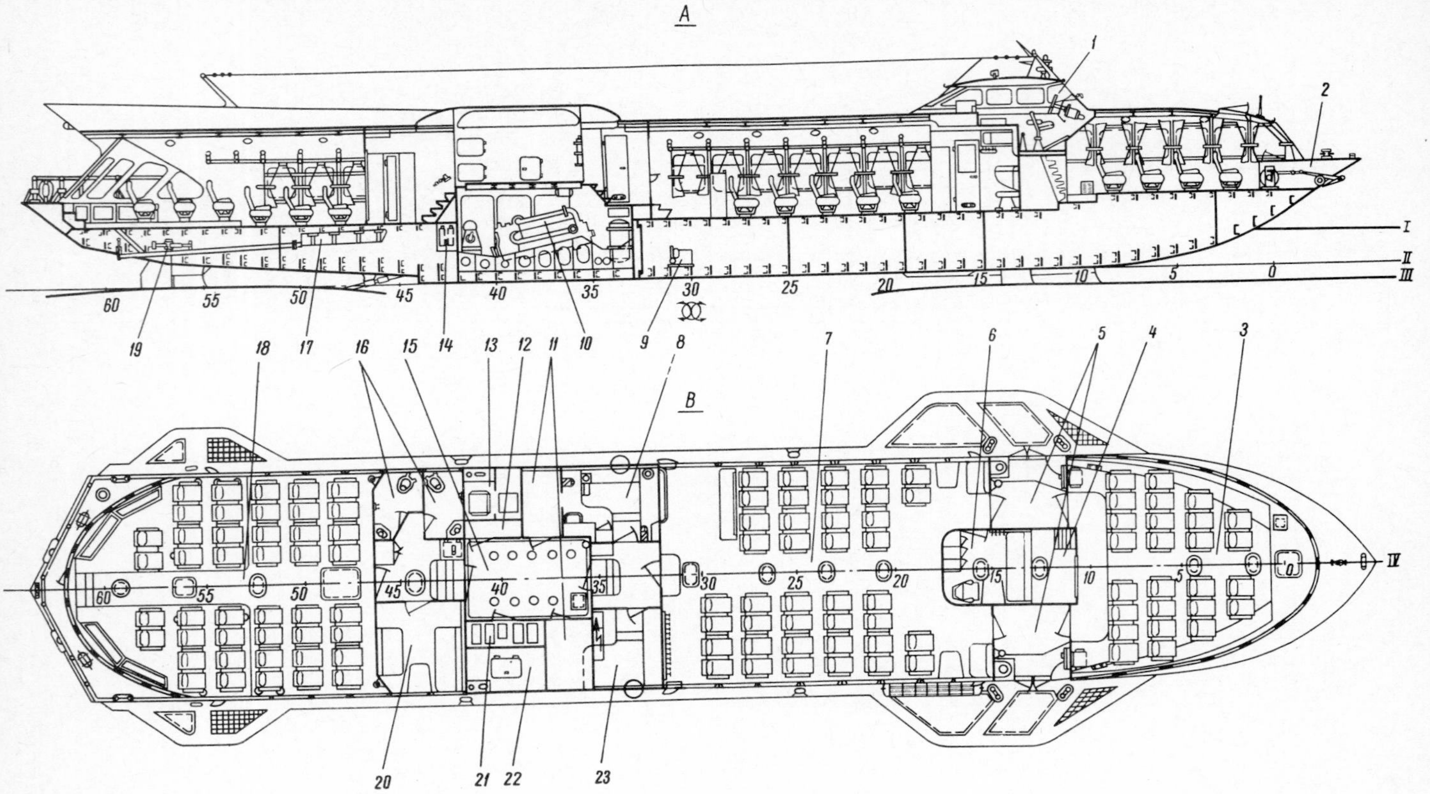

Meteor. General Arrangement
A. Inboard profile; B. main deck plan. I. waterline hullborne; II. hull base line; III. waterline foilborne; IV. longitudinal centreline. 1. wheelhouse; 2. anchor compartment; 3. forward passenger saloon, 26 seats; 4. luggage compartment; 5. embarkation companionway; 6. crew duty room; 7. midship passenger saloon, 42 seats; 8. bar; 9. refrigeration unit; 10. engine room; 11. pantry; 12. boatswain's store; 13. calorifies; 14. fire fighting equipment; 15. promenade deck; 16. WCs; 17. tank; 18. aft passenger saloon, 44 seats; 19. tiller gear; 20. four-seat passenger cabin; 21. storage batteries; 22. hydraulic units; 23. main switchboard

stop mechanism, closing feed cocks of the fuel tanks, recharging the hydraulic system accumulator and the ship's siren.
FIREFIGHTING: Remote system for fighting outbreak in engine room, with automatic light and sound indicator operating in wheelhouse. Hand-operated foam and CO_2 extinguishers provided in passenger saloons and wheelhouse.
DIMENSIONS
Length overall: 34·5m (112ft 2¼in)
Beam overall: 9·5m (31ft 2in)
Height foilborne above water surface: 6·8m (22ft 3¾in)
Draft hullborne: 2·4m (7ft 10½in)
foilborne: 1·2m (3ft 11¼in)
WEIGHTS
Light displacement: 37·2 tonnes
Fully loaded: 54·3 tonnes
PERFORMANCE
Cruising speed, calm water: 65km/h (35 knots)
Limiting sea states:
foilborne: Beaufort Force 3
hullborne: Beaufort Force 4

MOLNIA

This popular six-seat hydrofoil sports runabout was derived from Alexeyev's original test craft. Many hundreds are available for hire on Russian lakes and rivers. In slightly modified form, and renamed Volga, the type is being exported to 44 different countries. The craft is navigable in protected off-shore water up to 2 miles from the land and has particular appeal for water-taxi and joy-ride operators.

Molnia is no longer in production, having been replaced by the Volga. Details of the Molnia can be found in *Jane's Surface Skimmers 1976-77* and earlier editions.

NEVKA

This light passenger ferry and sightseeing craft is in series production at a Leningrad shipyard and the first units have been supplied to Yalta for coastal services on the Black Sea. A multi-purpose runabout, it is intended to cope with a variety of duties including scheduled passenger services, sightseeing, VIP transport and crew-boat. The standard version seats a driver and 14 passengers.

In service in growing numbers as a light passenger ferry and sightseeing craft, the Nevka is about to be offered on the export market. The standard model seats a driver and up to 14 passengers

An export model is expected to be available from the spring of 1979 onwards.

The craft, which is designed to operate in waves up to 1m (3ft) high, is the first small hydrofoil in the Soviet Union to employ surface-piercing V foils, and also the first to employ a diesel engine in conjunction with a Z-drive.

In December 1971 a waterjet-propelled variant made its first cruise along the Crimean coast. The 16-mile trip from Yalta to Alushta was made in half an hour.
FOILS: Bow and stern foils are of fixed V surface-piercing configuration and made of solid aluminium magnesium alloy.
HULL: Glass fibre reinforced plastic structure assembled in four basic sections. The outer hull is assembled with the transom, the deck with the rib of the windscreen, the cabin/cockpit with the engine air intakes and afterpeak, and the inner hull with the companionway at the aft of the cabin.

The lower hull is subdivided by watertight bulkheads into four compartments.

The hull contours are designed to facilitate easy transition from hull to foilborne mode and minimise structural loadings due to wave impact. Two transverse steps are incorporated.
ACCOMMODATION: The craft can be supplied with an open cockpit and folding canopy, as a cabin cruiser with a solid top or as a sightseeing craft with a transparent cabin roof. As a cabin cruiser, the craft is equipped with bunks, a galley and toilet. The driver's stand can be located either at the forward end of the cabin or in a raised position amidships.
POWER PLANT: Power is supplied by a single

3D20 four-cycle, six-cylinder diesel, developing 235hp at 2,200rpm. The engine, located aft, drives a three-bladed propeller via a DK-300 Z-drive.

CONTROLS: Craft heading is controlled by a single balanced rudder in solid aluminium alloy mounted aft of the rear foil main strut and operated by a steering wheel via a mechanical linkage. Other controls include a footpedal to control engine speed, and a reverse lever.

SYSTEMS, ELECTRICAL: Power is 24V dc. A 1kW engine-mounted generator supplies power while the craft is operating. Two 12V acid storage batteries, each of 180Ah capacity and connected in series to give 24V, supply power during stops.

FIREFIGHTING: An independent fluid fire fighting system of aircraft type is installed in the engine bay and is operated remotely from the driving seat.

DIMENSIONS
Length overall: 10·9m (35ft 11in)
Hull beam: 2·7m (8ft 11in)
Beam overall: 4m (13ft 2in)
Draft, hullborne: 1·7m (5ft 3in)
Draft, foilborne: 0·9m (2ft 9in)

WEIGHTS
Max take-off displacement: 5·9 tons
Displacement unloaded: 4·1 tons
Payload: 1·05 tons

PERFORMANCE
Cruising speed: 30 knots
Normal cruising range: 160 miles
Diameter of turn at max speed: 109m (357ft)
Take-off time: approx 30 seconds
Max permissible wave height in foilborne mode: 1m (3ft 3in)
Fuel and lube oil endurance: 6 hours
Fuel consumption per hp at cruising rating: 178g/h

This particular model of the Nevka is fitted with trapeze foils instead of the V-foils which appear to be standard on the export model. Power is supplied by a 235hp 3D20 diesel which drives a three-bladed propeller via a Z-drive

PCHELA (BEE)

This military derivative of the Strela is in service with the KGB for frontier patrol duties in the Baltic, Black Sea, Caspian and various other sea areas. The craft is equipped with a full range of search and navigation radar and is reported to have a speed of about 35 knots. Twenty-five were built between 1965-1972. The craft carry depth charges and two twin machine gun mounts.

RAKETA

The prototype Raketa was launched in 1957 and was the first multi-seat passenger hydrofoil to

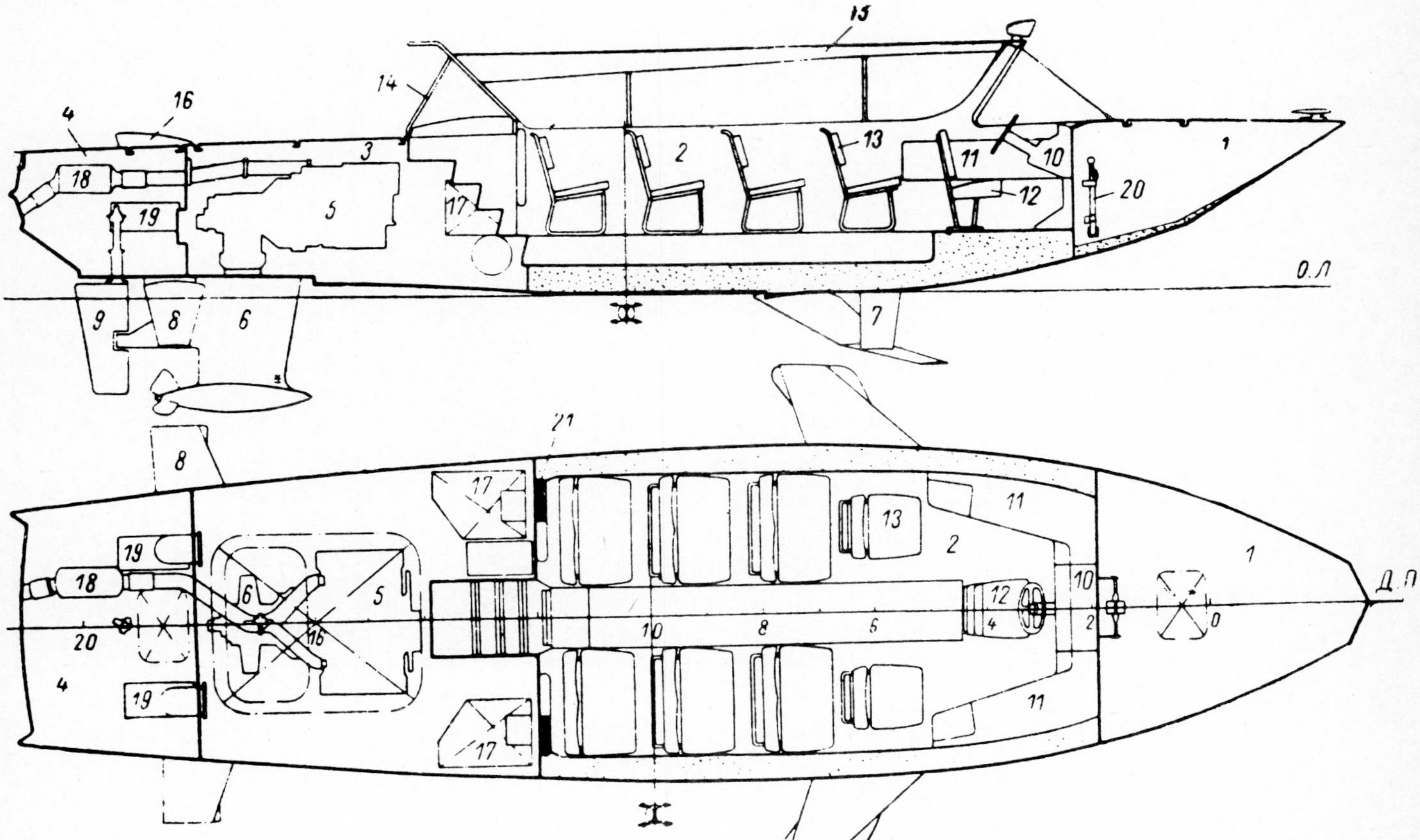

Internal arrangements of the standard Nevka, seating a driver and 14 passengers, (a) inboard profile; (b) deck plan. 1. forepeak; 2. passenger cabin; 3. engine bay; 4. afterpeak; 5. 235hp 3D20 four-cycle six-cylinder diesel; 6. DK-300 Z-drive; 7. bow foil; 8. rear foil; 9. rudder; 10. control panel; 11. lockers; 12. driver's seat; 13. passenger seat; 14. guard rail; 15. detachable awning; 16. engine air intakes; 17. fuel tank; 18. silencer; 19. storage batteries; 20. anchor; 21. lifebelt

employ the Alexeyev shallow draft submerged foil system. Several hundred are now in service on all the major rivers of the USSR.

In January 1973 it was announced that more than three hundred Raketas were being operated on rivers and lakes in the Soviet Union, including sixty-six in service with the Volga United River Shipping Agency.

Variants include the standard non-tropicalised Raketa M seating 64 passengers; the current export model, the 58-seat Raketa T, which is both tropicalised and air-conditioned, and finally the Raketa TA, modified in London by Airavia Ltd, and licensed by the UK Department of Trade to carry up to 100 passengers (58 seated) on high density commuter and tourist routes on sheltered waters such as Westminster—Greenwich.

A substantial number of Raketas have been exported. Examples are currently in service in Romania, Hungary, Finland, Czechoslovakia, Yugoslavia, Austria, Bulgaria and the Federal Republic of Germany.

Production of the Raketa has now stopped and yards previously involved in their fabrication and assembly are building Voskhod and other designs.

The description that follows applies to the Raketa T, the standard export variant, powered by an M-401A diesel and with a cruising speed of about 58km/h (32 knots).

The vessel is designed for high-speed passenger ferry services during daylight hours on rivers, reservoirs and sheltered waters in tropical climates. It meets the requirements of the Soviet River Register Class 'O' with operation restricted to 0·8m (2ft 7in) waves when foilborne and up to 1·5m (4ft 11in) when hullborne.

The passenger saloon is provided with natural and induced ventilation and seats 58. The crew comprises a captain, engineer, deckhand and barman.

FOILS: The foil system comprises one bow foil, one aft foil and two dart-like planing sub-foils, the tips of which are attached to the trailing edges of the outer bow foil struts. Foils, sub-foils and struts are in welded stainless steel. The bow foil, which incorporates sweepback, and the straight aft foil, are both supported by three vertical struts.

The base of the centre strut aft provides the end bearing for the propeller which is located beneath the foil.

HULL: The hull is framed on longitudinal and transverse formers and all the main elements—plating, deck, partitions, bulkheads, platforms and wheelhouse—are in riveted duralumin. The stem is fabricated in interwelded steel strips. Below the freeboard deck the hull is divided into six watertight compartments employing web framing.

ACCOMMODATION: The passenger saloon seats 58 in aircraft-type, adjustable seats. At the aft end of the saloon is a bar. The saloon has one exit on each side leading to the promenade deck and one forward, leading to the forecastle. Aft of the saloon is the engine room, promenade deck with additional seats, two toilets, a storeroom and a companionway leading up to the wheelhouse.

The craft carries a full range of life-saving and fire fighting equipment. There are 62 life jackets stowed in the passenger saloon and four for the crew in the wheelhouse and under the embarkation companionway. Two lifebelts are provided on the embarkation platform and two on the promenade deck. Fire fighting equipment includes four foam and four CO_2 fire extinguishers, two fire axes, two fire buckets and two felt cloths.

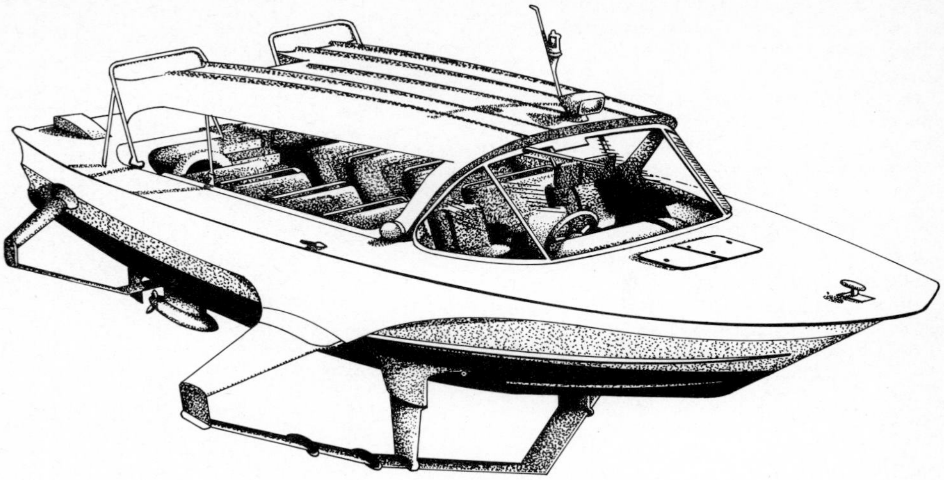

Perspective drawing of the export model of the 15-seat Nevka showing foil details

Raketa M operated on the Rhine by the Köln-Düsseldorfer Shipping Company between Cologne and Koblenz

Raketas in one of the locks on the Irtysh River in the Kazakh republic

POWER PLANT: Power is supplied by a single M-401A water-cooled, supercharged 12-cylinder V-type diesel, with a normal service output of 900hp. The engine drives via a reverse gear and inclined stainless steel propeller shaft a three-bladed cast bronze propeller. The fuel system comprises two fuel tanks with a total capacity of 1,400kg, a fuel priming unit, and a hand fuel booster pump. A compressed air system, comprising a propeller shaft-driven air compressor and two 40-litre compressed air bottles is provided for main engine starting, emergency stopping, operating the foghorn and scavenging the water intake.

The diesel generator unit comprises a Perkins P3.152 diesel engine employed in conjunction with a Stamford C20 alternator.

CONTROLS: The wheelhouse is equipped with a hydraulic remote control system for the engine, reverse gear and fuel supply. The balanced rudder, made in aluminium-magnesium alloy, is controlled hydraulically by turning the wheel. A hand tiller is employed in an emergency. Employment of gas exhaust as a side-thruster to assist mooring is permitted at 850rpm.

SYSTEMS, ELECTRICAL: A 3kW generator, rated at 27·5V and coupled to the main engine is the main source of power while the vessel is under way. A 50Hz, 230V, 1,500rpm three-phase alternator supplies ac power. Four 12V acid storage batteries, each with a 132Ah capacity and connected in series to give 24V, supply power during short stops.

HYDRAULICS: The hydraulic system for controlling the main engine, reverse gear and fuel supply, consists of control levers located in the wheelhouse and on the main engine, power cylinders located on the engine, a filler tank, pipelines and fittings.

HEATING AND VENTILATION: Passenger saloon and wheelhouse are provided with natural ventilation, using ram inflow when the boat is in motion. Norris warming air-conditioning is fitted for use in hot weather. One conditioner is installed in the wheelhouse and eight are installed in the passenger saloon and bar. The cooled air is distributed throughout the saloon by electric fans installed on the ceiling. One is provided in the wheelhouse. A radio-telephone with a range of about 30km (19 miles) is installed for ship-to-shore and ship-to-ship communication. The vessel also has a public address system and intercom speakers linking the engine room, wheelhouse and forecastle.

DIMENSIONS

Length overall: 26·96m (88ft 5in)

Beam amidships: 5m (16ft 5in)

Freeboard: 0·8m (2ft 7½in)

Height overall (excluding mast): 4·46m (14ft 8in)

Draft, hullborne: 1·8m (5ft 11in)

foilborne: 1·1m (3ft 7¼in)

WEIGHTS

Displacement, fully loaded: 27·09 tonnes

light: 20·31 tonnes

PERFORMANCE

Service speed: about 58km/h (32 knots)

Max wave height, foilborne: 0·8m (2ft 8in)

hullborne: 1·5m (4ft 11in)

Turning diameter, hullborne: 3-4 boat lengths

foilborne: 15-16 boat lengths

Pchela fast patrol boat of the KGB frontier guard. Note the surface-piercing trapeze foils

SPUTNIK

The 100-ton Sputnik was the first of the Soviet Union's large hydrofoils. On its maiden voyage in November 1961, the prototype carried 300 passengers between Gorki and Moscow in 14 hours. Although a heavy autumn storm was encountered en route the craft was able to continue under way at a cruising speed of 40 knots through several large reservoirs with waves running as high as 8ft.

FOILS: The foil system comprises a bow and rear foil with the outer struts of the bow assembly carrying two additional planing subfoils.

HULL: The hull is welded in AlMg-61 aluminium magnesium alloy. Adoption of an all-welded unit construction facilitated prefabrication of sections at the Sormovo shipyard and elsewhere, the parts being sent to other yards in the USSR for assembly. One yard used for assembling Sputniks is at Batumi, on the Caspian Sea.

POWER PLANT: Power is supplied by four 850hp M-50 water cooled, supercharged V-type diesels, each driving its own propeller shaft and controlled electro-hydraulically from the forward wheelhouse.

ACCOMMODATION: Passengers are accommodated in three saloons, a well-glazed fore compartment seating 68, and central and aft compartments each seating 96. On short, high frequency services, the seating is increased to 108 in the latter compartments by the substitution of padded benches instead of adjustable aircraft-type seats. Two separate off-duty cabins are provided for the 5-man crew. The cabins are attractively finished in pastel shades and fully insulated against heat and sound. Full fire fighting and other emergency provisions are made and in addition to lifebelts for all passengers and members of the crew, two inflatable rubber boats are carried.

DIMENSIONS

Length overall: 47·9m (157ft 2in)

Beam overall: 9m (29ft 6in)

Draft, hullborne: 1·3m (4ft 3in)

foilborne: 0·9m (2ft 10in)

WEIGHTS

Displacement fully loaded: 110 tons

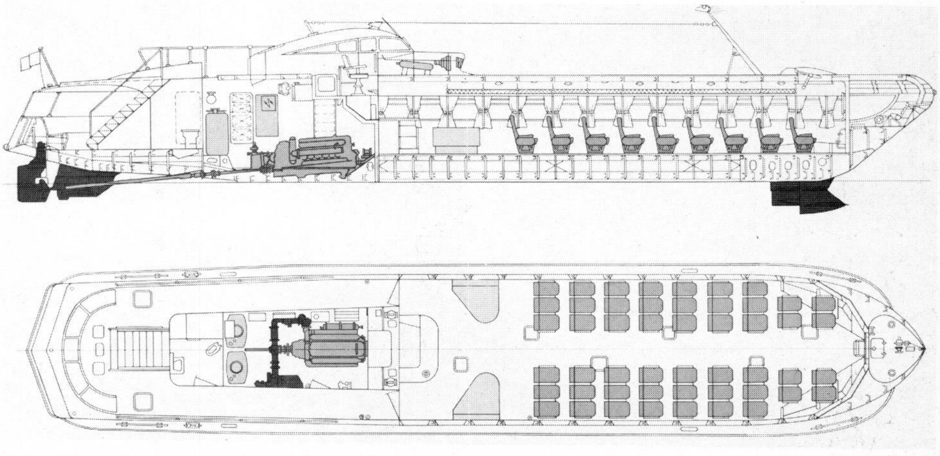

Inboard profile and plan view of the standard 50-seat Raketa. On short-range commuter services, additional passengers are seated around the promenade deck aft, and others are permitted to stand. The high density traffic version accommodates up to 100 passengers

The bow foil and planing stabiliser foils of the 50-seat Raketa

PERFORMANCE
Cruising speed: 75km/h (41 knots)

STRELA

Developed from the Mir and intended for services across the Black Sea, the prototype Strela (Arrow) completed its acceptance trials towards the end of 1961. The craft, which was designed and built in Leningrad, was first put into regular passenger service between Odessa and Batumi, and later between Yalta and Sevastapol. More recently a Strela 3 has been operating a service between Leningrad and Tallinn. It covers the distance in four hours, ninety minutes faster than the express train service connecting the two ports.

Two 970hp 12-cylinder V-type M-50 F3 diesels driving twin screws give the Strela a cruising speed of 75km/h (40 knots). The craft has trapeze type surface-piercing bow foils with a horizontal centre section between the main struts, and can operate in sea state 4.

It carries 82-94 passengers in airliner type seats.

DIMENSIONS
Length overall: 29·3m (96ft 1in)
Beam overall: 8·3m (26ft 4in)
Draft, hullborne: 2·25m (7ft 7in)
foilborne: 1·2m (3ft 11in)

WEIGHTS
Displacement, fully loaded: 46 tons

PERFORMANCE
Cruising speed: 40 knots
Sea state capability: 1·22m (4ft) waves
Range of operation: 740km (460 miles)
Time to reach service speed from stop: 130 seconds
Distance from full speed to stop: 234m (713ft)
Full speed ahead, to full speed astern: 117m (356ft)

Aft foil assembly comprising the foil, three supporting struts and bearing for the inclined propeller shaft of the Raketa passenger ferry

The 100-ton Sputnik, first of the Soviet Union's large hydrofoil passenger ferries

The prototype Strela during trials off the Yalta coast

VIKHR (WHIRLWIND)

Seagoing version of the 100-ton Sputnik, Vikhr employs the same hull and is one of the most powerful passenger hydrofoils operating today. Described as a "Coastal liner", it is designed to operate during hours of daylight on inshore services on the Black Sea up to 50km (31 miles) from the coast. The craft was launched in 1962 and is currently in service on the Odessa-Herson route.

FOILS: Compared with the Sputnik, innovations include more sharply swept back foils, a form of stability augmentation, and an amidship foil, in addition to those fore and aft, to increase seaworthiness and stability. The bow and rear foils and their struts are in stainless steel, foil and stabiliser are made in aluminium magnesium alloy.

HULL: Similar to the Sputnik. Two steps are aligned with the flare of the sides. Hull and superstructure are of welded AlMg-61 aluminium magnesium alloy.

ACCOMMODATION: There are three passenger saloons, seating a total of 268 passengers. The forward saloon seats 78, the central saloon seats 96, and the aft 94. At the rear of the central cabin is a large buffet and bar, beneath which is the engine room. From the bar double doors lead to the off-duty quarters for the seven-man crew.

In high seas, passengers board from the stern, across the promenade deck. In normal conditions, embarkation takes place through a wide passageway across the vessel between the fore and middle saloons. Seats are arranged in rows of four abreast across each cabin with two aisles, each 1m (3ft 4in) wide, between, to ease access to the seats.

POWER PLANT: Power is supplied by four 1,200hp M50-F3 diesel engines, with DGKP (diesel generator, compressor pump) auxiliary engines. Each engine drives a three-bladed propeller via a reverse gear and its own inclined stainless steel shaft. The central shafts are inclined at 12° 20′ and the side shafts at 13° 13′.

An overriding control valve is fitted to the control systems of the main engines, so that the fuel gauges of all four can be controlled simultaneously. This makes it possible to maintain a uniform load on the engines immediately the craft becomes foilborne, thus increasing the life of the engines. The craft can operate satisfactorily with one engine out.

CONTROLS: The wheelhouse is equipped with an electro hydraulic remote control system for the engines, reverse gear, fuel supply etc. Twin balanced rudders are hydraulically operated by two separate systems—main and emergency.

SYSTEMS, ELECTRICAL: Power supply is 24V dc. A 1kW dc generator is attached to each of the engines and these supply power when operating. Two KG-5·6, 5·6kW generators are included in the auxiliary unit and supply power when at rest. They can also be used when under way for supplying the heating plant or when the 1kW generators are inoperative. Four 12V acid storage batteries, each of 180Ah capacity and connected in series to provide 24V, supply power during stops.

COMMUNICATIONS: A radio transmitter/receiver is installed in the wheelhouse for ship-shore and inter-ship communication on r/t, also a receiver. A ship's broadcast system is also installed with speakers in the passenger saloons.

NAVIGATION: Equipment includes radar, and a radio direction finding unit, both with displays in the wheelhouse.

DIMENSIONS

Length overall: 47·54m (156ft)

Beam: 9m (29ft 6in)

Height of hull to awning deck: 5·54m (18ft 2in)

Draft hullborne: 4·1m (13ft 6in)

foilborne: 1·5m (4ft 11in)

WEIGHTS

Displacement, fully loaded: 117·5 tons

PERFORMANCE

Max speed: 78km/h (43 knots)

Cruising speed: 66km/h (35·8 knots)

Cruising range: 386km (240 miles)

Max wave height in foilborne condition: 1·5m (4ft 11in)

Time to reach service speed from stop: 190 seconds

Distance from full speed to full stop: 300m (984ft)

Distance from full speed ahead to full speed astern: 224m (735ft)

VOLGA 70

First export version of the Molnia sports hydrofoil, the Volga 70 incorporates various design refinements including a completely redesigned bow foil.

Powered by a 90hp Volvo Penta diesel engine it was introduced at the end of 1972. The cruising

The Vikhr employs the same hull as the Sputnik and is designed for regular year round services on the Black Sea

Volga 70, a six-seat hydrofoil taxi and runabout powered by a 106hp Volvo Penta diesel. Volgas have been exported to 44 countries since 1972. Production is officially stated to have run into "several thousand"

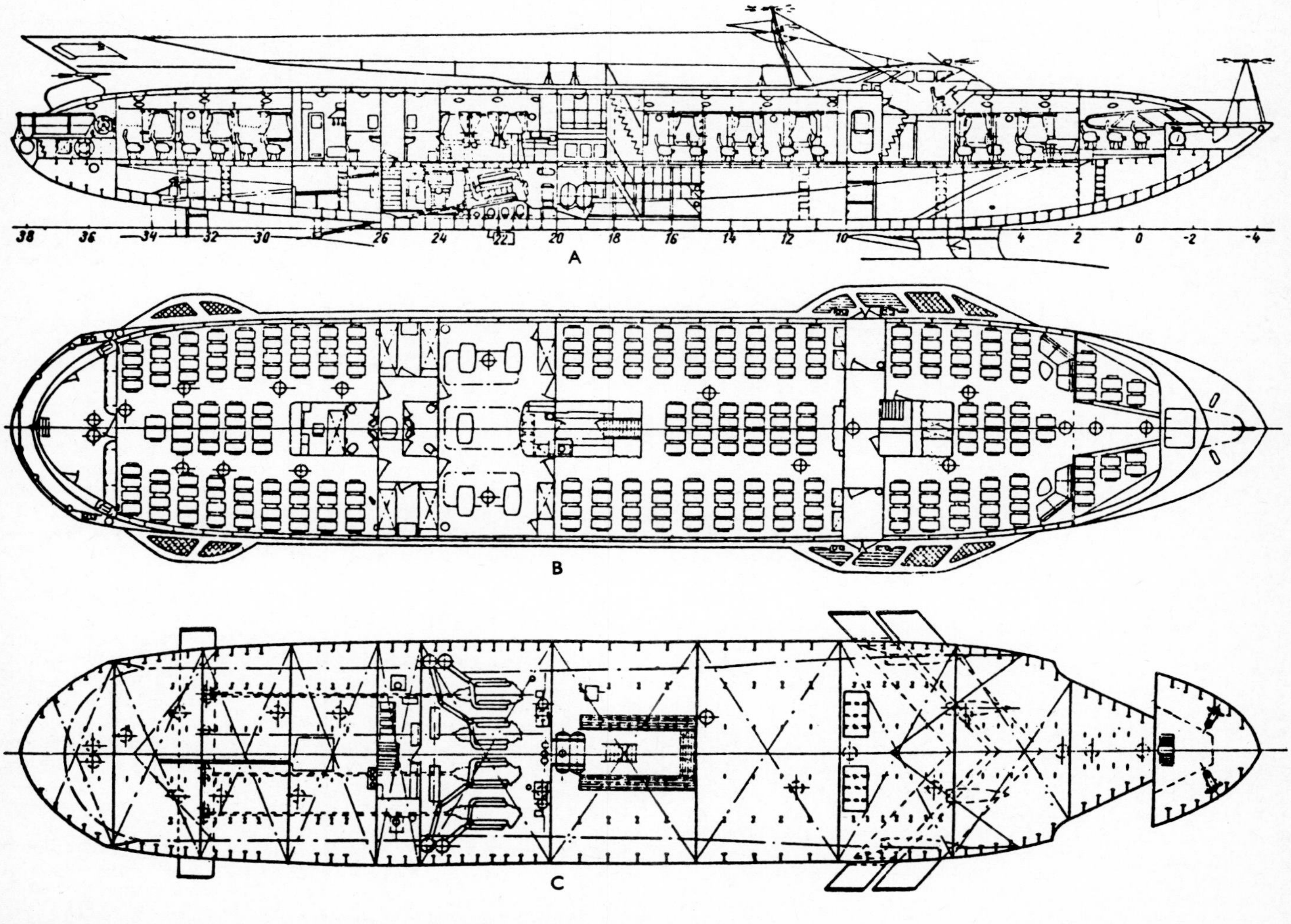

Internal arrangement of the Vikhr. a. profile; b. main deck plan; c. holds

speed is four km/h slower than that of the earlier model, but engine maintenance is easier and the acquisition of spares is simplified in many parts of the world. This model has been purchased by companies and individuals in the USA, West Germany, Sweden, Netherlands and Singapore.

A new export model of the Volga is due to be introduced in 1979. It will succeed both the Volga 70 and the Volga-275 described in *Jane's Surface Skimmers 1978.*

FOILS: The foil system consists of a bow foil with stabilising sub-foil and a rear foil assembly. The foils are of stainless steel.

HULL: Built in sheet and extruded light alloy, the hull is divided into three compartments by metal bulkheads. The forepeak is used for stores, the midship compartment is the open cockpit and the aft compartment houses the engine and gearbox.

ACCOMMODATION: Seats are provided for six—a driver and five passengers. The controls, instruments, magnetic compass and radio receiver are grouped on a panel ahead of the driver's seat. A full range of safety equipment is provided, including life jackets for six, life line, fire extinguisher and distress flares. A folding awning can be supplied.

POWER PLANT: Power is supplied by a single Volvo Penta AQD 32A/270TD diesel with a steerable outboard drive delivering 106hp at 4,000rpm. Fuel capacity is 120 litres (26·4 gallons), sufficient for a range of 150 miles.

SYSTEMS, ELECTRICAL: 12V dc. Starting, instrument and navigation lights and siren, are provided by an engine-mounted generator and an acid stowage battery.

DIMENSIONS
Length overall: 8·55m (28ft 1in)
Beam: 2·1m (6ft 10⅝in)
Height above water when foilborne: 0·98m (3ft 2⅝in)
Draft hullborne: 0·92m (3ft)
foilborne: 0·52m (1ft 8½in)

WEIGHTS
Loaded displacement: 1,930kg (4,255lb)
Light displacement: 1,350kg (2,977lb)

PERFORMANCE
Max speed: 30 knots
Cruising speed: 28 knots
Range: 241km (150 miles)

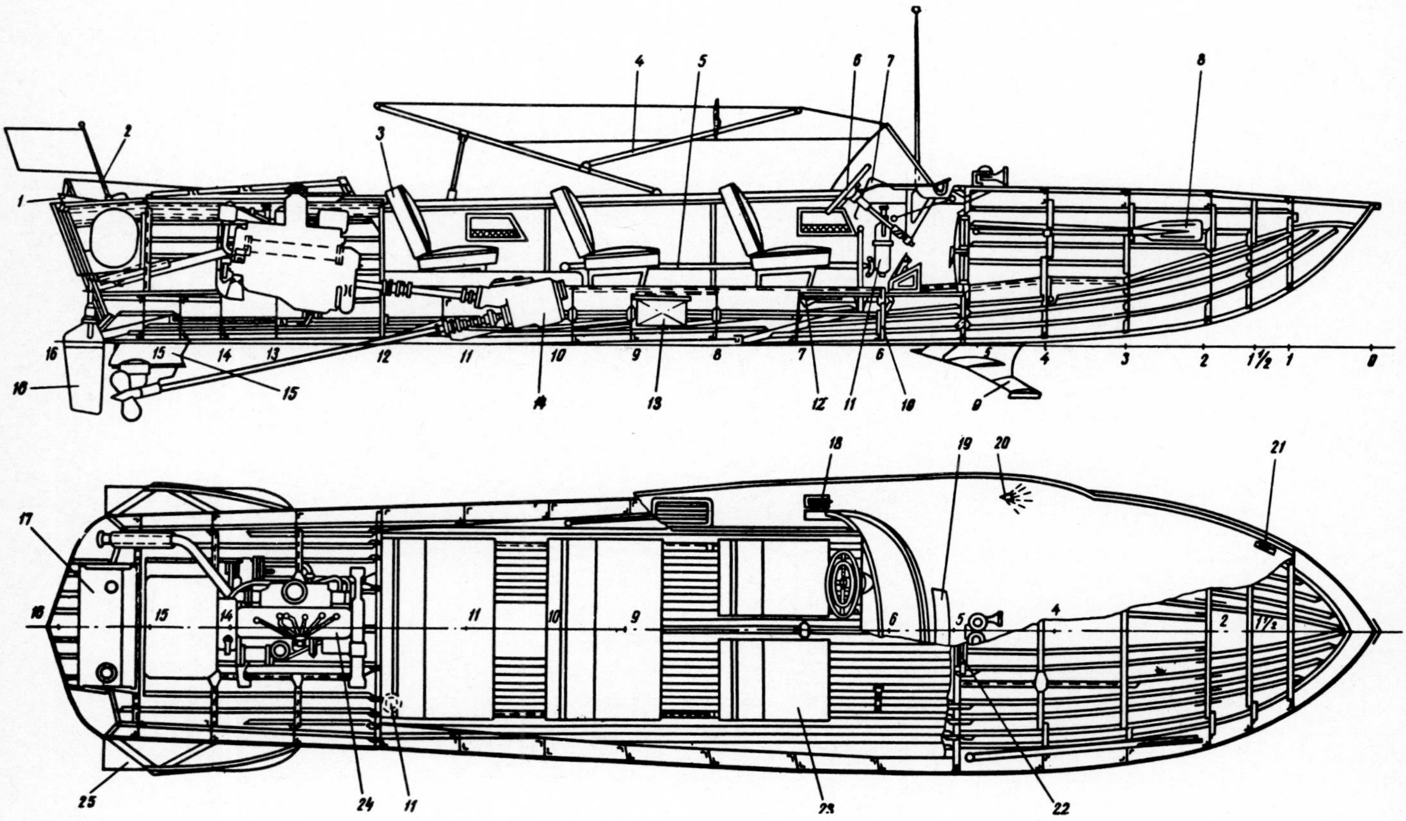

Inboard profile and plan of the Volga
1 stern light; 2 flag pole; 3 bench seat; 4 awning; 5 dog hook; 6 steering column; 7 instrument panel; 8 oar; 9 bow foil assembly; 10 anchor line; 11 fire extinguisher OY-2; 12 anchor; 13 storage battery; 14 reduction and reverse gear; 15 rear foil assembly; 16 steering and rudder gear; 17 fuel tank; 18 cleat; 19 air intake; 20 side running light; 21 fairlead; 22 cover of first bulkhead hatch; 23 seat; 24 M652-Y six-cylinder automotive engine; 25 foilguard

UNITED STATES OF AMERICA

BOEING MARINE SYSTEMS

A Division of the Boeing Company

Head Office: PO Box 3707, Seattle, Washington 98124, USA
Telephone: (206) 655 3200
Officials:
Robert E Bateman, *Vice President and General Manager, Boeing Marine Systems*

Boeing Marine Systems, now a separate operating division of the Boeing company, was formed in 1959 to conduct research, development, design, manufacture and the testing of high performance marine vehicles systems. Boeing's entry into the hydrofoil field was announced in June 1960, when the company was awarded a US $2 million contract for the construction of the US Navy's 120-ton PCH-1 High Point, a canard design which was the outcome of experiments with a similar arrangement in the US Navy test craft Sea Legs.

Boeing has also built a jet-driven hydroplane, the HTS, for testing foil models at full-scale velocity; the Fresh-1, a manned craft for testing superventilating or supercavitating foils at speeds between 60–100 knots and a waterjet test vehicle, Little Squirt. Descriptions of Fresh-1 and Little Squirt appear in *Jane's Surface Skimmers 1970-71* and earlier editions. The company also completed a highly successful waterjet-propelled gunboat, the PGH-2 Tucumcari, for the US Navy's Ship Systems Command. Its operational trials included several months of combat evaluation in Vietnam as part of the US Navy's coastal surveillance force. Data provided by the vessel assisted the design and development of the NATO/PHM, which is a 'scaled up' Tucumcari, and the Jetfoil commercial hydrofoil.

High Point was modified by Boeing during 1972 to incorporate a new automatic control system, new struts and foils, a new diesel for hullborne propulsion and a steerable forward strut to provide improved manoeuvrability. The craft was returned to the US Navy in a new configuration, identified as Mod-1, in March 1973. In its revised form it is employed as a testbed for hydrofoil weapons compatability.

On 4 April 1975, the PCH was operated by the US Coast Guard for one month as part of a continuing research and development programme to evaluate high-speed water craft for the US Coast Guard use. Operating in Puget Sound and around San Francisco, the craft was employed on fisheries patrol, marine environmental protection and search and rescue missions.

On 19 January 1973, the keel was laid for the first 110-ton 250-seat Model 929-100 Jetfoil passenger ferry. The hull was assembled in a former 727 assembly building at Renton, Washington, and the first craft was launched on 29 March 1974 on Lake Washington, which is adjacent to the plant. Ten Jetfoils of this type are in commercial service. Jetfoil 0011, which was launched in June 1978, is the first of five additional Jetfoils of improved design now under construction. Most of the improvements in this new version, known as the Model 929-115, are based on operating experience over the past three years and will add to the Jetfoil's performance, payload and reliability.

An order for the first fast patrol craft version of the Jetfoil was placed by the Royal Navy in 1978. This is basically a modified commercial Jetfoil, designated Patrol Hydrofoil 0001, PH01, and will be built on the commercial Jetfoil production

Pegasus, first of the Boeing/NATO PHM (Patrol Hydrofoil Missile) class vessels, was commissioned into service with the US Navy on 9 July 1977, becoming the first hydrofoil to be officially designated a United States Ship (USS Pegasus). All other USN hydrofoils are operated by test commands and are not officially part of the fleet. Main armament comprises eight AGM-84A Harpoon anti-ship missiles and one rapid-fire 76mm cannon. Top speed is in excess of 50 knots

line. It is a 117-ton craft with the top passenger deck removed. Two Allison 501-K20A gas-turbines will be installed for foilborne operation and two Allison 8V92T1 diesels for hullborne operation, giving added time on-station and increased endurance. Launching is scheduled for July 1979 and delivery in October 1979.

The company is at present examining the possibility of exporting both civil and military versions of the Jetfoil on a modular basis, with the customer purchasing a basic hull, which would contain all the essential systems, and installing his own superstructure.

In April 1973, US Naval Ship Systems Command awarded the company a US $42,602,384 contract for the design and development of the 235-tonne NATO PHM missile-equipped patrol boat, under the terms of which Boeing was to build the lead craft for the US Navy for evaluation.

The PHM was the first US Navy craft to be designed on the basis of a co-operative technical interchange between the United States and its allies within NATO.

The first PHM, Pegasus, was launched on 9 November 1974. Delivery to the US Navy took place in late 1976 and the craft completed its acceptance trials at Seattle in early June 1977.

In August 1977 it was announced by the US Defense Secretary that the US Navy will receive five more PHMs between January 1981 and February 1982. US$85·2 million has been appropriated to date for PHM development and US$272·7 million for the procurement of the five follow-on craft. On delivery the vessels will be assigned to a PHM squadron operating with the Sixth Fleet in the Mediterranean and will specialise in anti-submarine warfare in coastal waters.

Interested observers in the PHM programme include the navies of Canada, Australia, Denmark, the Netherlands, France, Greece, Turkey and the United Kingdom.

Design studies are now being completed for bigger and faster hydrofoils including the 1,300–1,500-ton Destroyer Escort Hydrofoil (DEH), a vessel capable of open ocean missions and of crossing the Atlantic without refuelling.

PCH-1 HIGH POINT

General design of the PCH-1 High Point was specified by the US Navy's Bureau of Ships, with responsibility for detail design and construction assigned to Boeing. The ship was accepted by the US Navy in August 1963 and based at the Puget Sound Naval Shipyard at Bremerton, Washington. Since then it has been undergoing a wide range of tests to evaluate the performance of an inshore hydrofoil ASW system.

High Point had a major modification and overhaul by Boeing in 1972 and was returned to the US Navy in March 1973. The new configuration is identified as Mod-1. In its revised form it is employed as a weapons testbed to evaluate PHM missile ship equipment and weapons and ASW devices. Two RGM-84A-1 Harpoon blast test vehicles were successfully launched from the deck of the vessel while foilborne at 40 knots off British Columbia on the US-Canadian Nanoose range during December 1973–January 1974.

Both firings were conducted in normal sea conditions and moderate winds, the first being made while foilborne with the vessel straight and level, and the second while turning foilborne at 5 degrees/second. The dynamic stability of the craft was measured throughout the tests and the gas-turbine was monitored to establish any possible harmful effects caused by the blast of the Aerojet-General 300lb solid-propellant booster employed in the launch. The success of the test confirmed the suitability of the launch canister design for use on the PHM and other hydrofoils.

During April 1975, the PCH-1 was employed by the US Coast Guard in Puget Sound and off San Francisco. It undertook a number of duties, from fisheries patrol to search and rescue missions, as part of a programme to evaluate high-speed water craft for possible use by the US Coast Guard.

FOILS: Submerged fixed incidence canard foil system, with 68% of the foil area located aft, and trailing-edge flaps on all foils for lift control, is a scaled-up version of that employed on Sea Legs. The foil struts retract vertically into the hull. Foils are of built-up construction in HY-80 weldable steel, and struts are in HY-130 steel.

HULL: Hull and superstructure are of all-welded, corrosion resistant 5456 aluminium. Integral plate stiffener extrusions are extensively used for decks and portions of the sides not having excessive curvature.

ACCOMMODATION: A crew of 18 is carried to provide a three-section watch: on duty at any given time are one officer of the deck/helmsman, one lookout on bridge, one radar operator and one navigator required in combat information centre, and two engineers on watch in main control. The wheelhouse seats two operators on the port and the helmsman on the starboard side. In addition there are seats for two observers. Crew accommodation is ventilated and heated only. Entry is via four watertight doors in the deckhouse and two watertight hatches on main deck.

POWER PLANT: Foilborne propulsion is provided by two Proteus Model 1273 gas-turbines, each rated at 4,250hp maximum and 3,800hp continuous. The turbines are located aft and take air through the two towers housing the retracted foil struts. The exhaust is discharged directly aft through the transom. Each gas-turbine is coupled to a pair of contra-rotating, subcavitating five-bladed propellers, 34in in diameter, through two right-angle gearboxes one at the top of each aft strut and the others in each of the underwater nacelles.

Hullborne propulsion is supplied by a single GM 12-V-71 (N75) rated at 525hp for continuous operation. The engine is coupled to a 1,092mm (43in) diameter propeller through a retractable outdrive unit, which is steerable through 360 degrees and rotates about the axis of the horizontal shaft for retraction.

CONTROLS: Attitude and foilborne stability are controlled by an automatic control system, the heart of which is a computer. This governs motion of the trailing-edge flaps and the steerable forward strut in response to inputs from ultrasonic height sensors, position and rate gyros, accelerometers, feedback on control surface positions and helm commands. The system is active and all control surfaces are continuously moving in response to computer commands. On the bow foil, which is of single inverted tee (T) configuration, lift is varied by two trailing-edge flaps driven by a single actuator. The aft foil, of shallow M configuration, has two ailerons and two trailing-edge flaps. Each flap and its corresponding aileron are driven by a single hydraulic actuator.

Pitch is controlled by the flaps on the forward and aft foils. The gains in the control system were selected to provide automatic trim. Roll is controlled by differential operation of the flaps on the aft foil system. A roll to steer system causes the vessel to perform banked turns. Hullborne steering is accomplished by rotation of the hullborne propulsion unit about a vertical axis. This unit can also be rotated upward 87 degrees about a longitudinal axis to eliminate its drag during foilborne operation.

The attitude control is entirely automatic except for steering. The take-off procedure on the PCH-1 is simply to set the desired flying height, then advance the throttles. At a gross weight of 117 tons take-off occurs at 24 knots with 3,750 total horsepower delivered to the transmission system, the speed stabilising at 40 knots at that power setting. Minimum foilborne speed is 24 knots. At a cruising speed of 44 knots 4,400hp is required, with propellers turning at 1,350rpm.

SYSTEMS, ELECTRICAL: 100kW (450V, 60Hz 30).

HYDRAULICS: 3,000psi ship's service for hullborne steering, strut and foil extension/retraction, engineering auxiliaries, and separate 3,000psi system for foilborne control surfaces.

ELECTRONICS: Raytheon Pathfinder 1605 radar, UHF and HF radio transceivers.

ARMAMENT: Two fixed twin-tube Mk 32 torpedo tubes mounted on main deck at waist of ship.

DIMENSIONS

Length overall, hull: 35·28m (115ft 9in)
Length waterline, hull: 33·65m (110ft 5in)
Hull beam: 9·14m (30ft)
Beam overall with foilguards: 11·71m (38ft 5in)
Draft hullborne: 2·62m (8ft 7in)
Freeboard: 2·67m (8ft 9in)

WEIGHTS

Light displacement: 99·61 tons
Normal take-off displacement: 127·21 tons
Useful load (fuel, water, etc): 27·6 tons

PERFORMANCE

Max speed foilborne: 50 knots
Cruising speed foilborne: 30-40 knots
Max speed hullborne: 25 knots
Cruising speed hullborne: 8 knots

The PCH-1 High Point launching a McDonnell Douglas RGM-84A-1 Harpoon anti-ship missile during tests on the Joint US/Canadian Range, Nanoose, Canada, in January 1974

PCH-1 bearing the insignia of the US Coast Guard, which operated the vessel during the month of April 1975 as part of a continuing research and development programme to evaluate high-speed water craft for S & R missions, fisheries patrol and marine environmental protection

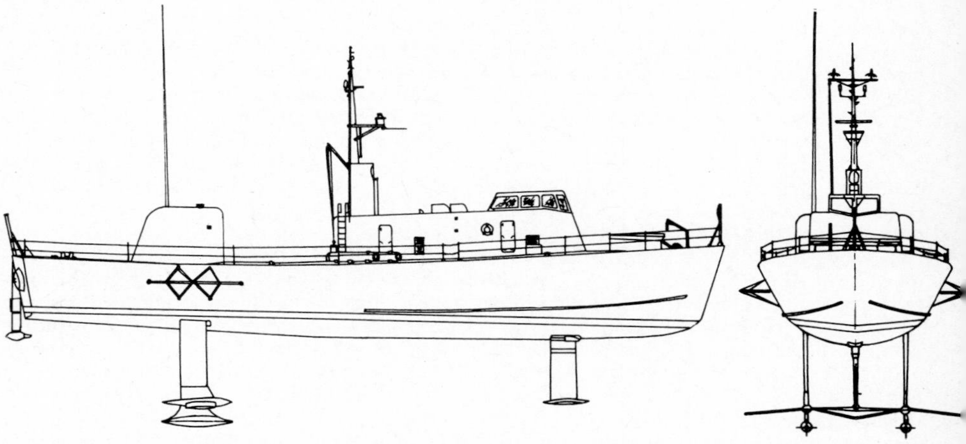

Outboard profile and bow-on view of the PCH-1 High Point in its new Mod-1 configuration. Note the shallow M aft foil, which has two ailerons and two trailing edge flaps. Output of each of the two Proteus 1273 gas-turbines has been uprated to 4,250shp

PGH-2 TUCUMCARI

A 58-ton waterjet-propelled hydrofoil gunboat, the PGH-2 was ordered from Boeing by the US Navy's Ship Systems Command in 1966, under a US $4 million, fixed price PGH (Patrol Gunboat Hydrofoil) programme. The craft was designed, constructed and tested in 23 months and delivered on schedule to the US Navy on 7 March 1968.

The craft operated with both the US Navy Pacific Fleet Amphibious Command, San Diego, and the Atlantic Amphibious Forces, Norfolk, Virginia. Its operational trials included several months of combat evaluation in Vietnam as part of the US Navy's 24-hour coastal surveillance force in Operation Market Time.

In 1971 the craft was deployed to Europe for operation with the US Sixth Fleet in the Mediterranean following a series of demonstrations for officials of NATO navies.

In November 1972, Tucumcari ran aground in the Caribbean, seven miles east of Puerto Rico, while conducting night-time operations with amphibious forces. No crewmen were killed or seriously injured. Due to damage sustained while removing the craft from the coral reef, the craft was struck from the list of active US Navy vessels and sent to the US Naval Research and Development Center where it has been employed for structural evaluation and fire containment tests. A full technical description of the vessel appeared in *Jane's Surface Skimmers 1974-75* and earlier editions.

BOEING NATO/PHM

The NATO Hydrofoil Fast Patrol Ship Guided Missile (NATO/PHM) originated in mid-1969 when C-in-C South presented to NATO a requirement for a large number of fast patrol boats to combat the threat posed by missile-armed fast patrol boats in the Mediterranean.

The concept of a common fast patrol boat was studied, and in September 1970 it was decided that the submerged foil craft of 140 tons proposed by the US Navy was the vessel most suited to NATO mission requirements. In October 1971, the United States indicated that it would proceed at its own expense with the design of the vessel and share the results of the studies with those nations wishing to purchase PHMs. It also offered to conduct all aspects of design and development, contracting and management in co-operation with governments entering into project membership. Costs would be reimbursed only by those nations engaged in the project.

Letters of intent, acknowledging design and cost scheduled obligations, were provided by Italy and West Germany in April and May 1972, respectively. Sudden and extreme changes in the US government's attitude regarding PHM production in recent years had a markedly negative effect on the continued programme participation by West Germany. Tentative moves were made by Congress to delete four of the five production craft from the programme early in 1976. When, in February 1977, the new Secretary of Defense announced to the West German Government that the United States was terminating the PHM programme, the West German navy decided it had no option but to terminate participatory effort in production design, called back its project office personnel and embarked on the ordering of conventional fast patrol craft. By the time Congress had completed its 1977 action refusing to rescind prior year appropriated PHM funding, the situation was irreversible and West Germany was no longer an active partner.

Statements made in mid-1978 suggest, however, that the US Departments of Defense and State are currently seeking to promote renewed participation in the PHM Programme by the USA's NATO allies. Although only three governments decided to participate actively in the initial stages, future project membership is not restricted. Interested observers include Canada, Denmark, the Netherlands, France and the United Kingdom. Greece and Turkey have also considered participation. Japan is also expressing interest in purchasing or building PHMs.

In November 1971, the US Navy awarded Boeing a US $5·6 million contract for the preliminary design of a 230-ton craft and the purchase of mechanical and electronic components for at least two of the vessels. Seventeen months later, Boeing was awarded a US $42,607,384 contract for the design and development of the PHM for NATO navies. Under the terms of the contract the first craft, the Pegasus, was built for the US Navy.

Pegasus was launched on 9 November 1974, and made its first foilborne flight on 25 February 1975. Pegasus achieved its classified designed speed, completed the Navy-conducted phase of testing its weapons, and then began operational evaluation in the San Diego area in the autumn of 1975.

It completed its acceptance trials during the first week of June 1977 and was commissioned

PHM-1 Pegasus underway hullborne, with foils extended. When the foils are fully retracted for long-range cruising and slow-speed manoeuvring, the craft is propelled by the two waterjet pumps of a hullborne propulsion system, powered by two 800hp Mercedes-Benz diesels

into service on 9 July 1977, becoming the first hydrofoil officially designated a United States Ship (USS Pegasus). Rear Admiral John Bulkely, USN, In-Service Trial President recorded that she had demonstrated 'superb reliability throughout her trial with no major or significant breakdowns or failures'.

In October 1977 it was announced that the US Navy will receive five more PHMs between January 1981 and February 1982. Designated Patrol Combatants — Missile (Hydrofoils), they will be assigned to a PHM squadron operating with the Sixth Fleet in the Mediterranean and will specialise in anti-submarine warfare in coastal waters.

The first squadron of PHMs will consist of the USS Pegasus and her five sister ships now under construction, plus the PHM Mobile Logistic Support Group (MLSG) and the Squadron commander's staff. An interim MLSG has been established to support Pegasus and comprises one officer and 28 enlisted personnel operating from six standard 40ft containers and three roadable trailers outfitted to provide shop, office and training space and stowage for spares and food stores. During the second phase of the squadron build-up a converted 1178 Class LST, to be known as a Hydrofoil Support Ship (AGHS) was to be made available. This would have provided all the facilities available from the van complex plus the basic fuel and other services now provided from ashore.

However the AGHS has been deleted from the US Navy budget, although the support need remains. One possible alternative would be the use of selected DD 963 Spruance Class destroyers to carry the PHM Mobile Logistics Support Group and equip the PHM to undertake portions of the DD 963 helicopter (LAMPS) mission. This would dramatically increase the surface warfare capability of each of the two classes of ship. It would release the PHM from any restrictions on its mobility and deployment and improve the all-weather ASW capability of the DD 963.

Four of the production craft will be armed with a 75mm OTO Melara dual-purpose rapid fire cannon and eight Harpoon anti-ship missiles in two four-tube lightweight canister launchers. The fifth, PHM-6, will be employed as a test craft and will not carry armament. Construction of PHM-2 Hercules began in May 1974 but was stopped in 1975. This will be the last to be delivered in March 1982. PHM-3, the first of the follow-on craft to be completed, is scheduled to be delivered in February 1981, followed by PHM-4 in April of that year, PHM-5 in October and PHM-6 in January 1982. All five craft will be built by Boeing Marine Systems at its hydrofoil assembly plant at Renton, Washington, adjacent to Lake Washington.

The PHM has sufficient design flexibility to allow for individual variations by any country. These variations will be primarily in the weapons systems installed, and the participating nations, current and future, can acquire the standard PHM carrying whatever combat equipment is determined necessary to meet national requirements.

PHM's potential in terms of strategic mobility was demonstrated between 30 September and 1 October 1975, when Pegasus completed the 1,225 nautical miles from Seattle to San Diego in the record-breaking time of less than 34 hours, which included a refuelling stop at Eureka, California.

With the aid of midway refuelling the craft is capable of crossing oceans with fast carrier task groups, convoys of merchant ships and amphibious assault groups. With three underway refuellings, it can cross the Atlantic from Massachusetts to the United Kingdom at an average speed of 30 knots in 4·2 days, or it could cross from Norfolk, Virginia to Cadiz in 4·6 days with four underway refuellings.

PHM is designed to be self-supporting at sea for a period of five days. For extended periods, or during intensive operations, it could be refuelled with either JP-5 or Naval Distillate (DFM) by oilers, major combatants and carriers.

It can be easily adapted for such roles as anti-submarine warfare, fisheries law enforcement and the protection of offshore resources.

The standard PHM is approximately 40m (131ft 2in) long, has a beam of 8·6m (28ft 2in) and a full load displacement of about 235 tonnes (231 tons). Foilborne range is in excess of 500n miles at speeds in excess of 40 knots in 8–12ft seas. The hull form and size, the major structural bulkheads and decks, foils and struts, waterjets, pumps, controls and main propulsion machinery are identical. The auxiliary equipment and arrangements, deckhouse and crew accommodation are also of standard design, but variations in the latter are possible to suit the manning requirements of individual countries.

FOILS: Fully-submerged canard arrangement with approximately 32% of the dynamic lift provided by the bow foil and 68% by the aft foil. The aft foil retracts rearwards and the bow foil retracts forward into a recess in the bow. Bow doors preserve the hull lines when the forward foil is either fully extended or retracted. The foils and struts are in 17-4 PH stainless high strength steel. Both forward and aft foils are welded assemblies consisting of spars, ribs, and skin. Flaps are fitted to the trailing edges to provide control and lift augmentation at take-off and during flight. The bow foil system incorporates a strut that rotates to provide directional control and reliable turning rates in heavy seas.

The shallow M or inverted double pi configuration of the aft foil is designed for improved hydroelastic and turning characteristics. The primary strut structure consists of spars, ribs and skin welded into watertight assemblies. The struts are designed as beam columns, and rigidly attached to the foil support structure at the hull.

The struts are attached to the hull with pivot pins that allow the foils to rotate clear of the water. Hydraulic actuators are used for retraction and extension, mechanical stops and position locks being employed to secure the foils in either position.

CONTROLS, FOILBORNE: The helm, throttle and an automatic control system (ACS) provide continuous dynamic control during take-off, foilborne operation and landing. Once take-off is complete, the ACS requires no attention on the part of the crew. It controls the craft by sensing craft attitude, motion rates and acceleration, then comparing them electronically with desired values. Any deviations are processed by analogue control computer which generates electrical commands causing hydraulic actuators to reposition the control surfaces, thus minimising detected errors. The foilborne control surfaces are trailing edge flaps on each of the foils, plus the rotating bow foil strut which acts as the foilborne rudder.

Manual controls and displays for both hullborne and foilborne conditions are concentrated at the helm station and include the wheel, a foil-depth selector, a foil-depth indicator, a ship-heading indicator and a heading holding switch.

CONTROLS, HULLBORNE: Steering control in the hullborne mode is provided by stern rudders which rotate electro-hydraulically in response to the wheel. An automatic heading control, similar to that employed for foilborne operation is incorporated, together with the necessary heading reference provided by the gyrocompass.

POWER PLANT, FOILBORNE: The foilborne propulsion system comprises a single 18,000shp, co-axial two-stage, two-speed waterjet, driven through two sets of reduction gears by a single General Electric LM 2500 marine gas-turbine, developed from the GE TF39, which powers the USAF's C-5 transport and the DC-10 Trijet.

Both the foilborne and hullborne propulsion systems were designed by Aerojet Liquid Rocket Company, Sacramento, California, under a Boeing contract.

The single foilborne propulsion pump is capable of handling 90,000 gallons/min and the two hullborne pumps will each operate at approximately 30,000 gallons/min.

Engine installation and removal for overhaul is accomplished through hatches located in the main deck between the deckhouse and exhaust outlet.

The vessel is capable of operation on JP-5 or diesel fuel.

POWER PLANT, HULLBORNE: Twin Aerojet waterjet pumps powered by two 800hp Mercedes-Benz 8V331TC80 diesels propel the vessel when hullborne. Each waterjet propulsor has nozzle steering and reversing buckets. The hullborne system provides long-range cruising and slow speed manoeuvring, while the gas turbine is available when required for high-speed foilborne operation.

Pegasus launching a test missile during operational and technical evaluation. The firing, conducted by the US Navy at Port Hueneme, California, was to test the structure of the PHM's Harpoon anti-ship missile system. The evaluation included the testing of the Mk 94 fire control system and the 76mm Oto Melara dual-purpose rapid-fire cannon

Pegasus during an operational exercise. A Boeing three-axis automatic control system regulates the height of the PHM's hull above the waves. The ACS also introduces the correct amount of bank and steering to coordinate turns in full

Impression of a projected Coast Guard variant of PHM. Hydrofoils of this type can easily be converted to perform such roles as anti-submarine warfare, fisheries law enforcement and the protection of off-shore resources

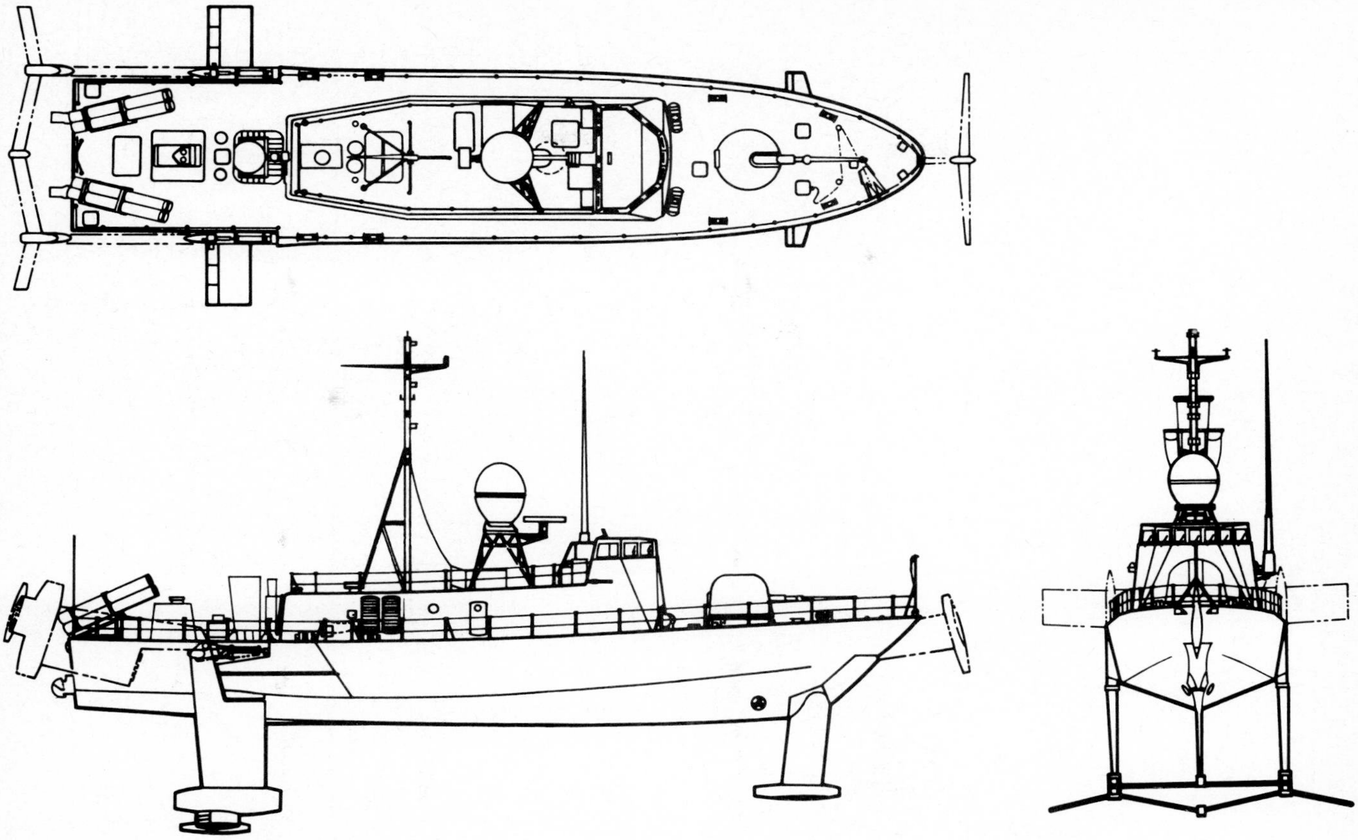

General arrangement of the NATO PHM

HULL: Hull and deckhouses are all-welded structures in AL 5465 alloy.

ACCOMMODATION: Crew will average 21 officers and men, but will vary according to the armament carried. Accommodation on the US Navy version is provided for four officers—the commanding officer has a separate cabin—three chief petty officers and 14 enlisted men. The superstructure accommodates the bridge, which contains steering and engine control consoles and is elevated to provide a 360 degree view. A short ladder from the bridge leads down to the command and surveillance deckhouse that accommodates the fire control, radar, communications and navigation equipment. The size of the deckhouse provides flexibility in accommodating various national equipment requirements. The space aft of the superstructure and forward of the foilborne engine exhaust is used to erect rigging for replenishment and refuelling.

Below the main deck, about one third of the PHM's length is devoted to crew accommodation, the forward third is occupied by the primary gun, automatic loader mechanism, ammunition storage and forward foil, and the after third is occupied by the unmanned machinery spaces.

All manned spaces are equipped with a recirculating air conditioning system to give a maximum air temperature of 27°C at 55% relative humidity in summer, and a minimum inside temperature of 18°C in winter. The officers' staterooms, crew quarters and lounge/messing area are fully air-conditioned, the temperature being controlled by individual thermostats in the spaces concerned.

SYSTEMS, ELECTRICAL: Ship's service electric plant comprises two AiResearch Ship Service Power Units (SSPUs), with ME831-800 gas-turbines as prime movers driving 250kVA, 400Hz, 450V generators. Each SSPU also drives an attached centrifugal compressor for starting the LM 2500 engine and two hydraulic pumps for the ship's hydraulic system. One is capable of handling the entire electrical load, the second is provided as a standby. Through the use of static power conversion equipment, limited three-phase, 60Hz ac power and 28V dc is available for equipment requirements. In port, the craft can utilise shore power, or use its own auxiliary power unit for this purpose as well as battery charging and emergency use of navigation and radio equipment.

Jet Caribe, one of two Boeing Jetfoils in service with Turismo Margarita in Venezuela

HYDRAULICS: 3,000psi to actuate the hullborne and foilborne controls, foil retraction and hullborne engine starting. Dual hydraulic supply is provided to each service with sub-system isolation fore and aft in the event of major damage.

FIRE EXTINGUISHING: Dry chemical equipment throughout craft, and a fixed total flooding-type Freon 1301 system.

WEAPONS/FIRE CONTROL: Either WM-28 radar and weapons control system or American model, the Mk 92. Both systems embody a combined fire control and search antenna system, mounted on a single stabilised platform and enclosed in a fibreglass radome. The Italian Argo system can also be installed.

TARGETING/MISSILE WARNING: Automatic classification ESM (electronic warfare support measures) set is installed for missile warning and over-the-horizon targeting of enemy surface units.

GUNS: Standard primary gun is the Oto Melara 76mm gun, which is unmanned and automatically controlled by the fire control system. The craft can also be delivered with secondary guns. If specified two Mk 20 Rh 202 20mm AA cannon can be provided, one each, port and starboard, adjacent to the fire control antenna structure.

MISSILES: The prototype carries eight Harpoon missiles in two four-tube lightweight canister launchers, but Exocet, Otomat, Tero or any smaller missile system can be installed. Space is provided aft to accommodate the four launchers, port and starboard, in parallel pairs. The launchers are deck-fixed in elevation and azimuth.

Armament of the standard US Navy version will be eight McDonnell Douglas AGM-84A Harpoon anti-ship missiles in lightweight container launchers; one Mk 75 Mod 1 76mm cannon and one Mk 92 Mod 1 GFCS (Mk 94 on

PHM-1) and two Mk 34 Chaff launchers.

COMMAND, CONTROL AND COMMUNICATIONS: True motion navigation radar; OMEGA navigation equipment; gyro compass; dead reckoning tracer; Tactical and Navigation Collision Avoidance System (TANCAV); speed log; depth sounder/recorder; AN/SPA-25B repeater consoles (2); integrated intercom/announcing/exterior communications system; HF, UHF and VHF communications (teletype and voice) IFF system, ESM system.

The basic PHM design allows for a growth of approximately five tons in full load displacement to enhance mission capability. Areas under consideration include sonar, torpedoes, improved surface-to-surface missiles and low-light-level TV, all of which appear to be feasible without having an adverse effect on its current capabilities.

The following details apply to the model under construction for the US Navy.

DIMENSIONS

Length overall,
- foils extended: 40m (131ft 2in)
- foils retracted: 45m (147ft 6in)

Beam max, deck: 8·6m (28ft 2in)

Max width across foils: 14·5m (47ft 6in)

Draft,
- hullborne, foils retracted: 1·9m (6ft 3in)
- hullborne, foils extended: 7·1m (23ft 2in)
- foilborne, normal: 2·7m (8ft 11in)

WEIGHTS

Displacement, full load including margins: 235 tonnes

PERFORMANCE

Max speed foilborne: in excess of 50 knots

Cruising speed,
- foilborne, sea state 0–5: in excess of 40 knots
- hullborne: 11 knots

Sea state: can negotiate 8ft 2in seas at speeds in excess of 40 knots

Foilborne range: in excess of 600n miles

Hullborne range: in excess of 1,800n miles

Flying Princess, a Jetfoil operated by P & O Jet Ferries

Passenger accommodation is fully air-conditioned and arranged on two decks. This photograph was taken in the upper passenger saloon of Jetfoil 002 Madeira, one of the five Jetfoils operated by Far East Hydrofoil Co, Hong Kong, on its Hong Kong-Macao service. Seats are provided on this particular model for 284 passengers. Cruising speed is 45 knots (83·3km/h; 51·8mph)

BOEING JETFOIL 929-100

This is a 110-ton waterjet-propelled commercial hydrofoil for services in relatively rough waters. It employs a fully-submerged, automatically-controlled canard foil arrangement and is powered by two 3,710hp Allison 501-K20A gas-turbines. Normal foilborne cruising speed is 42 knots.

Typical interior arrangements include a commuter configuration with up to 400 seats and a tourist layout for 190-250 tourists plus baggage.

The company is also evaluating various utility models with open load decks suitable for search and rescue duties, offshore oil-rig support and firefighting. Two utility derivatives for offshore rig crew and priority/emergency cargo support are showing great potential. They are 50 and 100 seat crew/supply boat versions with considerable cargo capacity for supporting rigs within 50–250n miles from shore.

Ten Jetfoils are currently in service: five with Far East Hydrofoil Co, Hong Kong; two with Turismo Margarita CA, Venezuela; two with Sado Kisen Kaisha, Japan and one with P & O Ferries, London.

In addition, at the time of going to press, the Washington State Ferry System was conducting a demonstration on a charter basis to investigate the feasibility of operating various routes on Puget Sound.

During 1978, Boeing announced an order by B & I Lines of Dublin, Ireland, for a Jetfoil to operate between Dublin and Liverpool, starting in April 1980, and an order from the Royal Navy in the United Kingdom for a modified Offshore Jetfoil to be used in the fisheries protection role in the North Sea.

By 20 August 1978, Jetfoils had logged 178,389,734 passenger miles during 41,873 underway hours, with a dispatch reliability of 98·6%.

Keel-laying of the first Jetfoil took place at the company's Renton, Washington, plant on 19 January 1973, and the craft was launched on 29 March 1974. After testing on Puget Sound and in the Pacific, the craft was delivered to Pacific Sea Transportation Ltd for inter-island services in Hawaii. High speed foilborne tests began in Puget Sound in mid-July and it was reported that the vessel attained a speed of 48 knots during its runs.

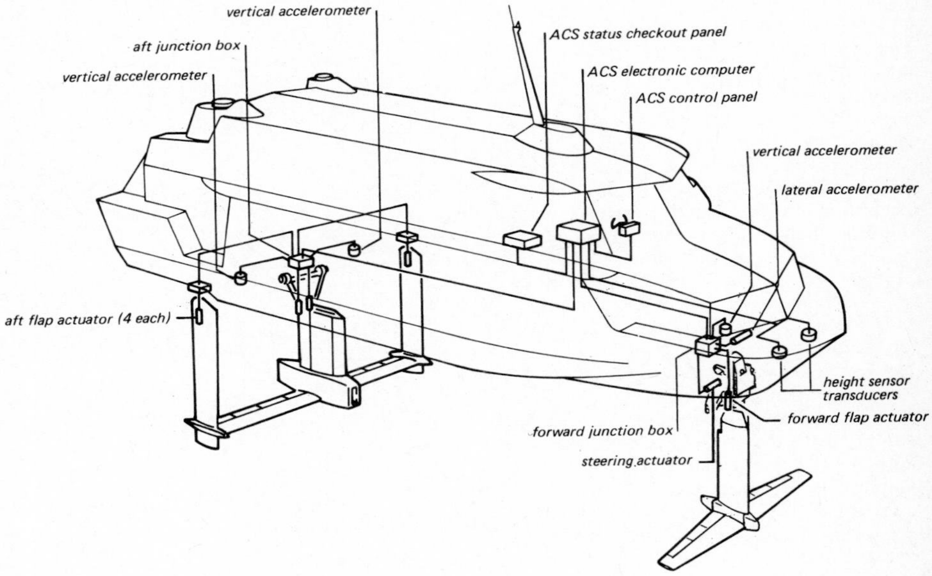

Jetfoil 929-100 automatic control system

During a rigorous testing programme to prove the boat's design and construction, Jetfoil One operated for 470 hours, including 237 hours foilborne. The latter phase of testing was conducted in the rough waters of the straits of Juan de Fuca and the Pacific Ocean, where it encountered wave swells as high as 30ft, winds gusting up to 60 knots and wave chop averaging six feet high.

The first operational Jetfoil service was successfully initiated on 25 April 1975 by Far East Hydrofoil Co, of Hong Kong, with Jetfoil 002, Madeira. Prior to this, the Jetfoil received its ABS classification, was certificated by the Hong Kong Marine Department and passed US Coast Guard certification trials, although a US Coast Guard certificate was not completed since the craft would not be operating in US waters.

The first US service began in Hawaii on 15 June 1975 with the first of three Jetfoils, 003 Kamehameha, starting inter-island runs. By the end of the summer all five Jetfoils were in service. The tenth Jetfoil was launched in May 1977. An active world-wide marketing programme is under way to sell these high-speed craft, which are currently priced at US $8·5 million.

Jetfoil 0011, which was launched in June 1978, is the first of five additional Jetfoils of improved design now under construction. Many of the improvements incorporated in this new version, the Model 929-115, are based on operating experience accrued over the past three years and will add to the Jetfoil's performance, payload and reliability.

The main external differences between the 929-100 and the new 929-115 are indicated in the accompanying illustration. These and the basic internal changes are listed in a separate entry for the Model 929-115.

FOILS: Fully submerged canard arrangement with a single inverted tee strut/foil forward and a three-strut, full-span foil aft. The forward foil assembly is rotated hydraulically through 7 degrees in either direction for steering. All foils have trailing-edge flaps for controlling pitch, roll and yaw and for take-off and landing. Hydraulically-driven foil flap actuators control the variation in flap positions through linkages between actuators and flap hinge points. Foils and struts retract hydraulically above the water-line, the bow foil forward, and the rear foil aft. All structural components of the foil/strut system are in 15·5PH corrosion resistant all-welded steel construction.

CONTROLS: The craft is controlled by a three-axis automatic system while it is foilborne and during take-off and landing. The system senses the motion and position of the craft by gyros, accelerometers and height sensors, signals from which are combined in the control cumputer with manual commands from the helm. The resulting computer outputs provide control-surface deflections through electro-hydraulic servo actuators. Lift control is provided by full-span trailing edge flaps on each foil. Forward and aft flaps operate differentially to provide pitch variation and height control. Aft flaps operate differentially to provide roll control for changes of direction.

The vessel banks inwardly into all turns, to ensure maximum passenger comfort. The ACS introduces the correct amount of bank and steering to coordinate the turn in full. Turn rates of up to 6 degrees per second are attained within 5 seconds of providing a heading change command at the helm.

Three basic controls only are required for foilborne operation. The throttle is employed to set the speed, the height command lever to set the required foil depth, and the helm to set the required heading. If a constant course is required, a "heading hold" circuit accomplishes this automatically.

For take-off, the foil depth is set, the two throttles advanced, and the hull clears the water in about 60 seconds. Acceleration continues, until the craft automatically stabilises at the command depth and the speed dictated by the throttle setting. The throttle setting is reduced for landing, the craft settling as the speed drops. The speed normally diminishes from 45 knots (cruising speed) to 15 knots in about 30 seconds. In emergencies more rapid landings can be made by the use of the height command lever to provide hull contact within two seconds.

HULL: Hull and deckhouse in marine aluminium. Aircraft assembly techniques are used, including high-speed mechanised welding processes.

POWERPLANT: Power for the waterjet propulsion system is supplied by two Allison 501-K20A free-power gas-turbines, each rated at 3,300shp at 27°C (80°F) at sea level. Each is connected to a Rocketdyne Powerjet 20 axial-flow pump through a gearbox drive train. The two turbine/pump systems are located in their own bays, port and starboard, separated by the slot in the hull into which the central water strut retracts for hullborne operation. The system propels the craft in both foilborne and hullborne modes. When

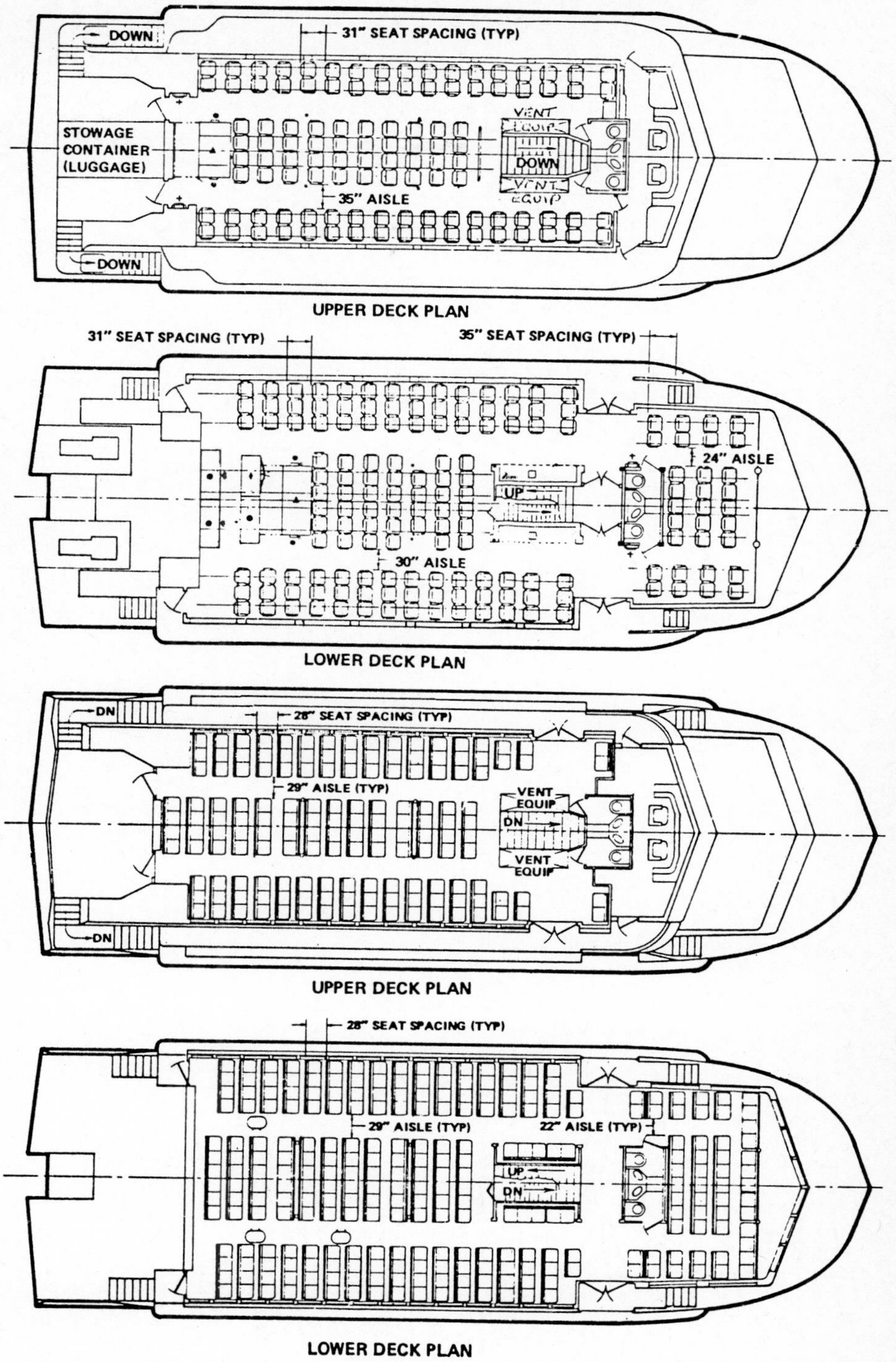

Typical interior arrangements on the Jetfoil include a commuter configuration with 420 seats. Seats are track mounted to facilitate spacing changes, removal or replacement. Food and beverage service units can be installed

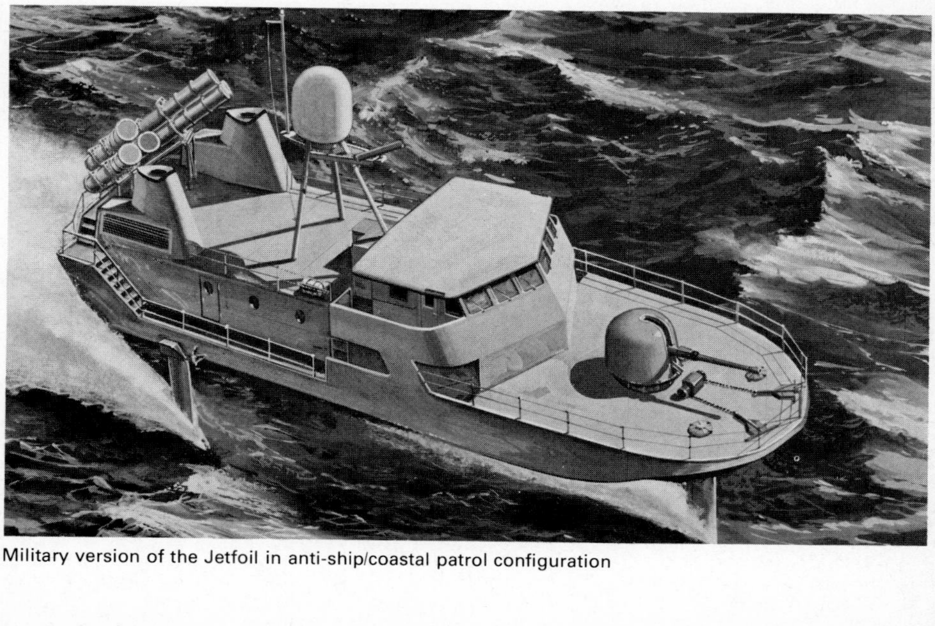

Military version of the Jetfoil in anti-ship/coastal patrol configuration

foilborne, water enters through the inlet located at the forward lower end of the aft centre foil strut. At the top of the duct, the water is split into two paths and enters into each of the two axial flow pumps. It is then discharged at high pressure through nozzles in the hull bottom.

The water path is the same during hullborne operations with the foils extended. When the foils are retracted, the water enters through a flush inlet located in the keel. Reversing and steering for hullborne operation only are accomplished by reverse-flow buckets located immediately aft of the water exit nozzles. A bow thruster is provided for positive steering control at low forward speeds.

A 15,140 litre (4,000 gallon) integral fuel tank supplies the propulsion turbine and diesel engines. Recommended fuel is Diesel No 2. The tank is fitted with a 5cm (2in) diameter fill pipe and fittings compatible with dockside refuelling equipment. Coalescent-type water separating fuel filters and remote-controlled motor-operated fuel shut-off valves are provided for fire protection.

ACCOMMODATION: Passenger accommodation is fully air-conditioned and arranged on two decks, which are connected by a wide, enclosed stairway. The cabins have 91·4cm (3ft) wide aisles and 2·06m (6ft 9in) headroom. In the commuter configuration 1·58m³ (56ft³) per passenger is provided and 1·87m³ (66ft³) in the tourist configuration. Floors are carpeted and 61cm (2ft) seats are provided. Lighting is indirect and adjustable from the wheelhouse. Interior noise is near conversation level (below 68 dB SIL). Passengers are entertained and informed by a public announcement system. Each deck level has two wc/washbasin units. Drinking water dispensers are located on each passenger deck.

Quality of the ride in the craft is comparable with that of a Boeing 727 airliner. The vertical acceleration at the centre of gravity is designed to be no more than 0·04 G, with lateral acceleration less than that of the vertical. Angles of pitch and roll will be less than 1 degree RMS. Passenger discomfort in an emergency landing is prevented by a 'structural fuse', which limits deceleration to less than 0·4 G longitudinally and 0·8 G vertically so that a passenger would not be thrown from his seat in the event of the craft striking a major item of floating debris at full speed. The 'structural fuse', when actuated, causes the foil and strut to rotate backwards, protecting the system from sustaining significant damage. The fuses can be reset while under way in some cases, depending on the degree of impact.

Crew comprises a captain and first officer plus cabin attendants.

SYSTEMS, ELECTRICAL: 60Hz, 440V ac electrical system, supplied by two diesel-driven generators rated at 62·5kVA each. Either is capable of supplying all vital electrical power. 90kVA capacity shore connection facilities provided, and equipment can accept 50Hz power. Transformer rectifier units for battery charging provide 28V dc from the ac system.

HYDRAULICS: 210·9kg/cm² (3,000psi) system to actuate control surfaces. Each pump is connected to a separate system to provide split system redundancy in the event of a turbine, pump, distribution system or actuator malfunctioning.

EMERGENCY: Craft meets all applicable safety regulations of the US Coast Guard and SOLAS. Hull provides two-compartment subdivision and a high degree of stability. Life rafts and life jackets are provided.

NAVIGATION: Equipment includes radar. A low-light-level television system covering potential collision zone is available as an optional extra.

DIMENSIONS

Length overall, foils extended: 27·4m (90ft)
 foils retracted: 30·1m (99ft)
Beam overall, max: 9·5m (31ft)
Draft hullborne,
 foils retracted: 1·5m (4ft 10in)
 foils extended: 5m (16ft 4in)

WEIGHTS

Displacement: 110 tons

PERFORMANCE

Max speed: 50 knots
Normal service speed: 42 knots
Turning radius at 45 knots: less than 304·8m (1,000ft)
Normal endurance at cruising speed: 4 hours
Max endurance: 8 hours
Max wave height foilborne: 3·65m (12ft)

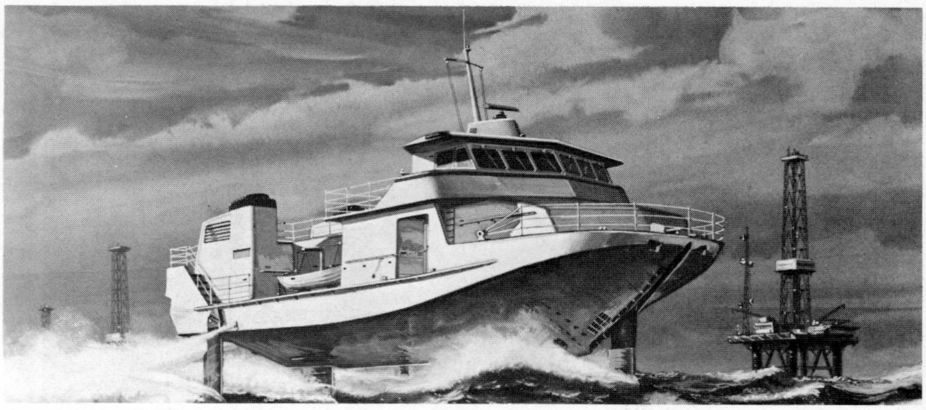

Jetfoil with superstructure designed for law and treaty enforcement applications

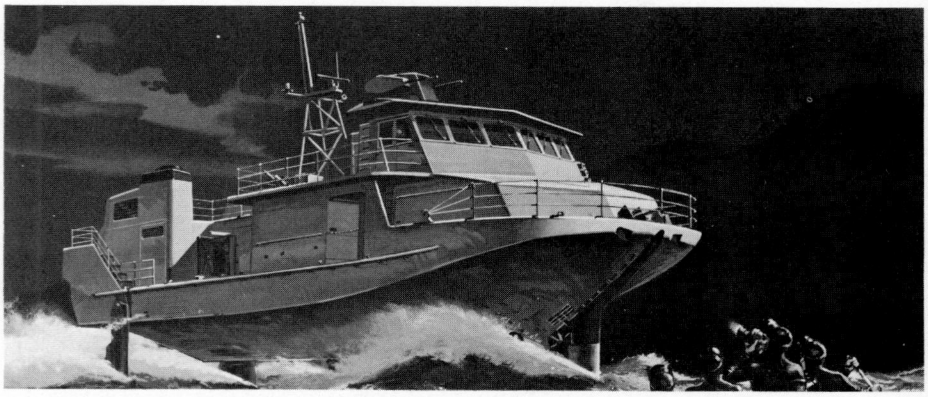

In the counter-insurgency role, the Jetfoil would carry two fully-equipped twelve-man SEAL (sea-air-land) teams. A twin 30mm rapid-fire cannon would provide defensive armament

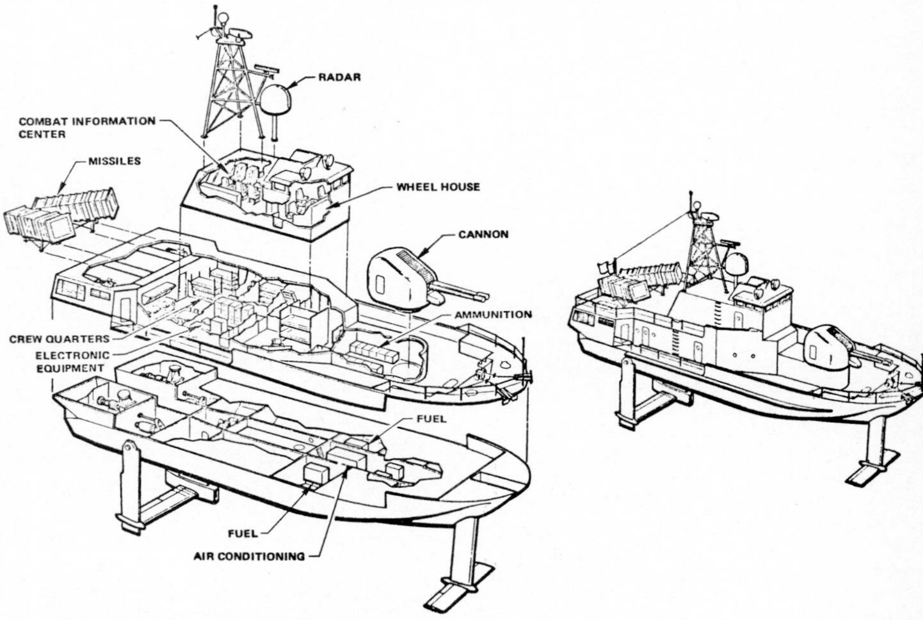

Projected 117-ton fast patrol boat version of the Jetfoil. The company is examining the possibility of exporting the Jetfoil on a modular basis with the customer purchasing a basic hull, which will contain the power plant and all the necessary systems, and installing his own superstructure

BOEING 929-115

The last of the Jetfoil 929-100 series was the 0010 "Flying Princess II". The first of the improved 929-115 series, Jetfoil 0011 "Mikado", was launched at Renton, Washington on 29 June 1978, and after undergoing engineering tests on Puget Sound, was due to be shipped to the operator Sado Kisen during the autumn of 1978.

The chief external differences between the two models are shown in the accompanying illustration. A number of detail changes have been made in order to comply with the new international novel craft code, but most have been made in the light of operating experience over the past three years. As a result the new model Jetfoil will have an increased payload, greater reliability and be easier to maintain. Some of the modifications are listed below.

FOILS: External stiffeners on the foil struts have been eliminated; the retracted angle of the aft foil has been raised in order to lift the foil 330mm (13in) clear of the calm water level at 111 long tons, and the bow foil has been changed from constant section to tapered planform for improved performance. Stress levels have been reduced for extended life.

CONTROLS: Heading hold (autopilot) installed as basic equipment. Automatic control system "Autotrim" is improved to reduce steady state pitch and depth errors to negligible values. This

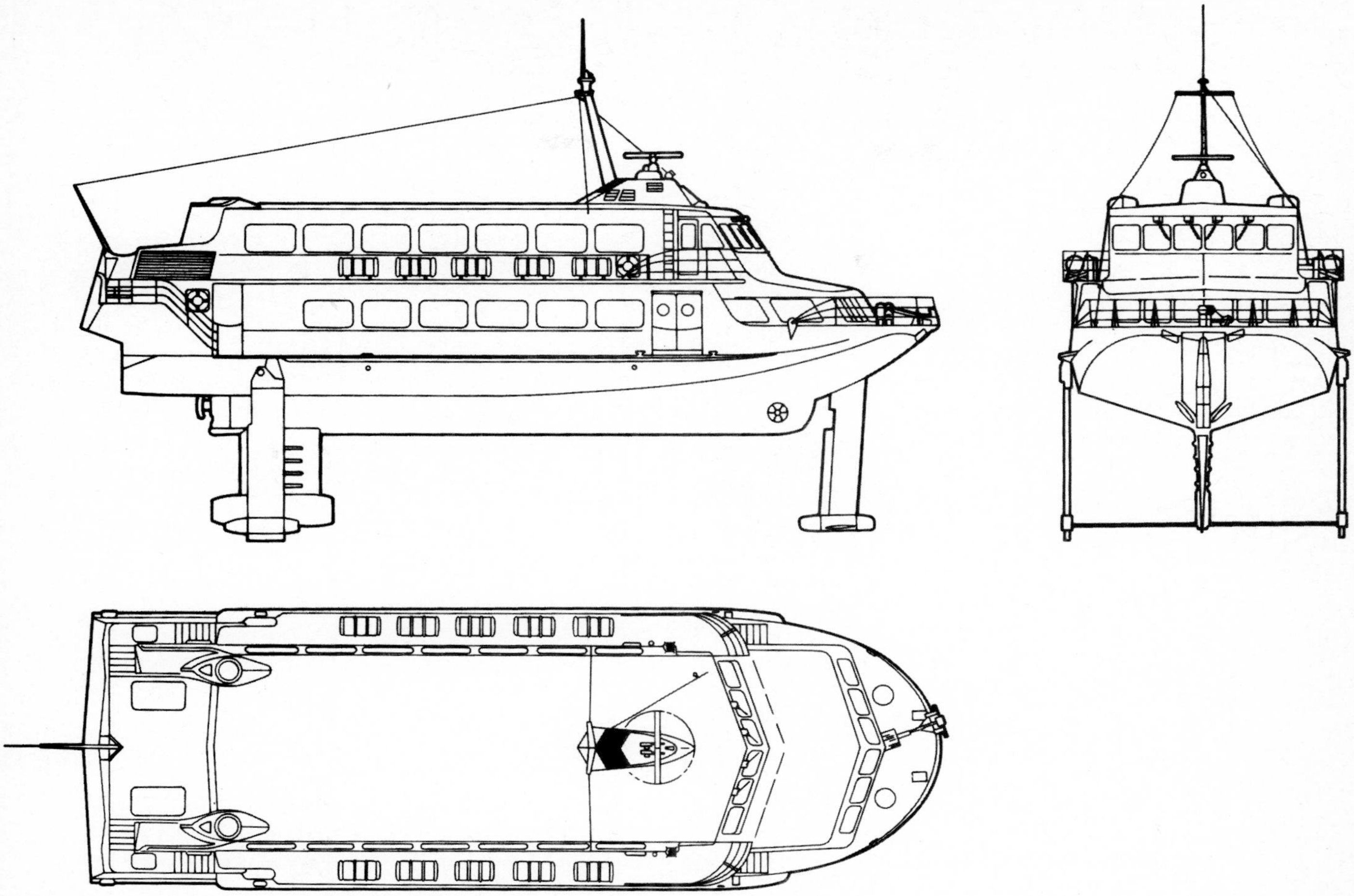

General arrangement of the new Boeing Jetfoil Model 929-115 passenger ferry

reduces or completely eliminates the need for foil angle of incidence adjustments. A higher thrust bow-thruster is fitted and the navigation radar is now installed on a pedestal between the captain and first officer so that it can be swivelled for viewing from either position.

HULL: The bow structure design has been simplified to provide equivalent strength with increased payload and bulkhead 2 has been revised for decreased stress levels. Based on a seven-minute evacuation time in case of fire the following fire protection provisions have been made:

Fibreglass is used for thermal insulation where required throughout the passenger accommodation areas.

Aluminium ceiling panels, window reveals and air conditioner sleeves are employed throughout, together with aluminium doors and frames.

One-half inch thick Marinite is employed in machinery spaces, with US Coast Guard-type felt added wherever required for insulation to comply with 30 minute fire test.

Carpet, seat fabrics and lining materials meet low flame spread, toxicity and smoke requirements of US Coast Guard and Department of Trade, United Kingdom.

POWERPLANT: The propulsion system has been uprated to operate at 2,200 maximum intermittent pump rpm with an increase of 3 tons in maximum gross weight.

ACCOMMODATION: Seats of revised design are fitted; environmental control unit has been located forward to increase payload and aid servicing, stairway to upper deck has a round handrail for better grip.

SYSTEMS, ELECTRICAL: DC system is now located in the wheelhouse to comply with new dynamically supported craft rules. AC panels relocated to be closer to equipment served to reduce wire runs. Redundant power sources are provided from either diesel generator for services to 24V dc emergency loads and loads essential for foilborne operation. Emergency 24V dc lights have been added in lavatories and aft machinery areas. Daylight signalling lamps with self-contained batteries are provided.

HYDRAULICS: System is now consolidated

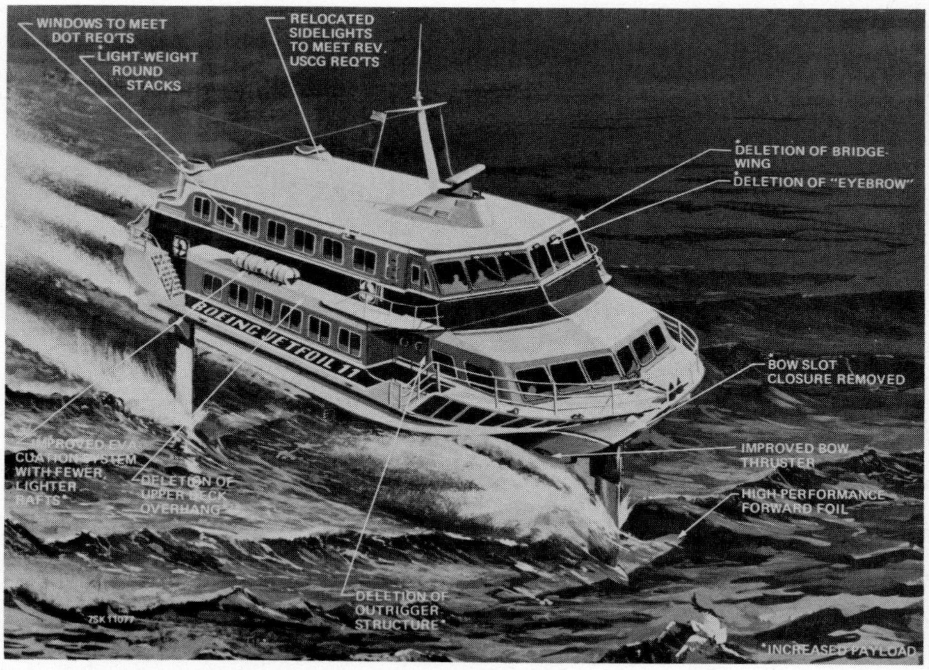

External modifications introduced on the Jetfoil Model 929-115

Jetfoil 0011 "Mikado", first of the 929-115 models, (foreground) undergoing engineering tests on Puget Sound accompanied by Jetfoil 0010 "Flying Princess II" while conducting a seven-week demonstration for the Washington State Ferry System

with one manifold and reduced piping.
AIR CONDITIONING: Machinery moved forward to space above the main stairway and forward machinery space to improve operation and servicing.
DIESEL FUEL SYSTEM: Separate fuel systems have been provided for the propulsion engines and diesel generators. This allows alternate fuels to be used in the turbines and greatly simplifies the plumbing system.
SEAWATER SYSTEM: Cooling water for the propulsion system has been separated from the remainder of the system. This simplifies the system and improves its reliability.
MISCELLANEOUS: Originally the hull corrosion prevention system was based on the isolation of dissimilar metals and ship-to-shore grounding. The new approach uses dockside impressed current, resistance-controlled shorting of struts and foils to the hull, additional pod anodes and electrical isolation. Other changes include a changeover to titanium seawater piping, a change in seawater pump materials and protective painting added to the hydraulic system.
DIMENSIONS
Length overall, foils extended: 27·4m (90ft)
Beam, max: 9·5m (31ft)
Draft,
foils extended: 5·2m (17ft)
foils retracted: 1·7m (5ft 6in)
Height (without retractable mast),
hullborne, above mean waterline: 12·8m (42ft)
foilborne, at 2·4m (8ft) foil depth: 15·5m (51ft)
WEIGHTS
Fully loaded displacement: 115 long tons
PERFORMANCE
Design cruising speed: 43 knots (80km/h; 50mph)

JETFOIL PATROL HYDROFOIL (ROYAL NAVY)

The first Jetfoil patrol hydrofoil has been ordered by the Royal Navy for use in the fisheries protection role in the North Sea. Basically, the craft is a modified Model 929-115 commercial Jetfoil and will be built on the commercial Jetfoil production line. Power for foilborne operation will be provided by two Allison 501-K20A gas-turbines and two Allison 8V92T1 diesels will be installed for hullborne operation, giving increased on-station time and endurance.

Externally the craft will resemble the projected Boeing Offshore Jetfoil, with the top passenger deck removed to provide an open deck measuring 4·87 × 7·31m (16 × 24ft) which will be occupied by two semi-inflatable dinghies on davits. Light weapons will be carried. Displacement will be 117 tons.

Launching is scheduled to take place in July 1979 with delivery in October 1979.
DIMENSIONS: As for Jetfoil Model 929-115.

MILITARY JETFOIL

Five new military variants of the Jetfoil were announced by the Director of Military Sales and Marketing at Boeing during 1977, as follows:

TROOP TRANSPORT

In this configuration the Jetfoil can fly 250 troops and their equipment 300n miles in 7 hours. Since it draws only 1·8m in the hullborne mode with foils retracted, it can use most docking facilities.

CARGO CARRIER

Up to 30 tons of high-priority cargo can be flown up to 250n miles without refuelling. With seats and carpeting removed the lower deck provides 230m³ of storage space. Access is through forward and aft doors on both sides of the superstructure. The forward doors are 2m high by 1·5m wide and the aft doors 2m high by 1m wide. A special door 2m high by 3·5m wide is optional. In addition to lower deck cargo, up to 96 troops can be seated on the upper deck.

Jetfoil Patrol Hydrofoil 0001, PH01, on order by the Royal Navy for use in the fisheries protection role in the North Sea. A modified commercial Jetfoil, it will be built on the commercial Jetfoil production line and is due to be delivered in October 1979.

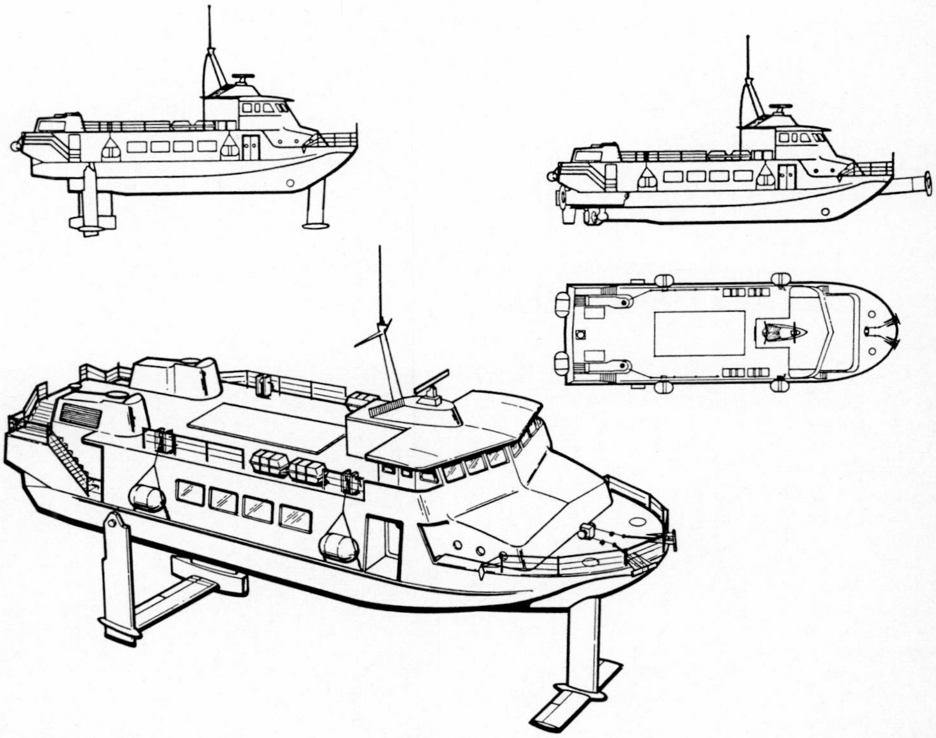

Outboard profiles and main deck view of the offshore oil rig support model of the Boeing Jetfoil Model 929-100

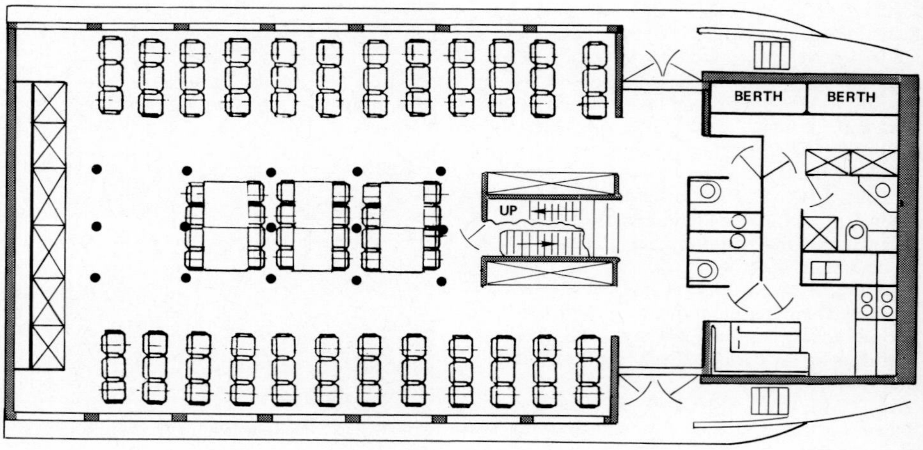

MEDICAL EVACUATION

Up to 213 litter cases with their attendants can be evacuated at a time. Special facilities are provided on board for the treatment of emergency cases while underway. Conversion from the standard Jetfoil configuration can be accomplished in 4 hours. Seats are removed and replaced with litter stanchions from a medical evacuation kit which can be stowed aboard for emergency use.

FISHERIES AND OFFSHORE RESOURCES PROTECTION

This version, which can be either sea- or shore-based can be equipped for search and rescue duties, law and treaty enforcement, anti-smuggling patrol and similar missions.

COUNTER INSURGENCY VEHICLE

Two fully equipped twelve-man patrols, complete with inflatable dinghies can be carried by this variant. Its defensive armament, mounted above bridge level for maximum field of fire, comprises a twin 30mm rapid fire cannon.

ANTI-SHIP/COASTAL PATROL CRAFT

Intended as a fast, economical weapons platform, this version is armed with six anti-ship missiles on two triple-tube lightweight launchers plus a single Oto Melara 76mm rapid fire cannon for air defence, together with launchers for rapid blooming off-board chaff (RBOC). The combat system level of automation, similar to that of the PHM, is such that one man, unassisted, can simultaneously engage air and surface targets with guns and missiles respectively. A 12-man crew would be carried.

MODULAR JETFOIL

In November 1974 Boeing announced that consideration was being given to the export of Jetfoils on a modular basis. One approach would be to supply operators, both commercial and military, with the basic Jetfoil hull, complete with foils, powerplant and control system, and the operator would arrange to install his own superstructure.

This would give them access to craft embodying the latest developments in hydrofoil technology and permit them to add superstructure tailored to their own particular needs. Variants would range from passenger ferries and utility craft for offshore marine operations, to coastguard patrol vessels and missile gunboats.

The modular concept is expected to appeal in particular to lesser developed countries, since by completing the craft locally, a useful saving in hard currency could be realised. A substantial amount of the superstructure could be riveted together by fairly low-skilled labour. The cost per hull unit, once production is established, is expected to be about US $6 million.

Maintenance requirements are expected to be reasonably low. The Allison 501-K20A gas-turbines have a life of 18,000 hours, and the Boeing autopilot, the most sensitive part of the system, has a life expectancy of 3–4 years under normal operating conditions, allowing 3,000 hours in service each year.

Allison is willing to negotiate contract rates for servicing the gas-turbines at a fixed-rate per operating hour.

Boeing states that modifications could be made to the design to allow the installation of alternative engines, such as the Rolls Royce Tyne or Proteus, should countries like the United Kingdom prefer them.

Weapons suitable for the military models include the Oto Melara 76mm rapid-fire cannon and the Emerson 30mm cannon, the Argo control system and the Otomat, Exocet, Penguin and Gabriel anti-ship missiles.

Another Boeing concept is the regional final assembly centre, a number of which would be established around the world in order to supply customers with complete vessels made up from imported hulls and superstructures. At the same time the arrangement would meet the growing demand in lesser developed areas for greater participation in industrial programmes.

The centres, which would not be owned or operated by Boeing, would simply be involved with their importation, assembly and marketing. Likely areas for the establishment of these centres include the Caribbean, Greece, Iran, Japan, Taiwan, Indonesia and Scandinavia.

DAK HYDROFOILS

PO Box 1747, Sausalito, California 94965, USA
Officials:
David A Keiper, *Proprietor and Chief Designer*

Dak Hydrofoils is currently designing and developing simple low-cost hydrofoil conversion kits for outboard powerboats. These are based on those available from the company for existing racing catamarans.

The arrangement employs identical lateral foils, positioned in a similar location, plus a fully-submerged stern foil. Lighter craft will have a simple foil beneath the outboard engine. Heavier craft, of up to 680·38kg (1,500lb) loaded weight, have a retractable 152mm (6in) chard foil supported by twin struts.

The propeller is lowered by a combination of engine shaft extension or extensions, and/or lowering the engine by means of parallel bars.

A 12ft dinghy equipped with DAK hydrofoils for an owner in New Zealand. Power is supplied by a 9·5hp engine

DEPARTMENT OF THE NAVY, NAVAL SEA SYSTEMS COMMAND (NAVSEA)

Headquarters: Washington DC 20362, USA
Office Address: US Naval Sea Systems Command, Advanced Technology Systems Division (Code 0322), National Center Building 3, Room 10E54, Washington DC 20362, USA
Officials:
James L Schuler, *Advanced Ship Development Manager*

The Research and Technology Directorate of the US Naval Sea Systems Command (NAVSEA) is a primary technical sponsor for all US Navy hydrofoil and hovercraft programmes. The programme manager responsible for the development of all types of high performance ship concepts is James L Schuler (Code 032).

Technical manager of the US Navy Advanced Hydrofoil Systems Development Programme is Robert Johnston of the David W Taylor Naval Ship Research and Development Centre. The Amphibious Assault Landing Craft (AALC) Programme is being managed by J Benson (NAVSEA 032J). The AALC Programme includes the construction of two air cushion vehicles of about 160 tons design all-up weight. The craft are the JEFF (A) being built by the Aerojet General Corporation and the JEFF (B) being developed by the Bell Aerosystems Corporation.

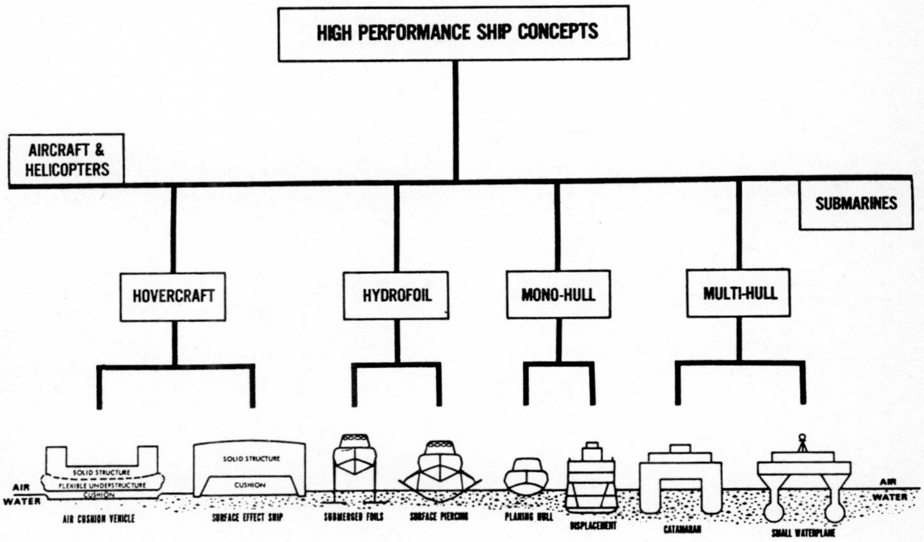

High performance ship concepts under development by US Naval Sea Systems Command

DYNAFOIL INC

881 West 16th Street, Newport Beach, California 92660, USA
Telephone: (714) 645 3201
Officials:
David J Cline, *Chairman*
James M Dale, *Secretary/Treasurer*
Paul D Griem, *Executive Vice President*

Dynafoil, Inc was formed in December 1971 to develop the Dynafoil sport craft. The development of this vehicle began in late 1970 with the construction of IRMA 1, the foil configuration of which has been the foundation for all subsequent work. Patents for the foil configuration have been applied for in all the main consumer countries, and have been granted in the USA.

DYNAFOIL MARK I

This fibreglass-hulled sports hydrofoil is a marine counterpart to the motorcycle and snowmobile. The bow foil is mounted at the base of a handlebar-equipped steering head and the handling characteristics are similar to those of a motor-cycle. Production began in June 1975.

FOILS: Canard configuration with a fully submerged main foil located aft and bearing 60% of the load and small incidence-controlled twin-delta foil forward. The angle of incidence is controlled mechanically by a curved planing control foil to achieve a constant flying height. Both the control foil and the bow foils rotate on pitch axes located forward of their centre of hydrodynamic lift. In normal flight the trailing edge of the control foil skims the water surface, while the twin delta bow and foil maintains its designed angle of incidence. If the bow rises too high above the mean water line, the control foil pitches upwards, allowing the foils to operate in a neutral position, in which it generates little or no lift. Conversely, downward pitch at the bow decreases the angle of attack of the control foil, which, through a linkage system causes the bow foils to increase its incidence angle, thus restoring normal flight. The aft foil has anhedral to prevent tip breeching and ventilation and is set above the propeller. The foils are in cast 356-T6 aluminium while the struts are of fibreglass. Both foils retract fully, the bow foil rotating upwards and rearwards, the aft foil rearwards and upwards against the transom.

CONTROLS: Steering is accomplished by turning the front foil strut. All turns enter a fully co-ordinated bank.

HULL: Two-stage deep V hull comprises two fibreglass mouldings bonded together at the beltline. After bonding, all voids not employed for functional components are filled with 2lb density polyurethane foam providing 600lb of buoyancy.

ACCOMMODATION: Open cockpit with a motorcycle pillion-style seat for two.

POWER PLANT: The Mark I is available with a choice of two engines—either a 340cc, 26hp, or a high performance 440cc, 36hp, two-cylinder, two-stroke Xenoah engine. Power is delivered to the outdrive through a 90 degree gearbox mounted inboard. The overall gear ratio is 1·75:1. Final drive is through a bevel gear at the base of the rear strut. The propeller, made by Michigan Wheel, is of three-bladed subcavitating design in cast aluminium. A single 18·92 litre (5 US gallon) fuel tank is located amidships, with a refuelling neck on the outside hull at the bow.

DIMENSIONS

Length overall, hull: 2·13m (7ft)
  foils retracted: 2·43m (8ft)
  foils extended: 2·13m (7ft)
Beam overall,
  foils retracted: 1·06m (3ft 6in)
  foils extended: 1·06m (3ft 6in)
Draft hullborne,
  foils retracted: 304mm (1ft)
  foils extended: 914mm (3ft)
Draft foilborne: 457mm (1ft 6in)
Freeboard: 355mm (1ft 2in)
Height overall: 1·06m (3ft 6in)
  hullborne: 609mm (2ft)

WEIGHTS

Light displacement: 158·75kg (350lb)
Normal take-off displacement: 272·14kg (550lb)
Max take-off displacement: 362·85kg (800lb)

PERFORMANCE

Max speed, foilborne: 64·36km/h (40mph)
  hullborne: 8·04km/h (5mph)
Cruising speed,
  foilborne: 48·28km/h (30mph)
  hullborne: 8·04km/h (5mph)
Designed endurance and range at cruising speed, approx: 104·6km (65 miles)
Turning radius at cruising speed: 4·57m (15ft)
Fuel consumption at max speed: 9–22·7 litres/hour (2–5 gallons/hour)

SEA TEST: Craft has been tested in 3-4ft chop and 8-10ft swells.

PRICE: $1,995, plus options.

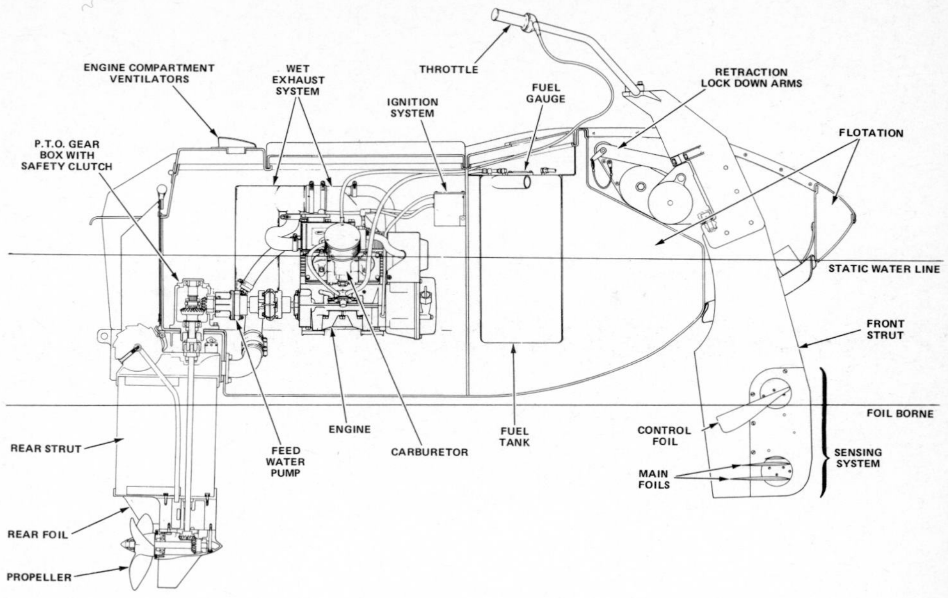

Inboard profile of the Dynafoil Mark I showing the power plant and transmission arrangements

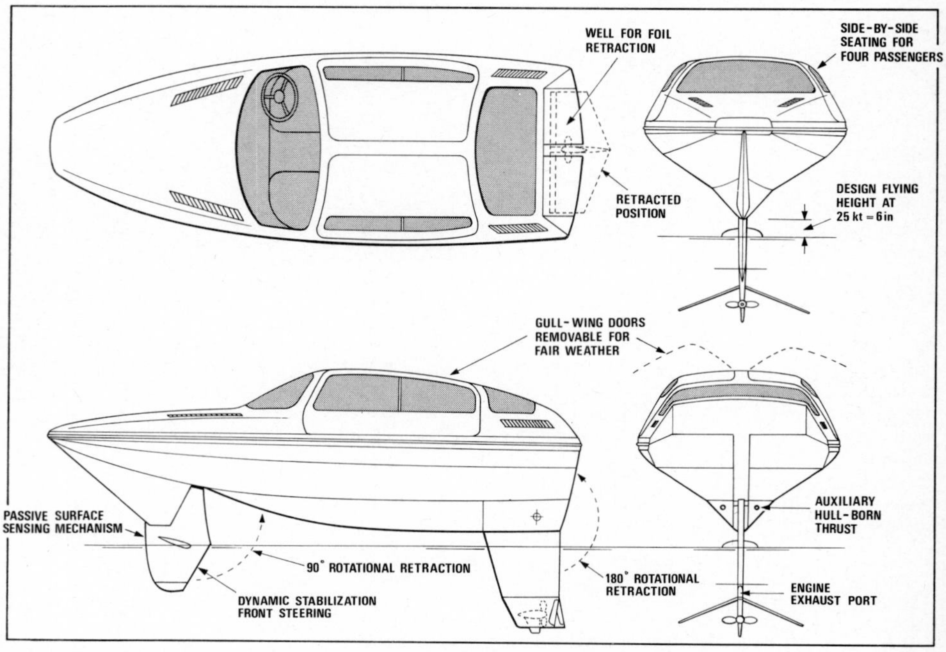

Dynafoil Mk II—a four-seater employing the same basic foil configuration as the Dynafoil Mk I. The gull-wing doors of the fully enclosed cabin can be removed for fair weather operation. Both foils are fully retractable

The Dynafoil Mark I two-seat sports hydrofoil

MILITARY DYNAFOIL

Tentative interest has been shown in a military version of the Dynafoil Mk II. Feasibility studies are being undertaken by the company but no construction timetable has yet been established. Power would be supplied by a 700hp turbo-charged V-8 automotive engine. Hydraulic foil retraction is envisaged.
DIMENSIONS
Length overall: 7·62m (25ft)
WEIGHTS
Max take-off displacement: 2,722kg (6,000lb)
Light displacement: 1,814kg (4,000lb)
PERFORMANCE
Cruising speed: 96km/h (60mph)

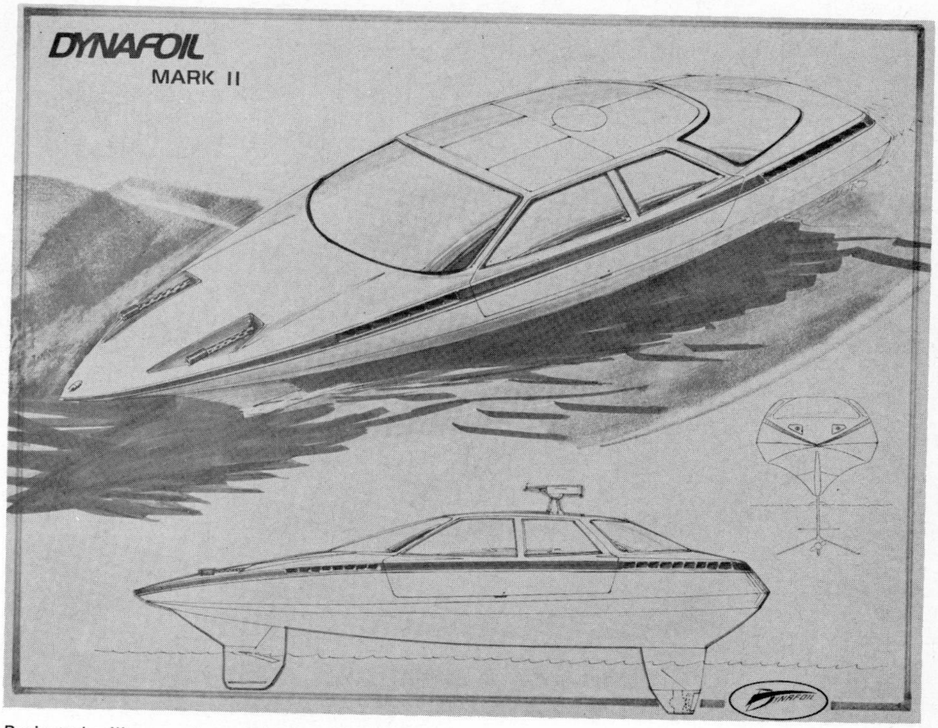

Projected military variant of the Dynafoil Mk II

EDO CORPORATION, GOVERNMENT PRODUCTS DIVISION

13-10 111th Street, College Point, New York 11356, USA
Officials:
L M Swanson, *Director, Air MCM Applications*

Edo Corporation has developed a foil-equipped catamaran MCM system which speeds the process of magnetic mine clearance and reduces the hazards of mine sweeping operations. The system, the Edo Mark 105, is designed to be towed by the US Navy's RH-53D Sea Stallion and other heavy-lift helicopters of similar size and performance. The first unit formed to operate Mk 105 Airborne Minesweeping Gear was the HM-12 helicopter mine countermeasures squadron, which operated off North Vietnam to clear mines from the entrance to the port of Haiphong and undertook the aerial sweeping of the Suez Canal during the spring of 1974. The operation—code named Nimbus Star—was said to have been a complete success.

It has been stated that a mine can be detonated almost immediately beneath the Mk 105 without the craft sustaining major structural damage.

If required the equipment can be towed behind a BHC BH.7 amphibious hovercraft or other suitable ACV. Tests with this arrangement have been undertaken in the UK and USA.

It is reported that ten RH-53D Sea Stallions, together with towed sweeping equipment, have been supplied to the Naval Air Transport Battalion, Iran.

Advantages claimed for the system include the following: lower acquisition and maintenance costs; fewer operating personnel required; low equipment vulnerability and bigger areas cleared within a given time.

Normally the helicopter/seasled combination is conveyed to the affected area aboard an amphibious assault craft. The helicopter lifts-off with the sled at the end of a line, lowers it into the water, extends its foils, and sets off to sweep the minefield.

The towline, which is 137·16m (450ft) long, also serves as an electric cable for carrying control signals to the sled, and as a fuel transfer line in the case of extended operations.

A portable winch in the helicopter is used to handle the craft, the sweep cables and the towing cable during launching and retrieval. The system can be operated from either ships or shore bases

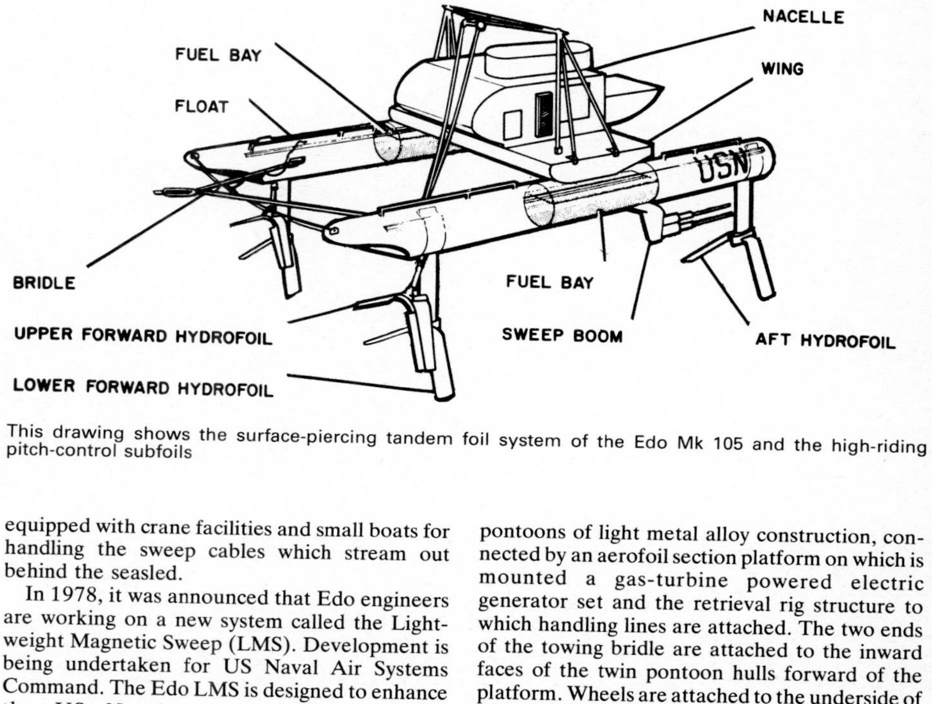

This drawing shows the surface-piercing tandem foil system of the Edo Mk 105 and the high-riding pitch-control subfoils

equipped with crane facilities and small boats for handling the sweep cables which stream out behind the seasled.

In 1978, it was announced that Edo engineers are working on a new system called the Lightweight Magnetic Sweep (LMS). Development is being undertaken for US Naval Air Systems Command. The Edo LMS is designed to enhance the US Navy's airborne minesweeping capabilities now provided by the Edo Mk 105. It is said to offer a substantial advance in performance compared with previous systems.

MK 105 AIRBORNE MINESWEEPING GEAR

The Mk 105 is a helicopter-towed, magnetic minesweeping system mounted on a 8·38m (27ft 6in) long catamaran seasled. Foils are fitted to permit high speed operation and provide improved seakeeping performance. Aboard the craft is a turbogenerator which provides energy for the magnetic sweep cables and powers a hydraulic pump for foil retraction.

FOILS: Surface-piercing tandem configuration with two inverted V foils forward and two aft, balancing the loading between them. High-riding pitch control subfoils of similar configuration are located ahead of the two bow foils. Bow and stern foils are rotated for retraction and extension by a self-contained hydraulic system.

HULL: Catamaran hull comprising two tubular pontoons of light metal alloy construction, connected by an aerofoil section platform on which is mounted a gas-turbine powered electric generator set and the retrieval rig structure to which handling lines are attached. The two ends of the towing bridle are attached to the inward faces of the twin pontoon hulls forward of the platform. Wheels are attached to the underside of the pontoons to facilitate deck handling. Fuel for the turbogenerator set is carried in two centrally located tanks, one in each pontoon.

TOWING AND OPERATION: The 137·16m (450ft) long towing cable terminates in an electrical connector and fuel fitting. As well as providing the towing links between the platform and the helicopter, all electrical commands and supplementary fuel pass through the cable. The cable consists of an electrical core containing 19 individual conductors, around which is a double layer of steel wire. Surrounding this is a hose, and fuel flows through the annular space between the inner diameter of the hose and the steel wire reinforcement.

The 27ft 6in long sled is generally carried aboard an Amphibious Assault Ship (LPH) or Amphibious Transport Dock (LPD), which also act as a mobile base for the helicopters. The helicopter lifts the sled off the deck then lowers it into the water to enable the sweepgear streaming operation to be completed.

The tow cable is then picked up and the sled is

The Edo Mk 105, probably the most sophisticated of all mine countermeasures systems, has been under development for some years. It comprises a helicopter and a towed hydrofoil sea sled, on which is mounted a turbogenerator that energises magnetic sweep cables, thus simulating the magnetic field of a ship

towed, foilborne, into the sweep area. Once in the area, the sled can be towed at lower speeds, hullborne, to simulate a displacement vessel and its magnetic (or in the case of the Mk 106, combined magnetic and acoustic) signature.

SYSTEMS: A gas-turbine generator set, mounted within a nacelle on the platform provides energy for the generation of the magnetic field. The complete power pack comprises a gas-turbine driven ac generator, a rectifier, a controller containing the waterborne electronics and batteries to power the electronics system.

MAGNETIC SWEEP CABLE: This is attached to the after end of the sweep boom located on the underside of the port pontoon. It comprises an upper electrode attached to the end of a trailing cable and a lower electrode fitted to the boom fin. The potential between the electrodes, employing the water as a conductor, produces a magnetic field which simulates that of a ship.

CONTROL PROGRAMMER: Located in the helicopter this is the only manned station employed in the system. It contains the airborne electronics and all the controls and instrumentation necessary.

The console contains the fuel transfer control panel, turbine indicators, hydrofoil and sweep boom actuators and the generator controls and indicators.

From the console the operator can start and stop the turbine, raise and lower the foils and control the magnetic influences generated through the conductor cables trailed behind the sled.

DIMENSIONS
Length overall: 8·38m (27ft 6in)
Beam,
catamaran structure only: 3·53m (11ft 7in)
across foils: 6·4m (21ft)
Height, foils extended,
to top of retrieval rig: 5·26m (17ft 3in)
to top of nacelle: 4·11m (13ft 6in)
foils retracted, to base of wheels: 3·5m (11ft 6in)

WEIGHTS
Empty: 2,504kg (5,522lb)
Gross: 2,917kg (6,432lb)

PERFORMANCE
Towing speeds and sea state capability: not available

MARK 106

An earlier airborne minesweeping system was the Mk 104, which can also be carried, towed and recovered by helicopters. This is used to detonate acoustic mines. It comprises a venturi tube and a water-activated turbine which rotates a disc to reproduce a ship's acoustic signature. The latest model in the series combines the duties of the Mk 104 and 105 to provide both acoustic and magnetic influences and is known as the Mk 106.

GRUMMAN AEROSPACE CORPORATION

Head Office: Bethpage, New York 11714, USA
Telephone: (516) 752 3681, Management and technical staff
(516) 575 2735, Marketing
Telex: GRUMAIRBETHPAGENY 961430
Officials:
G M Skurla, *Chairman and President*
R S Mickey, *Senior Vice President*
W G Wohleking, *Director Marine Programs*
C G Pieroth, *Deputy Director, Navy & Product Development Programs*
W D Brown, *Deputy Director, M161 Program*
J M Semmens, *Manager, Business Operations*
D L Walsh, *Director, Marketing*
C R Rabel, *Manager, International Marketing*

Grumman entered the hydrofoil field in 1956 when it acquired Dynamic Developments Inc, producer of the experimental XCH-4, built for the Office of Naval Research in 1955. Powered by two aircraft engines with air propellers, this 8-ton vessel established a world speed record for hydrofoil craft by exceeding 145km/h (78 knots). In 1958 Grumman designed and built the XCH-6 Sea Wings, also for the Office of Naval Research. Sea Wings was the first hydrofoil to employ both supercavitating foils and a supercavitating propeller and attained speeds in excess of 60 knots.

In 1960, Grumman was awarded a contract by the Maritime Administration for the design and construction of the HS Denison, an 80-ton open ocean research vessel which was launched in June 1962. This craft (described in the 1967-68 edition) was operated at speeds above 60 knots, demonstrated good foilborne manoeuvrability and seakeeping ability in rough water.

Grumman also completed the guidance design for the 328-ton, 64·6m (212ft) AGEH Plainview for the US Navy. The foils for this ship were the forerunners of those used on the Dolphin and the more recent PGH-1 Flagstaff.

The primary purpose of Plainview is to establish the possibility of operating large hydrofoils in high sea states, and explore many possible mission assignments including ASW, hydrographic data collection, surveillance, search and rescue and escort duties.

In December 1972, it was equipped with a single missile container and launched three NATO-configured Sea Sparrow missiles during rough water trials off the coast of Washington.

An overhaul of Plainview was completed in 1977, and the vessel scheduled to be used in the evaluation of platform and weapon systems for future large hydrofoils of the US Navy. However, due to budget limitations, de-activation was to begin in late June 1978.

Two Dolphin I class hydrofoils were built for Grumman by Blohm & Voss, Hamburg, but development of this class has now discontinued. In September 1968, the PGH-1 Flagstaff, the Grumman designed and built hydrofoil gunboat, was delivered to the US Navy. Between April and June 1971, it was employed on 152mm (6in) gun-firing trials.

A series of underwater explosion tests were also conducted with the Flagstaff in an experiment aimed at obtaining data on the shock responses of hydrofoil craft. The Flagstaff was the first and is so far the only hydrofoil to have undergone such tests. The vessel is currently in service with the US Coast Guard.

The company is now concentrating on the development of improved variants of Flagstaff and Dolphin class hydrofoils for use by both foreign navies and Coast Guards as well as domestic interests, and on large combatant hydrofoil ships for the US Navy.

In 1975, an updated and stretched version of PGH-1 was announced—the Flagstaff Mk II. With an overall length of 25·74m (84ft 5in), 3·04m (10ft) longer than the PGH-1, this model can accommodate a variety of the latest naval weapon systems. Main propulsion is supplied by either an Allison 501 KF or a Rolls Royce RM-2D Tyne marine gas-turbine. Maximum foilborne speed is 50 knots. This military design has been followed by the commercial variant, the Dolphin II, with seats for up to 200 passengers. The Dolphin II uses many of the Flagstaff Mk II components including the foils, foilborne propulsion system, hydraulics and foilborne automatic control system. High speed utility and crew boat configurations for servicing offshore facilities are available.

In December 1977, a contract was awarded to Grumman for the detail design and construction of two 96-tonne missile patrol craft, variants of the Mk II design. While details of the programme are classified, the design variant has been designated M161.

Grumman's PGH-I Flagstaff hydrofoil patrol gunboat equipped with 152mm howitzer

WPGH-I Flagstaff bearing the insignia of a US Coast Guard Cutter. The craft was transferred permanently to the US Coast Guard in October 1976 and is currently in service in Coast Guard District 1 (New England area) where it is undergoing further evaluation and augmenting fisheries patrol

PGH-1 FLAGSTAFF

The 67·5 ton PGH-1 Flagstaff hydrofoil gunboat was launched on 9 January 1968. It underwent preliminary trials in July 1968, and was delivered and placed in service at West Palm Beach in September 1968.

For five and a half months it underwent operational trials in South Vietnam. Between 1 September 1969 and 19 February 1970, Flagstaff was employed on various missions in Phase II of "Opeval" and "Market Time", operating from Da Nang.

Between November and December 1970 the craft was modified to mount a 152mm M551 gun from a Sheridan light tank on its foredeck. The gun fires conventional 6in shells or Shillelagh missiles and has a laser range-finder giving instant accurate ranging. It is capable of hitting a target at a range of up to 6·43km (4 miles).

Between November 1974 and February 1975 the vessel underwent evaluation by the US Coast Guard in a number of missions including: enforcement of laws and treaties; fisheries and contraband enforcement; search and rescue; marine environmental protection; servicing aids to navigation and marine science activities.

In October 1976, the PGH-1 was transferred permanently to the US Coast Guard and recommissioned as a US Coast Guard cutter. Now designated WPGH-1, the Flagstaff is currently in service in Coast Guard District 1 (New England area) where it is being employed to evaluate further the use of hydrofoils for Coast Guard missions and to augment the fisheries patrol in that area.

FOILS: Fully submerged system of conventional configuration, split forward, and a single foil aft. About 70% of the weight is supported by the twin forward foils and 30% by the aft foil. Foil section is sub-cavitating, 16 series. All three foils are incidence-controlled and operated by an AiResearch hydropilot. The stern foil strut rotates ±3 degrees for steering and all three retract completely clear of the water. Foils (by Potvin Kellering) are forged 6061-T652 aluminium and struts (by Blohm & Voss) are 4130 and HY80 steel. Foil area is 9·29m² (100ft²).

HULL: The hull structure is of combined welded and riveted corrosion resistant 5456 aluminium. The pilot house roof is of fibreglass sandwich. All frames and bulkheads are welded assemblies and transverse framing is used throughout.

POWER PLANT: The main engine is a 3,550hp Rolls-Royce Tyne Mk 621/10 gas turbine, flat rated to 90°F. Power is transmitted through a mechanical right-angle drive to a KaMeWa 1·14m (45in) diameter, three-bladed supercavitating, controllable pitch propeller. Nominal rpm at cruising speed, 1,000. Hullborne power is supplied by two 202hp GM 6V diesels driving twin Buehler 419mm (1ft 4½in) diameter waterjets, equipped with ±35 degree steering and reversing nozzles.

SYSTEMS, ELECTRICAL: Ship's service generator sets: twin GM 4-53N diesels with Delco 120V, 50kW, 62-5kVA, three-phase Delta, 60Hz at 1,800rpm. Emergency power (generators inoperable): 2 sets batteries 200Ah, 24V, for autopilot, gyroscope and navigation lights, all automatically switched.

RADIO: VHF and HF transceivers.

RADAR AND NAVIGATION: Decca TM626 at navigator's station and repeater at commander's station. Bendix ADF-162A automatic direction finder, Raytheon 726 depth sounder, Arma Mk 26 hydrocompass, Chesapeake EM-log speed log, Bendix prototype DRAI and DRT navigation system.

FIREFIGHTING AND DAMAGE CONTROL: Diesel-driven 50 gallons/min bilge pump, plus 50 gallons/min diesel-driven deck service pump, portable electric 250 gallons/min pumps and hand pump. Deck SW connection for fighting fires on other craft. Walter Kidde central CF BR fire extinguishing system in two 251lb cylinders. Four portable 2½lb Ansul Foray Combo Pacs.

ARMAMENT: Main battery (until November 1970): single 40mm Mk 3 Mod 0 rapid firing cannon. Machine guns: two twin mounts .50 calibre Mk 56 Mod 0. Mortar: One 81mm Mk 2 Mod 0. Small arms: M16 rifles (11), .38 calibre pistols, 12 gauge shotguns. New main gun battery to June 1973: 152mm M551 howitzer, firing conventional 6in shells or Shillelagh missiles. Laser range finder. Main gun battery has been removed. Current Coast Guard armament consists of single .50 calibre mount forward and small arms.

DIMENSIONS

Length overall, hull: 22·2m (73ft)
 foils extended: 23·36m (86ft 6in)
 foils retracted: 27·1m (89ft)
Hull beam: 6·5m (21ft 5in)
Extreme beam, foils retracted tip-to-tip: 11·28m (37ft 1in)
Draft, foils extended, static: 4·26m (13ft 11in)
Nominal draft foilborne: 1·72m (5ft 8in)

WEIGHTS

Displacement, fully loaded, as delivered: 67·5 long tons
 1971, with 152mm howitzer: 72 long tons

PERFORMANCE

Cruising speed, foilborne: in excess of 40 knots
 hullborne: in excess of 7 knots

FLAGSTAFF Mk II

This new model has been designed for a variety of naval and military roles and can be fitted with a wide range of weapons. A number of variants are available with differing payloads and endurances. The chief differences between this craft and its predecessor lie in the installation of a more modern, higher horsepower gas-turbine; a longer hull; an improved foil system and the installation of new foilborne automatic control and foilborne transmission systems. The fully loaded displacement has been increased to 92 tonnes. Maximum useful load (payload and fuel) is over 32 tonnes. It is reported that negotiations have begun with a number of navies for the construction of variants.

FOIL SYSTEM: Fully submerged system of conventional configuration, comprising twin inverted T foils forward and a single inverted T foil aft. Approximately 70% of the load is supported by the two forward foils and 30% by the aft foil. All three foils are incidence controlled and operated by an ACS employing electro-hydraulic actuators. The stern foil power strut, together with the propeller, rotates ±5 degrees for steering and all three foil/strut units retract completely clear of the water for hullborne manoeuvring. The foils are of machined aluminium and the struts are in HY130 steel. Break joints are incorporated on the two forward struts, so that should either of them strike large items of debris each would break clean at the point of its connection to its yoke. A shear bolt releases the aft strut permitting it to rotate rearwards and upwards above the transom.

HULL: Fabricated in 5086 and 5456 aluminium alloys. Frames and bulkheads are welded assemblies. Bottom, side, and deck plating consists of large panels of wide-ribbed extrusions welded to the frames and bulkheads.

ACCOMMODATION: Ship manning varies with the mission and weapons fitted. Minimum operating crew normally comprises three to four men; helmsman, engineer, deck officer/navigator and, if needed, a look-out. A nominal crew complement of 15 can be accommodated in terms of berthing, and messing facilities. All normally manned spaces are fully heated and air conditioned. The forward superstructure accommodates the bridge, which contains steering and engine control consoles and is elevated to give a 360 degree view. Entry to the deckhouse is via two 660mm × 1·52m (2ft 2in × 5ft) watertight doors, one port, one starboard. An emergency exit is located aft, behind the pilothouse on the weather deck. Escape hatches are provided in the living spaces.

POWER PLANT: FOILBORNE: Either a 3,980hp (continuous) Allison 501 KF or a 4,680hp (continuous) Rolls Royce RM-2D-Tyne marine gas-turbine. Power is transmitted to a supercavitating controllable pitch propeller through a Grumman Z drive transmission. Overall reduction 14 : 1.

HULLBORNE: Two GM 6V53N diesels rated at 216bhp each. Propulsors can be either retractable outdrives or waterjet pumps depending on customer preference.

FUEL: All installed prime movers will operate on JP-5, diesel No 2 or equivalent fuel. Tank for 16·1 tonnes (19,600 litres) of fuel normally provided; though in extended range variant designs more fuel can be accommodated. Underway refuelling facilities can be incorporated.

SYSTEMS, ELECTRICAL: Electrical power is supplied by two 95kW, 440V, 60Hz three-phase generators driven by GM 4-71 diesels. Each generator is capable of supplying normal ship electrical load and can be operated in parallel during battle conditions. A 400Hz system, included for installed electronics, is supplied by a motor generator. A dc system is incorporated for engine starting and emergency operations.

HYDRAULICS: A 3,000psi system, driven by four pumps located on both the hullborne and foilborne prime movers, provides control power for hullborne and foilborne operation and turbine starting.

CONTROLS: An automatic control system stabilises the Mk II in foilborne operations. This system consists of: dual radar height sensors, an inertial sensor, a digital processor, displays and controls. Both flat or co-ordinated turns and platforming or contouring modes can be selected by the helmsmen.

Flagstaff Mk II with four Gabriel missiles, Emerlec 30mm gun and two twin 20mm cannon mounts in port and starboard gun tubs

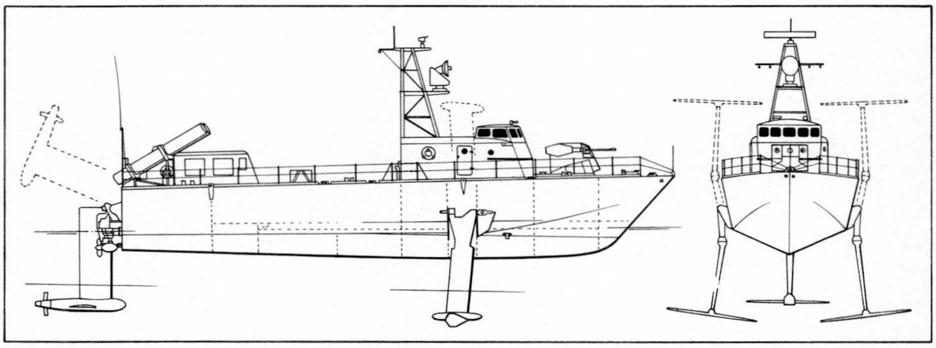
Outboard profile, Grumman Flagstaff Mk II (single 3,980hp Allison 501KF or single 4,680hp Rolls Royce RM-2D type marine gas-turbine)

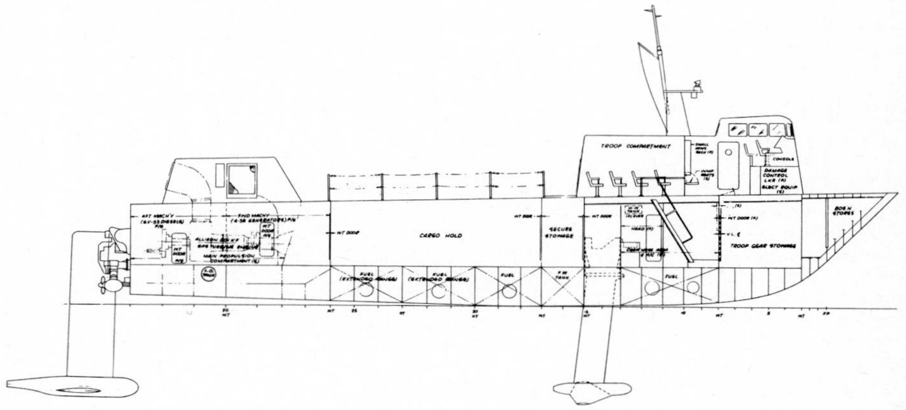

Inboard profile of a military transport variant of the Flagstaff Mk II

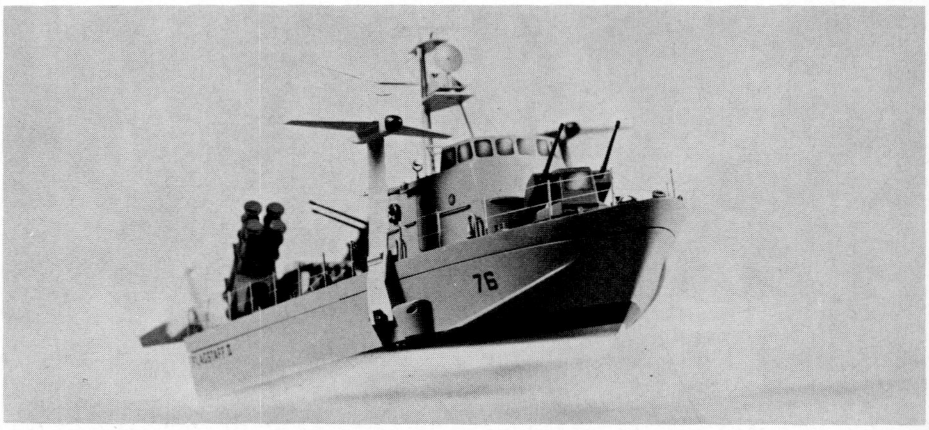

Model of Flagstaff Mk II with foils retracted. Armament of this variant comprises eight Harpoon missiles and two twin 30mm gun mounts

FIRE EXTINGUISHING: A manual over-ride automatic Freon extinguishing system is installed in machinery spaces.

ELECTRONICS: Navigation and communications equipment will vary with specific customer preferences. A true motion radar, a stable ele-

ment gyro-compass, hullborne and foilborne speed logs and fathometers are recommended.
ARMAMENT: Typical armament would include surface-to-surface missiles of the Harpoon, Gabriel, Otomat, Exocet or Penguin type, either one or two 30mm to 40mm gunmounts; sensors and fire control equipment and an integrated control centre.
DIMENSIONS
Length, overall (hull moulded): 25·74m (84ft 5in)
between perpendiculars: 23·4m (76ft 9in)
overall (foils retracted): 30·56m (100ft 3in)
overall (foilborne): 29·81m (97ft 10in)
Beam, hull moulded: 7·32m (24ft)
foils retracted (extreme): 12·95m (42ft 6in)
foilborne (extreme): 12·45m (40ft 10in)
Draft (full load), foils system retracted: 1·45m (4ft 9in)
foils system extended: 4·83m (15ft 10in)
foilborne (nominal): 1·7m (5ft 7in)
Surface search radar height, hullborne: 9·99m (32ft 10in)
foilborne: 12·13m (39ft 10in)
WEIGHTS
Light displacement: 59·8 tonnes
Full load displacement: 92 tonnes
Normal fuel load: 16·1 tonnes
Variable loads and combat system payload: 16·1 tonnes
PERFORMANCE
Max intermittent speed: 52 knots
Most economical speed: 42 knots
Foilborne operating envelope (normal): 35-48 knots
Max hullborne speed: 9 knots
Range at 42 knots: 850n miles
Range at 8 knots: 2,600n miles
Specific range at 42 knots: greater than 52n miles per tonne

DOLPHIN Mk II

The Dolphin Mk II is the commercial version of the Flagstaff Mk II. The two designs share common hydrofoil systems developed on the well proven performance of the original Flagstaff and Dolphin designs. Dolphin Mk II is being developed to satisfy commercial requirements for reliable high-speed passenger transportation on unsheltered open ocean routes.

Current configurations which can be tailored to suit a wide range of requirements, include a 200 passenger version designed for two-hour inter-urban services with refuelling scheduled for alternate round trips. Maximum speed is 50 knots continuous, the best range speed being 42 knots. Foilborne range is up to 600n miles.

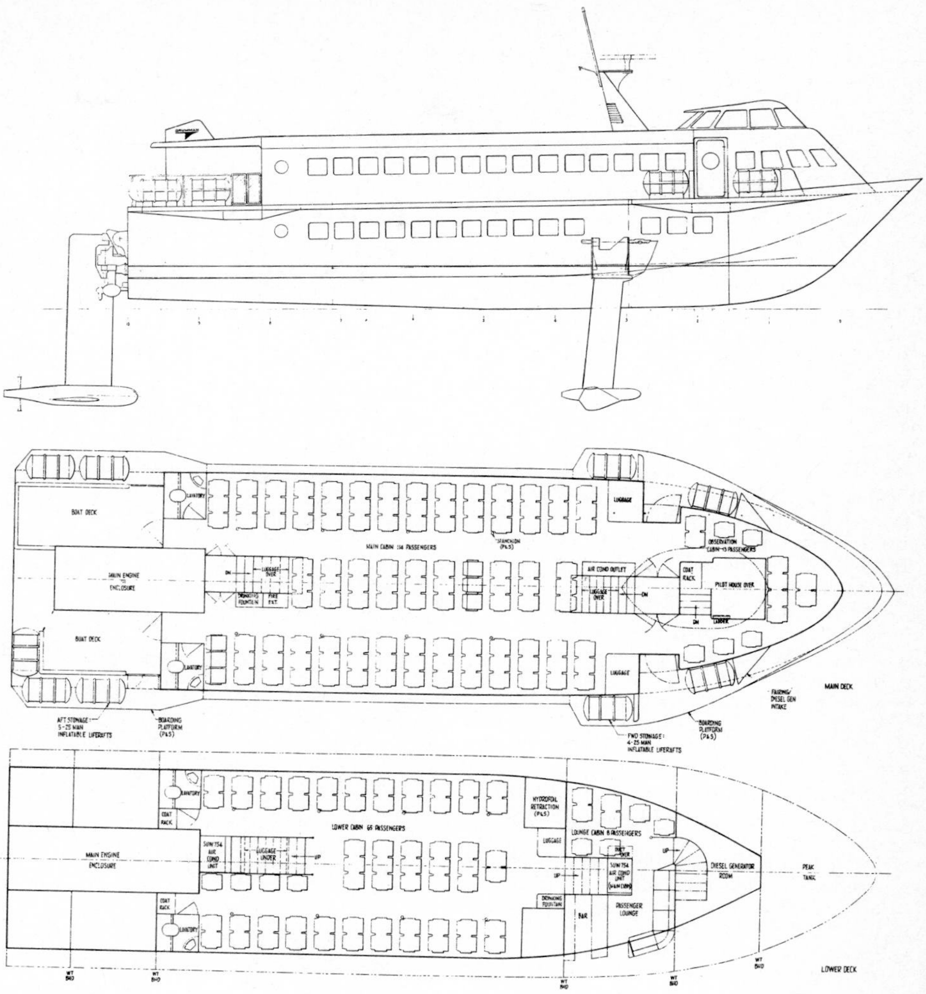

Outboard profile and deck plans of the Grumman Dolphin Mk II 50-knot open ocean passenger ferry

AG(EH)-1 PLAINVIEW

The 320-ton AG (EH)—the designation means auxiliary general experimental hydrofoil—was built by the Lockheed Shipbuilding & Construction Company, Seattle, Washington. It has been used by the US Navy's Hydrofoil Systems Testing Unit, Bremerton, Washington to investigate the performance of a large seagoing hydrofoil under operational conditions. The guidance design and preparation of contract specifications were undertaken by Grumman under the direction of the Bureau of Ships.

A contract for detailed design and construction was awarded to Lockheed Shipbuilding and Construction Company in June 1963 and the hull was launched in June 1965. The craft successfully completed her maiden flight on 21 March 1968 at Puget Sound and was officially delivered to the US Navy on 1 March 1969. It was given the US Navy classification "In Service, Special" in March 1969 and US Navy research and development trials are continuing. Due to budget limitations, de-activation was due to begin in late July 1978.

FOILS: The foil system is fully submerged and automatically controlled by a Hamilton Standard autopilot system similar to that used in High Point. The foil arrangement is of conventional type with 90% of the weight carried on the two main foils and the remainder on the aft foil. The three foils, which have considerable sweep and taper, are geometrically similar with an aspect ratio of three. The swept back leading edges help to delay cavitation and facilitate the shedding of seaweed and other neutrally buoyant debris. They also reduce impact loads associated with water entry after foil broaching. The main foils have some dihedral while the tail foil is flat.

Total foil area is 509ft², and foil loading is 1,460lb/ft² maximum. Foils are constructed in welded HY80 steel.

In February 1976, Grumman Aerospace deli-

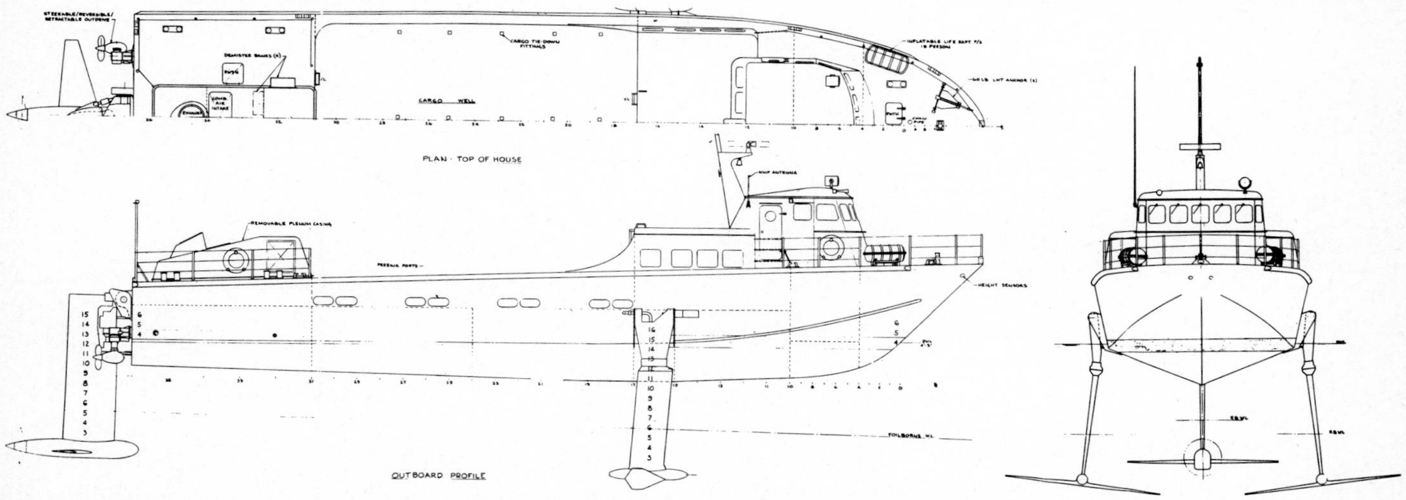

General arrangement of the Grumman Dolphin Mk II, a 50-knot utility and crew boat for servicing off-shore oil rigs

vered a new tail strut fabricated in HY130 steel. HY130 is being considered by the US Navy as a material for future large hydrofoils.

The main foils are extended, retracted and locked in each terminal position by means of a hydraulically-operated activating arm connected to the upper part of the strut. The two foils are synchronised to be raised and lowered together in the transverse plane. The aft foil operates in a similar manner, but can be raised and lowered independently.

Foil lift variation is by change in the incidence angle; each can move through +11 degrees to —4 degrees. The single aft foil controls pitch angle.

The aft foil strut rotates for use as a rudder. Steering can be flat (rudder only) or fully coordinated, using differential main foil angles for banked turns, with the aft strut trailing.

HULL: The hull is almost completely fabricated in 5456 aluminium alloy. All deck, side and bottom plating is made from integrally stiffened, aluminium extruded planks. The hull is predominantly welded construction with the exception of the pilot house and certain longitudinal hull seams that act as crack stoppers.

The hull shape is designed to minimise the structural loadings due to wave impact and the bow shape has been developed for this specific purpose. Bottom deadrise is carried to the transom with the same objective.

ACCOMMODATION: Crew of 25, comprising 4 officers and 21 enlisted men. The pilothouse, CIC compartment, living, messing and berthing spaces are air-conditioned. Sanitary and washroom areas, galley, displacement and main engine room are all mechanically ventilated. In the wheelhouse, the pilot's position is on the left, with the principal instrumentation; the co-pilot is on the right, and the observer between and slightly aft. Entry to the deckhouse is via three standard US Navy quick-acting aluminium doors—one aft port and one forward starboard on the main deck, and one aft on the lower deck. Emergency equipment includes seven-man liferafts, seven life-rings, four aircraft markers, one kapok heaving line and emergency scuttles, port and starboard.

POWER PLANT: Foilborne propulsion is supplied by two General Electric LM 1500s (marine version of the J-97), each of 14,500hp continuous rating, connected by shafting and gearing to two four-bladed 1·52m (5ft) diameter supercavitating titanium propellers at the end of the propulsion pods on the main foils. The hydrodynamic design of the propellers was undertaken by Hydronautics Inc, and they were built by Hamilton Standard. The blades are bolted to the hubs and each blade is replaceable. The air inlet for the main turbines is introduced at the top of the deckhouse. Because of the need to prevent ingestion of water or saltspray into the gas turbines, there are lowered deflectors over the inlet opening, followed by a bank of sheet metal spray separators.

There is a dam for solid water separation and four right angle turns before the air reaches the engine bellmouths.

The hullborne powerplants are two General Motors V12-71 diesels each rated at 500hp. Each diesel drives aft through a shaft to a right angle gear drive resembling a large outboard motor, mounted on the side of the hull. Each of these right angle drives is retractable about a horizontal axis and steerable about a vertical axis through 360 degree rotation. A 1·34m (4ft 5in) diameter five-bladed subcavitating propeller is mounted at the end of each right angle drive.

Auxiliary power is supplied by two GMC V8-71 engines driving two 100kW generators.

AIR CONDITIONING: The pilothouse, CIC compartment, living, messing and berthing spaces are air-conditioned during the cooling season by a 15-ton capacity Trane type compressor system. Sanitary and washroom areas, galley, displacement engine room, main engine room, windlass room and the engineer's control booth are all mechanically ventilated.

HYDRAULICS: 3,000psi operates foils, steering, extension, retraction and locking of struts

AGEH-I Plainview, 328-ton US Navy ocean-going hydrofoil warship research vessel, moored in Puget Sound with foils retracted. Two four-bladed propellers at the end of the pods on the main foils struts propel the vessel when foilborne

Maximum foilborne speed of the Plainview, which is powered by two 14,500hp GE LM1500s, is in excess of 50 knots. It is designed to operate in sea state 5 conditions and has undergone trials in 2·43-3·04m (8-10ft) waves off Victoria, British Columbia

In the interests of weight economy, the Plainview's hull is built largely from specially extruded aluminium planks, each 12·19m (40ft) in length and 0·635m (2ft 1in) in width. Struts and foils are built in HY80 and HY100 steel alloys. The bow shape is designed to minimise structural loadings due to wave impact

New AG (EH)-I Plainview aft foil assembly, comprising strut, pod and foil

and anchor windlass and starts propulsion diesels.

ELECTRONIC SYSTEMS: Raytheon Pathfinder radar with AN/SPA-25 repeater, AN/WRC-1B Bendix radio, AN/URC-58 radio RF Comm Inc, two AN/ARC-52X Collins radios.

ARMAMENT: Six Mk 32 torpedo tubes in two tri-mounts, port and starboard, aft of the deckhouse. One Mk 44 torpedo stowed in each tube. Single missile canister fitted in late 1972 for demonstration launching of three NATO-configured Sea Sparrow missiles.

DIMENSIONS

EXTERNAL

Length overall, hull: 64·61m (212ft)
  foils retracted: 68·17m (223ft 8in)
  foils extended: 66·75m (219ft ½in)
Length waterline, hull: 62·48m (205ft 1¾in)
Hull beam: 12·31m (40ft 5in)
Beam overall, foils retracted: 25·19m (82ft 8in)
  foils extended: 21·59m (70ft)
Draft hullborne, foils retracted: 1·9m (6ft 3in)
Freeboard,
  forward: 4·72m (15ft 6in)
  aft: 2·29m (7ft 6½in)
Height to top of mast: 16·69m (54ft 9½in)

WEIGHTS

Light displacement: 265 tons
Normal take-off: 290 tons
Max take-off: 328 tons

PERFORMANCE

Max speed foilborne: in excess of 50 knots
Cruising speed foilborne: 42 knots
Max speed hullborne: 13·4 knots
Cruising speed hullborne: 12 knots
Max permissible sea state and wave height in foilborne mode: (design sea state) Beaufort 5, Sea state 5

OCEAN HYDROFOIL COMBATANT

Since September 1974, Grumman Aerospace Corporation has been involved in the exploration of the potential of hydrofoil ships to fulfill the role of ocean combatants for the US Navy.

Preliminary designs have been completed for ships ranging in displacement from 1,330 to 1,625 tonnes. A variety of foil configurations have been investigated including fixed and totally retractable systems. Foilborne ranges in the order of 3,000n miles, speeds in excess of 50 knots and continuous operations in sea state six are being considered. Sustained operation will be possible from zero to maximum foilborne speed.

Foilborne power for the designs under consideration will be provided by twin General Electric LM 2500 gas-turbines, with optional gas turbines for hullborne operation. Power is transmitted through mechanical Z-drives to supercavitating CP propellers for foilborne operation and CRP

Project for a 1,330-ton ocean going hydrofoil frigate with a fixed fully submerged foil system

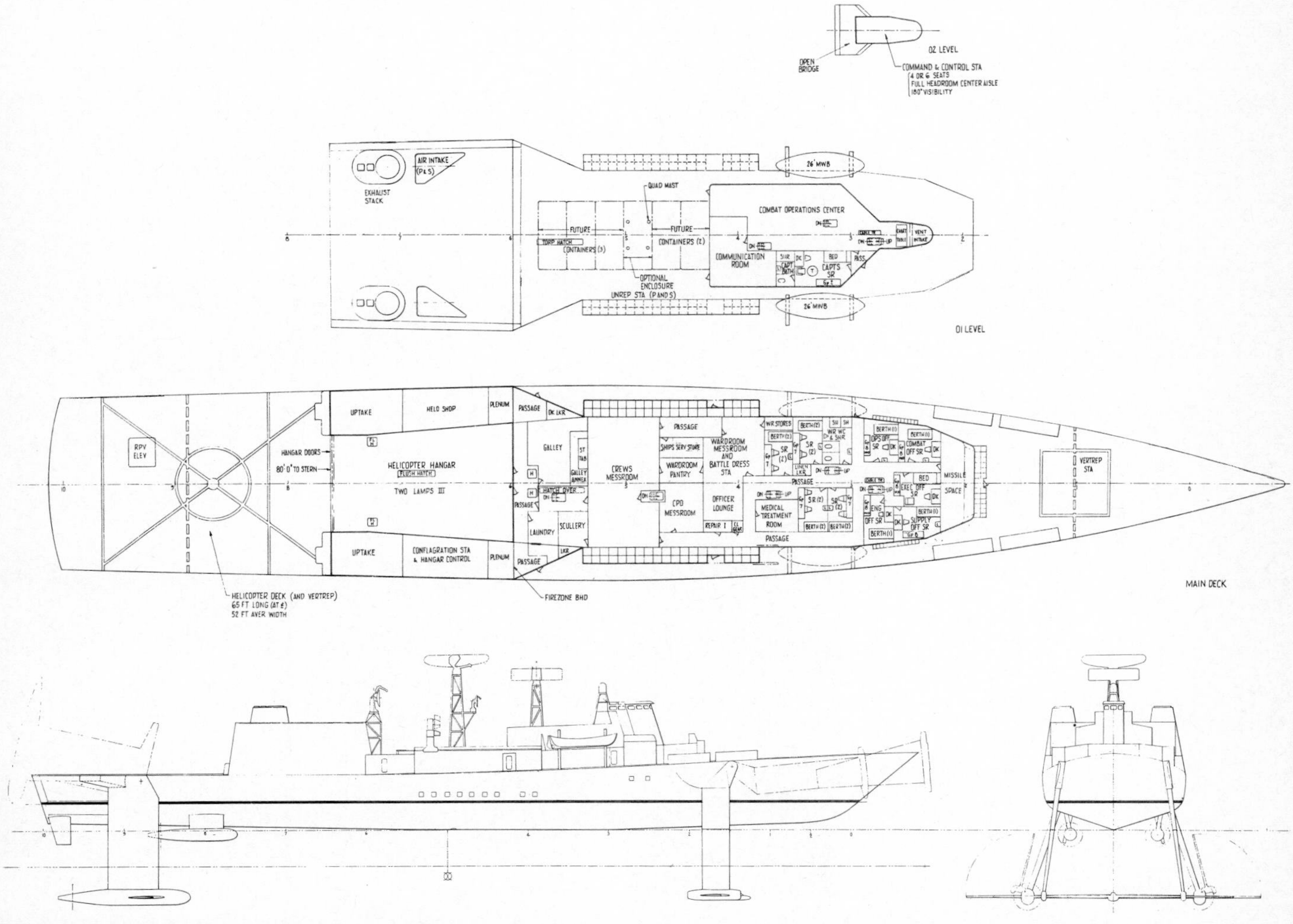

Outboard profile and deck views of a projected 2,400 ton air capable hydrofoil warship. This design accommodates a variety of weapon systems, and provides for the operation of two LAMPS III ASW helicopters and the launching and recovering of RPVs

propellers when hullborne. Hull construction is all-welded aluminium. Foil and struts are in HY 130 steel. New composite material is under consideration for foil fabrication.

Multiple combat systems are under study, including vertical launch missiles and air capability. The larger designs under study may employ VTOL aircraft to provide long-range identification for shipboard missiles and surveillance up to 400 nautical miles from the ship.

2400 MT AIR CAPABLE HYDROFOIL

In March 1977 Grumman delivered to the US Navy the conceptual design of a 2,400 tonnes air capable hydrofoil ship. This design accommodates a variety of weapon systems and provides for the launching, retrieving, and servicing of two LAMPS III helicopters.

FOILS: Fully submerged canard arrangement with approximately 40% of the load carried by the bow foil and 60% by the aft foil. Fuel burnoff increases the percentage of the load on the bow foil, assisting the maintenance of favourable pitch stability throughout the loading range. For hullborne operation the bow foil rotates forwards and upwards clear of the waterline and the rear foil rotates aft.

POWER PLANT: Foilborne power is provided by two Turbo Power and Marine Systems Inc FT9 Marine gas turbines, each rated at 43,000shp maximum intermittent and 37,000shp maximum continuous at 4,000rpm and 27°C (80°F). Hullborne power is supplied by a single General Electric LM500 gas-turbine, rated at 5,100shp maximum intermittent and 4,650shp maximum continuous at 7,000rpm at 27°C (80°F). All three units are located aft of amidship and drive four propellers, two foilborne and two hullborne, through a combined transmission. All four propellers are identical in blade design to facilitate servicing and replacement. The hullborne propellers are reversible and variable in pitch to reduce take-off drag, while the foilborne propellers are variable in pitch to reduce drag when operating hullborne.

An impression of Grumman's proposal for a 2,400-tonne air capable hydrofoil for the US Navy

HULL: Incorporates continuous main (weather) and second decks and a partial lower platform deck. Hold beneath the load deck is divided into 13 major watertight compartments.

ACCOMMODATION: Crew will vary according to the nature of the missions for which the craft is employed and the type of weapons installed. Accommodation is provided for 155 officers and enlisted personnel, allowing for the in-service growth of the crew by 15 members above the anticipated initial manning of 140. All accommodation is located amidships in the area of least motion.

SYSTEMS, ELECTRICAL: Three Lycoming T35 gas-turbines are fitted, each rated at 2,800shp continuous at 15,000rpm, two to drive generators for normal ship's services, one for emergency use and anchor operation.

WEAPONS: Two LAMPS III helicopters operated from pad aft of superstructure. Pad is also employed for launching and recovering remotely piloted vehicles (RPVs). Vertically launched weapons, located principally in mounts located fore and aft, along both sides of the hull and inboard, amidship.

DIMENSIONS

Length between perpendiculars (hull): 97·54m (320ft)

Length overall, foils retracted: 111·17m (364ft 9in)

foils extended: 106·85m (350ft 7in)

Beam overall, foils retracted (tips folded): 24·69m (81ft)

foils extended: 35·62m (116ft 10½in)

Operational draft, foils retracted: 5·72m (18ft 9in)

hullborne, foils extended: 13·41m (44ft)

Draft (nominal), foilborne: 5·43m (17ft 10in)

Max beam (hull): 15·87m (52ft 1in)

Radar height above water (nominal):

foilborne: 24·99m (82ft)

hullborne: 17·07m (56ft)

HYDROFOILS INCORPORATED

PO Box 115, Red Bank, New Jersey 07701, USA
Telephone: (201) 842 1260
Officials:
Kenneth E Cook, *President*

Hydrofoils Incorporated has designed a fibreglass-hulled two-seater, the Mirage, for powerboat racing. The company, in conjunction with the American Power Boat Association, is examining the possibility of establishing a new racing class which would lead to the inception of a water counterpart to multi-turn Grand Prix road racing.

One of the company's latest projects is a 8·53m (28ft) patrol hydrofoil employing foils of similar configuration to those of Mirage.

Work is also under way on a new craft, powered by a 1,500hp engine, which will attempt to establish a world hydrofoil speed record during 1979.

Performance of the Mirage is said to compare favourably with that of other high performance craft. At the time of going to press, production quantities and the retail price were in the process of being settled. Preliminary details are given below.

Note the novel canard arrangement incorporating an inverted V main foil with a conventional V foil forward. Wing-shaped stabilisers on the main foils limit the degree of immersion of the main foil thereby maintaining the hull at a negative angle of attack, and preventing the craft from blowing over at high speed

The two-seat Mirage racing hydrofoil during tests

MIRAGE

This novel recreational craft is intended as a water-borne equivalent to a two-seater sports car. One major objective has been to produce a craft capable of tight, high-speed turns, thus permitting boats of this type to race on relatively small courses. The prototype is fitted with a 350in³ Chevrolet automobile engine, but a wide range of alternative petrol engines can be fitted.

FOILS: Surface-piercing canard configuration. About 75% of the load is borne by the inverted V foil aft and the remainder on the small conventional V foil at the bow. Wing-shaped stabiliser foils are attached to the inverted V main foil at calm water line level to limit the degree of foil immersion, maintaining the hull at a negative angle of attack to prevent kiteing and blowover at high speed. Foils are of supercavitating design and fabricated in high strength aluminium. Small rudder surfaces are attached at right angles to

main foil. Various sizes available. Rudder design is a compromise between maximum steering capability and optimum fin effect to limit yaw, roll and drift in high speed turns. The aft foils hinge upwards for towing, reducing the overall beam to conform with state trailer laws.
HULL: Planing type hull. Moulded fibreglass structure with aluminium frames and sitka spruce stringers.
ACCOMMODATION: Open cockpit with twin upholstered bucket seats for driver and one passenger.
POWER PLANT: Single 350in³ Nicson marine conversion engine installed aft of the cockpit. Output is transferred via a Casalle vee-drive to a Stellings chrome-plated high-performance two-bladed propeller. Drive is air, water and oil-cooled and provides forward and neutral quick-change. Ten different gear ratios are available from 1·03:1 to 1·37:1. Total fuel capacity is 15 gallons.
CONTROLS: Craft heading is controlled by twin rudders operated from the cockpit by a steering wheel. There is also a foot-operated throttle and a gear shift lever. The boat is equipped with an automatic bilge pump.
SYSTEMS, ELECTRICAL: 12V dc starter, alternator and voltage regulator.
DIMENSIONS
Length overall, hull: 5·02m (16ft 6in)
Beam overall: 3·96m (13ft)
hull: 2·43m (8ft)
Draft, hullborne: 0·91m (3ft)
foilborne: 457mm (1ft 6in)
WEIGHTS
Displacement: 816·42kg (1,800lb)
PERFORMANCE
Max speed: 129km/h (80mph)
PRICE: The Mirage is available both as a complete craft or in kit form. A kit information package is available at US$7.

28ft PATROL HYDROFOIL

Hydrofoils Incorporated is completing a design study for the Department of Fisheries, Canada, for a 8·53m (28ft) patrol hydrofoil, with living and sleeping accommodation for a crew of four. Foil configuration is similar to that of the Mirage. Power will be supplied by either a single or twin engines driving marine propellers through V-drive shafts or retractable outboard drives.

A provisional three-view drawing accompanies this entry.
DIMENSIONS
Length overall, hull: 8·53m (28ft)
foils retracted: 9·14m (30ft)
foils extended: 9·14m (30ft)
Hull beam: 3·63m (11ft 11in)
Beam overall, foils extended: 5·79m (19ft)
Draft static, foils retracted: 0·609m (2ft)
foils extended: 2·13m (7ft)
Draft foilborne: 0·67m (2ft 6in)
Height overall, foilborne: 3·04m (10ft)
static: 1·82m (6ft)

Hull of the Mirage is in moulded glassfibre with an aluminium frame

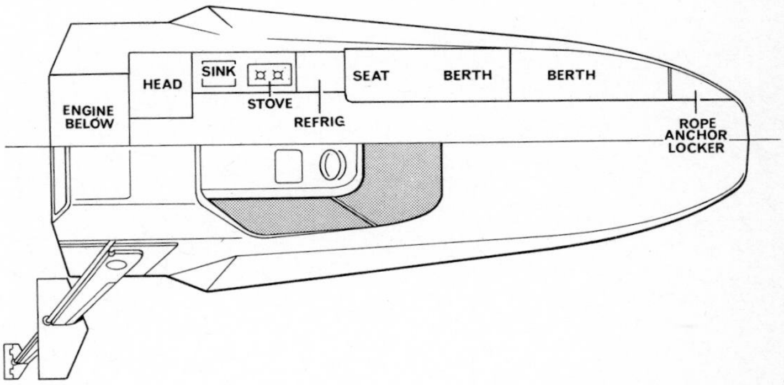

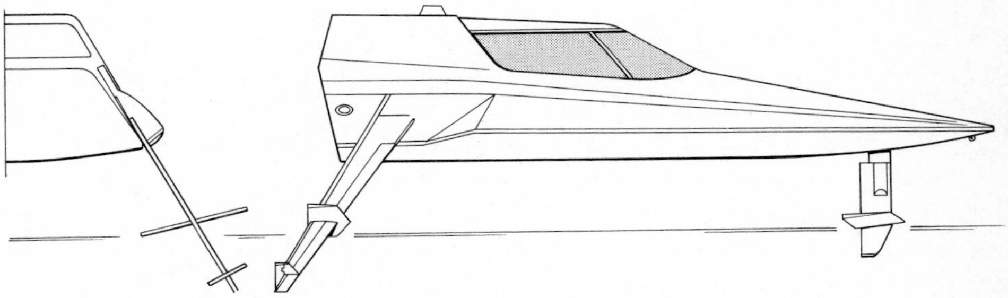

Design studv for a 8·53m (28ft) patrol hydrofoil completed by Hydrofoils Inc

40ft FERRY

Work has started on a 20 passenger, 40ft long light ferry which could also be employed to service off-shore oil rigs.

SAILING SKIMMERS

JAPAN

KANAZAWA INSTITUTE OF TECHNOLOGY

Department of Mechanical Engineering, Kanazawa Institute of Technology, PO Kanazawa-South, Ishikawa-Ken 921, Japan
Telephone: 0762 48 1100
Officials:
Yutaka Masuyama, *Researcher*

The Department of Mechanical Engineering, Kanazawa Institute of Technology, has been studying sailing hydrofoil craft since 1975. Two experimental craft have been built. Ichigo-Tei was completed in 1975 and tested in 1976, and employing data obtained from this craft, Hi-Trot II was built and tested in 1977.

ICHIGO-TEI

This is a basic test rig to investigate the manoeuvrability, stability and balance of sails and foil systems. The Ichigo-Tei has a specially designed catamaran hull, to which two surface-piercing bow foils and one stern foil are attached.

FOILS: The bow foils are of three-rung ladder configuration with removable outer rungs. The stern foil is of trapeze configuration with the rudder mounted immediately aft. Foil loading during a normal take-off is bow foils 60% and stern foil 40%. The foils, struts and rudder are fabricated in glass fibre and polyester resin. Foil section throughout is Göttinger 797, with 170mm (6·7in) chord.

HULL: Marine plywood sheathed with glass fibre and polyester resin.

SAIL: Sloop rig with a 10·2m² (110ft²) mainsail borrowed from the Hobie-cat 14, and a jib sail of 3·7m² (40 ft²) borrowed from the Snipe.

DIMENSIONS

Length overall:	4·46m (14ft 8in)
Length waterline:	4·2m (13ft 9in)
Hull beam:	2·2m (7ft 3in)
Width overall across foils:	4·3m (14ft 1in)
Draft afloat (fixed foils):	0·96m (3ft 2in)
Draft foilborne:	0·5-0·4m (1ft 8in-1ft 4in)

WEIGHTS

Empty:	140kg (309lb)

PERFORMANCE

Take-off speed: 6 knots with an 11-knot wind.
Max speed foilborne: 9 knots with a 14-knot wind.

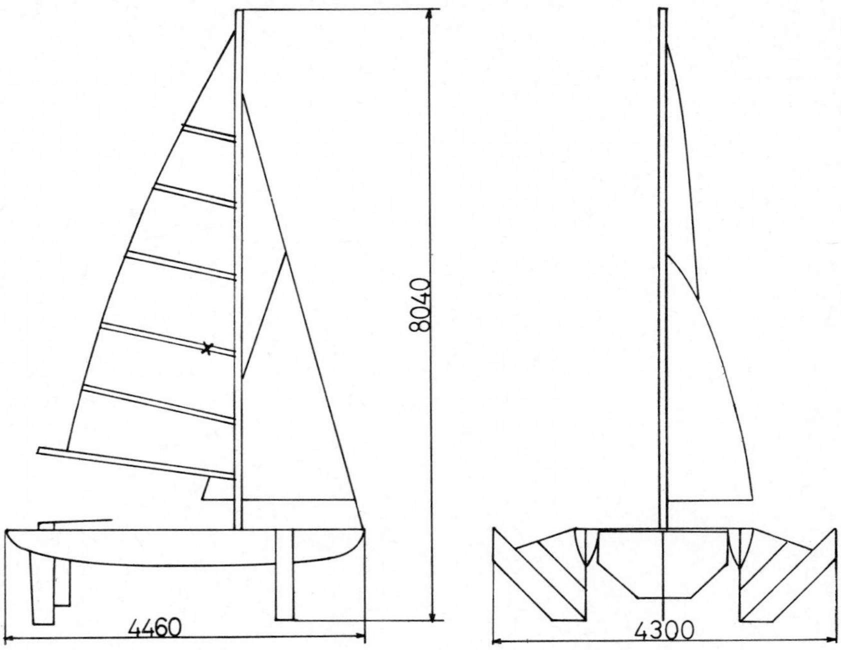

General arrangement of the Ichigo-tei sailing hydrofoil

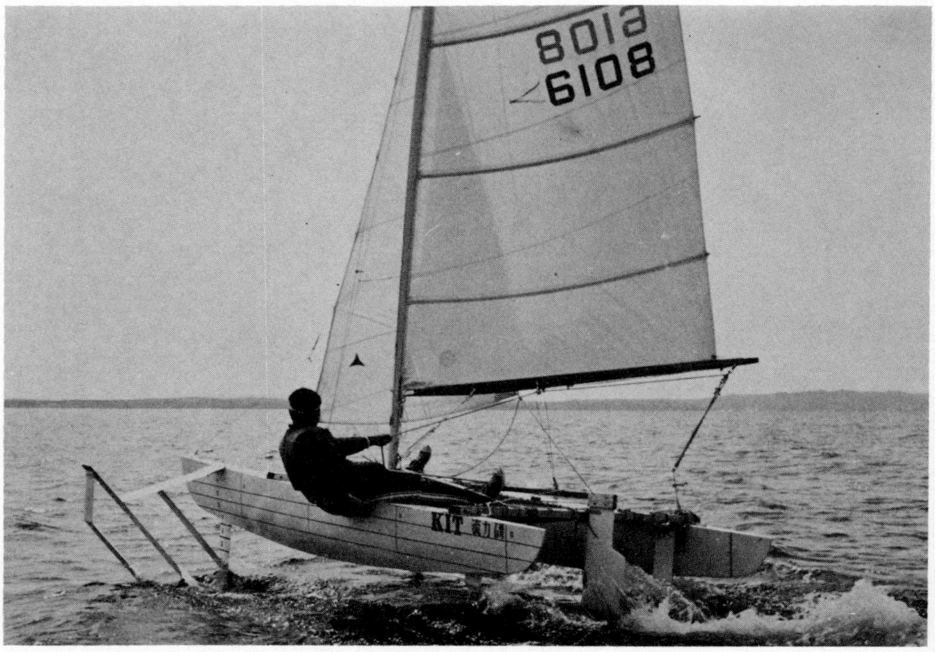

Ichigo-tei, Kanazawa Institute's test craft, during trials. Take-off speed is 7 knots

HI-TROT II

Employing data gathered during the test programme conducted with Ichigo-tei, the Kanazawa Institute of Technology design team built the Hi-Trot II. The hull is longer than that of the earlier craft, but the chief difference, apart from the adoption of a simpler foil system, is the use of a rotating sail rig.

FOILS: The split bow foil is of surface-piercing V-type, with cantilevered extensions, set at 40 degrees dihedral, at the apex. The bow foil section is ogival, with 250mm (9·8in) chord and a 12% thickness-to-chord ratio. The aft foil is of inverted T type and the complete foil and strut assembly rotates for use as a rudder. About 80% of the load is carried by the bow foils, and the remaining 20% by the stern foil. Foils, struts and rudder are all fabricated in glass fibre, carbon fibre and epoxy resin.

HULL: Plywood structure sheathed with glass fibre and epoxy resin.

SAIL: Comprises three sail panels in parallel, each 4·2m², mounted in parallel. An air rudder automatically adjusts the attack angle of the sails to the wind. Each panel has a wing section, and though the section is symmetrical, it can form a camber on either side by bending at 40% chord length. The leading edge of each wing is covered with thin aluminium sheet while the trailing edges are covered with terylene cloth. Wing frames are of plywood and polystyrene foam sandwich and provide the necessary buoyancy to prevent the craft from capsizing should it turn on its side. The surface of each wing is spray painted with polyurethane paint.

Hi-Trot foilborne. Note the air rudder attached to the central sail panel which automatically adjusts the attack angle of all three sails to the wind

DIMENSIONS

Length overall:	5·1m (16ft 9in)
Length waterline:	4·95m (16ft 3in)
Hull beam:	2·68m (8ft 10in)
Beam, overall (fixed foils):	5·45m (17ft 11in)
Draft afloat (fixed foils):	1·1m (3ft 7in)
Draft foilborne:	0·55-0·4m (1ft 10in-1ft 4in)

WEIGHTS

Empty:	250kg (551lb)

PERFORMANCE

Take-off speed: 7 knots with 15 knots wind

Max speed foilborne: 11 knots with 17 knots wind

SEA TEST: The craft has been tested in 10-20 knot winds. Due to mechanical problems, tests could not be undertaken in wind speeds exceeding 20 knots. Improvements are being made to remedy this.

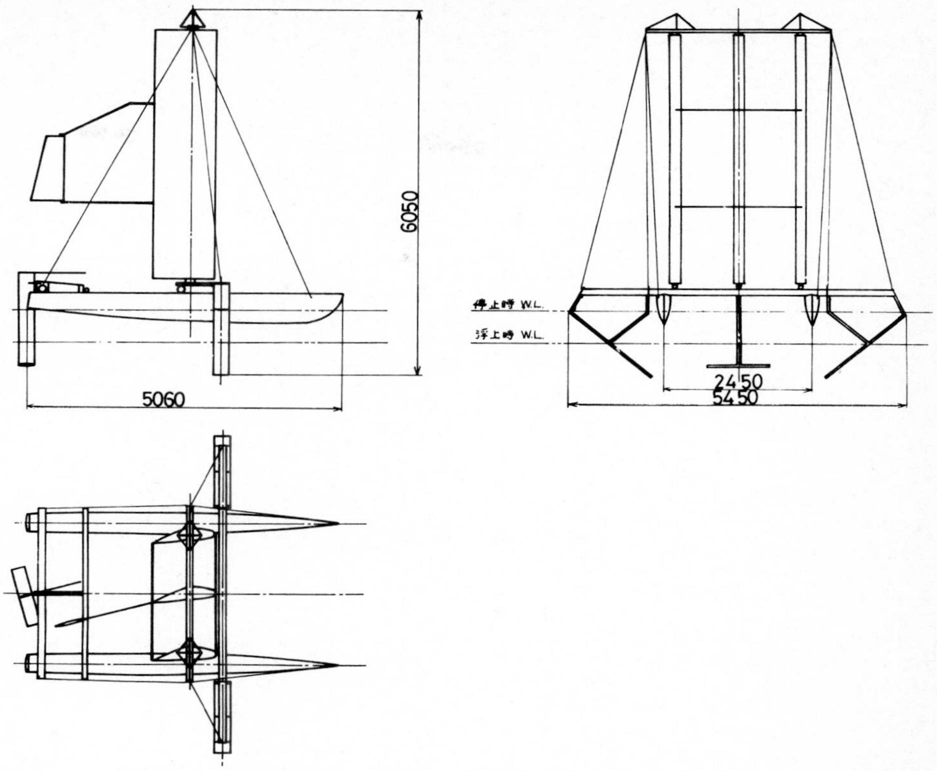

General arrangement of Hi-Trot, Kanazawa's rotating sail hydrofoil test craft

POLAND

INSTYTUT LOTNICTWA (AVIATION INSTITUTE)

02-256 Warszawa, Al Krakowska 110/114, Poland
Telephone: 460993
Telex: 81-537

Dr Jerzy Wolf is employing an ultra-light wing, constructed by the Aviation Institute while undertaking research on agricultural aircraft, as a sail for an experimental "skimmer" sailing craft.

The wing raises the hull above the water surface and also acts as a sail.

The object of Dr Wolf's experiments is to develop a sailing vessel which offers a higher speed than that attained by current sailing hydrofoils.

The wing, which has inherent directional and lateral stability, is hinged to the mast top, slightly ahead of the centre of pressure, and pulls the craft obliquely, in a similar way to a kite of high lift/drag ratio. The angles of attack and roll are controlled by lines or push-pull rods connected to a control cross-bar. Craft heading is controlled by a conventional water rudder.

Dr Wolf's Z-70 and Z-71 sailwing craft are described in *Jane's Surface Skimmers 1976-77* and earlier editions.

ZAGLOSLIZG (SAILING SKIMMER)

Developed from the Z-70 and Z-71, the Z-73 employs a modified Cadet class dinghy hull, equipped with a high aspect ratio centreboard and rudder.

During 1974, several further modifications were made to the sailwing, including the addition of a bow stabiliser to assess the advantages of a canard configuration, and a horizontal stabiliser surface to assess the value of a conventional configuration.

The mast was moved aft of the cockpit, and foot-operated rudder bar steering was installed.

Based on the test results, a further development model—the Z-76—is being built, the wing of which will also be used as an ultra-light, tailless hang-glider.

The wing, covered in dacron, incorporates a light vertical stabiliser, and has inherent directional and lateral stability.

Altitude control is based on a combination of incidence and heel angle control. Excessive

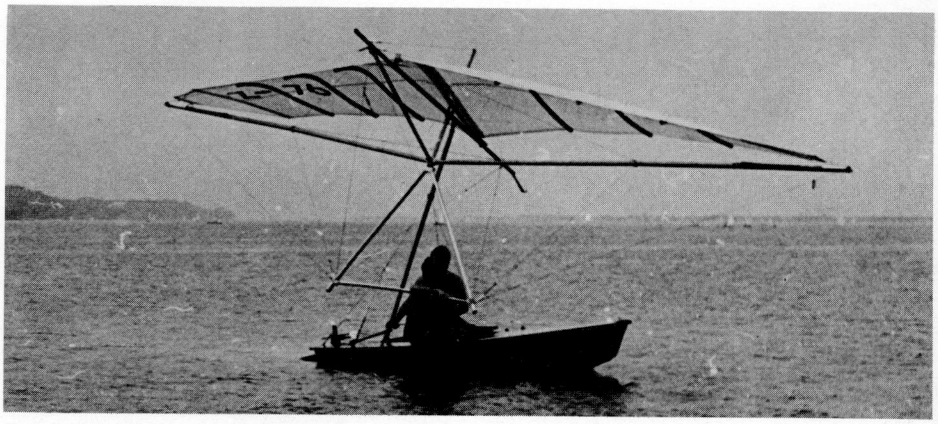

Z-76 Sailing Skimmer undergoing tests

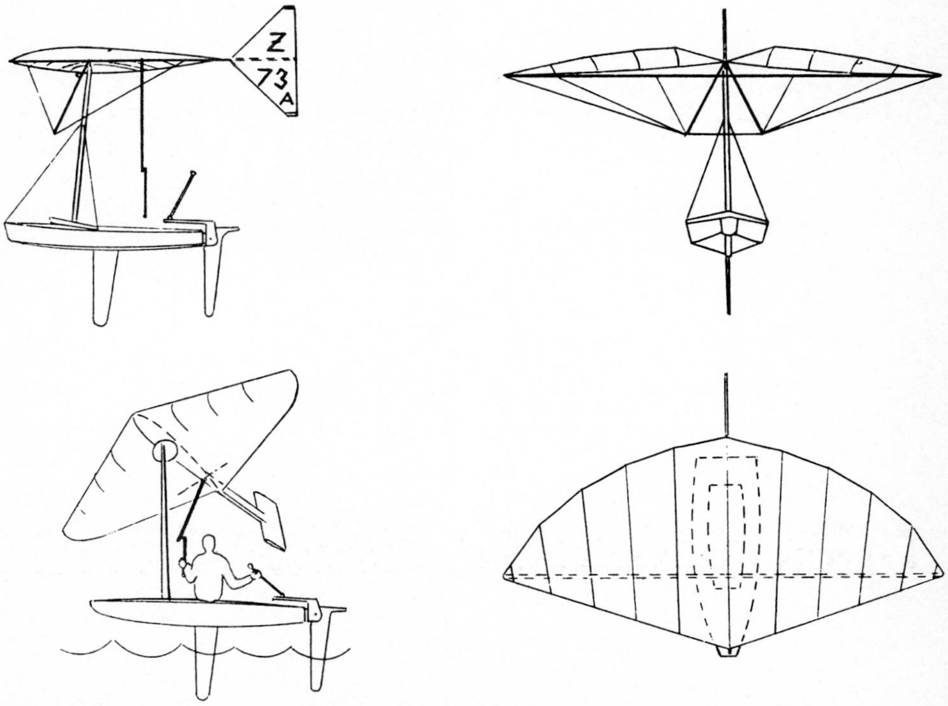

General arrangement of the Z-73A, incorporating a sketch showing the control arrangements

altitude results in increased drift and a loss of speed and lift. This leads to a restoration of normal trim, with the hull riding at a predetermined height above the water level. The restoring forces are described as being similar to those of a V-foil sailing hydrofoil.

DIMENSIONS
Length overall, hull: 3·2m (10ft 6in)
Beam: 1·3m (4ft 3in)
Draft, centreboard lowered: 1·2m (3ft 11in)
Sailwing span: 6·5m (21ft 4in)
Aspect ratio: 4·7:1
Stabiliser area: 1·2m² (13ft²)

WEIGHTS
Empty: 68kg (150lb)
Gross: 150kg (330lb)
Sailwing: 10kg (22lb)

PERFORMANCE (Design)
Lift/drag ratio, sailwing: approx 8:1
Max angle of wing setting: 60 degrees
Horizontal lift/drag ratio for 45 degree heel: 3·5:1
Lift/drag ratio of centreboard and rudder: 2·1:1
Wind velocity for take-off: 6·5m/s (21ft/s)
Minimum speed for take-off: 45km/h (27mph)
Optimum airborne speed: 60km/h (36mph)

UNITED STATES OF AMERICA

DAK HYDROFOILS

PO Box 1747, Sausalito, California 94965, USA
Officials:
David A Keiper, *Proprietor and Chief Designer*

Design of the Williwaw, the world's first seagoing sailing hydrofoil, began in 1963. Construction of the craft, which is based on a specially designed trimaran hull, began in May 1966 and tests started in November 1967.

After nearly three years of trials along the California coast, Williwaw, manned by David Keiper and one other crew member, successfully completed a 16-day passage between Sausalito, California and Kahului Harbour, Maui, Hawaii, in September 1970—the first ocean crossing by the hydrofoil sailboat.

Heavy seas and strong winds were encountered on the first two days of the voyage, during which the craft made 200 miles per day. At times the craft attained 25 knots, but light winds in mid-ocean prevented the craft from making the passage in record time.

The craft entered chartered sailing yacht service in March 1971, operating from Hanalei, Hawaii and before returning to Sausalito, California, completed about 2,000 miles of inter-island sailing around Hawaii, mainly in open sea conditions.

Williwaw was entered in the Pacific Multihull Association speed trials held in Los Angeles Harbour on 9 May 1975. Average speed was determined over a 229m (250yd) course, planned so that the true wind was approximately 10 to 20 degrees aft of the beam. On one run, with a reasonably steady wind of 17 knots, Williwaw averaged 17·5 knots over the course. On another run, with a stronger wind of 24 knots, under gusty and turbulent conditions with a 1½ft very short wave chop, Williwaw averaged 18·5 knots.

The foils stabilised the craft perfectly. The bow kept up high in all runs, while various racing catamarans of 14 to 38ft experienced serious problems with bow burying. Two catamarans capsized. The three-man crew on Williwaw stood on the windward deck, holding onto the shrouds, while the crews of the catamarans had to lie down and hold on tight to avoid being thrown overboard.

Various modifications to the craft were undertaken during 1974-75, and in the summer of 1975 a second series of sea trials were undertaken in the South Pacific, to test these modifications.

Williwaw sailed to Hawaii again in June 1975. Wind was generally light until deep within the tradewind region. In heavy tradewind squalls with the boat running down steep 15ft seas, the foils were found to stabilise perfectly and the bow was never submerged.

On a run from Hanalei, Hawaii to Whangaroa, New Zealand, made between November and December 1975, with stopovers in Samoa and Tonga, moderate trade winds were experienced during the first 2,000 miles of the voyage and generally light winds during the last 2,000 miles. During the first 12 days of the voyage, the foils were left set continuously. Over one ten-day period, the craft completed 1,650 miles, including a doldrums crossing. Self-steering was used for most of the way, with the helm tied. Only the working sail area of 380ft² was used.

The return trip from New Zealand to Hawaii was made via Rarotonga and Penrhyn in the Cook Islands. When the craft left New Zealand, a disturbed south west air stream was generating 35 knot squalls, day and night. Seas were very irregular and the boat would occasionally slam into walls of water at speeds in excess of 20 knots. About 500 miles from the New Zealand coast one freak wave encountered was 35-40ft high, and had a slope greater than 45 degrees. The trough was flat-bottomed, with no rounding between the slope and the trough. Descending the slope, the bow was well above the surface. After impact there was no tendency for the stern to lift. The bow remained under for about two seconds before it emerged and the boat started moving again. Waves such as this have been known to pitchpole yachts, monohull and multihull, but the hydrofoil trimaran showed no such tendency.

Williwaw has now operated sailing excursions from Hanalei, Hawaii, during the summers of 1971, 1975 and 1976. By the end of August, 1976, it had completed 19,000 miles of sailing.

Dak Hydrofoils is currently developing simple low-cost hydrofoil conversion kits for existing racing catamarans with lengths ranging from 3·65-6·9m (12-20ft). These were test marketed between 1972-1974. Economic conditions permitting, Dak Hydrofoils hopes to begin the full-scale marketing of ready-to-install foil sets for a variety of multihulls in 1979.

The design of 16, 35 and 40ft hydrofoil trimarans is continuing, and complete boats will be built to order. A modified conversion kit introduced in 1974 is also suitable for outboard powerboats.

Williwaw sailing in San Francisco Bay before her historic trans-ocean voyage to New Zealand

Demonstrating the stability of Williwaw while foiling in gusty conditions

WILLIWAW

A prototype sailing hydrofoil, Williwaw has a specially designed trimaran hull attached to which are four foils—a deep V-foil at the bow, a ladder foil at the stern, and one laterally outboard of each of the port and starboard pontoons. The stern foil pivots and serves as a rudder when hullborne.

The craft accommodates 2-3 passengers, together with cruising supplies.

It is able to remain fully foilborne for unlimited distances in moderate seas as long as there is adequate wind power.

Various modifications and improvements were made to the craft during 1974-75. These included the addition of streamlined fairings at the four main intersections of the lifting surfaces and struts on the bow foil the installation of a retractable leeboard for improved windward performance in light airs, and the facing of various aluminium foil fittings with stainless steel to prevent wear and tear around the shear/fastening bolts.

FOILS: The bow foil, of surface-piercing V configuration, is mounted between the pontoon bows and that of the main hull. Foils, supporting struts and sub-foil elements, are of welded aluminium, with a protective coating of vinyl. Foil section is NACA 16-510 with 152·4mm (6in) chord throughout the system. The foils have fairly high aspect ratio. Foil loading during a normal take-off is: bow foil 40%, stern foil 20% and leeward lateral foil 40%, depending on sail heeling forces. Dihedral of the bow foil is 30-50 degrees.

The lateral foils, which are not as deep as the bow and stern foils, are of four-rung ladder type, and have 35 degrees dihedral. The stern foil is of three-rung ladder configuration with zero dihedral at rest, but craft heel gives it 10-15 degrees dihedral. Under most conditions the rungs are fully submerged. The entire stern foil pivots for steering action. Shear bolts protect bow and stern foils from damage if debris is struck.

Foil retraction arrangements are as follows:

After the removal of shear bolts the bow foil swings forward and upwards through 90 degrees; the lateral foils swing outwards and over, and are laid flat on the deck through a second pivot axis, and the stern foil swings aft and over through 180 degrees. Retraction of the bow and lateral foils is achieved through the use of a simple block and tackle.

CONTROL: A tiller-operated, combined stern foil and rudder controls direction in foilborne mode; paired struts, also tiller operated, provide rudder control when hullborne.

HULL: Lightweight, but robust trimaran hull with small wing deck to avoid aerodynamic lift. Marine ply structure sheathed with glass fibre. Built-in attachment points for foils. Mast supported by main frame.

ACCOMMODATION: The craft is designed for two to three people, with cruising supplies, but has flown with nine aboard. The deep cockpit accommodates the helmsman and one crew member. The cockpit, which provides adequate shelter from the strong winds developed by high-speed sailing, forms the entrance to main and stern cabins. The main cabin seats four comfortably. There are two berths in the main cabin and one in the stern cabin. The main cabin also includes a galley, shelving and a marine head. There is generous stowage space in the pontoon hulls.

SAIL AND POWERPLANT: Sail power alone on prototype, but a small outboard auxiliary engine can be fitted if required. Total sail area is 35·3m² (380ft²).

SYSTEMS, ELECTRONICS: Radio direction finder normally carried.

DIMENSIONS

EXTERNAL

Length overall, hull: 9·54m (31ft 4in)
Length waterline, hull: 8·53m (28ft)
Length overall, foils retracted: 10·05m (33ft)
Length overall, foils extended: 9·75m (32ft)
Hull beam:
Main hull at water line: 0·91m (3ft)

Williwaw in Auckland harbour, with foils retracted

Outboard profile of the Pacific Express 35

Hull overall, foils retracted: 4·97m (16ft 4in)
Beam, overall, foils extended: 7·62m (25ft)
Draft afloat, foils retracted: 0·4m (1ft 4in)
Draft afloat, foils extended: 1·21m (4ft)
Draft foilborne: 0·45-0·76m (1ft 6in-2ft 6in)
Freeboard: 0·61m (2ft)
Pontoon deck: 475-762mm (1ft 6in-2ft 6in)
Main hull deck: 762mm-1·06m (2ft 6in-3ft 6in)
Height overall to masthead: 11·88m (39ft)

INTERNAL

Cabin (Wheelhouse, galley, toilet included):
length: 8·53m (28ft)
max width: 4·87m (16ft)
max height: 1·62m (5ft 4in)
volume: 13·78m³ (480ft³)

WEIGHTS

Light displacement: 997·88kg (2,200lb)
Normal take-off displacement: 1,360kg (3,000lb)
Max take-off displacement: 1,632kg (3,600lb)
Normal payload: 362·8kg (800lb)
Max payload: 635kg (1,400lb)

PERFORMANCE (in steady wind and calm water, with normal payload)

Take-off speed: normally 12 knots. Craft is able to take-off with a 12-knot beam wind and accelerate to 18-20 knots
Max speed foilborne: 30 knots
Cruising speed foilborne: 12-25 knots
Max permissible sea state and wave height in foilborne mode: sea state almost unlimited at 12 knot average speed with wind aft of beam. Foils well behaved in all conditions met so far. Sails reefed down in heavy conditions to maintain comfort and ease of handling. Craft shows no tendency to pound.
Turning radius at cruising speed: 45·72m (150ft)
Number of seconds and distance to take-off: 5 seconds in strong wind, two boat lengths
Number of seconds to stop craft: 8 seconds, turning dead into wind
SEA TESTS: Craft operated in strong winds and breaking seas including steep 15-20ft seas in Pacific en route to New Zealand and one freak wave 35-40ft high with 45-50 degree slope. It has completed a return voyage from the California coast to Hawaii, and a second Pacific voyage from California to New Zealand and back to Hawaii. By the end of August 1976, the craft had covered 19,000 miles.

Speed is significantly more than wind speed in conditions of steady wind and calm water. The craft can match wind speed in moderate seas, but not in heavy seas. In heavy seas, broad reaching or beam, it has averaged 15 knots for hours at a time, winds gusting to Force 5 and 6. Speeds may climb to 30 knots or drop to 5 knots, depending upon local wind and waves. Acceleration and decelerations are gradual and not objectionable. The ride is far smoother than that of displacement multihulls.

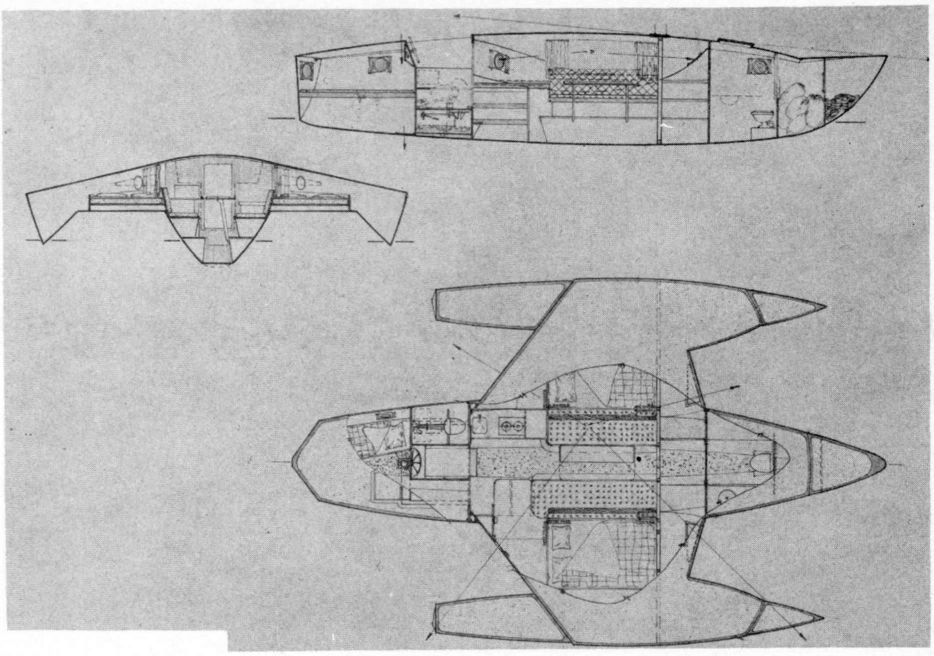

Inboard profile and deck plan of the Pacific Express 35 hydrofoil racing/cruising Trimaran

PACIFIC EXPRESS 35

Successor to Williwaw, the Pacific Express is a second generation hydrofoil cruising trimaran. It is designed to be sailed solo when necessary, and avoid many of the problems inherent in conventional trimarans—pounding, broaching, tunnel interference, quick motion, pitchpoling, poor control and poor self-steering in heavy seas.

The craft is wider than its predecessor, has fully buoyant float hulls, is equipped with a more efficient hydrofoil system and has a slightly greater load-carrying capacity.

It is designed to operate in a wide variety of conditions, from heavy storm seas to light airs. In heavy seas, with foils set, it is exceptionally stable and capable of high speeds.

The length, 10·66m (35ft), is the shortest in which it is convenient to have full standing headroom as well as a flush deck. Through its proportionately wider hulls, it should be able to exceed true wind speed more substantially than Williwaw and be able to fly fully foilborne at about 50 degrees from the true wind. The boat should be able to beat to windward with complete comfort for the crew.

In light airs and calms, with foils retracted, the craft makes the most of the available wind.

FOILS: Configuration similar to that of Williwaw. Foils have a 152mm (6in) chord and are fabricated in heavily anodised aluminium extrusions. Bolts, washers, etc, are in stainless steel. Bow and lateral foil are fixed while sailing. Tiller-operated combined stern foil and rudder controls craft direction when foilborne. All four foils retract manually after the removal of sheer bolts.

Hobie-16 Dak-foil conversion with foils retracted

HULL: Main hull bottom and topside, triple diagonal wood strips, remainder in plywood. All wood saturated with epoxy.
SAIL: Sail area as a cutter 650ft². Sloop working sail area 485ft².
DIMENSIONS
Length, overall: 10·66m (35ft)
Length waterline, static: 9·65m (31ft 8in)
Beam, foils retracted: 6·7m (22ft)
Mast height: 12·19m (40ft)
Draft, foils retracted: 457mm (1ft 6in)
Draft (static) foils extended: 1·52m (5ft)
Outboard projection of lateral foils: 1·21m (4ft)
WEIGHTS
Normal loaded displacement: 1,814kg (4,000lb)
PERFORMANCE
Top speed, strong wind, flat water: 45 knots
Normal foilborne speed range: 13-30 knots
Speed to become fully foilborne: 13 knots
Speed to become half foilborne: 9 knots
Wind required to become fully foilborne, in flat water: 11-12 knots
in average seas: 12-15 knots
Average hull clearance at high speed: 0·6m (2ft)
Max sea state for foilborne operation: unlimited
In heavy seas, sails are reefed in order to obtain a good balance between speed, comfort and safety.

DONALD NIGG

7924 Fontana, Prairie Village, Kansas 66208, USA
Telephone: (913) 642 2002

Development of the Flying Fish began in 1963 at Lake Quivira, an inland lake in Kansas. Donald Nigg believed that if the pitchpole moment and vertical stability problems could be solved, the front-steering three-point suspension system typical of the modern ice-yacht offered several advantages. Previous craft had often used three-point suspension, but all appear to have used rear steering. To develop this new approach, Exocoetus, an experimental platform was built. It was evolved through three distinct versions during 1964-67 and established the basic feasibility.

Interest in the experiments resulted in numerous requests for plans, but although the craft was ideal as a development platform, it was not a design suitable for home construction. In response to these requests the Flying Fish was developed.

To keep the costs to a minimum, the craft is designed to carry a sail area of 100-150ft². It was anticipated that most of those interested in building a sailing hydrofoil would be small boat sailors, owning a boat carrying a mainsail of this size. The design thus allows the builder to share the sail and rigging with an existing dinghy.

A true development class of sailing hydrofoil has been slow to emerge, but the Flying Fish may mark the beginning of such a class. The Amateur Yacht Research Society, Hermitage, Newbury, Berkshire, England, is promoting the design as a development class.

Sets of plans for the Flying Fish have been supplied to potential builders in many countries, including Brazil, Canada, Greece, Australia, the USA and the United Kingdom.

FLYING FISH

First of a development class of sailing hydrofoils, the Flying Fish has been specially developed for home builders. Built mainly in wood and with a length overall of 5·02m (16ft 6in), it has a maximum foilborne speed of more than 30 knots.

The estimated cost of constructing a craft of this type, less sail and rigging (the 125ft² mainsail and rigging from a Y-Flyer were used for the prototype illustrated), is US$250.

FOILS: The foil configuration is surface piercing and non-retractable with 16% of the weight supported by the V bow foil and the remaining 84% by the outrigged main foils. The latter are also of the V type, with cantilevered extensions at the apex. Total foil area is 1·42m² (15·3ft²) and the foil loading is 300lb/ft² max at 30 knots. The front foil and its supporting strut are built in aluminium and oak, and the main foil is in oak only.

STEERING: A basic feature of the design is the use of front rather than rear steering. Directional control is provided by the movement of the hinged bow foil.

HULL: This is an all-wooden structure built in fir plywood, ¼in thick and sealed. Torque load is carried by the skin, and bending loads are carried by the skin and the internal beam structure.

The crossbeam provides stability when in dock and in a displacement condition at low speeds. At 2-3 knots the horizontal safety foils at the top of the V of the rear foils provide interim foil stabilisation up to the take-off speed of 5 knots and prevent dragging an end of the crossbeam in the water. At foilborne speeds the safety foils preclude the possibility of an end of the crossbeam being driven into the water by sudden heeling.

RIG: A cat rig of 9·2-13·9m² (100-150ft²) area is recommended.

DIMENSIONS

Length overall, hull (plus boom overhand at rear, dependent on sail plan): 5·02m (16ft 6in)
Length waterline, hull: 4·87m (16ft)
Beam: 6·09m (20ft)
Draft afloat (fixed foils): 1·06m (3ft 6in)
Draft foilborne: 12-30in over operating speed range
Height, approx: 7·3m (24ft)

PERFORMANCE

Max speed foilborne: over 30 knots
design cruise range: optimised for 20-30 knots
Max speed hullborne: 5 knots
Minimum wind for take-off: 10 knots
Number of seconds and distance to take-off (theoretically approx): 3s with 15·2m (50ft) run in favourable wind
Number of seconds and distance to stop craft (theoretically approx): can land from 20 knots in 45·6m (150ft) in about 6 seconds

SEA TEST: The craft has been tested in 10-25 knot winds, on both sheltered inland lakes and on ocean bays, with a maximum chop of about 18in. Speeds up to approximately 30 knots have been attained.

Topping 20 knots on a close reach in a light wind

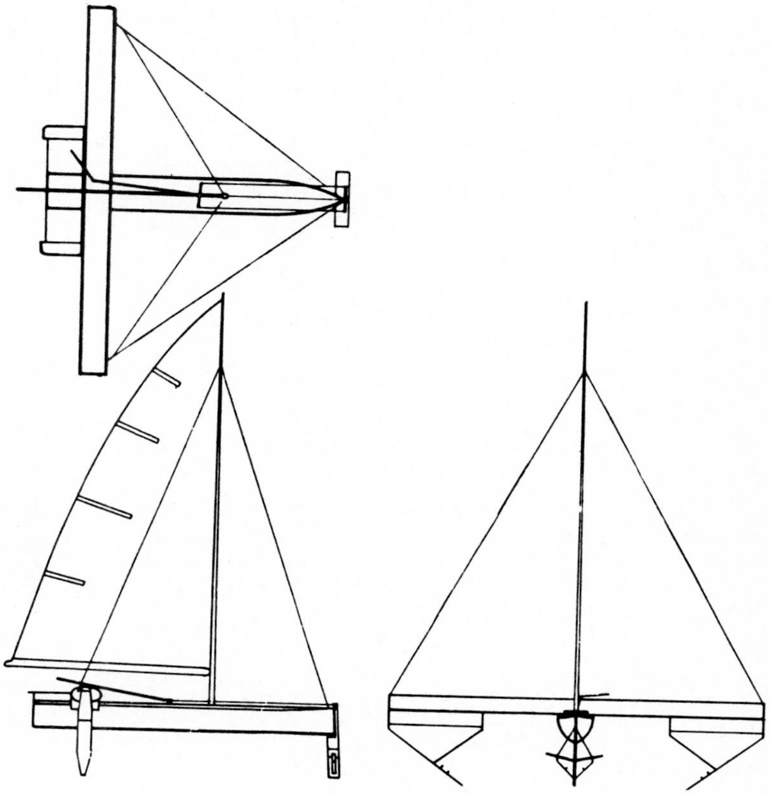

The Nigg Flying Fish

HYDROFOIL OPERATORS

ALBANIA
ALBANIAN NAVY

Type(s): Hu Chwan (White Swan) Class, 30 (Shanghai)
Operating areas: Coastal waters

ARGENTINA
ALIMAR SanciyF

Avda Cordoba 1801 (Esq Callao), Codigo Postal 1120, Buenos Aires, Argentina
Telephone: 42-4498
Telex: 121510 Almar
Type(s): PT 50, 3 (Rodriquez)
Route: Buenos Aires-Colonia-Montevideo

AUSTRALIA
PUBLIC TRANSPORT COMMISSION OF NEW SOUTH WALES

Head Office: Ferry Division, No 2 Jetty, Circular Quay, Sydney, New South Wales 2000, Australia
Telephone: 27 9251
Telex: NSWTC AA25702
Terminal Offices: No 2 Jetty, Circular Quay
Telephone: 27 9251
Manly Wharf, Manly. Telephone: 97 3028
Officials:
T F Gibson, *General Manager*
W Heading, *Superintendent Engineer*

OPERATIONS: Routes served and frequency. Sydney to Manly, 7 miles, every 20 minutes between 7am and 7pm

Approximate number of passengers carried during year: 1·5 million.

CRAFT OPERATED
PT 50 (Rodriquez) "Fairlight", 140 passengers, built 1966
PT 50 (Rodriquez) "Long Reef", ex "Freccia di Mergellina", 140 passengers, built 1968
PT 50 (Rodriquez) "Palm Beach", ex "Patane", 140 passengers, built 1969
PT 50 (Rodriquez) "Dee Why", 140 passengers, built 1970
RHS 140 (Navaltecnica) "Curl Curl", 140 passengers, built 1972

TIRES PTY LTD TD

Corner Junction Road and Gray Terrace, Rosewater, Outer Harbour, South Australia, Australia
Type(s): Aquavion Waterman, 1.
Route(s): Port Adelaide to Outer Harbour. Hourly service. Also educational and scenic tours of Port River, Adelaide.

AUSTRIA
SCHIFFSWERFT KORNEUBURG

Korneuburg, Austria
Type(s): Raketa, 1 (Sormovo)
Route(s): Danube

BAHAMAS
BAHAMAS HYDROFOIL CRUISES, INC

903 South American Way, Port of Miami, Florida 33132, USA
Type(s): PT 150, 3 (Westermoen)
Route(s): Miami—Nassau; Miami—Freeport; Freeport—Nassau.

BOLIVIA
CRILLON TOURS LTD

PO Box 4785, Av Comacho 1223 Ed, Krsul, La Paz, Bolivia
Telephone: 50363/40102/20222
Telex: BX 5296
Cables: Critur
Officials:
Darius Morgan, *General Manager*
Helmut Kock, *Hydrofoil Designer and Consultant*
Type(s): Albatross (Honold) 4, modified by Helmut Kock; Bolivia Arrow (Kock-Crillon Tours) 1; Seaflight H-57, 1.
Route(s): Lake Titicaca

BRAZIL
AEROBARCOS DO BRASIL, Transtur

Transportes Maritimos e Turismo SA, Transtur, Avenida Amaral Peixoto, 71 Conj 1009, Niteroi—R-J, Brazil
Telephone: 722-5546
Telex: 217171 JTMH BR
Type(s): PT 20, 3 (Rodriquez); RHS 110, 1 (Navaltecnica)

BULGARIA
KORABOIMPEX

128 D Blagoev Blvd, Varna, Bulgaria
Type(s): Kometa, 11; Raketa, 1; Meteor, 4 (Sormovo)
Route(s): Bourgas-Nesetow-Varna; Danube, between Rousse and Silistra

CHINA (PEOPLE'S REPUBLIC)
NAVY OF THE CHINESE PEOPLE'S REPUBLIC

Type(s): Hu Chwan Class, 60 plus (Shanghai)
Operational areas: Coastal waters

CUBA
MAR-PORT

Calle 21 y O, Vedado, Havana, Cuba
Type(s): Kometa M, 5 (Sormovo)
Route(s): Batabano—Nueva Gerona

CYPRUS
WONDER SHIPPING LTD

Head Office: c/o Hanseatic Ship Management/Jeropoulov & Co, Limassol, Cyprus
Type(s): PT 50, 1 (Rodriquez)
Route(s): Larnaca-Lebanon-Syria

Boeing Jetfoil 0011 "Mikado", first of the 929-115 models, undergoing tests on Puget Sound accompanied by Jetfoil 0010 "Flying Princess II" during a seven week demonstration for the Washington State Ferry Systems. Sado Kisen Kaisha, Niigata, Japan, currently operates one Jetfoil from Niigata to Ryotsu on Sado Island. "Mikado" will operate over the same route, starting in May 1979. By August 1978 Jetfoils in service had logged 178,389,734 passenger miles during 41,873 underway hours

DENMARK

A/S DAMPSKIPSSELSKAPET ORESUND

Havnegade 49, DK-1058 Copenhagen, Denmark
Telephone: 01 14 77 70, 01 12 80 88
Telex: 45-27502 Sundet DK
Type(s): PT 50, 6 (5 Rodriquez, 1 Westermoen)
Route(s): Copenhagen-Malmö, Sweden

EGYPT

THE GENERAL NILE COMPANY FOR RIVER TRANSPORT

39 Kasr El-Nil Street, Cairo, Egypt
Telephone: 54517/18
Cables: Naknahri Cairo
Type(s): PT 20, 3 (Rodriquez)
Route(s): Abu Simbel-Asswan

FINLAND

PAIJANTEEN KANTOSIIPI OY

Type(s): Raketa, 1 (Krasnoye Sormovo)
Route(s): Lahti-Jyvaskyla, across Lake Paijane

FRANCE

VEDETTES ARMORICAINES

Ier Eperon, 56 rue d'Aiguillon, 29N Brest, France
Type(s): Kometa, 1 (Sormovo)

GERMANY, DEMOCRATIC REPUBLIC

SCHIFFACOMMERS

Doberaner Str 44-47, Rostock 1, German Democratic Republic
Type(s): Kometa, 3 (Sormovo)

GERMANY, FEDERAL REPUBLIC

WATER POLICE

Type(s): PT 4, 3 (German shipyard)
Route(s): Patrol service on the Rhine

KÖLN DÜSSELDORFER SHIPPING CO

Frankenwerft 25, D-5000 Cologne 1, Federal Republic of Germany
Type(s): Raketa, 1 "Rhine Arrow" (Sormovo)
Route(s): Cologne—Koblenz

GREECE

CERES HELLENIC SHIPPING ENTERPRISES LTD

Akti Miaouli 69, Piraeus, Greece
Companies: Ceres Flying Hydroways Ltd, Ceres Hydrofoils Limited and Ceres Express Ltd.
Type(s): Kometa-M, 9 plus 6 (Sormovo)
Route(s): Piraeus to islands in the Cyclades group.

SOLAM HELLAS

Piraeus, Greece
Type(s): Kometas (Sormovo)
Route(s): Piraeus to Hydra, Spetiai, Syros, Paros, Antiparos, Amagos, Asypalea, Nissyros, Symi and Rhodes.

HONG KONG

HONG KONG MACAO HYDROFOIL CO

Han Seng Bank Building, 77 de Voeux Road Central, Hong Kong
Type(s): PT 50, 4 (Rodriquez); RHS 140, 5 (Navaltecnica)

FAR EAST HYDROFOIL CO LTD

36th Floor, Connaught Centre, Connaught Road, Hong Kong
Telephone: H-243176
Telex: 74200
Officials:
Stanley Ho, *Managing Director*
K B Allport, *Group Manager*
D Hay, *Technical Manager*
Type(s): PT 50, 4, Guia, Penha, Taipa, Balsa (Hitachi Zosen);
RHS 110, 4, Cerco, Praia, Barca, Cacilhas (Navaltecnica);
RHS 160, 1, Lilau (Navaltecnica);
PTS 75 Mk III, 2, Rosa (Vosper Thornycroft), Patane (Supramar Pacific Shipbuilding Co Ltd);
Jetfoils, 5, Madeira, Santa Maria, Flores, Corvo and Pico (Boeing).
Route(s): Hong Kong-Macao, distance 36n miles by the Southern Route. Services half-hourly, sunrise to sunset, ie 15,400 trips per annum. Approximate total number of passengers carried per year, 1,450,000.

HUNGARY

MAHART MAGYAR HAJÓZASIRT

Apáczai Csere Yános utca 11, H-1052 Budapest V, Hungary
Type(s): Raketa; Meteor, 1; Voskhod (Krasnoye-Sormovo)
Route(s): Budapest-Vienna

INDONESIA

SUNDAHARYA CORP, JAKARTA

Type(s): PT 20 (Rodriquez)
Route(s): Indonesian coast

IRAN

MINISTRY OF DEFENCE

Type(s): Kometa, 2 (Sormovo)
Operating area: Persian Gulf

IRELAND

B & I LINES

Dublin, Ireland
Type(s): Jetfoil 929-115, 1 (Boeing)
Route(s): Dublin-Liverpool

ISRAEL

ISRAEL NAVY

Type(s): Flagstaff, 4 (Grumman)
Duties: Coastal patrol, convoy escort
A licence for the series production of these craft in Israel is being negotiated. Once her own needs have been met, Israeli-built craft would be made available for export.

ITALY

ITALIAN NAVY

Type(s): Sparviero Class, 1 plus 6 on order (Alinavi)
Route(s): Coastal patrol.

ALISCAFI SNAV, SpA

Cortina del Porto, IS XI, 98100 Messina, Italy
Type(s): PT 20, 7; PT 50, 8 (Rodriquez)
Route(s): Messina-Reggio-Isole-Lipari and Naples-Capri-Ischia.

ACHILLE ONORATO

Via A De Gasperi 55, 80133 Naples, Italy
Type(s): PT 50, 2 (Westermoen); PT 20, 1 (Rodriquez); Kometa and Kometa M,20 (Sormovo).
Route(s): Naples Bay, Naples-Capri, Naples-Capri-Ischia

SAS, TRAPANI

Via Evrialo 9, 91100 Trapani, Italy
Type(s): PT 50, 1; PT 20, 3 (Rodriquez)
Route(s): Trapani-Egadi Islands

ADRIATICA DI NAVIGAZIONE SpA

Zattere 1411, 30123 Venice, Italy.
Telephone: 704322
Telex: 41045 Adrianav
Type(s): PT 50, 1 (Rodriquez); RHS 160, 1 (Navaltecnica)
Route(s): Termoli-Isole Tremiti; Ortona-Vasto-Isole Tremiti

MINISTRY OF TRANSPORT, MILAN

Via L Ariosto 21, 20145 Milan, Italy
Type(s): PT 20, 2 (Rodriquez); RHS 70, 1 (Navaltecnica); RHS 150, 1 (Navaltecnica)
Route(s): Lake Garda

COMPAGNIA DI NAVIGAZIONE

Viale F Baracca 1, 23041 Arona, Italy
Type(s): PT 20, 2 (Rodriquez); RHS 70, 2 (Navaltecnica)
Route(s): Lake Maggiore

COMPAGNIA DI NAVIGAZIONE

Piazza Volta No 44, 22100 Como, Italy
Type(s): PT 20, 2 (Rodriquez); RHS 70, 2 (Navaltecnica)
Route(s): Lake Como

G & R SALVATORI, NAPLES

Type(s): PT 50, 2 (Westermoen)
Route(s): Naples-Capri

CAREMAR COMPAGNIA REGIONALE MARITIMA SpA

Molo Beverello 2, Naples, Italy
Type(s): RHS 140, 1; RHS 160, 2 (Navaltecnica)

SIREMAR SICILIA REGIONALE MARITIMA SpA

Via Crispi 120, Palermo, Sicily
Telephone: 240801/211916
Telex: 91135 Siremar
Type(s): RHS 160, 2 (Navaltecnica)
Route(s): Palermo—Ustica

TOREMAR TOSCANA REGIONALE MARITIMA SpA

Scali del Corso 5, Livorno, Italy
Type(s): RHS 140, 1 (Navaltecnica)

AGIP SpA

S Donato Milanese, Milan, Italy
Telephone: 53531
Telex: 31246 ENI
Type(s): PT 20, 1; PT 50, 1 (Rodriquez)

JAPAN

BOYO KISEN CO LTD

Type(s): PT 50, 1 (Hitachi); PT 20, 1 "Shibuki No 2" (Hitachi)
Route(s): Yanai—Matsuyama

ISIZAKI KISEN CO LTD

Fukae, Ohaki-cho, Saeki-gun, Hiroshima-ken, Japan
Type(s): PT 50, 1 "Kosei" (Hitachi)
Route(s): Hiroshima-Kure-Matsuyama
Type(s): PT 50, 1 (Hitachi)
Route(s): Hiroshima-Kure-Matsuyama
Type(s): PT 20, 1 "Kinsei" (Hitachi)
Route(s): Onomichi-Matsuyama
Type(s): PT 20, 1 "Tsobasamaru" (Hitachi)
Route(s): Hiroshima-Kure-Matsuyama
An additional PT 50 was delivered to the company during 1977.

MAYEKAWA TRADING CO LTD

3-22-1 Aobadai, Meguru-ku, Tokyo, Japan
Type(s): Kometa, 1 (Sormovo)

MEITETSU KAIJO KANKOSEN CO

99-1 Shin-miyazaka-cho, Atsuta-ku, Nagoya, Japan
Type(s): PT 50, 1 "Osyo" (Hitachi)
Route(s): Nagoya-Toba-Gamagori-Nishiura-Irako
Type(s): PT 20, 2 "Taihomaru" and "Hayabusamaru" (Hitachi)
Route(s): Nagoya-Toba-Irako-Gamagori-Shinojima and Kowa-Shinojima-Irako-Toba-Nishiura

NICHIMEN CO LTD (KINKOWAN FERRY CO LTD)

Type(s): PT 50, 1 "Otori No 3" (Hitachi)
Route(s): Kajiki-Kagoshima-Ibusuki

NISSHO-IWAI CO LTD (HANKYU LINES CO LTD)

Type(s): PT 50, 2 "Zuiho" and "Houo" (Hitachi)
Route(s): Koke-Tokushima

HANKYU LINES CO LTD

Type(s): PT 20, 2 "Amatsu" and "Kasugano" (Hitachi)
Route(s): Kobe-Naruto

HITACHI ZOSEN

Type(s): PT 20, 1; ST 3, 1 (Rodriquez)
Route(s): Japanese coast

SADO KISEN KAISHA

Niigata, Japan
Type(s): Jetfoil 929-100, 1; Jetfoil 929-115, 1 (Boeing)
Route(s): Niigata, Honshu Island and Ryotsu, Sado Island, Sea of Japan.
Route distance: 63km (34n miles)

SETONAIKAI KISEN CO LTD

Ujina Kaigani-chome, Hiroshima, Japan
Type(s): PT 50, 3 "Wakashio", "Otori No 1" and "Otori No 2" (Hitachi)
Route(s): Onomichi-Sètoda-Imabari and Hiroshima-Kure-Matsuyama
Type(s): PT 50, 1 "Kondoru" (Hitachi)
Route(s): Hiroshima-Kure-Matsuyama
Type(s): PT 50, 1 (Hitachi)
Route(s): Onomichi-Setoda-Imbari
Type(s): PT 50, 4 "Hibiki No 1", "No 2" and "No 3" and "Shibuki No 1" (Hitachi)
Route(s): Onomichi-Setoda-Omishima-Imbari and ("Shibuki No 1") Yanai-Matsuyama

KOREA (REPUBLIC OF)

HAN RYEO DEVELOPMENT CO LTD

25-5 1-Ka, Chungmu-Ro, Chung-ku, Seoul, Republic of Korea
Telephone: 23-8532/28-7145
Telex: Keico K27273
Type(s): PT 20, 1 (Rodriquez)

MOROCCO

CIE MARITIME D'HYDROFOILS "TRANSTOUR"

Tangier, Morocco
Type(s): Kometa, 3 (Sormovo)
Route(s): Tangier-Algeciras, Tangier-Marbella

NEW ZEALAND

KERRIDGE ODEON CORPORATION

Type(s): PT 20, 1 (Rodriquez)
Route(s): Auckland-Waiheke Island

NORWAY

DE BLA OMNIBUSSER A/S

Type(s): PT 20, 2 (Westermoen)
Route(s): Oslofjord

DET STAVANGERSKE DAMPSKIBS-SELSKAB

PO Box 40, N-4001 Stavanger, Norway
Telephone: 200 20
Telex: 33022 DSDP N
Type(s): PT 50, 1; PT 20, 1 (Rodriquez); RHS 140, 1 (Navaltecnica)
Route(s): Stavanger-Haugesund-Bergen

HARDANGER SUNNHORDELANDSKE DAMPSKIBSSELSKAB

Box 268, N-5001 Bergen, Norway
Telephone: 215070
Telex: 42607 HSD N
Type(s): PT 20, 1 (Westermoen); RHS 140, 1 (Navaltecnica)
Route(s): Bergen-Tittelsness

PAKISTAN

PAKISTAN NAVY

Type(s): Hu Chwan, 6 (Shanghai)
Duties: Coastal patrol and strike missions

PHILIPPINES

BATAAN MANILA FERRY SERVICES

Manila, Philippines
Type(s): Raketa TA, 1 (Sormovo/Airavia)

TOURIST HOTEL AND TRAVEL CORPORATION

Type(s): PT 20, 2 (Rodriquez)
Route(s): Manila-Corregidor

PHILIPPINE NAVY

Headquarters, Roxas Boulevard, Manila, Philippines
Type(s): PT 20, 2 (Rodriquez); PT 32, 2 "Bontoc", "Baler" (Hitachi)
Route(s): Coastal patrol

POLAND

NAVIMOR

Ul Matejkl 6, Gdansk, Poland
Type(s): Kometas, 10; Meteors, 4; Raketas, 3
Route(s): Szczecin-Swinoujscie; Szczecin-Stralsund, Copenhagen, Malmö and Strassuitz, also Kolobrzez and Stralsund

ROMANIA

INDUSTRIALEXPORT

Bucharest, Romania
Type(s): Kometa 2; Raketa, 6 (Sormovo)

ROMANIAN NAVY

Type(s): Hu Chwan, 10
Operating area: Coastal waters

SRI LANKA

SRI LANKAN NAVY

Type(s): Waterman, 1 (International Aquavion)
Duties: Communications and patrol

SWEDEN

SVENSKA REDERIAKTIEBOLAGET ORESUND

PO Box 177, S-20121 Malmö 1, Sweden
Telex: 32632 SROMT 5
Type(s): PT 50, 2 (Rodriquez); RHS 140, 1 (Navaltecnica)
Route(s): Copenhagen-Malmö

TANZANIA

TANZANIA NAVY

Dar es Salaam, Tanzania
Type(s): Hu Chwan, 4 (Shanghai)
Duties: Coastal patrol

TURKEY

SEJIR DENIZYOLLARI LTD

34-A Canbulat, Sokak, Girne, Mersin 10, Turkey
Type(s): PT 20, 1; PT 50, 1 (Rodriquez)
Route(s): Turkey-Cyprus

MED SHIPPING

Type(s): Kometa-M, 2 (Sormovo)
Route(s): Turkey-Cyprus

UNION OF SOVIET SOCIALIST REPUBLICS

MINISTRY OF THE RIVER FLEET

The Soviet Ministry of the River Fleet operates hydrofoil passenger ferries on practically all the major rivers, lakes, canals and reservoirs from Central Russia to Siberia and the Far East.

In 1958, when hydrofoils were first introduced to the rivers of the USSR, they carried ten thousand passengers. By 1968 the number of passengers carried had grown to three million. During the 1969-70 navigation season there were 80 hydrofoil services on the Volga alone, operated by vessels of the Raketa, Meteor, Sputnik and Burevestnik series. There are now more than 150 hydrofoil passenger services in the Soviet Union and it was stated that during 1972 the 200 craft operating these services carried about 20 million passengers.

In addition to craft on inland waterways employing the Alexeyev shallow draft submerged foil system, Strela-type craft, with surface-piercing foils, operate in the Gulf of Finland, and supported by Kometas and Vikhrs, provide year-round services between ports on the Black Sea.

Four new hydrofoil passenger ferry designs are being put into production—the Cyclone, a seagoing, waterjet-propelled ferry with seats for 250 and capable of 40 knots, the Typhoon, a gas-turbine powered 90-seat vessel with fully submerged, autostabilised foils, the Voskhod (Sunrise), a Raketa replacement and the Albatros. The Voskhod provides greater comfort and improved facilities for passengers and crew and air-conditioning will be installed. As with the Raketa, a family of variants will be available to suit a wide variety of operating and traffic conditions. Fastest of the series is reported to be the Voskhod-3, powered by a gas-turbine and capable of 43 knots.

The Albatros has the same overall dimensions as the Kometa, but its engines will be mounted aft, its foils will be controlled by an automatic control system and the standard version will seat 150 passengers.

The Raketa has given excellent service and has extremely low operating costs. The cost of carrying passengers on the craft is stated to be lower than that of either displacement-type passenger ferries or automobiles. Similar low-cost operation is demonstrated by the 260-passenger Sputnik on the Moscow-Astrakhan route. It has been found that the cost of operating a Sputnik on this service is only 8% of that of the latest displacement-type passenger ferry of the United Volga Steamship Line. Time saving is one of the most important considerations. In many cases, hydrofoils take passengers to their destinations faster than trains. For example, a Raketa service covers the 800km (516 miles) from Gorky to Kazan in 12 hours, while trains take 20 hours for the same journey. Price of the ticket is the same, however, whether the journey is undertaken by hydrofoil or rail.

The Meteor service from Moscow to Sormovo takes 13 hours 40 minutes to cover 900km (559

"Curl Curl" an RHS 140 operated by the Ferry Division of the Public Transport Commission of New South Wales, Australia, on the route Sydney to Manly. Four PT 50s and the RHS 140 carry a total of 1·5 million passengers between them annually

miles). A conventional passenger ship requires about three days to cover this distance.

In 1976 sea trials confirmed that the Kometa can operate successfully in Arctic waters. Tests conducted off the Kola Peninsula and Kamchatka, in the Soviet Far East, demonstrated that the craft is capable of navigating through areas with broken ice without sustaining damage.

A number of Russian commercial hydrofoils are now being equipped for night operations.

In 1977 it was announced that the number of hydrofoils operating on Soviet waterways exceeded 3,000. Nearly two-thirds of these are likely to be Molnia and Volga hydrofoils which are used throughout the Soviet Union as water taxis.

SOVIET FRONTIER POLICE

Some twenty-five Pchela patrol hydrofoils, derived from the Strela passenger ferry, are in service with the KGB Frontier Police in the Baltic, Caspian and the Black Sea areas.

SOVIET NAVY

First hydrofoil warship to enter service with the Soviet Navy was the wooden-hulled P 8-class torpedo boat, which was equipped with bow foils and a gas-turbine booster engine. These have now been retired. In the spring of 1973, the first sightings were made of a larger craft, a 190-ton fast patrol boat given the NATO code-name Turya. This vessel, which is equipped for ASW work, is based on the hull of the Osa missile craft. The design employs a fixed surface-piercing bow foil only. Powered by three 4,330hp diesels it has a top speed of about 45 knots under calm conditions. Production is in hand at three Soviet naval shipyards.

Latest hydrofoils to be built for the Soviet Navy are the Sarancha, a 330-350 tonne missile-armed fast strike craft and the Babochka, a 400-tonne fast patrol boat equipped for anti-submarine warfare. Babochka is the world's biggest and most powerful hydrofoil warship.

Bolivia Arrow, designed by Helmut Kock, and operated by Crillon Tours on Lake Titicaca, Bolivia

Diomedea, a Navaltecnica RHS 160 operated by Adriatica di Navigazione SpA

UNITED KINGDOM
CHANNEL ISLANDS
CONDOR LTD

4 North Quay, St Peter Port, Guernsey
Telephone: 0481 24604
Telex: 41275 (a/b Dilig G)
Type(s): PT 50, 1 (Rodriquez); RHS 140, 2 (Navaltecnica); RHS 160 (Navaltecnica)
Route(s): Guernsey-Jersey-St Malo

P & O
JET FERRIES

World Trade Centre, East Smithfield, London E1 9AA, England
Telephone: 01-481 4033
Officials:
Ian Churcher, *Chairman*
Type(s): Jetfoil 929-115, 2 (Boeing). 259 seats each.
Route(s): Hays Wharf, London Bridge—Ostend

JETLINK FERRIES LTD (SEAJET)

18 Westminster Palace Gardens, Artillery Row, London SW1P 1RL, England
Telephone: 01 222 6464/67
Officials:
Leslie Colquhoun, *Operations Director*
Roy Veysey, *Marketing and Sales*
Type(s): Jetfoil 929-115, 1 (Boeing). Option on Jetfoil 929-115 015.
Route(s): Brighton Marina-Dieppe. Three return crossings per day, beginning 27 April 1979.

RED FUNNEL STEAMERS LTD.

12 Bugle Street, Southampton, Hampshire SO9 4LJ, England
Telephone: 0703 22042
Telex: 47388 Chamcom G (Attn Red Funnel)
Type(s): RHS 70, 2 (Navaltecnica)
Route(s): Southampton-Cowes

ROYAL NAVY

The first Jetfoil patrol hydrofoil has been ordered by the Royal Navy for use in the fisheries protection role in the North Sea. Basically the craft is a modified Model 929-115 commercial Jetfoil, designated Patrol Hydrofoil 0001, PH01, and will be built on the commercial Jetfoil production line. It is a 117-ton craft with the top passenger deck removed. Two semi-inflatable dinghies will be carried together with light weapons. Launching is scheduled to take place in July 1979 with delivery in October 1979.

UNITED STATES OF AMERICA
DEPARTMENT OF THE NAVY, NAVAL SEA SYSTEMS COMMAND (NAVSEA)

The Boeing/NATO PHM, Patrol Hydrofoil, Guided Missile, is a NATO project, sponsored by the US Navy. It is being developed by NAVSEA PMS 303.

The first craft, the PHM-1 Pegasus, was accepted by the US Navy's Board of Inspection and Survey in June 1977. A further five PHMs are scheduled for delivery to the US Navy over the thirteen month period between January 1981 and February 1982. On delivery to the US Navy they will be employed as a squadron with the US Sixth Fleet in the Mediterranean.

SEA WORLD

1720 South Shores Road, Mission Bay, San Diego, California 92109, USA
Telephone: (714) 222 6363
This company operates three 28-seat hydrofoils, Sea World II, III and IV (Sprague Engineering Co) on seven minute sightseeing tours around Mission Bay. The craft were the first built on the West Coast to be licensed by the US Coast Guard for commercial use.

US COAST GUARD

Coast Guard District 1, New England
Type(s): WPGH-1 Flagstaff (Grumman).
Craft transferred permanently to US Coast Guard from US Navy and recommissioned as a USCG cutter.
Duties: Coast guard missions and augmentation of fisheries patrol.

US NAVAL SHIP RESEARCH AND DEVELOPMENT CENTER

Type(s): High Point, PCH-1; Plainview AGEH-1
Purpose: US Navy hydrofoil development programme

VENEZUELA
COMPANIA SHELL

Type(s): PT 20, 3 (Werf Gusto)
Route(s): Offshore oil drilling operations on Lake Maracaibo

TOURISMO MARGARITA, CA

Type(s): Jetfoil, 2 (Boeing)
Route: Puerto La Cruz-Isle of Margarita

YUGOSLAVIA
SPLIT AIRPORT/INTEREXPORT

Split, Yugoslavia
Type(s): Kometa, 11 (Sormovo)
Route(s): Adriatic coastal services; tourist and passenger ferry services between Italy and Yugoslavia

CENTROTOURIST

Beograd, Yugoslavia
Type(s): Raketa, 2 (Sormovo)
Route(s): Adriatic coastal services

RUDNAP

Beograd, Yugoslavia
Type(s): Meteor, 4 (Sormovo)
Route(s): Adriatic coastal services

ZAIRE
NAVAL FORCE

Bases: Matadi and Lake Tanganyika
Type(s): Hu Chwan, 3 (Shanghai)

POWER PLANTS AND PROPULSION SYSTEMS

CANADA

PRATT & WHITNEY AIRCRAFT OF CANADA LTD

PO Box 10, Longueuil, Quebec, Canada

Officials:

D C Lowe, *President*

R H Guthrie, *Vice President, Industrial and Marine Division*

E L Smith, *Vice President, Operations*

K H Sullivan, *Vice President, Marketing*

E H Schweitzer, *Vice President, Product Support*

L D Caplan, *Vice President, Finance and Administration*

J P Beauregard, *Vice President, Materials and Procurement*

R G Raven, *Vice President, Helicopter and Systems Division*

A L Tontini, *Vice President, Personnel*

V W Tryon, *Vice President*

E A Clifford, *Engineering Manager, Industrial and Marine Division*

P Henry, *Director of Communications*

In addition to its compact range of low-power aircraft turbines (eg the PT6A turboprop, PT6B, PT6T and T400 turboshafts, and JT15D turbofan), Pratt & Whitney Aircraft of Canada Ltd also manufactures a marine derivative of the PT6, the ST6 series of turboshafts. These engines are rated at 550shp and upwards, and are installed in a number of ACV and hydrofoil vessels. The US prototype Surface Effect Ship SES-100B is equipped with three ST6J-70s to power its eight lift fans, and two ST-60 series engines power the Canadian research hydrofoil Proteus. Two ST6T-75 Twin-Pac turbines power the Bell Aerospace Canada Voyageur hovercraft and a single ST6T-75 provides power in that company's Viking craft. A series of larger Voyageurs for the US Army designated LACV-30 are powered by ST6T-76 engines.

Including aero-engine installations, over 13,000 of this series of gas-turbines have been delivered. Between them they have accumulated running experience in excess of 25 million hours.

ST6 MARINE GAS-TURBINE

ST6 marine gas-turbines are designed and manufactured by Pratt & Whitney Aircraft of Canada Ltd. Details of the engine specifications are given below:

TYPE: A simple cycle free turbine engine with a single spool gas generator and a multi-stage compressor driven by a single stage turbine. Burner section has an annular combustion chamber with

ST6 gas-turbine

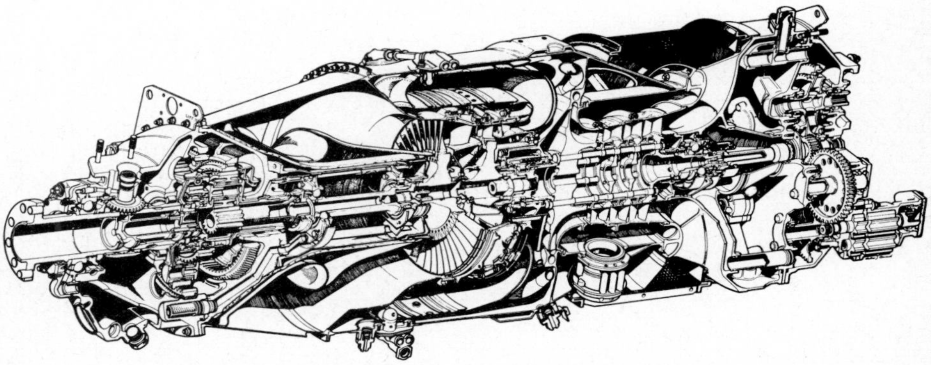

Cutaway of the ST6-70. The model illustrated, the ST6J-70, differs from the ST6K-70 only in the main reduction gearbox

ST6-J77 seen from above

ST6 ENGINE DATA SUMMARY

Sea Level Standard Pressure at 15°C (59°F) Inlet Temperature

IMPERIAL MEASURE

Model	*Maximum*		*Intermediate*		*Normal*		*Output*	*Length*	*Width*	*Height*	*Weight*
	SHP	*SFC**	*SHP*	*SFC**	*SHP*	*SFC**	*RPM (max)*	*(in)*	*(in)*	*(in)*	*(lb)*
ST6J-70	620	0·64	580	0·65	510	0·67	2,200	62	19	19	350
ST6K-70	620	0·64	580	0·65	510	0·67	6,230	60	19	19	317
ST6L-77	811	0·589			654	0·62	33,000	52·2	19	19	306
ST6J-77	750	0·608	650	0·631	550	0·66	2,200	62	19	19	379
ST6K-77	690	0·62	620	0·64	550	0·66	6,230	60	19	19	350
ST6L-80	1,065	0·58	955	0·60	840	0·62	30,000	59·4	19	19	360
*ST6T-75	1,700	0·62	1,500	0·63	1,300	0·65	6,600	66·4	44·4	31·6	730
*ST6T-76	1,850	0·615	1,645	0·627	1,440	0·65	6,600	66·4	44·4	31·6	730

METRIC MEASURE

Model	*Maximum*		*Intermediate*		*Normal*		*Output*	*Length*	*Width*	*Height*	*Weight*
	kW	*SFC**	*kW*	*SFC**	*kW*	*SFC**	*RPM (max)*	*(mm)*	*(mm)*	*(mm)*	*(kg)*
ST6J-70	463	0·389	433	0·395	380	0·407	2,200	1,575	483	483	159
ST6K-70	463	0·389	433	0·395	380	0·407	6,230	1,524	483	483	144
ST6L-77	605	0·358			488	0·377	33,000	1,326	483	483	139
ST6J-77	560	0·371	485	0·384	410	0·401	2,200	1,575	483	483	172
ST6K-77	515	0·377	463	0·389	410	0·401	6,230	1,524	483	483	159
ST6L-80	794	0·353	712	0·365	627	0·377	30,000	1,509	483	483	164
*ST6T-75	1,268	0·377	1,119	0·383	970	0·395	6,600	1,687	1,128	803	332
*ST6T-76	1,380	00·374	1,227	0·381	1,074	0·395	6,600	1,687	1,128	803	332

*SFC = lb/hp/h (imperial)
= kg/kWh (metric)

downstream injection. The single stage-free turbine is connected to the output shaft via a reduction gearbox.

The ST6T-75 and ST6T-76 Twin Pac TM are dual engines with the two engines mounted side-by-side and coupled to a twinning reduction gear.

AIR INTAKE: Annular air intake at rear of engine with intake screen.

COMPRESSOR: Three axial-flow stages, plus single centrifugal stage. Single-sided centrifugal compressor with 26 vanes, made from titanium forging. Axial rotor of disc-drum type with stainless steel stator and rotor blades. Stator vanes are brazed to casing. The rotor blades are dove tailed to discs. Discs through-bolted with centrifugal compressor to shaft. Fabricated one-piece stainless steel casing and radial diffuser.

COMBUSTION CHAMBER: Annular reverse-flow type of stainless steel construction, with 14 Simplex burners. Two glow or spark plug igniters.

GAS GENERATOR: Single-stage axial. Rotor blades mounted by fir tree roots.

POWER TURBINE: Single or dual-stage axial. Rotor blades mounted by fir tree roots.

BEARINGS: Gas generator and power turbine supported by one ball bearing and one roller bearing each.

SHAFT DRIVE: Single, or two-stage planetary reduction gear or direct drive, depending on engine model. Torque measuring system incorporated with reduction gearing.

FUEL GRADE: Diesel Nos 1 and 2 and Navy diesel or aviation turbine fuel.

JET PIPE: Single port exhaust discharging vertically upwards or at 60 degrees port or starboard of vertical. Alternatively twin ports discharging horizontally on some models.

ACCESSORY DRIVES: Mounting pads on accessory case including for starter or starter-generator and tacho-generator. Also tacho-generator drive on power section.

LUBRICATION SYSTEM: One pressure and four scavenge gear type pumps driven by gas generator rotor. Integral oil tank.

OIL SPECIFICATIONS: Type 2 synthetic lube oil PWA-521 MIL-L-23699.

FRANCE

CLUB FRANÇAIS DES AÉROGLISSEURS

41 and 43 rue Aristide Briand, 45130 Meung sur Loire, France

Club Français des Aéroglisseurs is marketing special propulsion units for high performance lightweight air cushion vehicles. The units, given the name Diagloo, comprise adapted 600 and 1200cc Citroen air-cooled, automotive engines, driving a 1·4m (4ft 7⅛in) diameter, two-bladed Merville propeller via a reduction and reverse gearbox. Engine outputs are 32·5bhp (33cv) and 56cv at 5,750rpm.

The 33cv units weigh 100kg (220lb) and the 56cv unit 160kg (352 lb). Each is supplied complete with an aerodynamically profiled hood. Series production has begun.

The Diagloo propulsion unit for light sports ACVs

SOCIÉTÉ TURBOMÉCA

Head office and works: Bordes 64320 Bizanos (Pyrénées Atlantiques), France

Paris office: 1 rue Beaujon, 75008 Paris, France

Officials:

J R Szydlowski, *President and Director General*

The Société Turboméca was formed in 1938 by MM Szydlowski and Planiol to develop blowers, compressors and turbines for aeronautical use.

In 1947 the company began development of gas-turbines of low power for driving aircraft auxiliaries and for aircraft propulsion.

Many of Turboméca's production series aircraft turbines have been adapted to industrial and marine duties including installation in French air cushion vehicles of various types. General descriptions follow of the main Turboméca turbine engines at present in production or under development. Reference is also made to air cushion vehicle and hydrofoil installations.

Turboméca Turmo 1,300shp IIIC free-turbine turboshaft, two of which will power the projected Aérospatiale SA 800 mixed-traffic hydrofoil ferry

TURBOMÉCA ARTOUSTE

The Artouste is a single-shaft turboshaft engine which has been manufactured in quantity in two versions, the 400shp Artouste IIC and the 563shp Artouste IIIB. The 590shp Artouste IIID has also been developed. More than 1,500 of the earlier Artouste II were built to power the Sud-Aviation Alouette II helicopter. The Artouste II has a single-stage centrifugal compressor, annular reverse-flow combustor and two-stage axial turbine. In the second generation Artouste III in which the pressure ratio is increased from 3·88 : 1 to 5·2 : 1, a single-axial stage compressor has been added ahead of the centrifugal impeller. The turbine also has an additional stage.

A single Artouste drives the two propulsion airscrews on the Naviplane BC 8.

The following description refers to the Artouste IIIB.

TYPE: Single-shaft axial-plus-centrifugal turboshaft.

COMPRESSOR: Single-stage axial plus single-stage centrifugal compressor. Two diffusers, one radial and the other axial, aft of compressor. Pressure ratio at 33,500rpm at S/L 5·2 : 1. Air mass flow 4·3kg/sec (9·5lb/sec) at 33,500rpm at S/L.

COMBUSTION CHAMBER: Annular type, with rotary atomiser fuel injection. Torch igniters.

TURBINE: Three-stage axial type. Blades integral with discs. Row of nozzle guide vanes before each stage.

JET PIPE: Fixed type.

STARTING: Automatic with 4,000W starter-generator. Two Turboméca igniter plugs.

DIMENSIONS

Length: 1,815mm (71·46in)

Width: 520mm (20·47in)

Height: 627mm (24·68in)

WEIGHT: Dry equipped: 182kg (401lb)

PERFORMANCE RATING: 563shp at 33,500rpm

FUEL CONSUMPTION at T-O and max continuous rating: 322g (0·71lb) ehp/h

TURBOMÉCA TURMO

The Turmo is a free-turbine engine available in both turboshaft and turboprop versions spanning the 1,200 to 2,000shp power bracket. First generation Turmo IIIC and E series have a single-stage axial plus single-stage centrifugal compressor, annular reverse-flow combustor, two-stage axial compressor-turbine, and mechanically-separate single- or two-stage power turbine. Second-generation Turmo XII engines have an additional axial compressor stage and other refinements. By December 1977 more than 1,916 Turmo engines had been built.

Main versions of the Turmo at present in production or under development include: Turmo $IIIC_7$: Derived from the Turmo IIIB, this model (with two-stage power turbine) has a 1,610shp at maximum contingency rating and powers early Sud-Aviation SA 321 Super-Frelon three-engined military helicopters. Two will power the projected Aérospatiale 46-ton patrol boat hydrofoil under development for the French navy.

The Turmo IIIF also powers the Turbotrains of SNCF.

Turmo IVC: based on the Turmo IIIC, this is a special version with a single-stage power turbine and powers the Sud-Aviation SA 330 Puma twin-engined military helicopter. The engine has a maximum contingency rating of 1,558shp.

Turmo $IIIC_7$: this model (which reverts to the standard two-stage power turbine) is in the same series as the Turmo IIIC and E and has a maximum emergency rating of 1,610shp. It is installed in Sud Aviation SA 321 F and J Super-Frelon civil three-engined helicopters.

Turmo $IIIC_2$: embodies new materials for the gas generator turbine, and offers an emergency rating of 1,610shp.

Turmo $IIIE_3$: two, each rated at 1,282shp, power the Bertin/Société de l'Aérotrain Orléans 250-80 tracked air cushion vehicle. Both engines drive a ducted seven-bladed 2·3m (7ft 7in) diameter Ratier-Figeac FH-201 hydraulically operated reversible-pitch propeller for propulsion. The Turmo IIIE is rated at 1,580shp.

Turmo IIIF: this model has been in production since 1970 to power the production version of the SNCF Turbotrain operating on the Paris-Caen-Cherbourg, Lyon-Nantes, Lyon-Strasbourg, Lyon-Bordeaux and Bordeaux-Toulouse runs.

In the United States it is employed in the AMTRAK locomotives on the Chicago-St Louis run and in Iran it is employed on locomotives on the Teheran—Mashed line.

Turmo $IIIN_8$: rated at 1,250shp, this version powers the twin-engined SEDAM Naviplane N300 marine air cushion vehicle. The engines are cross-coupled to drive two three-bladed 3·6m (11ft 10in) diameter Ratier-Figeac FH 195-196 hydraulically-operated variable-pitch propellers for propulsion and two 11-bladed 1·85m (6ft 3in) diameter Ratier-Figeac FD 155 hydraulically-operated variable-pitch axial fans for lift.

Turmo XII: developed from the Turmo IIIC this second-generation model has a two-stage axial compressor ahead of the centrifugal stage. With a maximum continuous rating of 1,610shp, the Turmo XII is in operation on an RTG Turbotrain in France.

Two Turmo IIIC series engines with a combined installed power of 2,564shp, are to power the projected Sud-Aviation SA800 second-generation hydrofoil.

TURMO $IIIC_7$

TYPE: Free-turbine axial-plus-centrifugal turboshaft.
AIR MASS FLOW: 6·2kg (13·7lb)/s
DIMENSIONS
Length: 1,976mm (77·8in)
Width: 693mm (27·3in)
Height: 717mm (28·2in)
WEIGHT Dry with standard equipment: 325kg (715lb)
PERFORMANCE RATINGS
T-O: 1,550shp
Max continuous: 1,292shp
FUEL CONSUMPTION
At T-O rating: 273g (0·6lb)/shp/h
At max continuous rating: 291g (0·64lb)/shp/h

TURBOMÉCA MARBORE

The Marbore single-shaft turbojet has been built in greater numbers than any other Turboméca engine. By December 1977 over 9,000 400kg (880lb) thrust Marbore IIs and 480kg (1,058lb) thrust Marbore VIs had been manufactured by Turboméca and its licensees for trainer aircraft and target drone applications. Of this total, 5,395 Marbore engines were manufactured by Turboméca. In both these versions the engine comprises a single-stage centrifugal compressor, annular reverse-flow combustor and single-stage axial turbine.

Two Marbores will power the SA 890 hydrofoil test platform currently under development by Aérospatiale for the French Ministry of National Defence.

A Marbore II powers the lift system of the SEDAM Naviplane BC8 marine ACV. The exhaust gases are ducted along channels designed to entrain additional air to augment the efflux.

MARBORE VI

DIMENSIONS
Length, with exhaust cone but without tailpipe: 1,416mm (55·74in)
Width: 593mm (23·35in)
Height: 631mm (24·82in)
WEIGHT Dry equipped: 140kg (309lb)
PERFORMANCE RATINGS
T-O: 480kg (1,058lb) st at 21,500rpm
Cruising: 420kg (925lb) st at 20,500rpm
SPECIFIC FUEL CONSUMPTION
At T-O rating: 1·09
At cruising rating: 1·07

TURBOMÉCA ASTAZOU

The Astazou is another of the later generation Turboméca engines, incorporating the experience gained with earlier series and making use of new design techniques. It has an extremely small gas-producer section and has been developed both as a turboshaft and as a turboprop driving a variable-pitch propeller.

The compressor consists of one or two axial stages followed by a centrifugal stage, with an annular combustion chamber and three-stage turbine. Accessories are mounted on the rear of the main intake casing. Pressure ratio is 6:1 and air mass flow 2·5kg/s (5·5lb/s) for the two-stage compressor engines, and 8 : 1 and 3·4kg/s (7·4lb/s) for the three-stage compressor engines respectively. In the turboshaft version, the rpm of the output shaft is 5,922.

Well over 1,900 Astazou engines of various types have been built. The following are the main Astazou variants:

Astazou II. This is a 535hp turboprop (with two-stage compressor) which powers a version of the Naviplane N 102.

Astazou IIA. A 523shp turboshaft (two-stage compressor) version powering the Sud-Aviation SA 318C Alouette II Astazou helicopter. A 450 shp Astazou provides power for the integrated lift and propulsion system of the SEDAM Naviplane N 102 marine ACV. The engine drives a 1·7m (5ft 7in) diameter axial lift fan and two three-bladed variable-pitch propellers for propulsion.

Astazou IIIN. Rated at 592hp, this is the definitive version (two-stage compressor).

Astazou IV. New version especially designed for industrial duty and in particular to form, associated with a Jeumont-Schneider ac generator, a 300kW generating set. It is installed in the RTG turbotrains made in France, USA and Iran. It is also being tested by the French Navy.

Astazou XIV (alias AZ14). Current major production turboshaft version (with three-stage compressor) rated at 852shp. The engine is the standard power plant for the Naviplane N 102.

The B version is installed in the Alouette III helicopter and the H version in the SA 342 Gazelle helicopter.

Astazou XVI (alias AZ16). First Turboméca production engine to embody the company's new air-cooled turbine. Rated at 913shp for Jetstream aircraft and the FMA IA 58 Pucará counter-insurgency aircraft of the Argentine Air Force.

Astazou XVIII. An uprated version of the Astazou XVI with take-off power of 1,554ehp and sfc of 232g (0·512lb)/ehp/h.

A turboshaft version is installed in the SA 360

Turboméca Turmo XII which has an additional axial compressor stage

The 889shp Turboméca Turmastazou XIV free-turbine turboshaft

TYPE	PERFORMANCE I.S.A. CONDITIONS: Max. thermo-dynamic power (shp)	S.F.C. (lb/shp.hr)	Shaft power at max. contingency rating (shp)	Shaft power at take-off (shp)	Shaft power at max. continuous (shp)	Residual thrust (kg)	Total equivalent power at take-off (eshp)	S.F.C. at take-off related to total equivalent power (lb/eshp.hr)	COMPRESSOR CHARACTERISTICS (at take-off): Number of stages: Axial	Centrif.	Air mass flow (kg/s)	Pressure ratio	R.P.M.	TURBINE: Number of stages: Gas generator	Free turbine	Power off-take/ propeller R.P.M.	OVERALL DIMENSIONS (mm): Length	Width	Height	WEIGHT (equipped engine) (kg)
TURBOSHAFT ENGINES																				
ARTOUSTE III B	858	0.659	–	562(1)	542	–	–	–	1	1	4.5	5.35	33 500	3	–	5 773	1 815	522	665	182
ASTAZOU II A	523	0.646	–	523	473	–	–	–	1	1	2.5	5.8	43 500	3	–	5 922	1 427	516	560	142
ASTAZOU III	590	0.644	–	590	590	–	–	–	1	1	2.5	5.7	43 500	3	–	6 179	1 433	483	508	147
ASTAZOU XIV H	858	0.559	–	590(1)	590(1)	–	–	–	2	1	3.33	7.5	43 000	3	–	6 334	1 470	500	565	158
ASTAZOU XVIII A	1 032	0.570	–	873(3)	805	–	–	–	2	1	3.33	7.5	43 000	3	–	5 830	1 419	533	711	173
ASTAZOU XX A	1 295	0.510	–	1 004(2)	1 004	–	–	–	3	1	4.2	9.5	42 000	3	–	5 855	1 526	533	716	185
TURMO III C7	1 610	0.635	1 610	1 548	1 274	–	–	–	1	1	6.2	5.9	33 800	2	2	5 915	1 975	693	718	325
TURMO IV C	1 558	0.635	1 558	1 496	1 262	–	–	–	1	1	6.2	5.9	33 800	2	1	22 840	2 184	637	719	227
ARRIEL	680	0.581	680	641	592	–	–	–	1	1	2.4	8	52 600	2	1	6 000	1 200	420	627	109(7)
MAKILA	1 908	0.478	1 908	1 775	1 627	–	–	–	3	1	–	–	33 600	2	2	22 840	2 000	570	570	238
TURBOPROP ENGINES																				
ASTAZOU XVI D	912	0.559	–	912	785	63	968	0.525	2	1	3.33	8	43 089	3	–	1 783	1 556	581	581	205(7)
ASTAZOU XVI G	965	0.557	–	965	878	63	1 021	0.525	2	1	3.33	8	43 000	3	–	1 970	1 556	645	645	228
ASTAZOU XX	1 381	0.510	–	1 381	1 217	72	1 444	0.485	3	1	4.2	9.5	42 000	3	–	–	1 677	580	580	–
BASTAN VI C4	1 085	0.631	–	1 085	1 085	84.5	1 164	0.588	1	1	4.5	5.8	33 500	3	–	1 588	1 772	710	852	322
BASTAN VII	1 361	0.559	–	1 045(2)	1 045	100	1 460	0.521	2	1	5.85	6.8	32 000	3	–	1 517	1 911	736	802	370

TYPE	PERFORMANCE I.S.A. CONDITIONS: Thrust at take-off (kg)	Thrust at max. continuous (kg)	Ducted Fan: Dilution ratio	Ducted Fan: L.P. compressor pressure ratio	S.F.C. (kg/kg.hr): Take-off	S.F.C. (kg/kg.hr): Max. continuous	COMPRESSOR CHARACTERISTICS (at take-off): Number of stages: Axial	Centrif.	Air mass flow (kg/s)	Pressure ratio	R.P.M.	TURBINE: Number of stages	OVERALL DIMENSIONS (mm): Length	Width	Height	WEIGHT (equipped engine) (kg)
TURBOJET ENGINES																
ARBIZON III	380	330	–	–	1.12	1.11	1	1	6	5.5	33 000	1	1 361	410	410	115
ARBIZON IV	367	336	–	–	1.05	1.03	1	1	–	–	–	1	960	330	330	60
MARBORE II	400	400	–	–	1.15	1.15	–	1	8	3.85	22 600	1	1 566	567	684	159
MARBORE VI	480	480	–	–	1.11	1.11	–	1	9.6	3.72	21 500	1	1 416	594	631	159
AUBISQUE I A	742	625	2	1.5	0.618	0.6	1-1	1	22.2	6.9	33 000	1	2 288	650	750	292
ADOUR Mk 804 (8)	2 386(4)	2 028(10)	0.8	2.48(10)	0.77(10)	0.73(10)	2-5	–	42.7(10)	11	15 650	1-1	2 970	795	1 137	766
LARZAC 04 (9)	1 345	1 250	1.13	–	0.714	0.675	2-4	–	27.1	10.65	22 560	1-1	1 343	600	760	290
ASTAFAN II G	700	700	8.8	1.3	0.38	0.38	1-2	1	36	9	43 000	3	1 980	665	665	285
ASTAFAN III	790(5)	715	7.7	1.32	0.365	0.359	1-2	1	31	–	43 000	3	2 030	665	665	–
ASTAFAN IV	1 150(6)	1 020	7	1.34	0.31	0.305	1-3	1	39	–	42 000	3	2 218	780	780	–

(1) Up to + 55° C, or 4,000 m
(2) Up to + 40° C, or 2,500 m
(3) Up to + 35° C, or 2,000 m
(4) 3 629 kg with reheat lit
(5) 850 kg with water injection
(6) 1 230 kg with water injection
(7) Without starter generator
(8) In cooperation with ROLLS-ROYCE
(9) In cooperation with S.N.E.C.M.A.
(10) Ref. values

December 1977

Table of Turboméca's current range of gas-turbine engines

Dauphin helicopter. Thermodynamic power: 1,032shp, sfc of 260g (0·57lb)/shp/h.

Astazou XX. This later version has an additional axial compressor stage, and is rated at take-off at 1,445ehp for an sfc of 204g (0·45lb)/ehp/h.

Turboshaft version has 1,295shp thermodynamic power, with sfc of 230kg (0·51lb)/shp/h.

ASTAZOU IIIN

DIMENSIONS
Length: 1,433mm (40·7in)
Basic diameter: 460mm (18·1in)
WEIGHT Dry equipped engine: 147·5kg (325lb)
PERFORMANCE RATINGS
T-O: 592shp at 43,500rpm
Max continuous: 523shp at 43,500rpm
FUEL CONSUMPTION
At T-O rating: 284g (0·627lb)/shp/h
At max continuous rating: 292g (0·644 lb)/shp/h

TURBOMÉCA BASTAN

A compact single-shaft turboprop in the 1,000 to 2,000shp power bracket, the Bastan has its main application in the Nord 262. The 1,065ehp Bastan VIC powering the original 262 series aircraft, comprises a single-stage axial compressor plus single-stage centrifugal compressor, annular reverse-flow combustor and three-stage axial turbine, and is equipped with water-methanol injection. A new version of the Bastan VIC4 is under development with a rating of 1,085shp. The higher rated Bastan VII is capable of maintaining its 1,135ehp T-O power up to an ambient temperature of 40°C. This version is entering production to power the new 262C and incorporates an additional axial compressor stage.

BASTAN VII

DIMENSIONS
Length: 1,911mm (75·2in)
Width: 550mm (21·7in)
Height: 802mm (31·6in)
WEIGHT Dry basic engine: 290kg (639lb)
PERFORMANCE RATINGS: T-O and max continuous: 1,135ehp
FUEL CONSUMPTION: At T-O and max continuous ratings: 259kg (0·572lb)/shp/h

TURBOMÉCA TURMASTAZOU

This is a new free-turbine direct-drive turboshaft comprising the Astazou XIV single-shaft gas generator section provided with a mechanically-independent power turbine. The Astazou turbine has two stages in place of its normal three, and the power turbine has two stages also. Development is underway of the 889shp Turmastazou XIV with a view to its use in twin-engined helicopters. The engine has also been proposed for the Bertin/Société de l'Aérotrain Orléans tracked ACV.

Turmastazou XVI. This version introduces the Turboméca air-cooled turbine, and gives a take-off rating of 1,015shp for an sfc of 231g (0·51lb)/shp/h.

TURMASTAZOU XIV

DIMENSIONS
Length: 1,371mm (54in)
Width: 440mm (17·3in)
Height: 553mm (21·8in)
WEIGHT Dry equipped engine: approx 155kg (341lb)
PERFORMANCE RATINGS
T-O: 889shp
Max continuous: 792shp

GERMANY, FEDERAL REPUBLIC

MTU

Motoren-und Turbinen-Union Friedrichshafen GmbH

Olgastrasse 75, Postfach 2040, D-7990 Friedrichshafen, Federal Republic of Germany

Telephone: (07541) 2071
Telex: MTUFH 0734360
Officials:
Dr Oec Dipl Ernst Zimmermann, *President*
Dr Ing Hans Dinger, *Executive Vice President*
Hubert Dunkler, *Director*
Dr Ing Wolfgang Hansen, *Director*
Gunther Welsch, *Director*

The MTU-group of companies, formed in 1969 by MAN AG and Daimler-Benz AG, consists of MTU-München GmbH and MTU-Friedrichshafen GmbH.

MTU-Friedrichshafen comprises the two plants of the previous Maybach Mercedes-Benz Motorenbau GmbH at Friedrichshafen and is owned by MTU-München GmbH. MTU-München, in turn is owned equally by MAN and Daimler-Benz.

MTU-Friedrichshafen is today the development and production centre for high-performance diesel engines of Maybach, MAN and Mercedes-Benz origin and as such embodies the experience of these companies in diesel engine technology. In addition to diesel engines, MTU-Friedrichshafen is responsible for sales and application of industrial and marine gas-turbines.

For application in hydrofoils MTU-Friedrichshafen offers the following engines:

331 engine family
652 engine family
538 engine family

The areas of responsibility of the two MTU companies are as follows:

MTU-München:

Development, production and support of lightweight, advanced-technology gas turbines mainly for aircraft applications.

MTU Friedrichshafen:

Development, production and application of high-performance diesel engines.

The following table specifies hydrofoil propulsion engines available within MTU's engine delivery programme.

Output characteristics of operational engines usually depend on the special demands of the hydrofoil, from the operating profile to the application, and therefore will be specified for each system.

Reference conditions:
Intake air temperature 27°C
Seawater temperature 27°C (no influence on 331 TC. These engines have integrated change-air cooler)
Barometric pressure: 1000 m bar

MTU projects and delivers, as a supplement to their diesel engine programme, complete propulsion systems, comprising diesels and marine gas-turbines. This enables selection of either CODOG or CODAG arrangements.

MTU diesel engines for hydrofoil propulsion

Engine model	Speed rpm	MCR Maximum continuous rating (overload capacity for transition to foil borne operation) kW	hp	Engine weight (dry) kg	lb
6 V 331 TC 82	2180	480	650	1880	4144
8 V 331 TC 82	2180	640	870	2278	5003
12 V 331 TC 82	2180	960	1300	3250	7163
12 V 538 TB 81	1710	1470	2000	5250	11571
12 V 538 TB 82	1710	1640	2230	5250	11571
16 V 538 TB 81	1710	1960	2670	6850	15097
16 V 538 TB 82	1710	2185	2970	6850	15097
20 V 538 TB 81	1710	2455	3340	9080	20023
20 V 538 TB 82	1710	2730	3715	9080	20023
12 V 652 TB 81	1400	1270	1725	4790*	10557
16 V 652 TB 81	1400	1690	2300	6213*	13314

1) Ratings are dependent on type of vessel.
*Weight of engine with light alloy housing.

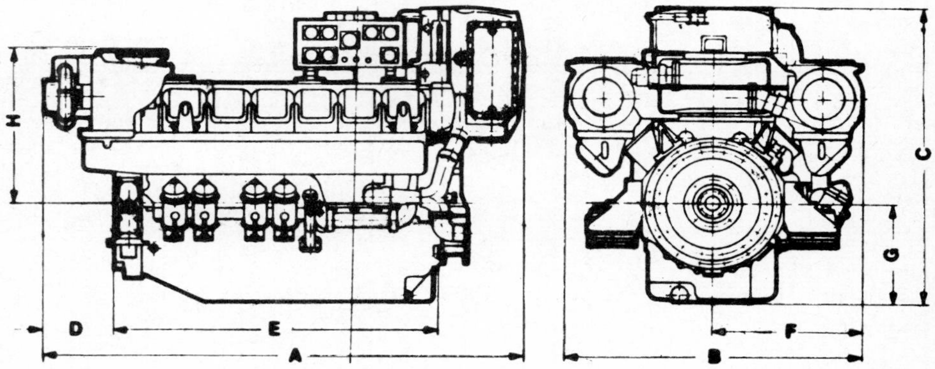

Engine	A	B	C	D	E	F	G	H
6V 331 TC 82	1580	1420	1280	257	1027	735	475	745
8V 331 TC 82	1884	1404	1414	261	1255	720	475	745
12V 331 TC 82	2438	1446	1605	319	1711	761	442	779

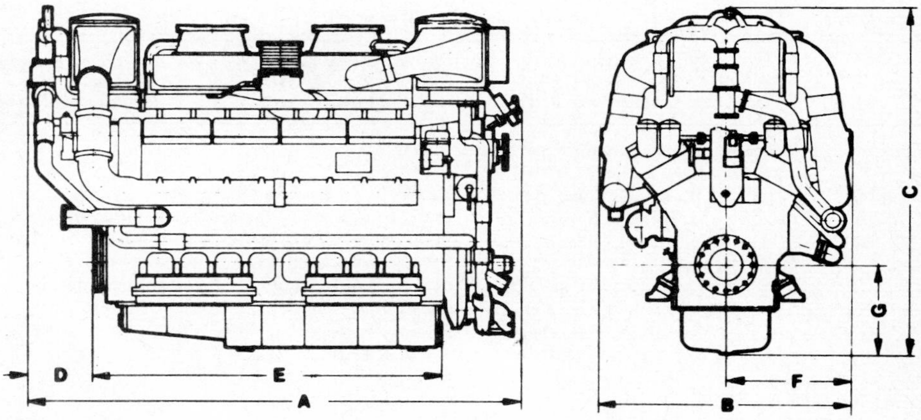

Engine type	A	B	C	D	E	F	G
12V 652 TB 81	2450	1747	2230	225	1900	748	550
16V 652 TB 81	2950	1791	2265	243	2500	984	625

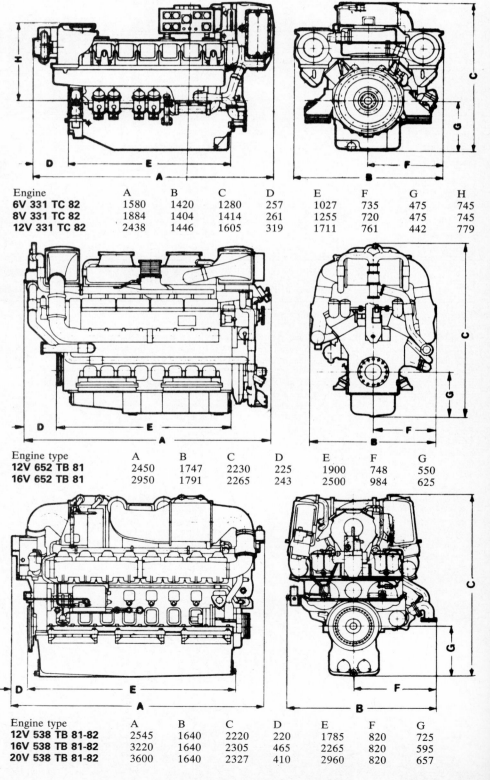

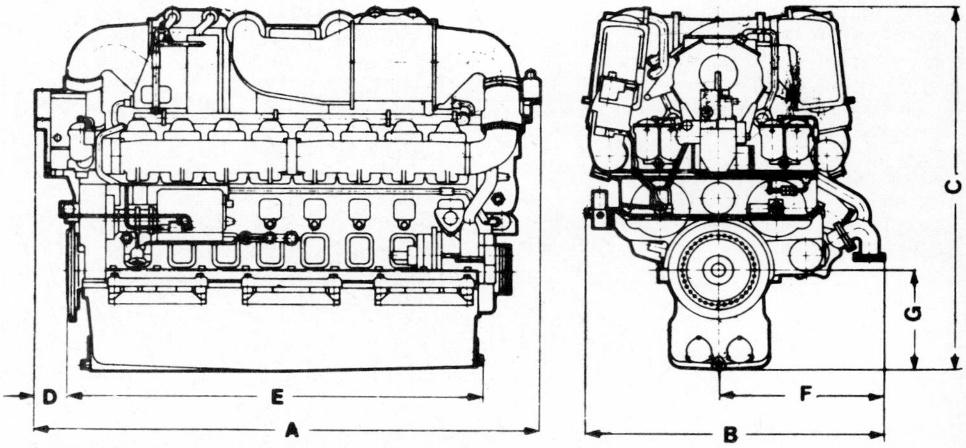

Engine type	A	B	C	D	E	F	G
12V 538 TB 81-82	2545	1640	2220	220	1785	820	725
16V 538 TB 81-82	3220	1640	2305	465	2265	820	595
20V 538 TB 81-82	3600	1640	2327	410	2960	820	657

RHEIN-FLUGZEUGBAU GmbH

Postfach 408, D-4050 Mönchengladbach 1, Federal Republic of Germany
Telephone: (02161) 66 20 31
Telex: 08 525 06

Officials:
Dipl Volksw W Kutscher, *Commercial Director*
Dipl Ing A Schneider, *Technical Director*

RFB has developed a fan thrust pod module for wing-in-ground-effect machines, gliders, air cushion vehicles and air-propelled boats.

By combining rotary engines of the Wankel type with a ducted fan, the company has produced an extremely compact power unit which can be mounted on either a fuselage or a wing in much the same way as gas-turbine pods. The air cooling system permits prolonged ground running when necessary with full throttle.

The system has been fitted to the L13 Blanik glider and also to boats.

RFB Fan Pod Type SG 85

SG 85

Length: 1,200mm (3ft 11½in)
Width max: 750mm (2ft 5½in)
Height, including 200mm connection: 1,000mm (3ft 3⅜in)
Inside shroud diameter: 650mm (2ft 1⅜in)
Weight: 58kg (127·8lb)
Power: 50hp
Static thrust at 5,400rpm (with muffler installed): 90kg (198·4lb)
Noise level with full throttle at 304·8m (1,000ft) altitude: 54 dB (A)
Rotor: 3-blades-rotor in fibre-reinforced plastic with erosive protection.
Shroud: plastic.
Engine cowling: glass-fibre reinforced plastic.
Engine: Rotary engine KM 914/2V-85 ('Wankel' system; two coupled engines 25hp each) with electric starter 12V, generator, exhaust-gas system and complete assembly sets ready for installation.
Connection: Metal-construction as pylon having a connection-part.
Fuel: mixture 1:30
Fuel consumption:
full throttle 5,500rpm: 15 litres/h (3·3 gallons/h)
cruising speed 5,000rpm: 11·5 litres/h (2·5 gallons/h)

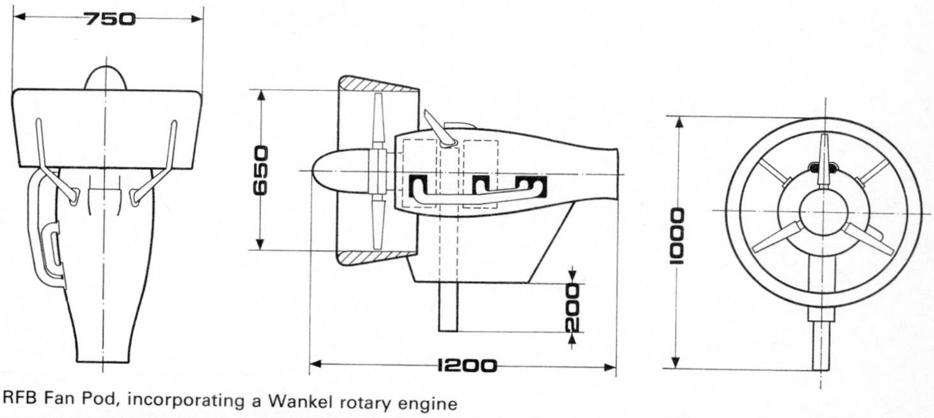

RFB Fan Pod, incorporating a Wankel rotary engine

SG 85 thrust pod mounted on an Espadon Canot 422 inflatable dinghy, built by Etablissements Georges Hennebutte

VOLKSWAGEN (GB) LIMITED
(Incorporating Audi NSU (GB) Limited)

Volkswagen House, Brighton Road, Purley, Surrey CR2 2UQ, England
Telephone: 01 668 4100
Telex: 263226

TYPE 122

The air-cooled petrol engines powering over 20 million Volkswagen cars and vehicles are also produced as industrial power units in which role they have been proved reliable and economical in millions of hours running. There are three versions available, the Type 122 developed from the 1,192cc Volkswagen car engine; the 1,584cc Type 126A developed from the 1,500cc van engine; and the 1,795cc Type 127 developed from the 1,700 car engine.

TYPE: Air-cooled four-cylinder, horizontally-opposed four-stroke petrol engine available with or without governor.

CYLINDERS: Four separate cylinders of special grey cast iron, with integral cooling fins. Cast aluminium heads, one for each two cylinders, with shrunk-in sintered steel valve seats and bronze valve guides. Bore 77mm (3·032in). Stroke 64mm (2·52in). Cubic capacity 1,192cc (72·74 in³). Compression ratio 7·3 : 1.

CRANKCASE: Two-part magnesium pressure casting with enclosed oil sump and flange for mounting the engine on machine or pedestal.

CRANKSHAFT: Forged, with hardened journals, mounted in three aluminium bearings and one three-layer, steel-backed bearing (No 2).

CONNECTING RODS: Forged steel, I-section shank. Three-layer, steel-backed, lead-bronze big-end bearing shells with white metal running surfaces.

PISTONS: Aluminium with steel inserts, two compression rings and one scraper ring.

CAMSHAFT: Grey cast iron, with three steel-backed, shell-type bearings in crankcase, driven by helical gears.

VALVES: One inlet and one exhaust valve per cylinder. Exhaust valves have special armoured seating surfaces. 'Rotocap' valve rotating devices can be fitted on request.

COOLING: Radial fan, driven by belt from crankshaft. Protective grille on fan intake.

LUBRICATION: Forced feed gear-type pump. Full flow, flat tube oil cooler in fan airstream. Oil capacity 2·5 litres (4·4 pints).

CARBURETTOR: Downdraft Solex 26 VFIS on engine with governor. Downdraft Solex 28 PCI with accelerator pump, on engine without governor. Both have choke for cold starting.

IGNITION: Magneto, fully waterproofed and suppressed.

PLUGS: Bosch W145 T1.

FUEL: RON 87.

STARTING: Hand cranking lever or electric starter.

GOVERNOR: Centrifugal type, operating on

carburettor throttle, driven by toothed belt.
EXHAUST SYSTEM: Cylindrical muffler located transversely at bottom of engine, with exhaust pipes from cylinders and damper pipe with short tail pipe.
MOUNTING: By four bolts in the crankcase flange.
COUPLING: Engine is connected to driven shaft by a clutch or flexible fixed-coupling.
PEDESTALS AND TRANSMISSIONS: Suitable flange pedestals, with or without couplings or clutches, can be supplied as well as gearboxes with direct drives or drives of various ratios for clockwise or anti-clockwise rotation.
DIMENSIONS
Length: 740·5mm (29·2in)
Width: 748mm (29·4in)
Height: 665·5mm (26·2in)
WEIGHT Dry with standard equipment: approx 93·5kg (205lb)
PERFORMANCE RATINGS: Continuous rating: 34bhp DIN at 3,600 output rpm
FUEL CONSUMPTION
At 20bhp at 2,000 output rpm: 242g (0·534lb)/bhp/h
At 30bhp at 3,600 output rpm: 268g (0·59lb)/bhp/h
OIL CONSUMPTION: Approximately 20 to 35cc/h at 3,000 output rpm

TYPE 126A

TYPE: Air-cooled four-cylinder, horizontally-opposed four-stroke petrol engine available with or without governor. Construction generally similar to Type 122 with following exceptions:
CYLINDERS: Bore 85·5mm (3·543in). Stroke 69mm (2·717in). Cubic capacity 1,584cc (96·5in³). Compression ratio 7·7 : 1.
CARBURETTOR: Downdraft Solex 26 or 28 VFIS on engine with governor. Downdraft Solex 32 PCI on engine without governor.
DIMENSIONS
Length: 723mm (28·5in)
Width: 760mm (29·9in)
Height: 675·5mm (26·5in)
WEIGHT Dry with standard equipment: approx 100kg (220lb)
PERFORMANCE RATINGS: Continuous rating: 46bhp DIN at 3,600 output rpm
FUEL: 90 octane minimum

Volkswagen Type 127 industrial engine

FUEL CONSUMPTION
At 28bhp at 2,000 output rpm: 225g (0·496lb)/bhp/h
At 44bhp at 3,600 output rpm: 255g (0·562lb)/bhp/h
OIL CONSUMPTION: Approximately 25 to 40 cc/h at 3,000 output rpm

TYPE 127

TYPE: Air-cooled, four-cylinder, horizontally-opposed four-stroke petrol engine of low profile design.
CYLINDERS: Bore 93mm (3·74in). Stroke 66mm (2·165in). Cubic capacity 1,795cc (109·53in³). Compression ratio 7·3 : 1.
CRANKCASE: Aluminium, pressure die cast.
COOLING: Radial fan on crankshaft.
CARBURETTOR: Downdraft Solex 32 PCI or two Downdraft Solex 34PDSIT.
IGNITION: 12 volt battery.
DIMENSIONS
Length: 829mm (32·64in)
Width: 960mm (37·8in)
Height, without air cleaner: 556mm (12·89in)
WEIGHT Dry with standard equipment: 124kg (273lb)
PERFORMANCE RATINGS
Max continuous ratings at 4,000rpm:
single carburettor: 62bhp DIN
twin carburettor: 68bhp DIN
FUEL: 90 octane minimum.
FUEL CONSUMPTION
At 3,000 output rpm: 230g (0·506lb)/bhp/h
At 4,000 output rpm: 255g (0·561lb)/bhp/h

ITALY

CRM FABRICA MOTORI MARINI

Via Manzoni 12, 20121 Milan, Italy
Telephone: 708 326/327
Telex: 26382 CREMME
Cables: Cremme
Officials:
Ing G Schisani, *Director*
Ing B Piccoletti, *Director*
Ing S Rastelli, *Director*
S Sussi, *Director*

CRM has specialised in building lightweight diesel engines for more than twenty years. The company's engines are used in large numbers of motor torpedo boats, coastal patrol craft and privately-owned motor yachts. More recently, the engines have also been installed in hydrofoils.

During the 1960s the company undertook the development and manufacture of a family of 18-, 12- and 9-cylinder diesel engines of lightweight high-speed design, providing a power coverage of 300bhp to 1,350bhp. These comprise the 18-cylinder CRM 18D/2 and 18 D/S-2 of 1,050 to 1,350bhp with mechanically-driven supercharging and turbo-driven supercharging respectively and its cylinders arranged in an unusual W arrangement of three banks of six cylinders each; the 12-cylinder CRM 12 D/S-2 of 900bhp with two banks of six cylinders and first in the new series to introduce turbo-charging; and the 715bhp CRM 9 D/S-2 with a W arrangement of three banks of three cylinders and offering the option of turbo-charging or natural aspiration.

All engines available in a magnetic version, the disturbance of their magnetic field being reduced to insignificant amounts, for special applications.

Details of these engines are given below.

CRM 18

First in CRM's new series of lightweight high-speed diesels, the CRM 18 is an 18-cylinder unit with its cylinders arranged in a W form comprising three banks of six cylinders. Maximum power is 1,050bhp at 1,900rpm with mechanically driven supercharging and 1,350bhp at 2,075rpm with exhaust gas turbo-charging. One 1,050bhp 18D/2 engine powers the Finnish Tehi 70-passenger Raketa-type hydrofoil.

The following description relates to the mechanically supercharged CRM 18 D/2 and turbo-supercharged CRM 18 D/S.

TYPE: 18-cylinder in-line W type, four-stroke, water-cooled mechanically-supercharged (CRM 18 D/2) or turbo-supercharged (CRM 18 D/S) diesel engine.
CYLINDERS: Bore: 150mm (5·91in). Stroke 180mm (7·09in). Swept volume 3·18 litres (194·166in³) per cylinder. Total swept volume: 57·3 litres (3,495in³). Compression ratio: 16·25 : 1. Separate pressed-steel cylinder frame side members are surrounded by gas-welded sheet metal water cooling jacket treated and pressure-coated internally to prevent corrosion. Cylinders are closed at top by a steel plate integral with side wall to complete combustion chamber. Lower half of cylinder is ringed by a drilled flange for bolting to crankcase. Cylinder top also houses a spherical-shaped pre-combustion chamber as well as inlet and exhaust valve seats. Pre-combustion chamber is in high-strength, heat and corrosion resistant steel. A single cast light alloy head, carrying valve guides, pre-combustion chambers and camshaft bearings bridges each bank of cylinders. Head is attached to cylinder bank by multiple studs.
PISTONS: Light alloy forgings with four rings, top ring being chrome-plated and bottom ring acting as oil scraper. Piston crowns shaped to withstand high temperatures especially in vicinity of pre-combustion chamber outlet ports.
CONNECTING RODS: Comprise main and secondary articulated rods, all rods being completely machined I-section steel forgings. Big-end of each main rod is bolted to ribbed cap by six studs. Big-end bearings are white metal lined steel shells. Each secondary rod anchored at its lower end to a pivot pin inserted in two lugs protruding from big-end of main connecting rod. Both ends of all secondary rods, and small ends of main rods have bronze bushes.
CRANKSHAFTS: One-piece hollow shaft in nitrided alloy steel, with six throws equi-spaced at 120 degrees. Seven main bearings with white metal lined steel shells. Twelve balancing counterweights.
CRANKCASE: Cast light alloy crankcase bolted to bed plate by studs and tie bolts. Multiple integral reinforced ribs to provide robust structure. Both sides of each casting braced by seven

cross ribs incorporating crankshaft bearing supports. Protruding sides of crankcase ribbed throughout length.
VALVE GEAR: Hollow sodium-cooled valves of each bank of cylinders actuated by twin camshafts and six cams on each shaft. Two inlet and two outlet valves per cylinder and one rocker for each pair of valves. End of stem and facing of exhaust valves fitted with Stellite inserts. Valve cooling water forced through passage formed by specially-shaped plate welded to top of cylinder.
FUEL INJECTION: Pumps fitted with variable speed control and pilot injection nozzle.
PRESSURE CHARGER: Two mechanically-driven centrifugal compressors on CRM 18 D/2, or two exhaust gas turbo-driven compressors on CRM 18 D/S-2.
ACCESSORIES: Standard accessories include oil and fresh water heat exchangers; fresh water tank; oil and fresh water thermostats; oil filters, fresh water, salt water and fuel hand pumps; fresh water and oil temperature gauges; engine, reverse gear and reduction gear oil gauges; prelubrication, electric pump and engine rpm counter. Optional accessories include engine oil and water pre-heater, and warning and pressure switches.
COOLING SYSTEM: Fresh water.
FUEL: Fuel oil having specific gravity of 0·83 to 0·84.
LUBRICATION SYSTEM: Pressure type with gear pump.
OIL: Mineral oil to SAE 40 HD, MIL-L-210GB.
OIL COOLING: By salt water circulating through heat exchanger.
STARTING: 24 volt 15hp electric motor and 85A, 24 volt alternator for battery charge, or compressed air.
MOUNTING: At any transverse or longitudinal angle tilt to 20 degrees.
REVERSE GEAR: Bevel crown gear wheels with hydraulically-controlled hand brake.
REDUCTION GEAR: Optional fitting with spur gears giving reduction ratios of 0·561 : 1, 0·730 : 1 and 0·846 : 1. Overdrive ratio 1·18 : 1.
PROPELLER THRUST BEARING: Incorporated in reduction gear or in overdrive. Axial thrust 3,003kg (6,620lb) at 1,176rpm.
DIMENSIONS
Length: 2,960mm (116·5in)
Width: 1,350mm (53·15in)
Height: 1,304mm (51·33in)
WEIGHTS
DRY
Engine: 1,665kg (3,690lb)
Reverse gear, generator and starter: 410kg (900lb)
Reduction gear or overdrive, with propeller thrust bearing: 150kg (330lb)
Total: 2,225kg (4,920lb)
PERFORMANCE RATINGS
CRM 18 D/S-2:
Max power: 1,350bhp at 2,075rpm
Intermittent service: 1,250bhp at 2,020rpm
Continuous service: 1,040bhp at 1,900rpm
FUEL CONSUMPTION: CRM 18 D/S-2 at continuous service rating: 0·17kg (0·37lb)/bhp/h
OIL CONSUMPTION: CRM 18 D/S-2 at continuous service rating: 0·003kg (0·007lb)/h

CRM 12D/S-2

Second in the new CRM series of lightweight diesels is the 900bhp 12-cylinder 12 D/S-2 with two banks of six cylinders set at 60 degrees to form a V assembly. The bore and stroke are the same as in the CRM 18 series, and many of the components are interchangeable, including the crankshaft, bedplate, cylinders and pistons. The crankcase and connecting rod-assemblies are necessarily of modified design; the secondary rod is anchored at its lower end to a pivot pin inserted on two lugs protruding from the big-end of the main connecting rod. The fuel injection pump is modified to single block housing all 12 pumping elements located between the cylinder banks.

A major innovation first developed on the 12 D/S (and later provided for the other engines in the series) was the introduction of an exhaust gas driven turbo-charger. This involved a complete revision of the combustion system and all components comprising the cylinder heads. Conversion to turbo-charging avoided the mechanical power loss expended in driving the blower, and enabled a greater volume of air to be forced into the cylinders. The effect on specific fuel consumption was a reduction to around 160 to 170g (0·35 to 0·37lb)/bhp/h in conjunction with exhaust temperatures not exceeding 530°C (986°F) at maximum rpm. Two Holset turbochargers are fitted.

CRM 18 D/S-2 marine diesel rated at 1,350bhp at 2,075rpm

CRM 12D/S-2 marine diesel engine rated at 900hp at 2,035rpm

TYPE: 12-cylinder in-line V type, four-stroke water-cooled, turbo-supercharged diesel engines.
DIMENSIONS
Length: 2,530mm (99·6in)
Width: 1,210mm (47·64in)
Height: 1,204mm (47·4in)
WEIGHTS
DRY
Engine: 1,240kg (2,735lb)
Reverse gear, generator and starter: 410kg (900lb)
Reduction gear or overdrive, with propeller thrust bearing: 150kg (330lb)
Total: 1,800kg (3,965lb)
PERFORMANCE RATINGS
Max power: 900bhp at 2,035rpm
Intermittent service: 850bhp at 2,000rpm
Continuous service: 750bhp at 1,900rpm
FUEL CONSUMPTION: At continuous service rating: 0·18kg (0·4lb)/bhp/h

CRM 12D/SS

As a development of 12D/S-2, the 12D/SS is available for applications where a high rating is required, but space is limited.

Dry sump and wet sump versions are available for installation in engine-rooms with limited space available.
TYPE: Twelve cylinder V-60°, four stroke water-cooled, turbo-supercharged and intercooled diesel engine.
DIMENSIONS
Length: 2,642mm (104in)
Width: 1,210mm (47·63in)
Height, dry sump: 1,299mm (51·14in)
Height, wet sump: 1,427mm (56·18in)
WEIGHTS
DRY
Engine: 1,340kg (2,953lb)
Reverse gear, generator and electric starter: 410kg (903·9lb) (compressed air starter option)
Reduction gear: 150kg (330·6lb) (optional)
PERFORMANCE RATINGS
Max power: 1,265bhp at 2,050rpm
Intermittent power: 1,150bhp at 1,985rpm
Continuous power: 1,000bhp at 1,900rpm
FUEL CONSUMPTION: At continuous service rating: 0·175kg (0·38lb)/bhp/h

CRM NON-MAGNETIC DIESEL ENGINES

Non-magnetic versions of all CRM diesel engines are also available. These have extremely low magnetic perturbation fields.

FIAT/AIFO

Applicazioni Industriali Fiat OM

Via Carducci 29, Milan, Italy

Telephone: 877 066/8

AIFO Carraro V12SS, 700hp 12-cylinder diesel engines are installed in the H57 60-passenger hydrofoil ferries built by Seaflight, Messina.

CARRARO V12SS

TYPE: Pre-chamber injection, V-form 12-cylinder, turbocharged and inter-cooled four-stroke diesel engine.

OUTPUT: Basic engine, 700bhp; maximum shaft output 650hp at 1,500rpm.

BORE AND STROKE: 142 × 180mm (5·59 × 7·09in).

FUEL INJECTION: Bosch type pumps and centrifugal governor; fuel feeding pumps; fuel cartridge filters.

ENGINE COOLING: By fresh water into closed circuit with thermostatic control valve.

OIL COOLING: By salt water circulating through a heat exchanger.

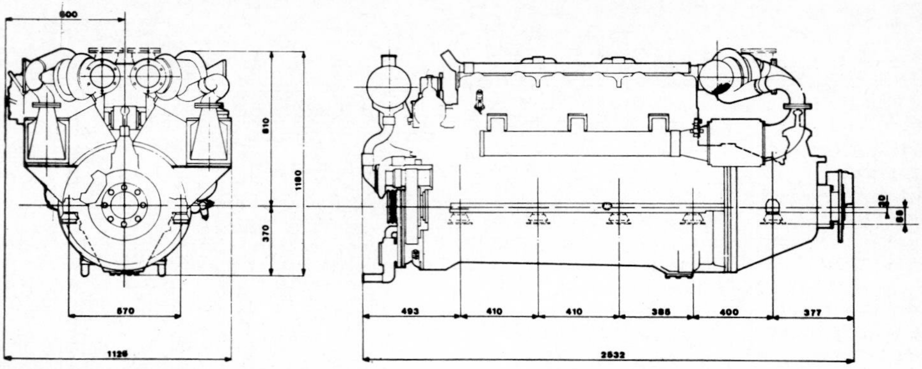

Fiat-Carraro V12SS 700hp marine diesel. Two of these 12-cylinder water-cooled and supercharged engines power the Seaflight H57 hydrofoil passenger ferry

STARTING: 6hp starting motor and 600W generator for battery charging.

LUBRICATION: By gear pump.

REVERSE GEAR: Hydraulically operated, with brake on transmission.

REDUCTION GEAR: Standard ratios, 1·5 : 1-2 : 1.

WEIGHT Dry: 2,200kg (4,120lb)

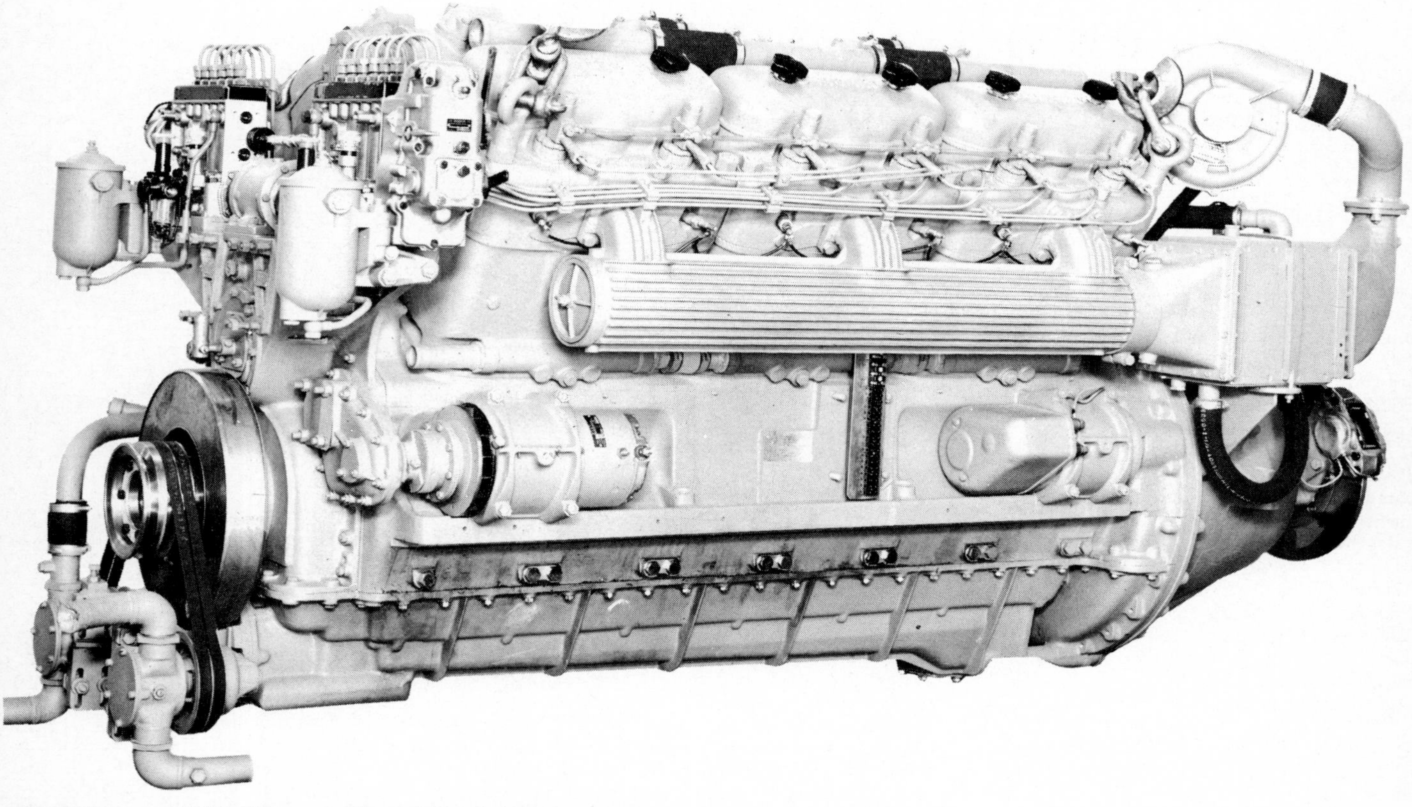

AIFO/FIAT-Carraro V12SS, 700hp supercharged 12-cylinder marine diesel engines

UNION OF SOVIET SOCIALIST REPUBLICS

A. IVCHENKO

This design team headed by the late general designer Ivchenko is based in a factory at Zaporojie in the Ukraine, where all prototypes and pre-production engines bearing the 'AI' prefix are developed and built. Chief designer is Lotarev and chief engineer Tichienko. The production director is M Omeltchenko.

First engine with which Ivchenko was associated officially was the 55hp AI-4G piston-engine used in the Kamov Ka-10 ultra-light helicopter. He later progressed via the widely used AI-14 and AI-26 piston-engines, to become one of the Soviet Union's leading designers of gas-turbine engines.

Two AI-20s in de-rated, marinised form and driving two three-stage waterjets power the Burevestnik, the first Soviet gas-turbine hydrofoil to go into series production, and a single AI-24 drives the integrated lift/propulsion system of the Sormovich 50 passenger ACV.

IVCHENKO AI-20

Ivchenko's design bureau is responsible for the AI-20 turboprop engine which powers the Antonov An-10, An-12 and Ilyushin Il-18 airliners and the Beriev M-12 Tchaika amphibian.

Six production series of this engine had been built by the spring of 1966. The first four series, of which manufacture started in 1957 were variants of the basic AI-20 version. They were followed by two major production versions, as follows:

AI-20K. Rated at 3,945ehp. Used in Il-18V, An-10A and An-12.

AI-20M. Uprated version with T-O rating of 4,190ehp (4,250 ch e). Used in Il-18D/E, An-10A and An-12.

Conversion of the turboprop as a marine power unit for hydrofoil waterjet propulsion (as on the Burevestnik) involved a number of changes to the engine. In particular it was necessary to hold engine rpm at a constant level during conditions of varying load from the waterjet pump—and it was also necessary to be able to vary the thrust from the waterjet unit from zero to forward or rearwards thrust to facilitate engine starting and vessel manoeuvring.

Constant speed under variable load was achieved by replacing the engine's normal high pressure fuel pump with a special fuel regulator pump—and the waterjet pump was modified to have a variable exit area and was fitted with an air valve enabling a variable amount of air to be passed into the intake just ahead of the pump rotor. With less air passing through the waterjet, unit load on the engine increased, and vice versa if the air flow was increased by opening the air valve.

The fuel regulator pump was designed to maintain engine rpm constant and to regulate output while the AI-20 was driving the waterjet unit. Steady running conditions were shown to be satisfactorily maintained by the engine under all operating conditions—and rpm and turbine temperature were held within the limits laid down for the aircraft turboprop version: engine rpm did not fluctuate outside ±2·5% of its set speed when loading or unloading the waterjet unit.

During development of the marinised AI-20, the normal aircraft propeller and speed governor were removed and the turboprop was bench tested over the full range of its operating conditions. This demonstrated that the engine performed in a stable manner throughout, from slow running to normal rpm. These tests were run initially using aviation kerosene Type TS-1 fuel, and then diesel fuels Types L and DS.

Following satisfactory results on the bench, the test engine was mounted on a self-propelled floating test bed equipped with a waterjet propulsion unit. Further tests with this configuration were also satisfactorily concluded, including starting checks with varying degrees of submersion of the pump section of the waterjet unit.

Electrical starting of the engine up to slow running speed (equal to approximately 25% of rated rpm) was shown to take 70 to 85 seconds. For starting and ignition at ambient conditions below 10°C, fuel pre-heating is employed and modified igniters are fitted. With this equipment, starts have been achieved down to minus 12°C.

Based on this experience, the marinised AI-20 for the twin-engined Burevestnik was rated at 2,700hp at 13,200rpm. At this power output, the hydrofoil achieved speeds of up to 97km/h (60mph). Specific fuel consumption was 320-330g (0·71-0·73lb)/hp/h.

Testing with the Burevestnik revealed a number of operating characteristics of the vessel: when the two AI-20s were running while the vessel was moored or manoeuvring, residual exhaust thrust from the turbines occurred and this is required to be balanced by a negative, or reverse thrust from the waterjet by partially closing the unit's nozzle flaps. This increased the load on the engine however, and caused a rise in fuel consumption.

Also, experience showed that with a normal start following a series of wet starts, any fuel which has accumulated in the jet pipe became ignited. This resulted in a sharp rise in turbine temperature and back pressure, and flame emerged from the ejection apertures into the engine compartment and exhaust nozzle. To circumvent this, the ejection apertures were covered with a metal grid, and a spray of water is provided at the exhaust nozzle prior to starting.

Based on an overhaul life for the turboprop AI-20 of several thousand hours, special techniques have been applied to the marinised version

1,750hp Ivchenko AI-23-CI marine gas-turbine

to increase its service life. These include the use of high quality assembly procedures for the engine, efficient design of the air intake and exhaust duct, adoption of appropriate procedures for starting and on-loading of the main and auxiliary turbines at all ambient temperature conditions—and by the utilisation of highly-skilled servicing methods of the installation during operation.

The AI-20 is a single-spool turboprop, with a ten-stage axial-flow compressor, cannular combustion chamber with ten flame tubes, and a three-stage turbine, of which the first two stages are cooled. Planetary reduction gearing, with a ratio of 0·08732 : 1, is mounted forward of the annular air intake. The fixed nozzle contains a central bullet fairing. All engine-driven accessories are mounted on the forward part of the compressor casing, which is of magnesium alloy.

The AI-20 was designed to operate reliably in all temperatures from −60°C to +55°C at heights up to 10,000m (33,000ft). It is a constant speed engine, the rotor speed being maintained at 21,300rpm by automatic variation of propeller pitch. Gas temperature after turbine is 560°C in both current versions. TBO of the AI-20K was 4,000 hours in the spring of 1966.

WEIGHT
DRY
AI-20K: 1,080kg (2,380lb)
AI-20M: 1,039kg (2,290lb)

PERFORMANCE RATINGS
Max T-O:
AI-20K: 4,000ch e (3,945ehp)
AI-20M: 4,250ch e (4,190ehp)
Cruise rating at 630km/h (390mph) at 8,000m (26,000ft):
AI-20K: 2,250ch e (2,220ehp)
AI-20M: 2,700ch e (2,663ehp)

SPECIFIC FUEL CONSUMPTION
At cruise rating:
AI-20K: 215g (0·472lb)/hp/h
AI-20M: 197g (0·434lb)/hp/h

OIL CONSUMPTION Normal: 1 litre (1·75 pints)/h

IVCHENKO AI-24

In general configuration, this single-spool turboprop engine, which powers the An-24 transport aircraft, is very similar to the earlier and larger AI-20. Production began in 1960 and the following data refers to engines of the second series, which were in production in the spring of 1966.

A single marinised version, developing 1,800shp, drives the integrated lift/propulsion system of the Sormovich 50-passenger ACV.

An annular ram air intake surrounds the cast light alloy casing for the planetary reduction gear, which has a ratio of 0·08255 : 1. The cast magnesium alloy compressor casing carries a row of inlet guide vanes and the compressor stator vanes and provides mountings for the engine-driven accessories. These include fuel, hydraulic and oil pumps, tacho-generator and propeller governor.

The ten-stage axial-flow compressor is driven by a three-stage axial-flow turbine, of which the first two stages are cooled. An annular combustion chamber is used, with eight injectors and two igniters.

The engine is flat-rated to maintain its nominal output to 3,500m (11,500ft). TBO was 3,000 hours in the spring of 1966.

LENGTH (overall): 2,435mm (95·87in)
WEIGHT Dry: 499kg (1,100lb)
PERFORMANCE RATING: Max T-O with water injection: 2,859ch e (2,820ehp)

SUDOIMPORT

ul. Kaliaevskaja 5, Moscow K-6, USSR

Soviet industry has developed a variety of marine diesel engines, selected models of which have been installed in the Krasnoye Sormovo series of hydrofoil craft. Most popular of these are the 1,100hp M401 powering the Kometa hydrofoil, and the 1,200hp M50 powering the Byelorus, Chaika, Meteor, Mir, Raketa, Sputnik, Strela and Vikhr hydrofoils. A third marine diesel engine is the 3D12 with a continuous rating of 300hp. A version of this engine is installed in the Nevka hydrofoil, now in series production in Leningrad.

These and other marine diesels are available through Sudoimport, USSR marine export, import and repair organisation.

TYPE M 400

TYPE: Water-cooled, 12-cylinder, V-type four-stroke supercharged marine diesel engine.

CYLINDERS: Two banks of six cylinders set at 30 degrees, each bank comprising cast aluminium alloy monobloc with integral head. Pressed-in liner with spiral cooling passages comprises inner alloy steel sleeve with nitrided working surface, and outer carbon steel sleeve. Each monobloc retained on crankcase by 14 holding-down studs. Bore 180mm (7·09in). Stroke 200mm (7·87in). Cubic capacity 62·4 litres (381in³). Compression ratio 13·5 : 1.

SUPERCHARGING: Single-stage centrifugal supercharger, mechanically driven and providing supercharging pressure of at least 1·55kg/cm² (22lb/in²) at rated power.

CRANKCASE: Two-part cast aluminium alloy case with upper half carrying cylinder monoblocs, and transmitting all engine loads.

CYLINDER HEADS: Integral with cylinder monoblocs.

CRANKSHAFT: Six-crank seven-bearing crankshaft in nitrided alloy steel with split steel shells, lead bronze lined with lead-tin alloy bearing surface. Spring damper at rear end reduces torsional vibrations.

CONNECTING RODS: Master and articulated rods, with master connected to crankshaft by split big end with lead bronze lining. Articulated rods connected by pin pressed into eye of master rods.

PISTONS: Forged aluminium alloy with four rings, upper two of which are of trapeziform cross-section. Alloy steel floating gudgeon pin. Piston head specially shaped to form combustion chamber with spherical cylinder head.

CAMSHAFTS: Two camshafts acting direct on valve stems.

VALVES: Four valves in each cylinder, two inlet and two exhaust. Each valve retained on seat by three coil springs.

COOLING: Forced circulation system using fresh water with 1 to 1·1% potassium bichromate added. Fresh water pump mounted on forward part of engine. Fresh water, and lubricating oil leaving the engine are cooled by water-to-water and water-to-oil coolers, in turn cooled by sea water circulated by engine-mounted sea water pump.

SUPERCHARGING: Single-stage centrifugal supercharger, mechanically driven and providing supercharging pressure of at least 1·55kg/cm² (22lb/in²) at rated power.

LUBRICATION: Comprises delivery pump together with full-flow centrifuge; twin-suction scavenge pump, double gauze-type strainers at inlet and outlet to oil system; and electrically-driven priming pump to prime engine with oil and fuel.

FUEL INJECTION: Closed-type fuel injection with hydraulically-operated valves, giving initial pressure of 200kg/cm² (2,845lb/in²). Each injector has eight spray orifices forming 140 degree conical spray. High pressure 12-plunger fuel injection pump with primary gear pump. Two filters in parallel filter oil to HP pump.

STARTING: Compressed air system with starting cylinder operating at 75 to 150kg/cm² (1,067

to 2,134lb/in²) two disc-type air distributors and 12 starting valves.
GOVERNOR: Multi-range indirect-action engine speed governor with resilient gear drive from pump camshaft. Governor designed to maintain pre-set rpm throughout full speed range from minimum to maximum.
EXHAUST SYSTEM: Fresh water-cooled exhaust manifolds fastened to exterior of cylinder blocs. Provision made for fitting thermocouple or piezometer.
REVERSING: Hydraulically-operated reversing clutch fitted to enable prop shaft to run forwards, idle or reverse with constant direction of crankshaft rotation.
MOUNTING: Supports fitted to upper half of crankcase for attaching engine to bedplate.
DIMENSIONS
Length: 2,600mm (102·36in)
Width: 1,220mm (48·03in)
Height: 1,250mm (49·21in)
PERFORMANCE RATINGS
Max: 1,100hp at 1,800rpm
Continuous: 1,000hp at 1,700rpm
FUEL CONSUMPTION: At continuous rating: not over 193g (0·425lb)/hp/h
OIL CONSUMPTION: At continuous rating: not over 6g (0·013lb)/hp/h

TYPE 3D12

TYPE: Water-cooled, 12-cylinder, V-type, four-stroke marine diesel engine.
CYLINDERS: Two banks of six cylinders in jacketed blocks with pressed-in steel liners. Bore 150mm (5·9in). Stroke 180mm (7·09in). Cubic capacity 38·8 litres (237in³). Compression ratio 14 to 15 : 1.
CRANKCASE: Two-part cast aluminium alloy case with upper half accommodating seven main bearings of steel shell, lead bronze lined type. Lower half carries oil pump, water circulating pump and fuel feed pump.
CYLINDER HEADS: Provided with six recesses to accommodate combustion chambers. Each chamber is connected via channel to inlet and outlet ports of cylinder bloc.
CRANKSHAFT: Alloy steel forging with seven journals and six crankpins. Pendulum anti-vibration dampers fitted on first two webs to reduce torsional vibration.
CONNECTING RODS: Master and articulated rods of double-T section forged in alloy steel. Master rod big-end bearings have steel shells, lead bronze lined. Small end bearings of master rods and both bearings of articulated rods have bronze bushes.
PISTONS: Aluminium alloy.
CAMSHAFTS: Carbon steel camshafts with cams and journals hardened by high frequency electrical current.
COOLING: Closed water, forced circulation type incorporating centrifugal pump, self suction sea water pump and tubular water cooler.
LUBRICATION: Forced circulation type with dry sump, incorporating three-section gear pump, oil feed pump, wire-mesh strainer with fine cardboard filtering element and tubular oil cooler.
FUEL INJECTION: Rotary fuel feed pump, twin felt filter, plunger fuel pump with device to stop engine in event of oil pressure drop in main line. Closed-type fuel injectors with slotted filters. Plunger pump carries variable-speed centrifugal governor for crankshaft rpm.
STARTING: Main electrical starting system, with compressed air reverse system.
REVERSE-REDUCTION GEAR: Non-co-axial type with twin-disc friction clutch and gear-type reduction gear giving optional ratios, forwards, of 2·95 : 1, 2·04 : 1 or 1·33 : 1, and 2·18 : 1 astern.
DIMENSIONS
Length: 2,464mm (97·01in)
Width: 1,052mm (41·42in)
Height: 1,159mm (45·63in)
WEIGHT Dry fully equipped: 1,900kg (4,189lb)
PERFORMANCE RATING: Continuous: 300hp at 1,500rpm

Sudoimport M400

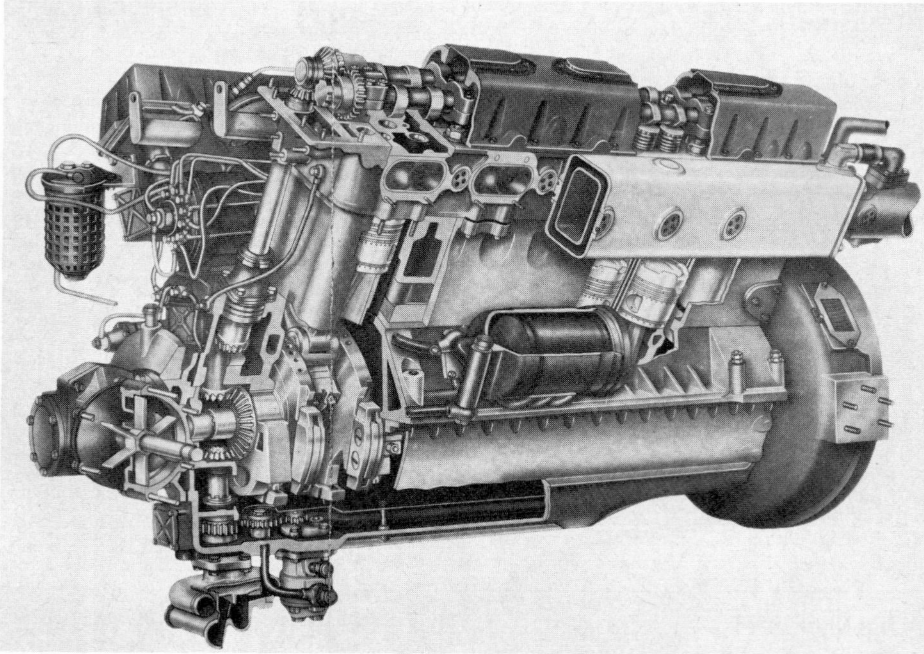

Sudoimport 3D12

FUEL CONSUMPTION: At continuous rated power: 176g (0·388lb)/hp/h
OIL CONSUMPTION: At continuous rated power: Not over 9g (0·02lb)/hp/h

M401A

The M401A, fitted to the new Voskhod and the latest variants of the Kometa and Raketa, is based on the M50. The new engine is more reliable than its predecessor and its development involved the redesigning of a number of units and parts, as well as the manufacturing of components with a higher degree of accuracy, which necessitated the employment of the latest engineering techniques.

The engine is manufactured in left hand and right hand models. These differ by the arrangement on the engine housing of the fresh water pump drive and the power take-off for the shipboard compressor.

TYPE: Water-cooled, 12-cylinder, V-type four-stroke supercharged marine diesel.
CYLINDERS: Two banks of six cylinders set at 60 degrees. Monobloc is a solid aluminium casting. Pressed into monobloc are six steel sleeves with spiral grooves on the outer surface for the circulation of cooling water. Bore 180mm (7·09in). Stroke 200mm (7·87in). Compression ratio 13·5 : 0·5.
CRANKCASE: Two piece cast aluminium alloy case with upper half carrying cylinder monoblocs and transmitting all engine loads.
CYLINDER HEADS: Integral with cylinder monobloc.
CRANKSHAFT: Six-crank, seven bearing crankshaft in nitrided alloy steel with split steel shells, lead-tin bronze lined with lead tin alloy bearing surface.
CONNECTING RODS: Master and articulated rods, with master connected to the crankshaft by split big end, lined with lead tin bronze. Articulated rod connected to crankshaft by a pin pressed into its eye ring.
PISTONS: Forged aluminium alloy with five

rings. Top two steel rings, one cast iron of rectangular section and the two bottom rings, in cast iron and steel, are oil control rings fitted in a common groove.
CAMSHAFTS: Two, acting directly on valve stems.
VALVES: Four in each cylinder, two inlet and two exhaust. Each retained on seat by three coil springs.
SUPERCHARGING: Two, Type TK-18H superchargers, each comprising an axial-flow turbine and a centrifugal compressor mounted on a common shaft with a vane diffuser and volute. A silencer can be installed on the compressor air inlet. Turbine casing cooled with fresh water from the diesel engine cooling system.
GOVERNOR: Multi-range indirect action engine speed governor with resilient gear drive from pump camshaft. Designed to maintain preset rpm throughout full speed range.
LUBRICATION: Delivery pump with full-flow centrifuge, scavenge pump, double gauge strainers and electrically driven priming pump to power engine with oil and fuel.
COOLING: Double-circuit forced circulation system using fresh water with 1 to 1·1% potassium bichromate to GOST2652-71. Fresh water pump mounted on engine. Fresh water and lubricating oil leaving engine are cooled by water-to-water and water-to-oil coolers in turn cooled by sea water circulated by engine-mounted sea water pump.
STARTING: Compressed air system with two disc-type air distributors and twelve starting valves.
REVERSING: Hydraulically operated reversing

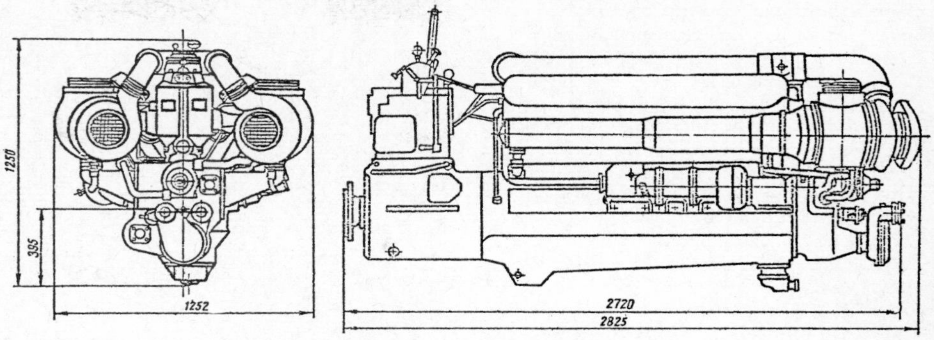

M401A water cooled 12-cylinder, V-type four-stroke supercharged marine diesel

clutch to enable propeller shaft to run forwards, idle or reverse. Manual control available in emergency.
Rated power at ahead running under normal atmospheric conditions and at rated rpm: 1,000hp
Rated rpm at ahead running: 1,550
Max hourly power at maximum rpm: 1,100hp
Max rpm at ahead running: 1,600
Max power at astern running: 250hp
Minimum rpm at astern running (with the diesel engine control lever at reverse stop): 750
Max specific fuel consumption at rated power (with operating generator, hydraulic pump and the power take-off for compressor): 172 g/ehp/h+ 5%
Maximum specific oil burning losses at rated power: 5 g/ehp/h
Fuel:
Diesel fuel Grade (GOST 4749—49) Oil
MC-20 (GOST 4749—49) with additive (GOST 8312-57) 3% in weight
Sense of power take-off flange rotation (if viewed from turbo-supercharger):
of right hand diesel engine: clockwise
of left hand diesel engine: counter-clockwise
Operating life (until major overhaul): 2,500 hours
Diesel engine dimensions:
length: (with muffler at intake) 2,825mm (111·1in)
length: (without muffler at intake) 2,720mm (107in)
width: 1,252mm (49·29in)
height: 1,250mm (49·21in)
Weight (dry) with all units and pipe lines mounted: 2,000kg (4,409lb)

UNITED KINGDOM

PAXMAN DIESELS LIMITED
(a management company of GEC Diesels Limited)

Hythe Hill, Colchester, Essex CO1 2HW, England

Manufactured at the Colchester Works of Ruston Paxman Diesels are three of the world's most advanced diesel designs; the V-form 'Ventura', built in 6, 8, 12 and 16-cylinder sizes covering 450 to 2,400bhp, the RP200 built in 8, 12 and 16-cylinder sizes covering 1,000-4,500bhp, and the Paxman 'Deltic'—an 18-cylinder engine of unique triangular configuration—in powers from 1,500 to 4,000shp. These engines, with their compact overall dimensions and low unit weight, are particularly suitable for the propulsion of high-speed craft including hydrofoils and hovercraft.

The 'Ventura' is being incorporated in several current designs for hydrofoils and rigid sidewall ACVs.

Paxman 18-cylinder Valenta marine diesel developing 4,500bhp

VENTURA (YJ) AND VALENTA (RP200) DIESELS

TYPE: Ventura engines: Direct injection 60 degree, V-form 6, 8, 12 and 16-cylinder, turbocharged or turbocharged and after-cooled four stroke diesel engine. Valenta engines: Direct injection, V-form 8, 12, 16 and 18-cylinder, turbocharged and water-cooled, four-stroke engine.
OUTPUT: Ventura engines: 450-2,400bhp, 1,000-1,600rpm. Valenta engines: 1,000-4,000bhp, 1,000-1,600rpm.
BORE AND STROKE: 197 × 216mm (7·75 × 8·5in).
SWEPT VOLUME (per cylinder): 6·57 litres (401in^3).
HOUSING: Fabricated high quality steel plate.
CRANKSHAFT AND MAIN BEARINGS: Fully nitrated shaft carried in aluminium tin pre-finished steel-backed main bearings. Engine fully balanced against primary and secondary forces.
CONNECTING RODS: Fork and blade type with steel-backed, aluminium tin lined large end (forked rod) and steel-backed, lead bronze lined, lead tin flashed bearings (blade rod).
PISTONS: Conventional aluminium alloy, oil cooled with Alfin bonded insert for top ring. Three compression rings and one oil control ring (Ventura): Three compression rings and one oil control ring (Valenta).
CYLINDER HEAD: High grade casting carrying four valve direct injection system.
LINERS: Wet type seamless steel tube, chrome plated bore and water side surface honeycombed for surface oil retention.
FUEL INJECTION: External Monobloc pumps located below air manifolds (Ventura); single unit pumps (Valenta). Pump plungers and camshaft lubricated from main engine pressure system. Feed and injection pump driven from engine drive and gear train; a fuel reservoir and air bleed system fitted. Injectors of the multi-hole type spray fuel into the toroidal cavity in the top of piston. Injectors retained by clamp and are external to head cover (Ventura); sleeved connection inside cover (Valenta).
GOVERNOR: Standard hydraulic 'Regulateurs Europa' unit with self-contained lubricating oil system; mechanical, electrical or pneumatic controls. Alternative makes available.
PRESSURE CHARGING AND INTERCOOLING: Napier water-cooled exhaust-gas-driven turboblowers mounted above engine. Air to water intercooler of Serck manufacture for after-cooled versions.
LUBRICATION: Pressure lubrication to all bearing surfaces; separate pressure and cooling pumps (Ventura): single pump system (Valenta). Oil coolers mounted externally and integral with

engine (fresh water-cooled (Ventura); sea water cooled (Valenta)). Full flow single or duplex oil filter can be supplied. Centrifugal filters fitted as standard (Ventura).
FRESH WATER COOLING: Single pump at free end, shaft-driven from drive end gear train. Thermostatic control valve mounted above pump, giving quick warm-up and even temperature control of water and oil circuits (Ventura); oil thermostat (Valenta).
EXHAUST: Single outlet from turboblower(s). Dry type manifolds (Ventura); watercooled manifolds (Valenta).
STARTING: Air, electric or hydraulic starting.
FUEL: Gas oil to BS.2869/1970 Class A1 and A2 or equivalent, and certain gas turbine fuels. Other classes of fuel subject to specification being made available.
LUBRICATING OIL: Oils certified to MIL-L-46152 (with a TBN of not less than nine).
OPTIONAL EXTRA EQUIPMENT: Gearboxes, starting control systems, and all associated engine ancillary equipment necessary for marine applications.

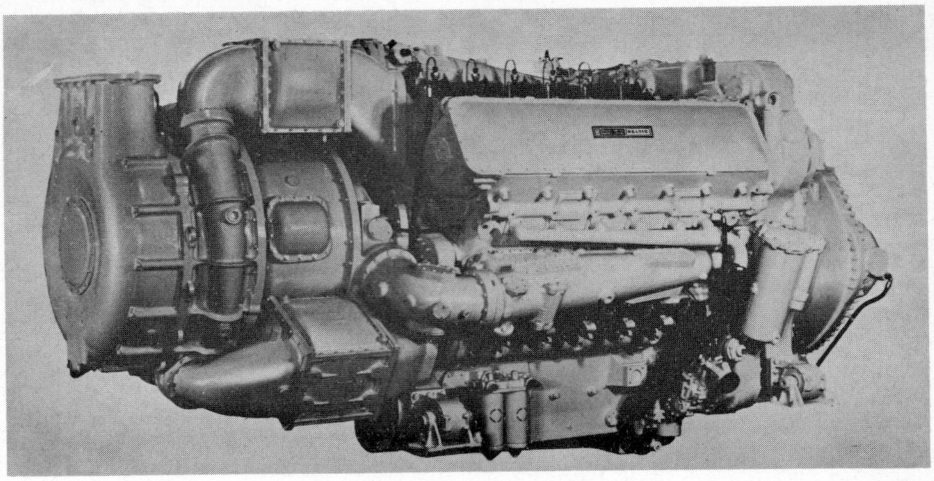

Deltic charge-air cooled, turbo-charged diesel engine with integral reverse reduction gear, developing 4,000shp

DELTIC DIESEL

TYPE: 18-cylinder, opposed piston, liquid cooled, two-stroke, compression ignition. Three banks of six cylinders in triangular configuration.
OUTPUT: Covers horsepower range of 1,500-4,000shp. Charge-cooled engine rating up to 3,000shp continuous at 1,800rpm. Half hour sprint rating up to 4,000shp at 2,100rpm. Weight/power ratio 3·94lb/shp.
BORE AND STROKE: Bore 130·17mm (5·125in). Stroke 184·15mm × 2 (7·25in × 2) (opposed piston).
SWEPT VOLUME: (total): 88·3 litres (5,284in³).
COMBUSTION SYSTEM: Direct injection.
PISTONS: Two piece—body and gudgeon pin housing. Gudgeon pin housing with fully floating gudgeon pin shrunk into body and secured with taper seated circlip. Body skirt and gudgeon pin housing in light alloy, piston crown in 'Hidurel' material. Oil cooled. Three gas, two oil control and one scraper ring.
CONNECTING RODS: Fork and blade type with steel backed, lead bronze, lead flashed, indium infused thin-wall bearings. Manufactured from drop forgings, machined and polished all over.
CRANKSHAFTS: Three crankshafts machined from forgings and fully nitrided. Each shaft fitted with viscous type torsional vibration damper. Each crankpin carries one inlet and one exhaust piston, thus the loading on all crankpins is identical and reciprocating forces are balanced within the engine.
CRANKCASES AND CYLINDER BLOCKS: Three crankcases and three cylinder blocks arranged in the form of an inverted equilateral triangle all of light alloy construction. Crankcases substantially webbed and carrying each crankshaft in seven, thin-wall, steelbacked, lead bronze, lead flashed indium infused main bearings. Cylinder blocks each carry six 'wet' type liners, have integrally cast air inlet manifolds and mount the injection pumps camshaft casings.
CYLINDER LINERS: 18 'wet' type liners machined from hollow steel forgings, bores chrome plated with honeycomb process applied, finished by lapping. Coolant side flash tin plated. In areas of liquid contact with exhaust coolant-area, flash chrome plated.
TURBOCHARGER: Geared-in type, single stage, axial flow turbine and single-sided centrifugal compressor mounted on common shaft. Light alloy main castings. Charge-cooled engines have charge-air coolers (one for each cylinder block) incorporated within the overall dimensions of the turbocharger unit.
PHASING GEAR: To combine the output from the three crankshafts. A light alloy gear casing containing an output gear train linked to the crankshafts by quill-shafts and passing the torque to a common output gear. All gears hardened and ground and carried in roller bearings. Gear train also provides drives for auxiliary pumps and engine governor.
FUEL SYSTEM: Pressurised system from engine driven circulating pump supplying 18 'jerk' type fuel injection pumps one per cylinder mounted in banks of six on camshaft casings secured to each cylinder block. Each pump supplies a single injector per cylinder.
LUBRICATION: Dry sump system with engine driven pressure and scavenge pumps. Twin pressure oil filters engine mounted.
COOLING: Closed circuit system with engine driven circulating pump. Engine mounted circulating pumps for sea-water system for cooling coolant heat exchanger and oil cooler, also for charge-air coolers.
STARTING: Air starting to six cylinders of one bank.
MOUNTING: Four points by resilient mounting units.
REVERSE GEAR: Marine reverse reduction gearbox incorporating a hydraulic friction clutch can be supplied as an integral unit.

ROLLS-ROYCE LIMITED
(Industrial & Marine Division)

PO Box 72, Ansty, Coventry, Warwickshire CV7 9JR, England
Telephone: 0203 613211
Telex: 31637

In April 1967 Rolls-Royce Limited formed a new division merging the former industrial and marine gas-turbine activities of Rolls-Royce and Bristol Siddeley. The new division was known as the Industrial & Marine Gas-Turbine Division of Rolls-Royce.

In May 1971 the present company, Rolls-Royce Limited, was formed combining all the gas-turbine interests of the former Rolls-Royce company.

It offers a wider range of industrial and marine gas-turbines based on aero-engine gas generators than any other manufacturer in the world. It has available for adaptation a large selection of the gas-turbines being developed and manufactured by the Rolls-Royce Derby Engine Division, the Bristol Engine, and Small Engine Divisions. Marinised gas-turbines at present being produced and developed by the Company include the Gnome, Proteus, Tyne, Olympus and Spey.

Over 1,799 of these marine and industrial engines are in service or have been ordered for operation around the world. Twenty-three navies and nine civil operators have selected the company's marine gas-turbines to power naval craft, following the initial orders from the Royal Navy in the late 1950s.

Tyne RM2 configuration

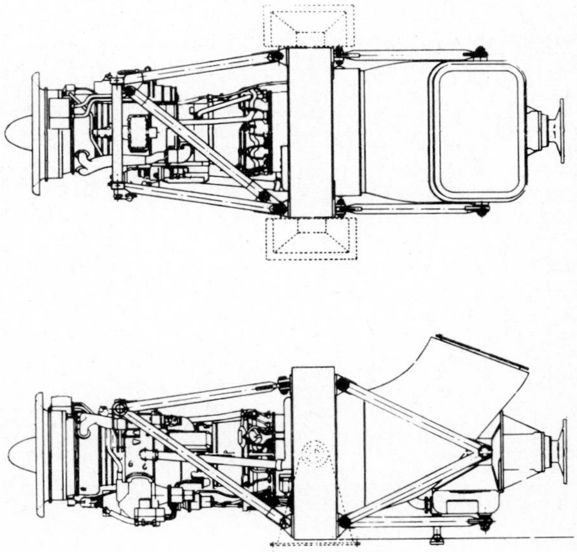

Rolls-Royce Marine Tyne RM2D rated at 5,800bhp

HYDROFOILS: The Boeing PCH High Point is powered by two Proteus gas-turbines while single Proteus turbines power the CNR-Alinavi Swordfish. A Tyne powers the Grumman designed PG(H)-1 Flagstaff and the Super Flagstaff. Rolls-Royce marine gas-turbines can also be specified as alternative power plants for the modular version of the Boeing Jetfoil.
HOVERCRAFT: The Gnome powers the BHC SR.N5 and SR.N6. The Proteus powers the SR.N4, the BH.7 and the new Vosper Thornycroft VT 2.

MARINE GNOME

TYPE: Gas-turbine, free-turbine turboshaft.
AIR INTAKE: Annular. 15°C.
COMBUSTION CHAMBER: Annular.
FUEL GRADE
DERD 2494 Avtur/50 Kerosene.
DERD 2482 Avtur/40 Kerosene.
Diesel fuel: BSS 2869 Class A, DEF 1402 or NATO F75
TURBINE: Two-stage axial-flow generator turbine and a single-stage axial-flow free power turbine.
BEARINGS: Compressor rotor has a roller bearing at the front and a ball bearing at the rear. Gas generator turbine is supported at the front by the compressor rear bearings, and at the rear by a roller bearing.

Single stage power turbine is supported by a roller bearing behind the turbine disc and by a ball bearing towards the rear of the turbine shaft.
JET PIPE: Exhaust duct to suit installation.
ACCESSORY DRIVES: Accessory gearbox provides a drive for : the fuel pump, the hydromechanical governor in the flow control unit, the centrifugal fuel filter, the dual tachometer and the engine oil pump.
LUBRICATION SYSTEM: Dry sump.
OIL SPECIFICATION: DERD 2487.
MOUNTING: Front: three pads on the front frame casing, one on top, one on each side. Rear: without reduction gearbox, mounting point is the rear flange of the exhaust duct centre-body. With reduction gearbox mounting points are provided by two machined faces on the reduction gearbox.
STARTING: Electric.
DIMENSIONS
Length: 1,667mm (72·8in)
Width: 462mm (18·2in)
Height: 527mm (20·75in)
PERFORMANCE RATINGS
Max: 1,050bhp
Continuous: 900bhp
Ratings are at maximum power-turbine speed, 19,500rpm. A reduction gearbox is available giving an output speed of 6,650rpm.
SPECIFIC FUEL CONSUMPTION
Max: 283g (0·625lb)/bhp/h
Continuous: 295g (0·65lb)/bhp/h
OIL CONSUMPTION
0·67 litres (1·2 pints)/h
Power turbine: 0·84 litres (1·5 pints)/h

MARINE OLYMPUS

Gas generator and single stage power turbine. Powered by the Marine Olympus the TM33 module is a fully equipped enclosed power unit used for high speed operation by navies for modern warships.
TYPE: Gas-turbine, two-shaft turbojet.
AIR INTAKE: Annular 15°C.
COMBUSTION CHAMBER: Eight.
FUEL GRADE: Diesel fuel BSS 2869 Class A. DEF 2402 or NATO F75.
TURBINE
ENGINE: Two stage, each stage driving its own respective compressor—5 stage low pressure or 7 stage high pressure.
POWER: Single stage axial flow.
BEARINGS: Compressor rotor forward end supported by a roller bearing and rear end by a duplex ball bearing.

The power turbine rotor assembly and mainshaft are supported as a cantilever in two white metal bearings housed in a pedestal.
JET PIPE: Exhaust duct to suit installation.
ACCESSORY DRIVES: Power turbine. Accessories are mounted on the main gearbox which is a separate unit transmitting the turbine's power output to the propeller shaft. These include pressure and scavenge oil pumps. Speed signal generator, iso-speedic switch and rpm indicator are driven by the pedestal-mounted accessory gearbox.
LUBRICATION SYSTEM: The gas generator has its own integral lubrication system which is supplied with oil from a 122·74 litre (27 gallon) tank. Components in the system are: a pressure pump, main scavenge pump, four auxiliary scavenge pumps and an oil cooler.

Power Turbine: Bearings are lubricated and cooled by a pressure oil system.
OIL SPECIFICATION: Gas generator: D Eng RD 2487. Power turbine: OEP 69.
MOUNTING: The mounting structure depends on the customer's requirements for a particular application.
STARTING: Air or electric.
DIMENSIONS
GAS GENERATOR
Length: 3·6m (11ft 9in)
Width: 1·29m (4ft 3in)
POWER TURBINE
Length: 3·9m (12ft 9in)
Width: 2·4m (8ft)
Height: 3m (9ft 9in)
COMPLETE UNIT
Length: 6·8m (22ft 3in)
Width: 2·4m (8ft)
Height: 3m (9ft 9in)
WEIGHTS
Gas generator: 2,948·35 kg (6,500 lb)
Complete unit: 20·32 tonnes (20 tons)
PERFORMANCE RATING: Max: 28,000bhp at max power-turbine speed of 5,660rpm.
SPECIFIC FUEL CONSUMPTION: Max: 226g (0·478lb)/bhp/h
OIL CONSUMPTION
GAS GENERATOR
Max: 0·84 litres (1·5 pints)/h
Power turbine: 0·84 litres (1·5 pints)/h

MARINE PROTEUS

TYPE: Gas-turbine, free-turbine turboprop.
AIR INTAKE: Radial between the compressor and turbine sections of the engine. 15°C.
COMBUSTION CHAMBERS: Eight, positioned around the compressor casing.
FUEL GRADE: DEF 2402—Distillate diesel fuel.
TURBINE: Four stages coupled in mechanically independent pairs. The first coupled pair drive the compressor, the second pair form the free power turbine, which drives the output shaft.
BEARINGS: HP end of compressor rotor is car-

BOEING PCH-1 HIGH POINT

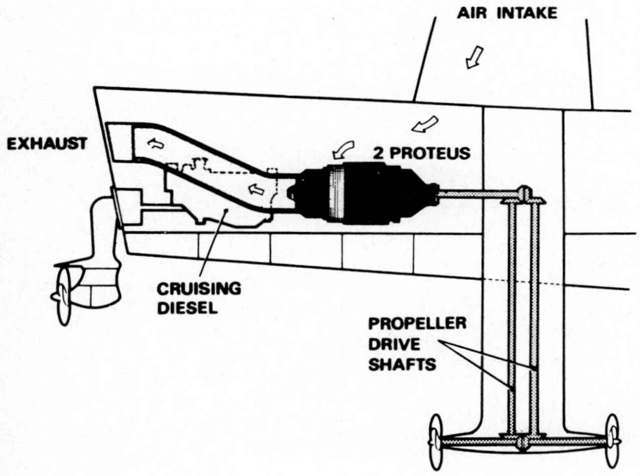

GRUMMAN PGH-1 FLAGSTAFF

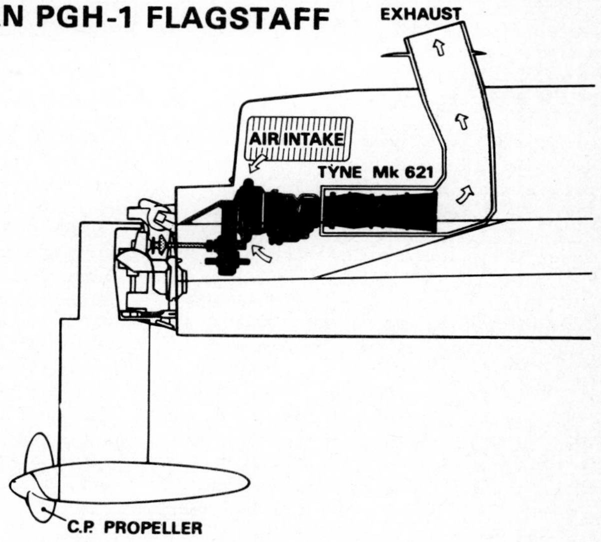

ITALIAN NAVY SWORDFISH

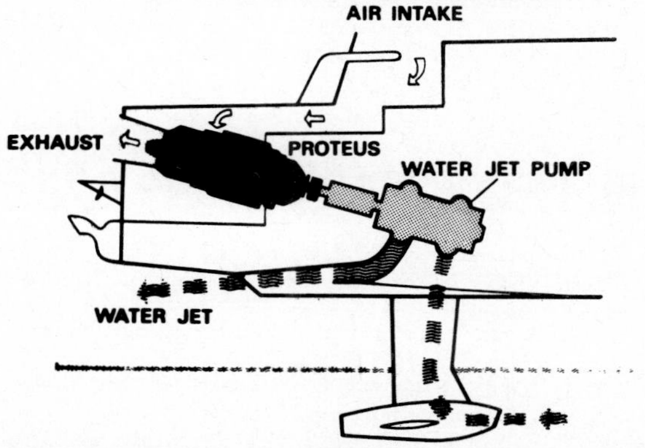

Rolls-Royce marine gas-turbines are employed on the PCH-1 High Point, the PGH-1 Flagstaff and the Swordfish hydrofoils

ried by roller bearing, the rear end by a duplex ball bearing. Compressor turbine rotor shaft is located by a ball thrust bearing, as is the power turbine rotor.
JET PIPE: Exhaust duct to suit installation.
ACCESSORY DRIVES: All accessories are driven by the compressor or power turbine systems. Compressor driven accessories are: compressor tachometer generator, fuel pump and centrifugal oil separator for the breather. The power turbine tachometer generator and governor are driven by the power turbine. The main oil pressure pump and also the main and auxiliary scavenge pumps are driven by both the compressor and power turbines through a differential gear.
LUBRICATION SYSTEM: The engine is lubricated by a single gear type pump connected by a differential drive to both the compressor and power turbine systems.
OIL SPECIFICATION: OEP 71. DERD 2479/1 or DERD 2487 (OX 38).
MOUNTING: Three attachment points comprise two main trunnions one on each side of the engine close to the diffuser casing and a steady bearing located beneath the engine immediately aft of the air intake. Engines are supplied with integrally-mounted reduction gears giving maximum output shaft speeds of 5,240, 1,500 or 1,000rpm depending on the gearbox selected.
DIMENSIONS
Length: 2,870mm (113in)
Diameter: 1,067mm (42in)
WEIGHT Dry: 1,414kg (3,118lb)
PERFORMANCE RATINGS
Max: 4,500bhp
95% power: 4,250bhp
80% power: 3,600bhp
SPECIFIC FUEL CONSUMPTION: At max rating: 253g (0·565lb)/bhp/h
OIL CONSUMPTION: Average: 0·28 litres (0·5 pints)/h

MARINE TYNE RM2D

Gas generator and two-stage power turbine.
TYPE: Gas-turbine, two-shaft turboprop.
AIR INTAKE: Annular. 15°C.
COMBUSTION CHAMBER: Cannular containing ten flame tubes.
FUEL GRADE: Diesel fuel Grade A. DEF 2402B AVCAT.
TURBINE
ENGINE: Two stage, each stage driving its own respective compressor—six-stage low pressure and nine-stage high pressure.
POWER: Two-stage, axial flow free turbine.
BEARINGS: Compressor rotor forward end supported by a roller bearing and at the rear end by a thrust ball location bearing.
The power turbine front stubshaft is supported on a roller bearing and the rear on a thrust bearing.
JET PIPE: Exhaust duct to suit installation.
ACCESSORY DRIVES: Engine and power turbines accessories are mounted on the external wheelcase of the engine and the primary gearbox accessories gearcase.
LUBRICATION SYSTEM: The gas generator lubricating oil system comprises fuel pump, scavenge pumps, filters, and magnetic plugs. The primary gearbox is also fed from the gas generator lubricating oil system.
OIL SPECIFICATION: DERD 2487
MOUNTING: The forward engine mounting comprises two cantilever frames constructed of tubular members, one each side of the engine.

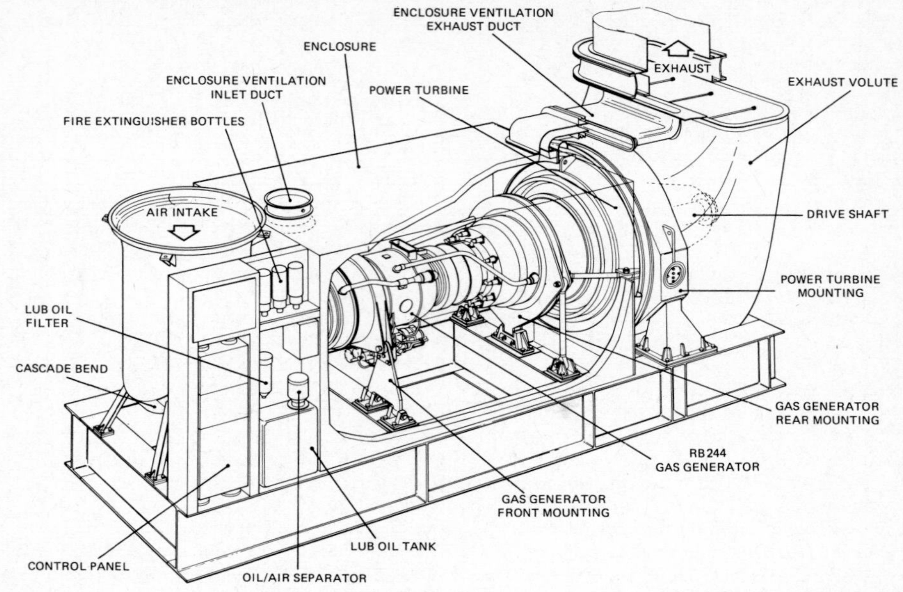

Rolls-Royce SM1A Marine Module rated at 17,100bhp

The frames are joined by a diagonal strut across the uppermost members.
The reduction gearbox is supported in a similar way by three tubular steel supports, one either side and one beneath the gearbox. The ends of the engine and gearbox supports are attached to the central main engine support frame by means of spherical bearings. The centre of the unit is supported through a dogged ring into the main central frame.
STARTING: Air or electric.
DIMENSIONS
Length: 4,013mm (158in)
Width: 1,270mm (50in)
Height: 1,400mm (54in)
WEIGHT: 2,815kg (6,200lb)
PERFORMANCE RATINGS
Max 5,800bhp (5,880cv) at max power turbine speed of 14,500rpm (primary gearbox output speed 3,600rpm).
SPECIFIC FUEL CONSUMPTION
Max: 209g (0·461lb)/bhp/h

MARINE SM1A AND SM2B

The Marine SM1A and SM2B power units have been based on the Rolls-Royce RB244 gas generator derived from the Spey aero engine.
Both units offer high efficiency (in excess of 34%) and up to date features. They have been designed to fill the gap in the range of current marine gas turbines, and cater for a wide range of marine propulsion applications in the 1980s.
The SM1A unit has been designed for the longer vessel, such as frigates, cruisers, destroyers etc, and the SM2B is for the lighter craft, such as hydrofoils, hovercraft and patrol boat applications.
The SM series of marine gas turbine has been under development since 1972 in a programme sponsored by the British Ministry of Defence.
TYPE: Marine gas-turbine, incorporating two independently driven compressors, an axial-flow free-power turbine and exhaust volute, all on a lightweight mounting frame.
GAS GENERATOR CHARACTERISTICS
AIR INTAKE: Direct entry, fixed, without intake guides.
LP COMPRESSOR: 5 axial stages.
HP COMPRESSOR: 11 axial stages.
COMBUSTION SYSTEM: Turbo-annular type with ten interconnected straight flow flame tubes.
TURBINES: Impulse reaction, axial-type. Two HP and two LP stages.
EXHAUST: Fixed volume.
STARTING: Air/gas starter motor.
FUEL SYSTEM: Hydromechanical high pressure system with automatic acceleration and speed control.
FUEL GRADE: Diesel fuel Grade 'A', DEF 2402 or NATO F75.
LUBRICATION SYSTEM: Self-contained gear pump filters and chip detectors.
POWER TURBINE: Two-stage free axial-flow turbine.
DIMENSIONS
SM1A UNIT
Length: 7·46m (22ft 9in)
Width: 2·286m (7ft 6in)
Height: 3·073m (10ft 7in)
SM2B UNIT
Length (air intake flare to drive coupling): 6·063m (19ft 10½in)
Height: 2·678m (9ft 1in)
Width: 2·286m (7ft 6in)
GAS GENERATOR CHANGE UNIT DRY
Length: 2·677m (8ft 9in)
Max diameter: 910mm (2ft 11·82in)
WEIGHTS
Estimated weight
SM1A: 19,295kg (42,500lb)
SM2B: 9,080kg (20,000lb)
Estimated dry weight of gas generator change unit: 1,406kg (3,100lb)
NOMINAL PERFORMANCE
*Max power: 17,100bhp (12·75MW)
*Specific fuel consumption: 0·239kg/kWh (0·393lb/bhp/h)
Based on LCV of fuel of 43,125kJ/kg (18,540btu/lb)
No power off-takes
No intake or exhaust duct losses
Ambient air temperature of 15°C (59°F) and a pressure of 101·3kPa (14·7lbf/in²)

UNITED STATES OF AMERICA

AVCO LYCOMING

Avco Lycoming Division of Avco Corporation

550 South Main Street, Stratford, Connecticut 08497, USA
Officials:
George L Hogeman, *President of Avco Corporation*
Joseph S Bartos, *General Manager, Lycoming Division*
Seymour L Rosenberg, *Vice President, Controller, Lycoming Division*
James F Shanley, *Vice President, Administration, Lycoming Division*
E Louis Wilkinson, *Vice President, Factory Operations, Lycoming Division*
Michael S Saboe, *Vice President, Engineering and Development, Lycoming Division*
Martin J Leff, *Vice President, Product Support and Marketing, Lycoming Division*
Michael Cusick, *Manager, Marine Marketing, Lycoming Division*
William C Pappas, *Manager, Industrial Marketing, Lycoming Division*

K M Austin, *UK Manager, Avco International Overseas Corporation*

The Avco Lycoming Division, Stratford, is the turbine engine manufacturing division of the Avco Corporation.

Avco Lycoming is mainly producing two families of gas-turbine engines. Designated T53 and T55, these are both of the free-turbine type and are available in turboshaft, turbofan and turboprop form. The T53 in particular has been built in large numbers to power US Army helicopters. Industrial and marine versions of the T55 are designated Super TF 25, TF 35 and TF 40. Avco Lycoming has also initiated investigations into the possible application of the AGT-1500 gas turbine unit (which was originally designed for the US Army's new main battletank—XM-1) in air-cushion vehicles and hydrofoils.

SUPER TF25 AND SUPER TF35

These engines are developments of the T55 aircraft engine.

Current production and development versions are as follows:

TF25. High-speed shaft-turbine engine, with output shaft speed equal to power turbine speed. Integral oil tank and cooling system. An earlier TF25 powers the Vosper Thornycroft VT1, the Coastal Patrol Interdiction Craft (CPIC-X) and the Mitsui MV-PP15 155-seat hover ferry.

TF35. Uprated, redesigned version of the TF25. New turbine section with four stages and variable-incidence inlet guide vanes. First two compressor stages transonic. New atomising fuel nozzles. Earlier TF35s power a number of six-engined Patrol Ship Multi-Mission craft (PSMM); a number of tri-engined waterjet ferries for the San Francisco Bridge and Highway Authority off the coast of California and the Aerojet-General SES-100A surface effect test craft. This 100-ton vessel employs four TF35 engines, each rated at 3,300shp (maximum).

AIR INTAKE: Side inlet casting of aluminium alloy supporting optional reduction gearbox and front main bearings. Provision for intake screens.

COMPRESSOR: Seven axial stages followed by a single centrifugal stage. Two-piece aluminium alloy stator casing with one row of inlet guide vanes, fixed on TF25, variable on TF35, and seven rows of steel stator blades, bolted to steel alloy diffuser casing to which combustion chamber casing is attached. Rotor comprises seven stainless steel discs and one titanium impeller mounted on shaft supported in forward thrust ball bearings and rear roller bearing. TF25 pressure ratio 6 : 1 and 6·5 : 1 for TF35.

COMBUSTION CHAMBER: Annular reverse flow type. Steel outer shell and inner liner. Twenty-eight fuel burners with downstream injection.

FUEL SYSTEM: Woodward fuel control system. Gear-type fuel pump, with gas producer and power shaft governors, flow control and shut-off valve.

FUEL GRADE: MIL: J-5624 grade JP-4, JP-5, MIL-F-46005 or marine diesel standard and wide-cut kerosene.

TURBINE: Two mechanically-independent axial-flow turbines. First turbine with single-stage on TF25 and two-stages on TF35 drives compressor, has cored-out cast steel blades and is flange-bolted to outer co-axial drive shaft. Hollow stator vanes. Second, two-stage turbine drives output shaft, has solid steel blades and is mounted on inner co-axial drive shaft.

EXHAUST UNIT: Fixed area nozzle, with inner cone, supported by six radial struts.

ACCESSORIES: Electric, air or hydraulic starter. Bendix-Scintilla TGLN high-energy ignition unit. Four igniter plugs.

LUBRICATION: Recirculating type. Integral oil tank and cooler.

OIL GRADE: MIL-L-17808, MIL-L-23699.

DIMENSIONS

Length

Super TF25: 1·27m (50·1in)

Super TF35: 1·32m (52·2in)

Width, Super TF25, 35: 0·87m (34·4in)

Height, Super TF25, 35: 1·11m (43·8in)

Avco Lycoming Super TF25 marine/industrial gas turbine engine of 2,500shp

Avco Lycoming Super TF 35 direct drive two-stage, free-power marine/industrial gas turbine, rated at 3,500shp continuous and 4,050shp boost power

WEIGHT Dry

Super TF25: 600kg (1,324lb)

Super TF35: 641kg (1,414lb)

PERFORMANCE RATINGS

Max intermittent (peak):

Super TF25: 3,000shp

Super TF35: 4,050shp

Max continuous (normal):

Super TF25: 2,500shp

Super TF35: 3,500shp

FUEL CONSUMPTION At max continuous rating:

Super TF25: 0·62sfc 198 US gallons/h

Super TF35: 0·56sfc 223 US gallons/h

SUPER TF40

The TF40 engine is a scaled-up TF35 with higher mass flow. It has a four stage turbine section and variable-incidence inlet guide vanes. The first two compressor stages are transonic, and new atomising fuel nozzles are fitted.

Both the Jeff A (Aerojet General) and Jeff B (Bell Aerospace) AALCs employ TF40s. Jeff A employs six, each developing 3,350shp continuous. Four drive individual, steerable ducted propellers, and the remaining two drive separate centrifugal lift fans. In the case of Jeff B, the six engines are arranged in two groups of three, located port and starboard. Each trio drives a single propeller and lift system through integrated gears.

Other craft now powered by TF40s include the SEDAM N.500, which employs two for lift and three, mounted in separate nacelles, for propulsion, a twin hull waterjet ferry now in service in Scandinavia, two PSMM Mk 5 CODAG gunboats for Taiwan, each equipped with three TF40s and three DDA 12V 149 diesel engines, and two private yachts.

AIR INTAKE: Side inlet casting of aluminium alloy housing internal gearing and supporting power producer section and output drive shaft. Integral or separately mounted gears are operational. Provision for intake filters and/or silencers.

COMPRESSOR: Seven axial stages followed by a single centrifugal stage. Two-piece aluminium alloy stator casing, with one row of variable inlet guide vanes, and seven rows of steel stator blades bolted to steel alloy casing diffuser, to which combustion chamber casing is attached. Rotor comprises seven stainless steel discs and one

titanium impeller mounted on shaft supported in forward thrust ball bearing and rear roller bearing. TF40 pressure ratio is 7·2 : 1.
COMBUSTION CHAMBER: Annular reverse flow type. Steel outer shell and inner liner. Twenty-eight fuel burners with downstream injection.
FUEL SYSTEM: Woodward fuel control system. Gear-type fuel pump, with gas producer and power shaft governors, flow control and shut-off valve.
FUEL GRADE: MIL-T-5624, JP-4, JP-5; MIL-F-16884 diesel, standard and wide-cut kerosene.
TURBINE: Two mechanically-independent axial-flow turbines. First turbine, with two stages, drives compressor. It has cored-out cast steel blades and is flange-bolted to outer co-axial drive shaft. Hollow stator vanes. Second two-stage turbine drives output shaft. It has solid steel blades and is mounted on inner co-axial drive shaft. (Other features include: integral cast first turbine nozzle, cooled first turbine blades in both first and second stages, second turbine vane cooling, second turbine disc and blade cooling, and a modified third stage nozzle shroud).
EXHAUST UNIT: Fixed area nozzle, with inner cone, supported by six radial struts.
ACCESSORIES: Electric, air or hydraulic starter. Bendix-Scintilla TGLN high-energy ignition unit. Four igniter plugs.
LUBRICATION: Recirculating type. Integral oil tank and cooler.
OIL GRADE: Synthetic base oils.
DIMENSIONS
Length: 1·32m (52·2in)
Width: 0·88m (34·4in)
Height: 1·11m (43·8in)
PERFORMANCE RATINGS
Max intermittent (at 15°C (59°F)—sea level): 4,600shp
Max continuous (at 15°C (59°F)—sea level): 4,000shp
FUEL CONSUMPTION: At max continuous rating: 0·54sfc/255 US gallons/h
OIL CONSUMPTION: 454g/h (1lbh)

Cutaway of the Avco Lycoming Super TF40 marine/industrial gas turbine rated at 4,000shp continuous, 4,600shp 'boost' power

AGT-1500 ARMY GROUND TURBINE

This is a new recuperative cycle, 1500shp ground turbine engine which was designed from the outset as a ground vehicle turbine for the US Army's new main battle tank, XM-1. Recently Avco Lycoming has initiated investigations with general US builders into the possibilities of installing the AGT-1500 in various sizes of ACVs and SEVs.
INTAKE: An axial air inlet from the vehicle plenum which is fitted into a single stage inertial air filter with barrier-filters behind it.
COMPRESSOR: Twin-spool, axial/centrifugal compressor. Air flows through variable inlet guide vanes and through a five-stage axial flow low pressure spool of decreasing diameter. It then enters the counter-rotating high pressure spool, which consists of four decreasing diameter axial stages, followed by a single centrifugal timing stage. The latter stage performs the transition to the radial diffuser and turns the air 90 degrees for flow through the recuperator, where it picks up additional heat. Overall pressure ratio is 14·5 : 1.
RECUPERATOR: A stationary cylindrical cross-flow heat exchanger constructed of a series of formed steel wave plates. Plates are welded identical pairs, with depressions on the face and holes of various shapes to permit axial airflow and radial hot gas flow.

Avco Lycoming AGT-1500 army ground turbine

COMBUSTOR: A single cam, tangential scroll combustor receives pre-heated air from the recuperator at approximately 566°C.
TURBINE:
COMPRESSOR: Two axial stages, comprising an air-cooled high pressure stage which drives the high pressure compressor and an air-cooled second stage, which drives the low pressure compressor via an inner co-axial shaft. Turbines inlet temperature is 1,193°C.
POWER: A variable geometry nozzle provides controllable power to two free power turbines which drive the output shaft to an aft-mounted gearbox. The power turbine wheels are shrouded with the shroud cut in alternate groupings of five and nine blades for dampening.
EXHAUST: Gases pass through the recuperator and exit vertically in the rear of the engine.
REDUCTION GEARBOX: Rear drive single stage planetary reduction with concentric output drive shaft to power turbine shaft with output speed of 3,000rpm.
FUEL SYSTEM: Integrated gear pump and hydromechanical fuel control, with electronic controls for sequencing starting, and for power turbine speed governing. (Full authority electronic control is under development).
STARTERS: A truck-type electric starter cranks through the accessory gear train. An additional drive pad is available for hydraulic pump etc.
DIMENSIONS
Length: 1·6m (63in)
Width: 1·02m (40in)
Height: 0·71m (28in)
WEIGHT: 1,100kg (2,475lb)

BRIGGS AND STRATTON CORPORATION

Milwaukee, Wisconsin 53201, USA

Central Service Distributors for Great Britain and Ireland:

Autocar Electrical Equipment Co Ltd, 16 Rippleside Commercial Estate, Ripple Road, Barking, Essex, England

Briggs & Stratton is a major American supplier of low-power four-stroke gasoline engines, an important application of which is in motor lawn mowers of both US and European manufacture. Several installations of Briggs & Stratton in ACVs have been made. These include the American Bartlett M-8 Flying Saucer, a small lightweight craft powered by a single 3hp Briggs & Stratton engine mounted above a central plenum chamber driving a two-bladed Banks-Maxwell Mod 30-14 30in diameter pusher propeller; and Coelacanth Gemco's Pluto two-seat test vehicle which has two 7hp Briggs & Stratton engines each driving 42in fans, one for lift and a second for propulsion.

CATERPILLAR TRACTOR CO

Industrial Division, Peoria, Illinois 61602, USA

Caterpillar Tractor Ltd is a leading US manufacturer of diesels, which has supplied engines worldwide equivalent to hundreds of millions of diesel horsepower. Engines are sold for marine, electrical power and industrial applications, and are supported by more than 900 Caterpillar dealer facilities for parts and service; more than 14,000 dealer servicemen provide a 24-hour service to diesel operators. The engines are designed to give a high degree of component interchangeability.

MODELS 3304T, 3306T and 3306TA

TYPE: Four and six cylinder, straight in-line, four-stroke, water cooled, turbo-charged, (plus after cooling on 3306TA) diesel engines. Counterclockwise rotation when viewed from the rear.
CYLINDERS: Bore 121mm (4·75in). Stroke 152mm (6in). Total swept volume 3304 6·9 litres (425in³), 3306T and 3306TA 10·5 litres (638in³). Compression ratio 17·5 : 1. Cylinder liners cast from Molybdenum alloy iron, induction hardened full depth water cooling and specifically designed to give life equal to engine.
TURBO CHARGER AND AFTER COOLER: Single stage centrifugal air compressor driven by single stage centripetal turbine energised by exhaust gases. 3306TA has watercooled after cooler interposed between compressor air delivery and cylinder manifold. Complete system doubles air flow rate to cylinders and reduces exhaust temperature.
ACCESSORIES: Include fuel priming pump, 24 or 30-32 volt alternator, starter, hydraulic starting, air starting etc.
STARTING AND CONTROL SYSTEMS: Mechanical governor charging alternator 12 volt, electric start 12 volt.
GEAR RATIOS
3304 1·97:1; 2·96:1; 3·79:1; 4·48:1.
3306 2:1; 2·95:1; 3·83:1; 4·50:1.
DIMENSIONS
WITH GEAR
3304T
Length: 1,613mm (63·5in)
Width: 913mm (36in)
Height: 1,051mm (41·4in)
3306T
Length: 2,125mm (83·7in)
Width: 924mm (36·4in)
Height: 1,217mm (47·9in)
3306TA
Length: 2,019mm (79·5in)
Width: 934mm (36·8in)
Height: 1,108mm (43·6in)
PERFORMANCE RATINGS
3304T
Max intermittent: 160hp (shaft)
Max continuous: 121hp (shaft)
3306T
Max intermittent: 243hp (shaft)
Max continuous: 184hp (shaft)
3306TA
Max intermittent: 281hp (shaft)
Max continuous: 228hp (shaft)
FUEL CONSUMPTION
AT MAX CONTINUOUS RATING
3304T: 28·8 litres/h (7·6 US gallons/h)
3306T: 41·6 litres/h (11 US gallons/h)
3306TA: 50·7 litres/h (13·4 US gallons/h)

Caterpillar 3406 Marine Generator set

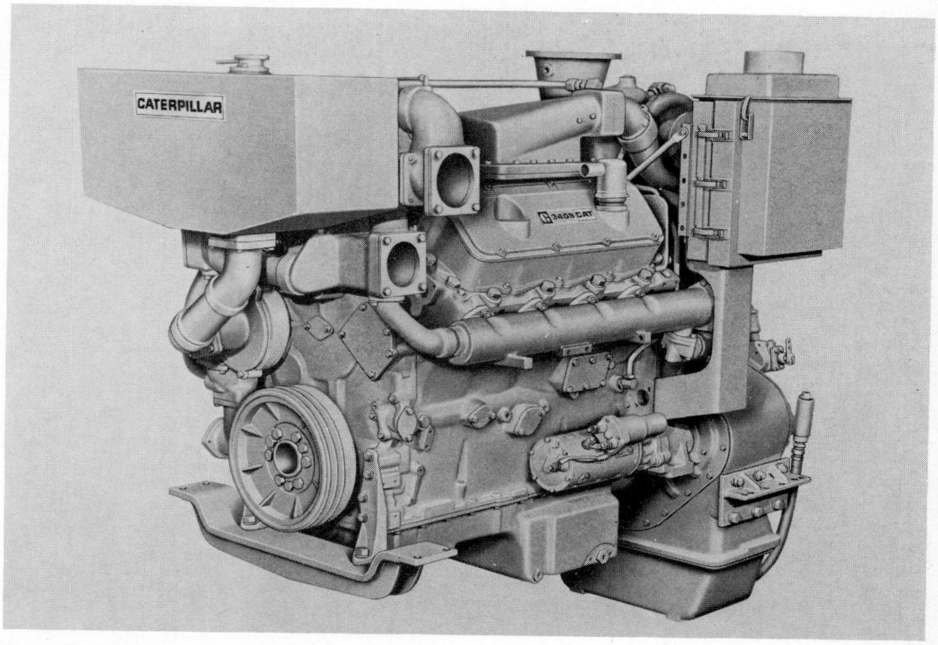

Caterpillar Model 3412 marine diesel engine

MODELS 3406T and TA, 3408T and TA, 3412T & TA

The basic features of these models are in general similar to the D330 and D333 series, with the following main differences.
TYPE: Eight and twelve 65 degree V in-line (3412 and 3408) and six cylinder straight in-line 3406 four-stroke, water-cooled, turbo-charged, after-cooled diesel engines. Counter-clockwise rotation when viewed from the rear.
CYLINDERS: Bore 137mm (5·4in). Stroke 152mm (6in); except **3406** at 165mm (6·5in). Total swept volumes **3412** 2·7 litres (1649in³); **3408** 18 litres (1,099in³): **3406** 14·6 litres (893in³).
TURBO-CHARGER AND AFTER-COOLER: As for Model 3306.
STANDARD EQUIPMENT: Hydro-mechanical governor. Fuel, oil pressure, temperature and service hour gauges. Gear-driven fuel priming, fuel transfer and water jacket pumps.
ACCESSORIES: These include heat exchangers, sea water pumps, air starting, hydraulic starting, 24 or 32 volt starting generator and glow plugs.
COOLING SYSTEM: Water jacket with pump.
CRANKSHAFT: Unique **3408** offset crankshaft produces smooth even spaced 90 degree V type power delivery from 65 degree V layout.
GEAR RATIOS
3412 2·0:1; 2·94:1; 3·54:1; 4·0:1; 4·67:1; 5·88:1; 7·08:1
3408 2:1; 2·5:1; 3:1; 3·5:1; 4·5:1; 6:1
3406 2:1; 2·5:1, 3:1; 3·5:1; 4·5:1; 6:1
DIMENSIONS
WITH GEAR
3412TA
Length: 3,309mm (130·3in)
Width: 1,270mm (50in)
Height: 1,647mm (64·9in)
3408TA
Length: 2,188mm (86·1in)
Width: 1,231mm (48·5in)
Height: 1,481mm (58·3in)
3406TA
Length: 2,385mm (93·9in)
Width: 1,011mm (39·8in)
Height: 1,562mm (61·5in)
WEIGHTS
TOTAL WITH GEAR
3412TA: 3,809kg (8,400lb)
3408TA: 2,371kg (5,228lb)
3406TA: 2,046kg (4,510lb)
PERFORMANCE RATINGS
SHAFT
3406T
Max intermittent: 315hp
Max continuous: 242hp
3406TA
Max intermittent: 364hp
Max continuous: 267hp
3408T
Max intermittent: 412hp
Max continuous: 291hp
3408TA
Max intermittent: 460hp
Max continuous: 354hp
3412T
Max intermittent: 436hp
3412TA
Max continuous: 504hp
FUEL CONSUMPTION
3406T: 53·8 litres/h (14·2 US gallons/h)
3406TA: 59·9 litres/h (15·8 US gallons/h)
3408T: 59·2 litres/h (15·6 US gallons/h)
3408TA: 75·6 litres/h (20 US gallons/h)
3412T: 89·3 litres/h (23·6 US gallons/h)
3412TA: 110·5 litres/h (29·2 US gallons/h)

MODEL D348

Basic features of these models are in general similar to the earlier series, with the following main differences.

TYPE: Twelve cylinder 60 degree V in-line four-stroke, water-cooled, turbo-supercharger-aftercooled diesel engine. Counterclockwise rotation viewed from rear.

CYLINDERS: Bore 137mm (5·4in). Stroke 165mm (6·5in). Total swept volume 29·3 litres (1,786in^3). Compression ratio, 16·5 : 1. One-piece nickel-chrome alloyed grey iron cast cylinder block, precision bored and milled. Conventional studs on V models are complemented by extra length studs extending into bearing saddle area.

TURBO-SUPERCHARGER AND AFTER-COOLER: Turbo-charger similar to 3304 and 3306 models with addition of water-cooled aftercooler interposed between compressor air delivery and cylinder manifold. System doubles rate of airflow to engine and lowers exhaust temperatures.

ACCESSORIES: Hydro-mechanical governor gear-driven fuel priming and transfer pumps, gear-driven jacket-water pump.

COOLING SYSTEM: Jacket water pump minimum flow 22·1 litres/s (350 gallons/min).

GEAR RATIOS: **D348** 2·00 : 1, 2·94 : 1, 3·54 : 1, 4·00 : 1, 4767:1, 5:88:1 and 7·07:1, **D349** 2 : 1, 2·94 : 1, 3·54 : 1, 4·67 : 1. All ratios at 1,800 engine continuous rpm.

DIMENSIONS

WITH GEAR

D348

Length: 2,963mm (116·4in)

Width: 1,527mm (60·12in)

Height: 1,938mm (76·3in)

WEIGHTS

DRY WITH GEAR

D348: 5,146kg (11,335lb)

PERFORMANCE RATINGS

D348

Max at 2,000rpm: 920hp (flywheel)

Continuous at 1,800rpm: 725hp (flywheel)

FUEL CONSUMPTION: D348: 144 litres/h (38gallons/h) at 725hp

MODEL 3208

TYPE: Eight cylinder 90 degree V in-line, four-stroke, water-cooled naturally separated diesel engine.

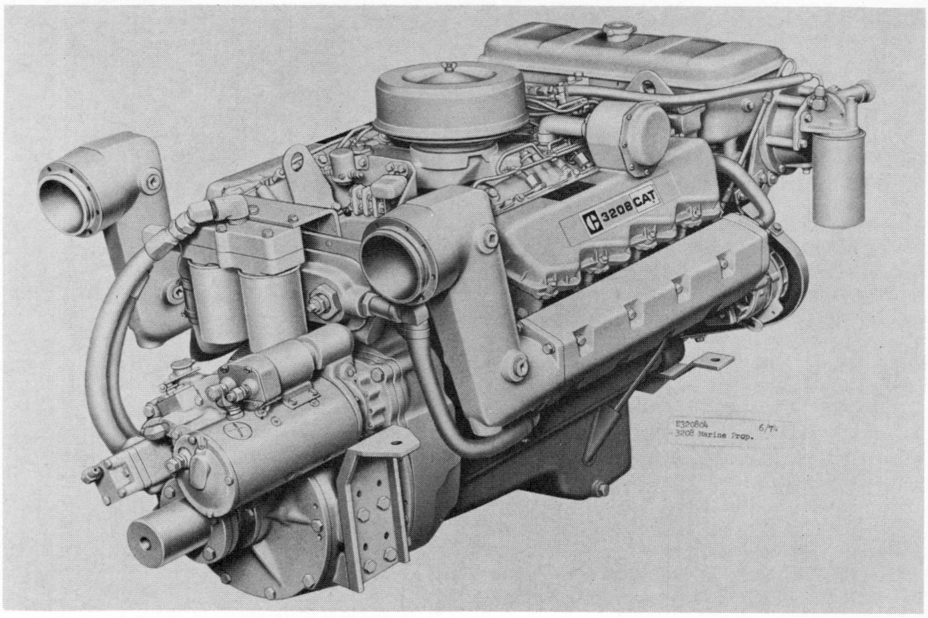

Caterpillar Model 3208 marine diesel engine

CYLINDERS: Bore 114mm (4·5in). Stroke 127mm (5in). Total swept volume 10·4 litres (636in^3). Compression ratio 16·5 : 1.

CRANKSHAFT: Forged, lightened, total hardened, 90 degree V results in balanced power strokes for smooth running. Regrindable at overhaul if needed.

CONNECTING RODS: Forged H-section rods. Computer-controlled grinding to precise balance.

FUEL SYSTEM: Fuel is fed from low pressure transfer pump to manifold. Separate pumps plunger for each cylinder driven by own crankshaft. System incorporates priming pump fuel filter and automatic variable timing.

COOLING SYSTEM: Water jacket cooling plus expansion tank with copper/nickel tube sea water exchanger. Jacket and sea water pumps are incorporated.

LUBRICATION SYSTEM: Gear driven six lobe oil pump passes oil through cooler and filters to oil gallery, supplying direct lubrication to all bearing surfaces. The system employs positive crankshaft ventilation.

STARTING AND CONTROL SYSTEMS: 12 volt electric start and charging. Mechanical governor.

ACCESSORIES: Include marine gears, exhaust risers, 24 volt charging and starting system, gauges and instruments.

GEAR RATIOS: 1·50 : 1; 1·97 : 1; 2·50 : 1; 2·96 : 1 or 1·54 : 1; 2·00 : 1; 2·47 : 1 which are limited to pleasure craft applications.

DIMENSIONS

WITH GEAR

Length: 1,504mm (59·2in)

Width: 928mm (36·5in)

Height: 920mm (36·2in)

WEIGHT

Total: 816kg (1,800lb)

PERFORMANCE RATING

Max intermittent: 203hp (shaft)

Max continuous: 146hp (shaft)

FUEL CONSUMPTION: At max continuous rating: 29·9 litres/h (7·9 US gallons/h).

CUMMINS ENGINE COMPANT INC

Cummins Engine Company Inc, 1000 Fifth Street, Columbus, Indiana 47201, USA

Cummins Engine Company Ltd, Coombe House, St Georges Square, Maldon Road, New Maldon, Surrey, England

The Cummins Engine Company was formed in 1919 in Columbus, Indiana. It produces a wide range of marine diesel engines which are now manufactured and distributed internationally. In addition to manufacturing plants in the United States, the company also produces diesel engines in Brazil, India, Japan, Mexico and the United Kingdom. All these plants build engines to the same specifications thus ensuring interchangeability of parts and the same quality standards.

Cummins marine diesels power the Seaflight 46 (two VT8N-370-Ms) hydrofoil, and the Hovermarine HM.2 Mk 3 sidewall hovercraft.

On the latter, two VT8-370-Ms, each derated to 320bhp, supply propulsive power, and a single V-504-M, derated to 185bhp, drives the lift fans.

MODEL V-555-M

Horsepower: 240

Governed rpm: 3,300

Number of cylinders: 8

Bore and stroke: 117×104mm (4⅝×4⅛in)

Piston displacement: 9·095 litres (555in^3)

Operating cycles: 4

Crankcase oil capacity: 22·73 litres (5 gallons)

Coolant capacity: 44 litres (9·5 gallons)

Net weight (engine less gear): 839·2kg (1,850lb)

BEARINGS: Precision type, steel backed inserts.

CAMSHAFT: Single camshaft controls all valve and injector movement. Induction hardened alloy steel with gear drive.

CAMSHAFT FOLLOWERS: Roller type for long cam and follower life.

CONNECTING RODS: Drop forged, 170·7mm (6·72in) centre to centre length. Taper piston pin end reduces unit pressure.

COOLER, LUBRICATING OIL: Tubular type, jacket water cooled.

CRANKSHAFT: High tensile strength steel forging. Bearing journals are induction hardened.

CYLINDER BLOCK: Alloy cast iron with removable wet liners. Cross bolt support to main bearing cap.

CYLINDER HEADS: Two, one each bank. All fuel lines are drilled passages. Individual intake and exhaust porting for each cylinder. Corrosion resistant inserts on intake and exhaust valve seats.

DAMPER, VIBRATION: Compressed rubber type.

FUEL SYSTEM: Cummins self adjusting system with integral flyball type governor. Camshaft actuated injectors.

GEAR TRAIN: Heavy duty, located rear of cylinder block.

LUBRICATION: Force feed to all bearings. Gear type pump.

PISTONS: Aluminium, cam ground, with two compression and one oil ring.

PISTON PINS: 38·1mm (1½in) diameter, full floating.

THERMOSTAT: Dual, modulating by-pass type.

VALVES: Dual intake and exhaust each cylinder. Each valve 41·3mm (1⅝in) diameter.

STANDARD EQUIPMENT:

CORROSION RESISTOR: Mounted, Cummins spin-on type, checks rust and corrosion, controls acidity, and removes impurities from coolant.

DIPSTICK, OIL: Port side when viewing engine from drive end.

ELECTRICAL EQUIPMENT: 12V, 58A ac system. Includes starting motor, alternator, regulator, magnetic switch and starting switch.

EXCHANGER, HEAT: Tubular type, mounted.

FILTERS: Cummins. Lubricating oil full flow paper element type, mounted. Fuel, spin-on, mounted.

FLYWHEEL: For reverse and reduction gear.

GOVERNOR: Mechanical variable speed type.

HOUSING, FLYWHEEL: SAE No 3

INTAKE AIR: Silenced.

MANIFOLD, EXHAUST: Two, fresh water cooled.

PAN, OIL: Aluminium, rear sump type, 5 US gallon capacity.

PUMP, COOLANT: Belt driven, centrifugal type, 80gallons/min at 3,300rpm.

PUMP, RAW WATER: Belt driven rubber impeller type, 48gallons/min at 3,300rpm.

SUPPORT, ENGINE: Marine type, front and rear.

MODEL V-903-M

Horsepower: 295
Governed rpm: 2,600
Number of cylinders: 8
Bore and stroke: 139·7×120·6mm (5½×4¾in)
Piston displacement: 14·8 litres (903in³)
Operating cycles: 4
Oil pan capacity: 5 US gallons
Engine coolant capacity: 54·5 litres (12 gallons)
Net weight with standard accessories: 2,800lb

BEARINGS: Precision type, steel backed inserts. Five main bearings, 95·2mm (3¾in) diameter. Connecting rod 79·3mm (3⅛in) diameter.
CAMSHAFT: Single camshaft controls all valve and injector movement. Induction hardened alloy steel with gear drive.
CAMSHAFT FOLLOWERS: Roller type for long cam and follower life.
CONNECTING RODS: Drop forged. Taper piston pin end provides superior load distribution and maximum piston crown material.
COOLER, LUBRICATING OIL: Tubular type, jacket water cooled.
CRANKSHAFT: High tensile strength steel forging. Bearing journals are induction hardened. Fully counterweighted.
CYLINDER BLOCK: Alloy cast iron with removable wet liners.
CYLINDER HEADS: Two, one each bank. All fuel lines are drilled passages. Individual intake and exhaust porting for each cylinder.
DAMPER, VIBRATION: Compressed rubber type.
FUEL SYSTEM: Cummins wear-compensating system with integral, flyball type, mechanical variable speed governor. Camshaft actuated injectors.
LUBRICATION: Force feed to all bearings. Gear type pump.
MAIN BEARING CAPS: Cross bolted for rigidity.
PISTONS: Aluminium, cam ground, with two compression and one oil ring.
PISTON PINS: 95·2mm (1¾in) diameter, full floating.
THERMOSTAT: Single unit, modulating bypass type.
VALVES: Dual intake and exhaust each cylinder. Each valve 47·9mm (1⅞in) diameter. Heat and corrosion resistant face on all valves.
STANDARD EQUIPMENT
CLEANER, AIR: Silencer type.
CORROSION RESISTOR: Cummins. Mounted. Throw-away unit. Checks rust and corrosion, controls acidity, and removes impurities from coolant.
DIPSTICK, OIL: Port side when viewing engine from drive end.
ELECTRICAL EQUIPMENT: 12V, 55A ac system. Includes starting motor alternator, regulator, and starting switch.
EXCHANGER, HEAT: Tubular type, mounted.
FILTERS: Cummins. Lubricating oil, full flow replaceable paper element type, mounted. Fuel, paper element throw-away type, mounted.
FLYWHEEL: For reverse and reduction gear.
GEAR, MARINE: Capitol 4HE-10200, 2:1 reverse and reduction gear with propeller shaft companion flange.
GOVERNOR: Mechanical variable speed type.
HOUSING, FLYWHEEL: SAE No 2.
MANIFOLD, AIR INTAKE: Two, located on inside of engine Vee.
MANIFOLD, EXHAUST: Two, fresh water cooled, with outlet to rear.
PAN, OIL: Aluminium, front sump type, 5 US gallon capacity.
PUMP, COOLANT: Gear driven, centrifugal type, 78 gallons/min at 2,600 rpm.
PUMP, RAW WATER: Gear driven, 61 gallons/min at 2,600 rpm.
SUPPORT, ENGINE: Marine type, 571mm (22½in) centres.

MODEL KTA-1150-M

Power rating, max: 388kW (520bhp)
Governed rpm: 1,950

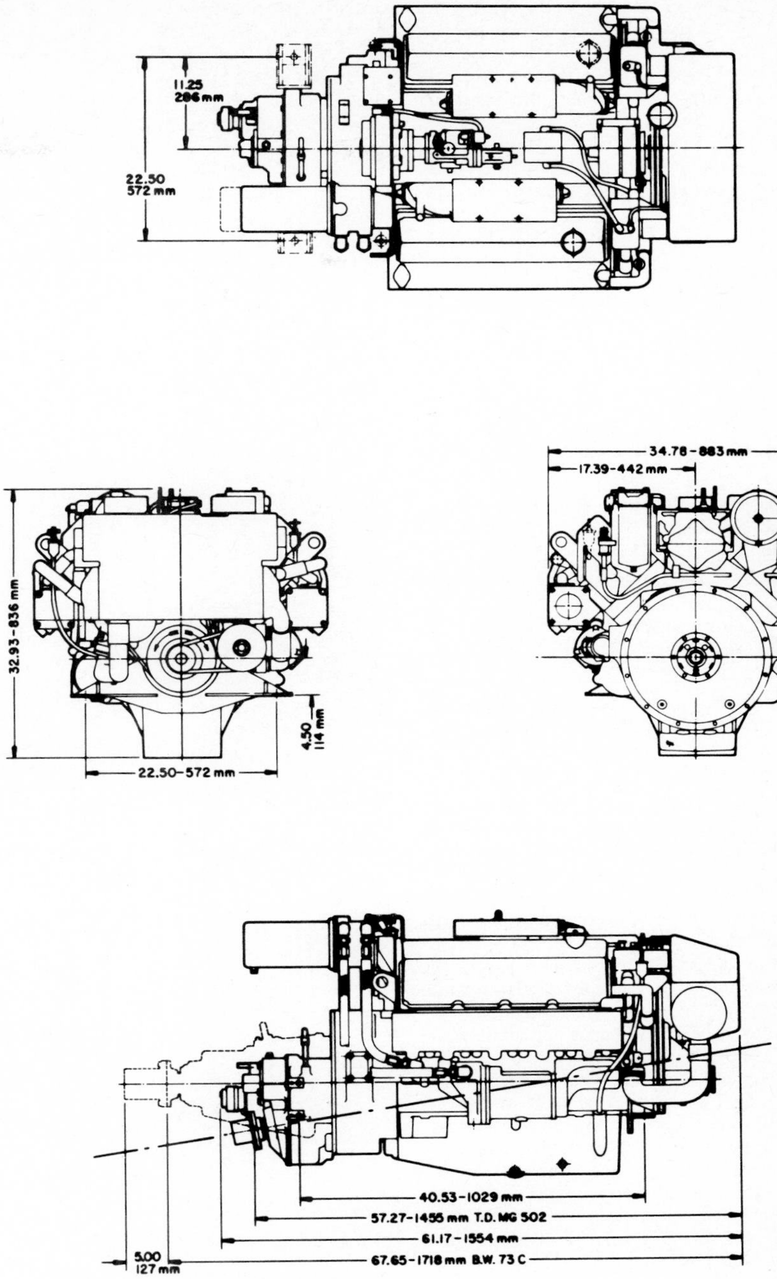

Cummins 8-cylinder V-555-M diesel, rated at 240hp

Power rating, continuous: 350kW (470bhp)
Governed rpm: 1,800
Number of cylinders: 6
Bore and stroke: 159 × 159mm (6¼ × 6¼in)
Piston displacement: 18·86 litres (1,150in³)
Operating cycles: 4
Lube system oil capacity: 59 litres (15·5 US gallons)
Coolant capacity: 34·9 litres (9 US gallons)
Net weight, dry: 1,725kg (3,800lb)

AFTERCOOLER: Two. Jacket water cooled.
BEARINGS: Precision type, steel backed inserts. Seven main bearings 140mm (5½in) diameter. Connecting rod 102mm (4in) diameter.
CAMSHAFT: Single camshaft controls all valve and injector movement. Induction hardened alloy steel with gear drive.
CAMSHAFT FOLLOWERS: Roller type for long cam and follower life.
CONNECTING RODS: Drop forged 290mm (11·4in) centre to centre length. Rifle drilled for pressure lubrication of piston pin. Taper piston pin end reduces unit pressures.
CRANKSHAFT: High tensile strength steel forging. Bearing journals are induction hardened. Fully counterweighted.
CYLINDER BLOCK: Alloy cast iron with removable, wet liners.
CYLINDER HEADS: Individual cylinder heads. Drilled fuel supply and return lines. Corrosion resistant inserts on intake and exhaust valve seats.
FUEL SYSTEM: Cummins PT™ self adjusting system with integral flyball type governor. Camshaft actuated injectors.
GEAR TRAIN: Heavy duty, induction hardened, located at front of cylinder block.
LUBRICATION: Force feed to all bearings, gear type pump. All lubrication lines are drilled passages, except pan to pump suction line.
PISTONS: Aluminium, cam ground, with two compression and one oil ring. Oil cooled.
PISTON PINS: 61mm (2·4in) diameter, full floating.
TURBOCHARGER: Scroll diffuser, side mounted.
VALVES: Dual intake and exhaust each cylinder. Each valve 56mm (2·22in) diameter. Heat and corrosion resistant face on intake and exhaust valves.
STANDARD EQUIPMENT:
AIR CLEANER: Two stage dry type for vertical mounting.
COOLER, LUBRICATING OIL: Plate type, jacket water cooled.
CORROSION RESISTOR: Fleetguard, mounted, dual spin-on type.

DAMPER, VIBRATION: Viscous type.
DIPSTICK, OIL: Mounted on either port or starboard side of engine.
DRIVE, ALTERNATOR: High capacity, poly-v belt arrangement driven from accessory drive pulley.
ELECTRICAL EQUIPMENT: 24 or 32 volt positive engagement starting motor and 24 or 32 volt ignition proof alternators with built-in voltage regulators.
EXHAUST OUTLET CONNECTIONS: Straight or 90 degree turbo exhaust connection for adapting 127mm (5in) piping.
EXCHANGER, HEAT: Copper-nickel tubular type, engine mounted.
FILTERS: Fleetguard. Lubricating oil: spin-on, full flow, paper element type, mounted on either port or starboard side of engine and by-pass type, not mounted. Fuel: dual spin-on, paper element type, mounted.
FLYWHEEL: For 356 to 457mm (14 to 18in) over centre clutch, reverse and reduction gear.
GEAR, MARINE: Twin Disc MG-521: 2·19 : 1, 3·03 : 1, 4·09 : 1. Twin Disc MG-527: 3·86 : 1, 5·18 : 1. Capitol HP 6900 : 2·5 : 1. Capitol HP 7700 : 3·5 : 1, 4·5 : 1. Capitol HP 28000: 5·16 : 1, 6 : 1.
GOVERNOR: Mechanical variable speed.
HOUSING, FLYWHEEL: SAE O with marine mounting pads.
MANIFOLD, EXHAUST: Water cooled.
PAN, OIL: Aluminium, rear sump type, 37·9 litres (10 US gallon) capacity.
PANEL, INSTRUMENT: Not mounted. Includes ammeter, tachometer or hour meter, lube oil temperature gauge, oil pressure gauge and engine water temperature gauge.
POWER TAKE-OFF: Front mounted. Twin Disc clutch models SP-114 for up to 112kW (150hp) and SL-214 for up to 161kW (215hp).
PUMP, COOLANT: Gear driven, centrifugal type 700 litres/min (185gallons/min) at 1,950rpm.
SHIELD, BELT: For alternator drive.
STARTING AID: Manual ether cold start aid.
SUPPORT, ENGINE: Three point marine type, front cover, and marine gear.

DETROIT DIESEL ALLISON
(Division of General Motors Corporation)

General Offices: PO Box 894, Indianapolis, Indiana 46206, USA
Telephone: (317) 244 1511

Detroit Diesel Allison International Operations
(Division of General Motors Corporation)
25200 Telegraph Road, Southfield, Michigan 48075, USA

General Motors Power Products—Europe
(Division of General Motors Corporation)
PO Box 6, London Road, Wellingborough, Northamptonshire NN8 2DL, England

Detroit Diesel Allison has been active in the development of gas-turbines for aircraft, industrial and marine use for many years. Production of the first Allison gas-turbine began in the 1940s, when the company built the power plant for the P-59, the first jet-powered aircraft to fly in the United States.

Later, the Allison T56 turboprop aircraft engine was developed. It demonstrated outstanding reliability and the same basic design has been adapted for industrial and marine applications. In the early 1960s, the first Allison 501-K gas-turbine powered electric powerplant went into service. Today, almost 660 501-K industrial series engines are used not only in electric powerplants but also in industrial and marine applications. The two-shaft marine engine powers the Boeing Jetfoil, Halter crewboats and more recently has been installed in Westermoen catamarans and the Grumman M161 hydrofoil for primary propulsion.

ALLISON 501-K SERIES

The Allison 501-K series industrial gas-turbine incorporates a 14-stage axial-flow compressor, with bleed valves to compensate for compressor surge.

Of modular design, it comprises three main sections: the compressor, combustor and turbine. Each section can be readily separated from the other. Modular design provides ease in handling and servicing of the engine.

The first stage of the four-stage turbine section is air-cooled, permitting the engine to be operated at higher than normal turbine inlet temperatures.

The combustor section of the 501-K consists of six combustion chambers of the through-flow type, assembled within a single annular chamber. This multiple provides even temperature distribution at the turbine inlet, thus eliminating the danger of hot spots.

The 501-K Series engines are available in either single-shaft or free turbine design.

The lightweight, compact size of the 501-K lends itself to multiple engines driving a single shaft through a common gearbox, or as a gas generator driving a customer-furnished power turbine.

The engine can be operated on a wide range of liquid fuels. Designation of the marine model is 501 KF, a brief specification for which follows. Dimensions are shown on the accompanying general arrangement drawing.

Detroit Diesel Allison 501-KF two-shaft marine gas turbine

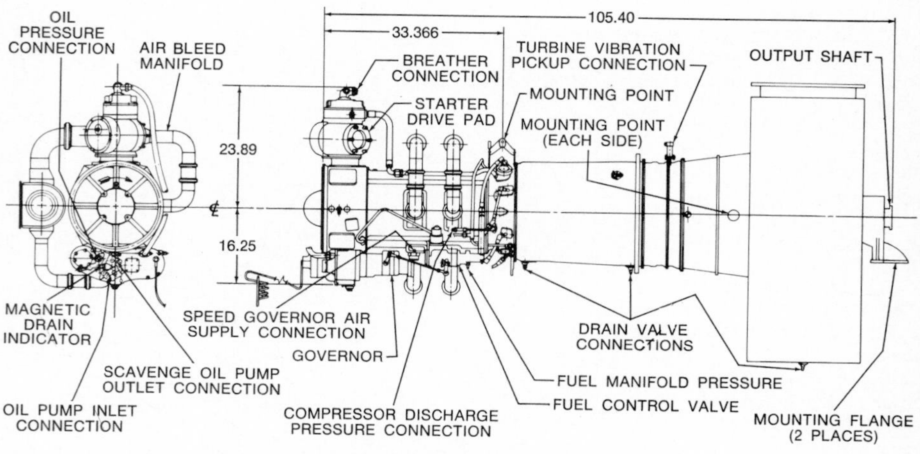

General arrangement of the Allison 501-KF two-shaft marine gas-turbine

Allison 570-K series gas-turbine designed as a prime mover for the industrial and marine markets

Exhaust gas temperature: 535°C (994°F)
Inlet air flow: 26,000cfm
Exhaust air flow: 81,000cfm
Engine jacket heat rejection: 6,000 Btu/min
Lube heat rejection (Gasifier): 1,270 Btu/min
Max liquid fuel flow: 6,365 litres (360ghp)
Liquid fuel: DF-1, DF-2 per Allison EMS66
Lubricant: Synthetic oil per Allison EMS 35 and 53
Specific fuel consumption: 0·24 litre (0·503lb)/hp/h
Required Auxiliaries:
25hp starter
20-29V dc electrical power
Power take-off shaft and couplings
Temperature and speed controls from engine-furnished signals
Oil cooler
Auxiliary lube pump
Compressor inlet sensor
Gauge panel, meters and associated components
Engine exhaust diffusing tailpipe

ALLISON 570-K

A new 7,000hp gas turbine designed as a prime mover in the industrial and marine fields, the 570 series is a front drive, two-shaft gas turbine. It is currently in full operation and entered production in 1978. The model 570 represents General Motors' newest entry in the industrial & marine markets and is a derivative of the US Army's heavy lift helicopter (HLH) engine.

The 570 engine uses a variable geometry, 13-stage, axial flow compressor with a compression ratio of 12·1:1; the inlet guide vanes and the first five stages of status are variable. The compressor is directly coupled to a two-stage axial flow turbine and the vanes and blades of both stages are air-cooled. A power turbine drives the output shaft at the front end of the engine through a torque senser assembly located on the engine's centreline. The air foils of the power turbine are solid and do not require air cooling.

The 570 is operated by a full authority electronic control which features automatic starting sequence, speed governing, turbine temperature limiting, vibration sensing etc.

All production 570 engines will be fully marinised using materials and coatings selected after more than ¼ million hours of marine experience with Boeing Jetfoils and DD963 'Spruance' class destroyers.

The 570-K engine incorporates many technological advances and these have resulted in the unit having the lowest specific fuel consumption (SFC) of any turbine in its hp class. At maximum rated power of 7,170hp, the engine's SFC is 0·46lb/hp/h. This low level is maintained over a wide range of output power and speed; at 50% power the SFC increases by only 7%.

A larger version, designated the model 570-KB will enter production in mid-1980. A three-stage power turbine will be used and the unit will have a maximum power rating of 8,312hp with an SFC of 0·405lb/hp/h.

570-KA (two-stage) and 570-KB (three-stage) Gas Turbines

	Maximum		*Continuous*	
	570-KA	*570-KB*	*570-KA*	*570-KB*
Power (shp)				
15°C (59°F)	7,170	8,312	6,445	7,665
26·7°C (80°F)	6,610	7,644	5,890	6,876
Fuel Consumption (59°F)				
g/hp/h	210	184	209	186
lb/hp/h	0·462	0·405	0·460	0·409
Power Turbine Temperature				
°C	850	837	802	802
°F	1,562	1,538	1,477	1,475
Compression Ratio	12·1	12·8	11·3	12·3
Corrected Airflow				
kg/sec	19·4	20·1	18·1	19·6
lb/sec	42·8	44·3	40·0	43·3
Power Turbine Speed (rpm)	11,500	11,500	11,500	11,500
Weight				
kg	612	676	612	676
lb	1,350	1,490	1,350	1,490
Length				
m	1·83	1·90	1·83	1·90
in	72	75	72	75

Performance is subject to 5% guarantee factors.

DOBSON PRODUCTS CO

2241 South Ritchey, Santa Ana, California 92705, USA
Telephone: (714) 557 2987
Officials:
Franklin A Dobson, *Director*

Franklin Dobson has been building and marketing light ACVs in kit and factory-built form since 1963.

His company is now specialising in the design and construction of light ACV components evolved after a more thorough engineering approch. The components include reversible-pitch propellers and fans—the main purpose of which is to provide light craft with adequate braking—and suitable ducts, screens, etc.

Preliminary details of the company's first 0·91m (3ft) diameter, variable-pitch two-bladed propeller are given below.

DIMENSIONS
Diameter: 0·91m (36in)
Chord: 104mm (4·25in)
Blades: 2
Solidity (at 0·6 radius): 0·125
Pitch range: 60 degrees (nom +40, −20)
Max shaft diameter: 28mm (1·25in)
Design rpm: 3,000
Max rpm: 3,250
Horsepower required: 7-10
Max static thrust (with shroud): 34·01kg (75lb) (forward or reverse)
Max thrust at 60mph: 22·67kg (50lb)

A duct with integral screen, suitable for use with this propeller, is also under development.

THE GARRETT CORPORATION

AiResearch Manufacturing Company of Arizona

111 South 34th Street, Phoenix, Arizona 84010, USA
Telephone: (602) 267 3011
Officials:
Jack Marinick, *Vice-President and Manager*
Donald I Cauble, *Assistant Manager*
Malcolm E Craig, *Sales Manager*

The Garrett Corporation is the world's largest manufacturer of small gas-turbine engines for commercial, military, marine and industrial application, as well as a leading producer of air turbine starters, air motors, pneumatic valves and control systems for aircraft and aerospace applications.

ME990-3

The Garrett ME990-3 is a fully marinised gas-turbine, rated at 6,250shp maximum. A free turbine, it has been designed for propulsion, pump and compressor drives and to power generator sets for primary and secondary power. Features are ease of maintenance and facilities for the replacement of modules in situ. Fitted with optional shock mounts, it satisfies the shock requirements of MIL-S-901C, Grade A, Class III.

TYPE: Simple cycle, two-shaft, free turbine.
COMPRESSOR: Two-stage centrifugal.
COMBUSTION CHAMBER: Single, annular.
TURBINE: Two-stage axial gas generator. Three-stage axial power turbine.
FUEL GRADES: VV-F-800, DF-A, DF-1 or DF-2; ASTM-D-975, 1-D or 2-D; ASTM-D-2880, 1-GT or 2-GT; ASTM-D-1655, Jet A, Jet Al or Jet B; MIL-T-5624, JP4 or JP5.
ACCESSORIES: Integral within the gearbox.
DIMENSIONS
Length: 3·04m (120in)
Width: 1·60m (63in)
Height: 1·21m (48in)

WEIGHT Dry: 2,835kg (6,250lb) including integral gearbox and accessories, insulation blankets and electronics package. Shock mounts (optional) 454kg (1,000lb)
PERFORMANCE RATING
At ISO standard conditions with accessory power losses and no inlet or exhaust pressure losses normal power is 5,600shp at 7,200rpm power turbine speed.
System Output Speed: 3,600rpm

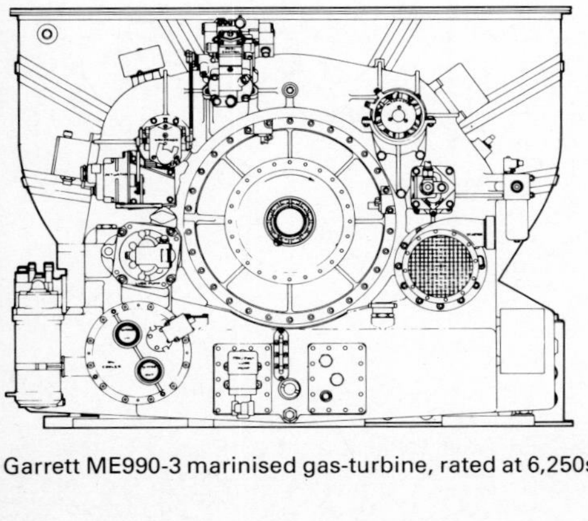

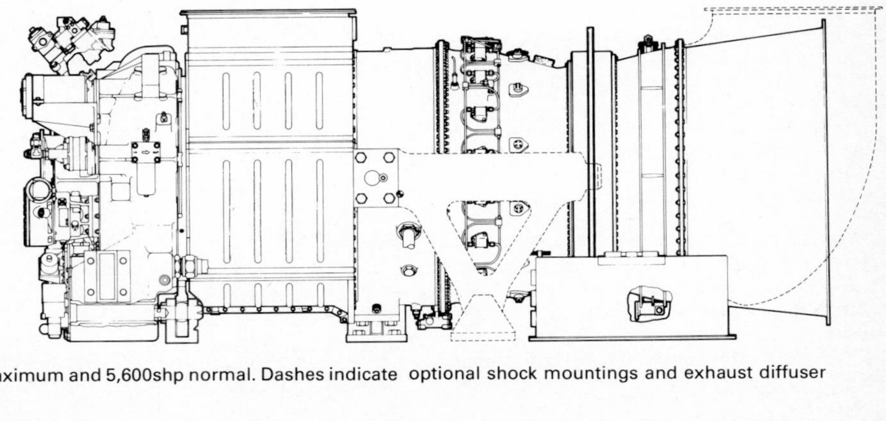

Garrett ME990-3 marinised gas-turbine, rated at 6,250shp maximum and 5,600shp normal. Dashes indicate optional shock mountings and exhaust diffuser

831-800

Garrett also has a fully marinised gas-turbine engine with a continuous power rating of 690shp and an intermittent rating of 800shp. This unit, designated 831-800, is currently in service on the Boeing PHM hydrofoil, providing secondary power. It is also in use in several other commercial and military applications.
TYPE: Simple-cycle, single shaft.
COMPRESSOR: Two-stage centrifugal.
COMBUSTION CHAMBER: Single, reverse-flow.
TURBINE: Three-stage axial.
FUEL GRADES: DF1 and DF2 per ASTM-D-975, VV-F-800, MIL-F-16884 and MIL-R-46005, Jet A, A-1 and B per ASTM-D-1665; JP-4 and JP-5 per MIL-F-5624 and VV-K-211.
DIMENSIONS
Length: 1,829mm (72in)
Width: 991mm (39in)
Height: 864mm (34in)
WEIGHT Dry: 680·4kg (1,500lb)
POWER RATING
Continuous SLS: 690shp
Standby: 800shp
Rated rotor speed: 41,730rpm (max)
System output speed constant speed, two output pad speed of 8,000rpm and two at 3,600rpm

GENERAL ELECTRIC COMPANY AIRCRAFT ENGINE GROUP

1000 Western Avenue, West Lynn, Massachusetts 01910, USA

Officials:

Fred O MacFee, Jr, *Vice President and Group Executive*
J W Sack, *Counsel*

The General Electric Company's Dr Stanford A Moss operated the first gas turbine in the United States in 1903 and produced the aircraft turbosupercharger, first flown in 1919 and mass-produced in World War II for US fighters and bombers.

The company built its first aircraft gas-turbine in 1941, when it began development of a Whittle-type turbojet, under an arrangement between the British and American Governments.

Since that time, General Electric has produced and licensed over 82,000 aircraft gas turbine engines with more than 135 million hours of operation.

Three General Electric gas-turbines have been marinised for marine service, the LM100, the LM1500 and the LM2500. The LM100 powers the Bell SK-5 air cushion vehicle, the LM1500 powers the 300 ton AGEH-1 Plainview and 17 US Navy patrol gunboats and the LM2500 is specified for powering various classes of ships in ten navies around the world.

LM2500

The LM2500 marine gas turbine is a two shaft, simple cycle, high efficiency engine, derived from the GE military TF 39 and civil CF6 high by-pass turbofan engines for the US Air Force C-5 transport and DC-10, 747 and A300B commercial jets. The engine incorporates the latest features of compressor, combustor, and turbine design to provide maximum progression in reliability, parts life, and time between overhaul. The engine has a simple cycle efficiency of more than 35% which is due to the most advanced cycle pressures temperatures and component efficiencies in marine gas turbine production today.

The LM2500 marine gas turbine has been specified for the foilborne power of the joint US Navy/NATO Patrol Hydrofoil Missile (PHM), six ships being built by the Boeing Company, Seattle, Washington. The engine is also specified for the base line propulsion and lift engines for the US Navy's 3,000 ton 3KSES. Rohr Marine Inc, has been awarded the contract for the detailed design of this large Surface Effect Ship.

Other world naval applications of the LM2500 include: US Navy's DD-963 Spruance-class destroyers, FFG-7 Perry-class frigates, Australian Navy FFG-7 frigates, Iranian DD-963 destroyers, Italian, Venezuelan and Peruvian LUPO-class fast frigates, West German Navy frigates, a South Korean Navy frigate, and Patrol gunboats and corvette size ships for the Indonesian, Saudi Arabian and Danish navies.

Two LM2500s power the Gas Turbine Ship (GTS) Admiral William M Callaghan roll-on/roll-off cargo vessel. The ship has over 80,000 operating hours to date with the LM2500 engine.
TYPE: Two-shaft, axial flow, simple cycle.
AIR INTAKE: Axial, inlet bellmouth or duct can be customised to installation.
COMBUSTION CHAMBER: Annular.
FUEL GRADE: Kerosene, JP4, JP5. Diesel, heavy distillate fuels and natural gas.
TURBINE: Two-stage gas generator, six-stage power.
JET PIPE: Vertical or customised to fit installation.

GE LM2500 gas turbine

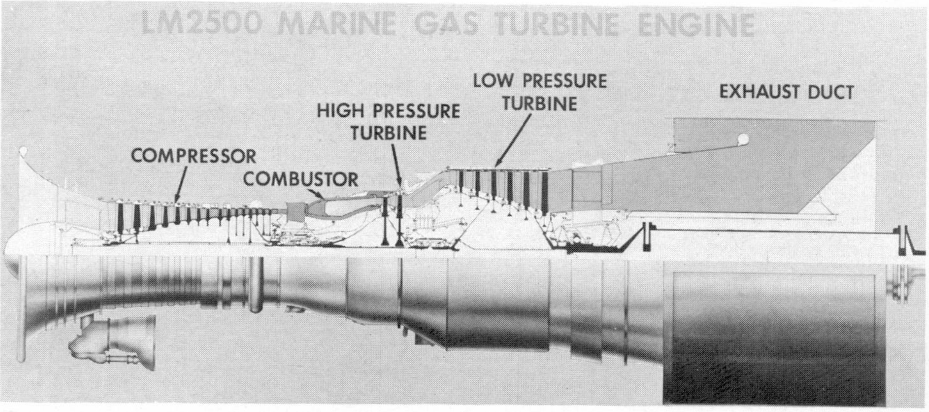

Internal arrangements of the GE LM2500 marine gas-turbine

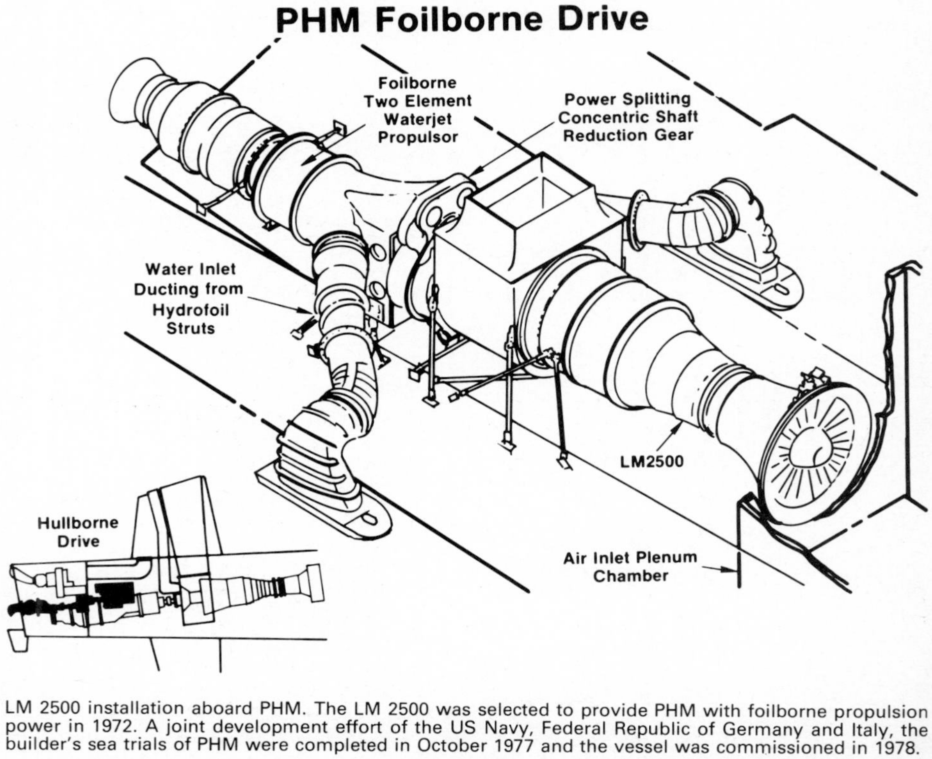

LM 2500 installation aboard PHM. The LM 2500 was selected to provide PHM with foilborne propulsion power in 1972. A joint development effort of the US Navy, Federal Republic of Germany and Italy, the builder's sea trials of PHM were completed in October 1977 and the vessel was commissioned in 1978.

OIL SPECIFICATION: Synthetic Turbine Oil (MIL-L-23699) or equal.
MOUNTING: At power turbine and compressor front frame.
STARTING: Pneumatic, hydraulic.

DIMENSIONS
Length: 6,630mm (261in)
Width: 2,133mm (84in)
Height: 2,133mm (84in)

PERFORMANCE RATINGS: 30,000shp at 15°C (59°F) at sea level
SPECIFIC FUEL CONSUMPTION: 0·171kg (0·376lb)/hp/h

NORTHROP CORPORATION
Ventura Division

1515 Rancho Conejo Boulevard, Newbury Park, California 91320, USA
Telephone: (213) 553 6262

In 1972 Northrop Corporation acquired the rights to this engine from McCulloch Corporation. The 4318 series continues to be made and sold by Ventura Division, which uses the engine to power the Basic Training Target (BTT), also known in the United Kingdom as the MQM-36 Shelduck.

MODEL 4318F

TYPE: Four-cylinder horizontally-opposed air-cooled two-stroke.
CYLINDERS: Bore: 80·8mm (3³/₁₆in). Stroke 79·4mm (3⅛in). Displacement 1·6 litres (100in³). Compression ratio 7·8 : 1. Heat-treated die-cast aluminium cylinders with integral heads, having hard chrome plated cylinder walls. Self-locking nuts secure cylinders to crankcase studs.
PISTONS: Heat-treated cast aluminium. Two rings above pins. Piston pins of case-hardened steel.
CONNECTING RODS: Forged steel. 'Free-roll' silver-plated bearings at big-end. Small-end carries one needle bearing. Lateral position of rod controlled by thrust washers between piston pin bosses and small-end of rod.
CRANKSHAFT: Four-throw one-piece steel forging on four anti-friction bearings, two ball and two needle, one with split race for centre main bearing.
CRANKCASE: One-piece heat-treated permanent-mould aluminium casting, closed at rear end with cast aluminium cover which provides mounting for magneto.
VALVE GEAR: Fuel mixture for scavenging and power stroke introduced to cylinders through crankshaft-driven rotary valves and ported cylinders.
INDUCTION: Crankcase pumping type. Diaphragm-type carburettor with adjustable jet.
FUEL SPECIFICATION: Grade 100/130 aviation fuel mixed in the ratio 20 parts fuel with one part 40SAE two-cycle outboard motor oil (or 30 parts fuel to one part Super Red oil).
IGNITION: Single magneto and distributor. Directly connected to crankshaft through impulse coupling for easy starting. Radio noise suppressor included. BG type RB 916S, ac type 83P or Champion REM-38R spark plugs. Complete radio shielding.
LUBRICATION: Oil mixed with fuel as in conventional two-stroke engines.
PROPELLER DRIVE: RH tractor. Keyed taper shaft.
STARTING: By separate portable hydraulic starter.
MOUNTING: Three mounting lugs provided with socket for rubber mounting bushings.
DIMENSIONS
Length: 686mm (27in)
Width: 711mm (28in)
Height: 381mm (15in)

Northrop Model 4318F 4-cylinder, horizontally opposed 2-stroke

WEIGHT Dry: Less propeller hub: 34·9kg (77lb)
POWER RATING: Rated output: 84-96hp at 4,100rpm
SPECIFIC CONSUMPTION: Fuel/oil mixture: 0·408kg (0·9lb)/hp/h

ROCKETDYNE DIVISION ROCKWELL INTERNATIONAL

6633 Canoga Avenue, Canoga Park, California 91304, USA
Telex: 698478
Officials:
Hal Oquist, *Director, Division Propulsion Programmes*
John Lauffer, *Programme Manager, Powerjet 16, 20, 24 Programme*
H Lee Barham, *Marketing Manager, Waterjet Propulsion*

The technology gained in the design and manufacture of high-performance pumps for the US space programme has enabled Rocketdyne to develop a new family of waterjet propulsion systems, called Powerjet 16, 20 and 24. These propulsion systems employ advanced-design, axial-flow pumping elements to produce a compact, lightweight waterjet propulsor. Simplicity of design minimises the number of components necessary in the units, while allowing accessibility for servicing or replacement of seals and bearings. All system components, which are designed to meet American Bureau of Shipping requirements, have been built in materials selected for their resistance to cavitation damage, and sea-water and galvanic corrosion.

Rockwell 20s power the nine Boeing Jetfoils currently in service. On each Jetfoil, dual PJ20s, each driven by a Detroit Diesel Allison 501-K20A gas-turbine rated at 3,500hp deliver a 22,000 gallons/min water flow.

Jetfoils operate regularly at a cruising speed of 45 knots in 12ft seas to transport and passengers between Hong Kong and Macao; Margarita Island and Puerto la Cruz, Venezuela; Sado Island and Niigata in Japan and London to

Zeebrugge, Belgium.

The eight vessels in service have carried 1,500,000 passengers over 147 million passenger miles, during which the Powerjet 20 units have logged in excess of 73,000 pump hours.

Another new vessel to employ Rocketdyne Powerjets is the American Enterprise, the world's first turbine/waterjet-powered fast offshore crew and supply boat, which has achieved speeds in excess of 35 knots during trials. Power is supplied by two Powerjet 16 waterjet pumps driven by Detroit Diesel Allison Model 16V-92T engines, developing 860shp each, and one Powerjet 24 pump on the centreline driven by a Detroit Diesel Allison Model 501-KF gas-turbine, rated at 5,430hp maximum output. The aluminium-hulled American Enterprise is designed to carry 60-90 passengers and up to 30 long tons of high priority cargo at speeds not previously associated with conventional planing hull crew/supply boats.

POWERJET 20

TYPE: Single-stage, axial-flow.

APPLICATION: Designed for hydrofoils and high-speed craft at 3,500hp and medium- to high-speed craft at lower horsepower. Two Powerjet 20 propulsion units, each of which is driven by an Allison 501-K20A gas-turbine through a 6·37:1 reduction gearbox, power the Boeing 929 Jetfoil, 106-ton, 45-knot passenger-carrying hydrofoil. In this application, the gearbox is used in conjunction with an over/under configuration, which results in a compact installation. Input horsepower to the gearbox is 3,700 at 13,250rpm.

ACCESSORY DRIVE: For the Boeing Jetfoil, Powerjet 20 is coupled to a gearbox that provides two pads for accessory drive. The first pad supplies power for the boat's hydraulic system, while the second directs power to gearbox, pump, and turbine lubrication and scavenge pump.

PRIME MOVERS: Diesels and gas-turbines up to 3,700hp.

LUBRICATION SYSTEM: External recirculating supply, with 2·5 to 3·5 gallons/min flow at 55 to 70psi provided by a gerotor-type pump that contains both pressure and scavenge cavities.

Powerjet 20, designed for hydrofoils and high-speed craft with diesels and gas-turbines developing up to 3,700hp. Pump flow rate is 23,150 gallons/min

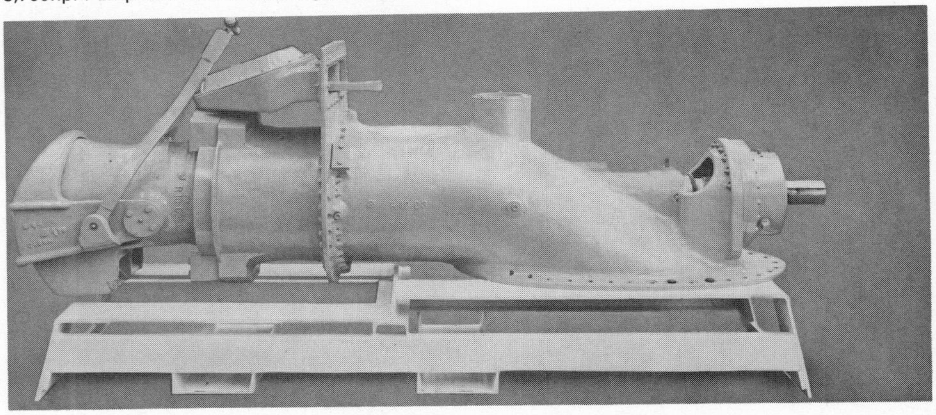

Powerjet 16, single-stage axial-flow waterjet pump for diesels and gas turbines developing between 700 and 1,575hp

Twin Powerjet 16 and Powerjet 24 installed on the crewboat 'American Enterprise'

LUBE OIL GRADE
MIL-L-23699
MIL-L-2106
Diesel crankcase oil—API (D Series)
Automobile differential oil—API (M Series)
SPECIFICATION
Operating range:
Input hp: 3,840 (4,320hp also available)
Input shaft speed: 2,145rpm
Total inlet head: 7·92m (26ft)
Pump flowrate: 24,750 gallons/min
Propulsion pump weight:
Dry: 707·6kg (1,560lb)
Wet: 961·6kg (2,120lb)

POWERJET 16

TYPE: Single-stage, axial-flow.
APPLICATION: Designed for high propulsive efficiency at moderate speeds in all types of hull configurations.
PRIME MOVERS: Diesels and gas-turbines developing between 700 and 1,500hp. Three inducer trims are available for direct coupling to most marine diesels.
LUBRICATION SYSTEM: Integrated recirculating system.
LUBE OIL GRADE:
MIL-L-23699
MIL-L-2105
Diesel crankcase oil—API (D Series)
Automobile differential oil—API (M Series)
SPECIFICATION
Operating Range:

	Trim Number 1	2	3	4
Max hp, up to:	1,575	1,575	1,575	1,306
Input shaft speed rpm, up to:	2,310	2,530	2,630	2,650
Nominal input direct drive, hp:	1,025	900	800	815
Nominal input shaft speed, rpm:	2,000	2,100	2,100	2,260
Total inlet head, ft, minimum:	30·1	22	22	22
Pump flowrate (at 30 knots), gallons/min:	18,200	16,700	16,700	16,700

Propulsion pump weight:
Dry: 1,027kg (2,265lb)
Wet: 1,141kg (2,515lb)
Steering vector: ±22 degrees
Reverse thrust: 50% of forward gross thrust to a maximum of 1,025hp

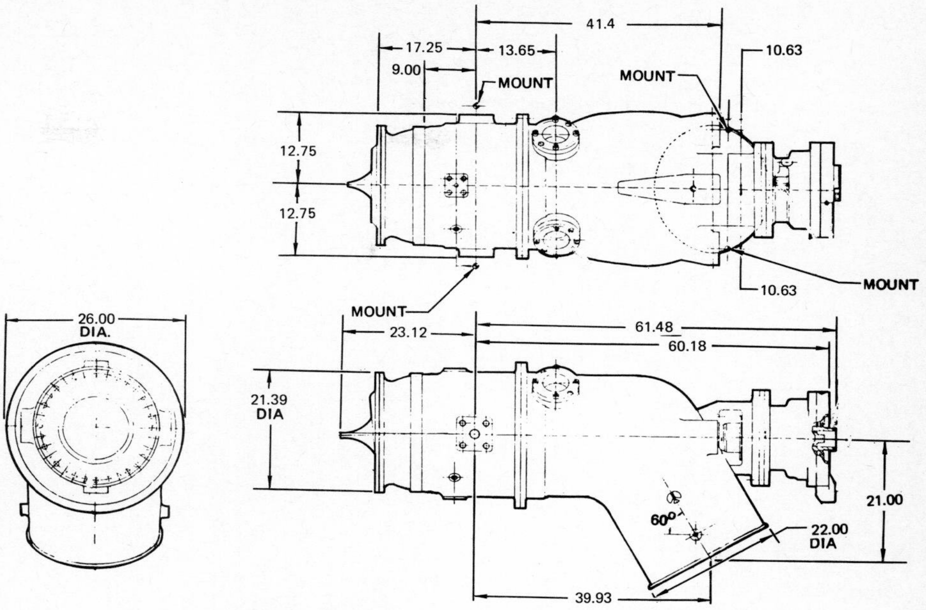

General arrangement of the Powerjet 20, two of which are installed on the Boeing Jetfoil

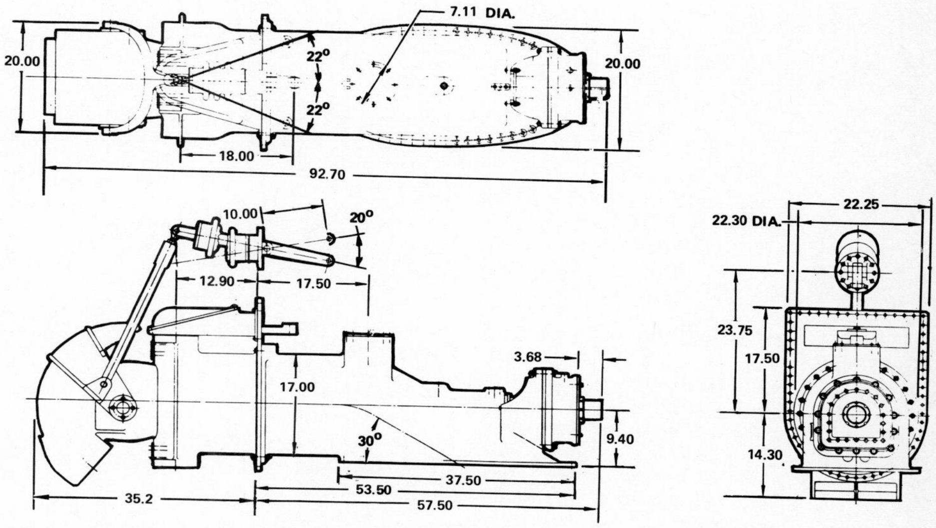

The Powerjet PJ16, for diesels and gas-turbines delivering between 700 and 1,500shp

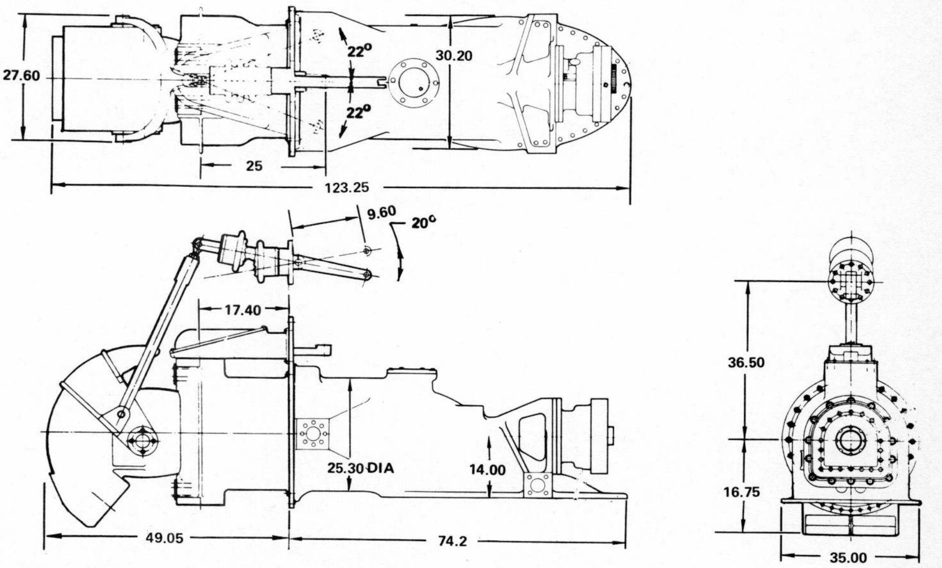

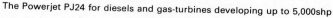

The Powerjet PJ24 for diesels and gas-turbines developing up to 5,000shp

POWERJET 24

TYPE: Single-stage, axial-flow.
APPLICATION: Designed for high-propulsive efficiency at moderate speeds.
PRIME MOVERS: Diesels and gas turbines developing up to 5,790hp.
LUBRICATION SYSTEM: External recirculating supply requiring 3·8 to 4·2 gallons/min flow at 55 to 70psi.
LUBE OIL GRADE
MIL-L-23699
MIL-L-2105
Diesel crankcase oil—API (D Series)
Automobile differential oil—API (M Series)
SPECIFICATION
Operating range:
Input: 5,790hp
Input shaft speed: 1,853rpm
Total inlet head: 13·1m (43ft) at 1,640rpm
Pump flowrate (at 30 knots): 45,000 gallons/min
Propulsion pump weight
Dry: 1,769kg (3,900lb); 2,358kg (5,200lb) heavy duty
Wet: 2,177kg (4,800lb); 2,767kg (6,100lb) heavy duty
Steering vector: ±22 degrees
Reverse thrust: 50% of forward gross thrust to a maximum of 1,830hp

Powerjet PJ24 unit

SCORPION INC.

Crosby, Minnesota 56441, USA
Telephone: (218) 546 5123
Telex: 294452
Officials:
Charles A Srock, *OEM and Export Manager*

The company is now manufacturing and marketing the Cuyuna range of axial-fan cooled twin-cylinder engines, developing 29-40hp.

The engines are serviced through a network of 2,000 independent service outlets and central distributors throughout the USA and Canada.

CUYUNA AXIAL-FAN TWIN-CYLINDER ENGINES

Models 295, 340, 400 and 440

Features of this range include a standard mounting for all models to ease installation; low engine profile with built-in shrouding; lightweight construction to reduce overall vehicle weight and high interchangeability of all parts. Crankshafts, crank cases, blower assemblies, magnetos, recoil starters and hardware items are fully interchangeable, thus reducing spare parts inventory requirements and lowering maintenance costs. Specifications for the four standard productions are given in the accompanying table.

Type	Twin Cylinder Axial-Fan Cooled			
Model	295	340	400	440
Bore	2·185in	2·362in	2·559in	2·658in
Stroke	2·362in	2·362in	2·362in	2·362in
Displacement	290cc	339cc	389cc	428cc
Compression Ratio	12·5 : 1			
Max Torque	6,500 rpm			
Brake hp/rpm	29hp 6,500/7,000rpm	32hp 6,500/7,000rpm	38hp 6,500/7,000rpm	40hp 6,500/7,000rpm
Base Mounting Hole Thread	7/16—14 UNC			
Cylinder	Aluminium with Cast Iron Sleeve			
Connecting Rod Bearing Upper	Needle			
Connecting Rod Bearing Lower	Needle			
Connecting Rod Material	Forged Steel			
Main Bearing	4 Heavy Duty Ball Bearings (1 Dual Row Bearing, PTO)			
Ignition	Bosch			
Lighting Coil	12 volt, 150 watt			
Contact Breaker Gap	0·014in to 0·018in			
Ignition Setting Before TDC	0·102in to 0·112in (Cam Fully Advanced)			
Spark Plug Thread	14 × 1·25mm (3/4in) Reach			
Gap	0·016in to 0·020in			
Type	Bosch W-260-T-2 (or) Champion N-3			
Rotation	Counter-clockwise Viewed From PTO End			
Fuel-Oil Mixture	40:1 (1 pint to 5 gallons)			
Lubrication	Premium Gasoline & Cuyuna 2 Cycle Engine Oil			
Carburettor Type	2 15/16in Centre to Centre Bolt Dimension			
Starter	Rewind Type, Standard; Electric, Optional			
Rope Material	Nylon			
Weight	62lb			

Horsepower ratings established in accordance with specifications SAE-J 607.
Engines will produce no more than 78dB when used with Cuyuna approved carburettor/muffler/intake silencer systems, according to SAE-J192 specifications.

UNITED TECHNOLOGIES CORPORATION POWER SYSTEMS DIVISION

(Gas Turbine Operations)

1690 New Britain Avenue, Farmington, Connecticut 06032, USA
Telephone: (203) 677 4081
Officials:
Rolf Bibow, *President, Power Systems Division*
T S Melvin, *Vice President and General Manager, Gas Turbine Operations*
R F Nordin, *Director of Marketing*
D Caplow, *Manager, Industrial Sales*
J Paterson, *Manager, Utility Marketing*
D G Assard, *Director of Engineering*

United Technologies Power Systems Division (Turbo Power and Marine Systems Inc), designs and builds industrial and marine gas turbine power plants and related systems utilising the FT4 Modular Industrial Turbine. It also provides a systems support for each of its installations.

Canadian sales of the FT4 are handled by Pratt & Whitney Aircraft of Canada Limited, PO Box 10, Longueuil, Quebec, Canada, which also manufactures and sells the ST6 marine gas turbine.

Power Systems Division efforts have resulted in over 1,200 Modular Industrial Turbines supplied or on order in the USA and in 20 other countries. The turbines will supply more than 34 million hp for electric power generation, gas transmission and industrial drives as well as for marine propulsion.

MARINE GAS TURBINES

United Technologies (UTC) is currently offering the FT4 38,600shp gas turbines for marine propulsion.

UTC is also developing a new marine gas turbine for the US Navy. This new design incorporates the extensive operating experience of the FT4 turbine and the advanced features of the Pratt & Whitney Aircraft JT9D fan jet engine. Designated the FT9, it will have an initial marine rating of 33,000shp at 37°C (100°F) with inlet and exhaust duct losses of 4 and 6in of water. Advantages of the FT9 gas turbine will include modular construction for maintainability and low fuel consumption. Details of the FT9 are shown in the cross-section illustration.

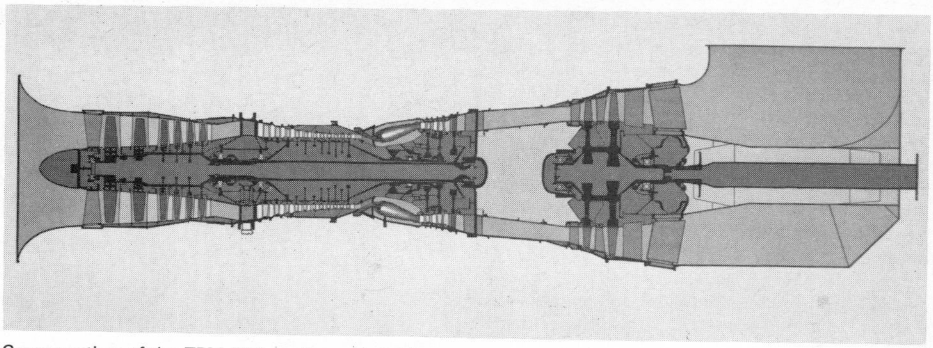

Cross-section of the TPM FT9 marine gas-turbine, rated at 33,000shp at 100°F

MARINE INSTALLATION

PSD's FT4 marine gas turbines were first used for boost power in military vessels, including two Royal Danish Navy frigates, twelve US Coast Guard Hamilton Class high endurance cutters and four Canadian Armed Forces DDH-280 Iroquois Class destroyers. Another boost power application of the FT4 is in the Fast Escort and ASW vessel Bras d'Or also built for the Canadian Armed Forces. Another application is for two new 12,000 ton Arctic ice breakers for the US Coast Guard. With three FT4 marine gas turbines, these vessels are capable of maintaining a continuous speed of three knots through ice 6ft thick, and are able to ram through ice 21ft thick.

PSD's marine gas turbines are used for both the main and boost propulsion in the four Canadian DDH-280 destroyers. These are the first military combatant vessels to be designed for complete reliance on gas turbine power. PSD's marine gas turbines are also used in a military surface effect ship programme.

Four 32,000 ton container ships with marine gas turbines are in trans-Atlantic service with Seatrain Lines. These vessels are Euroliner, Eurofreighter, Asialiner and Asiafreighter. All four ships are burning treated residual fuel.

Another commercial vessel where FT4 gas turbines are used as the main propulsion unit is the FINNJET, a high-speed Finnlines passenger liner. The Finnjet has completed its first year of service and has cut the Baltic crossing time in half, routinely maintaining 30 knots, with over 200 Baltic crossings, engine availability over 99%.

UTC/PSD Marine Power Pac with an FT4 Modular Industrial Turbine

UTC/PSD MARINE POWER PAC

The photograph shows an FT4 marine gas turbine completely packaged as a marine power pac ready for installation, with the minimum of interface connections to be made. Each is built upon a rigid mounting frame and includes a housing and gas turbine mounting system, together with controls, accessory equipment, wiring and piping. A remote control system is also provided. Installation is simple. Since all the equipment is pretested at the factory before shipment, time required for checkout after installation is minimised.

The gas generator portion of the gas turbine is easily removed for servicing. With a spare gas generator to replace the one removed for servicing, the ship's power plant can be changed in a matter of hours.

The FT4 gas turbine comprises the gas generator and the power (free) turbine. The independent power turbine accepts the kinetic energy of the gas generator and converts it to mechanical energy through a shaft which extends through the exhaust duct elbow.

GAS GENERATOR

TYPE: Simple cycle two spool turbine. A low pressure compressor is driven by a two stage turbine and a high pressure compressor is driven by a single turbine. The burner section has eight burner cans which are equipped with duplex fuel nozzles.

Current production model of the FT4 marine gas-turbine, rated at 48,300shp maximum intermittent and 38,600shp base load

AIR INTAKE: Cast steel casing with 18 radial struts supporting the front compressor bearing and equipped with a bleed air anti-icing system.
LOW PRESSURE COMPRESSOR: Nine stage axial flow on inner of two concentric shafts driven by two stage turbine and supported on ball and roller bearings.
HIGH PRESSURE COMPRESSOR: Seven stage axial flow on outer hollow shaft driven by single stage turbine and running on ball and roller bearings.
COMBUSTION CHAMBER: Eight burner cans located in an annular arrangement and enclosed in a one piece steel casing. Each burner has six duplex fuel nozzles.
TURBINES: Steel casing with hollow guide vanes. Turbine wheels are bolted to the compressor shafts and are supported on ball and roller bearings. A single stage turbine drives the high compressor and a two stage turbine drives the low compressor.
POWER TURBINE: The gas turbine is available with either clockwise or counter-clockwise rotation of the power turbine. Desired direction of rotation specified by customer. Power turbine housing is bolted to gas generator turbine housing. The three stage turbine shaft assembly is straddle mounted and supported on ball and roller bearings. The output shaft is bolted to the hub of the power turbine rotor and extends through the exhaust duct.
BEARINGS: Anti-friction ball and roller bearings.
ACCESSORY DRIVE: Starter, fluid power pump, tachometer drives for low compressor, high compressor and free turbine.
LUBRICATION SYSTEM: Return system and scavenge pumps with internal pressure, 3·09 kg/cm² (45 psi).
LUBRICATING OIL SPECIFICATIONS: Type 2 synthetic lube oil PWA-521.
MARINE APPLICATIONS: Meets installation, high shock and ships seaway motion requirements.
STARTING: Pneumatic or hydraulic.
DIMENSIONS
Length: 8,788mm (346in)
Width: 2,438mm (96in)
Height: 2,794mm (101in)

FT4 gas turbines provide main propulsion for the high-speed Finnish passenger liner "Finnjet"

PERFORMANCE DATA: FT4 MARINE GAS TURBINE

Rating	*Power Output* (1)	*Specific Fuel Consumption* (2)
Max Intermittent	48,300shp	197g (0·435lb)/shp/h
Max Continuous	43,800shp	200g (0·440lb)/shp/h
Normal	38,600shp	204g (0·450lb)/shp/h

(1) All ratings at 3,600rpm shaft speed, 15°C (59°F) and sea level.
(2) Based on fuel with LHV of 18,500 Btu/lb.

FUEL SPECIFICATIONS
Light Distillate (Naphtha): PWA-532(1)
Aviation Grade Kerosene: PWA-522(1)
Marine Diesel: PWA-527(1)
Heavy Distillate: PWA-539
(1) Covered by TPM-FR-1 for series engine
Treated crude and residual oil refer to manufacturer.

SELECTED AMATEUR-BUILT HOVERCRAFT

R. CRESSWELL

184 St Bernards Road, Solihull, West Midlands B92 7BJ, England

ECCLES

This craft was completed in April 1977 at a cost of about £800 and has since shown itself to be an extremely successful design. Its owner is the current Over 500cc champion in the British Hovercraft Championships. In some 55 events entered in the 1977 season he achieved 51 wins.

LIFT AND PROPULSION: A single JLO 250cc engine, rated at 9bhp at 3,800rpm, driving direct a 559mm (22in) diameter, five-bladed, Multi-wing axial fan provides lift. The blades of this fan are set at 30 degrees. For propulsion a single Kohler 440 2AS, twin cylinder 436cc engine, rated at 42bhp at 7,600rpm, is employed. This drives via toothed belts a pair of 584mm (23in) diameter, five-bladed, ducted Multi-wing fans fitted with 45 degree pitch blades. This unit supplies 78kg (173lb) of static thrust. The craft carries 24·8 litres (5½ gallons) of fuel. Cushion pressure in its normal racing configuration with one person is 35kg/m² (7·2lb/ft²).

CONTROLS: The propulsion engine is controlled by a twistgrip throttle and a thumb-lever acts as the lift engine throttle. A pair of handlebars activate the craft's two flat rudders located at the rear of the thrust ducts via Teli-flex cable.

HULL: The craft hull is constructed from glass reinforced plastics and has a buoyancy box located beneath the driving seat and in the rear chamber. Additional buoyancy in the form of two buoyancy bags provides the craft with a total buoyancy equivalent to 150% of craft normal all-up weight. A distinctive extended segment skirt is fitted to the craft and the front twenty segments are individually fed. The segments are made from 1,831g/m² (6oz/yd²) nylon impregnated with PVC.

"Eccles", built and operated by Richard Cresswell, pictured during a Hoverclub race meeting

ACCOMMODATION: Craft seating is for a maximum of two persons sitting in-line, motorcycle style.

DIMENSIONS

Length, overall: 3·56m (11ft 8in)

Width, overall: 1·93m (6ft 4in)

Height, hovering: 1·22m (4ft)

at rest: 0·97m (3ft 2in)

WEIGHTS

Empty: 145kg (320lb)

Normal payload: 86kg (190lb)

Normal all-up: 231kg (510lb)

PERFORMANCE

Max speed (estimated): 96km/h (60mph) over land, 55 knots over water

Endurance: 1¾h

Obstacle clearance: 25cm (10in)

M. MARTYN JONES

47 Rosebank Cottages, Westfield Square, Woking, Surrey

KIPPER

This light hovercraft runabout was built at a cost of about £400 by Mike Martyn-Jones and was completed in May 1975. Since that date the craft has been entered in a number of Hoverclub meetings in various parts of Britain. The craft is designed for use in the hover-cruising role rather than for racing events.

LIFT AND PROPULSION: A single JLO 250cc engine, rated at about 15bhp, supplies power direct to a 610mm (24in) diameter, five-bladed axial fan which uses 30 degree pitch blades. For propulsion the craft has a JLO 440cc engine, rated at 40bhp, and this drives, via vee-belts, a pair of 610mm (24in) diameter ducted fans. These are five-bladed fans using 45 degree pitch blades. Cushion pressure of the craft loaded is about 48·82kg/m² (10lb/ft²).

CONTROLS: A twist-grip throttle on the control handlebars governs the thrust unit whilst a simple lever acts as lift throttle. Moving the handlebars activates rudders in the thrust ducts for directional control.

HULL: The glass reinforced plastic hull contains large airtight buoyancy chambers amounting to a high percentage excess buoyancy. A loop and segment skirt made from a lightweight material is fitted.

ACCOMMODATION: Seating 'in-line' is available for three persons.

DIMENSIONS

Length overall: 3·81m (12ft 6in)

Width overall: 1·98m (6ft 6in)

Height overall, hovering: 1·21m (4ft)

on pads: 0·99m (3ft 3in)

WEIGHTS

Not available.

PERFORMANCE

Estimated max speed: 56·32km/h (35mph)

Obstacle clearance: 228mm (9in)

NEWARK C OF E HIGH SCHOOL

Barnby Road, Newark, Nottinghamshire

MILADY

This simple yet successful light hovercraft is the second to be built by pupils of the School, and despite its very modest engine power, the craft has demonstrated a very satisfactory performance over land and water. The hovercraft was completed early in July 1976 and is estimated to have cost only £50 to build.

LIFT AND PROPULSION: A single Rowena Stihl 137cc engine rated at 8½bhp provides power for both lift and thrust functions. The engine drives a single 610mm (24in) Multi-wing ducted fan with approximately one-third of the air going into the cushion and two-thirds being used for propulsion. The fan is fitted with five blades, each of 30 degree pitch.

CONTROLS: A pair of handlebars provide the craft driver with directional controls for a single rudder in the rear of the thrust duct. The thrust engine is controlled by a twist-grip arrangement on the handlebars.

HULL: The craft has a simple tray-shaped hull made from glass-reinforced plastic with buoyancy bags strapped onto the inner sides of the hull to provide reserve buoyancy. A simple bag skirt design is used on the craft and is fitted to the outer edge of the hull. The skirt is made from lightweight 1,831g/m² (6oz/yd²) material.

ACCOMMODATION: Seating is provided for one person in an open cockpit.

DIMENSIONS

Length overall: 2·74m (9ft)

Width overall: 1·52m (5ft)

Height hovering: 0·86m (2ft 10in)

at rest: 0·76m (2ft 6in)

WEIGHTS

Empty: 68kg (150lb)

All-up weight, one person: 136kg (300lb)

PERFORMANCE

Estimated max speed over land and water: 40·2km/h (25mph)

B SHERLOCK

35 Combewell Close, Garsington, Oxford, England

SATURN 1

Completed in March 1975 at an estimated cost of £160, this craft showed great promise during the Hoverclub's 1975 Racing Programme.

LIFT AND PROPULSION: A JLO 98cc engine, rated at 5bhp at 3,500rpm, drives direct a 482mm (19in) diameter, five-bladed, 35 degree pitch axial fan. Propulsion is supplied by a Triumph T100A engine of 500cc, rated at 40bhp at 6,000rpm. This drives, via toothed belts, a pair of 610mm (24in) diameter, five-bladed, 45 degree pitch ducted thrust fans. A static thrust of 77·1kg (170lb) is obtained with this arrangement. The craft carries three gallons of fuel. Cushion pressure is estimated at 34·18kg/m² (7lb/ft²).

CONTROLS: Movement of the control joystick backwards regulates the thrust engine and a twist grip operates the lift engine throttle. A single rudder in each thrust duct provides the craft with directional control.

HULL: Construction of the hull and superstructure is of glass-reinforced plastic with eight buoyancy chambers built into the hull. A deep bag skirt system is made from 1,526g/m² (5oz/yd²) coated nylon material.

ACCOMMODATION: Side-by-side seating for two persons is provided in an open cockpit.
DIMENSIONS
Length overall: 3·35m (11ft)
Width overall: 1·68m (5ft 6in)
Height, hovering: 1·14m (3ft 9in)
  at rest: 0·914m (3ft)
WEIGHTS
Empty: 131·54kg (290lb)
All-up (with two persons): 276·68kg (610lb)
PERFORMANCE
Max speed, estimated
  land: 56·33km/h (35mph)
  water: 30 knots
Endurance: 2 hours
Obstacle clearance: 228·6mm (9in)

"Saturn I", driven by Bill Sherlock, has a Triumph 500cc thrust engine and a ILO lift unit

T SHERLOCK

14 Collinwood Road, Risinghurst, Oxford, England

SATURN 3

Completed in April 1976 at an estimated cost of £120, this light hovercraft, the second to be built by Terry Sherlock, has proved a good performer during the Hoverclub's 1978 race season.

LIFT AND PROPULSION: A single BSA Bantam 125cc engine, rated at 6bhp at 3,300rpm, provides power for a 0·48m (19in) diameter axial fan, fitted with five 30 degree pitch blades. Propulsion is supplied by a single Triumph 5TA 498cc motorcycle engine, rated at 28bhp at 6,000rpm, which drives, via a toothed belt, a 0·53m (21in) diameter, ten-bladed ducted fan, fitted with 45 degree pitch blades. This arrangement gives the craft a static thrust of 59kg (130lb). Fuel capacity of the craft is 13·3 litres (3 gallons) and with one person being carried the craft's cushion pressure is 43·9kg/m² (9lb/ft²).
CONTROLS: A twist-grip throttle is used for the propulsion engine and a choke lever for the lift unit. Engine controls are mounted on handlebars which also activate twin rudders in the thrust duct.
HULL: The complete hull of the craft, with the exception of the engine frame, constructed from 1 × 1 × 8⅛in angle iron, is in glass reinforced plastic. Eight separate chambers in the side sections of the craft provide 150% buoyancy. A bag skirt is employed, made from 5493g/m² (18oz/yd²) nylon/PVC material.
ACCOMMODATION: The craft can carry two persons sitting astride the central section of the hull.
DIMENSIONS
Length, overall: 3·35m (11ft)
Width, overall: 1·67m (5ft 6in)
Height, overall, hovering: 1·27m (4ft 2in)
  on pads: 1·06m (3ft 6in)
WEIGHTS
Empty: 136kg (300lb)
All-up: 249·46kg (550lb)
Normal payload: 113·39kg (250lb)
PERFORMANCE
Estimated max speed: 64·37km/h (40mph)
Obstacle clearance: 203mm (8in)
Endurance: 15n miles (racing) or 30n miles (cruising)

Saturn 3, the Triumph motorcycle-engined hovercraft built by Terry Sherlock of Risinghurst, Oxford for £120. *(Photo: Neil MacDonald)*

ACV and HYDROFOIL LICENSING AUTHORITIES

ARGENTINA
ACVs and Hydrofoils
Prefectura Naval Maritima
Paseo Colon 533
Buenos Aires
Argentina

AUSTRALIA
ACVs and Hydrofoils
Department of Transport
GPO Box 1839Q,
Melbourne,
Victoria 3001,
Australia

State Licensing Authorities
New South Wales
Ministry of Motor Transport
Rothchild Avenue,
Roseberry,
Sydney,
New South Wales 2000,
Australia

Queensland
Department of Harbours and Marine
Edward Street,
Brisbane,
Queensland 4000,
Australia

South Australia
Department of Marine and Harbours
211 Victoria Square West,
Adelaide,
South Australia 5000,
Australia

Tasmania
Navigation and Survey Authority of Tasmania
1 Franklin Wharf,
Hobart,
Tasmania 7000,
Australia

West Australia
Harbour and Light Department
Crane House,
185-187 High Street,
Fremantle,
West Australia 6000,
Australia

AUSTRIA
ACVs and Hydrofoils
Bundesministerium für Handel Gewerbe und Industrie
Stubenring 1,
Vienna 1,
Austria
Telephone: 57 66 55

BELGIUM
ACVs and Hydrofoils
Ministry of Communications
Administration de la Marine et de la Navigation Intérieure
rue Belliard 30,
B-1040 Brussels,
Belgium
Telephone: 02/230 02 57

CANADA
ACVs
Chief, Air Cushion Vehicle Division Marine Safety Branch
Canadian Coast Guard,
Transport Canada,
Tower A,
Place de Ville,
Ottawa,
Ontario K1A ON5,
Canada

DENMARK
ACVs
Handelsministeriet
3 Afdeling,
Slotsholmsgade 12,
DK-1216 Copenhagen K,
Denmark

Hydrofoils
Government Ships Inspection Service
Snorresgade 19,
DK-2300 Copenhagen S,
Denmark

EGYPT
ACVs
The Arab General Organisation for Air Transport
11 Emad El Din Street,
Cairo,
Egypt

FIJI
ACVs and Hydrofoils
Director of Marine
Marine Department,
PO Box 326,
Suva,
Fiji

FINLAND
Board of Navigation
Vurorimiehenkatu 1,
PO Box 158,
SF-00141 Helsinki 14,
Finland

FRANCE
ACVs and Hydrofoils
Secrétariat Général de la Marine Marchande
3 Place de Fontenoy,
75700 Paris,
France
Telephone: (1) 567 55 05
Telex: 250 823 Minimar Paris

GAMBIA
ACVs and Hydrofoils
Ministry of Works and Communications
Banjul,
Gambia

GERMANY (Federal Republic)
ACVs and Hydrofoils
See-Berufsgenossenschaft
Ships Safety Department
Reimerstwiete 2,
D-2000 Hamburg 11,
Federal Republic of Germany

GHANA
The Shipping Commissioner
Ministry of Transport and Communications,
PO Box M.38,
Accra,
Ghana

GREECE
ACVs and Hydrofoils
Ministry of Mercantile Marine
Merchant Ships Inspection Services,
Palaiologou 1 str,
Piraeus,
Greece

HUNGARY
Közlekedési Es Postaügyi Minisztérium
Kpm Hajozási Föosztály,
Budapest V, Apáczai Csere J-u 11,
Hungary

ICELAND
Directorate of Shipping
PO Box 484,
Reykjavik,
Iceland

INDIA
ACVs and Hydrofoils
Directorate General of Shipping
Bombay,
India

INDONESIA
ACVs and Hydrofoils
Department of Transport, Communications and Tourism
8 Medan Merdelka Barat,
Jakarta-Pusat,
Indonesia

IRELAND
ACVs and Hydrofoils
Department of Tourism and Transport
Kildare Street,
Dublin 2,
Ireland

ISRAEL
ACVs and Hydrofoils
Ministry of Transport
Division of Shipping and Ports,
102, Ha'atzmauth Road,
PO Box 33993,
Haifa,
Israel

ITALY
ACVs and Hydrofoils
Ministero Della Marina Mercantile
Ispettorato Tecnico,
Viale Asia,
00100 Rome,
Italy

IVORY COAST
ACVs and Hydrofoils
Ministère des Travaux Publics et des Transports
BP V6,
Abijan,
Ivory Coast

JAMAICA
The Collector General's Department
Newport East,
Kingston,
Jamaica

JAPAN
ACVs and Hydrofoils
Japanese Ministry of Transportation
2-1-3 Kasumigaseki,
Chiyoda-ku,
Tokyo,
Japan

KOREA (REPUBLIC OF)
Ministry of Transportation
1-3 Do-dong,
Choong-ku,
Seoul,
Republic of Korea

KUWAIT
ACVs and Hydrofoils
Department of Customs and Ports
PO Box 9,
Kuwait

LEBANON
ACVs and Hydrofoils
Ministère des Travaux Publics
Direction des Transports,
Beirut,
Lebanon

LUXEMBOURG
ACVs
Ministère des Transports et de l'Energie,
19-21 boulevard Royal,
Luxembourg
Telephone: 2 19 21

MADAGASCAR
ACVs and Hydrofoils
Ministère de l'Amina
Jement du Territoire,
Anosy,
Antananarivo,
Madagascar

MALAWI
The Ministry of Transport and Communications
Private Bag 322,
Capital City,
Lilongwe 3,
Malawi

MALAYSIA
The Ministry of Communications
Jalan Gurney,
Kuala Lumpur,
Malaysia
Telephone: 20 4044
Cables: Transport

MEXICO
ACVs and Hydrofoils
Departamento de Licencias
Direction de Marina Mercante,
Dr Mora No 15,
3er Piso,
Mexico 1,
Mexico

MOROCCO
Ministère des Travauxs Publics
Rabat,
Morocco

NETHERLANDS
ACVs and Hydrofoils
Ministerie van Verkeer en Waterstaat
Directoraat-Generaal van Scheepvaart
Afdeling Scheepvaartinspectie,
NW Buitensingel 2,
2518 PA 's-Gravenhage (The Hague),
Netherlands

NEW ZEALAND
ACVs and Hydrofoils (Certificates of Construction and Performance)
Operating approval and licences:
Ministry of Transport
Marine Division,
Private Bag,
Wellington 1,
New Zealand

Hovercraft regulations currently being drafted. Among other things these will require hovercraft over a certain size to be licenced for commercial operation. The administration of all legislation for hovercraft and hydrofoils is the responsibility of the above.

NORWAY
ACVs and Hydrofoils
Norwegian Maritime Directorate
Thv. Meyersgt 7,
PO Box 8123,
Oslo 1,
Norway

SOUTH AFRICA
Department of Transport
Private Bag X193
Pretoria 0001,
South Africa

SPAIN
ACVs and Hydrofoils
The Subsecretaria de la Marina Mercante
Ruiz de Alacron No 1,
Madrid 14,
Spain

SWEDEN
ACVs and Hydrofoils
The National Board of Shipping and Navigation
Sjofartsverket,
Fack,
S-102 50 Stockholm,
Sweden

SWITZERLAND
Cantonal licensing authorities for ACVs and Hydrofoils

Lake Zurich
Seepolizei/Schiffahrtskontrolle des Kantons Zürich
Seestrasse 87,
CH-8942 Oberriden,
Switzerland

Seepolizei-und Gewässerschutzkommissariat der Stadt Zurich
Bellereivestrasse 260,
CH-8008 Zurich,
Switzerland

Lake Constance
Polizeidepartement des Kantons Thurgau,
Regierungsgebaude,
CH-8500 Frauenfeld,
Switzerland
Polizeidepartement des Kantons St Gallen,
Schiffahrts-und Hafenverwaltung,
CH-9400 Rorschach,
Switzerland

Lake Lucerne
Schiffsinspektorat des Kantons Luzern
Gibraltarstrasse 3,
CH-6002 Lucerne,
Switzerland

Lake Geneva
Departement de Justice et Police Service de la Navigation
Place Bourg-de-Four 1,
CH-1200 Geneva,
Switzerland

Departement de la Justice, de la Police et des Affaires Militaire,
Service de la Police Administrative,
Place du Château 6,
CH-1001 Lausanne,
Switzerland

Lake Lugano
Ufficio Cantonale de Polizia
VC Ghiringhelli 27b,
CH-6500 Bellinzona,
Switzerland

Lake Neuchatel
Departement de Police
CH-2000 Neuchatel,
Switzerland

Lake Thoune and Lake Brienz
Direktion für Verkehr, Energie- und Wasserwirtschaft des Kantons Bern
Verkehrsamt,
Rathausplatz 1,
CH-3011 Bern,
Switzerland

TURKEY
ACVs and Hydrofoils
T C Ulastirma Bakanligi
Liman ve Deniz Isleri Dairesi Baskanligi,
Ankara,
Turkey

UNITED KINGDOM
Hovercraft – Certification and Maintenance, Type Certificates; approval of components and equipment.
Issue of Safety and Experimental Certificates; Certificates of Construction and Performance.
Approval of persons or organisations from whom the CAA may accept reports on the design, construction, maintenance or repair of hovercraft or elements thereof.
Publication of "British Hovercraft Safety Requirements"
Technical enquiries to:
Hovercraft Department
Airworthiness Division
Civil Aviation Authority,
Brabazon House,
Redhill,
Surrey RH1·1SQ,
England
Telephone: Redhill 65966
Telex: 27100

Publications:
Printing and Publication Services
Greville House,
3 Gratton Road,
Cheltenham,
Gloucestershire GL50 2BN,
England

Hovercraft and Hydrofoils
Hovercraft Operating Permits and Hydrofoil Passenger Certificates
Department of Trade
Marine Divison,
Sunley House,
90-93 High Holborn,
London WC1V 6LP,
England
Telephone: 01-405 6911
Telex: 264084

UNITED STATES OF AMERICA
ACVs and Hydrofoils
Department of Transportation
Commandant (G-MMT-4),
US Coast Guard,
Washington DC 20590,
USA

VENEZUELA
Ministerio de Communicaciones
Dirección General de Transporte y Tránsito Maritimos
Esquina Carmelitas,
Edifico Ramia,
Caracas 101,
Venezuela

YUGOSLAVIA
Yugoslav Federal Economic Secretariat
Transport Department,
Bulevar AVNOJ-a 104,
Belgrade,
Yugoslavia

ACTIVE UK CIVIL ACV REGISTRATIONS

Registration Number	*Craft Type and Production No*	*Manufacturer*	*Operator, Owner or Charterer*
GH-2004	SR.N4-002	British Hovercraft Corp	Hoverlloyd Ltd
GH-2005	SR.N4-003	British Hovercraft Corp	Hoverlloyd Ltd
GH-2006	SR.N4-001	British Hovercraft Corp	British Rail Hovercraft Ltd
GH-2007	SR.N4-004	British Hovercraft Corp	British Rail Hovercraft Ltd
GH-2008	SR.N4-005	British Hovercraft Corp	Hoverlloyd Ltd
GH-2009	SR.N5-001*	British Hovercraft Corp	Hoverwork Ltd
GH-2010	SR.N6-022	British Hovercraft Corp	Hovertravel Ltd
GH-2011	SR.N6-024	British Hovercraft Corp	Hovertravel Ltd
GH-2012	SR.N6-026	British Hovercraft Corp	Hovertravel Ltd
GH-2013	SR.N6-130	British Hovercraft Corp	Hovertravel Ltd
GH-2014	SR.N6-009	British Hovercraft Corp	Westland Charters Ltd
GH-2015	SR.N6-011	British Hovercraft Corp	Westland Charters Ltd
GH-2017 (lapsed)	HM.2-007	Hovermarine Transport Ltd	Overseas operator
GH-2018	HM.2-305	Hovermarine Transport Ltd	International Hoverservices
GH-2019	HM.2-312	Hovermarine Transport Ltd	International Hoverservices
GH-2020	HA5 MkIIIW(101)	Hover Air Ltd	Lord Hotham (Contract Hover)
GH-2022 (lapsed)	SR.N6-028	British Hovercraft Corp	Destroyed
GH-2023	HM.2-002	Hovermarine Transport Ltd	Hovermarine Transport Ltd
GH-2024 (lapsed)	HM.2-303	Hovermarine Transport Ltd	International Hoverservices
GH-2025	HQ-007	Robin Parkhouse	Messrs Warman & Pott
GH-2026	SH.2-004**	Sealand Hovercraft Ltd	Sealand Hovercraft Ltd
GH-2031	SR.N6-031	British Hovercraft Corp	British Hovercraft Corp
GH-2032	SH.2-006**	Sealand Hovercraft Ltd	—
GH-2034	SH.2-013**	Sealand Hovercraft Ltd	Airgo Ltd
GH-2035	SR.N6-055†	British Hovercraft Corp	Hovertravel Ltd
GH-2037	SH.2-001**	Sealand Hovercraft Ltd	—
GH-2040	SH.2-020**	Sealand Hovercraft Ltd	—
GH-2041	SR.N5-006	British Hovercraft Corp	Hoverwork Ltd
GH-2046	SR.N6-037	British Hovercraft Corp	Overseas operator
GH-2049	VT.2-001	Vosper Thornycroft Ltd	Vosper Thornycroft Ltd
GH-2050	HM.2-435	Hovermarine Transport Ltd	Overseas operator
GH-2051	HM.2-310	Hovermarine Transport Ltd	Secretary of State for Industry
GH-2053	Nimbus Mk III	Surface Craft Ltd	B & B Enterprises
GH-2054	SR.N4-006	British Hovercraft Corp	Hoverlloyd Ltd
GH-2055	SR.N6-005	British Hovercraft Corp	Destroyed
GH-2058	HM.2-317	Hovermarine Transport Ltd	Hovermarine Transport Ltd

* Although originally built by BHC, this craft (GH-2009) was re-built by Air Vehicles Ltd and is known as an SR.N5A.
** The ownership of many SH.2 craft is uncertain following the demise of Sealand in mid-1976. New registrations are awaited for them.
† This craft has been constructed from components from other SR.N6 and SR.N5 hovercraft by Hovertravel, Hoverwork and Air Vehicles personnel under supervision from BHC.

LIGHT HOVERCRAFT REGISTERED WITH THE HOVERCLUB OF GREAT BRITAIN

This list, compiled with assistance from the Hoverclub of Great Britain, presents the numbers, names and operators/owners of recreational light hovercraft registered with the Hoverclub of Great Britain Ltd. Some of the craft included in this list have undergone changes in ownership or name since registration and others have been destroyed or scrapped.

Key:
Craft ownership/existence uncertain *
Craft destroyed or scrapped **

Craft No	*Craft Name*	*Craft Owner/Operator*
01	—	—
02	Guinea Pig**	Grant Wickington
03	Olympic Runner	Ian Massey
	Mistral*	P Smith & Tony Larosa
04	Mod Rider*	P Smith
05	Highbury Hoverer*	Keith Oakley
06	Bumbly Two*	Chris Fox Robinson
	Number Six*	Manchester Hoverclub
07	Avenger 1*	Graham Porter
	Hover Hornet*	Capt John Prendergast
08	Hover Imp	Cecil Blankley
09	Hoverscout Mk 2*	Colin Knight
10	Air Raiser*	C Maddocks
11	Jimbo**	Jim Rowbotham
	Doufa*	Brian Wavell
12	Crested Wren*	W Parkin
13	—	—
14	Phoop*	Nick Low
15	Unknown*	Ian Hall
16	Caliban 1*	Don Draper
	Bullet**	Barry Oakley
17	Loflya	Mike Weller
18	Blue Streak**	P Howell
19	K.B.1*	Ken Burtt
20	Poof*	Phil Conron
21	Pinkushion*	Dave McClunan
22	Hoveranne 2*	Keith Oakley
23	G.T.3*	Peter Garbutt
24	Humbug	John Gifford
25	Express Air Rider*	John Vass
	Dair-E-Goes Mk 2	Job's Dairy Sports & Social Club
26	Yellow Peril**	Malcolm Saunders
27	Snoopy*	Barry Wilkinson
28	Avenger 1 (as No. 7)	Graham Porter
29	Aries*	R Aubrey
30	Dunnit	Poundswick School
31	Vulcan*	Ron Shepherd
32	Unknown*	E Betty
33	Cheshire Cat*	Colin Burley
34	Atlast 2*	Wellington School
	Unknown	H Ratcliffe
35	Unknown*	Cowes Secondary School
36	Aerostyle*	P Hall
37	Jet Hover**	John Trulock
38	Blowfly*	Terry Brazier
39	114 Squadron ATC*	114 Squadron ATC Ruislip & Norwood
40	J.4**	Hovercraft Development Ltd
41	—	—
42	Project 69*	Teddington Secondary School
	JR.5	Rev G Spedding & Jeff Green
43	Express Air Rider*	St Margaret Mary Secondary School
44	Norvil*	Norton Villiers Ltd.
45	Aquarius*	L Scarr
46	Nefaettiti*	Venerable Francis Levenson School
47	Cyclone 1	John Scriven
48	Dragonfly*	D Gubbins
49	Blue Devil*	Robert Dee (Netherlands)
50	Ariel*	J Adlington & C Felton
51	Superdocious*	Ernie Lamerton
52	Cyclone 2*	Nigel Beale
53	Horatio*	Mark Prentice
54	Air Lubri-Cat 2*	Roy Barnes
55	Philibuster	Phil Conron
56	Calibug**	Nigel Beale
57	Rocket*	G R Stephenson
58	Unknown*	Eric Sangster
59	Aeolus*	Brian Wavell
60	Typhoon	Peter Mayer
61	Rowena*	Tony Billing

Craft No	*Craft Name*	*Craft Owner/Operator*
62	JD.600*	Job's Dairy Sports & Social Club
63	Daffydol*	Ted Naylor
64	Unknown	Rev G Spedding
65	Simo*	Jack Simpson
66	Ranger 1*	Colin Knight
67	Ranger 1*	P Smith
68	Vulcan 3*	David Ibbotson
69	Caliban 4*	Geoff Kent
70	Nodis 1	Don Ison
71	Peanuts	David Waters
72	Gee Whizz	Grant Wickington
73	Cyclone 3	Colin Saunders
74	Chinook*	Nick Horn & Alan Bliault
75	Skima 2S	Pindair Ltd
76	Skima 4	Pindair Ltd
77	Skima	Tony Billing
78	Excalibur*	Bill Gough
79	Unknown*	A Provost
80	Mistral*	Robert Trillo
81	Gryphon	Ken Kennaby
82	Nodis 1	Don Ison
83	Discorde**	Jim Batten
84	Eureka**	Keith Oakley
85	Vulcan IV	David Ibbotson & Greg Peck
86	Windmill	Warriner School
87	Scarab Noir	Jim Lyne
88	Hoverminx*	Alan Stanley
89	Scarab 1	Graham Nutt
90	Pushover*	Rex Camp
91	Caspar**	Greg Peck
92	Air Lubri-Cat 3*	Roy Barnes
93	—	—
94	Aggro*	Tony Wilcox
95	Pooline	149 (Poole) Squadron ATC
96	Caliban 5*	Geoff Kent
97	Buzzard*	Robert Raven
98	AH.5*	Peter Dance
99	Hoverking Experimental*	Colin Knight
100	—	—
101	Marander**	Aleks Murzyn
102	G.T.4*	Peter Garbutt
103	Tellstar	Malcolm Harris
104	Paddywack	Guy Rackham
105	Hoverfly*	Geoff Kent
106	Snoopy Too	Barry Wilkinson
107	Nimbus	R Gerring
108	Arrowspeed*	Richard Cresswell
109	Skyboy**	Bob Hall
110	Greenfly**	Bill Baker
111	Blood, Sweat & Tears*	Terry Sherlock
112	Tango	Westfield School
113	—	—
114	Wasp*	Lindsay Gatward
115	—	—
116	Wotsit 6	Geoff Harding
117	Tornado	Alan Stanley
118	Buzzard 2	Lindsay Gatward
119	Tentando	Heles School
120	Marander	Aleks Murzyn
121	Hoverfly 2*	Geoff Kent
122	Jayfour	Mike Turner
123	—	—
124	—	—
125	Ere -'E-Cums	Peter Ball
126	Streaker	Roy Barnes
127	Go-Tune-One	Gordon Harker
128	Swift	Bourne Valley School
129	Scarab III/B	Hoverservices
130	Saturn 1	Bill Sherlock
131	Woodstock	Alan Bliault
132	Swallow	Bourne Valley School
133	Unknown	Rudheath School
134	Aggro II	Tony Wilcox
135	Bluebottle	Danny Sherlock
136	GP Too	Grant Wickington
137	Matilda	Newark School
138	Blue Scarab	Royal Grammar School, Newcastle
139	Draftee	D Bennett
140	Bora	Heles School
141	Unknown	Reeds School
142	Unknown	Churchill School
143	Be-off*	Dennis Shrimpton
144	Tri-A-Fly	Dave Council
145	Mistrale 1	Nick Low
146	Kipper	Mike Martyn-Jones
147	No-name**	Dennis Wilson
148	Talisman*	Lewis Sharp
149	Volitat	Tony Groves

Craft No	*Craft Name*	*Craft Owner/Operator*
150	Bullet	Chris & Anne English
151	Torvic	Victor Garman
152	Tempest	Roy Smart
153	Splinter*	Bill Congdon
154	Viking	M Scott
155	Saturn 2	Derek Preston
156	Grasshopper	13th Nuneaton Scout Group
157	N.R. S.4 (?)	Wrockwardine School
158	Snagglepuss*	Keith Smallwood
159	Hum-Bolt	John Gifford
160	Nasus**	Barry Oakley
161	Scarab 10	Bill Baker
162	Unknown	B Howarth
163	Saturn 3	Terry Sherlock
164	—	Graham Nutt
165	Treboreus	Bob Hall
166	RH.1	Richard Hale School
167	Stardust*	Dennis Wilson
168	Red Baron	Heles School
169	Alicart	K Allen
170	Half Pint	S Allen
171	Simple Cyclone	Nigel Beale
172	Spirit of Snodland	Keith Oakley
173	Gale Force	R Lang & K Norton
174	Barrycuda	Barry Horsman
175	Peek-A-Boo	Roger Peek
176	Armadillo	Roger Porter
177	The Custard Beast	Bill Congdon
178	What's it called	Churchill School
179	Deep Purple	Alan Vaughn
180	Lynx	Westfield School
181	Milady	Newark School
182	Kestrel	Hayes Grammar School
183	Krak-A-Long	Ian & David Cook
184	Nima	Nick Horn
185	Blo-Fly	Roger Lee
186	Stratus	Lindsay Gatward
187	Fantasy	Lindsay Gatward
188	Skidka	R Penny
189	Chaos	Trevor Griffiths
190	Tempest II	Roy Smart
191	Ventura	Wyvern Hovercraft Services (H Ashley)
192	Wyvern Bug	Wyvern Hovercraft Services (H Ashley)
193	JR6	Rev G Spedding & Jeff Green
194	Halcyon	Philip Greenfield
195	Scarab 10	Bill Baker
196	Rubber Duck	Roger Lang
197	Wombat	Tom Hanson
198	Bover	Bob Hill
199	Aries	Matthew Tulley
200	Eccles	Richard Cresswell
201	Padingtun**	Keith Smallwood
202	Morninglay	P Stettner
203	—	W D Bolt
204	Mallot 1	A L Thompson
205	Overdraft	Ben Mullett
206	—	Malcolm Sanders
207	Kestrel	Kip McCollum
208	RSP	R S Pooley
209	Scarab 10	Brian Bucknall
210	Unconfirmed	—
211	Popcorn	Jeremy Kemp
212	Wyvern Bug 2	Hal Ashley
213	Bee-Off 2	Dennis Shrimpton
214	—	R Fowler
215	The Fuzz	M I Dougall
216	Buccaneer	Lindsay Gatward
217	Victor	P Swanborough
218	Herbie	M Reynolds
219	Penny	Ian Crombie
220	Dougal	Dennis Wilson
221	Unconfirmed	—
222	Skima 3S	Pindair Ltd
223	Unconfirmed	—
224	Unconfirmed	—
225	Simplicity	Barry Oakley

ACV CLUBS AND ASSOCIATIONS

THE HOVERCLUB OF GREAT BRITAIN LTD

As Britain's national organisation for light hovercraft, the Hoverclub exists to encourage the construction and operation of light, recreational hovercraft by private individuals, schools, colleges, universities and other youth groups. The Hoverclub's major role in recent years has been its organisation of several national race meetings at sites throughout Britain. At these events forty or more light hovercraft may compete for National Championship points over land and water courses at meetings held in the grounds of stately homes, or at reclaimed gravel workings.

In addition to national race meetings, the Hoverclub also performs the important task of providing its own members and prospective hovercraft builders with useful advice and information. This information, largely collected by the Club through the vast range of experience accumulated by its members during twelve years of hovering, is made available through technical articles in the Hoverclub's monthly magazine, "Light Hovercraft", the annually published "Light Hovercraft Handbook", or through various booklets dealing with specific areas of hovercraft construction and operation. Club members can also contact a technical enquiries officer within the Hoverclub.

The "Light Hovercraft Handbook" has been regularly up-dated and expanded since it was first launched a few years ago, and it is now acknowledged as the prime reference book for the design, construction and safe operation of small recreational hovercraft.

Recently the club has added two other publications to its series; one is the "Guide to Model Hovercraft" and the other, "Light Hovercraft Design, Construction and Safety Requirements".

A growing activity within the Hoverclub has been the pastime of hovercruising which involves travelling by single or more usually multi-seat light hovercraft along rivers, canals, lochs or coastlines. Many hovercraft constructors see this activity as one offering the ability to explore areas which are not accessible by other means of transport. Hovercruises and holidays have been arranged in Scotland and Wales.

HOVERCLUB COUNCIL 1978/79

G G Harding, *President*
K Oakley, *Chairman*
M Drake, *Treasurer*
Mrs A English, *Hon Secretary*
C C A Curtis
C English
N MacDonald
K Kennaby
J Lyne
W Sherlock
Mrs M Smart
R Smart
Mrs J Waddon
K Waddon

The Hoverclub's main address for initial enquiries related to membership and publication is:
Mrs J Waddon, Hoverclub Information Officer,
45 St Andrews Road, Lower Bemerton,
Salisbury, Wilts
Telephone: 0722 3424
Addresses of the various branches of the Hoverclub throughout Britain are listed below:

CHILTERNS
J Lyne,
Berkshire College of Agriculture, Hall Place, Burchetts Green, nr Maidenhead, Berks

EAST ANGLIAN
B Hill,
10 Fenland Road, Reffley Estate, Kings Lynn, Norfolk

LONDON
B Horsman,
5 Beeches Close, Uckfield, Sussex

MIDLANDS
Mrs B Kemp,
10 Long Acre, Bingham, Notts

NORTH WEST
Rev W G Spedding,
26 Milverton Close, Lostock, Bolton, Lancs

SCOTTISH
W S Sharp
1 Coates Place, Edinburgh EH3 7AA

SOUTH WESTERN
D Moorhead,
24 Canford Cliffs Road, Parkstone, Poole, Dorset

WELSH
Miss M Hughes,
4 Barry Walk, Rogerstone, Newport, Gwent

WESSEX
Mrs J Waddon,
45 St Andrews Road, Lower Bemerton, Salisbury, Wilts

OTHER BODIES

ESSEX
E W Sangster,
53 Elm View Road, Benfleet, Essex SS7 5AR

ISLE OF WIGHT
M Prentice,
1 Kingston Farm Cottages, Kingston Farm Lane, East Cowes, Isle of Wight

SOUTHERN HOVERCLUB
A Bliault,
17 Southampton Road, Paulsgrove, Hants

NATIONAL SCHOOLS HOVERCRAFT ASSOCIATION

The National Schools Hovercraft Association was formed in 1975 to provide a focal point for the growing interest from schools and colleges in building and operating recreational hovercraft. Each year the Schools Association, together with BP Oil Ltd and the Hoverclub of Great Britain, organise a National Schools Hovercraft Championship. This competition allows many light hovercraft built by school groups to be evaluated over land and water circuits.

D Hale, *Secretary*
Brookmead, Rimpton, nr Yeovil, Somerset
Telephone: 093 585 241

Stanford Hall 1978. Light hovercraft built by British enthusiasts pictured at the start of a major race. National Race Meetings are organised by The Hoverclub of Great Britain and take place at sites throughout England and Wales. They attract up to 45 craft and provide useful experience and development for makers of small hovercraft intended for recreational or light utility tasks. *(Photograph: Neil MacDonald)*

THE UNITED KINGDOM HOVERCRAFT SOCIETY

Rochester House, 66 Little Ealing Lane, London W5 4XX, England
Telephone: 01-579 9411
Officers:
Sir Christopher Cockerell, *President*
R L Wheeler, *Vice President*
J E Rapson, *Vice President*
W F S Woodford, OBE, *Chairman*
P H Winter, *Treasurer*
P A Bartlett, *Secretary*

Formed in 1971, the United Kingdom Hovercraft Society (UKHS) is the UK constituent member of the 'International Air Cushion Engineering Society'. Its membership is drawn from ACV manufacturers, ferry operators, design groups, government departments and agencies, financial and insurance organisations, consultants, journalists and universities. Membership of the Society is open to persons engaged in hovercraft related fields in the UK and overseas. Currently the UKHS has over 250 members.

In addition to its programme of regular meetings, at which papers are presented on the technical, commercial, design, operating and military aspects of hovercraft and aircushion devices, the UKHS also produces a regular monthly "UKHS Bulletin". This publication contains the latest up-to-date information on hovercraft activities throughout the world. From time to time the Society also organises visits to hovercraft manufacturing or component factories for its members.

At the Society's headquarters in London a collection of hovercraft films is held, together with a library of books, periodicals, papers and reports on the subject of hovercraft.

THE HOVERCLUB OF AMERICA INC

Box 234, Uniontown, Ohio 44685, USA

Directors (1977-78):
Dennis N Benson
Mike Klare
Paul Esterle
Chris Fitzgerald
Wayne Moore
Bob Windt

Officers:
Paul Esterle, *President*
Chris Fitzgerald, *Vice-President & Public Relations*
Dennis N Benson, *Secretary & Treasurer*

Membership of the HoverClub of America, Inc, is available at US $10 pa.

Following a general meeting of the members of the American Hovercraft Association on 29 May, 1976, it was agreed to reorganise the Association into the HoverClub of America, Inc. Subsequently the HoverClub of America has been incorporated under the State Laws of Indiana and six national directors appointed and elected to serve for one year.

In the United States the HoverClub of America organises race meetings, rallies and other events for members possessing hovercraft, and also publishes a monthly newsletter.

INTERNATIONAL HOVERCLUBS

HOVERCLUB OF GREAT BRITAIN LTD
Mrs A English, *Hon Sec*
17 Abbotts Road, Newbury, Berks, England

HOVER CLUB OF AUSTRALIA
H B Standen, *Hon Sec*
GPO Box 1882, Brisbane, Queensland 4001, Australia

HOVERCLUB OF AMERICA
Box 234, Uniontown, Ohio 44685, USA

FÉDÉRATION FRANÇAIS DES CLUBS d'AÉROGLISSEURS
41-43 rue Aristide, 45130 Meung-sur-Loire, France
Member Clubs:

CLUB FRANÇAIS DES AEROGLISSEURS
41-43 rue Aristide-Briand, 45130 Meung-sur-Loire, France

SUD-EST AÉROGLISSEURS
Les Aloes B, avenue Saint-Jean-du-Désert, 13012 Marseille, France

AÉROGLISSEURS D'ILE DE FRANCE
232 rue des Pyrénées, 75020 Paris, France

CENTRE AÉROGLISSEURS
64 Levée des Tuileries, 41000 Blois, France

COUSS' AIR TOURAINE
81 rue Michelet, 37000 Tours, France

AÉROGLISSEURS D'Oc
51 avenue Louis Abric, 34400 Lunel, France

ANJOU-BRETAGNE AÉROGLISSEURS
83 Résidence Keranoux, 22300 Ploubezere-Lannian, France

HOVER CLUB OF TRINIDAD & TOBAGO
N Seal, *President*
1 Richardson Street, Point Fortin, Trinidad.

HOVERCRAFT CLUB OF NEW ZEALAND
K F Leatham, *Hon Sec*
MacDonald Road, Pokeno, New Zealand

HOVER CLUB OF CANADA
R Fishlock
103 Doane Street, Ottawa, Ontario K2B 6GY, Canada

HOVER CLUB OF JAPAN
Information from Masahiro Mino, Senior Director, Aerodynamics Section, Nihon University at Narashino, 7-1591 Narashinodai, Funabashi, Chiba-Ken, Japan

SWEDISH HOVERCLUB
(Svenska Svävarklubben)
Garry Olsson, *Sec*
Odensalvägen 72, S-19500 Marsta, Sweden

THE INTERNATIONAL HYDROFOIL SOCIETY

17 Melcombe Court, Dorset Square, London NW1, England
Telephone: 01-935 8678
President: Dott Ing Leopoldo Rodriquez

The International Hydrofoil Society publishes a regular newsletter and holds meetings at which hydrofoil topics are discussed.

ACV AND HYDROFOIL CONSULTANTS

ACV CONSULTANTS

LIECHTENSTEIN

Surflight SA

General Trust Company, Vaduz, Liechtenstein
Officials:
Dr Güggi
A De Weck
J De Chollet

Surflight SA provides technical consultancy, applications studies, and economic analyses for any type of operation involving air cushion systems in Africa. It also provides marketing facilities and general support services for amphibious ACVs in Africa, south of Sahara.

NIGERIA

Hovermarine Services (Nigeria) Ltd

PO Box 116, 19th Floor, Western House, Broad Street, Lagos, Nigeria
Officials:
El Haji Waziri Ibrahim, *Chairman*
J Tunde Johnson, *Director*
J B Oluntunde, *Director*
Prince A Dusonnu

General consultancy services for ACVs, route surveys, route proving, applications studies, performance assessments. Agents for Hovermarine Transport Ltd.

UNITED KINGDOM

Air Cushion Equipment (1976) Ltd

15-35 Randolph Street, Shirley, Southampton SO1 3HD, England
Telephone: 0703 776468
Telex: 477537
Officials:
J D Hake, *Chairman*
R J Howling, *Director*
L A Hopkins, *Director*
R C Gilbert, *General Manager*
R R Henvest, *Works Manager*

Air Cushion Equipment (1976) Ltd offers its services as design engineers and technical consultants for air cushion and for water cushion systems. Past experience has involved investigations into systems using both water and air as the cushion fluid.

Water cushions have involved investigating skirt systems up to 15 bar and the various effects of these systems for operating within the industrial sector. Air cushion and skirt systems have been studied with cushion pressures up to 0·75 bar having skirt geometries which can be fitted to structures of various types.

An air cushion oil storage tank movement service is offered on a world wide basis together with an additional tank stressing service to verify structural integrity.

The company offers its own services and those of its licensed contractors for the movement of heavy, dense and awkward structures as well as its manufacturing facilities for the production of flexible structures and skirt systems.

Air Vehicles Ltd

Head Office: 1 Sun Hill, Cowes, Isle of Wight, England
Yard: Dinnis' Yard, High Street, Cowes, Isle of Wight, England
Telephone: 098 382 3194 & 4739
Officials:
P H Winter, MSc, *Director*
C D J Bland, *Director*
C B Eden, *Director*

Air Vehicles Ltd, formed in 1968, has a wide experience of all types of hovercraft and hovercraft operation, and can offer a full range of services as consultants.

Particular fields where Air Vehicles Ltd has specialised knowledge are:

1. manufacture and operation of small hovercraft up to 14 seats. Several craft have been built and the latest AV Tiger is also offered for charter;
2. design and construction of ducted propellers. Sizes have ranged from 4ft 6in diameter used on AV Tiger, ducts for SR.N6 and two large ducts of 9ft overall diameter delivered to the USA early 1976;
3. design, operation and site surveys for hoverbarges, particularly for ship-to-shore cargo. The first 350-ton hoverbarge on the Yukon River in Alaska was designed and commissioned by Air Vehicles Ltd.

Approved by the Civil Aviation Authority, the company can design and undertake modifications to larger craft. Typical of this work is the conversion to hoverfreighter configuration of SR.N5 and SR.N6. The company also offers two SR.N5 hovercraft for charter as well as the AV Tiger eight to ten seat hovercraft and the new Tiger S, 12-14 seater.

The company's association with Hoverwork Ltd enables it to call on the company's world-wide experience of hovercraft operations. A special feature of Air Vehicles' consultancy is a complete on-site survey and a feasibility study of all types of hovercraft which is undertaken for a fixed fee. Several of these have been completed for hoverbarge projects in various parts of the world.

British Rail Hovercraft Limited

Royal London House, 22-25 Finsbury Square, London EC2P 2BQ, England
Telephone: 01-628 3050
Officials:
J M Lefeaux, *Managing Director*
A J Tame, *Marketing Director*
P A Yerbury, *Chief Engineer*
Capt D Meredith, *Operations Manager*

British Rail Hovercraft Limited is the most experienced commercial hovercraft operator in the world. It is the only company to have operated commercially both amphibious and non-amphibious craft on estuarial and open water services.

Studies have been conducted on behalf of clients in many parts of the world and the company is able to provide a route costing and viability appraisal service based on "real time" operating experience.

Leslie Colquhoun and Associates

7 Daryngton Avenue, Birchington, Kent, England
Telephone: 0843 43085

Leslie Colquhoun and Associates was formed in 1973 to provide a hovercraft transport consultancy service using the unique experience of L R Colquhoun who has been closely associated with the hovercraft industry since 1959. This experience involved the testing, development and marketing of Vickers Ltd hovercraft projects from 1959-1965, and from 1966-1973 the setting up and running of Hoverlloyd's Ramsgate to Calais hovercraft service with the SR.N6 and SR.N4. Mr Colquhoun was Managing Director of the company when he resigned in December 1972 to set up the consultancy.

The consultancy is contracted to Hoverlloyd and has completed on their behalf a report on the company's SR.N4 cross-Channel operations for the SESPO PM17 office of the Department of the US Navy.

Further work has been contracted in UK, France, Hungary, America, Iran and Malaysia.

The consultancy also provides assistance to International Hoverservices Ltd.

Through a close association with Comasco International Ltd the consultancy is involved in pollution and waste disposal schemes using both chemical and incineration processes.

Peter G Fielding, CEng, FRAeS

Branches:
United Kingdom: 20 Warmdene Road, Brighton, East Sussex BN1 8NL, England
Telephone: 0273 501212
Dock House, Niton Undercliff, Ventnor, Isle of Wight PO38 2NE, England
Telephone: 0983 730 252
USA: 1701 North Fort Myer Drive, Suite 908, Arlington, Virginia 22209, USA
Telephone: (703) 528 1092
7910 Woodmont Avenue, Suite 1103, Bethesda, Maryland 20014, USA
Telephone: (301) 656 5991

Consultant in air cushion systems, air cushion operations, and air cushion technology since 1959 to the US Army, the US Navy, US Department of Defense, the Advanced Research Projects Agency-DOD, US Department of Commerce-Maritime Administration, the Office of Naval Research, the US Naval Ships Research and Development Center, the US Army TRECOM, the Executive Office of the President USA, the US Navy-Chief of Naval Operations, the US Marine Corps, the Institute for Defense Analysis, the Center for Naval Analysis, the Bell Aerosystems Corporation, the Aerojet Corporation, the Research Analysis Corporation, Science Applications Incorporated, Hoverlift Applications Incorporated, Booz-Allen Applied Research Incorporated, Associated Consultants International Inc, and SeaSpan Inc. Services for the above organisations have included state of the art reports, technical and economic analysis, route surveys, environmental impact studies, subsystem analysis, operational plans, test plans, mission studies, advanced technology estimates, test site selection, cost analysis, structural and materials analysis and market research.

Assignments completed include:

1. Review and assessment of the Arctic SEV advanced technology programme for the Advanced Research Projects Agency, US Dept of Defense.
2. Analysis of "paddle wheel" propulsion and sealing systems for SES, for SA Inc McLean, Virginia, USA.
3. 'The Surface Effect Vehicle (SEV) in Search and Rescue Missions in Alaska'—for the Research Analysis Corporation, McLean, Virginia, USA.
4. 'An Assessment of the Technological Risk and Uncertainty of Advanced Surface Effect Vehicles (SEV) for the Arctic'—for the US Naval Ships Research and Development Center, Carderock, Maryland, USA.
5. 'An Evaluation of Advanced Surface Effect Vehicle Platforms Performing Military Missions in the Arctic'—for Science Applications Inc, La Jolla, California, and Arlington, Virginia, USA.
6. 'An Exhaustive Bibliography of Air Cushion Subjects' for the Research Analysis Corporation, McLean, Virginia, USA.
7. 'Preliminary Findings of the Economic Suitabilities of the Surface Effect Ship to Various Routes in the US'—for SEASPAN Inc, Washington DC, USA.
8. 'Appraisal of Heavy Lift Systems for Commercial Applications'—for Hoverlift Applications Inc, Arlington, Virginia, USA.
9. Results and Implications of the Advanced Projects Agency, US Department of Defense, Surface Effect Vehicles Programme—for Science Applications Inc, Arlington, Virginia, USA.

Hovercraft Development Ltd

Head Office: Kingsgate House, 66-74 Victoria Street, London SWIE 6SL, England
Telephone: 01-828 3400
Telex: 23580
Technical Office: Forest Lodge West, Fawley Road, Hythe, Hampshire SO4 6ZZ, England
Telephone: 0703 84 3178
Officials:
T A Coombs, *Chairman*
Prof W A Mair, *Director*
J E Rapson, *Director*
P N Randell, *Director*
D Anderson, *Director*
B Bailey, *Secretary*

Hovercraft Development Ltd was established by the National Research Development Corporation in 1959 to develop and exploit the hovercraft patents of Christopher Cockerell. The Technical Group of the company was set up in 1960. It provided technical services for the company's hovercraft manufacturing licensees until that part of HDL was taken over by Mintech (now the Department of Industry). HDL has continued to provide these services and its Technical Unit has specialised in cushion and skirt design requirements. It offers a consultancy to the hovercraft industry and has recently accepted assignments from British and overseas government departments. The Technical Unit also advises HDL on technical matters associated with development projects and the craft designs of prospective licensees.

Hoverwork Limited

12 Lind Street, Ryde, Isle of Wight PO33 2NR, England
Telephone: 0983 5181
Telex: 86513 (A/B Hoverwork Ryde)
Officials:
C D J Bland, *Managing Director*
D R Robertson, *Director*
E W H Gifford, *Director*
A C Smith, *Director*
R G Clarke, *Director*

Hoverwork Limited is a subsidiary of Hovertravel Limited and was formed in 1966. The company provides crew training and charter facilities for all available types of ACVs, thus bridging the gap between the operators and manufacturers.

Hoverwork and its parent, Hovertravel, own the largest fleet of hovercraft available for charter in the world. Types include the SR.N6, the SR.N6 freighter, SR.N5 passenger/freighter and the AV.2. In recent years the company has concentrated on providing craft for seismic, gravity and hydrographic survey work in shallow water areas and terrain impossible to other forms of transport.

The company, jointly with Hovertravel Limited, offers a route feasibility investigation service.

P N Structures Limited

Marine and Engineering Division
30A Sackville Street, Piccadilly, London W1X 1DB, England
Telephone: 01-734 2578
Telex: 261709
Officials:
Theo Pellinkhof, *Chairman*
Karin M Adeler, *Director*
David J Rimmer, *Secretary*
José Romero Sánchez, *Associate*

Consultancy in the fields of economic transport systems and air cushion applications, including air-supported structures (airdomes).

Selection and indication of solutions for various transport problems. Also the selection of amphibious craft, hydrofoils, catamarans and a variety of types from a range of planing hulls to more conventional hull designs, to meet clients' specific requirements.

Selection of air cushion platforms and conveyor belts to facilitate cost-saving load moving.

A wide area of industrial and technological resources will be made available to clients.

R A Shaw

(Managing Director Hoverprojects Limited)
Fell Brow, Silecroft, Millom, Cumbria LA18 5LS, England
Telephone: 0657 2022

Consultancy services to governments, local authorities and private enterprise on all aspects of fast transport with special emphasis on hovercraft and hydrofoils. Services include financial, economic and operational assessments in all conditions and new designs to meet particular requirements.

Contracts have included:

1. A study for the State of Washington to assess the feasibility of introducing hovercraft and hydrofoils into the Puget Sound ferry system.
2. A feasibility appraisal of proposed hovercraft operations in British Columbia.
3. Reporting to a local authority on prospects of establishing a hoverport within their borough.
4. A study for the Greater London Council on fast passenger services on the Thames.
5. Three independent studies on the potential for hovercraft in the Venetian lagoon.
6. Examination of world potential market for hovercraft.
7. Design and economics of 1,000-ton river hovercraft.
8. Planning and operating consultancy for Airavia Ltd and Speed Hydrofoils Ltd for hydrofoils on the River Thames.

Robert Trillo Limited

Broadlands, Brockenhurst, Hampshire SO4 7SX, England
Telephone: 05902 2220,
Officials:
R L Trillo, CEng., FIMechE, FRAeS, AFAIAA, AFCASI, *Managing Director,* Author and Distributor "Marine Hovercraft Technology" (ISBN 0 249 44036 9) and Editor "Jane's Ocean Technology Yearbook" (ISBN 0 354 00553 7).
A U Alexander, *Secretary*

Operating since 1969 as a consultancy, engaging principally in air cushion vehicle technology and economics, the firm has worked for industry and government departments in a number of countries and has undertaken transport feasibility studies, preliminary design investigations, design of light hovercraft and experimental investigations. Other work has been concerned with the aerodynamic design of five ducted propeller installations including the SR.N6 and Skima 12 hovercraft, and the Aerospace Developments AD 500 airship. Research into skirt wear and the design of skirts has also been undertaken. Commissions have included work in Canada for the National Research Council, Ottawa, and in Australia for the Department of Aboriginal Affairs. The firm publishes bi-monthly bibliography services on air cushion and hydrofoil systems and on high speed ground transportation and urban rapid transit systems. (ISSN 0306-0594, ISSN 0306-0586).

Affiliate member of Northern Associates Reg'd, Canada, Canadian Arctic consulting group.

Representatives:
Canada:
Vice Admiral K L Dyer, RCN Rtd, Dyer & Associates, Suite 708, 77 Metcalfe Street, Ottawa K1P 5L6, Canada

Denmark:
Leif Hansen, A B C Hansen Comp A/S, Hauchsvej 14, DK-1825 Copenhagen V, Denmark

UNITED STATES OF AMERICA

Aerophysics Company

3500 Connecticut Avenue NW, Washington DC 20008, USA
Telephone: (202) 244 7502
Officials:
Dr Gabriel D Boehler, *President*
William F Foshag, *Chief Engineer*

Aerophysics Company was formed in 1957 to conduct fundamental research of the ground effect principle. Dr Boehler had previously performed private feasibility work with M Beardsley. Since then, Aerophysics has undertaken work in various areas of ACV design, including skirt design, control techniques, parametric analysis, conceptual and design studies, studies of ACV lift air systems including various types of blowers and propulsion systems.

Booz-Allen & Hamilton Inc

245 Park Avenue, New York, New York 10017, USA

General management consulting, computer systems and software; market and social science research; industrial engineering systems; pollution and environmental resources management; defence and space research; product, process and equipment development; transportation and airport planning and engineering.

Davidson Laboratory
Stevens Institute of Technology

Castle Point Station, Hoboken, New Jersey 07030, USA
Telephone: (201) 792 2700
Officials:
Dr J P Breslin, *Director*
Daniel Savitsky, *Deputy Director*

Organised in 1935 as the Experimental Towing Tank, the Laboratory is active in basic and applied hydrodynamic research, including smooth water performance and manoeuvrability; seakeeping, propulsion and control of marine vehicles including ACV, SES and hydrofoil craft. Special model test facilities are available to investigate the dynamic behaviour of ACV, SES and hydrofoil craft in smooth water and waves.

Doty Associates, Inc

416 Hungerford Drive, Rockville, Maryland 20850, USA
Telephone: (301) 424 0270
Officials:
Donald L Doty, *President and Technical Director*
James H Herd, *Vice President and Director, Cost and Economic Analysis Division*
Eugene H Brown, *Director, Management Support Division*
Ralph W Christy, *Attorney – Austin, Miller & Gaines*
Ernest S Fritz, *Director, Operations Analysis Division*

Doty Associates, Inc is a privately-owned, small business firm founded in 1968. The firm specialises in financial management, project control, weapon system analysis, test planning and evaluation, operations research, cost and economic analyses for Department of Defense and other government and state agencies.

Since its founding, the firm has been engaged in providing engineering services to the US Navy on a number of high technology programmes. These programmes include both the 2K and 3K Surface Effect Ship (SES) designs, the PHM Hydrofoil, the Sea Control Ship and the Vertical Support Ship (VSS). In addition, the firm is actively involved in Naval V/STOL aviation studies.

Forrestal Laboratory

Princeton University, Princeton, New Jersey, USA
Officials:
T E Sweeney

Research prototypes (ACVs).

Gibbs & Cox

40 Rector Street, New York, New York 10006, USA
Telephone: (212) 487 2800
Arlington Office: 2341 Jefferson Davis Highway, Arlington, Virginia 22202, USA
Telephone: (703) 979 1240

Project management, co-ordination and consultation on conceptual and preliminary designs, contract drawings and specifications and construction drawings for commercial or naval ships of the SES/ACV or submerged hydrofoil systems, destroyers, escorts, frigates, corvettes and VTOL/Helo carriers.

Global Marine Inc

811 West 7th Street, Los Angeles, California 90017, USA
Telephone: (213) 680 9550
Officials:
R C Crooke, *President*
R B Thornburg, *Senior Vice President*
R G Longaker, *General Manager*
M R Bade, *Operations Manager*

Arctic Engineers & Constructors
1770 St James Place, Suite 504, Houston, Texas 77027, USA
Telephone: (713) 626 9773

Global Marine Inc was incorporated in 1959, and is engaged primarily in offshore drilling and engineering. However, in 1968 the company undertook an engineering feasibility study directed towards developing equipment and techniques for drilling in Arctic areas. This engineering study led to the selection of ACT (Air Cushion Transport) units as the most feasible for operating in the area, and it has a continuing design programme directed towards various size ACT (Air Cushion Transport) drilling rigs with various drilling capabilities. This design work is handled by Global Marine Inc (Los Angeles), and the sales and operational aspects, with respect to the Arctic, are handled by Arctic Engineers & Constructors (see above). Arctic Engineers & Constructors is a wholly-owned subsidiary of Global Marine Inc.

AEC constructed the ACT-100 in Canada in 1971. This unit was test operated in the Arctic during 1971, and was test operated by the Canadian government in connection with the Mackenzie River Highway and by Imperial Oil Ltd in connection with its offshore winter drilling operations in 1973-74. Design work on larger ACV drilling rigs continues.

Hydronautics, Incorporated

7210 Pindell School Road, Howard County, Laurel, Maryland 20810, USA
Telephone: (301) 776 7454
Officials:
Marshall P Tulin, *Chairman of the Board*
Phillip Eisenberg, *President and Chief Executive Officer*
Virgil E Johnson, Jr, *Senior Vice President*
Alex Goodman, *Senior Vice President*
Philip A Weiner, *Vice President and Secretary*
Harvey Post, *Treasurer*

The company was founded in July 1959, and has undertaken research, development and design of air cushion vehicles, hydrofoil craft and other high speed marine vehicles as well as advanced propulsion systems, under US Government and industrial contacts. Hydronautics has its own ship model basin and high speed water channel suitable for the evaluation of air cushion vehicles and hydrofoils.

Institute for Defense Analyses (IDA)

400 Army-Navy Drive, Arlington, Virginia 22202, USA
Telephone: (703) 558 1000

Performs interdisciplinary studies and analysis for agencies of the US Government, systems analysis, operations research, economics, policy analysis and studies of advanced technology and its applications.

E K Liberatore Company

567 Fairway Road, Ridgewood, New Jersey 07450, USA
Officials:
E K Liberatore, *Head*

A J Piccolo,

Formed in 1964, the company specialises in systems engineering, vehicle design and in operations in the fields of ACVs, SESs and VTOL aircraft. Work includes requirements, integration, analysis, design, costing, FAA and other certification, route and market surveys and methodology. Current projects in the areas of helicopter development; proposal preparation; development of non-expendable energy systems for pumping water and generating electricity, and experimental installations for California City, California, and Cantil Ranch, Cantil, California using hydraulic air compression principles.

George E Meese

194 Acton Road, Annapolis, Maryland 21403, USA
Telephone: (301) 263 4054
Cable: Meesmarine Annapolis

SES structures.

M Rosenblatt & Son, Inc

350 Broadway, New York, New York 10013, USA
Telephone: (212) 431 6900
Officials:
Lester Rosenblatt, *President*
P W Nelson, *Vice President, Operations*
E F Kaufman, *Vice President and Manager, Western Division*
N M Maniar, *Vice President and Technical Director*
L M Schlosberg, *Vice President and Design Manager*
F K Serim, *Vice President and Manager, Washington Area Branch*

M Rosenblatt & Son, Inc is an established naval architectural and marine engineering firm with over 30 years of proven experience in all phases of ship and marine vehicle design.

With offices in 10 US cities and abroad, the firm is close to the entire shipbuilding community and has a thorough understanding of its problems and needs. Its experience covers programme management and inspection of construction, as well as design.

A major portion of the company's design activities has been and is for the US Navy. Completed assignments are of the broadest possible variety covering research and development, feasibility studies, and conceptual and detail design for all classes of major combatants, auxiliaries, and high performance craft. In addition, the company has provided extensive design services for the conversion, overhaul, and repair of naval combatants, auxiliaries, submarines, amphibious warfare supply and landing craft.

The service to the maritime industry includes a wide variety of tasks covering the new and modification design of oceanographic ships, containerships, tankers, general cargo ships, dredges, bulk carriers, drilling platforms and ships, survey vessels, pipe-laying barges, and a great variety of supporting craft.

Typical ACV assignments include:

1. ARPA Advanced Surface Effect Vehicles

Conceptual studies, parametric studies and propulsion machinery analysis for phase 'O' studies of Advanced Surface Effect Vehicles for Advanced Research Project Agency. Work performed for American Machine and Foundry Company.

2. JSESPO Surface Effect Ship Testcraft

Conceptual and feasibility design studies of candidate SES vehicles for the JSESPO sizing study for second generation SES testcraft in the 1,000 to 3,000-ton range. The work included studies of various candidate versions of SES to identify and evaluate their unique operational and design capabilities; technological assessment of various structural materials and systems; preparation of a proposed development programme with required supporting research and development. Work performed for Joint Surface Effect Ship Program office.

3. Amphibious Fleet Conceptual Studies

Conceptual design studies of various types of ships for future amphibious fleets, including submarine, displacement, planing hydrofoil and ACV type ships. Studies included technological assessment of performance of the concepts, taking into account various operational capabilities, including speed, propulsion systems, manning, weapons, materials, payloads and costs. Work performed for Stanford Research Institute under basic contract with ONR.

4. The Surface Effect Ship, Advanced Design and Technology

A 283 page text book covering drag, structure, propulsion, transmission, propulsors, stability, lift systems, seals, auxiliaries, weights, parametric analysis, and sample problems. Each topic is discussed including design procedures and equations. The book was prepared for the US Navy Surface Effect Ships Project Office.

5. 2,000-ton Surface Effect Ship

Trade-off studies, system design parameters, equipment selection, system diagrams, hullborne stability in connection with a complete design proposal. The scope of work included hullborne structural design criteria, electrical power generating and distribution, heating, ventilating, air conditioning, hull appurtenances, piping systems, hotel and auxiliary machinery arrangements. Work performed for the Lockheed Missiles and Space Co, and the Surface Effect Ship Project Office.

6. ACV Amphibian

Conceptual design of a 20-ton capacity air cushion lighter, with retractable wheels, for US Army Mobility Equipment Research and Development Center.

Science Applications, Inc

1200 Prospect Street, La Jolla, California 92037, USA
Telephone: (714) 459 0211

Science Applications, Inc provides technical consulting, systems integration, and operations services in a wide range of fields in defence, energy and environment. In the field of air cushion vehicles, the company has experience in field operations, engineering consulting, and control systems. The company specialises in applications studies and economic analyses for any type of operation involving air cushion systems and heavy lift helicopter operations. The company employs 1,500 technical specialists and has 50 offices throughout the United States.

Stanford Research Institute

Menlo Park, California 90425, USA
Telephone: (415) 326 6200
Officials:
Robert S Ratner, *Director Transportation Center*

Operational trade-off studies; optimising vehicles with missions; demand studies; economic evaluations; system and facilities planning; simulation studies.

Martin Stevens

Woodhull Cove, Oldfield Village, Setauket, Long Island, New York, USA

Mechanical design, drive systems.

Systems Exploration Inc

3687 Voltaire Street, San Diego, California 92106, USA
Telephone: (714) 223 8141
Officials:
Dale K Beresford
Erwin J Hauber

Consultants to the US Navy on ACV, SES and hydrofoil test and development programmes. Developed high aspect ratio displacement (HARD) hydrofoil concept.

Water Research Company

3003 North Central Avenue, Suite 600, Phoenix, Arizona 85012, USA
Telephone: (602) 265 7722
Officials:
Richard R Greer, *President, Member of American Society of Naval Engineers*

The Water Research Company was formed in 1972 to consolidate activities surrounding the patents held or applied for by Richard R Greer relating to various aspects of water-borne vehicles. The company has subsequently prepared conceptual studies on a class of winged surface effect vessels (WSEV) intended to fill a variety of US Navy and commercial freight applications. The conclusions of this study were published in the *Naval Engineers' Journal, April 1974,* and further comprehensive conclusions also setting forth energy savings and use of alternate fuels were published in *Jane's Surface Skimmers 1975-76* . Present efforts are directed to providing assistance in related research activities and further research studies.

Wheeler Industries Inc

Executive Office: Board of Trade Building, Suite 403, 1129 20th Street NW, Washington DC 20036, USA
Telephone: (202) 659 1867
Telex: 89 663
Systems Research Center: Longfellow Building, Suite 800, 1201 Connecticut Avenue NW, Washington DC 20036, USA
Telephone: (202) 223 1938
Other offices: Hayes Building, Suite 618, 2361 South Jefferson Davis Highway, Arlington, Virginia 20362, USA
Telephone: (703) 521 5005
Presidential Building, Suites 618/635, Prince George's Center, 6525 Belcrest Road, Hyattsville, Maryland 20782, USA
Telephone: (301) 779 2060
Officials:
E Joseph Wheeler, Jr, *President and Chief Executive Officer*
George W Glatis, *Vice President, Corporate Development*
James W Wine, *Vice President, Energy and Environment*
James S Tassin, *Vice President, Contracts and Administration*
Samuel A Mawhood, *Director, Advanced Systems Development*
Scott E Terrill, Jr, *Director, Systems Research Center*
Roy G Shults, *Associate Director, Systems Research Center*

Wheeler Industries Inc, is a privately-owned, small business firm that was founded in 1966 and specialises in systems engineering for ship, air, electronic, and deep ocean systems, as well as oceanographic and environmental research. Since its establishment, the company has continuously provided technical, engineering, and management support, primarily in the ship acquisition areas, to the US Navy. This support has encompassed a wide range including top level management plans, ship acquisition plans, technology assessments and forecasts, subsystem analysis and trade-offs, development and acquisition requirements and specifications, programme budgeting, development of hydrofoil design data, and hydrofoil strut/foil hydrodynamic load criteria and data. Currently, the company has one of the largest high speed surface ship teams in the United States. A team of experienced engineers has been assembled which is fully capable of providing the engineering, technical, design, and management services associated with hydrofoils. During the past year, the company has expanded its organisation to provide technical and management services to the US Navy for air cushion vehicles and surface effect ships.

The technical and operational functions and capabilities are co-ordinated by the System Research Center. Under the Director of the Center, permanently assigned Project Managers (for ship, electronic, and oceanographic systems) form engineering task teams for the duration of a contract or included task(s), supported as necessary by technical support (clerical, graphics, editorial, and reproduction) personnel. This approach provides maximum management visibility and control over each task, and provides optimum response to customers while minimising costs.

HYDROFOIL CONSULTANTS

SWITZERLAND

Dr Ing E G Faber

Weinberglistrasse 60, CH-6000 Lucerne, Switzerland
Telephone: (041) 44 33 20
Telex: 78 670 DATAG-CH

Consultant in marine engine plant planning, marine engineering and marine technology, with special emphasis on high-speed and hydrofoil craft.

GENERAL: Feasibility studies, cost estimates, specifications, plant descriptions, project co-ordinations.

CONCEPTUAL AND PRELIMINARY DESIGNS: Engine and auxiliary plants, piping systems and hydraulics, electrical and monitoring systems, ventilation and air conditioning systems, noise insulation.

TECHNICAL EXPERTISE: Speed estimates and hydrodynamics problems, waterjet propulsion, analysis of ship structure, vibration and shock isolation, acceptance tests and damage survey.

Supramar AG

Ausserfeld 5, CH-6362 Stansstad, Switzerland
Telephone: (041) 61 31 94
Telex: 78228
Officials:
Hussain Najadi, *Chairman*
Baron Hanns von Schertel, *Director*
Martin Furrer, *Board Member*
Heinrad Schnueriger, *Board Member*
Baron Hanns von Schertel, *Research and Development*
Dipl Ing Eugen Schatté, *Research and Development*
Dipl Ing Georg Chvojka, *Technical Advisor for Hull Machinery and Foils*

Supramar was founded in Switzerland in 1952 to develop on a commercial basis the hydrofoil system introduced by the Schertel-Sachsenberg Hydrofoil Syndicate and its licensee, the Gebrüder Sachsenberg Shipyard.

From this early date Supramar have provided a consultancy service on a world-wide basis covering not only their hydrofoil vessels but also other aspects of fast marine transportation. Their scientists have delivered papers to most of the world's leading professional bodies.

The company has been under contract to many Governments and military services.

UNITED KINGDOM

H H Snowball

30 Lismore Road, Croydon, Surrey, England

Founder, in 1968, of Airavia Ltd, the first company to represent Sudoimport hydrofoils in the West. Founder, Speed Hydrofoils Ltd, which introduced Raketa hydrofoils on scheduled services on the River Thames in 1974. Consultant Bataan-Manila Ferry Services, Hydrofoil Exploration Services, etc. Crew training arranged, also feasibility studies of projected hydrofoil routes.

P N Structures Ltd

Marine and Engineering Division

See main entry under ACV consultants.

UNITED STATES OF AMERICA

Davidson Laboratory Stevens Institute of Technology

See main entry under ACV consultants.

Doty Associates, Inc

See main entry under ACV consultants.

Gibbs & Cox

See main entry under ACV consultants.

W A Graig

307 Troy Towers, Union City, New Jersey 07087, USA
Telephone: (201) 864 3993

W A Graig, Ingénieur Civil de l'Aéronautique (Ecole Nationale Supérieure de l'Aéronautique, France). Registered Prof Engineer (Ohio, USA).

W A Graig (formerly Grunberg) is the inventor of the Grunberg foil system, first patented in 1935. His approach provided the basis for the Aquavion series and many other designs, and his influence is still to be found in vessels in production today.

The Grunberg principle of inherent angle of attack variation is fully compatible with Forlanini's concept of area variation. Both can be incorporated in the same structure and in a number of modern hydrofoils the two principles work in association.

Mr Graig's more recent developments include several foil systems which provide lateral stability without impinging on the original Grunberg concept. Directional control ensures co-ordinated turns.

Hoerner Fluid Dynamics

PO Box 342, Brick Town, New Jersey 08723, USA
Officials:
S F Hoerner
Dr Ing Habilitatus

Hydrodynamicist of hydrofoils "Sea Legs" and "Victoria", since 1951.

Author of "Fluid-Dynamic Drag" (1965) and "Fluid-Dynamic Lift" (1975).

Hydronautics Incorporated

See main entry under ACV consultants.

M Rosenblatt & Son Inc

See main entry under ACV consultants.

Typical hydrofoil assignments include:

AG(EH)

Preliminary design and naval architectural services for preparation of proposal for design and construction of 300-ton AG(EH) Hydrofoil Research Vessel—for Lockheed Aircraft Corp.

Hydrofoil (LVH)

Provided naval architectural services, including development of lines, powering predictions, stability curves and loading criteria for design and development of a 37ft Landing Force Amphibious Support Vehicle Hydrofoil (LVH)—for Lycoming Division, Avco Corporation.

Hydrofoil Amphibian

Conceptual design of a 60-ton capacity hydrofoil lighter with retractable wheels for US Army Mobility Equipment Research and Development Center.

Stanford Research Institute

See main entry under ACV consultants.

Systems Exploration, Inc

See main entry under ACV consultants.

Water Research Company

See main entry under ACV consultants.

Wheeler Industries Inc

See main entry under ACV consultants.

GLOSSARY

ACS. Automatic control system. See **foil systems, submerged.**

ACV. Air cushion vehicle.

AMPS. Arctic Marine Pipelaying System. Method of laying pipelines in ice-covered Arctic waters employing a skirted air-cushion barge as an icebreaker. System was devised after Arctic Engineers successfully and continuously broke ice up to 0·68m (27in) thick using the 250-ton ACT-100 platform. On contact with the ice sheet, the skirt rises above it, maintaining its seal. As the ice sheet enters the cushion zone, the water level beneath it is depressed by the air pressure. Having lost flotation support, the ice becomes a cantilevered ledge and when it reaches its critical length, it breaks off into the water below. The broken ice is then thrust aside by a plough-like deflector.

APU. Auxiliary power unit.

AQL. Aéroglisseur à quille latérale. Term employed in France for a ship-size seagoing air-cushion vehicle employing rigid sidewalls and flexible seals fore and aft to contain the air cushion.

ASW. Anti-submarine warfare.

abeam. Another craft or object seen at the side or beam.

actuator. Unit designed to translate sensor information and/or computer instructions into mechanical action. Energy is transferred to control surfaces hydraulically, pneumatically or electrically.

A to N. Aids to navigation.

aeration. See **air entry.**

aerodynamic lift. Lifting forces generated by a vehicle's forward speed through the atmosphere due to the difference in pressure between upper and lower surfaces.

Aerofoil boat. Name given by the late Dr Alexander M Lippisch, the inventor and aircraft designer, to his range of aerodynamic ram-wing machines.

aéroglisseur. Air-glider. Name given to range of passenger-carrying amphibious ACVs designed in France by Société Bertin & Cie in conjunction with Société d'Études et de Développement des Aéroglisseurs Marins (SEDAM). The name **Aérobac** is given to mixed passenger/car ferries and freighters designed by Bertin and SEDAM.

aeroplane foil system. Arrangement in which the main foil is located forward of the centre of gravity to support 75% to 85% of the load, and the auxiliary foil, supporting the remainder, is located aft as a tail assembly.

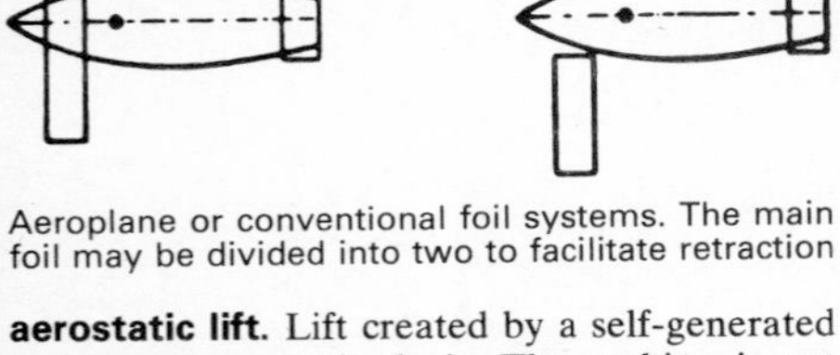

Aeroplane or conventional foil systems. The main foil may be divided into two to facilitate retraction

aerostatic lift. Lift created by a self-generated cushion of pressurised air. The cushion is put under pressure by a fan or fans and contained beneath the vehicle's structure by flexible seals or sidewalls.

aérosuspendu. Air-suspended. Form of suction-suspended monorail designed in France by Maurice Barthalon for mass public transportation on urban and suburban routes. The vehicle is suspended from its track by an air lift system in which the pressure is sub-atmospheric. Propulsion is by linear induction motor, qv.

Aerotrain. Generic name for a range of tracked air cushion vehicles under development in France by Société de l'Aérotrain.

aft. At, near or towards the stern of the craft.

air bleed (hyd). See **air stabilisation.** Occasionally used instead of aeration or air entry.

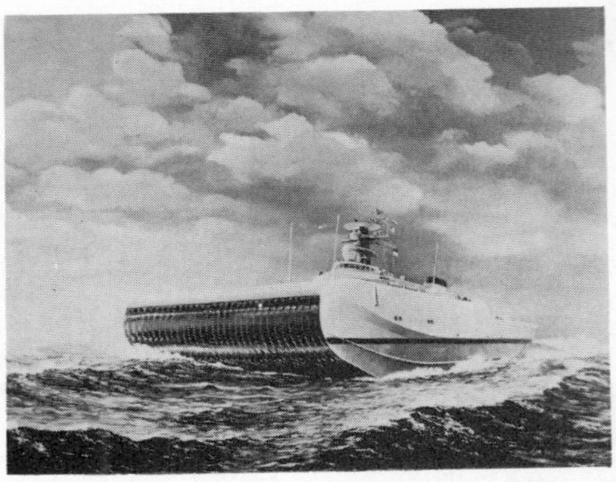

Four aerostatic-type air cushion vehicles. Each is supported by air put under pressure by a fan or fans and contained beneath the vehicles by flexible skirts or sidewalls. **Left to right**: the projected 3,000-ton Rohr 3KSES; the 220-ton Soviet Aist and **below** (upper picture) the 300-ton BHC SR.N4 Mk III and (lower) Sedam's 240-ton N500

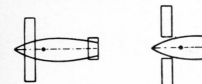

air bleed (ACV). One method of preventing "plough in" on a skirted ACV is to bleed air from the cushion through vent holes on the outer front of the skirt to reduce its water drag by air lubrication.

air cushion vehicle. A vehicle capable of being operated so that its weight, including its payload, is wholly or significantly supported on a continuously generated cushion or 'bubble' of air at higher than ambient pressure. The air bubble or cushion is put under pressure by a fan or fans and generally contained beneath the vehicle's structure by flexible skirts or sidewalls. In the United States large or ship size air-cushion vehicles are called **surface effect ships** or **surface effect vessels.** Broadly speaking, there are two main types of air-cushion vehicle, those supported by a self-generated cushion of air and those dependent on forward speed to develop lift. The former are designated aerostatic, and the latter, aerodynamic.

Aerodynamic craft include the *ram-wing*, the *channel-flow wing* and the *wing-in-ground-effect*. The *ram-wing* (a) can be likened to a short-span wing with sidewalls attached to its tip. The wing trailing edge and the sidewalls almost touch the water surface. At speed, lifting forces are generated by both the wing and the ram pressure built up beneath. One of the first concepts utilising a *channel-flow* wing (b) was the Columbia, designed in the USA by Vehicle Research Corporation in 1961 (*Jane's Surface Skimmers 1967-68*). The design featured a peripheral jet sidewall system for use at low speeds and an aerofoil shaped hull to provide lift at high speeds during forward flight. The side curtains of the peripheral jet were to be retained to seal the high pressure "channel" of air developed beneath from the low pressure airflow above and along the sides of the craft, down to the water surface. A 30ft long manned model of the Columbia was successfully tested in 1964.

The *wing-in-ground-effect* (c) is essentially an aircraft designed to fly at all times in close proximity to the earth's surface, in order to take advantage of the so-called "image" flow that reduces induced drag by about 70%. In the Soviet Union this type of machine is known as an

Ekranoplan.

Aerostatic-type air cushion vehicles can be divided into two categories—plenum chamber craft and peripheral or annular jet craft. *Plenum chamber craft* (d) employ the most simple of surface effect concepts. Air is forced from the lift fan directly into a recessed base where it forms a cushion which raises the craft. The volume of air pumped into the base is just sufficient to replace the air leaking out beneath the edges.

Variants of this category include the *skirted plenum craft* (e), in which a flexible fabric extension is hung between the metal structure and the surface to give increased obstacle and overwave clearance capability. The Naviplane and Terraplanes designed by Bertin and SEDAM employ separately fed multiple plenum chambers, each surrounded by lightweight flexible skirts. Skirted plenum chamber types are also favoured by builders of light air cushion vehicles because of their relatively simple design and construction.

Another variant is the *sidewall* ACV (f), in which the cushion air is contained between solid sidewalls or skegs and deflectable seals, either solid or flexible, fore and aft. Stability is provided by the buoyancy of the sidewalls and their planing forces. Sidewall craft are also known as captured air bubble vessels *(CABs)* a term used widely in the United States. One of the derivatives of the sidewall type is the *Hydrokeel* (g) which is designed to plane on the after section of its hull and benefit to some degree from air lubrication.

In *peripheral* or *annular jet craft* (h) the ground cushion is generated by a continuous jet of air channelled through ducts or nozzles around the outer periphery of the base. The flexible skirts fitted to this type can take the form either of an extension to the outer wall of the duct or nozzle only, or an extension to both outer and inner walls. In the latter form it is known as a *trunked annular jet* (i).

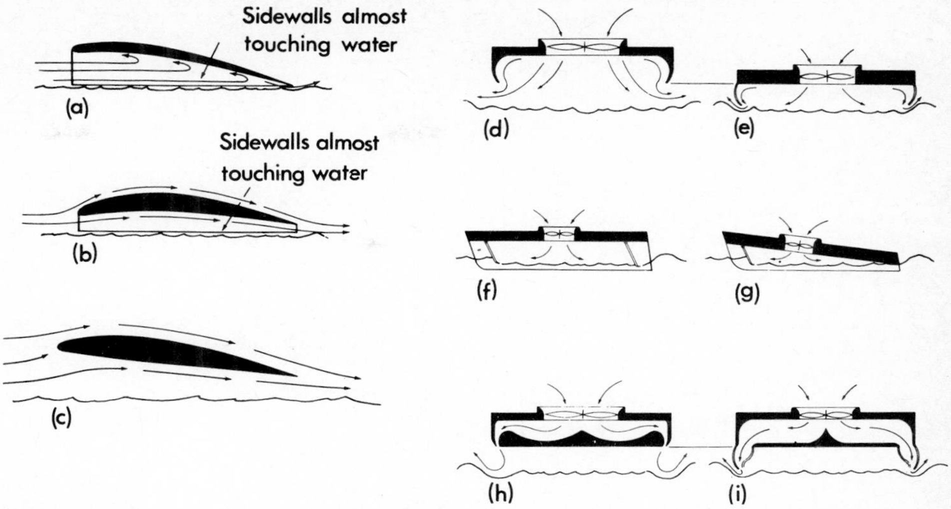

(a) ram wing; (b) channel-flow wing; (c) wing-in-ground-effect; (d) plenum chamber; (e) plenum chamber with skirt; (f) captured air bubble; (g) hydrokeel; (h) annular jet; (i) trunked annular jet

air entrainment. See **air entry.**

air entry. Entry of air from the atmosphere that raises the low pressures created by the flow due to a foil's cambered surface.

air gap; also daylight gap, daylight clearance and **hover gap.** Distance between the lowest component of the vehicle's understructure, eg skirt hem, and the surface when riding on its cushion. **air gap area:** area through which air is able to leak from a cushion.

air pad. Part of an air pallet assembly into which compressed air is introduced and allowed to escape in a continuous flow through communicating holes in the diaphragm.

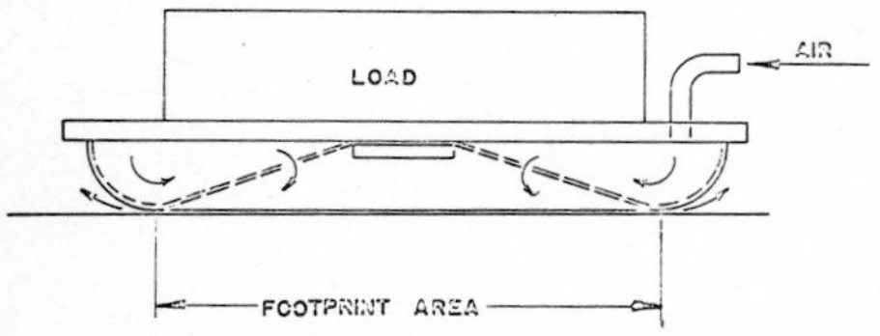

An air pad with a flexible plastic diaphragm

air pallet, also **hoverpallet.** Air cushion supported, load-carrying structure, which bleeds a continuous low pressure volume of air between the structure and the reaction surface, creating an air film.

air-port system, also **thrust port.** See **puff port.**

air-rider. Alternative generic name for air cushion vehicles or weight carrying structures lifted off the surface by a cushion or film of air.

air stabilised foils. See **foil systems.**

amidships. (1) Midway between the stem and stern of a hull. (2) abbreviated to **midships** and meaning the rudder or helm is in a mid-position.

amphibarge. Name given to a range of amphibious air cushion barges designed in France by SEDAM. The craft can be either self-propelled or towed.

Sedam Amphibarges

angle of attack. The angle made by the mean chord line of an aero- or hydrofoil with the flow.

angle of incidence. The angle made by the mean chord line of a hydrofoil in relation to the fixed struts or hull.

Aquavion type foil. Adapted from the Grunberg system. About 85% of the load is carried by a mainfoil located slightly aft of the centre of gravity, 10% by a submerged aft stabiliser foil, and the remainder on a pair of planing sub-foils at the bow. The planing subfoils give variable lift in response to wave shapes, whether skimming over them or through them, and so trim the angle of the hull in order to correct the angle of attack of the main foil.

articulated air cushion vehicle. A modular type load-carrying platform designed by Charles Burr of Bell Aerospace. A number of skirted platforms can be joined to form a variety of ACVs of different load carrying capacities. An application envisaged for craft of this type is the movement of containers and other heavy machinery in the American arctic and middle north.

aspect ratio. (1) the measure of the ratio of a foil's span to its chord. It is defined as

$$\frac{\text{span}^2}{\text{total foil area}}$$

(2) for ACVs it is defined as $\frac{\text{cushion beam}}{\text{cushion length}}$

athwart, athwartship. Across the hull in a transverse direction from one side of the craft to the other.

axial-flow lift fan. A fan generating an airflow for lift that is parallel to the axis of rotation.

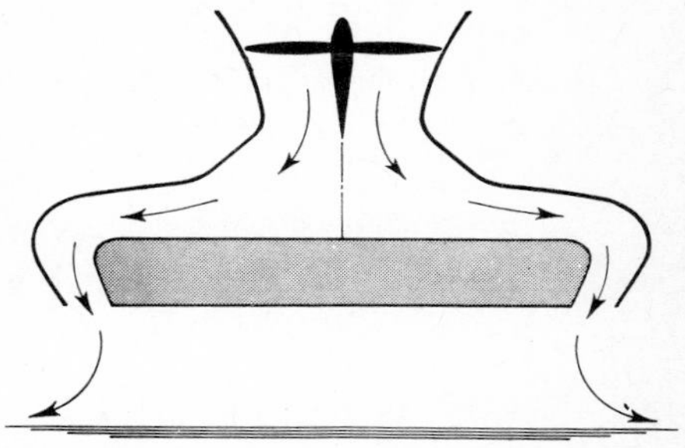

Axial flow lift fan

bhp. Brake horse power.

backstrap. A fabric strap used to secure a lift jet exit nozzle in a flexible skirt at the correct angle.

baffle plates. See **fences.**

ballast. Fuel, water or solids used to adjust the centre of gravity or trim of a craft.

ballast system. A method of transferring water or fuel between tanks to adjust fore and aft trim. In Mountbatten class ACVs, four groups of tanks, one at each corner of the craft, are located

Three aerodynamic air cushion vehicles. Like aeroplanes, these craft depend upon forward speed to develop lift. A dynamic air cushion is formed between the vehicle and its supporting surface below. **Left to right**: The Soviet ESKA-1, two-seat river rescue craft; the Lippisch Rheinflugzeugbau X 113 Am and a large Soviet experimental wing-in-ground-effect machine said to have been built at Gorky, and which is undergoing tests

in the buoyancy tanks. A ring main facilitates the rapid transfer of fuel between the tanks as ballast and also serves as a refuelling line.

ballast tank or box. Box or tank containing the liquids or solids used to trim a craft.

base ventilated foil. A system of forced ventilation designed to overcome the reduction in lift/drag ratio of a foil at supercavitating speeds. Air is fed continuously to the upper surface of the foil un-wetting the surface and preventing the formation of critical areas of decreased pressure. Alternatively the air may be fed into the cavity formed behind a square trailing edge.

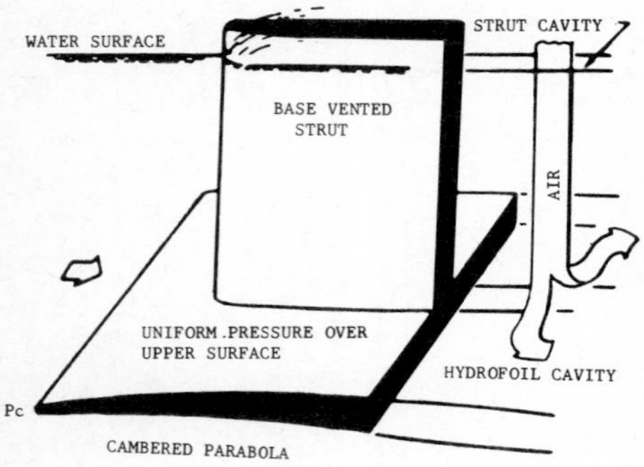

Base ventilated foil

beam. Measurement across a hull at a given point.

Beaufort Scale. A scale of wind forces described by name and range of velocity and classified as from force 0 to force 12, or in the case of strong hurricanes to force 17. Named after Admiral Sir Francis Beaufort, 1774-1857, who was responsible for preparing the scale.

Beaufort Force Number	*State of Air*	*Description*	*Wind Velocity in Knots*
0	calm	Smoke ascends vertically. Sea mirror-like	Less than 1
1	light air	Wind direction shown by smoke. Scale-like ripples on surface but no crests	1-3
2	slight breeze	As force 1, but wavelets more pronounced	4-6
3	gentle breeze	Flags extended. Short pronounced wavelets; crests start to break, scattered white horses	7-10
4	moderate breeze	Small waves, lengthening. Frequent white horses	11-16
5	fresh breeze	Waves more pronounced and longer form. More white horses some spray	17-21
6	strong breeze	Larger waves and extensive white foam crests. Sea breaks with dull rolling noise. Spray	22-27
7	moderate gale	White foam blown in streaks in direction of wind. Spindrift appears. Noise increases	28-33
8	fresh gale	Moderately high waves breaking into spindrift; well marked foam	34-40
9	strong gale	High waves and dense streaks of foam along direction of wind. Sea begins to roll	41-47
10	whole gale	Sea surface becomes white. Very high waves with over-hanging crests. Rolling of sea heavy. Visibility affected	48-55
11	storm	Waves exceptionally high. Visibility affected	56-65
12	hurricane	Air full of foam and spray. Visibility seriously affected	above 65

bilge. Point of the hull where the side and the bottom meet. Also water or fuel accumulated in the bilges.

bilge system. A pumping system devised to dispose of water and other fluids which have accumulated in the bilges. In air cushion vehicles bilge systems are installed to clear the buoyancy tanks. Small craft generally have a hand operated pump which connects directly to pipes in the tanks. In larger craft, like the 200-300-ton BHC Mountbatten, because of the large number of buoyancy compartments, four electrically driven pumps are provided, each of which can drain one compartment at a time.

block speed. Route distance divided by block time.

block time, also **trip time.** Journey time between lift off and touchdown.

boating. Expression used to describe an air cushion vehicle when operating in displacement condition. The boating or **semi-hover** mode is used in congested terminal areas, when lift power and spray generation is kept to a minimum. Some craft have water surface contact even at full hover for stability requirements.

bow. Forward part of a craft. The stem.

bow-up. Trim position or attitude when a craft is high at the bow. Can be measured by eye or attitude gyro.

breast, to. To take waves at 90 degrees to their crests.

Breguet range. The approximate range of a craft based upon the average values of propulsion efficiency, specific fuel consumption and the ratio of initial to final gross weight, assuming a constant lift-to-drag ratio. Named after L Breguet who first suggested the simplified formula.

bridge. Elevated part of the superstructure, providing a clear all round view, from which a craft is navigated and steered.

broach, to. Sudden breaking of the water surface by a foil, or part of a foil, resulting in a loss of lift due to air flowing over the foil's upper surface.

to broach to. Nautical expression meaning to swing sideways in following seas under wave action.

bulkheads. Vertical partitions, either transverse or longitudinal, which divide or sub-divide a hull. May be used to separate accommodation areas, strengthen the structure, form tanks or localise fires or flooding.

buoyancy. The reduction in weight of a floating object. If the object floats its weight is equal to (or less than) the weight of fluid displaced.

buoyancy chamber. A structure designed in such a way that the total of its own weight and all loads which it supports is equal to (or less than) the weight of the water it displaces.

buoyancy, reserve. Buoyancy in excess of that required to keep an undamaged craft afloat. See **buoyancy.**

buoyancy tubes. Inflatable tubular members providing reserve buoyancy. May be used as fenders if fitted to the outer periphery of a craft.

CAA. Civil Aviation Authority.

CAB. Captured Air Bubble. See **air cushion vehicle.**

CIC. Combat information centre.

cp. Centre of pressure.

CP shifter. A control system which moves the centre of pressure of an air cushion to augment a craft's natural stability in pitch and roll.

CPIC. Coastal patrol interdiction craft.

CWL. Calm water line.

camber. (1) A convexity on the upper surface of a deck to give it increased strength and/or facilitate draining. (2) The convex form on the upper surface of a foil. The high speed flow over the top surface causes a decrease in pressure and about two-thirds of the lift is provided by this surface.

canard foil system. A foil arrangement in which

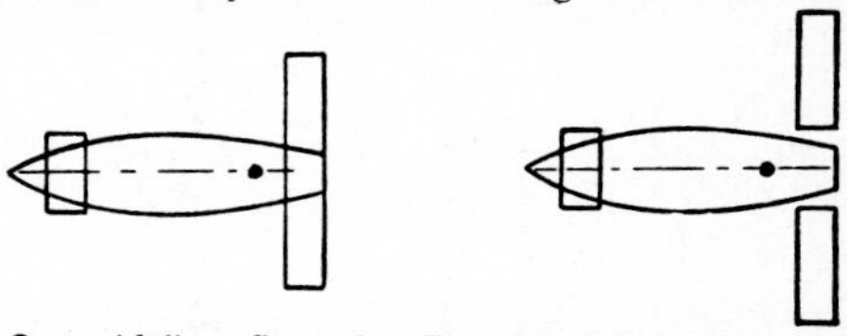

Canard foil configuration. The main foil area may be divided into two to facilitate retraction

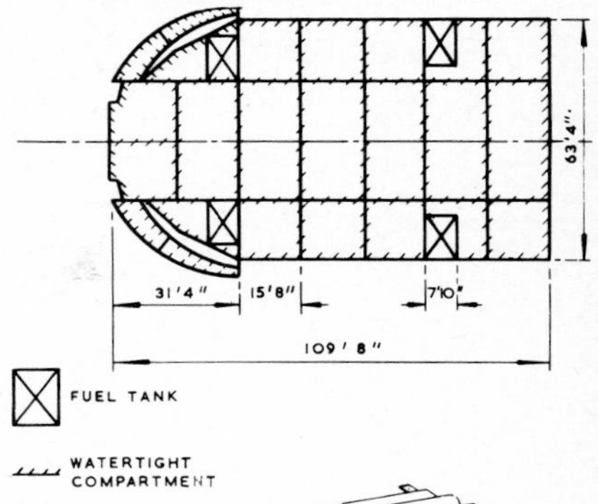

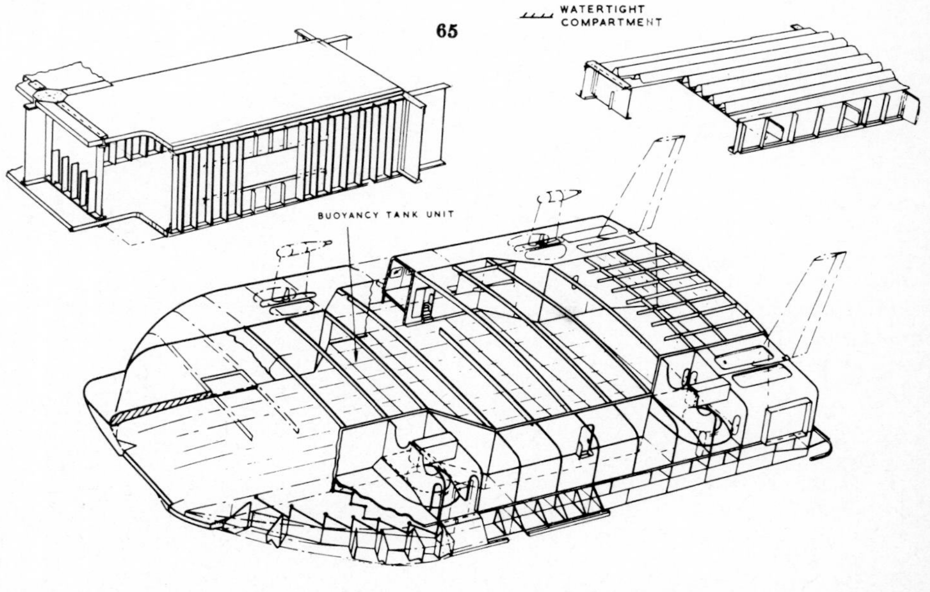

Typical buoyancy tank unit on the SR.N4. The basic structure of the SR.N4 is the buoyancy chamber, built around a grid of longitudinal and transversal frames, which form twenty four watertight sub-divisions for safety. Below, the SR.N4 buoyancy tank layout

the main foil of wide span is located near the stern, aft of the centre of gravity, and bears about 65% of the weight, while a small central foil is placed at the bow.

captain. Senior crew member aboard a hovercraft. Defined as the person designated by the operator to be in charge of a hovercraft during any journey, under the UK government's "The Hovercraft (Application of Enactments) Order 1972". Equivalent in rank to airliner or ship's captain. Alternative terms: pilot, driver, helmsman, coxswain and ACV operator.

captured air bubble craft (see also **sidewall craft** and **surface effect ship).** Vessel in which the cushion (or air bubble) is contained by rigid sidewalls and flexible bow and stern skirts. Occasionally used for any air cushion craft in which the air cushion (or air bubble) is contained within the cushion periphery with minimal air leakage.

cavitation. Cavitation is the formation of vapour bubbles due to pressure decrease on the upper surface of a foil or the back of a propeller's blades at high speeds, and falls into two categories, unstable and stable. Non-stable cavities or cavitation bubbles of aqueous vapour form near the foil's leading edge and extend down stream expanding and collapsing. At the points of collapse positive pressure peaks may rise to as high as 20,000psi. These cause erosion and pitting of the metal. Cavitation causes an unstable water flow over the foils which results in abrupt changes in lift and therefore discomfort for those aboard the craft.

Foil sections are now being developed which either delay the onset of cavitation by reduced camber, thinner sections, or sweepback, or if the craft is required to operate at supercavitating speeds, stabilise cavitation to provide a smooth transition between sub-cavitating and supercavitating speeds.

centrifugal flow lift fan. A cushion lift fan which generates an airflow at right angles to the axis of rotation.

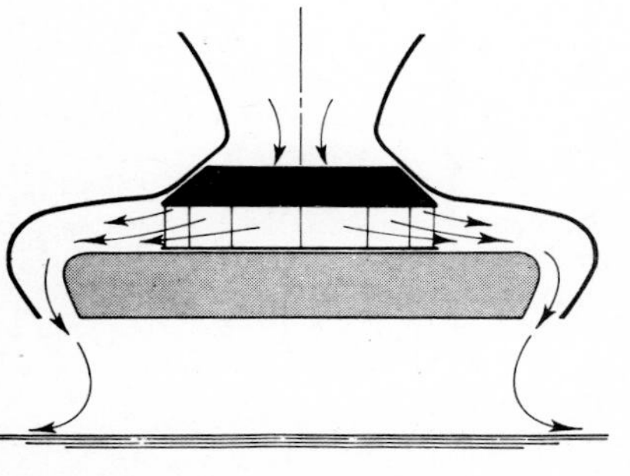

Centrifugal flow lift fan

chain ties. Chains used to maintain the correct shape of an air jet exit nozzle on a flexible skirt.

chord. The distance between the leading and trailing edges of a foil section measured along the chord-line.

chord-line. A straight line joining the leading and trailing edges of a foil or propeller blade section.

classification. Seagoing and amphibious craft for commercial application are classified by mode and place of construction, in the manner of the registration system started in the City of London by Edward Lloyd, and continued since 1760 by Lloyd's Register of Shipping. Outside the British Isles classification societies now include Registro Italiano Navale, Germanischer Lloyd, Det Norske Veritas, American Bureau of Shipping and the Japanese Ministry of Transport.

A classification society's surveyors make a detailed examination of craft certificated by them at regular intervals to ensure their condition complies with the particular society's requirements.

continuous nozzle skirt. See **skirt.**

contour, to. The motion of an air cushion vehicle or hydrofoil when more or less following a wave profile.

craft. Boats, ships, air cushion vehicles and hydrofoils of all types, regardless of size.

crew. Those responsible for manning a craft of either boat or ship size, including the officers. The company of an ACV or hydrofoil.

cross-flow. The flow of air, transversally or longitudinally within an air cushion.

cryogenics. Science of refrigeration, associated in particular with temperatures of —260°C and lower.

cushion. A volume of higher than ambient pressure air trapped beneath the structure of a vehicle and its supporting surface causing the vehicle to be supported at some distance from the ground.

cushion area. Area of a cushion contained within a skirt or sidewall.

cushion beam. Measurement across an air cushion at a given point.

cushion borne. A craft borne above the sea or land surface by its air cushion.

cushion length. Longitudinal cushion measurement.

cushion length, mean. Defined as:

$$\frac{\text{cushion area}}{\text{cushion beam}}$$

cushion pumping. see **wave pumping.**

cushion seal. Air curtains, sidewalls, skirts, water-jets or other means employed to contain or seal an air cushion to reduce to a minimum the leakage of trapped air.

cushion thrust. Thrust obtained by the deflection of cushion air.

DWL. Displacement water line.

daylight clearance. See **air gap.**

daylight gap. See **air gap.**

deadrise. The angle with the horizontal made at the keel by the outboard rise of a vessel's hull form at each frame.

delta wing. A triangular-shaped aircraft wing, as in fourth letter of Greek alphabet Δ, corresponding to D. Designed and developed by Dr Alexander Lippisch and applied in supersonic configuration on the Me 163B rocket-propelled interceptor, the fastest military aircraft of World War II. More recently the delta wing has been employed by Dr Lippisch in his series of Aerofoil Boats. Applied also in Soviet Union because of its high aerodynamic qualities and stability for a range of Ekranoplan aerodynamic ram-wings.

diesel engine. An internal combustion engine which burns a relatively inexpensive oil of similar consistency to light lubricating oil. Invented by Rudolf Diesel, 1858-1913. Fuel oil is pumped into the cylinder then compressed so highly that the heat generated is sufficient to ignite oil subsequently injected, without an electric spark.

diffuser-recirculation. See **recirculation system.**

direct operating cost. Cost of operating a craft, excluding company overheads and indirect costs.

displacement. The weight in tons of water displaced by a floating vessel. Light displacement is the craft weight exclusive of ballast.

ditch, to. An emergency landing on water while under way due to a local navigation hazard, loss of cushion air or failure of a powerplant.

Doppler, navigator. An automatic dead reckoning device which gives a continuous indication of position by integrating the speed derived from measuring the Doppler effect of echoes from directed beams of radiant energy transmitted from the vessel.

down-by-the-head. Trim or sit of a craft with its bow more deeply immersed than the stern. The opposite expression is 'down-by-the-stern'.

draft, draught. Depth between the water surface and the bottom of a craft. Under the Ministry of Transport Merchant Shipping (Construction) rules, 1952, draught is defined as the vertical distance from the moulded base line amidships to the sub-division load waterline.

draft, draught marks. (1) marks on the side of a craft showing the depth to which it can be loaded.

(2) figures cut at the stern and stem to indicate draft and trim.

drag. (1) ACVs—aerodynamic and hydrodynamic resistances encountered by an air cushion vehicle resulting from aerodynamic profile, gain of momentum of air needed for cushion generation, wave making, wetting or skirt contact.

(2) hydrofoils—hydrodynamic resistances encountered by hydrofoils result from wave making, which is dependent on the craft shape and displacement, frictional drag due to the viscosity of the water, the total wetted surface and induced drag from the foils and transmission shafts and their supporting struts and structure, due to their motion through the water.

drift angle. Difference between the actual course made and the course steered.

ESKA. Russian. Ekranolytny Spasatyelny Kater Amphibiya (screen-effect amphibious lifeboat). Name given to series of small wing-in-ground-effect machines developed by the Central Laboratory of Lifesaving Technology, Moscow. Also known as **Ekranolyet** or **Nizkolet** (skimmer).

Ekranoplan. Russian. Composite word based on *ekran*, a screen or curtain, and *plan*, the principal supporting surface of an aeroplane. Employed almost exclusively to describe types of ACVs in the Soviet Union raised above their supporting surfaces by dynamic lift. Western equivalent, wing-in-ground-effect machines (WIG) and aerodynamic ram-wing.

elevator. Movable aerodynamic control surface used on small hovercraft to provide a degree of fore and aft trim control. Elevator surfaces are normally located in the slipstream of the propulsive units in order to provide some control at low speed.

FPB. Fast patrol boat.

FWL. Foilborne water line.

fathom. A depth of 6ft.

fences. Small partitions placed at short intervals down the upper and lower surfaces of a hydrofoil tending to prevent air ventilation passing down to destroy the lift. They are attached in the direction of the flow.

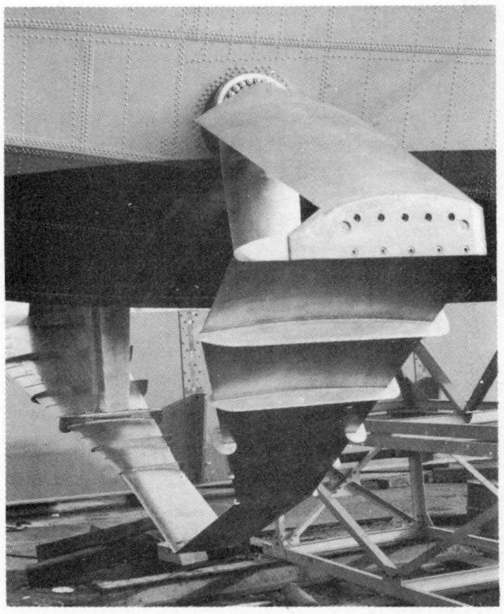

Fences on the bow foil of a Supramar hydrofoil

ferry. A craft designed to carry passengers across a channel, estuary, lake, river or strait.

fetch. The number of miles a given wind has been blowing over open water or the distance upwind to the nearest land.

finger skirt. See **skirts.**

fire zone. A compartment containing a full supply and ignition source which is walled with fire resisting material and fitted with an independent fire warning and extinguishing system.

fixed annual cost. Major component of a vehicle's direct operating cost. This comprises depreciation, craft insurance and operating and maintenance crew salaries, all of which are incurred regardless of whether the craft is operated or not.

flare. Upward and outward curvature of the freeboard at the bow, presenting additional, rising surface to oncoming waves.

flexible skirt. See **skirt.**

flying bridge. A navigating position atop the wheel or chart house.

foilborne. A hydrofoil is said to be foilborne when the hull is raised completely out of the water and wholly supported by lift from its foil system.

foil flaps. Foils are frequently fitted with (a) trailing edge flaps for lift augmentation during take-off and to provide control forces, (b) upper and lower flaps to raise the cavitation boundary.

foil systems. Foil systems in current use are generally either **surface piercing, submerged** or **semi-submerged.** There are a number of craft with hybrid systems with a combination of submerged and surface piercing foils, recent examples being the Supramar PT.150 and the De Havilland FHE-400.

surface piercing foils are more often than not V-shaped, the upper parts of the foil forming the tips of the V and piercing the surface on either side of the craft. The V foil, with its marked dihedral is area stabilised and craft employing this configuration can be designed to be inherently stable, and, for stability, geometry dependent.

The forces restoring normal trim are provided by the area of the foil that is submerged. A roll to one side means the immersion of increased foil area, which results in the generation of extra lift to counter the roll and restore the craft to an even keel.

Equally, a downward pitching movement at the bow means an increase in the submerged area of the forward foil, and the generation of extra lift on this foil, which raises the bow once more. Should the bow foil rise above its normal water level the lift decreases in a similar way to restore normal trim. This type of foil is also known as an **emerging foil system.**

As the V-foil craft increases its speed, so it generates greater lift and is raised further out of the water—at the same time reducing the wetted area and the lift. The lift must be equal to the weight of the craft, and as the lift depends on the speed and wetted foil area, the hull rides at a predetermined height above the water level.

ladder foils. Also come under the heading surface piercing, but are rarely used at the present time. This is one of the earliest foil arrangements and was used by Forlanini in his 1905 hydro-aeroplane, which was probably the first really successful hydrofoil. In 1911 Alexander Graham Bell purchased Forlanini's patent specifications and used his ladder system on his Hydrodomes, one of which, the HD-4, set up a world speed record of 61·5 knots in 1919. Early ladder foils, with single sets of foils beneath the hull, fore and aft, lacked lateral stability, but this disadvantage was rectified later by the use of two sets of forward foils, one on each side of the hull. The foils were generally straight and set at right angles to their supporting struts, but were occasionally of V configuration, the provision of

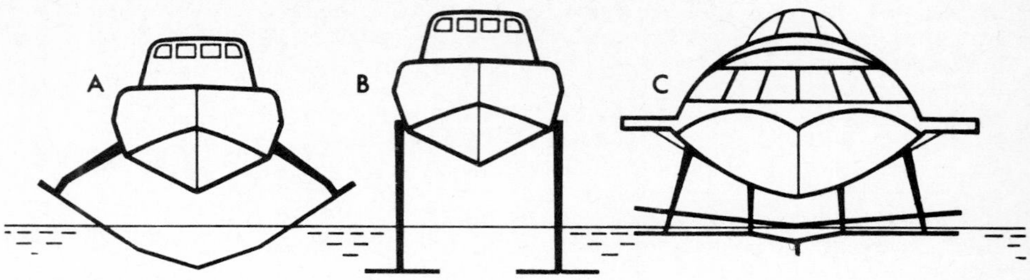

Foil systems in current use. A surface piercing, B submerged and C shallow draft submerged

dihedral preventing a sudden change of lift as the foils broke the surface. Both the V foil and the ladder systems are self-stabilising to a degree. The V foil has the advantage of being a more rigid, lighter structure and is less expensive.

Primary disadvantages of the conventional surface-piercing systems in comparison with the submerged foil system are: (a) the inability of V-foil craft without control surfaces to cope with downward orbital velocities at wave crests when overtaking waves in a following sea, a condition which can decrease the foil's angle of attack, reducing lift and cause either wave contact or a stall; (b) on large craft the weight and size of the surface-piercing system is considerably greater than that of a corresponding submerged foil system; (c) restoring forces to correct a roll have to pass above the centre of gravity of the craft, which necessitates the placing of the foils only a short distance beneath the hull. This means a relatively low wave clearance and therefore the V foil is not suited to routes where really rough weather is encountered.

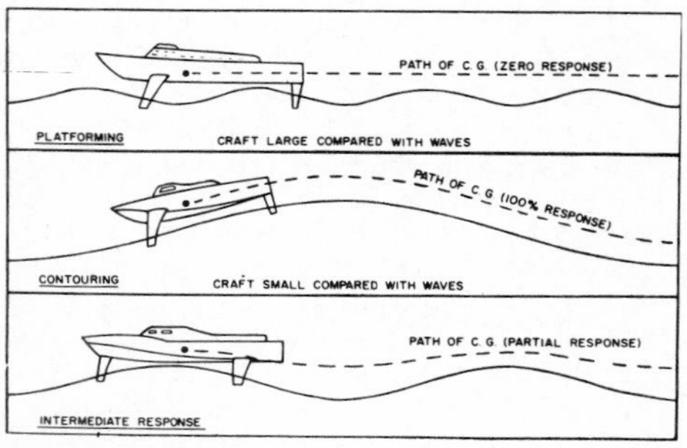

Comparison of platforming and contouring modes, and the intermediate response of a craft equipped with fully submerged, automatically controlled foil system

shallow-draft submerged foil system. This system which incorporates the Grunberg angle of attack variation approach, is employed almost exclusively on hydrofoils designed and built in the Soviet Union and is intended primarily for passenger carrying craft used on long, calm water rivers, canals and inland seas. The system, also known as the immersion depth effect system, was evolved by Dr Rostislav Alexeyev. It generally comprises two main horizontal foils, one forward, one aft, each carrying approximately half the weight of the vessel. A submerged foil loses lift gradually as it approaches the surface from a depth of about one chord, which prevents it from rising completely to the surface. Means therefore have to be provided to assist take-off and prevent the vessel from sinking back into the displacement mode. Planing subfoils, port and starboard, are therefore provided in the vicinity of the forward struts, and are so located that when they are touching the water surface, the main foils are submerged at a depth of approximately one chord.

submerged foils. These have a greater potential for seakeeping than any other, but are not inherently stable to any degree. The foils are totally immersed and a sonic, mechanical or air stabilisation system has to be installed to maintain the foils at the required depth. The system has to stabilise the craft from take-off to touch-down in heave and all three axes—pitch, roll and yaw. It must also see that the craft makes co-ordinated banked turns in heavy seas to reduce the side loads on the foil struts; ensure that vertical and lateral accelerations are kept within limits in order to prevent excessive loads on the structure and finally, ensure a smooth ride for the passengers and crew.

The control forces are generated either by deflecting flaps at the trailing edge of the foil or varying the incidence angle of the entire foil surface. Incidence control provides better performance in a high sea state.

The key element of a typical automatic control system is an acoustic height sensor located at the bow. The time lag of the return signal is a measure of the distance of the sensor from the water.

Craft motion input is received from dual sonic ranging devices which sense the height above the water of the bow in relation to a fixed reference; from three rate gyros which measure yaw, pitch and roll; from forward and aft accelerometers which sense vertical acceleration fore and aft and from a vertical gyro which senses the angular position of the craft in both pitch and roll. This information is processed by an electronic computer and fed continuously to hydraulic actuators of the foil control surfaces, which develop the necessary hydrodynamic forces for stability producing forces imposed by wave action manoeuvring and correct flight.

mechanical incidence control. The most successful purely mechanically operated incidence control system is the Hydrofin autopilot principle, designed by Christopher Hook, who pioneered the development of the submerged foil. A fixed, high-riding crash preventer plane is mounted ahead of and beneath the bow.

The fixed plane, which is only immersed when the craft is in a displacement mode, is also used as a platform for mounting a lightweight pitch control sensor which is hinged to the rear.

The sensor rides on the waves and continuously transmits their shape through a connecting linkage to vary the angle of incidence of the main foils as necessary to maintain them at the required depth. A filter system ensures that the

These military hydrofoil designs illustrate three different foil systems. **Left to right:** The De Havilland Canada MP-100, a 100-ton missile craft with its inherently stable 'canard' surface-piercing system, incorporating a trapeze configuration main foil aft; the 83·5 ton Flagstaff II with incidence-controlled fully submerged foils in "aeroplane" configuration and the Boeing NATO/PHM. The latter has a fully submerged canard system with 32% of the dynamic lift provided by the bow foil and 68% by the aft foil. Lift control is provided by trailing edge flaps on each foil

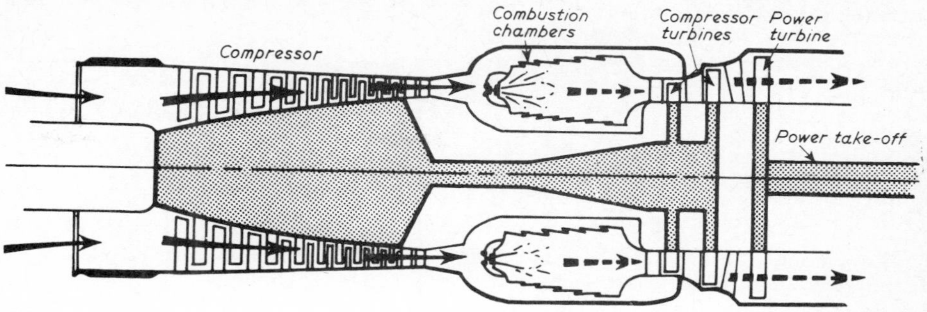

Free power turbine

craft ignores small waves and that the hull is flown over the crests of waves exceeding the height of the keel over the water.

Two additional sensors, trailing from port and starboard immediately aft of the main struts, provide roll control. The pilot has overriding control through a control column, operated in the same manner as that in an aircraft.

air stabilisation system. A system designed and developed by Baron Hanns von Schertel of Supramar AG, Lucerne. Air from the free atmosphere is fed through air exits to the foil upper surface and under certain conditions the lower surface also (ie into the low pressure regions). The airflow decreases the lift and the flow is deflected away from the foil section with an effect similar to that of a deflected flap, the air cavities extending out behind producing a virtual lengthening of the foil profile. Lift is reduced and varied by the quantity of air admitted, this being controlled by a valve actuated by signals from a damped pendulum and a rate gyro. The pendulum causes righting moments at static heeling angles. If exposed to a centrifugal force in turning, it causes a moment, which is directed towards the centre of the turning circle, thereby avoiding outside banking (co-ordinated banking). The rate gyro responds to angular velocity and acts dynamically to dampen rolling motions.

following sea. A sea following the same or similar course to that of the craft.

force time effectiveness. Time to land an effective landing force ashore.

fore peak. The space forward of the fore collision bulkhead, frequently used as storage space.

forward. Position towards the fore end of a craft.

frames. The structure of vertical ribs or girders to which a vessel's outside plates are attached. For identification purposes the frames are numbered consecutively, starting aft.

freeboard. Depth of the exposed or free side of a hull between the water level and the freeboard deck. The degree of freeboard permitted is marked by load lines.

freeboard deck. Deck used to measure or determine loadlines.

free power turbine. A gas-turbine on which the power turbine is on a separate shaft from the compressor and its turbine.

full hover. Expression used to describe the condition of an ACV when it is at its design hoverheight.

furrowing. The condition of foilborne operation of a hydrofoil caused by contact of the lower part of the hull and keel with the crests of the larger waves. The contact is brief and does not prevent the craft from remaining foilborne. See also **hull cresting.**

g. Gravitational acceleration.

grp. Glass-reinforced plastics.

gas-turbine engine. Engine in which expanding gases are employed to rotate a turbine. Its main elements are a rotary air compressor with an air intake, one or a series of combustion chambers, a turbine and an exhaust outlet.

GEM. Ground effect machine.

gross tonnage. Total tonnage of a vessel, including all enclosed spaces, estimated on the basis of $100ft^2$ = 1 ton.

ground effect machine. Early generic term for air cushion vehicles of all types.

ground crew and **ground staff.** Those responsible for craft servicing and maintenance. Also those responsible for operational administration.

Grunberg Foil System. First patented in 1936, the Grunberg principle of inherent angle of attack variations comprises a "stabiliser" attached to the bow or a forward projection from the latter, and behind this a "foil". Both foil and stabiliser can be "split" into several units. The lift curve of the stabiliser, plotted against its draft, is considerably steeper than its corresponding foil lift curve. Hence as the operational conditions (speed, weight, CG travel) change, the foil sinks or rises relative to the stabiliser, automatically adjusting its angle of attack. The "foil" is set at an appropriate angle of incidence in order to prevent it from approaching the interface. The system is fully compatible with Forlanini's concept of area variation and both can be incorporated in the same structure.

HDL. Hovercraft Development Ltd.

hp. Horsepower.

HYSWAS. Hydrofoil small waterplane area ship.

Hz. Unit of wave frequency employed especially in acoustics and electronics. 1 hertz = 1 cycle per second. Named after Heinrich Hertz (1857-1894), German physicist.

hard chine. Hull design with the topsides and bottom meeting at an angle, rather than curving to a round bilge.

head sea. A sea approaching from the direction steered.

heave. Vertical motion of a craft in response to waves.

heel. (a) To incline or list in a transverse direction while under way. (b) Lower end of a mast or derrick. (c) Point where keel and stern post meet.

Helibarge. System devised by Walter A Crowley (USA) combining a helicopter with an air-cushion barge. The downwash of the helicopter rotor pressurises the air-cushion.

hourly running cost. That part of the direct operating cost incurred when the craft is operated, ie, fuel, maintenance and overhauls.

hoverbarge. Fully buoyant, shallow-draft hovercraft built for freight carrying. Either self-propelled or towed.

hovercraft. (a) Originally a name for craft using the patented peripheral jet principle invented by Sir Christopher Cockerell, in which the air cushion is generated and contained by a jet of air exhausted downward and inward from a nozzle at the periphery at the base of the vehicle. (b) Classification in the USA for skirted plenum chamber and annular jet-designs. (c) In the British Hovercraft Act 1968, a hovercraft is defined as a vehicle which is designed to be supported when in motion wholly or partly by air expelled from the vehicle to form a cushion of which the boundaries include the ground, water or other surface beneath the vehicle.

hover gap. See **air gap.**

hover height. Vertical height between the hard structure of an ACV and the supporting surface when a vehicle is cushion-borne.

hover-listen. Expression covering ACVs employed for anti-submarine warfare while operating at low speeds to detect a target.

hover pallet. See **air pallet.**

hoverplatform. Non self-propelled hovercraft designed primarily to convey heavy loads across terrain impassable to wheeled and tracked vehicles under load.

hoverport. Defined by the British Hovercraft Act, 1968 as any area, whether land or elsewhere, which is designed, equipped, set apart or commonly used for affording facilities for the arrival and departure of hovercraft.

hoversled. Vehicle designed for northern latitudes combining features of an air cushion vehicle with skis or pontoons. The first vehicle of this type was designed in Finland by Mr Erkki Peri. Because of the contact between the vehicle's skis and the supporting surface beneath, directional control is a great improvement on that of most conventional skirted ACVs while operating over ice and snow.

A Mackace 50-ton hoverplatform

hovertrailer. A steel structure platform around which is fitted a flexible segmented skirt, cushion lift being provided by fans driven by petrol or diesel engines on the platform. The system, devised by Air Cushion Equipment Ltd and UBM Hover-Systems, is designed to increase the load capacity of tracked and wheeled vehicles many times. In cases where it is impossible for a tow vehicle to operate, the trailer can be winched.

A hovertrailer. Payload at $100lb/ft^2$ is 6·7 tons

hull cresting. Contact of a hydrofoil's hull with the waves in high seas. The term **hull slamming** qv, or slamming, is used if the hull contact is preceeded by foil broaching.

hull slamming. Contact of a hydrofoil's hull with the water following a foil broach. See **broach, to.**

hump. The "hump" formed on the graph of resistance against the speed of a displacement vessel or ACV. The maximum of the "hump" corresponds to the speed of the wave generated by the hull or air depression.

hump speed. Critical speed at which the curve on a graph of wave making drag of an ACV tends to hump or peak. As speed is increased, the craft over-rides its bow wave; the wave making drag diminishes and the rate of acceleration rapidly increases with no increase in power.

hydrofoils. Small wings, almost identical in section to those of an aircraft, and designed to generate lift. Since water has a density some 815 times that of air, the same lift as an aeroplane wing is obtained for only $^1/_{815}$ of the area (at equal speeds).

Hydrofoil small waterplane area ship. Projected hybrid vessel comprising a single submerged hull with a fully submerged foil system and an upper hull structure supported by a vertical strut or struts. At low speeds the craft is supported by the buoyancy of its submerged hull, the strut, and the lower section of the upper hull. At speed the dynamic lift generated by the foil system raises the upper hull out of the water with a reduction of the waterplane area of the strut.

hydroskimmer. Name given originally to experimental air cushion vehicles built under contract to the US Navy Bureau of Ships. Preference was given to this name since it gave the craft a sea-service identity.

IOT&E. US Navy. Initial operational testing and evaluation.

inclined shaft. A marine drive shaft used in small V foil and shallow-draft submerged foil craft, with keels only a limited height above the mean water level. The shaft is generally short and inclined at about 12-14 degrees to the horizontal. On larger craft, designed for operation in higher waves, the need to fly higher necessitates alternative drive arrangements such as the vee drive and Z-drive, the water jet system or even air propulsion.

indirect operating cost. Costs incurred apart from running a craft. Includes advertising, buildings, rents, rates and salaries for terminal staff other than those employed for craft maintenance.

induced wave drag. Drag caused by the hollow depressed in the water by an ACV's air cushion. As the craft moves forward the depression follows along beneath it, building up a bow wave and causing wave drag as in a displacement craft until the hump speed has been passed.

integrated lift-propulsion system. An ACV lift and propulsion system operated by a common power source, the transmission and power-sharing system allowing variation in the division of power.

JP-4. Liquid fuel, based on kerosene, used widely in gas-turbines.

keel. (a) The "backbone" of a hull. (b) An extension of an ACV's fore-and-aft stability air jet, similar in construction and shape to a skirt, and taking the form of an inflated bag.

knitmesh pads. Thick, loosely woven pads, in either metal or plastic wire fitted in the engine's air intake to filter out water and solid particles from the engine air.

knot. A nautical mile per hour.

LIMRV. Linear Induction Motor Research Vehicle.

land, to. At the end of a run hydrofoils and ACVs are said to "settle down" or "land".

landing pads, also **hard points.** Strengthened areas of the hull on which an ACV is supported when at rest on land. These may also provide attachment points for towing equipment, lifts and jacks.

leading frequency of sea waves. See **significant wave height.** Sea waves are composed of different frequencies. The sea wave of greatest energy content is called the sea wave of leading frequency.

leakage rate. Rate at which air escapes from an air cushion, measured in cubic metres or cubic feet per second.

lift fan. See also **axial flow lift fan** and **centrifugal flow lift fan.** A fan used to supply air under pressure to an air cushion, and/or to form curtains.

lift off. An ACV is said to lift off when it rises from the ground on its air cushion.

linear induction motor. Linear induction motors show considerable promise as a means of propulsion for tracked skimmers, and are now under development in France, the United Kingdom, West Germany, Italy, Japan, the United States and USSR. An attractive feature of this method of electric traction is that it does not depend upon the vehicle having contact with the track or guideway.

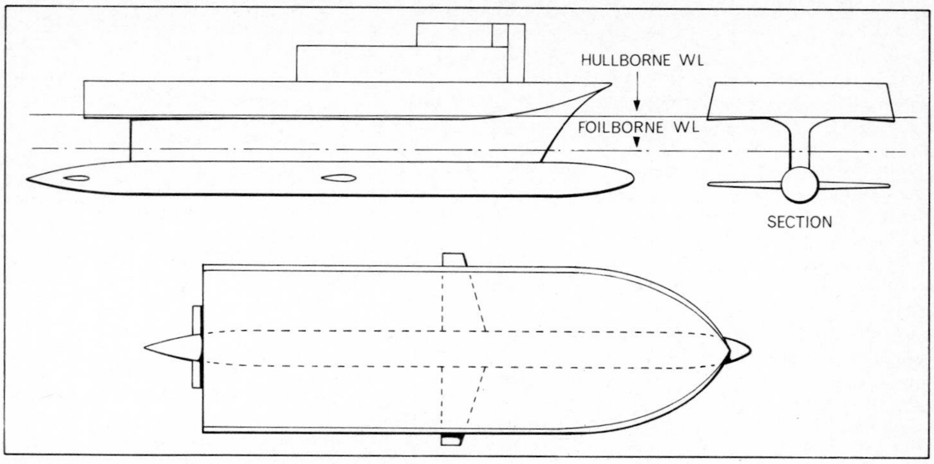

Hydrofoil small waterplane area ship (HYSWAS)

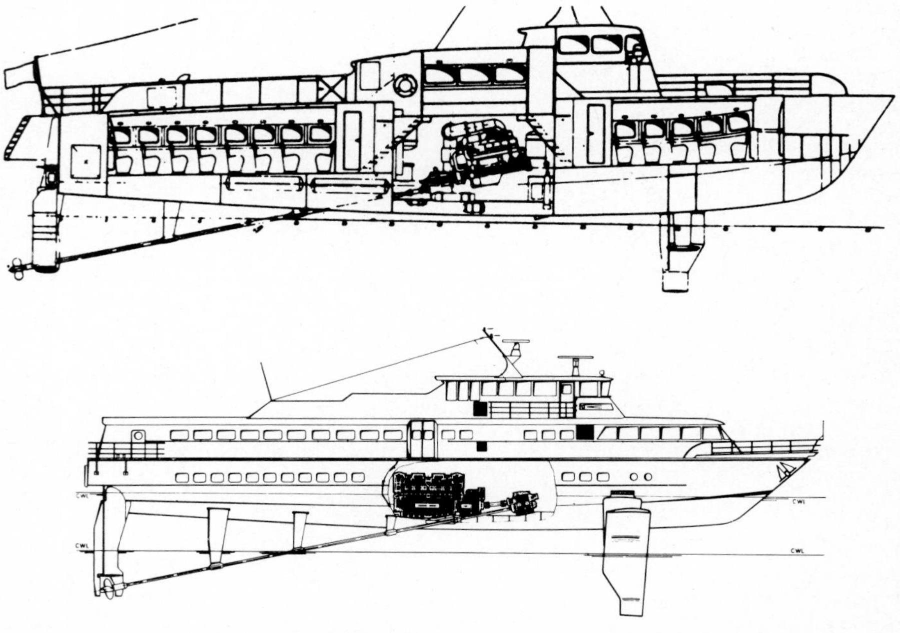
Sectional views showing the inclined shaft **(top)** on the PT 50 and the vee drive system employed on the PT 150

The motor can be likened to a normal induction motor opened out flat. The "stator" coils are attached to the vehicle, while the "rotor" consists of a flat rail of conductive material which is straddled by the stator poles. The variable frequency multi-phase ac current required for the linear motor can either be generated aboard the vehicle or collected from an electrified track.

Although the mounting of the stators on the vehicle appears to be preferred in Europe at present they can also be built into the guideway. In this case the rotor, in the form of a reaction rail, would be suspended from the vehicle. It would be of sufficient length to span several of the fixed stators simultaneously to avoid jerking.

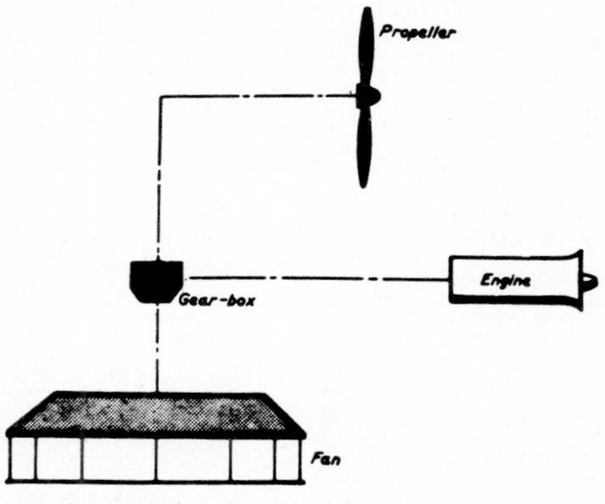

Integrated lift-propulsion system

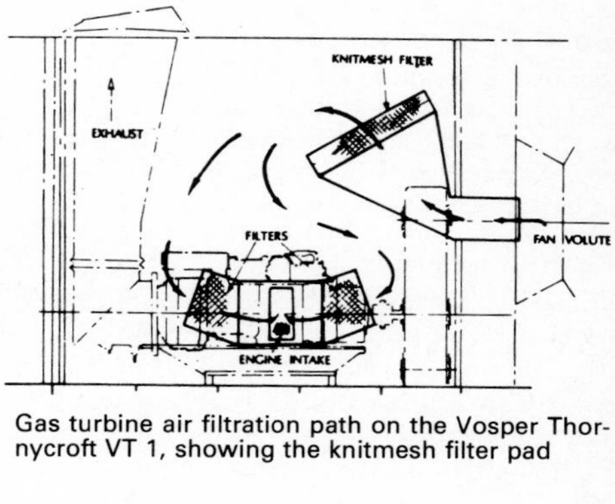

Gas turbine air filtration path on the Vosper Thornycroft VT 1, showing the knitmesh filter pad

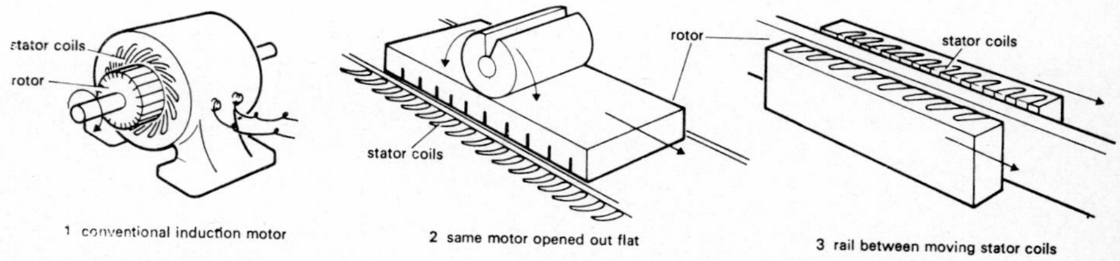

Principle of the linear induction motor

load factor. Relationship between the payload capacity available, and the capacity filled.

logistics. Science of transporting, accommodating and supplying troops.

longitudinal framing. Method of hull construction employing frames set in a fore and aft direction or parallel to the keel.

MCM. Mine countermeasures.

maglev. Magnetic levitation.

multiple skirt. System devised by the late Jean Bertin, employing a number of separate flexible skirts for his system of individually fed, multiple air cushions.

nautical mile. A distance of 6,080ft or one minute of latitude at the equator.

Naviplane. Name for the overwater or amphibious air cushion vehicles developed in France by SEDAM.

net tonnage. Total tonnage of a craft based on cubic capacity of all space available for carrying revenue-producing cargo less allowance for the engine room, crew quarters, water ballast, stores and other areas needed to operate the craft.

OPEVAL. US Navy. Operational evaluation.

orbital motion. Orbital or circular motion of the water particles forming waves. The circular motion decreases in radius with increasing depth. It is the peculiar sequence of the motion that causes the illusion of wave translation. In reality the water moves very little in translation. The circular directions are: up at the wave front, forward at the crest, down at the wave back and back at the trough.

PAR. Power augmented ram-wing.

PTO. See **power take-off unit.**

payload weight. Weight of revenue earning load, excluding crew and fuel.

peripheral jet. See **air curtain** and **hovercraft.**

peripheral jet cushion system. A ground cushion generated by a continuous jet of air issued through ducts or nozzles around the outer periphery of the base of a craft. The cushion is maintained at above ambient pressure by the horizontal change of momentum of the curtain.

peripheral trunk. See **skirt.**

pitch. Rotation or oscillation of the hull about a transverse axis in a seaway. Also angle of air or water propeller blades.

pitch angle. Pitch angle a craft adopts relative to a horizontal datum.

platform, to. Approximately level flight of a hydrofoil over waves of a height less than the calm water hull clearance.

plenum. Space or air chamber beneath or surrounding a lift fan or fans through which air under pressure is distributed to a skirt system.

plenum chamber cushion system. The most simple of air cushion concepts. Cushion pressure is maintained by pumping air continuously into a recessed base without the use of a peripheral jet curtain.

"plough in". A bow down attitude resulting from the bow part of the skirt contacting the surface and progressively building up a drag. Unless controlled this can lead to a serious loss of stability and possibly an overturning moment.

With the skirt's front outer edge dragging on the water towards the centre of the craft (known as 'tuck under') there is a marked reduction in righting moment of the cushion pressure. As the downward pitch angle increases, the stern of the craft tends to rise from the surface and excessive yaw angles develop. Considerable deceleration takes place down to hump speed and the danger of a roll over in a small craft is accentuated by following waves which further increase the pitch angle.

Solutions include the provision of vent holes on a skirt's outer front to reduce its drag through air lubrication, and the development of a bag skirt which automatically bulges outwards on contact with the water, thereby delaying tuck under and providing a righting moment.

porpoising. Oscillatory motion in pitch and heave of a high speed planing hull craft caused by incorrect trim rather than wave action.

power augmented ram-wing. Wing-in-ground-effect machine designed so that the propulsion system exhaust is directed into the space between the wing and the surface to lift the wing clear of the water at zero speed. Current research is also aimed at employing power augmentation in conjunction with end plates to provide a low speed or hover capability. Advantages include the avoidance of the high hydrodynamic drag experienced by craft with relatively high wing loadings during take-off and the high impact loadings encountered during take-off and landing. Use of the PAR system would also provide surface mobility over short ranges or under high sea state conditions which would normally prevent take-off. The system is expected to avoid the need for large hydrodynamic hulls for WIGs since the wing volume on winged hull types and others with deep aerofoil sections, could also be used for buoyancy.

power take off unit. Unit for transmitting power from the main engine or engines, generally for auxiliary services required while a craft is under way, such as hydraulics, alternators and bilge pumps.

pvc. Polyvinylchloride.

puff ports. Controlled apertures in a skirt system or cushion supply ducting through which air can be expelled to assist control at low speeds.

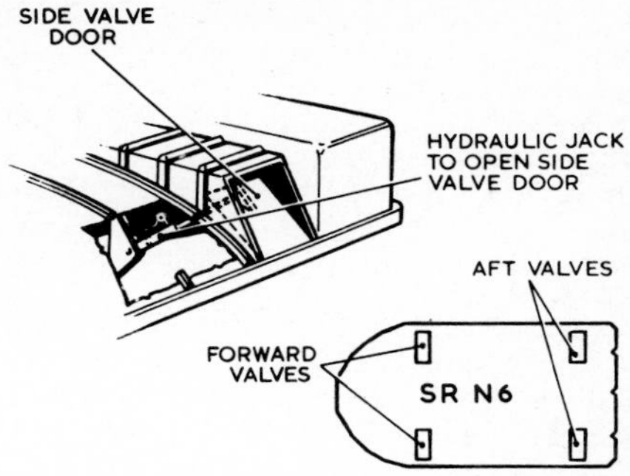

Puff port arrangement on the BHC SR.N6

ram wing. See **air cushion vehicles.**

recirculation system. An air curtain employing a recirculating air flow, which is maintained within and under the craft.

reliability factor. Percentage relationship between the number of trips scheduled and those achieved.

Ro-ro. Roll-on roll-off. Applied to ships and air cushion vehicles with decks providing straight through loading facilities, ie with cargo ramps or loading doors fore and aft.

roll. Oscillation or rotation of a hull about a longitudinal axis.

roll attitude. Angle of roll craft adopts relative to a longitudinal datum.

running time. Time during which all machinery has been in operation, including idling time.

SAR. Search and rescue.

SES. See **surface effect ship.**

SEV. Surface effect vehicle. Currently used in the USA to describe air cushion vehicles of all types. In the Soviet Union, the term is employed to describe large sea- or ocean-going wing-in-ground-effect machines.

SSP. Semi-submerged platform craft.

SSPU. Ship's service power unit.

SWATH. Small waterplane area twin-hull craft.

Savitsky flap. Hinged vertical control flaps employed for foil lift variation, attached to the trailing edge of the foil struts, and canted out at an angle. The flaps are attached mechanically to the trailing-edge flaps on the foil. At the normal flying height only the lower part of the Savitsky flap is submerged.

As more of the flap becomes submerged due to increased wave height, the moment of the flap increases causing it to raise the foil flap, thus increasing lift and restoring normal inflight attitude and flying height. The system can be adjusted to react only to lower-frequency layer waves. The system is employed on the Atlantic Hydrofoils Flying Cloud and Sea World. It was

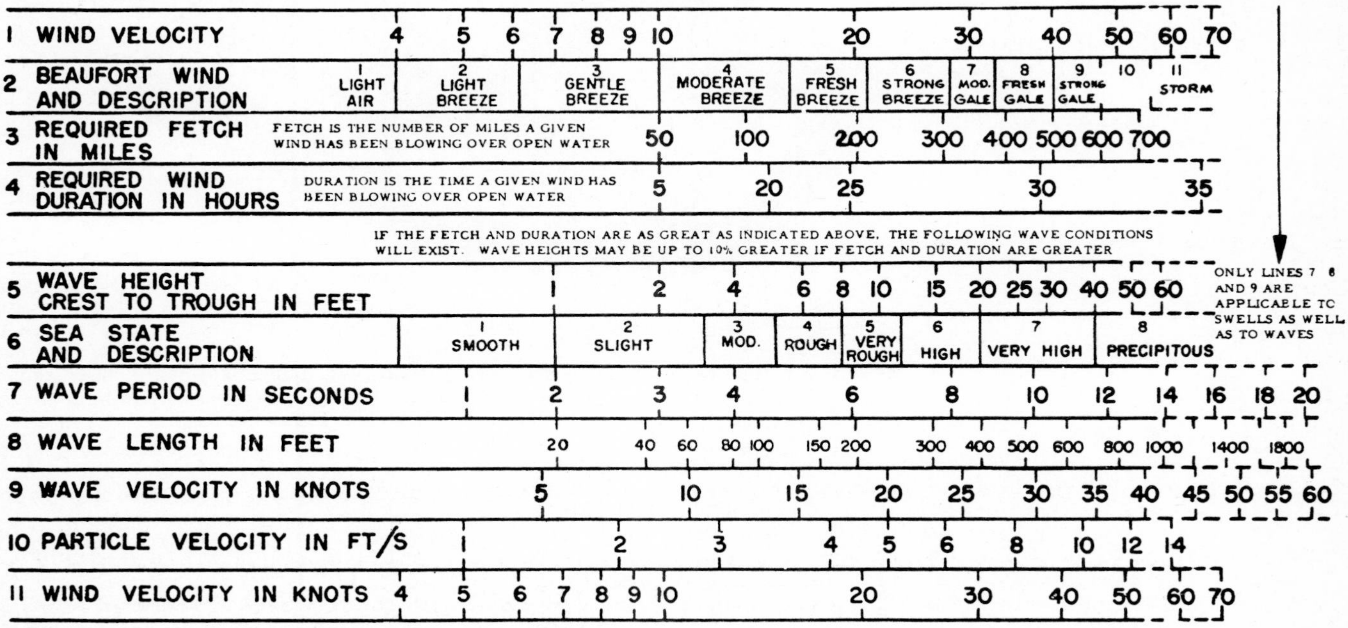

Chart of sea state conditions. Corresponding values lie on a vertical line

invented by Dr Daniel Savitsky of the Davidson Laboratory.

sea loiter aircraft. Aircraft capable of loitering on or under the sea for extended periods of time are currently being investigated by the US Navy which foresees a significant operational potential for this type of machine. Several kinds of operation do not require altitude while loitering and it is these for which the sea loiter aircraft is felt to be suitable. Applications would include anti-submarine warfare, command, communications and control and strategic missile carrier.

seal. See **cushion seal.**

sea state. A scale of sea conditions classified from state 1, smooth, to state 8, precipitous, according to the wind duration, fetch and velocity, also wave length, period and velocity.

semi-submerged propeller. A concept for the installation of a partially submerged, super-cavitating propeller on ship-size air cushion vehicles, driven through the sidewall transom. The advantages of this type of installation include considerable drag reduction due to the absence of inclined shafts and their supporting structures, and possibly the elimination of propeller erosion as a result of appendage cavity impingement.

service speed. Cruising speed obtained by an average crew in an average craft on a given route.

set down. To lower an air cushion vehicle onto its landing pads.

sidewall vessel. An ACV with its cushion air contained between immersed sidewalls or skegs and transverse air curtains or skirts fore and aft. Stability is provided by the buoyancy of the sidewalls and their planing forces.

significant wave height. Sea waves are composed of different frequencies and have different wave heights (energy spectrum). A wave with the leading frequency of this spectrum and energy content is called the significant wave. It is from this wave that the significant wave height is measured.

single shaft gas-turbine. A gas-turbine with a compressor and power turbine on a common shaft.

Single shaft gas turbine

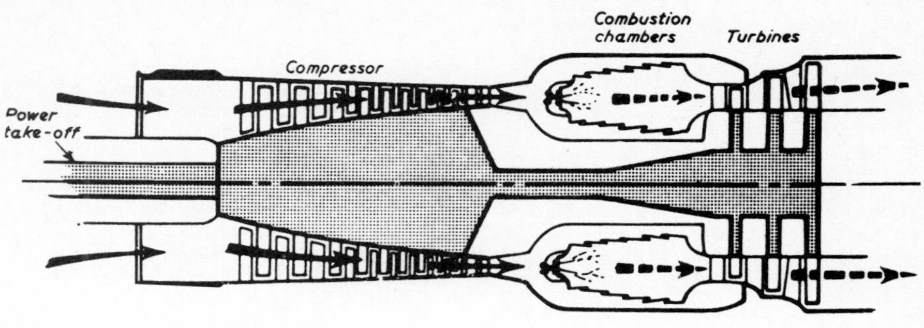

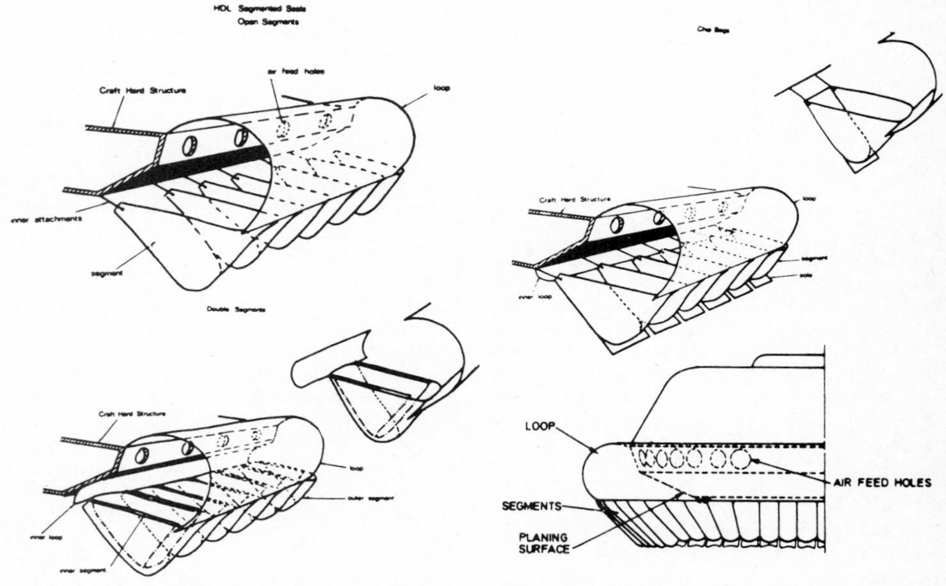

Segmented skirt developed by Hovercraft Development Ltd and employed on the HD.2. The separate segments occupy the full depth of the cushion between the hard structure and the supporting surface

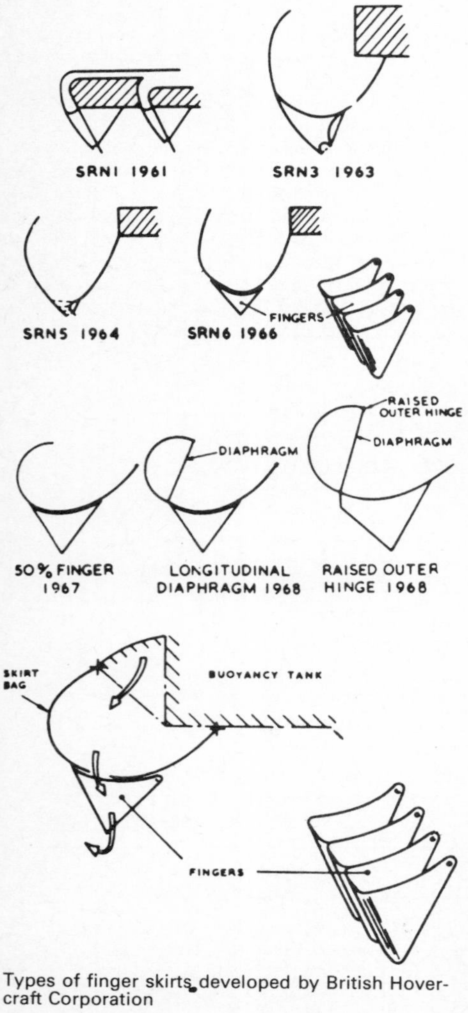

Types of finger skirts developed by British Hovercraft Corporation

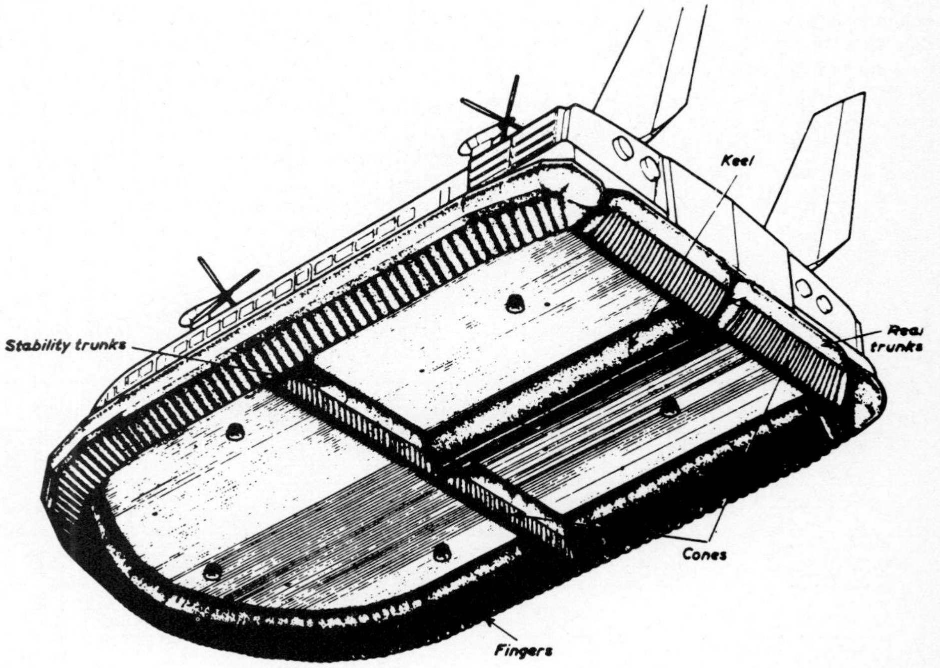

Underside of the SR.N4 showing stability skirts

skirt. Flexible fabric extension hung between an ACV's metal structure and the surface to give increased obstacle and overwave clearance capability for a small air gap clearance and therefore reduced power requirement. The skirt deflects when encountering waves or solid obstacles, then returns to its normal position, the air gap being increased only momentarily. On peripheral jet ACVs the skirt is a flexible extension of the peripheral jet nozzle with inner and outer skins hung from the inner and outer edges of the air duct and linked together by chain ties or diaphragms so that they form the correct nozzle profile at the hemline.

skirt, bag. Simple skirt design consisting of an inflated bag. Sometimes used as transverse and longitudinal stability skirts.

skirt, finger. Skirt system designed by British Hovercraft Corporation, consisting of a fringe of conically shaped nozzles attached to the base of a bag or loop skirt. Each nozzle or finger fits around an air exit hole and channels cushion air inwards towards the bottom centre of the craft.

skirt, segmented. Conceived by Hovercraft Development Ltd's Technical Group, this skirt system is employed on the HD.2, Vosper Thornycroft VT1, VT2 and many new craft either under design or construction. It is also being employed for industrial applications, including hoverpallets and hovertrailers.

The flexible segments are located around the craft periphery, each being attached to the lower edge of a sheet of light flexible material, which inflates to an arc shape, and also to the craft hard structure.

The system enables the craft to clear high waves and obstacles as the segments occupy a substantial part of the full cushion depth. No stability skirts or other forms of compartmentation are necessary. A smooth ride is provided as the skirt has good response due to low inertia.

The cushion area can be the same as the craft hard structure plan area. The skirt inner attachment points can be reached without jacking the craft up from its off-cushion position, simplifying maintenance.

skirt shifting. A control system in which movement of the centre of area of the cushion is achieved by shifting the skirt along one side, which has the effect of tilting the craft. Pitch and roll trim can be adjusted by this method.

split foil. A main foil system with the foil area divided into two, either to facilitate retraction, or to permit the location of the control surfaces well outboard, where foil control and large roll correcting moments can be applied for small changes in lift.

stability curtain. Transverse or longitudinal air curtains dividing an air cushion in order to restrict the cross flow of air within the cushion and increase pitch and roll stability.

stability skirt. A transverse or longitudinal skirt dividing an air cushion so as to restrict cross flow within the cushion and increase pitch or roll stability.

strake. (a) a permanent band of rubber or other hard wearing material along the sides of a craft to protect the structure from chafing against quays, piers and craft alongside. (b) lengths of material fitted externally to a flexible skirt and used to channel air downwards to reduce water drag.

submerged foil system. A foil system employing totally submerged lifting surfaces. The depth of submergence is controlled by mechanical, electronic or pneumatic systems which alter the angle of incidence of the foils or flaps attached to them to provide stability and control. See **foil systems.**

supercavitating foil. A general classification given to foils designed to operate efficiently at high speeds while fully cavitated. Since at very high speeds foils cannot avoid cavitation, sections are being designed which induce the onset of cavitation from the leading edge and cause the cavities to proceed downstream and beyond the trailing edge before collapsing. Lift and drag of these foils is determined by the shape of the leading edge and undersurface.

surf. The crests of waves that break in shallow water on a foreshore.

surface effect ship. Term implying a large ship-size ACV. Generally applied in the United States and United Kingdom to large sidewall craft.

The various surface effect ship concepts are illustrated. For further definitions see **air cushion vehicles.**

surface piercing acv A craft with rigid sidewalls that penetrate the water surface. The air cushion is contained laterally by the sidewalls and at the bow and stern by flexible seals. See **sidewall air cushion vehicles** or **surface effect ships**.

surf zone. Area from the outer waves breaking on the shore to the limit of their uprush on a beach.

TECHEVAL US Navy. Technical evaluation.

TLACV. Track-laying air cushion vehicle. Air cushion vehicle employing looped caterpillar-like tracks for propulsion. The air cushion and its seals may be located between the flexible tracks, as in the case of the Soviet MVP-3 series, or it can take the form of a broad belt or track that loops round the complete air cushion. The latter approach is being developed by the Ashby Institute, Belfast.

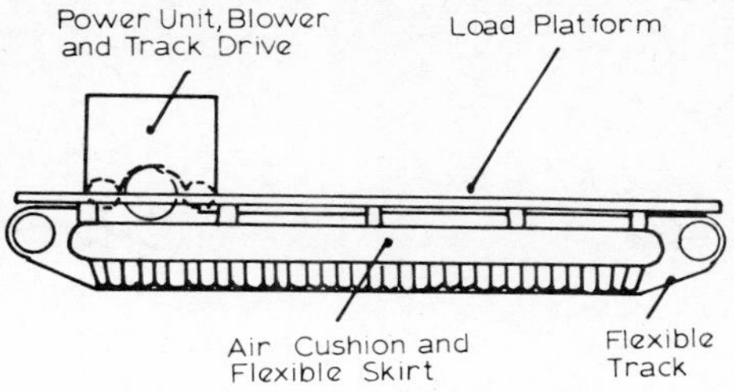

Track laying air cushion vehicle operating on a broad track that loops around the air cushion. This approach is being developed at the Ashby Institute, Belfast

TLRV. Tracked Levitated Research Vehicle.

take-off speed. Speed at which the hull of a hydrofoil craft is raised clear of the water, dynamic foil lift taking over from static displacement or planing of the hull proper.

tandem foils. Foil system in which the area of the forward foils is approximately equal to that of the aft foils, balancing the loading between them.

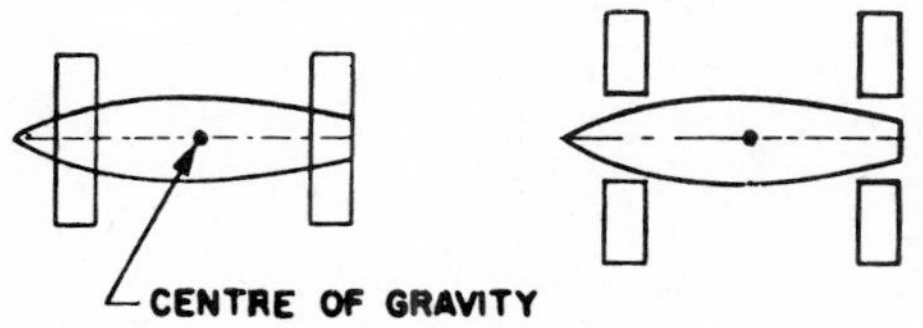

Tandem foil system. The foil areas can be "split" into two to facilitate retraction

terramechanics. Study of the general relationship between the performance of an off-road vehicle and its physical environment.

thickness-chord ratio. Maximum thickness of a foil section in relation to its chord.

thruster. Controlled aperture through which air or water can be expelled to assist control at low speeds.

Tietjens-type foil. Named after Professor Tietjens, this system was based on a forward swept (surface piercing) main foil located almost amidships and slightly ahead of the centre of gravity. It was intended that the pronounced sweep of the V foils would result in an increasing area of the foil further forward coming into use to increase the bow up trim of the craft when lift was lost. The considerable length of unsupported hull ahead of the centre of gravity meant the craft was constantly in danger of "digging in" in bad seas and it was highly sensitive to loading arrangements.

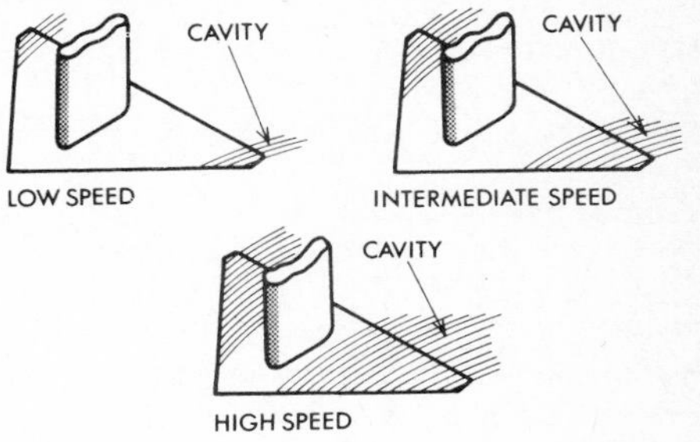

Transit foil operation

transcavitating foil. Thin section foil designed for smooth transition from fully wetted to supercavitating flow. By loading the tip more highly than the root, cavitation is first induced at the foil's tip, then extends spanwise over the foil to the roots as speed increases.

transisting foil. See **transcavitating foil.**

transit foil. See **transcavitating foil.**

transom. The last transverse frame of a ship's structure forming the stern board.

transverse framing. Steel frames running athwartships, from side to side, instead of in a fore and aft direction.

trapped air cushion vehicle. A concept for a skirt-type surface effect ship with 20ft skirts

SURFACE EFFECT SHIP CONFIGURATIONS

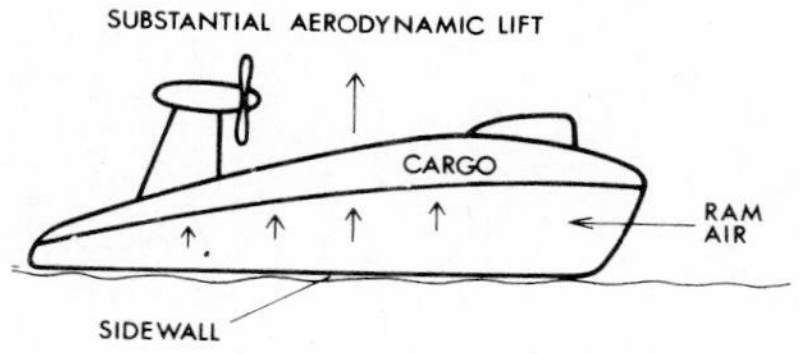

Ram wing SES

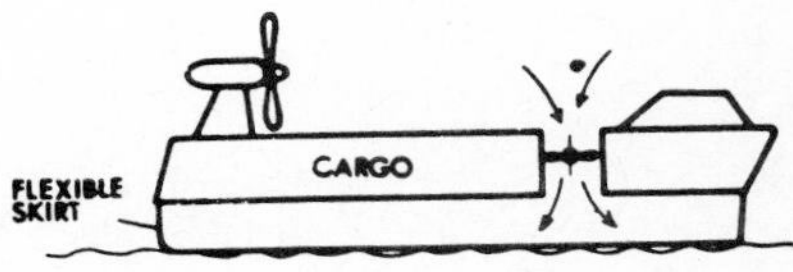

Air-propelled amphibious SES

Wing-in-ground-effect

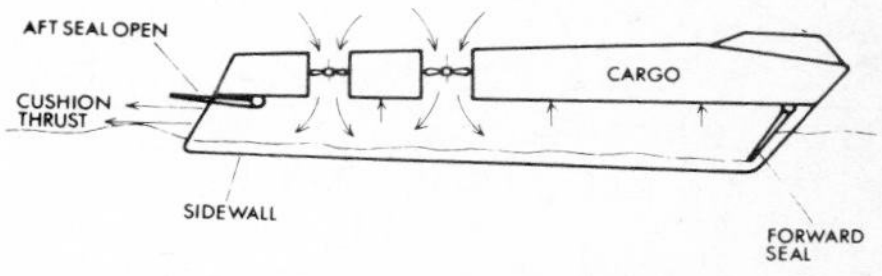

Airjet SES, propelled by cushion thrust

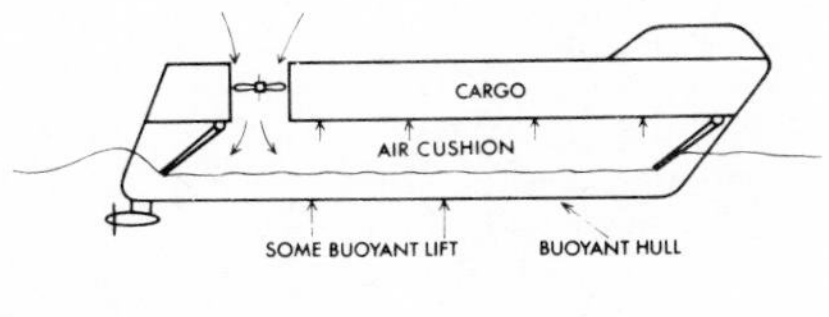

Aircat SES with wide buoyant hulls

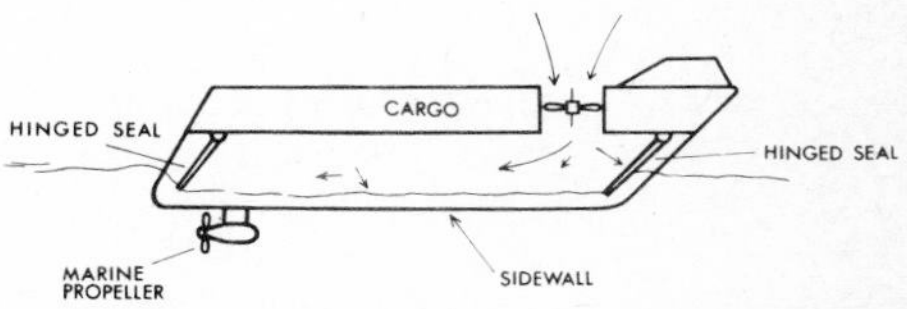

Sidewall SES. Also known as a Captured Air Bubble or CAB Type

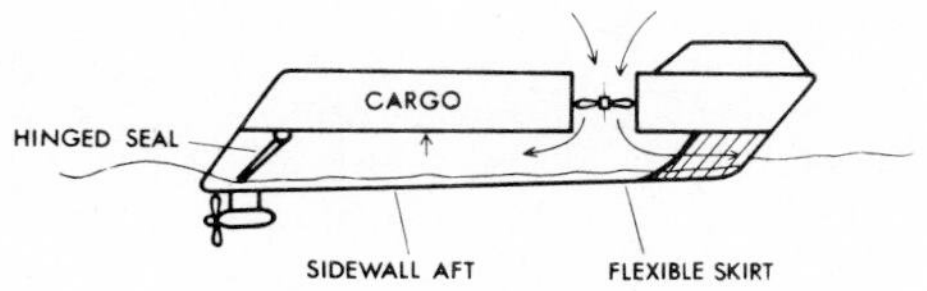

Hybrid SES with rigid sidewalls and bow skirt

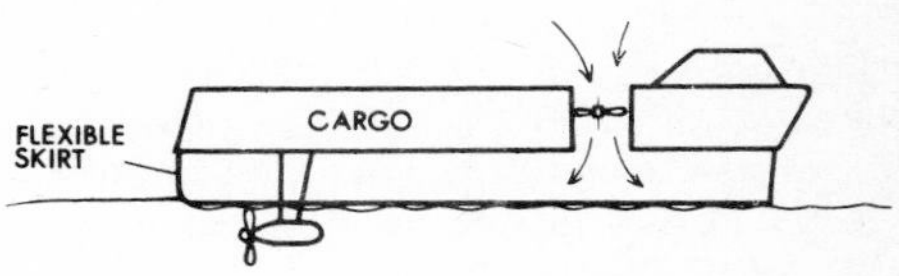

Water propelled, semi-amphibious SES

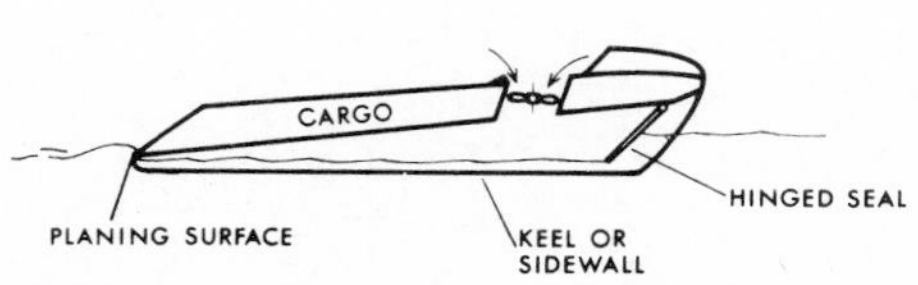

Air lubricated hull or hydrokeel SES

separated from the water surface by a thin film of air lubrication.

trim. Difference between drafts forward and aft in a displacement vessel and by extension of the general idea. ACV and hydrofoil hull attitude relative to the line of flight.

tunnel hull. Racing boat with tunnel-shaped hull designed to employ the advantages of aerodynamic lift as in a ram-wing or channel-flow wing ACV.

turnround time. Time from doors open to doors closed between trips.

utilisation. Operating hours timed from doors closed to doors open, including manoeuvring time.

utilisation, annual. Annual total of utilisation time.

variable-pitch propeller. A propeller with blades which can be rotated about their longitudinal axes to provide forward or reverse thrust.

ventilation. See **air entry**.

water wall ACV. A craft employing a curtain of water to retain its air cushion instead of an air curtain.

waterjet propulsion. A term now applied to a propulsion system devised as an alternative to supercavitating propellers for propelling high speed ship systems. Turbines drive pumps located in the hull, and water is pumped through high velocity jets above the water line and directed astern. The system weighs less than a comparable supercavitating propeller system and for craft with normal operating speeds above 45 knots it is thought to be competitive on an annual cost basis. First high speed applications include the Soviet Burevestnik and Chaika hydrofoils, the Aerojet-General SES-100A testcraft and two products of the Boeing Company—the PGH-2 hydrofoil gunboat and the NATO PHM Fast Patrol Ship Guided Missile.

Waterjets are also being employed for propulsion at relatively low speeds. In the Soviet Union the Zarya shallow-draught waterbus (24 knots) and the Gorkovchanin sidewall ACV are propelled by waterjets. In the USA the PGH-1 and PGH-2 hydrofoils use waterjets for hullborne propulsion. The jet can be turned easily to give side propulsion to facilitate docking which is not so easy for a normal propeller.

wave height. The vertical distance from wave trough to crest or twice the wave amplitude.

wave length. The horizontal distance between adjacent wave crests.

wave pumping. The alternating increase and decrease of the volume of pressurised air in an ACV's cushion, caused by the passage of waves or other objects through the cushion.

wave velocity. Speed at which a wave form travels along the sea surface. (The water itself remaining without forward movement).

weights. The subject of weights involves definition of format, nomenclature, and units. There are no generally accepted standards with respect to ACV and SES weights, except that small ACVs tend to follow aircraft practice and large types follow ship practice. The hydrofoil concepts are ship orientated. A consistently used format aids in evaluating the concept and permits usage on, or direct comparison with other designs. Format 1, below is according to US Naval practice and is suitable for all sizes of ACVs, SESs, and hydrofoils. The actual terminology used for the totals is optional, so that the nomenclature can be consistent with the size of the vessel. In presenting results, the units (short tons, long tons, metric tons, pounds, etc) should be clearly indicated.

Format 2 is used by the Hovercraft industry in the United Kingdom. This emphasises equipment options, and by breaking down the expendable or useful load, the payload/range performance can be readily determined. It is also useful in defining first costs and operating costs.

winged hull. Alternative name given by the late Dr Alexander M Lippisch to his range of aerodynamic ram-wing machines. See also **Aerofoil boat.**

wing-in-ground-effect. See **air cushion vehicle.** An aerodynamic-type air cushion vehicle which depends upon forward speed in order to develop lift. At speed lifting forces are generated both by the wing and a dynamic cushion of air built up beneath the vehicle and its supporting surface.

yaw angle. Rotation or oscillation of a craft about a vertical axis.

yaw-port. See **puff port.**

Z-drive. A drive system normally employed on hydrofoils to transmit power from the engine in the hull to the screw. Power is transmitted through a horizontal shaft leading to a bevel gear over the stern, then via a vertical shaft and a second bevel gear to a horizontal propeller shaft, thus forming a propeller "Z" shape.

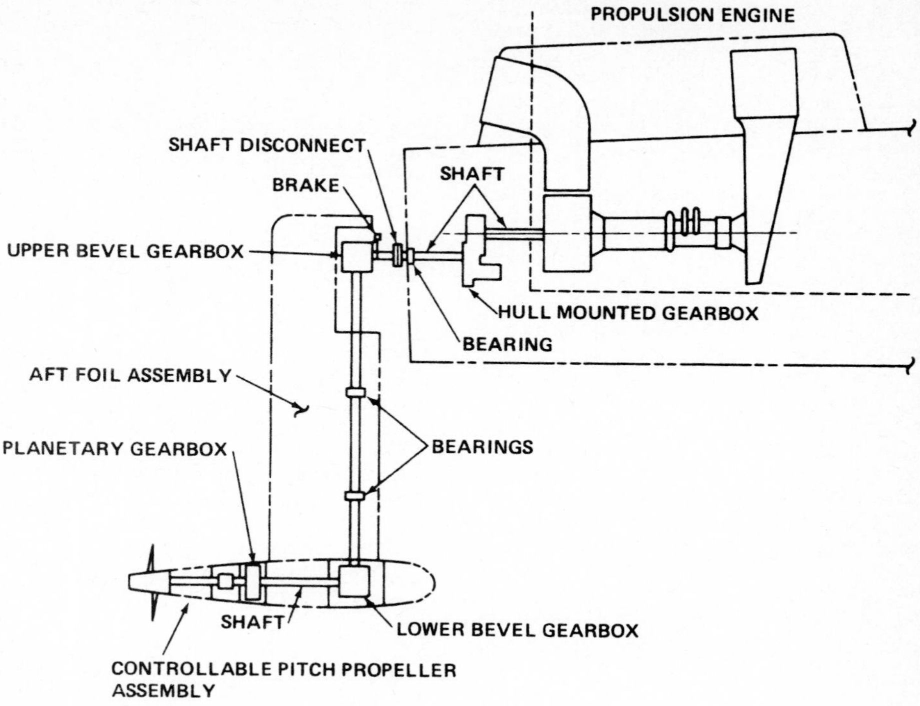

Z-drive system on the Grumman Flagstaff II

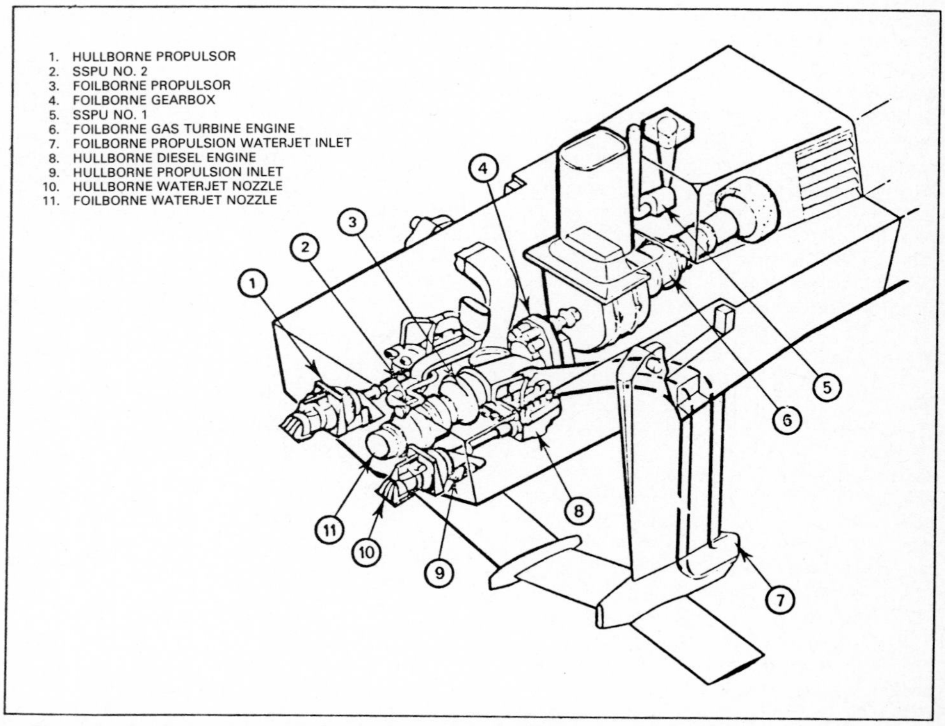

Waterjet propulsion system employed on the Boeing/NATO PHM missile-armed fast patrol craft in service with the US Navy

HOVERCRAFT WEIGHT TERMS

Format 1

Group	*Typical Items*
1 Hull (or structure)	Basic structure, planting, frames, stringers, scantlings, decks, foundations, fittings, superstructure, doors and closures.
2 Propulsion	Engines, turbines, propellers, fans, gearboxes, shafting, drive systems, associated controls, nuclear plant, associated fluids.
3 Electrical	Power generation, switching, lighting, load canters, panels, cable.
4 Communication and Control	Communications (internal, external) and navigation equipment, military electronics, computers, displays (note ship controls are in Group 5).
5 Auxiliary Systems	Fuel, heating, ventilation, fresh water, ship controls, rudder, cushion seal (flexible or articulated), plumbing, oil, fire extinguishing, drainage, ballast, mooring, anchoring, hydrofoils distilling plant.
6 Outfit and Furnishings	Hull fittings, marine hardware, ladders, furnishings, boats, rafts, preservers, stowages, lockers, painting, deck covering, hull insulation, commissary equipment, radiation shielding (other than at reactor area).
7 Armament	Weapons, mounts, ammunition stowage, handling systems, special plating.
Total: Light Ship or Light Displacement or Empty Weight	(sum of the above items).
Variable Load or Useful Load	Operating personnel and effects, cargo, freight, fuel, passengers, baggage, water, ammunition, aircraft, stores, troops, provisions.
Full Load Displacement or Load Displacement or Gross Weight or All Up Weight	(sum of empty weight and useful load).

Format 2

Standard Bara Weight

(1) Weight of structure, power plants & systems considered to be integral parts of the standard craft
(2) Oil (turbine engines only)
(3) Full hydraulic/pneumatic/cooling etc systems
(4) Essential standard equipment common to all customer requirements
(5) Unusable fuel
(6) Other unconsumable liquids

Customer Equipment Weight

(1) Flight crew seats
(2) Flight crew emergency equipment
(3) Soundproofing, trim, partitions, floor covering etc in payload areas
(4) Passenger seats, tables, lockers and other furnishings
(5) Heating, ventilating and air conditioning
(6) Toilet and washing facilities
(7) Galley facilities
(8) Domestic water supply (inc toilet)
(9) Fire precautions in payload areas
(10) Marine equipment
(11) Life rafts and containers
(12) Life jackets and stowages
(13) Emergency equipment (axes, first aid etc)
(14) Radio
(15) Radar
(16) Navaids
(17) Intercommunication and internal broadcasting
(18) Racking (for 14-17)
(19) Weapon and system installations
(20) Signalling equipment, distress flares etc
(21) Environmental equipment
(22) Long range tankage and system

Basic Weight

Variable Load

(1) Crew
(2) Crew's baggage and equipment
(3) Purser's equipment
(4) Role equipment
(5) Non-consumable liquid ballast

Operating Weight

Expendable Load (other than usable fuel)

(1) Oil (piston engines only)
(2) Domestic, humidifying, windscreen water
(3) Other liquid/gaseous consumables
(4) Ammunition, missiles, etc
(5) Food, drink, bonded stores, etc
(6) Boarding parties and their equipment

Payload

(1) Passengers
(2) Vehicles
(3) Freight

Zero Fuel Weight

Usable Fuel

(1) Main fuel
(2) Reserve fuel
(3) Long range fuel

All-up Weight

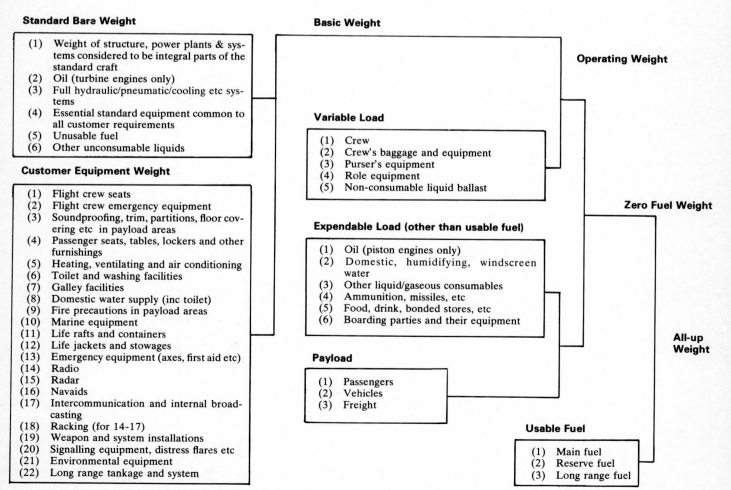

BIBLIOGRAPHY

AIR CUSHION VEHICLES

ACVs IN NORTH AMERICA

ACV Icing Problems, J R Stallabras and T R Ringer (National Research Council). Seventh Canadian Symposium on Air Cushion Technology, June 1973.

ACV potential in New York, C Leedham (New York City Commissioner for Marine and Aviation). *Hoverfoil News,* Vol 5 No 6, 14 March 1974.

Air Cushion Technology: the Prospects for Canadian Industry, Dr P A Sullivan (Institute for Aerospace Studies, University of Toronto). Sixth CASI Symposium on Air Cushion Technology, Ontario, June 1972.

Air-Cushion Vehicles, Operational use in the Arctic, G Ives. *Petroleum Eng,* Vol 45 No 1, January 1974.

Air Cushion Vehicles and Soil Erosion, P Abeels. International Society for Terrain-Vehicle Systems 5th International Conference, Detroit, Houghton, Michigan, June 1975.

Arctic Development Using Very Large ACVs, J L Anderson (NASA Lewis Laboratories). Seventh Canadian Symposium on Air Cushion Technology, June 1973.

Arctic Operational Experience with SR.N6 engaged in Hydrographic Survey and Cushioncraft CC-7, L R Colby and G M Yeaton (Polar Continental Shelf Project, DEMR). Fourth Canadian Symposium on Air Cushion Technology, 1970. publ Canadian Aeronautics and Space Institute.

Arctic Transportation, Operational and Environmental Evaluation of an ACV in Northern Alaska, G Abele and J Brown (US Army Cold Region Research and Engineering Laboratory). ASME Conference, Mexico City, September 1976. Paper 76-Pet-41 ASME. (Also in *Transactions of Journal of Pressure Vessels Technology,* Vol 99, February 1977, pp. 176-182).

The Arctic Surface Effect Vehicle Program, J V Kordenbrock and C W Harry. 59th Annual Meeting of American Society of Naval Engineers, Washington DC, May 1976.

Continuing Advances with Air Cushion Icebreaking, M A Ball, (Transport Canada). Tenth CASI Symposium on Air Cushion Technology, October 1976.

Dynamic Performance of an Air-Cushion Vehicle in a Marine Environment, J A Fein, A H Magnuson and D D Moran (Naval Ship Research and Development Center, Bethesda, Maryland), AIAA/SNAME Advanced Marine Vehicle Conference, San Diego, California, February 1974.

Development of the Canadian Air-Cushion Vehicle Industry, R G Wade (Ministry of Transport, Ottawa). AIAA/SNAME Advanced Marine Vehicle Conference, San Diego, California, 25-28 February 1974.

Effects of Hovercraft Operation on Organic Terrain in the Arctic, Gunars Abele (US Army Cold Regions Research and Engineering Laboratory). Hovering Craft, Hydrofoil and Advanced Transit Systems Conference, Brighton, May 1974.

Environmental Effects of ACV and other Off-Road Vehicle Operations on Tundra, G Abele and W E Rickard (US Army Cold Region Research and Engineering Laboratory). Seventh Canadian Symposium on Air Cushion Technology, June 1973.

Heavy Goods Transport by Air-Cushion Vehicles. C A R Eastman. *The Society of Engineers Journal* (UK) Vol LXIV, Nos 2 and 3, April/June and July/September 1973.

High Speed Method of Air Cushion Icebreaking, R W Robertson (Transport Canada). Tenth CASI Symposium on Air Cushion Technology, October 1976.

Hovercraft Operations in the Arctic, the Activities of Voyageur 003 Between Hay River, Northwest Territories, Canada and Umiat, Alaska, N Ray Sumner Jr (Science Applications, Inc), 1651 Old Meadow Road, McLean, Virginia 22101, USA. November 1974.

Icebreaking with Air-Cushion Technology, Report National Research Council of Canada, NRC Associate Committee on Air-Cushion Technology, 1975.

Improvements in Ice-breaking by the use of Air Cushion Technology, R G Wade, R Y Edwards and J K Kim. Eastern Canada Section of SNAME Symposium Ice Tech 75, Montreal, April 1975.

Marine Transportation and Air-Cushion Vehicles North of 60. L R Montpetit. *Canadian Min & Met Bulletin* 68, pp 78-81, January 1975.

Model Tests of an Arctic Surface Effect Vehicle over Model Ice, E J Lecourt, T Kotras and J Kordenbrock. Eastern Canadian Section of SNAME Ice Tech 75 Symposium, Montreal, April 1975.

NCTL's Voyageur Experience, B Meade (Northern Transportation Co). Seventh Canadian Symposium on Air Cushion Technology, June 1973.

Operational Evaluation of the SK-5 in Alaska, R A Liston and B Hanamoto (US Army Cold Region Research and Engineering Laboratory). Seventh Canadian Symposium on Air Cushion Technology, June 1973.

Requirements for the La Crete Ferry—An ACV Proposal, A R Rogers (Alberta Transportation). Tenth CASI Symposium on Air Cushion Technology, October 1976.

Small Air Cushion Vehicle Operation on Floating Ice under Winter Condition, R J Weaver and R O Romseier (Dept of the Environment). Seventh Canadian Symposium on Air Cushion Technology. June 1973.

AIR CUSHION LANDING SYSTEMS

ACLS for a Commercial Transport, T D Earl (Bell Aerospace Textron). Society of Automotive Engineers Meeting, 30 April-2 May 1974.

Air-Cushion Landing Systems Development on a Buffalo Aircraft, C J Austin (The De Havilland Aircraft Co of Canada Ltd). CASI Flight Test Symposium, Edmonton, Alberta, March 1975.

The Development and Flight Testing of the XC-8A Air Cushion Landing Systems, D J Rerez (US Air Force Wright Patterson Base). SAE Aerospace Engineering & Manufacturing Mtg, November 29-December 2, 1976. Paper 760920.

Elastically Retracting ACLS Trunks, T D Earl (Bell Aerospace Textron). *Canadian Aeronautics and Space Journal,* Vol 21 No 5, pp 169-173, May 1975.

Further Developments in Surface Effect Take-Off and Landing System Concepts, A E Johnson, F W Wilson and W B Maguire (NSRDC). Sixth CASI Symposium on Air Cushion Technology, Ontario, June 1972.

Landing on a Cushion of Air, J H Brahney (Wright Patterson Air Force Base). *Astronautics & Aeronautics,* pp 58-61, February 1976.

Tests on the Air Cushion Landing System Buffalo Aircraft, Captain T Clapp (US Air Force). Tenth CASI Symposium on Air Cushion Technology, October 1976.

The Potential of an Air Cushion Landing Gear in Civil Air Transport, T D Earl (Bell Aerosystems Co). Second Canadian Symposium on Air Cushion Technology, 1968. publ Canadian Aeronautics and Space Institute.

AIR CUSHION LOAD CARRIERS

A 1,000-ton River Hovercraft, R A Shaw, V E Barker and D M Waters (Hoverprojects Ltd). Hovering Craft, Hydrofoil and Advanced Transit Systems Conference, Brighton, May 1974.

Air and Water Cushion Lift Systems, G Parkes (Hoverlift Systems Ltd). Tenth CASI Symposium on Air Cushion Technology, October 1976.

Aircraft Recovery, G M Parkes (Hovertrailers International Ltd). Hovering Craft, Hydrofoil and Advanced Transit Systems Conference, Brighton, May 1974.

Air Cushion Towed Raft Evaluation Project—Current Trials, J E Laframboise (Transportation Development Agency). Seventh Canadian Symposium on Air Cushion Technology, June 1973.

An Amphibious Hover Platform for Civil Engineering uses, D G W Turner (Mackace Ltd). Hovering Craft, Hydrofoil and Advanced Transit Systems Conference, Brighton, May 1974.

A Track Laying Air-Cushion Vehicle. R Wingate Hill (NSW Dept of Agriculture, Agricultural Engineering Centre, Glenfield, NSW, Australia). *Journal of Terramechanics,* Vol 12 No 3/4, 1975, pp 201-216.

Development of a Track Laying Air Cushion Vehicle, J R Goulburn and R B Steven (University of Belfast). Hovering Craft, Hydrofoil and Advanced Transit Systems Conference, Brighton, May 1974.

Movement of Drill Rigs Using an Air Cushion Platform, R L Wheeler (British Hovercraft Corporation). Fourth Canadian Symposium on Air Cushion Technology, June 1970. publ Canadian Aeronautics and Space Institute.

Movement of Heavy Loads, L A Hopkins (Air Cushion Equipment Ltd). Seventh Canadian Symposium on Air Cushion Technology, June 1973.

On the Applications of Air Cushion Technology to Off-Road Transport, Dr J Y Wong (Carleton University). Sixth CASI Symposium on Air Cushion Technology, Ontario, June 1972.

River Crossing Problems Posed by the Mackenzie Highway and a Possible Solution, R G Wade (Canadian Ministry of Transport). Seventh Canadian Symposium on Air Cushion Technology, June 1973.

The Role of the Non-Self Propelled Air Cushion Vehicle, L A Hopkins (Air Cushion Equipment Ltd). Sixth CASI Symposium on Air Cushion Technology, Ontario, June 1972.

Towed Air Cushion Rafts, J Doherty, G Morton and C R Silversides (National Research Council of Canada). NRC Associate Committee on Air-Cushion Technology, Ottawa, Canada, 1975.

AIR LUBRICATED HULLS

The Application of the Air Cushion Principle to Very Large Vessels—A Case for Further Research, J W Grundy, Naval Architect. Hovering Craft, Hydrofoil and Advanced Transit Systems Conference, Brighton, May 1974.

COMMERCIAL OPERATION

A Successful Operation, E Jones (Hoverlloyd Ltd). Second International Hovering Craft and Hydrofoil Conference, Amsterdam, May 1976.

Air Cushion Vehicles in the Gulf Offshore Oil Industry: A Feasibility Study, J M Pruett (Louisiana State University, Baton Rouge). Final Report on Sea Grant Project (NOAA Contract 04-3-158-19), December 1973.

Air Cushion Vehicles in the Search and Rescue Role, Commander B W Mead (Canadian Coast Guard). Third Canadian Symposium on Air Cushion Technology, June 1969. publ Canadian Aeronautics and Space Institute.

Air Cushion Vehicles in Support of the Petroleum Industry, Wilfred J Eggington and Donald J Iddins (Aerojet-General Corporation). American Petroleum Institute Meeting, Shreveport, Louisiana, March 1969.

Commercial Operation of Hovercraft, J Lefeaux (BR Seaspeed). Second International Hovering Craft and Hydrofoil Conference, Amsterdam, May 1976.

ACV PROJECTS

ACV Technology Programs at Aerojet-General, R W Muir (Aerojet-General Corporation). Third Canadian Symposium on Air Cushion Technology, June 1969. publ Canadian Aeronautics and Space Institute.

Control of a Single Propeller Hovercraft, with Particular Reference to BH.7, R L Wheeler (British Hovercraft Corporation Ltd). Fourth Canadian Symposium on Air Cushion Technology, June 1970. publ Canadian Aeronautics and Space Institute.

Development of Surface Effect Technology in the US Industry, John B Chaplin (Bell Aerospace Company). AIAA/SNAME/USN Advanced Marine Vehicles Meeting, Annapolis, Maryland, July 1972.

Future Hovercraft, J M George (British Hovercraft Corporation). TIMG Presentation, London 1977.

New Advanced Design ACVs, Jean Bertin (Bertin et Cie). Third Canadian Symposium on Air Cushion Technology, June 1969. publ Canadian Aeronautics and Space Institute.

Stretching the Hovermarine HM.2, A J English (Hovermarine Transport Ltd). *Hovering Craft and Hydrofoil,* Vol. 16 No 5, February 1977.

Operational Experience on VT1s, R D Hunt (Hovercraft Division, Vosper Thornycroft Ltd). Institute of Production Engineers, Second International Hovercraft Conference, April 1971.

Shore-to-Shore Lightering with the Voyageur, R W Helm (Bell Aerospace Canada Textron). Tenth CASI Symposium on Air Cushion Technology, October 1976.

The 260-tons French Amphibious Hovercraft 'Naviplane N.500', P F Guienne (SEDAM). AIAA/SNAME Advanced Marine Vehicles Conference, San Diego, April 1978.

The VT.2 100-ton Amphibious Hovercraft, A Bingham (Vosper Thornycroft Ltd). Second International Hovering Craft and Hydrofoil Conference, Amsterdam, May 1976.

Voyageur Trials and Operating Experience, T F Melhuish (Bell Aerospace Canada). Seventh Canadian Symposium on Air Cushion Technology, June 1973.

1976—A Significant Year for UK Hovercraft, J E Rapson (Hovercraft Development Ltd). Tenth CASI Symposium on Air Cushion Technology, October 1976.

DESIGN

A Comparison of Some Features of High-Speed Marine Craft, A Silverleaf and F G R Cook (National Physical Laboratory). Royal Institution of Naval Architects, March 1969.

A Linearised Potential Flow Theory for the Motions of Air-Cushion Vehicles in a Seaway, T K S Murthy (Portsmouth Polytechnic). Ninth Symposium on Naval Hydrodynamics, Paris, August 1972.

A method for the preliminary sizing of Lift Fan Systems, Applicable to Large Hovercraft, W B Wilson (Webb Institute of Naval Architecture, Glen Cove, New York). Naval Ship Engineering Center of the US Navy, Propulsion Systems Analysis Branch, Technical Report 6144E-75-126, February 1975.

A Theoretical Note on the Lift Distribution of a Non-Planar Ground Effect Wing, T Kida and Y Miyai (University of Osaka, Japan). *The Aeronautical Quarterly,* Vol 24, August 1973. Part 3.

Development of the Axial-flow Surface Effect Vehicle, A M Jackes (AirSeamobile Co, Santa Ana, California). Advanced Marine Vehicle Meeting, AIAA/SNAME/USN, Annapolis, Maryland, July 1972.

FANS

Aerodynamic Challenges for the Faster Interface Vehicles, P R Shipps (Rohr Corporation). Sixth CASI Symposium on Air Cushion Technology, Ontario, June 1972.

The Design of a Ram Wing Vehicle for high speed ground Transportation, E A Tan (E I Dupont Co), W P Goss and D E Cromack (University of Massachusetts). International Conference on High Speed Ground Transportation, Arizona State University, January 1975.

The Design, Fabrication and Initial Trials of a Light Amphibious Arctic Transporter, J H Kennedy and A M Garner, Jr (Transportation Technology Inc). Fourth Canadian Symposium on Air Cushion Technology, 1970. publ Canadian Aeronautics and Space Institute.

Lateral Stability of a Dynamic Ram Air Cushion Vehicle, P V Aidala (Transportation Systems Center, Cambridge, Massachusetts). DOT-TSC-FRA-74-6. FRA-ORD/D-75-6. PB-236-516/1WT, August 1974.

A Method for Generating Aerodynamic Sideforces on ACV Hulls, Dr R J Kind (Carleton University). Sixth CASI Symposium on Air Cushion Technology, Ontario, June 1972.

On the Determination of the Hydrodynamic Performance of Air-Cushion Vehicles, S D Prokhorov, V N Treshchevski and L D Volkov (Kryloff Research Institute, Leningrad). Ninth Symposium on Naval Hydrodynamics, Paris, August 1972.

On the Prediction of Acceleration Response of Air-Cushion Vehicles to Random Seaways and the Distortion Effects of Cushion Inherent in Scale Models, D R Lavis and R V Bartholomew (Aerojet-General Corporation). Advanced Marine Vehicle Meeting, AIAA/SNAME/USN, Annapolis, Maryland, July 1972.

Ram-Wing Surface Effect Boat, Capt R W Gallington (USAF, US Air Force Academy, Colorado). Advanced Marine Vehicle Meeting, AIAA/SNAME/USN, Annapolis, Maryland, July 1972.

Resultats d'Exploitation des Aéroglisseurs Marins "Naviplane", P F Guienne (Bertin et Cie). Seventh Canadian Symposium on Air Cushion Technology, June 1973.

Some Aspects of Optimum Design of Lift Fans, T G Csaky (NSRDC). Sixth CASI Symposium on Air Cushion Technology, Ontario, June 1972.

Some Design Aspects of Air Cushion Craft, Peter J Mantle. International Congress of Subsonic Aeronautics, New York Academy of Sciences, April 1967.

Some Design Aspects of an Integrated Lift/Propulsion System, D Jones (Jones, Kirwan and Associates). Sixth CASI Symposium on Air Cushion Technology, Ontario, June 1972.

Trade-Off Methodology for Evaluation of Design Alternatives of Air Cushion Vehicles, O Gokcek and J H Madden (Aerojet General Corporation). Sixth CASI Symposium on Air Cushion Technology, Ontario, June 1972.

Vortex Shedding from the Ram Wing Vehicle, Technical Progress Report, R Gallington, Air Force Acadamy, Colorado, January-July 1973. AD-767234. August 1973. Available N T I S

Design and Operation of Centrifugal, Axial-flow and Crossflow fans. Translated from German, Edited by R S Azad and D R Scott, Pergamon Press 1973.

EXTERNAL AERODYNAMICS

The External Aerodynamics of Hovercraft, Professor E J Andrews (College of Aeronautics, Cranfield). Royal Aeronautical Society Rotorcraft Section, April 1969.

INDUSTRIAL APPLICATIONS

Hoverpallets for Material Handling, A J I Poynder (British Hovercraft Corporation). Institution of Production Engineers, International Hovercraft Conference, April 1968.

Industrial Applications of Air Cushion Technology, P H Winter (Air Vehicle Developments Ltd). Third Canadian Symposium on Air Cushion Technology, June 1969. publ Canadian Aeronautics and Space Institute.

LIGHTWEIGHT ACVs

Amphibious Hovercraft: The Little Ones are growing up, M A Pinder (Pindair Ltd). *Hovering Craft and Hydrofoil,* Vol 14 No 9, pp 5-9, June 1975.

Control and Guidance of Light Amphibious Hovercraft up to a Gross Weight of 5,000lbs, R L Trillo (Robert Trillo Ltd). Seventh Canadian Symposium on Air Cushion Technology, June 1973.

Small Hovercraft Design, P H Winter (Air Vehicle Developments). Institution of Production Engineers (Southampton Section). International Hovercraft Conference, 1968.

Small Hovercraft Structure, A J English (Sealand Hovercraft Ltd). Hovering Craft, Hydrofoil and Advanced Transit Systems Conference, Brighton, May 1974.

The Evaluation of Light Hovercraft, B J Russell. *Hovering Craft and Hydrofoil,* Vol 17 No 4, pp 8-12, January 1978.

MILITARY APPLICATIONS and OPERATING EXPERIENCE

ACV Military Applications—Experience and Potential, J B Chaplin (Bell Aerosystems Company). Third Canadian Symposium on Air Cushion Technology, June 1969. publ Canadian Aeronautics and Space Institute.

Air Cushion Vehicles in a Logistical Role, Col H N Wood (Ret) (US Army Combat Development Command Transportation Agency). Fourth Canadian Symposium on Air Cushion Technology, 1970. publ Canadian Aeronautics and Space Institute.

BH.7 Mk 2—Experience during the first 2,000 hours of Operation, Cdr L G Scovell (Dept of Trade and Industry, UK). Seventh Canadian Symposium on Air Cushion Technology, June 1973.

Development of the SR.N6 Mk 5 Vehicle-carrying Hovercraft, Major M H Burton (Dept of Trade and Industry, UK). Seventh Canadian Symposium on Air Cushion Technology, June 1973.

Military Experience, Commander D F Robbins, RN (Interservice Hovercraft Unit). Institution of Production Engineers (Southampton Section). International Hovercraft Conference, April 1968.

Military Hovercraft, R Old (British Hovercraft Corporation Ltd). Second International Hovering Craft and Hydrofoil Conference, Amsterdam, May 1976.

A Review of British Army Hovercraft Activity 1967-72, Major G G Blakey (Royal Corps of Transport). Sixth CASI Symposium on Air Cushion Technology, Ontario, 1972.

SES-100 Test Program, C Raleigh (SESTF). AIAA/SNAME Conference, 1976. Paper 76-860.

Seakeeping Characteristics of the Amphibious Assault Landing Craft, A H Magnuson and R F Messal. AIAA/SNAME Conference, 1976. Paper 76-865.

Some Military Applications of Small Hovercraft, G W Shepherd (SAS Developments Ltd). Second International Hovering Craft and Hydrofoil Conference, Amsterdam, May 1976.

UK Military Hovercraft, Commander N T Bennett, AFC, RN (Interservice Hovercraft Unit). Institute of Production Engineers, Second International Hovercraft Conference, April 1971.

The Amphibious Hovercraft as a Warship, R L Wheeler (British Hovercraft Corporation). RINA Small Warship Symposium, London, March 1978.

The US Army LACV-30 Program, J Sargent (US AME R & D Command) and C Faulkner (Bell). AIAA/SNAME Conference 1976. Paper 76-866.

US Army ACV Operations, Major D G Moore (US Army Air Cushion Vehicle Unit). Third Canadian Symposium on Air Cushion Technology, June 1969. publ Canadian Aeronautics and Space Institute.

The US Navy Surface Effect Ship Acquisition Project, E H Handler. *Hovering Craft and Hydrofoil,* Vol 17 No 3, pp 4-10, December 1977.

The US Navy 3000-LT Surface Effect Ship Programme, G D McGhee (Rohr Marine Inc). 85th Meeting of SNAME, New York, November 1977.

LEGISLATION and REGULATIONS

The Air Registration Board and Hovercraft, S Gardner (Air Registration Board). Second Canadian Symposium on Air Cushion Technology, June 1968. publ Canadian Aeronautics and Space Institute.

Canadian Air-Cushion Vehicle Legislation and Regulation, J Doherty (Ministry of Transport Canada). Ninth Canadian Symposium on Air Cushion Technology, Ottawa, October 1975.

Operating Legislation for ACVs, Captain J Doherty (Department of Transport). Second Canadian Symposium on Air Cushion Technology, June 1968. publ Canadian Aeronautics and Space Institute.

United States Requirements for Commercial Surface Effect Ships, W A Cleary Jr and Lt D H Whitten (US Coast Guard). Second Canadian Symposium on Air Cushion Technology, June 1968. publ Canadian Aeronautics and Space Institute.

A Review of the Report of the ARB Special Committee on Hovercraft Stability & Control, J G Wrath (Civil Aviation Authority). Tenth CASI Symposium on Air Cushion Technology, October 1976.

POWERPLANTS

Gas Turbine Power for Large Hovercraft, P A Yerbury (BR Seaspeed). *Proc Symposium Gas Turbines,* London, pp 117-124, February 1976.

Gas Turbine Installations for Air Cushion Vehicle Lift and Propulsion Power, G H Smith (Avco Lycoming). ASME Gas Turbine Conference, Philadelphia, March 1977. Paper 77-GT-71.

The Selection of the Optimum Powerplant for the Air Cushion Vehicle, R Messet (United Aircraft of Canada Ltd). Fourth Canadian Symposium on Air Cushion Technology, June 1970. publ Canadian Aeronautics and Space Institute.

Some Aspects of Free Turbine Engine Hovercraft Control, W Bloomfield and T B Lauriat (AVCO Corporation Lycoming Division). Institute of Production Engineers, Second International Hovercraft Conference, April 1971.

PRODUCTION

Hovercraft from a Shipbuilder, A E Bingham (Vosper Thornycroft Ltd). Hovering Craft, Hydrofoil and Advanced Transit Systems Conference, Brighton, May 1974.

The Production of Air Cushion Vehicles, E F Gilberthorpe (British Hovercraft Corporation). Institution of Production Engineers (Southampton Section), International Hovercraft Conference, April 1968.

RESEARCH and DEVELOPMENT

Air Appraisal of Present and Future Large Commercial Hovercraft, R L Wheeler (British Hovercraft Corporation Ltd). Royal Institution of Naval Architects, October 1975.

CAA Paper 75017, Report of the ARB Special Committee on Hovercraft Stability and Control, Civil Aviation Authority, London, 1975.

Conceptual Study for a new Winged Surface Effect Vehicle System, J H McMasters and R R Greer. *Naval Engineers Journal,* Vol 86, pp 41-51, April 1974.

A Decade of Development—The SR.N6 Family of Hovercraft, R L Wheeler (British Hovercraft Corporation). Hovering Craft, Hydrofoil and Advanced Transit Systems Conference, Brighton, May 1974.

Development of Hovermarine Transport Vehicles, E G Tattersall (Hovermarine Transport Ltd). Institute of Production Engineers, Second International Hovercraft Conference, April 1971.

The Development of Marine Hovercraft with special reference to the Construction of the N500, P F Guienne, (SEDAM). Second International Conference Transport-Expo, Paris, April 1975.

The Drag of a Sidewall ACV over Calm Water, R Murao (Ministry of Transport, Japan). Second International Hovering Craft and Hydrofoil Conference, Amsterdam, May 1976.

General Survey of the Studies and Testing Techniques that led to the definition of N500 Performance, G Herrouin and Y Boccarodo (SEDAM). Second International Hovering Craft and Hydrofoil Conference, Amsterdam, May 1976.

Hovercraft Research and Development, R L Wheeler (British Hovercraft Corporation Ltd). Institute of Production Engineers, Second International Hovercraft Conference, April 1971.

Investigation of the static lift capability of a Low-Aspect-Ratio Wing operating in a powered ground-effect mode, J K Huffman and C M Jackson. NASA TM X-3031, July 1974.

Optimum Speed of an Air Cushion Vehicle—A Naviplane N500 Application, P F Guienne (SEDAM). *Hovering Craft and Hydrofoil,* Vol 16 No 9-10, 1977.

Minimum Induced Drag of a Semi-Circular Ground Effect Wing, H Mamada (Aichi University of Education) and S Ando (Nagoya University). *Journal of Aircraft,* Vol 10 No 11, November 1973.

Recent Developments in Hovercraft Performance Testing, B J Russell (Interservice Hovercraft Unit, HMS Daedalus). Hovering Craft, Hydrofoil and Advanced Transit Systems Conference, Brighton, May 1974.

Research and Development Work Associated with the Lift and Propulsion of Air Cushion Vehicles, J G Russell (Dowty Rotol Ltd). Hovering Craft, Hydrofoil and Advanced Transit Systems Conference, Brighton, May 1974.

Research into the Profitability of the Design and Construction of the N.500, P F Guienne (SEDAM). Second International Hovering Craft and Hydrofoil Conference, Amsterdam, May 1976.

Response of Air Cushion Vehicles to random seaways and the inherent distortion in scale models., D R Lavis, R J Bartholomew and J C Jones. *Journal of Hydronautics,* Vol 8, p 83, July 1974.

Some Aspects of Hovercraft Dynamics, J R Richardson (NPL Hovercraft Unit). Institution of Production Engineers, Second International Hovercraft Conference, April 1971.

Study of Materials and Nonmetallic coatings for erosion and wear resistance, (In French), G Sertour, M Armbruster, H Bernard and P Renard (Soc Nationale Industrielle Aérospatiale, Paris). Association Technique Maritime et Aéronautique Bulletin No 74, p 357-367, 1974.

The Definition of Sea State for Hovercraft Purposes, NPL Hovercraft Sea State Committee Report 2, National Physical Laboratory (HU Report 8), April 1969.

STRUCTURAL DESIGN

A Method of Testing Models of Hovercraft on Open Waters, Prof L Koblinski and Dr M Krezelewski (Ship Research Institute, Technical University of Gdansk). Institute of Production Engineers, Second International Hovercraft Conference, April 1971.

Static and Dynamic Analysis of the 3KSES Hull Structure, Messrs Havel, Dent, Phillips & Chang (Bell Aerospace). AIAA/SNAME Conference, 1976. Paper 76-858.

Prediction of Hydrodynamic Impact Loads Acting on SES and ACV Structure, E G U Band, D R Lavis and J G Giannotti. AIAA/SNAME Conference, 1976. Paper 76-868.

SYSTEMS

An Accumulator Control System for Alleviating SES Craft Heave motions in waves, P Kaplan and T P Sargent (Oceanics Inc) and James L Decker (US Navy Surface Effect Ships Project Office, Washington DC). Advanced Marine Vehicle Meeting AIAA/SNAME/USN, Annapolis, Maryland, July 1972.

An Investigation of the Roll Stiffness Characteristics of three Flexible Slanted Cushion Systems, Messrs Sullivan, Hinchey and Delaney (Toronto University, Institute for Aerospace Studies). UTIAS Report No 213, 1977.

Characterisation and Testing of Skirt Materials, Dr R C Tennyson and J R McCullough (Toronto University, Institute for Aerospace Studies). Seventh Canadian Symposium on Air Cushion Technology, June 1973.

The Design and Operating Features of Vosper Thornycroft Skirts, R Dyke (Vosper Thornycroft Ltd). Second International Hovering Craft and Hydrofoil Conference, Amsterdam, May 1976.

Deterioration of Hovercraft Skirt Components on Craft Operating over Water, M D Kelly, J Morris and E R Gardner (Avon Rubber Co Ltd). Hovering Craft, Hydrofoil and Advanced Transit Systems Conference, Brighton, May 1974.

Evolution of Integrated Lift, Propulsion and Control in the Aeromobile ACV, Dr W R Bertelsen (Bertelsen Manufacturing Co). Third Canadian Symposium on Air Cushion Technology, June 1969. publ Canadian Aeronautics and Space Institute.

Experience of Using the Gas Turbine Engine for the Propulsion of the Fully Amphibious Air Cushion Vehicle, M L Woodward (Rolls-Royce (1971) Ltd). Sixth Canadian Symposium on Air Cushion Technology, Ontario, June 1972.

The French Technique of Aéroglisseurs Marins, C Marchetti (SEDAM). Second Canadian Symposium on Air Cushion Technology, June 1968. publ Canadian Aeronautics and Space Institute.

Hovercraft Skirts, R L Wheeler (British Hovercraft Corporation). Hovering Craft, Hydrofoil and Advanced Transit Systems Conference, Brighton, May 1974.

Iceater 1-The Air Cushion Icebreaker, J C Snyder (Global Marine) and M Ball (Canadian Coast Guard). Offshore Technology Conference, Houston, May 1977.

The Influence of Plenum Chamber Obstructions on the Performance of a Hovercraft Lift Fan, G Wilson, Dr D J Myles and G Gallacher (National Engineering Laboratory). Third Canadian Symposium on Air Cushion Technology, June 1969. publ Canadian Aeronautics and Space Institute.

Jets, Props and Air Cushion, Propulsion Technology and Surface Effect Ships, Alfred Skolnick and Z G Wachnik (Joint Surface Effect Ships Program Office). The American Society of Mechanical Engineers. Gas Turbine Conference and Products Show, March 1968.

Low Temperature Effects on the Abrasion Behaviour of Coated Fabrics, R C Tennyson and A A Smailys (University of Toronto, Institute for Aerospace Studies). Tenth CASI Symposium on Air Cushion Technology, October 1976.

Pneumatic Power Transmission Applied to Hovercraft, J F Sladey Jr and R K Muench (United States Naval Academy and Naval Ship Research and Development Centre). Sixth CASI Symposium on Air Cushion Technology, Ontario, June 1972.

Power Optimization of the Captured Air Bubble Surface Effect Ship, K F Richardson (Naval Postgraduate School). AD-A039341, December 1976.

Power Transmission System of Hovercraft MV-PP1, MV-PP5 and MV-PP15, T Yamada, O Tamano, T Morita, K Horikiri, H Hirasawa and M Fujiwasa (Mitsui Shipbuilding & Engineering Co). Proc International Symposium on Marine Engineering, Tokyo, November 1973. Technical Paper Vol Ser 2-4, pp 13-23. publ Marine Engineers Society in Japan, Tokyo, 1973.

Seakeeping Trials of the BH.7 Hovercraft, A H Magnusson. Naval Ship R & D Report SPD-574-01, August 1975.

Surface Effect Vehicle Propulsion: A Review of the State of the Art, J B Chaplin, R G Moore and J L Allison (Bell Aerospace). Sixth Canadian Symposium on Air Cushion Technology, Ontario, June 1972.

Water-Jet Propulsion, S Kuether and F X Stora (Tamco Ltd, US Army Mobility Equipment, R & D Center). Second Canadian Symposium on Air Cushion Technology, 1968. publ Canadian Aeronautics and Space Institute.

Waterjet Propulsion for High Speed Surface Ships, P Duport, M Visconte and J Merle (SOGREAH). Ninth Symposium on Naval Hydrodynamics, Paris, August 1973.

SURFACE EFFECT SHIPS

An Analysis of Desired Manoeuvring Characteristics of Large SEVs, W Zeitfuss Jr and E N Brooks Jr (Naval Ship Research and Development Centre, Washington DC). Advanced Marine Vehicle Meeting, AIAA/SNAME/USN, Annapolis, Maryland, July 1972.

Crew/Combat System Performance Requirements in the Operational Environment of Surface Effect Ships, A Skolnick. *Naval Engineers Journal,* Vol 86 No 6, pp 15-32, December 1974.

Current State-of-the-Art of Waterjet Inlet Systems for High Performance Naval Ships, R A Barr and N R Stark. Hydronautics Inc, Tech Rep 7224-5, December 1973.

Domain of the Surface Effect Ship, W J Eggington and N Kobitz. Eighty-third Annual Meeting of SNAME, New York, November 1975. Paper NB 11.

Large High Speed Surface Effect Ship Technology, P J Mantle (Aerojet-General Corporation). Hovering Craft, Hydrofoil and Advanced Transit Systems Conference, Brighton, May 1974.

The Nuclear Powered Ocean-Going SES, E K Liberatore (Aeromar Corporation). *Jane's Surface Skimmers, 1971-72.*

Ocean-Going Surface Effect Ships, W F Perkins (Ocean Systems Div, Lockheed Missiles & Space Co). Northern California Section of SNAME and Golden Gate Section of ASNE Meeting at Treasure Island Naval Station, 1974.

On the Wave Resistance of Surface Effect Ships, J C Trotinclaux. Eighty-third Annual Meeting of SNAME, New York, November 1975. Paper No 3.

SES Programme, Civil Application, J J Kelly (Bell-Halter). *Hovering Craft and Hydrofoil,* Vol 17 No 4, pp 26-36, January 1978.

Some Special Problems in Surface Effect Ships, Robert D Waldo (Aerojet-General Corporation). *Journal of Hydronautics.* July 1968. publ American Institute of Aeronautics and Astronautics.

Study of Heave Acceleration/Velocity Control for the Surface Effect Ship, AD-009 302/1WT. US Grant, Naval Postgraduate School, Monterey, California, December 1974.

Surface Effect Ship Habitability Familiarisation, W F Clement and J J Shanahan (Systems Technology Inc). Interim Tech Rep STI-1041-1, November 1973.

The US Navy's Large Surface Effect Ship, Commander Jerome J Fee and Eugene H Handler (US Navy). Tenth CASI Symposium on Air Cushion Technology, October 1976.

Surface Effect Ships in the Surface Navy, R C Truax. *US Navy Institute Proceedings,* Vol 99 No 12/850, pp 50-54, December 1973.

TRACKED AIR CUSHION VEHICLES

A Comparative Study of the Ride Quality of TRACV Suspension Alternatives, R A Lums (Wright-Patterson Air Force Base). AFIT-C1-78-2 AD-AO46 565/8WT, September 1977.

Aérotrain Tridim for Urban Transportation, Jean Bertin and Jean Berthelot (Bertin & Cie and Sté Aérotrain). Hovering Craft, Hydrofoil and Advanced Transit Systems Conference, Brighton, May 1974.

The Air-Cushion at High Speeds, F Steiner (Société de l'Aérotrain). Second International Conference Transport-Expo, Paris, April 1975.

Applications du Coussin d'Air Aux Transports en Zones Urbaines, André Garnault (Société de l'Aérotrain). June 1973.

Canadian Research Activities Applicable to Tracked Levitated Vehicle Systems, P L Eggleton (Transportation Development Agency). Seventh Canadian Symposium on Air Cushion Technology, June 1973.

Current Collection for High-Speed Transit Systems, Messrs Appleton, Bartam, MacMichael and Fletcher (International Research & Development Co Ltd). Second International Hovering Craft and Hydrofoil Conference, Amsterdam, May 1976.

High Speed Ground Transportation, Documentation of Preliminary Engineering, Los Angeles International Airport and the San Fernando Valley, Kaiser Engineers, Los Angeles, California, April 1972.

LIM—Suspension Interaction, J H Parker and R J Charles (Ministry of Transportation & Communications, Ontario). Second Intercity Conference on Transportation, Denver, Colorado, September 1973. ASME Paper No. 73-ICT-116.

Linear Propulsion by Electromagnetic River, Prof E R Laithwaite (Imperial College of Science and Technology). Hovering Craft, Hydrofoil and Advanced Transit Systems Conference, Brighton, May 1974.

A New Linear Air Turbine Vehicle—TACV, Dr Yau Wu (Virginia Polytechnic Institute and State University). Sixth CASI Symposium on Air Cushion Technology, Ontario, June 1972.

The Operational Performance and Economics of URBA, M E Barthalon and L Pascual (SETURBA). Hovering Craft, Hydrofoil and Advanced Transit Systems Conference, Brighton, May 1974.

The Pendair Suspension System, D S Bliss (Pendair Ltd). Hovering Craft, Hydrofoil and Advanced Transit Systems Conference, Brighton, May 1974.

Problems Posés à Propos des Technologies non Conventionnelles de Transports Rapide au Sol, Jean Bertin (Président Directeur Général de la Société de l'Aérotrain). June 1973.

Status of "Transrapid" Development Programme, G Winkel (Krauss-Maffei, Augsburg). Second Intercity Conference on Transportation, Denver, Colorado, September 1973.

Tracked Air-Cushion Research Vehicle Dynamics Simulation Program User's Manual Final Report, E Magnani, R Lee and R Coppolino (Grumman Aerospace Corp). PB-219 984/2, October 1972.

Tracked Air Cushion Vehicle Research and Development by the US Department of Transportation, A F Lampros and C G Swanson (Mitre Corporation). Hovering Craft, Hydrofoil and Advanced Transit Systems Conference, Brighton, May 1974.

Tracked Air-Cushion Vehicle Suspension Models: Analysis and Comparison, D P Garg (Duke University, North Carolina) and B E Platin (MIT, Cambridge). *Vehicle System Dynamics (Holland),* Vol 2 No 3, November 1973.

ACV PUBLICATIONS, BOOKS and GENERAL LITERATURE
GENERAL INTEREST

This is the Hovercraft, Hugh Colver. publ Hamish Hamilton.

Hovercraft and Hydrofoils, Roy McLeavy. Blandford Press Ltd, Link House, West Street, Poole, Dorset BH15 1LL, 80pp col.

Hovercraft & Hydrofoils Work Like This, Egon Larsen. publ J M Dent.

The Hovercraft Story, Garry Hogg. publ Abelard-Schuman.

Hydrofoils and Hovercraft, Bill Gunston. publ Aldus Books.

Jane's Surface Skimmers (annual) edited by Roy McLeavy. publ Macdonald & Jane's.

TECHNICAL

Hovercraft Design and Construction, Elsley & Devereax. publ David & Charles.

An Introduction to Hovercraft and Hoverports, Cross & O'Flaherty. publ Pitman Publishing/Juanita Kalerghi.

Light Hovercraft Handbook, (ed) Neil MacDonald. publ Hover Club of Great Britain Ltd (available from 45 St Andrews Road, Lower Bemerton, Salisbury, Wilts).

A Guide to Model Hovercraft, (ed) Neil MacDonald. publ Hover Club of Great Britain Ltd.

Marine Hovercraft Technology, Robert Trillo. publ Leonard Hill Books.

Light Hovercraft Design Handbook, (ed) Dave Waters. publ Loughborough University.

HOVERCRAFT PERIODICALS

Air-Cushion and Hydrofoil Systems Bibliography Service, (bi-monthly) Robert Trillo Ltd, Broadlands, Brockenhurst, Hants SO4 7SX.

Hovering Craft & Hydrofoil, (monthly) Kalerghi Publications, 51 Welbeck Street, London W1M 7HE.

Light Hovercraft, (monthly) The Hover Club of Great Britain Ltd, 45 St Andrews Road, Lower Bemerton, Salisbury, Wilts.

UKHS Bulletin, (monthly) The United Kingdom Hovercraft Society, Rochester House, 66 Little Ealing Lane, London W5 4XX.

Air Cushion Review, (monthly) Aristos Publications, 17 Southampton Road, Paulsgrove, Hants PO6 4SA.

SPECIAL INTEREST

The Law of Hovercraft, L J Kovats. publ Lloyd's of London Press Ltd, 1975.

HYDROFOILS
BOOKS

Hydrofoils, Christopher Hook and A C Kermode. publ Sir Isaac Pitman & Sons Ltd, London.

Hydrofoil Sailing, A J Alexander, J L Grogono and Donald J Nigg. Kalerghi Publications, 51 Welbeck Street, London WIM 7HE.

PAPERS, ETC
COMMERCIAL OPERATION

Jetfoil Progress Report 2: Test and Commercial Service, B Michael (Boeing Marine Systems). Second International Hovering Craft and Hydrofoil Conference, Amsterdam, May 1976.

Operational Experience with USSR Raketa Hydrofoils on the River Thames, H Snowball (Hovermarine Transport Ltd). Second International Hovering Craft and Hydrofoil Conference, Amsterdam, May 1976.

Operating the PT150 Hydrofoil, J Presthus (Johns Presthus Rederi). Second International Hovering Craft and Hydrofoil Conference, Amsterdam, May 1976.

Running and Maintenance of Supramar Hydrofoils in Hong Kong, D Hay and N J Matthew (Institute of Marine Engineers). April 1970.

The US Gets Serious about Hydrofoils, R B Aronson. *Machine Design,* Vol 45 No 25, 18 October 1973.

DESIGN

Bending Flutter and Torsional Flutter of Flexible Hydrofoil Struts, P K Beach, Y N Liu (US Naval Ship Research and Development Centre). Ninth Symposium on Naval Hydrodynamics, Paris, August 1972.

Canadian Advances in Surface Piercing Hydrofoils, N E Jeffrey and M C Eames (Defence Research Establishment Atlantic, Dartmouth, Nova Scotia). Advanced Marine Vehicle Meeting, AIAA/SNAME/USN, Annapolis, Maryland, July 1972.

A Comparison of Some Features of High-Speed Marine Craft, A Silverleaf and F G R Cook (National Physical Laboratory). Royal Institute of Naval Architects, March 1969.

Design Optimization of Waterjet Propulsion Systems for Hydrofoils, R P Gill, M S Theseis (Massachusetts Institute of Technology). May 1972.

Flow Separation, Re-attachment and Ventilation of Foils with Sharp Leading Edge at Low Reynolds Number, R Hecker and G Ober. Naval Ship Research & Development Center Report 4390, III, May 1974.

A High-Speed Hydrofoil Strut and Foil Study, R Wermter and Y T Shen (Naval Ship Research & Development Center, Bethesda, Maryland). AIAA/SNAME Advanced Marine Vehicle Conference, San Diego, California, February 1974. Paper 74-310.

Hydrodynamics and Simulation in the Canadian Hydrofoil Program, R T Schmitke and E A Jones (Defence Research Establishment Atlantic, Canada). Ninth Symposium on Naval Hydrodynamics, Paris, August 1972.

Hydroelastic Design of Sub-Cavitating and Cavitating Hydrofoil Strut Systems, Naval Ship Research & Development Center, Maryland, USA. NSRDC Report 4257. April 1974.

Hydrofoil Craft Designers Guide, R Altmann, Hydronautics Inc, Technical Report 744-1, March 1968.

Laminar Boundary-Layer Induced Wave Forces on a Submerged Flat-Plate Hydrofoil, *Journal of Hydronautics,* Vol 8 No 2, pp 47-53, April 1974.

Large Hydrofoil Ships Feasibility Level Characteristics, James R Greco (Naval Ship Engineering Center, Hyattsville, Maryland). Advanced Marine Vehicle Meeting, AIAA/SNAME/USN, Annapolis, Maryland, July 1972.

Navaltecnica Hydrofoils, Dott Ing Leopoldo Rodriquez (Navaltecnica) and Dott Ing Maurizo Piatelli (SMA), *Hovering Craft and Hydrofoil,* Vol 17 No 8-9, pp 4-12, May-June 1978.

Production PHM Hull Structure Productivity Design, Ottis R Bullock and Bryan Oldfield (Boeing Co). *Hovering Craft and Hydrofoil,* Vol. 16, No. 9-10, 1977.

Prospects for very High Speed Hydrofoils, A Conolly. San Diego Section of the Society of Naval Architects and Marine Engineers/The American Society of Naval Engineers joint meeting, 20 November 1974. Available from: Section Librarian, Cdr R Bernhardt, US Coast Guard, Code 240, Box 119, US Naval Station, San Diego, California 92136.

Special Problems in the Design of Supercavitating Hydrofoils, G F Dobay and E S Baker (Naval Ship Research and Development Center, Bethesda, Maryland). AIAA/SNAME Advanced Marine Vehicle Conference, San Diego, California, February 1974. Paper 74-309.

Typhoon—A Seagoing Vessel on Automatically Controlled Submerged Foils, I I Baskalov and V M Burlakov *(Sudostroyeniye). Hovering Craft and Hydrofoil,* October 1972.

A Universal Digital Autopilot for a Hydrofoil Craft, Pierre Dogan and Frederick Gamber (Massachusetts Institute of Technology). Advanced Marine Vehicle Meeting, AIAA/SNAME/USN, Annapolis, Maryland, July 1972.

NAVAL CRAFT

High Speed and US Navy Hydrofoil Development, D A Jewell (Naval Ship Research and Development Center, Bethesda, Maryland). AIAA/SNAME Advanced Marine Vehicle Conference, San Diego, California, February 1974. Paper 74-307.

HMCS Bras d'Or—Sea Trials and Future Prospects, M C Eames and T G Drummond (Defence Research Establishment Atlantic, Canada). Royal Institution of Naval Architects, April 1972.

Military Hydrofoils, Baron H von Schertel, Dipl Ing Egon Faber and Dipl Ing Eugen Schatté (Supramar AG). *Jane's Surface Skimmers 1972-73.*

Military Hydrofoils, G Myers (Boeing Marine Systems). *Hovering Craft and Hydrofoil,* Vol 17 No 1, pp. 32-35, October 1977.

The NATO PHM Programme, Cdr Karl M Duff, USN (Naval Ship Systems Command, Washington DC). Advanced Marine Vehicle Meeting, AIAA/SNAME/USN, Annapolis, Maryland, July 1972.

The Operational Evaluation of the Hydrofoil Concept in US Coast Guard Missions, R E Williams (US Coast Guard and Development Center). Second International Hovering Craft and Hydrofoil Conference, Amsterdam, May 1976.

PHM Hullborne Wave Tests, C J Stevens (Institute of Technology, Hoboken, New Jersey). Stevens Institute of Technology, Davidson Lab Rep R-1759, June 1974.

Research on Hydrofoil Craft, Prof Dr Siegfried Schuster (Director Berlin Towing Tank). International Hydrofoil Society Winter Meeting, 1971, *Hovering Craft and Hydrofoil,* December 1971.

Sparviero-'Swordfish'-Type Multi-Role Combat Hydrofoil, Dott Ing Francesco Cao (Cantieri Navali Riuniti). Mostra Navale Italiana, Genoa, Italy, May 1978.

The Role of the Hydrofoil Special Trial Unit (HYSTU) in the US Navy Hydrofoil Program, R E Nystrom (US Navy). Second International Hovering Craft and Hydrofoil Conference, Amsterdam, May 1976.

The "Swordfish" Type Hydrofoil Design Criteria and Operational Experience, M Baldi (Cantieri Navali Riuniti). Second International Hovering Craft and Hydrofoil Conference, Amsterdam, May 1976.

SEAKEEPING CHARACTERISTICS

Prediction of the Seakeeping Characteristics of Hydrofoil Ships, Irving A Hirsch (Boeing Company). AIAA/SNAME Advanced Marine Vehicles Meeting, Norfolk, Virginia, May 1967. Paper 67-352.

A Synthesis of AALC Program ACV Seakeeping Data, A Gersten,

NSRXAC, AD-AO40122 SPD-765-01, April 1977.

Wave Impacts on Hydrofoil Ships and Structural Indications, Messrs Drummond, Mackay and Schmitke. 11th Symposium on Naval Hydrodynamics, London 1976.

SYSTEMS

Heaving Motions of Ventilated Trapezoidal Hydrofoils, L F Tsen and M Guilbaud (University of Poitiers). Fourth Canadian Congress of Applied Mechanics, CANCAM '73, 28 May—1 June 1973, Ecole Polytechnique, Montreal.

The Longitudinal Behaviour of a Hydrofoil Craft in Rough Seas, M Krezelewki (Institute of Ship Research, Gdansk University). Hovering Craft, Hydrofoil and Advanced Transit Systems Conference, Brighton, May 1974.

On the Design of Propulsion Systems with Z-Drives for Hydrofoil Ships, A A Rousetsky (Kryloff Research Institute, Leningrad). Ninth Symposium on Naval Hydrodynamics, Paris, August 1972.

RESEARCH AND DEVELOPMENT

A Theory for High Speed Hydrofoils, D P Wang and Y T Shen. Naval Ship R & D Centre Report SPD-479-14, June 1975.

The Design of Waterjet Propulsion Systems for Hydrofoil Craft, J Levy, Soc Naval Architects and Marine Engineers, *Marine Technology,* 2, 15-25 41, January 1965.

The Development of Automatic Control Systems for Hydrofoil Craft, R L Johnston and W C O'Neill (Naval Ship Research Development Centre, Bethesda, Maryland). Hovering Craft, Hydrofoil and Advanced Transit Systems Conference, Brighton, May 1974.

The Economics of an Advanced Hydrofoil System, A M Gonnella and W M Schultz (Hydrofoil Systems Organisation, The Boeing Company). *Hovering Craft & Hydrofoil,* November 1970.

The Effect of Nose Radius on the Cavitation Inception Characteristics of Two-Dimensional Hydrofoils, D T Valentine, Naval Ship Research & Development Center Report 3813, VI, July 1974.

An Examination of the Hazards to Hydrofoil Craft from Floating Objects, Christopher Hook. Society of Environmental Engineers Symposium, The Transport Environment, April 1969.

Key Problems Associated with Developing the Boeing Model 929-100 Commercial Passenger Hydrofoil, William Shultz (Boeing International Corporation). Hovering Craft, Hydrofoil and Advanced Transit Systems Conference, Brighton, May 1974.

The Large Commercial Hydrofoil and its limits in Size and Speed, Baron H von Schertel (Supramar). Second International Hovering Craft and Hydrofoil Conference, Amsterdam, May 1976.

Machinery of the PT 150 DC Hydrofoil, E Faber (Supramar). *Marine Engineer and Naval Architect,* January 1968.

Model Resistance Data of Series 65 Hull Forms Applicable to Hydrofoils and Planing Craft, H D Holling and E N Hubble. Naval Ship Research & Development Center Report 4121, V, May 1974.

Nine Years' History of the Hitachi-Supramar Hydrofoil Boat, *Hovering Craft & Hydrofoil,* November 1970.

Parametric Survey of Hydrofoil Stunt Flutter, P K Besch and E P Rood. Naval Ship R & D Center Report 76-0050, March 1976.

Preliminary Propulsion Performance Estimates for an 80ft Hydrofoil Craft, D L Gregory. Naval Ship R & D Center Evaluation Report SPD-606-01, June 1975.

PGH Tucumcari: Successful Application of Performance Specification, Gene R Myers (The Boeing Company). *Naval Engineers Journal,* June 1970.

Selection of Hydrofoil Waterjet Propulsion Systems, Ross Hatte and Hugh J Davis (The Boeing Company). *Journal of Hydronautics,* Vol 1 No 1, 1967. publ American Institute of Aeronautics and Astronautics.

Survey of French Hydrofoil Programmes (in French), J L Vollot, *Bulletin de l'Association Technique Maritime et Aéronautique,* No 72, pp 229-248, 1972.

Twenty Years of Hydrofoil Construction & Operation, L Rodriquez (Cantiere Navaltecnica). Second International Hovering Craft and Hydrofoil Conference, Amsterdam, May 1976.

Waterjet Propulsion for Marine Vehicles, V E Johnson, Jr. AIAA Paper 64-306, 1964. publ American Institute of Aeronautics and Astronautics.

Waterjet Propulsion for Marine Vehicles, J Traksel and W E Beck. AIAA Paper 65-245, 1965. publ American Institute of Aeronautics and Astronautics.

SAILING SKIMMERS

The Basic Mechanics of Sailing Surface Skimmers and Their Future Prospects, Dr Jerzy Wolf (Aviation Institute, Warsaw). *Hovering Craft & Hydrofoil,* March 1972.

Hydrofoil Ocean Voyageur "Williwaw", David A Keiper, PhD, Hydrofoil Sailing Craft. Third AIAA Symposium on the Aero/Hydronautics of Sailing, November 1971.

Hydrofoil Sailing, James Grogono. Hovering Craft, Hydrofoil and Advanced Transit Systems Conference, Brighton, May 1974.

Mayfly—A Sailing Hydrofoil Development, J Grogono and J B Wynne. *The Naval Architect,* pp 131-132, July 1977.

A Self-Tending Rig with Feedback and Compass Course, C Hook. *Hovering Craft & Hydrofoil,* Vol 14 No 10, pp 26-31, July 1975.

Why Sailing Hydrofoils? Christopher Hook. Ancient Interface IV Symposium, American Institute of Aeronautics and Astronautics, January 1973.

ADDENDA

AIR CUSHION VEHICLES

CHINA (PEOPLE'S REPUBLIC)

SHANGHAI 708 RESEARCH INSTITUTE

Prior to constructing the experimental passenger ferry illustrated on page 21, the Shanghai 708 Research Institute appears to have built a 1/3 scale model powered by two air-cooled radial engines. In elevation the craft is not unlike a scaled-down SR.N5 with the two radials mounted on the twin fins, each driving a two-bladed propeller. However, the power sharing arrangement is unique. A shaft with a universal joint extends from each of the two propeller hubs and both meet in a mixing gearbox and right-angle drive above a horizontally-mounted centrifugal lift fan located behind the cabin. The skirt is of fingered bag configuration, similar to that of the N5.

Among other ACVs under development in China is a rigid sidewall passenger ferry similar to the HM.2 in overall appearance, but with a higher length-to-beam ratio and employing diesel-powered waterscrew propulsion, and what is thought to be a naval sidewall type. Somewhat smaller than the passenger craft, the naval patrol craft is waterjet-propelled.

FRANCE

LA SOCIETE ANGEVINIERE

PSL 003

La Société Angevinière, previously specialising in inflatable life rafts, life jackets etc, has developed a mini hovercraft capable of carrying three persons. During its development, the PSL 003 was tested on three notable expeditions, across the Himalayas in 1972, through the waters of the Yucatan in 1975 and through the rapids of the River Tarn, France in 1976. Designed for use over rough terrain, as well as over marsh and water, the PSL 003 is expected to be employed by immigration, port surveillance and fire fighting services.

PROPULSION: Thrust is supplied by an air-cooled two-cylinder 980cc BMW engine of 60hp, driving a four-bladed propeller. It is capable of speeds of up to 34 knots on water and 96·56km/h (60mph) over land. With a fuel capacity of 15 litres (3·3 gallons), its endurance is between 2-3 hours.

CONTROLS: Craft direction is controlled by stick-operated hinged rudders situated behind the propeller.

DIMENSIONS

Length: 3·796m (13ft)

Width: 2·2m (7ft 2in)

WEIGHTS

Empty: 220kg (485lb)

Payload: 240kg (529lb)

INDONESIA

LAPAN

LEMBAGA PENERBANGAN DAN ANTARIKSA NASIONAL

(The National Institute of Aeronautics and Space)

Head Office: Jalan Pemuda Persil No 1, Jakarta Timur, Indonesia

Mailing Address: PO Box 3048, Jakarta, Indonesia

Telephone: (021) 48 28 02; (021) 48 51 25

Telex: 45675 LAPAN IA

Cable: LAPAN JAKARTA

Officials:

Air Vice Marshal J Salatum, *Chairman*

Prof Wiranto Arismunandar, *Vice Chairman*

PUSAT TEKNOLOGI DIRGANTARA (Aerospace Technology Centre)

Rumpin Airfield, Bogor, West Java

Dr Haryono Djojodohardjo, *Head, Aerospace Technology Centre*

Ir Jaidun Kromodihardjo, *Manager, Aerospace Technology Development*

Lapan was established in 1963 with the object of pioneering indigenous capabilities in aeronautics and space in support of the National Five Year Plan. At the beginning of 1978 Lapan had 527 personnel, out of which there were 195 university graduates and bachelors of science, divided into the Space Applications Centre (Jakarta), the Aerospace Technology Centre (Rumpin Airfield near Bogor), the Atmospheric and Space Research Centre (Bandung) and the Aerospace Study Centre (Jakarta).

Starting in 1977 Lapan undertook the design and construction of an experimental hovercraft designated XH-01.

LAPAN XH-01

Lapan's first research craft is a two-seater with a moulded fibreglass hull. Trials were due to begin at Rumpin Airfield, the site of Lapan's Aerospace Technology Centre, in September 1978.

LIFT AND PROPULSION: A McCullough 6hp engine drives a 70mm (2ft 3½in) fan at 6,000rpm for cushion lift. Propulsion is supplied by two 6hp McCullough engines aft, each driving a 60cm (1ft 11½in) ducted fan for propulsion.

CONTROLS: A single rudder in each thrust duct provides the craft with directional control.

HULL: Moulded glass reinforced plastic with integral buoyancy.

ACCOMMODATION: Side-by-side seating for two persons is provided in an open cockpit.

DIMENSIONS

Length overall: 3m (9ft 10in)

Lapan XH-01 two-seat research hovercraft

Beam overall: 1·5m (4ft 11in)

WEIGHTS

Empty: 250kg (550·66lb)

Max all-up: 370kg (814·97lb)

PERFORMANCE: Not available at the time of going to press.

UNION OF SOVIET SOCIALIST REPUBLICS

KRASNOYE SORMOVO

Gorky, USSR

The Central Scientific Research Institute has completed the design of a new sidewall ACV ferry, the Turist (Tourist). The vessel, which is based on extensive experience gained from the operation of the Zarnitsa, Orion, and Rassvet, is virtually a scaled-up version of the latter. It has a design speed of 36 knots and is intended for use along waterways of limited depth and unsuitable for hydrofoils. Two variants are projected, a 250-300 seat passenger ferry and a mixed traffic variant for 10-15 cars and 100-120 passengers.

Recent reports suggest that, as a result of detailed assessments undertaken in the Soviet Union over a period of years, a range of large sidewall hovercraft is being developed for the conveyance of freight. It appears that designs of 2,000 to 4,000 tons are under consideration.

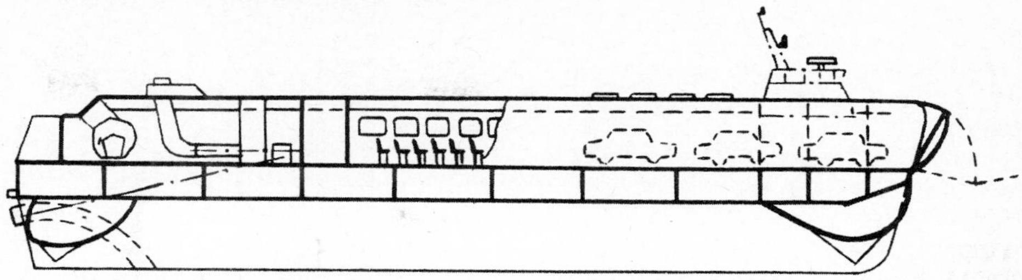

Inboard profile of the car ferry version of the Turist rigid sidewall hovercraft. Propulsion thrust appears to be supplied by two gas-turbine driven waterjets, one in each sidewall. Note the fingered bag skirts fore and aft

UNITED STATES OF AMERICA

ALASKA HOVERCRAFT

7133, Arctic Unit 14, Anchorage, Alaska 99502, USA

Telephone: (907) 344 6719

TIGER SHARK

Alaska Hovercraft has introduced a four-seat utility ACV, the Tiger Shark, which is currently in series production at Anchorage, Alaska. The craft, which has been under development for two years, is fully amphibious and will operate across land, tundra, water, ice and snow. Thrust is supplied by an air propeller driven by an engine mounted immediately aft of the cockpit. Twin aerodynamic rudders control craft heading. The main physical characteristics of the craft are seen in the accompanying photograph.

DIMENSIONS, WEIGHTS, PERFORMANCE: No details were available at the time of going to press.

Tiger Shark, a utility four-seater built in Anchorage, Alaska by Alaska Hovercraft

BELL AEROSPACE TEXTRON

PO Box 29307, New Orleans, Louisiana 70189, USA

AALC JEFF (B)

Following manufacturers' trials the Bell Aerospace Textron Jeff (B) was delivered to the US Navy's Coastal Systems Center, Panama City, Florida, on 28 July 1978, The craft, together with the Aerojet-General Jeff (A), has been designed to demonstrate the military effectiveness of air cushion vehicles in amphibious assault operations. Although both craft employ very different technical approaches, particularly in areas of lift, propulsion and control, both are designed to meet the same set of performance requirements and to operate from the well decks of amphibious ships. The specification calls for a nominal speed of 50 knots in sea state 2 and the ability to accommodate 60-75 tons in palletised supplies and/or equipment and vehicles up to the size of one of the US Army's main battle tanks.

On the completion of tests, which are being conducted by the US Navy's AALC Experimental Trials Unit, the best features of Jeff (A) and Jeff (B) will be incorporated in a production craft. The follow-on design and procurement will be accomplished under the new Landing Craft, Air Cushion (LCAC) Acquisition Programme.

During tests in the Gulf of Mexico, Jeff (B) reached a speed of 62 knots and demonstrated its ability to make the transition from the sea through the surf and across the beach to offload cargo, including men, vehicles and equipment, on hard ground. The craft also demonstrated its ability to operate at cruising speed with two of its six engines shut down.

During November 1978 Jeff (B) completed three days of interface trials with the Landing Ship Dock USS Spiegel Grove (LSD-32), an 11,270-ton vessel designed specially to carry assault landing craft. During the tests, the Spiegel Grove was ballasted with 6ft of water in its well deck. Jeff (B) was moved into the well using the ship's amphibious in-haul device (AID) to ensure

LC JEFF (B) seen during trials in the Gulf of Mexico

LC JEFF (B) being moved into the well deck of USS Spiegel Grove using the ship's amphibious in-haul device (AID)

positive directional control. AID is a prototype system, developed under the AALC programme and installed on the Spiegel Grove to provide positive control of a landing craft from the time it crosses the ship's stern gate until it moves forward and is finally positioned in the well.

Tests were conducted inside the ship's well deck for 2½ days to determine the temperature and the noise level at various engine powers. The purpose of the tests was to establish design criteria for a projected new amphibious ship, the LSD-41 class, and also to demonstrate that the 14·32m (47ft) wide Jeff (B) could manoeuvre successfully within the 14·63m (48ft) wide well of an LSD.

ACV TRAILERS AND HEAVY LIFT SYSTEMS

UNITED KINGDOM

AVON INDUSTRIAL POLYMERS (MELKSHAM) LIMITED

Melksham, Wiltshire, England
Telephone: 0225 703101
Telex: 44142
Officials:
B Stacey, *Managing Director*
D Gale, *Director*
D Wisely, *Director*
B Rowley, *Director*
Dr J Harwood, *Director*
D Pawlyn, *Director*
D Wisely, *Business Manager, Flexible Fabrications*
D Fisher, *Commercial Manager*
E F Lane, *Sales Manager, Flexible Fabrications*

Avon has been a designer and manufacturer of hovercraft skirt materials since 1966 and is now the leading international supplier to manufacturers of commercial and military hovercraft, industrial over platforms and transporters.

Avon Industrial Polymers, a division of the Avon Rubber group, started at Limpley Stoke in Wiltshire in 1885 with 22 employees. In 1890 it moved to Melksham, the present headquarters of the group, which has more than 7,000 employees. Tyres, industrial products and processed rubber are produced at Melksham on a 28-acre site. The group has several other factories within the United Kingdom, manufacturing industrial products, engineering components, synthetic sports surfaces, processed materials for the tyre industry, inflatable craft and sterile disposable medical products.

The company undertook a substantial research and development contract awarded by the British Government Department of Trade and Industry on behalf of Britain's hovercraft industry to look into ways and means of improving the performance of hovercraft skirt materials. Avon conducted a programme of laboratory and operational tests over a five-year period on fabrics to achieve a decrease in skirt operational costs.

Avon is also a manufacturer of ACV components and offers a detailed design service. It supplies hovercraft skirt systems to numerous operators in both commercial and industrial fields. The company is a major supplier to both British Rail Hovercraft Limited and Hoverlloyd, the cross-Channel operators, and earlier this year won a one million dollar order from Hoverlloyd for replacement components for its four Mountbatten-class SR.N4 hovercraft.

Avon has also been involved with Mackace Limited, Funtley, Hants, in supplying skirt materials for a giant 750-ton hover transporter working in the Persian Gulf; specially-developed coated fabric and components for two hoverbarges operating on the Alaskan pipeline project; a specially formulated skirt system for a hover platform drilling for potash in the Dead Sea, and rubber skirts for an icebreaking hover platform operating on the Illinois River in the United States.

Sea Pearl, the largest hover transporter in the world, lifting off at Abu Dhabi. The craft, 180ft × 80ft wide and fitted with Avon skirts, was used to carry LNG plant to Das Island, 110 miles away

Mackley Ace hover platform fitted with Avon hovercraft skirts, in operation in the Dead Sea where a search for deposits of potash is underway

Among other projects in which Avon has become involved are producing the entire skirt system for the military prototype hovercraft, the Vosper Thornycroft VT 2; designing and making the skirt system for the EM-2 amphibious freight hovercraft, now on trials with the Greek Navy, and undertaking detailed design work on the skirt systems for the Hovermarine HM.5.

Avon has also produced the materials for a hover ferry service for road transport on the Peace River in Northern Alberta, Canada. A similar ferry, also manufactured by Hoverlift Systems Limited of Calgary, is to be commissioned in British Columbia in the spring of 1979.

A new 44,000ft² factory is currently under construction at Chippenham, Wiltshire, to house the entire manufacture of Avon's flexible fabrications operation. Production was moved to the new factory from Melksham during the early part of 1979.

MACKACE LTD

(A subsidiary of British Hovercraft Corporation)
Funtley Road, Funtley, Fareham, Hampshire PO17 5ED, England
Telephone: 0329 285541
Telex: 86518 Machov G

WATER BUFFALO

An amphibious heavy-duty hover platform, the Water Buffalo is a standard Mackace hoverbarge equipped with BHC propulsion units. Intended for use in remote areas unsuitable for conventional craft, it will be available in two sizes, the larger with a 160-ton payload capacity, the smaller with a 100-ton capacity. Normal operating speed will be between 10-13 knots. The craft is designed for operation over water or relatively flat terrain; winches would be supplied to enable the craft to negotiate difficult gradients and obstacles. Endurance is 2·5 hours.

LIFT AND PROPULSION: Power for the lift fans will be supplied by twin diesel engines. Thrust will be supplied by two gas-turbines driving two four-bladed, variable and reversible pitch 5·79m (19ft) diameter propellers of the type employed on the SR.N4. One major difference will be the employment of propeller ducts.
CONTROLS: Craft heading is controlled by rudders hinged to the rear of the two propeller ducts and, when operating over water, by a drop keel. Differential pitch is employed for steering at low speeds and reversed pitch for braking.
HULL: Mild steel construction.
SKIRT: Segmented type, 1·21m (4ft) deep.
ACCOMMODATION: Cabin for crew and an elevated bridge.

PRICE: £3 million.
DELIVERY: 6-9 months, ex-works.

Impression of the Mackace Water Buffalo, a self-propelled heavy-duty hoverbarge for use in remote areas

UNITED STATES OF AMERICA

MARIDYNE

116 East Ash Avenue, Fullerton, California 92631, USA
Telephone: (714) 992 1620

MARIDYNE ACV-4000 BACKHOE

The Backhoe is basically an air cushion platform equipped with a hydraulically-operated backhoe. The prototype has been designed and built for the mechanised harvesting of oyster beds in the trial areas within Puget Sound, requiring raking, light digging and lifting, but it can also be employed for trenching, dredging or light excavating on mudflats, marshes or shoreline areas which cannot be reached by conventional machines because the footing is too soft. On level surfaces the craft, which is 5·5m (18ft) long and weighs 1,814kg (4,000lb), can be moved without difficulty by two men.

LIFT: Cushion air is supplied by a single Wisconsin petrol engine, developing 37hp at 2,400rpm, driving a 60·96cm (24in) diameter Rotafoil centrifugal fan. Cushion pressure is 17lb/ft^2 and the airflow is 12,000ft^3/min. Fuel is carried in a single 72·7 litre (16 gallon) tank.

PROPULSION: Tests have shown that the backhoe itself can be employed for locomotion. Alternative methods of propulsion include one or two persons pushing; the use of a winch or hydraulically-driven capstan with a 2,000lb maximum line pull for steep slopes; hydraulically-driven rear-mounted wheels fitted with soft tyres and, for overwater use, a 50hp outboard motor fitted on a retractable mounting bracket.

CONTROLS: All air cushion, propulsion and backhoe controls at operation console.

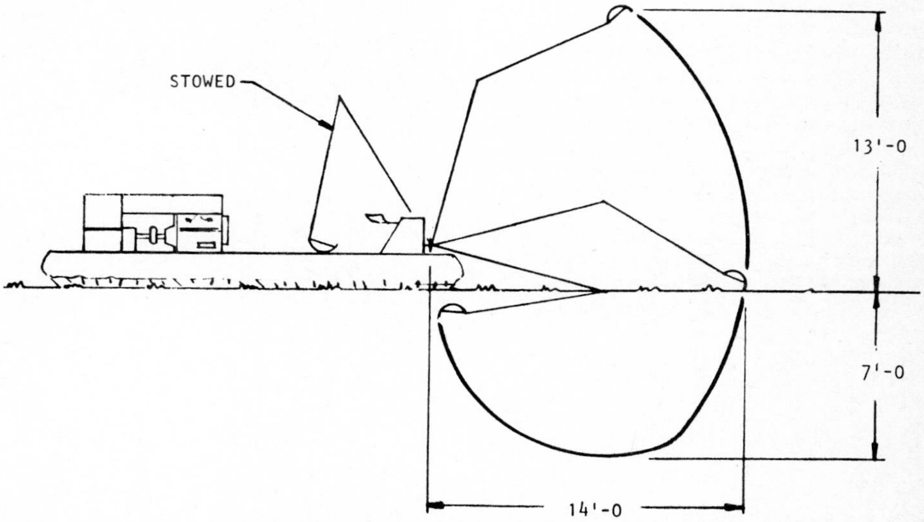

Maridyne's ACV-4000 Backhoe, designed for trenching, dredging or light excavating on mudflats, marshes or shoreline areas which cannot be reached by conventional machines

HULL: Raft type structure in aluminium with foam for additional bouyancy. The side sections are of fibreglass construction and are removable to reduce the overall width for transport by road.

SKIRT: Loop and segment type in neoprene or nylon fabric. Hull clearance 305mm (12in). Total of 120 peripheral fingers, all independently replaceable.

DIMENSIONS
Length: 5·5m (18ft)
Width: 4·57m (15ft)
Reach from swing mast: 4·27m (14ft)
Digging depth (max): 2·13m (7ft)
Swing arc: 270 degrees
Transport width, side sections removed: 2·39m (7ft 10in)
length 5·5m (18ft)
height 2·44m (8ft)

HYDROFOILS

BOLIVIA

HELMUT KOCK

PO Box 491, Lome Linda, California 92354, USA

Helmut Kock, designer of the Honald Albatross hydrofoil, which operated New York's first commercial hydrofoil service, and former chief engineer of International Hydrolines Inc, has designed and built a 47ft hydrofoil ferry for Crillon Tours of La Paz, Bolivia. The craft, the Bolivia Arrow, was built during 1976 at Huatajata, on the shore of Lake Titicaca (12,000ft) and entered service in February 1977.

All materials, equipment, engines, tools and machinery were imported from the United States. The entire craft is of welded aluminium and was built by Helmut Kock with the aid of a few Bolivian Indians who, in order to undertake the work, were first taught how to use modern hand and electric tools and automatic welding techniques.

Helmut Kock is currently negotiating for the construction of a 65ft hydrofoil for use by one operator in California and one on the Eastern seaboard of the United States. Interest is also being displayed in a 113ft design.

Bolivia Arrow cruising at 32 knots across Lake Titicaca, Bolivia

BOLIVIA ARROW

Crillon Tours Ltd, La Paz, Bolivia, has operated four of Helmut Kock's 20-seat Albatross craft on tourist routes across Lake Titicaca since the late 1960s. The need to cope with increasing tourist traffic and to provide a craft capable of crossing the full length of the lake led to a decision by Darius Morgan, Crillon's chief executive, to build a craft tailored to the company's requirements on the shore of the lake. Construction of the Bolivia Arrow began on 1 December 1975 and it was launched in September 1976. Very little adjustment was required before the craft entered service in February 1977. The craft is designed for medium range fast ferry services on rivers, bays, lakes and sounds.

FOILS: Surface-piercing trapeze foil system with W configuration pitch stability subfoil. Welded aluminium construction designed by Helmut Kock, US patent no 3,651,775.

POWER PLANT: Twin Cummins VT8-370 diesels, each developing 350shp at sea level and oversize to compensate for loss of power due to altitude. Each engine drives its own propeller via an inclined shaft. Engine room is amidships, after the third row of seats.

ACCOMMODATION: Crew comprises a captain, deckhand and a tourist guide. The captain is accommodated forward in a raised wheelhouse. His seat is on the hull centreline with the wheel, engine controls and main instrumentation in front. Passengers are accommodated in a single saloon equipped with seats for 40. Seats are arranged in ten rows of two abreast, separated by a central aisle. A washbasin/WC unit is provided and also a luggage compartment. All void spaces are filled with polyurethane foam.

Bolivia Arrow, showing the new foil system designed by Helmut Kock

DIMENSIONS
Length overall: 15·24m (50ft)
Hull beam: 3·55m (11ft 8in)
Width across foils: 4·87m (16ft)
Draft, hullborne: 2·28m (7ft 6in)

WEIGHTS
Displacement fully loaded: 14 tons

PERFORMANCE
Cruising speed: 32 knots

INDEX

Printed in England by Netherwood Dalton & Co. Ltd., Huddersfield